NEW PERSPECTIVES ON

Adobe® Photoshop® CS6

COMPREHENSIVE

NEW PERSPECTIVES ON

Adobe® Photoshop® CS6

COMPREHENSIVE

Jane Hosie-Bounar
Mitch Geller
Kelly Hart

Australia • Brazil • Japan • Korea • Mexico • Singapore • Spain • United Kingdom • United States

New Perspectives on Adobe Photoshop CS6, Comprehensive

Vice President, Career and Computing: David Garza

Director of Development: Marah Bellegarde

Executive Editor: Donna Gridley

Associate Acquisitions Editor: Amanda Lyons

Senior Product Manager: Kathy Finnegan

Product Managers: Leigh Hefferon, Julia Leroux-Lindsey

Senior Brand Manager: Elinor Gregory

Market Development Managers: Gretchen Swann, Kristie Clark

Developmental Editor: Mary Pat Shaffer

Senior Content Project Manager: Jennifer Goguen McGrail

Composition: GEX Publishing Services

Art Director: Marissa Falco

Text Designer: Althea Chen

Cover Designer: Roycroft Design

Cover Art: © Deb Casso/OJO Images/Getty Images

Copyeditor: Karen Annett

Proofreader: Brandy Lilly

Indexer: Rich Carlson

Library of Congress Control Number: 2013932030

ISBN-13: 978-1-133-52631-5

ISBN-10: 1-133-52631-4

Course Technology
20 Channel Center Street
Boston, MA 02210
USA

Cengage Learning is a leading provider of customized learning solutions with office locations around the globe, including Singapore, the United Kingdom, Australia, Mexico, Brazil, and Japan. Locate your local office at:
international.cengage.com/global

Cengage Learning products are represented in Canada by Nelson Education, Ltd.

To learn more about Course Technology, visit **www.cengage.com/course technology**

To learn more about Cengage Learning, visit **www.cengage.com**

Purchase any of our products at your local college store or at our preferred online store **www.cengagebrain.com**

Printed in the United States of America
1 2 3 4 5 6 7 17 16 15 14 13

Preface

The New Perspectives Series' critical-thinking, problem-solving approach is the ideal way to prepare students to transcend point-and-click skills and take advantage of all that Adobe Photoshop CS6 has to offer.

In developing the New Perspectives Series, our goal was to create books that give students the software concepts and practical skills they need to succeed beyond the classroom. We've updated our proven case-based pedagogy with more practical content to make learning skills more meaningful to students.

With the New Perspectives Series, students understand *why* they are learning *what* they are learning, and are fully prepared to apply their skills to real-life situations.

"The format of the text lends itself to easy-to-follow explanations and step-by-step processes assisting students in reviews for concept assessments. The hands-on exercises reinforce the concepts covered, the ProSkills sections bring reality into the classroom and coursework, and the problems at the end of each chapter give variety and relevance to all elements presented."

—Joyce Porter
Weber State University

About This Book

This book provides complete coverage of the new Adobe Photoshop CS6 software, and includes the following:

- Hands-on instruction of essential digital editing concepts, such as file formats, color modes, raster versus vector graphics, and the new CS6 features such as Content-Aware Move, layer filtering, and vector layers
- Coverage of important skills including drawing and using work paths; and filling text and objects with images, gradients, and patterns using selections and clipping masks
- Highlights of Adobe Photoshop innovations such as adjustment layers, layer comps and styles, painting and drawing tools, non-destructive editing techniques, filters, and masks
- Instructions for editing images using the auto correction tools, the Threshold and Curves adjustments, and the Dodge, Burn, and Sponge tools
- Coverage of how to use color management tools to edit camera raw files and create various outputs for desktop, printing, and the Web

New for this edition!

- Coverage of the new Content-Aware Move feature
- New hands-on instruction of new layer filtering
- Introduction of the new Properties panel

System Requirements

This book assumes a typical installation of Adobe Photoshop CS6 and Microsoft Windows 7 Ultimate using an Aero theme. You will need a graphics card that supports OpenGL 2.0. The browser used for any steps that require a browser is Internet Explorer 9.

"The clear step-by-step instructions, real-world data files, and helpful figures make New Perspectives texts excellent for courses taught in the classroom, the hybrid/blended format, or entirely online."
—Sylvia Amito'elau
Coastline Community College

The New Perspectives Approach

Context
Each tutorial begins with a problem presented in a "real-world" case that is meaningful to students. The case sets the scene to help students understand what they will do in the tutorial.

Hands-on Approach
Each tutorial is divided into manageable sessions that combine reading and hands-on, step-by-step work. Colorful screenshots help guide students through the steps. **Trouble?** tips anticipate common mistakes or problems to help students stay on track and continue with the tutorial.

VISUAL OVERVIEW

Visual Overviews
New for this edition! Each session begins with a Visual Overview, a new two-page spread that includes colorful, enlarged screenshots with numerous callouts and key term definitions, giving students a comprehensive preview of the topics covered in the session, as well as a handy study guide.

PROSKILLS

ProSkills Boxes and Exercises
New for this edition! ProSkills boxes provide guidance for how to use the software in real-world, professional situations, and related ProSkills exercises integrate the technology skills students learn with one or more of the following soft skills: decision making, problem solving, teamwork, verbal communication, and written communication.

KEY STEP

Key Steps
New for this edition! Important steps are highlighted in yellow with attached margin notes to help students pay close attention to completing the steps correctly and avoid time-consuming rework.

INSIGHT

InSight Boxes
InSight boxes offer expert advice and best practices to help students achieve a deeper understanding of the concepts behind the software features and skills.

TIP

Margin Tips
Margin Tips provide helpful hints and shortcuts for more efficient use of the software. The Tips appear in the margin at key points throughout each tutorial, giving students extra information when and where they need it.

REVIEW
APPLY

Assessment
Retention is a key component to learning. At the end of each session, a series of Quick Check questions helps students test their understanding of the material before moving on. Engaging end-of-tutorial Review Assignments and Case Problems have always been a hallmark feature of the New Perspectives Series. Colorful bars and brief descriptions accompany the exercises, making it easy to understand both the goal and level of challenge a particular assignment holds.

REFERENCE
TASK REFERENCE
GLOSSARY/INDEX

Reference
Within each tutorial, Reference boxes appear before a set of steps to provide a succinct summary and preview of how to perform a task. In addition, a complete Task Reference at the back of the book provides quick access to information on how to carry out common tasks. Finally, each book includes a combination Glossary/Index to promote easy reference of material.

www.cengage.com/ct/newperspectives

Our Complete System of Instruction

BRIEF
INTRODUCTORY
COMPREHENSIVE

Coverage To Meet Your Needs

Whether you're looking for just a small amount of coverage or enough to fill a semester-long class, we can provide you with a textbook that meets your needs.

- Brief books typically cover the essential skills in just 2 to 4 tutorials.
- Introductory books build and expand on those skills and contain an average of 5 to 8 tutorials.
- Comprehensive books are great for a full-semester class, and contain 9 to 12+ tutorials.

So if the book you're holding does not provide the right amount of coverage for you, there's probably another offering available. Go to our Web site or contact your Course Technology sales representative to find out what else we offer.

CourseCasts – Learning on the Go. Always available...always relevant.

Want to keep up with the latest technology trends relevant to you? Visit our site to find a library of podcasts, CourseCasts, featuring a "CourseCast of the Week," and download them to your mp3 player at http://coursecasts.course.com.

Our fast-paced world is driven by technology. You know because you're an active participant—always on the go, always keeping up with technological trends, and always learning new ways to embrace technology to power your life.

Ken Baldauf, host of CourseCasts, is a faculty member of the Florida State University Computer Science Department where he is responsible for teaching technology classes to thousands of FSU students each year. Ken is an expert in the latest technology trends; he gathers and sorts through the most pertinent news and information for CourseCasts so your students can spend their time enjoying technology, rather than trying to figure it out. Open or close your lecture with a discussion based on the latest CourseCast.

Visit us at http://coursecasts.course.com to learn on the go!

Instructor Resources

We offer more than just a book. We have all the tools you need to enhance your lectures, check students' work, and generate exams in a new, easier-to-use and completely revised package. This book's Instructor's Manual, ExamView testbank, PowerPoint presentations, data files, solution files, figure files, and a sample syllabus are all available on a single CD-ROM or for downloading at login.cengage.com.

Acknowledgments

I'd like to thank the following reviewers, who provided invaluable feedback to help make the book the best it can be. Their experience teaching Photoshop in the classroom was very helpful: DeAnnia Clements, Joyce Porter, and Samantha Brodie. I'd also like to thank everyone on the New Perspectives Team, including Kathy Finnegan, who encouraged me to write the book in the first place, and Leigh Hefferon, who managed all the moving parts with patience and expertise. Special thanks go to Mary Pat Shaffer, my editor, whose insights and eye for detail are always invaluable. Thanks also to Khaled, who didn't mind being "Photoshopped," Anya and Cyn, who provided some of the photos, and Maya, who gave me an excuse to go to Italy and take pictures.
– Jane Hosie-Bounar

We want to thank Mark Chapman for his unique assistance in tracking Adobe developments and changes, the staff and management of Meshnet.com, and the staff of the Sid Richardson Museum and Store (www.sidrichardsonmuseum.org/store) for their support and generosity in allowing us to use images from their catalog and collection. I would like to thank Edyie and Joe Geller, Pam, Gregg, and the rest of the family for their love and support . . . you guys rock! He would also like to thank John Knecht, John Orentlicher, and Don Little.
– Mitch Geller

I would like to thank Mary O'Brien for much needed C8H10N4O2 infusions and linguistic reality checks, Robin Romer for always answering the phone, along with the rest of the Nu-Design.com team, Tika and Matt, for their support.
– Kelly Hart

BRIEF CONTENTS

PHOTOSHOP

Tutorial 1 Getting Started with Adobe Photoshop . . . . PS 1
Introducing Graphics and Photoshop CS6

Tutorial 2 Working with Image Files. . . . . PS 59
Working with File Sizes, Color Modes, and Image Adjustments

Tutorial 3 Layering Content to Compose Images . . . . PS 115
Working with Layers in Compositions

Tutorial 4 Adding Content. . . . . PS 171
Adding Content and Working with Color

Tutorial 5 Selecting and Modifying Content . . . . PS 239
Compositing Photos

Tutorial 6 Designing with Text . . . . PS 313
Using Text and Text Effects

Tutorial 7 Correcting, Adjusting, and Retouching . . . . PS 329
Adjusting and Retouching Photographic Images

Tutorial 8 Advanced Input/Output and Color Management . . . . PS 393
Working with the Camera Raw Plug-In and Color Management Tools

Tutorial 9 Planning, Creating, and Delivering a Complete Project . . . . PS 451
Creating a Web Banner Ad Campaign

Glossary/Index **REF 1**

Task Reference **REF 13**

TABLE OF CONTENTS

Preface v

PHOTOSHOP LEVEL I TUTORIALS

Tutorial 1 Getting Started with Adobe Photoshop CS6
Introducing Graphics and Photoshop CS6........ **PS 1**

SESSION 1.1 .... **PS 2**

Introducing Graphics and Photoshop CS6 .... PS 4

How Graphics Are Used to Enhance Communications .... PS 4

The Role of Photoshop in Professional Production .... PS 4

Bitmap vs. Vector Graphics .... PS 5

Starting Photoshop and Touring the Photoshop Workspace .... PS 7

Opening a File .... PS 8

Touring the Photoshop Workspace .... PS 10

Menu Bar .... PS 10

Tools Panel .... PS 10

Options Bar .... PS 11

Document Window .... PS 11

Panels .... PS 11

Getting Help in Photoshop .... PS 11

Working with Multiple Files .... PS 13

Saving a File with a New Name .... PS 14

Navigating and Arranging File Windows .... PS 15

Navigating Open File Windows and Changing Tab Order .... PS 15

Arranging File Windows .... PS 17

Closing Files .... PS 20

Exiting Photoshop .... PS 21

Session 1.1 Quick Check .... PS 21

SESSION 1.2 .... **PS 22**

Viewing and Changing Photoshop Preferences ..... PS 24

Restoring Default Photoshop Preferences .... PS 26

Working with Panels .... PS 27

Displaying and Closing a Panel .... PS 29

Minimizing, Hiding, and Redisplaying Panels .... PS 32

Moving and Stacking Panels .... PS 33

Stacking Panels .... PS 34

Preset Workspaces .... PS 35

Using the Rulers, Guides, and Grid .... PS 38

Showing the Rulers .... PS 38

Adding Guides .... PS 39

Showing and Hiding the Grid .... PS 42

Using Tools in the Tools Panel .... PS 44

Selecting and Using Tools .... PS 44

Using the Options Bar to Change Tool Settings .... PS 45

Adding Content to the Canvas and Using Tool Presets .... PS 47

Session 1.2 Quick Check .... PS 52

Review Assignments .... PS 53

Case Problems .... PS 54

Tutorial 2 Working with Image Files
Working with File Sizes, Color Modes, and Image Adjustments.............................. **PS 59**

SESSION 2.1 .... **PS 60**

Understanding File Formats and Their Uses .... PS 62

Changing File Type, File Size, and Resolution ...... PS 63

Optimizing an Image .... PS 63

Changing Image Resolution .... PS 68

Managing Multiple Image Files with Adobe Bridge and Mini Bridge . . . PS 72
Understanding Color Modes and Intensities . . . PS 75
Understanding the RGB Color Mode . . . PS 76
Understanding the CMYK Color Mode . . . PS 77
Understanding Indexed Colors . . . PS 78
Understanding the Grayscale Color Mode . . . PS 79
Understanding How Bit Depth Combined with Color Mode Affects File Size . . . PS 80
Changing Color Modes . . . PS 81
Creating a New File . . . PS 83
Placing an Image in a New File . . . PS 83
Creating a Custom Document Preset . . . PS 86
Session 2.1 Quick Check . . . PS 89
SESSION 2.2 . . . PS 90
Making Image Adjustments . . . PS 92
Working with the Canvas . . . PS 97
Zooming and Panning an Image . . . PS 102
Zooming an Image . . . PS 102
Panning an Image . . . PS 103
Rotating and Flipping an Image . . . PS 107
Session 2.2 Quick Check . . . PS 109
Review Assignments . . . PS 110
Case Problems . . . PS 111

Tutorial 3 Layering Content to Compose Images
Working with Layers in Compositions . . . **PS 115**
SESSION 3.1 . . . PS 116
Understanding Layers . . . PS 118
Understanding Layer Positioning . . . PS 119
Selecting and Deselecting Layers . . . PS 121
Selecting and Deselecting Single Layers . . . PS 121
Selecting and Deselecting Multiple Layers . . . PS 123
Adding and Duplicating Layers . . . PS 125
Adding an Empty Layer . . . PS 125
Adding a Vector Layer and an Effects Layer . . . PS 126
Creating a New Layer by Cutting or Copying and Pasting a Selection . . . PS 128
Duplicating a Layer . . . PS 129
Changing Layer Properties . . . PS 131
Displaying Layer Edges . . . PS 133
Moving a Layer in the Layers Panel to Change Its Visibility . . . PS 135
Moving a Layer to Change Its Position on the Canvas . . . PS 137
Aligning and Distributing Layers . . . PS 138
Hiding and Redisplaying Layers . . . PS 141
Deleting a Layer . . . PS 143
Placing, Resizing, and Positioning an Image on a Layer . . . PS 143
Rotating a Placed Image . . . PS 146
Session 3.1 Quick Check . . . PS 147
SESSION 3.2 . . . PS 148
Locking and Unlocking Layer Content . . . PS 150
Working with Layer Comps . . . PS 152
Working with Blending Modes and Opacity . . . PS 155
Applying Blending Modes . . . PS 155
Changing Opacity . . . PS 158
Creating Layer Groups . . . PS 159
Finalizing Layers . . . PS 160
Merging Layers . . . PS 160
Flattening an Image . . . PS 161
Session 3.2 Quick Check . . . PS 162
Review Assignments . . . PS 163
Case Problems . . . PS 164

Tutorial 4 Adding Content

Adding Content and Working with Color . . . . **PS 171**

SESSION 4.1 . . . . PS 172

Understanding the Effect of Color . . . . PS 174

Using the Color Selection Tools . . . . PS 176

Setting the Foreground Color with the Eyedropper Tool . . . . PS 177

Setting the Foreground Color in the Color Panel . . . . PS 180

Changing the Background Color . . . . PS 185

Working with the Swatches Panel . . . . PS 187

Adding Colors to the Swatches Panel . . . . PS 190

Saving Modified Swatches as a Preset. . . . . PS 191

Working with the Styles Panel . . . . PS 192

Using the Layer Style Dialog Box. . . . . PS 194

Session 4.1 Quick Check . . . . PS 197

SESSION 4.2. . . . . PS 198

Adding Fill Layers . . . . PS 200

Creating a Solid Color Fill Layer. . . . . PS 202

Creating a Gradient Layer . . . . PS 203

Creating a Pattern Layer. PS 205

Adding Shape Layers vs. Filling Pixels on a Layer . . . . PS 206

Specifying Fill and Stroke Options for a Vector Shape . . . . PS 207

Adding a Shape Layer (Vector Objects). . . . . PS 209

Using Fill Pixels (Bitmap/Raster Objects). . . . . . . PS 218

Using the Brush Tool . . . . PS 220

Choosing Brush Settings and Adding Brushstrokes . . . . PS 221

Working with Brush Presets . . . . PS 225

Loading Other Presets . . . . PS 226

Using a Brush Preset to Stroke a Path . . . . PS 227

Creating a Custom Preset . . . . PS 229

Session 4.2 Quick Check. . . . . PS 231

Review Assignments . . . . PS 232

Case Problems . . . . PS 233

Tutorial 5 Selecting and Modifying Content

Compositing Photos. . . . . **PS 239**

SESSION 5.1 . . . . PS 240

Selecting Content for Compositing . . . . PS 242

Selecting with the Rectangular or Elliptical Marquee Tool . . . . PS 244

Specifying a Fixed Ratio or Fixed Size Selection. . . . . PS 246

Modifying a Selection. . . . . PS 249

Applying an Adjustment to a Selection . . . . PS 251

Creating Complex Selections . . . . PS 254

Selecting a Color Range . . . . PS 257

Undoing and Redoing Actions . . . . PS 262

Stepping Backward and Forward. . . . . PS 263

Reverting to a Previous State Using the History Panel. . . . . PS 265

Using the History Brush Tool . . . . PS 270

Session 5.1 Quick Check . . . . PS 275

SESSION 5.2. . . . . PS 276

Working with the Lasso Tools, Fills, and the Content-Aware Move Tool . . . . PS 278

Filling a Selection Using the Content-Aware Fill Feature . . . . PS 278

Moving a Selection Using the Content-Aware Move Tool. . . . . PS 280

Selecting Content with the Magnetic Lasso Tool. . . . . PS 284

Saving and Reloading a Selection. . . . . PS 288

Selecting with the Quick Selection Tool. . . . . PS 289

Stroking a Selection . . . . PS 293

Working with Filters and Masks . . . . PS 295
Understanding Masks. . . . . PS 296
Using the Liquify Filter . . . . PS 297
Working with the Filter Gallery . . . . PS 301
Session 5.2 Quick Check. . . . . PS 305
Review Assignments . . . . PS 306
Case Problems . . . . PS 307

Tutorial 6 Designing with Text
Using Text and Text Effects . . . . **PS 313**

SESSION 6.1 . . . . PS 314

Introducing Text Layers. . . . . PS 316
Adding and Modifying Point Type . . . . PS 318
Working in the Typography Workspace. . . . . PS 321
Scaling Text Using the Character Panel . . . . PS 325
Scaling Text Using the Move Tool . . . . PS 326
Working with Vertical Point Type . . . . PS 328
Adjusting the Tracking of Vertical Text . . . . PS 331
Working with Paragraphs . . . . PS 333
Checking Spelling and Replacing Text. . . . . PS 340
Session 6.1 Quick Check. . . . . PS 343

SESSION 6.2. . . . . PS 344

Creating Unique Text . . . . PS 346
Applying a Style to Text. PS 346
Scaling and Tracking Text to Achieve Balance. . . PS 348
Specifying a Baseline Shift. . . . . PS 353
Warping Text . . . . PS 354
Adding Text Along a Path. . . . . PS 358
Filling Text with an Image, Pattern, or Gradient. . . . PS 361
Session 6.2 Quick Check. . . . . PS 365
Review Assignments . . . . PS 366
Case Problems . . . . PS 367
ProSkills Exercise: Teamwork . . . . PS 373

Tutorial 7 Correcting, Adjusting, and Retouching
Adjusting and Retouching Photographic Images . . . . **PS 377**

SESSION 7.1 . . . . PS 378

Photoshop as Digital Darkroom . . . . PS 380
Straightening and Cropping . . . . PS 380
Cropping with the Crop Tool . . . . PS 380
Straightening an Image . . . . PS 384
Cropping and Altering the Perspective of an Image . . . . PS 388
Moving and Removing Objects in an Image Using Content-Aware Tools . . . . PS 390
Patching an Image . . . . PS 394
Auto Correction Tools. . . . . PS 396
Correcting Images with the Adjustments Panel. . . . PS 402
Using Auto Adjustments in Adjustment Layers . . . . PS 403
Using the Threshold Adjustment . . . . PS 405
Enhancing Images with the Curves Adjustment. . . . . PS 409
Session 7.1 Quick Check . . . . PS 417

SESSION 7.2. . . . . PS 418

Repairing and Retouching Images . . . . PS 420
Repairing Images with the Spot Healing Brush Tool. . . . . PS 420
Repairing Images with the Healing Brush Tool. . . . . PS 422
Retouching with the Dodge Tool. . . . . PS 426
Retouching with the Burn Tool. . . . . PS 428
Retouching with the Sponge Tool . . . . PS 429
Retouching with the Sharpen Tool. . . . . PS 431
Transforming an Image using the Blur Gallery of Filters . . . . PS 432
Working with the Lab Color Mode. . . . . PS 439
Session 7.2 Quick Check. . . . . PS 444

Review Assignments . . . . .PS 445

Case Problems . . . . .PS 446

Tutorial 8 Advanced Input/Output and Color Management
Working with the Camera Raw Plug-In and Color Management Tools . . . . **PS 453**

SESSION 8.1 . . . . PS 454

Working with Camera Raw Files . . . . .PS 456

The Photoshop Camera Raw Plug-in . . . . .PS 456

Exploring the Camera Raw Workspace . . . . .PS 457

Specifying Workflow Options. . . . . .PS 462

Saving Adjustments to a Camera Raw File. . . . . . . .PS 464

Making Basic Adjustments to RAW Images . . . . . . .PS 469

Understanding the Histogram . . . . .PS 470

Lighting Concepts . . . . .PS 473

White Balancing an Image . . . . .PS 473

Making Basic Tonal Adjustments . . . . .PS 476

Clarity, Vibrance, and Saturation Adjustments . .PS 479

Opening JPEG and TIFF Files in Camera Raw . . . . .PS 481

Saving Camera Raw Files as DNG files. . . . . .PS 482

Session 8.1 Quick Check. .PS 483

SESSION 8.2. . . . . PS 484

Creating Successful Output . . . . .PS 486

Basic Color Management .PS 487

Calibrating Your Monitor . . . . .PS 488

Setting Your View for Soft Proofing. . . . . .PS 494

Understanding Color Profiles. . . . . .PS 497

Setting Profiles and Color Management Policies . . . . .PS 497

Using Bridge to Synchronize Color Settings . . . .PS 499

Converting a Color Profile . . . . .PS 500

Printing at Home. . . . . .PS 502

Printing at a Professional Print Shop. . . . . .PS 503

Creating Images for the Web . . . . .PS 504

Creating Video Output and Preparing Images for Video . . . . .PS 507

Session 8.2 Quick Check. .PS 509

Review Assignments . . . . .PS 510

Case Problems . . . . .PS 511

Tutorial 9 Planning, Creating, and Delivering a Complete Project
Creating a Web Banner Ad Campaign . . . . **PS 519**

SESSION 9.1 . . . . PS 520

Planning and Delivering a Professional Project . . . .PS 522

Planning a Design Project. . . . . .PS 522

Understanding the Client's Vision . . . . .PS 523

Establishing Goals for the Project . . . . .PS 524

Ascertaining the Target Audience . . . . .PS 527

Defining Project Scope and Determining Project Deliverables . . . . .PS 530

Creating a Master Planning Document . . . . .PS 530

Conducting Research . . . . .PS 532

Studying the Target Audience and the Competition . . . . .PS 532

Reviewing the Client's Branding, Identity, and Marketing Materials . . . . .PS 534

Determining Output Specifications . . . . .PS 538

Session 9.1 Quick Check . . . . .PS 539

SESSION 9.2. . . . . PS 540

Designing a Project. . . . . .PS 542

Gathering or Acquiring Materials . . . . .PS 542

Developing a Concept and Metaphor . . . . .PS 543

Creating a Layout . . . . .PS 544

Balance and Space . . . . .PS 545

Rhythm and Unity. . . . . .PS 547

Creating a Wireframe of Your Layout. . . . . .PS 548

Selecting Colors . . . . PS 551
Selecting Harmonious Colors. . . . . PS 552
Additional Guidelines for Color Selection . . . . . . PS 557
Using the Kuler Panel . . . . PS 559
Adding Colors to Your Composition . . . . PS 566
Selecting Fonts and Adding Text . . . . PS 567
Selecting the Appropriate Typographical Style . . . . PS 568
Selecting Typefaces and Font Styles . . . . PS 568
Creating a Graphic Style. . . . . PS 572
Selecting a Photographic Style. . . . . PS 581
Creating Output Files and Wrapping Up . . . . PS 587
Session 9.2 Quick Check. . . . . PS 588
Review Assignments . . . . PS 589
Case Problems . . . . PS 590
ProSkills Exercise: Decision Making . . . . PS 597
GLOSSARY/INDEX . . . . REF 1
TASK REFERENCE . . . . REF 13

TUTORIAL 1

Getting Started with Adobe Photoshop CS6

Introducing Graphics and Photoshop CS6

PHOTOSHOP

OBJECTIVES

Session 1.1

- Understand the role of Photoshop in professional production
- Define raster versus vector graphics
- Start and exit Photoshop, and explore the workspace
- Examine Photoshop Help
- Open, rename, and close files
- Navigate and arrange file windows

Session 1.2

- Set Photoshop Preferences
- Work with the Photoshop interface, tools, and tool presets
- Work with panels and use the panel menu
- Choose a preset workspace
- Display and use rulers, guides, and the grid
- Add content to the canvas

Case | *Mirabeau Media*

Mirabeau Media is a consulting firm in Burlington, Vermont, that was founded in 2010 by Sarah Alward, a 2008 college graduate with a double major in journalism and graphic design. Sarah spent two years working for a local news organization, but decided her interest really lay in using her skills to help clients promote their products and companies through brochures, print ads, and Web-based media.

Sarah's firm uses Adobe Photoshop along with the other applications in the Adobe Creative Suite to create logos, flyers, brochures, catalogs, and online advertising for various clients in the Burlington area. You have recently been hired by Sarah to help in all areas of the company's activities, from design to production. Sarah knows you don't have experience using Photoshop, but based on your interview, she has decided that you are a quick learner with a lot to offer.

STARTING DATA FILES

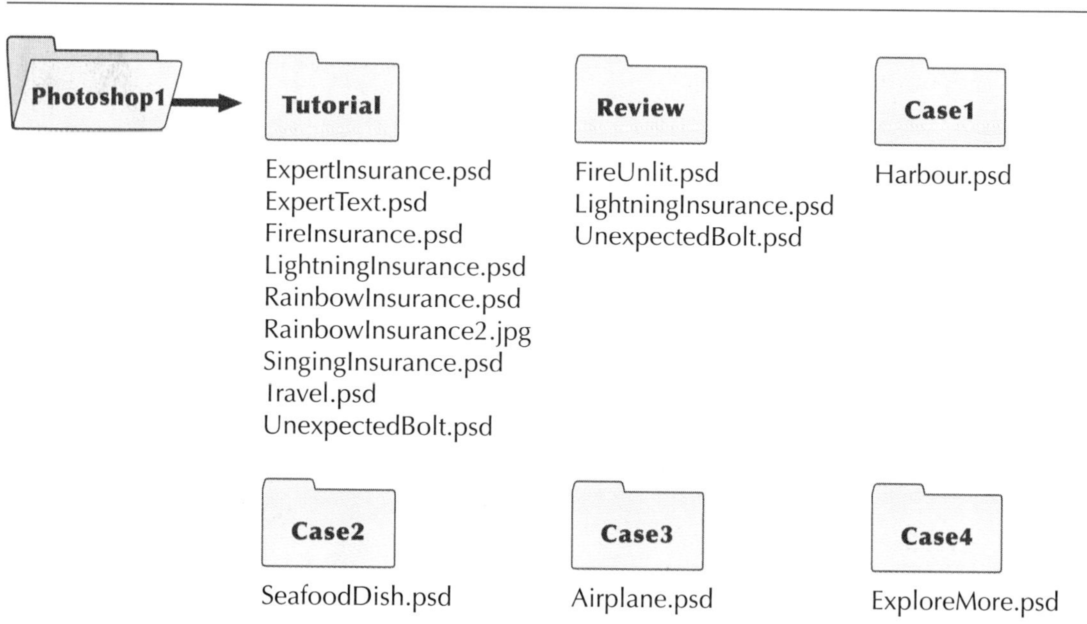

SESSION 1.1 VISUAL OVERVIEW

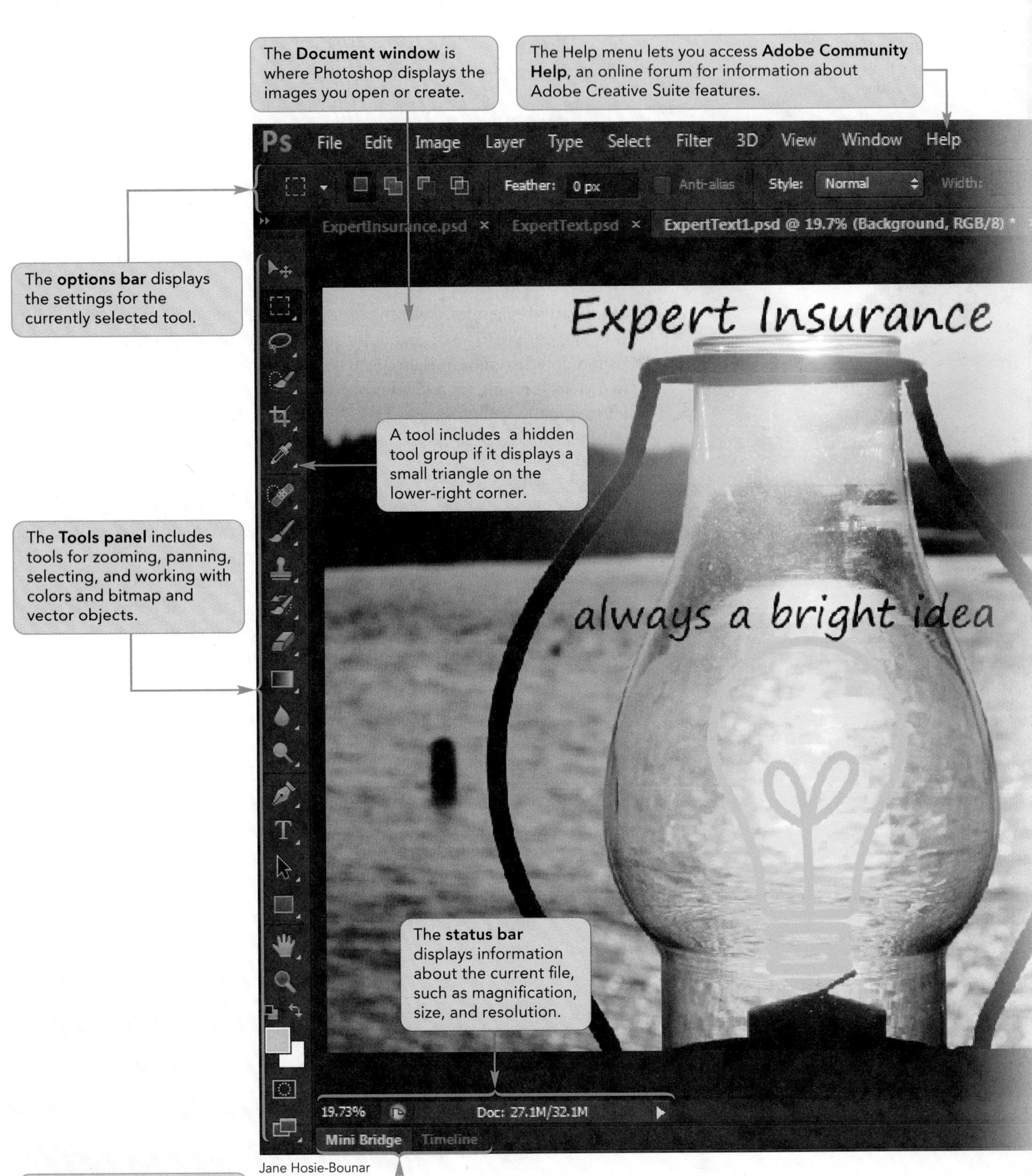
The **Document window** is where Photoshop displays the images you open or create.
The Help menu lets you access **Adobe Community Help**, an online forum for information about Adobe Creative Suite features.
The **options bar** displays the settings for the currently selected tool.
A tool includes a hidden tool group if it displays a small triangle on the lower-right corner.
The **Tools panel** includes tools for zooming, panning, selecting, and working with colors and bitmap and vector objects.
The **status bar** displays information about the current file, such as magnification, size, and resolution.
You can click a **panel tab** to display and access the tools in a panel.
Ps File Edit Image Layer Type Select Filter 3D View Window Help
Feather: 0 px Anti-alias Style: Normal Width:
ExpertInsurance.psd ExpertText.psd ExpertText1.psd @ 19.7% (Background, RGB/8) *
Expert Insurance
always a bright idea
19.73% Doc: 27.1M/32.1M
Mini Bridge Timeline

Jane Hosie-Bounar

PHOTOSHOP PROGRAM WINDOW

When you have multiple files open, the Document window displays each filename on a tab.

Panels can be collapsed to icons.

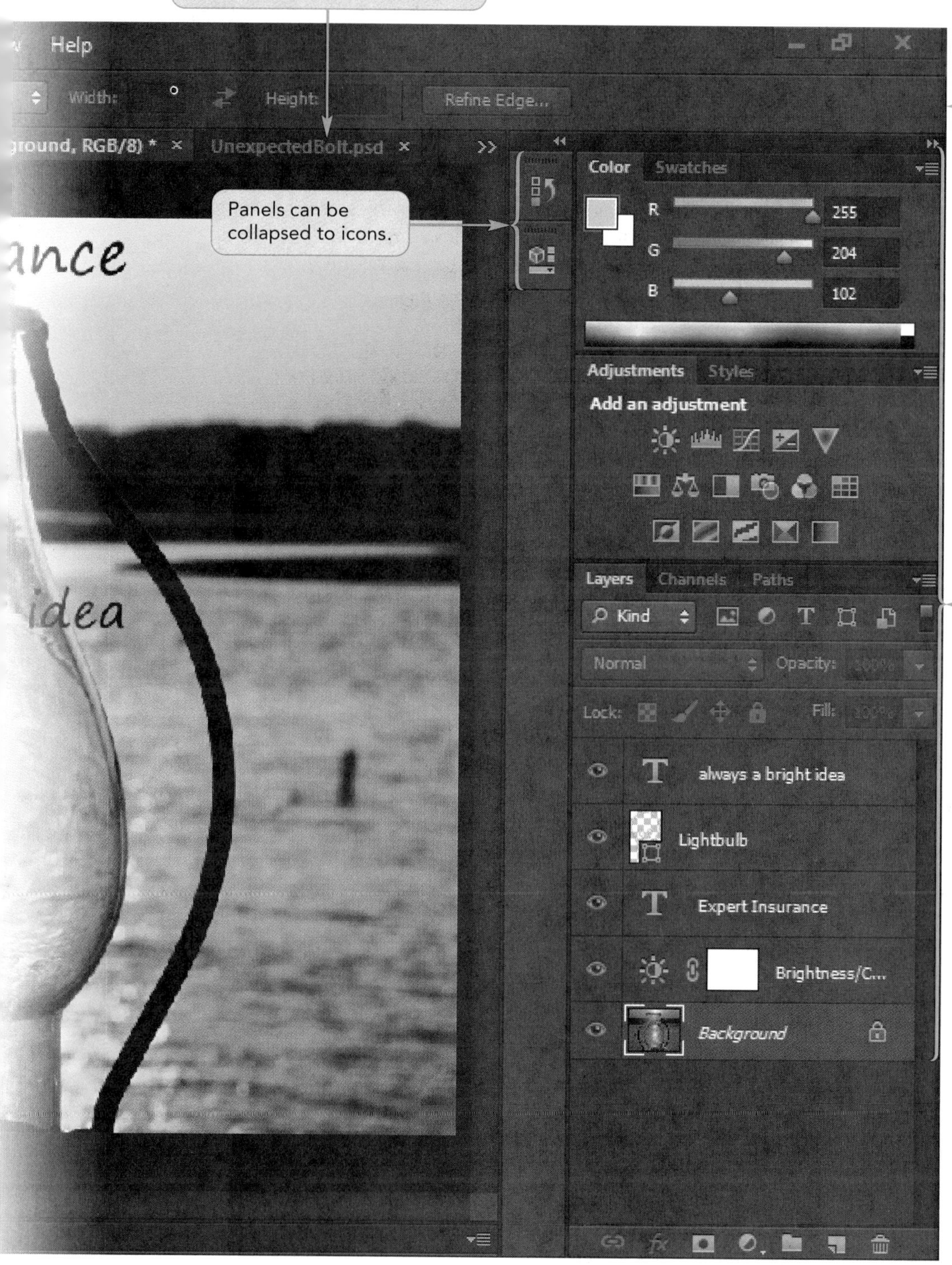

If your screen resolution is higher than 1024 × 768, the Workspace Switcher button appears here; you can use it to access the same commands that are available via the Window/Workspace commands on the menu bar.

Panels consist of groups of related tools.

Introducing Graphics and Photoshop CS6

Over 20 years ago, Photoshop 1.0 was released exclusively for the Macintosh operating system. It has since become a standard for both Mac and PC image editing, and it is widely used by graphics professionals at advertising and graphic design agencies, news organizations, educational institutions, nonprofit organizations, and countless other businesses. Over the years, the product's name has even morphed from a noun to a verb, and graphics professionals now routinely *Photoshop* images to sell products, market ideas, and educate consumers.

How Graphics Are Used to Enhance Communications

Think for a moment about how images are used every day in print and Web media. You might use an image to add interest to a printed page by illustrating a story or by showing a product. You might also use an image to teach the mechanics of something—for example, an image of someone kneading bread dough in a cookbook or of someone changing an oil filter in a how-to book on car repair. Images are an important part of how we communicate—and they always have been, from cave drawings to digital photography. This fact explains a great deal about the appeal of Photoshop. Using Photoshop, you can remove the flaws in an image, refine its color and contrast, and modify it in a variety of other ways. You can also compose something completely new by combining digital photographs, text, and other artwork—all in Photoshop. And with the popularity of mobile devices and apps, you can instantly share your composition with relatives, friends, or colleagues—a feat that was unimaginable only a decade ago.

The Role of Photoshop in Professional Production

Since its inception, Photoshop has grown from a relatively straightforward digital image-editing program to a multifaceted, powerful tool used in many industries, from professional photography to Web design to advertising. A **digital image** is a photograph or drawing in electronic form—in other words, a digital image can be displayed on a computer monitor or on the LCD screen of a camera or mobile device. An **image-editing program** is software that lets you manipulate a digital image and then save it with the changes you have made. Many enhancements and adjustments can be achieved with the click of a mouse. Figure 1-1 shows two versions of a photograph enhanced merely by adding an adjustment and applying a filter. Furthermore, Photoshop lets you save images in different file formats—using different color settings and different resolutions depending on whether your output will be print or digital media.

Figure 1-1 **Image enhanced in Photoshop**

a simple adjustment and filter can dramatically alter a photograph

original photograph

Jane Hosie-Bounar

Mirabeau Media's newest client is a small, local insurance company interested in running an ad campaign that will help it expand its business nationally. Sarah has asked you to learn the basics of digital photography and Photoshop so you can help her mock up a series of proposed ads for the business.

Bitmap vs. Vector Graphics

Digital images consist of two types of graphics—bitmap and vector. A **bitmap** graphic (also called a **raster** graphic) consists of closely spaced rows of pixels, the smallest element in a digital image. Each **pixel** (short for *picture element*) is a square that defines a color. Multiple pixels laid out in a rectangular grid give the illusion of continuity and smoothness in an image. They are the building blocks of any image. The human eye cannot distinguish between pixels unless the image is enlarged so much or the quality is so poor that the individual pixels and the spaces between them are visible. See Figure 1-2.

Resolution is the level of detail in an image, and it is measured in pixels per inch (ppi). The higher the resolution (the more pixels per inch), the sharper the image appears. The default resolution for a Web image is 72 ppi, which is also the default resolution for a new file created in Photoshop. If you plan to use an image for anything other than a Web page, you should create your new Photoshop file with a higher resolution. For example, the resolution required for a professional-quality printed photograph is usually around 300 ppi.

Figure 1-2 Comparing pixels in an enlarged bitmap image

square pixels spaced closely together provide the illusion of continuity
pixels can be seen as squares or jagged edges in an image when it is enlarged

The **file size** of a digital image is dependent both on its resolution and on its physical dimensions. For example, a 300-ppi photo that is 4 by 6 inches has a smaller file size than a 300-ppi photo that is 8 by 12 inches. Photoshop calculates file size by multiplying the number of pixels running across an image by the number of pixels running down an image. Because there are usually millions of pixels in an image, we often use the term **megapixel** (mega means millions) when we talk about file size.

A **vector** graphic is a collection of points, lines, curves, and shapes stored as a set of mathematical instructions. You can create vector graphics in a drawing program such as Adobe Illustrator, but you can also create them in Photoshop, which includes a number of vector tools in its Tools panel. The mathematical instructions in a vector graphic define the lines and curves that make up the graphic. They also define the object's colors and its position on the screen. Text is one example of a vector graphic. You can compose images in Photoshop that include both vector and bitmap graphics. Because of the way vector graphics are stored on a computer, you can resize them proportionally and maintain their quality. See Figure 1-3.

Figure 1-3 Enlarged bitmap loses quality but vector stays crisp

when enlarged, the vector image remains crisp, whereas the bitmap image becomes blurry
bitmap and vector images are both clear at the proper resolution

PROSKILLS

Decision Making: Knowing When Enough Is Enough

Photoshop is a fun program to work with, and by using its features correctly and in moderation you can create interesting and exciting compositions. However, because Photoshop's image-editing possibilities are limitless, it is easy to get carried away. As a Photoshop user in the business world, it will be your responsibility to decide when an image is finished. For example, if you are providing artwork for a repair manual, your photographs should be clear representations of the device and its workings. Fancying up a repair manual with special effects photography would be counterproductive and a waste of your time. On the other hand, sometimes altering a photograph or combining it with another actually makes it stronger. For example, a photograph might be in need of minor color or brightness adjustments to improve its appearance. An image for an advertisement might need to be altered drastically so that the product you are showcasing stands out. As you decide how to manipulate an image in Photoshop, you should keep three things in mind: the message, the client, and the intended audience. Careful decision making will produce positive results.

Now that you have a better sense of what kinds of graphics you can work with in Photoshop, Sarah suggests that you start Photoshop and explore the workspace.

Starting Photoshop and Touring the Photoshop Workspace

TIP

You can restore Photoshop's defaults by pressing and holding the Ctrl+Alt+Shift keys while starting the application.

When you start Photoshop CS6 for the first time, it opens with the default workspace displayed. In subsequent sessions, restarting Photoshop will display the workspace and settings that were in effect when you exited your last session. The **workspace** includes every element of the Photoshop program window, including the Document window, panels, and other elements that you'll explore in this tutorial.

TIP

Depending on your screen resolution, some elements may have a different appearance in your Photoshop window.

To start Photoshop and view the Photoshop program window:

1. Click the **Start** button on the taskbar, click **All Programs**, and then click **Adobe Photoshop CS6** while pressing and holding the **Ctrl+Alt+Shift** keys. When you are prompted to delete the Adobe Photoshop settings, click **Yes**.

   Trouble? If you see an Adobe Creative Suite name, such as Adobe Design Premium CS6, listed before Adobe Photoshop CS6 on the All Programs menu, click the suite name and then click Adobe Photoshop CS6.

   Trouble? If you can't find Adobe Photoshop CS6 on the All Programs menu, navigate to the Adobe folder in the Program Files folder on your hard drive, double-click the Adobe Photoshop CS6 folder, and then double-click Photoshop.exe.

   Trouble? If a User Account Control dialog box appears asking if you want to allow Photoshop to make changes to your computer, click No. Then, restart Photoshop, making sure to press and hold the Ctrl+Alt+Shift keys immediately *after* clicking Adobe Photoshop CS6 so you are prompted to delete the Photoshop settings file.

   Trouble? If the Adobe Product Activation dialog box opens, click the appropriate option button, click Continue, enter the information requested, and then click the Register button. If you do not know your serial number or need additional assistance, ask your instructor or technical support person for help.

Trouble? If you see a message about a problem with the display driver on your computer, click the OK button.

The Photoshop program window opens and displays the default workspace, which is called Essentials. The largest area of the workspace, the Document window, is empty.

TIP

If you're working at a resolution greater than 1024 × 768, you can also click the Workspace Switcher button on the right side of the options bar to access the Workspace commands.

2. On the menu bar, click **Window**, point to **Workspace**, and then click **Reset Essentials** to reset the default workspace layout. On the far left side of the options bar, right-click the **Rectangular Marquee Tool** button, and then click **Reset All Tools**. When you are asked if you want to reset all tools to the default settings, click the **OK** button.

3. If necessary, click the **Maximize** button on the title bar to maximize the Photoshop program window. See Figure 1-4.

Figure 1-4 **Photoshop program window**

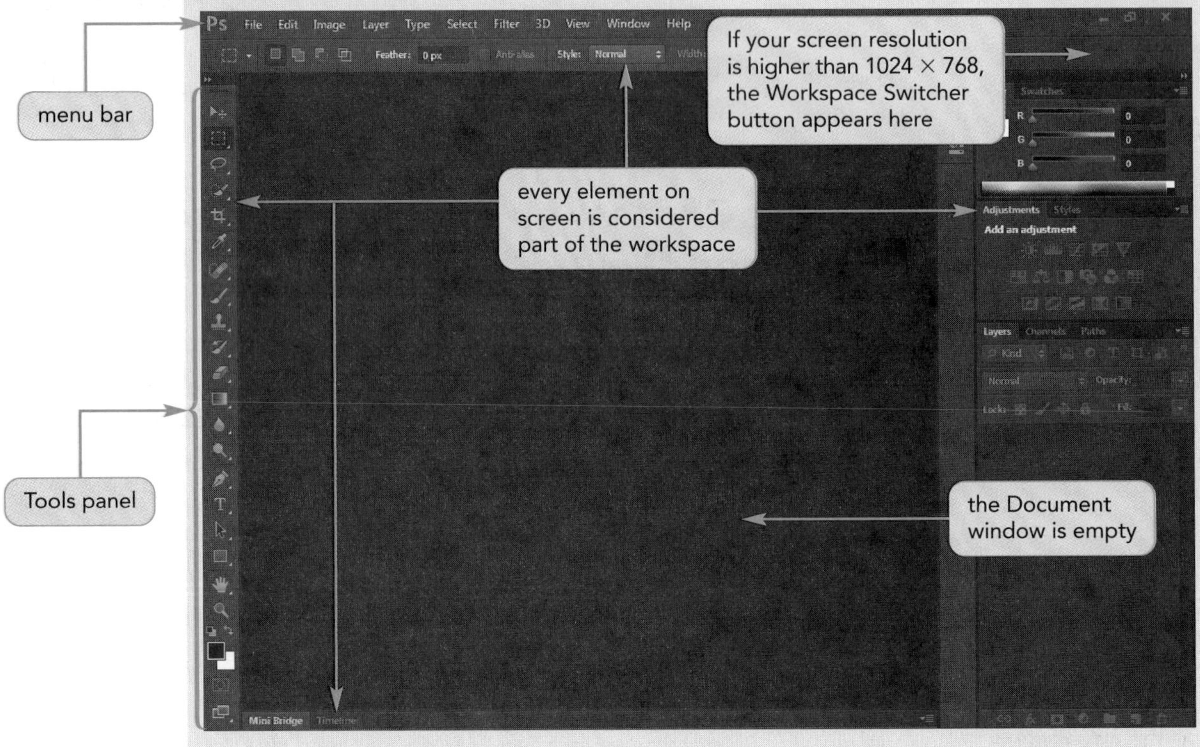
menu bar
Tools panel
If your screen resolution is higher than 1024 × 768, the Workspace Switcher button appears here
every element on screen is considered part of the workspace
the Document window is empty

Opening a File

You open a file in Photoshop using the File command on the menu bar. Sarah has given you two Photoshop files that you can open to begin exploring Photoshop.

To open the files and tour the Photoshop workspace:

1. On the menu bar, click **File**, and then click **Open**. The Open dialog box opens.

2. Navigate to the Photoshop1\Tutorial folder included with your Data Files, click **LightningInsurance.psd** in the files list, and then click the **Open** button. The LightningInsurance document opens in the Document window.

   Trouble? If you don't have the starting Data Files, you need to get them before you can proceed. Your instructor will either give you the Data Files or ask you to obtain them from a specified location (such as a network drive). In either case, make a backup copy of the Data Files before you start so that you will have the original files available in case you need to start over. If you have any questions about the Data Files, see your instructor or technical support person for assistance.

   So that you can see how Photoshop handles multiple open files at a time, you'll also open a second file.

3. On the menu bar, click **File**, and then click **Open**. The Open dialog box opens.

   Because the last file you opened was in the Photoshop1\Tutorial folder, the Open dialog box opens to the Photoshop1\Tutorial folder.

4. Double-click **ExpertInsurance.psd**. The ExpertInsurance file opens on a new tab in the Document window, but you can still see the LightningInsurance file's tab behind the current tab. See Figure 1-5.

Figure 1-5 Most recently opened file is visible

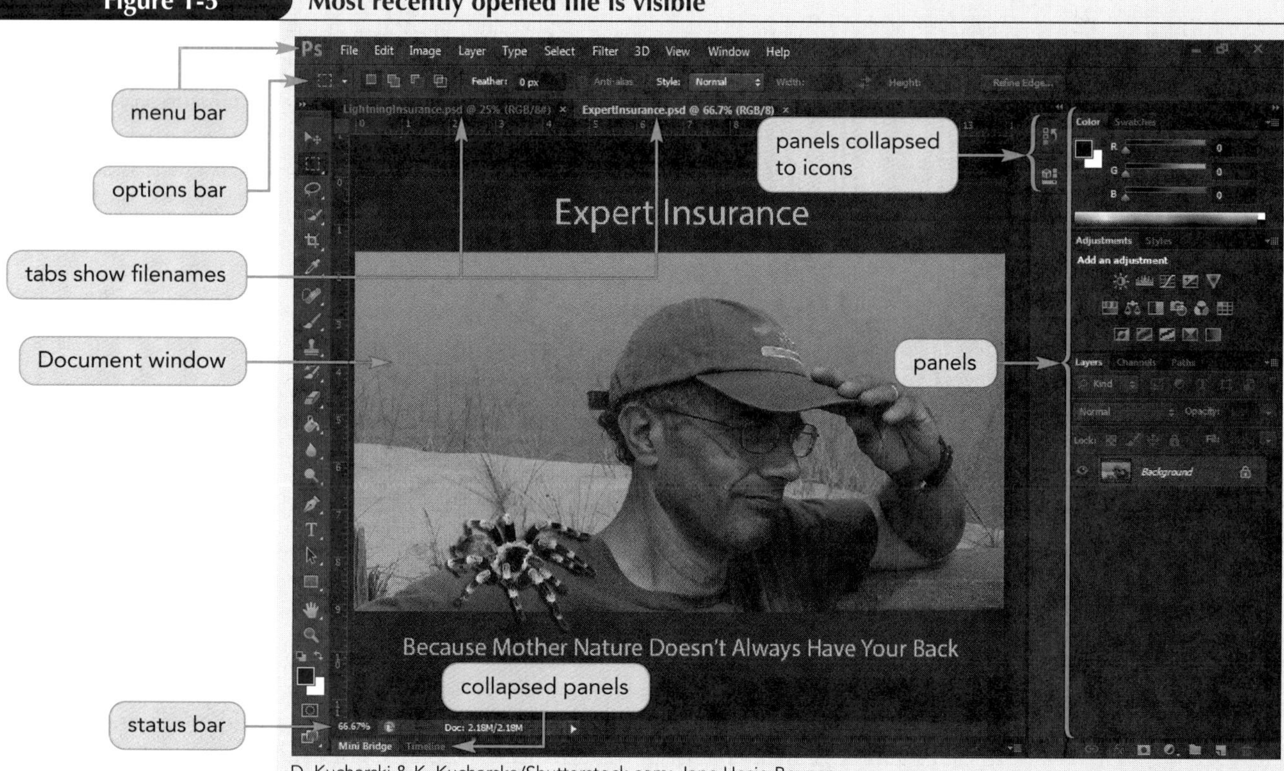

D. Kucharski & K. Kucharska/Shutterstock.com; Jane Hosie-Bounar

You opened two files so that you could see how the Photoshop tools and panels are laid out around the Document window, which contains the images you'll be working with. Now you'll tour the Photoshop workspace so you understand the function of its different elements.

Touring the Photoshop Workspace

The main components of the Photoshop workspace are the menu bar, the Tools panel, the options bar, the Document window, and any panels displayed in the currently selected workspace. In the Essentials workspace, the default panels are Color, Swatches, Adjustments, Styles, Layers, Channels, and Paths. The History and Properties panels also appear, but they are collapsed. (The Properties panel is new to Photoshop CS6 and is covered in detail in Tutorial 2.) At the bottom of the Photoshop workspace, the Mini Bridge and Timeline panels appear, also collapsed. You'll explore all of these panels in later sessions as you work toward becoming a Photoshop expert.

Menu Bar

The menu bar displays a list of 11 commands that open drop-down menus, similar to the menus you find in other applications. To select a menu command, you can either click the command, or press the Alt key and then press the key for the letter you see underlined on the menu bar. Figure 1-6 describes the commands found on the menu bar.

Figure 1-6 **Menu bar**

Menu Name	Use To
File	Browse files in Bridge and Mini Bridge; open, close, and save files; import and export files; print and perform other file-related commands; and exit Photoshop
Edit	Undo and redo changes; cut, copy, and paste objects; transform and format objects; assign and convert color profiles; and adjust user preferences
Image	Change the color mode; apply image adjustments; adjust image and canvas size; rotate, crop, and trim an image; and use other analysis tools
Layer	Add, duplicate, arrange, group, and ungroup layers; merge layers; align and distribute layers; and create layer-based slices for the Web; among other things
Type	Work with characters, paragraphs, fonts, and languages on text layers
Select	Save, edit, refine, and transform selections
Filter	Apply a filter to a layer or a selection; and browse online for additional filters
3D	Work with 3D layers and effects
View	Work with proofing tools; adjust the zoom level of a displayed image; change the screen modes; and display and hide rulers and guides
Window	Arrange windows; switch workspaces; and display and hide different panels
Help	Access local and online help; get software updates; and participate in online Photoshop community discussions

Tools Panel

TIP

To display the Tools panel in two columns, click the double arrows directly above the panel. To go back to a one-column display, click the double arrows again.

The Tools panel contains tools for creating vector images such as geometric shapes, selecting portions of a document, adding text, adding brushstrokes, and modifying pixels in bitmap images. Related tools are grouped in the panel. For example, tools for selecting pixels and colors appear in the top section. You can display the Tools panel as a single column (the default) or in two columns. When you point to a tool in the Tools panel, Photoshop displays a **tooltip**, which includes the name of the tool plus any shortcut key for selecting the tool. For example, the shortcut key for selecting the Zoom tool is Z.

The Tools panel also includes hidden tools. In fact, any tool with a small triangle displayed in the lower-right corner has other tools hidden beneath it, as shown in the Session 1.1 Visual Overview. To display a list of hidden tools, point to the top-level tool in the Toolbar, click and hold the mouse button, and then click the tool you want to make active.

Options Bar

The options bar includes the controls, or options, for the current tool. For example, if you select the Horizontal Type tool in the Tools panel, Photoshop displays options for text orientation, font, style, and size, among others. If you are working at a resolution higher than 1024 × 768, the options bar also displays the Workspace Switcher, which you use to create a new workspace, delete a workspace, reset a workspace, or switch to a different workspace.

Document Window

The Document window displays the current file. When you have multiple files open, the Document window displays each filename on a tab along the top of the window by default. Clicking a tab displays the document named on the tab. You can also use the Arrange command on the Window menu to display open files tiled in a grid or side by side vertically or horizontally. As soon as you open a file in the Document window, the status bar appears near the lower-left corner of the window. By default, the status bar displays the current zoom percentage as well as the document size (in kilobytes or megapixels). You can change what is displayed on the status bar by clicking the arrow to the right of the document size, and then clicking the information you want to display (for example, the document dimensions or the name of the currently selected tool).

Panels

Panels consist of groups of related tools. For example, the Swatches panel displays samples of colors available in the current color mode and stores the most frequently used colors. You can change the set of swatches displayed in the panel or add your own swatches to an existing set. The Adjustments panel lets you modify your images by adjusting different settings, such as brightness and contrast, or by changing a photograph from color to black and white. You'll explore panels and how to arrange them in Session 1.2.

Sarah suggests you make use of Photoshop's Help system to help you master the features of Photoshop. You decide to spend time exploring Help now so that you can use it efficiently in the future.

Getting Help in Photoshop

Photoshop includes an online Help system that lets you access information posted by Adobe as well as information posted by members of **Adobe Community Help**, a forum where you can find resources such as tips, videos, and other information from professional photographers and designers willing to share their insights. Some of the topics are written by Adobe and Adobe partners, but others are not. To access Help, you can use the Photoshop Online Help command on the Help menu, or you can press the F1 key.

When you first open Adobe Help using the Photoshop Online Help command, Photoshop displays a list of topics in the browser window. You can explore Adobe-authored Help by clicking the links. You can also search for specific information by typing a term in the Search Help box on the left. When you click a link, the relevant information is displayed.

You'll explore Help to find more about workspaces in Photoshop.

TIP

You can also press the F1 key to access Photoshop Help.

To get help in Photoshop:

1. On the menu bar, click **Help**, and then click **Photoshop Online Help**. The Photoshop Help/Help and tutorials window opens in your browser. See Figure 1-7.

Figure 1-7 Adobe Community Help

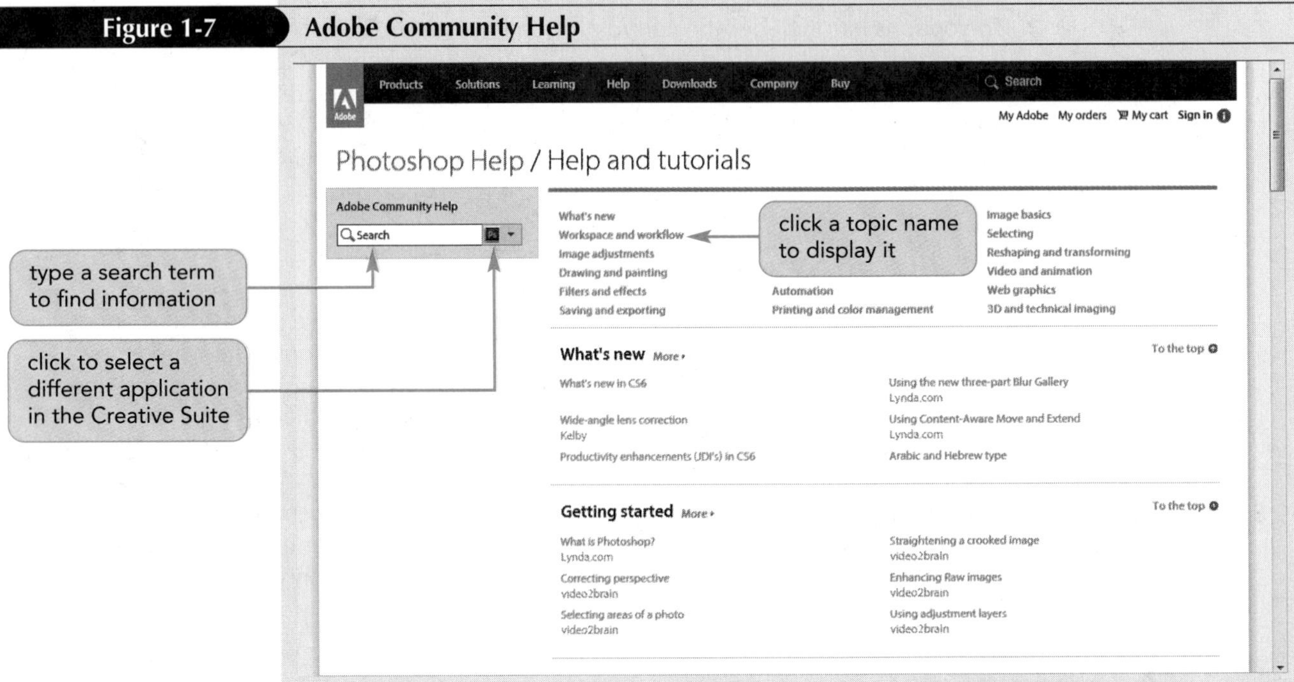

2. In the list of topics on the right, click **Workspace and workflow**, and then click **Workspace basics**.

3. Click **Manage windows and panels**. Photoshop displays detailed information about managing windows and panels. See Figure 1-8.

Figure 1-8 Help topic

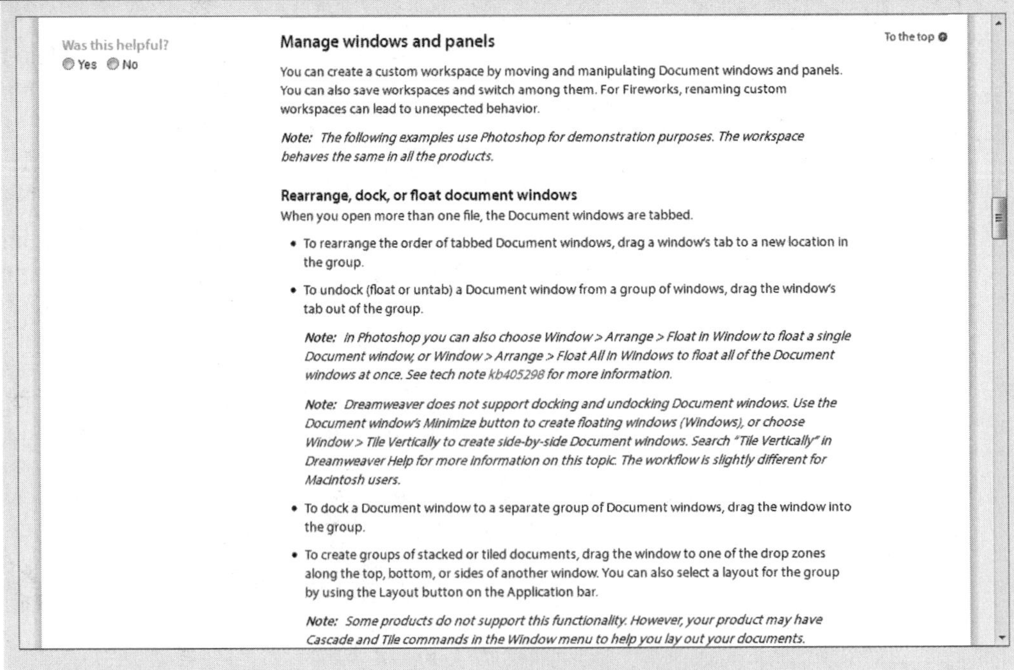

4. Scroll through and read the **Rearrange, dock, or float document windows** topic. Photoshop shows detailed information about working with Document windows. Notice that some of the information presented is about other products in the Adobe Creative Suite. Once you know how to manage the elements in Photoshop, you will recognize many of the same elements in other Adobe products, such as Dreamweaver.

5. Click the Close button [X] on the Adobe Community Help window title bar to close your browser. The Help system closes, and the Photoshop program window is now displayed.

INSIGHT

Searching for Information and Using External Help

You can use the Help system to search the Web for information on using Adobe Photoshop. To do so, at the top of the Help browser window, type a term in the Search box and then press the Enter key. Keep in mind that when you do this, the information you find is not necessarily approved by Adobe (even though it appears in the Search results) and, therefore, might not be as accurate as the information within the Help system itself. For the most reliable help, click the Only Adobe content option button above the list of search results.

Now that you have a sense of how to find information about any tool you need to use in Photoshop, you'll practice working with multiple files.

Working with Multiple Files

Photoshop not only allows you to edit and transform existing images, but it also lets you combine elements to create a completely new photo composition. When you do this kind of complex work, you will most likely need to have multiple files open at one time. You open, save, and close Photoshop files in the same way you perform file-handling tasks in many other applications, so some of the commands might be familiar to you.

REFERENCE

Opening Multiple Files at Once

- On the menu bar, click File, and then click Open (or press the Ctrl+O keys).
- To open contiguous files (files listed next to each other), click the first filename, press and hold the Shift key, click the last filename, and then release the Shift key.
- To open noncontiguous files, click the first filename, press and hold the Ctrl key, and then click any other file(s) in the list.
- Click Open (or press the Enter key).

Sarah has given you a number of photographs and photo compositions that she wants you to review so that you can better understand the power of Photoshop.

To open multiple files:

1. On the menu bar, click **File**, and then click **Open**. The Open dialog box opens. You can select multiple files and apply the Open command to all of them at once.

Be sure to press the Ctrl key and not the Shift key. If you press the Shift key, all the files in between will be selected as well.

2. Navigate to the Photoshop1\Tutorial folder included with your Data Files, if necessary. Click **FireInsurance.psd**, press and hold the **Ctrl** key, scroll down the files list, if necessary, and then click **UnexpectedBolt.psd**.

3. Click the **Open** button. Photoshop opens both files at once, each on its own tab in the Document window. See Figure 1-9.

Figure 1-9 **Multiple open files**

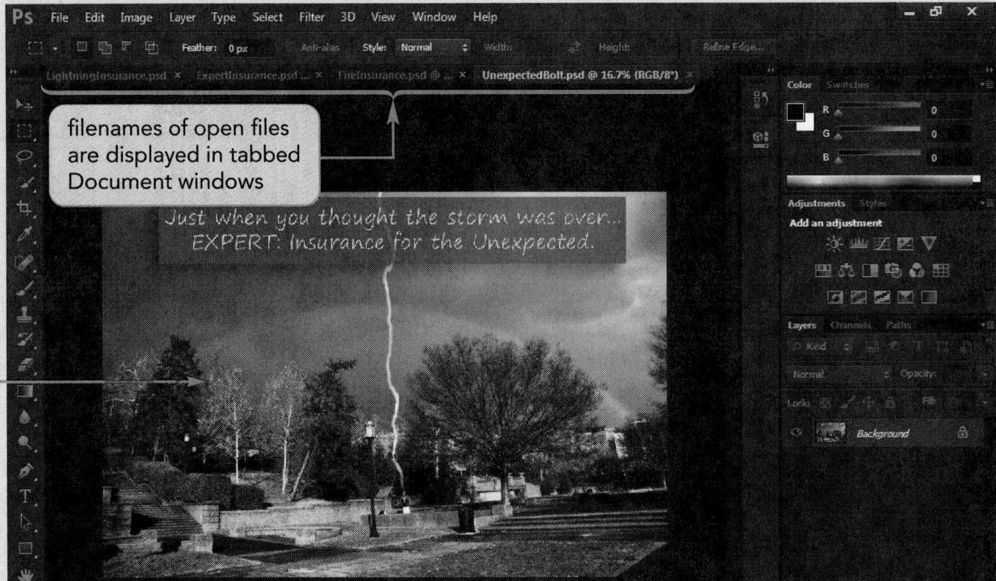
filenames of open files are displayed in tabbed Document windows
the last file you selected is visible
Just when you thought the storm was over...
EXPERT: Insurance for the Unexpected.

© 2012 Chadwick Cipiti/DCNature.com

The last file you selected, UnexpectedBolt, is visible. The other file you selected, FireInsurance, is behind it, as are the two files you opened previously, ExpertInsurance and LightningInsurance.

Sarah explains that because you will often modify files in Photoshop, it is best to preserve the original file so that you can reuse it or backtrack if you make and then save unwanted changes. Therefore, she asks you to save the UnexpectedBolt file with a new name.

Saving a File with a New Name

When you save files in Photoshop, you have many different options. You can save a file with the same name and file format (for example, JPEG), which overwrites the original file. You can save a file with a new name in the same file format. You can also save a file with a new name in a new format. No matter which option you choose, it is best to save your work often in Photoshop so you don't lose your changes should something unexpected occur.

TIP

You can also press the Shift+Ctrl+S keys to open the Save As dialog box.

To save a file with a new name:

1. Make sure the **UnexpectedBolt** tab is selected in the workspace, and then on the menu bar, click **File**, and then click **Save As**. The Save As dialog box opens. You can save the file in a different format, or as a copy of the original file. You'll explore a number of these save options in later tutorials, but for now, you'll save the file in the same format, with a new name.

Trouble? If the Photoshop Format Options dialog box opens, click the OK button to accept the default options to maximize compatibility.

2. Select the text in the File name box, and then type **NewUnexpected** to overwrite the existing filename. You don't need to type the .psd file extension because Photoshop automatically adds the selected file type's extension to the filename.
3. Click the **Save** button. Photoshop saves the file with a new name. To confirm that the original file is still intact, you can open the Open dialog box.
4. Press the **Ctrl+O** keys, navigate to the Photoshop1\Tutorial folder and then scroll to the bottom of the files list, if necessary. Notice that the new file, NewUnexpected, and the original file, UnexpectedBolt, both appear in the files list in the Tutorial folder. Any changes that you make to the newly saved file will not affect the original.
5. Click the **Cancel** button to close the Open dialog box.

Now that you've practiced opening and saving files, Sarah explains that you need to learn how to best arrange the Document windows and navigate through open files so you can work efficiently in Photoshop.

Navigating and Arranging File Windows

Photoshop provides many different ways to navigate through and arrange the files you are working with. You can navigate by clicking the Document window tabs, or you can use predefined key combinations. You can also use a menu to select a file and switch to it.

Navigating Open File Windows and Changing Tab Order

You can move from one open file to another by clicking the Document window tabs. Photoshop also provides two key combinations for navigating open files. Pressing the Ctrl+Tab keys cycles through the open files in the order in which they were opened. Pressing the Ctrl+Shift+Tab keys cycles through the open files in reverse.

To navigate the open file windows:

1. Click the **LightningInsurance** Document window tab. Photoshop displays the LightningInsurance photograph.
2. Click the **ExpertInsurance** tab.
3. Press the **Ctrl+Tab** keys. Photoshop displays the FireInsurance document.
4. Press and hold the **Ctrl+Shift** keys, and then press the **Tab** key two times. Photoshop cycles through the files in reverse order.
5. On the menu bar, click **File**, click **Open Recent**, and then click **UnexpectedBolt.psd**. Because you have more files open in the Document window than Photoshop has room to display tabs, a new window element appears on the right side of the tab area—a double arrow pointing to the right.
6. Click the **double arrow** >>. Photoshop displays a list of all open files. The active file has a check mark next to the filename. See Figure 1-10.

Trouble? Your view might vary depending on the size and resolution of your monitor. Such differences shouldn't cause problems as you complete these steps. However, if you don't see the double arrow », read but don't perform Step 6.

Figure 1-10 Open file list displayed

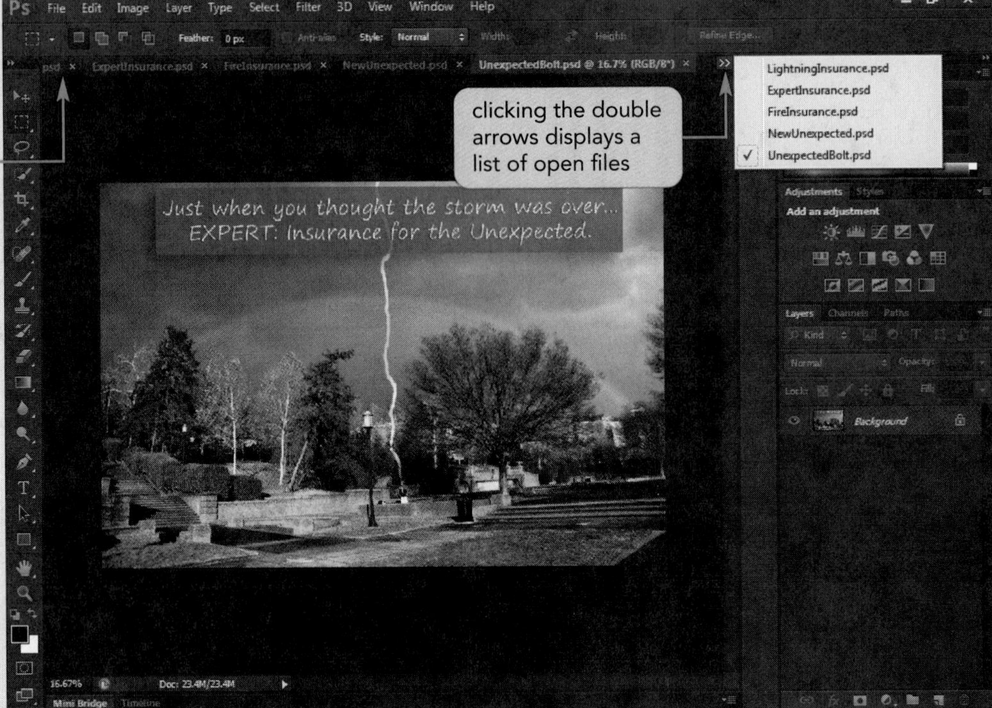
the workspace window does not have room to completely display all of the tabs for the open files
clicking the double arrows displays a list of open files
File Edit Image Layer Type Select Filter 3D View Window Help
LightningInsurance.psd
ExpertInsurance.psd
FireInsurance.psd
NewUnexpected.psd
UnexpectedBolt.psd
Just when you thought the storm was over...
EXPERT: Insurance for the Unexpected.

© 2012 Chadwick Cipiti/DCNature.com

You can display an image by clicking its name on the list.

7. In the list of open files, click **LightningInsurance**, which is the file whose tab you cannot see. Photoshop displays the LightningInsurance image.

You might want to change the order of tabs in the Document window so you can navigate more easily between related files. You can change the tab order by clicking and dragging the tabs with the mouse.

To change the tab order:

1. Point to the **LightningInsurance** tab, click and hold the mouse button, and then drag to the right along the tab bar until the LightningInsurance tab appears to the right of the FireInsurance tab. See Figure 1-11.

Figure 1-11 Moving a tab

the LightningInsurance tab now appears to the right of the FireInsurance tab

2. Release the mouse button.

   Dragging a tab changes its position, but it does not change the order in which you cycle through the files using the shortcut keys. They will always cycle from first opened to last opened when you press the Ctrl+Tab key combination.

Arranging File Windows

You can arrange file windows so that multiple files appear in the Document window at one time. You can display images in floating Document windows and drag them around the workspace, or you can arrange the files using the commands on the Arrange Documents menu.

Next, you'll explore how to work with floating Document windows, and then you'll arrange the windows in one of the arrangement choices provided by Photoshop.

To float the Document window:

1. Point to the **ExpertInsurance** tab, click and hold the mouse button, drag the tab down to the middle of the workspace, and release the mouse button. The Document window "detaches" from the other tabs and appears in its own free-floating Document window. See Figure 1-12.

Figure 1-12 **Free-floating Document window**

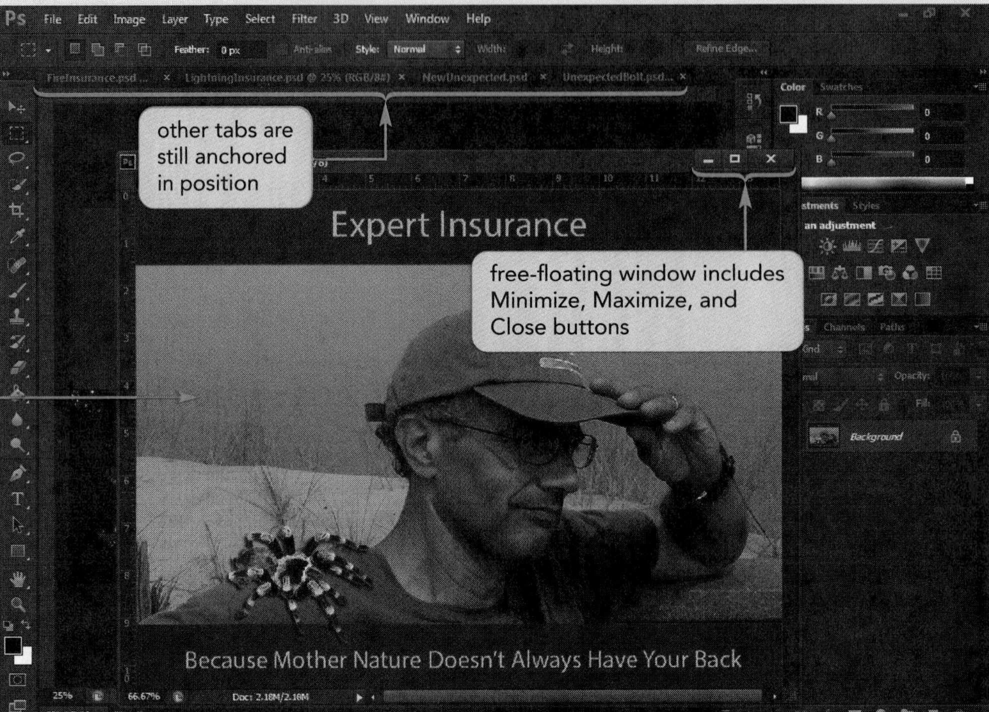

2. Click the **Minimize** button in the floating Document window title bar. The ExpertInsurance window seems to disappear from the Photoshop program window.
3. Point to the **Photoshop** program icon on the Windows 7 taskbar, and you will see that the ExpertInsurance document is still there, but minimized. Click the thumbnail. The ExpertInsurance Document window is restored to its floating size.
4. Click the **Maximize** button for the ExpertInsurance file. The file is maximized in its own window and covers the Photoshop program window.
5. Click the **Restore** button. The file again floats in its own Document window.
6. Point to the title bar of the floating Document window, click and hold the mouse button, and then drag the Document window up to the tabs until the window is surrounded by a blue outline. Release the mouse button. The ExpertInsurance Document window is now one of the tabbed windows.

Photoshop also provides a variety of predefined arrangements for viewing your open documents. You can find the different choices on the Arrange Documents menu.

To arrange the documents using the Arrange Documents menu:

1. On the menu bar, click **Window**, and then point to **Arrange**. Photoshop displays a menu of options with icons, each representing a window arrangement, as well as a series of commands for displaying your files in the Document window. The available options change based on the number of open files. For example, notice that the 6-up command is grayed out because you have fewer than six windows open. The default arrangement is Consolidate All to Tabs, which is the arrangement you have been working in.
2. Click **Tile**. Photoshop arranges the Document window so that all open files are visible. Notice that Photoshop does not change the zoom levels for any of the images. It merely fits each file in a smaller window so that less of each image is visible.
3. On the menu bar, click **Window**, point to **Arrange**, and then click **2-up Vertical** . Photoshop arranges the topmost file and the next file in the tab order into two windows in the Document window. You can view the other open files by clicking the double arrow to display the files list. See Figure 1-13.

Figure 1-13 2-up Vertical arrangement

click the double arrow to see the list of open files

click to access the Arrange command for window arrangement options

the 2-up Vertical arrangement shows two Document windows side by side

D. Kucharski & K. Kucharska/Shutterstock.com; Jane Hosie-Bounar; A. H. Bounar

4. On the menu bar, click **Window**, point to **Arrange**, and then click **Float All in Windows**. Photoshop stacks all of the files in free-floating Document windows. To navigate these windows, you click their title bars.
5. Click the **LightningInsurance** title bar. The LightningInsurance Document window moves to the front. See Figure 1-14.

Figure 1-14 Stacked floating windows

click a window title bar to display the file; your file arrangement might be different

© 2012 Brian Gratwicke/DCNature.com; D. Kucharski & K. Kucharska/Shutterstock.com; Jane Hosie-Bounar

Although you can no longer see the title bars of the other files, and there is no double-headed arrow displayed, you can still access these files using the Window menu.

6. On the menu bar, click **Window**, and then click **ExpertInsurance** in the list of files at the bottom of the menu. The ExpertInsurance window is now on top.
7. On the menu bar, click **Window**, point to **Arrange**, and then click **Consolidate All to Tabs** to return to tabbed windows.

Now that you have spent time exploring the Photoshop workspace and have learned some of the basics of working with files and file windows, Sarah suggests you close all the files you have opened.

Closing Files

After you finish working on a file, you should close it. This saves system resources on your computer.

To close all the open files:

1. On the menu bar, click **File**, and then click **Close**. The top file closes.

   Trouble? If you are prompted to save the file, you might have inadvertently changed the file while you were exploring the workspace. Click No to close the file without saving it.

2. Click the **Close** button on the current Document window tab. The file closes.
3. On the menu bar, click **File**, and then click **Close All** to close the rest of the open files. The Photoshop window is now empty. You can open additional files, or you can exit Photoshop.

Exiting Photoshop

If you are no longer working in Photoshop, you should exit the application. This saves system resources as you work in other programs. You can also exit Photoshop without first closing the files. When you do, Photoshop asks you if you want to save any modified files before they are closed.

To exit Photoshop:

1. On the menu bar, click **File**, and then click **Exit**. Photoshop closes.

In this session, you learned how to start Photoshop, and you explored the program window. You also learned how to open and close files, how to find the information you need in Help, how to arrange windows, and how to exit Photoshop.

Now that you know the basics of working with files and Document windows, Sarah asks you to spend time learning about some additional features of Photoshop. In the next session, you will explore preference settings, panels, grids, and guides.

REVIEW

Session 1.1 Quick Check

1. Photoshop is a(n) ______________ program.
2. Explain how a bitmap graphic is different from a vector graphic.
3. The smallest unit in a bitmap graphic is called a(n) ______________.
4. What is the name of the default workspace in Photoshop?
5. The ______________ panel on the left side of the program window provides options for creating and modifying vector graphics and modifying the pixels in bitmap graphics in your Photoshop file.
6. True or False. You can only have one Photoshop file open at a time.
7. The ______________ command on the Window menu lets you tile open documents within the Document window.

SESSION 1.2 VISUAL OVERVIEW

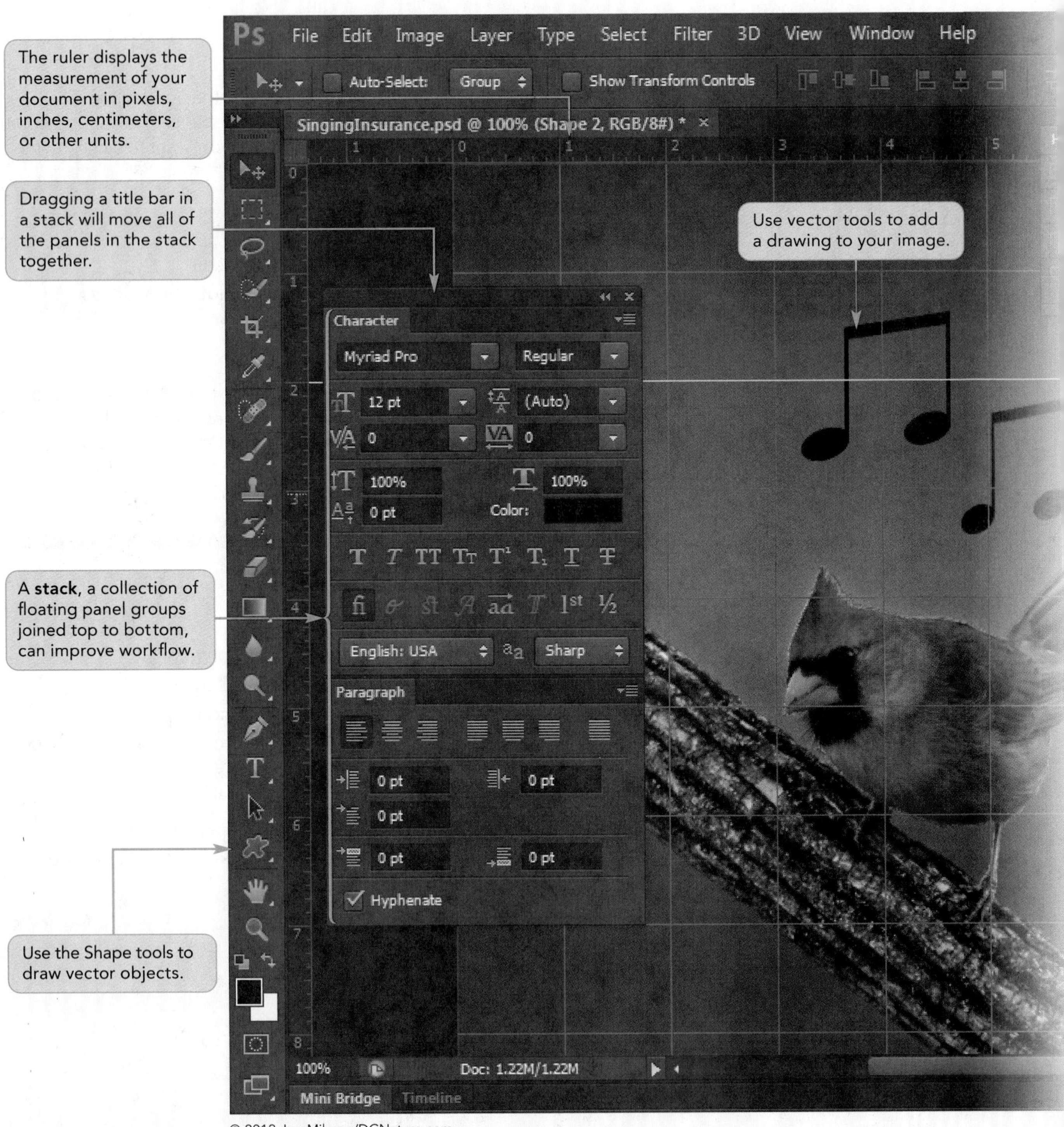
The ruler displays the measurement of your document in pixels, inches, centimeters, or other units.
Dragging a title bar in a stack will move all of the panels in the stack together.
A **stack**, a collection of floating panel groups joined top to bottom, can improve workflow.
Use the Shape tools to draw vector objects.
Use vector tools to add a drawing to your image.
File
Edit
Image
Layer
Type
Select
Filter
3D
View
Window
Help
Auto-Select:
Group
Show Transform Controls
SingingInsurance.psd @ 100% (Shape 2, RGB/8#) *
Character
Myriad Pro
Regular
12 pt
(Auto)
0
0
100%
100%
0 pt
Color:
English: USA
Sharp
Paragraph
0 pt
0 pt
0 pt
0 pt
0 pt
Hyphenate
100%
Doc: 1.22M/1.22M
Mini Bridge
Timeline

GRIDS, GUIDES, AND PANELS

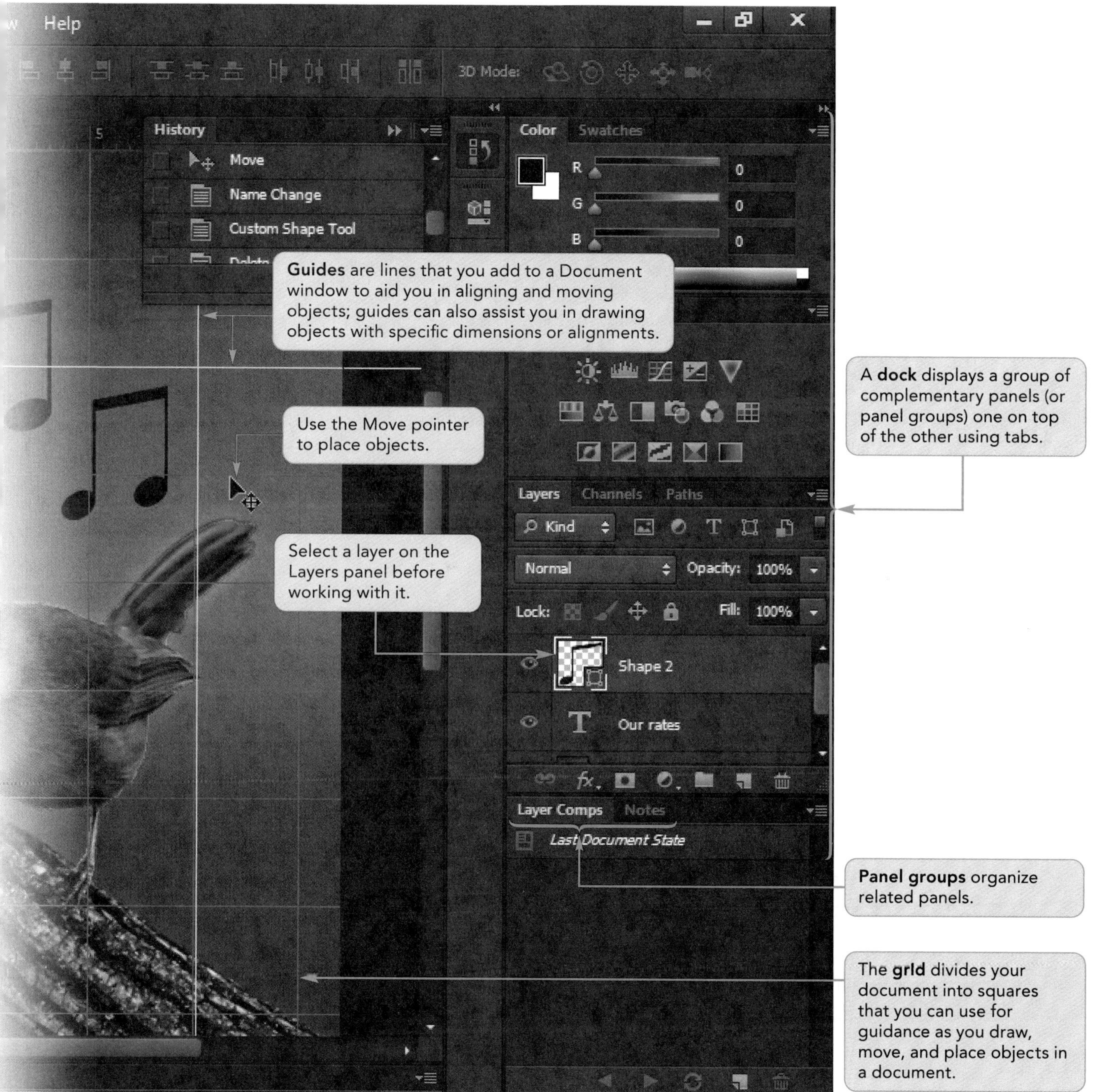

Guides are lines that you add to a Document window to aid you in aligning and moving objects; guides can also assist you in drawing objects with specific dimensions or alignments.

Use the Move pointer to place objects.

Select a layer on the Layers panel before working with it.

A **dock** displays a group of complementary panels (or panel groups) one on top of the other using tabs.

Panel groups organize related panels.

The **grid** divides your document into squares that you can use for guidance as you draw, move, and place objects in a document.

Viewing and Changing Photoshop Preferences

Once you have some experience working with Photoshop, you will find that you develop certain preferences for how the program window is set up. Photoshop lets you customize those preferences and save them for different tasks.

Now that you understand how to arrange and manipulate the display of files in the Document window, Sarah suggests you learn about Photoshop Preferences.

REFERENCE

Setting Photoshop Preferences

- On the menu bar, click Edit, point to Preferences, click General, and then click the Next button until you reach the panel you want to work with.
- Set preferences in the panel, and click the OK button to close the panel and save the preferences, or click the Next button or the Prev button to display the next or previous Preferences panel.

or

- On the menu bar, click Edit, point to Preferences, and then click the name of the panel you want to work with.
- Set preferences in the panel, and click the OK button to close the panel and save the preferences, or click the Next button or the Prev button to display the next or previous Preferences panel.

Photoshop includes plenty of options for customizing its tools, performance, file handling, and interface. Many of those options are covered in later tutorials, but it's important to know that they exist and where to access them so you can use them as your expertise in Photoshop grows.

Sarah suggests that you begin to explore the preferences in Photoshop by changing one of the Preferences settings.

To set Photoshop Preferences:

1. Start Photoshop while pressing the **Ctrl+Alt+Shift** keys. When you are prompted to delete the Adobe Photoshop Settings File, click **Yes**. On the menu bar, click **Window**, point to **Workspace**, and then click **Reset Essentials** to reset the default workspace layout. On the options bar, right-click the **Rectangular Marquee Tool** button, and then click Reset All Tools. When you are asked if you want to reset all tools to the default settings, click the **OK** button.
2. Navigate to the Photoshop1\Tutorial folder, and open the file **SingingInsurance.psd**.
3. On the menu bar, click **Edit**, point to **Preferences**, and then click **General**. All of the preferences are available in different panels of the Preferences dialog box. See Figure 1-15.

Figure 1-15 Preferences dialog box

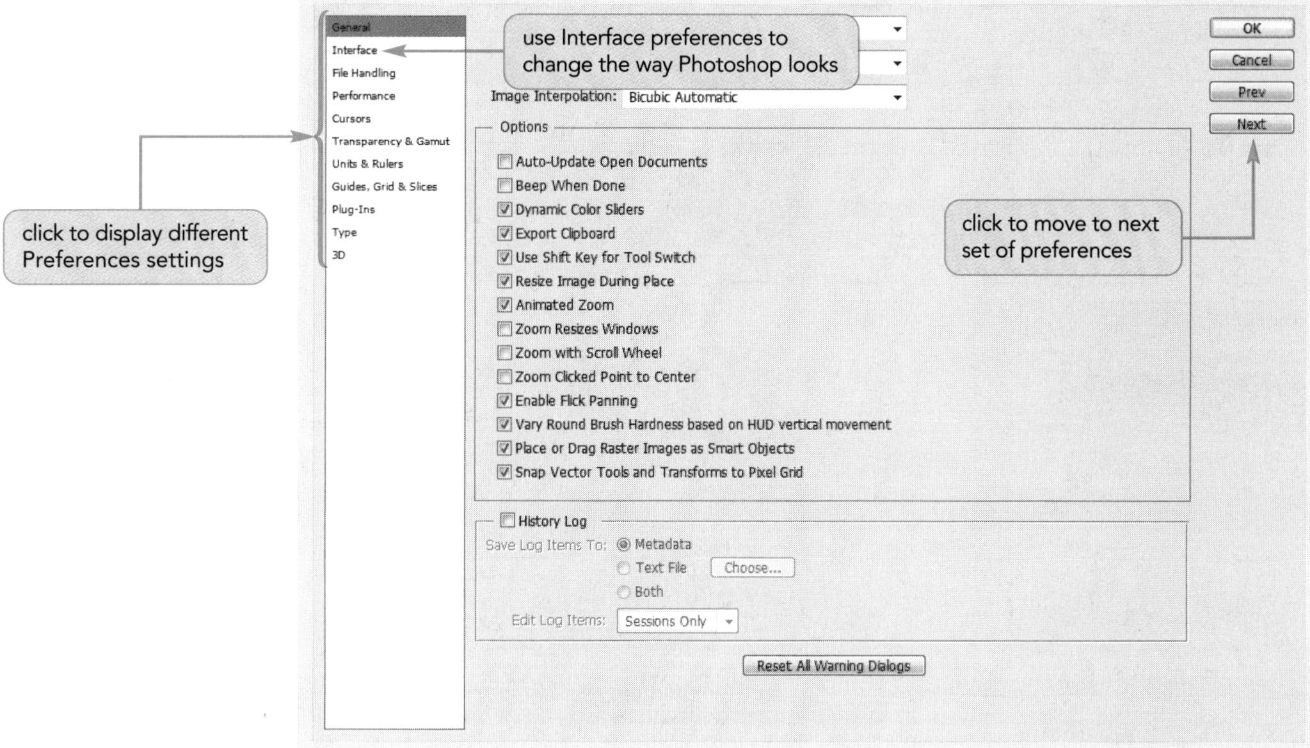

You change panels by clicking panel names in the left pane of the dialog box, or by clicking the Next button or the Prev button in the right pane.

4. In the left pane of the dialog box, click **Interface**. The Interface settings let you change the way Photoshop looks. You will change the color of the standard screen, which is the area that appears around a file.

5. In the Appearance section, click the **Standard Screen Mode Color arrow**, click **Light Gray**, and then click the **OK** button. The area around the document in the Document window is now light gray. See Figure 1-16.

Figure 1-16 Changing an Interface setting

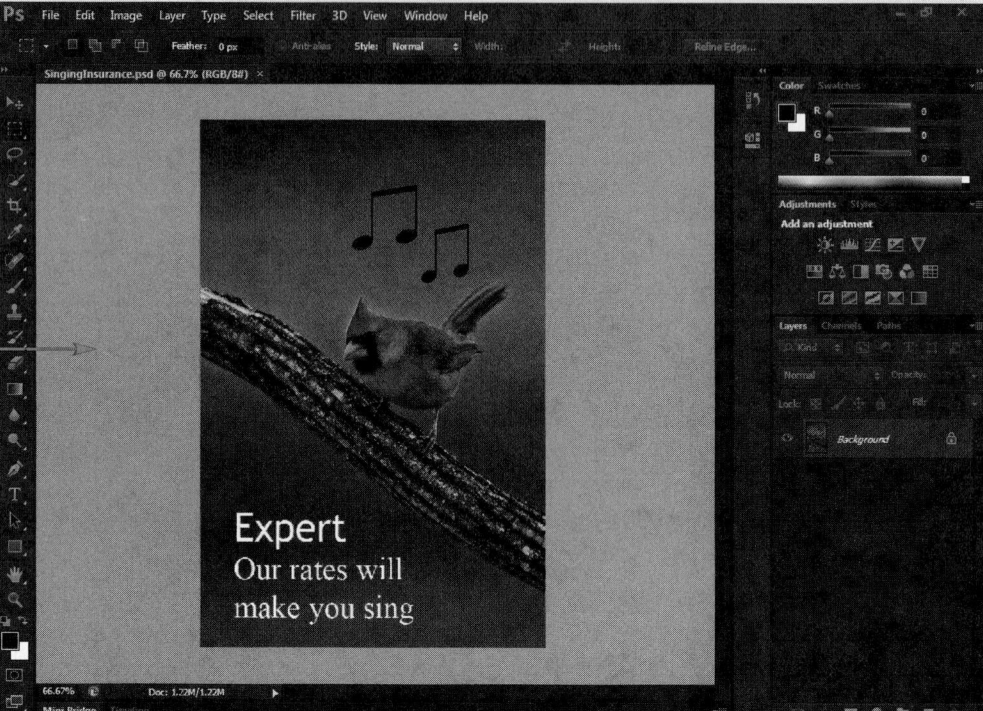
Document window area is light gray instead of dark gray
Expert
Our rates will make you sing

6. On the menu bar, click **Edit**, point to **Preferences**, and then click **Interface**.
7. In the Appearance section, click the **Standard Screen Mode Color arrow**, click **Default**, and then click the **OK** button. The area around the file in the Document window is now dark gray, the default setting.

INSIGHT

Understanding File Handling Preferences

Photoshop CS6 has new file-handling preference settings that let users define how, where, and how often files and file backups are saved. The Save in Background option in the File Handling section of the Preferences dialog box ensures that even in the case of a crash or power failure, you won't lose your work. The Save in Background freature also allows you to continue working while Photoshop is saving a large file. In addition, you have the option to auto-save your work as frequently as every 5 minutes—another safeguard against losing the image-editing effects you may have spent hours trying to achieve.

Restoring Default Photoshop Preferences

If you make changes to Photoshop Preferences but later decide you want to restore the defaults, you do not have to go back to the individual Preferences panels and undo each change individually. Instead, you can simply exit Photoshop and restart it while pressing and holding the Ctrl+Alt+Shift keys. When you are prompted to delete the Adobe Photoshop Settings File, click Yes. When Photoshop opens, the default preferences will be restored.

Working with Panels

You have seen how you can arrange Document windows in different ways. You can also customize the workspace by rearranging the panels in the workspace or by opening panels that don't appear by default in a particular workspace. Furthermore, you can increase your work area by hiding and collapsing panels or by floating panels and then dragging them out of the way. See Figure 1-17.

Figure 1-17 Panel groups and docks

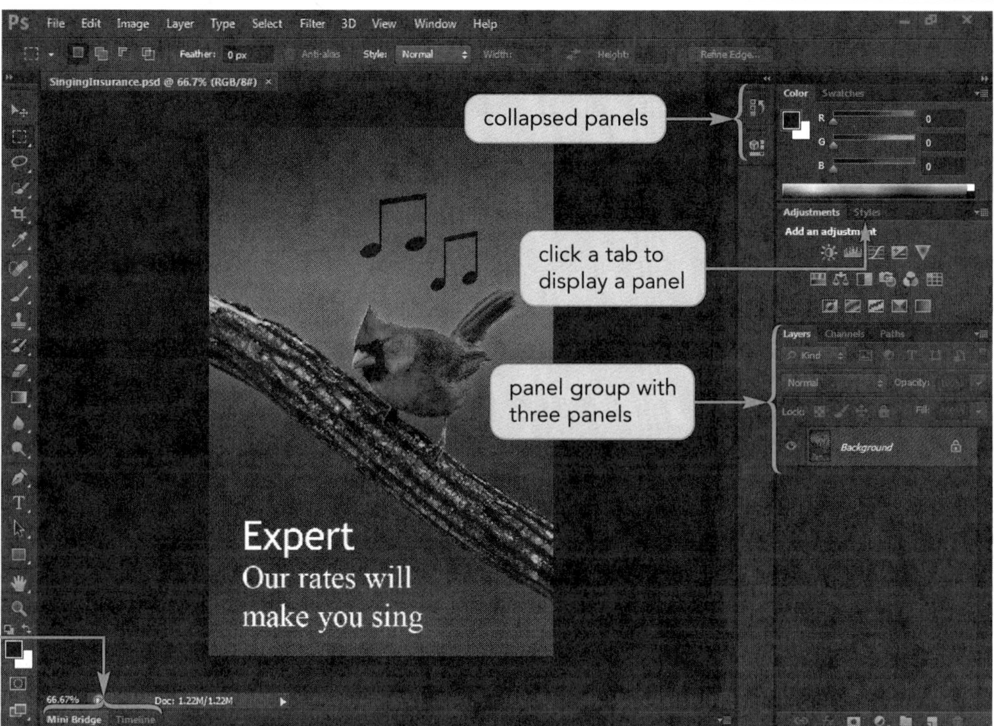

Each panel in Photoshop is a collection of related tools and settings, and panel groups organize related panels. Beyond that, groups of panels are often collected in docks. For example, in the Essentials workspace, the Layers, Channels, and Paths panels are displayed in a group by default because those panels are often used together. In turn, they are docked with two other panel groups: Adjustments and Styles, and Color and Swatches. Two collapsed panels, History and Properties, are also docked on the left side of the Color and Swatches panel group in the Essentials workspace. An additional panel group, Mini Bridge and Timeline, appears at the bottom of the window, collapsed. The default Essentials workspace also includes the Tools panel to the left of the Document window. You move from one docked panel to another by clicking the tabs.

Panels can also be displayed in stacks, which are collections of floating panel groups. The panels in a stack share a title bar, and you can drag the title bar to move the stack anywhere in the Photoshop window. See Figure 1-18.

Figure 1-18 Panel stack

drag title bar to move the stack anywhere in the Photoshop window
shared title bar
two panel groups are stacked
Expert
Our rates

As you become more familiar with Photoshop, you will develop a preference for how you want your panels displayed, depending on what you are working on.

The way you work with the tabs in open panels is similar to the way you work with Document window tabs: You click a panel tab to move from one panel to the next in a group.

Now that you have a general idea of how a Photoshop workspace is set up, Sarah wants you to practice rearranging the Photoshop interface and working with some of the tools.

To choose a tab in an open panel:

1. Open **UnexpectedBolt.psd**, located in the Photoshop1\Tutorial folder. The file opens on top of the SingingInsurance file in the Essentials workspace. The workspace includes four panel groups, two collapsed panels, and the Tools panel. The top panel group includes the Color and Swatches panels.
2. In the top panel group, click the **Swatches** tab. The Swatches panel displays a set, or palette, of frequently used colors.
3. In the middle panel group, click the **Styles** tab. The Styles panel displays options for formatting layers in the current file.
4. On the menu bar, click **Window**, point to **Workspace**, and then click **Reset Essentials**. The Essentials workspace returns to its default settings, with the Color panel on top in the top panel group, and the Adjustments panel on top in the middle panel group.

Displaying and Closing a Panel

You do not always have to work with the default panels provided in a workspace. You can open and close panels at will. To access any of the panels not displayed in the current workspace, click Window on the menu bar to display a list of available panels, including panels for working with color, text, and brushes.

Sarah wants you to explore some of the panels that are not open by default in the Essentials workspace so you can learn how to open and close panels as you need them when working on projects in the future.

To display and close panels:

1. On the menu bar, click **Window**. The Window menu includes commands for arranging the windows and changing the workspace. It also includes a list of panels ranging from 3D to Tool Presets. The options bar and the Tools panel are listed separately at the end of the list of panels. Finally, the Window menu displays a list of open files. See Figure 1-19.

Figure 1-19 Window menu

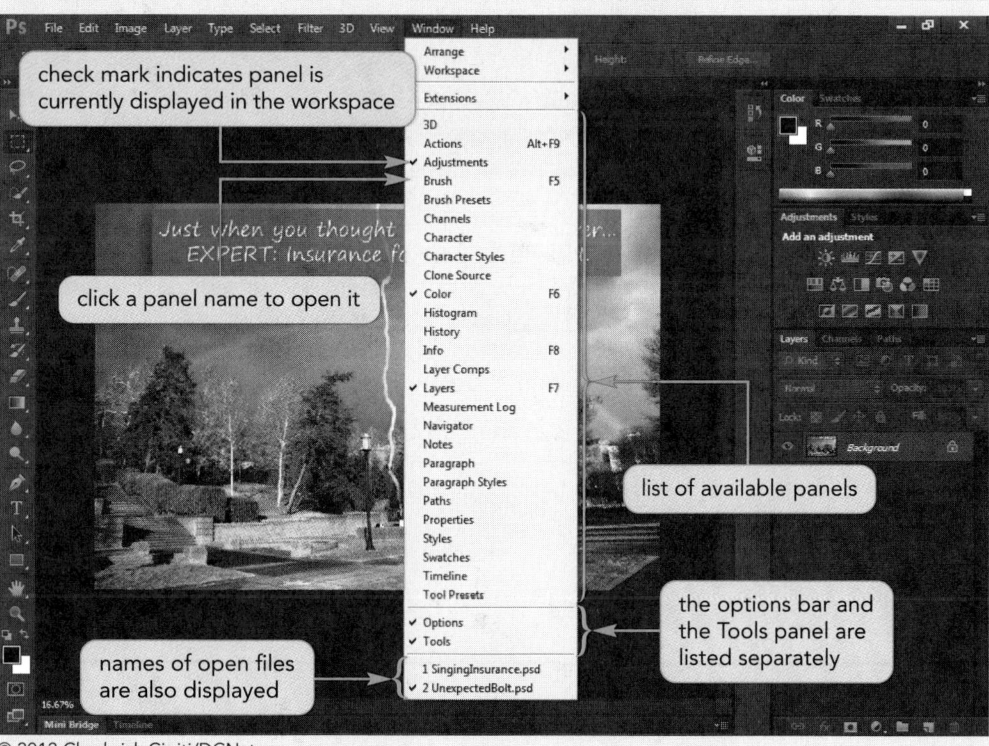

Any panel name preceded by a check mark is currently open in the workspace. To open a panel that isn't visible in the workspace, click its name.

2. Click **Brush**. The Brush panel opens in the workspace. See Figure 1-20.

TIP

You can also open the Brush panel by pressing the F5 shortcut key.

Figure 1-20 Brush panel

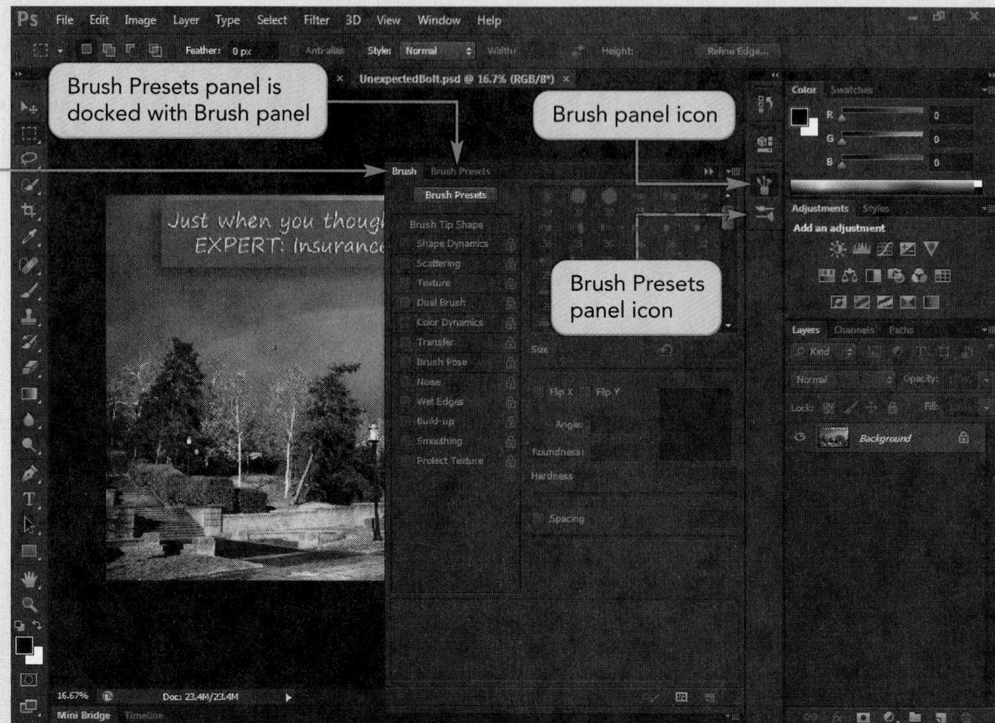
Brush Presets panel is docked with Brush panel
Brush panel icon
Brush panel appears expanded, but also docked, with collapsed panel icons to the right
Brush Presets panel icon

Most panels open in logical groups when you select one of the panels from the Window menu. In this case, the Brush Presets panel opens with the Brush panel. Notice that Photoshop has docked the panel to the left of the Adjustments panel, and that a Brush panel icon appears to the right of the Brush panel. Below that icon is the Brush Presets icon.

3. On the menu bar, click **Window**, and then click **Character**. Photoshop collapses the Brush panel, and the Character panel opens in a dock, with the Paragraph panel behind it. Panel icons for the Character and Paragraph panels also appear to the left of the default panels. See Figure 1-21.

Figure 1-21 **Character panel**

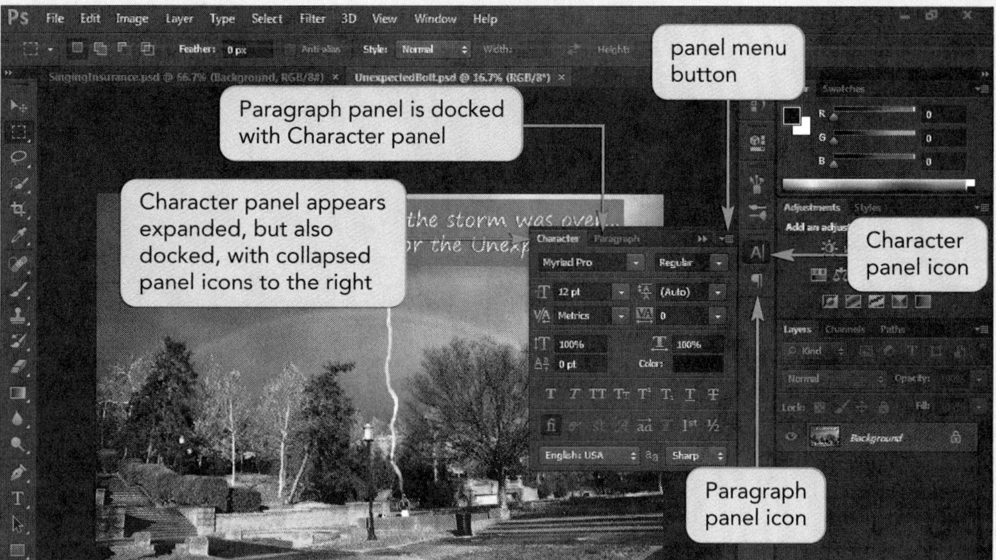

© 2012 Chadwick Cipiti/DCNature.com

4. In the Character panel, click the **panel menu** button, and then click **Close** to close the panel. The Character panel closes, but the Paragraph panel, which was docked with it, remains open.

5. In the Color panel, click the **panel menu** button, and then click **Close Tab Group**. The Color panel group closes. See Figure 1-22.

Figure 1-22 **Closing a panel group**

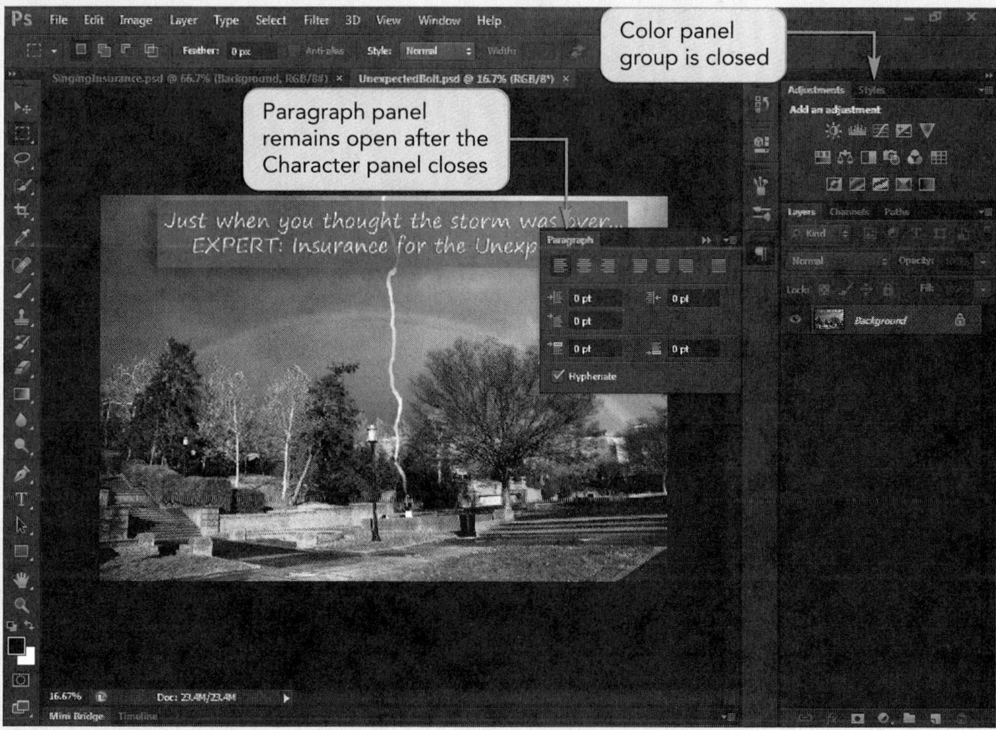

© 2012 Chadwick Cipiti/DCNature.com

You can also use the Window menu to close a panel.

6. On the menu bar, click **Window**, and then click **Tools** to deselect the panel and remove the check mark. The Tools panel closes, and the Document window fills the space on the left side of the window.
7. Click Window on the menu bar, point to **Workspace**, and then click **Reset Essentials** to reset the workspace. All of the default panels reopen, and the Paragraph panel closes.

Sarah suggests that you experiment with minimizing, hiding, and redisplaying panels before you tackle a project.

Minimizing, Hiding, and Redisplaying Panels

As you work in Photoshop, you'll often find that you want more of the workspace area to display your file, and you'll also come to realize that you don't need all of the panels that might be displayed in the current workspace all of the time. To save real estate on your screen, you can minimize open panels or even hide them temporarily. This flexibility streamlines your work in Photoshop, and lets you work the way that suits you best.

To minimize, hide, and redisplay panels:

1. On the right side of the title bar for the docked panels, click the **Collapse to Icons** button. The panels collapse, and the Document window expands to fill the space. See Figure 1-23.

Figure 1-23 Collapsed panel groups

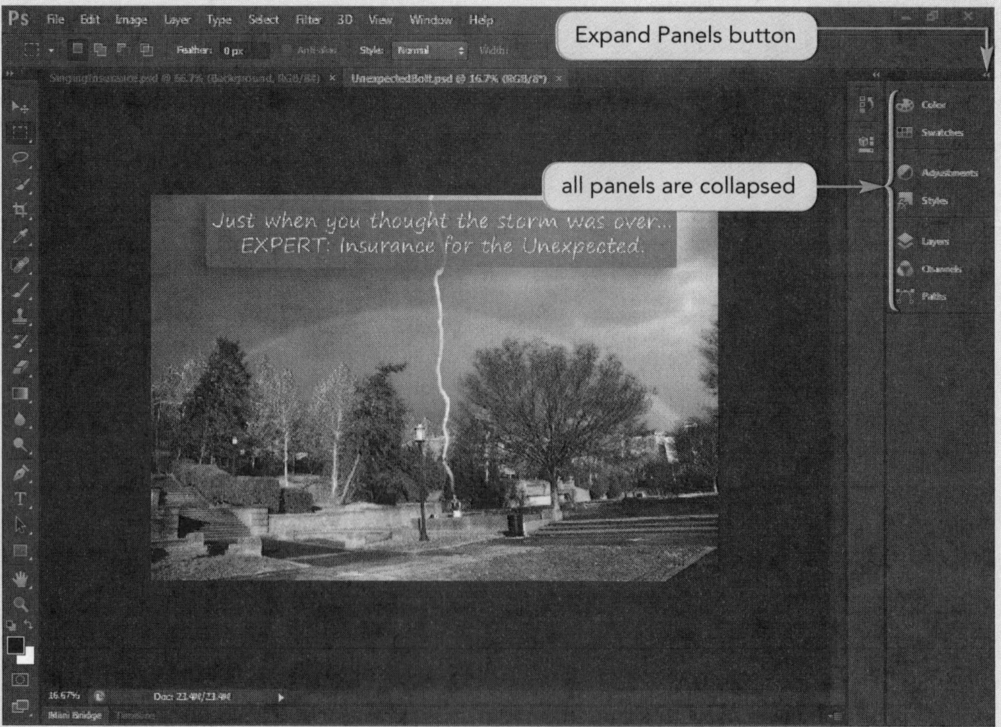

2. On the right side of the title bar for the collapsed panels, click the **Expand Panels** button to restore the panels to their original display.

Trouble? If you click the wrong Expand Panels button, the History and Properties panels will expand. To correct this, click the Collapse to Icons button for those panels, and then click the Expand Panels button on the right side of the screen.

For even more screen real estate, you can temporarily hide all panels.

3. Press the **Tab** key. All of the panels in the workspace are now hidden. Only the menu bar and the status bar are visible. See Figure 1-24.

Figure 1-24 **Hiding all panels**

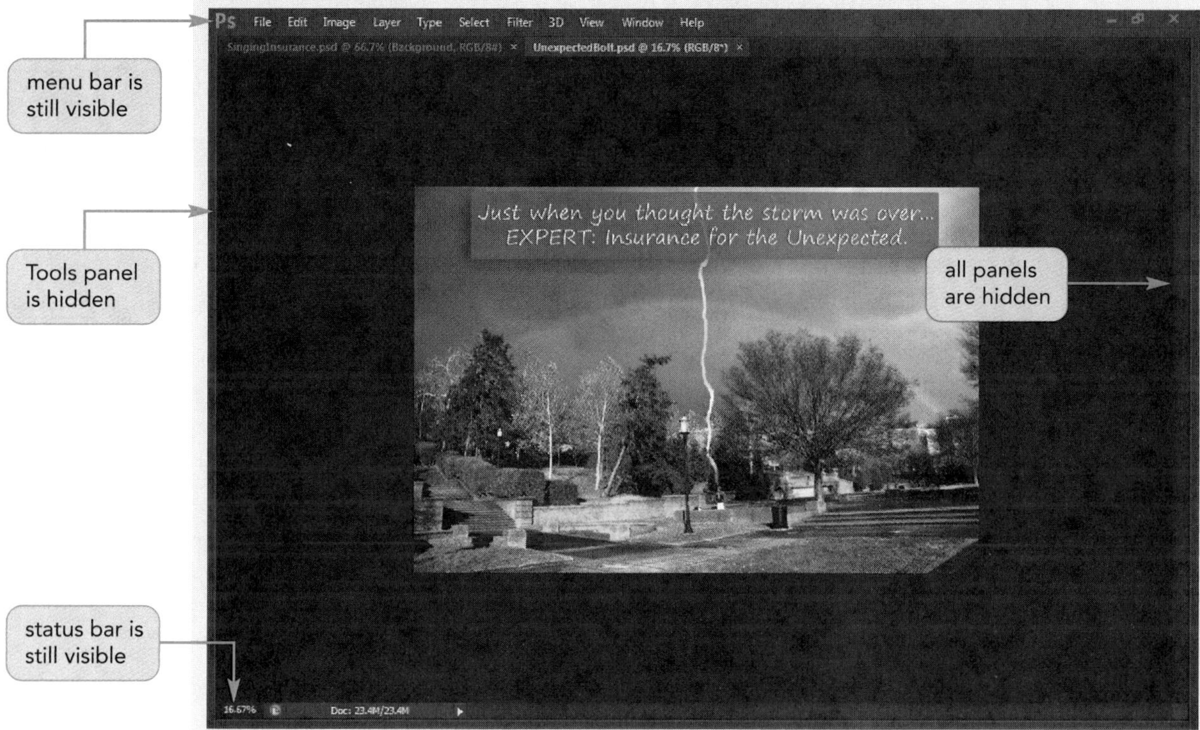

© 2012 Chadwick Cipiti/DCNature.com

4. Press the **Tab** key. All of the hidden panels are now visible.

Sarah has explained that you will sometimes want to group panels in ways that are different than the groupings in any of Photoshop's predefined workspaces. Because of this, she would like you to experiment with moving and stacking panels.

Moving and Stacking Panels

Because everyone has different work habits and preferences, Photoshop provides even more ways to manipulate panels. For example, you can move panels in the workspace, and you can create custom groups of panels by stacking them.

To move the panels:

1. On the menu bar, click **Window**, and then click **Brush** to open the Brush panel group.
2. Point to the **panel bar** to the right of the Brush Presets tab.

3. Click and hold the mouse button, and drag the panel group to the left and then up, into the Document window. A "ghost" version of the panel appears, and a blue border indicates the original location of the panel. See Figure 1-25.

Figure 1-25 **Moving a panel group**

when the ghosted image turns solid, the panel is undocked

drag panel to the left and then up

blue border indicates original location

When the ghosted version and the blue border disappear and a "solid" version of the panel appears, you have dragged the panel far enough from the dock to undock it so that it floats in the Document window. At that point, you can release the mouse button.

4. Release the mouse button. The panel is now floating in the middle of the Document window. Notice that the floating panel now has its own title bar that includes a Collapse to Icons button and a Close button.

Stacking Panels

By stacking panel groups, you can move multiple panels and panel groups as a single unit. Next, you'll experiment with stacking panels so you can move groups of panels together around the Photoshop program window as you work.

To stack panels:

1. In the Layers, Channels, and Paths panel group, point to the right of the word Paths, click the **panel bar**, and drag the **Layers, Channels, and Paths** panel group to the left and under the Brush panel group until you see a blue line between the two panel docks. See Figure 1-26.

Figure 1-26 **Stacking panels**

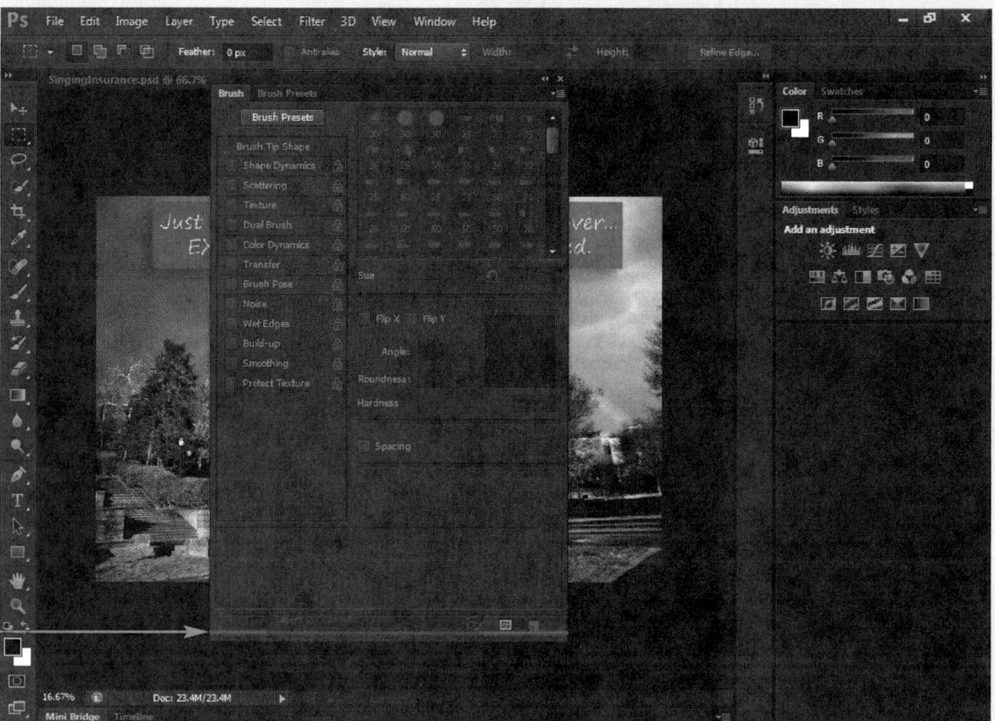

blue line indicates where panels will be stacked

2. Release the mouse button. The panels are now stacked.
3. Point to the stacked panels title bar, click the mouse button, and drag the stack up and to the right. The entire stack moves as you drag.

Preset Workspaces

As you have seen, the Photoshop workspace is customizable so you can change the way it appears based on your preferences. As you become more comfortable in Photoshop, you might find that you prefer one layout to another, depending on the task at hand. So far, you have been working in and modifying the default Essentials workspace. However, Photoshop also comes with a number of other predefined workspaces that you will explore throughout this book. For example, the Painting workspace opens six panels on the right side of the screen: Swatches, Navigator, Brush Presets, Layers, Channels, and Paths. It also displays collapsed History, Brush, Clone Source, and Tool Presets panels. These panels give you many different options for painting in Photoshop, including brush shape, color, and texture. The Typography workspace displays the Character and Paragraph panels, which give you multiple text formatting options when you add text to a file, as well as the Paragraph Styles and Character Styles panels, which let you create and save styles that you can apply to other text in your files. It also displays Layers, Channels, Paths, History, Info, Swatches, and Styles panels, all useful for working with text. Unless otherwise noted, the figures in this book show the workspace in the default Essentials layout.

Photoshop comes with seven preset workspaces. You can switch workspaces at any point in an editing session, and then switch back, depending on your current task. To switch workspaces, you click Window on the menu bar, click Workspace, and then click a workspace on the menu. See Figure 1-27 for a description of all the available preset workspace layouts.

Figure 1-27 **Workspace layouts**

Workspace Layout	Description
Essentials	Displays the most frequently used panels for accomplishing basic tasks in Photoshop, such as manipulating layers and channels, working with paths, applying image adjustments, and setting colors
New in CS6	Displays the new CS6 panels, as well as panels with new features, and highlights new commands on the menu
3D	Displays panels for working with imported 3D objects and converting 2D layers to 3D objects; 3D features are only available in Photoshop Extended
Motion	Displays panels that let you create motion effects and animate 3D objects
Painting	Displays panels with tools and settings for working with painting features, such as brushes, brush presets, and colors
Photography	Displays advanced panels for making fine adjustments to photographs, including modifying color balance, hue, and saturation; applying filters; and mixing color channels
Typography	Displays panels for working with type, including the Character and Paragraph panels, which allow you to make quick formatting changes to text, and the Character Styles and Paragraph Styles panels, which let you save text formatting and quickly apply it to new text

Sarah explains that depending on what your focus will be in an editing session, you might find you need to work in a different workspace. She suggests that you explore some of the other available workspaces.

TIP

If you're working at a resolution greater than 1024 × 768, you can also click the Workspace Switcher button and then click Typography.

To choose a preset workspace:

1. On the menu bar, click **Window**, point to **Workspace**, and then click **Typography**. Panels specific to working extensively with text appear. See Figure 1-28.

Figure 1-28 Typography workspace

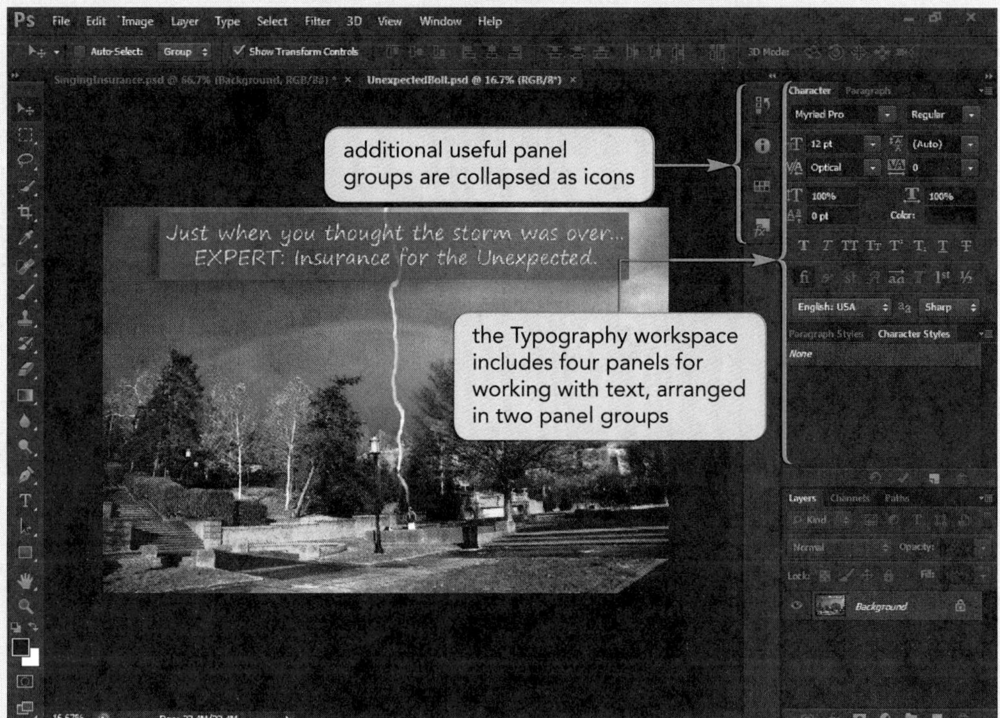
additional useful panel groups are collapsed as icons
Just when you thought the storm was over...
EXPERT: Insurance for the Unexpected.
the Typography workspace includes four panels for working with text, arranged in two panel groups

Trouble? If you can't see the Window menu, drag the panel stack down. If your window doesn't look like the figure, then click Window, point to Workspace, and then click Reset Typography.

2. On the menu bar, click **Window**, point to **Workspace**, and then click **Painting**. The workspace changes again to include tools and settings that are most helpful for working with the various brush and pencil tools in the Tools panel. Notice that in addition to the Brush Presets panel, which is docked by itself, the Brush panel appears collapsed to the left of the Swatches panel.
3. Click the **Brush Tool** button in the Tools panel. The Brush Presets panel display changes to show active settings appropriate for the Brush Tool.

You have explored a number of the workspaces Photoshop provides by default, but now you'll explore the other workspace options you might need in your work for Mirabeau Media.

INSIGHT

Saving, Redisplaying, and Deleting a Custom Workspace

In Photoshop, you can save **custom workspaces** to display the panels and tools you need for specific tasks, such as working on a photograph for a brochure or designing a poster. To create a custom workspace, make the changes you want—for example, by opening additional panels, closing panels you don't want, and rearranging the docks or stacks to your liking. When you have designed the workspace you want, click Window on the menu bar, point to Workspace, and then click New Workspace, or click the Workspace Switcher and then click New Workspace. Type a name for the new workspace, and then click the Save button. The next time you display the Workspace menu, your new workspace will be displayed in the workspace list. By using custom workspaces, you can improve your work flow and become more efficient.

Using the Rulers, Guides, and Grid

Photoshop provides a number of tools for keeping track of the measurements of your document, as well as guiding you as you make selections or add and position objects. For example, you might use the rulers to help you position an element in your composition. In addition, if you are adding an object such as text or a vector drawing to an image, you can first draw guides so you can place the object exactly at their intersection. **Smart Guides** are lines that appear automatically on the Document window as you move an object on one layer to align it with an object on another layer. For example, if you are aligning a small rectangle with a large rectangle, a Smart Guide runs through the center of the large rectangle as you drag the small rectangle, or appears when the bottom of the small rectangle is exactly aligned with the bottom of the large rectangle. You can also display another tool, called the grid, to help you quickly align multiple objects added to an image.

Sarah has suggested you experiment with rulers, guides, and the grid as you continue to experiment with other tools in Photoshop.

Showing the Rulers

You can display rulers so that you can measure objects in the Document window. The rulers show inches by default, but you can change the unit of measurement on the rulers by right-clicking a ruler and then clicking another unit of measurement, for example Pixels or Centimeters.

Sarah has provided you with a photograph of a pelican that she intends to use in one of her print ads for a travel agency. You'll use that image to experiment with the rulers and guides.

To show the rulers:

1. Close all open files, display the Essentials workspace, and then reset it.
2. Open **Travel.psd**, located in the Photoshop1\Tutorial folder included with your Data Files.
3. On the menu bar, click **View**, and then click **Fit on Screen**. The image fills the available area on the screen.
4. On the menu bar, click **View**, and then click **Rulers**. Two rulers appear around the Document window, one along the top, and one along the left side. See Figure 1-29.

TIP

You can also press the Ctrl+R keys to display and hide the rulers.

Figure 1-29 **Displaying rulers**

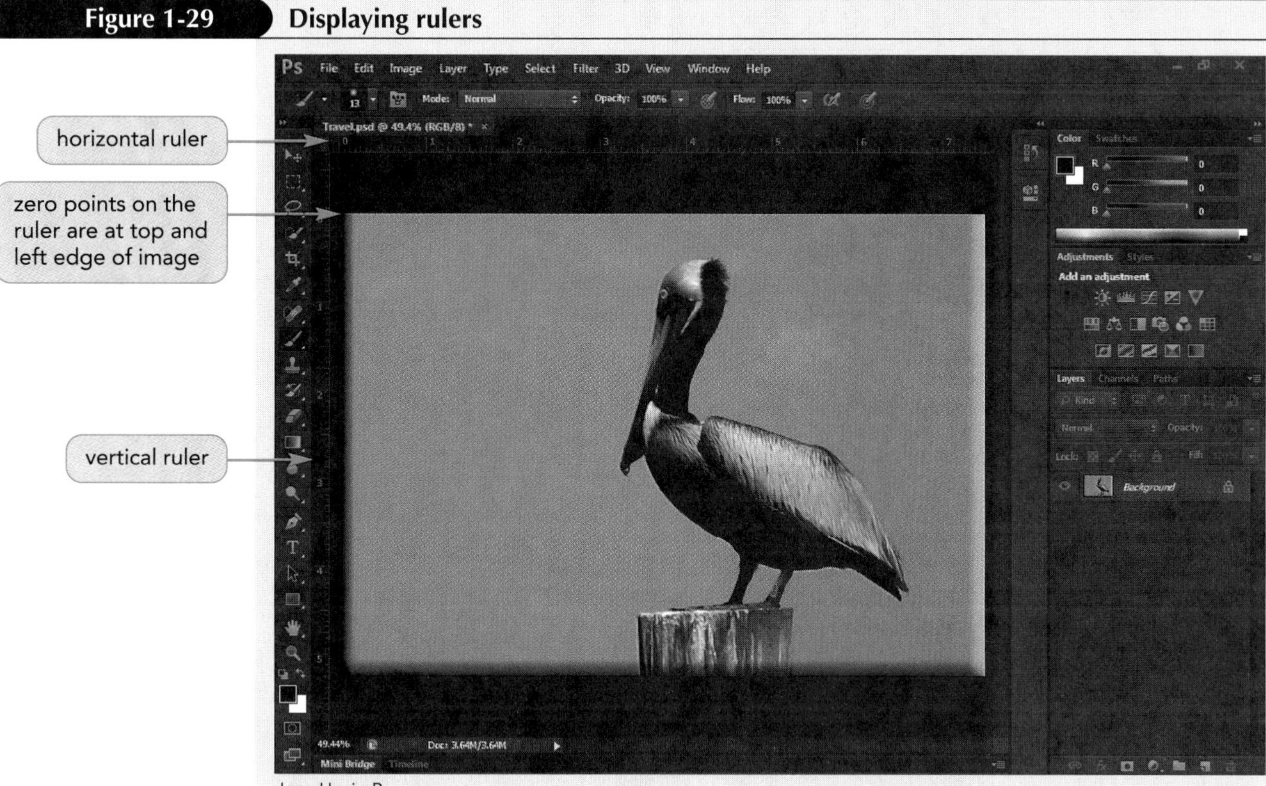

Jane Hosie-Bounar

By default, the rulers' zero points are at the upper-left corner of the document.

Adding Guides

Guides are another tool for measuring or aligning objects in an image. You can customize the location of guides and place them exactly where you want them. There are two ways to place guides in your document. You can use the View command on the menu bar, or you can drag guides from the rulers.

You'll experiment with guides as you continue to improve your Photoshop skills.

To add guides:

1. On the menu bar, click **View**, click **New Guide**, click the **Horizontal** option button, if necessary, type **.5** in the Position box, and then click the **OK** button. A horizontal guide appears at the half-inch mark on the vertical ruler and runs from one side of the Document window to the other.

   You can also add a guide by dragging from the ruler. To add a vertical guide, you drag from the vertical ruler. To add a horizontal guide, you drag from the horizontal ruler.

2. Point to the **horizontal ruler**, click and hold the mouse button, and then drag down toward the bottom of the pelican's beak, to about the **3-inch mark** on the vertical ruler.

3. Release the mouse button. Photoshop adds a horizontal guide to the Document window. See Figure 1-30.

Figure 1-30 Adding guides

Jane Hosie-Bounar

Using the guides and the ruler, you can see that from the top of the pelican's head to the tip of its beak is about 2 ½ inches.

4. On the menu bar, click **View**, and then click **Actual Pixels**.
5. Drag the vertical scroll bar up until you can see the top guide and the top of the pelican's head, and drag the horizontal scroll bar to the right so that the beak nearly touches the vertical ruler. See Figure 1-31.

Figure 1-31 Actual pixels display size

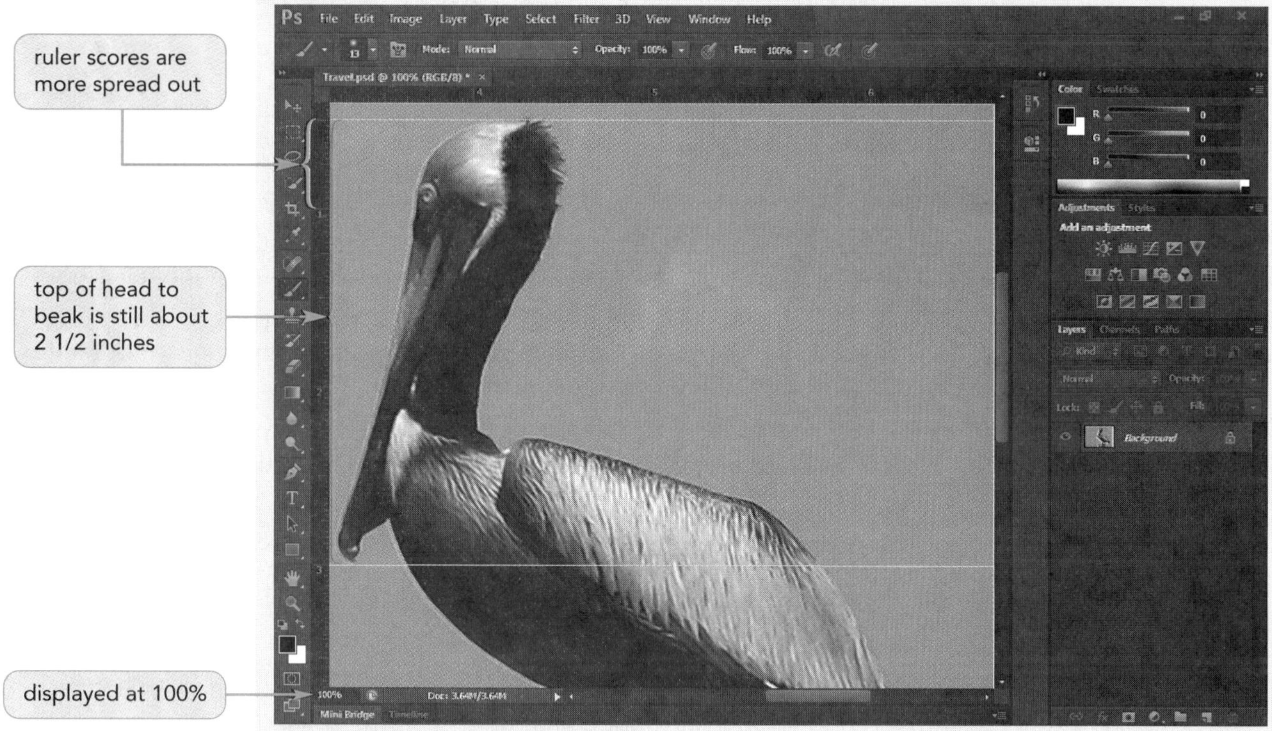

ruler scores are more spread out

top of head to beak is still about 2 1/2 inches

displayed at 100%

Jane Hosie-Bounar

The picture is enlarged to 100% of its size. Notice that the ruler markings are more spread out, and that the measurement from the top of the head to the bottom of the beak is still about 2 ½ inches.

6. Move the mouse pointer around the Document window. Notice that dotted lines slide along both rulers to indicate the position of the mouse pointer as you move it. This feature is helpful in determining the exact point at which you begin making a selection or drawing a vector object.

7. On the menu bar, click **View**, point to **Show**, and then click **Guides** to remove the check mark and turn off the display of the guides. Turning off the display of the Guides hides them, but does not delete them from the file. You can repeat this command to redisplay the guides at any time.

   You can delete a guide by pointing to the guide until the mouse pointer changes to ‡ or ⟺ and then dragging the guide either up over the ruler, or to the left or right until it is off the image. You can also click View, and then click Clear Guides.

8. Save the file as **TravelGuides.psd**, and then close it. When you close a file, the rulers and any guides disappear from the workspace. Since the rulers were displayed when the TravelGuides file was saved, the next time you open that file, they will be redisplayed.

You can change the **origin** of the rulers (where the number 0 appears) by pointing to the intersection of the rulers until a crosshair pointer appears, and then dragging diagonally down and to the right. The crosshairs indicate the new intersection of the rulers, and 0 appears at the spot where you release the mouse button. To reset the ruler, double-click the intersection of the rulers.

You can also work with the grid to help you align objects in a document, which you'll do next.

Showing and Hiding the Grid

The grid helps you align multiple objects or arrange them exactly where you want them in your document. It can also help you make an exact selection. You show and hide the grid using commands on the View menu.

To show and hide the grid:

1. Open **ExpertText.psd**, located in the Photoshop1\Tutorial folder, and then save it as **ExpertText1.psd**.
2. Click **View** on the menu, click **Fit on Screen**, and make sure the rulers are displayed.

   Trouble? If Photoshop displays a message about missing fonts, click the OK button and let Photoshop make a substitution.
3. On the menu bar, click **View**, point to **Show**, and then click **Grid**. Photoshop displays a pattern of equally spaced horizontal and vertical lines. These lines can be especially useful if you want to align two or more objects exactly. Notice that the major gridlines appear as solid dark gray lines, and the minor gridlines appear as dashed white lines.

   You'll modify the Preferences to display only the major gridlines to make them easier to work with.
4. On the menu bar, click **Edit**, point to **Preferences**, and then click **Guides, Grid & Slices**. In the Grid section of the Preferences dialog box, select the text in the Subdivisions box, type **1**, and then click the **OK** button. The grid-lines are now spaced one inch apart. See Figure 1-32.

Figure 1-32 Turning off the minor gridlines

change the display of the gridlines by modifying the Preferences via the Edit menu
major gridlines appear at every inch
Expert Insurance
always a bright idea

Jane Hosie-Bounar

Photoshop uses the Layers panel to store different elements in a composition on layers that can be edited and manipulated separately. You'll select a layer in the Layers panel to move it, using the grid to guide the placement of the layer.

5. In the Layers panel, click the **Layers** tab, if necessary, to expand the Layers panel, and then click the **Expert Insurance** layer to select it. You must always select a layer before you can work with it in Photoshop.
6. In the Tools panel, click the **Move Tool** button, if necessary, and then move the mouse pointer over the document. The move pointer appears.
7. Point to the **Expert Insurance** text, click and hold the mouse button, and then drag the text to the right so that the *E* is aligned with the fifth vertical gridline, resting on the first horizontal gridline. Notice that Photoshop provides additional guidance in the form of arrows and numbers that appear in a black box as you drag, indicating how many inches you have dragged an object from its original location, and in what direction.
8. In the Layers panel, click the **Lightbulb** layer, point to the **lightbulb** on the canvas, and drag it to the left and up slightly so that the bottom of the bulb is centered on the horizontal and vertical gridlines that intersect at the bottom of the candle wick.
9. In the Layers panel, click the **always a bright idea** layer to select it. The Move tool is still active.
10. Point to the **always a bright idea** text on the canvas, click and hold the mouse button, and then drag the text to the left and up so that the first *a* in *always* is aligned with the same vertical gridline as the *E* in *Expert*, resting on the horizontal gridline at the top of the lightbulb. See Figure 1-33.

TIP

You can also press the V key to select the Move tool.

Figure 1-33 **Aligning objects on the grid**

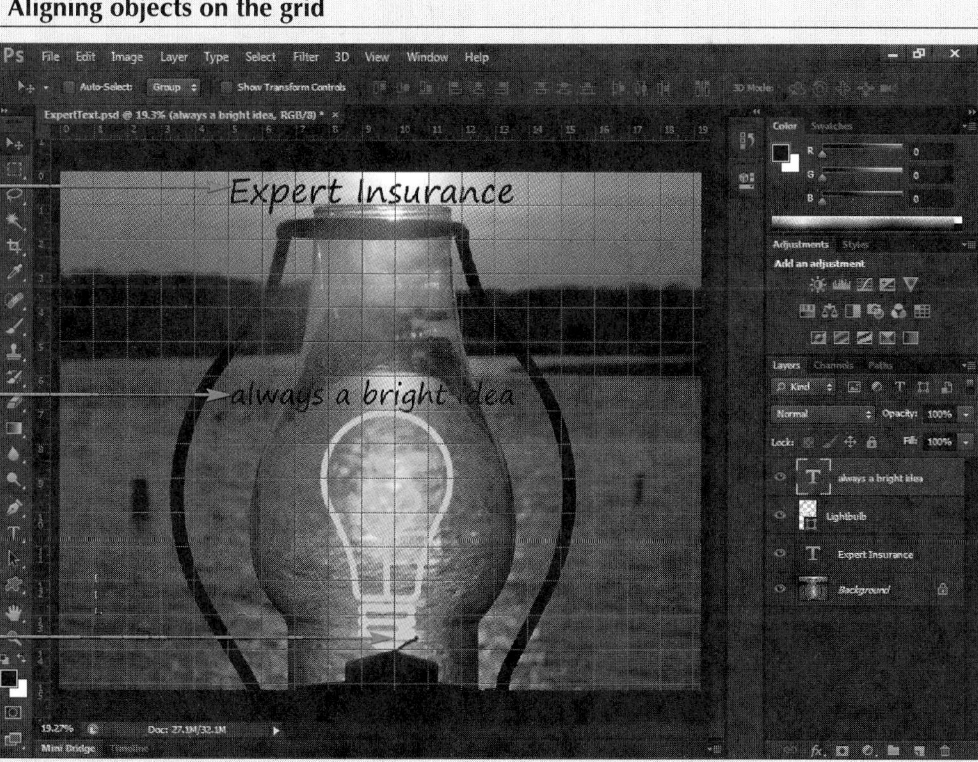
E is aligned with fifth vertical gridline
a is aligned with *E* in *Expert*
lightbulb is centered on same gridlines as candle wick
Expert Insurance
always a bright idea

Jane Hosie-Bounar

11. Press the **Ctrl+'** keys to turn off the grid, and then save and close the file.

INSIGHT

Snapping to the Grid and Guides

Photoshop includes a **Snap To** feature that lets you easily align objects with gridlines or guides. Snap To "magnetizes" the lines so that when you drag a selection or shape, or move an object, the object aligns to the closest gridlines or guides. You can turn the Snap To feature on and off by clicking View on the menu bar, clicking Snap To, and then clicking the choice you want to turn on or off.

Using Tools in the Tools Panel

You might have noticed while you were working with panels earlier in this tutorial that there is one panel, the Tools panel, that appears on the left side of the window, whereas all of the other panels appear on the right by default. As you become more familiar with Photoshop, you'll use the Tools panel constantly; having it appear in a consistent place no matter what workspace you're currently working in makes it convenient to find the tools you use over and over again. Because Photoshop provides so many tools in its Tools panel, some of the tools are grouped to improve your work flow. The triangle on the lower-right corner of a tool in the Tools panel indicates that there are additional tools, called a **tool group**, hidden beneath the tool you see in the panel. You display the hidden tools either by right-clicking the top tool (the tool that is displayed in the panel) or by pointing to the tool and clicking and holding the mouse button until a menu of additional tools appears.

Sarah notes that much of your work will involve fine-tuning images and that this kind of work might require you to zoom in and pan an image. She explains that you can find the tools for this kind of work in the Tools panel.

Selecting and Using Tools

You select a tool in the Tools panel by clicking it with the mouse. Some tools also have shortcut keys assigned. For example, earlier in this tutorial, you saw that pressing the V key activates the Move tool. When you select a tool, the mouse pointer changes to reflect the selection.

To select and use a tool:

1. Open **RainbowInsurance.psd**, located in the Photoshop1\Tutorial folder included with your Data Files, and turn off the ruler display if necessary. Notice on the status bar that the photograph is displayed in the Document window at a low zoom percentage, depending on your monitor.
2. Click the **Zoom Tool** button in the Tools panel, and then move the mouse pointer over the photograph. The mouse pointer changes to the Zoom In pointer, a magnifying glass with a plus sign in the center.

TIP

You can also press the Z key to select the Zoom tool.

3. Click the center of the photograph. The photograph is enlarged in the window and centered at the place you clicked.
4. On the status bar in the lower-left corner of the Document window, click in the **zoom percentage** box, double-click the current zoom percentage to select it, type **300**, and then press the **Enter** key. The image zooms in again. Because the zoom percentage is so high, the image looks blurry, or pixelated.
5. Click the **Hand Tool** button in the Tools panel. The Hand tool lets you drag a file within the Document window to display different areas.
6. Point to the center of the **lightning bolt**, and then drag the image all the way to the right until the lightning is no longer visible.
7. Click the **Zoom Tool** button, press and hold the **Alt** key, and point to the center of the Document window. The Zoom In pointer changes to the Zoom Out pointer when you press the Alt key.
8. Click the **center** of the document. The image zooms out.
9. Press the **Ctrl+1** keys. The image zooms to 100%.
10. Press the **Ctrl+0** keys. The image now fits on the screen.

TIP

Pressing the Spacebar while using any other tool changes the pointer temporarily to the Hand tool pointer.

INSIGHT

Changing the Zoom Level

When you work to modify individual pixels in an image—for example, to change their color—the zoom feature will be an important tool for your work. The maximum zoom percentage for an image is 3200%. You will rarely need to zoom in this much, but if you are doing extremely precise work—for example, pixel-by-pixel corrections on an image—the ability to zoom in this much is an advantage. You might also find that you need to zoom way out (decrease the zoom percentage) on a very large image in order to see the overall effect of changes you have made. The minimum zoom percentage is .36%, which you'll probably never use. However, it is often helpful to have this much flexibility in zooming in and zooming out on an image.

Using the Options Bar to Change Tool Settings

Many tools in the Tools panel let you modify the default options using the options bar, which appears beneath the menu bar in the Photoshop window. The options bar changes depending on which tool is selected in the Tools panel. Using the options bar, you can define custom settings for the tool.

Now that you're comfortable with the Photoshop environment, Sarah asks you to try modifying some elements on the canvas. She would like you to start by erasing the faint lightning bolt in the RainbowInsurance file.

To use the options bar:

1. In the Layers panel, click **Layer 1** to select it, and then click the **Eraser Tool** button in the Tools panel. The options bar displays the default settings for the Eraser tool or the settings in effect the last time the tool was used.

2. On the left side of the options bar, right-click the **Eraser Tool** button, and then click **Reset Tool**. This command ensures that the default settings are in effect.
3. On the options bar, click the **Brush Preset picker** button (to the right of the number 13) to open the Brush Preset picker. See Figure 1-34.

   Trouble? If the Brush Preset picker button isn't visible, confirm that the mode is set to Brush and not Pencil or Block. To change the mode, click the Mode button on the options bar, and then click Brush.

Figure 1-34 Eraser tool settings and Brush Preset picker

© 2012 Chadwick Cipiti/DCNature.com

You can change the diameter of the brush by dragging the Size slider, by typing in the Size box, or by selecting one of the **brush presets**, which are commonly used Photoshop brush sizes. Presets are discussed later in this tutorial.

4. Select the text in the Size box, and then type **100**.
5. Click the **Brush Preset picker** button again to close the Brush Preset picker. You are now ready to use the Eraser Tool.
6. Position the **Eraser Tool** pointer over the bottom of the faint lightning bolt, and then click. The lightning disappears where you clicked.
7. Drag the **Eraser Tool** pointer over the lightning image until it has disappeared entirely. If you miss any parts of the lightning bolt, you can drag over the area again. The faint lightning bolt has been removed from the image. See Figure 1-35.

Figure 1-35 **Using the Eraser tool**

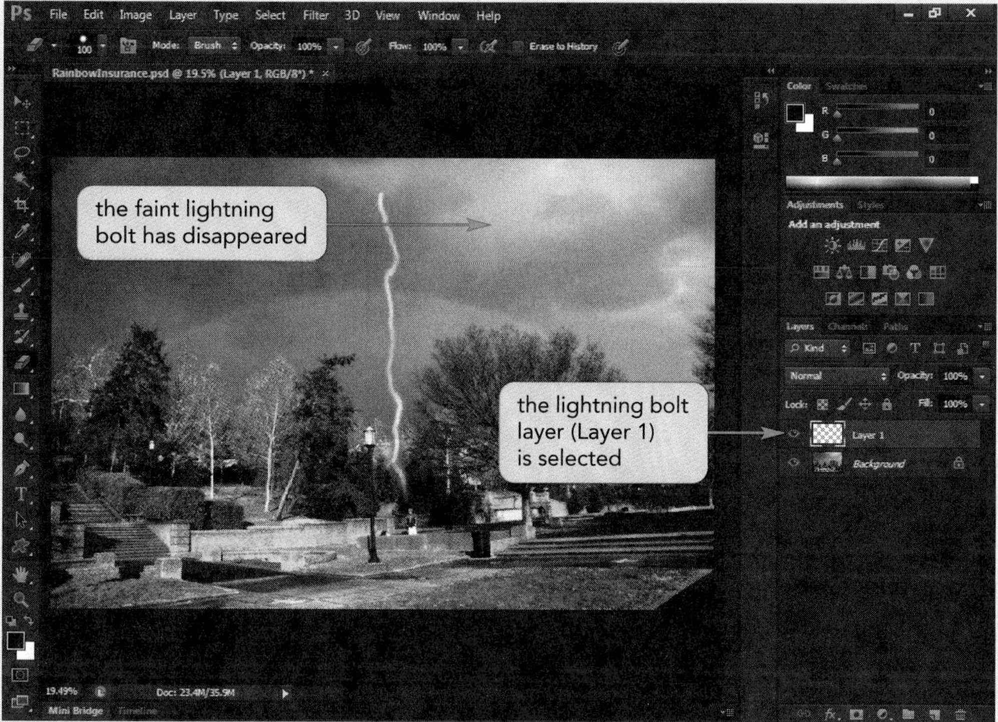

8. Save the file as **OneBolt.psd** in the Photoshop1\Tutorial folder, and then close it.

Adding Content to the Canvas and Using Tool Presets

You can use the drawing tools in the Tools panel to add content to the canvas. **Tool presets** are custom settings for tools that you can save to use again and again. For instance, you might want specific text—for example, a company name—to always appear in the same font and font color, no matter what document you are working in. You can set these options on the options bar for the Horizontal Type tool and then save the settings as a preset. When you need the settings again, you can open the preset after you select the tool. Photoshop also comes with its own presets. For example, when you used the Eraser tool earlier, you saw that it had brush size presets associated with it.

Sarah wants you to learn how to work with custom shapes and add them to the canvas. She gives you the image of the rainbow you used earlier and asks you to add a vector lightning bolt to the image for the insurance company campaign she's working on. To draw a lightning bolt, you can use the Custom Shape Tool, which is hidden under the Rectangle tool in the Tools panel.

To add content to the canvas:

1. Open **RainbowInsurance2.jpg**, located in the Photoshop1\Tutorial folder included with your Data Files.

2. In the Tools panel, point to the **Rectangle Tool** button, and then click and hold the mouse button. Photoshop displays a list of hidden tools.
3. Click the **Custom Shape Tool** button.
4. On the left side of the options bar, right-click the **Custom Shape Tool** button and then click **Reset Tool**. The options bar displays the default settings for the Custom Shape Tool.
5. On the right side of the options bar, click the **Custom Shape picker** button to open the Custom Shape picker. See Figure 1-36.

Figure 1-36 Custom Shape picker

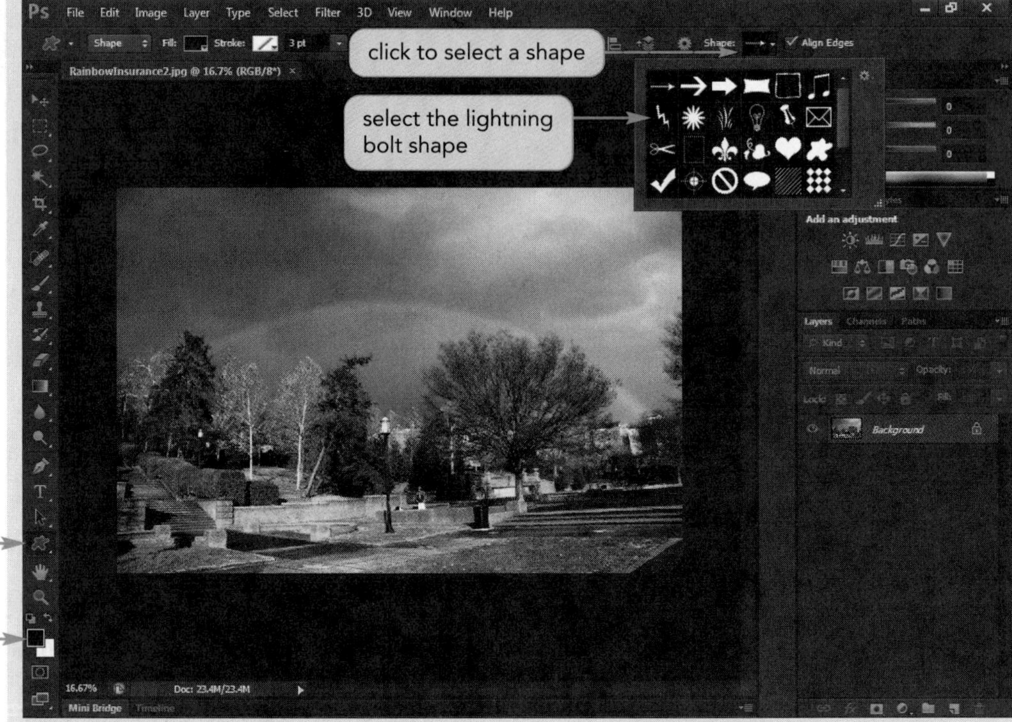

6. Double-click the **lightning bolt** in the first column, second row of the picker, to select that shape. You can now set the color for the shape.
7. On the options bar, click the **Fill** button to open a palette of fill colors.
8. Click a **yellow** box. See Figure 1-37.

Figure 1-37 Fill color palette

yellow is added to the Recently Used Colors list and appears as the Fill color on the options bar
click to select yellow

© 2012 Chadwick Cipiti/DCNature.com

9. On the options bar, click the **Fill** button to close the palette. The lightning bolt brush is now set to paint in yellow.
10. Drag from slightly to the left of the top center of the photograph down to the top of the person in the image, and then release the mouse button. You added a custom shape to the file. See Figure 1-38.

Figure 1-38 Brush panel

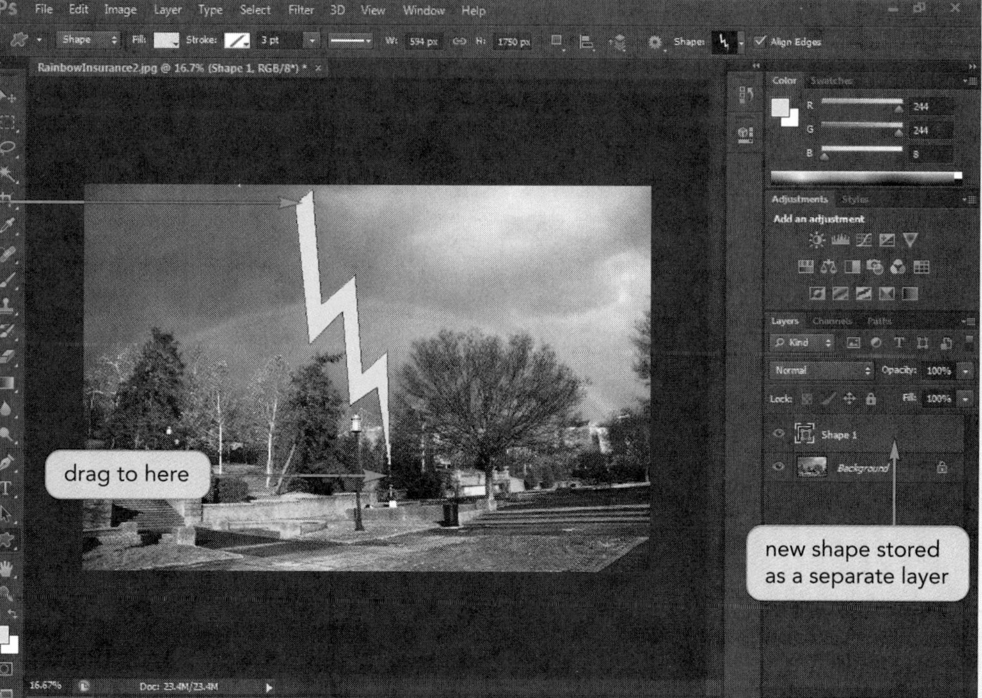
start dragging here
drag to here
new shape stored as a separate layer

© 2012 Chadwick Cipiti/DCNature.com

The new shape is stored as a new layer on top of the Background layer.

When you set the options for the lightning bolt, you were making changes to the options bar for the lightning shape that you can now save as a tool preset.

To save a tool preset:

1. On the options bar, click the **Tool Preset picker** button, and then click the **Create new tool preset** button to the right of the preset list. The New Tool Preset dialog box opens. See Figure 1-39.

Figure 1-39 New Tool Preset dialog box

2. Type **Bolt preset** in the Name box, click the **Include Color** check box to select it, if necessary, and then click the **OK** button. The preset is added to the Tool Preset picker list. See Figure 1-40.

Figure 1-40 Tool preset added to Tool Preset picker list

The next time you choose the Custom Shape Tool, the options will be set to a yellow lightning bolt.

3. Click the **Tool Preset picker** button again to close the list.

You might use a custom tool preset frequently while working on a particular project, but then find that you no longer need it once the project is finished. In that case, you can easily delete the custom tool preset from the Tool Preset picker list.

To delete a tool preset:

1. On the options bar, click the **Tool Preset picker** button .
2. Click the **Bolt preset** on the list, click the **Manage Tool Presets** button to the right of the preset list, and then click **Delete Tool Preset**.
3. Save the file as **Rainbow.psd** in the Photoshop1\Tutorial folder, and then close it.
4. Exit Photoshop.

In this session, you learned how to set Photoshop Preferences and then to restore the default preferences. You also worked with different elements of the Photoshop interface, including panels, workspaces, and tools. You learned how to display and use rulers, guides, and the grid; how to customize and save a workspace; and how to define and use tool presets. You also added content to the canvas.

PROSKILLS

Decision Making: Understanding Permissions

If you don't have a photograph that's appropriate for the job you need to accomplish, the Web provides a limitless supply—or does it? Just because an image is easy to download from the Web, does that mean it is free to use in any way you want? Think about it. If you're writing a paper for a class, you may easily find online sources, but can you copy paragraphs wholesale and not give credit to the original author?

As you acquire images, keep in mind that copyright law also applies to photographs (as well as video, music, and sound files). You should always operate under the assumption that every image on the Web is protected by copyright. Therefore, before you use someone else's work, you may need to obtain permission for its use, give credit or **attribution**, and, in some cases, pay a fee. You might be required to pay a **royalty** each time you use an image. Images that are **royalty-free** may still require payment, but usually it's a one-time fee. Some photographers assign a flexible copyright license that allows others to use their work. This might seem like an easy agreement to follow, but even a color correction would be considered an alteration, and would constitute copyright infringement if the photographer did not grant you the right to modify the photograph. Some government images and older works that are no longer protected by copyright law are in the **public domain**, and can be used however you want.

As you search for images to use in your work, you need to keep all of these issues in mind and make sure to read any licensing agreements or conditions posted by the owner of the photograph before you download an image. Two of the best resources for finding images you might be able to use are morgueFile and Creative Commons. Finally, if you plan to use one of your own photographs in any work, and would like to ensure that people understand that you hold the copyright, you can simply add the word *Copyright* or the copyright symbol ©, followed by the year. You can place this information directly on a photograph using the Text tools, or you can add it as a caption above or beneath the photograph.

By taking the time to understand copyright law and any pertinent licensing agreements, you can make the right decisions about the images you use in your projects.

REVIEW

Session 1.2 Quick Check

1. The Preferences command is found on the ____________ menu.
2. A ____________ displays a group of panels one on top of the other using tabs.
3. A ____________ is a collection of panels or panel groups joined top to bottom and sharing a title bar.
4. You can modify a predefined workspace in Photoshop and save it as a ____________ workspace.
5. What is a grid, and why would you use it in a Photoshop document?
6. ____________ are lines that you can add to the Document window to aid you in aligning and moving objects.
7. True or False. Any image that you can download from the Web is free to use in any manner.

Practice the skills you learned in the tutorial using the same case scenario.

PRACTICE

Review Assignments

Data Files needed for the Review Assignments: FireUnlit.psd, LightningInsurance.psd, UnexpectedBolt.psd

Sarah has given you some files that she plans to include in the Expert Insurance campaign so you can use them to familiarize yourself with the Photoshop interface, toolbars, and commands. She would also like you to create an image—using a photograph of a campfire—that she can use to present to her client as an idea for a new ad. Complete the following steps:

1. Start Photoshop while pressing the Ctrl+Alt+Shift keys. When you are prompted to delete the Adobe Photoshop Settings File, click Yes. Reset Photoshop to the Essentials workspace, and then reset all tools.
2. Open the **FireUnlit.psd**, **LightningInsurance.psd**, and **UnexpectedBolt.psd** files located in the Photoshop1\Review folder provided with your Data Files.
3. Save UnexpectedBolt as **RevUnexpected.psd** and FireUnlit as **FireLit.psd** in the Photoshop1\Review folder.
4. Switch to a 2-up Horizontal view of the files, and then switch back to the Consolidate All to Tabs view to view a single file in the Document window.
5. Open the original files, **UnexpectedBolt.psd** and **FireUnlit.psd**, so that you have five files open in the Document window.
6. Switch to the FireLit file.
7. Rearrange the tabs so the UnexpectedBolt file and the RevUnexpected file are next to each other and the FireUnlit file and the FireLit file are next to each other. Press the Alt+Print Screen keys to capture an image of the current Photoshop window; then open WordPad, which is available on the Accessories menu of the All Programs menu in Windows 7; and press the Ctrl+V keys to paste the image into a new file. Save the WordPad file as **PSTabs.rtf** in the Photoshop1\Review folder provided with your Data Files.
8. Display FireUnlit in a free-floating Document window.
9. Stack the Color panel group on top of the Layers panel group on the left side of the Document window. Press the Alt+Print Screen keys to capture an image of the current Photoshop window, switch to WordPad, and then press the Ctrl+V keys to paste the image into the PSTabs file you created in Step 7.
10. Consolidate all of the documents in the Document window to tabs with the FireLit file on top, and then switch to the Photography workspace.
11. Change the Guides, Grid & Slices preferences so that the Grid color is Medium Blue, and then display the grid.
12. Switch to the Essentials workspace, and reset the workspace.
13. Display the rulers; then, in the FireLit file, add a horizontal guide at 4 ½ inches on the vertical ruler and add a vertical guide at 6 inches on the horizontal ruler. Use the Custom Shape tool to add a shape that looks like fire on top of the wood. (*Hint*: Use the Grass 2 custom shape, which is in the second row, third column of the Custom Shape picker, and assign it an orange color to look like fire.)
14. With the Shape 1 layer selected, select the Move tool, and on the options bar, click to select the Show Transform Controls check box. Use the Move tool to center the drawing at the intersection of the horizontal and vertical guides. Press the Alt+Print Screen keys to capture an image of the current Photoshop window, switch to WordPad, and press the Ctrl+V keys to paste the image into the PSTabs file you created in Step 7.
15. Save your work in the **PSTabs.rtf** file, and then close WordPad.
16. Save your work in the **FireLit.psd** file, and then exit Photoshop.
17. Submit the results of the preceding steps to your instructor either in printed or electronic form, as requested.

Use your skills to create a magazine ad for an investment firm.

APPLY

Case Problem 1

Data File needed for this Case Problem: Harbour.psd

Safe Harbour Securities Maria Velasco, the marketing manager at Safe Harbour Securities, wants to place an ad for the company in a travel magazine. She asks you to create a mock-up for a magazine ad that would appeal to readers of a travel magazine. Complete the following steps:

1. Start Photoshop while pressing the Ctrl+Alt+Shift keys. When you are prompted to delete the Adobe Photoshop Settings File, click Yes. Reset Photoshop to the Essentials workspace, and then reset all tools.
2. Open **Harbour.psd**, located in the Photoshop1\Case1 folder provided with your Data Files, and then save the file as **SafeHarbour.psd** in the same folder.
3. Fit the image on the screen, and show the rulers.
4. Add guides at 6 inches on the horizontal ruler and at 2 inches and 4 inches on the vertical ruler.
5. Select the Background layer and then use the Custom Shape tool to draw an orange banner (Banner 3) that is 2 inches high and 6 inches wide, within the boundaries of the three guides on the left side of the screen.
6. Select the text layer, and use the Move tool to position the "Safe Harbour Securities..." text on top of the banner.
7. Add guides at 5 inches on the vertical ruler and 3 inches on the horizontal ruler.
8. Select the Background layer, and then use the Custom Shape tool to add a red heart below the banner, centered at the intersection of the two guides you just added.
9. Turn off the display of the guides to see what your ad will look like in final form.
10. Turn on the grid, and then turn the guides back on.
11. Save your work, and then exit Photoshop.
12. Submit the results of the preceding steps to your instructor, either in printed or electronic form, as requested.

Use Help to learn about and use tools to modify a photograph for a restaurant.

CHALLENGE

Case Problem 2

Data File needed for this Case Problem: SeafoodDish.psd

Yaya's Restaurant Yaya Venizia, the owner of Yaya's Restaurant, wants to modify a photograph of a lobster dish and change the image background for an upcoming ad. She wants you to help her make the necessary changes. Yaya thinks the Smudge tool will do what she wants, but she asks you to research the tool in Help before using it. Complete the following steps:

1. Start Photoshop while pressing the Ctrl+Alt+Shift keys. When you are prompted to delete the Adobe Photoshop Settings File, click Yes. Reset Photoshop to the Essentials workspace, and then reset all tools.
2. Open **SeafoodDish.psd**, located in the Photoshop1\Case2 folder provided with your Data Files. Fit the image on screen, and then save the file as **Yayas.psd** in the same folder.
3. **EXPLORE** Search Adobe Community Help for information on the Smudge Tool. Read the information provided by Adobe. (*Hint*: The topic should be called "Smudge image areas.")
4. **EXPLORE** Select the Seafood layer, and select the Smudge Tool. (*Hint*: The Smudge tool is hidden beneath the Blur tool in the Tools panel.) Set the brush size to 50 pixels and make sure Sample All Layers and Finger Painting check boxes on the options bar

are not selected. Using Figure 1-41 as a guide, smudge the edges of the image so that the photograph blends with the red border along all four sides of the photo image. Smudge every part of the seafood image except the lobster body and its claws so that the food looks as if it's surrounded by paint. (*Hint*: If you make a mistake, press the Ctrl+Z keys to undo your last action or click Edit on the menu bar and then click Step Backward.)

Figure 1-41 **YaYa's Restaurant image**

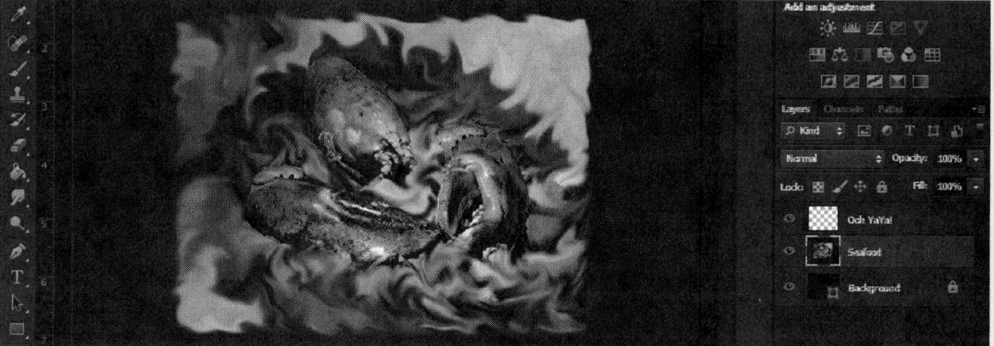

Jane Hosie-Bounar

5. Display the rulers and add guides at 5 ½ inches on the horizontal ruler and 8 inches on the vertical ruler.
6. Select the Ooh YaYa! layer, and then select the Move tool.

EXPLORE

7. Select the Show Transform Controls check box on the options bar, if necessary, and make the text ½ inch taller by dragging the center top control up. Press the Enter key to accept the size change.
8. Drag the text down so that the center bottom control is on the intersection of the two guides.

EXPLORE

9. Select the Paint Bucket tool in the Tools panel. (*Hint*: The Paint Bucket tool is hidden beneath the Gradient tool in the Tools panel.) Select the Seafood layer in the Layers panel, and then click the red border band surrounding the seafood with the Paint Bucket tool pointer to change the red border to black.
10. Save your work, and then exit Photoshop.
11. Submit the results of the preceding steps to your instructor, either in printed or electronic form, as requested.

Using Figure 1-42 as a guide, enhance a photograph for a placement agency.

CREATE

Case Problem 3

Data File needed for this Case Problem: Airplane.psd

Career Centers Fiona Friedman runs a career placement agency and wants to create a new brochure to promote her company. She asks you to modify a photograph that includes the company's trademark phrase so she can use the new image as the cover for the brochure. Figure 1-42 shows the final result.

Figure 1-42 **Career Centers image**

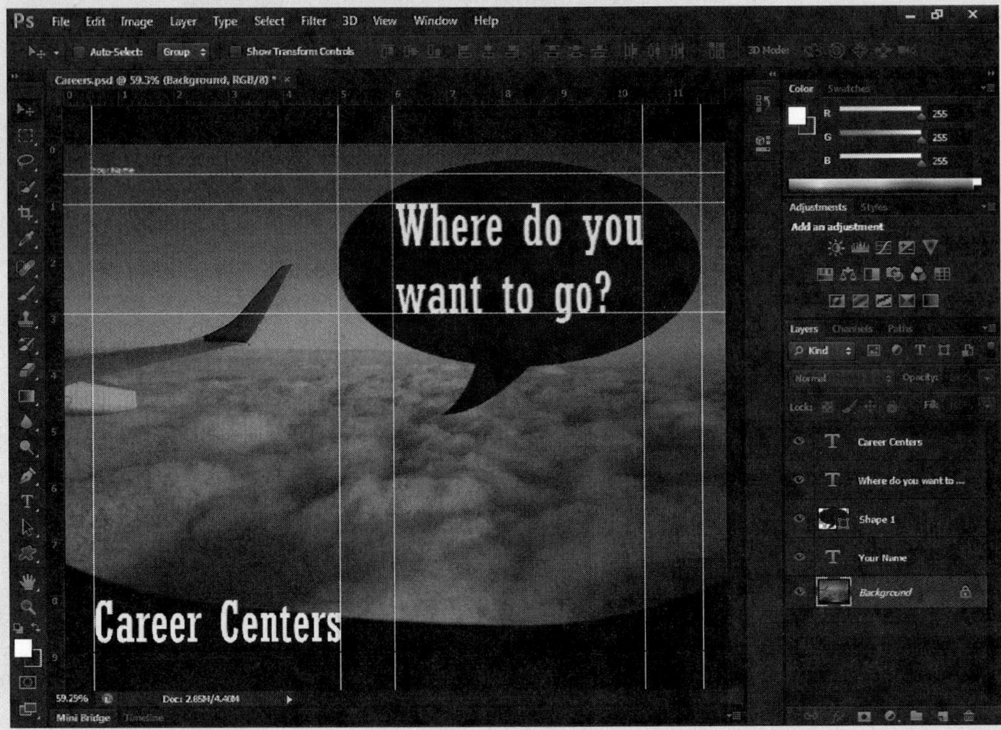

A. H. Bounar

Complete the following steps:

1. Start Photoshop while pressing the Ctrl+Alt+Shift keys. When you are prompted to delete the Adobe Photoshop Settings File, click Yes. Reset Photoshop to the Essentials workspace, and then reset all tools.
2. Open **Airplane.psd**, located in the Photoshop1\Case3 folder provided with your Data Files, and then save the file as **Careers.psd** in the same folder.
3. Zoom the image to fit on the screen.
4. Show the rulers, and add guides to the Document window, as shown in Figure 1-42.
5. Select the Background layer, and then add the blue shape shown in the figure.
6. Save the shape settings as a preset named **Bubble**.
7. Drag the "Where do you want to go?" text so that it is centered in the blue shape. Use the guides to position the text as shown in the figure.
8. Reset all of the tools.
9. Drag the "Career Centers" text to position it as shown in the figure, and then select the Background layer.

10. Select the Horizontal Type tool in the Tools panel, reset the tool, and make sure the foreground color is white. Click in the upper-left corner of the image, and then type your name. Drag your name so that it starts at the guide that is at the half-inch mark on the horizontal ruler and rests on the guide that is at the half-inch mark on the vertical ruler.
11. Delete the Bubble tool preset.
12. Save your work, and then exit Photoshop.
13. Submit the results of the preceding steps to your instructor, either in printed or electronic form, as requested.

Using Figure 1-43 as a guide, enhance a photograph for a travel agency.

CREATE

Case Problem 4

Data File needed for this Case Problem: ExploreMore.psd

Explore More Travel Hamid Brahim has hired you to help him with a new advertising campaign for his travel agency. He asks you to add text and drawings to a photograph that he has already "posterized," or adjusted to look like a painting rather than a photograph. Figure 1-43 shows the final result.

Figure 1-43 Explore More Travel image

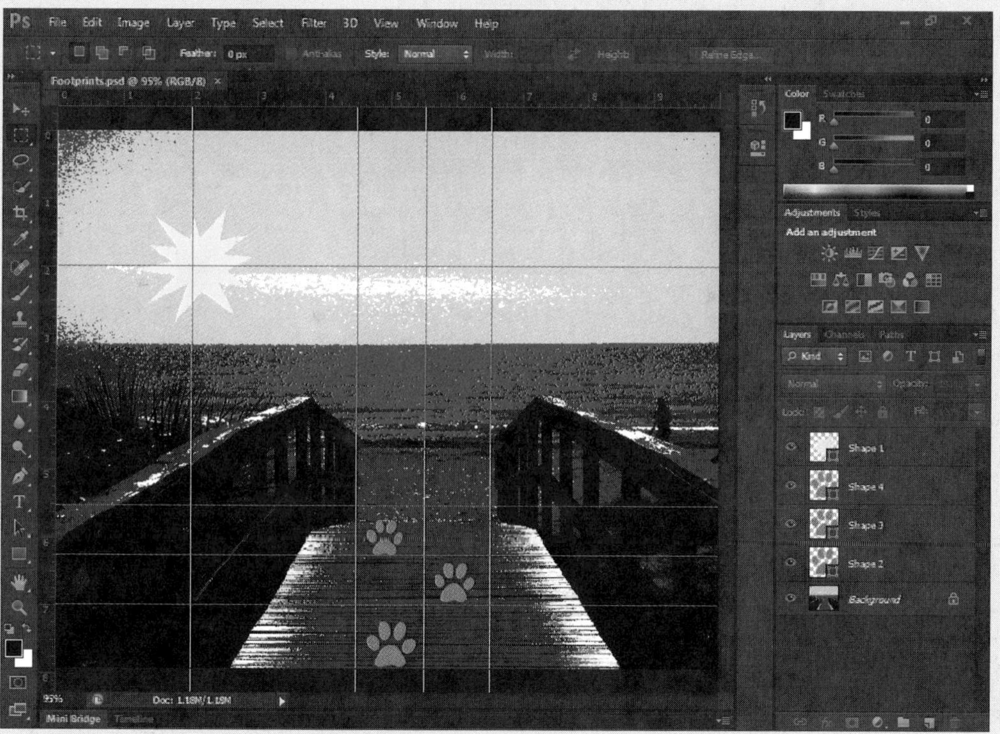

A. H. Bounar

Complete the following steps:

1. Start Photoshop while pressing the Ctrl+Alt+Shift keys. When you are prompted to delete the Adobe Photoshop Settings File, click Yes. Reset Photoshop to the Essentials workspace, and then reset all tools.
2. Open **ExploreMore.psd**, located in the Photoshop1\Case4 folder provided with your Data Files, and save the file as **Footprints.psd** in the same folder.
3. Zoom the image so it fills the Document window, and show the rulers, if necessary.

4. Change the Preferences so that the color of guides is Light Red, and then add guides to the Document window, as shown in Figure 1-43.
5. Draw a yellow starburst at the position indicated by the guides in the figure.
6. Draw three footprints at the positions indicated in the figure. Choose a color that you think works well with the image.
7. Zoom the image to 300%, and then pan until the starburst is at the center of the screen.
8. Press the Alt+Print Screen keys to capture an image of the current Photoshop window, then open WordPad and press Ctrl+V to paste the image into a new file. Save the file as **Starburst.rtf** in the Photoshop1\Case4 folder provided with your Data Files. Close WordPad.
9. Change the zoom to 95%.
10. Save your work, and close the file.
11. Submit the results of the preceding steps to your instructor either in printed or electronic form, as requested.

ENDING DATA FILES

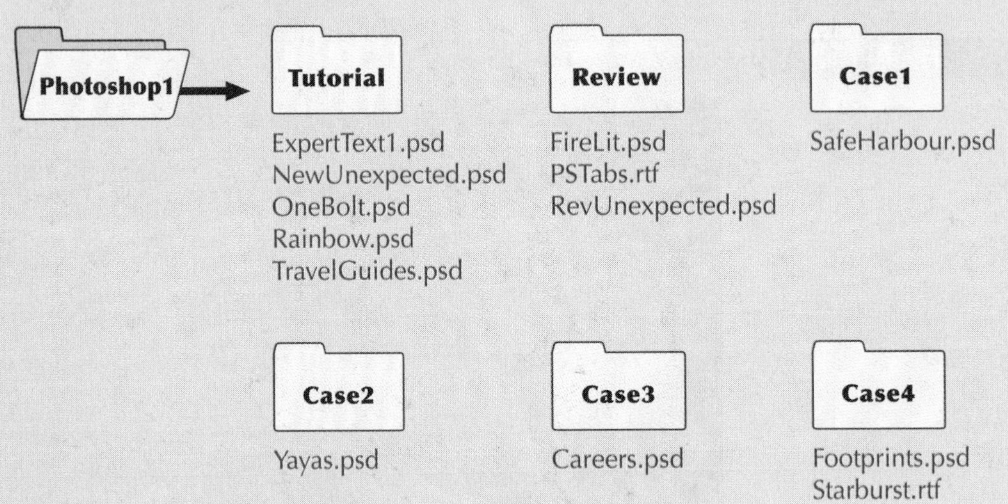

TUTORIAL 2

Working with Image Files

Working with File Sizes, Color Modes, and Image Adjustments

PHOTOSHOP

OBJECTIVES

Session 2.1
- Learn about file formats and their uses
- Change file type, file size, and resolution
- Examine Bridge and Mini Bridge
- Understand and change color modes
- Create new files using document presets and custom settings
- Place an image in a new file

Session 2.2
- Modify an image using adjustment layers
- Change canvas size
- Zoom and pan an image
- Rotate and flip an image

Case | *GreenHouse Construction*

GreenHouse Construction, an environmental construction firm in Fort Myers, Florida, was founded in 1992 by C. J. Kohl. The company designs "green" homes and buildings, so its building plans usually include features such as photovoltaic (solar) panels, automatic dimming fluorescent lights, double-paned windows, rooftop gardens, and plenty of natural lighting.

In the past, C. J. has created his own promotional materials. However, he thinks he needs help updating the materials to broaden his client base. He wants you to work with him on campaigns for both Web and print advertising. As you do, you'll explore various file sizes and color modes and determine which resolutions are best for which media. You'll also place images in files, make adjustments to images, and modify canvas and image size.

STARTING DATA FILES

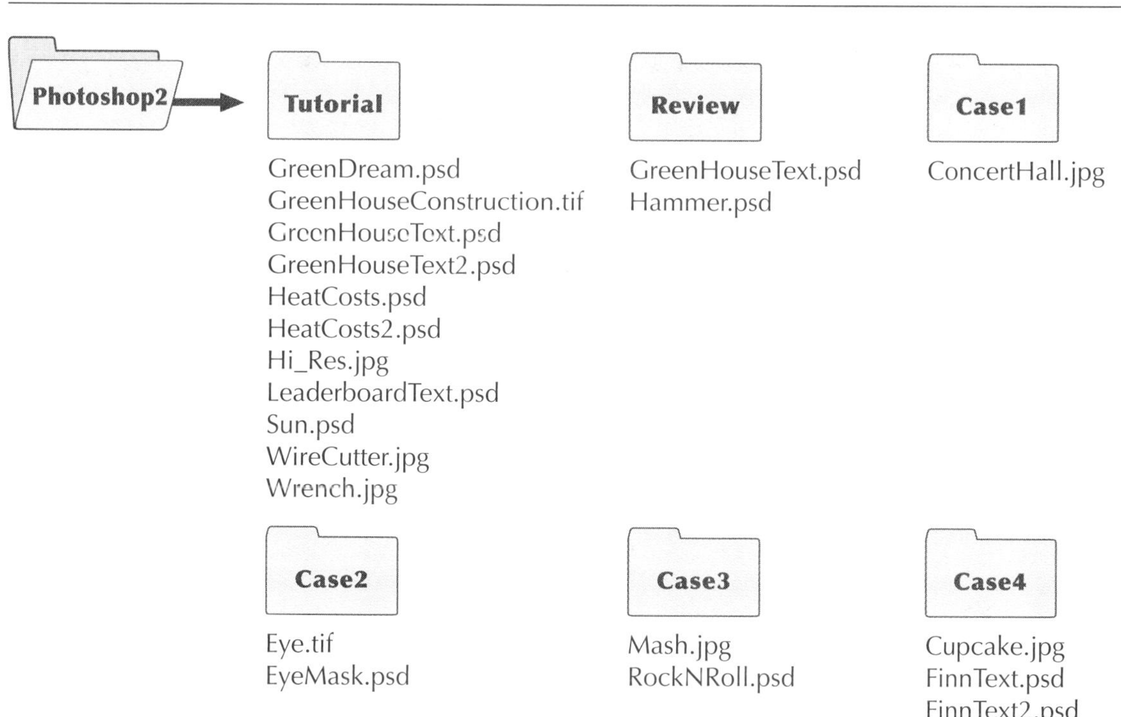

SESSION 2.1 VISUAL OVERVIEW

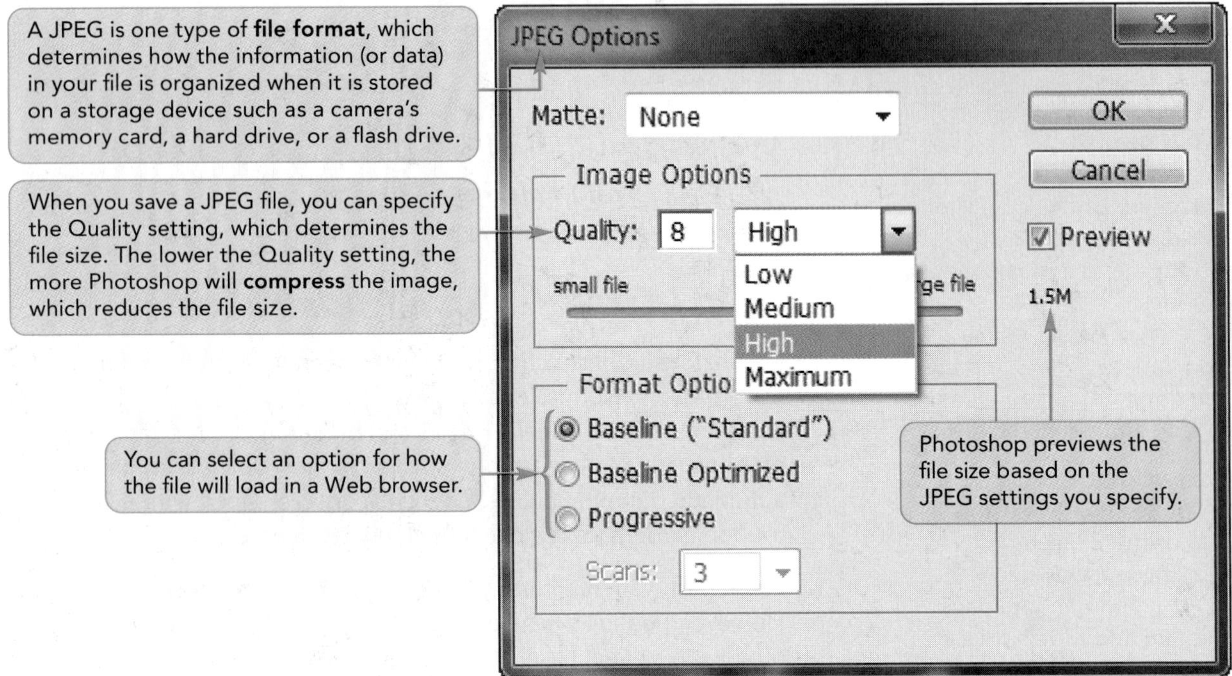

A JPEG is one type of **file format**, which determines how the information (or data) in your file is organized when it is stored on a storage device such as a camera's memory card, a hard drive, or a flash drive.
When you save a JPEG file, you can specify the Quality setting, which determines the file size. The lower the Quality setting, the more Photoshop will **compress** the image, which reduces the file size.
You can select an option for how the file will load in a Web browser.
Photoshop previews the file size based on the JPEG settings you specify.
JPEG Options
Matte: None
OK
Pixel Dimensions: 6.19M
Cancel
Image Options
Quality: 8 High
Preview
small file
Low
Medium
High
Maximum
1.5M
Format Optio
Baseline ("Standard")
Baseline Optimized
Progressive
Scans: 3

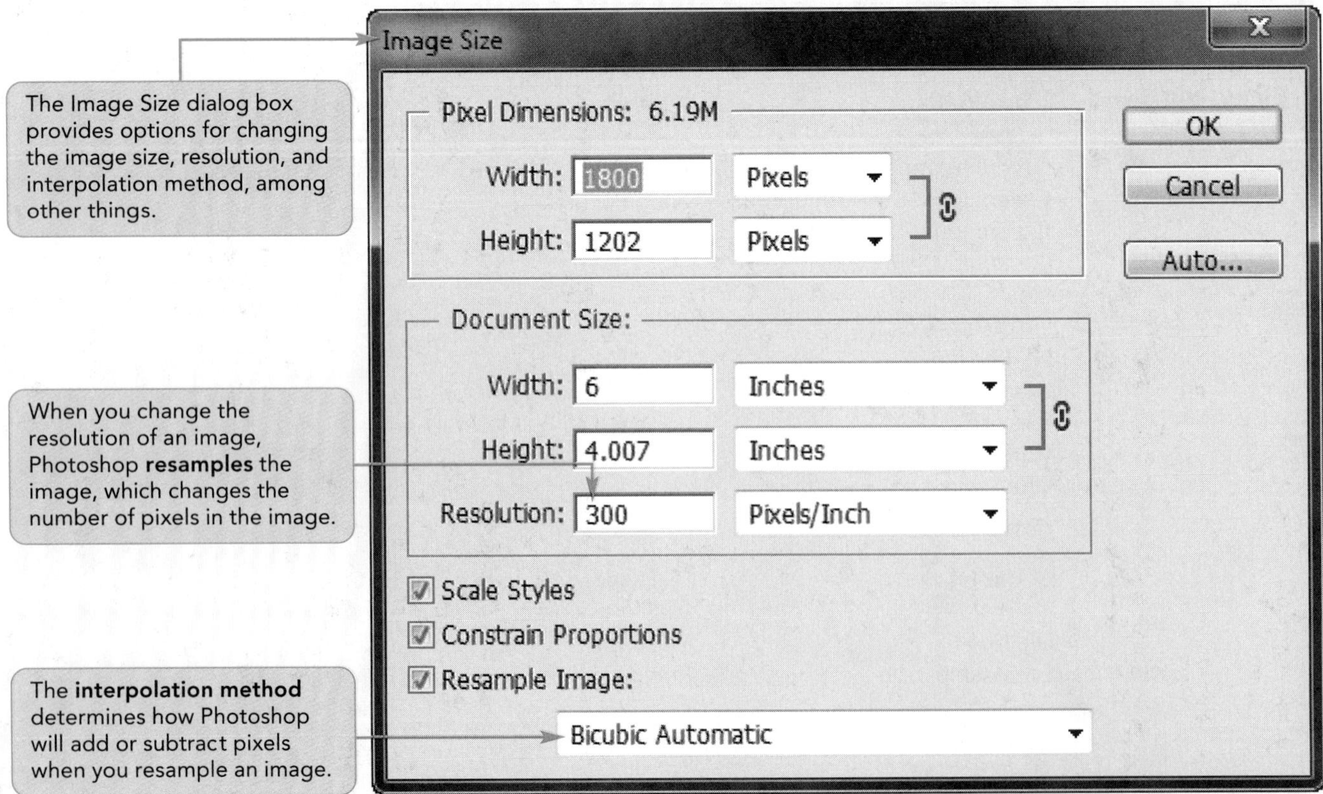

The **interpolation method** determines how Photoshop will add or subtract pixels when you resample an image.

FORMAT AND SIZE OPTIONS

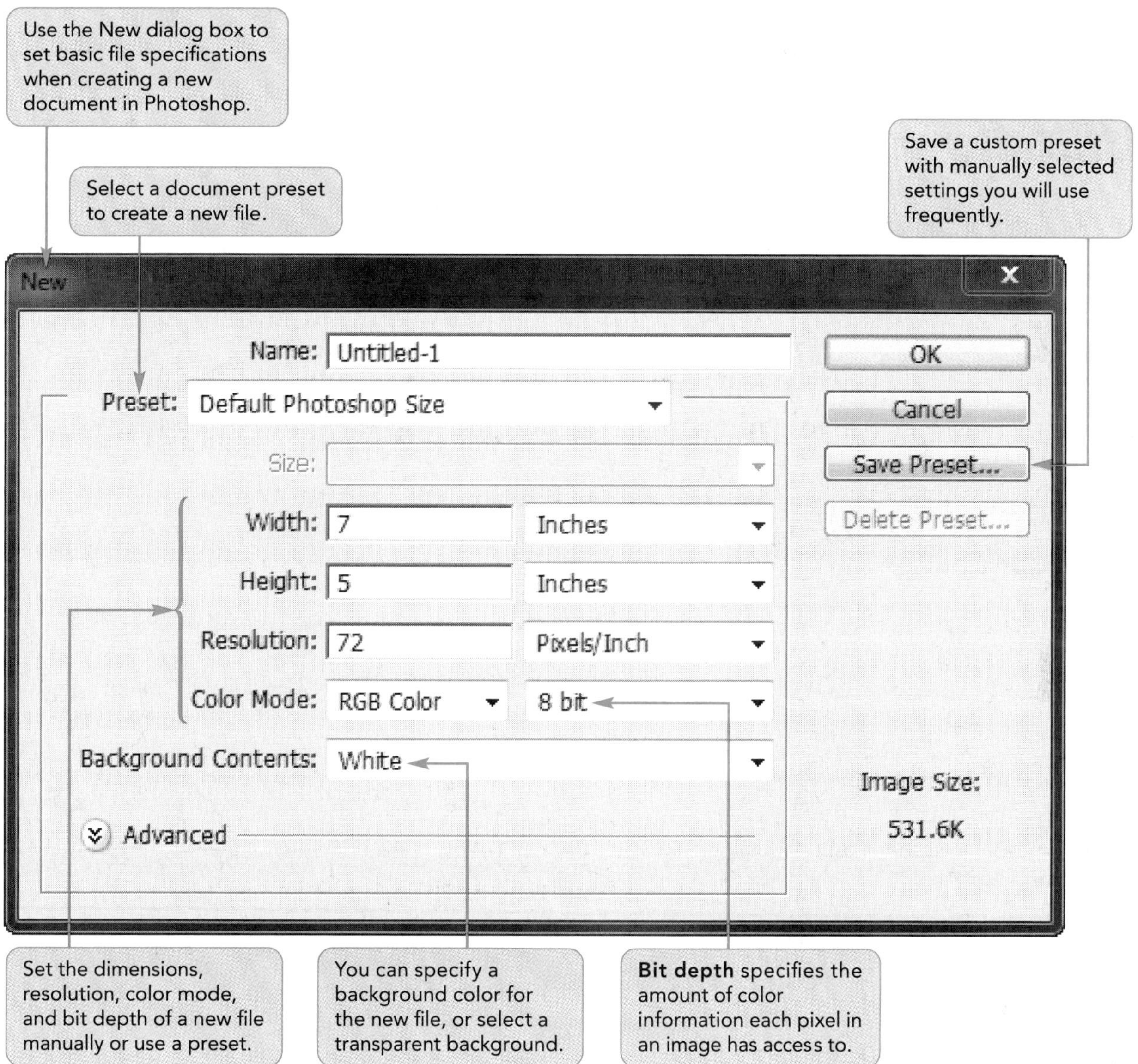
Use the New dialog box to set basic file specifications when creating a new document in Photoshop.
Select a document preset to create a new file.
Save a custom preset with manually selected settings you will use frequently.
New
Name: Untitled-1
Preset: Default Photoshop Size
Size:
Width: 7 Inches
Height: 5 Inches
Resolution: 72 Pixels/Inch
Color Mode: RGB Color 8 bit
Background Contents: White
Advanced
OK
Cancel
Save Preset...
Delete Preset...
Image Size:
531.6K
Set the dimensions, resolution, color mode, and bit depth of a new file manually or use a preset.
You can specify a background color for the new file, or select a transparent background.
Bit depth specifies the amount of color information each pixel in an image has access to.

Understanding File Formats and Their Uses

You can open and save images in Photoshop in well over a dozen file formats. In an image-editing program like Photoshop, the file format, or file type, determines how much space an image takes up in memory, how it handles color, and how it is printed as output.

Although files with different formats might look the same in the Photoshop Document window, certain characteristics of each format can affect upload time on the Web, the print quality of a finished piece, and even the Photoshop features you can use to manipulate the file. The number of file formats might seem overwhelming at first, but as you continue to work with Photoshop, you'll find that choosing the right file format will eventually become second nature. Figure 2-1 summarizes some commonly used file formats.

Figure 2-1 File formats

Format	Details
Bitmap (BMP)	Bitmap image file format for Windows; does not support CMYK color
Encapsulated PostScript (EPS)	File format that supports both vector and bitmap graphics; can be used for high-quality printouts on a PostScript printer; and can also be read by most graphics, illustration, and layout programs
Graphics Interchange Format (GIF)	Lossless format for bitmap images; suitable for Web images
Joint Photographic Experts Group (JPEG or JPG)	Lossy file format for bitmap images; suitable for Web images; supports CMYK, RGB, and Grayscale
Photoshop format (PSD)	File format that supports all Photoshop features and is easily imported by other Creative Suite applications; can include both vector and bitmap graphics
Photoshop Raw (RAW)	File format that allows you to transfer images between different applications and operating systems; includes metadata, including camera type and exposure, but cannot contain layers
Portable Document Format (PDF)	File format that can display images in different applications and operating systems
Portable Network Graphics (PNG)	Lossless file format for bitmap images; suitable for Web images
Tagged Image File Format (TIFF, TIF)	File format for bitmap images; allows you to transfer images between different applications and operating systems; supports layers in Photoshop, but not in other applications
Digital Imaging and Communications in Medicine (DICOM)	Medical scan file format; each frame or slice of a scan is converted to a layer in Photoshop, which can then be edited or adjusted using Photoshop tools
Digital Negative (DNG)	File format that contains raw image data, including metadata
Large Document Format (PSB)	File format that supports large documents—up to 300,000 pixels
Desktop Color Separations (DCS)	File format that saves the color separations in a file; related to the EPS format, it saves vector and bitmap graphics and is used for high-quality printouts
OpenEXR	High-quality file format used in movie production
Cineon	File format developed by Kodak that lets you import a file from film to digital and then output it back to film
Targa (TGA)	An RGB format developed for use with TrueVision technology

Each file format has its own advantages and disadvantages. Some file formats support only vector graphics, whereas others support only bitmap graphics. **PSD**, the default Photoshop format, stands for Photoshop document. The PSD format, which can hold both vector and bitmap data, stores multiple image components and enhancements on separate elements called **layers** so you can make changes to one part of a composition while leaving the other parts intact. **GIF** (Graphics Interchange Format), **PNG** (Portable Network Graphics), and **JPEG** (Joint Photographic Experts Group, sometimes written as JPG) formats are **flat formats** consisting of single layers of bitmap data. These file types work best for the Web because they tend to have smaller file sizes, so they upload more quickly. Other file types, such as **TIFF** (Tagged Image File Format) and **EPS** (Encapsulated PostScript), contain a great deal of data and are used to output high-quality print pieces.

Some file formats are **proprietary**, meaning they can only be edited in the program in which they were created. For example, the PSD file type is a proprietary file type; the .psd extension indicates a file is **native** to—or created in—Photoshop. PSD files can be easily manipulated in other Adobe applications such as Adobe Illustrator, Adobe Flash, and Adobe Fireworks, but many drawing, Web design, and image-editing programs do not support the PSD file format. If you need to use a PSD file in a program that doesn't support the PSD format, you must save it in a compatible format so you can open and manipulate it in the other application. When you convert a file to another format, you might lose some features—for example, Photoshop layers—that are supported in the original file. However, you also gain some benefits, such as the ability to use a file in many different applications. You can save an image in different formats for use in different media, such as in a four-color printed piece, on a Web page, or in a newspaper advertisement.

Changing File Type, File Size, and Resolution

In Photoshop, you have the flexibility to change the properties of a file not only by changing its file type, but also by changing its file size and its resolution. You can do this in a number of different ways, including by compressing a file and by resampling a file. As you learn the nuances of the different file types in Photoshop, you'll be able to achieve the results you want for each project by using the appropriate file type, size, and resolution.

Optimizing an Image

When you edit or enhance images in Photoshop, each layer of editing you add can increase the size of a file by many megabytes. Larger file sizes are a necessity if you want to print high-quality images; to achieve the most accurate colors and the sharpest printout, you need the layers of detail and color data stored with an image. However, on the Web, large image file sizes can result in painfully slow download times for the end user, as well as file storage challenges. Because of this, images on Web sites are often compressed to allow for quicker download times. Finding the right balance between image quality and file size is called **optimization**.

The three image file formats most commonly used on the Web—GIF, JPEG, and PNG—all use compression to optimize images and reduce the size of image files. The JPEG format uses **lossy compression** to reduce file size by throwing out, or "losing," some of the original data in an image. For example, it reduces the number of colors in an image and uses a process called **dithering** to replace the discarded colors with colors from the new, smaller color palette. A file format that uses lossy compression is called a **lossy file format**. The GIF file format is a **lossless file format**; it uses **lossless** compression, which means it doesn't discard data when it compresses the file. Instead, it stores data more efficiently—for example, by mapping all colors to a color table instead of storing each pixel's color information with the pixel itself.

It's wise to make edits to an image file while working in a high-resolution, non-lossy format. Doing so gives you more editing options. Then, when you have finished editing the image, you can optimize it by saving it in a file format, such as JPEG, that is better suited to Web use. When you save a file as a JPEG, the JPEG Options dialog box opens, as shown in Figure 2-2.

Figure 2-2 JPEG Options dialog box

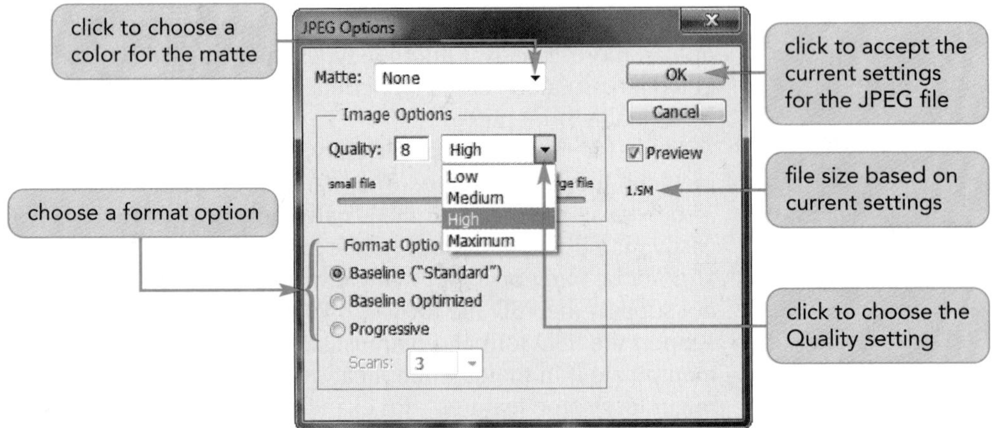

In the JPEG Options dialog box, you can select the **matte**, which is the color that will appear in the background of an image as it downloads while a user is trying to view it on the Web. You can also specify the quality of the image. The lower the quality, the smaller the file size and the faster the download time; however, you should always confirm that you haven't compromised the image quality on your Web site for the sake of a smaller file size. The JPEG Options dialog box offers three format options, including Baseline ("Standard"), which saves the file in a format most browsers can read. Baseline Optimized optimizes the color and results in a smaller than standard file size; however, not all browsers support optimized images. The Progressive format option results in an image that will initially be displayed with little detail, and then increase in detail as the file loads. In other words, it will appear as the ghost of an image, and then be filled in as the file loads. With the Progressive format option, you can specify three, four, or five **scans**, or stages, that the viewer will see before the image has finished loading. If you select the Preview check box, Photoshop calculates the approximate size of the file based on the selections you have made and displays it beneath the check box.

TIP

Always keep a copy of the original, unedited image file so it is available for other projects.

C. J. has an image that he'd like to use on the company's Web site. He asks you to save the file in a format that is suitable for Web use. You'll save the file as a JPEG and then use the JPEG Options dialog box to see the effect that compression has on file size.

To save the file in a lossy file format:

1. Start Photoshop while pressing the **Ctrl+Alt+Shift** keys. When you are prompted to delete the Adobe Photoshop Settings File, click **Yes**. On the menu bar, click **Window**, point to **Workspace**, and then click **Reset Essentials** to reset the default Essentials workspace layout. On the options bar, right-click the **Rectangular Marquee Tool** icon, and then click **Reset All Tools**. When you are asked if you want to reset all tools to the default settings, click the **OK** button.
2. On the menu bar, click **File**, click **Open** to display the Open dialog box, and then navigate to the Photoshop2\Tutorial folder included with your Data Files.

3. In the Open dialog box, click the **View Menu** button, and then click **Details** to select it, if necessary.

4. Click **GreenHouseConstruction.tif**. Scroll to the right, if necessary, to see the Size column. Notice that this file is large, over 19 megabytes (MB).

   Trouble? If the Size column does not appear in the Open dialog box, right-click any column header and then click Size on the context menu to add the Size column to the dialog box.

5. Click the **Open** button. The GreenHouseConstruction.tif file opens in the Photoshop Document window.

   The TIFF file has several layers, including a shape layer and a text layer with special effects. Preserving these layers in a TIFF file lets you modify them at a later point. You'll learn more about layers in Tutorial 3.

   Trouble? If you get a message about missing fonts, click the OK button, and let Photoshop make the substitution.

6. On the menu bar, click **File**, and then click **Save As**. The Save As dialog box opens with the Layers check box selected, indicating that the file includes layers.

7. Click the **Format** arrow, and then click **JPEG (*.JPG;*.JPEG;*.JPE)** in the list of available image file formats. The filename changes to GreenHouseContruction.jpg. See Figure 2-3.

Figure 2-3 Save As dialog box

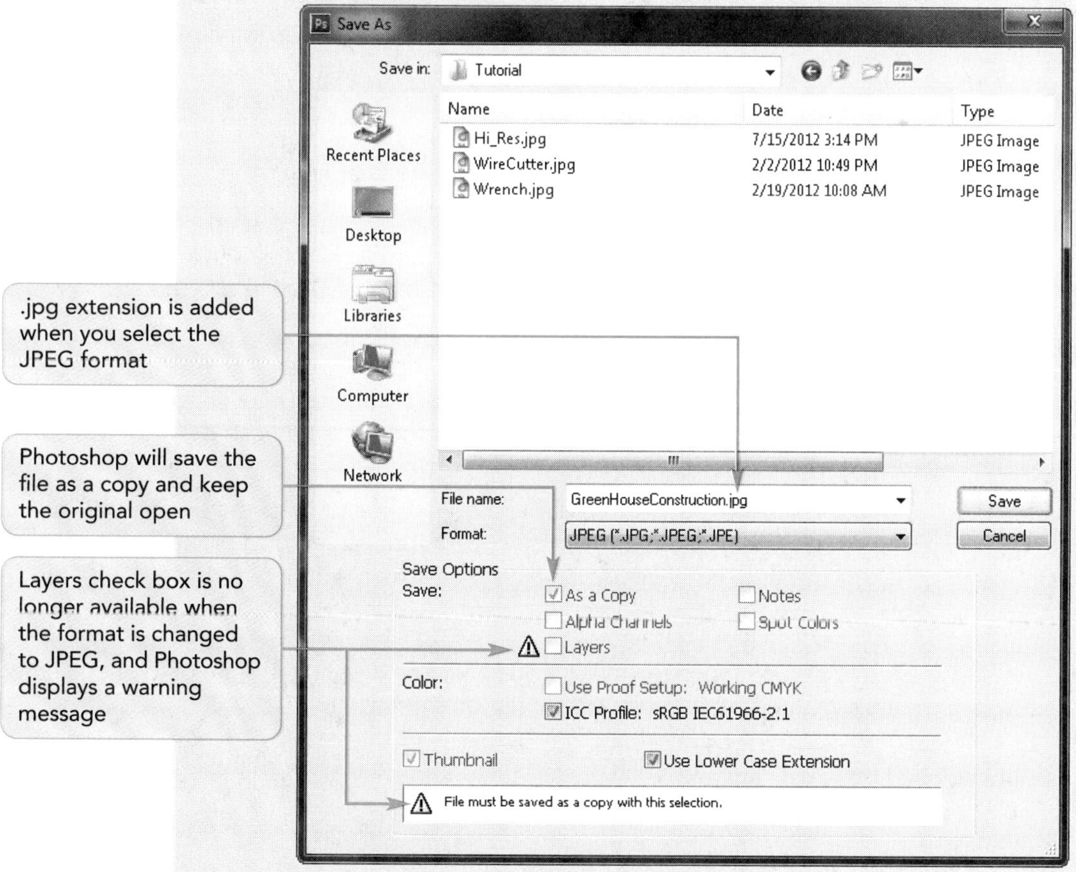

When you select JPEG as the file format, the Layers check box is cleared and is no longer available; at the bottom of the dialog box, next to an exclamation point, Photoshop displays a message indicating the file must be saved as a copy. When Photoshop saves the file, it will save it with the same name plus a .jpg extension in the current folder, but it will keep the original TIFF file open. To see the saved file, you'll need to open it in Photoshop.

8. Navigate to the Photoshop2\Tutorial folder, if necessary, and click the **Save** button. The JPEG Options dialog box opens, as shown in Figure 2-4.

Figure 2-4 **Changing JPEG options when saving**

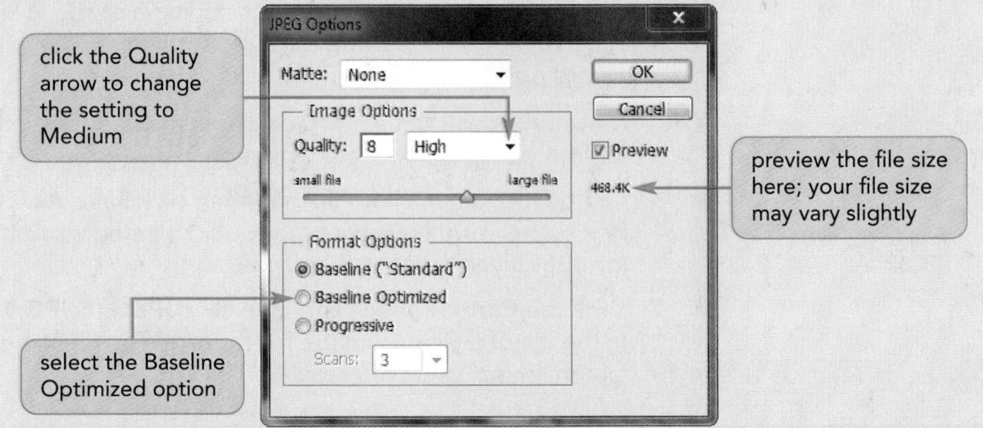

If you save the file with the default JPEG settings, the file size is reduced to around 468.4 kilobytes (KB), as shown under the Preview check box in the JPEG Options dialog box. This is a fraction of the original TIFF file size (which was over 19 MB). Next, you'll see what effect changing the Quality and Format Options has on file size.

Trouble? If you can't see the file size in the JPEG Options dialog box, click the Preview check box to select it and show the file size.

9. Click the **Quality** arrow, click **Medium**, and then, under Format Options, click **Baseline Optimized**. Photoshop previews the file size at around 295 KB.

The new file size is only about 60 percent as large as the file size that results from using the default settings in the JPEG Options dialog box. It is also less than 2 percent of the size of the original file. This difference should give you a very clear idea of how important optimization can be when you prepare images for the Web.

10. Click the **OK** button. Photoshop saves a copy of the file in JPEG format. The original version of the file, in TIFF format, remains open. To view the JPEG version, you need to open the new file.

Next, you'll open the file so you can show C. J. that in spite of the huge difference in file size, the images look very similar on screen.

To compare the two GreenHouseConstruction files:

1. On the menu bar, click **File**, and then click **Open**. The Open dialog box opens.

   Notice that the size of the GreenHouseConstruction.jpg file is even smaller than it was in the preview, and is listed at around 284 KB. This is because when Photoshop saves the file to disk, it compresses it even more. When you open it, it will expand slightly in memory for better display, and return to about 295 KB. (Your file sizes may vary slightly.)

2. Double-click the **GreenHouseConstruction.jpg** file to open it. Notice in the Layers panel that this file consists of a single layer labeled *Background*.
3. On the menu bar, click **Window**, point to **Arrange**, and then click **2-up Vertical** .
4. Press the **Tab** key to hide all panels so the images appear larger.
5. On the status bar of the GreenHouseConstruction.jpg window, type **35** in the zoom percentage box, and then press the **Enter** key to zoom GreenHouseConstruction.jpg to 35%.
6. On the status bar of the GreenHouseConstruction.tif window, type **35** in the zoom percentage box, and then press the **Enter** key to zoom GreenHouseConstruction.tif to 35%. See Figure 2-5.

Figure 2-5 **JPEG and TIFF files displayed side by side**

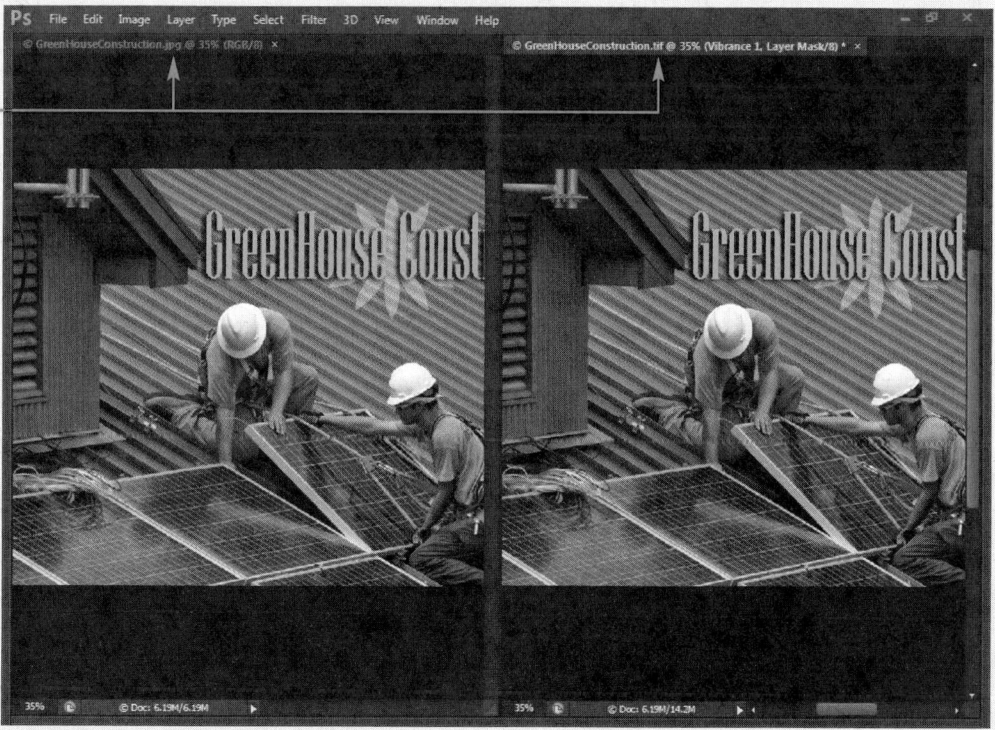

Even though the JPEG file is a small fraction of the size of the TIFF file, the two files look identical on screen at a 35% zoom setting.

7. Press the **Ctrl+1** keys to zoom the TIFF file to 100%, click the **GreenHouseConstruction.jpg** tab, and then press the **Ctrl+1** keys to zoom the JPEG file to 100%. Although the JPEG file has been compressed and is slightly less crisp than the TIFF file at such a high zoom percentage, it is still suitable for viewing on a computer monitor.

   Given that images on Web pages take up only a fraction of the display area available on a monitor, you can be sure that this file will work well on C. J.'s Web site.

8. Close GreenHouseConstruction.tif. Leave the GreenHouseConstruction.jpg file open, and press the **Tab** key to redisplay the panels.

Changing Image Resolution

Because different projects require files with different resolutions, Photoshop gives you the option of changing the resolution of a file. To change resolution, you open the Image Size dialog box and type in a new value. See Figure 2-6.

Figure 2-6 Image Size dialog box

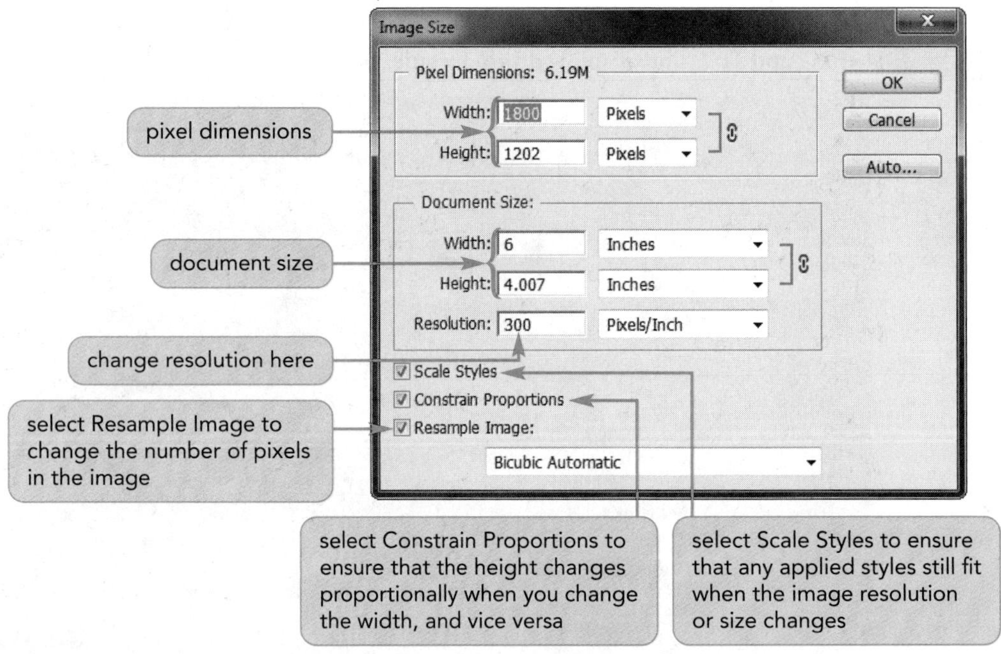

TIP

You can upsample a low-resolution image to increase the dimensions of a photo, but you'll achieve better results if you simply start with a high-resolution image.

Remember that resolution is measured in pixels per inch, so when you change an image's resolution, you are changing the number of pixels per inch. Photoshop uses a process called resampling to achieve the new resolution. You can resample an image in two different directions, depending on whether you want to decrease or increase the resolution. If you **upsample** an image, Photoshop adds pixels to the image so that there are more pixels per inch. It does this using a mathematical algorithm that uses interpolation to calculate what each added pixel should look like based on the surrounding pixels. The different interpolation methods are outlined in Figure 2-7.

Figure 2-7 **Interpolation methods**

Method	Details
Nearest Neighbor	Makes exact copies of pixels when upsampling; can result in jagged edges
Bilinear	Averages the color values of surrounding pixels to create new pixels
Bicubic	Uses complex calculations to determine values for new pixels; higher quality than Nearest Neighbor or Bilinear
Bicubic Smoother	Uses more complex calculations to calculate values for new pixels; higher quality than Nearest Neighbor, Bilinear, or Bicubic
Bicubic Sharper	Sharpens an image using a calculation similar to Bicubic Smoother; can result in edges that are too sharp
Bicubic Automatic	The default interpolation method; automatically chooses the best resampling method for you based on the resizing options you choose

Upsampling can't improve the quality of a blurry image because the interpolation algorithm can only use the information already contained in the file. If the existing pixels display an imperfect image, the upsampled image will be imperfect as well.

If you **downsample** an image by decreasing the resolution, Photoshop throws out pixels to keep the document the same physical dimensions—for example, 6 × 4 inches. What do you think might happen to the size of a file if you decrease the number of pixels per inch by downsampling? Rather than thinking in terms of pixels, think of a high-resolution photograph as a bucket of pebbles—with dozens of evenly spaced pebbles completely covering the bottom of the bucket. Now consider what happens to the weight of the bucket when you take some pebbles out so that the remaining pebbles are still evenly spaced, but no longer touching—the bucket will be lighter. When you downsample, you are decreasing the resolution (you have fewer pixels per inch), which results in a "lighter" file.

INSIGHT

PPI vs. DPI

Note that *ppi*, or pixels per inch, is different from the *dpi* (dots per inch) setting used to describe printer resolution. On a printer, one pixel can be created by multiple dots, depending on the resolution of your printer. In other words, there is not a one-to-one correspondence between ppi and dpi. A resolution of 300 ppi is excellent for a high-quality print piece, but 300 dpi could result in a grainy-looking printout if an image includes many different color gradations. An image with a resolution of 300 pixels per inch printed on a high-resolution printer might very well have 1200, or even 2880, dots per inch. It is a good idea to make sure everyone involved in a project is using these terms correctly so the final output quality meets the project's requirements.

You can also decrease the resolution of an image without resampling to increase the physical dimensions of your image. For example, you can change the resolution of a 4 × 6-inch photograph from 300 ppi to 150 ppi. If you deselect Resample Image in the Image Size dialog box, Photoshop will achieve the new resolution by spreading out the pixels over a larger area. Cutting the resolution in half will result in an image that is twice the dimensions of the original—or, using this example, 8 × 12 inches. This decrease in resolution will *not* result in a smaller file size because the image will still have the same number of pixels. If we return to the bucket analogy, you'll be carrying around a bucket with the same number of pebbles in it, but the bucket itself will be twice the size of the original, and the pebbles will be more spread out. Depending on your needs, this method might produce an acceptable image. However, if you plan to use the image in a printed piece, remember that spreading out pixels can result in poorer image quality.

REFERENCE

Changing Image Resolution Using Resampling

- On the menu bar, click Image, and then click Image Size.
- Confirm that the Resample Image check box is selected in the Image Size dialog box.
- Type a new value in the Resolution box.
- Click the OK button to change the resolution.
- Save the file with a new filename.

You'll experiment with different resolution settings so you are familiar with the different options available for the various advertising media C. J. plans to use.

To change the resolution of the GreenHouseConstruction.jpg image using resampling:

1. Make sure that the GreenHouseConstruction.jpg file is open in Photoshop at 100% magnification.
2. On the menu bar, click **Image**, and then click **Image Size**. The Image Size dialog box opens. It displays the pixel dimensions of the image (1800 pixels wide × 1202 pixels high). It also displays the document size, which is the size at which the image is currently set to print. At present, the document size is about 6 × 4 inches.
3. Click the **Resample Image** check box to select it, if necessary. Highlight **300** in the Resolution box to select it, and then type **150**. Leave the default interpolation method, Bicubic Automatic, unchanged. See Figure 2-8.

Figure 2-8 **Changing the resolution**

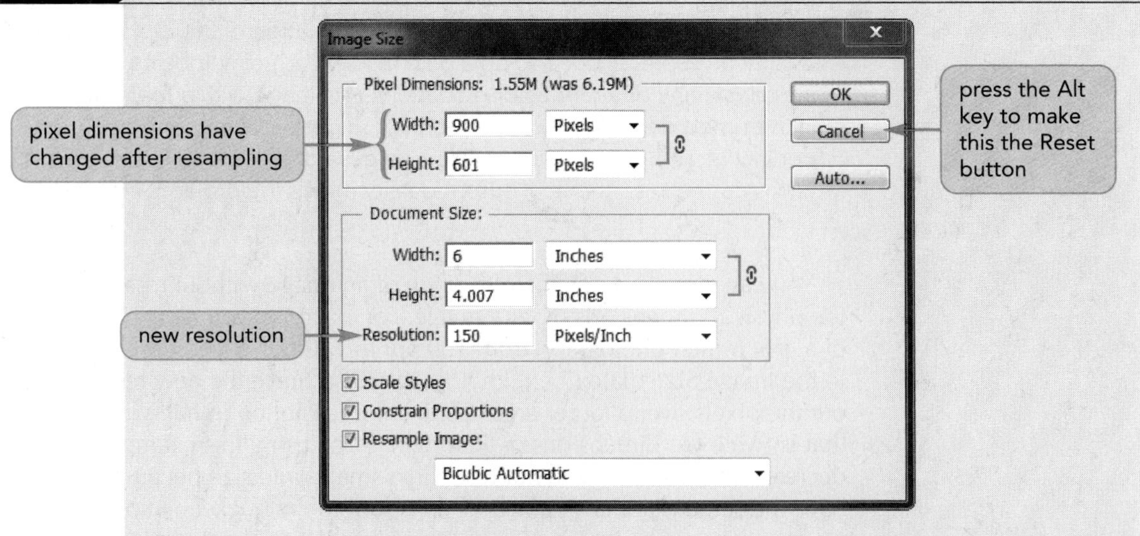

Trouble? If you make a mistake while working in the Image Size dialog box, press and hold the Alt key and then click the Reset button in the dialog box to return to the original settings.

When the Resample Image option is selected, Photoshop throws out pixels to reach the lower resolution (fewer pixels per inch). The pixel dimensions are now 900 × 601, or exactly half the pixel dimensions of the 300 ppi image.

4. Click the **OK** button, and then press the **Ctrl+0** keys to fit the image on the screen.

   Trouble? If the Open dialog box appears, you pressed the letter O instead of the number zero. Click the Cancel button to close the dialog box and press the Ctrl+0 keys.

5. Save the file as **GreenHouseConstruction150ppi.jpg** in the Photoshop2\Tutorial folder, and then click the **OK** button to accept the settings in the JPEG Options dialog box.

   A resolution of 150 ppi will be appropriate for a newspaper ad or for a 4 × 6-inch photograph printed on your home printer. You can also resave the file at a lower resolution appropriate for Web graphics.

Be sure to save the file with the new name so you still have a copy of the original high-resolution file, which you'll need for later steps.

6. On the menu bar, click **Image**, and then click **Image Size**.
7. Highlight **150** in the Resolution box to select it, and then type **72**. The pixel dimensions are now 432 × 289, or a little less than half the pixel dimensions of the 150-ppi image. This resolution will be sufficient for displaying the construction image on the Web.
8. Click the **OK** button to close the Image Size dialog box, and then save the file as **GreenHouseConstruction 72ppi.jpg** in the Photoshop2\Tutorial folder using the current JPEG settings.
9. Close GreenHouseConstruction 72ppi.jpg.

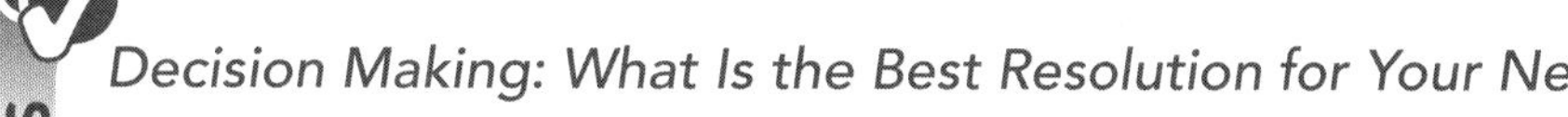

PROSKILLS

Decision Making: What Is the Best Resolution for Your Needs?

You already know that the resolution you need for an image is determined by how you plan to use the image, but which resolutions are best for which needs? If you are going to display the image on the Web, a relatively low resolution of 72 ppi is the standard. If your image will appear in black and white in a newspaper, 150 ppi is acceptable. If you are going to print an image on your color printer and want it to look good enough to frame, the resolution should be 240 ppi or above. Finally, if your image will appear in a magazine or professional journal, 300 ppi is your safest bet. At a lower resolution, you risk having your image look grainy. A resolution higher than 300 ppi adds many megabytes to the file size, but not much in terms of quality.

These guidelines can help you make decisions about which images you'll use for a project, but you also need to decide in advance whether you'll manipulate resolution in Photoshop, or whether you'll start with a file that already fits the bill. Many factors will go into making this decision, including time constraints (you are on a deadline), client needs (you are required to use the images provided), and budget (the client cannot afford to send a photographer into the field to shoot a new image or cannot afford to purchase a different image). Familiarizing yourself with all of your options ahead of time will ensure that you make the best decision to meet the needs of any given project.

Managing Multiple Image Files with Adobe Bridge and Mini Bridge

After you have worked with Photoshop for a while, you are bound to have dozens or even hundreds of different image files on your computer, but how do you organize them? Photoshop ships with a file management application called Adobe Bridge that simplifies storing, finding, sorting, and filtering your images. You work with Bridge outside of Photoshop, and you can use it in much the same way you use Windows Explorer to navigate folders on your computer. See Figure 2-9.

Figure 2-9 Adobe Bridge

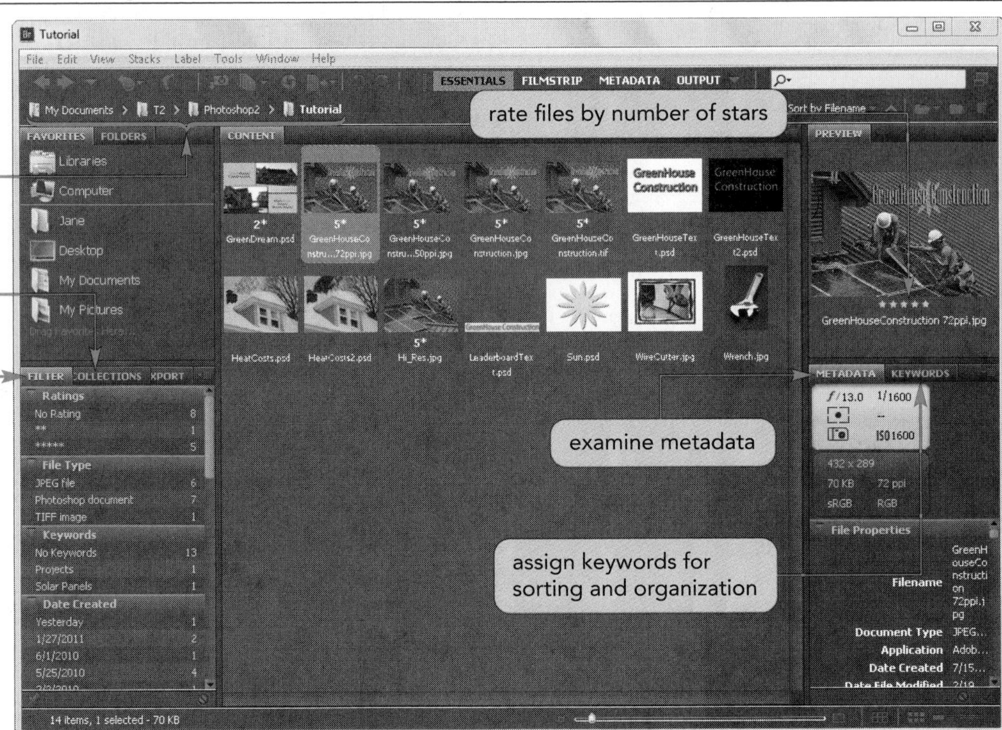
navigate through the folder hierarchy on your computer
organize your photos by selecting them and storing them in a named collection
filter the contents of a folder
rate files by number of stars
examine metadata
assign keywords for sorting and organization
Tutorial
ESSENTIALS FILMSTRIP METADATA OUTPUT
FAVORITES FOLDERS
CONTENT
PREVIEW
FILTER COLLECTIONS EXPORT
METADATA KEYWORDS
14 items, 1 selected - 70 KB

C.H. Gorman; © 2009 Alex Snyder/Wayne National Forest; Jane Hosie-Bounar; © 2009 Alex Snyder/Wayne National Forest; Garsya/Shutterstock.com

Bridge also has powerful tools that let you use metadata and keywords to categorize your images. In general terms, **metadata** is data about data—for example, information describing how data is formatted or how it was collected. In Bridge, metadata information could include details about the camera that a photographer used to shoot a photograph, the lighting conditions in which a photograph was taken, the date a file was created, the date a file was modified, file dimensions, resolution, color mode, bit depth, and copyright information, among other things. You can use the tools in Bridge to categorize your images with **keywords**, or words that describe your photographs in some way. For example, you might assign the keyword *People* to all photographs of people. You can also rate your photographs using a system of stars. A five-star image is better than a two-star image. You can then use this information to filter a folder containing photographs. A **filter** hides all files except those specified by the filter. So, you could filter by keyword so that only photos assigned the keyword *People* are listed, or you could filter by rating to display only the five-star photographs. You can also sort your images by rating, by filename, by file type, or by a number of other sort options. Another feature in Bridge lets you select files from many different folders and then add them to a custom object called a collection. A **collection** allows you to access photos stored in multiple locations with the click of a mouse. Bridge is fully integrated with Photoshop, so it is easy to switch between the two applications.

Photoshop also includes a stripped-down version of Bridge called Mini Bridge that opens directly in Photoshop. Adobe Mini Bridge is the "pocket-sized" version of Adobe Bridge. It has some, but not all, of the features of Bridge. For example, you can't assign a rating to a file in Mini Bridge, but you can view ratings, navigate folders, filter images, and search for and preview images without leaving the Photoshop workspace. You can also preview a file in Full Screen mode before you open it in Photoshop or see a slide show of all of the files in a folder before opening them. Review Mode displays the currently selected image in a new window, with the other images in the folder stacked behind it. You can navigate through those images using navigation buttons. You can also use Review mode to add photos to a named collection, or to zoom in on different areas of an image.

When it first opens, Mini Bridge displays the folder path of the current Windows user in the navigation area on the left. You can display a list of recently used folders by clicking the Computer button in the navigation area and then clicking Recent Folders. You can also click Recent Files to display a list of recently used files. When you do, the navigation area displays the names of any Creative Suite applications you have installed. When you click an application name such as Photoshop, the preview area displays a list of the digital image files you have recently worked with in Photoshop.

TIP

You can also click the Browse in Mini Bridge command on the File menu to expand Mini Bridge.

To use Mini Bridge:

1. Click the **Mini Bridge** tab at the bottom of the Photoshop window. The Mini Bridge panel expands under the Document window and displays a message indicating that Bridge must be open in order to use Mini Bridge.
2. In the Mini Bridge panel, click the **Launch Bridge** button. Photoshop displays the message "Waiting for Bridge CS6." Then Mini Bridge displays the navigation area on the left and the preview area on the right. By default, the navigation area displays a Computer button and a list of the drives on your computer. You can click the Computer button to display Favorites and recently visited folders.
3. In the navigation area on the left, click the **Computer** button, and then click **Favorites**. Mini Bridge displays a list of favorites in the navigation area including Computer, Desktop, My Documents, and My Pictures. If you have specified any Favorites in Windows, it displays those folders as well.

   Trouble? If the button in the navigation area is labeled something other than Computer, clicking it will still display the current user's main Windows folder, Favorites, Recent Folders, Recent Files, and Collections.
4. In the Favorites list, click **My Pictures**. Mini Bridge displays the contents of the My Pictures library.
5. In the navigation area click the **Favorites** button, click **Recent Files**, and then click **Photoshop**. See Figure 2-10.

Figure 2-10 Adobe Mini Bridge

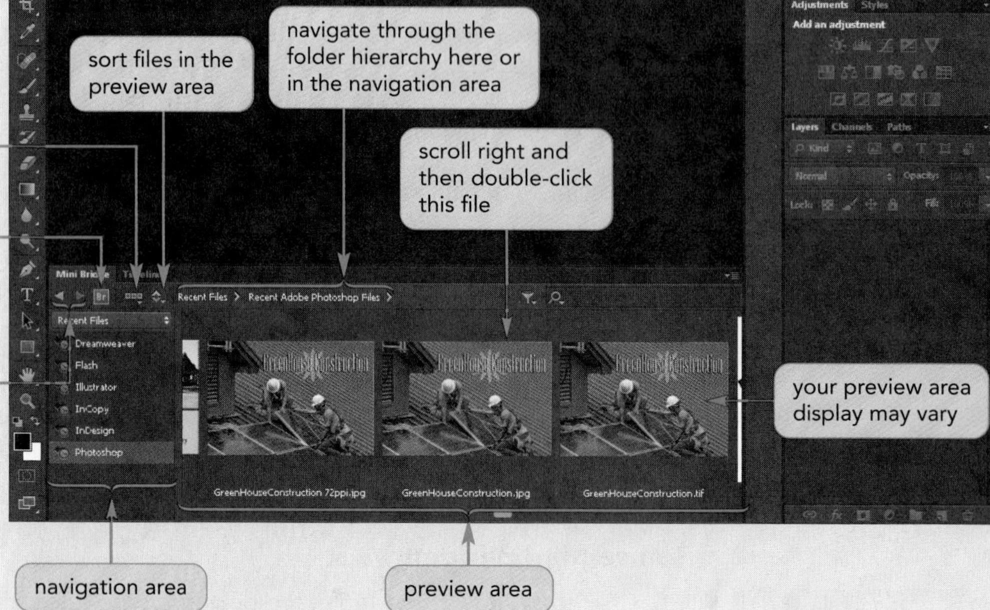

sort files in the preview area
navigate through the folder hierarchy here or in the navigation area
select files or change their viewing mode
scroll right and then double-click this file
click to display current folder contents in Bridge
navigate through the files in the folder or among folders in the folder hierarchy
your preview area display may vary
navigation area
preview area

C.H. Gorman; © 2009 Alex Snyder/Wayne National Forest

TIP

You can also open a file by dragging it from Mini Bridge into the Document window.

6. In the preview area, scroll right if necessary, and then double-click **GreenHouseConstruction.jpg**. The GreenHouseConstruction.jpg file opens in the Document window.
7. Double-click the **Mini Bridge** tab. The Mini Bridge panel collapses.
8. On the menu bar, click **File**, and then click **Browse in Bridge**. In Bridge, click **File** on the menu bar, and then click **Exit**. Bridge closes.

Now that you have a good understanding of file formats, resolution, and file size, and know how to find and sort files in Mini Bridge, C. J. asks you to spend some time learning about the different color modes available in Photoshop so you'll be able to meet the needs of his advertising campaign on the Web, in four-color printed pieces, and in black-and-white newspapers.

INSIGHT

Adding User Information and Metadata in the File Info Dialog Box

Photoshop offers many options for viewing and adding metadata to a file. You have already seen that you can categorize and add metadata to files using Bridge. You can also open the File Info dialog box from the File menu to view camera and image data and add metadata such as keywords, ratings, and descriptions. You can view camera data such as camera model, image resolution, image size, and exposure, and if your camera has GPS capabilities, you can view GPS information for an image. If you are working with a medical image, you can use the DICOM tab to enter information such as a patient's name, ID number, and date of birth. Whether you choose to use the File Info dialog box or Bridge, it is always a good idea to enter as much information about a file as possible in case you need to reference it later.

Understanding Color Modes and Intensities

Color mode is an important setting that you must take into consideration when preparing an image in Photoshop. The color modes in Photoshop are based on a variety of industry-standard color models. A **color model** is a set of mathematical values that numerically represent color. Each color model consists of a few **primary**, or starting, colors (for example, red, green, and blue) that you can combine in different intensities to create hundreds of thousands, or even millions, of other colors. Common color models are RGB, CMYK, and grayscale. To understand how many color choices you can end up with using different combinations of only a few colors, consider the RGB model. The RGB color model uses only three colors—red, green, and blue—but each of these colors can be assigned a value from 0 (for no color) to 255 (for maximum color intensity). In Photoshop, **intensity** simply refers to the value you have assigned to one of the primary colors. That means you have 256 choices—or intensities—for red (remember that 0 is a choice), 256 choices for green, and 256 choices for blue. That's 256 × 256 × 256 color possibilities, or about 16.7 million choices. See Figure 2-11.

Figure 2-11 **Differing color intensities**

the red brush stroke on the right has these RGB intensity values
three different red colors with different intensity values

You can think of intensity in terms of paint. If you dip your brush in red paint and then paint on a canvas, you'll get one version of red paint. However, if you first put a bit of blue paint on your brush, and then dip the brush in the red paint, you'll get a different red with a different intensity. Finally, if you first dip your brush in a bit of green and then dip it in the red paint, you get still another version of the color red. Now imagine that you mix that first deep color of red thoroughly with a deep blue, but no green. You'll get a color that is neither red, nor blue, nor green, but a combination of red and blue. Or perhaps you combine it with green, but not blue. You'll get a different color.

Photoshop lets you specify the intensity of colors using numbers. Each color mode uses a different numbering system, but the results are similar: You start with a few color settings, but you wind up with a seemingly unlimited palette of colors to choose from. Different media require different color modes, and although the orange color you see on screen and the orange color you see on a printed page might look identical, they are created in completely different ways, by combining different colors in different color modes.

Understanding the RGB Color Mode

By default, new files in Photoshop use the RGB color mode, which is based on the RGB color model. The **RGB** (red, green, blue) color mode is an additive color mode. As you might expect, an **additive color mode** adds colors together to create a different color. See Figure 2-12.

Figure 2-12 **RGB color mode**

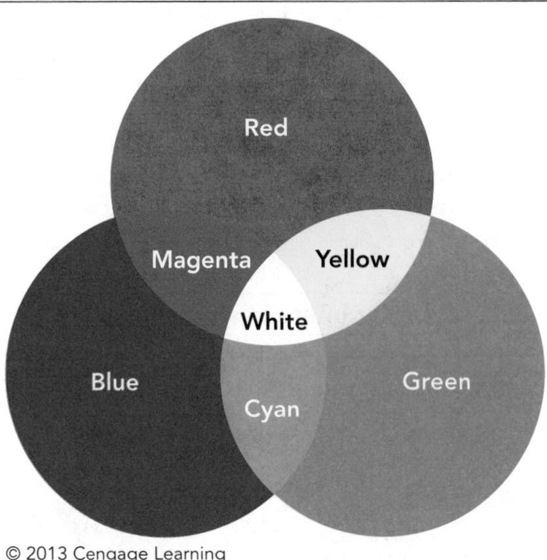

Combining the three primary colors in varying intensities results in the colors cyan, magenta, and yellow. For example, in Photoshop, a red setting of 142, a green setting of 61, and a blue setting of 151 results in an intense magenta. A red setting of 255, a green setting of 255, and a blue setting of 0 results in a yellow color, as shown in the color sliders in Figure 2-13.

Figure 2-13 **Color values**

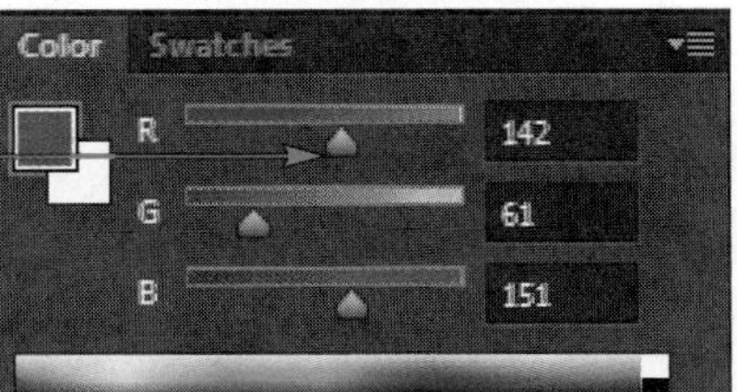

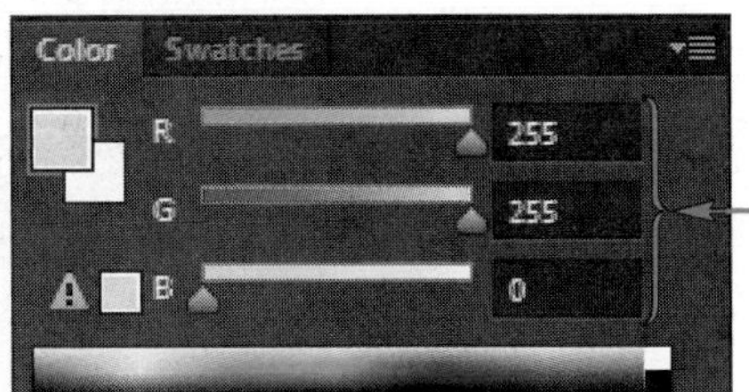

You have seen that red, green, and blue additive colors can create cyan, magenta, and yellow, but where do the colors white and black come from? If you have ever taken a physics course, you know that white light contains all of the colors in the color spectrum, and black is the absence of color. In fact, the RGB color mode follows the laws of physics; combining all three colors at their maximum intensities (255, 255, 255) results in white. Specifying a setting of 0 for all three colors (0, 0, 0) results in the color black.

Understanding the CMYK Color Mode

CMYK (cyan, magenta, yellow, key) is a color mode specifically meant for printed output. CMYK is a **subtractive color mode** because each color subtracts the light from the white page on which it's printed. Because printed output involves putting ink on white paper, the CMYK mode might make more sense to you than RGB. You don't need to have studied physics to understand CMYK. In fact, you learned all you need to know about this mode in kindergarten, where you discovered that mixing two paint colors together results in a third color, but mixing all paint colors together results in black. See Figure 2-14.

Figure 2-14 **CMYK color mode**

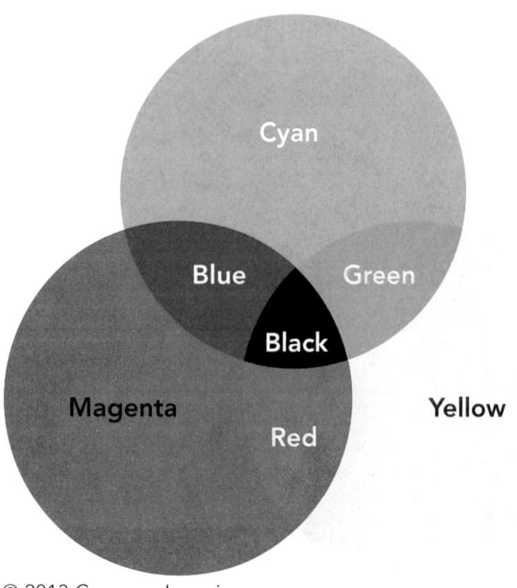

In the CMYK color mode, you specify color combinations in terms of percentages rather than intensity values, but CMYK still involves combining the primary colors of the mode, which in this case are cyan, magenta, yellow, and black.

You might wonder why the mode is called CMYK (for key) instead of CMYB (for black). In the CMYK color mode, *key* does refer to black, which is the color used on the key plate in the four-color printing process. The **key plate** is the plate in the printing process used to print the details in an image. To understand how printed output might look without the color black (and to understand why black is "key"), see Figure 2-15.

Figure 2-15 **Image with and without black, a "key" color**

black adds detail
and contrast to
shadows and light

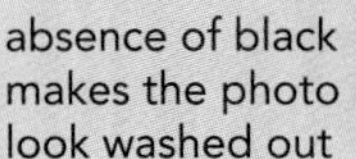
absence of black
makes the photo
look washed out

Jane Hosie-Bounar

> **TIP**
>
> Some inkjet printers print in RGB color mode rather than CMYK. Although the quality of these printers is not sufficient for a professional project, it is usually acceptable for home use.

The photograph on the top of the figure includes the key color (black). The photograph on the bottom shows the image as it would look without any black. You can see that the key color is essential to a crisp, clean image.

Because CMYK involves one more color than RGB, the file size of a CMYK image can be about 50 percent larger than its RGB counterpart, depending on optimization settings. Therefore, if you are only using a file for the Web, it's wise to use RGB.

Understanding Indexed Colors

The 8-bit Indexed color model uses a palette of 256 colors, which might seem limited given the millions of colors available in other models. However, for many uses, such as for Web animations and Web pages, 256 colors are more than enough. The advantage of using an Indexed color model rather than RGB is smaller file size. When you convert a file to the Indexed color model, Photoshop analyzes the colors in the image and then creates a **color lookup table (CLUT)** of 256 colors. The CLUT can consist of any of the colors in the image you are converting. For example, if you are converting from RGB, Photoshop creates the CLUT using just 256 of the 16.7 million color choices. See Figure 2-16.

Figure 2-16 **Color lookup table (CLUT)**

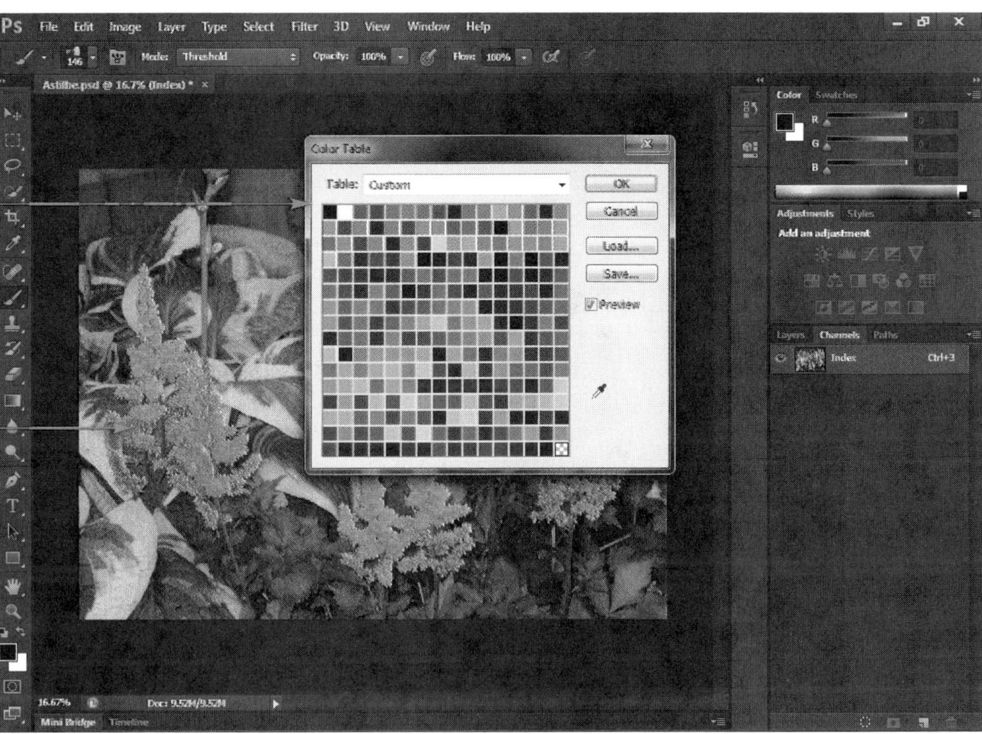
the CLUT includes only 256 of the 16.7 million colors available to the RGB image
even with limited colors, the image quality is acceptable
File Edit Image Layer Type Select Filter 3D View Window Help
Color Table
Table: Custom
OK
Cancel
Load...
Save...
Preview

Jane Hosie-Bounar

If a color in the image matches a color stored in the table, Photoshop maps the pixel to that cell in the table. If a color has no matches in the table, Photoshop chooses the closest color from the table, or maps it to two or more indexed colors to simulate the color needed in the image. Switching an image to the Indexed color model in Photoshop is another way to optimize an image. Furthermore, the Indexed color model is supported by many different applications and, therefore, "travels" well from application to application. Your challenge is to ensure that the reduction of color choices doesn't result in a reduction in image quality.

Understanding the Grayscale Color Mode

When you convert an image from one of the other Photoshop color modes to Grayscale mode, Photoshop translates every intensity or shade of every color to a different shade, or **tone**, of gray. White is 0 percent, and black is 100 percent gray. See Figure 2-17.

Figure 2-17 Grayscale color percentages

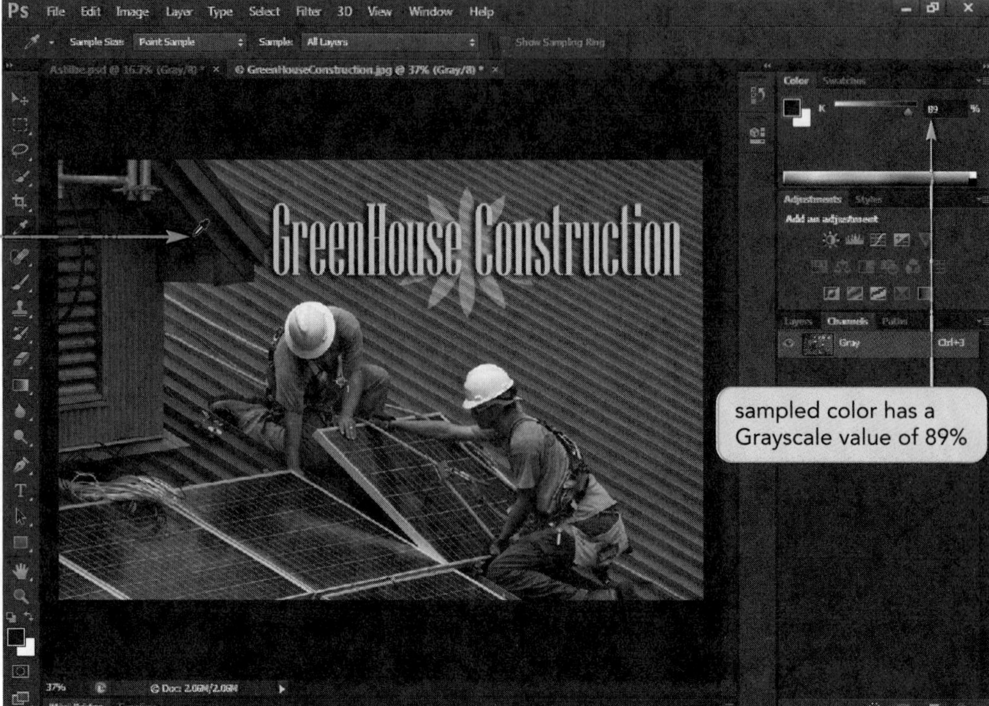
gray color sampled from here
sampled color has a Grayscale value of 89%
GreenHouse Construction

© 2009 Alex Snyder/Wayne National Forest

You can modify the tones of gray in an image converted to Grayscale mode—in other words, make them lighter or darker—but you cannot get the original color back once you save the file and close it. Converting the color mode to Grayscale in Photoshop is an example of **destructive editing**—all of the original color information is discarded when you save and close the file. Therefore, when you convert a file to Grayscale mode, you should immediately save it with a new name so you do not overwrite your original color file with the grayscale file.

Understanding How Bit Depth Combined with Color Mode Affects File Size

Each pixel in an image represents a single color. When the eye views hundreds or thousands of pixels together, the colors blend together and appear to transition smoothly from one part of the image to the next. Images with higher bit depths result in more realistically colored images because they have more available colors for shading and variations. Figure 2-18 explains the relationship between bit depth and color mode for some of the most commonly used Photoshop color modes.

Figure 2-18 Bit depth and color mode

Color Mode	Bit Depth	Number of Colors
Black and White	1	Each pixel in a black-and-white image has two possible values, black (0) or white (1), resulting in 2^1 possible colors—in other words, two.
Grayscale	8	The bit depth of a grayscale image in Photoshop is 8, which allows you to access 2^8, or 256 shades of gray.
RGB	8	An RGB image with a bit depth of 8 has a possible 16.7 million colors, 2^8 (or 256) choices of red, times 2^8 (or 256) choices of green, times 2^8 (or 256) choices of blue.
CMYK	8	A CMYK image with a bit depth of 8 has 256 times the number of colors available in an RGB image. In other words, it has over 4.2 billion possible colors (256 × 256 × 256 × 256).

Photoshop also supports 32-bit and 16-bit images, but not all of its features are available at these bit depths. Typically, you would use a 32-bit image, also called a **high dynamic range** or **HDR image**, in a computer graphics scene that requires a high level of detail and great contrast between dark and light areas; you might also use 32-bit images in 3D imagery. HDR image files are very large, and if you're using Photoshop for print pieces and Web ads, you are safe sticking with 8-bit imagery.

Changing Color Modes

You can change color mode in Photoshop based on your needs. For example, if you have a CMYK image that you would also like to use on the Web, you can switch from CMYK mode to RGB mode. To do so, you use the Mode command on the Image menu. If you switch from CMYK or RGB to the Indexed color mode, Photoshop will confirm that you want to flatten your image because Indexed color doesn't support layers; when you flatten an image, Photoshop merges all the layers into one. If you switch from any color mode to Grayscale, Photoshop will display a warning asking you to confirm that you want to discard the color information in the file.

C. J. wants you to save his GreenHouseConstruction.jpg image so that it is suitable for a newspaper ad. To do so, you'll convert it to Grayscale mode and decrease the resolution.

To change the color mode and decrease the resolution of the GreenHouseConstruction.jpg image:

1. Press the **Ctrl+0** keys to fit the photo on screen, and then save GreenHouseConstruction.jpg as **BWGreenHouse.jpg** in the Photoshop2\Tutorial folder, selecting **High** quality and **Baseline ("Standard")** in the JPEG Options dialog box.
2. On the menu bar, click **Image**, point to **Mode**, and then click **Grayscale**. Photoshop displays a dialog box prompting you to confirm that you want to discard color information. See Figure 2-19.

Figure 2-19 Discarding color information

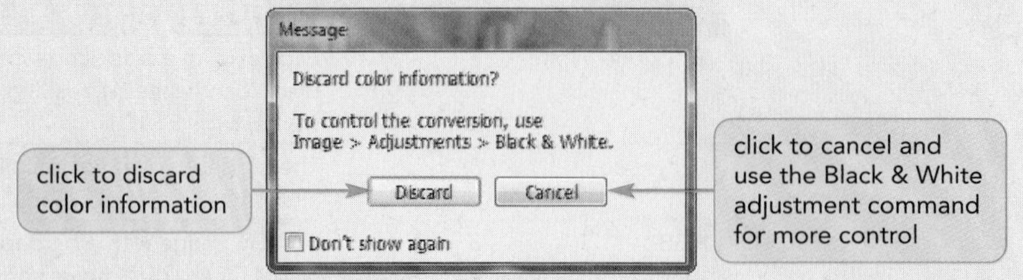
Message
Discard color information?
To control the conversion, use Image > Adjustments > Black & White.
Discard
Cancel
Don't show again
click to discard color information
click to cancel and use the Black & White adjustment command for more control

The dialog box also informs you that if you want more control over how each color is converted to grayscale, you can use the Black & White adjustment command instead. In this case, a simple conversion is fine for your needs.

3. In the dialog box, click **Discard**. See Figure 2-20.

Figure 2-20 Discarding color information

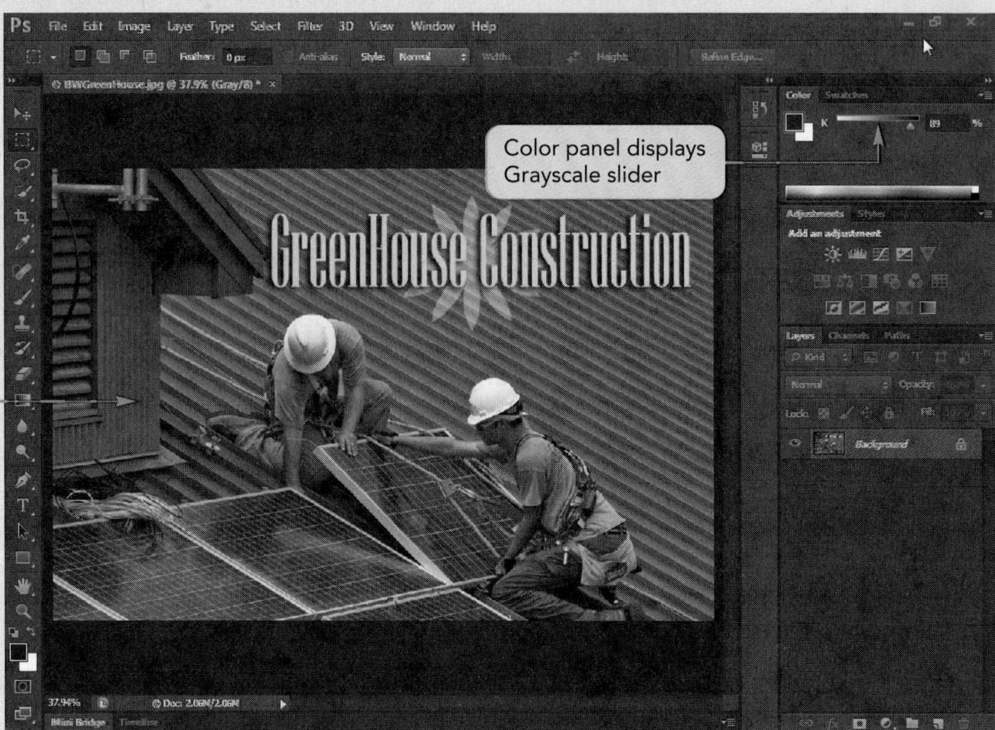
File Edit Image Layer Type Select Filter 3D View Window Help
GreenHouse Construction
Color panel displays Grayscale slider
all colors have been assigned to gray tones

© 2009 Alex Snyder/Wayne National Forest

The photograph is now in grayscale. However, it is still 300 ppi, which is a larger file size than you need for a newspaper ad.

4. On the menu bar, click **Image**, click **Image Size**, and then change the resolution to **150** pixels per inch. Leave the other image size settings intact, and click the **OK** button to accept the changes.
5. Press the **Ctrl+1** keys to display the image at 100% zoom. The image now has the proper color mode and resolution for a newspaper ad.
6. Save BWGreenHouse.jpg, and then close it.

C. J. wants you to experiment with creating a few new files of your own so you are more familiar with the options available in Photoshop, and so you can feel confident making choices based on project needs.

Creating a New File

So far, you have only opened existing files in Photoshop. However, it's easy to open a new blank file in Photoshop and create your own composition. Before you create a new file in Photoshop, you should decide on the document's size, resolution, and background color based on the needs of your project. You can always modify a file's specifications later, but it will save you time and effort to set them up properly in advance. See Figure 2-21.

Figure 2-21 **Default settings for a new file**

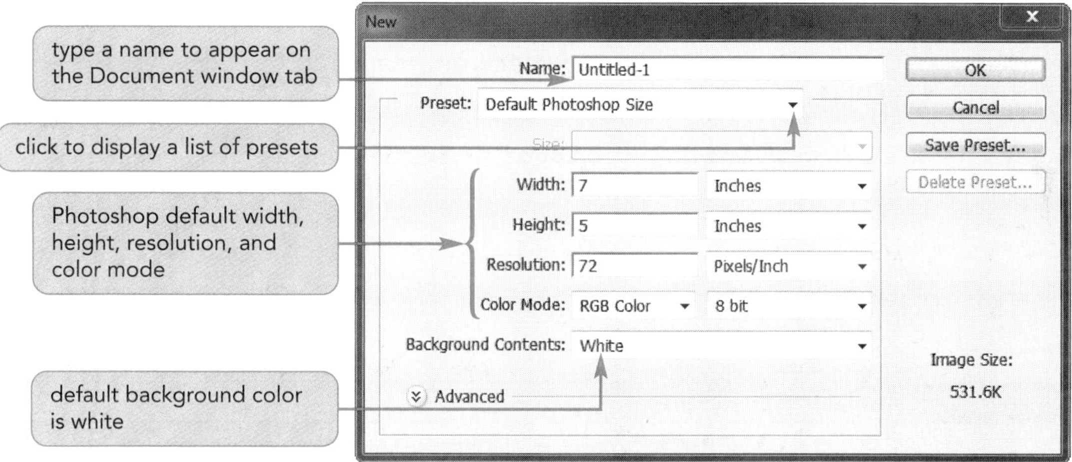

By default, Photoshop will create a new 7 × 5-inch file—using the RGB color mode, a bit depth of 8, and a white background. Once you have created the new file, you can add to it using the tools in the Tools panel, or you can copy an image from another file and paste it into the Document window. You can also place an image in the file.

Placing an Image in a New File

When you create a new file, you can think of yourself as an artist starting with a blank canvas. The **canvas** in Photoshop is the blank area in the middle of the Photoshop Document window, on which you can "paint" with bitmap images, vector graphics, and text. You can use vector drawing tools to paint on the canvas, but you can also copy and paste bitmap images or vector objects, or place them on the canvas. When you **place** an image in Photoshop, you import a copy of the image file that is still linked to the original. If you open and then edit the original file—for example, if you adjust a dark image by increasing its brightness—that change is reflected in the placed image in your new document file as well. You can open the original image file using the File command, or you can double-click the thumbnail of the placed image in the Layers panel.

A placed object is an example of a Photoshop feature called a **Smart Object**, which gives you the flexibility to transform the *placed* object in some way—for example, you can **transform** a placed image by rotating it or distorting it by making it wider or taller—without affecting the *original* object. To place an image file in a Photoshop document, you use the Place command on the File menu.

REFERENCE

Creating a New File Using a Preset

- On the menu bar, click File, and then click New. The New dialog box opens.
- In the Name box, type a name for the new file.
- Click the Preset arrow, and select the desired preset.
- Click the OK button to create the new file.

C. J. has asked you to create three new files, each based on a different design need. First, you'll create a variation of the company's logo for a Web-based campaign, using two separate files. You will not be making any changes to the placed images.

To create a new file and place an image:

1. On the menu bar, click **File**, and then click **New**. The New dialog box opens.
2. In the Name box, type **Logo1**. This is the name that will appear on the Document window tab. It will also appear as the default filename in the Save As dialog box, although you can choose to change the filename prior to saving it.
3. Click the **Preset** arrow. Photoshop displays a list of available presets. See Figure 2-22.

Figure 2-22 **Available new file presets**

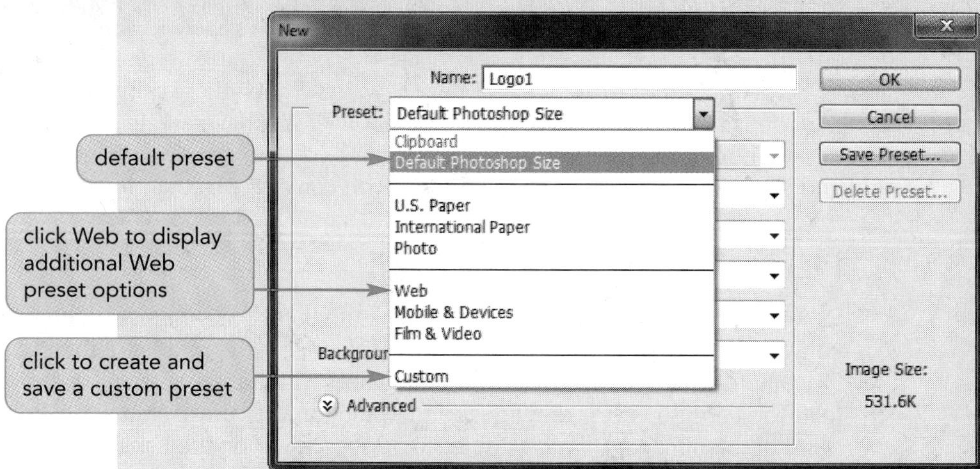

4. Click **Default Photoshop Size**, if necessary. The Default Photoshop Size preset creates a document that is 7 × 5 inches, with a resolution of 72 ppi.
5. Click the **OK** button. Photoshop creates the new file and displays the blank canvas at 100% zoom in the Document window.
6. On the menu bar, click **File**, and then click **Place**. The Place dialog box opens.
7. Navigate to the Photoshop2\Tutorial folder, click **Sun.psd**, click the **Place** button, and then press the **Enter** key. The sun image is placed at the center of the new file. Next, you'll place text on top of this image.

8. On the menu bar, click **File**, and then click **Place**. Navigate to the Photoshop2\Tutorial folder, click **GreenHouseText.psd**, click the **Place** button, and then press the **Enter** key. See Figure 2-23.

Figure 2-23 **Default new Photoshop file with placed images**

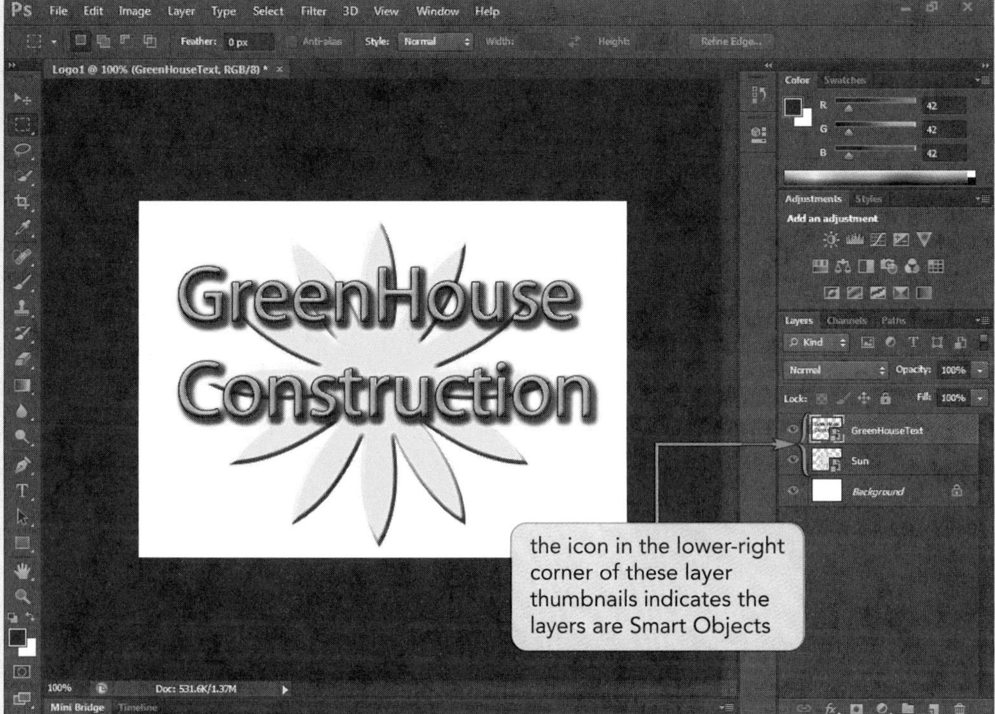
GreenHouse
Construction
the icon in the lower-right corner of these layer thumbnails indicates the layers are Smart Objects

You created a new file using the default Photoshop settings and placed two images in it. You'll save this file and present it to C. J. as a possible new logo for the company's Web site.

9. Save the file as **Logo1.psd** in the Photoshop2\Tutorial folder, and then close the file.

You can also create a new file using a Web preset, which will create a file with dimensions suitable for displaying in a Web browser. Photoshop includes Web presets for low-resolution monitors (640 pixels by 480 pixels), high-resolution monitors (1600 pixels by 1200 pixels), and many resolutions in between. It also includes file sizes appropriate for navigation bars and **leaderboards**, which are advertising banners that often appear at the top of a Web page.

C. J. wants you to create a leaderboard for the company name. You'll create a new file with the proper dimensions and then place the text on the canvas.

To create the file using the Leaderboard Web preset:

1. On the menu bar, click **File**, and then click **New**. The New dialog box opens.
2. In the Name box, type **Leaderboard**.
3. Click the **Preset** arrow, and then click **Web**.
4. Click the **Size** arrow, click **Leaderboard, 728 x 90**, and then click the **OK** button to create the new file.

5. On the menu bar, click **File**, and then click **Place**.
6. Navigate to the Photoshop2\Tutorial folder, click **LeaderboardText.psd**, click **Place**, and then press the **Enter** key. The text is now placed in the new file. See Figure 2-24.

Figure 2-24 **Leaderboard file with placed image**

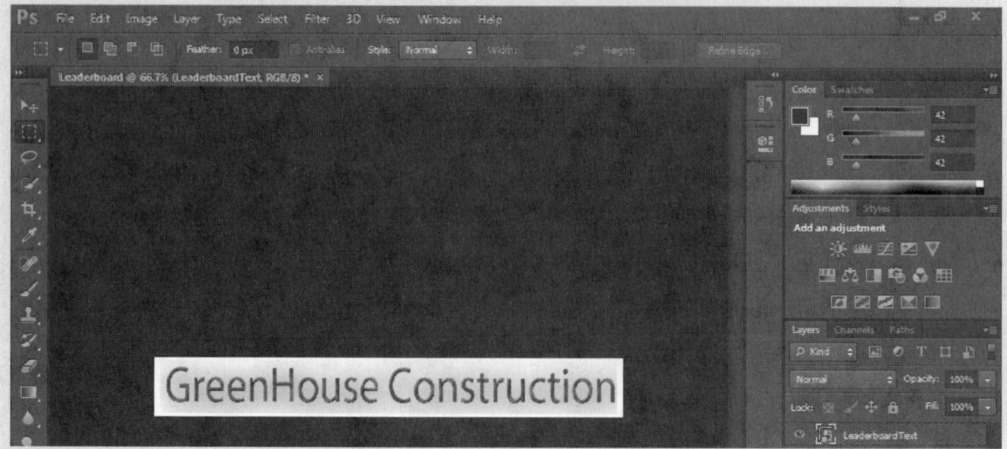

7. Save the file as **Leaderboard.psd** in the Photoshop2\Tutorial folder, and close the file.

C. J. will be able to use this file as an advertising banner on a Web site.

PROSKILLS

Decision Making: Using a Standard or a Nonstandard Size for a Photoshop Document

Photoshop gives you the flexibility to create documents using any dimensions. It provides presets for the Web or for printing photographs, but you might want to create a brochure with three panels, and no preset exists for that. You can easily create a new file using any dimensions you want, but it is wise to first check with your commercial printer to see if they have a standard size for a three-panel brochure. If they do, you need to decide whether following your original vision is worth the extra expense you're sure to incur if you use a nonstandard size for your piece. By exploring the options available in Photoshop and conferring with your printer before you start a project, you can ensure that you will make a decision about the size of your final document that results in a visually appealing marketing piece, while staying within your project budget.

C. J. frequently creates images that he then makes into posters for use at trade shows, so he asks you to create a document preset that you can use for trade show posters. You'll create and save a custom document preset for this project.

Creating a Custom Document Preset

You might find that the new document presets that come with Photoshop aren't exactly what you need for a particular project. You can specify custom options in the New dialog box and then save them as presets. Once you save a preset, it is listed along with all of the other presets in the New dialog box. If at any time you decide you will no longer use a particular custom preset, you can delete it.

REFERENCE

Saving a Custom Document Preset

- On the menu bar, click File, and then click New. The New dialog box opens.
- In the Name box, type a name for the new file.
- In the Width box, type a width for the canvas, and then specify the unit of measurement (such as pixels or inches).
- In the Height box, type a value for the height of the canvas.
- In the Resolution box, enter the resolution.
- Click the Save Preset button. The New Document Preset dialog box opens.
- Name the preset, and then select the necessary options in the New Document Preset dialog box.
- Click the OK button to save the custom preset.

To save a custom document preset for trade show posters:

1. On the menu bar, click **File**, and then click **New**. The New dialog box opens.
2. In the Name box, type **PosterPresetExample**.
3. Click the **Width** arrow, click **Inches**, if necessary, and then type **24** in the Width box. Notice that the setting for Height also changes to Inches.
4. In the Height box, type **36**.
5. In the Resolution box, type **300**.
6. Click the **Save Preset** button. The New Document Preset dialog box opens. See Figure 2-25.

Figure 2-25 Saving a new file preset

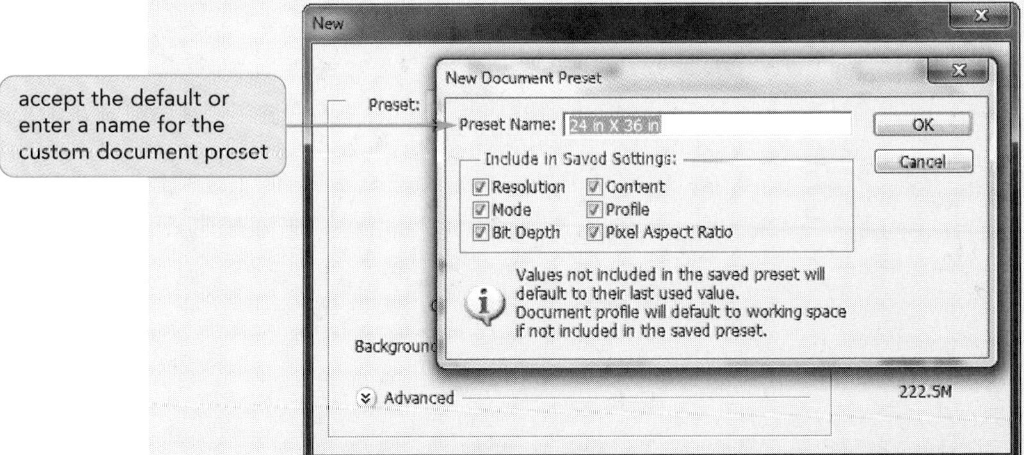

You can leave the default preset name, which is the dimensions of the new document, or you can type a new name.

7. In the Preset Name box, type **PosterPreset**, accept the default settings (all check boxes checked) so that every setting is saved with the preset, and then click the **OK** button.

8. In the New dialog box, click the **Preset** arrow.

   The new preset name appears in the Preset list. It will be available for all your future Photoshop sessions unless you delete it.

9. Click **PosterPreset**, and then click the **OK** button. Photoshop opens the blank canvas with the custom dimensions and resolution you entered.
10. On the menu bar, click **File**, and then click **Place**.
11. Navigate to the Photoshop2\Tutorial folder, click **Logo1.psd**, click **Place**, and then press the **Enter** key to place the logo. Use the Move tool to center the logo at the top of the poster.
12. Save the file as **PosterPresetExample.psd** in the Photoshop2\Tutorial folder, and then close the file.

You have shown your preset to C. J., and he wants to change it substantially. Because you will not be using this preset again, you can delete it to prevent a cluttered preset list.

REFERENCE

Deleting a Custom Document Preset

- On the menu bar, click File, and then click New.
- Click the Preset arrow, and then click the custom preset you want to delete.
- Click the Delete Preset button, and then click Yes in the dialog box to confirm that you want to delete the preset.
- Click the OK button.

To delete the custom preset:

1. On the menu bar, click **File**, and then click **New**.
2. In the New dialog box, click the **Preset** arrow, and then, if necessary, click **PosterPreset**, which is the preset you want to delete.
3. Click the **Delete Preset** button. A dialog box opens asking you to confirm that you want to delete the preset.
4. Click **Yes**. Photoshop deletes the PosterPreset custom preset.
5. Click the **OK** button, close the open file without saving it, and then exit Photoshop.

REVIEW

Session 2.1 Quick Check

1. Name one advantage of using the PSD file format.
2. The higher the resolution, the ______________ the file size.
3. Finding the right balance between image quality and file size is called ______________.
4. True or False. A JPEG version of an image is larger than a PSD version of the same image.
5. The default resolution for a new Photoshop file is ______________ ppi.
6. True or False. Resampling does not alter the number of pixels in the image.
7. ______________ specifies the amount of color information for each pixel in an image.

SESSION 2.2 VISUAL OVERVIEW

Open the Image menu to access the Image Rotation command; you can rotate your image or flip it horizontally or vertically on the canvas.

Rotate your image using presets of 90 degrees clockwise and counterclockwise.

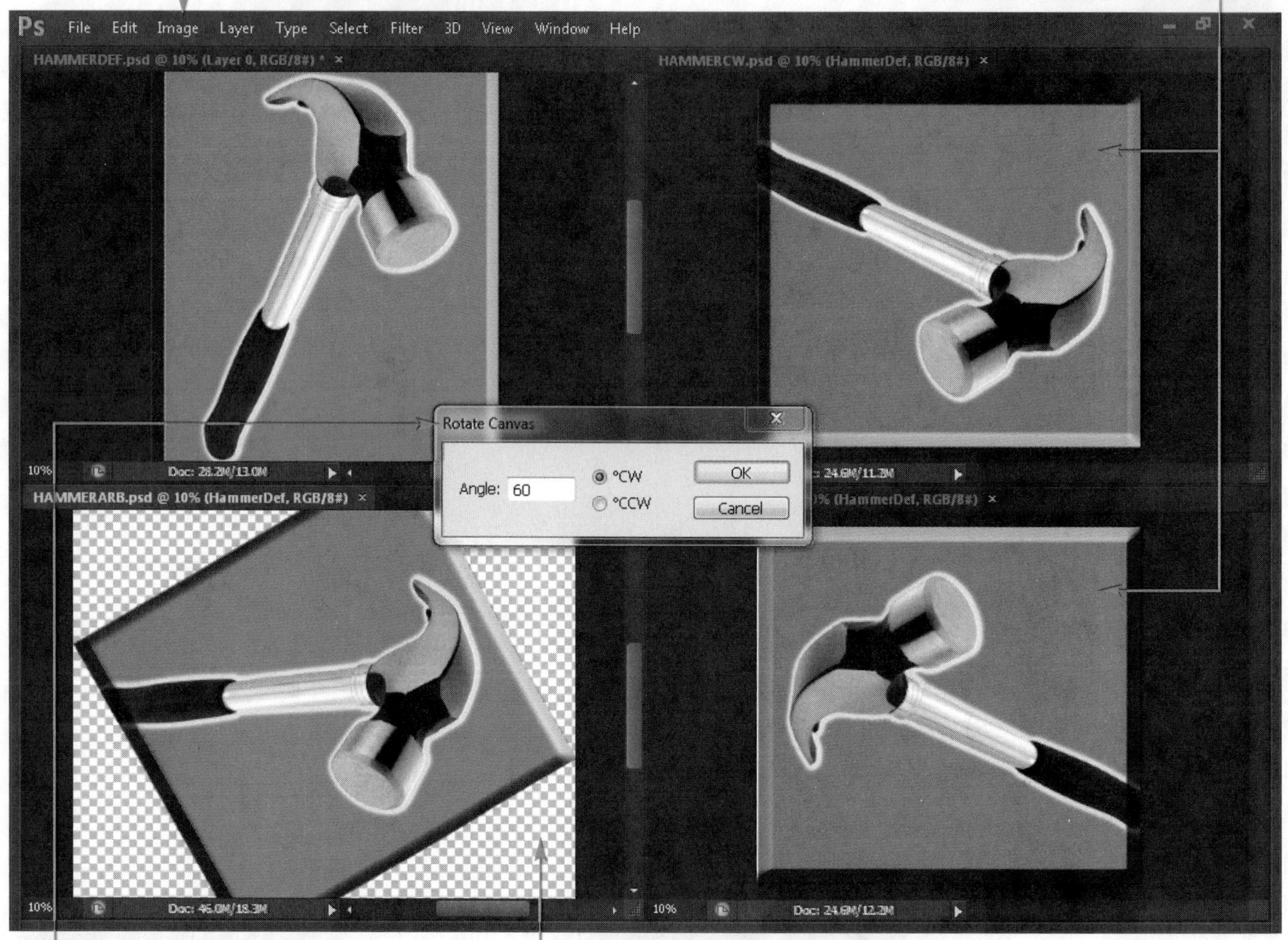

Use the Rotate Canvas dialog box to specify an angle of rotation, and whether to rotate clockwise or counterclockwise.

If you rotate your image by an **arbitrary angle**, which is an angle that you specify, Photoshop increases the dimensions of the canvas to compensate for the change.

Fotonic/Shutterstock.com

ADJUST, VIEW, AND ROTATE IMAGES

Many image adjustments include multiple presets for you to choose from.

The **Properties panel** is a new feature in Photoshop CS6 that lists the **properties**, or settings, of the adjustment layer selected in the Layers panel.

The Brightness/Contrast adjustment lets you change the lighting and modify the contrast between dark and light in your image.

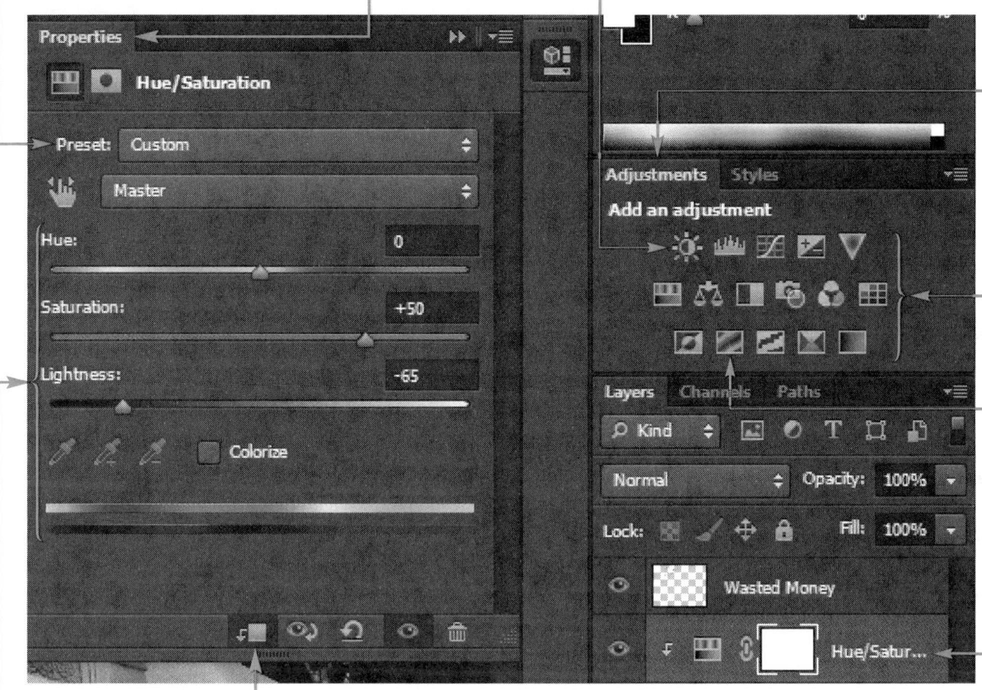

The **adjustments** feature in Photoshop lets you easily manipulate an image and preview an adjustment as you make it.

Clicking any of these adjustments adds an adjustment layer to your file.

The Posterize adjustment turns an image into a stylized painting that resembles a poster.

An **adjustment layer** changes your image in a nondestructive way.

You can modify preset properties for even more adjustment options.

You can click the Clip to layer icon to **clip** an adjustment to the layer directly beneath the adjustment layer so that other layers are unaffected by the adjustment.

In the Navigator, you can **pan** your image, which means to move the image within the Document window so that a different part of the image is visible.

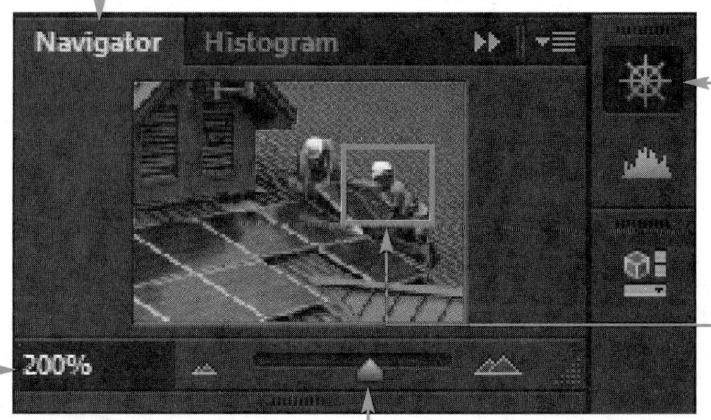

The Navigator can be collapsed to an icon.

The **view box** outlines the area of the image that is displayed in the Document window.

Type the zoom percentage in this zoom box or in the zoom box on the status bar.

Drag the Zoom slider to change the zoom setting.

Making Image Adjustments

As you work with digital images, you'll often find that an image is *almost* what you're looking for, but not quite. For example, perhaps the colors are a bit off or the image is overexposed. Maybe you'd prefer more shadows, or more light, or even a red door on a house instead of a blue door. Using Photoshop's adjustments feature, you can easily modify an image by making changes to the color and tone, among other things. If you make an image adjustment using the Adjustment command on the Image menu, the adjustment is made directly on the selected layer. This kind of adjustment is called a **destructive image adjustment** because it actually changes the pixels in the image. Once you save a file with this kind of adjustment, you have permanently changed the file. Unless you save the adjusted file with a different name, there is no way to return to the original. If this makes you nervous, it should. However, Photoshop has a feature called nondestructive image editing that should put you at ease. **Nondestructive image adjustments** are stored as layers on top of the original image. They are applied to the image, but rather than altering the pixels in the image, they are overlaid on the image as separate layers. As a result, you can easily turn them on or off or even delete them without harming the image itself. This session gives you a brief introduction to the Adjustments panel. As with many of the features in Photoshop, the Adjustments panel offers countless possibilities for editing your images, including adjusting the brightness and contrast of an image using the Brightness/Contrast adjustment.

The Adjustments panel includes icons for 16 different adjustments. Each adjustment has its own set of options, which appear on its Properties panel when you first select the adjustment or if you later select the adjustment layer to modify it. Some adjustments have additional presets, which also appear in the Properties panel. For example, if you select the Levels adjustment (the second icon in the first row), Photoshop adds an adjustment layer called Levels 1 and displays the Properties panel for that new layer. See Figure 2-26.

Figure 2-26 **Adjustment panel icons and Properties panel for an adjustment layer**

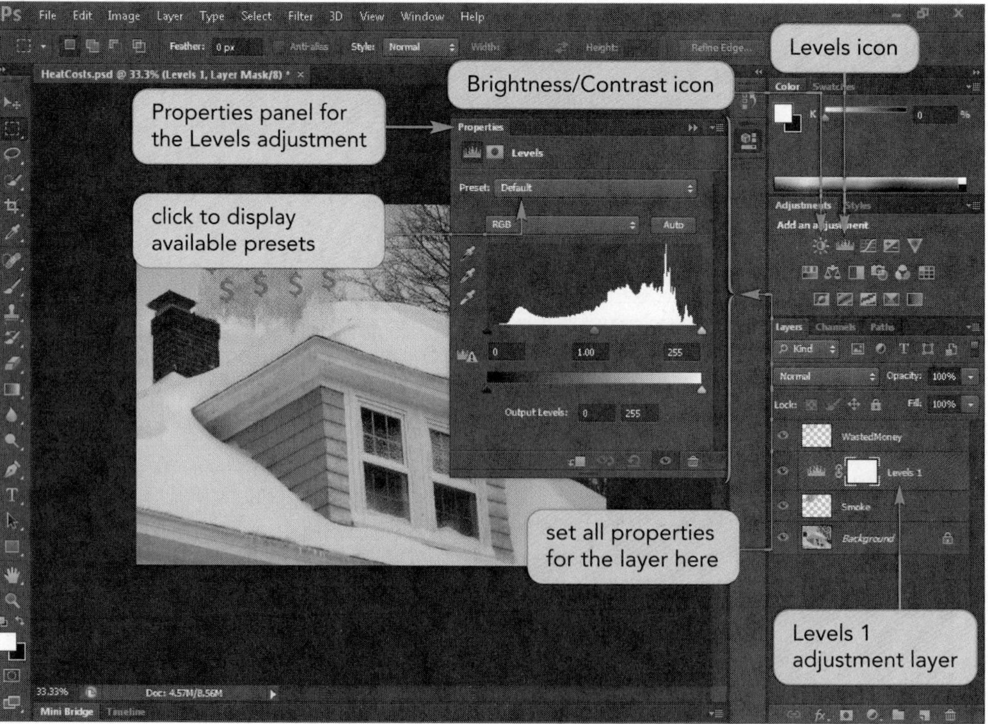

Jane Hosie-Bounar

The Properties panel displays the default settings for the Levels adjustment, but it also includes multiple presets that you can display by clicking the Preset arrow, and then clicking the name of the preset you want to apply.

C. J. is working on a campaign to persuade consumers to switch from gas and oil heat to solar and geothermal heat. He has started to compose an image meant to convince people that continuing with their current heating plans will cost them money and have a negative effect on the environment. He would like you to adjust the image so it has more impact. You'll experiment with brightness, contrast, and levels settings to see if those changes make the image stronger. You'll also experiment with a black-and-white preset to see how dramatic the change would be.

To add the Brightness/Contrast adjustment layer:

1. Start Photoshop while pressing the **Ctrl+Alt+Shift** keys, and click **Yes** to delete the Settings File when prompted. Reset Photoshop to the default Essentials workspace layout, and then reset all tools.
2. Navigate to the Photoshop2\Tutorial folder, and open **HeatCosts.psd**.
3. In the Layers panel, click the Background layer, if necessary, and then click the **Brightness/Contrast** icon. Photoshop adds an adjustment layer above the Background layer, and the Properties panel for the Brightness/Contrast adjustment opens. See Figure 2-27.

TIP

You can also work with adjustment layers using the New Adjustment Layer command on the Layer menu.

Figure 2-27 Brightness/Contrast settings

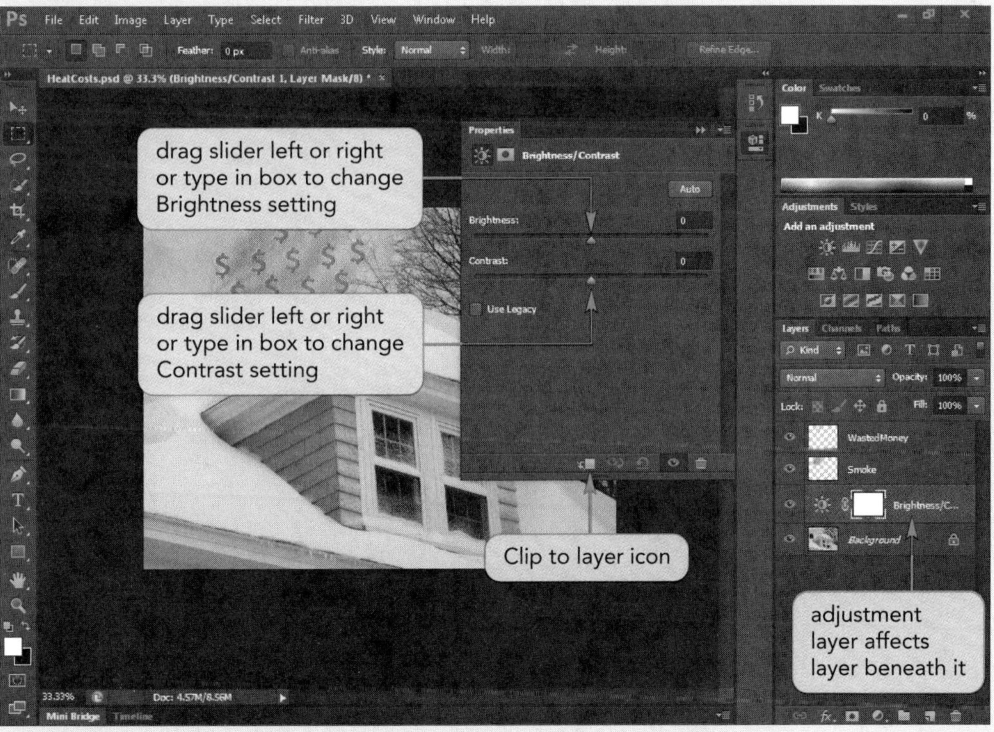

Jane Hosie-Bounar

An adjustment layer affects any layers beneath it in the Layers panel by default. If you have multiple layers beneath an adjustment layer but only want to affect the layer directly beneath the adjustment, you can clip it to that layer by clicking the Clip to layer icon at the bottom of the Properties panel.

Next, you'll use the slider to adjust the Brightness of the image, and you'll type a new Contrast value to see the effect of these changes.

4. In the Properties panel for the Brightness/Contrast adjustment, drag the **Brightness** slider to the left until the value reads **-45**.
5. In the Contrast box, type **85**.

   Notice that the color of the smoke hasn't changed because the Smoke layer is above the adjustment layer.
6. Click the **Smoke** layer to select it. Notice that the Properties panel is now blank because only adjustment layers have properties.

Be sure to select the Clip to layer icon. If you don't, the adjustment will also be applied to the Background layer, which you don't want to change.

7. In the Adjustments panel, click the **Hue/Saturation** icon, and then in the Properties panel, click the **Clip to layer** icon to direct Photoshop to clip the adjustment to the selected layer.

   The Clip to layer icon changes to .
8. In the Properties panel, click the **Preset** button, click **Strong Saturation**, and then drag the **Lightness** slider to the left until the box reads -65. See Figure 2-28.

Figure 2-28 Hue/Saturation adjustment layer clipped to Smoke layer

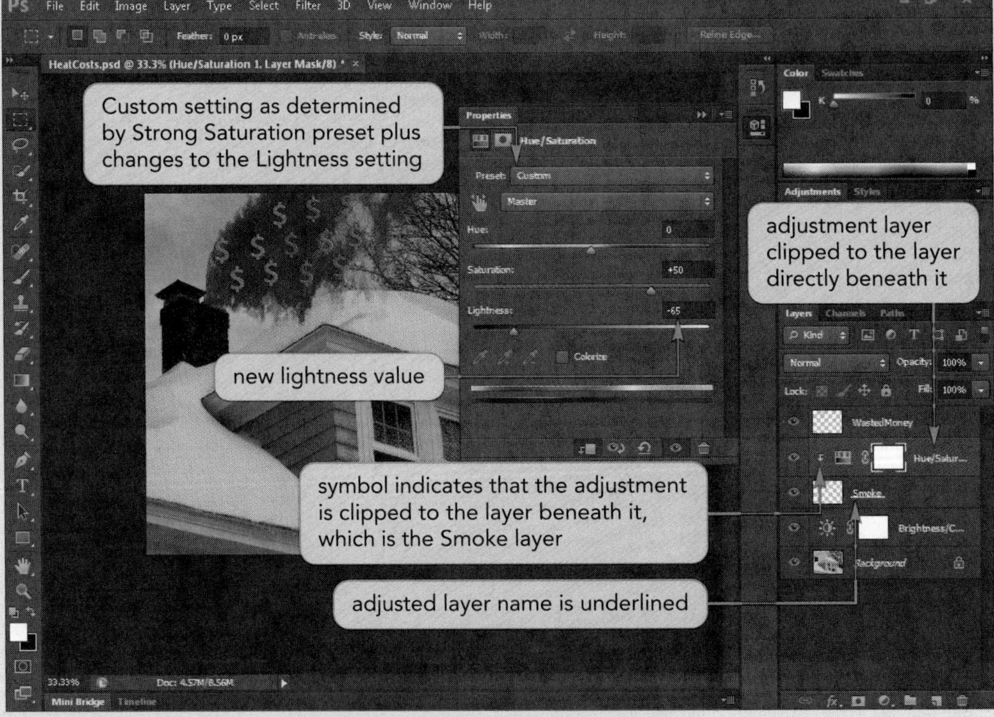

Jane Hosie-Bounar

The Smoke layer is now much darker, but because the adjustment was clipped only to that layer, the rest of the image is unchanged.

9. Save the file as **AdjustHeatCosts.psd** in the Photoshop2\Tutorial folder.

After seeing the changes you made to this image, C. J. has decided that the original brightness and contrast of the Background layer looks fine, so you'll delete the Brightness/Contrast layer.

To delete the adjustment:

1. In the Layers panel, click the **Hue/Saturation** layer, drag it to the lower-right corner of the Layers panel until it is over the Delete layer icon, and then release the mouse button. See Figure 2-29.

Figure 2-29 Dragging the adjustment layer to delete it

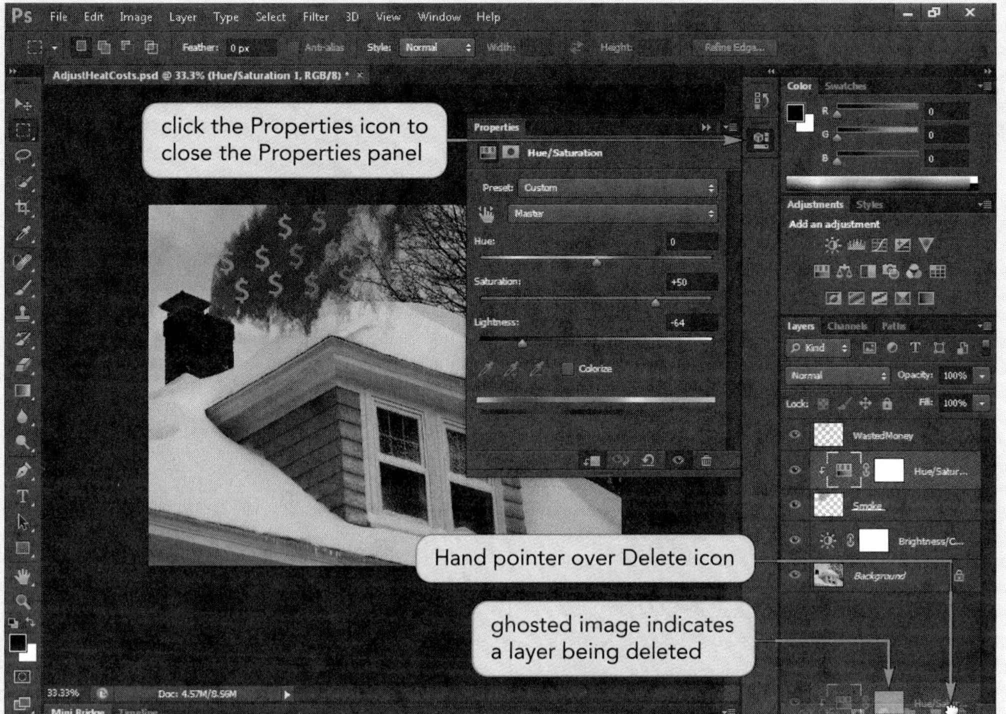

Jane Hosie-Bounar

The Hue/Saturation layer is deleted and the smoke returns to its original color. However, this is not the layer you really want to delete, so you'll undo the deletion and select the Brightness/Contrast layer to delete it.

2. Press the **Ctrl+Z** keys to undo the deletion. The smoke is now the darker, adjusted color.
3. In the Layers panel, click the **Brightness/Contrast** layer, and then press the **Delete** key to delete that layer. The Background layer reverts to its original brightness and contrast levels.
4. Click the **Properties panel** icon to close the Properties panel, and then save the file and close it.

You can also use adjustment layer presets as is, without any modifications, to get an entirely new effect with the click of a button. Next, you'll use a black-and white preset to see if it will convey the message of your image more powerfully.

TIP

It is a good practice to clip adjustment layers when you apply them so they only affect the layers you want them to affect.

To use the Black & White adjustment layer preset:

1. Navigate to the Photoshop2\Tutorial folder, and open **HeatCosts2.psd** and then in the Layers panel, click the **Background** layer to select it, if necessary.
2. In the Adjustments panel, click the **Black & White** icon, and in the Properties panel, click the **Preset** button to see a list of Black & White presets.
3. Click **High Contrast Red Filter** to apply the preset, click the **Clip to layer** icon, and then close the Properties panel. See Figure 2-30.

Figure 2-30 **Black & White adjustment applied to the Background layer**

adjustment not applied to the Smoke layer or the WastedMoney layer
Background layer is black and white
symbol shows that the adjustment was applied to the Background layer

Jane Hosie-Bounar

Most of the image changes to black and white. Notice that the Smoke layer and the WastedMoney layers are unaffected by this adjustment because they are above the Black & White adjustment layer in the Layers panel.

4. Save the file as **BWHeatCosts2.psd** in the Photoshop2\Tutorial folder, and then close the file.

PROSKILLS

Problem Solving: Acquiring an Image from a Scanner

You might have a project that requires you to acquire photographs taken before the days of digital imaging. In fact, what if the ideal photograph for your project was taken in 1959? How can you get that image into Photoshop and use it in your work? The fact is that you don't have to start with a digital file to end up with a digital file. You can use a scanner to scan a printed photograph directly into Photoshop, or you can scan the image to a storage device on your computer and then open the file in Photoshop. (Keep in mind that you shouldn't scan a copyrighted photo without obtaining permission.) If the scanner uses its own software to scan the image to your hard drive, make sure to specify the file format you want. If you have a scanner that includes a Photoshop plug-in such as TWAIN, make sure to install the plug-in software. You can then import the file directly into Photoshop. If your scanner has a preview option, it's a good idea to preview the image before you scan it because previewing lets you adjust scanner settings such as dimensions, color mode, and resolution, and saves you time and effort.

A scanner works by illuminating, or shining light at, a photograph you place face down on the glass surface of the scanner. When you start the scan, the scan head moves across the photo one or more times and uses reflected light and two or more mirrors to direct image information to a lens that then converts the information into digital format. In simple terms, a scanner takes a digital photograph of your printed photograph and then transfers the digital data it to your computer.

Once you scan an image, you haven't necessarily finished with the file. You might find that the image needs adjusting to make it work in your project. With Photoshop's image-adjustment features, your problem is solved: Not only have you performed magic by digitizing an image that was made before the digital age, you have actually repurposed the image to suit your needs using Photoshop's image-editing features. In fact, being required to use an old photograph for a project isn't much of a problem at all. Scanning the photograph to digitize it, and then manipulating it with Photoshop, can bring any photograph, no matter how old, into the twenty-first century.

Working with the Canvas

You saw earlier in this tutorial that when you create a new file, you often start with a blank canvas. As you create your composition, you might find that you need more or less room on the canvas to finalize your work. To enlarge the canvas, you can use the Canvas Size command on the Image menu to open the Canvas Size dialog box.

In the Canvas Size dialog box, you specify the new dimensions for your canvas. If you select the Relative check box, you can specify the width and height measurements you want to add to the canvas, rather than the final dimensions of the canvas. You can also select an anchor position for your image. The **anchor** determines whether the existing content on the canvas will remain in the center of the extended canvas, or whether it will be aligned with an edge or a corner of the canvas.

You have created a mock-up for a postcard campaign based on a sketch that C. J. provided, and you need to increase the canvas size so you can add a border around the composition.

REFERENCE

Extending the Canvas

- With an image file open, on the menu bar, click Image, and then click Canvas Size. The Canvas Size dialog box opens.
- With the Relative check box deselected, specify the final Width and Height measurements for the canvas.
- Click an Anchor setting to determine where the existing image will appear on the larger canvas.
- Click the Canvas extension color arrow, click an option and then click the OK button.

or

- With the Relative check box selected, specify the additional Width and Height measurements you want to add to the canvas size.
- Click an Anchor setting to determine where the existing image will appear on the larger canvas.
- Click the Canvas extension color arrow, click an option, and then click the OK button.

To extend the canvas:

1. Navigate to the Photoshop2\Tutorial folder, and open **GreenDream.psd**. The file opens in the Document window. The image consists of the composition (photographs, text, and rectangles) and a white Background, which is not visible because it is covered by the other elements in the document. The image size and the canvas size are identical.
2. On the menu bar, click **Image**, and then click **Canvas Size**. The Canvas Size dialog box opens showing the Current Size, which is a little less than 9 inches × 6 inches. See Figure 2-31.

Figure 2-31 **Canvas Size dialog box**

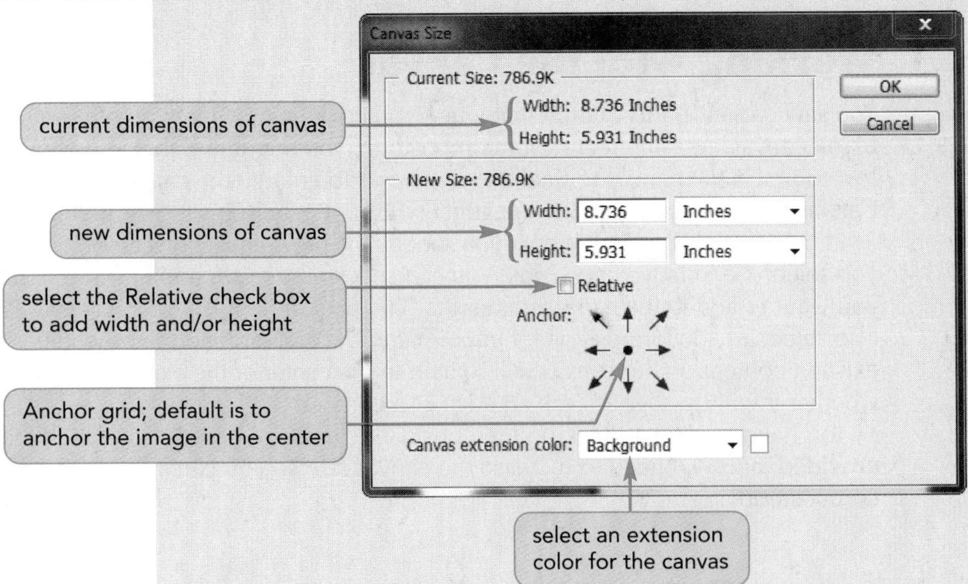

You need to add a half-inch border around the postcard image. To do so, you must increase the canvas size one inch in height and one inch in width.

3. Click the **Relative** check box to select it. When the Relative check box is selected, you can specify the width and height you want to add to the canvas, rather than the final width and height. Notice that under New Size, the Width and Height settings are now both 0 because you haven't yet specified what dimensions you want to add.
4. Verify that Inches is selected, and in the Width box, type **1**, and then in the Height box, type **1**. This will make the canvas ½ inch larger on all four sides of the current composition.

   If you wanted to anchor the image at the top, bottom, or side of the larger canvas, you could click one of the anchor buttons. Because you want to create a border of equal width around all four sides of the image, leave the anchor setting in the center. You also want the extension to be black, so you'll change the Canvas extension color setting.
5. Click the **Canvas extension color** arrow, click **Black**, and then click the **OK** button.

   The canvas increases in size with the image anchored in the middle of the canvas. The canvas extension color is black. See Figure 2-32.

Figure 2-32 **Extending the canvas**

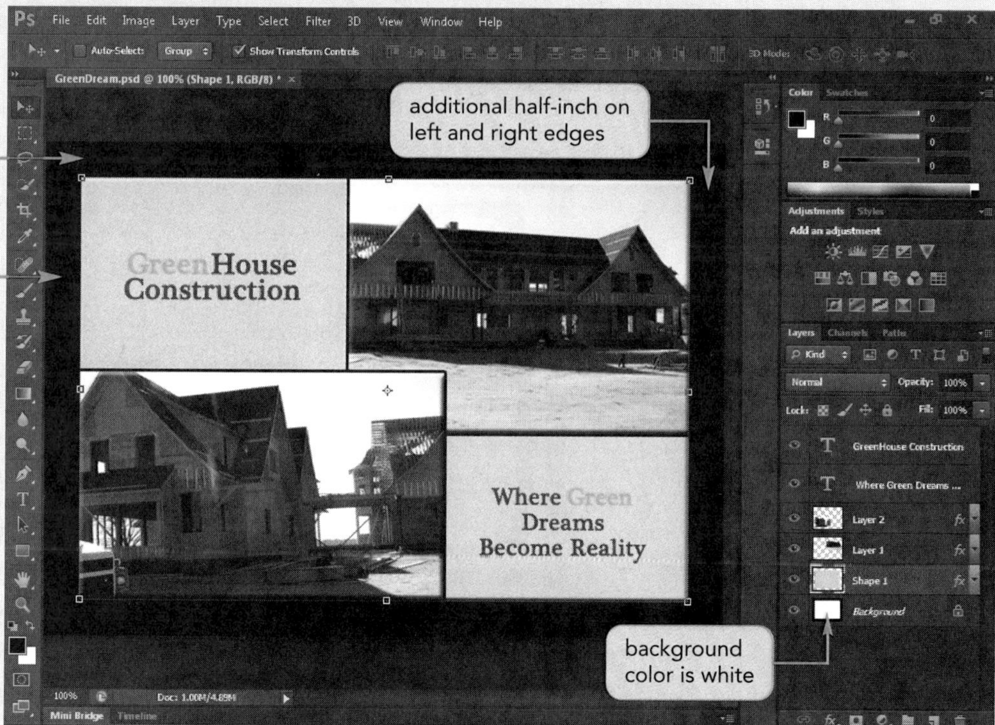

C.H. Gorman

6. Save the file as **CanvasSize.psd** in the Photoshop2\Tutorial folder, and close the file.

You can also trim a canvas to make an image smaller. Choosing Trim from the Image menu opens the Trim dialog box, where you can specify the color on which you want to base the trim, as well as indicate whether you want Photoshop to trim the top, bottom, left, or right of the image, or some combination of these choices.

C. J. has given you a second file for a solar panel advertising campaign that he would like you to trim so there's no white space around the image.

REFERENCE

Trimming the Canvas

- On the menu bar, click Image, and then click Trim. The Trim dialog box opens.
- Click the option button for the pixel color on which to base the trim—Transparent Pixels, Top Left Pixel Color, or Bottom Right Pixel Color.
- Specify which areas to trim by selecting or deselecting check boxes in the Trim Away section.
- Click the OK button to trim the image.

To trim the canvas:

1. Navigate to the Photoshop2\Tutorial folder, and open **WireCutter.jpg**. Notice that the image has extra white space on all sides.
2. On the menu bar, click **Image**, and then click **Trim**. The Trim dialog box opens. See Figure 2-33.

Figure 2-33 Trimming the canvas

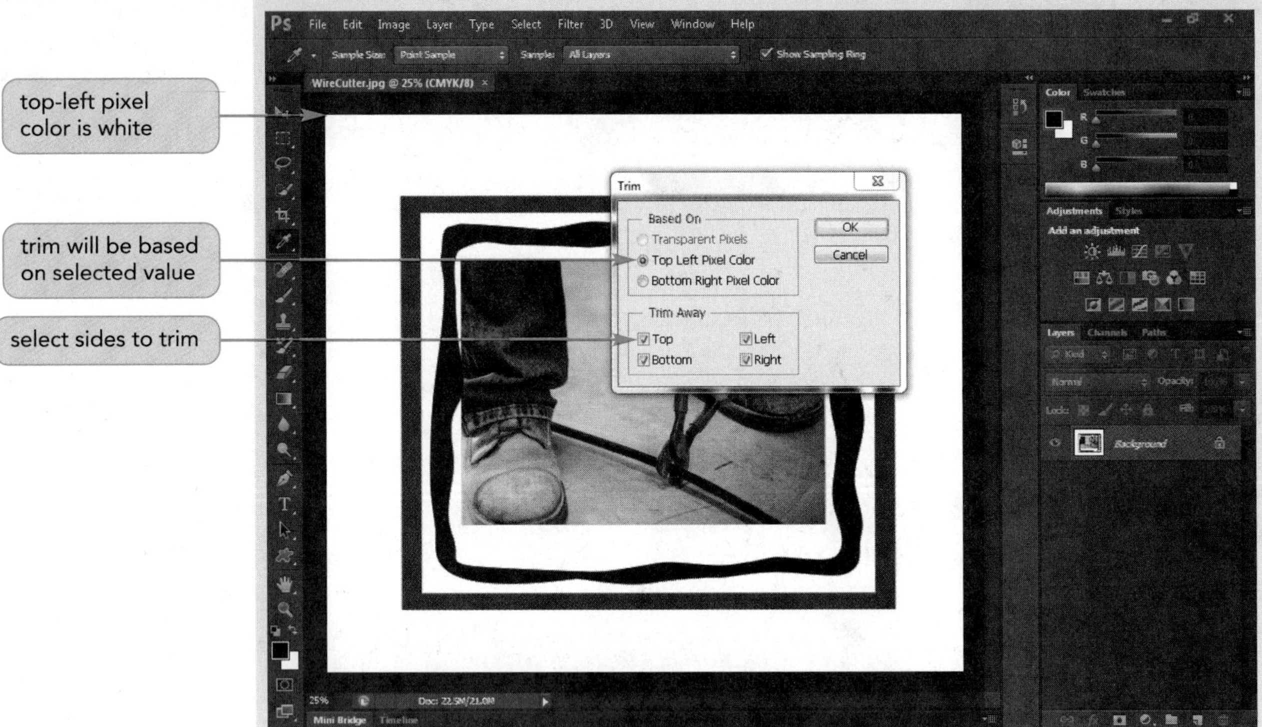

You can trim an image based on pixel colors. Photoshop will start trimming at the edges of the image based on either transparent pixels (if any), or the top-left or bottom-right pixel color. In this case, the top-left and bottom-right pixel colors are both white.

3. Click the **Top Left Pixel Color** option button to select it, if necessary. You can trim the top, left, bottom, or right part of the canvas, or any combination of those choices. For this image, you want to trim all sides of the image, so leave all four check boxes selected.
4. Click the **OK** button. Photoshop trims the canvas. See Figure 2-34.

Figure 2-34 Trimming the canvas

white pixels have been trimmed from all sides

© 2009 Alex Snyder/Wayne National Forest

5. Save the file as **Trim.jpg** in the Photoshop2\Tutorial folder using the current JPEG settings, and then close the file.

INSIGHT

Trimming vs. Cropping

When you trim an image, you are cutting out image data by removing pixels in the image based on the criterion you specify in the Trim dialog box. For example, you can specify that Photoshop will trim away transparent pixels or that it will trim away pixels the color of the corner pixels in the image. When you **crop** an image, you can choose to delete the cropped pixels or save them. You can also control additional features. For example, you can specify the dimensions of the crop, rotate the cropping marquee, or straighten the image. In addition, you can control whether or not you want to transform the perspective of an image. When you **transform perspective**, you remove the distortion produced by taking a photograph at an angle. For example, you have probably seen a photograph of a tall building shot directly in front of the building, looking up. The photograph makes the building appear wider at the bottom than at the top. The Crop tool lets you correct this distortion and square the corners of the building so that it appears that the photograph was shot straight on, rather than at an angle. There will be times when you want this kind of detailed control over the image you're working with, and you'll choose to crop rather than trim.

Zooming and Panning an Image

As you spend more time working in Photoshop, you'll find that you use its zoom feature frequently. You can zoom in on an image to select, copy, or modify individual pixels. Zooming gives you the flexibility to fine-tune an image in ways not possible if you were always looking at a photograph displayed at its actual screen or print size. Panning lets you keep the image at a high magnification while quickly moving to the next area of the image you want to modify.

Zooming an Image

There are many ways to zoom an image in or out in Photoshop, and a number of these are available on the Zoom tool options bar. When the Zoom tool is selected, the options bar changes to reflect available zoom settings, as shown in Figure 2-35.

Figure 2-35 Zoom options

Option	Details
	Indicates currently selected tool; click the arrow to open the Tool Preset picker.
	Select to zoom in.
	Select to zoom out.
Resize Windows to Fit	Resizes the window automatically when you zoom in or out.
Zoom All Windows	When you have multiple documents open, zooming one image zooms all the other images the same amount.
Scrubby Zoom	Only available with an Open GL video card; drag to the left to zoom out, or drag to the right to zoom in.
Actual Pixels	Shows the image at 100% magnification.
Fit Screen	Fits the image in the Document window.
Fill Screen	Fills the document window top to bottom; if the image is taller than it is wide, there will be space on either side of the image; if the image is wider than it is tall, the sides of the image will not show in this view.
Print Size	Displays the file in the size at which it will print.

TIP

You can also press the Ctrl++ keys to zoom in on the image and the Ctrl+- keys to zoom out.

To use the Zoom In pointer (a magnifying glass with a plus sign), position the pointer over the area on which you want to zoom in, and then click. How much the image is zoomed depends on your monitor size and the starting zoom percentage. For example, for an image displayed at a 25% zoom on a 19-inch monitor, clicking the Zoom In pointer once increases the zoom percentage to 33.33%. (The zoom percentage is also called the magnification level.) Clicking it a second time increases the zoom to 50%. Additional clicks result in 66.67% and then 100% zoom settings.

If you have a video card that supports OpenGL and if you have selected Animated Zoom in the General Preferences, you can zoom continuously rather than zooming in increments. When you zoom continuously, you achieve the same effect you see when you use your digital camera's zoom feature to zoom in on a scene to get a close-up photograph. To zoom continuously in Photoshop when the Zoom tool is active, point to the area of the image you want to zoom in on, and then press and hold the mouse button until you zoom to the level you want. If you press and hold the Alt key while zooming, you can achieve a similar animated zoom effect while zooming out continuously.

Photoshop provides another useful way to examine an image close up. Dragging a zoom selection marquee simplifies the zooming process and is often more practical than clicking the image repeatedly with the Zoom In pointer. To zoom in on a specific rectangular area of an image, activate the Zoom tool and then position the Zoom In pointer over the area on which you want to focus and drag a box, called a **selection marquee**, around the area. Photoshop zooms the image so the area inside the marquee is centered in and fills the Document window. If your computer is equipped with a video card that supports OpenGL, dragging the pointer will zoom continuously rather than draw a marquee.

When the Zoom tool is selected, you can also zoom an image using Zoom preset buttons on the options bar, including Actual Pixels, Fit Screen, Fill Screen, and Print Size. Zoom In, Zoom Out, Fit on Screen, Actual Pixels, and Print Size are also available on the View menu.

To zoom the image using presets:

1. Navigate to the Photoshop2\Tutorial folder, and open **Hi_Res.jpg**, display the rulers, and change the zoom setting to 50%, if necessary.
2. In the Tools panel, click the **Zoom Tool** button to display the zoom options on the options bar.
3. On the options bar, click the **Actual Pixels** button to display the image at a 100% zoom setting.

   If you have a large monitor, the inches on the rulers might appear wider than the inches on a real ruler. Because this image has a resolution of 240 pixels per inch and is five inches wide, what you see on screen is 1200 pixels across the width of the Document window. (5 inches times 240 pixels per inch equals 1200 pixels.) If you have a smaller monitor, or if you haven't maximized the Photoshop window, the inches on the ruler might appear smaller than real inches.
4. Click the **Print Size** button on the options bar. The image is now displayed at a lower zoom setting. Again, the actual setting depends on the size of your monitor. Notice that the ruler measurements are closer together. When the zoom is set to Print Size, an inch on the ruler is a true inch.
5. Click the **Fit Screen** button on the options bar. Photoshop enlarges the image so it is as large as possible but still fits on screen.
6. Click the **Fill Screen** button on the options bar. The image fills the Document window area.

Because zooming often hides parts of an image with which you might want to work, sometimes you need to pan an image to see an area that was previously hidden.

Panning an Image

TIP

You can temporarily turn off the panning feature by pressing the Ctrl key to change the pointer to the Zoom In pointer, or by pressing the Alt key to change it to the Zoom Out Pointer.

When you are doing detail work on an image and have zoomed in to a high magnification level, there will often be large parts of the image that you can't see. To move from one part of the image to another, you could zoom out, find the area of the photo you want to work with, and then zoom in again. However, it is much simpler to pan the image so that you can see a different area of the image.

Panning an image is like looking at a photograph on your desk using a magnifying glass. You can only see a part of the image at the high magnification the magnifying glass provides. To see another area, you can either slide the photo across the desk, or move the magnifying glass to a different part of the photo. Either way, you are panning the image.

The Hand tool in the Tools panel is one of the most convenient ways to pan an image. To use the Hand tool, click it in the Tools panel; the pointer takes the shape of a hand. You can click the mouse button and drag in the direction you want to pan the photo. As you drag, a different part of the image comes into view. If you drag to the right, the left part of the image comes into view. If you drag to the left, the right part of the image comes into view. Dragging up displays the bottom of the image, while dragging down displays the top.

C. J. is working on a new stationery letterhead, and thinks it would be interesting to use the grid of solar panels as part of the company logo. You'll use the Hand tool to pan the image when it is zoomed in and then you'll select the solar panels and copy them to use in a new file.

To use the Hand tool to pan the Hi_Res.jpg image:

1. Press the **Ctrl++** keys to zoom to 200%.
2. Click the **Hand Tool** button in the Tools panel.

   Trouble? If you can't see the Hand Tool button, click the Rotate View Tool button, hold down the mouse button until you see the tools list, and then click the Hand Tool button.
3. Move the mouse pointer over the Document window. When it is over the Document window, the pointer changes to a hand.
4. Click the mouse button and drag to the right until the coil of wires is completely visible.
5. Point to the coil of wires, click the mouse button, and drag up until the wires are no longer visible.
6. Click the **Rectangular Marquee Tool** button and drag a selection marquee over part of the solar panel, as shown in Figure 2-36.

Figure 2-36 Making a selection

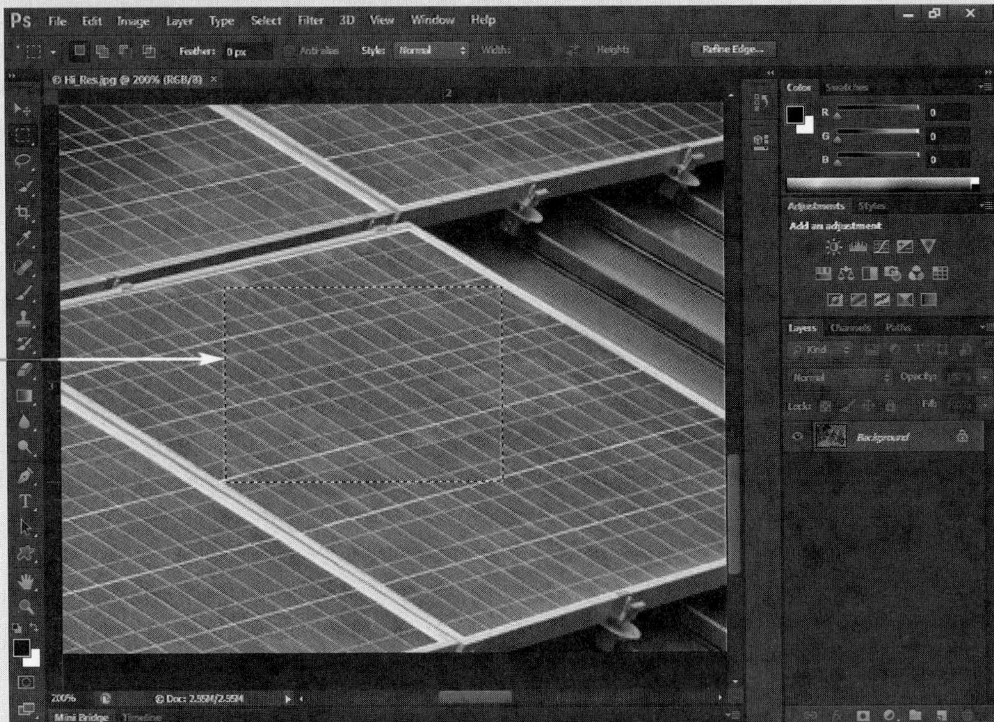

7. Press the **Ctrl+C** keys to copy the selection to the Clipboard.
8. On the menu bar, click **File**, and then click **Open**.
9. Navigate to the Photoshop2\Tutorial folder, and open **GreenHouseText2.psd**. In the Layers panel, click the **Background Layer**, and then press the **Ctrl+V** keys to paste the copied solar panel into the file.
10. Use the Move tool to move the copied panel so it is centered below the text.
11. Save the file as **SolarText.psd** in the Photoshop2\Tutorial folder, and then close the file.

The Navigator is another excellent tool for zooming and panning an image. It is especially useful because it displays a thumbnail of the entire image so you can easily choose your next "destination," or the place on the image to where you want to pan. You access the Navigator from the Window menu.

You'll work with the Navigator to become more comfortable focusing on different areas of a complex image. This skill will come in handy when you do detailed pixel-editing work for C. J. in the future.

To use the Navigator to pan and zoom the image:

1. Hi_Res.jpg should still be open at 200% in the Document window. On the menu bar, click **Select**, and then click **Deselect** to deselect the solar panel selection.
2. On the menu bar, click **Window**, and then click **Navigator**. The Navigator opens to the left of the Adjustments panel group. It is grouped with the Histogram panel. Notice the thumbnail of the open photograph and the red box, called the proxy preview area or view box, which outlines the portion of the image currently displayed in the Document window. The size of the view box changes based on the magnification. The lower the magnification, the larger the box because a larger part of the image is being displayed in the Document window.
3. Drag the **view box** in the Navigator up and to the right so that it encloses the man on the right. See Figure 2-37.

Figure 2-37 Using the Navigator

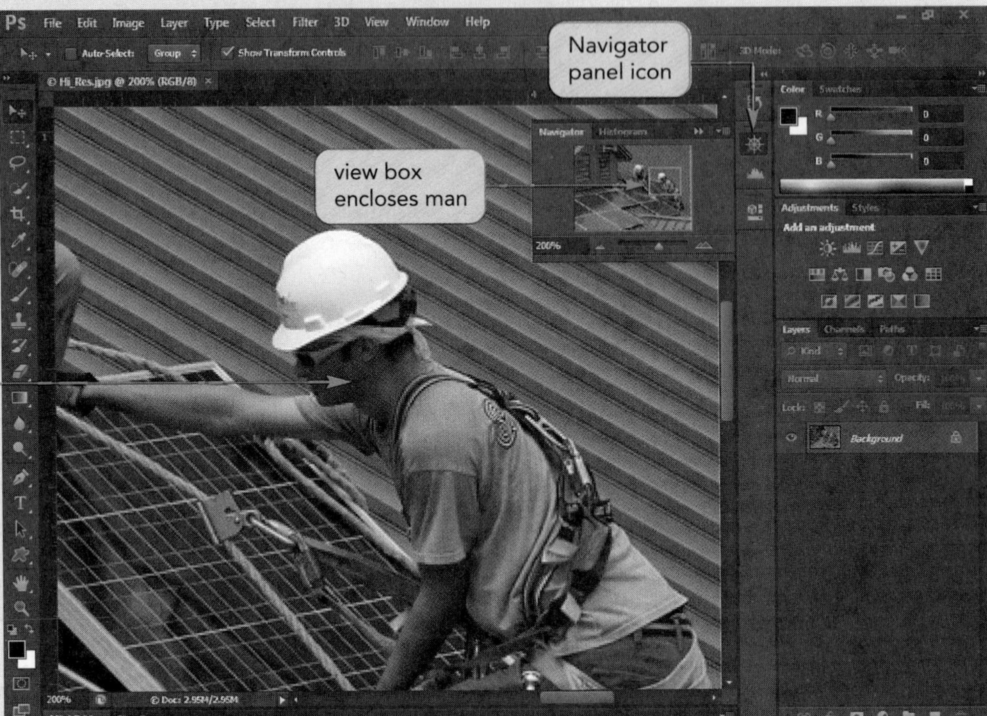

Dragging the view box pans the image.

4. Press the **Ctrl++** keys to change the zoom percentage to 300%. Notice that the view box has gotten smaller in the Navigator because a smaller portion of the image appears in the Document window.
5. Click the **Zoom Tool** button, if necessary, and then on the options bar, click the **Fit Screen** button. The view box in the Navigator is as large as the document in the Document window because the entire image is visible.
6. Click the **Actual Pixels** button on the options bar. The view box appears smaller on the thumbnail because by zooming in, you are viewing a smaller part of the image.

   You can also use the settings in the Navigator to zoom your image.
7. In the box in the lower-left corner of the Navigator, type **500**, and then press the **Enter** key. The image in the Document window zooms to a 500% magnification level. The view box on the thumbnail decreases substantially in size.
8. Drag the **Zoom** slider at the bottom of the Navigator all the way to the left, and then all the way to the right. The maximum zoom setting allowed by Photoshop is 3200%. Notice that the view box has nearly disappeared because you are focused on such a small part of the image.
9. Close the file without saving it, click **Window** on the menu bar, point to **Workspace**, and then click **Reset Essentials**.

Rotating and Flipping an Image

TIP

If you want to rotate the view while you are working, but don't want to permanently rotate the photo and alter the pixels, you can use the Rotate View tool if you have an OpenGL video card.

There might be times when you have the perfect image for a project—with one small problem: The door of the house needs to be on the right, not the left, or the photographer took the photograph with the camera held sideways in order to fit a tall person in the photo. As a result, the orientation is wrong. Or maybe you have photographs of two different people that you want to put in a composition so that they are facing each other. Unfortunately, each person is facing to the left. What can you do to fix this problem so the two people are facing each other? You can rotate or flip one of the images. It's important to note that rotating and flipping an image is a destructive form of editing: That is, it permanently alters the pixels in the photograph.

Photoshop provides a number of options for rotating and flipping images. You can access the rotation commands on the Image menu by clicking Image Rotation and then making a selection. Figure 2-38 shows the six options available for image rotation.

Figure 2-38 **Image rotation options**

Option	Details
180°	Flips the image so it is upside down and facing in the opposite direction
90°CW 90°CCW	Rotates the image 90 degrees clockwise or 90 degrees counterclockwise, respectively
Arbitrary	Lets you specify an angle of rotation for your image and whether you want to rotate the image clockwise or counterclockwise; when you rotate an image at an angle other than 90° or 180°, Photoshop increases the size of the canvas to accommodate the image
Flip Canvas Horizontal	Flips the image around an imaginary vertical line drawn through the center of the image
Flip Canvas Vertical	Flips the image around an imaginary horizontal line drawn through the center of the image

C. J. wants you to experiment with rotating and flipping an image of a wrench so that you are prepared to manipulate other images as needed on future projects.

To rotate and flip the image of the wrench:

1. On the options bar, reset all tools. Navigate to the Photoshop2\Tutorial folder, and open **Wrench.jpg**, display the rulers, if necessary, and fit the image on the screen. A photograph of a wrench that is about 8 1/2 inches wide and 13 inches high appears in the Document window.
2. On the menu bar, click **Image**, and then click **Image Rotation**. Photoshop displays the commands for rotating an image.
3. Click **90°CW**. See Figure 2-39. The photograph is now 13 inches wide by about 8 1/2 inches high.

Figure 2-39 Rotated image

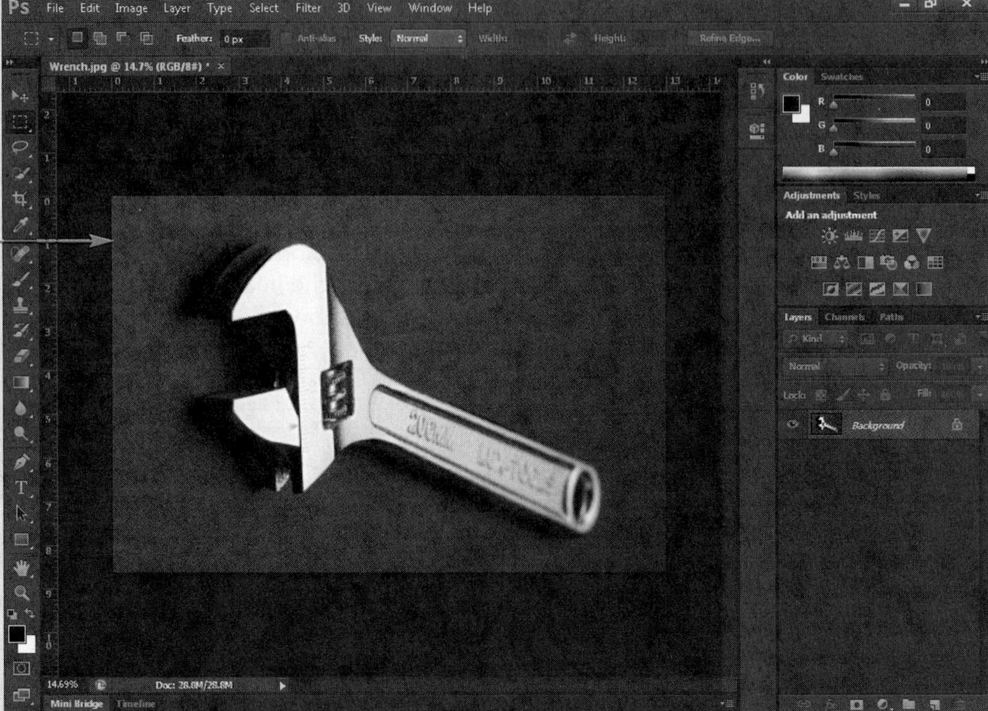
image is now 13" wide and about 8 1/2" high
Wrench.jpg @ 14.7% (RGB/8#)

Garsya/Shutterstock.com

4. On the menu bar, click **Edit**, and then click **Undo Rotate Canvas**.
5. On the menu bar, click **Image**, click **Image Rotation**, and then click **Arbitrary**. The Rotate Canvas dialog box opens. You can specify the angle and direction (clockwise or counterclockwise) of the rotation.
6. In the Angle box, type **60**, click the **°CCW** option button to rotate the image 60 degrees counterclockwise, and then click the **OK** button. The image rotates 60 degrees counterclockwise, and Photoshop expands the dimensions of the canvas to accommodate the rotation.
7. In the Tools panel, click the **Zoom Tool** button, if necessary, and then click the **Fit Screen** button on the options bar. See Figure 2-40.

Figure 2-40 **Extended canvas accommodates rotation**

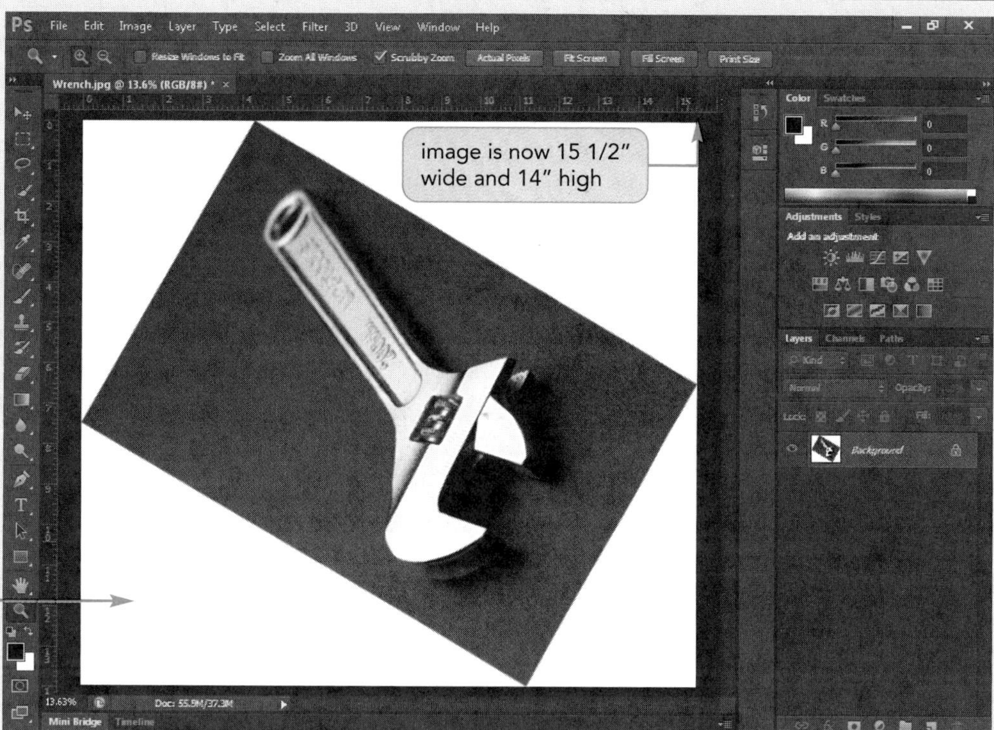
image is now 15 1/2" wide and 14" high
Photoshop extends the canvas to accommodate the rotation

Garsya/Shutterstock.com

The canvas is now 15 1/2 inches wide and 14 inches high, and Photoshop has added to the canvas to accommodate the new angle of the image.

8. Save the file as **WrenchRotate.jpg** in the Photoshop2\Tutorial using the current JPEG settings, close the file, and then exit Photoshop.

In this session, you learned how to use the Adjustments panel to quickly make adjustments to an image. You also learned how to pan and zoom an image and how to rotate an image.

REVIEW

Session 2.2 Quick Check

1. What is the difference between destructive image edits and nondestructive image edits?
2. Nondestructive image edits are stored in the ______________ panel.
3. Brightness/Contrast settings for an image can be found in the ______________ panel.
4. When you drag an image within the Document window to see an area that was previously hidden, you are ______________ the image.
5. True or False. The keyboard shortcut Ctrl+- increases the zoom magnification of an image.
6. The ______________ provides a convenient way to zoom and pan an image.
7. The Image Rotation command can be found on the ______________ menu.

Practice the skills you learned in the tutorial using the same case scenario.

PRACTICE

Review Assignments

Data Files needed for the Review Assignments: Hammer.psd, GreenHouseText.psd

C. J. wants you to continue exploring Photoshop on your own so that you become more comfortable working with and making adjustments to images. He suggests you work with an image of a hammer that he is thinking of including on a postcard he plans to send to his customers. Complete the following steps:

1. Start Photoshop while pressing the Ctrl+Alt+Shift keys, and click Yes to delete the Settings File when prompted. Reset Photoshop to the default Essentials workspace layout, and then reset all tools.
2. Open **Hammer.psd**, located in the Photoshop2\Review folder provided with your Data Files.
3. Add a Hue/Saturation adjustment layer to the Hammer layer, and select the Cyanotype preset. Clip the adjustment to the layer.
4. Add a Brightness/Contrast adjustment layer so it adjusts all the layers in the image. (*Hint*: The Brightness/Contrast layer should appear at the top of the Layers panel, and it should not be clipped to any other layers.) Set the Brightness to 100 and the Contrast to 30. Save the file as **HammerAdjust.psd** in the Photoshop2\Review folder.
5. Delete the Brightness/Contrast layer, and collapse the Properties panel.
6. Rotate the image 90° clockwise.
7. Increase the canvas size half an inch on every side, and set the Canvas extension color to gray.
8. Save the file as **HammerExtend.psd** in the Photoshop2\Review folder.
9. Save the file again as **HammerExtend.jpg** in the Photoshop2\Review folder using Medium quality and 3 Progressive scans.
10. Open **HammerExtend.jpg** and view both files in 2-up Vertical view. Zoom both files to 100% view, and then fit them on screen. Close **HammerExtend.jpg**.
11. Delete the Hue/Saturation layer in the **HammerExtend.psd** file, and then change **HammerExtend.psd** to Grayscale mode and flatten it. Save the file as **GrayHammer.psd**.
12. Zoom the image to 110%, and use the Navigator to center the face of the hammer (the part that hits the nail) in the Document window.
13. Reduce the zoom to 45%, and then pan to display the entire head of the hammer in the Document window. Close the Navigator tab group.
14. Use the Rectangular Marquee tool to select the portion of the image that appears in the window, and then copy the selection to the Clipboard.
15. Create a new file using the Clipboard preset and a black background and paste the portion of the image you copied into the file. (*Hint*: Press the X key before you open the New dialog box to change the background color to black.) Save the new file as **HammerHead.psd** and close it.
16. Zoom to 20% in the GrayHammer.psd file. Place **GreenHouseText.psd**, located in the Photoshop2\Review folder, at the top of **GrayHammer.psd** so that it fits in the top black canvas area without overlapping the hammer.
17. Save **GrayHammer.psd**, and exit Photoshop.
18. Submit the results of the preceding steps to your instructor either in printed or electronic form, as requested.

Use your skills to modify a photograph for a presentation.

APPLY

Case Problem 1

Data File needed for this Case Problem: ConcertHall.jpg

Sound Plan Engineering Sound Plan Engineering is an organization of acoustic, audio, and noise control consultants in Santa Fe, New Mexico. The firm specializes in acoustic and audiovisual system design. The firm was founded by Manuel Ramirez in 2002 and has grown from 10 employees to 150 in less than a decade. You have been tasked with preparing variations on an image of the firm's most recent work to present at a meeting with board members. Complete the following steps:

1. Start Photoshop while pressing the Ctrl+Alt+Shift keys, and click Yes to delete the Settings File when prompted. Reset Photoshop to the default Essentials workspace layout, and then reset all tools.
2. Open **ConcertHall.jpg**, located in the Photoshop2\Case1 folder provided with your Data Files, and fit the image on the screen.
3. Trim the image based on the top-left pixel color. Do not trim away the bottom part of the image, as this is where text for the final piece will go.
4. Select the Zoom tool, and drag a zoom selection marquee around the piano and the chairs surrounding it. (*Hint*: If your computer is equipped with a video card that supports OpenGL, dragging the pointer will zoom continuously rather than draw a marquee. Zoom so that you can see the area described in Step 4.)
5. Open the Navigator. Press the Alt+Print Screen keys to capture an image of the current Photoshop window, then open WordPad, which is available on the Accessories menu of the All Programs menu in Windows 7, and press the Ctrl+V keys to paste the image into a new file. Save the WordPad file as **Marquee.rtf** in the Photoshop2\Case1 folder.
6. Use the Navigator to pan to the seats in the audience on the lower-right side of the image. Press the Alt+Print Screen keys to capture an image of the current Photoshop window, switch to WordPad, create a new file, and press the Ctrl+V keys to paste the image into the new file. Save the WordPad file as **Navigator.rtf** in the Photoshop2\Case1 folder.
7. Collapse the Navigator. Fit the image on screen, and then apply the Black & White adjustment using the Neutral Density preset.
8. Zoom out to fit the image on screen and then save the file as **BWConcertHall.jpg** using Maximum quality and the Baseline ("Standard") format option.
9. Delete the black-and-white adjustment layer.
10. Add a Brightness/Contrast adjustment, and change the Brightness setting to -15 and the Contrast setting to 10.
11. Save the file as a JPEG image named **ConcertHallAdjust.jpg** in the Photoshop2\Case1 folder, using the same JPEG options you used in Step 8. Remember that saving a file as a JPEG merges all of the layers into a single layer, so when you open this file later, you'll see that it only has one layer.
12. Close ConcertHall.jpg without saving it, and exit Photoshop.
13. Submit the results of the preceding steps to your instructor either in printed or electronic form, as requested.

Use your skills to create an image for an online costume company.

APPLY

Case Problem 2

Data Files needed for this Case Problem: EyeMask.psd, Eye.tif

FrightSite Darron Murtha owns FrightSite, an online costume company specializing in exotic masks, based in Columbus, Ohio. Darron recently hired you to work in FrightSite's Marketing Department. Currently, you are working on a composition that will combine an image of a mask with an image of an eye, and you want to use Photoshop to achieve the creepy effect you're looking for. Complete the following steps:

1. Start Photoshop while pressing the Ctrl+Alt+Shift keys, and click Yes to delete the Settings File when prompted. Reset Photoshop to the default Essentials workspace layout, and then reset all tools.
2. Open **EyeMask.psd**, located in the Photoshop2\Case2 folder provided with your Data Files.
3. EXPLORE Place **Eye.tif**, located in the Photoshop2\Case2 folder, on top of the Background layer, and resize and move the image so that it fits in the eye socket on the left. (*Hint*: Click the Show Transform Controls check box on the options bar when using the Move tool, and press the Shift key when resizing to constrain proportions if desired.)
4. EXPLORE Deselect Show Transform Controls, if necessary, and add adjustments to create a creepy effect for the eye. (*Hint*: To adjust only the eye, make sure you clip the adjustment to the Eye layer. For a creepy effect, try adjusting the hue and saturation.) If you are unhappy with an adjustment, you can delete it from the Layers panel.
5. Adjust the text layer by changing its Brightness to 120.
6. Place another copy of **Eye.tif** in the file and resize it and move it so that it fits between the two lines of text. (*Hint*: The Eye layer should appear at the top of the Layers panel.) Adjust the eye by changing its hue to 95 and its saturation to 90.
7. Merge each layer and its adjustment. (*Hint*: Select the first Eye layer and its adjustment, by clicking the Eye layer and then pressing and holding the Ctrl key and then clicking the adjustment layer. Then, right-click and then click Merge Layers on the context menu. Do the same for the two other layers and their adjustment layer.)
8. Switch the image to RGB mode and flatten the image.
9. Change the image size to 5 inches wide, and constrain the proportions to ensure that the height and width change proportionally. Change the resolution to 72 ppi, select Scale Styles, and resample the image using the Bicubic (best for smooth gradients) interpolation method.
10. Zoom the image to 100%, and then change the canvas size to 4 inches wide, anchoring the image at the center. (*Hint*: Allow clipping when prompted, and make sure to deselect the Relative check box if necessary.)
11. Save the file as **Fright.jpg** in the Photoshop2\Case2 folder, using Medium quality, and a Baseline ("Standard") for optimization.
12. Close the file, and exit Photoshop.
13. Submit the results of the preceding steps to your instructor either in printed or electronic form, as requested.

Use your skills to create different versions of a profile photo.

APPLY

Case Problem 3

Data Files needed for this Case Problem: Mash.jpg, RockNRoll.psd

MashMatch Music MashMatch Music is an online site for sharing original music and creating mashups with other musicians. You have joined the site as a solo musician, and want to post a profile photo showcasing your instrument. You plan to use the same composition for a newspaper ad and for a poster that you'll hang up around town. Complete the following steps:

1. Start Photoshop while pressing the Ctrl+Alt+Shift keys, and click Yes to delete the Settings File when prompted. Reset Photoshop to the default Essentials workspace layout, and then reset all tools.
2. Open **Mash.jpg**, located in the Photoshop2\Case3 folder provided with your Data Files.
3. Change the size of the image to 15 × 10 inches.
4. Change the Saturation setting of the image to –20 to tone down the bright red of the guitar.
5. Extend the canvas to add two inches to the bottom only, and make the extension color black.
6. Place the file **RockNRoll.psd**, located in the Photoshop2\Case3 folder in the file, and position the text so it is centered in the black area at the bottom of the image.
7. Apply a Posterize adjustment to the Background layer using the default settings.
8. Save the file as **Poster.jpg** in the Photoshop2\Case3 folder, using Medium quality and Baseline ("Standard") format.
9. Delete the Posterize adjustment layer.
10. Change image size to 5 × 4 inches at 72 ppi. When you resize, scale styles, constrain proportions, and resample the image using the default settings. Zoom the image to 100%.
11. Save the resized image as **WebProfile.jpg** at Medium quality with an optimized baseline.
12. Change the color mode to Grayscale, rasterize and flatten the image, and discard color information.
13. Save the file as **GrayRock.jpg** with the current JPEG settings in the Photoshop2\Case3 folder, close the file, and exit Photoshop.
14. Submit the results of the preceding steps to your instructor either in printed or electronic form, as requested.

Use the skills you learned, plus some new skills, to modify a photograph and add text.

CHALLENGE

Case Problem 4

Data Files needed for this Case Problem: Cupcake.jpg, FinnText.psd, FinnText2.psd

Finnegan's Cakes You are the sole proprietor of Finnegan's Cakes, a neighborhood bakery in Northport, New York. You are just learning Photoshop, and want to use your new skills to modify an image for the cover of the menu. You'll create a color menu for in-house customers and a black-and-white menu for takeout. Complete the following steps:

1. Start Photoshop while pressing the Ctrl+Alt+Shift keys, and click Yes to delete the Settings File when prompted. Reset Photoshop to the default Essentials workspace layout, and then reset all tools.
2. Open **Cupcake.jpg**, located in the Photoshop2\Case4 folder provided with your Data Files.
3. Zoom in on one of the blue confetti circles on the cupcake.

EXPLORE

4. Change the background color in Photoshop to the blue from the confetti. (*Hint*: Click the blue confetti on the cake using the Eyedropper pointer. Then switch the foreground and background colors by pressing the X key so the confetti blue becomes the background color; the foreground color and background color squares in the Color panel will switch.)

5. Fit the image on screen. Extend the canvas by increasing the canvas by 4 inches in height, with no change in width. Leave the image anchored in the center, and use the Background color for the canvas extension. Fit the image on screen again, if necessary, so you can see the blue border at the top and bottom.
6. Place **FinnText.psd**, located in the Photoshop2\Case4 folder, in the blue rectangle at the top of the canvas.

EXPLORE

7. Use the Eyedropper tool, located in the Tools panel, to click the pink frosting on the cupcake to sample its color and assign it as the foreground color. The foreground color square in the Color panel should change to pink.
8. Use the Rectangle tool (*not* the Rectangular Marquee tool) to draw a pink rectangle over the blue rectangle at the bottom of the image so that it is as wide as the image, and about one inch tall. Center it vertically in the blue area.
9. Place **FinnText2.psd** located in the Photoshop2\Case4 folder, at the bottom of the canvas, centered on the pink rectangle.

EXPLORE

10. Display the Styles panel, and apply the Basic Drop Shadow style to the text you just placed at the bottom of the canvas. (*Hint*: Basic Drop Shadow is in the third row in the Styles panel, and is the last button on the right. You may need to scroll to see the button.)
11. Convert the image to CMYK mode, and rasterize and flatten it.
12. Save the file as **Menu.tif** in the Photoshop2\Case4 folder, using the default TIFF settings.
13. Change the color mode to Grayscale.
14. Adjust the Brightness to –10 and the Contrast to 75.
15. Save the file as **GrayCake.jpg** in the Photoshop2\Case4 folder, with the current JPEG settings. Close Menu.tif without saving, and exit Photoshop.
16. Submit the results of the preceding steps to your instructor either in printed or electronic form, as requested.

ENDING DATA FILES

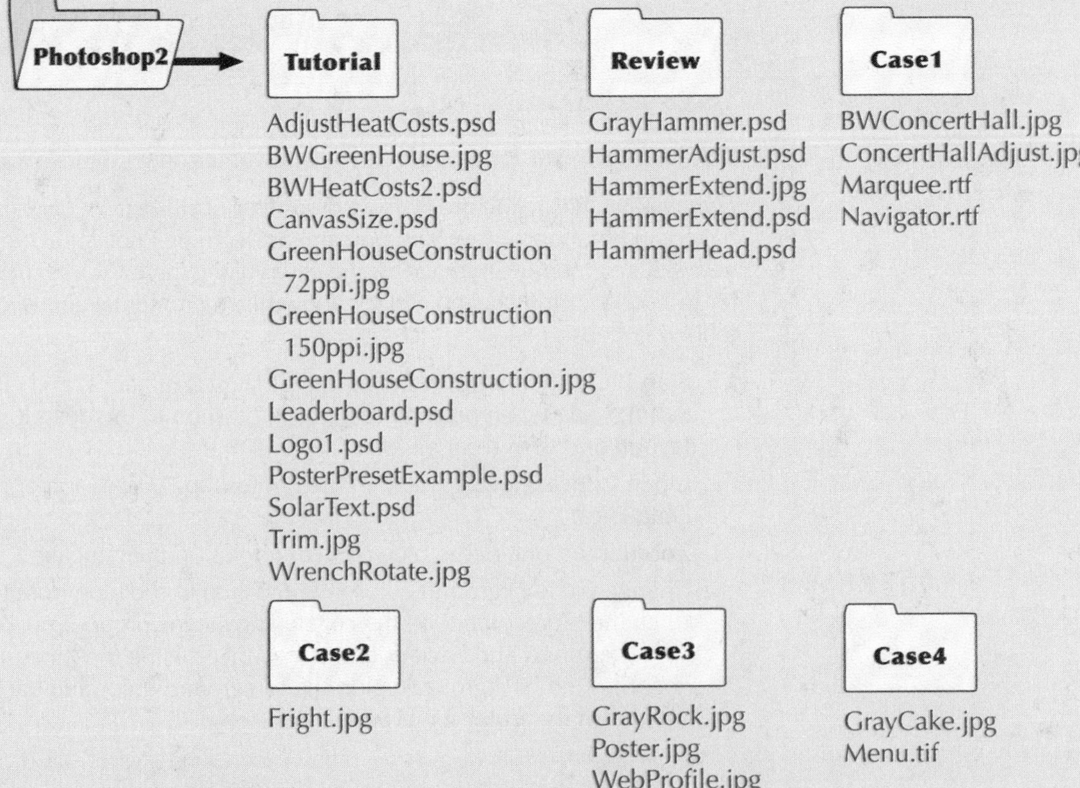

TUTORIAL 3

Layering Content to Compose Images

Working with Layers in Compositions

OBJECTIVES

Session 3.1

- Select, add, duplicate, and delete layers
- Change layer properties and visibility
- Move, align, and distribute layers
- Hide and redisplay layers
- Place, resize, and reposition an image on a layer

Session 3.2

- Lock layer content
- Work with layer comps
- Apply blending modes and adjust opacity
- Create layer groups
- Merge layers and flatten an image

Case | *Cooking the Books Publishing*

Cooking the Books Publishing is a small publishing house based in Madison, Wisconsin. The company was founded by Elena Genoa in 2008, and currently has 25 titles on its list. Upcoming titles include *The Fruit Fantastic: Recipes for the Adventurous Palate*, and *The New Old-Fashioned: 19th Century Recipes with a 21st Century Twist*. You are an assistant to Art Director Kaye Eastman. Because it's a small company, you and Kaye are tasked with creating all of the artwork for the publishing house, including illustrations and covers. Kaye has asked you to work on some cover and illustration ideas for the new titles. You'll use layers in Photoshop to develop a series of possible compositions to present to her at your next meeting.

STARTING DATA FILES

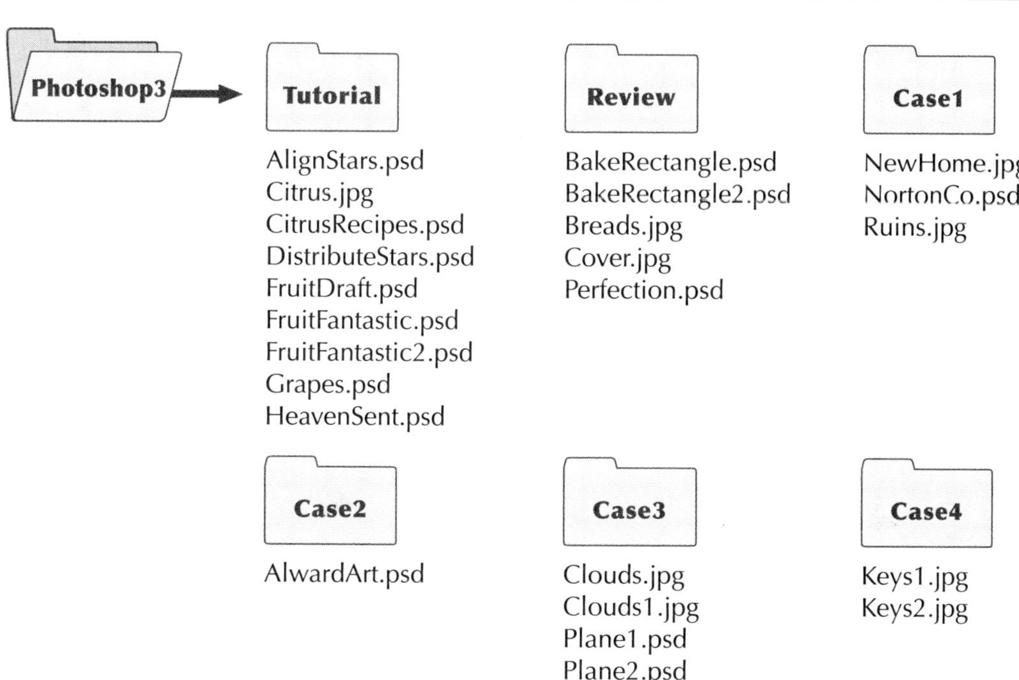

SESSION 3.1 VISUAL OVERVIEW

The Align icons on the options bar let you choose how to **align**, or line up, selected objects along their centers or edges.

Select the Show Transform Controls check box to see **transform controls**, the squares at each corner and along the sides of a selection that let you change the shape and size of an object.

Display **layer edges** to see where a layer begins and ends on the canvas.

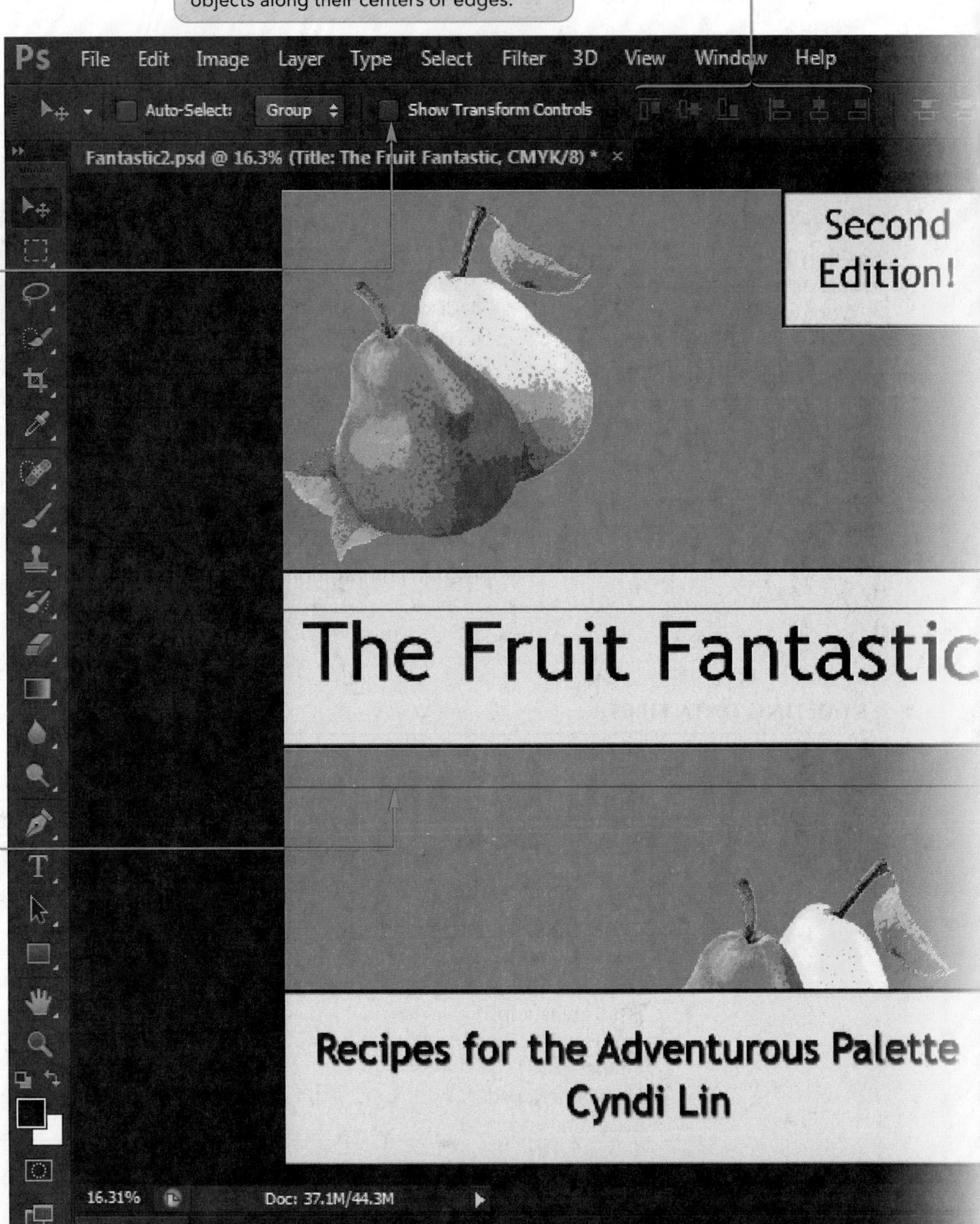

Anna Kucherova/Shutterstock.com

WORKING WITH MULTIPLE LAYERS

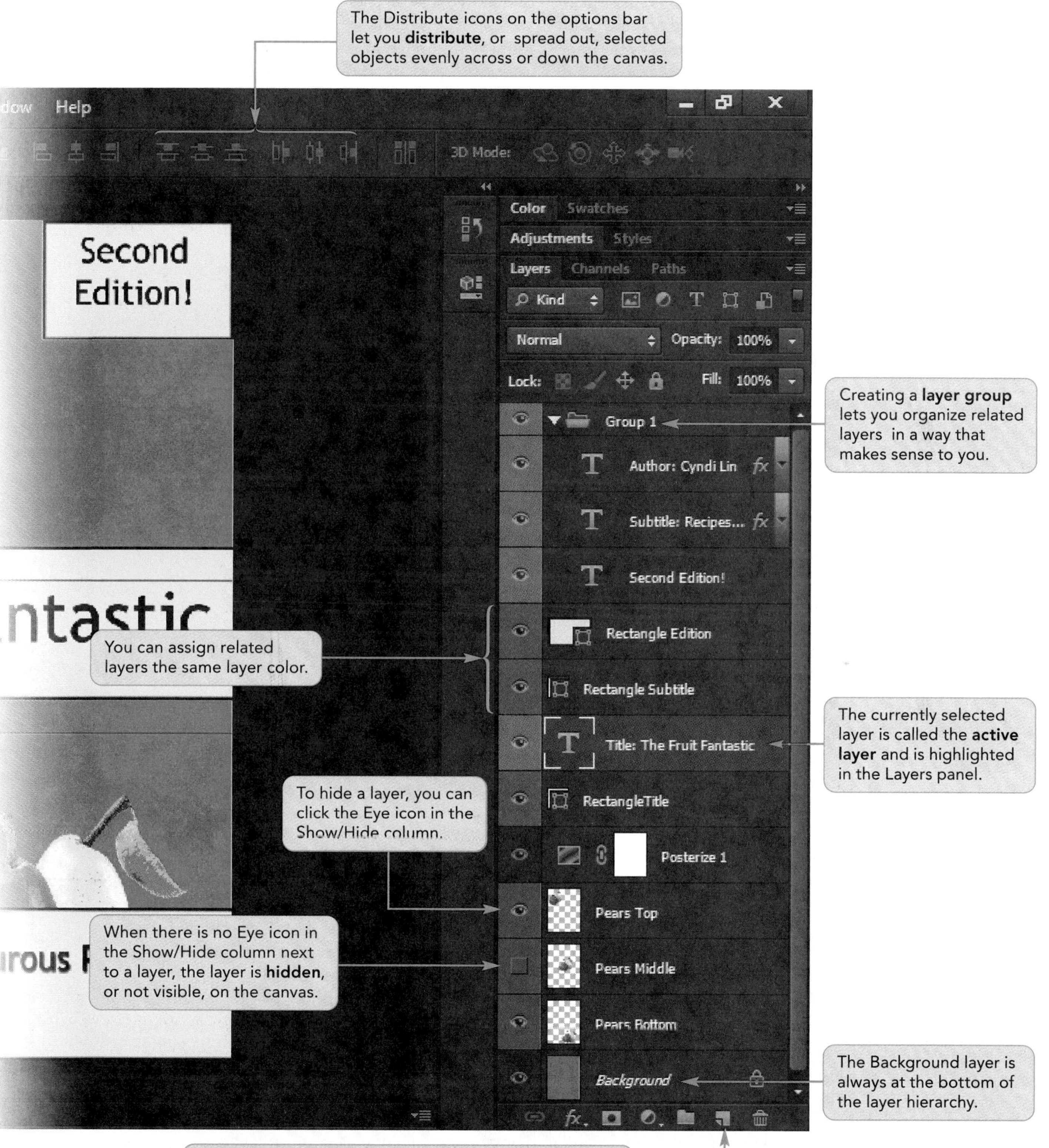
The Distribute icons on the options bar let you distribute, or spread out, selected objects evenly across or down the canvas.
Creating a layer group lets you organize related layers in a way that makes sense to you.
You can assign related layers the same layer color.
The currently selected layer is called the active layer and is highlighted in the Layers panel.
To hide a layer, you can click the Eye icon in the Show/Hide column.
When there is no Eye icon in the Show/Hide column next to a layer, the layer is hidden, or not visible, on the canvas.
The Background layer is always at the bottom of the layer hierarchy.
The Create a new layer icon lets you add a new layer to the file above the selected layer or, if no layers are selected, at the top of the layers list in the Layers panel.
Help
3D Mode:
Color
Swatches
Adjustments
Styles
Layers
Channels
Paths
Kind
Normal
Opacity:
100%
Lock:
Fill:
100%
Group 1
Author: Cyndi Lin
Subtitle: Recipes...
Second Edition!
Rectangle Edition
Rectangle Subtitle
Title: The Fruit Fantastic
RectangleTitle
Posterize 1
Pears Top
Pears Middle
Pears Bottom
Background
Second
Edition!
ntastic
urous

Understanding Layers

> **TIP**
>
> To hide a layer, click the Eye icon in the Show/Hide column to the left of the layer's thumbnail in the Layers panel. To redisplay a hidden layer, click the empty square to the left of the thumbnail.

You have already witnessed the power of layers in Photoshop. In Tutorial 2, when you placed an image in a file, it appeared on its own layer. When you added an image adjustment, you were actually adding it as a layer on top of the layer to which it was clipped. An adjustment layer changes the way an image looks, but it is a nondestructive edit; it does not alter the pixels in the image. Adding an adjustment layer is like placing a sheet of clear plastic over the original image with the changes etched on it. Through this virtual layer of plastic, it appears as if the image has changed in some fundamental way. However, if you want to restore that image to its original appearance, all you have to do is delete or hide the layer containing the adjustment—as if you were removing the sheet of plastic containing your changes. See Figure 3-1.

Figure 3-1 Nondestructive editing with an adjustment layer

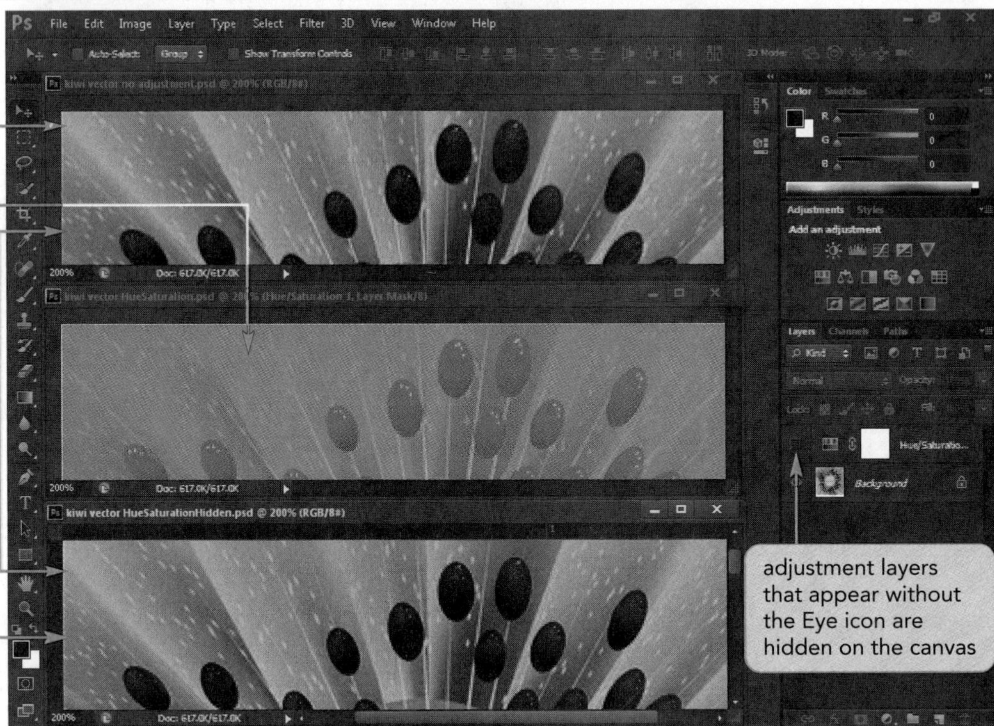

averych/Shutterstock.com

Figure 3-1 shows an image opened for the first time in Photoshop, then the same image with a Hue/Saturation adjustment layer applied, and a third version of the same image with the Hue/Saturation layer "turned off," or hidden. When the adjustment layer is visible, as shown in the middle image, it looks as if the underlying image itself has changed. However, when you hide the adjustment layer, you can see that the image pixels remain the same—with or without the adjustment layer.

If you do not make use of the layers functionality in Photoshop, any changes you make to an image are permanent after you save the file. If you haven't saved a backup of the original file, there is no way to go back to the original version of the file. With layers, however, you can experiment endlessly with a file by adding layer upon layer of changes, hiding layers, redisplaying layers, saving the file, working on it the next day and the next, and then deleting any layers you decide you don't want. Even with multiple changes, your original image remains intact—as long as you use layers to make those changes nondestructively.

Understanding Layer Positioning

As a rule, if no layer is selected in the Layers panel, any new layer that you add to a document appears at the top of the layers list in the Layers panel. If you first select a layer and then add a layer, the new layer appears directly above the selected layer. This is important to know because the order of layers in the Layers panel affects the way the image looks. Layers on top of other layers in the Layers panel appear on top of those layers in the composition itself. See Figure 3-2.

Figure 3-2 **The importance of layer order**

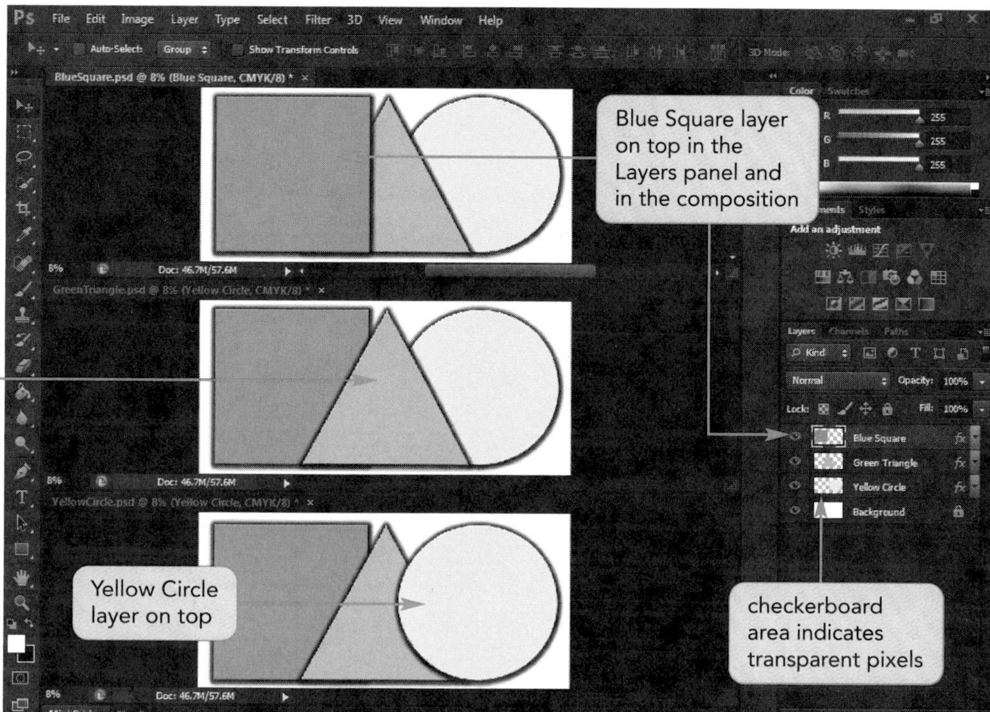

In the first file in Figure 3-2, the Blue Square layer is at the top of the list of layers in the Layers panel, followed by the Green Triangle layer and then the Yellow Circle layer. In the next file, the Green Triangle layer has been moved to the top of the list of layers, and appears on the top of the stacked objects in the document. In the third file, the Yellow Circle layer has been moved to the top of the Layers panel and appears on top in the document.

Notice that the thumbnail for each of these shapes in the Layers panel shows a checkerboard pattern around the shape. The checkerboard design in Photoshop indicates that the pixels in the checkerboard area are **transparent**, so you can see through them. Imagine that each of the shapes in Figure 3-2 has been painted on a rectangle of clear glass. Any area beneath the glass, except where the shape appears, is visible through the glass.

The position of adjustment layers in the Layers panel affects how the adjustments are applied to a file. An adjustment at the top of the Layers panel will affect all the layers beneath it, including the Background layer, unless it is clipped to a particular layer. As noted in Tutorial 2, when an adjustment is clipped to a layer in the Layers panel, it affects only that layer. See Figure 3-3.

Figure 3-3 **Adjustment clipped to one layer and clipped to all layers beneath it**

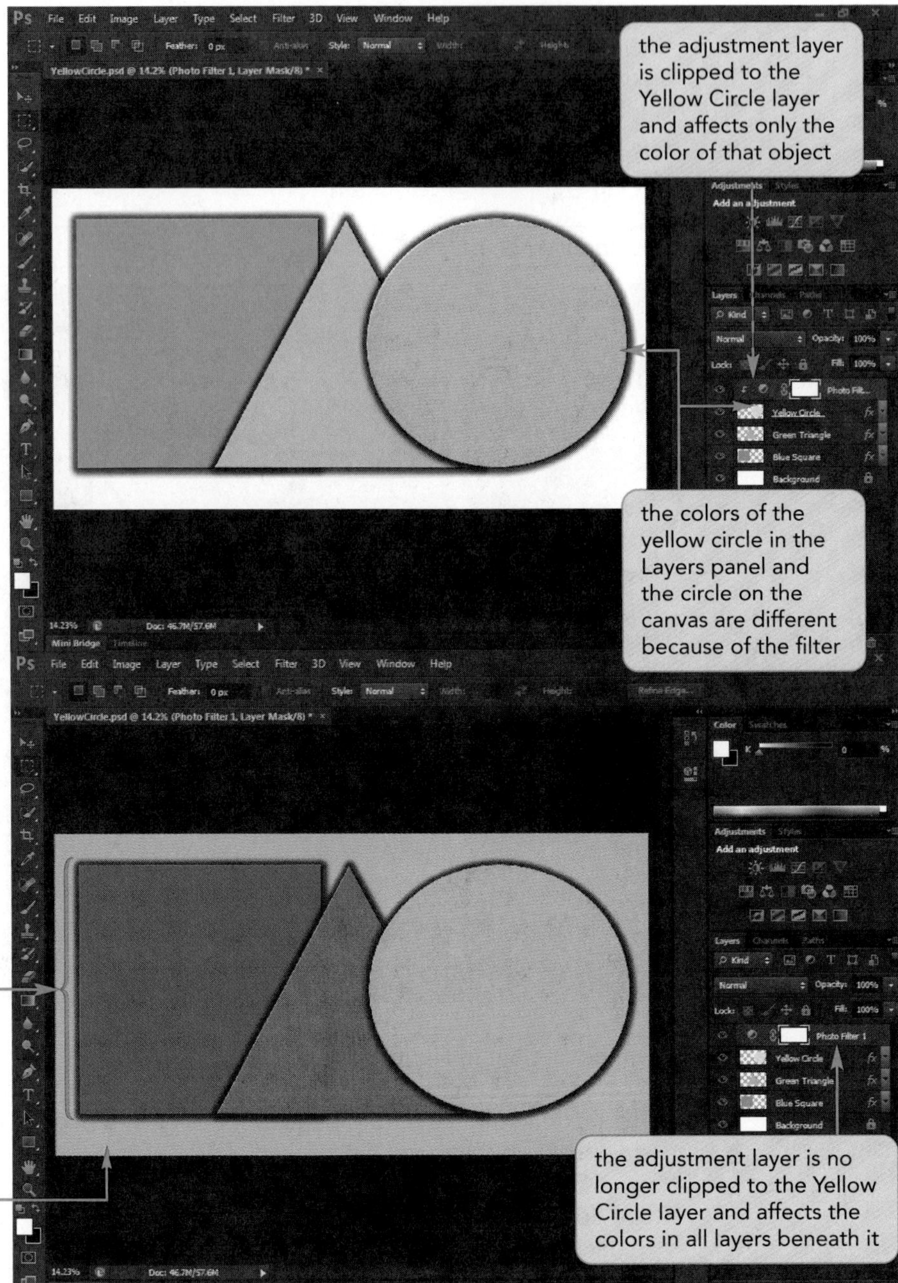

The Deep Red Photo Filter adjustment used in Figure 3-3 has the same effect on the colors in an image that putting a colored filter over your camera lens would have: It changes the colors of the objects in the image. In the top image, the Photo Filter adjustment layer is clipped to the layer beneath it (the yellow circle). As a result, the circle in the image appears orange rather than yellow. However, the color of the circle in the Layers panel thumbnail is still yellow. In the bottom image, the same Photo Filter adjustment layer has been unclipped from the Yellow Circle layer, so it affects *all* layers beneath it; each of the shapes and the background appear to have changed color.

You'll find that most of the work you do in a complex document involves layers. You will frequently add, duplicate, select, name, and move layers. You'll group layers in the Layers panel so their organization is logical, and you'll hide and redisplay them to compare their impact or effect. In this session, you'll learn many of the basic layer tasks you'll perform in Photoshop.

Selecting and Deselecting Layers

To work with any layer in a Photoshop file, you first need to select it so it becomes active. More than one layer can be active at a time, and a layer must be active if you want to work with it. It's a common mistake to start working on an image with a particular goal in mind only to realize that you are not actually working with the correct layer. See Figure 3-4.

Figure 3-4 **Trying to copy pixels in an unselected layer**

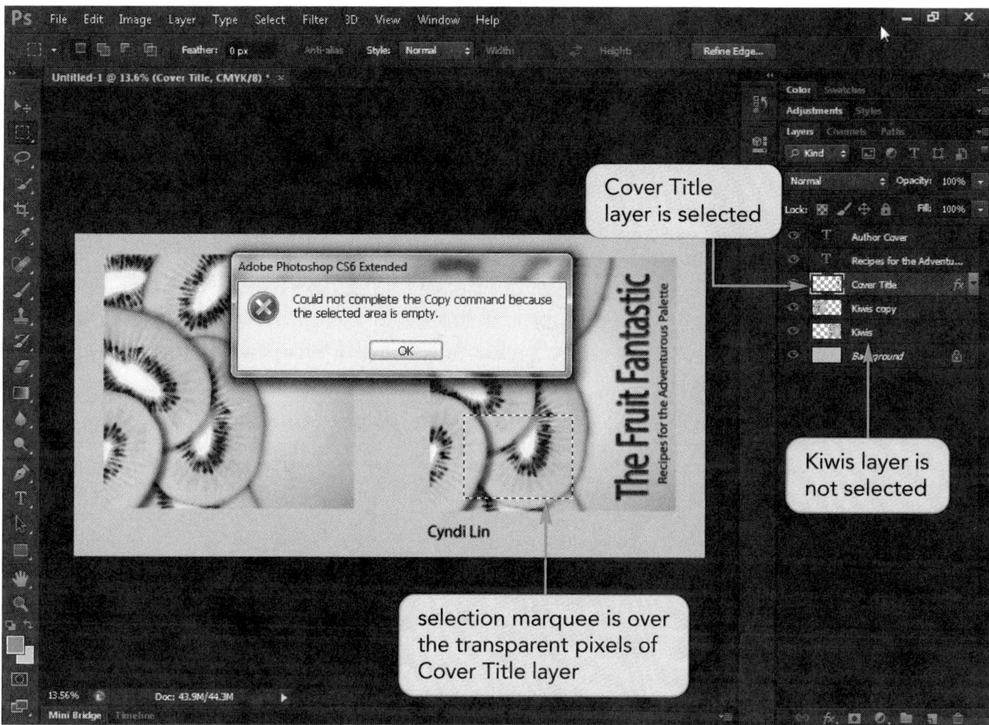

Subbotina Anna/Shutterstock.com

In Figure 3-4, the selection marquee appears around a portion of the image of the kiwi fruit. It is logical to think that you could use the Copy command on the Edit menu to copy the selection to the Clipboard. However, although the selection marquee is over the kiwi image, the Cover Title layer is the selected layer. If you hid all the layers except the Cover Title layer, you would see that the selected area consists of transparent pixels. In other words, there is nothing to copy. If you try to copy a selection that is empty, Photoshop displays the error message shown in the figure.

Selecting and Deselecting Single Layers

Often, you will need to select a single layer so you can make changes that affect that layer only. When you select certain layers in an image, a **bounding box** shows the borders of the layer; the transform controls are the squares on the sides and at each corner of the bounding box. Bounding boxes do not appear on **locked layers**, which are layers (such as the Background layer, which is locked by default) that you cannot move or resize. If you want to move or make changes to the locked Background layer, you can convert it to a regular layer by right-clicking the Background layer and selecting the Layer from Background option on the context menu.

Kaye has created a couple of mock-ups for the new *Fruit Fantastic* cookbook, and she wants you to experiment with the layers in her composition to see if you can improve on her ideas. You'll start by selecting and deselecting layers in order to make changes on a single layer at a time.

To select a single layer:

1. Start Photoshop while pressing the **Ctrl+Alt+Shift** keys, and click **Yes** to delete the Settings File when prompted. Reset Photoshop to the default Essentials workspace layout, and then reset all tools.
2. In the Tools panel, click the **Move Tool** button, and then click the Show Transform Controls check box to select it.
3. Click **File** on the menu bar, click **Open**, navigate to the Photoshop3\Tutorial folder included with your Data Files, open **FruitFantastic.psd**, and press the **Ctrl+0** keys to fit the image on the screen.
4. Minimize the **Color** panel group and the **Adjustments** panel group by double-clicking the panel tabs, and then expand the **Layers** panel, if necessary.

   The Layers panel lists all of the layers in the file, including text layers, image layers, an adjustment layer, and the Background layer. You'll select The Fruit Fantastic layer so you can change its font.
5. In the Layers panel, click the **Title: The Fruit Fantastic** layer to select it. The text layer is selected in the panel and in the document, as indicated by the bounding box and the transform controls. See Figure 3-5.

Figure 3-5 Text layer selected in the Layers panel and on the canvas

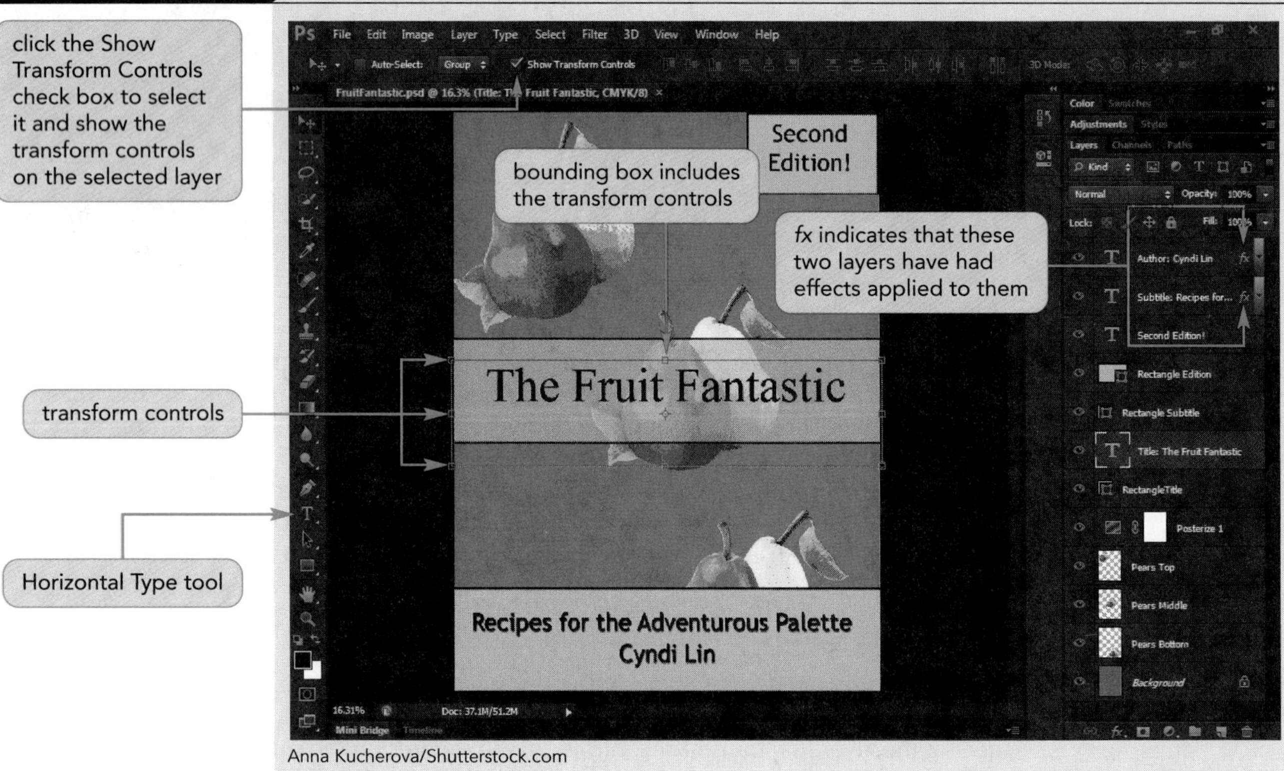

Anna Kucherova/Shutterstock.com

If you select the Horizontal Type tool to make changes to one or more text layers, the options for the Horizontal Type tool appear on the options bar, indicating that Photoshop is in text-edit mode. In **text-edit mode**, you can modify text on a layer by changing the font style and color, among other things. You'll make a change to the font on one of the text layers next.

To make changes to a single layer and deselect a layer:

1. In the Tools panel, click the **Horizontal Type Tool** button, and then on the options bar, click the **Set the font family** arrow.
2. In the font list, scroll down, if necessary, and then click **Trebuchet MS**. The title font changes to Trebuchet MS.

   Trouble? If Trebuchet MS does not appear on the font list, click a different font.
3. In the Tools panel, click the **Move Tool** button, and then in the Layers panel, click the **Pears Top** layer. The text layer is deselected, and the layer with the image of the pears in the upper-left corner of the composition is selected in the Layers panel and in the document, where a bounding box appears around the layer.
4. In the Layers panel, click the **Background** layer. The Background layer is selected in the Layers panel, but no bounding box appears in the document. This is because the Background layer is a locked layer and can't be moved or resized (as indicated by the lock icon that appears in the Layers panel).
5. In the Layers panel, click the **Posterize 1** layer. The Posterize 1 layer is selected in the Layers panel, but there is no selection in the document. This is because the Posterize 1 layer is an adjustment layer. It affects the layers beneath it, but doesn't appear as an object in the composition. However, it can be moved in the Layers panel so that it affects different layers in the composition.
6. On the menu bar, click **Select**, and then click **Deselect Layers**. Now there are no layers selected in the Layers panel.

TIP

You can also press and hold the Ctrl key and then click a layer to deselect it.

To work more efficiently, you can change many layers in a file at one time. To do so, you'll select multiple layers at once.

Selecting and Deselecting Multiple Layers

You will often find that you want to apply the same effect to multiple layers in a document. You could select the first layer, apply the effect, select the next layer, apply the effect, and so on. However, it's faster to select multiple layers at the same time and apply an effect to all of them at once. You can apply an effect to many layers at the same time by selecting all of the layers you want to work with to make them all active. For example, you might want to add a style to some of the text layers in your composition using the same settings. The subtitle and author name shown in Figure 3-5 were selected together and then had the Basic Drop Shadow style applied to them at the same time.

REFERENCE

Selecting Multiple Layers

- To select contiguous layers, in the Layers panel, click the first layer, press and hold the Shift key, and then click the last layer.
- To select noncontiguous layers, in the Layers panel, click the first layer, press and hold the Ctrl key, and then click each additional layer.

or

- To select all of the layers in the Layer panel, on the menu bar, click Select, and then click All Layers.

You can also select similar layers using a filter. **Similar layers** are layers with common characteristics. For example, all adjustment layers in the Layers panel would be considered similar layers, as would all image layers and all text layers. In the Layers panel, you can use a filter to display only those layers that are similar in some way, and then to select and make changes to all of those layers at the same time. You can filter by layer kind (for example, adjustment layer, type [or text] layer, or vector layer), layer name (for example, layers with the word *Title* in their name), or layer effect (for example, a layer with a shadow or bevel effect). Other filter options include mode, attribute, and color, all of which you'll learn about later in this tutorial.

Kaye asks you to see what the composition will look like if all of the rectangles behind the text are a different color. Notice that currently in the Layers panel, the rectangle layers are not next to each other. You'll use a filter to make it easy to select all the rectangles in the file at the same time to make the change.

To filter and display similar layers:

1. At the top of the Layers panel, click the **Filter for shape layers** icon. Photoshop hides all of the layers in the Layers panel except the three shape layers in the composition, the rectangles that are used as backgrounds for the text.
2. In the Layers panel, click the **Rectangle Edition** layer, press and hold the **Shift** key, and then click the **RectangleTitle** layer. All three rectangle layers are selected, so you can modify all three layers at the same time.
3. In the Tools panel, click the **Rectangle Tool** button, and then on the options bar, click the yellow **Fill** button. In the panel, click a bright green color for the rectangles, and then click the **Fill** button, which is now green, again to close the panel of swatches.

   The color of all three rectangles changes at the same time. See Figure 3-6.

Figure 3-6 **Filtering and modifying similar layers**

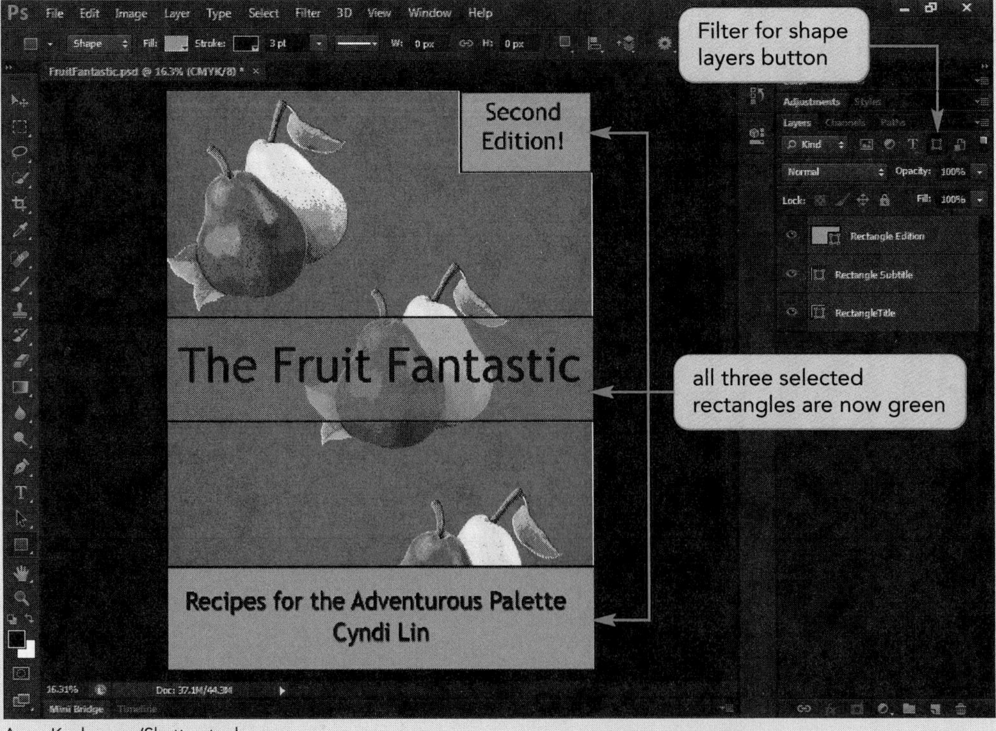

Anna Kucherova/Shutterstock.com

4. In the Layers panel, click the **Filter for shape layers** icon to deselect it and turn off layer filtering. All of the layers are redisplayed in the Layers panel.

   Next, you'll filter and select layers by name.

5. At the top of the Layers panel, click the **Kind** button, and then click **Name**. The layer Kind icons at the top of the Layer panel are replaced by a text box.
6. In the Name box, type **Pears**. Photoshop displays only the layers with the word *Pears* in their name.
7. In the Layers panel, click the **Turn layer filtering on/off** button to turn off filtering and redisplay all of the layers.
8. Save the file as **Fantastic2.psd** in the Photoshop3\Tutorial folder, and leave it open in the Photoshop workspace.

PROSKILLS

Teamwork: Knowing When to Call in Help

No matter how good your digital image-editing skills are, there will be times when you need to reach out to another person on your team to help you do your best work. Not only are teams useful for providing feedback on the work you do, but every good team has people who specialize in different areas. Being a Photoshop expert doesn't necessarily mean you have the artistic skills to create vector drawings at a professional level. Furthermore, although Photoshop's drawing tools might be sufficient for adding simple vector shapes to an image file, it is certainly not the best drawing tool for creating a professional composition—Illustrator is. When you need to create a challenging graphic for your composition, it is a good idea to call in a graphic designer or a visual artist if you need help. For example, if you need a vector drawing for a comp you are working on for a client, you could fumble around with the drawing tools in Photoshop and create a pretty good drawing—but why not shoot for excellent instead? Calling on an expert from your team for support will not only result in the best final product, but will also show that you have the decision-making and problem-solving skills necessary to get a job done right, the team player mentality to advance your organization's interests, and the potential to lead that team in the future.

Adding and Duplicating Layers

You can add a layer to a file in many ways. You can add an empty layer and then fill it with content. You can duplicate a selected layer so an exact copy of the layer appears in the Layers panel and in the composition. You can add a layer by drawing a vector object or by using the Type tools in the Tools panel. You can cut or copy a selection on one layer—or even in another file—and paste it into your composition to add it as a new layer. You can use the options in the Adjustments panel to add an adjustment layer. You can also add an **effects layer** by applying a style to a layer. In addition, you can add a fill layer to fill the background of a composition with a color, pattern, or gradient.

Adding an Empty Layer

To add a layer before adding any content or making an adjustment, use the Create a new layer icon at the bottom of the Layers panel. You can then place a photograph, enter text, or draw a vector object in the new layer, and it will appear on the canvas on top of the Background layer.

Kaye has asked you to develop some additional options for the *Fruit Fantastic* book cover by starting with a plain background and adding some new layers.

To add an empty layer and add a shape to the new layer:

1. Open **FruitDraft.psd**, located in the Photoshop3\Tutorial folder, and size it to fit the screen.
2. At the bottom of the Layers panel, click the **Create a new layer** icon. Photoshop creates a new layer, named Layer 1, above the Background layer.

   Next, you'll add a shape to the empty layer.
3. In the Tools panel, click the **Rectangle Tool** button, if necessary. The options bar changes to display settings for the Rectangle tool.
4. On the options bar, click the black **Fill** button. A swatches panel opens.
5. In the Swatches panel, click a pastel blue color, and then click the Fill button again to close the panel.
6. On the canvas, use the outer guides to draw a rectangle similar in size to the one shown in Figure 3-7.

Figure 3-7 Drawing a rectangle in an empty layer

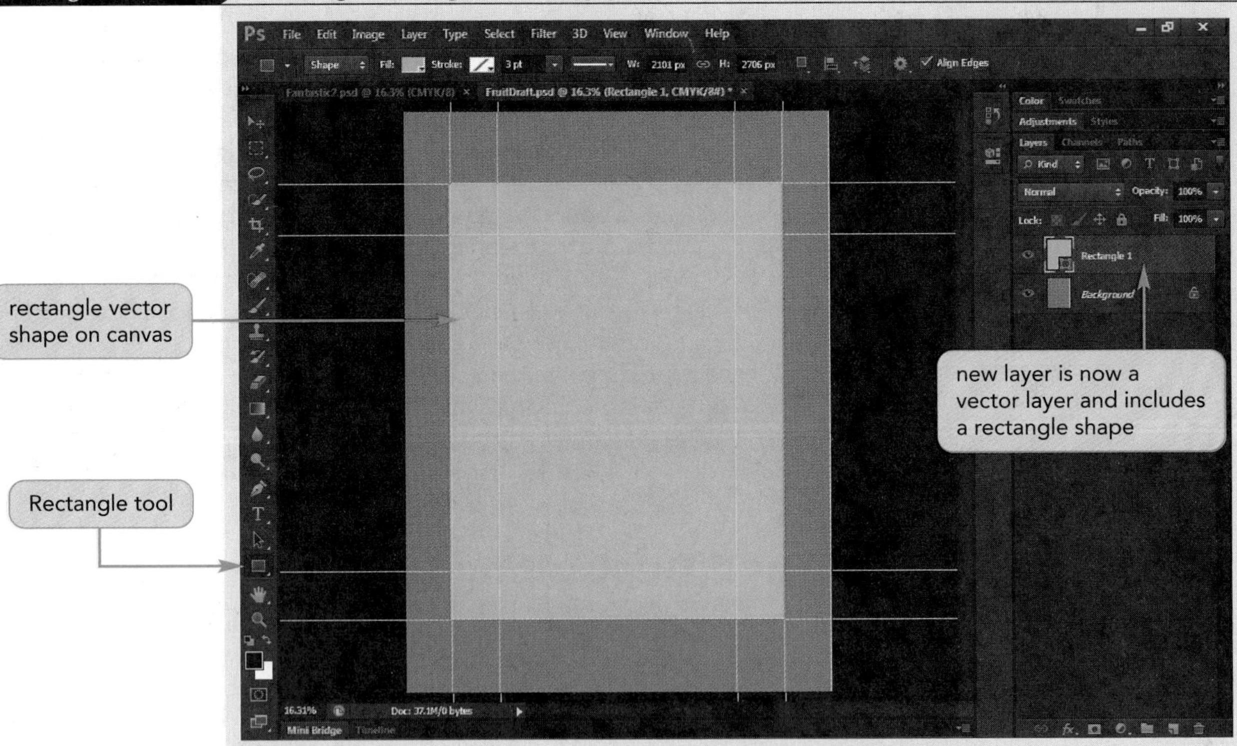

Adding a Vector Layer and an Effects Layer

When you use any of the vector drawing tools in the Tools panel when there are no layers selected, Photoshop places each vector object you draw on its own vector layer. When you modify the layer by adding an effect or applying a style, Photoshop adds an effects layer indented underneath the layer you are modifying and adds an ***fx*** designation next to the layer name. A **style** is a preset grouping of effects that are applied together. For example, a style might include a bevel and emboss effect as well as some sort of pattern or texture.

To add more interest to your cover design, you'll add another layer by drawing another shape in the file and then you'll apply one of the style presets to the new layer.

To add a vector layer and an effects layer:

1. Using the Rectangle tool and the inner guides, draw another rectangle inside the blue rectangle. Photoshop adds the rectangle to the document and places it on its own layer (Rectangle 2) in the Layers panel. You'll make the new rectangle stand out by applying a style to it.
2. Click the **Styles** tab behind the Adjustments tab to display the Styles panel.
3. In the Styles panel, click the **Tie-Dyed Silk (Texture)** icon to add the Tie-Dyed Silk style to the new layer. See Figure 3-8.

   Trouble? If you don't see the Tie-Dyed Silk (Texture) icon in the Styles panel, click the panel menu button, click Reset Styles, and then click the OK button to replace the current styles with the default styles. If prompted to save changes to the current styles before replacing them, click the No button. Repeat Step 3.

Figure 3-8 Tie-Dyed Silk effect applied to new layer

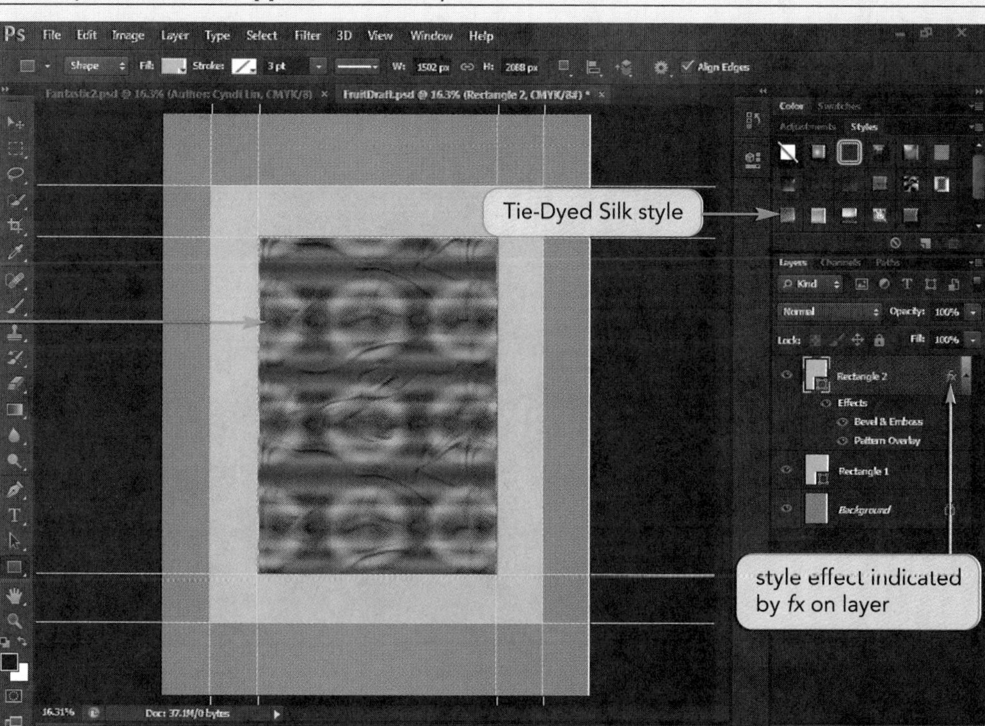

The Tie-Dyed Silk style includes two effects—a Bevel & Emboss effect, which gives the rectangle a three dimensional look, as if it is wrinkled, and a Pattern Overlay effect, which fills the rectangle with an image of tie-dyed silk.

4. Save the file as **FruitDraft2.psd** in the Photoshop3\Tutorial folder, and keep the file open.

Creating a New Layer by Cutting or Copying and Pasting a Selection

You might find that you want to reuse part or all of an image, either in the current composition or in another composition. To do so, you can use one of the selection marquee tools to select the part of an image that you want to reuse, and then copy or cut the selection to the Windows Clipboard, which stores the selection in memory so you can paste it into the current file or another file. When you paste a selection, Photoshop puts the object on a new layer in the Layers panel. You can then use the Move tool to position the object where you want it to appear on the canvas.

To continue creating your mock-up for the cookbook cover, you'll copy some grapes from a PSD file to the FruitDraft2 file and paste them on a new layer.

To create a layer by copying and pasting:

1. Open **Grapes.psd** from the Photoshop3/Tutorial folder, and then size it to fit the screen.
2. In the Tools panel, click the **Rectangular Marquee Tool** button, and then drag a marquee around some of the grapes in the bunch of grapes. See Figure 3-9.

Figure 3-9 Copying a rectangular marquee selection

Chianuri/Shutterstock.com

3. On the menu bar, click **Edit**, and then click **Copy**.
4. Switch back to the **FruitDraft2.psd** file.
5. On the menu bar, click **Edit**, and then click **Paste**. Photoshop pastes the selection in the file and on a new layer. Note that you selected and copied only the grapes, not the Posterize effect that was applied to them in the original file. See Figure 3-10.

TIP

You can also press the Ctrl+C keys to copy. You can press the Ctrl+V keys to paste.

Figure 3-10 Pasting a selection on the canvas

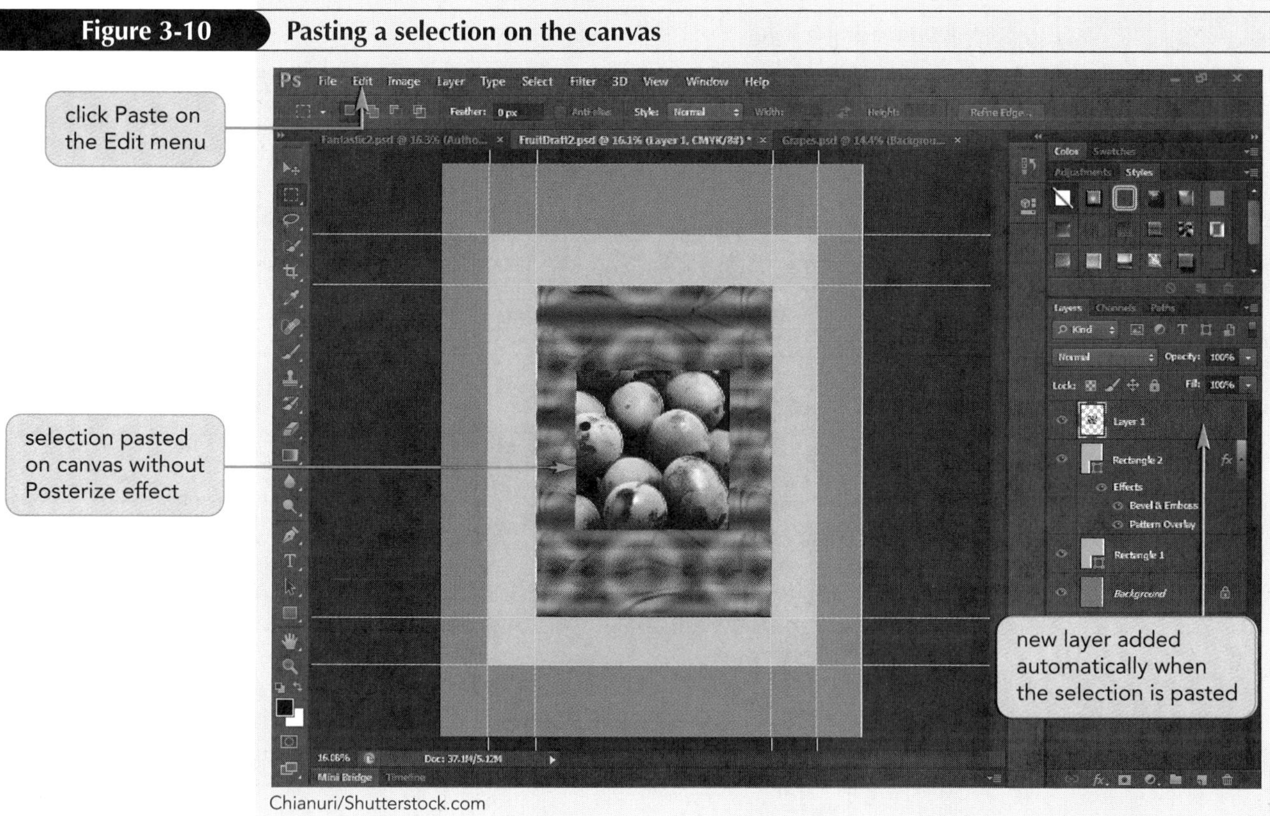

Chianuri/Shutterstock.com

Duplicating a Layer

When you duplicate a layer, you make an exact copy of its contents and any formatting or effects applied to it. For example, if you duplicate a shape layer that has a style applied to it, the new layer will include not only the vector shape but also the style. You can enter a name for the duplicate layer in the Duplicate Layer dialog box. You can also specify whether the duplicate should be added to the current file or another file, called a destination. A **destination file** can be any currently open file or a new file. You select the destination for a duplicate in the Duplicate Layer dialog box.

To duplicate a layer:

1. In the Layers panel, click the **Rectangle 2** layer to select it.
2. On the menu bar, click **Layer**, and then click **Duplicate Layer**. The Duplicate Layer dialog box opens. See Figure 3-11.

Figure 3-11 **Duplicating a layer**

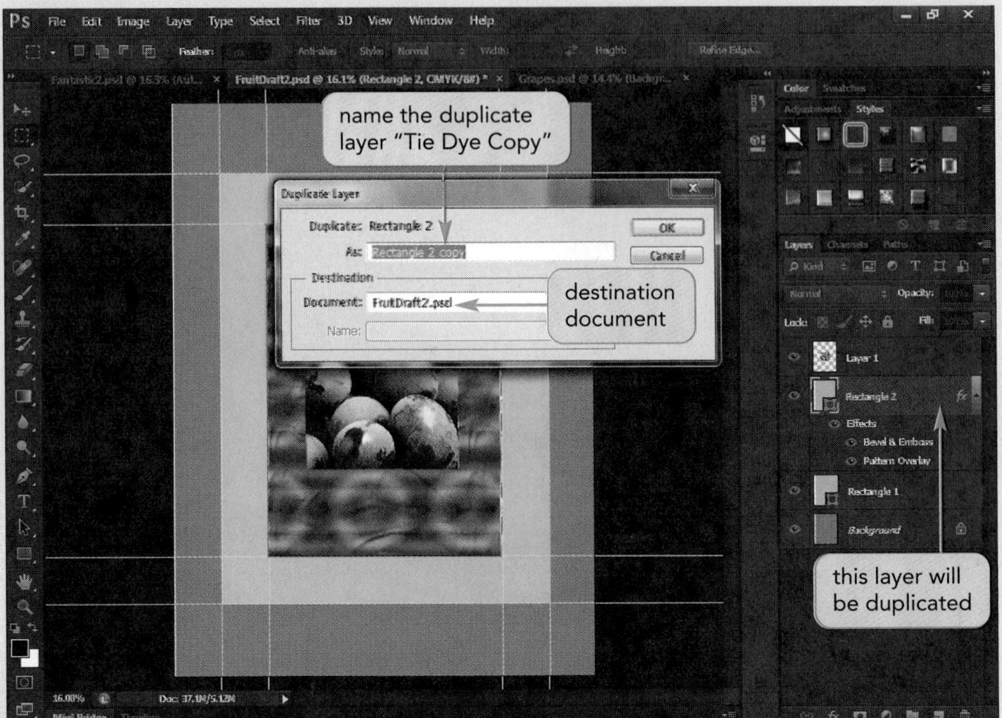

Chianuri/Shutterstock.com

3. In the As box, type **Tie Dye Copy**, confirm that the destination document is FruitDraft2.psd, and then click the **OK** button.

   Photoshop creates an exact copy of the Rectangle 2 layer, including the tie-dyed effect you added, and adds it to the Layers panel, with the name Tie Dye Copy. Because the duplicate is directly on top of the original layer on the canvas, you can't yet see it.

4. In the Tools panel, click the **Move Tool** button, point to the tie-dyed rectangle on the canvas, and then drag it up and to the top-left corner of the canvas.

5. In the Layers panel, right-click the **Tie Dye Copy** layer, and then click **Duplicate Layer** on the context menu.

6. Name the new layer **Tie Dye Copy 2**, and click the **OK** button. In the Document window, drag the new layer down and to the bottom-right corner of the canvas. See Figure 3-12.

Figure 3-12 **Document with two duplicate layers**

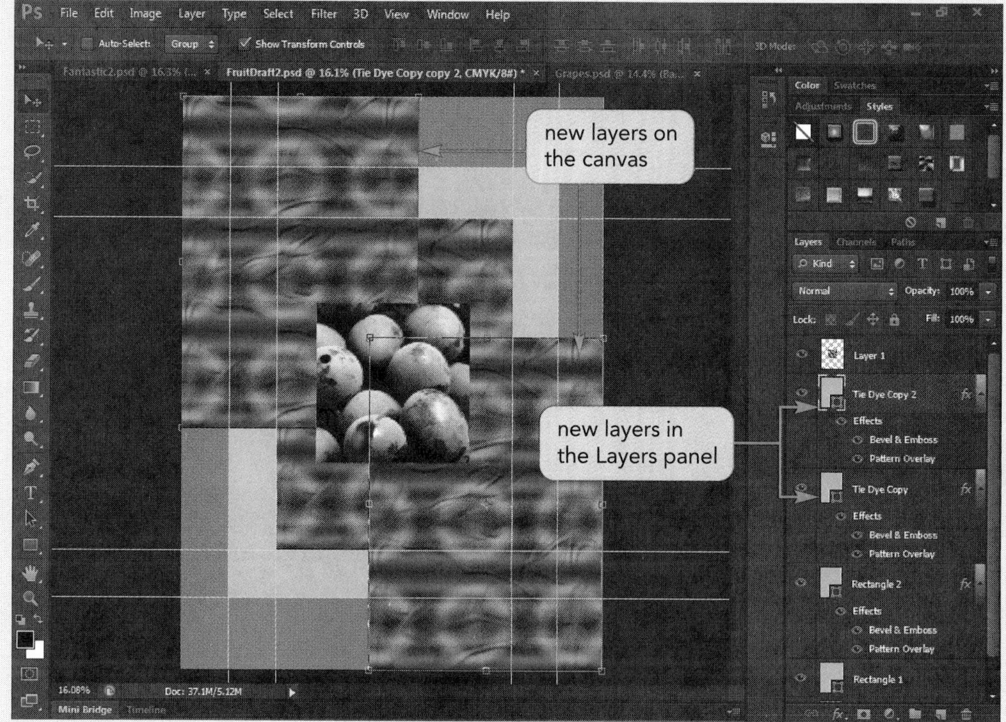

Chianuri/Shutterstock.com

Changing Layer Properties

When you are working in a file with many layers, it is helpful to give each layer a descriptive name that helps you remember its purpose or context. By default, Photoshop names generic layers by number: *Layer 1*, *Layer 2*, *Layer 3*, and so on. When you create a text layer, Photoshop names it using the actual text you have typed, and places a text icon (the letter *T*) in the thumbnail. When you draw a shape, Photoshop names the shape layer *Shape* 1, *Shape* 2, *Shape* 3, and so on. For example, when you draw a Rectangle, the first rectangle layer is given the name *Rectangle 1*. You can change the default name to make it more descriptive.

You can also change the color of a layer. Note that when you change the color of a layer, you are not changing the way the layer content looks on the canvas; rather, you are changing the color of the background of the Eye icon in the Show/Hide column in the Layers panel. If you assign the same color to related layers, you provide yourself with an easy visual overview of the organization of your document. For example, in the Session 3.1 Visual Overview, all text layers have a yellow color assigned to them, as does the group that contains the text layers; all digital images have been assigned a blue color; and all shape layers have been assigned a green color.

Kaye suggests that you organize your file by changing layer properties. You'll change the names and colors of the layers in your draft file so you can keep track of them more easily.

To change the name of a layer:

1. Press the **V** key to activate the Move tool, if necessary.
2. In the Layers panel, click **Layer 1** to select it, if necessary, and then point to the layer name, *Layer 1*, and double-click. The layer name appears highlighted in a box.
3. Type **Grapes** and then press the **Enter** key. Photoshop renames the layer.
4. In the Layers panel, click the **Rectangle 1** layer to select it. On the menu bar, click **Layer**, and then click **Rename Layer**.
5. Type **Blue Rectangle**, and then press the **Enter** key.
6. Change the name of the Rectangle 2 layer to **Tie Dye**, and then deselect all layers. Collapse the Adjustment and Styles panel group if necessary to see all of the layers in the Layers panel. See Figure 3-13.

Figure 3-13 **Renaming layers**

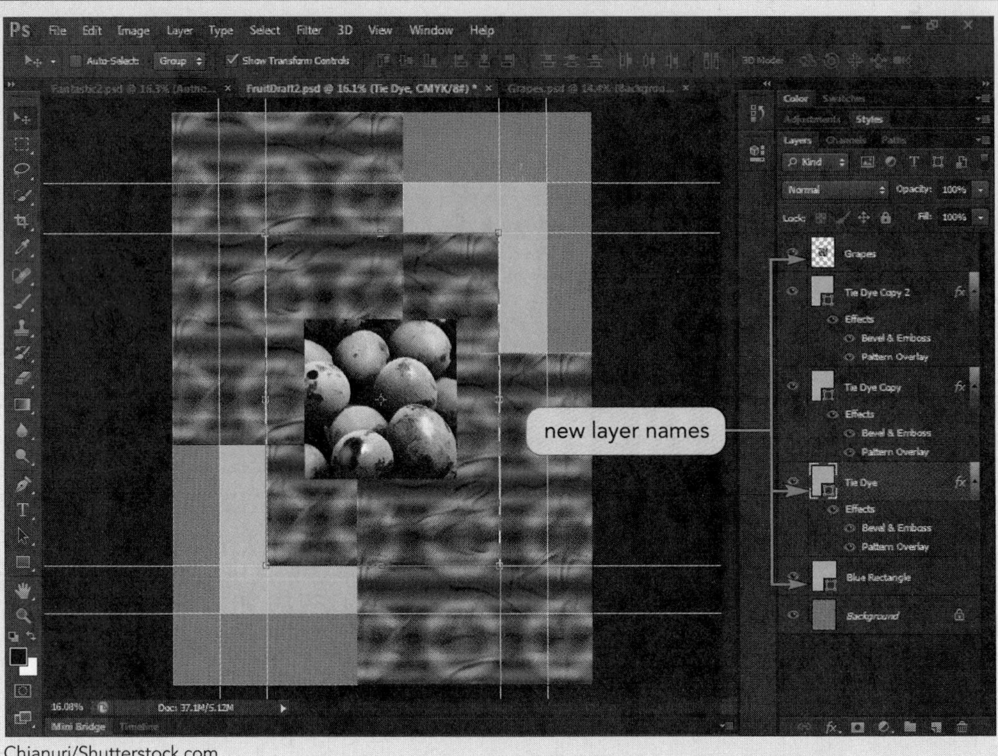

Chianuri/Shutterstock.com

The layers in the Layers panel now have names that help you identify them quickly. Next, you'll assign layer colors to the FruitDraft2.psd file to keep it organized.

To change the color of a layer:

1. In the Layers panel, right-click the **Grapes** layer, and then click **Violet**. Photoshop changes the color of the box in the Show/Hide column in the Layers panel to violet.
2. Change the color of all three Tie Dye layers to **Orange**. Photoshop assigns the orange color to the Tie Dye layers and their associated effects layers.
3. Change the color of the Blue Rectangle layer to **Blue**. See Figure 3-14.

Figure 3-14 **Changing layer colors**

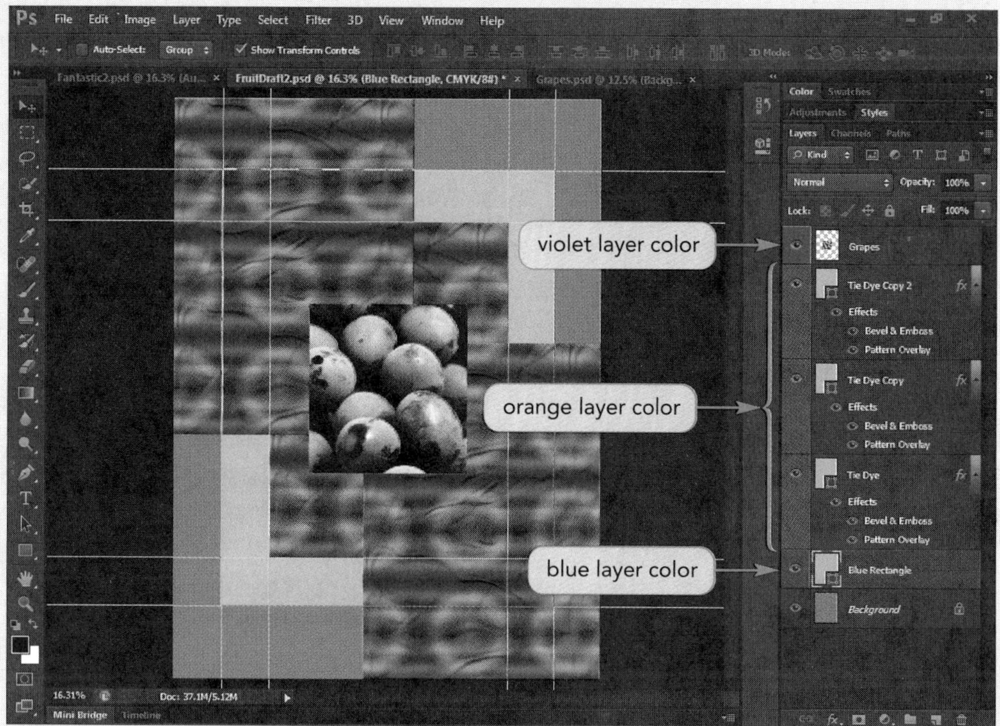

Chianuri/Shutterstock.com

4. Save FruitDraft2.psd in the Photoshop3\Tutorial folder, and then close the file. Close the Grapes.psd file without saving it.

INSIGHT

Keeping the Layers Panel Manageable

If you add many layers to your composition, and apply many adjustments to those layers, the Layers panel might become unwieldy. You can organize your layers by grouping them and color-coding them, but it can be tempting to go overboard when you do. For example, if you have one each of many different kinds of layers (shapes, text, adjustment), you should ask yourself whether it's worth the time and effort to change the color properties or even the names of each layer. Each composition will dictate its own best practice, and as you continue to familiarize yourself with Photoshop, you'll develop the insight you need to be able to determine which tools you should make use of in each situation.

Displaying Layer Edges

It is often helpful to be able to see where a layer begins and ends on the canvas. For some layers, you can see a bounding box when the layer is selected and you turn on the display of transform controls with the Move tool selected. When you select more than one layer, the bounding box expands to encompass the area enclosing all of the layers. When you turn on the display of layer edges, however, each layer selected in the Layers panel is enclosed in its own box in the Document window. To see the boundaries of all of the layers, select them all.

To display layer edges in the Fantastic2.psd file:

1. On the menu bar, click **Select**, and then click **Deselect Layers** to deselect all of the layers of the Fantastic2.psd file, if necessary.

   To make it easier to see the layer edges, you can turn off the Show Transform Controls setting.

2. Press **V** to activate the Move tool, if necessary, and then, on the options bar, click the **Show Transform Controls** check box to deselect it.
3. On the menu bar, click **View**, point to **Show**, and then click **Layer Edges**.
4. Fit the document on the screen if necessary, and then, in the Layers panel, click the **Pears Top** layer to select it.

   Layer edges appear as a blue box around the layer. You might have expected the edges to appear only around the picture of the pears, but the transparent pixels in the layer are also counted within the image boundaries.

5. In the Layers panel, click the **Title: The Fruit Fantastic** layer. Edges appear around the text layer.
6. On the menu bar, click **Select**, and then click **All Layers** to select all of the layers in the document except the Background layer. Photoshop displays the edges of all of the selected layers. See Figure 3-15.

Figure 3-15 **Showing layer edges**

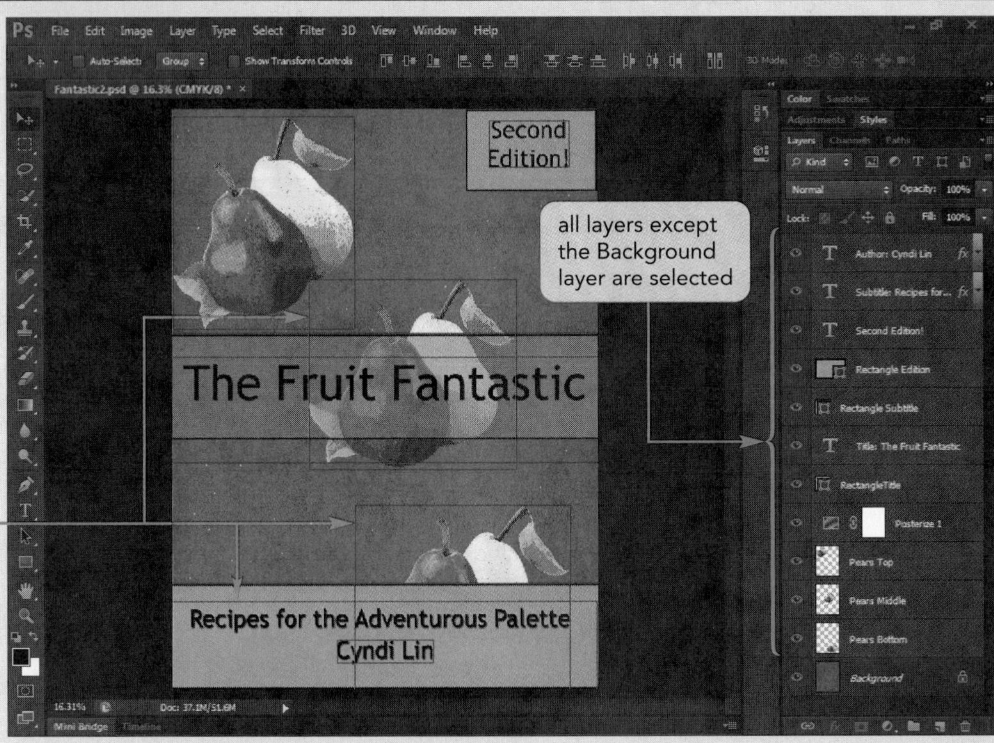

Anna Kucherova/Shutterstock.com

7. On the menu bar, click **View**, point to **Show**, and then click **Layer Edges** to turn off the display of layer edges.

Moving a Layer in the Layers Panel to Change Its Visibility

A layer's position in the Layers panel affects its appearance in the document. If it is near the bottom of the panel, it might be partially or completely hidden on the canvas by the layers above it. If a layer is at the top of the panel, it might obscure the layers underneath it.

REFERENCE

Moving a Layer in the Layers Panel to Change Its Visibility

- In the Layers panel, select a layer.
- Drag the layer down or up in the Layers panel to change its visibility on the canvas.

or

- On the menu bar, click Layer, click Arrange, and then click Bring to Front, Bring Forward, Send Backward, or Send to Back to change the position of the selected layer in the Layers panel. You can also click Reverse to reverse the order of two or more selected layers.

Kaye suggests that you experiment with the position of the layers in the Layers panel in the Fantastic2.psd file to see how changing their visibility affects the overall look of the composition.

TIP

You can also press the Ctrl+[keys to move the layer down or press the Ctrl+] keys to move the layer up in the Layers panel.

To move a layer in the Layers panel to change its visibility:

1. In the Layers panel, click the **Pears Middle** layer, and then drag it up. As you drag, a ghosted image of the Pears Middle layer indicates its new position in the Layers panel.
2. When the **Pears Middle** layer is above the Title: The Fruit Fantastic layer, release the mouse button.

   The Pears Middle layer appears above the Pears Top layer, the RectangleTitle layer, and the Title: The Fruit Fantastic layer in the Layers panel. Because of the change in layer order, the pears now obscure part of the book's title in the document. And because the Pears Middle layer is now also above the Posterize 1 adjustment layer in the Layers panel, it no longer has the Posterize adjustment applied to it. See Figure 3-16.

Figure 3-16 Moving a layer in the Layers panel

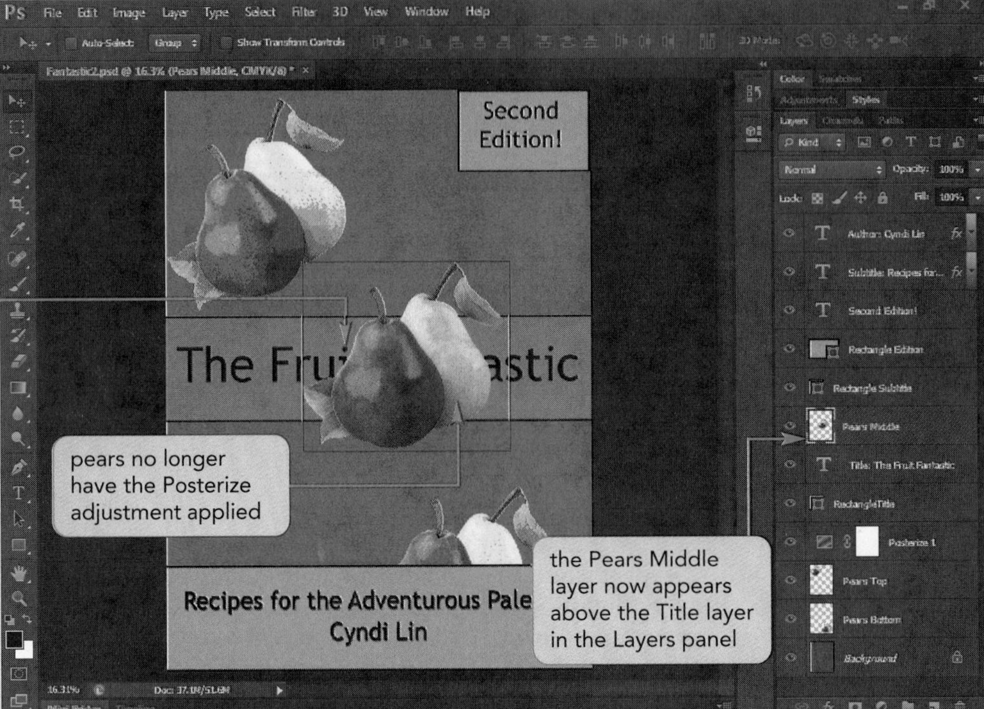
Second Edition!
The Fru astic
Recipes for the Adventurous Pale
Cyndi Lin
part of Title layer is hidden by the Pears Middle layer
pears no longer have the Posterize adjustment applied
the Pears Middle layer now appears above the Title layer in the Layers panel

Anna Kucherova/Shutterstock.com

3. On the menu bar, click **Edit**, and then click **Undo Layer Order**. The Pears Middle layer is once again beneath the title, the rectangle, and the Posterize adjustment.
4. Click the **Background** layer and drag it to the top of the Layers panel. As you drag, the mouse pointer changes to the unavailable pointer ⃠, which indicates the action you are trying to perform is not allowed. Because the Background layer is locked, you can't move it—unless you change it to a regular layer.
5. Release the mouse button. The Background layer remains at the bottom of the panel.
6. Drag the **Posterize 1** layer under the Pears Top layer. See Figure 3-17.

Figure 3-17 Dragging an adjustment layer

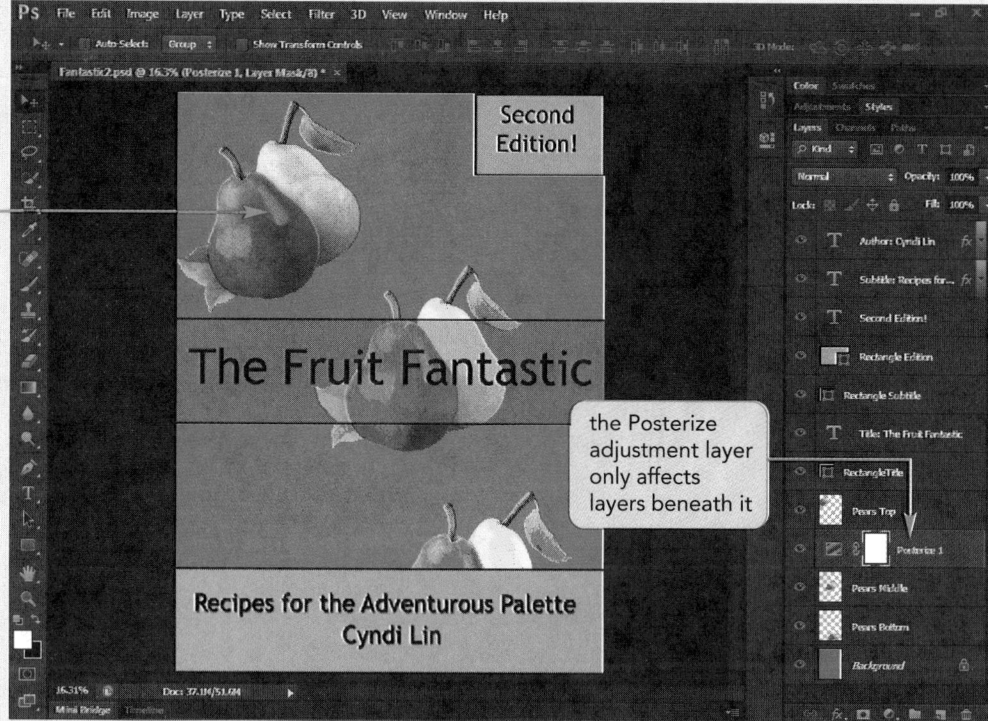
the Pears Top layer has no Posterize adjustment
Second Edition!
The Fruit Fantastic
Recipes for the Adventurous Palette
Cyndi Lin
the Posterize adjustment layer only affects layers beneath it

Anna Kucherova/Shutterstock.com

Dragging an adjustment layer changes which layers are affected by the adjustment. The Posterize adjustment is no longer applied to the Pears Top layer because it appears beneath it in the Layers panel. Only the Pears Middle, Pears Bottom, and Background layers are posterized.

7. On the menu bar, click **Edit**, and then click **Undo Layer Order** to move the Posterize 1 layer back to its original position.

Moving a Layer to Change Its Position on the Canvas

You can drag a layer to change its position on the canvas by selecting the layer in the Layers panel and using the Move tool to drag the image, drawing, or text to where you want it to appear on the canvas. If a portion of the layer ends up outside of the canvas area when you reposition it, that part will not show in the final composition and will be cropped when you finalize the image. You'll learn how to finalize an image later in this tutorial.

Kaye asks you to move some of the images on the canvas to see if you can improve the composition.

To move a layer to change its position on the canvas:

1. In the Layers panel, click the **Subtitle** text layer, point to the subtitle (Recipes for the Adventurous Palette) on the canvas, press the mouse button, and drag the text up so it is directly under the title.

2. In the Layers panel, click the **Author: Cyndi Lin** text layer, point to the name on the canvas, and then drag it until it is under the subtitle.
3. In the Layers panel, click the **RectangleTitle** layer, and then on the canvas, drag the green rectangle around the title down so the subtitle and author name also fit in it. See Figure 3-18.

Figure 3-18 Moving layers on the canvas

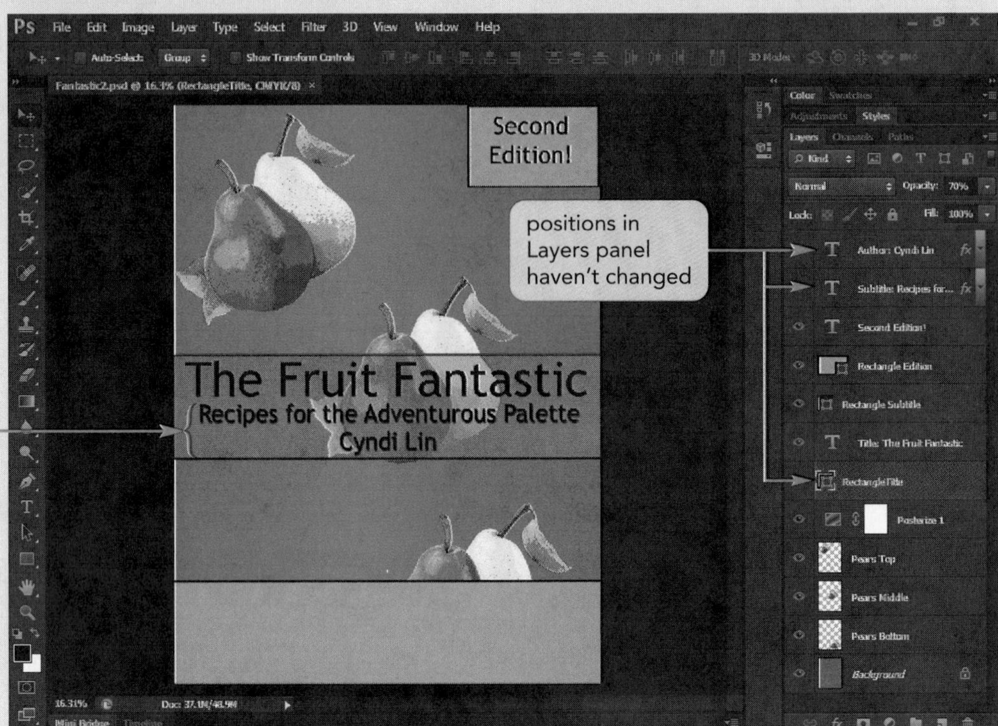

Anna Kucherova/Shutterstock.com

4. Save the file as **Fantastic3.psd** in the Photoshop3\Tutorial folder, and close the file.

Aligning and Distributing Layers

In Tutorial 1, you used the grid and guides to help you align and place images and text in a document. Photoshop offers a number of additional tools to help you align and place objects. To align or distribute selected layers, you can use commands on the Layers menu or icons on the Move tool options bar, shown in Figure 3-19.

Figure 3-19 Alignment and distribution icons and commands

Icon	Command
	Layer, Align, Top Edges
	Layer, Align, Vertical Centers
	Layer, Align, Bottom Edges
	Layer, Align, Left Edges
	Layer, Align, Horizontal Centers
	Layer, Align, Right Edges
	Layer, Distribute, Top Edges
	Layer, Distribute, Vertical Centers
	Layer, Distribute, Bottom Edges
	Layer, Distribute, Left Edges
	Layer, Distribute, Horizontal Centers
	Layer, Distribute, Right Edges

When you align layers, you can line them up along their top, bottom, left, or right edges, or you can align them based on their center points. When you distribute layers, you place them an equal distance apart along either an invisible horizontal or vertical axis.

REFERENCE

Aligning Layers in a Composition

- In the Layers panel, click the layers you want to align.
- On the menu bar, click Layer, point to Align, and then click an alignment option.

or

- With the Move tool selected, click one of the alignment icons on the options bar.

Kaye has given you a file of yellow star fruits on a green background. She'd like to create a logo to put next to any star fruit recipes in the book, but isn't sure how she wants to arrange the images. You'll experiment with aligning them to find the best arrangement.

To align the layers:

1. Open **AlignStars.psd**, located in the Photoshop3\Tutorial folder. Make sure the Move tool is selected in the Tools panel, and then click the Show Transform Controls check box on the options bar to select it. Turn on Layer Edges.
2. In the Layers panel, select the **Small Star Fruit**, **Medium Star Fruit**, and **Large Star Fruit** layers.

3. On the menu bar, click **Layer**, point to **Align**, and then click **Top Edges**. The top three star fruits are now aligned along the top edges of their layers.
4. In the Layers panel, select the **Small Star Fruit 2**, **Medium Star Fruit 2**, and **Large Star Fruit 2** layers.
5. On the options bar, click the **Align vertical centers** icon. The bottom three star fruits are now aligned along the vertical centers of their layers. See Figure 3-20.

Figure 3-20 Using the alignment options

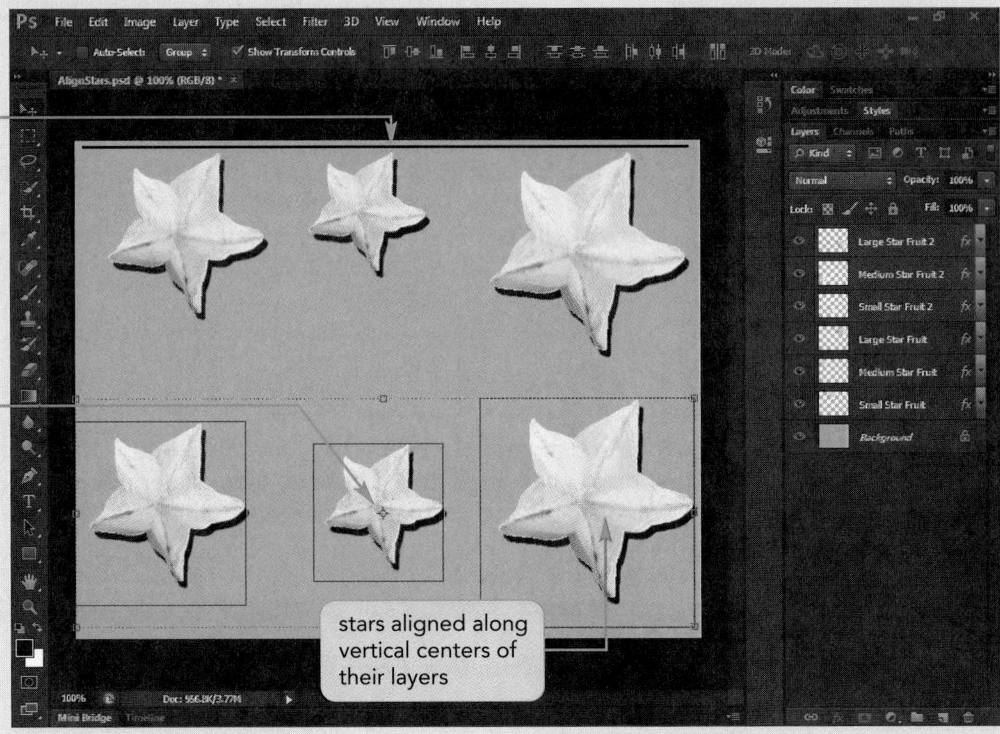

Viktar Malyshchyts/Shutterstock.com

6. Save the file as **StarsAligned.psd** in the Photoshop3\Tutorial folder, and then close the file.

Using the layer alignment options provided in Photoshop ensures that compositions you create are balanced and have the intended visual effect.

REFERENCE

Distributing Layers in a Composition

- In the Layers panel, click the layers you want to distribute. You must select at least three layers to distribute them.
- On the menu bar, click Layer, point to Distribute, and then click a distribute option.

or

- With the Move tool selected, click one of the distribute icons on the options bar.

Kaye has also given you a different star fruit file to see if you can come up with an idea for a logo to highlight or distinguish different elements in the book. This file includes three of the same size star fruits. You'll distribute them to see if the result is acceptable.

To distribute the star fruit layers:

1. Open **DistributeStars.psd**, located in the Photoshop3\Tutorial folder.
2. In the Layers panel, click the **Star Fruit 1** layer, press and hold the **Shift** key, and then click the **Star Fruit 3** layer to select all three Star Fruit layers.
3. On the menu bar, click **Layer**, point to **Distribute**, and then click **Vertical Centers**. Photoshop distributes the star fruits so they are evenly spaced.
4. Save the file as **StarsDistributed.psd** in the Photoshop3\Tutorial folder, and then close the file.

You'll show this image to Kaye for possible use on the chapter opener page for the star fruit recipes in the book or in the table of contents alongside the start fruit chapter title and contents.

Kaye has created another possible cover for *The Fruit Fantastic* book; this file contains even more layers and images in the composition. She wants you to decide whether the composition works with all of the different layers, or if some of the image layers should be deleted.

Hiding and Redisplaying Layers

In the Layers panel, the Eye icon in the Show/Hide column indicates that a layer is currently visible in the document. If you click the Eye icon, the icon disappears, and the layer is hidden on the canvas. If you click in the column again, the Eye icon reappears and the layer is redisplayed in the Document window.

To hide and redisplay a layer:

1. Open **FruitFantastic2.psd**, located in the Phostoshop3\Tutorial folder, and fit it on the screen. This file includes multiple images of fruit, three text layers, two shape layers, and a Posterize adjustment layer.
2. In the Layers panel, scroll down to the bottom of the list of layers, and then click the **Eye** icon in the Show/Hide column to the left of the Pears Middle layer. The Eye icon disappears, and the layer no longer appears on the canvas.
3. Click the empty **Eye** icon box in the Show/Hide column to the left of the Pears Middle layer. The Eye icon reappears and the middle photo of the pears reappears on the canvas.
4. In the Layers panel, click the **Eye** icon to the left of the Posterize 1 layer. The Eye icon disappears, and the posterize adjustment no longer affects the layers beneath it.
5. Click the empty **Eye** icon box. The Eye icon reappears and the Posterize adjustment is once again applied to the layers beneath it.

You can hide all of the layers but one by pressing and holding the Alt key and then clicking the Eye icon for the layer you want to stay visible. Photoshop hides all layers but the one you click. If you press and hold the Alt key and click the icon again, Photoshop redisplays the hidden layers. This is very convenient if you want to focus only on a single layer—to make detailed pixel corrections, for example, or to make a careful selection.

Next, you'll hide all of the layers except the Pears Middle layer.

To hide all but one layer and then redisplay all layers:

1. Click the **Pears Middle** layer, if necessary, press and hold the **Alt** key, and then click the **Eye** icon for the Pears Middle layer. All of the layers are hidden except the Pears Middle layer. See Figure 3-21.

Figure 3-21 Hiding all but one layer

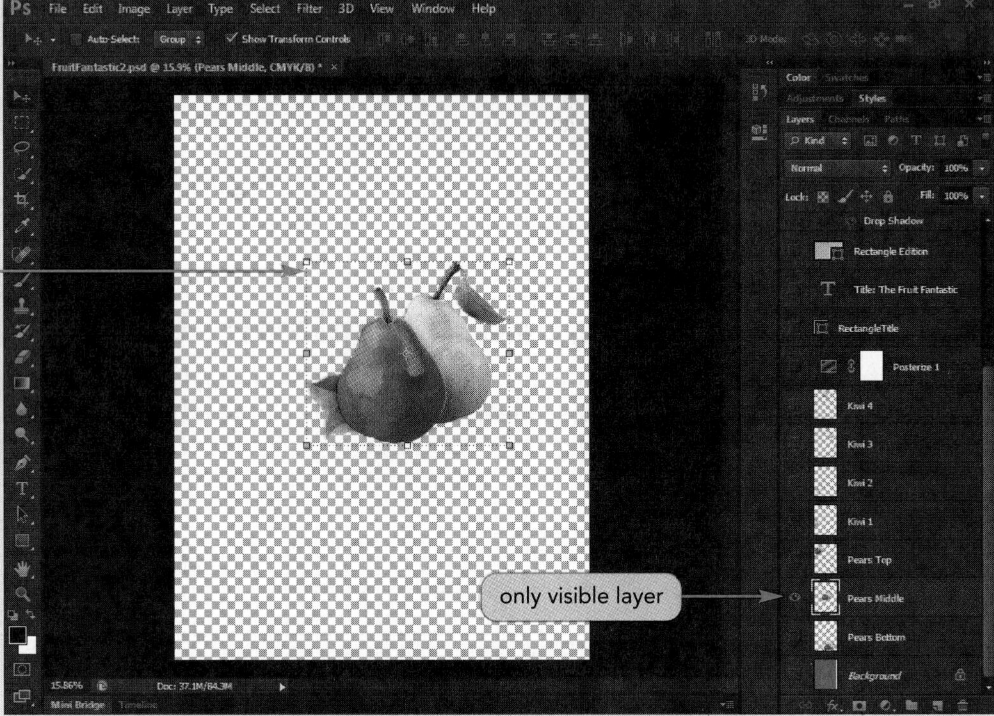

Anna Kucherova/Shutterstock.com

2. Alt-click the **Eye** icon to the left of the Pears Middle layer. The rest of the layers are redisplayed in the panel and on the canvas.

You can also drag down the Show/Hide column in the Layers panel. As you drag, the Eye icon for each layer disappears and the layer is hidden. To redisplay all of the layers, you can drag back over the column and the Eye icons reappear.

To hide and redisplay layers by dragging:

1. In the Layers panel, scroll up to the top of the list of layers, point to the **Eye** icon for the Author: Cyndi Lin layer, press and hold the mouse button, drag down the Show/Hide column to the Background layer, and then release the mouse button. All of the layers are hidden.

2. Point to the Show/Hide column to the left of the Background layer, press and hold the mouse button, drag up the column to the Author: Cyndi Lin layer, and then release the mouse button. All of the layers are redisplayed.

Now that Kaye has seen what the composition looks like with some of the layers hidden, she wants you to hide and then delete some layers so that they will no longer be saved with the file.

Deleting a Layer

One of the benefits of working with layers is that you can experiment with many different images, vector objects, and adjustments in the same composition, and then hide them, move them, and redisplay them to judge their effect. However, eventually you'll want your image to include only the layers that you want in the final composition. If you have added an adjustment, an image, or a vector object that you decide you no longer want to include, you can delete it from the Layers panel, which deletes it from the document.

To delete a layer:

1. In the Layers panel, scroll down, click the **Posterize 1** layer, and then press the **Delete** key. Photoshop deletes the adjustment layer without prompting you for confirmation.
2. Click the **Pears Middle** layer, and then click the **Delete layer** icon at the bottom of the Layers panel. Photoshop prompts you to confirm the deletion.
3. Click the **Yes** button to confirm the deletion. Photoshop deletes the Pears Middle layer. Save the file as **FruitFantastic3.psd** in the Photoshop3\Tutorial folder, and then close it.

Placing, Resizing, and Positioning an Image on a Layer

As you saw in Tutorial 2, you can place an image in a file to add it to your composition. When you place an image, Photoshop places the image on a new layer, positioned in the center of the canvas. The placed image is bounded by a box, and has diagonal lines running from corner to corner through a center point. You can use the options bar to change the placement and size of the image, as well as the angle at which it is rotated on the canvas. When you are satisfied with the placement of an image, you can click the Commit button on the options bar. See Figure 3-22.

Figure 3-22 **Placing an image**

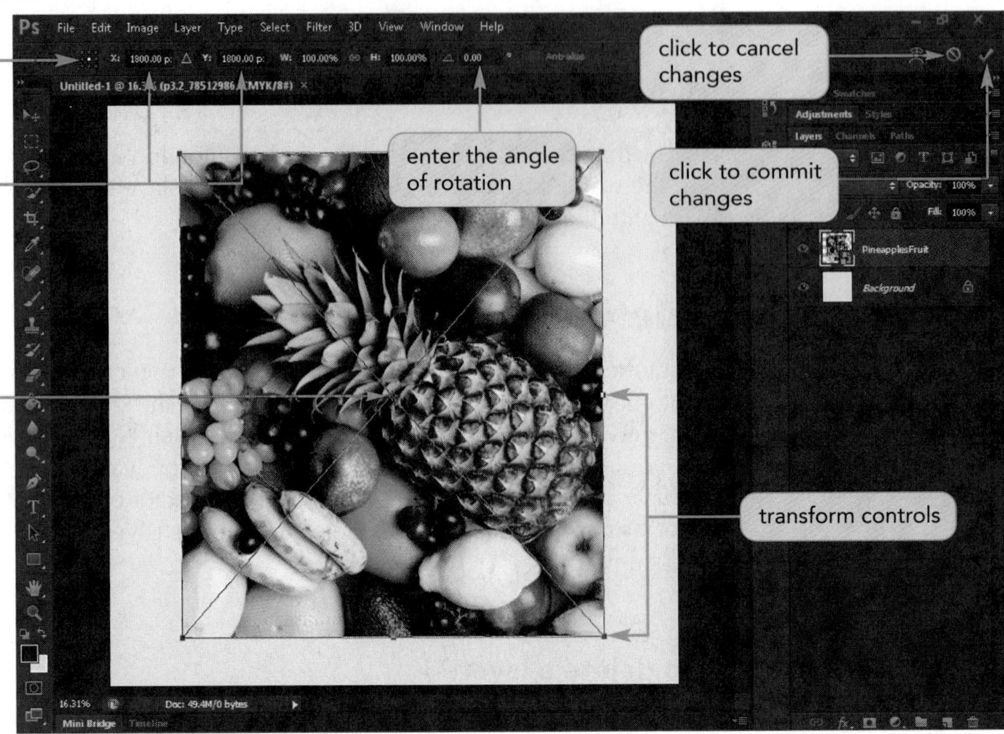

Shutter Lover/Shutterstock.com

In Photoshop, the **center point** is the point at which a placed image will rotate if you change its angle on the canvas. By default, the center point is located in the exact center of the image, but you can change its location by clicking a handle on the Center Point icon on the options bar, or by dragging the center point to a new location.

When you place an image, make sure it is the same resolution as the file into which you're placing it, or you'll see unexpected results. For example, a low-resolution file placed in a high-resolution file will be very small on the canvas, and a high-resolution file placed in a low-resolution file will be very large.

Kaye wants you to set up a chapter opener page for the section on citrus recipes. You'll place an image of oranges and kiwis on the canvas, and then you'll size and rotate it.

To place the image:

1. Open **CitrusRecipes.psd**, located in the Photoshop3\Tutorial folder.
2. On the menu bar, click **File**, and then click **Place**.
3. In the Place dialog box, select **Citrus.jpg**, located in the Photoshop3\Tutorial folder, and then click **Place**. Photoshop places the image in the center of the canvas.

   Right now, the image fills the entire canvas. See Figure 3-23.

Do not press the Enter key after you place the file. Doing so will place the image in the file without giving you any options to transform it or modify its placement.

Figure 3-23 Options bar for placing an image

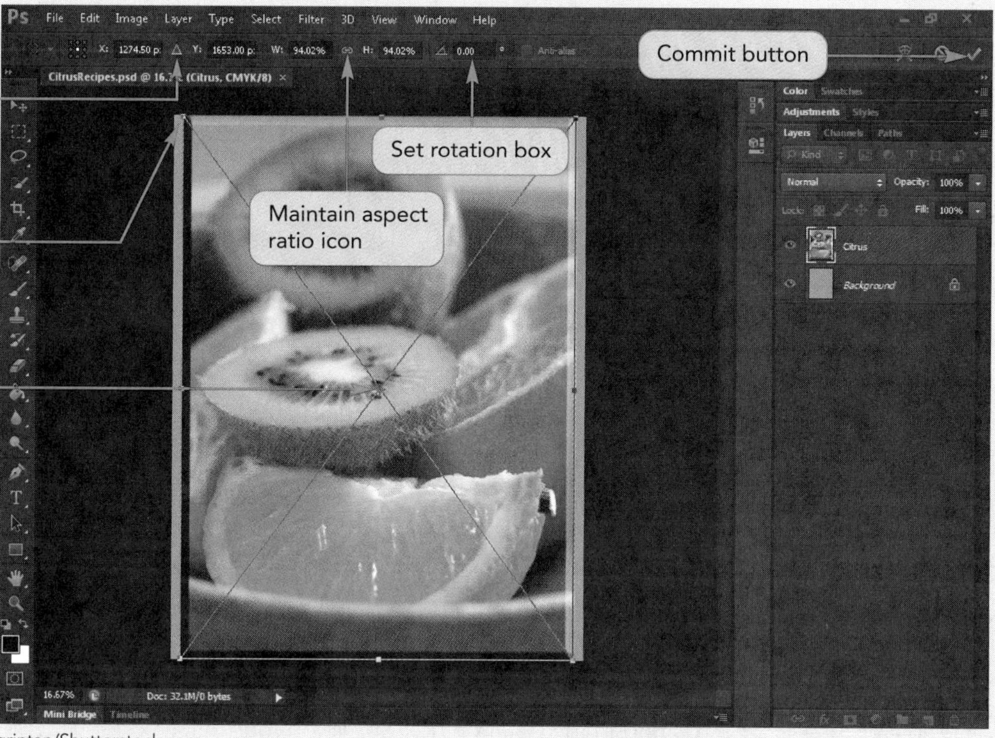

grintan/Shutterstock.com

You can resize a placed image using the width and height options on the options bar. To ensure that the image does not become distorted when you resize it, you need to maintain the aspect ratio. The **aspect ratio** is the relationship between the width and the height of an image. If the height of an image is two times greater than the width, it will still be two times greater than the width if you maintain the aspect ratio when resizing the image.

TIP

You can also press the Shift key while dragging a transform control to maintain the aspect ratio when resizing an image.

To resize the placed image:

1. On the options bar, click the **Maintain aspect ratio** icon to select it.
2. In the W box on the options bar, highlight the current value, type **50**, and then press the **Enter** key. You changed the width of the image to 50% of its original width, and because you chose to maintain the aspect ratio, the height of the image is also set to 50%.

To reposition a placed image, you can point inside the image with the mouse and drag the image to where you want it on the canvas. However, to place the image exactly, you can use the reference point on the canvas and the X, Y settings on the options bar.

The **reference point** is located at the (0,0) point on invisible x- and y-axes and is the point from which Photoshop will measure any change in position. If you have worked with graphs, you know that the (0,0) point is also called the origin. By default, Photoshop places the reference point in the upper-left corner of the document, as indicated in Figure 3-23. (This is also where it places the 0 mark on the rulers.) However, if you select the Use relative positioning for reference point icon on the options bar, the center point of the placed file becomes the new reference point.

To allow room for text to be added to the bottom of the chapter opener, Kaye suggests you move the image up one inch.

To reposition the placed image:

1. On the options bar, click the **Use relative positioning for reference point** icon to select it. The X and Y boxes on the options bar both change to zero values, indicating that the center point of the placed file is the new origin or reference point.
2. Right-click the **Y** box and then click **Inches** on the context menu to select it, if necessary.
3. In the Y box on the options bar, highlight the current value, type **-1**, and then press the **Enter** key. The image moves up one inch on the canvas.

Next, you'll rotate the placed image to see if that improves the effect.

Rotating a Placed Image

You can rotate a placed image around its center point in two ways. To rotate an image using the mouse, position the pointer outside of the image until it changes to a curved arrow, and then drag in the direction you want to rotate the image. This is called a **free transform** rotation. You can constrain a free transform rotation to 15-degree increments by pressing and holding the Shift key as you drag. You can also type a value for the rotation in the Rotation box on the options bar.

To rotate a placed image:

1. Place the mouse pointer outside of the image on the upper-right corner of the canvas until it turns into the rotate pointer.
2. Press and hold the **Shift** key and drag counterclockwise until the Set rotation box on the options bar reads -30.00.

   You can also rotate the image by an exact amount by entering the degrees rotation in the Set rotation box on the options bar.
3. In the Set rotation box on the options bar, select the value and then type **45**. The image rotates 45 degrees clockwise from its original position.
4. On the options bar, click the **Commit** button.
5. Save the file as **CitrusRecipes2.psd** in the Photoshop3\Tutorial folder, and then close the file and exit Photoshop.

The cover you've started has a completely different look than the covers you worked on previously, but it's an interesting one. Kaye would like you to present this possible cover image along with the other covers you've been working on at the next staff meeting so she can decide how to proceed with the book design.

You've spent a lot of time working with layers and should now have a good understanding of their benefits. You have also learned how nondestructive editing works in a Photoshop file. In the next session, you'll continue to work with and finalize the layers in the files that Kaye has given you, and you'll create some files of your own.

REVIEW

Session 3.1 Quick Check

1. What is nondestructive editing?
2. True or False. Adjustments in the Adjustments panel directly affect the image pixels.
3. A checkerboard display on the canvas or in a thumbnail in Photoshop is an indication of ______________ pixels.
4. True or False. When an adjustment is clipped to the layer beneath it, it affects all of the layers in the composition.
5. In Photoshop, the selected layer is also called the ______________ layer.
6. True or False. The Background layer is locked by default.
7. To move a layer on the canvas, you must first ______________ it in the Layers panel.
8. What does it mean to distribute layers?

SESSION 3.2 VISUAL OVERVIEW

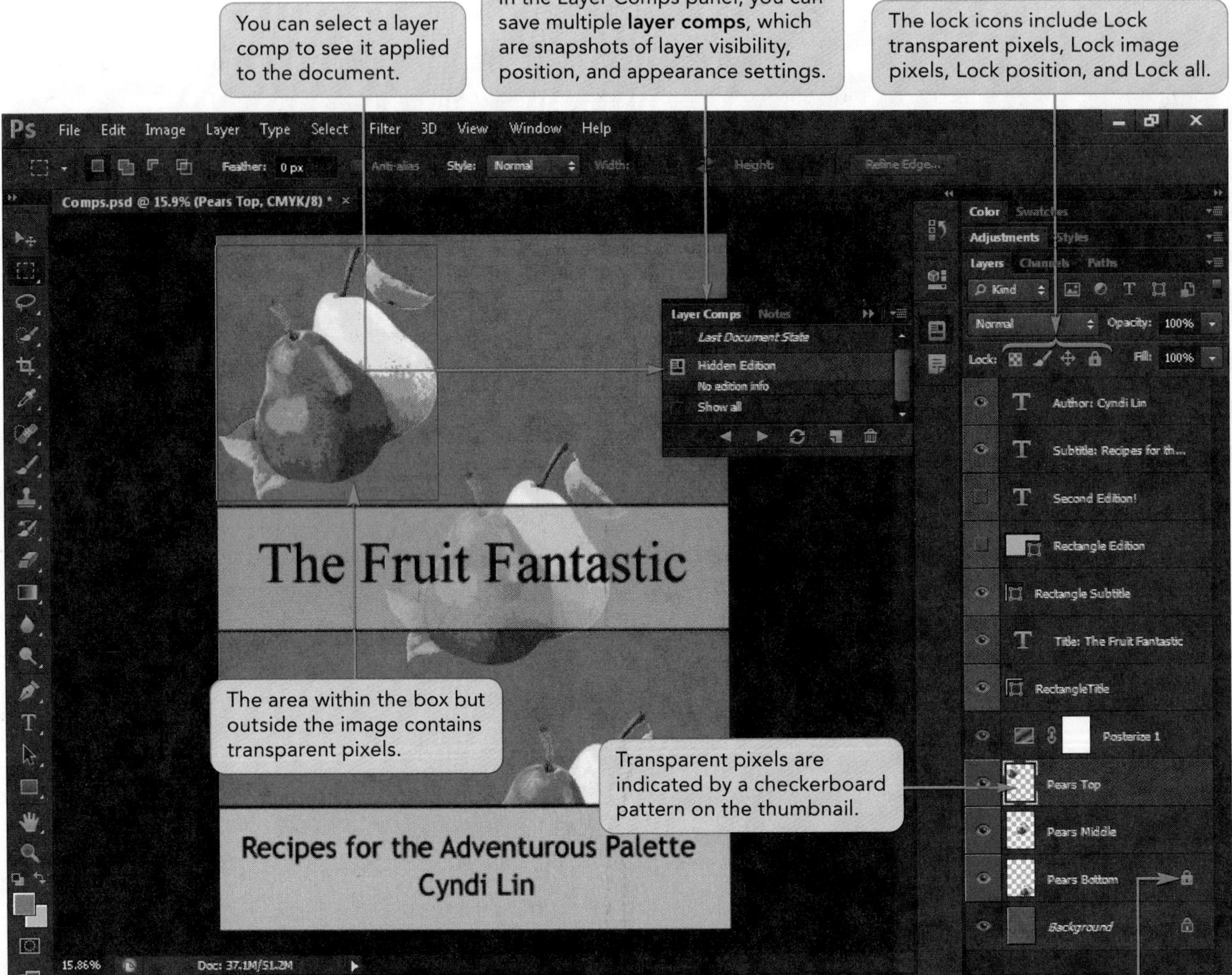
You can select a layer comp to see it applied to the document.
In the Layer Comps panel, you can save multiple **layer comps**, which are snapshots of layer visibility, position, and appearance settings.
The lock icons include Lock transparent pixels, Lock image pixels, Lock position, and Lock all.
File Edit Image Layer Type Select Filter 3D View Window Help
Comps.psd @ 15.9% (Pears Top, CMYK/8) *
Layer Comps Notes
Last Document State
Hidden Edition
No edition info
Show all
The Fruit Fantastic
Recipes for the Adventurous Palette
Cyndi Lin
Author: Cyndi Lin
Subtitle: Recipes for th...
Second Edition!
Rectangle Edition
Rectangle Subtitle
Title: The Fruit Fantastic
RectangleTitle
Posterize 1
Pears Top
Pears Middle
Pears Bottom
Background
The area within the box but outside the image contains transparent pixels.
Transparent pixels are indicated by a checkerboard pattern on the thumbnail.
The lock icon indicates that all or part of the layer is locked.

Anna Kucherova/Shutterstock.com

BLENDING AND FINALIZING LAYERS

The star fruit image is blended with the night sky image beneath it.

Blending modes are listed in the Layers panel; **blending modes** determine how the colors in a layer **blend**, or interact, with the colors in the layers beneath that layer.

You can set a layer's opacity here.

Each star fruit layer has a different blending mode applied; each mode is determined by a different mathematical **algorithm**, or formula.

Viktar Malyshchyts/Shutterstock.com; NASA

Locking and Unlocking Layer Content

After you have finished working with a layer, it is a good idea to lock it so you don't make any unintended changes to that layer. When locking a layer, you can choose among four options:

- You can lock the transparent pixels so nothing can be added in those areas.
- You can lock the image pixels so the image itself cannot be altered.
- You can lock a layer in position so it cannot be moved or resized.
- You can lock the entire layer: transparent pixels, image pixels, and image position.

To lock a layer, you select it, and then click one of the lock icons at the top of the Layers panel. See Figure 3-24.

Figure 3-24 **Locking layer content**

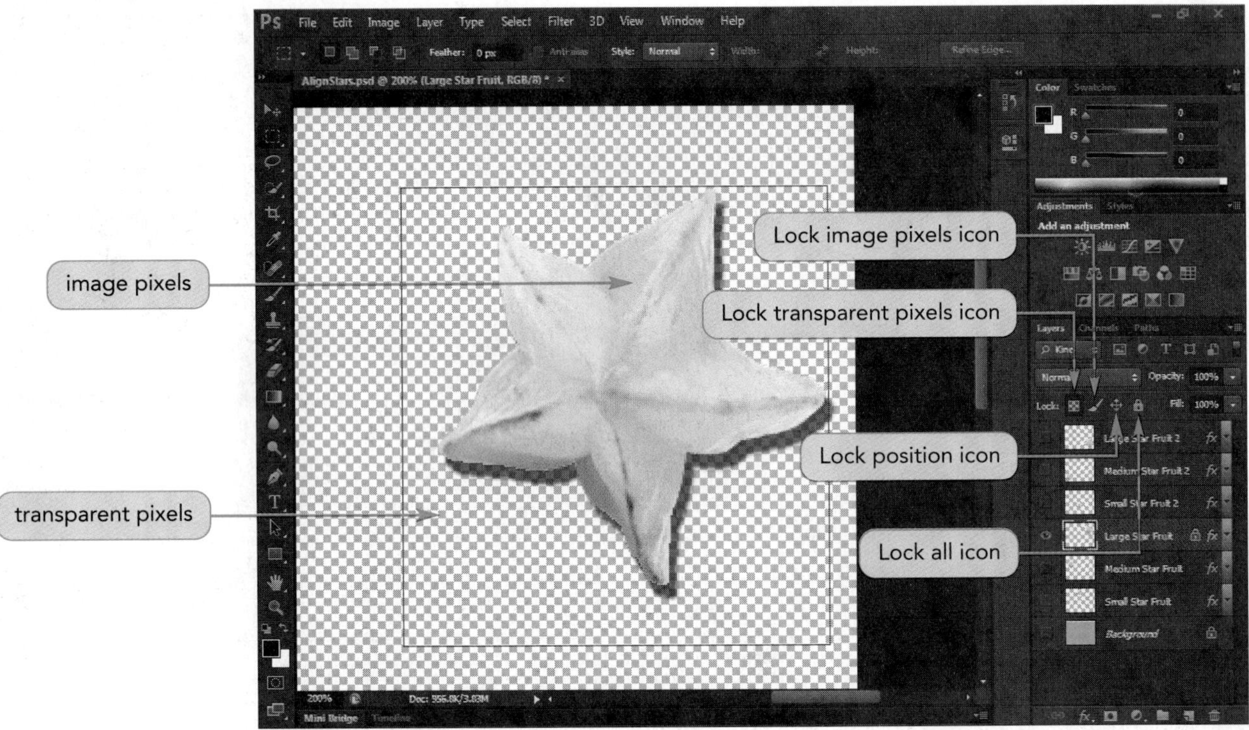

Viktar Malyshchyts/Shutterstock.com

You'll practice locking image pixels and position so you're prepared to work with and manipulate multiple layers in any future compositions you create for Kaye.

To lock pixels and position:

1. Start Photoshop while pressing the **Ctrl+Alt+Shift** keys, and click **Yes** to delete the Settings File when prompted. Reset Photoshop to the default Essentials workspace layout, and reset all tools.
2. Open **AlignStars.psd**, located in the Photoshop3\Tutorial folder, and then, in the Layers panel, click the **Large Star Fruit** layer.
3. On the menu bar, click **View**, point to **Show**, and then click **Layer Edges** to turn on the display of layer edges, and then zoom in and pan so the large star fruit is centered in the Document window.

4. Hide all of the other layers, and then in the Layers panel, click the **Lock transparent pixels** icon. The transparent pixels in the layer are now locked, but the image pixels are not.

   To see what it means to lock transparent pixels, you'll paint across the image area on the canvas using the Brush tool.

5. In the Tools panel, click the **Brush Tool** button, and then press the **D** key to reset the foreground and background colors to the default colors (black and white), if necessary.

6. On the options bar, click the **Brush Preset picker** button, click the second preset (**Hard Round**), and then type **50** in the Size box.

7. Point to the lower-left corner of the star fruit image area (within the Layer edges), press and hold the mouse button, and then drag to the upper-right corner of the image area. See Figure 3-25.

Figure 3-25 **Locking transparent pixels**

image pixels aren't locked
transparent pixels can't be changed

Viktar Malyshchyts/Shutterstock.com

Although you painted a brushstroke across the entire image, including transparent pixels, the brushstroke only appears on the star fruit, not on the locked transparent pixels.

8. Click the **Small Star Fruit** layer and unhide it, and then zoom out to 100%.

9. In the Layers panel, click the **Lock image pixels** icon.

10. Use the Brush tool to try to paint across the Small Star Fruit image. A dialog box opens, informing you that you can't complete the operation. You can't paint any part of the selected layer because the image pixels are locked. Click the **OK** button to close the dialog box.

11. Select and unhide the **Medium Star Fruit** layer, and then in the Layers panel, click the **Lock position** icon.

12. Press the **V** key to activate the Move tool, and then try to drag **Medium Star Fruit** to the right on the canvas. A dialog box opens with a message that says you can't complete the operation. You can't drag the layer because its position has been locked.
13. Click the **OK** button to close the dialog box.
14. Select the Brush tool again, and paint from one point of the Medium Star Fruit to another on the canvas. Because you only locked the layer's position, not the pixels, you can still paint over the pixels.
15. Click the **Background** layer. Notice that the Background layer is locked by default.
16. Save the file as **Locked.psd** in the Photoshop3\Tutorial folder, and close the file.

Kaye suggests that you learn about layer comps so you can present a few of your ideas to her at your next meeting using a single file.

Working with Layer Comps

One of the greatest benefits of layers in Photoshop is that they give you the ability to store and experiment with many different versions of a composition in a single file using layer comps. A **comp**, short for *composition*, is a mock-up or sketch of what a final design will look like. A layer comp is the electronic version of a graphic designer's comp. A Photoshop file can have multiple layer comps. You can use layer comps to save different draft versions of your layout before deciding on a final version or as a way to present several ideas to a client. See Figure 3-26.

Figure 3-26 Working with layer comps

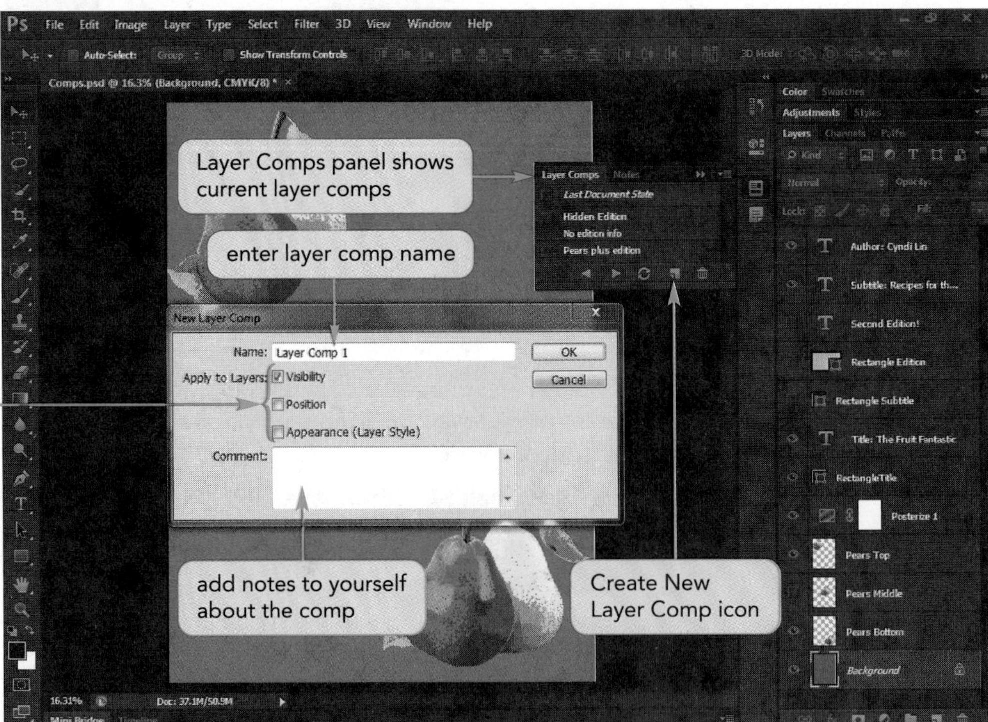

Anna Kucherova/ Shutterstock.com

In the New Layer Comp dialog box, you can give the composition a descriptive name and select the elements you want Photoshop to consider when creating the comp, including Visibility, Position, and Appearance (also called Layer Style). You can also add a comment to help you remember details about the comp—for example, notes on why you think a particular layer comp might be a good choice for the final composition, questions you might have for the client about the composition, or information about related comps.

To create a layer comp:

1. Open **FruitFantastic.psd**, located in the Photoshop3\Tutorial folder, fit the image on the screen, reset all tools, and collapse the Color and Adjustments panel groups.
2. Hide the **Second Edition!** Layer and the **Rectangle Edition** layer.
3. On the menu bar, click **Window**, and then click **Layer Comps** to open the Layer Comps panel.
4. At the bottom of the Layer Comps panel, click the **Create New Layer Comp** icon. The New Layer Comp dialog box opens.
5. In the Name box of the New Layer Comp dialog box, type **Hidden Edition**. Click the Visibility, Position, and Appearance (Layer Style) check boxes to select them, if necessary.
6. In the Comment box, type **No edition info**, and then click the **OK** button. The dialog box closes and Photoshop displays the new layer comp layout.

   Next, you'll redisplay all of the layers, and create a new layer comp called *All Visible*.
7. In the Layers panel, unhide the **Second Edition!** Layer and the **Rectangle Edition** layer.
8. At the bottom of the Layer Comps panel, click the **Create New Layer Comp** icon. Name the layer comp **All Visible**, and then click the **OK** button.

Next, you'll switch back to the Hidden Edition layer comp to see if you prefer that layout for the book cover.

To apply a layer comp to a file:

1. In the Layer Comps panel, click to the left of Hidden Edition to display that layout. See Figure 3-27.

Figure 3-27 Switching to a different layer comp

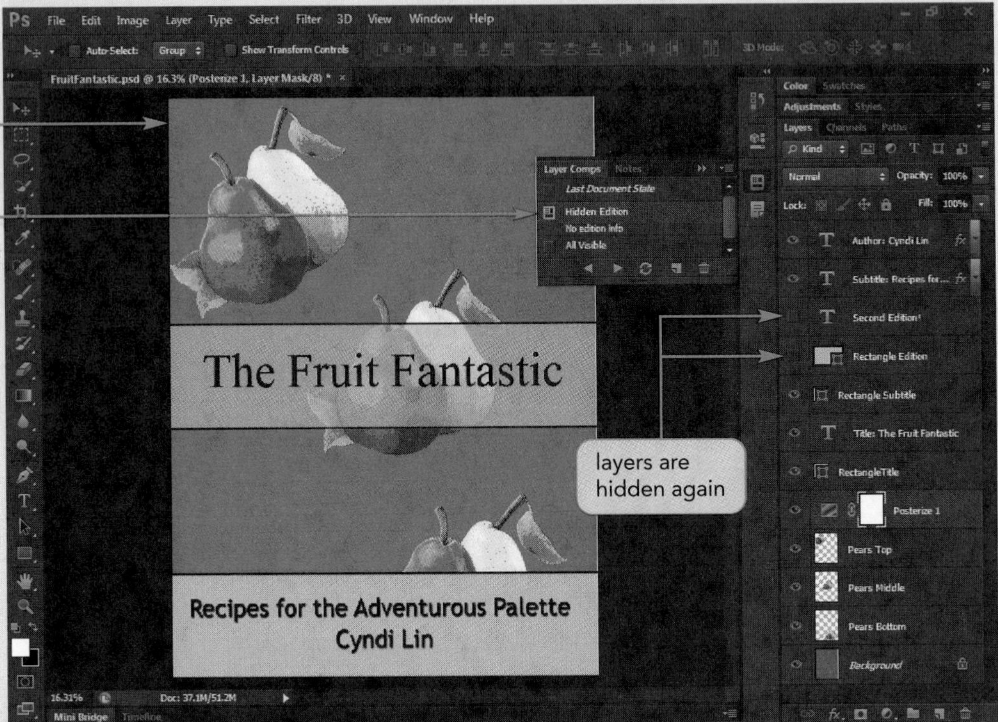
layout changes to new layer comp
click here to switch to Hidden Edition layer comp
layers are hidden again
The Fruit Fantastic
Recipes for the Adventurous Palette
Cyndi Lin

Anna Kucherova/Shutterstock.com

2. In the Layer Comps panel, click the **Apply Previous Selected Layer Comp** icon to display the **All Visible** layer comp.

After Kaye reviews your work, she decides that the layout of the Hidden Edition layer comp won't work for the cover, so you'll delete it from the file.

To delete a layer comp:

1. In the Layer Comps panel, click the **Hidden Edition** layer comp in the Layer Comps panel, and then click the **Delete Layer Comp** icon at the bottom of the Layer Comps panel.
2. Close the Layer Comps panel group.
3. Save the file as **Comps.psd** in the Photoshop3\Tutorial folder, and then close the file.

PROSKILLS

Teamwork: Using Layer Comps to Collaborate

If you work on a creative team that collaborates, layer comps can be a great tool to help you generate a final version of a composition. For example, team members can use the Comment field in a layer comp to critique a particular layout and make suggestions for improving it. They can also add text layers to a composition that include critiques or suggestions, or draw arrows and other vector objects to point out areas of the composition they would like to see changed. You can view their feedback by saving a layer comp with the comment layers visible, and then hiding the comments in a different layer comp. Alternatively, each team member can save a layer comp with his or her name in order to show the group their preferred layout, and the team can review the different options by selecting and then discussing each layer comp.

Reviewing a single file using various layer comps keeps your team's work in a single location and avoids any problems you might have with version control. Once the team has made its final decisions, you can delete any unnecessary layers and finalize the file. By using layer comps to collaborate with team members, you can create a final file that is the best it can be.

Now that you have spent some time working with layer comps, Kaye would like you to try to improve some of your compositions by experimenting with blending modes and opacity.

Working with Blending Modes and Opacity

As you have seen, the order of layers in the Layers panel affects how each layer appears in your composition. You can also change how a layer appears by blending it with the layer or layers beneath it to achieve an interesting effect. Photoshop comes with numerous blending modes.

You can also apply different opacity settings to an image to achieve additional effects. A setting of 100% means that a layer is completely opaque and nothing will show through. The lower the setting, the more transparent the layer becomes. An Opacity setting of 0% means that a layer is completely transparent.

Applying Blending Modes

When you apply a blending mode to a layer, you are specifying that you want the colors in the layer you are working with to interact in some way with all of the colors in the layers beneath it. When you work with blending modes, it helps to think of each different mode as a new experiment—such as in a chemistry class. Each mode blends the chemicals (or layer colors) of all of the layers together in a way that's unpredictable until you actually put them in the test tube and shake (apply the mode). If you make even the slightest change to one of the layers in the blend—for example, by modifying its color slightly, you have changed the chemicals in the test tube and will see a different result. See Figure 3-28.

Figure 3-28 **Different blending modes applied to same object**

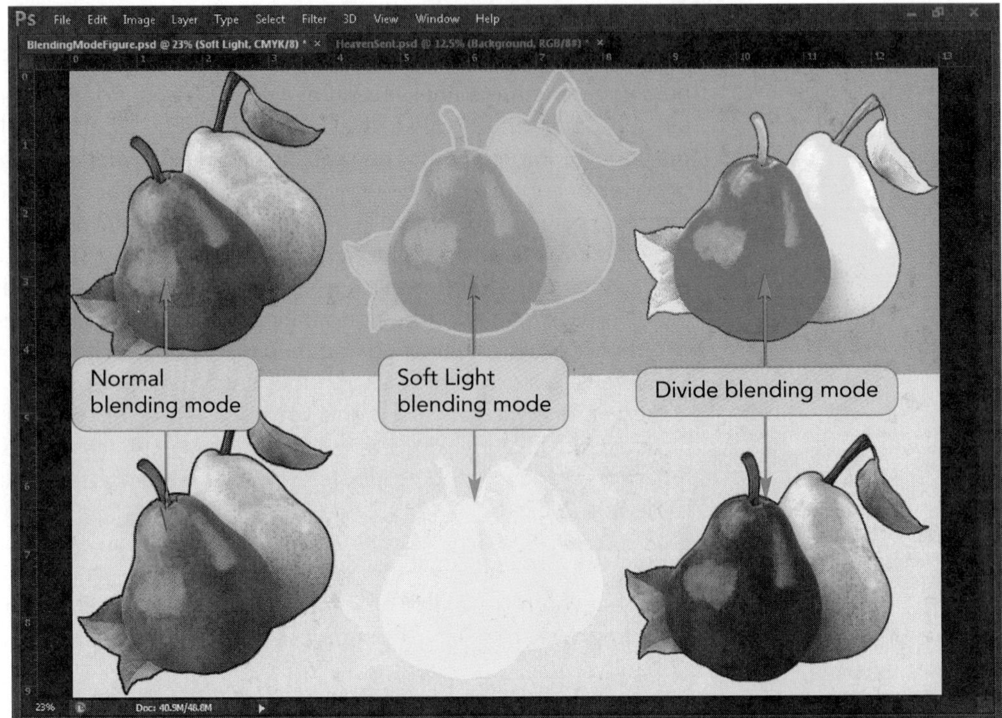

Anna Kucherova/Shutterstock.com

The upper-left and lower-left images in Figure 3-28 have the Normal blending mode applied, which is the default mode for any image you place on the canvas. With the Normal blending mode, a layer does not blend at all with the layers beneath it; the pixels in the image on the layer simply cover the pixels on any lower level layers. The middle two images have the Soft Light blending mode applied. Notice that they look completely different from each other because of the color of the layer beneath each image. The top image blends with the rose color of the rectangle layer beneath it while the bottom image blends with the yellow. The two images on the right have the Divide blending mode applied. Again, because the layers they are blending with are different colors, the result of applying the identical blending mode to identical images varies considerably. Blending modes can have dramatically different effects when applied to the same image, depending on the layers involved in the blend.

To apply a blending mode to a layer, click the layer in the Layers panel. When you do, the blending mode options become available. You can click the blending mode arrow in the Layers panel, and then choose a blending mode. After you have applied one blending mode to a layer, you can press the Ctrl key and the Down arrow key to apply the next blending mode on the list to that layer—without having to click the blending mode arrow. To go up the list, press the Ctrl key and the Up arrow key. You will often find that you need to experiment with many different blending modes to find the one you want.

You'll apply different blending modes to the artwork you're preparing for the cookbook section on star fruits to see what effects you can create.

To apply a blending mode:

1. Open **HeavenSent.psd**, located in the Photoshop3\Tutorial folder, and then show layer edges.
2. In the Layers panel, click the **Star 1** layer, and at the top of the Layers panel, click the **Set the blending mode for the layer** button and then click **Color Burn**.

   Color Burn darkens the base color and makes everything but the lightest color (the night stars) darker. However, it's probably too dark for the printed page.
3. Press and hold the **Ctrl** key, and then press the **Down arrow** key while Photoshop scrolls through the list of blending modes until **Color Dodge** is selected. Color Dodge brightens the base color and decreases the dark/light contrast.

   Trouble? If you pass Color Dodge by mistake, press and hold the Ctrl key and press the **Up arrow** key until you select Color Dodge.
4. In the Layers panel, apply the **Linear Light** blending mode to the Star 2 layer, and then apply the **Lighten** blending mode to the Star 3 layer. See Figure 3-29.

Figure 3-29 Blending modes applied

Viktar Malyshchyts/Shutterstock.com; NASA

Linear Light decreases the brightness of the star fruit's base color (the night sky). Lighten looks at the blend and base colors and selects whichever color is lighter to create the result. If a pixel is darker than the result color, Photoshop replaces it; if it's lighter, the pixel color doesn't change.

Each blending mode produces a very different effect. Next, you'll experiment with opacity settings in the Layers panel to see what other effects you can achieve when blending layers.

Changing Opacity

You can also use the Opacity setting in the Layers panel to blend layers. An Opacity setting of 100% means the layer is completely opaque or solid, with no pixels from the layer beneath it showing through. As you decrease the opacity, the layer becomes more and more transparent, showing some of the pixels on the layer beneath it. You can change the opacity by dragging the opacity slider, by typing a percentage value, or by scrubbing over the word *Opacity* in the Layers panel to change the setting. When you **scrub**, the mouse pointer changes to the scrub pointer. Scrubbing left decreases the setting, and scrubbing right increases the setting. In addition, you can press a number key to change the opacity. For example, pressing 2 changes the opacity to 20%, and pressing 5 changes the opacity to 50%.

In Figure 3-30, the first image shows the Star layer at 100% opacity. It completely hides the yellow layer beneath it. The second image shows the Star layer at 0% opacity, meaning that all of its pixels are completely transparent so the yellow layer is the only visible part of the image. In the third image, the Star layer's opacity is set to 50%, which lets some of the yellow in the Color Fill layer show through.

Figure 3-30 Changing opacity for blending effect

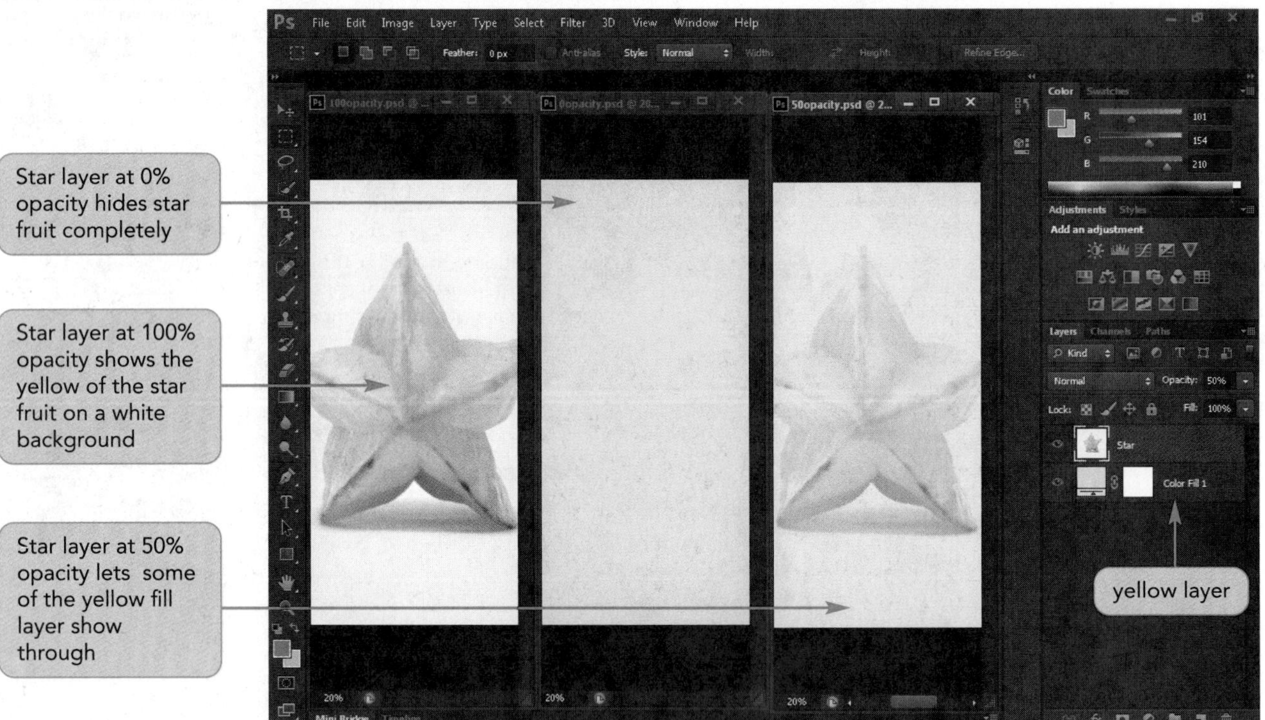
Star layer at 0% opacity hides star fruit completely
Star layer at 100% opacity shows the yellow of the star fruit on a white background
Star layer at 50% opacity lets some of the yellow fill layer show through
yellow layer
File Edit Image Layer Type Select Filter 3D View Window Help
50opacity.psd @ 2...
Star
Color Fill 1

Viktar Malyshchyts/Shutterstock.com

To change the opacity to blend an image:

1. Select the **Star 4** layer, and then in the Layers panel drag the scrub pointer to the left over the word *Opacity* until the Opacity setting at the top of the Layers panel is about **70%**. At this opacity setting, some of the stars in the NightSky layer begin to show through the star fruit.
2. Press the **4** key to change the Opacity setting to 40%. More of the stars in the NightSky layer show through the Star 4 layer.

INSIGHT

Combining Settings for a Unique Effect

You'll sometimes find that a blending mode is almost what you want as an effect, but not quite. To achieve the result you want, you can combine the blending mode with opacity settings. In addition, if an object has a shadow, you can change the Fill setting rather than the Opacity setting to maintain the intensity of the shadow, but reduce the opacity of the fill. In other words, with Photoshop layers, the possibilities for achieving different effects are almost limitless, and you should take the time to explore them.

Creating Layer Groups

Earlier in the tutorial, you learned how to organize layers by changing their order in the Layers panel, by giving each layer a meaningful name, and by changing the color of layers for a visual overview of layer organization. You can also group related layers into layer groups so you can easily change the style of multiple layers at the same time or show and hide a group as necessary as you work on your composition.

REFERENCE

Grouping Layers

- In the Layers panel, click the layers you want to group, and then, on the menu bar, click Layer, and then click Group Layers.

or

- Click the layers you want to group, and then press the Ctrl+G keys.

or

- Click the Create a new group icon at the bottom of the Layers panel. Photoshop creates a new group layer.
- Drag the layers you want to add to the new group folder.

You'll organize the layers by grouping them in the HeavenSent file so Kaye can easily understand how you laid out the composition. You'll also ungroup one of the groups.

To group and ungroup layers:

1. In the Layers panel, select the **Star 1**, **Star 2**, **Star 3**, and **Star 4** layers, and then on the menu bar, click **Layer**, and then click **Group Layers**. Photoshop moves all of the selected layers into a group called Group 1 and collapses the group.

2. Click the **triangle** ▶ to the left of the Group 1 folder to expand the group and view all of the layers.
3. Select the **Heaven Sent** and **NightSky** layers, and then press the **Ctrl+G** keys. Photoshop creates a new group called Group 2 and collapses the group.
4. In the Layers panel, click the **Group 2** layer group to select it, if necessary. On the menu, click **Layer**, and then click **Ungroup Layers**. The Heaven Sent and NightSky layers are no longer in a group.

TIP

You can also press the Shift+Ctrl+G keys to ungroup a selected group or right-click the group in the Layers panel and then click Ungroup Layers on the context menu.

Next, you will finalize your work in the HeavenSent file so it is ready to present to Kaye.

Finalizing Layers

After you have created many versions of a composition and shown different layer comps to a client, you will reach the point when you are ready to finalize your work. A file with multiple layers can take up many megabytes of storage space. However, you can do a number of things to reduce file size and ensure that your work can't be accidentally changed.

Merging Layers

You can merge an adjustment layer with an underlying content layer to permanently apply the adjustment to the image. You can also merge related layers to reduce file size. When you merge image layers, the pixels on the top layer replace the pixels on the layers beneath it. Reducing the number of pixels reduces file size. To merge selected layers, you can right-click the Layers panel and click Merge Layers on the context menu, or you can select Merge Layers on the Layer menu. You can also use the Merge Visible Layers command to merge only the visible layers in the Layers panel. Note that when you merge layers that have blending modes applied, the blending modes revert to Normal in a PSD file. To merge layers and maintain blending modes, you need to either flatten the file or save the file as a JPG or other single-layer file.

To merge selected layers and visible layers:

1. In the Layers panel, click the **Heaven Sent** layer.
2. Expand the Adjustments panel, and clip a Brightness/Contrast adjustment to the Heaven Sent layer. Change the Brightness setting to **105**, and then collapse the Properties panel. The words *Heaven Sent* are now a brighter color.
3. In the Layers panel, select the **Brightness/Contrast** and **Heaven Sent** layers. On the menu bar, click **Layer**, and then click **Merge Layers**. The two layers are merged into one layer. The name of the top layer, Brightness/Contrast1, is given to the new layer.
4. Change the name of the merged layer to **Heaven Sent**.
5. In the Layers panel, hide all of the layers except for **Heaven Sent** and **NightSky**, and then click the **NightSky** layer.
6. On the menu bar, click **Layer**, and then click **Merge Visible**. The Heaven Sent and NightSky layers are merged into a single layer. See Figure 3-31.

TIP

You can also merge visible layers by right-clicking a selected visible layer and then clicking Merge Visible on the context menu.

Figure 3-31 **Merging visible layers**

NASA

7. Unhide all of the layers.

INSIGHT

Stamping Layers vs. Merging Layers

When you stamp layers instead of merging them, Photoshop keeps the original layers intact and creates a new composite layer, called a **stamp**, with all of the selected or visible layers merged. To stamp selected layers, press the Ctrl+Alt+E keys. If you select a layer that is linked to other layers, pressing the Ctrl+Alt+E keys stamps the linked layers. You can also stamp visible layers by pressing Shift+Ctrl+Alt+E. You can use the stamp to sharpen or adjust the stamped part of the image as one layer.

Flattening an Image

TIP

When you save a PSD file in JPEG format, you flatten the image.

The final step you should take when finalizing any composition is to flatten it. If you think you might want to use the composition later and modify it, be sure to save a copy of the PSD file with all of its layers. Then flatten the image to reduce the file size and make the image portable to other file formats, such as JPEG. When you flatten an image, Photoshop merges all visible layers and throws out any hidden layers. It also replaces transparent pixels with white pixels. Once you save and close a flattened image, you cannot go back to the layered file, so it is essential that you are sure you have finished with the file before you take this last step.

As a final step before you show the HeavenSent file to Kaye, you'll flatten the composition so it has a manageable file size.

To flatten an image:

1. On the menu bar, click **Layer**, and then click **Flatten Image**. All of the layers have been flattened into a single layer called Background in the Layers panel.
2. Save the file as **FlatFile.psd** in the Photoshop3\Tutorial folder, and then close the file and exit Photoshop.

In this session, you learned how to work with layers. You selected, added, duplicated, and deleted layers and changed their properties and their visibility. You also moved, aligned, and distributed layers, and hid and unhid them. You learned how to lock layer content and how to work with layer comps and groups to improve your work flow. In addition, you learned about blending modes and opacity settings, and you finalized a file by merging layers and flattening it.

REVIEW

Session 3.2 Quick Check

1. What is a layer comp?
2. A ______________ works with the colors and opacity of one layer and combines it with the layer beneath it.
3. When you combine two or more layers into a single layer, you are ______________ the layers.
4. What is a layer group, and how would you use it?
5. You ______________ a layer by merging selected or visible layers into a new layer and leaving the original layers intact.
6. To finalize a file so it consists of only one layer, you ______________ it.

Practice the skills you learned in the tutorial using the same case scenario.

PRACTICE

Review Assignments

Data Files needed for the Review Assignments: Cover.jpg, Breads.jpg, Perfection.psd, BakeRectangle.psd, BakeRectangle2.psd

Kaye wants you to work on the graphics for another cookbook, *Baked to Perfection*. She supplies you with images to work with, and asks you to place them in a file and modify the file to develop ideas for the cover. You'll work with layers and layer comps as well as blending modes and opacity settings to create two files to present to Kaye as possible covers. Complete the following steps:

1. Start Photoshop while pressing the Ctrl+Alt+Shift keys, and click Yes to delete the Settings File when prompted. Reset Photoshop to the default Essentials workspace layout, and then reset all tools.
2. Open **Cover.jpg**, located in the Photoshop3\Review folder included with your Data Files, and save it as **BakeBook.psd** in the same folder.
3. Place **Breads.jpg**, located in the Photoshop3\Review folder, in the BakeBook.psd file. Move the image down 2.75 inches using a relative reference point.
4. Duplicate the Breads layer, using the default layer name. Move the duplicate image up to the top of the canvas so that it covers the background completely.
5. Place **Perfection.psd**, located in the Photoshop3\Review folder, in the BakeBook.psd file.
6. Place the file called **BakeRectangle.psd** in the BakeBook.psd file, and rotate it -45 degrees. Change the opacity of the BakeRectangle layer to 90%.
7. Place the file called **BakeRectangle2.psd** in the BakeBook.psd file, and change its opacity to 50%.
8. Apply the Hard Mix blending mode to the Breads copy layer, and apply the Divide blending mode to the Breads layer.
9. Save the current layer comp as **Blending Comp** and include Visibility, Position, and Appearance in the comp. Enter the comment **Blending experiment**.
10. Group the Rectangle layers, and then group the Bread layers.
11. Expand Group 2, and then ungroup the layers in that group.
12. Hide the BakeRectangle2 layer, and change the opacity of the other rectangle to 50%. Change the blending mode to Normal on both Breads layers.
13. Save the current layer comp as **No Blend** and enter the comment **Plain images**. Save BakeBook.psd.
14. Hide the Breads copy layer.
15. Draw a tan-colored rectangle on the canvas so it appears behind the *Baked to Perfection* title, and then duplicate the rectangle and move the duplicate on the canvas so it is behind the author's name at the bottom of the cover.
16. Filter the Layers panel for shape layers so only the Rectangle 1 and Rectangle 1 copy layers show. Change the name of the Rectangle 1 copy layer to **Author Background**, and then change the name of the Rectangle 1 layer to **Title Background**.
17. Display all of the layers in the Layers panel.
18. Hide the Author Background layer, merge all of the visible layers, and then delete the Breads copy layer and make the BakeRectangle2 layer visible.
19. Save the file as **BakeBook.jpg** in the Photoshop3\Review folder, using the default JPEG options. Close BakeBook.psd without saving it, and exit Photoshop.
20. Submit the results of the preceding steps to your instructor either in printed or electronic form, as requested.

Use your skills to create an interesting visual effect for an ad.

APPLY

Case Problem 1

Data Files needed for this Case Problem: NortonCo.psd, Ruins.jpg, NewHome.jpg

Norton & Company Emma Gottfried, lead architect of Norton & Company, a high-end architectural design firm, wants to launch a campaign with a "ruins to riches" theme using photo compositions of new homes rising out of ancient ruins. She gives you two photographs to work with and asks you to create a comp to present at your next meeting with her. Complete the following steps:

1. Start Photoshop while pressing the Ctrl+Alt+Shift keys, and click Yes to delete the Settings File when prompted. Reset Photoshop to the default Essentials workspace layout, and then reset all tools.
2. Open **NortonCo.psd**, located in the Photoshop3\Case1 folder, and save it as **NewRuins.psd** in the same folder. Use Figure 3-32 as a guide as you complete this exercise.

Figure 3-32 Riches from Ruins file and Layers panel

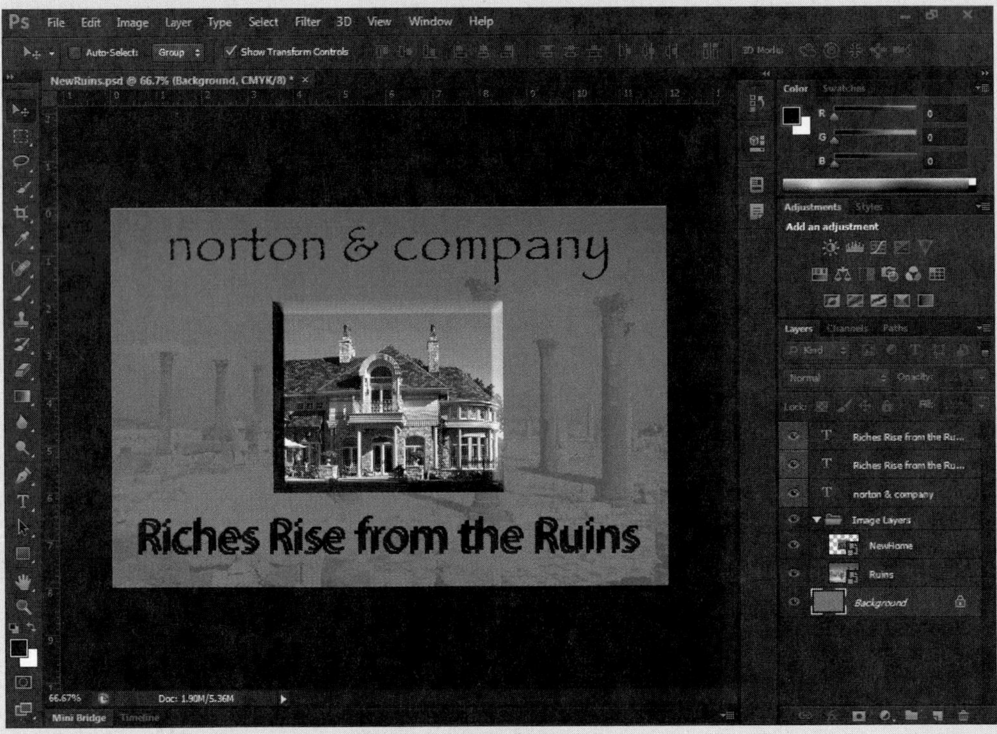

Aleksandar Tolorovic/Shutterstock.com; Ron Davey/Shutterstock.com

3. Place **Ruins.jpg**, located in the Photoshop3\Case1 folder, in the NewRuins.psd file.
4. Place **NewHome.jpg**, located in the Photoshop3\Case1 folder, on top of the Ruins image.
5. Change the Opacity of the Ruins layer to 50% and apply the Color Burn blending mode.
6. Using the Horizontal Type tool with a black Myriad Pro 72 point font, type **Riches Rise from the Ruins** at the bottom of the canvas. Use the Move tool to center the text layer below the image of the house.
7. Duplicate the text layer you just created, move it slightly down and to the left, and then change its opacity to 75%.

8. Select the Ruins layer, and using the Horizontal Type tool with any font type and size, type **norton & company** at the top of the canvas. Center the text layer above the image of the house. (*Hint*: To select a font size other than the sizes listed, you can type a value in the Set the font size box on the options bar.)
9. If necessary, rearrange the layers in the Layers panel so the text layers appear together and the image layers appear together, as shown in Figure 3-32.
10. Filter the Layers panel so that only the text layers appear, and then change the color of all of the text layers to red.
11. Turn off the filter, and put the image layers in a group called **Image Layers**.
12. Hide the Riches Rise from the Ruins copy layer, and then save the layer comp as **No Shadow**.
13. Redisplay the Riches Rise from the Ruins copy layer, and then save the layer comp as **All Layers**.
14. Save NewRuins.psd, close the file, and exit Photoshop.
15. Submit the results of the preceding steps to your instructor either in printed or electronic form, as requested.

Using Figure 3-33 as a guide, modify a composition by using what you know about layers and groups.

CREATE

Case Problem 2

Data Files needed for this Case Problem: AlwardArt.psd

Alward Art Museum You have been working on a logo for Director Guy Blanc at the Alward Art Museum. You'd like to present the file to Guy and give clear information about its organization so he can modify it as he sees fit. The file has many layers and effects, and you need to organize it so it is more manageable. Complete the following steps:

1. Start Photoshop while pressing the Ctrl+Alt+Shift keys, and click Yes to delete the Settings File when prompted. Reset Photoshop to the default Essentials workspace layout, and then reset all tools.
2. Open **AlwardArt.psd**, located in the Photoshop3\Case2 folder, and using Figure 3-33 as a guide, name and group the layers.

Figure 3-33 Alward Art file and Layers panel

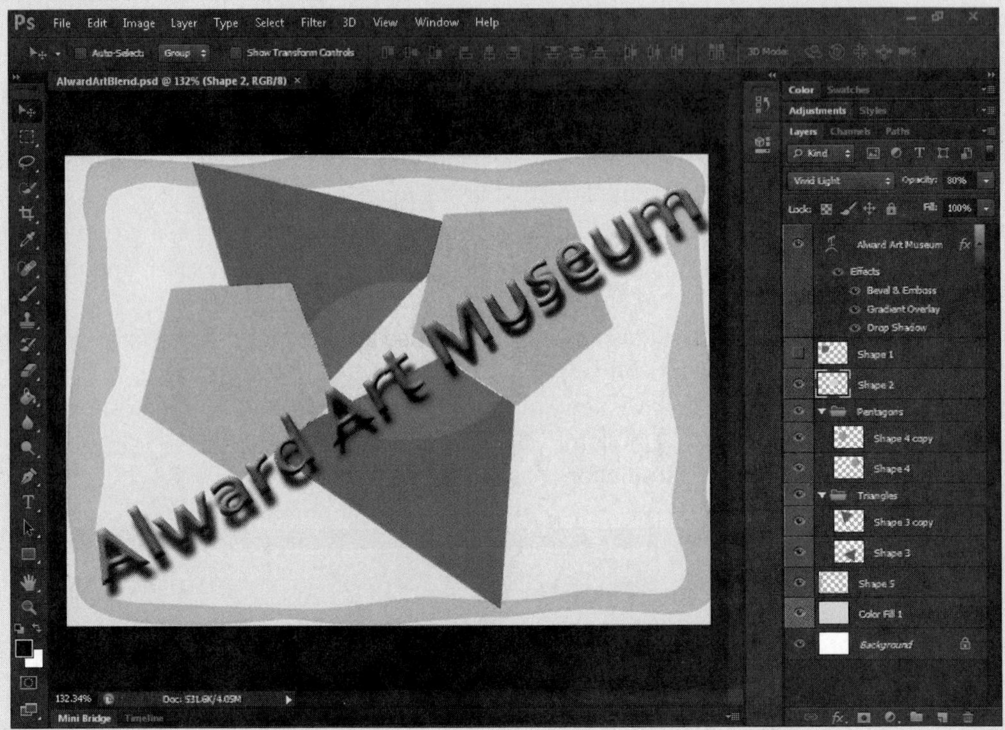

3. Move the layers so they appear in the order shown in the figure.
4. Hide layers as shown in the figure.
5. In the Layers panel, change the layer colors to match the figure.
6. Apply the blending mode and opacity shown in the Layers panel in the figure.
7. Save the file as **AlwardArtBlend.psd** in the Photoshop3\Case2 folder. Close the file, and exit Photoshop.
8. Submit the results of the preceding steps to your instructor either in printed or electronic form, as requested.

Create a unique composition by working with layers and effects.

CREATE

Case Problem 3

Data Files needed for this Case Problem: Clouds.jpg, Clouds1.jpg, Plane1.psd, Plane2.psd

Flight Plan, Inc. You are the owner of Flight Plan, Inc., a flight school in Dayton, Ohio. You will soon be meeting with an ad agency to present your ideas and launch a campaign that inspires people to learn how to fly. You'll use your Photoshop skills to combine images and work with blending modes, layers, and comps to present a couple of ideas to the agency so they will know what you want when they begin working on the campaign. Complete the following steps:

1. Start Photoshop while pressing the Ctrl+Alt+Shift keys, and click Yes to delete the Settings File when prompted. Reset Photoshop to the default Essentials workspace layout, and then reset all tools.
2. The Photoshop3\Case3 folder provided with your Data Files includes photographs of airplanes and clouds in the sky. You'll place the airplane and cloud images in a new file to create a unique composition with at least two layer comps. Use the two examples in Figure 3-34 as a reference, but use your own ideas to create the composition.

Figure 3-34 **Layer comps for Flight Plan campaign**

Jane Hosie-Bounar; Robert Spriggs/Shutterstock.com; ifong/Shutterstock.com

3. Create a new file using the dimensions and background color of your choosing.
4. Create a new layer and place one of the airplane images from the Photoshop3\Case3 folder on the new layer.
5. Create a new layer and place one of the cloud images from the Photoshop3\Case3 folder on the new layer.
6. Create another cloud layer and another airplane layer, using the remaining images in the Photoshop3\Case3 folder.
7. Apply blending modes and adjust the opacity of layers to achieve interesting effects. Your image does not need to match Figure 3-34.
8. Add at least two text layers and apply styles, colors, or blending modes to them. The text should include the company name and any catch phrase you think will work for the company. You can use different phrases for different layer comps.
9. Assign colors to layers to organize them, and create at least one logical group of layers in the Layers panel.
10. Lock at least two layers.

11. Hide and unhide layers to create at least two layer comps.
12. Save the file as **FlightPlan.psd** in the Photoshop3\Case3 folder.
13. Switch to your favorite comp, flatten the file, and then save it as **FlightPlan.jpg** in the Photoshop3\Case3 folder. Close the open file, and exit Photoshop.
14. Submit the results of the preceding steps to your instructor either in printed or electronic form, as requested.

Extend your skills to create a Web ad for an employment agency.

CHALLENGE

Case Problem 4

Data Files needed for this Case Problem: Keys1.jpg, Keys2.jpg

TempIT Sylvia Potter founded TempIT, an employment agency providing temporary clerical and administrative assistants to large corporations, five years ago in Denver, Colorado. You are Sylvia's administrative assistant but would like to take on more responsibility. You will use your Photoshop skills to create an interesting idea for a Web ad that you can present to Sylvia at the next staff meeting. Complete the following steps:

1. Start Photoshop while pressing the Ctrl+Alt+Shift keys, and click Yes to delete the Settings File when prompted. Reset Photoshop to the default Essentials workspace layout, and then reset all tools.
2. Create a new file of any size and background color and then extend the canvas using a second color for the extension. The extension should have room for three lines of text. Refer to Figure 3-35 for an example of a possible layer comp. Save the file as **HelpIT.psd**.

Figure 3-35 **A sample comp for TempIT**

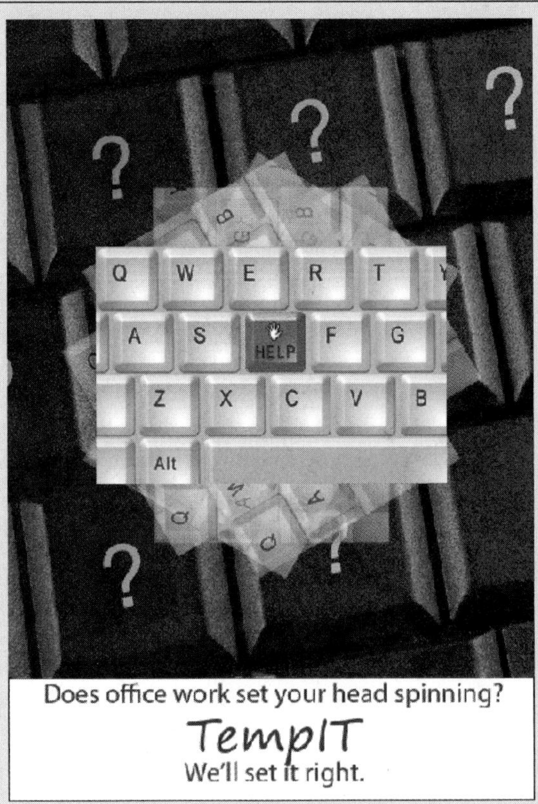

SCOTTCHAN/Shutterstock.com; keerati/Shutterstock.com

3. Use Mini Bridge to preview the images of keyboards in the Photoshop3\Case4 folder provided with your Data Files. Place one of the files in your composition, and resize it so the entire image fits in the center of the canvas.
4. Duplicate the layer containing the keyboard image, change the opacity setting, and apply a blending mode. Select the Move tool, if necessary, and using the transform controls, rotate the duplicate layer on the canvas. Create additional duplicates, and rotate each duplicate a different amount to achieve the effect of a spinning keyboard.
5. Rearrange the layers so the original keyboard layer is on top in the Layers panel and is displayed at 100% opacity.
6. Place the second keyboard file on the canvas; size and move it so it appears in the background, behind the spinning keyboards you created. Make it any size while leaving room for text at the bottom of the canvas.
7. Add text to the image on at least three layers. One layer should include the name of the company.
8. **EXPLORE** Duplicate the three text layers all at once. (*Hint*: Select similar layers and then apply the Duplicate Layer command to all three layers at the same time. You will not be able to assign unique names until after the duplication.)
9. Hide the original text layers.
10. **EXPLORE** Use the text style presets in the Styles panel to modify at least two of the duplicate layers. To display the presets, click the Styles panel menu button, click Text Effects 2 or Text Effects, and then replace the current styles with the Text Effects styles.
11. Apply at least two text styles to the duplicate text.
12. **EXPLORE** Use the Styles panel menu to replace the Text styles with the default styles.
13. Give some of the layers more descriptive names, and group or color-code related layers.
14. Create and save at least two layer comps. Make sure to experiment with text effects, blending modes, and opacity, and use different combinations for different layer comps.
15. Save the file as **HelpIT.psd** in the Photoshop3\Case4 folder. Close the file, and exit Photoshop.
16. Submit the results of the preceding steps to your instructor either in printed or electronic form, as requested.

ENDING DATA FILES

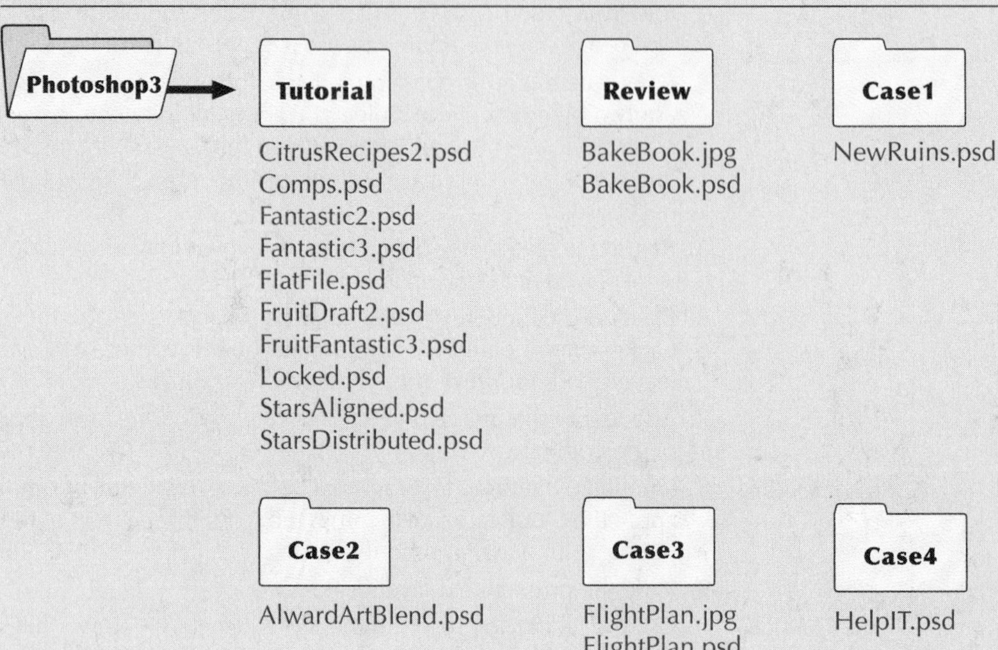
Photoshop3
Tutorial
CitrusRecipes2.psd
Comps.psd
Fantastic2.psd
Fantastic3.psd
FlatFile.psd
FruitDraft2.psd
FruitFantastic3.psd
Locked.psd
StarsAligned.psd
StarsDistributed.psd
Review
BakeBook.jpg
BakeBook.psd
Case1
NewRuins.psd
Case2
AlwardArtBlend.psd
Case3
FlightPlan.jpg
FlightPlan.psd
Case4
HelpIT.psd

TUTORIAL 4

Adding Content

Adding Content and Working with Color

PHOTOSHOP

OBJECTIVES

Session 4.1
- Understand the effect of color
- Sample and set colors using color selection tools
- Change background and foreground colors
- Work with the Swatches panel
- Assign and modify layer styles using the Styles panel

Session 4.2
- Add solid color, gradient, and pattern fill layers
- Add a shape layer
- Fill pixels on a layer
- Modify shapes by adding and subtracting
- Paint with the Brush tool
- Work with Brush tool presets
- Create a work path and apply a stroke

Case | *ReCycle Bike Shop*

ReCycle Bike Shop is a used bicycle shop in Concord, Massachusetts, that also offers bicycle repair classes and mountain biking lessons. Founded in 2006 by Lee duBois, ReCycle has five employees who handle the front-of-store business, teach classes, and give mountain biking lessons. For years, Lee has been doing all of the promotion and bookkeeping; however, because the business has been growing, she has hired you to help her develop promotional materials for the shop, including posters to hang in surrounding towns, Web ads for the local Chamber of Commerce Web site, and mailers for customers who have done business with the shop in the past. She is also interested in developing a logo for the shop that can appear on a sign above the door and on all of the promotional pieces.

You'll use the color selection tools, the Paint Bucket tool, and the drawing and painting tools in Photoshop for the projects Lee has in mind. You'll also add fill layers to an image and compose an image that places your proposed sign in an illustration of the shop so Lee can see what the finished product will look like.

STARTING DATA FILES

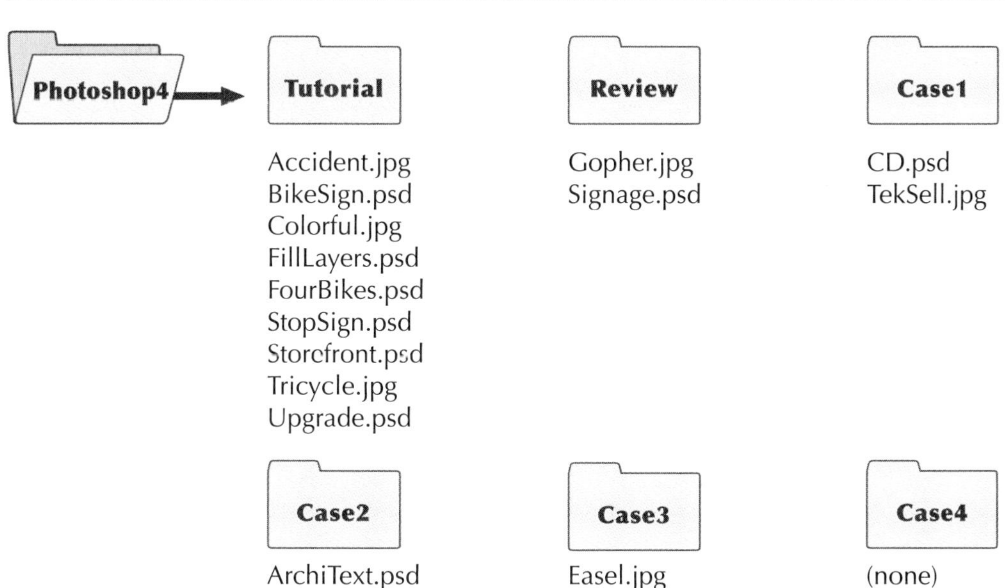

SESSION 4.1 VISUAL OVERVIEW

You can use the Eyedropper tool to **sample**, or copy the color of, pixels in an image so you can apply that color to another part of the image or to another image.

A **point sample** uses the color of a single pixel to set the color when you use the Eyedropper tool.

You can click the **foreground color** icon in the Color panel to open the Color Picker, where you can specify the color Photoshop uses when you work with the drawing tools.

Select the **background color** icon in the Color panel to specify the color used to extend the canvas or to create a gradient.

The Paint Bucket tool is hidden under the Gradient tool in the Tools panel.

The pointer takes the shape of an eyedropper when you sample a color.

Click the color ramp in the Color panel to select a foreground or background color and then adjust the color using the color sliders.

Losevsky Pavel/Shutterstock.com

CONTROLLING CONTENT COLOR

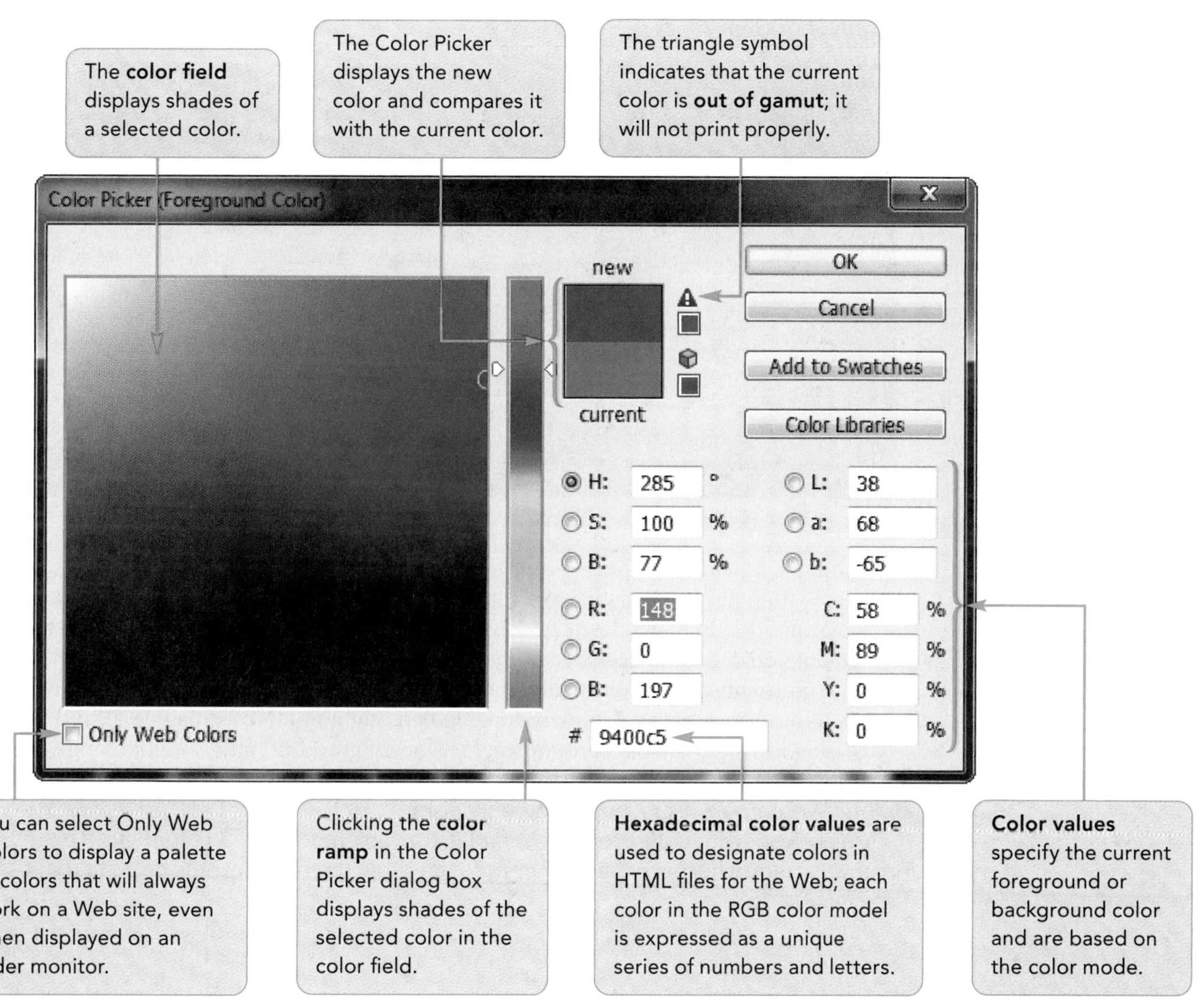
The color field displays shades of a selected color.
The Color Picker displays the new color and compares it with the current color.
The triangle symbol indicates that the current color is out of gamut; it will not print properly.
Color Picker (Foreground Color)
new
current
OK
Cancel
Add to Swatches
Color Libraries
H: 285 °
S: 100 %
B: 77 %
R: 148
G: 0
B: 197
L: 38
a: 68
b: -65
C: 58 %
M: 89 %
Y: 0 %
K: 0 %
9400c5
Only Web Colors
You can select Only Web Colors to display a palette of colors that will always work on a Web site, even when displayed on an older monitor.
Clicking the color ramp in the Color Picker dialog box displays shades of the selected color in the color field.
Hexadecimal color values are used to designate colors in HTML files for the Web; each color in the RGB color model is expressed as a unique series of numbers and letters.
Color values specify the current foreground or background color and are based on the color mode.

Understanding the Effect of Color

In the advertising world, certain brands are consistently identified with particular colors. For example, think of your favorite soft drink. Is its label red? blue? green? If your favorite soft drink has a red label, what might happen if the label were suddenly changed to yellow or pink? Would the identity of the brand change for you in some fundamental way? As you work to create the most effective compositions—that is, compositions that successfully convey your intended message or draw attention to a product you're trying to sell—you should spend some time considering the importance of color. Color can make or break a brand, can affect a viewer's mood, and can even help persuade someone to buy a product. See Figure 4-1.

Figure 4-1 **The effect of color**

PHOTOCREO Michal Bednarek/Shutterstock.com

Figure 4-1 provides a simple example of using color to create interest. Imagine that you're trying to sell the sneakers shown in the images. Which photograph draws the most attention to the shoes? Obviously, the grayscale image does not express the excitement you'd want to convey to a potential buyer. Not only does the color image generate more interest in the product, but the hot pink shoes convey a sense of adventure that, for example, pastel pink or forest green might not. Now imagine a third image, one in which the background isn't shades of gray, but rather bright orange or some other bright color. Would that additional color draw more attention to the shoes, or less? Would it be distracting? Would it clash?

As you work with color, you might find it convenient to keep a color wheel nearby. A **color wheel** is a diagram used to the show the relationships between colors. See Figure 4-2.

Figure 4-2 Sample color wheel

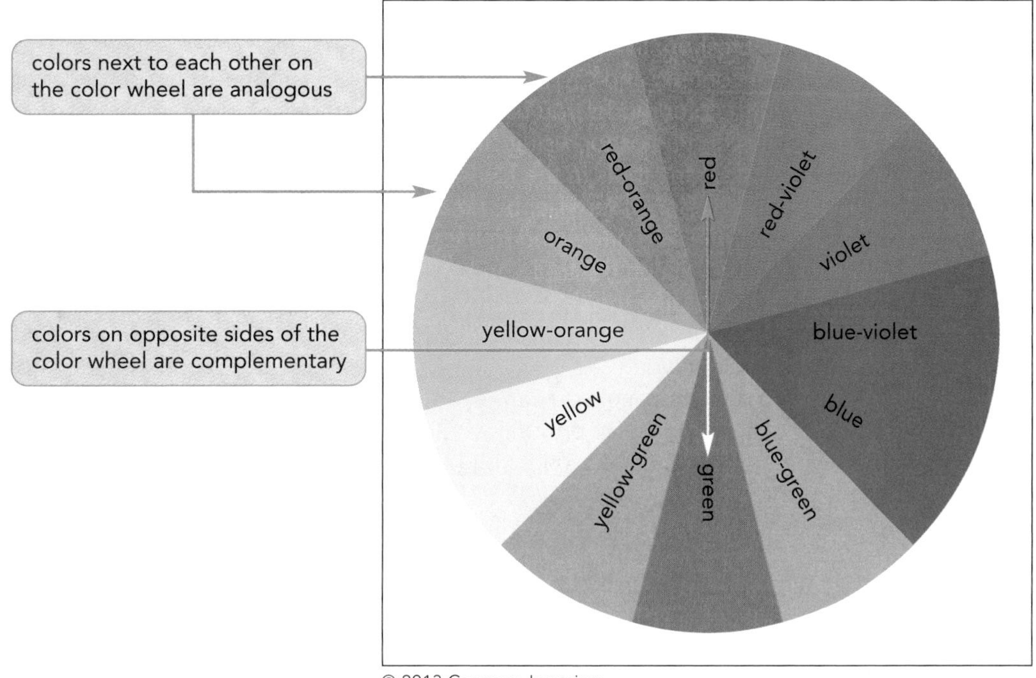

A color wheel can help you choose a **color scheme**, which is a combination of colors that work well together. Examples of color schemes include monochromatic, complementary, and analogous. A **monochromatic** color scheme uses different shades of a single color. A **complementary** color scheme includes colors that are on opposite sides of a color wheel. An **analogous** color scheme uses colors that are next to each other on a color wheel. Color schemes can also be described in terms of temperature. Certain colors, like red, orange, and yellow, convey a feeling of warmth, while others like blue and green are considered cool. **Neutral** colors are colors that aren't on a color wheel, such as browns and grays.

INSIGHT

The Psychology of Color

When working on a composition in Photoshop, you might find your choice of a color scheme dictated in part by the colors in a photograph you plan to use. However, you should also consider other factors, such as the message you want to convey, the emotions you want to elicit, or the audience you want to attract. To use color effectively, it is helpful to have some understanding of color psychology. Knowing how colors affect people—not only in your own culture, but also in other cultures—can help you convey a message or close a sale. For example, you might already know that wearing black makes you appear thinner, but did you know that it also gives you a look of authority or power? Red can elicit intense emotions, while blue and green can produce a calming effect. In certain cultures, green symbolizes paradise. Color is a powerful tool, and the more you know about it, the more effectively you'll use it. Photoshop offers a variety of tools that allow you to experiment with color to achieve the effect you want.

Using the Color Selection Tools

In Tutorial 2, you learned about different color models and the different color modes available in Photoshop. In particular, you focused on RGB, which is the standard color model for Web content, and CMYK, which is the standard model for printed output. No matter which color model you use, or which particular color mode you choose, you select colors in Photoshop using similar methods. In fact, before you use any of the drawing or painting tools in the Tools panel in Photoshop, you need to select the colors you want to use. Otherwise, by default, Photoshop will use the foreground color (shown in the Tools panel and in the Color panel) or the fill color selected on the options bar, depending on the tool you have selected. Photoshop includes many color selection tools, including the Color panel, the Color Picker dialog box, the Eyedropper tool, and the Swatches panel. Which selection tool you use depends on the task at hand. For example, if you want the color of a vector object you add to match one of the colors in a digital image, you can use the Eyedropper tool. If you want to ensure that a color is appropriate for printing, you can use the Color Picker or the Color panel, both of which display an icon to let you know if your color will be available when the image is printed.

In Photoshop, you can specify the foreground color and the background color. See Figure 4-3.

Figure 4-3 **Default foreground and background colors**

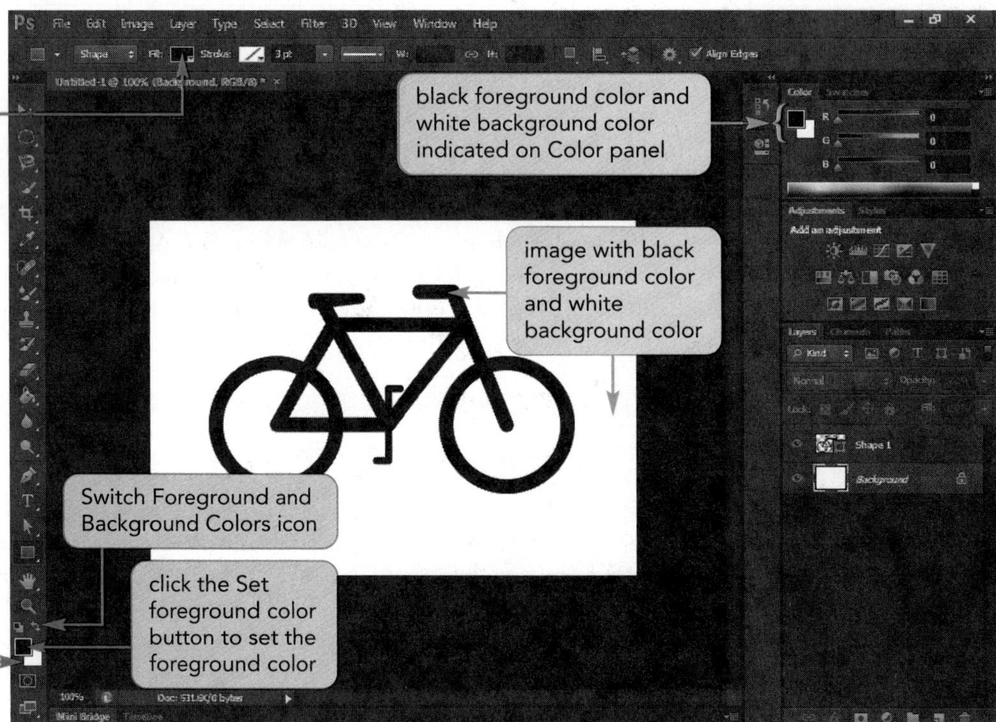
the default fill color for any drawn object is the foreground color unless you change it
black foreground color and white background color indicated on Color panel
image with black foreground color and white background color
Switch Foreground and Background Colors icon
click the Set foreground color button to set the foreground color
click the Set background color button to set the background color

Photoshop defaults to the foreground color when you work with the drawing tools in the Tools panel. By default, the foreground color of a new file created in Photoshop is black. The background color is the color Photoshop uses to extend the canvas or, when combined with the foreground color, to create a **gradient fill**, which is a gradual blending of the foreground and background colors or of other colors determined by a gradient preset. Photoshop also uses the background color to fill empty areas of an image. By default, the background color is white. You can change the foreground and background colors at any time, and unless you restore the defaults in your next Photoshop session, your changes will remain in effect from one session to the next.

Setting the Foreground Color with the Eyedropper Tool

If you are working on a composition and want to select a color for text or a vector object based on a color or colors in a photograph, the Eyedropper tool is a good choice for setting the foreground color. See Figure 4-4.

Figure 4-4 Sampling colors with the Eyedropper tool

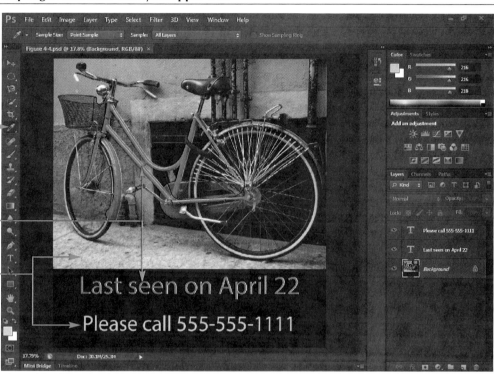

use the Eyedropper tool to sample a color
text color sampled from red bicycle
text color sampled from sidewalk
Last seen on April 22
Please call 555-555-1111

adam.golabek/Shutterstock.com

In the poster shown in Figure 4-4, the Eyedropper tool was used to sample the color of the bicycle for the top line of text. It was used again to sample the color of the sidewalk for the bottom line of text. When you sample a color, you pick up the color values for a single pixel, or for an average of pixel colors in a specified area. You can then use the sampled color to fill a vector object, to specify the color for text, or to fill a selection with the color.

You sample a color with the Eyedropper tool by selecting the layer that contains the color, activating the Eyedropper tool, and then clicking the location on the image where the color appears. To refine your selection, you can use the settings on the options bar to sample the color of a single pixel, called a point sample, or to sample the average of colors in an area of pixels, for example, a 3 × 3 pixel average or even a 101 × 101 pixel average, as shown in Figure 4-5.

TIP

You can also select a sample area by clicking the Eyedropper Tool button in the Tools panel, right-clicking the image, and then choosing a sample size from the context menu.

Figure 4-5 Sample size causes variations in color

color taken from 101 x 101 pixel sample size is closer to lavender because the sample includes the light background color
color taken from point sample is blue
sample location
101 x 101 layer
point sample layer

Losevsky Pavel/Shutterstock.com

Figure 4-5 shows the different results achieved by clicking the image at the same spot, but sampling areas of different dimensions. The first color sample includes only the blue of a single sampled pixel. The second sample is closer to lavender because the sample is 101 × 101 pixels, and includes the light-colored area around the bicycle. The sampled color can vary significantly at different sample sizes, so it's a good idea to experiment with a few settings if you aren't satisfied with the initial sampling.

You can also designate whether you want to sample the color on the current layer only, the current layer and the layers beneath it, or all of the layers in the document by clicking the Sample arrow on the options bar, and then clicking Current Layer, Current & Below, or All Layers. If you sample all layers, Photoshop combines the colors to come up with the sample. You can also determine whether or not Photoshop will include adjustment layers when it generates the sample color.

If you want to see the RGB and CMYK color values when you are sampling a color from an image, open the Info panel, and then, with the Eyedropper tool selected, move the mouse over different areas of the image. As you do, the numbers displayed in the Info panel change to reflect the color you are pointing to. You can open the Info panel by clicking Window on the menu bar and then clicking Info, or by pressing the F8 key.

REFERENCE

Using the Eyedropper Tool

- In the Tools panel, click the Eyedropper Tool button.
- On the options bar, click the Sample Size button to specify the size of the sample, and then click the Sample button to specify whether you want just the current layer or a combination of the image layers and adjustment layers to be used as the sample.
- Point to the area of the image from which you want to obtain a sample, and click the color you want to sample.
- Apply the sample using the Paint Bucket tool or another drawing or painting tool, or add it to the Swatches panel by clicking a blank area in the Swatches panel.

Lee is experimenting with ideas for a store logo and would like you to take one of her ideas a bit further. She has given you a simple graphic of four bicycles, currently filled with black or white, and she would like you to experiment by making them different colors. Her idea is that a multicolored image will emphasize the variety of bicycles available at the shop. You'll color the first bicycle using a color sample from the Eyedropper tool. You'll apply the sampled color to the bicycle with the Paint Bucket tool, which replaces the color of not only the pixel you click, but also all adjacent pixels with a similar color. In other words, if you click the white bicycle, the Paint Bucket tool will fill the pixel you click—plus all of the adjacent white pixels in that bicycle—with the new color, and it will leave the nonwhite pixels the same.

To sample a color using the Eyedropper tool:

1. Start Photoshop while pressing the **Ctrl+Alt+Shift** keys, and click **Yes** to delete the Settings File when prompted. Reset Photoshop to the default Essentials workspace layout, and then reset all tools.
2. Navigate to the Photoshop4\Tutorial folder provided with your Data Files, and open **Colorful.jpg** and **FourBikes.psd**.
3. Switch to the Colorful.jpg file, if necessary, and in the Tools panel, click the **Eyedropper Tool** button.
4. On the options bar, click the **Sample Size** button and select **Point Sample**, if necessary; confirm that **All Layers** is selected on the Sample button, and then click the green area near the bicycle spring, as shown in Figure 4-6.

Figure 4-6 **Color sampled in one image will be applied to another**

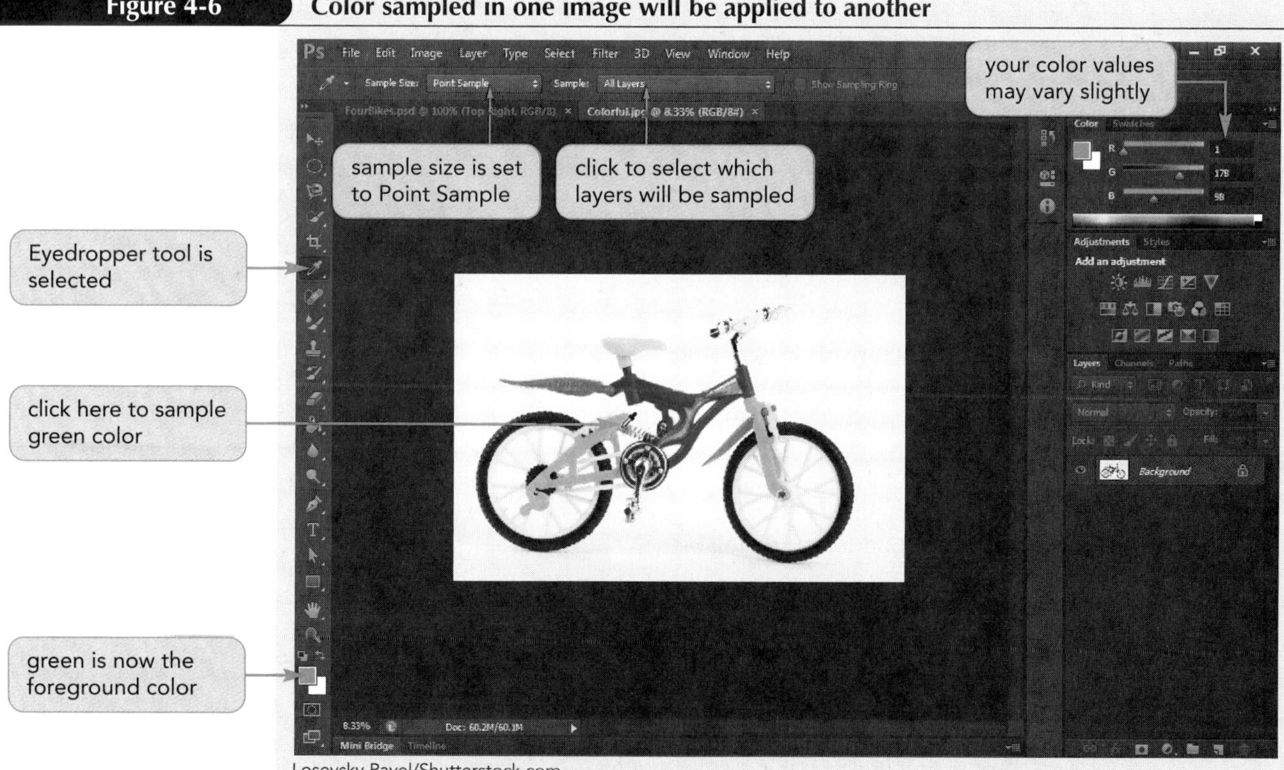

Losevsky Pavel/Shutterstock.com

The foreground color icon changes to green in the Tools panel and in the Color panel. (Don't be concerned if your color doesn't exactly match the color in the figure.)

Make sure you click the specified layer in this step and all other layer selection steps. Clicking an incorrect layer will apply the color to the wrong part of the image.

5. Switch to the **FourBikes** file, and in the Layers panel, click the **Lower Right** layer, if necessary, to make it the active layer.
6. In the Tools panel, click the **Paint Bucket Tool** button.

   Notice that the pointer shape changes to a paint bucket.

   Trouble? If you can't see the Paint Bucket Tool button, point to the Gradient Tool button in the Tools panel, click and hold the mouse button to display the hidden tool, and then click the Paint Bucket Tool button.
7. In the image, click the **lower-right bicycle**. Photoshop fills the bicycle with the sampled green color.

   Trouble? If the background or a different bicycle is filled with the green color when you click, you did not click the Lower Right layer, or you were pointing at the area around the bicycle rather than the bicycle itself. Press the Ctrl+Z keys, or click Edit on the menu bar and click Undo Paint Bucket to undo the change, and then repeat Step 7.
8. Save the FourBikes file as **FourColors.psd** in the Photoshop4\Tutorial folder, and keep it open for the next set of steps.

Setting the Foreground Color in the Color Panel

You can also use the Color panel to select a color for the foreground. In the Color panel, RGB color values are displayed if you're working in RGB mode; CMYK color values are displayed if you're working in CMYK mode. See Figure 4-7.

Figure 4-7 Color panel showing RGB color values

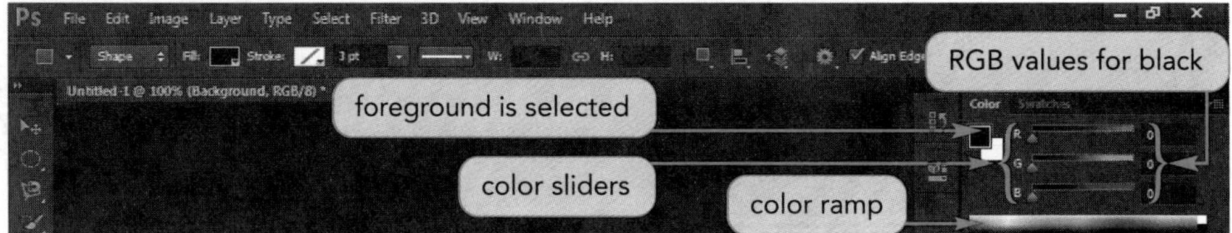

By default, the color values for the foreground color in RGB mode are R=0, G=0, and B=0 because those are the RGB values for black, the default foreground color. When you change the foreground color, those values change. You can modify the foreground color in the Color panel by entering new color values for R, G, and B; by dragging the color sliders for R, G, and B; by clicking a color in the color ramp; or by clicking the Set foreground color icon in the Color panel to open the Color Picker (Foreground Color) dialog box.

You can also use a combination of these methods to achieve the exact color you want. For example, you might click a green color in the color ramp, and then use the color sliders to adjust the levels to achieve the shade of green you want. Keep in mind, however, that some of your color manipulations might result in a color that won't print properly. You need to ensure that your color choice is within the **gamut**, or range of colors allowed by the CMYK mode. A color that won't print properly is considered out of gamut because it is a color not included in the complete set (or gamut) of print-safe colors. See Figure 4-8.

Figure 4-8 **Out-of-gamut color correction**

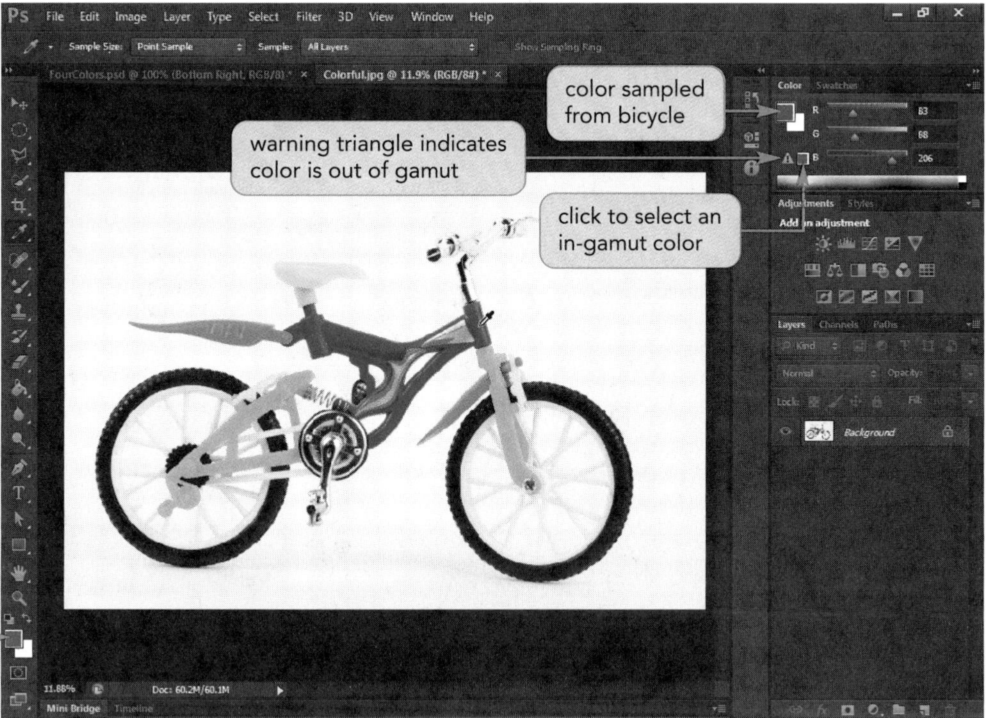
color sampled from bicycle
warning triangle indicates color is out of gamut
click to select an in-gamut color
new sampled foreground color

Losevsky Pavel/Shutterstock.com

In Figure 4-8, the selected foreground color is out of gamut for printing, as indicated by the triangle with the exclamation point. You can choose a new color yourself, or you can click the square to the right of the warning to have Photoshop substitute a similar color that is in gamut.

You'll use the Color panel to select a light blue color for the next bicycle.

REFERENCE

Specifying a Color in the Color Panel

- Enter color values in the boxes for R, G, and B if in RGB mode or in the boxes for C, M, Y, and K if in CMYK mode.

or

- Drag the color sliders for R, G, and B or for C, M, Y, and K.

or

- In the Color panel, click the Set foreground color icon to open the Color Picker dialog box.
- Select the color in the Color Picker dialog box, and then click the OK button.

To set a color using the Color panel:

1. In the Layers panel, click the **Lower Left** layer to select it.
2. In the Color panel, point to the **color ramp**. When the pointer is over the ramp, it changes to the Eyedropper pointer.
3. On the color ramp, click a **light blue** color. The foreground color icon changes to light blue in the Tools panel and in the Color panel.
4. Point to the **lower-left bicycle** in the image, and then click on the white area of the bicycle. Photoshop fills the bicycle with the light blue color. See Figure 4-9.

Figure 4-9 **Using the Color panel**

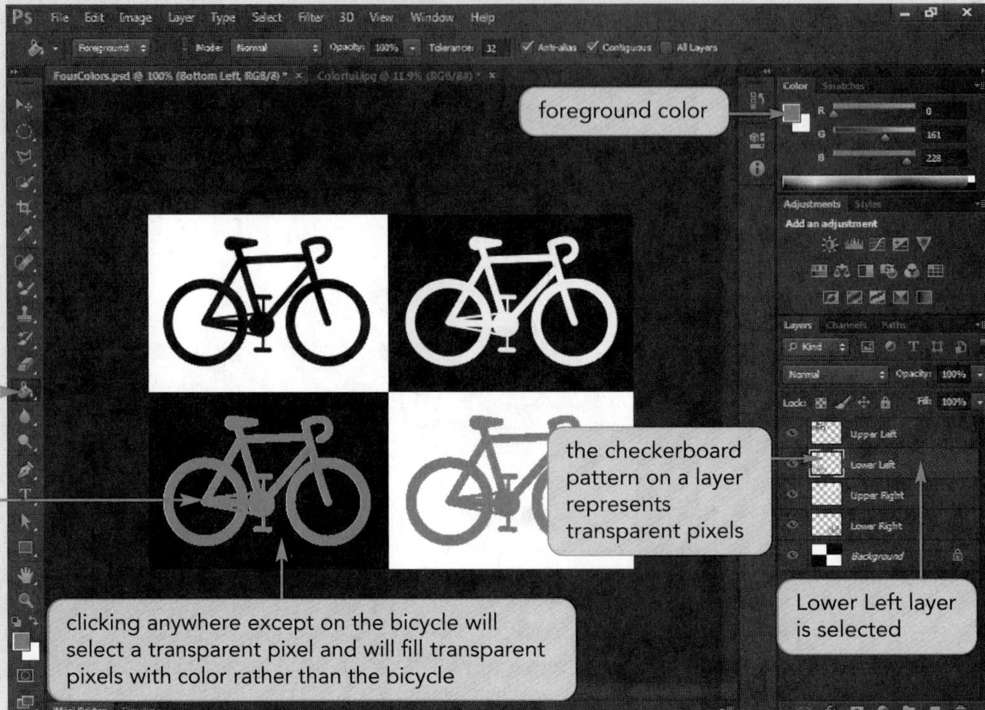
foreground color
Paint Bucket tool is selected
the bicycle is filled with the new color
the checkerboard pattern on a layer represents transparent pixels
clicking anywhere except on the bicycle will select a transparent pixel and will fill transparent pixels with color rather than the bicycle
Lower Left layer is selected

Black Images/Shutterstock.com

Trouble? If any part of the image other than the bicycle is filled with the light blue color, you have clicked a transparent part of the layer rather than the bicycle. Undo the change by pressing the Ctrl+Z keys, and then repeat Step 4.

Notice that the pointer shape is still a paint bucket because the Paint Bucket tool is still selected in the Tools panel.

INSIGHT

Understanding Web-Safe Colors

As you saw in Tutorial 2, today's color models can include millions of colors. However, in the not-so-distant past, computer monitors were limited to 256 colors. These 8-bit displays couldn't handle many of the colors available for Web design, and they used a process called dithering to mix two colors to achieve an approximation of any unavailable color. Dithering increased the time it took to upload images, and often made the Web experience less like surfing and more like a waiting game. In order to avoid dithering and slow upload times, Web designers could use **Web-safe colors**, colors that were available in any Web browser on any system. Photoshop still includes Web-safe options as color choices. For example, the Color Picker dialog box includes an Only Web Colors check box, and the Swatches panel includes palettes of Web-safe colors. Given that most computer monitors and mobile device displays can now display many more than 256 colors, you probably won't need to limit yourself to Web-safe colors, but it's good to know what they are.

You can also use the Color Picker to set a color for the foreground. To select a color in the Color Picker, click in the color ramp to display shades of that color in the color field. You can then use the color field to click a particular shade of the current color. See Figure 4-10.

Figure 4-10 **Color Picker (Foreground Color) dialog box**

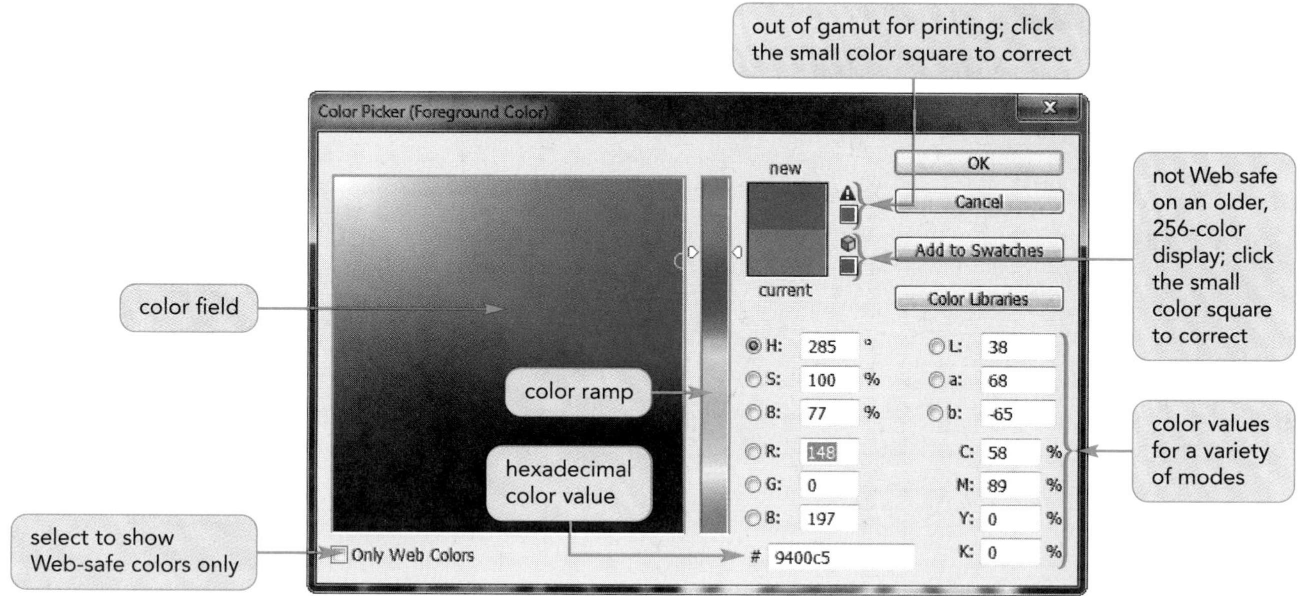

When you select the color, the Color Picker displays the color's values using different color modes, including HSB (Hue, Saturation, and Brightness), RGB, CMYK, and the color's hexadecimal color values. In a hexadecimal color value, the first pair of characters defines the red used in the color, and the next two pairs define green and blue, respectively. Hexadecimal color values are used to specify colors in **HTML (HyperText Markup Language)**, a programming language used to create Web pages. The Color Picker also displays Lab color mode values. **Lab color mode** describes colors as most people actually see them, rather than as they are interpreted by a device such as a monitor or a printer. Lab colors are considered **device independent** because a Lab color should look the same to the human eye no matter which device it's displayed on.

In addition to color values, the Color Picker displays icons that let you know if a color is either out of gamut, not Web safe, or both. To ensure that any color you choose will display correctly on an older 256-color monitor, select the Only Web Colors check box before selecting your color. If a color is out of gamut, click the "Click to select in gamut color" icon under the "Warning: out of gamut for color printing" icon to substitute a similar in-gamut color.

You'll use the Color Picker dialog box to select a yellow color for the third bicycle, and then you'll sample a color to assign to the final bicycle.

To set the foreground color using the Color Picker (Foreground Color) dialog box:

1. In the Layers panel, click the **Upper Right** layer.
2. In the Tools panel, click the **Set foreground color** icon ■. The Color Picker (Foreground Color) dialog box opens.
3. On the color ramp, click the **yellow color**, and then in the color field, click a **bright yellow**. See Figure 4-11. Note that your color values might not match the values shown in the dialog box.

Figure 4-11 Color Picker with Web-safe colors displayed

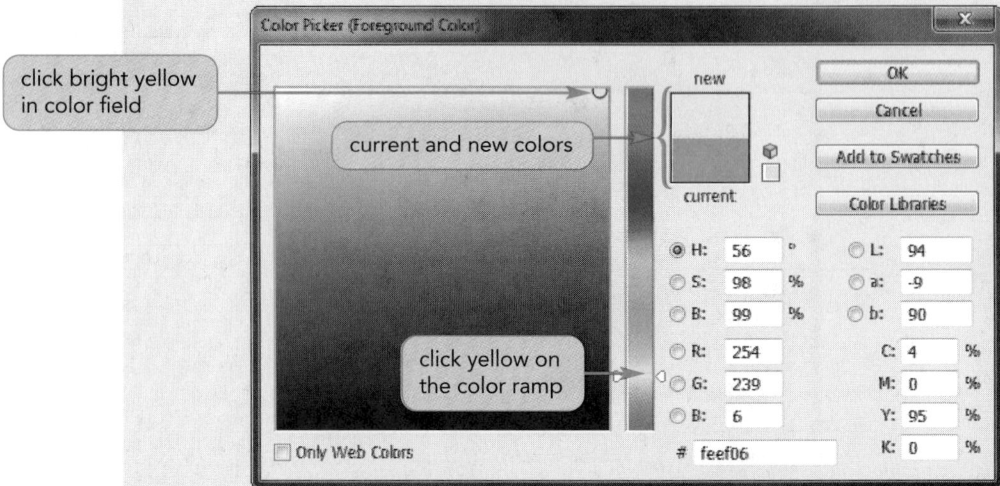

4. Click the **OK** button, and then click the **upper-right bicycle** in the image to apply the yellow color. The upper-right bicycle is now yellow.
5. Switch to **Colorful.jpg**, and sample the **red fender guard** color. In the Color panel, click the **Click to select in gamut color** icon, if necessary, and then switch back to **FourColors.psd**.
6. Click the **Upper Left** layer, click the **Paint Bucket Tool** button, and then click the **upper-left bicycle** to apply the sampled color from Colorful.jpg file.
7. Save **FourColors.psd**. See Figure 4-12.

Figure 4-12 Colors assigned to four bicycles

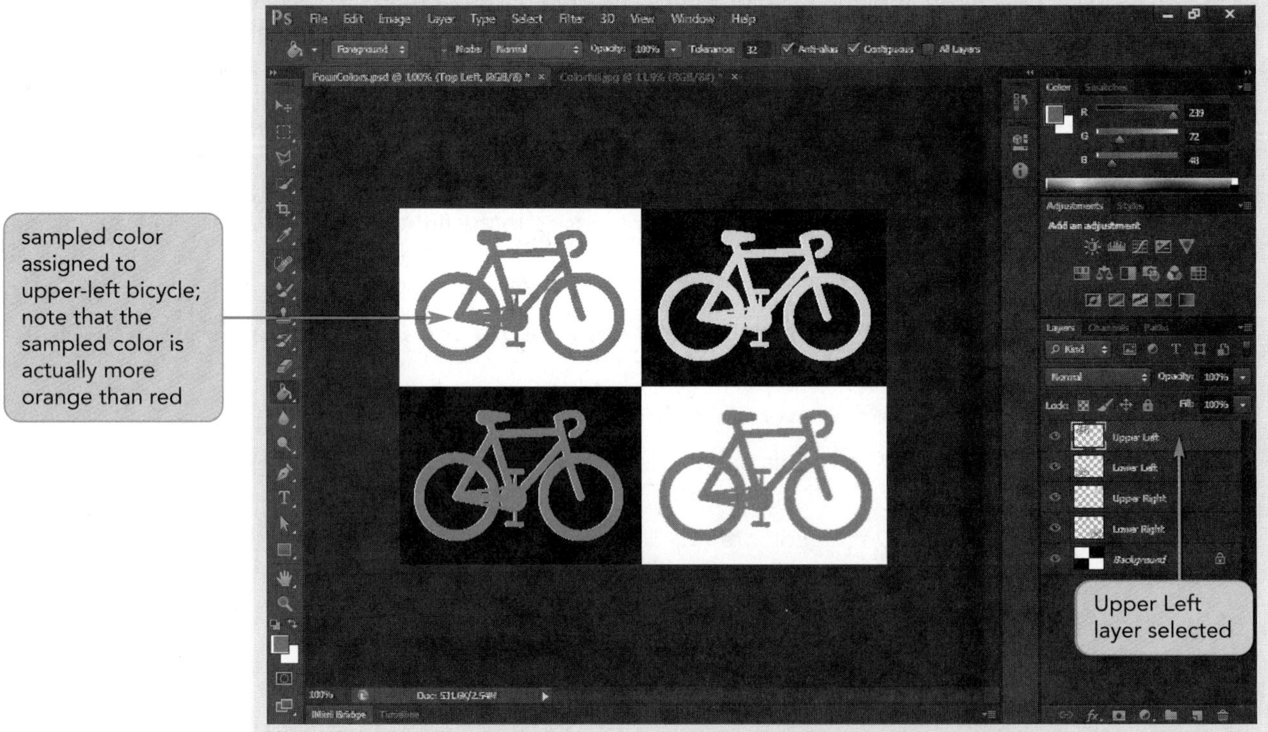

sampled color assigned to upper-left bicycle; note that the sampled color is actually more orange than red

Upper Left layer selected

Black Images/Shutterstock.com

All of the bicycles have been assigned a color. You'll continue to work with color by assigning a new background color and then using it to extend the canvas to see if you can add interest to the logo.

Changing the Background Color

Photoshop uses the background color in combination with the foreground color to create some of the gradient presets covered later in this tutorial. You can also use the background color when you increase the canvas size of a composition, as you did in Tutorial 2. However, Photoshop only provides a background color option for increased canvas size if your composition has a Background layer. When you create a new file, Photoshop uses the current background color if you select Background Color from the Background Contents list in the New dialog box.

You can specify the background color in Photoshop using the same methods you use to specify foreground color. You can use the Color Picker (Background Color) dialog box, the Color panel, or the Eyedropper tool.

You can easily switch foreground and background colors by clicking the Switch Foreground and Background Colors button in the Tools panel or by pressing the X key. You can reset Photoshop to the default foreground and background colors by clicking the Default Foreground and Background Colors button in the Tools panel or by pressing the D key.

Lee thinks that the four-bicycle logo idea might be overkill, but wants to see if adding a border to it helps unify the colors. She suggests that you increase the size of your poster by adding a border that alternates two of the colors you used on the bicycles. To do so, you'll use the Increase Canvas Size command two times, using a different method to choose a background color each time you do.

To change the background color:

1. In the Layers panel, click the **Background** layer to make it the active layer.
2. In the Color panel, click the **Set background color** icon, which is partially hidden by the Set foreground color icon. The color values for the current background color (white) are displayed.

   Trouble? If the Color Picker (Background Color) dialog box opens, click the Cancel button.
3. In the Tools panel, click the **Eyedropper Tool** button, and then click in the upper-right yellow bicycle. Because the sample includes all of the layers in the file, Photoshop samples the yellow from the bicycle, even though the Background layer is selected, not the bicycle layer. The background color icon changes to yellow.
4. On the menu bar, click **Image**, and then click **Canvas Size**.
5. In the Canvas Size dialog box, click the **Relative** check box to select it, if necessary, type **2** in the Width box, select **Inches** as the unit of measurement, if necessary, and then type **2** in the Height box. You'll leave the Anchor setting as is so the canvas is extended equally on all four sides of the image.
6. In the Canvas extension color list, click **Background** to select it, if necessary, and then click the **OK** button to close the Canvas Size dialog box. The canvas now has a border that uses the yellow color.
7. In the Tools panel, click the **Switch Foreground and Background Colors** icon. The background color icon changes to orange.

   Next, you'll extend the canvas again using the new background color.
8. On the menu bar, click **Image**, and then click **Canvas Size**.

TIP

You can also press the X key to switch the foreground and background colors.

9. In the Canvas Size dialog box, click the **Relative** check box to select it, if necessary, type **2** in the Width box, select **Inches**, if necessary, and then type **2** in the Height box.
10. In the Canvas extension color list, click **Background** to select it, if necessary, and then click the **OK** button to close the Canvas Size dialog box. Fit the image on the screen. The canvas now has a second border that uses the orange color. See Figure 4-13.

Figure 4-13 Extending the canvas with the background color

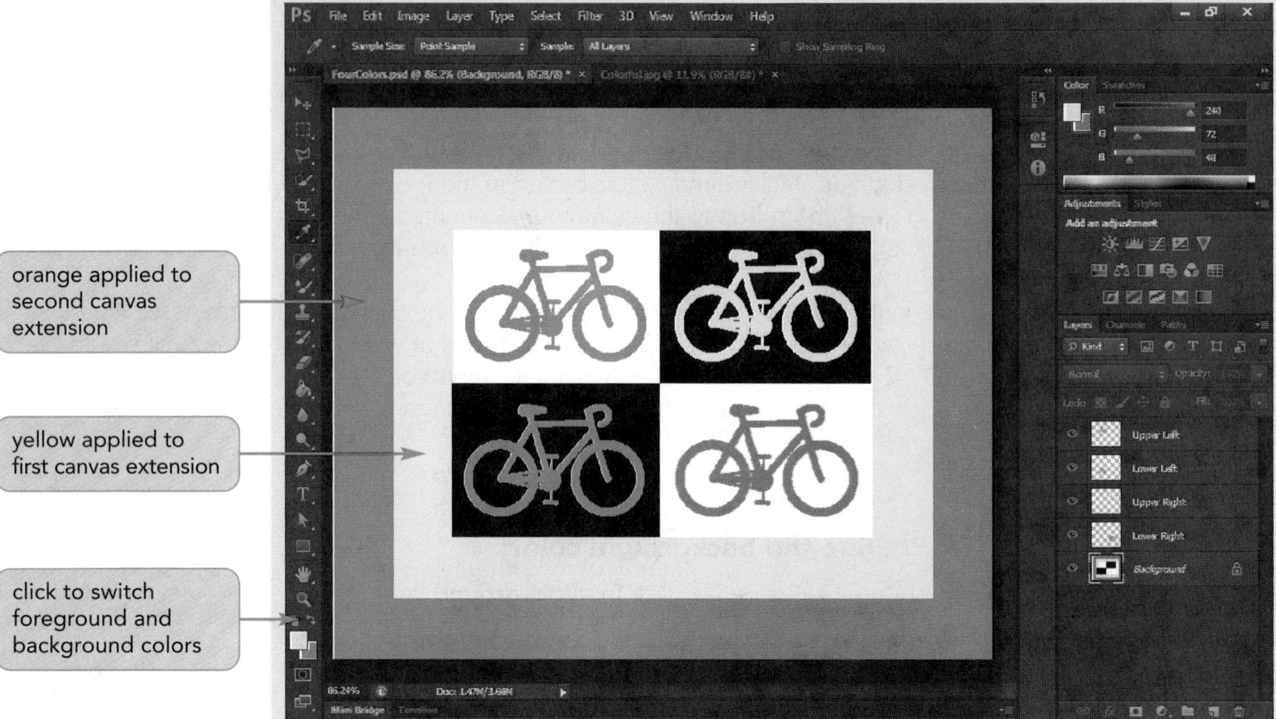

Black Images/Shutterstock.com

The canvas has been extended two times, once using yellow as the background color and then once again using orange. The image now has a border of alternating colors. You'll switch back to the default foreground and background colors before continuing your work.

11. Press the **D** key to return Photoshop to the default foreground and background colors, black and white.
12. Save the file as **FourColors.jpg**, using the default JPEG Options, in the Photoshop4\Tutorial folder. Photoshop saves the file as a JPEG and flattens the image into a single layer.
13. Close FourColors.psd without saving the file. Leave Colorful.jpg open.

PROSKILLS

Problem Solving: Making Your Work Accessible to the Color Blind

As someone using digital imaging to convey messages, you will often be faced with the challenge of trying to ensure that your work is accessible to the largest number of people possible. It's a good idea to keep in mind that some people are **color blind**, which means they don't see certain colors the same way the majority of the population sees them. There are many kinds of color blindness. Some color-blind people can't distinguish between red and green; others can't distinguish between blue and yellow; others don't see color at all (though this is extremely rare). You can create designs that accommodate the color blind in a number of ways:

- Avoid putting red and green or blue and yellow directly next to each other in a composition, if possible.
- Use textures in addition to colors to help distinguish between objects in a composition.
- Add borders to delineate separate areas in a composition or on a Web page.
- Underline text that you want to stand out, rather than relying solely on a color change.
- Vary the fonts for text that uses different colors.
- Use shapes as backgrounds for different parts of a composition.

These suggestions are helpful aids for reaching a color-blind audience, but they also present additional challenges, such as images that are too busy (because of multiple fonts and shapes), or images that aren't aesthetically pleasing to a wider audience. By following these guidelines and using the tools in Photoshop to help you solve other problems, you can create compositions that reach the widest possible audience.

Lee asks you to work on an ad that she has started for a Web campaign. She suggests you use the Swatches panel to try working with a different palette of colors.

Working with the Swatches Panel

The Swatches panel provides a library of commonly used colors that you can easily access to modify your images. The panel appears behind the Colors panel in the default Essentials workspace. You can also open the Swatches panel from any other workspace by clicking Swatches on the Window menu. See Figure 4-14.

Figure 4-14 **Default Swatches panel**

Ingvald Kaldhussater/Shutterstock.com

You can add colors to the Swatches panel so your customized palette of swatches gives you easy access to colors that you use often. To create a subset of colors with which to work, you can delete colors from the Swatches panel. You can also save the customized panel as a preset. In addition, Photoshop provides a long list of color palettes that you can choose to display in the Swatches panel based on your designing or printing needs.

TIP

To restore the default Photoshop swatches, click the panel menu button, and then click Reset Swatches.

You have the option of loading or replacing a swatches **library**, or palette of swatches, in the Swatches panel. When you load a library, it is added or **appended** to the current library of swatches at the bottom of the panel. When you replace a library, the new library takes the place of the current library in the panel, and you are prompted to save the current library if you have made any modifications to it. Whether you choose to load or replace a swatches library depends on the work you're doing. If you want to continue to work with the current swatches but need additional choices, loading a library is your best bet. If you want to restrict your choices to a single library, replace the current library. You can also customize the display of swatches in the Swatches panel to display small or large thumbnails, or to display the choices in a list.

Photoshop provides numerous libraries or color palettes that you can display in the Swatches panel. You choose a color palette based on your current project. For example, if you are creating graphics for a newspaper, you should consider displaying the ANPA color palette in the Swatches panel. ANPA stands for American Newspaper Publishers Association, and the ANPA palette displays colors commonly used in newspaper layout applications. If you are working on a printed piece, choose one of the PANTONE or other CMYK libraries. You can also display Web-safe swatches.

To select a color swatch, click a swatch to choose it as the foreground color, or press the Ctrl key and then click the swatch to choose it as the background color.

Lee wants you to revise an ad she's created for the local Chamber of Commerce Web site. She would like you to add colored rectangles behind the white text in the ad but also wants you to extend your Photoshop knowledge by working with a different palette of colors. You'll use the Swatches panel to see what a different palette looks like. You'll choose one that displays hexadecimal values for colors, which are the color values used by Web developers in their HTML code.

To customize the display of the Swatches panel:

1. Reset the Essentials workspace, click the **Swatches** panel tab, and then open **Upgrade.psd** from the Photoshop4\Tutorial folder. Photoshop displays the default Swatches panel presets using the Small Thumbnails display.
2. In the Swatches panel, click the **panel menu** button, and then click **Large List**. Photoshop displays the swatches in a list. Each swatch includes a thumbnail of the color, as well as the swatch name or color value.

Next, you'll change the Swatches panel palette to Web Spectrum to view the colors along with their hexadecimal values.

To change the color palette in the Swatches panel:

1. In the Swatches panel, click the **panel menu** button to display the list of presets, and then click **Web Spectrum**. Photoshop asks if you want to replace the current color swatches or append them to the swatches already in the panel.
2. Click the **OK** button to replace the colors in the panel with the Web Spectrum colors. The Swatches panel changes to display the new colors. Instead of names, the list displays a hexadecimal color value to the right of each swatch.

   Trouble? If you don't have the Web Spectrum palette, choose a different palette from the menu.

   Trouble? If Photoshop displays a message asking if you want to save changes to the current swatches before replacing them, click the No button.
3. Switch to the **Color** panel, click the **Set Foreground color** icon, and then switch back to the **Swatches** panel.

4. In the Swatches panel, drag the scroll box to just before the halfway point on the scroll bar, place the Eyedropper pointer over the green swatch that displays the hexadecimal values **#006600** for the green color, and then click. The foreground color changes to green.

   Trouble? If the background color changes instead of the foreground color, click the Color panel tab, and then click the Set foreground color icon in the Color panel. Switch back to the Swatches panel and repeat Step 4.

5. Click the **Background** layer to select it, if necessary. In the Tools panel, click the **Rectangle Tool** button and on the options bar, click the **Pick tool mode** button and then click **Shape**, if necessary.

6. Draw a rectangle over the "Time for an upgrade?" text. When you release the mouse button, a green rectangle appears. Because the Background layer was selected when you added the rectangle layer, the rectangle appears beneath the text on the canvas. See Figure 4-15.

Figure 4-15 **Shape layer under text layer**

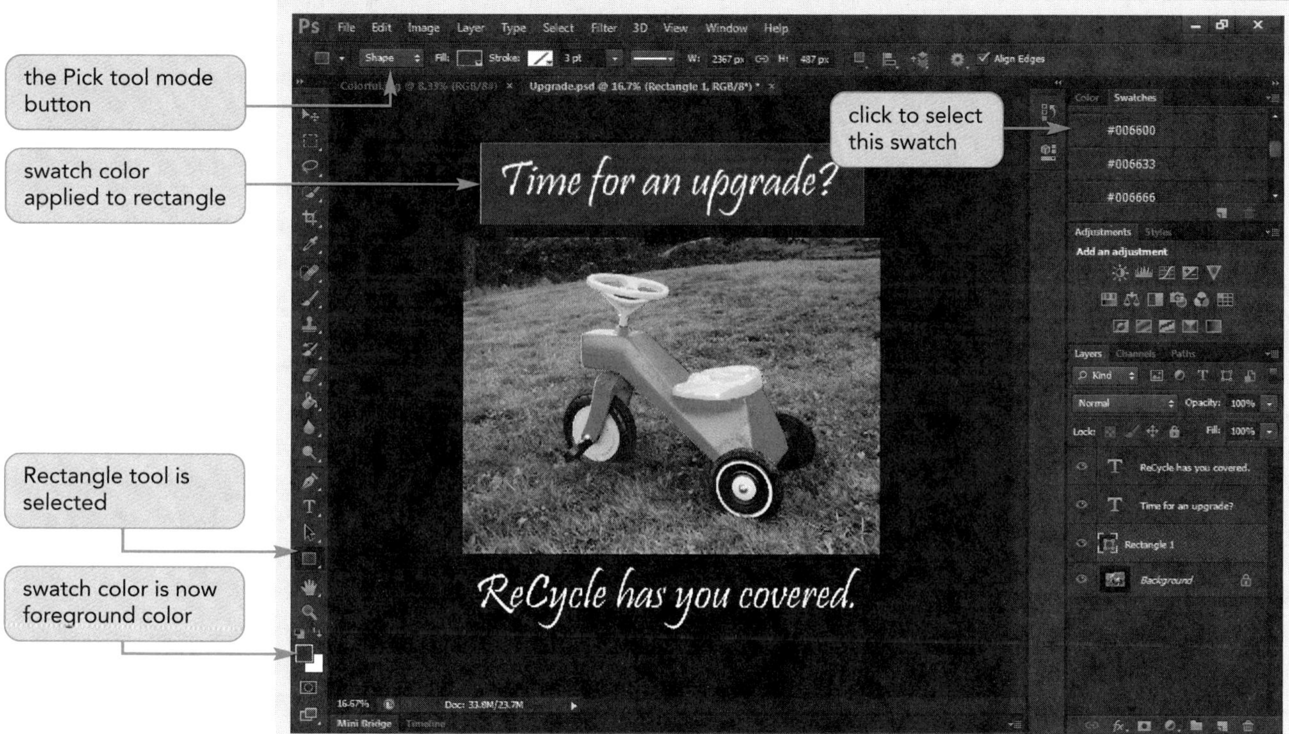
the Pick tool mode button
swatch color applied to rectangle
Rectangle tool is selected
swatch color is now foreground color
click to select this swatch
Time for an upgrade?
ReCycle has you covered.
#006600
#006633
#006666

Ingvald Kaldhussater/Shutterstock.com

Notice that the Rectangle 1 layer is now the active layer in the Layers panel.

7. Draw a rectangle over the "ReCycle has you covered" text. Because the Rectangle 1 layer was selected when you added the new rectangle layer, this rectangle also appears beneath the text on the canvas.

8. To restore the original swatches, click the **panel menu** button in the Swatches panel, click **Reset Swatches**, and then click the **OK** button.

9. Click the **panel menu** button again, and then click **Small Thumbnail** to reset the display of the Swatches panel to the default.

10. Save the file as **ColorUpgrade.jpg**, using the default JPEG Options, in the Photoshop4\Tutorial folder, and then close Upgrade.psd without saving it. Leave Colorful.jpg open for the next set of steps.

Adding Colors to the Swatches Panel

You can add the current foreground color to the Swatches panel by positioning the mouse pointer over a blank area of the Swatches panel; when the Paint Bucket pointer appears, click to add the color swatch to the panel. You can also use the Create new swatch of foreground color button at the bottom of the Swatches panel, or the New Swatch command on the panel menu. Once you add a color to the Swatches panel, you can apply it as you would apply any other color.

When you add a color to the panel, it is saved with the Swatches panel as a preference. If at some point you reset your preferences, you will lose any modifications to the Swatches panel. To save a modified Swatches panel permanently, you need to save it in a library.

Lee has given you a photograph that she plans to use in a number of different campaigns, and she would like you to save some of the colors in the photograph as swatches in the Swatches panel.

To add sampled colors to the Swatches panel:

1. Reset the default Essentials workspace, and then press the **D** key to restore the default foreground and background colors.
2. In the Tools panel, click the **Eyedropper Tool** button.
3. Click the **light green chain guard** on the bicycle.
4. Click the **Swatches** panel tab, if necessary, move the mouse pointer to a blank (gray) area at the bottom of the swatches area until it becomes a Paint Bucket pointer, and then click. The Color Swatch Name dialog box opens, as shown in Figure 4-16.

Figure 4-16 **Naming a color swatch**

5. Type **CoolGreen** in the Name box, and then click the **OK** button. The new swatch appears as the last swatch in the Swatches panel.
6. Place the mouse pointer over the new swatch until the tooltip CoolGreen appears. The new swatch has the name you assigned.
7. Sample the **yellow seat** on the bicycle and add it to the Swatches panel as **BrightYellow**. The new swatch appears to the right of the CoolGreen swatch in the panel.
8. Sample the **red fender guard** in the image and add it to the Swatches panel as **RedFender**. The new swatch appears to the right of the BrightYellow swatch in the panel.

You'll save the modified swatches as a preset so you can use the set again in the future.

Saving Modified Swatches as a Preset

If you have swatches that you plan to reuse, for example, swatches based on a color model that you will use consistently with one campaign or for one client, it is a good idea to save them as a preset so you can reload them at any time.

To save swatches as a preset and then load them:

1. In the Swatches panel, click the **panel menu** button, and then click **Save Swatches**. The Save dialog box opens.
2. Navigate to the Photoshop4\Tutorial folder, type **ReCycleSwatches** in the File name box, and then click the **Save** button. Photoshop saves the swatches with an .aco extension in the Tutorial folder.

   You'll replace the ReCycleSwatches palette with the default palette, and then practice opening the custom palette you created.
3. In the Swatches panel, click the **panel menu** button, click **Reset Swatches**, and then click the **OK** button. Photoshop reloads the default swatches.
4. Click the **panel menu** button again, click **Load Swatches**, navigate to the Photoshop4\Tutorial folder, click the **ReCycleSwatches.aco** file to select it, and then click **Load**. The saved customized swatches are appended to the default swatches in the Swatches panel.

You can delete colors that you don't need from the Swatches panel. When you delete a swatch from a library, you need to save the library for the deletion to be permanent. If you delete a swatch by mistake, close the library without saving it and then reopen it.

You'll delete two of the colors from the Swatches panel that you know you'll never use, and you'll keep the CoolGreen swatch in the customized library.

To delete a color from the Swatches panel:

1. Point to the **BrightYellow** swatch at the bottom of the Swatches panel, press the **Alt** key so a scissors pointer appears, and then click. The swatch is deleted from the Swatches panel.

   Trouble? If you delete a different swatch accidentally, reload the ReCycleSwatches library without saving changes to the open library.
2. Repeat Step 1 to delete the RedFender swatch.
3. Reset the swatches, and save changes to the current custom swatches before closing them. Saving your changes will ensure that the ReCycleSwatches custom library includes CoolGreen so you can use it in future Photoshop sessions.

   Trouble? If you are given the choice of replacing or appending the current swatches with the default, click the OK button.

   Trouble? If you are prompted to replace the existing ReCycleSwatches.aco file, click the OK button.
4. Close Colorful.jpg without saving it.

Working with the Styles Panel

You can take the time to apply individual effects to layers in Photoshop to achieve a certain look for text or a vector object, or you can choose from a library of professionally designed styles in the Styles panel. The Styles panel, which appears behind the Adjustments panel in the Essentials workspace, includes a library of layer presets that let you change the look of a layer by applying multiple effects with a single click of the mouse. Using a style is a quick and easy way to apply multiple effects at the same time—for example, a **bevel effect**, which gives an object the appearance of a third dimension, and a gradient or a shadow. See Figure 4-17.

Figure 4-17 Style applied from Styles panel

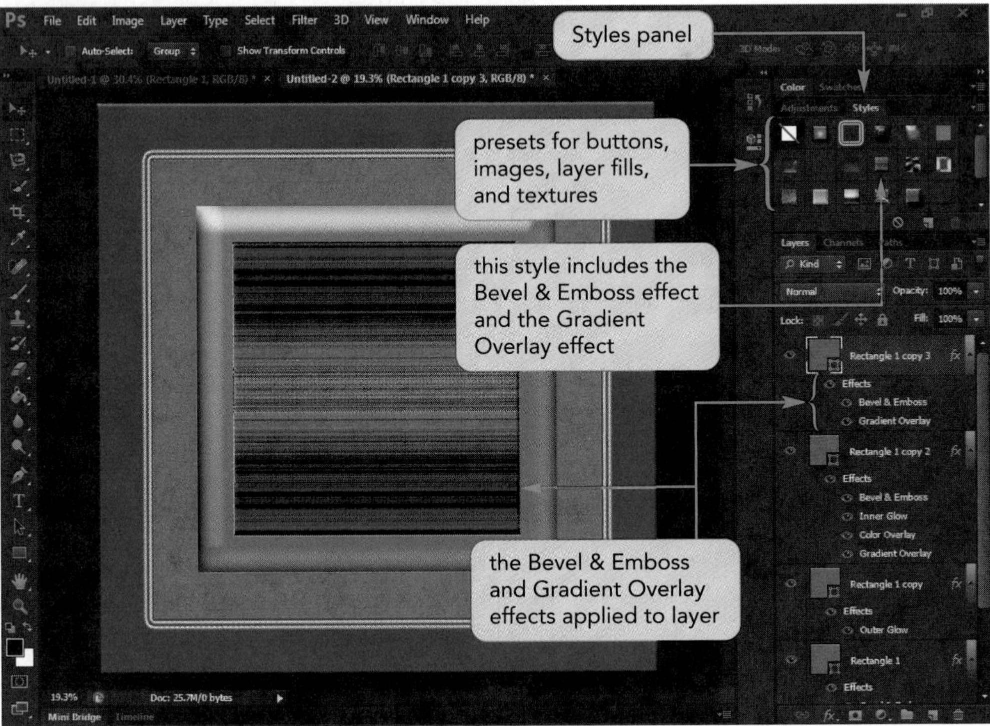

> **TIP**
>
> You can change the library of styles displayed in the Styles panel by selecting a new library of style presets from the Styles panel menu.

The default Styles panel library includes presets for buttons, images, layer fills, and textures. You can also choose a library with styles designed only for a particular object—for example, a library created solely for buttons or solely for text. When you assign a style to a layer, the letters *fx* appear to the right of the layer name, and the effects used in the style are listed beneath the layer in the Layers panel.

Lee would like her bicycle shop sign to be simple. She wants you to develop a sign that would consist of a bicycle silhouette that will appear on a hinged sign sticking out over the shop door—no words, just the sign. To show Lee the full effect of the sign you design, you'll place it in a vector drawing of the shop; later in the tutorial, you'll even draw the hinge that the sign will hang on.

To work with the Styles panel:

1. Reset the Essentials workspace, restore the default foreground and background colors, and then click the **Styles** tab in the Adjustments panel tab group to display the Styles panel.
2. In the Styles panel, click the **panel menu** button, click **Reset Styles**, and then click the **OK** button to replace the current styles with the default styles.

Trouble? If Photoshop displays a message asking if you want to save changes to the current styles before replacing them, click the No button.

If you hover over a style thumbnail, Photoshop displays the name of the style. However, it is difficult to tell from the names exactly what effects will be applied. To see what a style does, you need to apply it to a layer.

3. Open **BikeSign.psd**, located in the Photoshop4\Tutorial folder, display it at 100% magnification, and pan the image so the bicycle and the white background rectangle are near the center of the window.

   The file Lee provided you includes three layers: The background is a vector drawing of the storefront, the top layer is a plain bicycle silhouette on a transparent background, and the layer beneath the bicycle is a plain white rectangle.

4. In the Layers panel, click the **Bicycle** layer to select it.
5. Point to the first thumbnail in the Styles panel. Photoshop displays the style name, Default Style (None), when you point to the thumbnail. You can click this thumbnail at any point to undo any style you have applied to the layer.
6. Point to the thumbnail in the second row, fourth column, called **Blanket (Texture)**, and then click. Photoshop applies the Blanket style to the bicycle. Notice that *fx* appears to the right of the layer name in the Layers panel, and a list of effects appears indented under the layer name. Clicking a different style will replace this style with the new style.
7. Point to the thumbnail in the third row, fifth column, called **Sunset Sky (Text)**, and then click to apply this style to the bicycle. See Figure 4-18.

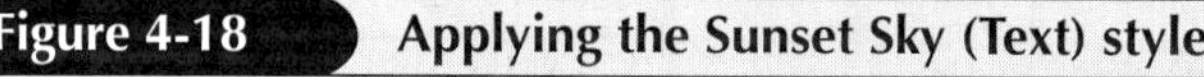

Figure 4-18 **Applying the Sunset Sky (Text) style**

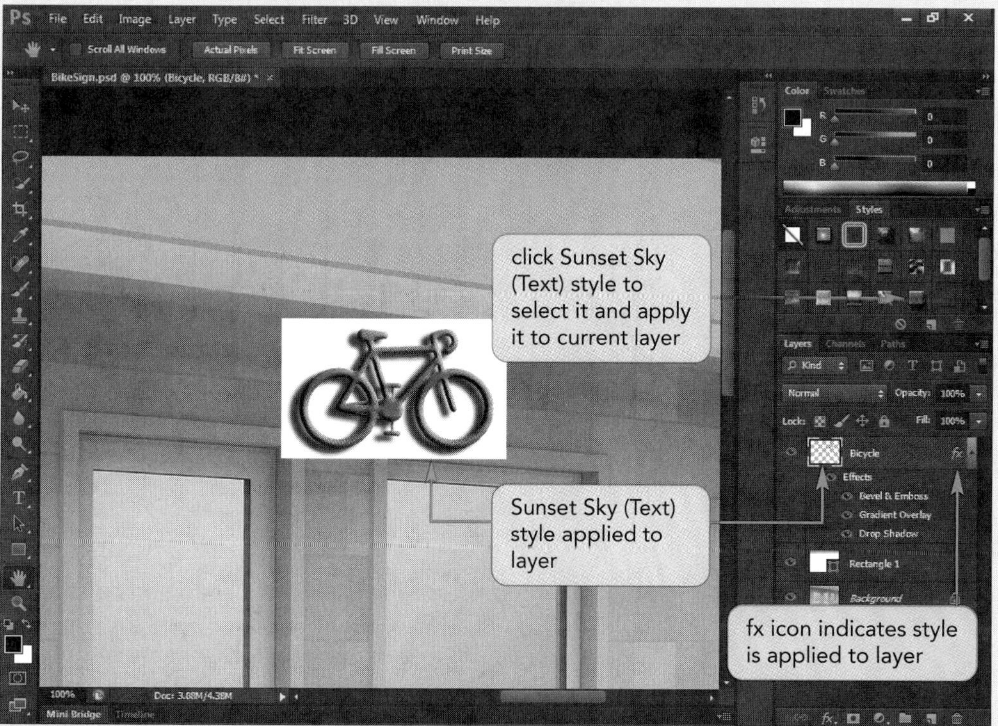

Shevchenko Nataliya/Shutterstock.com; Black Images/Shutterstock.com

Although this style was designed for text, it can be applied to any object. It includes three effects: Bevel & Emboss, Gradient Overlay, and Drop Shadow. You can hide any of these individual effects just as you can hide layers.

8. In the Layers panel, click the **Eye** icon to the left of Drop Shadow to hide that effect. The bicycle no longer has a shadow.
9. Click again in the same spot to turn the effect back on.
10. Hide the Gradient Overlay effect. The bicycle has returned to its original color, but with the Drop Shadow and Bevel & Emboss effects still applied.
11. Save the file as **SunsetBike.psd** in the Photoshop4\Tutorial folder.

You can leave a style preset as it is, or you can modify it to create a custom style preset. You'll modify the Sunset Sky (Text) style to see if you can achieve a better effect for the sign.

Using the Layer Style Dialog Box

You can modify a layer style using the Layer Style dialog box. For example, you might want to change the width of an outline (called a **stroke**) or the angle of a shadow. You can access the Layer Style dialog box by double-clicking the *fx* label to the right of the layer name, or through the Layer command on the menu bar. See Figure 4-19.

Figure 4-19 **Layer Style dialog box**

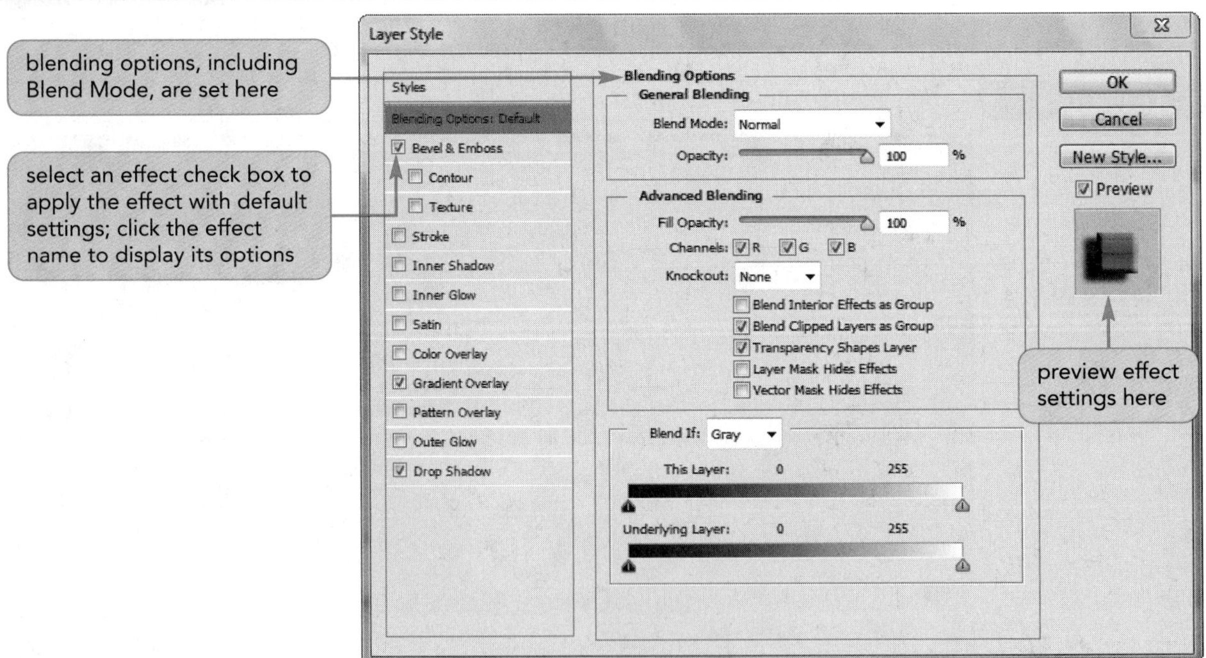

By default, the center of the Layer Style dialog box displays blending options, such as the blending modes discussed in Tutorial 3, and the fill opacity. However, the dialog box also includes a number of other options that are not visible when you first open the dialog box. In fact, the Layer Style dialog box behaves in ways you might not have seen before. On the left side of the dialog box, under the Blending Options: Default heading, you can click a check box to select an option such as Drop Shadow or Outer Glow and apply the default settings for that option. When you do, the effect is applied, but you are not given the opportunity to modify the effect. However, if you click the name of the effect rather than the check box, you select the effect and the center of the Layer Style dialog box changes to display options for the selected effect.

The effects available in the Layer Style dialog box are listed and described in the table in Figure 4-20.

Figure 4-20 **Effects in Layer Style dialog box**

Layer Style	Effect
Bevel & Emboss	Combines highlights and shadows to create a beveled effect that makes an object look three-dimensional
Stroke	Outlines the object—usually text—with a color, gradient, or pattern
Inner Shadow	Gives the layer an indented or recessed appearance by placing a shadow inside the edges of the layer content
Inner Glow	Adds a glow inside the layer content
Satin	Adds shading to the object's interior to give it the appearance of satin
Color Overlay	Fills the layer content with color
Gradient Overlay	Fills the layer content with a gradient
Pattern Overlay	Fills the layer content with a pattern
Outer Glow	Adds a glow outside the layer content
Drop Shadow	Places a shadow behind the layer; you can specify the angle and opacity of the shadow and its distance from the layer object, among the things

You've presented a draft of your sign to Lee, and she thinks it would be more effective without the gradient overlay and drop shadow. You'll experiment with different layer styles to see if you can achieve a better effect.

TIP

You can also double-click a layer thumbnail to open the Layer Style dialog box.

To use the Layer Style dialog box and save the new style:

1. In the Layers panel, double-click **fx** to the right of the Bicycle layer name. The Layer Style dialog box opens.
2. If necessary, drag the dialog box by its title bar up and to the right, and pan the document so you can see the bicycle.
3. In the Layer Style dialog box, click the **Gradient Overlay** check box to turn the effect back on. Because you clicked the check box and not the effect name, none of the Gradient Overlay effects is displayed in the right pane.

   Next, to see the options for an effect, you'll click the name of the effect rather than the check box.
4. Click **Drop Shadow**. The Drop Shadow settings are displayed in the right pane of the dialog box.

   You can change the blend mode of the shadow, its opacity, and its angle. If you would like the angle that you set to apply to all other effects so they are consistent, click the Use Global Light check box to select it. You can also change other shadow options, such as the distance from the object it is shadowing, and its size.
5. Decrease the Distance setting for the drop shadow from 10 pixels to **5** pixels. The shadow is now closer to the bicycle.
6. Click the **Drop Shadow** check box to deselect it. See Figure 4-21.

Figure 4-21 Deselecting Drop Shadow

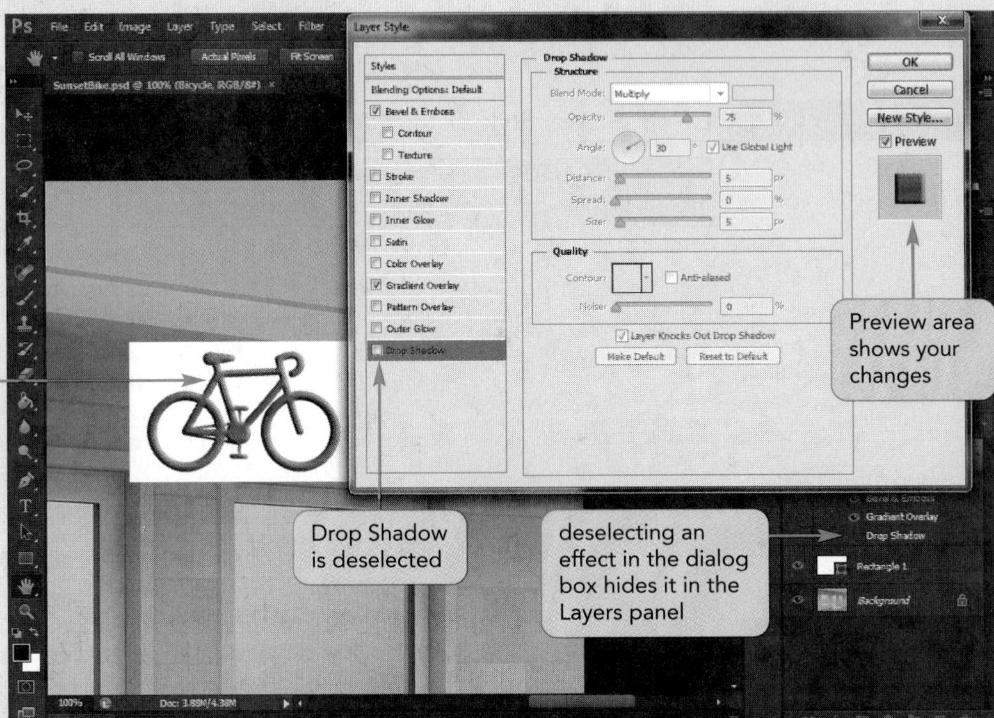

Shevchenko Nataliya/Shutterstock.com; Black Images/Shutterstock.com

In the Layer Style dialog box, the Preview area shows the effect without the drop shadow, and in the Document window, the bicycle on the sign no longer has the shadow.

7. Click the **Gradient Overlay** check box to deselect it. The bicycle appears in its original color, but it still has the Bevel & Emboss effect applied. You'll save this style so you can use it again in the future.
8. On the right side of the Layer Style dialog box, click the **New Style** button; the New Style dialog box opens.
9. Type **BikeSign** in the Name box, click the **Include Layer Effects** check box to select it, if necessary, and then click the **OK** button.
10. Click the **OK** button to close the Layer Style dialog box. The image of the bicycle on the sign now includes the new style you created.
11. Save the file as **EffectSign.jpg**, using the default JPEG Options, in the Photoshop4\Tutorial folder, close SunsetBike.psd without saving it, and then exit Photoshop.

In this session, you learned how to use the color selection tools, including the Color panel, the Color Picker, and the Eyedropper tool. You sampled colors, applied them to objects, and added them to the Swatches panel. You also worked with styles and made changes in the Layer Style dialog box to enhance parts of your image.

In the next session, you'll modify the image further so you can show Lee what your sign will look like hanging above the entrance of the store.

REVIEW

Session 4.1 Quick Check

1. By default, Photoshop uses the ____________ color when you draw or paint with one of the tools found in the Tools panel.
2. What tool in the Tools panel can you use to sample a color?
3. Define a color scheme, and give three examples of different types of color schemes.
4. ____________ is the process of mixing two colors to achieve an approximation of an unavailable color.
5. What does *gamut* mean?
6. Sometimes colors are defined by ____________ values, which are unique strings of six letters and numbers.
7. The ____________ panel displays a library of commonly used colors.

SESSION 4.2 VISUAL OVERVIEW

You can experiment with the angle of a fill to achieve different effects.

In the Gradient Fill dialog box, you can select the gradient, which can combine multiple colors.

The gradient fill style determines how the colors are laid out in the gradient. For example, they can be linear or **radial** (emanating out like a bull's eye).

Pattern fills include many different texture options.

A **fill layer** is a layer filled with a solid color, a pattern, or a gradient. This gradient fill uses multiple colors.

This gradient fill layer is transparent, and affects the Beach layer beneath it, but not the Rider layer.

A gradient fill layer blends the foreground color with transparent pixels, or it blends two or more other colors.

You can let underlying layers show through by setting the opacity of a fill layer.

sn4ke/Shutterstock.com; Jane Hosie-Bounar

FILL LAYERS, SHAPES, AND PAINTING

Use the options bar to set the **diameter**, or width, of the brush tip.
The Brush Presets panel lets you preview how brush tips will look when you stroke the canvas.
You can display the panel menu to choose from many different brush preset libraries.
To create an exact brushstroke, create a work path and then stroke the path.
Clicking once with a brush adds a single stroke.
Brush tip choices include leaves, flowers, and other natural objects.

Shevchenko Nataliya/Shutterstock.com; Black Images/Shutterstock.com

Adding Fill Layers

You can add a fill layer to a Photoshop file using the Create new fill or adjustment layer icon at the bottom of the Layers panel. You can use fill layers to colorize black-and-white photographs or to produce interesting effects—for example, placing an image so it has a gradient or patterned background. When you add a fill layer, you set its opacity to determine how much of an effect it will have on underlying layers. You can also move a fill layer in the Layers panel so it applies to some layers and not others, as shown in Figure 4-22.

Figure 4-22 Adding a solid color fill layer

an Opacity setting of 60% lets the background show through
Girl layer is unaffected by color fill
image with no fill layer applied
the mask is empty so the whole layer beneath the mask shows
green color fill layer only affects the layer beneath it

Jane Hosie-Bounar

Photoshop links every fill layer to a layer mask. A **layer mask** hides part of a layer so it doesn't show through. By default, the layer mask for a fill layer is empty so the whole layer shows through. You'll work with masks in Tutorial 5.

In Figure 4-22, the green, solid color fill layer is set at 60% opacity, and it has been placed beneath the Girl layer so it affects only the black-and-white Background layer, which is the only layer beneath it in the Layers panel. At this opacity, the fill layer makes the background photograph look as if it has been shot through a green-colored lens filter. If the fill layer were set to 100% opacity, it would completely hide the bottom layer.

You can add a gradient fill layer to produce an immediate and powerful effect in a composition without changing the pixels in any other layer. The default gradient combines the foreground color with transparent pixels; however, in the Gradient Fill dialog box, you can choose from many gradient presets, each with a different effect. You can also modify a gradient by making changes in the Gradient Fill dialog box. See Figure 4-23.

Figure 4-23 Gradient Fill dialog box

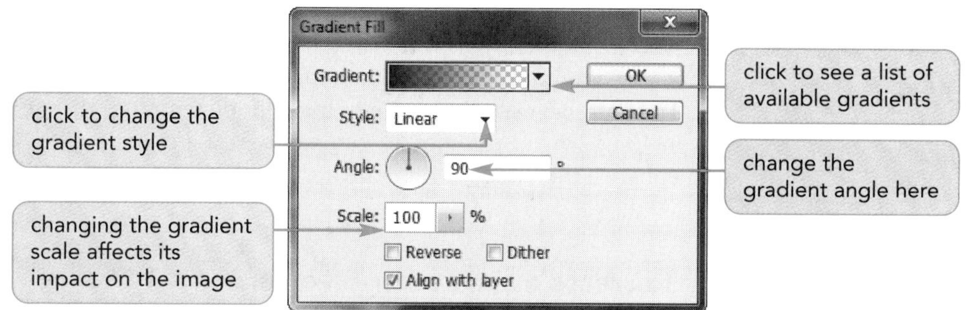

Given the number of options for changing a gradient fill, you could very easily spend hours playing with gradients to find the one that works best with your composition. Later in this session, you'll experiment with a few settings to see what works best in the image you're modifying.

A pattern fill layer works in much the same way both the solid fill and gradient fill layers work. When you add the pattern fill, it appears on its own layer in the Layers panel. Just as gradients and other layers in Photoshop include presets, so do pattern fill layers. When you first add a pattern fill layer, Photoshop applies the default pattern at 100% opacity. You can change the opacity, and you can drag the pattern fill layer in the Layers panel to change which layers it affects. To change the pattern, you use the Pattern Fill dialog box shown in Figure 4-24.

Figure 4-24 Pattern Fill dialog box

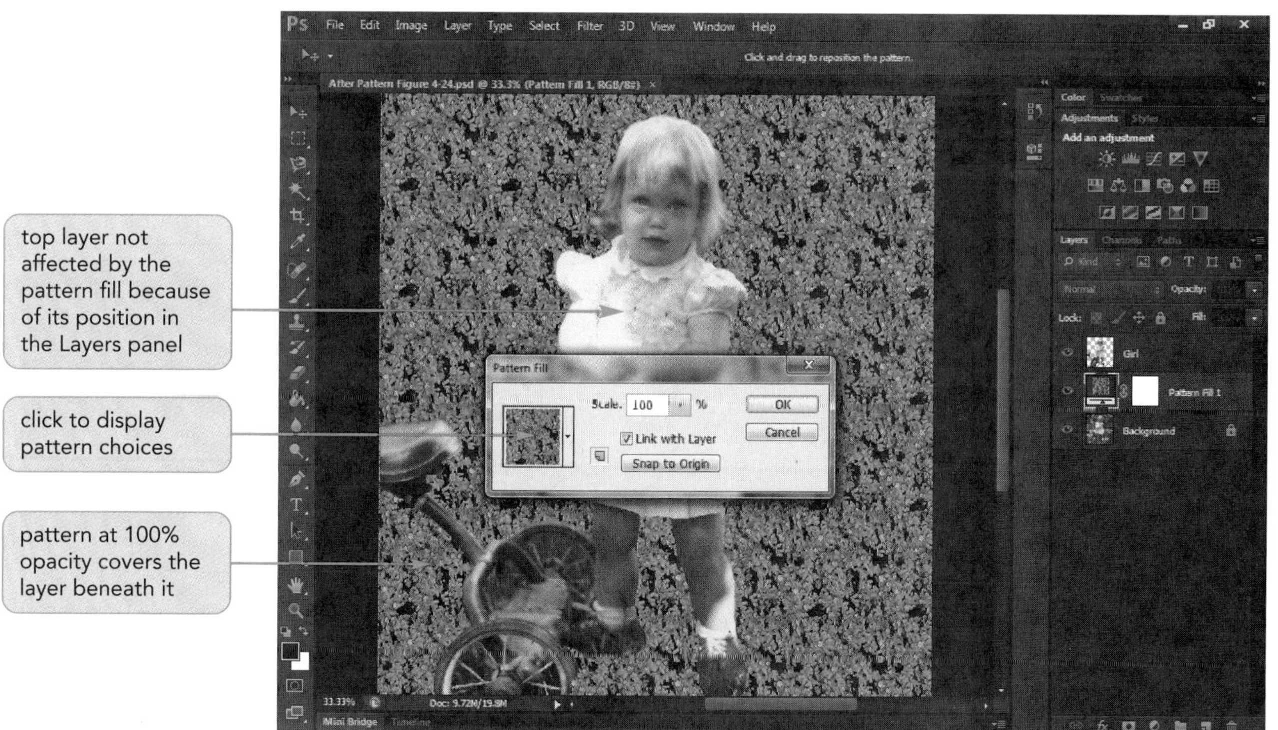

Jane Hosie-Bounar

You can choose from additional presets in the Pattern Fill dialog box by selecting a different preset group. For example, you can choose Rock Patterns, Nature Patterns, Color Paper, and different texture pattern sets. You can also modify the scale of a pattern. For example, if you modify the scale of a rock pattern, the size of the rocks in the pattern will increase by the percentage you specify in the dialog box.

Creating a Solid Color Fill Layer

Because a solid color fill layer is separate from the content it affects, it provides flexibility you wouldn't have by adjusting the color directly in the image itself. Once you add the layer, you can adjust its opacity and blending mode to achieve a variety of effects.

Lee has given you an image of the silhouette of a cyclist at a beach that she might want to use in her summer ad campaign. You'll experiment with a solid color fill layer to enhance the image and create a more dramatic effect.

To create a solid color fill layer:

1. Start Photoshop while pressing the **Ctrl+Alt+Shift** keys, and click **Yes** to delete the Settings File when prompted. Reset Photoshop to the default Essentials workspace layout, and then reset all tools.
2. Open **FillLayers.psd**, located in the Photoshop4\Tutorial folder, and then in the Layers panel, click the **Rider** layer.
3. At the bottom of the Layers panel, click the **Create new fill or adjustment layer** icon, and then click **Solid Color**. The Color Picker (Solid Color) dialog box opens. This dialog box is essentially the same as the Color Picker dialog boxes you worked with earlier.
4. In the Color Picker (Solid Color) dialog box, select any **blue** color, and then click the **OK** button. The color layer appears on top of the image so nothing shows through. You can change the opacity of the fill layer so the layers beneath it show through.
5. In the Layers panel, change the Opacity to **30%**. The rider shows through the blue layer; however, this effect would be more powerful if the layers were in a different order.
6. In the Layers panel, drag the **Color Fill 1** layer down below the Rider layer. See Figure 4-25.

Figure 4-25 Adding a fill layer

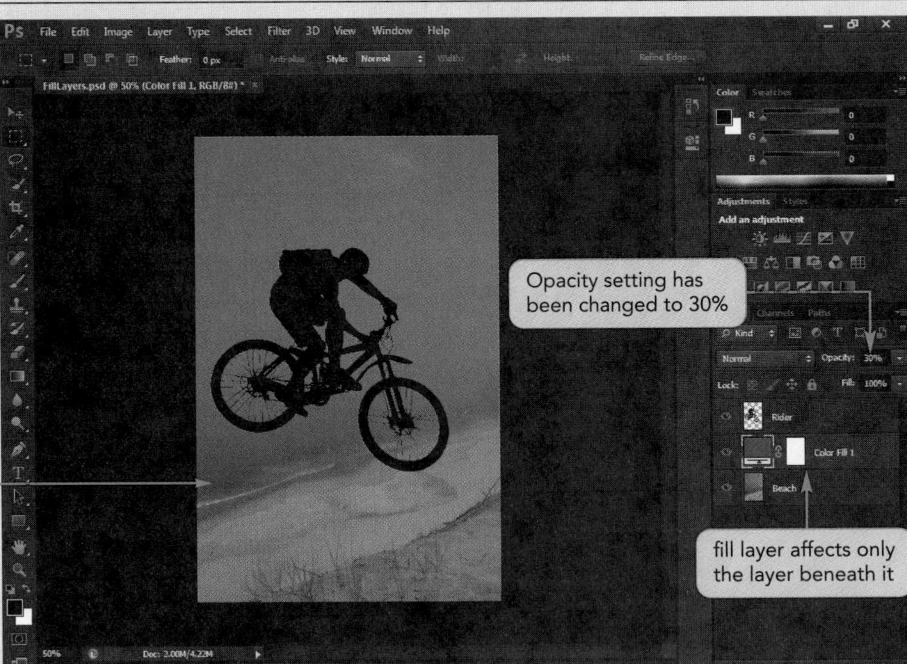
Opacity setting has been changed to 30%
lower opacity lets the background Beach layer show through
fill layer affects only the layer beneath it
File Edit Image Layer Type Select Filter 3D View Window Help
Rider
Color Fill 1
Beach

sn4ke/Shutterstock.com; Jane Hosie-Bounar

The image of the rider is now on top of the fill layer that you created, and the effect is more dramatic.

7. At the top of the Layers panel, click the **Set the blending mode for the layer** button, and then click **Divide**. The layer fill effect is brighter than it was using the Normal blending mode.
8. Save the file as **RiderEffects.psd** in the Photoshop4\Tutorial folder, and leave the file open.

Creating a Gradient Layer

You can also add a gradient layer to a composition. Gradients are an easy way to add dramatic effects to your compositions, as shown in Figure 4-26.

Figure 4-26 **Gradient effects**

sn4ke/Shutterstock.com

When you add a gradient layer, Photoshop opens the Gradient Fill dialog box. The default gradient combines the foreground color with transparent pixels, using a Linear style, with a 90-degree angle for the gradient. Changing any of these settings changes the look of the gradient. For example, you can change the Style setting to Radial, Angle, Reflected, or Diamond. You can also choose from other gradient presets by clicking the Gradient picker button in the dialog box to display the Gradient picker. See Figure 4-27.

Figure 4-27 Gradient picker on Gradient Fill dialog box

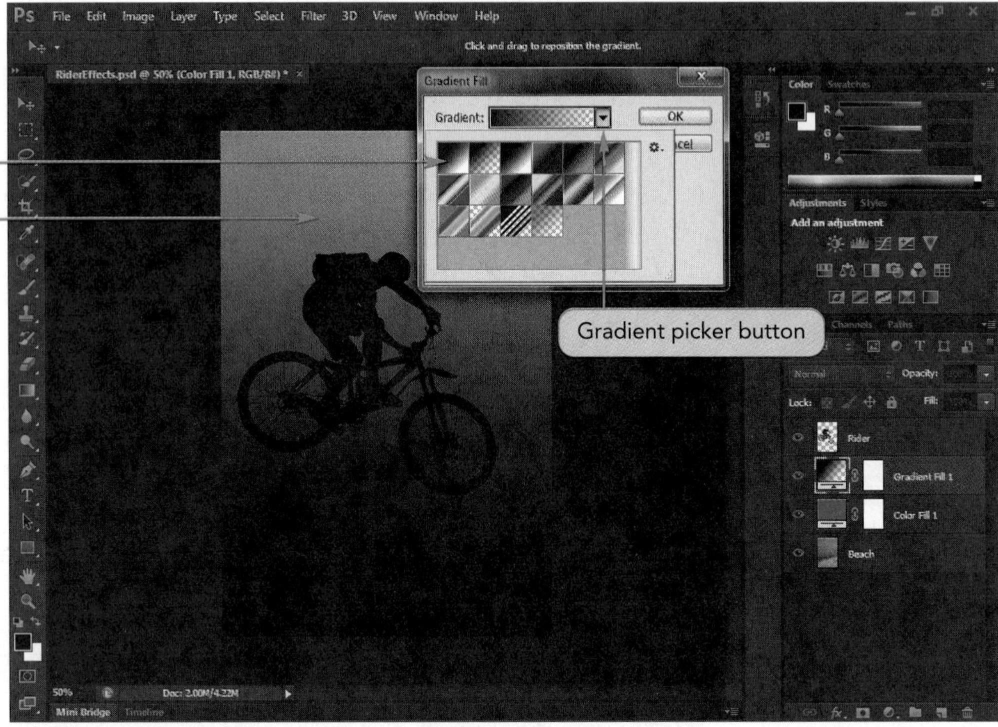

sn4ke/Shutterstock.com; Jane Hosie-Bounar

The Gradient picker displays a variety of gradient presets, some that use the background and foreground colors and others that have different color combinations, including foreground to transparent. If you apply a gradient and then decide you want to change it, you can double-click the gradient thumbnail on the gradient fill layer to reopen the Gradient Fill dialog box.

Next, you'll see if you can achieve a better effect using a gradient fill layer. You'll hide the solid fill layer so only the gradient affects the image.

To add a gradient layer:

1. In the Layers panel, hide the **Color Fill 1** layer, change the foreground color to any blue color, and make the background color black.
2. Click the **Beach** layer, click the **Create new fill or adjustment layer** icon at the bottom of the Layers panel, and then click **Gradient**. The Gradient Fill dialog box opens, and the default gradient is applied to the image.
3. In the Gradient Fill dialog box, click the **Gradient picker** button to display the Gradient picker. The first gradient choice on the list creates the gradient using the foreground color and the background color, in this case, blue and black.
4. Click the first gradient choice to see the effect. The effect is dramatic, but it completely covers the beach image and makes the cyclist hard to see. Changing the Opacity setting for the fill layer will allow more of the beach image to show through.
5. In the Gradient Fill dialog box, click the **OK** button, and then in the Layers panel, change the opacity of the layer to **30%**.

6. Double-click the **gradient thumbnail** on the Gradient Fill 1 layer. The Gradient Fill dialog box opens again. Click the **Gradient picker** button, click the **Spectrum** gradient (the first gradient in the third row), and then click the **OK** button. The Spectrum gradient is applied to the image using the gradient layer.
7. Save **RiderEffects.psd** and leave it open.

Next, you'll try a different effect by choosing from the pattern layers available in Photoshop.

Creating a Pattern Layer

Although there are only five patterns listed in the default Pattern Fill dialog box, there are many patterns to choose from if you select a different library of pattern presets. Pattern galleries include Artist Surfaces, Color Paper, Nature Patterns, and Rock Patterns, among others. When you select a pattern library, you are prompted to either replace the current patterns or append the list to the current pattern list, just as you were prompted to replace or append styles in Session 4.1.

You'll experiment with adding pattern layers to see the effects you can achieve.

To add a pattern layer:

1. In the Layers panel, hide the **Gradient Fill 1** layer, click the **Beach** layer, click the **Create new fill or adjustment layer** icon, and then click **Pattern**. The Pattern Fill dialog box opens, and Photoshop applies the default pattern fill to the image.
2. In the Pattern Fill dialog box, click the **pattern** thumbnail to open the Pattern preset picker, and then click the **More options** button to open the menu.
3. Click **Color Paper** on the menu, and then click the **OK** button to replace the current patterns with the selected patterns.

   Trouble? If you are prompted to save changes to the current patterns before replacing them, click the No button.

   The Color Paper patterns are displayed in the Pattern preset picker.
4. Scroll down the list and then click the **Red Textured** pattern to select it. See Figure 4-28.

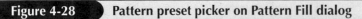

Figure 4-28 Pattern preset picker on Pattern Fill dialog

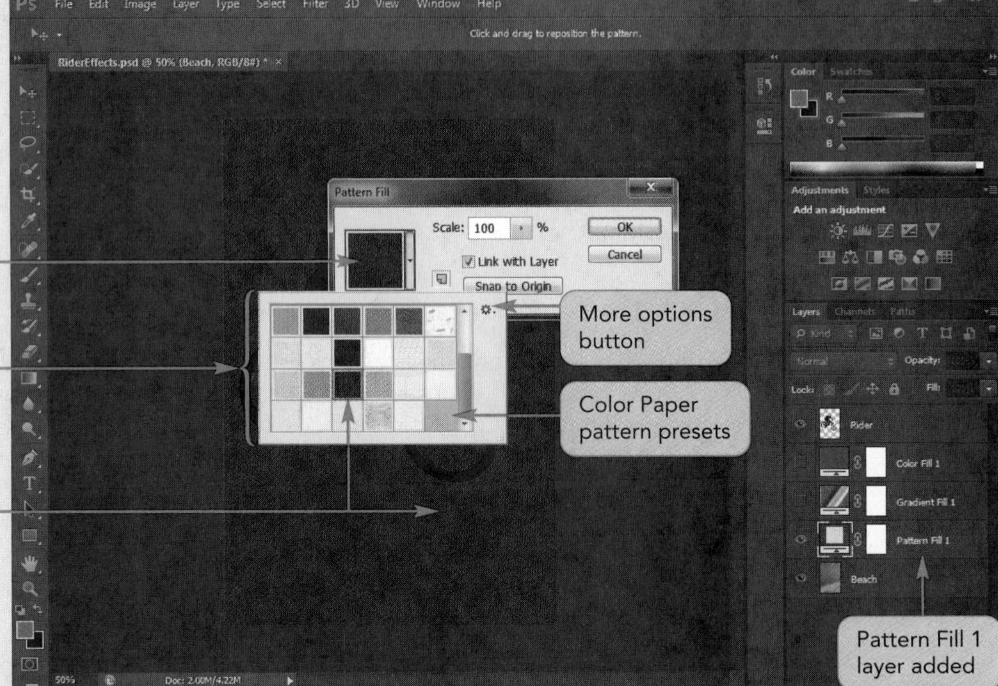

sn4ke/Shutterstock.com

The pattern appears in the dialog box and is applied to the image. The effect is interesting, but it's not the effect you had in mind. You'd like to add a sense of outdoor mountain adventure to the image.

5. Click the **More options** button to open the menu again, click **Rock Patterns**, and then click the **OK** button. The rock patterns replace the paper patterns.

6. Click **Stones** (the second pattern) to select it, change the scale to **200%**, and then click the **OK** button.

   Of the three layer fills you tried, the gradient fill best conveys the excitement that Lee wants for her summer ad campaign, so you'll hide the pattern fill layer and redisplay the gradient fill.

7. In the Layers panel, hide the Pattern Fill 1 layer, redisplay the Gradient Fill 1 layer, and then save **RiderEffects.psd** and close the file.

Adding Shape Layers vs. Filling Pixels on a Layer

You've already seen that Photoshop includes a number of drawing tools that you can use to enhance a composition. Now that you know what a fill layer is, and understand what a mask does, you can delve more deeply into options available to you when using the drawing tools. For example, you can choose to add a shape to an image by making a nondestructive edit (by adding a vector shape on a separate layer) or by making a destructive edit (by adding a raster shape, which fills in the pixels on a layer). See Figure 4-29.

Figure 4-29 Shape mode versus Pixels mode

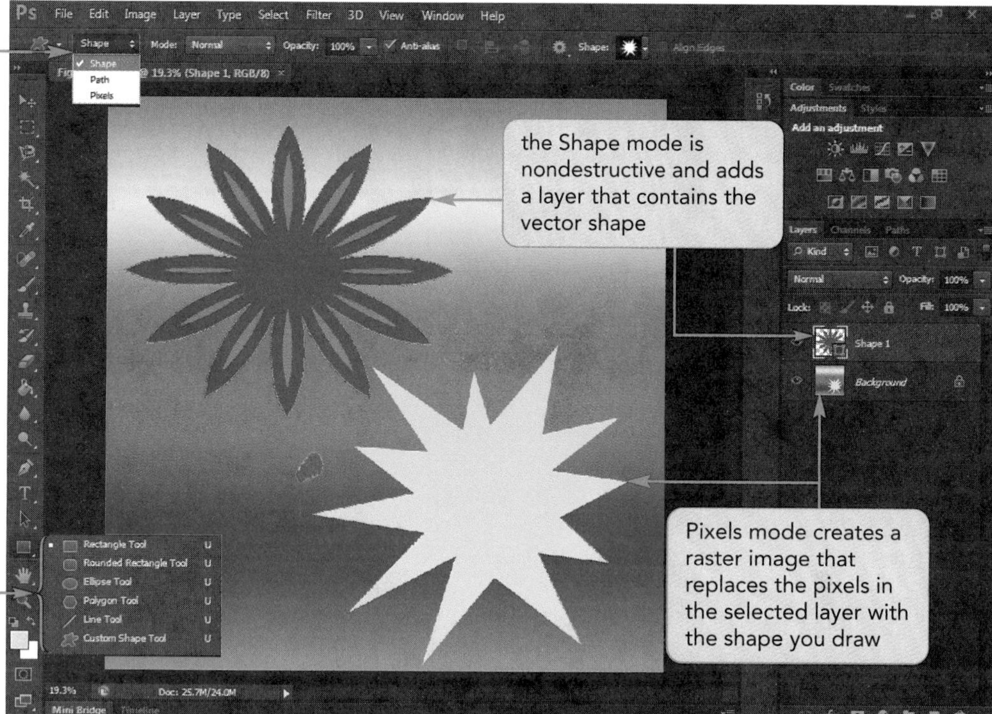
click to choose tool mode
the Shape mode is nondestructive and adds a layer that contains the vector shape
Pixels mode creates a raster image that replaces the pixels in the selected layer with the shape you draw
any of these tools adds a shape

When you draw a vector shape such as the rectangle you added in Session 4.1 or the purple flower shown in Figure 4-29, you are adding a shape layer. **Shape layers**, also called vector layers, are a form of nondestructive editing because they don't alter the pixels on the layer or layers beneath them. When you select the Shape tool mode on the options bar, you are choosing to add a vector shape on a shape layer. You can also add a raster shape to a layer using the same drawing tool but a different tool mode. Pixels mode places the shape you draw directly on a layer as a raster or bitmap object, overwriting the pixels beneath it. The yellow Starburst shape in Figure 4-29 appears directly on the multicolored Background layer that contains it. It consists of pixels that are painted over the original pixels on the layer. Adding the Starburst to the Background layer is an example of destructive editing.

The third option for adding a shape is the Paths option, which is covered later in this tutorial. If you draw a shape with the Paths option selected on the options bar, you are creating a temporary work path.

Specifying Fill and Stroke Options for a Vector Shape

When you add a shape using the Shape tool mode, you can specify the fill of a shape before you draw it, or, if it is selected, after you draw it. Like the layers you added earlier in this tutorial, a shape layer can be filled with a solid color, with no color (transparent), with a gradient, or with a pattern. To select the fill color, you click the Fill button on the options bar. See Figure 4-30.

Figure 4-30 **Shape fills**

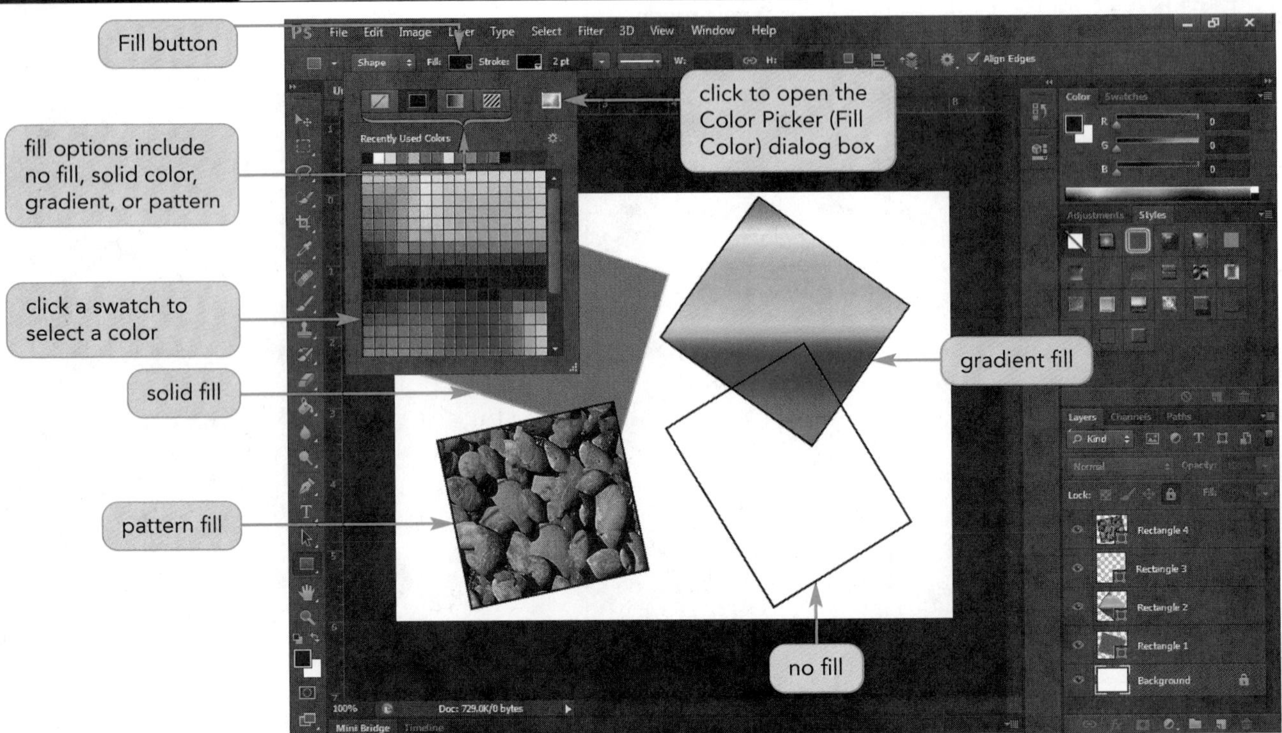

You also have a wide choice of settings for the stroke used to draw a vector shape. A stroke can be a solid color, or it can be transparent, a gradient, or a pattern. Other stroke options include width and line type (for example, solid, dashed, or dotted), as well as alignment, caps, and corner options. See Figure 4-31.

Figure 4-31 **Stroke options**

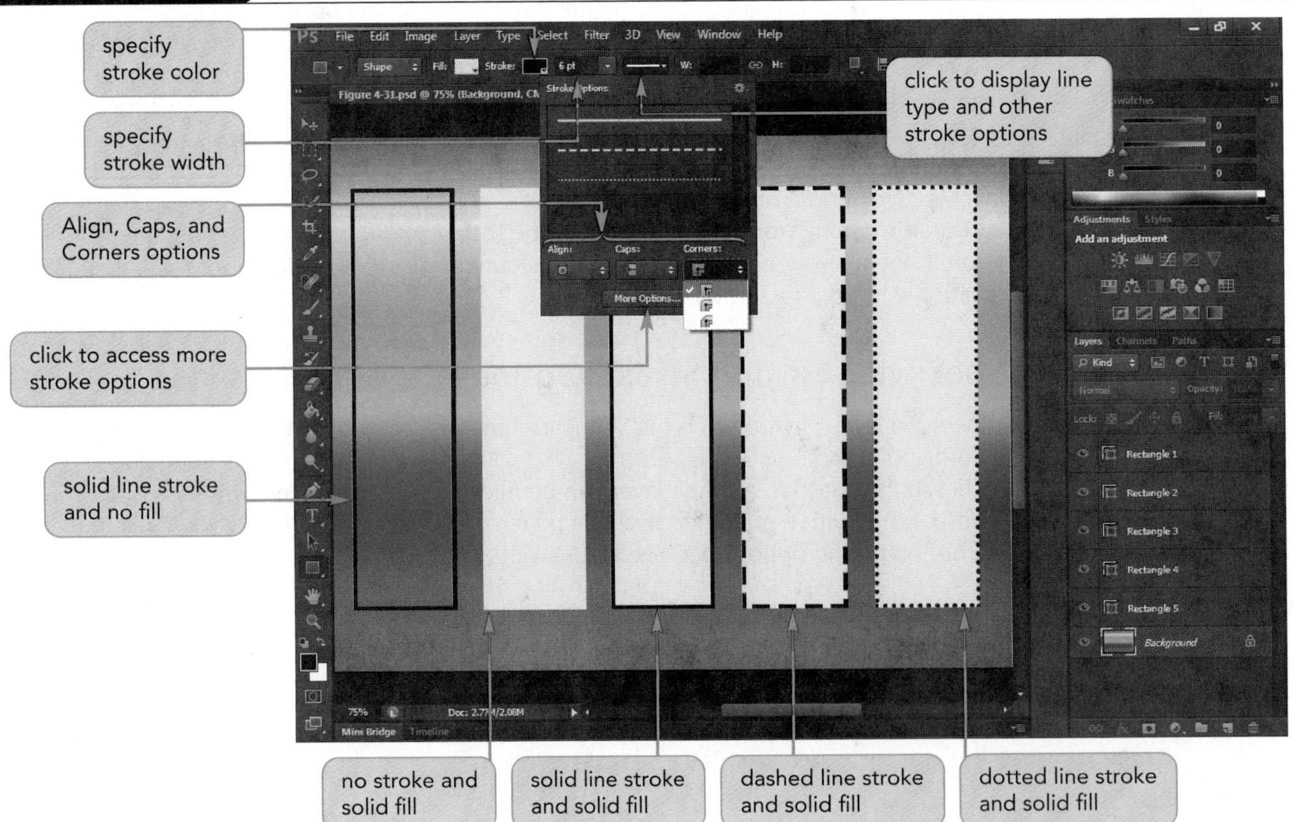

The Align options determine whether the stroke is aligned at the center of the path of the pointer as you drag, or inside or outside the path. The Caps settings let you specify how the ends of stroked paths are finished. Caps options include Butt, Round, or Square. The Corners setting determines whether a corner is mitered (square), rounded, or beveled. If you click the More options button in the Stroke Options panel, you can specify additional custom options, such as the distance between dots or dashes in a stroke, or the point size of the dots or dashes.

Adding a Shape Layer (Vector Objects)

You have already added a rectangle shape to an image. In this section, you'll learn about the different kinds of shapes you can add to a composition. To add a shape layer, click one of the shape tools in the Tools panel to select it. When the tool is selected, the options bar lets you choose to draw a shape layer (a vector object), to draw a path, or to fill the drawn object with pixels (a bitmap, or raster, object). Figure 4-32 describes the vector, path, and fill options on the options bar as well as the options for creating complex shapes by combining, intersecting, and excluding shapes as you draw.

Figure 4-32 **Shape options bar buttons**

Button	Name	Effect
	Shape	Specifies tool mode options, including Shape, Path, and Pixels
	Fill	Specifies the fill color as well as whether the fill is a solid color, pattern, or gradient
	Stroke	Specifies the stroke width
	Set shape stroke type	Specifies stroke type as a solid line, a dashed line, or a dotted line; also specifies stroke alignment, caps, and corners
W:	Set shape width	Specifies shape width and unit of measurement, either Pixels, Inches, Centimeters, Millimeters, Points, or Picas
	Link shape width and height	Constrains width and height proportions; if the width changes, the height changes proportionally, and vice versa
H:	Set shape height	Specifies shape height and unit of measurement, either Pixels, Inches, Centimeters, Millimeters, Points, or Picas
	Path operations	Specifies whether to put the shape on a new layer or to combine, subtract, intersect, exclude, or merge shapes in the same layer
	Path alignment	Specifies alignment and distribution options
	Path arrangement	Specifies arrangement of shapes on the canvas to control visibility, from front to back
	More options	Specifies whether a shape is unconstrained as it is drawn or has a fixed size or proportions and whether or not it is drawn from the center
	Align Edges check box	Aligns the edges of new shapes with existing shapes

To draw a shape, you must first activate the desired drawing tool in the Tools panel, and then select the Shape tool mode and stroke type on the options bar.

Before you begin to draw, click the Path operations button on the options bar and make sure New Layer is selected. As you drag the mouse pointer on the canvas, an outline of the object appears. When you release the mouse button, the object is filled with the fill color specified on the options bar, and the shape appears on its own layer in the Layers panel. To specify drawing options, click the More options button on the options bar to choose additional specifications. For example, if you are drawing a rectangle, you can constrain it to a square by selecting the Square option button. You can also specify a fixed or proportional size or select the From Center check box so you can start your drawing at the center and drag outward.

INSIGHT

Rasterizing a Vector Shape

Many of the digital image-editing tools in Photoshop manipulate pixels. What does this mean if you want to modify a vector shape using these tools? As you learned in Tutorial 1, a vector graphic is a collection of points, lines, curves, and shapes stored as a set of mathematical instructions. It is not pixel based. Therefore, to use the tools that manipulate pixels, you need to rasterize the image—or change it into a raster object. To rasterize a vector image, right-click the layer in the Layers panel, and then click Rasterize Layer. You can then use any of the pixel-editing tools to enhance or refine the shape on the layer.

Next, you'll add a vector shape to an image. Then, you'll copy the style that you created for the bicycle in the previous session and apply it to the sign in the image as well, so you can show Lee what your sign will look like over the doorway of the store.

To draw a vector shape:

1. Open **Storefront.psd**, located in the Photoshop4\Tutorial, display it at 50% magnification, and center the bicycle image in the Document window.
2. Restore the default background and foreground colors, press the **X** key to switch the background and foreground colors, and then click the **Background** layer in the Layers panel, if necessary.
3. In the Tools panel, click the **Rectangle Tool** button, and on the options bar, confirm that the fill color is white (the foreground color).
4. On the options bar, click the **Stroke** button, click the **Solid Color** icon, and click the **Black** color swatch (the last shape in the second row), if necessary.
5. On the options bar, highlight the current stroke width, type **2**, and then press the **Enter** key. The stroke width is now 2 points.
6. On the canvas, draw a rectangle so it contains the bicycle, as shown in Figure 4-33.

Figure 4-33 **Drawing a rectangle shape layer**

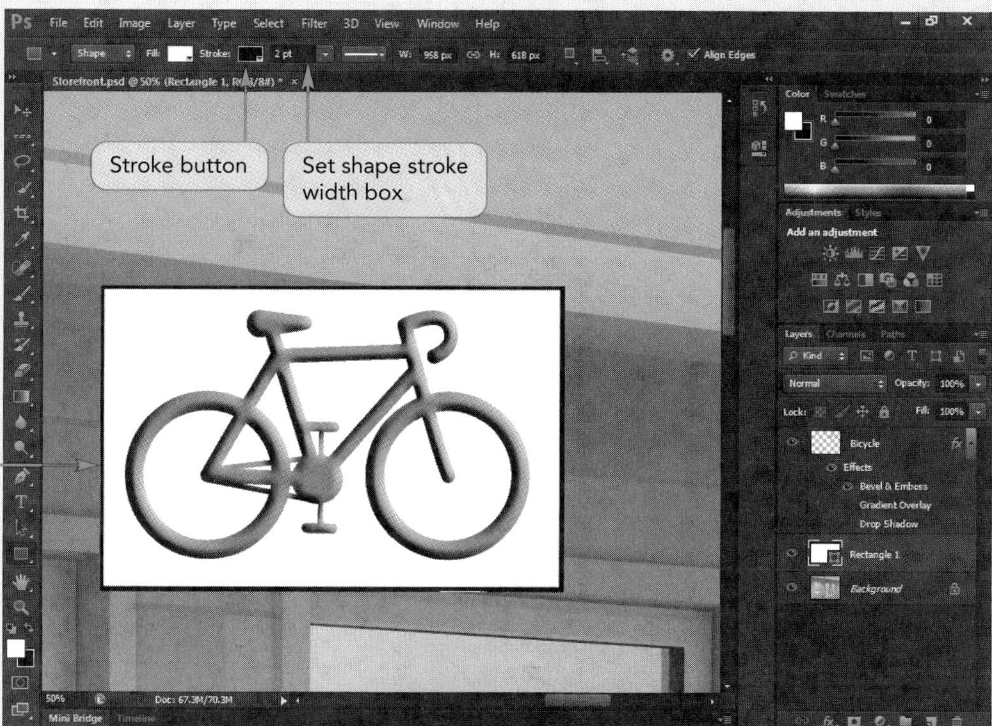

Shevchenko Nataliya/Shutterstock.com; Black Images/Shutterstock.com

7. Change the name of the new layer from Rectangle 1 to **Sign**.

   Next you'll copy the style applied to the Bicycle layer and paste it on the Sign layer.

8. In the Layers panel, right-click the **Bicycle** layer and then click **Copy Layer Style** on the context menu. Then, right-click the **Sign** layer and click **Paste Layer Style**. The sign now has the Bevel & Emboss effect that you applied to the bicycle. Note that the effects that were hidden for the Bicycle layer are still hidden for the Sign layer. Click to the left of Gradient Overlay to turn that effect on for the Sign layer. See Figure 4-34.

Figure 4-34 Copying and pasting the Bicycle layer style

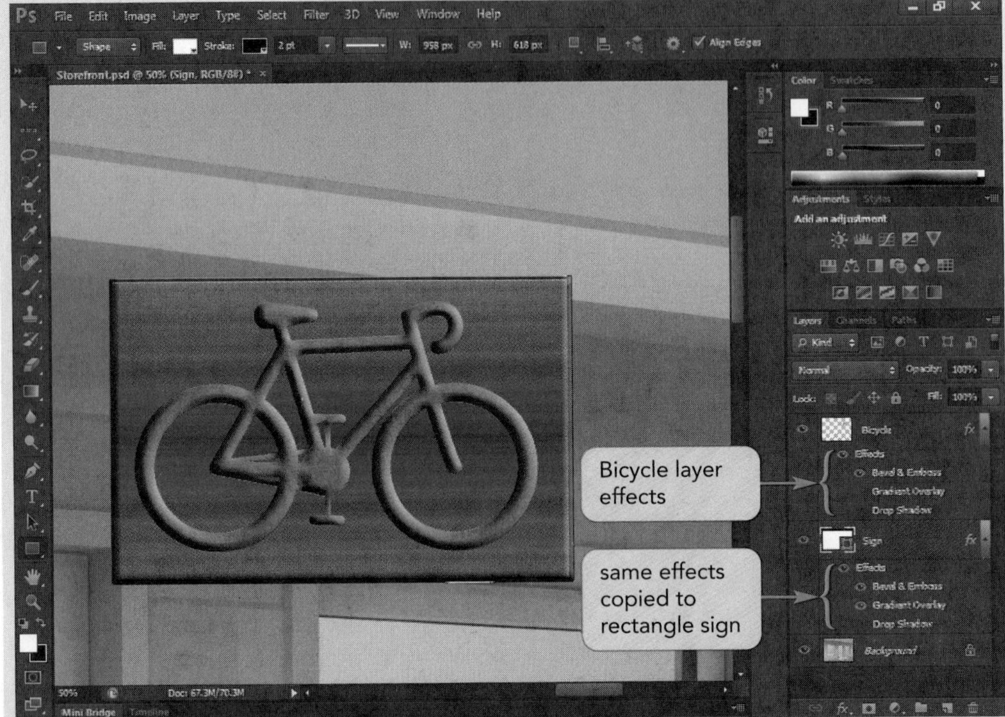

Shevchenko Nataliya/Shutterstock.com; Black Images/Shutterstock.com

9. Save the file as **BikeSignFinal.psd** in the Photoshop4\Tutorial folder, and leave the file open.

INSIGHT

Using the One-Click Method

If you select one of the shape tools in the Tools panel and click the canvas rather than drag to create the shape, the Create *Shape* dialog box opens, where *Shape* is the name of the shape you're drawing, for example, Polygon or Ellipse. In the Create *Shape* dialog box, you can specify a number of different shape attributes. For example, in the Create Polygon dialog box, you can specify the width, the height, and the number of sides of your polygon. You can also specify whether or not you want smooth corners. If the polygon you want to draw is a star, you can select the Star check box, and then specify a percentage value for the indents around the star. If you select the Custom Shape tool and then click the canvas, the Create Custom Shape dialog box includes From Center and Preserve Proportions check boxes, as well as Width and Height boxes. Once you have finished specifying shape settings in the Create *Shape* dialog box and have clicked the OK button, Photoshop draws the shape on the canvas at the location you clicked, and applies the settings you specified. The one-click method is yet another way Photoshop lets you work with vector objects, and it can be an excellent method for creating an object when you know its exact specifications.

To draw more complex shapes, you can modify existing vector layers using one of the Path operations options. See Figure 4-35.

Figure 4-35 **Excluding, subtracting, combining, and intersecting**

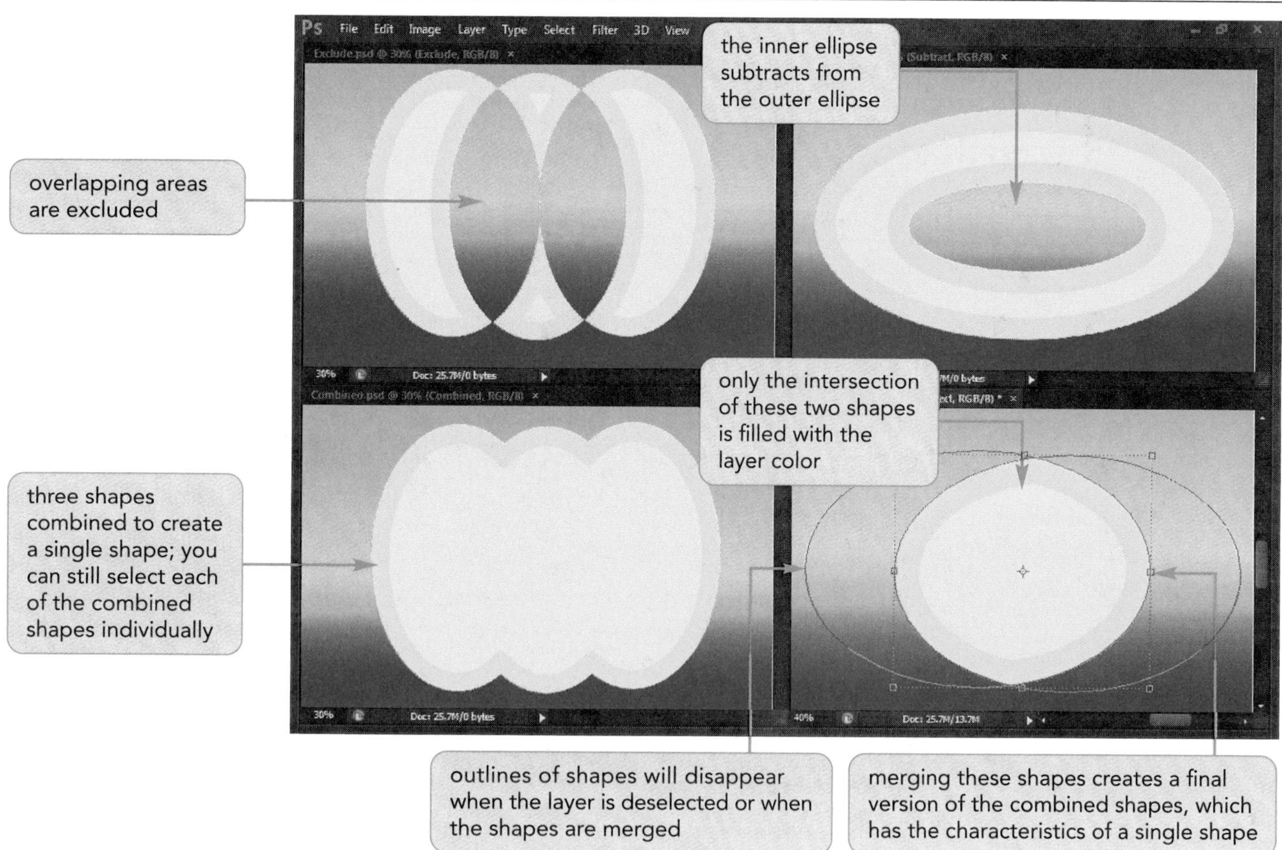
overlapping areas are excluded
the inner ellipse subtracts from the outer ellipse
only the intersection of these two shapes is filled with the layer color
three shapes combined to create a single shape; you can still select each of the combined shapes individually
outlines of shapes will disappear when the layer is deselected or when the shapes are merged
merging these shapes creates a final version of the combined shapes, which has the characteristics of a single shape

TIP

You can also leave the New Layer option selected and press the Shift key to add to the shape layer.

For example, to add to an additional vector object, select the Combine Shapes option on the Path operations menu, and then draw an additional shape. The new shape appears on the same layer as the existing shape, and the two shapes are combined to create a new shape. However, you can still select each of the combined shapes individually if you want to change the way they are arranged on the layer. To select individual shapes used in a combined shape, you use the Path Selection tool in the Tools panel, which functions much like the Move tool.

You can subtract from a shape you have drawn by clicking the Subtract Front Shape option on the Path operations menu, and then drawing a new shape on top of the original shape. When you release the mouse button, the new shape you drew is subtracted from the original shape so the color on the layer beneath it shows through. You can also achieve the same effect by leaving the New Layer option on the Path operations menu selected and pressing the Alt key to subtract from the shape layer.

You can click Intersect Shape Areas on the Path operations menu to create a shape that is the intersection of two or more shapes that you draw. If you click the Exclude Overlapping Shapes, intersecting areas are transparent, and areas outside of the intersections are opaque (or filled).

Finally, you can merge shapes after you have finished combining, subtracting, and intersecting separate shapes to create the final drawing. Once you merge shapes, they have the characteristics of a single shape and can no longer be selected individually using the Path Selection tool. To merge shapes into a final drawing, click the Merge Shape Components option on the Path operations menu.

Lee has asked you to stop work on the sign for now so you can work on an image of a tricycle that she needs immediately. She plans to use it in one of her ads, and wants you to frame the image using the drawing tools. You'll use the vector tools and options to create a frame around the tricycle.

To modify a vector shape by subtracting:

1. Open **Tricycle.jpg**, located in the Photoshop4\Tutorial folder, reset the Essentials workspace, restore the default foreground and background colors, and reset all tools.
2. In the Tools panel, click the **Eyedropper Tool** button, and then right-click in the image and click **31 by 31 Average** in the context menu. Then, sample the **red** color on the tricycle, near the pedal.

   Trouble? If the red color is assigned as the background color, press the D key to reset the colors, and then click the Set foreground color icon in the Color panel to make it active. Repeat Step 2.
3. In the Tools panel, click the **Rectangle Tool** button. On the options bar, click the **More options** button, click **Fixed Size**, and then specify a width of **8.5** inches and a height of **6** inches.
4. Click the canvas and start to drag. When you move the mouse pointer, Photoshop immediately adds a rectangle layer using the dimensions you specified. If necessary, use the Move tool to drag the rectangle so that it covers the canvas completely.
5. In the Tools panel, click the **Ellipse Tool** button.
6. On the options bar, click the **Path operations** button, and then click **Subtract Front Shape**.
7. On the options bar, click the **More options** button, click **Proportional**, enter a width to height proportion of **4** to **3**, and then click the **From Center** check box to select it.
8. In the Document window, display the rulers, and then place guides at 4.25 inches on the horizontal ruler and 3 inches on the vertical ruler.
9. Position the mouse pointer over the intersection of the guides. The mouse pointer now has a minus sign to the right of the crosshairs, indicating that the shape you draw will subtract from the previous shape.
10. Click at the intersection of the guides, and drag to draw an ellipse over the rectangle. Release the mouse button when the ellipse is about 1/4 inch from the top and bottom edges of the rectangle. The ellipse is subtracted from the rectangle when you release the mouse button, exposing the image underneath. See Figure 4-36.

Figure 4-36 **Subtracting a shape**

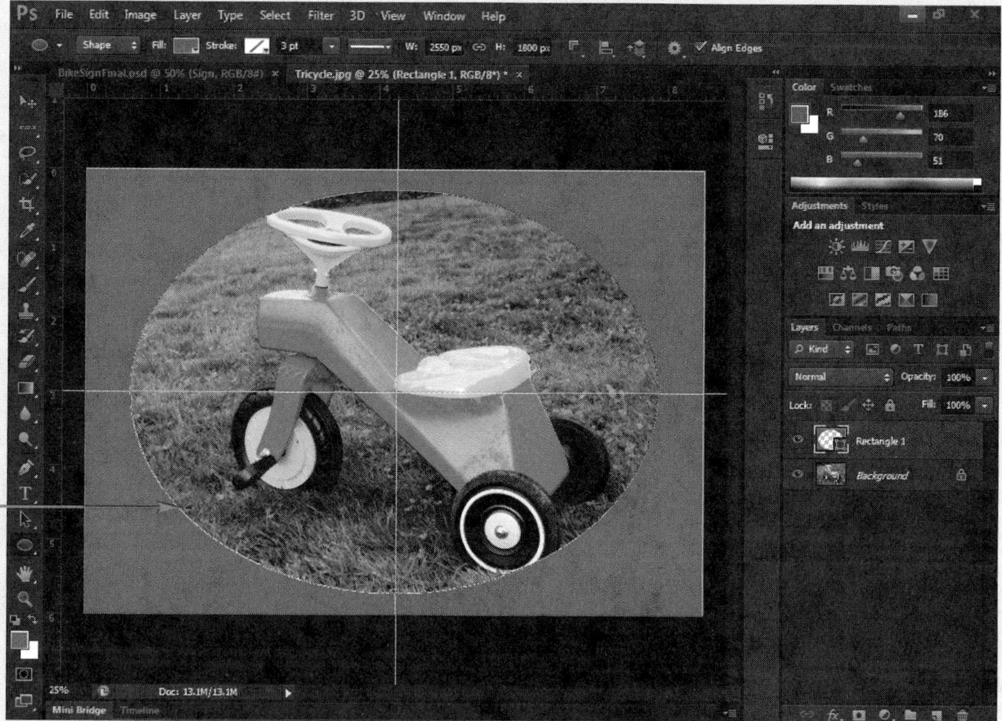
the ellipse is subtracted from the rectangle to expose the image beneath

Ingvald Kaldhussater/Shutterstock.com

11. In the Styles panel, click the **BikeSign** thumbnail (the last thumbnail on the Styles panel) to apply that style to the Rectangle 1 layer.
12. Save the file as **FrameTrike.psd** in the Photoshop4\Tutorial folder and then close the file.

You can switch from one option to another on the options bar as you draw to create a complex shape that is the result of adding, subtracting, and intersecting geometric objects. Next, you'll use a combination of standard shapes and add them together to create a shape that combines a Stop sign, a bicycle, and images of pedestrians. Lee wants to use it as one of the signs inside her store.

To modify a vector shape by subtracting and merging:

1. Open **StopSign.psd**, located in the Photoshop4\Tutorial folder, size it to fit the screen, and click the **Background** layer, if necessary.
2. In the Tools panel, click the **Polygon Tool** button.

   Trouble? If you can't find the Polygon Tool button, right-click the Ellipse Tool button, and then click the Polygon Tool button on the list of hidden tools.
3. On the options bar, select a **black** fill color, if necessary, a **black** stroke color, and then, in the Sides box, type **8**.

4. Click beneath the *T O* in STOP, press and hold the mouse button, and drag to draw an octagon. With the mouse button still depressed, drag left or right to rotate the polygon until its top edge runs parallel to the top of the canvas. Release the mouse button. The STOP text is not very visible because it is the same color as the octagon. See Figure 4-37.

   Trouble? If your octagon is not positioned correctly, use the Move tool to reposition it.

Figure 4-37 **Drawing a polygon**

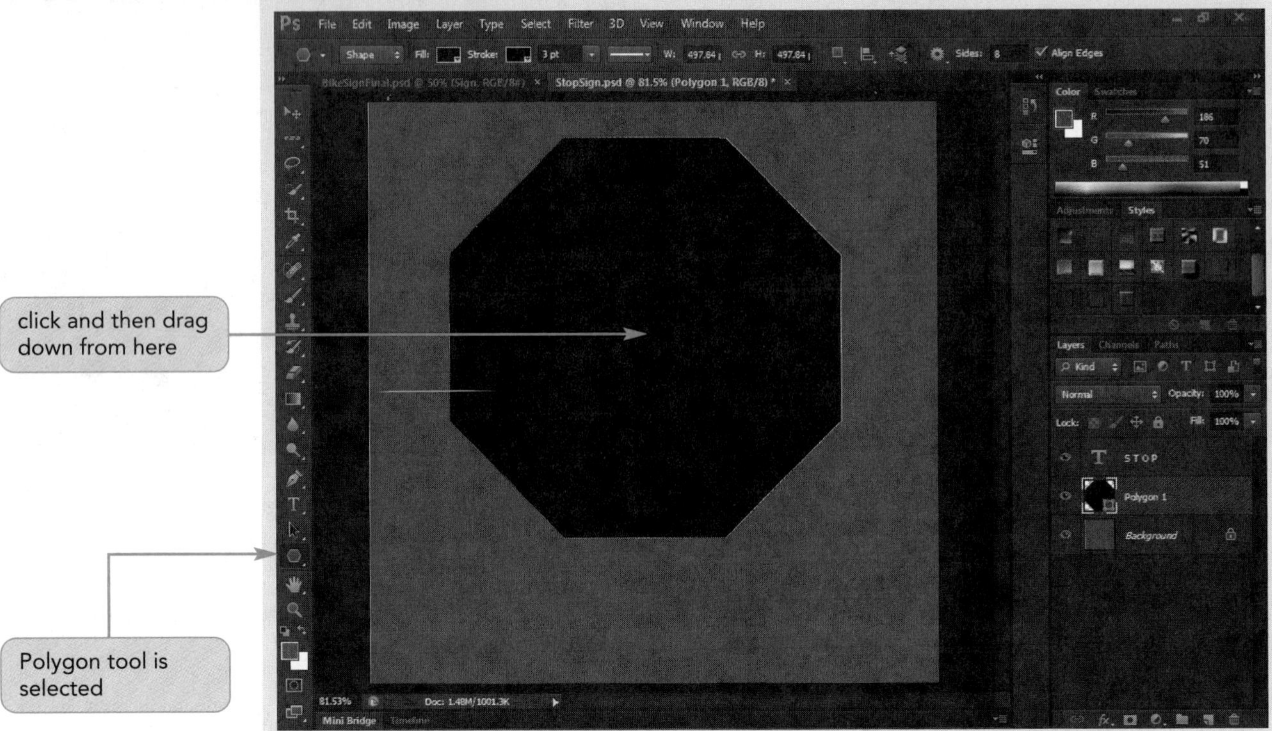

5. Click the **Polygon Tool** button in the Tools panel, if necessary, and then on the options bar, click the **Path operations** button, and click **Subtract Front Shape**. Click in the center of the octagon, and then drag to create another slightly smaller octagon on top of the original one. Drag left or right to rotate the polygon until its top edge runs parallel to the top of the canvas, but don't worry about centering it exactly. You'll adjust its position in the next step using the Path Selection tool, which lets you select a single shape on the layer, rather than the entire layer contents.

6. In the Tools panel, click the **Path Selection Tool** button, point to the second octagon, and then drag it into position. See Figure 4-38.

Figure 4-38 Placing the second octagon

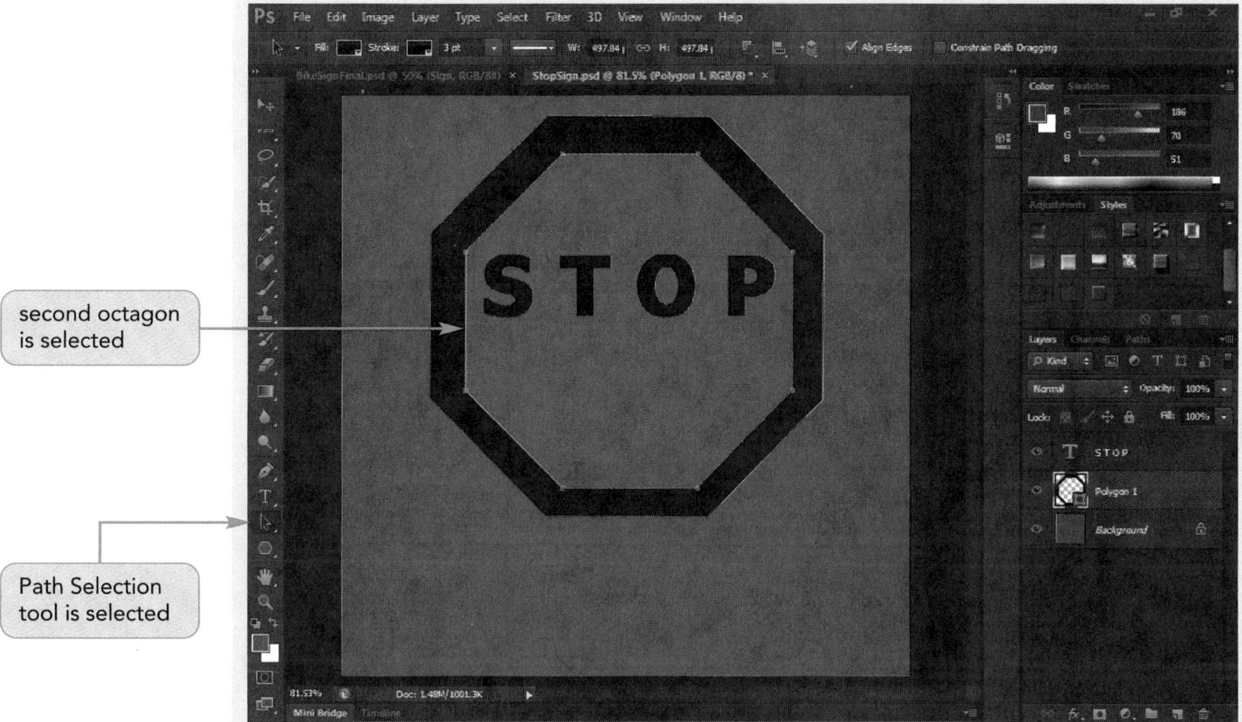
second octagon is selected
Path Selection tool is selected
STOP

Next, you'll merge two octagons on the layer so that they have the characteristics of a single shape.

7. With the **Polygon 1** layer selected, click the **Path operations** button on the options bar, and then click **Merge Shape Components**.
8. In the Tools panel, verify that the **Path Selection Tool** button is selected, click on a black area of the merged shapes, and drag. Press the **Ctrl+Z** keys to undo the move. Both shapes move together, indicating that they have been merged; Photoshop considers them a single shape, and you can no longer use the Path Selection tool to select them individually.

Next, you'll add two custom shapes to the drawing and combine them into a single shape.

To combine two custom shapes:

1. In the Layers panel, click the **Background** layer, and then in the Tools panel, click the **Custom Shape Tool** button. On the options bar, click the **Custom Shape picker** button, and then click the **More options** button. Photoshop comes with a variety of different custom shapes.
2. Click **Symbols**, and then click the **OK** button to replace the current shapes.

   Trouble? If Photoshop displays a message asking if you want to save changes to the current shapes before replacing them, click the No button.
3. In the Custom Shape panel, double-click the **School** shape (two people walking), the last shape in the second row.
4. On the options bar, click the **More options** button, and then click **Defined Proportions** to constrain the proportions of the people, and click the **More options** button again to close the list.

5. On the options bar, set the fill and stroke colors to **white**.
6. Click in the image under the *S* and drag down and to the right to add the symbol.
7. On the options bar, click the **Path operations** button and then click **Combine Shapes**. The next shape you draw will be added to the people shape that you already drew.
8. Click in the image under the *P* and drag down and to the left to add the symbol a second time. Press the **V** key to select the Move tool, and confirm that the Show Transform Controls check box is selected. Both symbols appear on a single layer and are treated as a single shape. Because they have not been merged, you can still move them individually on the canvas using the Path Selection tool. See Figure 4-39.

Figure 4-39 Combining shapes

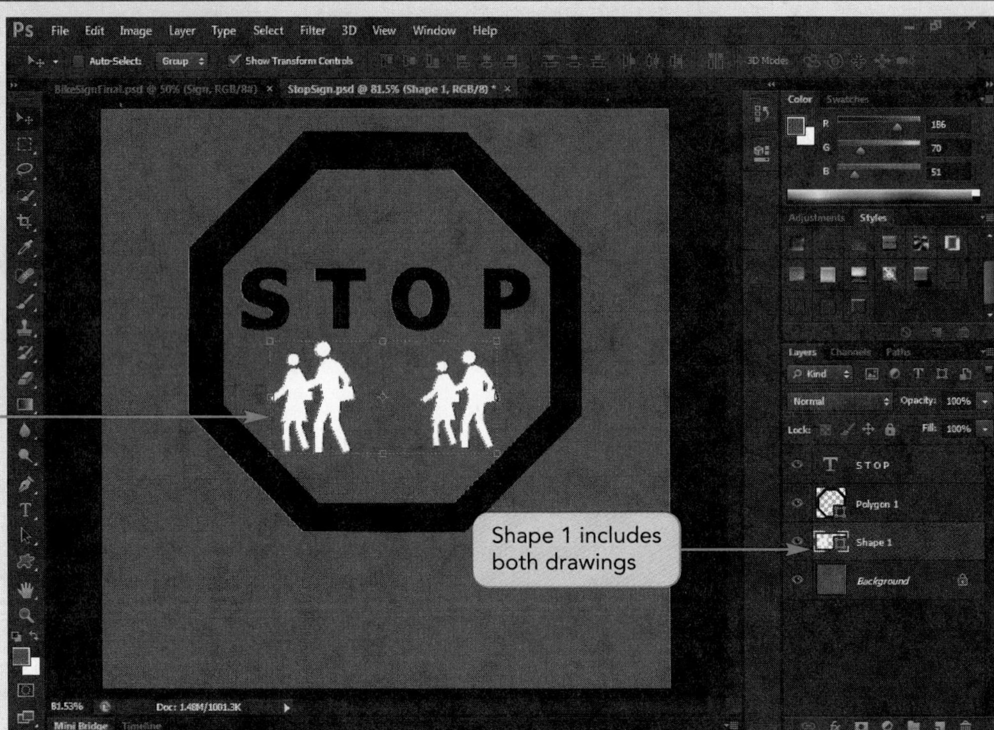
two drawings selected as a single shape
Shape 1 includes both drawings
STOP

9. Save the file as **Pedestrians.psd**, and close it. You'll show the sign to Lee to see if she wants to use it in the store.

Next, Lee wants you to add a symbol to a JPEG image she has put together for her latest campaign encouraging people to replace their old bicycles. You'll draw a bitmap shape over the background pixels to add a drawing without adding a new layer.

Using Fill Pixels (Bitmap/Raster Objects)

To draw a bitmap (or raster) shape, you select the tool with which you want to draw, for example, the rectangle or ellipse, and then select the Pixels tool mode on the options bar. As implied by the name, when you draw the shape using the Pixels tool mode, you are modifying the pixels in the area of your drawing by filling them with the foreground color. As such, you are making a destructive edit. When working in Pixels tool mode, you drag the mouse pointer on the canvas to draw the object. As you draw, an outline of the object appears. When you release the mouse button, the object appears filled with the foreground color on the current layer, replacing the pixels beneath it.

To draw a bitmap shape:

1. Open **Accident.jpg**, located in the Photoshop4\Tutorial folder, and save it as **IsItTime.jpg**, using the default JPEG Options, in the same folder.
2. Using the Eyedropper tool, take a point sample of the red text to set it as the foreground color.
3. In the Tools panel, click the **Custom Shape Tool** button.
4. On the options bar, click the **Custom Shape picker** button, and then double-click the **Question Mark** symbol (the second symbol in the second row).
5. On the options bar, click the **Pick tool mode** button, and then click **Pixels**. The pixels in the Background layer will be hidden by the pixels you add to the canvas as fill.
6. Click the **More options** button, click **Unconstrained**, and click the **From Center** check box to select it. Click the **More options** button again to close the list.
7. Click at the intersection of the two guides, and drag down and to the right to create a question mark. When you release the mouse button, the new pixels replace the original pixels on the Background layer. Once you save the file and close it, you will not be able to undo this change. See Figure 4-40.

Figure 4-40 **Drawing a bitmap shape**

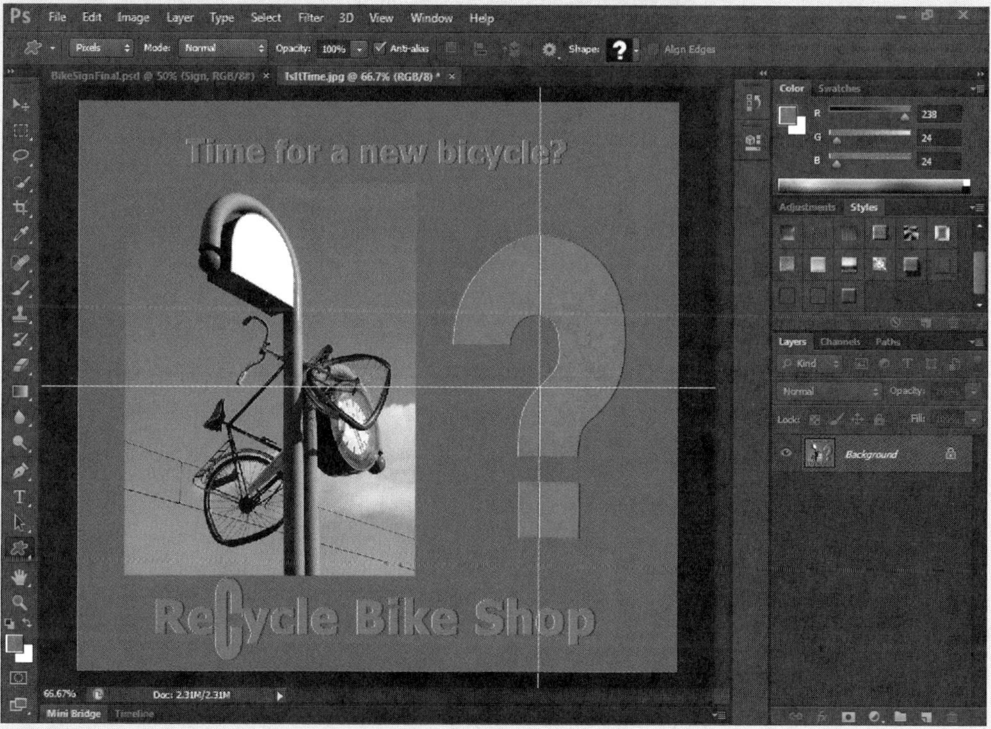

Björn Erlandsson/Shutterstock.com

8. Save **IsItTime.jpg**, and leave the file open.

Using the Brush Tool

The Brush and Pencil tools in Photoshop let you paint or draw on your images. If you are using a mouse, you have less control over your brushstrokes and pencil strokes than you would if you were using a Tablet PC with a **stylus**, which lets you write or draw directly on the screen. However, both tools are still valuable image-editing tools.

The Brush tool produces strokes that are **anti-aliased**—that is, even though you are working with pixels, your brushstrokes will have a smooth rather than a jagged appearance because Photoshop adds pixels to blend the edges into the background. Because anti-aliasing adds pixels, anti-alias settings increase file size. The **hardness** of the Brush tool is related to the amount of anti-aliasing applied to the brushstroke. A setting of 100% uses the least anti-aliasing, but still produces smooth edges. The Pencil tool is never anti-aliased; as a result, it can sometimes produce jagged or pixelated edges. See Figure 4-41.

Figure 4-41 **Brush and pencil strokes**

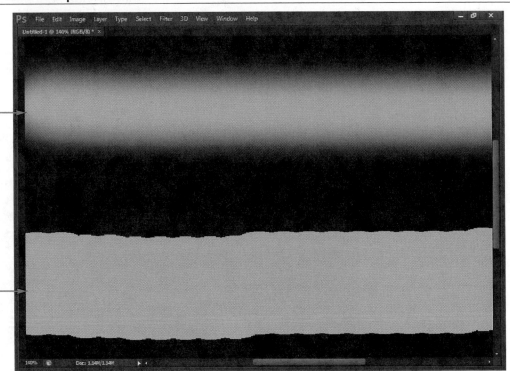

brushstroke is anti-aliased and smooth
pencil stroke is jagged, not smooth, with pixelated edges

In Figure 4-41, the top stroke was drawn with the Brush tool and the bottom stroke was drawn with the Pencil tool. Both strokes have identical diameter (width) and hardness settings. However, notice how different they look. The brushstroke is smooth because it is anti-aliased. The pencil stroke has hard edges and is not anti-aliased; in fact, you can distinguish the individual pixels along the edges. In this section, you'll focus on the Brush tool, but the skills you learn can also be applied to the Pencil tool.

Choosing Brush Settings and Adding Brushstrokes

When you select the Brush tool, the options bar displays the Brush tool options shown in Figure 4-42.

Figure 4-42 Brush tool options

Button	Name	Use To
	Tool Preset picker	Display the presets for the Brush tool, such as "Airbrush soft round 50% flow." You can choose to display presets for the current tool or for all of the tools.
	Brush Preset picker	Specify the size and the hardness for the brush or choose from a variety of presets, including Chalk, Dune grass, Stars, and certain preset brush hardness and size settings.
	Toggle the Brush panel	Expand and collapse the Brush panel display.
	Mode	Choose a painting mode for the brush.
	Opacity	Set brush opacity.
	Tablet pressure	Control brushstroke opacity based on the pressure you place on the tablet rather than via Brush panel opacity settings (this only applies when you are working on a tablet computer).
	Flow	Set the flow rate, or the amount of paint on the brush; a low percentage paints as if you have just dipped the brush lightly in paint, and a high percentage saturates the brush.
	Enable airbrush-style build-up effects	Turn on airbrush mode.
	Always use Pressure for Size	Control brushstroke size based on the pressure you place on the tablet rather than Brush panel opacity settings (this only applies when you are working on a tablet computer).

The Brush Preset picker displays a library of brush settings. You can set the diameter of the brush (measured in pixels) as well as the hardness of the brush. A brush with a high hardness setting will paint on the canvas in much the same way a physical paint brush with hard bristles will paint. Strokes will appear firm and full, with little space showing between the virtual bristles. A brush with a low hardness setting will paint like a brush with softer bristles. See Figure 4-43.

Figure 4-43 Working with brush presets

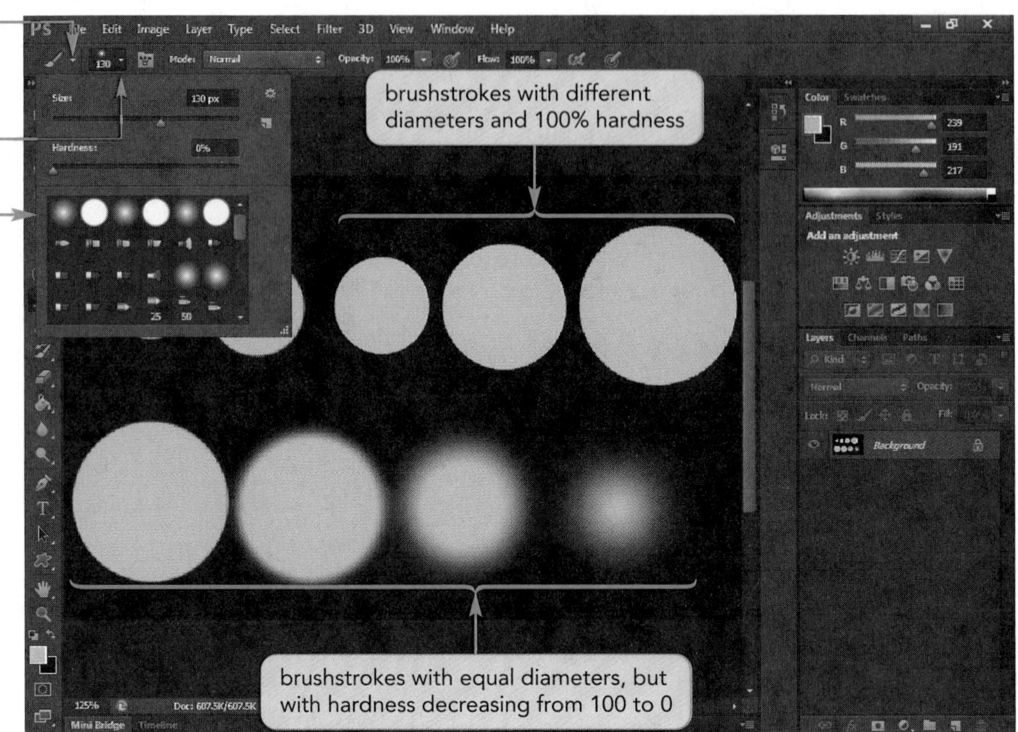

You can use the Brush Preset picker to choose from a variety of presets; however, the Brush Presets panel is a more convenient way to work with presets, and is covered later in this tutorial.

To paint with the Brush tool, set the foreground color you want to use, select the layer on which you want to paint, click the place you want to begin your brushstroke, and then drag the mouse to complete the stroke. When you have finished the first stroke, release the mouse button. You can repeat this procedure for each stroke in your composition.

You can also paint in straight lines with the Brush tool by using the click-Shift-click method. To draw a straight line, click the place on the canvas where you want to begin the stroke. Release the mouse button. Position the mouse over the point where you want to end the stroke and then Shift-click. Photoshop fills in the area between the first place you clicked and the last place you Shift-clicked with a straight brushstroke.

You'll use the Brush tool to add a chalky border to the image of the wrecked bicycle, much like the outline police might add at a crime scene. Lee wants to see if modifying that image will strengthen the material for her "Time for a Replacement?" campaign.

To paint using the Brush tool:

1. Ensure that IsItTime.jpg is open in the Document window.
2. In the Tools panel, click the **Brush Tool** button. The options for the Brush tool appear on the options bar.
3. Press the **X** key to switch the foreground and background colors and set the foreground color to white.
4. On the options bar, click the **Brush Preset picker** button. The Brush Preset picker displays the default size (13 pixels) and hardness (0%) for the Brush tool.

TIP

You can also press the B key to activate the Brush tool.

5. Change the brush size to **50** pixels, and then drag the brush pointer ◯ around the bicycle as if you are outlining the victim's body at a crime scene. See Figure 4-44.

Figure 4-44 Adding a brushstroke

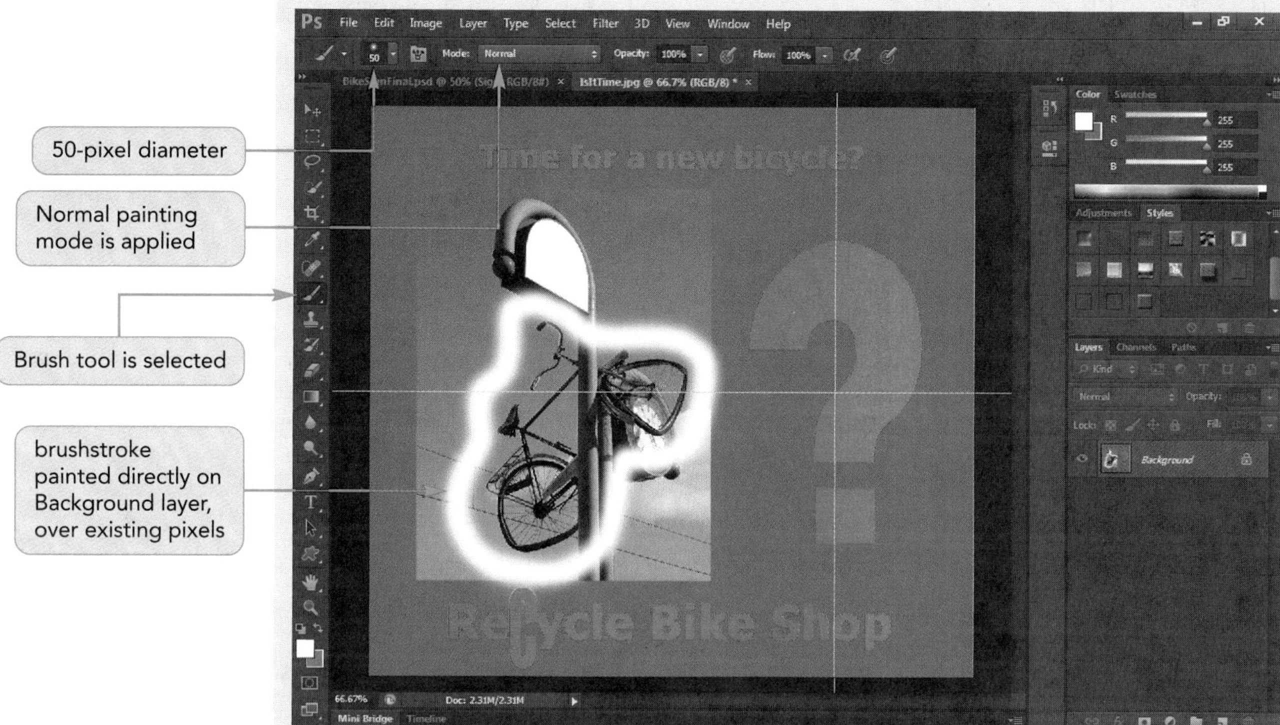
50-pixel diameter
Normal painting mode is applied
Brush tool is selected
brushstroke painted directly on Background layer, over existing pixels
Time for a new bicycle?
Recycle Bike Shop

Björn Erlandsson/Shutterstock.com

The brushstroke appears directly on the Background layer. The result is that the underlying pixels have been replaced, just as they were replaced when you used the Pixels tool mode to draw a shape.

6. Change the brush size to **30** pixels, click the **Mode** arrow, and then click **Dissolve**.
7. Drag slightly outside the stroke you just painted. Changing the mode results in a completely different effect.
8. Save **IsItTime.jpg** and then close it.

Now that you have had some practice working with brushstrokes, you'll switch back to the sign file so you can finish up that project for Lee. You'll use the Brush tool to add straight lines to your sign image to create a hinge to hang the sign. Because you'll add the lines to a layer that has a Bevel & Emboss effect, the lines you draw will also have a Bevel & Emboss effect.

To draw straight lines with the Brush tool:

1. Display **BikeSignFinal.psd** at 20% magnification in the Document window, pan the image so that the bicycle sign is at the right side of the Document window, and then select the **Bicycle** layer if necessary.

2. Press the **D** key to reset the foreground and background colors to the default, and reset all of the tools.
3. Open the **Brush Preset** picker and set the size of the brush to **90** pixels and the hardness to **100%**.
4. Position the brush pointer ◯ just to the left of the upper-left corner of the sign and then click. Photoshop adds the first point in the straight line you'll draw.
5. Position the brush pointer ◯ at the left of the lower-left corner of the sign, press and hold the **Shift** key, and then click.

   Photoshop draws a straight brushstroke along the left side of the sign. To "attach" the sign to the storefront, you'll draw another straight brushstroke from the upper-left corner to the storefront.
6. Position the brush pointer ◯ just to the left of the upper-left corner of the sign slightly overlapping the top of the brushstroke you just drew, and then click.
7. Position the brush pointer ◯ at the center of the wall above the door, press and hold the **Shift** key, and then click. The sign appears to be attached to the building by a wrought iron hanger. Because you added the brushstrokes to the Bicycle layer, the Bicycle layer style is applied to the brushstrokes. See Figure 4-45.

Figure 4-45 **Painting in a straight line**

the Bicycle layer style is applied to the brushstrokes
the click-Shift-click method was used to draw two straight lines
Bicycle layer is selected

Shevchenko Nataliya/Shutterstock.com; Black Images/Shutterstock.com

8. Save **BikeSignFinal.psd**, and keep the file open.

PROSKILLS

Verbal Communication: Understanding a Client's Needs Up Front

Before you begin working on a digital composition for a client, you must ensure that you fully understand what the client is looking for. To do so, you need to set up strong and reliable lines of communication, which will involve you not only offering your advice and expertise, but also listening to what the client is *really* saying. Helping your client clearly communicate his or her needs to you is essential before you dive into any project. For example, if your client asks you to create an ad for a magazine, that information should be just a starting point. You need to ask clarifying questions, such as: Is the ad aimed at a certain demographic or group? Is the magazine a conservative business magazine, an interior decorating magazine, or is it for teens—with an emphasis on pop culture? Are you trying to convey a certain mood? Should the text be in a particular font or color? Listen carefully, and give your client time to fully explain their vision for the ad. Even after your client has provided more details, it's a good idea to make sure you really understood what you were told. It can be helpful to use phrases such as "What I understood is" or "Let me see if I heard you correctly" to be sure you really know what's required.

By asking clarifying questions and restating your understanding of the client's needs, you can iron out many potential wrinkles ahead of time. That will save you time and effort in the short term, and in the long run, it will result in a happy client who will be more likely to request your services again—and recommend you to others.

Working with Brush Presets

The Brush and Pencil presets offer a great variety of brushstrokes and pencil shapes for you to choose from. The most convenient way to work with presets is to use the Brush panel or the Brush Presets panel. The Brush panel displays the brush tip shape and lets you modify size, angle, and roundness settings. The Brush Presets panel previews the brush tip shape and shows you what a brushstroke will look like. In this section, you'll work with the Brush Presets panel. It appears by default in the Painting workspace, so you'll switch to that workspace. See Figure 4-46.

Figure 4-46 Working with brush presets in the Painting workspace

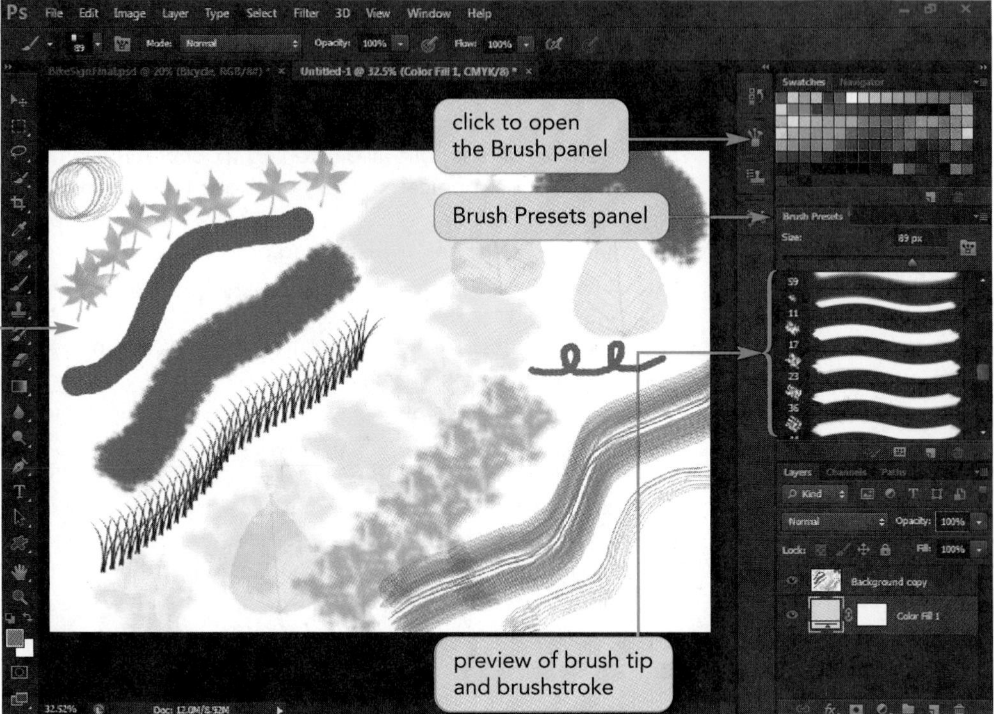

With the Brush tool, not only can you choose brush tips with different diameters and hardness settings, but you can also choose different paints as well. For example, you can choose a preset that mimics oil paint, one that mimics spray paint, or one that mimics chalk. You can also choose brush tips that paint leaves, spirals, butterflies, and other shapes.

Loading Other Presets

Photoshop provides numerous libraries of brush presets, and as a result, you have hundreds of choices for brushes. As you become more experienced in Photoshop, you'll develop a sense of which brushes you need for which effects, but as a novice, it's a good idea to experiment with as many presets and preset modifications as possible. Loading a brush preset library is basically the same as loading any other library. You do it from the panel menu, and, as with the Color, Swatches, and Styles panels you've already worked with, you need to determine whether you want to append the library to the current library, or use it to replace the current library. You can also modify any preset in any library and save it as a custom preset or, if you decide that you don't want to keep the changes you have made to a set of brush presets, you can reset the Brush panel by clicking Reset Brushes on the panel menu.

To load a preset library:

1. In the Layers panel, click the **Bicycle** layer, if necessary, click **Window** on the menu bar, point to **Workspace**, and then click **Painting** to display the most commonly used panels for painting. Click **Window** on the menu bar, point to **Workspace**, and then click **Reset Painting**, to reset the workspace.

   The Brush Presets panel is expanded above the Layers panel. The Brush panel is minimized to an icon.

2. In the Brush Presets panel, click the **panel menu** button, and then click **Assorted Brushes**.
3. Click the **OK** button to replace the current brushes with the new brushes. Click the **No** button if asked to save the current brushes.
4. In the Tools panel, click the **Brush Tool** button, and in the Brush Presets panel, scroll down until you see the Dashed Circle 2 preset shown in Figure 4-47, and then click the **Dashed Circle 2** preset to select it.

Figure 4-47 Selecting the Dashed Circle 2 brush preset

Shevchenko Nataliya/Shutterstock.com; Black Images/Shutterstock.com

The Dashed Circle 2 preset includes a brush diameter of 41 pixels; however, you can change the brush diameter to customize the preset.

5. In the Brush Presets panel, change the brush diameter to **330** pixels.
6. In the Tools panel, set the foreground color to white.
7. On the canvas, click in the front tire of the bicycle. The Dashed Circle 2 brush adds a white dashed circle to the image, which creates the appearance of tire spokes.
8. Click in the rear tire to add the dashed circle there as well.
9. Save the file.

Using a Brush Preset to Stroke a Path

When you draw a shape in Photoshop, you can use the Paths option on the options bar to specify that the shape is a temporary work path. A **work path** provides a temporary outline on a layer. You can use the outline to define a path for a variety of tasks, including erasing the area defined by the path, or stroking the path with the Brush or

Pencil tool. To create a work path and apply a stroke to it, you select the desired shape tool in the Tools panel, draw the shape, and then use the Stroke Path command on the context menu to display the Stroke Path dialog box and a list of tools you can use for the stroke. If you select the Brush option, Photoshop uses the current brush settings to draw a brushstroke around the work path. Once you have added the stroke, you can delete the work path from the Paths panel or save it for future sessions.

You'll create a circular work path and stroke it with a concentric circle brushstroke to show Lee an idea you have about painting a design on the store window.

TIP

To display a list of preset names rather than sample strokes, select the Text Only option from the Brush Presets panel menu.

To create a work path and apply a stroke:

1. In the Brush Presets panel, select the 32-pixel **Concentric Circles** preset (the fifth option in the list).
2. At the top of the Brush Presets panel, change the brush size to **200** pixels, and then in the Tools panel, set the foreground color to a **dark blue**.
3. In the Document window, zoom out to about **12.5%** and then click in the center of the store window on the left. Photoshop adds a single brushstroke to the window (a concentric circle).
4. Click two more times in exactly the same spot. Notice that the circles get darker, as if you are adding additional coats of paint.
5. In the Tools panel, select the **Ellipse Tool** button, and on the options bar, click the **Pick tool mode** button, and then click **Path**.
6. On the options bar, click the **More options** button, select the **Circle** and **From Center** options, and then click in the center of the circle you just painted and drag out to create the path.
7. Right-click the work path to open the path context menu. See Figure 4-48.

Figure 4-48 **Path context menu**

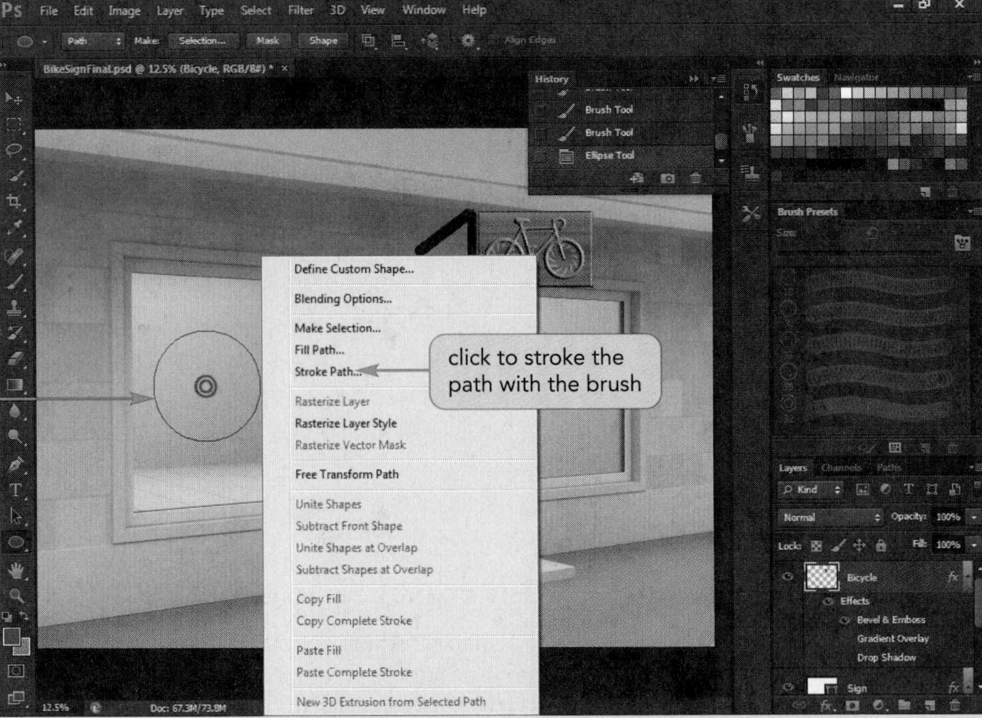

Shevchenko Nataliya/Shutterstock.com; Black Images/Shutterstock.com

Photoshop displays options for working with the work path. You can fill the path, make it a selection, or you can stroke it.

8. On the context menu, click **Stroke Path** to open the Stroke Path dialog box. Click the **Tool** arrow, click **Brush**, and then click the **OK** button to accept Brush as the tool you'll use to stroke the path.
9. Photoshop adds a brushstroke that follows the path of the circle you drew. In the Layers panel group, click the **Paths** tab. Photoshop lists a single work path in the Paths panel. Work paths are saved when a file is saved. Because you won't need this work path in the future, you'll delete it.
10. Select the **Work Path** path, if necessary, and then press the **Delete** key. The path is deleted from the panel and from the image, but the circular brushstroke remains. See Figure 4-49.

Figure 4-49 Brushstroke on path

Brush preset strokes the path
path is deleted from Paths panel

Shevchenko Nataliya/Shutterstock.com; Black Images/Shutterstock.com

Creating a Custom Preset

You can create a custom preset and save it so you can use it in future Photoshop sessions. To create a custom preset, select the brush preset you want to modify and change the settings, such as diameter and hardness, until you achieve the effect you want. When you are satisfied with your changes, you can use the New Brush Preset command on the panel menu for the Brush Presets panel to save the custom preset. You can then save a set of presets as a library using the Save Brushes options on the panel menu. Photoshop adds an .abr extension to any brush preset library you save. If you decide that you don't want to keep the changes you have made to a set of brush presets, you can reset the Brush panel without saving your changes.

Lee is happy with the work on the bike sign you have shown her so far and is planning to use your image of the storefront in an upcoming meeting with other members of the team. However, she would like you to add some color to the image to create some excitement. You'll use a customized preset to add azalea bushes to achieve a colorful effect.

To create a new brush preset:

1. Reset the Painting workspace, and reset the background and foreground colors to the default colors.
2. Fit the image to the screen, select the **Background** layer, set the foreground color to a **bright pink**, and then press the **B** key to activate the Brush tool.
3. In the Brush Presets panel, click the **panel menu** button, and click **Special Effect Brushes**, and then click the **OK** button. Click the **Azalea** preset (the first one on the list) to select it, and change the diameter to **150** pixels.
4. In the image, drag on the ground and in front of the building, avoiding the front step. See Figure 4-50.

Figure 4-50 Creating azalea bushes with brush preset

Shevchenko Nataliya/Shutterstock.com; Black Images/Shutterstock.com

5. In the Brush Presets panel, click the **panel menu** button, and then click **New Brush Preset**.
6. Type **150 px azalea** in the Name box, click the **Capture Brush Size in Preset** check box to select it, if necessary, and then click the **OK** button to save the new preset. Finally, you'll add a layer and apply a blending mode to give your illustration more depth.
7. In the Layers panel, click the **Bicycle** layer, if necessary, and add a **dark blue** fill layer. Set the opacity to **55%**, and add a **Soft Light** blending mode.
8. Save the **BikeSignFinal.psd** file, close it, and then exit Photoshop.

INSIGHT

Making a Brush Preset from an Image

You can create a custom brush preset by selecting part of an image and using the Define Brush Preset command on the Edit menu. For example, in a photograph of a pile of shells, you could select a single scallop shell and then use the Define Brush Preset command to save it as a preset. Photoshop adds the new preset to the Brush panel and shows a preview of the brushstroke at the bottom of the panel. Note that if you open an image but don't select an area, Photoshop uses the entire image as the preset, which might not be your intention. You might want to save a custom brush preset to create an effect that you plan to use in multiple files. Rather than repeating the same steps for every file, you can use the brush preset to add the desired effect.

In this session, you learned how to add color, gradient, and pattern fill layers to your compositions. You also learned how to add shapes to a layer and how to modify them by combining, excluding, and merging shapes. You worked with brushes and brush presets. In the next tutorial, you'll learn how to select, remove, and tweak content and work further with layer masks to create more sophisticated images.

REVIEW

Session 4.2 Quick Check

1. What is a gradient?
2. True or False. You cannot apply a blending mode to a Fill layer.
3. When you are drawing a shape such as a rectangle, what effect does the Proportional setting have?
4. To create a "hole" in a geometric shape that you draw, you can select the _______________ _______________ _______________ option on the Path operations menu.
5. True or False. If you use the Shape tool mode and draw directly on an image, you are altering the pixels on the layers beneath your drawing.
6. To draw or paint a straight line, you can click at the beginning of the line, press the _______________ key, and then click at the end of the line.
7. You can save the modifications you make to a brush as a brush _______________.

Practice the skills you learned in the tutorial using the same case scenario.

PRACTICE

Review Assignments

Data Files needed for the Review Assignments: Signage.psd, Gopher.jpg

Lee likes the sign you proposed for the entrance to her store, and would like you to submit some ideas for signs to place in various areas inside and outside the store. For starters, she'd like a sign to place above the bicycle rack in the parking lot. Because she thinks the bike shop sign worked well with no words, she would like you to do something similar for the new signs. Complete the following steps:

1. Start Photoshop while pressing the Ctrl+Alt+Shift keys, and click Yes to delete the Settings File when prompted. Switch to the Painting workspace, and then reset the Painting workspace. Reset all tools.
2. Open **Signage.psd** and **Gopher.jpg**, located in the Photoshop4\Review folder included with your Data Files, and arrange the Document windows so the files are displayed side by side.
3. Using a point sample of the yellow color from the gopher tortoise sign, fill the Signage file background with yellow. If the color is out of gamut, adjust it so it is in gamut.
4. Close Gopher.jpg without saving it. Save Signage.psd as **NoCars.psd** in the Photoshop4\Review folder.
5. Using Figure 4-51 as a guide and with the Shape tool mode selected on the options bar, draw a 'No' Sign shape with a 10-inch diameter, a red fill, and no stroke. (*Hint*: You can find the 'No' Sign custom shape in the Symbols shapes preset library for the Custom Shape tool.) Center the sign shape on the canvas, and apply the Blue Glass (Button) style to it. Hide the color Overlay effect and the Gradient Overlay effect.

Figure 4-51 **Sample sign for ReCycle Bike Shop parking lot**

6. Right-click the new shape layer, and then select the Rasterize Layer option. Then, open the Layer Style dialog box, and add a Drop Shadow effect with a Size setting of 10 pixels. Close the Layer Style dialog box.
7. Add a Car 1 custom shape inside the sign shape using a black fill and no stroke. (*Hint*: You can find the Car 1 custom shape in the Symbols shapes preset library.) Copy the layer style from the 'No' Sign layer to the car layer. If necessary, rearrange the layers in the Layers panel so that the car shape is behind the sign shape on the canvas, and then deselect all the layers.
8. Display the rulers, and add guides at 1/2 inch and 11 1/2 inches on the vertical ruler and at 1/2 inch and 13 1/2 inches on the horizontal ruler. Add a new empty layer, and then use the Rectangle tool to draw a path over the guides.
9. In the Tools panel, select the Brush tool, and switch to the Assorted Brushes presets. Select the Concentric Circles brush preset, and then sample the red used for the 'No' Sign, and set it as the foreground color.
10. Select the Rectangle tool again, right-click the path you created with the Rectangle tool, confirm that Brush is selected in the Stroke Path dialog box, and then click the OK button.
11. Delete the path, and clear the guides.
12. Select the car layer, and create the windows in the car by selecting the Subtract Front Shape path operation. (*Hint*: Make sure you are drawing a shape and not a path.)
13. Save the **NoCars.psd** file, and close the file.

Use your skills to create a composition for a technology business.

APPLY

Case Problem 1

Data Files needed for this Case Problem: TekSell.jpg, CD.psd

TekSell Founded in 2008, TekSell is an online technology retail business that sells computer hardware and software. TekSell's owner, Jose Ruiz, has hired you to create a new look for the company's Web site. For your initial meeting with Jose, you plan to present a few ideas for the page background and possible navigation buttons. In this exercise, you'll create two sample buttons and a proposed page background. Complete the following steps:

1. Start Photoshop while pressing the Ctrl+Alt+Shift keys, and click Yes to delete the Settings File when prompted. Reset Photoshop to the default Essentials workspace layout, and then reset all tools.
2. Open **TekSell.jpg**, located in the Photoshop4\Case1 folder provided with your Data Files, and save it as **TekSellWeb.psd**.
3. You'll start by creating the "look" you will propose for the Web page background. Add a gradient fill layer to the Background layer using the Color Harmonies 1 gradient preset library. Apply the Orange, Blue gradient from that group using a gradient angle of 180 degrees. Then, set the opacity of the gradient fill layer to 60%.

EXPLORE

4. Open **CD.psd**, located in the Photoshop4\Case1 folder, and arrange the two open files side by side. In the CD.psd file, select the CD Isolated layer, and drag it over the TekSellWeb.psd document window. After the CD Isolated layer has been added to the TekSellWeb.psd file, drag the CD Isolated layer above the Gradient Fill 1 layer, if necessary. Close the CD.psd file without saving it.

EXPLORE

5. Resize the image of the CD so it is 25% of its original size. (*Hint*: To resize the CD, select the Move Tool button, show the transform controls, click one of the transform controls in the Document window, click the Maintain aspect ratio icon on the options bar, and then type **25** in the Height box.) Then, move the individual CD to the left side of the canvas, toward the top of the extension color.

6. Apply the Striped Cone (Button) style to the CD layer. Your proposal will include using the image of the CD as a navigation button on the Web site. Modify the style you just applied so it has an Outer Glow with a size of 70 pixels.
7. Below the CD image you added, draw a circle shape with a red fill, and make it about the same size as the CD. Copy and paste the CD Isolated layer style you created onto the circle. This will be the selected state of the button you're proposing for the Web site.
8. Create a new layer above the Ellipse 1 layer, and select the Brush tool. Open the Brush Presets panel, switch to the Special Effect Brushes presets library, and select the Tumble Planets brush. Set the brush size to 250 pixels, change the foreground color to yellow, and then paint planets in one brushstroke down the side of the canvas, under the buttons.
9. Save the image, flatten it, and save it again as **TekSellWeb.jpg**, using the default JPEG settings, in the Photoshop4\Case1 folder. Submit the results of the preceding steps to your instructor either in printed or electronic form, as requested.

Use your skills to create two cover options for an architecture magazine.

APPLY

Case Problem 2

Data Files needed for this Case Problem: ArchiText.psd

ArchiText Meena Patel is the publisher of *ArchiText*, a magazine for architects, where you have recently been hired as a graphic designer. The fall issue of the magazine will include photographs and articles about a series of architecturally interesting buildings from a single city, anywhere in the world. Meena has presented a challenge to you and your colleagues: Submit a mock-up of a cover that uses a photograph of a city building and presents it in a unique way; the winner's work will be published on the cover of the fall issue. To stand out from the others who will be competing, you'll create a second version of the cover that uses mostly drawn objects instead of a photograph. Complete the following steps:

1. Start Photoshop while pressing the Ctrl+Alt+Shift keys, and click Yes to delete the Settings File when prompted. Reset Photoshop to the default Essentials workspace layout, and then reset all tools.
2. Open **ArchiText.psd**, located in the Photoshop4\Case2 folder provided with your Data Files, and save it as **ArchiText2.psd** in the same folder.
3. EXPLORE Open a Web browser of your choice and go to the MorgueFile or the Creative Commons Web site, or another site that supplies images for free for commercial purposes. If you use Creative Commons, click the Find CC-licensed works link and then, on the Search page, confirm that the "use is for commercial purposes," and the "modify, adapt, or build upon" check boxes are selected. (You can also use one of your own images.) Search the site for images of buildings from the city of your choice. For example, search for images of buildings in Chicago by using *Chicago* as your search term. Select an image in any format with which you would like to work. Before you download the image, check the licensing information to make sure that it can be remixed without attribution and used for commercial purposes. Download the image and save it as **CityShot.jpg** in the Photoshop4\Case2 folder.
4. Return to Photoshop, and place the **CityShot.jpg** image in the ArchiText2.psd file. Size the placed image so it fits properly in the composition, with the original text still showing. Apply any adjustment layers you think might be necessary.
5. Apply a style to the *ArchiText* text and modify it until it suits your composition. Save the modified style as ArchiStyle, and then apply it to *the city issue* text.
6. Add a Pattern or Gradient fill layer to the composition, change its settings as desired, and position the layer so it only affects the Background layer.

7. On a new layer, use the Brush tool to add brushstrokes or special effects to your cover using one or more brush presets. Make sure to position the layer so the strokes appear where you want them. Save ArchiText2.psd, and close it.
8. Create a new file with any background color using the same dimensions as the cover, 8 ½ × 11 inches. Use the CMYK color mode, 300-ppi resolution, and 8-bit color. Save the file as **ArchiText3.psd** in the Photoshop4\Case2 folder.
9. Use any combination of layers, brushstrokes, drawing tools, and color selection tools to create a page that you'll submit as an alternate cover idea. See Figure 4-52 as an example.

Figure 4-52 **Sample ArchiText cover**

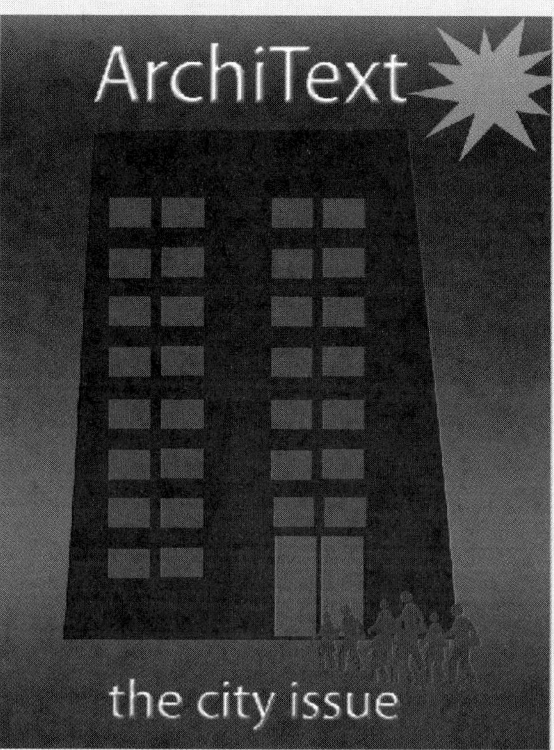

Your file should include a drawing that uses addition, subtraction, intersection, and exclusion. (*Hint*: Draw a building with windows and doors.) Be sure to include the magazine title and subtitle, as shown in Figure 4-52.

10. Flatten the image, and then save the file and close it.
11. Submit the results of the preceding steps to your instructor either in printed or electronic form, as requested.

Extend what you've learned to use the Mixer Brush to modify an image.

CHALLENGE

Case Problem 3

Data Files needed for this Case Problem: Easel.jpg

TeachOut David Jasper is the creative director for TeachOut, a company that provides distance learning solutions for schools, universities, and technical training centers. You have been hired to work with David on a series of ads that will emphasize TeachOut's goal of making learning fun. For your first project, you'll use the Mixer Brush to paint on an easel to produce an image reminiscent of a child's painting. Complete the following steps:

1. Start Photoshop while pressing the Ctrl+Alt+Shift keys, and click Yes to delete the Settings File when prompted. Reset Photoshop to the default Essentials workspace layout, and then reset all tools.
2. Open **Easel.jpg**, located in the Photoshop4\Case3 folder provided with your Data Files, and save it as **TeachOut.psd** in the same folder.
3. Add a shape layer with a white rectangle, sized to fit on the easel. Rasterize the rectangle, and then rotate it and position it so it appears to be a canvas sitting on the easel in the image. Add a shadow to the rectangle shape to give it depth and a more realistic look.
4. (EXPLORE) Use Photoshop Help to research the Mixer Brush. Make sure you understand the settings on the options bar, including Wet, Load, Mix, and Flow.
5. (EXPLORE) Create a new file with the default Photoshop settings to experiment with the Mixer Brush before you paint on the canvas in the TeachOut.psd file. Try different combinations of colors and different brushes until you understand how the options bar settings affect the mixture of colors. Save the file as **Scrap.jpg** in the Photoshop4\Case3 folder, and then close the file.
6. (EXPLORE) Switch back to TeachOut.psd, and using Figure 4-53 as a guide, paint an image in the style of a child's painting.

Figure 4-53 Sample TeachOut image

Fotocrisis/Shutterstock.com

Your painting should demonstrate that you understand how to mix colors with the Mixer Brush, and how to achieve different effects with different Wet, Load, Mix, and Flow levels. You should use at least five different colors, at least three color combinations (mixes), and three different brushes. (*Hint*: If you paint outside of the canvas by accident, use the Eraser tool to erase the paint so it is contained within the canvas edges.)

7. Change the dimensions of the document by extending the canvas one inch on all sides; sample one of the mixed colors as the canvas extension color.
8. When you are satisfied with your artwork, flatten the image and then save it.
9. Submit the results of the preceding steps to your instructor either in printed or electronic form, as requested.

Use your skills to create an original composition for a landscaping company.

APPLY

Case Problem 4

There are no Data Files needed for this Case Problem.

Prettyscapes Prettyscapes is a landscaping company with 15 employees in Boise, Idaho. Business has been growing lately, and Maya Morrisson, the owner, is interested in attracting creative talent. Maya has asked you to come up with a composition for a help wanted ad that conveys whimsy and creativity. She will provide the text. You'll use the color, drawing, and brush tools in Photoshop to show what a landscape designer might do when presented with an empty lot.

1. Start Photoshop while pressing the Ctrl+Alt+Shift keys, and click Yes to delete the Settings File when prompted. Reset Photoshop to the default Essentials workspace layout, and then reset all tools.
2. Create a new file with a white background of any dimensions.
3. Open a Web browser of your choice and go to the MorgueFile site or the Creative Commons site, or another site that supplies images for free for commercial purposes. If you use Creative Commons, click the Find CC-licensed works link and then, on the Search page, confirm that the "use is for commercial purposes," and the "modify, adapt, or build upon" check boxes are selected. (You can also use one of your own images.) In a later step, you will be adding a house to the image you download, so select an image with that in mind. Before you download the image, check the licensing information to make sure that it can be remixed without attribution and used for commercial purposes.
4. Download the image and save it as **Landscape.jpg** in the Photoshop4\Case 4 folder provided with your Data Files.
5. Return to Photoshop and place the Landscape.jpg image in your newly created file, and size it to fit.
6. On one part of the image, use the drawing tools to draw a house with windows and a door. To create the drawing, use at least two of the path operations options (creating a new layer, or combining, subtracting, intersecting, excluding, or merging shapes).
7. Use blending modes, opacity, styles, and other adjustments to modify the various shapes in your drawing. (*Hint*: For some effects, you might need to rasterize your drawn objects.)
8. EXPLORE Use any tools you choose to draw a brick walkway leading to the house.
9. EXPLORE Open one of the brush preset libraries you haven't yet used, and choose brush tips that will let you create bushes and flower beds around the house.
10. Add objects such as butterflies to your drawing using various brush presets. Make sure to vary your color choices.

11. Put any finishing touches on your composition that you'd like, flatten the image, and then save the file as **LandscapeWhimsy.psd** in the Photoshop4\Case4 folder.
12. Submit the results of the preceding steps to your instructor either in printed or electronic form, as requested.

ENDING DATA FILES

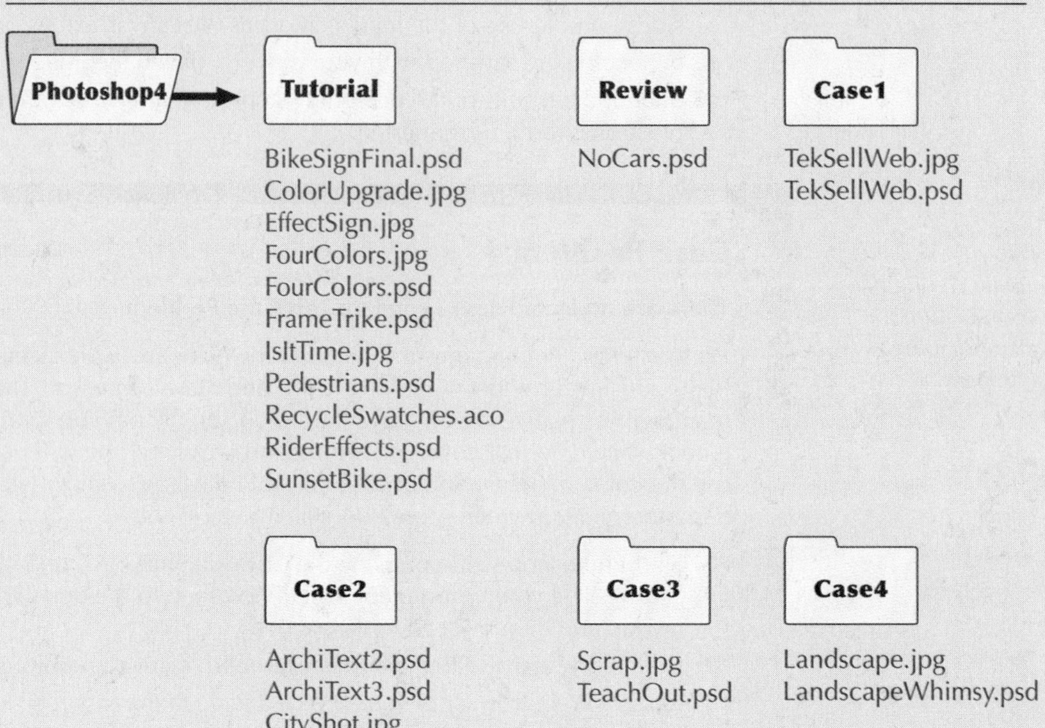

TUTORIAL 5

Selecting and Modifying Content

Compositing Photos

OBJECTIVES

Session 5.1

- Modify, grow, transform, and refine a selection
- Apply an adjustment to a selection
- Copy and paste a selection
- Create complex selections
- Select a color range in an image
- Step backward and forward
- Use the History panel and the History Brush tool

Session 5.2

- Use the Lasso tool, the Magnetic Lasso tool, and the Quick Selection tool
- Save and reload a selection
- Apply Content-Aware and other fills to a selection
- Use the Content-Aware Move tool
- Add a stroke to a selection
- Work with filters and masks

Case | *Food for Change*

Food for Change, a nonprofit organization in Hartford, Connecticut, brings sustainable food systems into urban areas. Its founder, Azar Miller, created the organization in 2002, after noticing that many city-owned dirt lots were not being used. He approached city leaders with a proposal: With the help of urban and suburban youth, he would transform the lots into fruit and vegetable gardens. At the same time, he would educate youth about good nutrition, and send them into the city schools to promote urban gardening and good nutrition.

You have been hired by Azar to transform some of his photographs into compositions that he can use in brochures and fund-raising materials and on the Food for Change Web site. To make the changes Azar wants, you'll explore several Photoshop selection tools. In addition to modifying and refining selections, you'll learn how to apply an adjustment to a selection. You'll will also learn how to undo and redo actions using the Edit menu, the History panel, and the History Brush tool. You'll examine Photoshop's Content-Aware fill feature, and you'll save and reload selections. Finally, you'll experiment with filters, fills, and masks.

STARTING DATA FILES

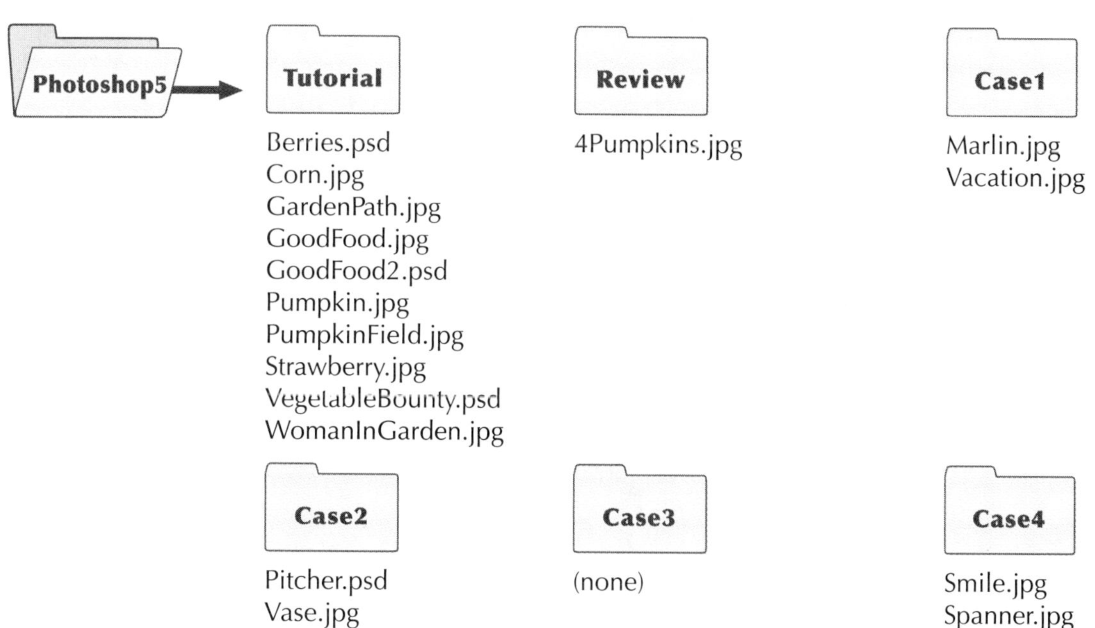

SESSION 5.1 VISUAL OVERVIEW

Use the commands on the Select menu to select all of the pixels on a layer, to deselect or reselect a selection, or to invert a selection.

Click one of the Marquee tools and then drag on the canvas to create an **active selection** enclosed by an animated series of dashed lines or curves called a selection marquee.

Using the History Brush tool, you can paint over your composition and uncover part of the history state that is set as the source in the History panel.

Making adjustments to an image or combining different image files (or parts of image files) and/or vector objects in a single file is called **compositing**.

Jane Hosie-Bounar; Teodora George/Shutterstock.com

SELECTING CONTENT

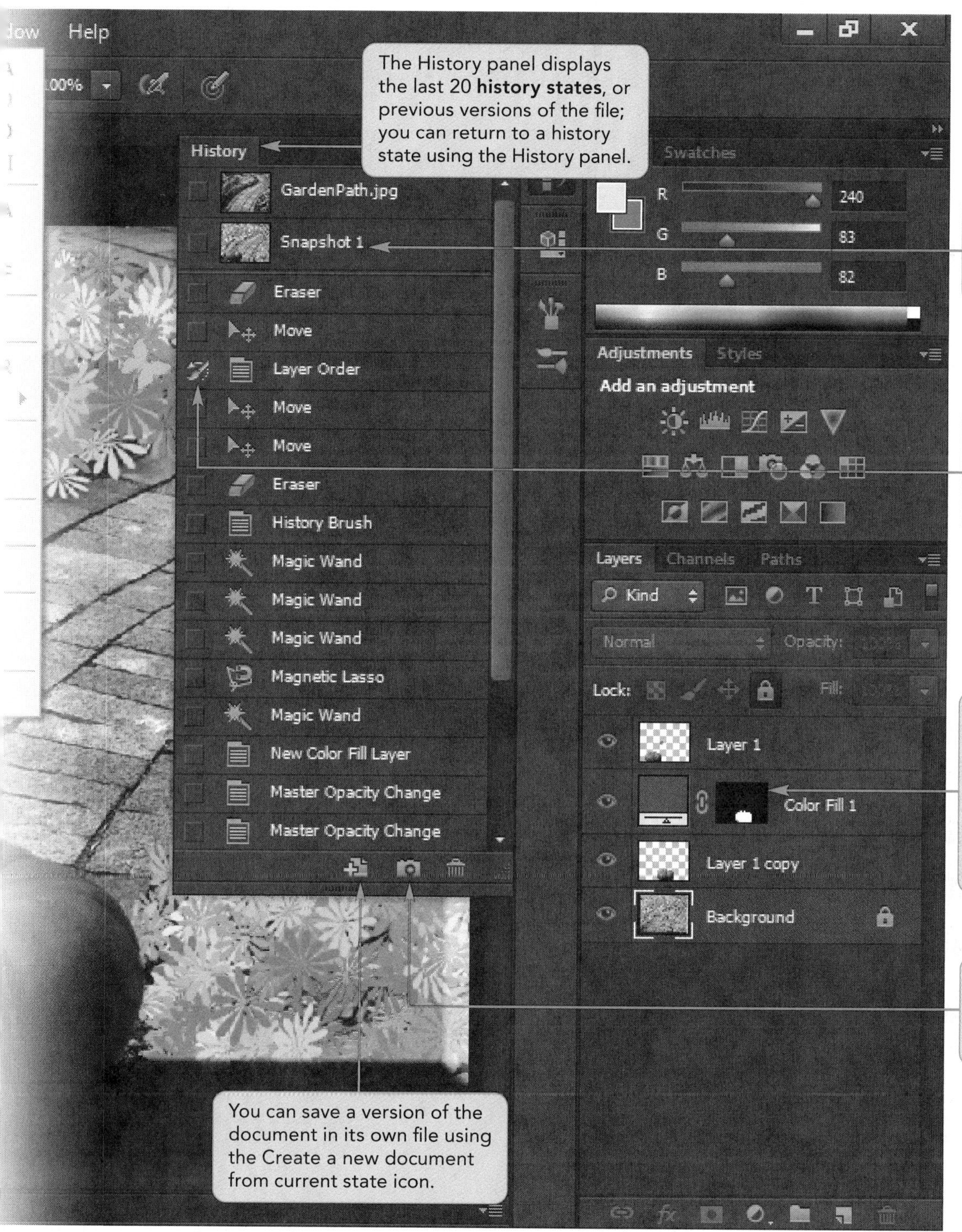

The History panel displays the last 20 **history states**, or previous versions of the file; you can return to a history state using the History panel.

You can save a **snapshot**, or a picture of what the composition looked like, at any given history state.

This history state is set as the **source** for the History Brush tool; you can use the source to revert part of an image to an earlier version.

You can make a selection, and then fill the selected pixels with color; the unselected area filled with black is the mask, which protects everything not included in the selection from changes.

Use the Create a new snapshot icon to produce a snapshot of the current history state.

You can save a version of the document in its own file using the Create a new document from current state icon.

Selecting Content for Compositing

When you work in Photoshop, much of your work will involve compositing, creating images by combining parts of different image files in a single file, or modifying an image to create a unique composition. For example, you might select a tree from one image and copy it to a photograph of an empty lot. If you do this repeatedly, you can grow a digital forest in no time. Or, you might put two people who appear in separate images into one image by selecting, copying, and pasting them into the same composition. You can also create a complex composition by starting with a single photograph to which you then apply multiple effects. Photoshop has numerous tools that let you select not only layers, but also areas of pixels in a layer. These selection tools allow you to apply different effects to different areas of an image. In Tutorial 3, you dragged a rectangular marquee around part of an image to select it, and then used the Copy and Paste commands to add your selection to another file. However, many more tools are available for making selections, as shown in Figure 5-1.

Figure 5-1 **Selection tools in Photoshop**

Icon	Tool	Use To
	Rectangular Marquee tool	Drag to select a rectangular area; select Fixed Ratio to draw a rectangle with a height/width ratio you specify, or select Fixed Size to specify the exact dimensions of the rectangle. You can also press the Shift key while drawing the selection to constrain the selection marquee to a square.
	Elliptical Marquee tool	Drag to select an elliptical area; select Fixed Ratio to draw an ellipse with a height/width ratio you specify, or select Fixed Size to specify the exact dimensions of the ellipse. You can also press the Shift key while drawing the selection to constrain the selection marquee to a circle.
	Single Row Marquee tool	Click once to select a row of pixels (one pixel high) across an image.
	Single Column Marquee tool	Click once to select a column of pixels (one pixel wide) down an image.
	Lasso tool	Drag on an image to make a freehand selection.
	Polygonal Lasso tool	Click on an image multiple times to create straight-edged selections to form the shape of a polygon.
	Magnetic Lasso tool	Drag a selection marquee whose border snaps to defined edges on an image—for example, a white object on a dark background.
	Quick Selection tool	Drag the pointer to paint your selection; as you drag, the selection grows. You can determine the sensitivity of the selection by specifying Tolerance.
	Magic Wand tool	Select an area based on a specific color; the Tolerance setting determines the color range that the tool will select.

In fact, the variety and power of the selection tools in Photoshop give you a great deal of creative license when you composite, or compose, an image. You can select an object in an image, cut it completely out of the image, and then fill in the cutout area with another object, a fill, or a gradient. You can also make a selection and apply filters and special effects only to the selection or to everything in the image *except* the selection. Figure 5-2 shows a composition created by selecting part of an image (the orange pumpkin in the middle).

Figure 5-2 Selecting, copying, and adjusting selected pixels

Teodora George/Shutterstock.com

The selection was copied to the Clipboard, pasted into the lower-left corner of the composition, and then resized to create the appearance of an additional pumpkin. While the new pumpkin was still selected, a Brightness/Contrast adjustment was applied only to the selection. Finally, the original pumpkin was copied and pasted again, and then dragged to the lower-right corner of the image. The end result is that an image that originally had one orange pumpkin now has three. As you can see from this simple example, the possibilities for working with selections in Photoshop are limitless.

PROSKILLS

Problem Solving: Using Photoshop to Communicate Critical Visual Data

Communicating critical visual data to clients, peers, and coworkers is an important—and sometimes challenging—task in a variety of industries, including technical fields, such as genetic research, architecture, and engineering. Using the tools in Photoshop, you can solve this problem by making adjustments to images that will focus a viewer's attention on the parts of an image that are most important. For example, imagine you are working with a researcher who will be presenting a lecture on mutations in the frog population near a hazardous waste dump. Some of the mutations are obvious, but others require a more trained eye to see. So how could you help the researcher solve the problem and make the mutations more visible to the audience? You could use the selection and adjustment tools in Photoshop to manipulate the image so that the physical features that need to be highlighted are more prominent. For example, you could darken the area around a feature, or change the contrast so that the feature stands out. Or, imagine that you're working for a structural engineer who is preparing a report that includes archived images of a building that collapsed in a minor earthquake. To highlight the weak areas of the design, you could select them and change their brightness or contrast to draw attention to them in the report. Photoshop offers a variety of tools to help solve the problem of needing to communicate critical visual data in technical and nontechnical fields. As you get more experience with Photoshop, you'll find you have more skills at your disposal to solve this type of problem in a variety of settings.

Azar would like you to work on a few compositions that show the bounty of the Food for Change program so he can present them at a government funding conference next month. He has some photographs from last summer, but he is concerned that some don't show the extent or variety of the food grown by the program, while others won't grab a viewer's attention. You'll work with the selection tools to enhance and compose images for the conference. You'll also work with the selection tools to apply effects to parts of your composition while leaving other parts unchanged.

Selecting with the Rectangular or Elliptical Marquee Tool

The Rectangular and Elliptical Marquee tools allow you to specify an exact rectangular or elliptical area by dragging on an image. These marquee tools should seem familiar to you; you use them to draw selections in much the same way you used the Rectangle and Ellipse tools to draw shapes in earlier tutorials. When you drag, Photoshop outlines the area you are selecting, and when you release the mouse button, a selection marquee indicates that the selection is active. You can press the Shift key as you drag to constrain the proportions of the selection marquee—for example, to constrain an ellipse to a circle or a rectangle to a square.

When you use either the Rectangular or Elliptical Marquee tool, you can specify settings on the options bar for the tool, as shown in Figure 5-3.

Figure 5-3 **Using Marquee tool options to create a complex selection**

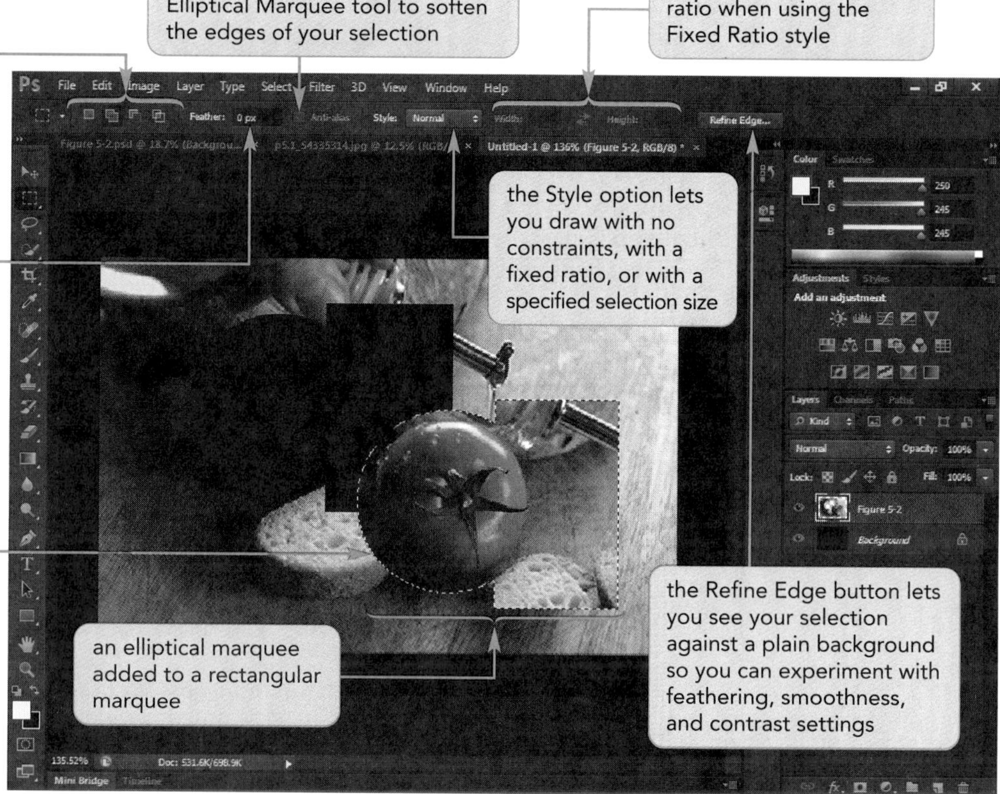

marco mayer/Shutterstock.com

The first group of settings should be familiar to you from Tutorial 4. The New selection, Add to selection, Subtract from selection, and Intersect with selection buttons behave like the New Layer, Combine Shapes, Subtract Front Shape, and Intersect Shape Areas commands you worked with when you created vector drawings. These buttons let you create complex selections by building on and subtracting from existing selections. For example, the selection in Figure 5-3 was created by drawing the first part of the selection (enclosing the tomato) with the Elliptical Marquee tool, clicking the Add to selection button on the options bar, and then using the Rectangular Marquee tool to add the rectangular area to the selection. The entire selection was then dragged down and to the right on the image, uncovering the black background beneath.

The next setting on the options bar is Feather, which you can use to soften or blur the edges of a selection. The higher the Feather setting, the softer the edges of the selection will be, which can help blend a selection into a composition. You can also modify the Feather setting in the Refine Edge dialog box to preview the setting before finalizing the selection.

The Anti-alias setting is available only with the Elliptical Marquee tool. Turning on this setting softens the pixelated edges of the curves in your selection. It is not available for the Rectangular Marquee tool because the edges of the rectangle are drawn horizontally and vertically along lines of pixels, so no jagged edges appear.

You can also specify the style of your selection. The default is the Normal style, which lets you drag a rectangle or an ellipse with no constraints. You can use Fixed Ratio to specify the width-to-height ratio of a selection. For example, a fixed ratio of Width 1 and Height 1 would draw a square or a circle. The Fixed Size option lets you specify the exact dimensions of the selection in pixels so when you click on the image, the selection marquee is created automatically. You can then drag it to its correct position. The last option on the Marquee tool options bar, Refine Edge, opens the Refine Edge dialog box, where you can fine-tune and preview your selection by modifying a number of options, including smoothness and feathering, all in one place.

Specifying a Fixed Ratio or Fixed Size Selection

As noted previously, with the Photoshop selection tools, you aren't confined to dragging on the canvas to create the selection marquee you need. You can instead specify a fixed ratio or fixed size selection when you have very specific needs, and then simply click the canvas and drag the selection marquee into position to create it. These fixed options allow you to be extremely precise.

REFERENCE

Specifying a Fixed Ratio Selection

- In the Tools panel, click the Rectangular Marquee Tool button or the Elliptical Marquee Tool button.
- On the options bar, click the Style button, and then click Fixed Ratio.
- Type ratio values in the Width and Height boxes.
- Click on the canvas, and drag to make your selection.
- Move the selection marquee to place it where you want it.

You'll work with a photograph of an arrangement of raw vegetables to create a unique, beveled image that Azar will use during his workshops around the city to emphasize that the work that Food for Change is doing is just one piece of a larger hunger and nutrition puzzle in urban areas.

To specify a fixed ratio selection:

1. Start Photoshop while pressing the **Ctrl+Alt+Shift** keys, and click **Yes** to delete the Settings File when prompted. Reset Photoshop to the default Essentials workspace layout, and reset all tools.
2. Navigate to the Photoshop5\Tutorial folder included with your Data Files, and open **VegetableBounty.psd**. Press **Ctrl+0** to fit the image to the screen.
3. Display the rulers, and then click the **Rectangular Marquee Tool** button in the Tools panel to select it, if necessary.
4. On the options bar, click the **Style** button, and then click **Fixed Ratio**. By default, Photoshop sets both the Width and Height boxes to 1, which would create a square.
5. Type **3** in the Width box, and then type **2** in the Height box. When you drag the selection, it will have a width-to-height ratio of 3 to 2.
6. In the Layers panel, select the **Vegetables** layer and then, starting at about 1" on the vertical ruler and 1" on the horizontal ruler, drag down and to the right until you're at about 5" on the vertical ruler. Photoshop creates a selection marquee with a width-to-height ratio of 3 to 2 that includes the red onion and most of the two tomatoes.
7. On the menu bar, click **Edit**, and then click **Cut**. The selection is cut from the image, and the black background shows through.
8. On the menu bar, click **Edit**, and then click **Paste**. The selection is pasted onto the center of the image on its own layer, named Layer 1.

9. In the Layers panel, double-click the **Layer 1** thumbnail to open the Layer Style dialog box, and then click **Bevel & Emboss** to select the style and display its properties.

10. In the Structure section, change the Structure Depth to **1000%**, set the Size to **100 px**, and then click the **OK** button. The cut-and-pasted selection now has a bevel and emboss effect. See Figure 5-4.

Figure 5-4 **Cutting and pasting a selection**

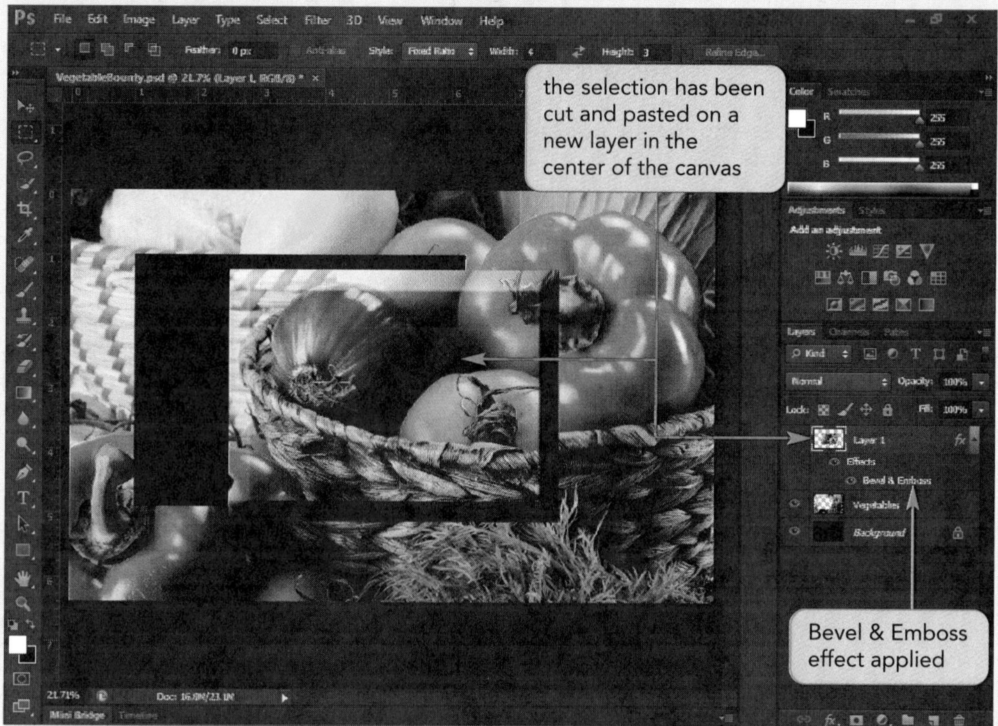
the selection has been cut and pasted on a new layer in the center of the canvas
Bevel & Emboss effect applied

monticello/Shutterstock.com

Trouble? If you can't see the Structure Depth option, you have selected the Bevel & Emboss check box, rather than clicking the Bevel & Emboss text. Click Bevel & Emboss, and then complete Step 10.

11. Save the file as **VegetableBevel.psd** in the Photoshop5\Tutorial folder, and then close it.

You selected an area of an image using the Rectangular Marquee tool with a fixed ratio setting. Next, you'll work with a fixed size selection.

REFERENCE

Specifying a Fixed Size Selection

- In the Tools panel, click the Rectangular Marquee Tool button or the Elliptical Marquee Tool button.
- On the options bar, click the Style button, and then click Fixed Size.
- Type the width and height values you want in the Width and Height boxes, making sure to specify *px* for pixels or *in* for inches.
- Click the canvas to draw the selection marquee.
- Move the selection marquee to place it where you want it.

Next, you'll use the Elliptical Marquee tool to select an area with a fixed size. You'll make a copy of one pumpkin and then paste it into the composition so an additional pumpkin appears in the image. Azar will use the before and after versions of the image to demonstrate that it is only with contributions from the public that the bounty at Food for Change can grow and multiply.

To specify a fixed size selection:

1. Open **Pumpkin.jpg**, located in the Photoshop5\Tutorial folder, and fit the image to the screen. In the Tools panel, click the **Elliptical Marquee Tool** button.

   Trouble? If you don't see the Elliptical Marquee Tool button in the Tools panel, click and hold the Rectangular Marquee Tool button to display the hidden tools, and then click the Elliptical Marquee Tool button.

2. On the options bar, change the Feather setting to **10 px**, select the **Anti-alias** check box, if necessary, click the **Style** button, and then click **Fixed Size**. The Width and Height boxes become available.

3. Type **800 px** in the Width box, and type **600 px** in the Height box.

   The ellipse you draw will have a width of 800 pixels and a height of 600 pixels. Because you selected Anti-alias, the edges of the selection will be smooth rather than jagged or pixelated.

Make sure you specify pixels (*px*) and not inches (*in*). Using inches will cause Photoshop to freeze up as it attempts to draw an ellipse well beyond the bounds of the canvas.

4. Click anywhere on the orange pumpkin. Photoshop immediately draws an elliptical selection marquee in the size you specified. Drag the **selection marquee** so it is centered over the pumpkin.

Notice that the selection marquee is smaller than the pumpkin. You can expand a selection using commands on the Select menu, which you'll do in the next section.

Modifying a Selection

Once you have made a selection, you can modify it. The Select menu includes many commands for changing the nature and dimensions of your selection. The Grow command selects adjacent pixels of a similar color. If some of the pixels are missed by the Grow command, you can use the Magic Wand tool and the Add to selection button on the options bar to select the missing pixels. The Grow command is a good choice when the object you are selecting is quite distinct from the background it is on, but may not work as well when the background has colors within range of the object's colors. You can use the Expand command, found in the Modify option menu, to expand the selection by a specified number of pixels. The Expand command is useful if the object you are selecting has a regular shape.

You can make a selection larger or smaller, or even distort or warp a selection, using the Transform Selection command on the Select menu. Photoshop encloses your selection in a rectangle with eight handles—one handle on each corner and one handle on each side. You can resize the selection by dragging the handles. To constrain the proportions of the selection so you don't distort it, press the Shift key while you drag. When you drag, the size of the selection marquee changes. You can accept the transformation by clicking the Commit button on the options bar or by pressing the Enter key.

REFERENCE

Expanding or Growing a Selection

- Use a tool from the Tools panel to make a selection.
- On the menu bar, click Select, point to Modify, and click Expand to open the Expand Selection dialog box.
- Type a pixel value in the Expand By box, and then click the OK button.

or

- Use a tool from the Tools panel to make a selection.
- On the menu bar, click Select, and then click Grow.

Next, you'll expand and then grow the current selection to encompass the whole pumpkin.

To expand and grow the selection:

1. On the menu bar, click **Select**, and then point to **Modify**. Photoshop displays a list of commands for modifying your selection.
2. Click **Expand**. The Expand Selection dialog box opens. You can enter a pixel value to specify the size of the expansion.
3. In the Expand By box, type **100**, and then click the **OK** button. The selection marquee expands to encompass more of the pumpkin. Because the selection is still not large enough to cover all of the pumpkin, you will try the Grow option next. Before you do so, make sure your expanded selection is still centered over the pumpkin so it does not include any of the green pumpkins in the background.
4. On the menu bar, click **Select**, and then click **Grow**. The selection expands to include most of the pumpkin. See Figure 5-5.

Figure 5-5 **Expanding and growing the selection**

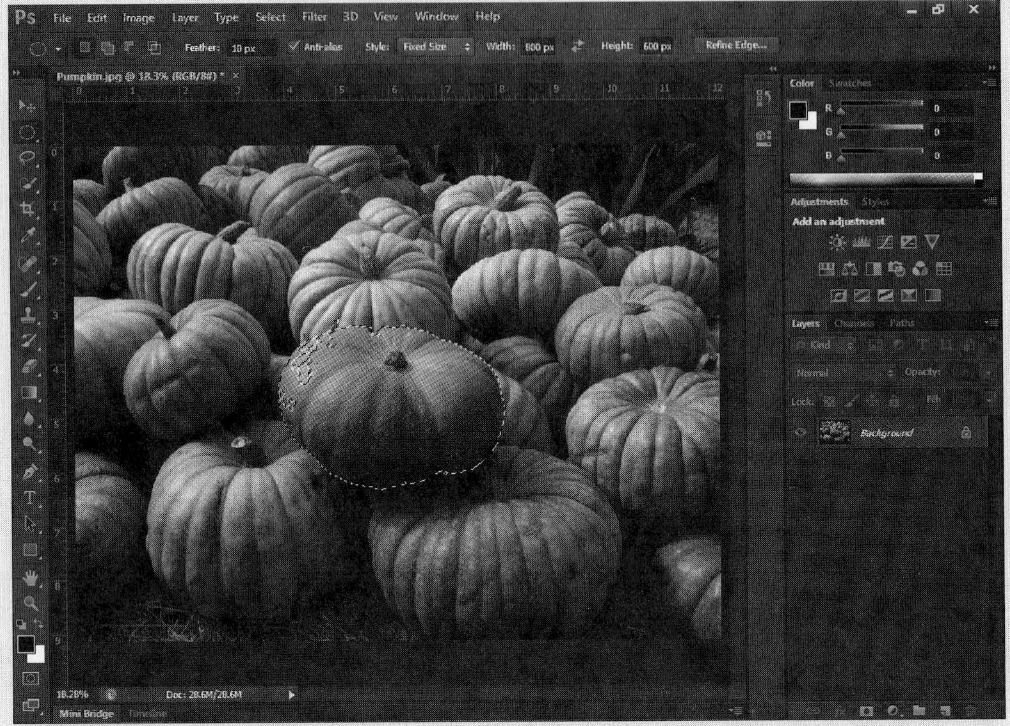

Teodora George/Shutterstock.com

Notice that the selection is no longer an ellipse because the Grow command grew the selection by finding similarly colored pixels. However, some small areas are still unselected. You'll use the Magic Wand tool to add those stray pixels to your selection.

To use the Magic Wand tool to add pixels to the selection:

1. In the Tools panel, point to the **Quick Selection Tool** button, press and hold the mouse button, and then click the **Magic Wand Tool** button.
2. On the options bar, change the Tolerance to **10**, and confirm that the **Anti-alias** and **Contiguous** check boxes are selected.

   Selecting Contiguous ensures that Photoshop selects only adjacent pixels that are the same color (orange) as the selection, rather than similarly colored pixels in the whole image.
3. On the options bar, click the **Add to selection** button. See Figure 5-6.

TIP

You can also press and hold the Shift key to temporarily select the Add to selection button. Press and hold the Alt key to temporarily select the Subtract from selection button.

Figure 5-6 **Adding pixels to the selection with the Magic Wand tool**

Add to selection button
the Anti-alias and Contiguous check boxes are checked
Magic Wand tool
click unselected pixels with the Magic Wand tool to add them to the selection

Teodora George/Shutterstock.com

4. Click on top of the pixels in the pumpkin that are not currently selected to add them to the selection. The wand pointer includes a plus sign, indicating that you are adding to the selection.

   All of the pixels in the pumpkin should now be selected.

   Trouble? If clicking the missing pixels doesn't add them to the selection, you have clicked one of the other options on the options bar, such as the Subtract from selection button. Click the Add to selection button, and then repeat Step 4.

   Trouble? If you select pixels that shouldn't be included in the selection, press the Ctrl+Z keys or click the Subtract from selection button on the options bar, and click until only the orange pumpkin is selected.

Applying an Adjustment to a Selection

In Tutorial 3, you applied adjustments to entire layers. Photoshop also lets you adjust individual areas of an image using selections. When a selection is active, you can apply an adjustment to it, and the adjustment will affect only the selected area of the image.

Next, you'll change the color balance of the selected pumpkin so the orange is intensified. You'll then copy and paste the selection so you have two pumpkins of different shades of orange.

To apply a Color Balance adjustment to the selection:

1. In the Adjustments panel, click the **Color Balance** icon.
2. In the Properties panel, drag the **Cyan Red** slider to the right so the value in the box is +**60**. The selection marquee disappears, but it is still active. The color of the pumpkin changes to a bright orange. The unselected area of the image is unchanged.
3. Collapse the Properties panel and then in the Layers panel, click the **Color Balance 1** layer, if necessary. In the Tools panel, click the **Move Tool** button.
4. Point to the pumpkin, press and hold the mouse button, and drag the **Color Balance** adjustment up and to the left, as shown in Figure 5-7.

Figure 5-7 Applying a color adjustment to a selection and moving the adjustment

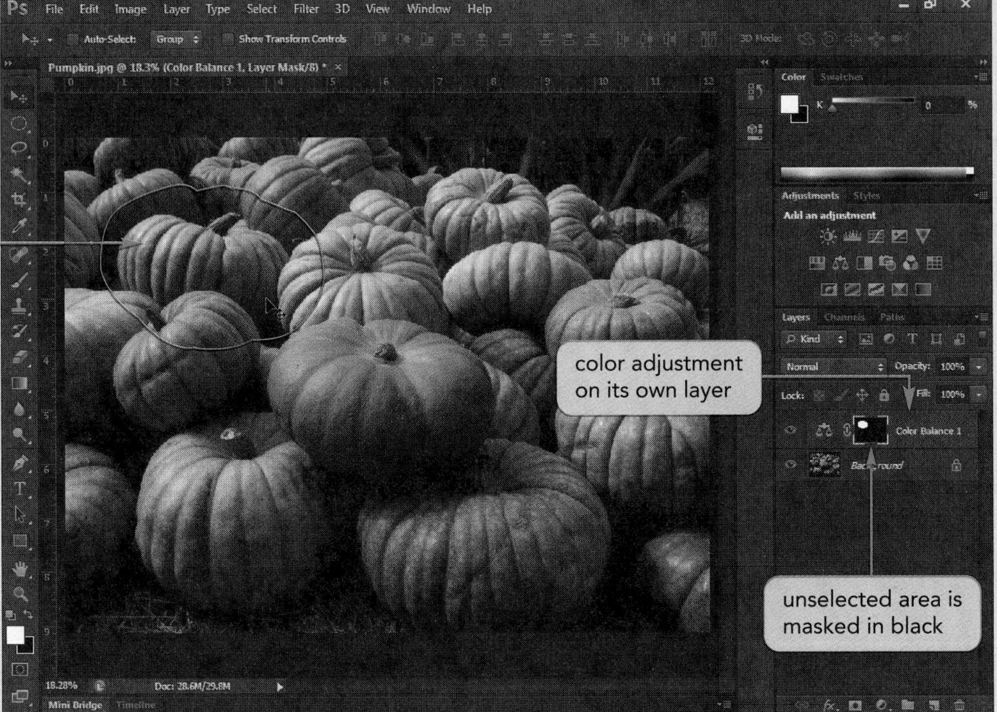
the color adjustment is not applied directly to the pixels; it is applied to the selection so it moves with the selection
color adjustment on its own layer
unselected area is masked in black
Pumpkin.jpg @ 18.3% (Color Balance 1, Layer Mask/8) *
Color Balance 1
Background

Teodora George/Shutterstock.com

The selection, along with the Color Balance adjustment, now appears above and to the left of the pumpkin. (The green outline around the Color Balance adjustment was added to Figure 5-7 to highlight the adjustment.) The colored adjustment has moved because the adjustment was applied to the selection, not to the pixels in the image.

When you made your selection and applied the adjustment, what you were actually doing was creating a mask. You can think of a mask as the inverse of a selection. A **mask** protects all of the pixels not included in the selection. As you can see on the Color Balance 1 layer, your selection (in the shape of the pumpkin) is shown in white on the thumbnail to the right in the Color Balance thumbnail. The rest of the thumbnail is black, indicating that anything you do to the selection will not affect the black areas.

You'll undo the move action you just performed, and then you'll reselect the pumpkin so you can copy and paste it in another part of the image.

To copy and paste the pumpkin selection:

1. On the menu bar, click **Edit**, and then click **Undo Move**. The Color Balance adjustment appears on top of the orange pumpkin again.
2. In the Layers panel, click the **Background** layer to select it.
3. On the menu bar, click **Select**, and then click **Reselect**. The Reselect command activates the most recent selection.
4. On the menu bar, click **Edit**, click **Copy**, click **Edit** again, and then click **Paste** to paste a second copy of the pumpkin onto the image; the copy appears on its own layer (Layer 1).
5. In the Layers panel, move the **Layer 1** layer above the Color Balance 1 adjustment layer.
6. Using the Move tool, point to the pumpkin and then drag it down and to the right. See Figure 5-8.

TIP

You can also press the Shift+Ctrl+D keys to reselect a selection. Press the Ctrl+D keys to deselect a selection.

Figure 5-8 Two versions of the same pumpkin

adjustment is not applied to copy of pumpkin
pumpkin copy layer is above the adjustment layer and not affected by it

Teodora George/Shutterstock.com

Notice that the copy of the pumpkin does not include the adjustment you made because it is no longer part of the selection. It retains the less-intense orange color of the original version of the pumpkin.

7. Save the file as **TwoPumpkins.psd** in the Photoshop5\Tutorial folder, and then close the file.

Now that you have added more interest to this image, you will give this file to Azar so he can use the image in his fund-raising presentation. In the next section, you will learn how to use selection tools to make more complex selections.

INSIGHT

Refining a Selection

Once you have made a selection, you can click the Refine Edge button on the options bar to further refine the selection. Using Refine Edge, you can better see if you have picked up any unwanted pixels in your selection, and you can fine-tune the selection. Clicking Refine Edge opens the Refine Edge dialog box, which shows your selection against a white background by default. You can change the View Mode setting to a black background or another option depending on the colors of the selection. You can also adjust edge settings, such as Smooth, Feather, and Contrast, and you can shift the edge to expand the selection or contract it.

Creating Complex Selections

As you continue to work in Photoshop, you'll find that many of the individual selection tools will work just fine in certain cases. But what happens if the area or areas you need to select are very complex? If they are, you might find that a single selection tool just won't do the job. Just as you did with the Magic Wand tool earlier, you can use the buttons on the options bar to add to and subtract from selections. This Photoshop feature is useful if you want to make a complex selection that includes irregularly shaped areas containing pixels with a variety of colors.

REFERENCE

Adding to a Selection to Create a Complex Selection

- Activate one of the selection tools in the Tools panel, and set its options on the options bar.
- Drag on the canvas to make the first selection.
- On the options bar, click the Add to selection button.
- Use the same tool or select a different one, and drag on the canvas to make a selection that will be added to the first.
- Repeat until you are satisfied with the final selection.

For one of your projects for Azar, you need to select just part of an image of a strawberry plant to use in a flyer. To do so, you'll create a complex selection using both the Rectangular Marquee tool and the Elliptical Marquee tool.

To create a complex selection and paste it into a new file:

1. Open **Strawberry.jpg**, located in the Photoshop5\Tutorial folder, fit the image on screen, reset all of the tools, press the **D** key, if necessary, to reset the default colors, and display the rulers, if necessary.
2. In the Tools panel, click the **Elliptical Marquee Tool** button, and on the options bar, confirm that the **New selection** button is selected and that the Feather setting is **0 px**.
3. On the options bar, click the **Style** button, and then click **Fixed Size**.
4. Specify a Width of **1000** pixels and a Height of **1100** pixels, click the canvas to create the selection, and then drag the selection until it is positioned as shown in Figure 5-9.

Figure 5-9 **Positioning a selection**

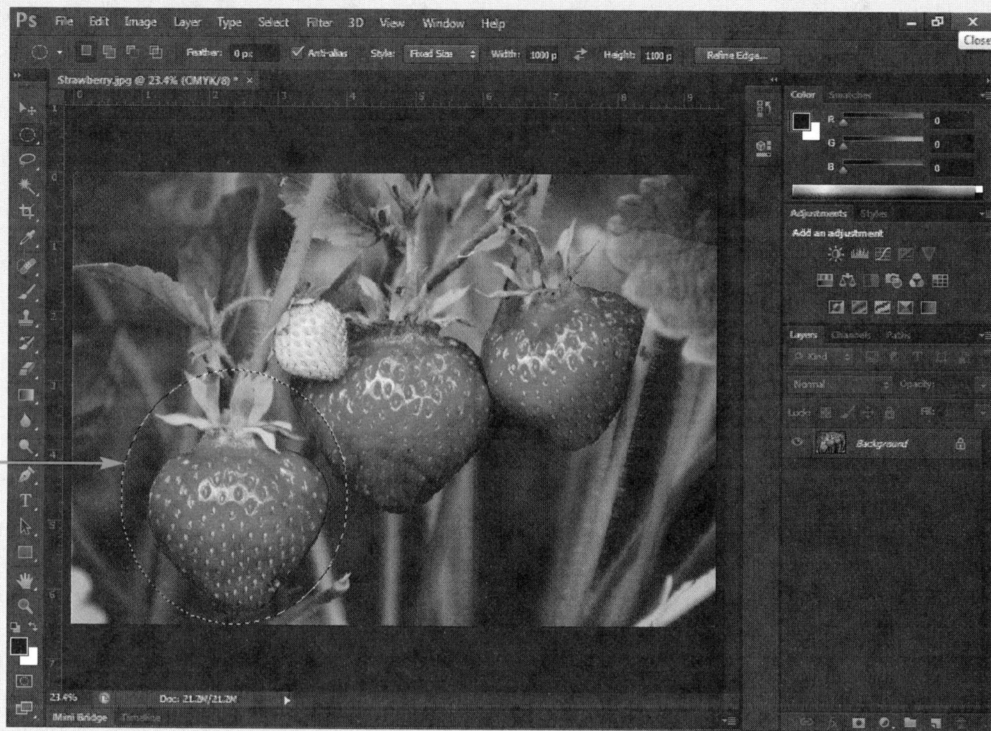
drag the selection marquee to this position

Catarina Belova/Shutterstock.com

5. In the Tools panel, click the **Rectangular Marquee Tool** button, and then on the options bar, click the **Add to selection** button. You can leave the default settings on the options bar.
6. Drag to create a rectangle, as shown in Figure 5-10.

Figure 5-10 **Adding to a selection**

Catarina Belova/Shutterstock.com

When you release the mouse button, the two selections are combined into a single selection.

7. On the menu bar, click **Edit**, and then click **Copy**.
8. Press the **X** key to switch the foreground and background colors so the background color is black.
9. On the menu bar, click **File**, click **New**, and then create a new file using the Default Photoshop Size preset, the CMYK Color mode, and a Resolution setting of 300 ppi. Click the **Background Contents arrow** ▾, and then click **Background Color** to create a black background. Click the **OK** button.
10. Fit the image to the screen, and then on the menu bar, click **Edit** and then click **Paste** to add your selection into the new file.

    The strawberry is pasted into the file as a new layer, labeled Layer 1.
11. In the Layers panel of the new file, double-click the **Layer 1** thumbnail to open the Layer Style dialog box. Apply an Outer Glow effect to the layer with **90%** opacity; in the Elements section, set the Size to **65** pixels, and then click the **OK** button. See Figure 5-11.

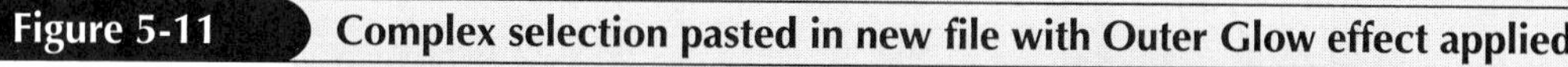

Figure 5-11 **Complex selection pasted in new file with Outer Glow effect applied**

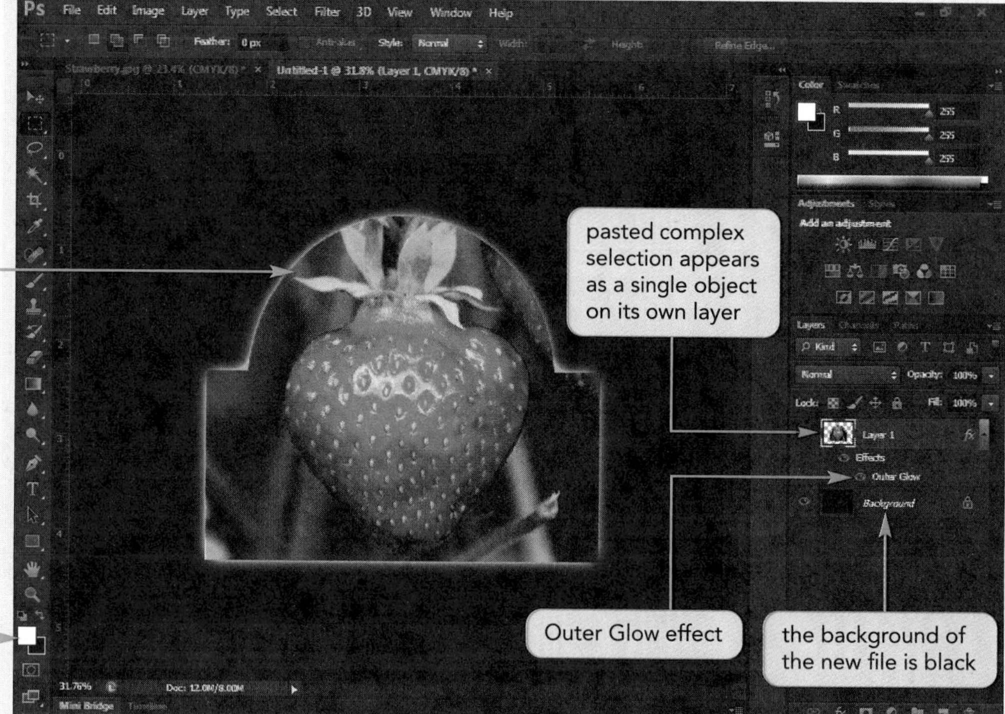

Outer Glow effect applied to layer
the default foreground and background colors have been switched
pasted complex selection appears as a single object on its own layer
Outer Glow effect
the background of the new file is black

Catarina Belova/Shutterstock.com

12. Save the new file as **StrawberryGlow.psd** in the Photoshop5\Tutorial folder, and then close the file. Close Strawberry.jpg without saving it.

Selecting a Color Range

There may be times when one of the colors in an image is not quite what you want it to be. To solve this problem, you can select a color range in an image, and then adjust the color of the pixels that are in that color range—without affecting any other part of the image. In the Color Range dialog box, you can select either a sampled color or any of the RGB (red, green, blue) or CMY (cyan, magenta, yellow) colors. When you use the Color Range command to select a color in an image, Photoshop surrounds the pixels containing the color with a selection marquee. See Figure 5-12.

Figure 5-12 **Selecting a color range in the Color Range dialog box**

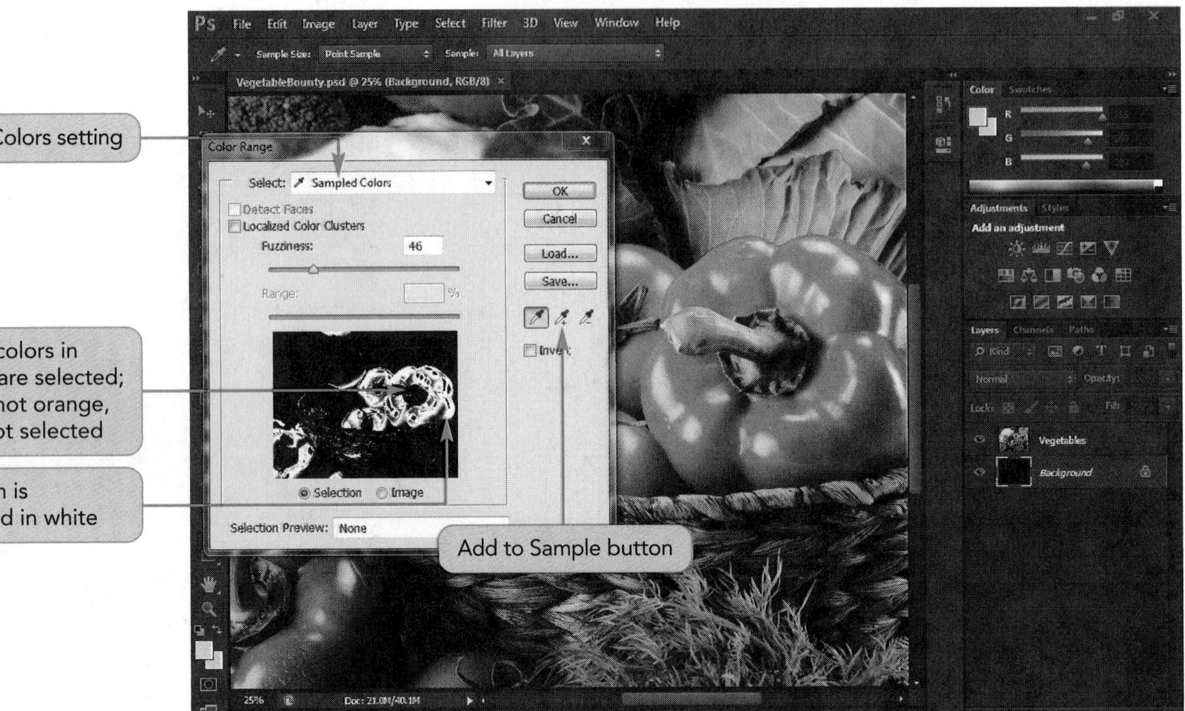

monticello/Shutterstock.com

Figure 5-12 shows a selection based on selecting a range of sampled orange colors. Notice that the selection shown in the Color Range dialog box is much more complex than a selection you could make yourself using the selection tools in the Tools panel. When you select a color range using sampled colors, you can expand your selection to include pixels that are variations in shades of the original sampled color, or even completely different colors. To do so, select the first color and then click the Add to Sample button in the Color Range dialog box. You can subtract from a sample by clicking the Subtract from Sample button and then clicking the color or shade on the canvas that you want to subtract from the selection. You can also click the Localized Color Clusters option to extend the selection only to pixels near the sampled color, and then use the Range slider to determine how near or far from the sample the selection will extend. A Range value of 100% includes the entire image. Increasing the Fuzziness setting increases the array of color values included in the selection. A low Fuzziness setting will select only colors that are very similar to the selected color. A high Fuzziness setting will select colors that are similar to the selected color—for example, oranges of different intensities. Once you select the colors you want, close the dialog box, and then modify the selection as desired—for example, by adjusting its hue, saturation, and brightness (HSB) or by applying an adjustment layer to the pixels that are part of the selection but not to the image as a whole.

Azar wants you to work with the image of the pumpkins to change it from a photograph of green pumpkins with one orange pumpkin on top to all orange pumpkins. He'd like to use the two images to show that in the Food for Change organization, every participant has an equal chance at success.

To select using a color range:

1. Open **Pumpkin.jpg**, located in the Photoshop5\Tutorial folder, display the image at a 10% zoom setting, hide the rulers, and reset all of the tools. Press the **D** key to return to the default foreground and background colors.
2. Click **Select**, and then click **Color Range**. The Color Range dialog box opens. Drag the dialog box to the right so the entire image is visible. See Figure 5-13.

Figure 5-13 Using the Color Range dialog box

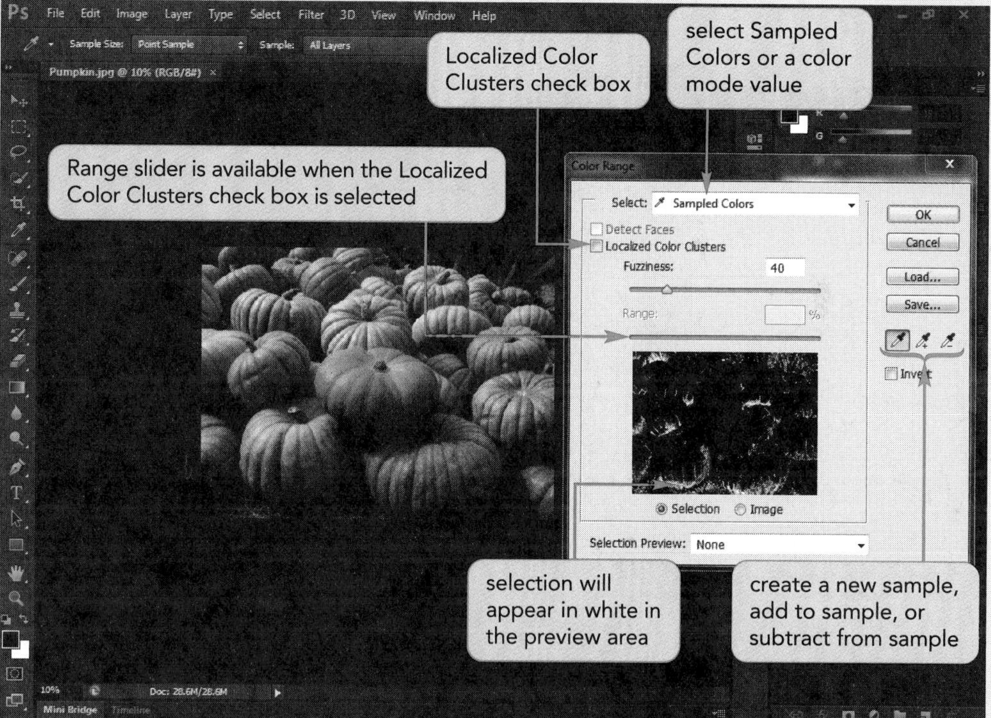

Teodora George/Shutterstock.com

3. Confirm that **Sampled Colors** is selected in the Select box at the top of the dialog box, and that the **Selection** option is selected under the preview box. The Fuzziness setting should be set at the default of **40**. Click different areas of the green pumpkins on the canvas. As you do so, the preview changes to show what areas of the image would be selected based on the sampled color. White areas show completely selected pixels, while gray areas show partially selected pixels.

   To see the effect of selecting localized color clusters, you'll select that option in the dialog box.

4. Click the **Localized Color Clusters** check box to select it, set the Range to **20%**, and then click one of the green pumpkins. Only a small area around the pumpkin you clicked shows a selection because you limited the range.
5. Drag the **Range** slider to the right until the setting is **100%**. The sampled color is once again selected in the entire image.
6. Change the Fuzziness setting to **170**. More pixels in the green pumpkins are selected.

7. Deselect the **Localized Color Clusters** check box. Notice that even more of the green pixels in the image are selected and the pixels appear white rather than gray, indicating that they are fully selected.
8. In the Color Range dialog box, click the **Select arrow** ▾, and then click **Reds**. The orange pumpkin, which includes a high red intensity value, is selected, but the green pumpkins are not.
9. Click the **Select arrow** ▾, and then click **Sampled Colors**. The green pumpkins are selected again.
10. Change the Fuzziness setting to **40**, click the **Add to Sample** button in the dialog box, and then on the canvas, click any areas of the green pumpkins that aren't selected in the dialog box. See Figure 5-14.

Figure 5-14 **Completing the selection**

Teodora George/Shutterstock.com

Trouble? If the ground and the green stems at the top of the image are selected and appear white in the preview instead of gray, click the Subtract from Selection button, and then click the ground on the canvas so that your dialog box resembles the dialog box in Figure 5-14. Note that you might need to subtract from and add to the selection a few times to get your selection to match the selection shown in the figure.

11. Click the **OK** button. Photoshop displays a complex selection marquee. See Figure 5-15.

Figure 5-15 Complex selection based on color

Teodora George/Shutterstock.com

You could continue to add to this selection to include additional pixels.

12. In the Adjustments panel, click the **Color Balance** icon.
13. In the Properties panel, make sure **Midtones** is selected for the Tone option, and adjust the settings to **+100** for Cyan Red, **-99** for Magenta Green, and **-100** for Yellow Blue.
14. Click the **Tone** button, select **Shadows**, and change the Cyan Red setting to **+49** and the Yellow Blue setting to **-55**. Collapse the Properties panel. See Figure 5-16.

Figure 5-16 Color Balance adjustment applied to selection

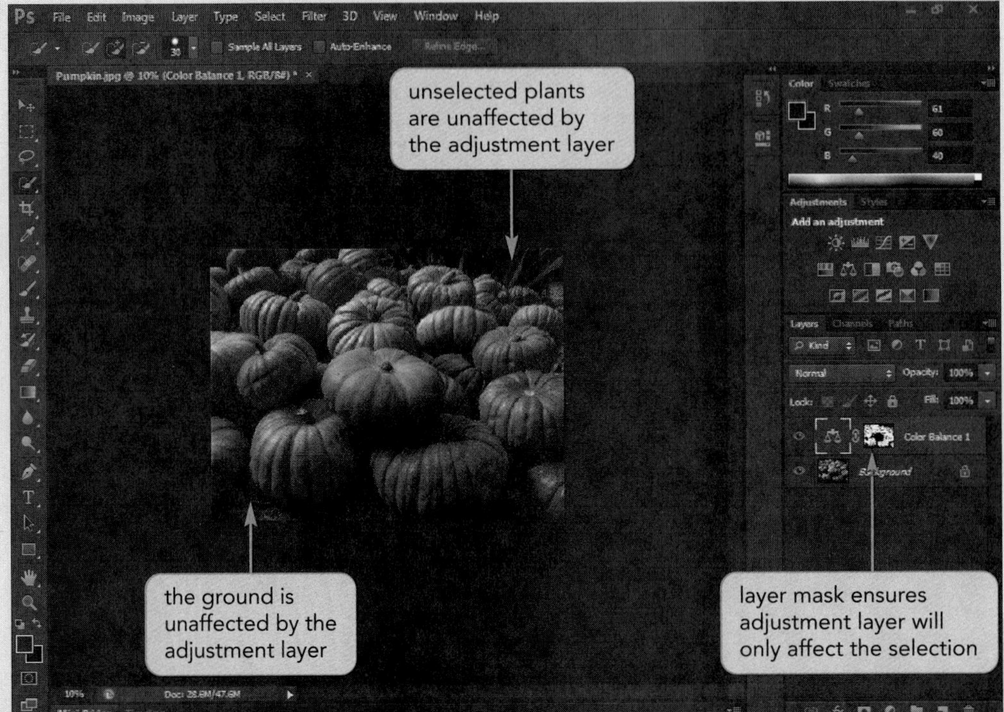
unselected plants
are unaffected by
the adjustment layer
the ground is
unaffected by the
adjustment layer
layer mask ensures
adjustment layer will
only affect the selection

Teodora George/Shutterstock.com

The layer mask thumbnail on the adjustment layer indicates which parts of the image are affected by the adjustment. The thumbnail displays the selection in white.

15. To see more clearly how the new adjustment layer has not altered the underlying pixels in the image, hide and then redisplay the **Color Balance 1** layer. The image beneath the adjustment layer is unchanged.
16. Save the file as **AllOrange.psd** in the Photoshop5\Tutorial folder, and then close it.

The tasks Azar is giving you are getting more and more complex. You'd like to make sure you can keep track of all of your changes to a composition and not alter any files permanently until you are happy with what you've done. You'll learn about and then use undo and redo techniques to keep track of your actions so you can proceed with confidence.

Undoing and Redoing Actions

Once you master selections, you have the tools to be more creative than ever. You can apply even more complex effects and adjustments to your compositions—not just to layers, but to pixels selected in a layer. With this newfound creative license, it is helpful to know how to undo some of your changes while preserving others.

Stepping Backward and Forward

When you make a change or an adjustment that you want to reverse, you can undo it by clicking the Undo command on the Edit menu. The actual name of the Undo command varies, depending on your most recent action. For example, if your most recent action was adding a new solid color fill layer, the command name is Undo New Color Fill Layer. If you have just drawn a rectangle on the canvas, the command name is Undo Rectangle tool. Using the Undo command, you can undo only the most recent action.

Photoshop has two additional commands on the Edit menu, Step Forward and Step Backward, that let you undo a series of changes, and then redo them to whatever point you want. Using these commands can help you determine if the modifications you've made to an image have the effect you had planned.

To step forward and backward in a file:

1. Open **Pumpkin.jpg**, located in the Photoshop5\Tutorial folder, and then zoom in to view the image at 50%. Pan the image, if necessary, so that the orange pumpkin appears at the center of the canvas, and press the **D** key to reset the foreground and background colors.
2. In the Tools panel, click the **Elliptical Marquee Tool** button, and click and drag to create an elliptical marquee that partially covers the orange pumpkin. Drag the selection to center it over the pumpkin, if necessary. Don't worry if the selection marquee doesn't encompass the entire pumpkin or if your selection marquee is too large.
3. On the menu bar, click **Select**, and then click **Transform Selection**. A rectangle appears around the selection, and handles appear on the rectangle.
4. Drag the handles on the rectangle until the ellipse covers most of the pumpkin but doesn't go beyond its edges, and then click the **Commit** button on the options bar.
5. In the Tools panel, click the **Brush Tool** button, and change the brush Size setting to **150** pixels. Paint three separate strokes over the selection, starting above the selection marquee and ending below the selection marquee. See Figure 5-17.

Figure 5-17 Altering the pixels within a selection marquee

Teodora George/Shutterstock.com

As you paint, notice that none of your painting spills over the selection border. The selection contains your actions, and only lets you affect the pixels within the selection marquee.

6. On the menu bar, click **Edit**. The top menu choice is Undo Brush Tool. The third choice is Step Backward. As you have seen, you can only undo one action (in this case, the last action taken using the Brush tool). However, you can step backward up to 20 times.
7. Click **Step Backward**. The last brushstroke you added disappears from the image.
8. On the menu bar, click **Edit**, and then click **Step Backward**. The previous brushstroke disappears.
9. On the menu bar, click **Edit**, click **Step Forward**, click **Edit**, and then click **Step Forward** again. Both brushstrokes reappear. You undid and then redid two actions.
10. On the menu bar, click **Edit**, and then click **Step Backward**. The last brushstroke to reappear disappears again.

TIP

You can also press the Alt+Ctrl+Z keys to step backward. Press the Shift+Ctrl+Z keys to step forward.

Using the Step Backward and Step Forward commands works well if you're only dealing with a few actions, but what happens when you've made multiple changes to a file, and want to quickly go back to a previous state? This is where the History panel comes in.

Reverting to a Previous State Using the History Panel

The History panel provides a more flexible way to reverse changes to a composition. By default, the History panel records your 20 most recent actions and lists them in order. Each item on the list is called a history state. A snapshot of the file's original state appears at the top of the list. As you work, you can create additional snapshots to make it easy to return to a particular history state after you have made a series of changes. If you perform more than 20 actions, the earliest history states drop off the History panel and are no longer visible or reversible. See Figure 5-18.

Figure 5-18 **Using the History panel**

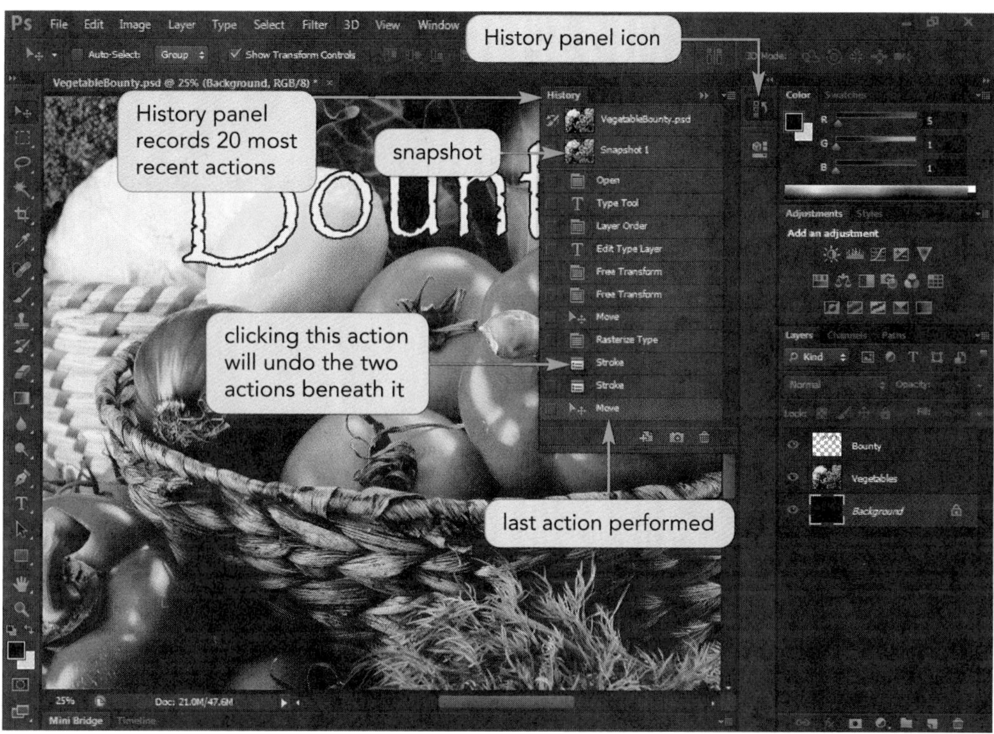

monticello/Shutterstock.com

You can click a history state in the History panel to revert your image to the state it was in when you performed that action. When you do, the states beneath that action appear dimmed in the History panel. However, they are still stored in memory, so if you want to redo all of the actions at once, you can simply click the bottom command on the panel. For example, in Figure 5-18, the last action on the list is Move. If you click the Stroke history state two rows up, Photoshop will undo the two actions beneath it in the panel. If you click the Move history state again, Photoshop will redo the final two actions in the History panel.

It's important to note, though, that if you select a history state and then perform a different action, all of the steps beneath the history state you selected are no longer in memory and are erased from the panel. Furthermore, once you close a document, all of the states and snapshots are erased and won't be available the next time you open the file.

REFERENCE

Reverting to a Previous History State Using the History Panel

- Click the History icon to the left of the Color panel, or on the menu bar, click Window, and then click History to open the History panel.
- Edit the image you are working with, and at the bottom of the History panel, click the Create new snapshot icon as needed to record specific history states.
- Click a history state or a snapshot to revert to that state.

You'll experiment with the History panel, and then modify the image of the pumpkin so Azar can use it in his nutrition presentation "Pumpkins: Not Just for Jack-o'-Lanterns," which is an outreach program that encourages schoolchildren to eat more vegetables.

To use the History panel to revert to history states, delete history states, and create snapshots:

1. Click the **History** icon to the left of the Color panel. The History panel opens, and a snapshot of the file's original state appears at the top of the list.

   Trouble? If you can't see the top of the list, drag the scroll bar up until you can.

2. Point to the bottom edge of the History panel until you see a double-headed arrow, and then, if necessary, drag down until all of the history states appear on the panel.
3. Add a horizontal brushstroke to the selection. See Figure 5-19.

Figure 5-19 **States recorded in the History panel**

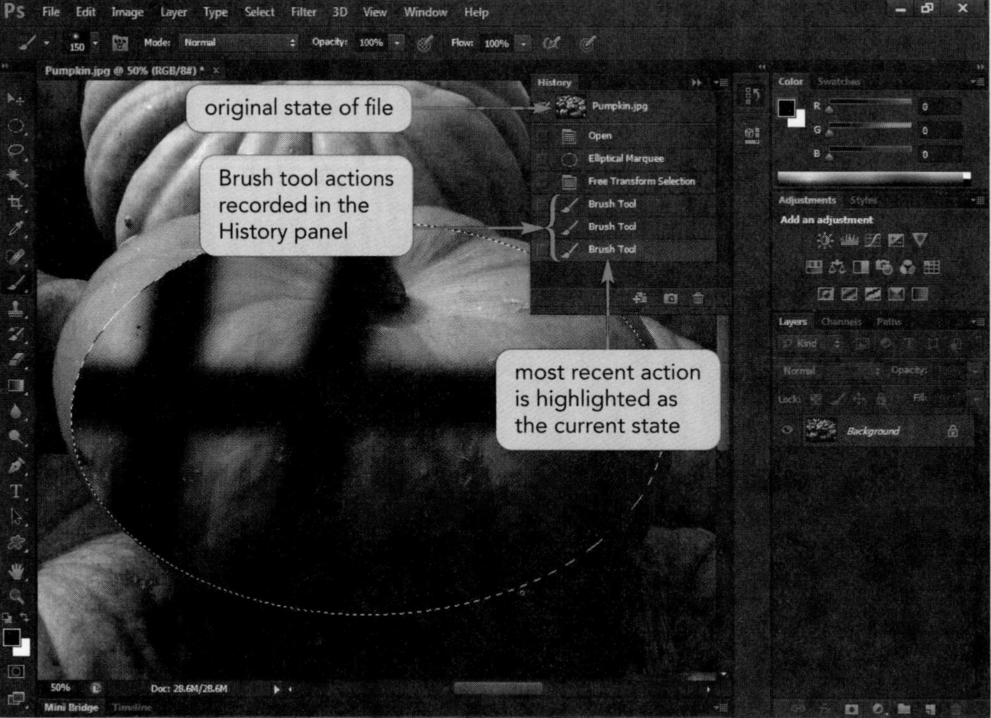

Teodora George/Shutterstock.com

Notice that an additional Brush tool history state now appears at the bottom of the panel. Because it is your most recent action, it is highlighted.

4. In the History panel, click the **Free Transform Selection** state. All of the Brush tool states appear dimmed in the History panel, and all of the brushstrokes disappear from the composition.
5. Click the **Pumpkin.jpg** snapshot at the top of the History panel. The file reverts to its original state, with no selection marquee.
6. Click the top **Brush Tool** state. One brushstroke appears on the image along with the selection marquee, but the other two brushstrokes are still not visible.
7. At the bottom of the History panel, click the **Create new snapshot** icon. A snapshot of the image in the selected state appears in the History panel beneath the image of the file in its original state. See Figure 5-20.

Figure 5-20 **Storing a state as a snapshot**

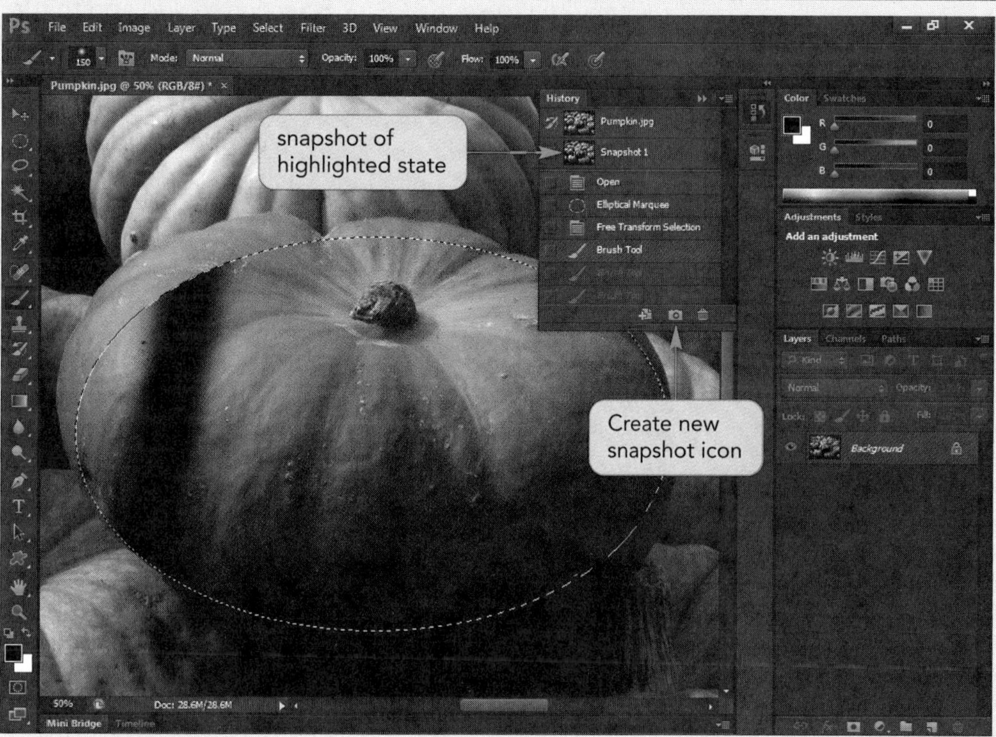

Teodora George/Shutterstock.com

You can click this snapshot at any time to revert to this state.

8. In the History panel, click the **Elliptical Marquee** state. The first brushstroke you painted disappears, and if you moved or resized the selection after you drew it, the selection marquee returns to its original location and size.
9. Click **Snapshot 1**. The document now reflects the history state of the selected snapshot.
10. Click the bottom **Brush Tool** state to select it, and then drag it to the Delete current state icon at the bottom of the panel. The Brush Tool state is deleted from the History panel, and the horizontal brushstroke is deleted from the image.
11. Click the top **Brush Tool** state in the History panel, click the **Delete current state** icon at the bottom of the panel, and then click the **Yes** button in the dialog box to confirm the deletion. Both of the remaining brushstrokes disappear from the image, and both of the Brush Tool states disappear from the History panel.

    You'll learn more about the Quick Selection tool in the next session, but for now, you'll use the Quick Selection tool to add to the selection, and then apply an effect to the inverse of the selection so the orange pumpkin stands out even more.
12. Collapse the History panel, and then in the Tools panel, click the **Quick Selection Tool** button, on the options bar, change the size of the Quick Selection pointer to **50** pixels, click the **Add to selection** button, and then click the unselected parts of the pumpkin until they are fully selected.

    Trouble? If you select more than the orange pumpkin, press the Ctrl+Z keys to undo the selection or click the Subtract from selection button on the options bar until only the orange pumpkin is selected.
13. On the menu bar, click **Select**, and then click **Inverse**. Press the **Ctrl+0** keys to fit the image on screen. Everything but the orange pumpkin is selected in the image.
14. Add a black Solid Color fill layer to the image with **75%** opacity. See Figure 5-21.

Figure 5-21 **Adding an effect to an inverse selection**

pumpkin unaffected by color fill
color fill is added to selected area
pumpkin is masked from color fill layer

Teodora George/Shutterstock.com

The orange pumpkin stands out even more, while the rest of the image is shaded in black.

15. Save the file as **SolePumpkin.psd** in the Photoshop5\Tutorial folder, and then close the file.

INSIGHT

Changing the Number of History States Stored by Photoshop

You can increase or decrease the number of history states Photoshop stores in memory. If you decrease the number of history states, you can improve your system performance by freeing up memory. If you increase the number of history states, you have more freedom to undo multiple changes, but your system may slow down. Photoshop stores history states for every file open in memory, so if you have five files open, you can have up to 100 history states in memory by default. You can change the number of history states Photoshop stores using the Preferences command on the Edit menu. The Performance option lets you change the number of history states. The number of states you decide to store ultimately depends on your work habits and your computer system.

You can also use the History Brush tool to return an image to a previous state—or even a partial version of a previous state.

Using the History Brush Tool

The History Brush tool works in tandem with the History panel to give you very detailed control over the edits you've made to a file. You might be familiar with the phrase *to airbrush history*. In historical terms, airbrushing history means deliberately hiding the parts of a historical record that you think are unfavorable. You can think of the History Brush tool in a similar way. Imagine that you have made multiple changes to a composition, and each change is recorded as a state in the History panel. Some of your changes are perfect; you want to keep them the way they are. Others work for some areas of the image but not for others. In Normal mode, the History Brush tool lets you paint over individual areas you want to revert to a previous state while leaving other areas alone. When you paint over those areas, the brush erases the state or states on top of the image to return to the state you have chosen as the source for your brush.

To use the History Brush tool, in the History panel, click in the empty box to the left of a state that you want to "uncover" with the brush. This sets the source for the History Brush tool. You can then choose a brush tip for your brush, set the diameter, and set the Opacity and Flow percentages. If you want to paint with the selected state exactly as it appeared before the additional changes, make sure that the Opacity and Flow settings are 100% and the Mode setting is Normal so all of the details revert to the way they looked in that state.

REFERENCE

Using the History Brush Tool to Return Part of an Image to a Previous History State

- Click the History icon to the left of the Color panel, or on the menu bar, click Window, and then click History to open the History panel.
- In the History panel, click to the left of a history state to mark it with the Sets the source for the history brush icon and to make that history state the source for the brush.
- In the Tools panel, click the History Brush Tool button.
- On the options bar, specify History Brush tool options such as brush diameter, mode, opacity, and flow.
- Paint over the part of the image you want to return to the source state.

Azar wants you to work with a photograph of a pathway to one of the organization's gardens to make it look magical so that he can include it in his presentation to a group of younger children he hopes will join the program.

To use the History Brush tool to return part of an image to a previous state:

1. Open **GardenPath.jpg**, located in the Photoshop5\Tutorial folder, reset the Essentials workspace, reset the foreground and background colors to the default colors, reset all tools, open the History panel, and drag the bottom edge of the History panel down to resize it so there is room to show multiple history states. Then, drag the entire History panel to the lower-right corner of the Document window so that it is beneath the Layers panel.
2. In the Tools panel, click the **Brush Tool** button.
3. On the menu bar, click **Window**, and then click **Brush Presets** to open the Brush Presets panel.
4. In the Brush Presets panel, click the **panel menu** button, click **Special Effect Brushes**, and then click the **OK** button to replace the current brushes with the Special Effect Brushes.

   Trouble? If you are prompted to save changes to the current brushes, click the No button.
5. In the Brush Presets panel, click the **Azalea** brush tip, and change the size of the brush to **200** pixels. Change the Opacity on the options bar to **100%** if necessary.
6. Press the **X** key to switch the foreground and background colors, and then set the foreground color on the Color panel to R=**230**, G=**50**, and B=**150**. The Azalea brush uses both the foreground and background colors in its strokes.
7. Click the **Brush Presets** icon to the left of the Color panel to collapse the Brush Presets panel.
8. Paint over the garden on the left side of the brick pathway, as shown in Figure 5-22, by dragging back and forth and up and down with the mouse pointer. Keep the mouse button depressed the entire time so only one Brush Tool state is recorded in the History panel.

Figure 5-22 Recording painting actions in the History panel

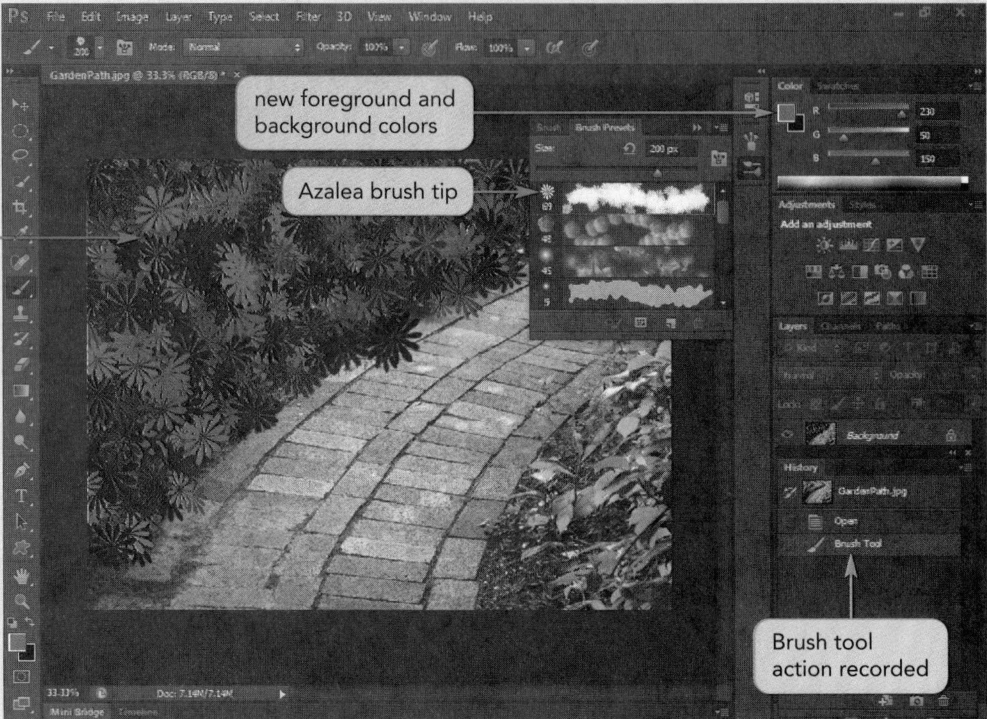

Jane Hosie-Bounar

Trouble? If you need to start over, either step backward to undo your actions, or delete the states in the History panel.

9. Click the **Brush Presets** icon to the left of the Color panel to expand the Brush Presets panel, scroll down if necessary, and then click the **Butterfly** brush tip. Set the size to **150** pixels, and change the Opacity on the options bar to **100%**, if necessary.
10. Set the foreground color to R=**140**, G=**200**, and B=**240**.
11. Keeping the mouse button depressed, drag up and down and side to side over the bed of azaleas you just painted until you've added many butterflies.

    You'll use the History Brush tool to uncover the azaleas and part of the original image.

TIP

You can also press the Y key to activate the History Brush tool.

12. In the Tools panel, click the **History Brush Tool** button, on the options bar, click the **Brush Preset picker** button, and then change the brush size to **100** pixels. Click the **Brush Preset picker** button again to close the Brush Preset picker.
13. On the options bar, confirm that the Opacity and Flow settings are 100%, and then drag down through the center of the flower bed. See Figure 5-23.

Figure 5-23 Using the History Brush tool

100-pixel width
100% opacity and flow
original image state uncovered because snapshot of original image is the source
History Brush
brush icon marks the source for the History Brush

Jane Hosie-Bounar

You uncovered the original image because by default, the History Brush tool uses the original image state as its source.

14. Expand the History panel, if necessary, and then, at the bottom of the History panel, click the **Delete current state** icon, and then click the **Yes** button to confirm the deletion.

    Next, you'll make the azaleas the source for the History Brush tool so it erases the butterfly brushstrokes, but not the flowers.

15. In the History panel, click to the left of the first Brush tool history state to mark it with the Sets the source for the history brush icon, and then drag over the flower bed with the brush until most of the butterflies have been painted over with the History brush. See Figure 5-24.

TIP

You can also take a snapshot of a history state, and then use that snapshot to set the source for the History Brush tool.

Figure 5-24 History erased to the state marked as the source

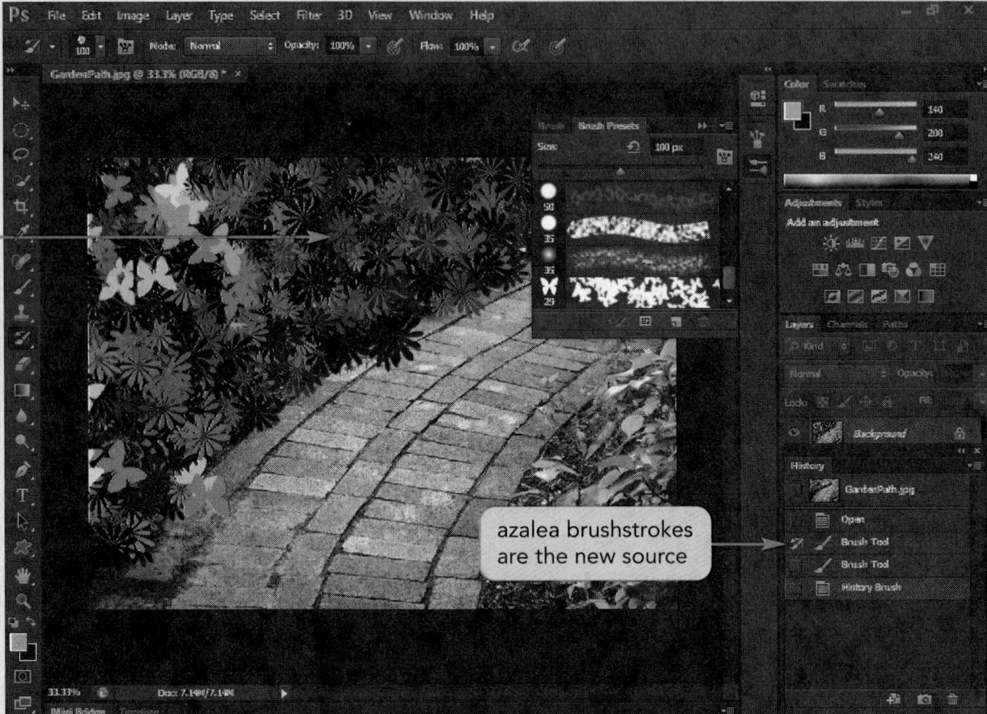
History Brush paints over the butterflies, but not the flowers
azalea brushstrokes are the new source

Jane Hosie-Bounar

The History Brush tool erases the butterfly brushstroke, but not the flower bed you painted. This is because you set the Azalea brushstroke state as the source for the brush.

16. Save the file as **Flowerbed.jpg**, using the default JPEG Options, in the Photoshop5\Tutorial folder, close the file, and then exit Photoshop.

INSIGHT

Using the Art History Brush Tool

The Art History Brush tool also uses history states to paint on an image, but the effect is completely different from the effect of the History Brush tool. The Art History Brush tool creates stylized artwork by essentially transforming a digital photograph into a painting using the colors of the source. Its results are often unpredictable, and if you choose to use the Art History Brush tool, you should take the time to experiment with different mode, opacity, style, and tolerance settings. Minor variations in any of these settings can create very different results.

In this session, you experimented with a variety of Photoshop selection tools. You learned how to apply an adjustment to a selection and how to copy and paste selections. You created complex selections, and explored how to select a color range in an image. You also spent time undoing and redoing actions with the Edit menu, the History panel, and the History Brush tool. In the next session, you'll explore additional selection tools, and work with filters, fills, and masks.

REVIEW

Session 5.1 Quick Check

1. A(n) ________________ encloses part of an image in a series of animated dashed lines or curves.
2. True or False. The Rectangular Marquee tool has an Anti-alias setting.
3. The ________________ setting on the options bar lets you specify a width and a height for your selection.
4. Which command increases the size of a selection by a specified number of pixels?
5. What is the purpose of a snapshot in the History panel?
6. True or False. When you save and close a file, all history states are saved with the file.
7. Which tool can you use in conjunction with the History panel to return part of an image to a previous state?

SESSION 5.2 VISUAL OVERVIEW

The Magnetic Lasso tool quickly selects the outline of a complex object on a high-contrast background and adds **fastening points** that define the selection marquee based on the frequency you specify; the **frequency** determines the distance between fastening points.

You can load a saved selection by selecting it from the Channel list.

An RGB image has a composite RGB color channel and three individual color channels (R, G, and B).

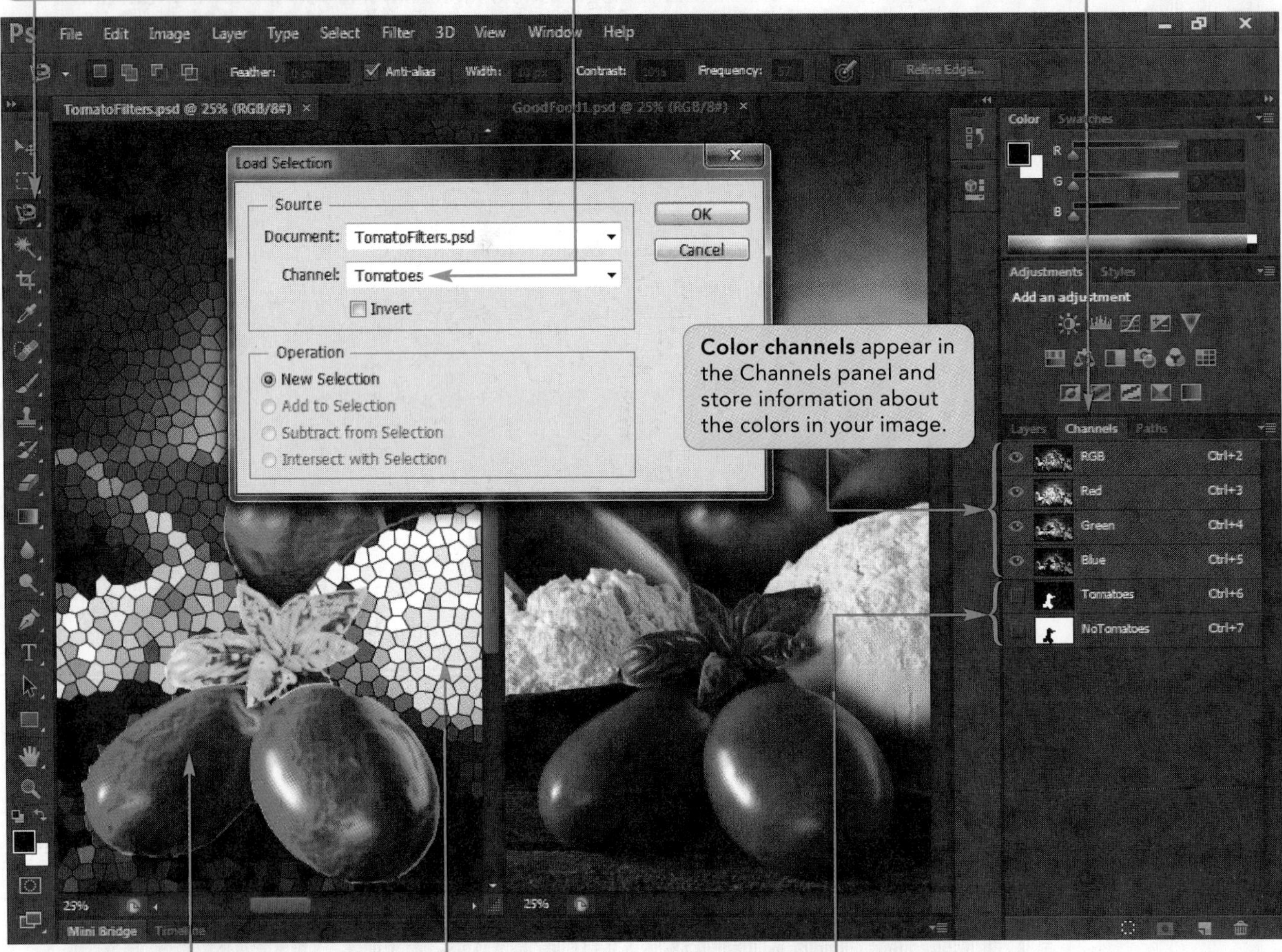

Color channels appear in the Channels panel and store information about the colors in your image.

The Diffuse Glow effect has been applied to the Tomatoes selection.

The Stained Glass effect has been applied to the NoTomatoes selection.

Selections can be saved as **alpha channels**, which store selections as masks; white indicates the selection, while black indicates the masked area.

marco mayer/Shutterstock.com

LASSO TOOLS AND FILTERS

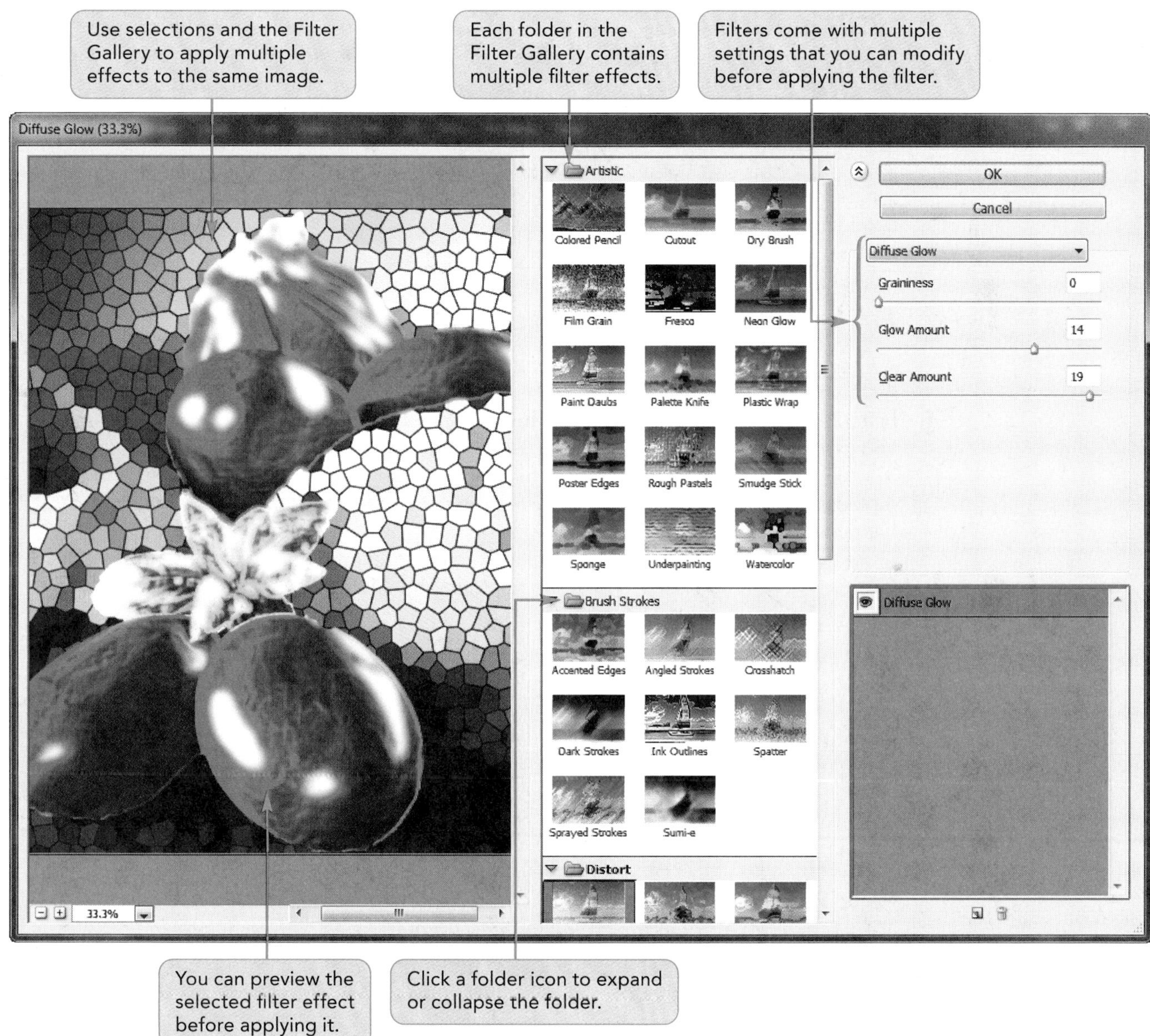

marco mayer/Shutterstock.com

Working with the Lasso Tools, Fills, and the Content-Aware Move Tool

The Lasso tools give you many options for selecting content on your canvas. Photoshop includes three Lasso tools, each with unique benefits. To use the Polygonal Lasso tool, click a starting point for your selection, and then continue to click around the selection. As you do, Photoshop connects the points you click with straight lines. You can close your selection and activate the selection marquee by double-clicking. The Magnetic Lasso tool is attracted to the defined edges of whatever object you first click on. As you move the mouse pointer, it adds points along the selection based on a frequency you specify. You can add extra points and change direction by clicking. You use the regular Lasso tool in much the same way you would draw with a brush or pencil. You simply drag on the image to create your free-form selection. When you release the mouse button, Photoshop creates the selection marquee. If you release the mouse button before returning to your starting point, Photoshop draws a straight line to the starting point from the point at which you stopped dragging to complete the selection. A selection made with the Lasso tool isn't as precise as other selection methods, but you'll find you use it often as a starting point. As you become more experienced with Photoshop, you'll be able to determine which particular tool is the best one for your selection needs.

Filling a Selection Using the Content-Aware Fill Feature

A Content-Aware fill allows you to remove objects from a photograph and replace them with similar versions of the surrounding pixels. For example, you might have a beautiful photograph of a sandy beach with a piece of trash right in the middle of it. You can use one of the Lasso tools to select the trash and some of the sand surrounding it. When you use the Content-Aware fill, Photoshop makes the trash disappear and replaces it with the sand. Because the feature generates the fill randomly, if you're not happy with the first result, you can repeat it.

Azar has given you a photograph of a tomato garden that he wants to use in his Live Green, Eat Green slide show. The photograph includes a woman, but he'd like to remove the woman and fill the area with tomato plants instead. You'll select the woman using the Lasso tool, and then you'll fill the selection using the Content-Aware fill.

To use the Lasso tool and fill the selection with content:

1. Start Photoshop while pressing the **Ctrl+Alt+Shift** keys, and click **Yes** to delete the Settings File when prompted. Reset Photoshop to the default Essentials workspace layout, and reset all tools.
2. Navigate to the Photoshop5\Tutorial folder included with your Data Files, and open **WomanInGarden.jpg**. Display the image at 25% zoom, and pan the image, if necessary, so the woman is completely in the Document window.
3. Click the **Lasso Tool** button in the Tools panel and drag a selection completely around the woman, and then release the mouse button.

   You don't need to be too exacting when you make the selection, but make sure the woman is completely selected, and that the selection includes some of the image area surrounding the woman.

A selection marquee appears around the woman. See Figure 5-25. (The green outline around the selection marquee was added to Figure 5-25 to highlight the selection marquee.)

Figure 5-25 **Selecting with the Lasso tool**

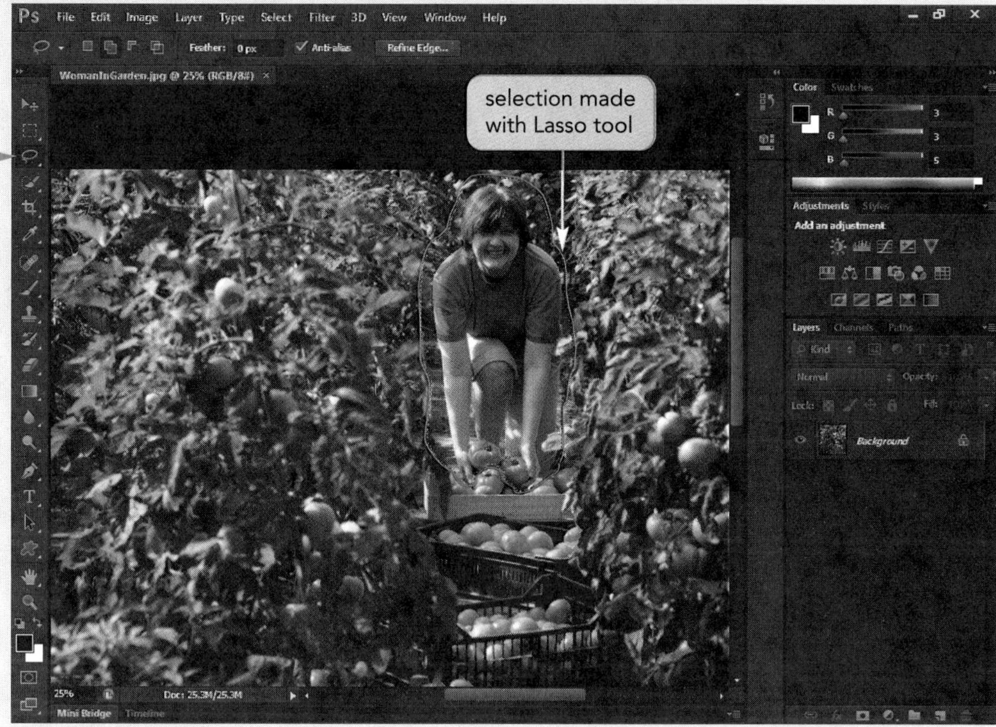

Fotokostic/Shutterstock.com

4. On the menu bar, click **Edit**, and then click **Fill**. The Fill dialog box opens.
5. In the Contents section, click the **Use** button, and click **Content-Aware**, if necessary. Set the Blending Mode to **Normal**, set the Opacity to **100%**, and then click the **OK** button. A progress bar appears while the selection is filled.
6. Press the **Ctrl+0** keys to fit the image on screen. See Figure 5-26.

Figure 5-26 **Selected area filled with surrounding content**

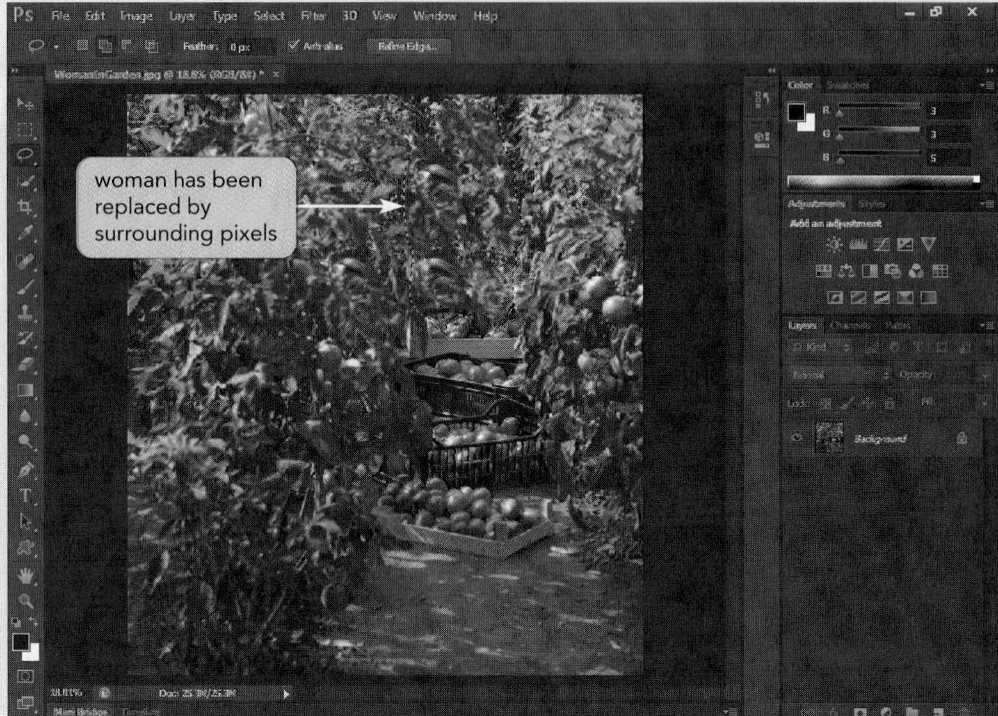

Fotokostic/Shutterstock.com

Photoshop uses the data in the area surrounding the selection to fill the selection.

7. On the menu bar, click **Select**, and then click **Deselect** to clear the selection.

   The image has been transformed from a photograph of a woman in a garden to just the garden. There is no evidence that the woman was ever there.

   Trouble? If you aren't satisfied with the way Photoshop filled in the area, repeat Steps 3 through 7. Because the results are randomly generated, the fill will look different every time.

8. Save the file as **TomatoGarden.jpg**, using the default JPEG Options, in the Photoshop5\Tutorial folder, and then close it.

Moving a Selection Using the Content-Aware Move Tool

In earlier versions of Photoshop, you could make a selection and move or cut the selected pixels, but when you did so, you were always left with an empty area on your canvas. Think back to what happened when you cut and pasted a selection in the last session: Cutting the pixels exposed the black Background layer underneath the strawberry layer because the remaining area contained only transparent pixels. Photoshop CS6 has a new tool hidden under the Spot Healing Brush tool on the Tools panel called the Content-Aware Move tool. The **Content-Aware Move tool** combines a typical move action with the magic of Content-Aware fill so that when you move a selection, the empty space left behind is automatically filled with pixels copied from the surrounding area. As a result, your image remains whole. See Figure 5-27.

Figure 5-27 Moving a selection with the Content-Aware Move tool

Dog on beach at sunset.jpg @ 12% (RGB/8) *
selection for the move operation includes pixels around the object to be moved
dog will be moved to this area
area where dog used to be is filled with pixels of surrounding sand
dog in new position
Doc: 28.6M/28.6M
12%
Doc: 28.6M/28.6M

Jane Hosie-Bounar

In Figure 5-27, the dog has been moved from the center of the image to the lower-left corner of the image using the Content-Aware Move tool. In the original photo, shown on the left, the dog and some of the surrounding sand were selected with the Lasso tool. Then, using the Content-Aware Move tool, the selection was dragged down and to the left. The space where the dog was originally lying was filled with pixels from the surrounding area—the sandy beach.

Azar would like you to modify an image of a pumpkin patch so there is room for advertising copy on the left side. He suggests you move the pumpkin in the foreground to the right.

To use the Content-Aware Move tool to move a selection:

1. Open **PumpkinField.jpg**, located in the Photoshop5\Tutorial folder, fit the image on the screen, and then, in the Tools panel, click the **Lasso Tool** button, if necessary, to select it.
2. Drag a selection around the pumpkin in the foreground and its shadow, as shown in Figure 5-28. (The green outline around the selection marquee was added to Figure 5-28 to highlight the selection marquee.)

Figure 5-28 Selecting the pumpkin to move

iKhai_TH/Shutterstock.com

3. In the Tools panel, click the **Content-Aware Move Tool** button. On the options bar, set the Mode to **Move**, and set the Adaptation to **Medium**, if necessary.

   Trouble? If you don't see the Content-Aware Move Tool button in the Tools panel, click and hold the Spot Healing Brush Tool button to display the hidden tools, and then click the Content-Aware Move Tool button.

4. Point to the selection. The pointer changes to . Press the mouse button, and then drag to the right until the pumpkin is in the location shown in Figure 5-29. Release the mouse button. As you drag, you can see two versions of the pumpkin.

   When you release the mouse button, you'll see a progress bar as Photoshop analyzes, moves, and replaces pixels, and then you'll see the pumpkin in its new location.

Figure 5-29 **Using the Content-Aware Move tool**

original location is filled based on surrounding pixels
pumpkin and shadow have been moved, and the selection is still active

iKhai_TH/Shutterstock.com

Trouble? If you're not satisfied with the result, step backward and then experiment with different-sized selections and options bar settings. Because of the complexity of the operation, results will vary not only by image, but also by the way you draw your selection.

5. Save the file as **PumpkinMoved.jpg** using the default JPEG options, and then close it.

Problem Solving: Using an Image Without a Model Release

Problem solving is the ability to identify—and close—a gap between an existing state and a desired state. It's a critical skill to develop because no matter what your career, you're bound to encounter problems that take a creative thinker (you) to solve them. For example, imagine that you have the perfect landscape photo for a travel ad you're creating. The image includes a stunning landscape, beautiful architecture, and an old man riding his bicycle along the cobblestone road. Can you use the photograph?

The answer isn't simple. Basically, it depends. If you're using the photograph for a commercial purpose, as in this travel ad example, you would need to ask the man to sign a model release form giving you permission to use his likeness in your piece. However, if the man isn't recognizable—for example, if you've photographed his back, or if his face is cloaked in shadow, you really don't need his permission. But, assume the man in the image is fully recognizable, and that using his image is a problem you need to solve. Even without his permission, you still have a number of options. You can modify the photograph so the man is unrecognizable—for example by using Photoshop to add shadows to his face. You can also use the Content-Aware fill feature to replace the man and his bicycle with pixels from the cobblestone road. In other words, when you're experienced in digital image editing, you'll find more than one way to solve any image problem you may encounter.

Selecting Content with the Magnetic Lasso Tool

The Magnetic Lasso tool is hidden under the Lasso tool in the Tools panel. It's aptly named because it appears to use a virtual magnet to select the edges of an object in an image. When you work with the tool, it is as if the object you are selecting is metal and the selection marquee is a magnet.

As the tool draws a selection marquee, it drops fastening points along the selection marquee to hold the selection in place. The frequency determines the distance between fastening points. On the options bar, you can specify a Frequency setting between 0 and 100. For a more refined selection, increase the frequency of the fastening points. You can also specify a detection Width, which is the distance from the pointer, in number of pixels, within which you want the tool to detect edges. The Contrast setting, which ranges from 1% to 100%, determines how sensitive the tool is to edges. A low Contrast setting detects low contrast edges, whereas a high setting detects edges with a sharp contrast. Unlike with the Lasso tool, you do not need to hold down the mouse button when making a selection using the Magnetic Lasso tool. You click to set the first fastening point, and then move the mouse pointer to outline the selection. As you do, Photoshop adds fastening points at the frequency you specified. You can add fastening points manually by clicking as you make your selection. You can delete the most recent fastening point by pressing the Backspace key. When you have finished making your selection, you can modify its pixels or fill it with surrounding content or with a pattern, color, or gradient. To fill a selection, you can use the Fill command on the Edit menu, which fills a selection on the current layer, rather than adding the fill to a separate layer as you did earlier in this tutorial. If you fill a selection with a pattern, you can choose a **scripted pattern**, which applies a special effect to the pattern you select, such as displaying it as a spiral or a weave.

REFERENCE

Using the Magnetic Lasso Tool

- In the Tools panel, click the Magnetic Lasso tool.
- On the options bar, click the New selection, Add to selection, Subtract from selection, or Intersect with selection button.
- Specify a Feather setting, and select or deselect the Anti-alias check box.
- Specify a Width for edge detection, the Contrast percentage for detecting either low-contrast or high-contrast edges, and the Frequency at which fastening points will appear.
- Click on the image to set the first fastening point, and then move the mouse pointer along the edges of your selection.
- Click at the last fastening point to close the selection marquee.

Azar has an image of corn that he wants to use in his presentation, where he includes various recipes, including many for corn. The image has a blue sky, and he has asked you to give the background a rainbow effect to support his slide text: *The gold at the end of the rainbow*. You'll select the corn cob, select its inverse to select the sky, and then apply a pattern fill to the selection.

To use the Magnetic Lasso tool and fill the selection with color:

1. Open **Corn.jpg**, located in the Photoshop5\Tutorial folder, and then, in the Tools panel, click the **Magnetic Lasso Tool** button.
2. On the options bar, confirm that the Feather setting is **0 px**, select the **Anti-alias** check box, if necessary, set the Width to **1 px**, set the Contrast to **10%**, if necessary, and set the Frequency to **80**. A frequency of 80 will drop fastening points very close together along the edges of the selection.
3. Start by clicking the tip of the corn cob, move the mouse pointer down and to the right until you reach the edge of the canvas, and then move the mouse pointer down until you reach the lower-right corner of the canvas. Stay at the edge, or even slightly outside of the image, so the fastening points are along the edges of the photograph.
4. Move the pointer to the left, and then up slowly along the edge of the ear of corn until you reach the top, and then click when you reach the first fastening point to close the selection marquee. The selection marquee encloses the corn cob in a selection. See Figure 5-30.

   Trouble? If you find that the selection marquee strays from the outlines of the corn cob, use the Magic Wand tool and the Add to selection button and the Subtract from selection button, as necessary, to refine your selection.

TIP

You can restart a selection by pressing the Esc key, and then clicking to create the first fastening point again.

Figure 5-30 Using the Magnetic Lasso tool

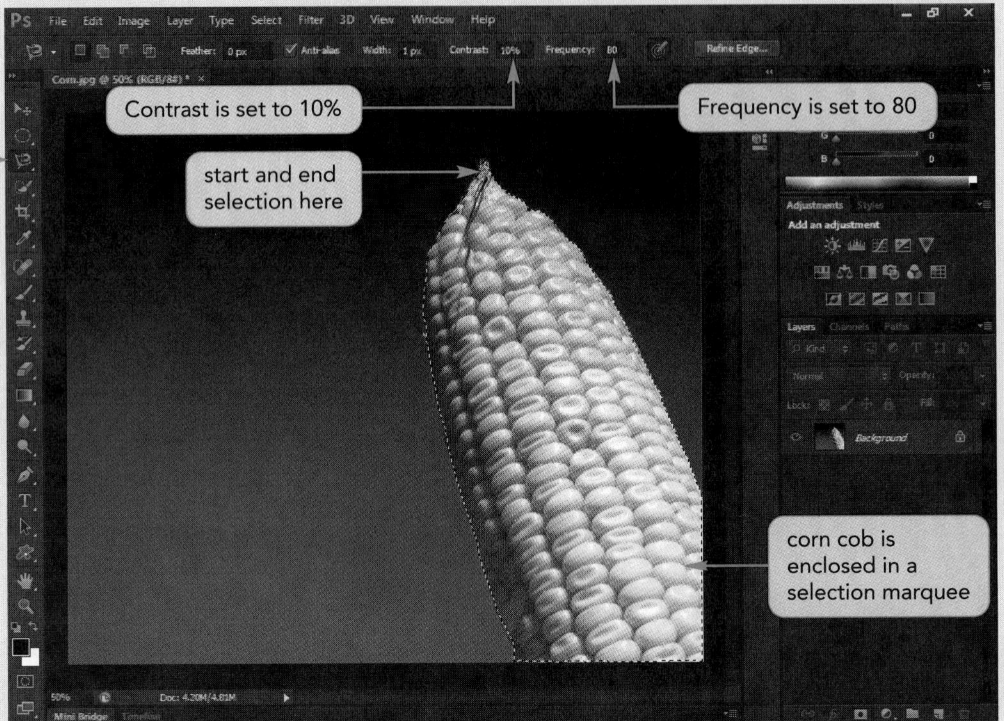

Zeljko Radojko/Shutterstock.com

Make sure you click to close the selection marquee. If you don't click, the tool will continue to drop fastening points, even outside of the canvas, and you'll be unable to choose any commands or tools.

5. On the menu bar, click **Select**, and then click **Inverse** to select every part of the image except the corn cob.
6. Click **Edit**, and then click **Fill**. In the Fill dialog box, click the **Use** button, and then click **Pattern**.
7. Click the **Custom Pattern arrow**, click the **Tie Dye thumbnail**, the second pattern in the first row, and then click the **Custom Pattern arrow** again to close the list.

   Trouble? If the Tie Dye thumbnail is not visible, click the More options button and then click Reset Patterns.
8. At the bottom of the Fill dialog box, click the **Scripted Patterns** check box to select it, click the **Script arrow**, click **Spiral**, and then click the **OK** button.
9. On the menu bar, click **Select**, and then click **Deselect** to clear the selection. See Figure 5-31.

Figure 5-31 Filling a selection with a scripted pattern

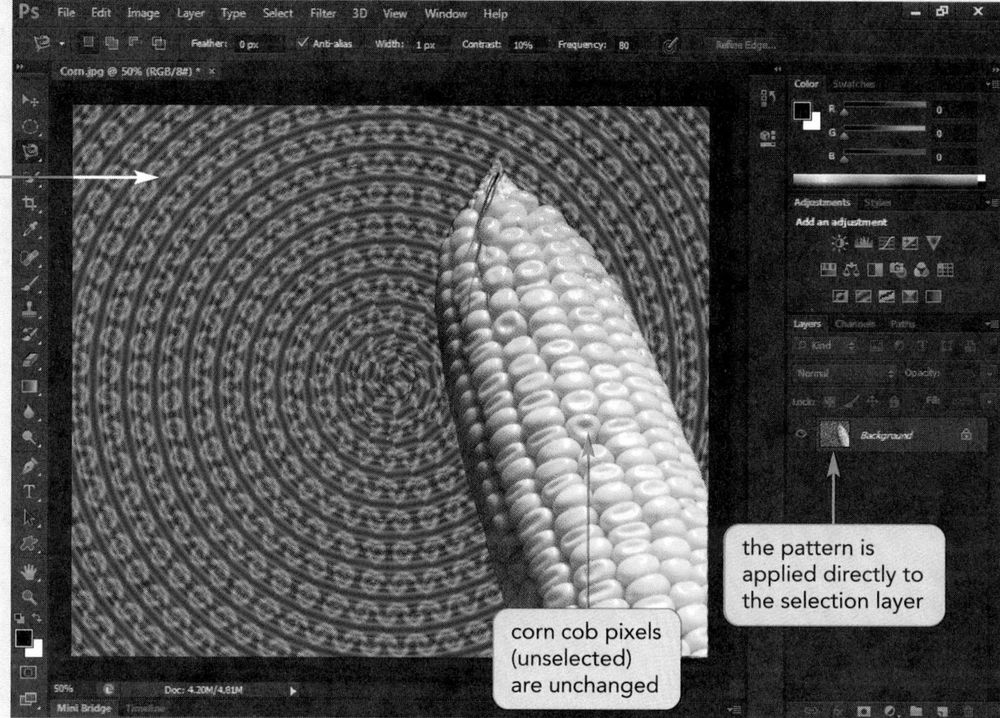
selection is filled with spiral pattern
the pattern is applied directly to the selection layer
corn cob pixels (unselected) are unchanged

Zeljko Radojko/Shutterstock.com

The sky has changed from blue to a colorful swirling effect because of the pattern fill you added to the selection. If you had been unable to isolate the selection, the pattern fill would have affected both the corn cob and the sky.

Notice that the Fill command added the pattern pixels to the current layer, and did not add a fill layer.

10. Save the modified file as **SwirledCorn.jpg** using the default JPEG options.

    Although you've created an interesting pattern, Azar wants you to try to achieve a rainbow effect behind the ear of corn.

11. Click **Edit** on the menu bar, and then click **Step Backward**, and then click **Edit** and **Step Backward** again. The pattern fill is removed from the image.

12. In the Layers panel, add a new Gradient fill layer to the Layers panel, and in the Gradient Fill dialog box, select the **Spectrum** gradient, set the Angle to **45** degrees, and then click the **OK** button. See Figure 5-32.

Figure 5-32 Creating a rainbow gradient fill

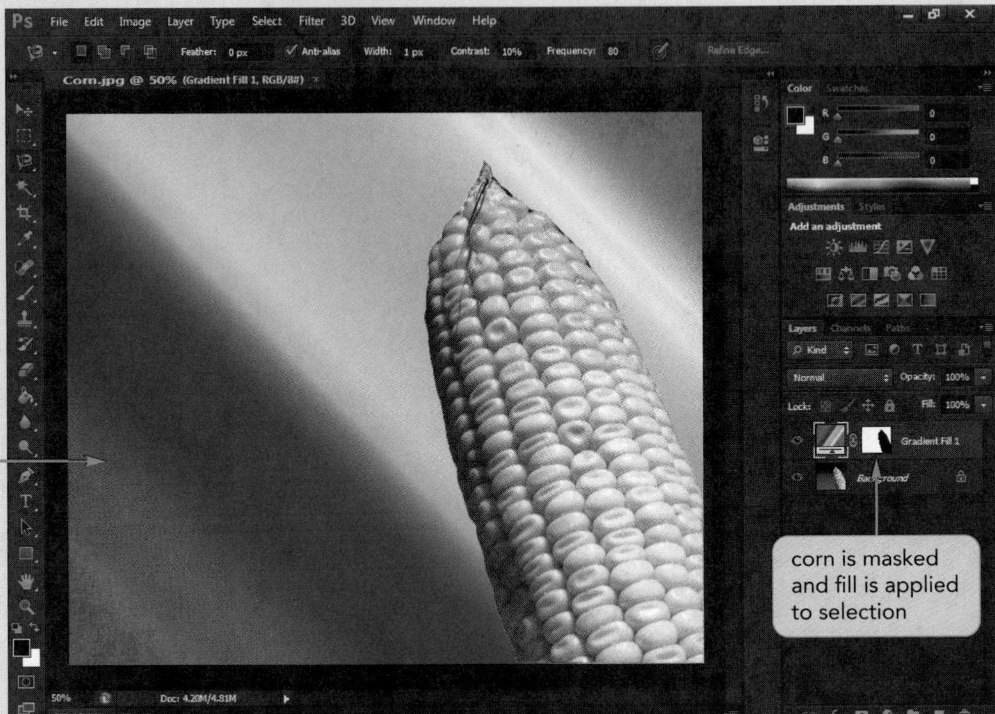
your gradient colors may vary slightly
corn is masked and fill is applied to selection

Zeljko Radojko/Shutterstock.com

The gradient fills the selected area, and provides a rainbow effect behind the ear of corn.

13. Save the file as **RainbowCorn.psd** and then close the file.

Saving and Reloading a Selection

You can save a selection with a file so you can use it the next time you open the file. For example, if you want to experiment with many different effects on a single selection, you can save the first effect in a file with a new name, reopen the original file, load the saved selection, and then try a different effect. Photoshop saves the selection as a new layer in the Channels panel, which you'll explore later in this tutorial. See Figure 5-33.

Figure 5-33 **Loading a selection**

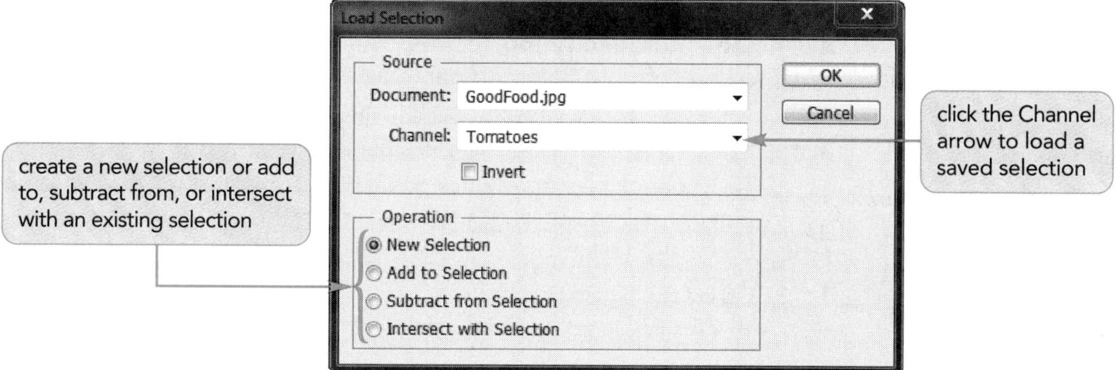

You can choose a selection from the Channel list in the Load Selection dialog box. You can use the saved selection to add to, subtract from, or intersect with an active selection. You can also simply load the selection you saved with the file.

REFERENCE

Saving and Loading a Selection

- In the Tools panel, activate any selection tool and make a selection on the image.
- On the menu bar, click Select, and then click Save Selection.
- In the Save Selection dialog box, type a name for the selection in the Name box, and then click the OK button.
- On the menu bar, click Select, and then click Load Selection.
- In the Load Selection dialog box, click the Channel arrow, and then click the name of the selection you want to load.
- In the Operation section of the Load Selection dialog box, click New Selection, Add to Selection, Subtract from Selection, or Intersect with Selection.
- Click the OK button.

Selecting with the Quick Selection Tool

You can select part of an image by painting it with the Quick Selection tool. The Quick Selection tool expands to select the edges of any object in an image that you paint over to enclose it in a selection marquee. It works well when you want to select areas with defined edges. It is also a good tool for adding pixels to a partial selection, as you did in the first session with the pumpkin. When you use the Quick Selection tool, you can specify its diameter. A larger diameter gives you less control over the tool, but if you are selecting a large area, it's more efficient. You can also select Sample All Layers to create the selection using all of the layers in the file rather than just the active layer. If you select Auto-Enhance, Photoshop automatically reduces the roughness around the border of the selection.

Azar has asked you to create two images that showcase the quality of last summer's tomato crop for Food for Change. To do so, you'll create two compositions. In one, you'll use the Quick Selection tool to make a selection and then select the inverse so you can change all of an image except the tomatoes to black and white to make them stand out. In the second composition, you'll place a stroke or outline around the tomatoes to make them stand out in the image.

To use the Quick Selection tool and save the selection:

1. Open **GoodFood.jpg**, located in the Photoshop5\Tutorial folder, and then zoom to about **35%** and pan it as necessary, so you can work with the tomatoes in the image.
2. Reset all of the tools, reset the Essentials workspace, and then, in the Tools panel, click the **Quick Selection Tool** button. By default, the New selection button is selected on the options bar, and the brush size is set to 30 pixels.
3. Open the Brush picker and drag the slider to the left to change the brush size to **20 px**. Close the Brush picker.
4. Point to the top of the tomato on the lower right, click and drag the mouse down to the bottom of that tomato. Photoshop selects most of the tomato, but it also selects some of the tabletop. See Figure 5-34.

TIP

You can also press the [key to reduce the brush size in 5-pixel increments.

Figure 5-34 Using the Quick Selection tool

marco mayer/Shutterstock.com

You need to select the other tomatoes as well, and then refine the selection to get rid of the areas that aren't part of the tomatoes. The Add to selection option has been automatically selected on the options bar so the next selection you make will be added to the current one.

5. Drag over the tomato on the left. Photoshop joins the selections, as shown in Figure 5-35.

Figure 5-35 **Selections are joined**

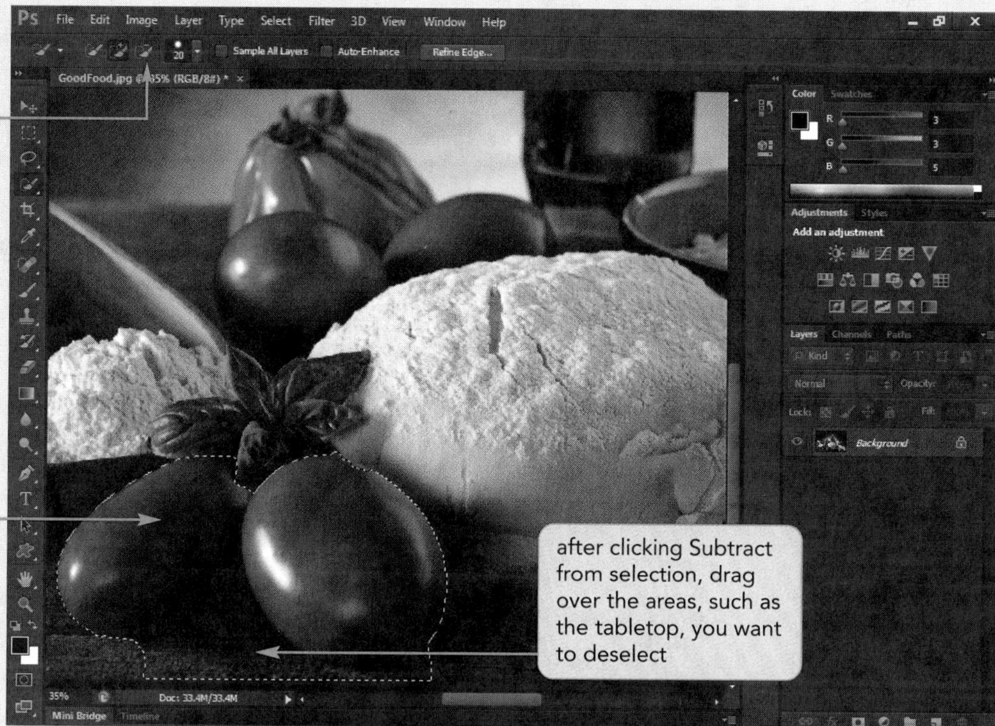
Subtract from selection button
any new areas you drag over are added to the selection
after clicking Subtract from selection, drag over the areas, such as the tabletop, you want to deselect

marco mayer/Shutterstock.com

You can subtract from your selection using the Subtract from selection button on the options bar.

6. On the options bar, click the **Subtract from selection** button, and then drag in the areas you want to deselect.

   Trouble? If you accidentally deselect part of one of the tomatoes, or if you were unable to select the complete tomato in your first selection, you can use the Add to selection button to add it back to the selection.

   Photoshop deselects the shadowed parts of the selection so now the selection marquee encompasses only the tomatoes.

7. Continue to add to the selection until you have selected all of the tomatoes and the basil leaves in the image, as shown in Figure 5-36. You'll save this selection to use later.

Figure 5-36 Selection is complete

marco mayer/Shutterstock.com

8. On the menu bar, click **Select**, click **Save Selection**, and then in the Save Selection dialog box, type **Tomatoes** in the Name box. Click the **OK** button. The selection is saved with the file so you can use it later.
9. Save the file as **GoodFood1.psd** in the Photoshop5\Tutorial folder.

Next, you'll select the inverse of the tomato selection so you can apply an effect that makes the tomatoes stand out.

To select the inverse of the selection:

1. Zoom out so you can see the entire image. On the menu bar, click **Select**, and then click **Inverse**. Photoshop changes the selection so all of the image *except* the tomatoes is now selected.
2. On the menu bar, click **Image**, click **Adjustments**, and then click **Black & White**.
3. In the Black and White dialog box, click the **OK** button to accept the default settings.
4. On the menu bar, click **Select**, and then click **Deselect**. See Figure 5-37.

Figure 5-37 Applying the Black and White adjustment to a selection

only the tomatoes and basil leaves appear in color

marco mayer/Shutterstock.com

All of the areas in the image except the tomatoes are now black and white. Using this kind of effect in a composition immediately draws attention to the area of the image on which you want the viewer's eyes to focus.

5. Save the file as **BlackWhiteRed.psd** in the Photoshop5\Tutorial folder, and close it.

Next, you'll work with the same image, and apply a different effect so you have two options to show to Azar at your next meeting.

Stroking a Selection

You can make a selection stand out by **stroking** it, or drawing a border around it. To do so, you select an area of the image with any of the selection tools—or load a saved selection—and use the Stroke option on the Edit menu. In the Stroke dialog box, you can specify the width, color, and location of the stroke, as well as its blending mode and opacity.

You'll add a stroke to the tomato selection you saved earlier to see if you like the effect.

To load the saved tomatoes selection and add a stroke to the selection:

1. Open **GoodFood1.psd**, located in the Photoshop5\Tutorial folder and zoom to **25%**. Photoshop displays the original image of the tomatoes. Although you can't see the selection you saved earlier, it has been saved with the file.
2. On the menu bar, click **Select**, and then click **Load Selection**.
3. Confirm that **Tomatoes** appears in the Channel box, and then click the **OK** button. Photoshop selects the tomatoes and basil in the image using the selection marquee you saved with the file. You'll expand the selection, and then you'll add a stroke to the selection to make it stand out.
4. On the menu bar, click **Select**, point to **Modify**, and then click **Expand** to open the Expand Selection dialog box.
5. In the Expand By box, type **20** and then click the **OK** button to expand the selection by 20 pixels.
6. On the menu bar, click **Edit**, and then click **Stroke**.
7. In the Stroke dialog box, specify a Width of **20 px**, and then click the Color box to open the Color Picker (Stroke Color) dialog box. Select a **yellow** color and then click the **OK** button to close the Color Picker (Stroke Color) dialog box.
8. In the Stroke dialog box, under Location, click the **Outside** option button. Under Blending, click the **Mode arrow**, and then click **Dissolve**. See Figure 5-38.

Figure 5-38 Stroking a selection

marco mayer/Shutterstock.com

9. Click the **OK** button, and then deselect the tomatoes. See Figure 5-39.

Figure 5-39 Selection with stroke added

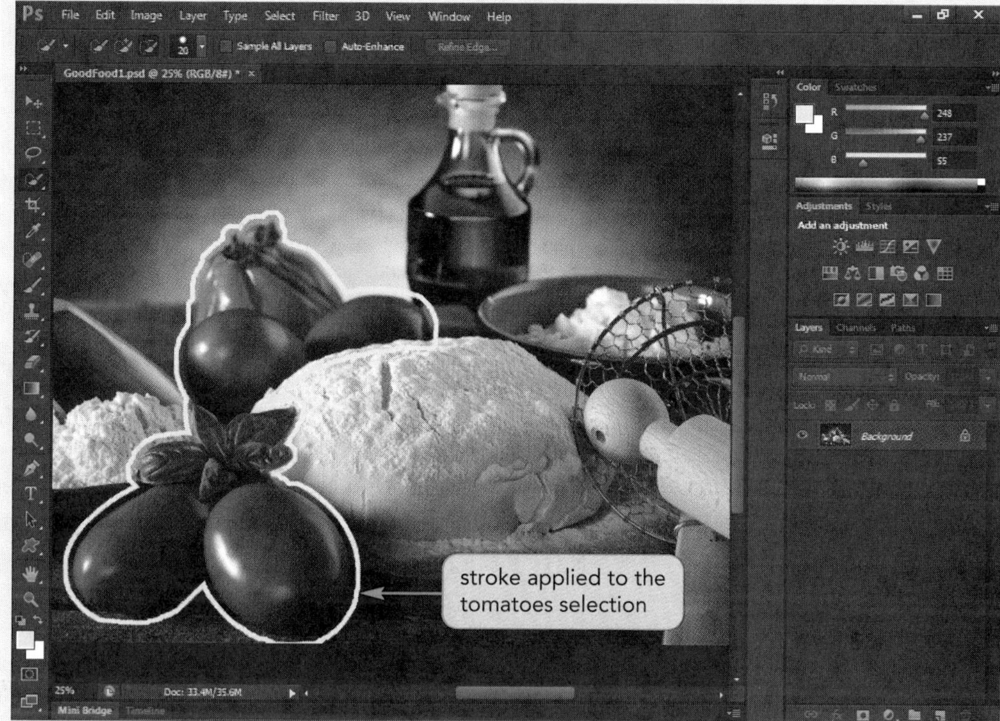
stroke applied to the tomatoes selection

marco mayer/Shutterstock.com

10. Save the file as **Stroke.psd** in the Photoshop5\Tutorial folder, and then close the file.

When you next meet with Azar, you'll show him the two versions of the file to see which one he prefers. Next, you'll explore filters and masks.

Working with Filters and Masks

Photoshop includes more than enough filter options to fill a book. In this session, you'll focus on just a few of the available filters. However, once you understand how to apply them, you'll be able to experiment with many more. You can access all of the available filters from the Filter menu. Some commands open a dialog box specific to the filter; other commands are applied when you click them. Still other commands open the Filter Gallery, where you can modify and preview different filters.

TIP

Some filters can only be applied to RGB images. If you are working on a piece for print, work on it in RGB mode and then switch to CMYK mode after you have applied any filters.

You can apply a filter effect to an entire image, to a layer, or to a selection on a layer. In this session, you'll apply different filters to different selections. When you apply an effect to a selection, you are actually working with a mask. The mask ensures that the filter is only applied to the selected area. Sometimes filter results can be a little over the top, but if you experiment with them, you'll see the variety and creativity you can achieve using these tools.

Understanding Masks

If you have ever painted a room, you know that there's a certain amount of preparation that has to take place before you actually put your paintbrush in the paint and the brush on the wall. Certain areas of the room—for example, the doors, windows, and molding—need to be protected, and to protect these areas, you'll most likely use masking tape. Photoshop carries the metaphor of masking tape into the digital image-editing world. Masking an area keeps it safe from any digital paint you apply. You saw a masking effect in Session 5.1 when you selected an area on an image, and then added brushstrokes: The brushstrokes were contained in the selection and did not spill over onto the rest of the image.

You might be wondering what a mask actually looks like in Photoshop. Masks are stored in the Channels panel, which appears behind the Layers panel in the Essentials workspace. See Figure 5-40.

Figure 5-40 **Channels panel**

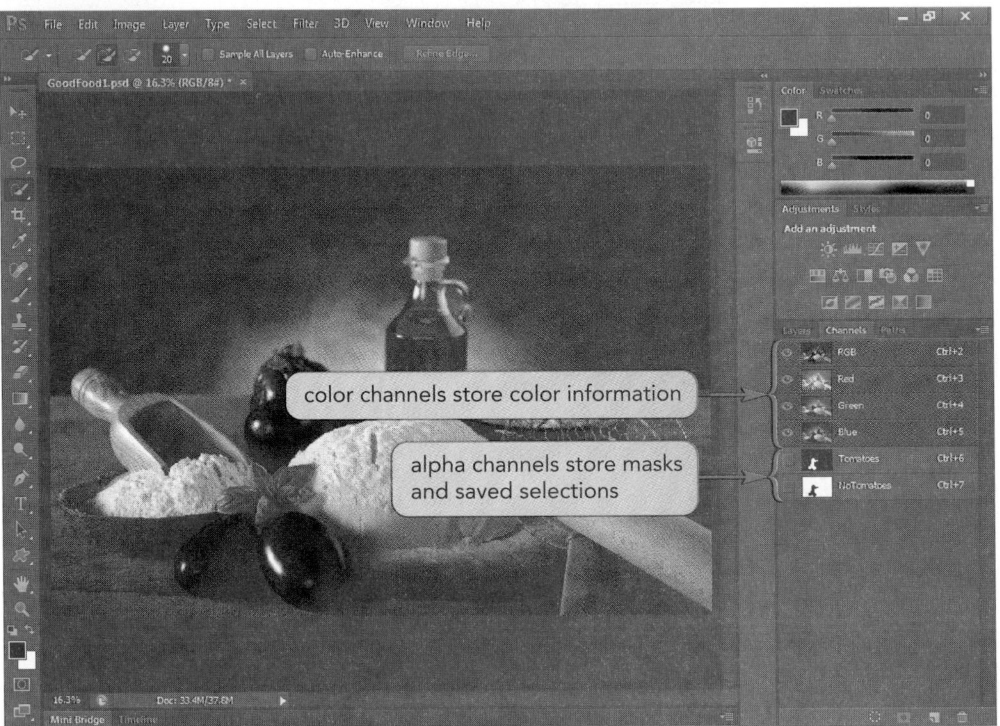

marco mayer/Shutterstock.com

The Channels panel stores a variety of information, including color information. In an RGB image, Red, Green, and Blue color channels appear, as well as the combined RGB channel. For a CMYK file, the Channels panel would display Cyan, Magenta, Yellow, and Black channels in addition to the CMYK channel. You can show and hide these color channels as you work with an image file.

When you saved a selection earlier in this tutorial, Photoshop saved it as a mask, also called an alpha channel, titled Tomatoes in the Channels panel. On any alpha channel thumbnail, the masked part of the image is black, indicating that it is protected, and the unmasked part of the image is white, indicating that it is editable. In Figure 5-40, notice that in addition to the color channels, there are two other channels. One, called Tomatoes in the figure, masks the tomatoes and basil. It was created by selecting the tomatoes and basil, and then saving the selection. The other channel in Figure 5-40 is called NoTomatoes, and it masks the rest of the Image. It was created by inverting the original selection, and then saving the new selection. You'll continue to work with masks in this tutorial as you apply filters from the Filter Gallery.

INSIGHT

Working with Color Channels

The color channels in the Channels panel give you a high level of control over color adjustments. You can use them to change the color balance in an image by modifying them individually. For example, you can modify the Red channel to achieve one effect or the Blue channel to achieve another. If you have a photograph with too much red in it, you can select the Red color channel in the Channels panel and modify its settings individually to reduce the red output. Having this kind of flexibility when you modify a photograph helps to ensure that you get exactly the effect you want.

Using the Liquify Filter

The Liquify filter is available directly from the Filter menu. You can use the Liquify filter to distort or correct an image. You can create swirls; you can stretch certain areas; you can even bloat or pucker the image. If you want to work with all of the options available in the Liquify dialog box, select the Advanced Mode check box. The advanced options let you modify the mask from within the dialog box itself, rather than returning to the image to change your selection. The tools on the left side of the dialog box give you a variety of options for using the Liquify filter, as shown in Figure 5-41.

Figure 5-41 **Liquify tools**

Icon	Name	Description
	Forward Warp tool	Pushes pixels ahead of the pointer as you drag
	Reconstruct tool	Undoes any distortion you've applied
	Twirl Clockwise tool	Twirls pixels clockwise; hold down the Alt key to twirl pixels counterclockwise
	Pucker tool	Moves pixels toward the center of the mouse pointer as you click
	Bloat tool	Moves pixels away from the center of the mouse pointer as you click
	Push Left tool	Moves pixels to the left when you drag up and to the right when you drag down
	Freeze Mask tool	Protects an area from changes
	Thaw Mask tool	Thaws an area with freeze mask applied
	Hand tool	Pans an image
	Zoom tool	Zooms in and out on an image

As you work, you can change tools to create different effects on different parts of an image. For example, you might use the Twirl Clockwise tool to create special effects in a cloudy sky or to add a whirlpool to still water.

The Freeze Mask tool in the Liquify dialog box is especially useful if you want to avoid liquifying parts of an image while working on other parts. It has a similar effect to inverting a selection to exclude it before applying an adjustment or effect. You use the Freeze Mask tool to paint a mask on the image. As with other masks in Photoshop, any area that is masked is protected. You can use the Zoom tool and the Hand tool to zoom and pan the image to paint an accurate mask. If you paint beyond the boundaries of the mask you want to create, you can "thaw" the mask by clicking the Thaw Mask tool and painting over the part of the mask you want to erase.

REFERENCE

Using the Liquify Filter

- Select the area you want to work with; if you want to liquify the whole layer, don't make any selection.
- On the menu bar, click Filter, and then click Liquify. In the Liquify dialog box, click the Advanced Mode check box to select it.
- Use the Freeze Mask tool to freeze any areas you don't want to liquify.
- Select a tool on the left side of the Liquify dialog box, and drag the mouse pointer over the image to warp, bloat, pucker, or otherwise liquify your image.
- Use the Thaw Mask tool to thaw any frozen areas, and use additional tools to add more liquify effects, if desired.
- Click the OK button to apply the effects, and close the dialog box.

Azar is planning a summer fund-raiser, and would like to send a postcard to patrons as an invitation. He supplies you with an image of strawberries, and asks you to apply an unusual eye-catching effect to the image. You'll use the Liquify filter to swirl the colors in the image around one of the strawberries.

To work with the Liquify filter:

1. Open **Berries.psd**, located in the Photoshop5\Tutorial folder, and save it as **SummerBerries.psd** in the same folder.
2. In the Layers panel, hide the Berry Fun!! layer, select the **Background** layer, and then use any of the selection tools you have learned about to select the strawberry on the left side of the image. Select only the berry, and not the leaves. Add to and subtract from the selection as necessary.

   Trouble? If you're having difficulty making exact selections, remember that you can refine your selection using the add and subtract buttons on the options bar.
3. On the menu bar, click **Select**, and then click **Inverse**. Everything but the strawberry on the left is selected in the image.
4. On the menu bar, click **Filter**, and then click **Liquify**. The Liquify dialog box opens.
5. Click the **Advanced Mode** check box to display all of the options, and then, at the bottom of the dialog box, click the **Mask Color** button, and then click **Magenta**. See Figure 5-42.

   Trouble? If the Mask Color button is unavailable, click that the Show Mask check box to select it.

Figure 5-42 **Liquify dialog box**

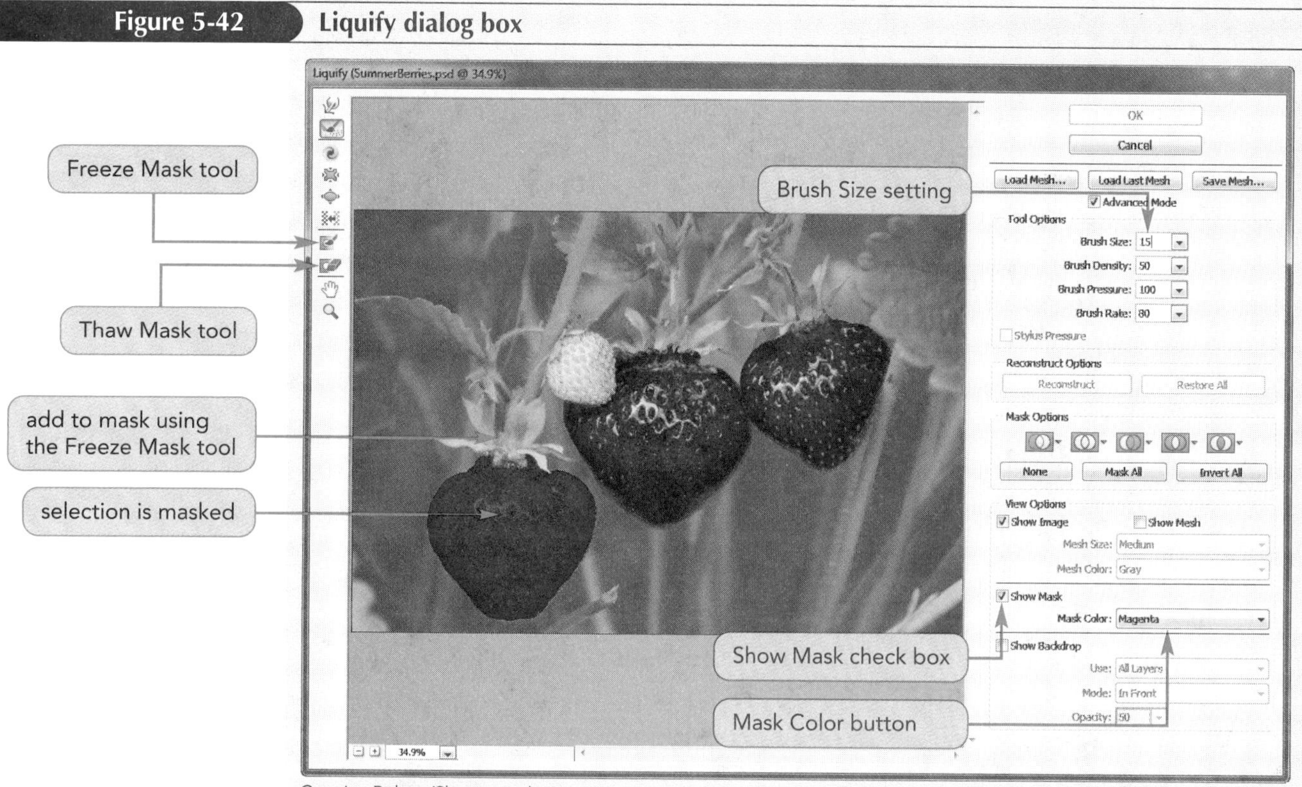

Catarina Belova/Shutterstock.com

The Liquify dialog box shows a preview of the image, with tools along the left side and settings for each tool along the right. By default, the strawberry was painted over with a red mask. The magenta color makes the mask easier to see. Your goal is to liquify the area around the strawberry to give it an impressionistic effect, while leaving one realistic berry image on the left side of the image.

In the figure, the mask of the strawberry is imperfect. You'll use the Freeze Mask tool to add the leaves to the selection, and then you'll correct any oversights on your mask.

6. In the Tools panel of the Liquify dialog box, click the **Freeze Mask Tool** button. The pointer shape for the Freeze Mask tool is a circle with a plus sign in the middle.
7. Change the Brush Size setting to **21**. You'll leave the other settings as is.
8. Drag over the leaves at the top of the strawberry to add them to the mask. As you paint, use the Hand tool and the Zoom tool to ensure that you paint every pixel of the strawberry and leaves to protect them from the filter changes. If the current brush size is inconvenient for you, use a different size.
9. If you make any errors while you paint, click the **Thaw Mask Tool** button and paint over your mistakes to erase them, and then click the **Freeze Mask Tool** button and continue painting. When you have finished applying the mask, your image should resemble Figure 5-43.

TIP

In the Liquify dialog box, you can also press the Ctrl++ keys and the Ctrl+- keys to zoom in and out, press the Ctrl+0 keys to fit the image in the dialog box, and press the Ctrl+1 keys to display the image at 100%.

Figure 5-43 Masked area in Liquify dialog box

Catarina Belova/Shutterstock.com

You are now ready to liquify the unmasked parts of your image.

10. In the Tools panel of the Liquify dialog box, click the **Forward Warp Tool** button, set the brush size to **65**, point to the upper-left side of the image, and then drag the mouse pointer to the right.

    The part of the image beneath the pointer is dragged to the right, as if it is made of putty.

    Trouble? If the warp uncovers part of the background, which is made up of transparent pixels, undo it using the Reconstruct tool.

11. Click the **Reconstruct Tool** button, and then drag to paint over the warp you just created. Continue to drag until the image returns to its original state. (It will take several passes with the Reconstruct tool to get back to the original state.)

    The Reconstruct tool works in much the same way the History Brush tool works. The history state you are reverting to is the state the image was in when you issued the Liquify command.

12. Click the **Twirl Clockwise Tool** button, and set the Brush Size to **105**.

13. Point to the middle of the strawberry on the right, and press and hold the mouse button. Look carefully inside the pointer: The image beneath the pointer has become a whirlpool and is rotating clockwise.

14. Change the Brush Rate to **100**, point to the right of the first whirlpool effect, and press and hold the mouse button. The pixels rotate more quickly than they did at a setting of 80.

15. Drag the pointer over the image, and watch the distortions take shape.

16. Continue to experiment with the different Liquify options by clicking different Liquify tools. If you are dissatisfied with a result, use the Reconstruct tool. If you would like to start over, use the Restore All button.

17. Click the **OK** button to liquify your image, and then deselect the selection. Unhide the **Berry Fun!!** layer. See Figure 5-44.

Figure 5-44 **Liquified image**

unmasked areas have been liquified
strawberry is unaffected by Liquify filter
Berry
Fun!!

Catarina Belova/Shutterstock.com

The area surrounding the strawberry has an oil paint effect, but the strawberry itself is unchanged by the filter because you masked it.

18. Save **SummerBerries.psd**, and then close it.

Working with the Filter Gallery

The Filter Gallery includes nearly 50 filters that you can apply to an image. The filters can provide artistic effects—for example, turning your image into a colored pencil drawing or pastel painting—or distortions—making your image appear to glow or to be covered by a pane of glass. Figure 5-45 shows just a few of the effects you can achieve with filters from the gallery. All of the filters have been applied to the same image.

Figure 5-45 **Four different filters applied to same image**

Diffuse Glow filter

Reticulation filter

Glowing Edges filter

Stained Glass filter

Jira Hera/Shutterstock.com

The Filter Gallery includes six categories of filter: Artistic, Brush Strokes, Distort, Sketch, Stylize, and Texture. Some filters, like the Sketch filters, use the current foreground and background colors to produce an effect. In addition, each filter has its own custom settings, which you can manipulate on the right side of the dialog box. You can also combine filters for unique effects by clicking the New effect layer icon at the bottom of the dialog box, or you can delete an effect by clicking the Delete effect layer icon. As you make changes to the filter or include additional filters, you can preview everything in the left pane of the dialog box. To see more or less of the image, you can click the Zoom Out or Zoom In icons at the bottom of the dialog box or type a zoom percentage. You can also pan the image by dragging the scroll boxes at the bottom and right side of the preview area.

To use the Filter Gallery:

1. Open **GoodFood2.psd**, located in the Photoshop5\Tutorial folder. Reset the default foreground and background colors, if necessary.
2. Click the **Channels** tab to display the Channels panel. This file includes a saved selection called Tomatoes. Notice that the tomato selection appears white on the channel thumbnail, and the rest of the image is black. This indicates that everything in the image except the tomato selection is masked.
3. On the menu bar, click **Select**, click **Load Selection**, confirm that **Tomatoes** is the selected Channel, and then click the **OK** button.
4. On the menu bar, click **Select**, click **Inverse**, click **Select** again, and then click **Save Selection**. In the Save Selection dialog box, type **NoTomatoes** in the Name box, and then click the **OK** button. Photoshop adds the new selection as an alpha channel in the Channels panel.

5. In the Channels panel, click the empty Eye icon box in the Show/Hide column to the left of the Tomatoes mask thumbnail so an Eye icon appears. Photoshop paints the masked area directly on the image using a translucent shade of red. See Figure 5-46.

Figure 5-46 Showing the mask on the image

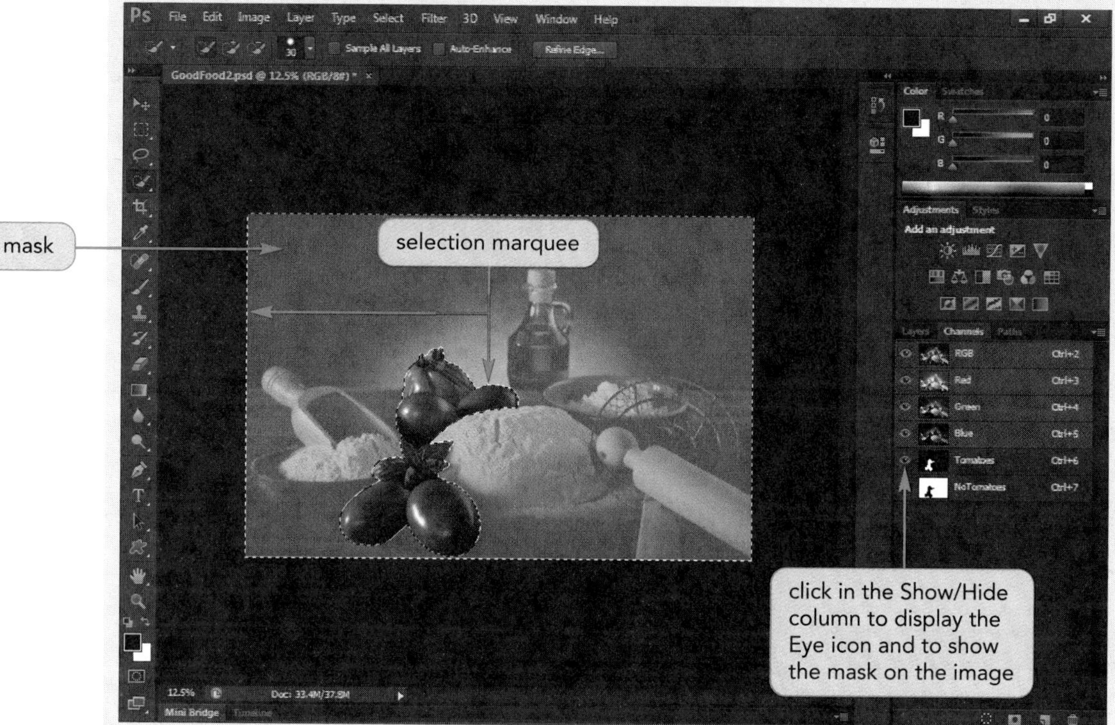
mask
selection marquee
click in the Show/Hide column to display the Eye icon and to show the mask on the image

marco mayer/Shutterstock.com

You can turn on this feature whenever you want to get a clearer image of the mask so you can make modifications.

6. In the Channels panel, click the **Eye** icon to the left of the Tomatoes mask thumbnail to hide the image mask.
7. On the menu bar, click **Filter**, and then click **Filter Gallery**. The Filter Gallery opens, and the image appears in a preview window. The filter that was applied the last time the Filter Gallery was open is applied to the selection.

   Trouble? If Filter Gallery appears twice in the Filter menu, click the second instance.
8. Click the **Zoom Out** button at the bottom of the Filter Gallery, if necessary, so you can see the entire image.
9. In the middle panel of the Filter Gallery, click the **Artistic** folder to see the options available.

   Trouble? If the Artistic folder isn't visible, click the Expand icon to the left of the OK button.
10. Click the various Artistic options to preview them in the gallery. Depending on the speed of your computer, it might take some time to display the filter result. If so, Photoshop displays a progress bar at the bottom of the dialog box to the right of the zoom box.

Each of the filters has its own additional settings on the right side of the dialog box. For example, for the Colored Pencil filter, you can specify the pencil width, stroke pressure, and paper brightness.

11. Click the **Texture** folder and experiment with the different available textures. You can change the Texture settings to see their effect.
12. Click the **Stained Glass** filter. On the right side of the Filter Gallery, set the Cell Size to **25**, the Border Thickness to **5**, and the Light Intensity to **2**, and then click the **OK** button to see the filter applied to the image in the Document window. The background appears with a stained glass effect, while the tomatoes and basil still resemble a photograph.
13. Invert the selection, and then open the Filter Gallery. Photoshop applies the Stained Glass effect to the new selection because the Filter Gallery keeps the settings of the previous filter. You'll change the effect.

    Trouble? If Photoshop applies a stained glass effect to the rest of the image without opening the gallery, you have selected the wrong Filter Gallery command. Photoshop lists your most recent filter command at the top of the Filter menu. Selecting it will just apply the same settings to the new selection. Undo the change, and then click the Filter Gallery command that is followed by ellipses (...).
14. Use the **Zoom Out** button ⊟ to zoom the image out to **25%**. In the Filter Gallery, click the **Accented Edges** filter in the Brush Strokes folder. Set the Edge Width to **10**, set the Edge Brightness to **50**, and set the Smoothness to **11**. See Figure 5-47.

Figure 5-47 **Image with two filters applied**

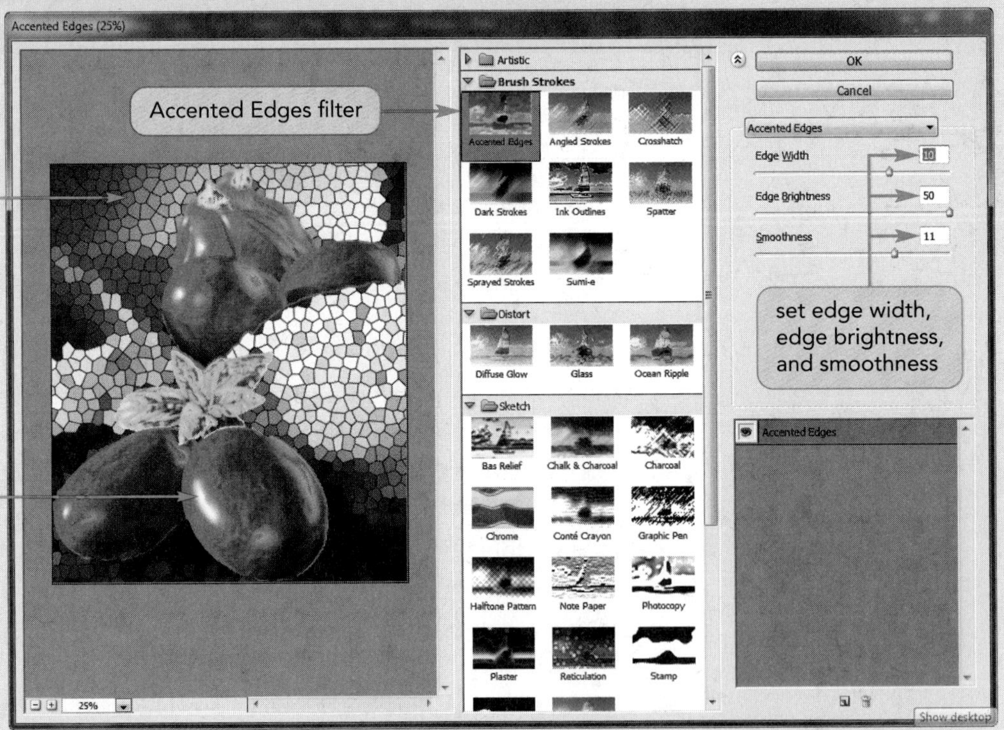

marco mayer/Shutterstock.com

15. Click the **OK** button to close the Filter Gallery.

You used selection masks, the Channels panel, and two filter effects to change a photograph into a completely different composition.

16. Deselect the tomatoes, save the file as **TomatoFilters.psd** in the Photoshop5\Tutorial folder, close the file, and exit Photoshop.

In this session, you learned how to use the Lasso tools and the Quick Selection tool to make selections. You learned how to save selections in the Channels panel and how to load selections to reuse them. You experimented with fills, including the Content-Aware fill, and you used the Content-Aware Move tool. You also learned how to work with masks and filters, including the Liquify filter and some of the filters in the Filter Gallery.

REVIEW

Session 5.2 Quick Check

1. Which tool lets you drag on the canvas to create a free-form selection marquee?
2. The ____________ fill feature lets you remove objects from an image and replace them with randomly generated versions of surrounding pixels.
3. What are fastening points?
4. True or False. Photoshop stores saved selections in the Layers panel.
5. The ____________ Selection tool works well if you want to select an area of an image with clearly defined edges.
6. To reuse a selection that you have saved, use the ____________ Selection command on the menu.
7. What does the Inverse command on the Select menu do?
8. Use the ____________ Mask tool in the Liquify dialog box to paint a mask on the part of an image you want to protect.

Practice the skills you learned in the tutorial using the same case scenario.

PRACTICE

Review Assignments

Data File needed for the Review Assignments: 4Pumpkins.jpg

Azar would like to include images in this year's annual report that emphasize his message that Food for Change not only unites urban and suburban youth, but also encourages cross-cultural understanding. He has given you an image of four pumpkins, and wants you to modify three of the pumpkins so each pumpkin has a different effect or filter, representing the variety of youth his program serves. He also wants you to create an image with two of the pumpkins that he can use for a postcard campaign at Halloween. Complete the following steps:

1. Start Photoshop while pressing the Ctrl+Alt+Shift keys, and click Yes to delete the Settings File when prompted. Reset Photoshop to the default Essentials workspace layout, and reset all tools.
2. Open **4Pumpkins.jpg**, located in the Photoshop5\Review folder provided with your Data Files.
3. Select the Background layer, if necessary, and then select the front pumpkin in the image, using the Elliptical Marquee tool with a fixed size of 1000 pixels by 1100 pixels. Then, use the Quick Selection tool to select the whole pumpkin. Don't include the stem when you make your selection.
4. Save the selection as **Pumpkin2**, and then deselect the pumpkin.
5. Select the pumpkin to the left of the first pumpkin you selected. Don't include any part of the first pumpkin you selected. Save the selection as **Pumpkin1**, and then deselect the pumpkin.
6. Select the pumpkin on the far right, but do not include any part of the first pumpkin you selected. Save the selection as **Pumpkin3**.
7. Load the Pumpkin1 selection, and on the Layers panel, add a new solid color fill layer with a green color fill at 50% opacity.
8. Open the History panel and take a snapshot of the current file.
9. Apply a Liquify filter to the second pumpkin using the Pumpkin2 selection. (*Hint*: Make sure to select the Background layer before you open the Liquify dialog box.) Try the Twirl Clockwise tool with a Brush Size of 225, a Brush Density of 100, a Brush Pressure of 100, and a Brush Rate of 100.
10. Load the Pumpkin3 selection, and apply the Chrome Filter (found in the Sketch folder) with a Detail setting of 7 and a Smoothness of 5.
11. Save the file as **Diversity.psd** in the Photoshop5\Review folder.
12. Revert the file to the snapshot you took in Step 8, then save the file as **GreenPumpkin.psd** in the same folder.
13. Load both the Pumpkin1 and Pumpkin2 selections. (*Hint*: When loading the second selection, make sure to select the Add to Selection option button in the Load Selection dialog box.) Then add to the combined selection by selecting the stems of the two pumpkins.
14. Select the Background layer, make the background color in the Tools panel black, and then copy the selection to the Clipboard.
15. Create a new file that is 10 inches wide and 8 inches high, select the Background Color as the Background Contents, and then click the OK button.
16. Paste the Clipboard contents into the new file.
17. Save the file as **2Pumpkins.psd** in the Photoshop5\Review folder, and then close both files.

Use your skills to select parts of an image to create interesting effects.

APPLY

Case Problem 1

Data Files needed for this Case Problem: Vacation.jpg, Marlin.jpg

Lake Shares Shirley Beaghan is the marketing director for Lake Shares, an online time-share company specializing in waterfront properties. She wants you to take two images and combine them to create a whimsical image for the Web site. You'll use selection tools and filter effects. Complete the following steps:

1. Start Photoshop while pressing the Ctrl+Alt+Shift keys, and click Yes to delete the Settings File when prompted. Reset Photoshop to the default Essentials workspace layout, and reset all tools.
2. Open **Vacation.jpg** and **Marlin.jpg**, located in the Photoshop5\Case1 folder provided with your Data Files.
3. In the Marlin.jpg file, select the marlin using the selection tools of your choice, copy it to the Clipboard and then, using Figure 5-48 as a guide, paste it into the Vacation image four times. Resize, rotate, and reposition three of the copies of the marlin so they appear to be jumping out of the water beyond the beach umbrella.

Figure 5-48 **Sample Lake Shares Web site image**

Danny Rehbein/Shutterstock.com; Paul Brennan/Shutterstock.com

4. Reposition the fourth copy of the marlin to the right of the top of the umbrella, and transform and rotate it so it is slightly larger than the fish in the water and appears to be jumping into the photograph from the right side of the image.
5. Select the Background layer, open the Liquify dialog box, and in Advanced Mode, use the Mask All button under Mask Options to mask the entire image. Thaw the part of the mask that covers the sky. (*Hint:* Remember that if you accidentally thaw outside the sky, you can use the Freeze Mask tool to repair the mask.)
6. Apply any of the Liquify filters to the sky.
7. Use the Color Range command to select some of the water tones, and add a bright green color fill layer to the selection. Make sure to lower the opacity so some of the texture of the water shows through.

8. Select the sand (but not the shadow on the sand) and fill it with a scripted pattern of your choosing.
9. Apply any other effects to other parts of the image, and then save the image as **BeachShow.psd** in the Photoshop5\Case1 folder.

Using Figure 5-49 as a guide, combine images in a single composition.

CREATE

Case Problem 2

Data Files needed for this Case Problem: Pitcher.psd, Vase.jpg

PierCeramics You are the owner of PierCeramics, a ceramics studio on Sanibel Island in Florida. You have many photographs of your work, and think you might be able to turn those photographs into digital art to sell along with your pottery. You'll experiment with selections, filters, and effects using two photographs of your pottery. Complete the following steps:

1. Start Photoshop while pressing the Ctrl+Alt+Shift keys, and click Yes to delete the Settings File when prompted. Reset Photoshop to the default Essentials workspace layout, and reset all tools.
2. Open **Pitcher.psd**, located in the Photoshop5\Case2 folder provided with your Data Files.
3. Apply a scripted pattern fill to the area around the pitcher, and apply a filter to the pitcher. Save the file as **PatternPitcher.psd** and close it.
4. Open **Vase.jpg**, located in the Photoshop5\Case2 folder.

Figure 5-49 Sample PierCeramics image

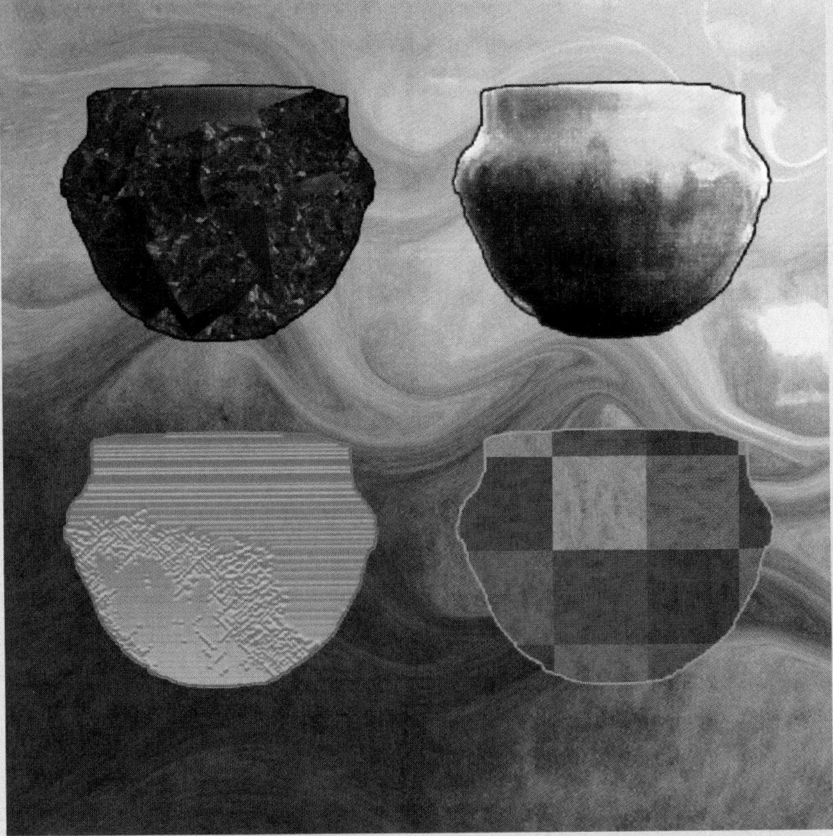

Jane Hosie-Bounar

5. Using Figure 5-49 as a guide, create a new file with a transparent background and the following settings: Width: 10 inches, Height: 10 Inches, Resolution: 180 ppi, and Color Mode: RGB.
6. Select the vase in Vase.jpg, and copy it into the new file five times. Change the size of the vase on the first layer so it extends beyond the edge of the canvas on all four sides and acts as a background for the other layers.
7. Apply a Liquify filter to the background vase.
8. Arrange and resize the other vases so that they are all visible on the canvas. (*Hint*: If you want them all to be the same size, select all four layers in the Layers panel before resizing.)
9. Apply different filters to two of the vases, and adjust the filter settings until you achieve the effects you want. (*Hint:* Some of the filters use the foreground and background color to achieve an effect, so experiment with different colors until you achieve the effect you want.)
10. Take a snapshot of the current state in the History panel.
11. Apply two different scripted fills to the other two vases. (*Hint:* Remember that you must select each vase on its layer before applying a fill or the whole layer will be filled.) In Figure 5-49, the lower-right vase uses a light marble cross weave fill. The upper-left vase uses a black marble random fill.
12. Add a 5-pixel stroke around each of the four vases. Use different colors for each of the strokes.
13. Save the file as **FilterVase.psd** in the Photoshop5\Case2 folder.
14. Return the file to the previous history state captured in the snapshot.
15. Create a new document based on the current history state. (*Hint:* Use the Create new document from current state icon at the bottom of the History panel.)
16. Flatten the new document image. Save the new file as **NoFill.psd**, and then close the file.
17. Return to the final history state by selecting the last entry in the History panel. Apply a Brightness/Contrast adjustment to lighten up the background to your liking, and then save FilterVase.psd in the Photoshop5\Case2 folder and close it.

Extend your skills to transform images for a bookstore.

CHALLENGE

Case Problem 3

There are no Data Files needed for this Case Problem.

GoBooks Gary Smith is the owner of a small bookstore in Shawano, Wisconsin. He has asked for your help in developing a poster he will display in the storefront window for the month of January that shows that books can take you anywhere—even when you're snowed in. Your focus for the first poster is children's books. You'll use one landscape image and at least two "character" images from the Web or your own collection to create the poster. Complete the following steps:

1. Start Photoshop while pressing the Ctrl+Alt+Shift keys, and click Yes to delete the Settings File when prompted. Reset Photoshop to the default Essentials workspace layout, and reset all tools.
2. Go to the MorgueFile or the Creative Commons Web site and search for a landscape or cityscape photograph with which you would like to work. Alternatively, use one of your own photographs of a landscape or cityscape. You'll be adding filters and effects to change a real landscape into a storybook landscape. Before you download any images, check the licensing information to make sure that they can be remixed without attribution and used for commercial purposes. Download the landscape image you have chosen.

3. Find images of at least two "characters" for your poster. Your characters can be animals, insects, plants, statues, tea pots—whatever you feel comfortable working with. Download the character images you have chosen.
4. Confirm that all the images you have downloaded are the same resolution before you combine them. If they aren't, change their resolution before combining the files.
5. Using WordPad, which is available from the Accessories menu of the All Programs menu in Windows 7, create a new document and keep a record of the steps you take to create the final image. You don't need to record steps that you later undo. Save the document as **Process.rtf** in the Photoshop5\Case3 folder.
6. Using the skills you learned in this tutorial, create a composition that you think would catch a customer's eye. The focus of this exercise is to mix realistic photographic images with images that have been altered to look painted or computer generated. Use selection tools, filters, fills, and the drawing tools for your composition. Use the Brush tools and the History Brush tool to refine your work.
7. In any font, add a headline to the poster that reads **Go Books Go Anywhere**.

EXPLORE

8. Warp the title text. To do so, click the Create warped text button on the options bar for one of the Text tools, and then click a Style setting such as Bulge.

EXPLORE

9. Transform or warp at least one of the characters you place in the landscape, either by resizing, rotating, or warping it. (*Hint*: To warp a selection, make an initial selection, click Select on the menu bar, and then click Transform Selection. On the options bar, click the Switch between free transform and warp modes button. When you are in warp mode, warp the selection by dragging one of the handles on the selection.)

EXPLORE

10. Use Puppet Warp to change the position of the limbs of one of your characters. (*Hint:* On the menu bar, click Edit, and then click Puppet Warp to add pins to one of the animals or objects in the poster and manipulate them. For example, click to place anchor pins in a knee joint or elbow, then click in a different spot to add a pin, and then drag that second pin to warp the limb.) In Figure 5-50, the wild turkey's legs have been manipulated with the Puppet Warp feature in all four copies of the turkey.

Figure 5-50 **Sample GoBooks poster**

Jane Hosie-Bounar

11. Save Process.rtf in the Photoshop5\Case 3 folder.
12. Save the file as **GoBooks.psd** in the Photoshop5\Case3 folder, and exit Photoshop.

Use your compositing skills to create an eye-catching image.

CREATE

Case Problem 4

Data Files needed for this Case Problem: Smile.jpg, Spanner.jpg

DBF Dental Aisha Gomez is the marketing manager for DBF Dental, a dental supply company in Chicago, Illinois. The company's customer base includes dentists and orthodontists in Iowa, Wisconsin, Indiana, and Minnesota. Recently, another dental supply company has moved into the area. However, there have been reports of inferior products from some of DBF's former customers who switched suppliers. Aisha wants you to develop a new campaign that addresses this issue and tries to win back the customers. You'll create an image that uses humor to address the topic. Complete the following steps:

1. Start Photoshop while pressing the Ctrl+Alt+Shift keys, and click Yes to delete the Settings File when prompted. Reset Photoshop to the default Essentials workspace layout, and reset all tools.
2. Create a new 300-ppi file with dimensions and a background color of your choosing. Place **Smile.jpg**, located in the Photoshop5\Case4 folder, on the canvas of your new file so it fits, and then rasterize the Smile layer. Flatten the image and then save the file as **DBFDental.psd**.
3. Use your compositing skills to create an image that uses the unexpected or the humorous to get your point across, as shown in the example in Figure 5-51. The sample image also uses the file called Spanner.jpg, included with your Data Files. You can use this file, or find another image to get your humorous message across.

Figure 5-51 **Sample DBF Dental ad**

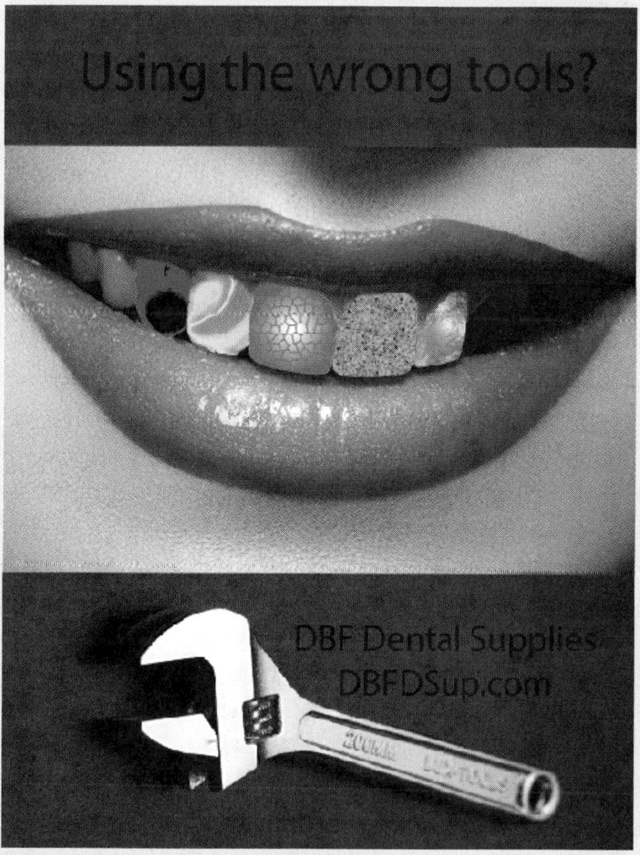

Seprimor/Shutterstock.com; Garsya/Shutterstock.com

4. Save your selections as channels and name them. For example, save each tooth as its own selection.
5. Save at least two layer comps that show different ideas or arrangements. If you want to create different fill effects for the same selection, make sure to apply the fill to its own layer so you can turn it on and off.
6. When you have finished editing the file, save it, and exit Photoshop.

ENDING DATA FILES

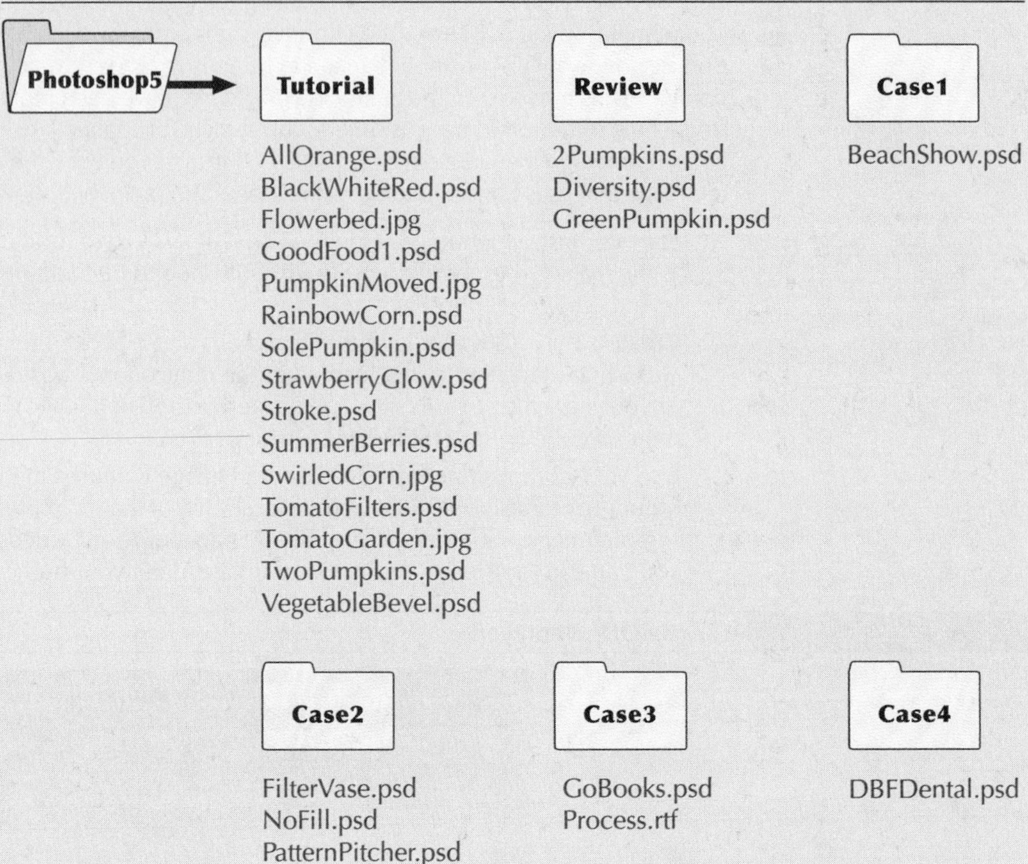

TUTORIAL 6

Designing with Text

Using Text and Text Effects

PHOTOSHOP

OBJECTIVES

Session 6.1

- Work with text layers and the Type tools
- Use the Typography workspace to enter and modify point type and paragraph type
- Assign fonts and other text formats
- Work with vertical text
- Check spelling, and find and replace text

Session 6.2

- Apply a style to text
- Set tracking and scaling for individual characters
- Specify a baseline shift
- Bend text to a closed path
- Apply a clipping mask to fill text with an image, pattern, and gradient

Case | *RC Investments*

You have taken a summer internship with a small investment firm called RC Investments, which was founded in 1979 by Rose Clarke's father, Richard. In 2009, Rose took over the company, which helps middle-income people manage their assets by developing an investment strategy best suited to their needs. Rose was the sole employee when she took over the firm, but word of mouth has helped her grow the firm to five investment professionals. She has asked you to create a marketing campaign to help her increase the firm's client base. You'll use the Photoshop Typography workspace and many of the text tools and features to create comps that you'll present to her for the proposed campaign. You'll add text to images and modify text fonts; you'll also adjust the scaling and tracking, alignment, and rotation of text. Finally, you'll apply styles to text and fill text with images, gradients, and color.

STARTING DATA FILES

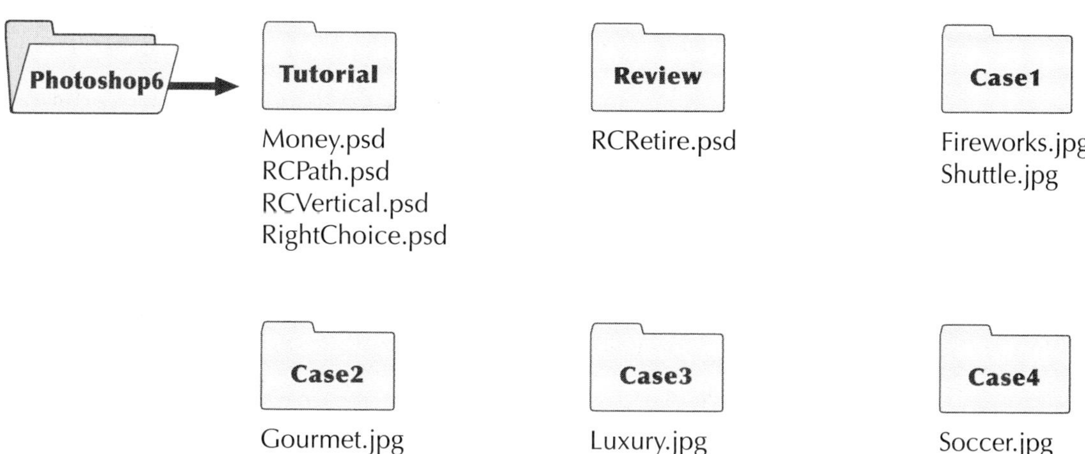

SESSION 6.1 VISUAL OVERVIEW

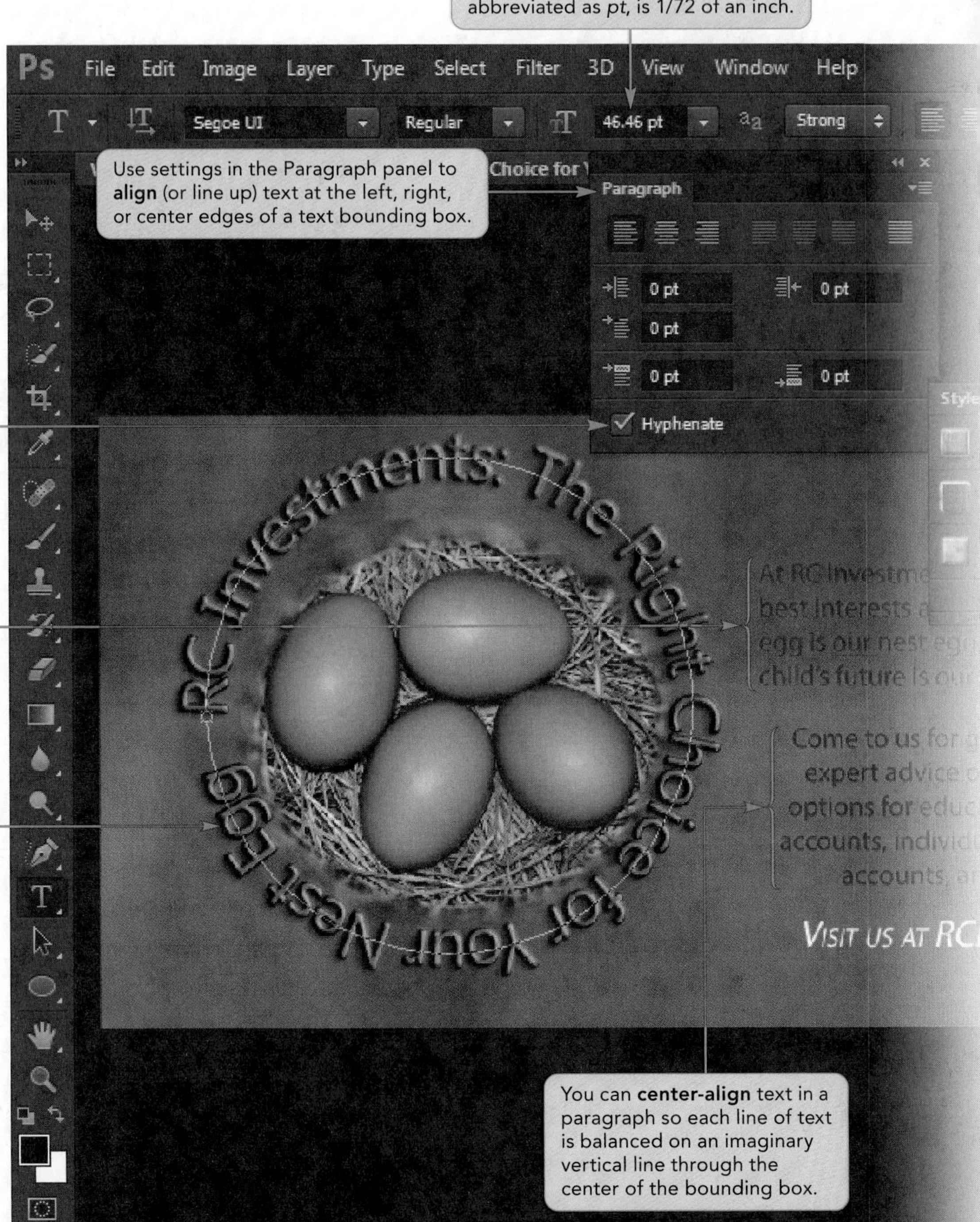

The **font size** is the height of the text measured in points. A **point**, abbreviated as *pt*, is 1/72 of an inch.
Use settings in the Paragraph panel to **align** (or line up) text at the left, right, or center edges of a text bounding box.
The Hyphenate setting determines whether a word breaks across two lines.
Left-aligned text lines up at the left edge of the text box you draw with the Horizontal Type tool.
To add interest to the copy in a composition, you can apply effects to the text; for example, this text has a style from the Styles panel applied.
You can **center-align** text in a paragraph so each line of text is balanced on an imaginary vertical line through the center of the bounding box.
File Edit Image Layer Type Select Filter 3D View Window Help
Segoe UI
Regular
46.46 pt
Strong
Paragraph
0 pt
Hyphenate
RC Investments: The Right Choice for Your Nest Egg
20%
Doc: 17.3M/33.2M

Steven Russell Smith Photos/Shutterstock.com

TEXT LAYERS AND PANELS

For more control, you can modify the **kerning**, which is the spacing between a pair of characters.

You can specify font family and font style in the Character panel.

To fine-tune the appearance of text, adjust the **tracking**, which is the spacing between all of the characters in selected text or a paragraph.

Quickly apply text effects by clicking a style button.

Scale text vertically or horizontally by changing the percentage settings.

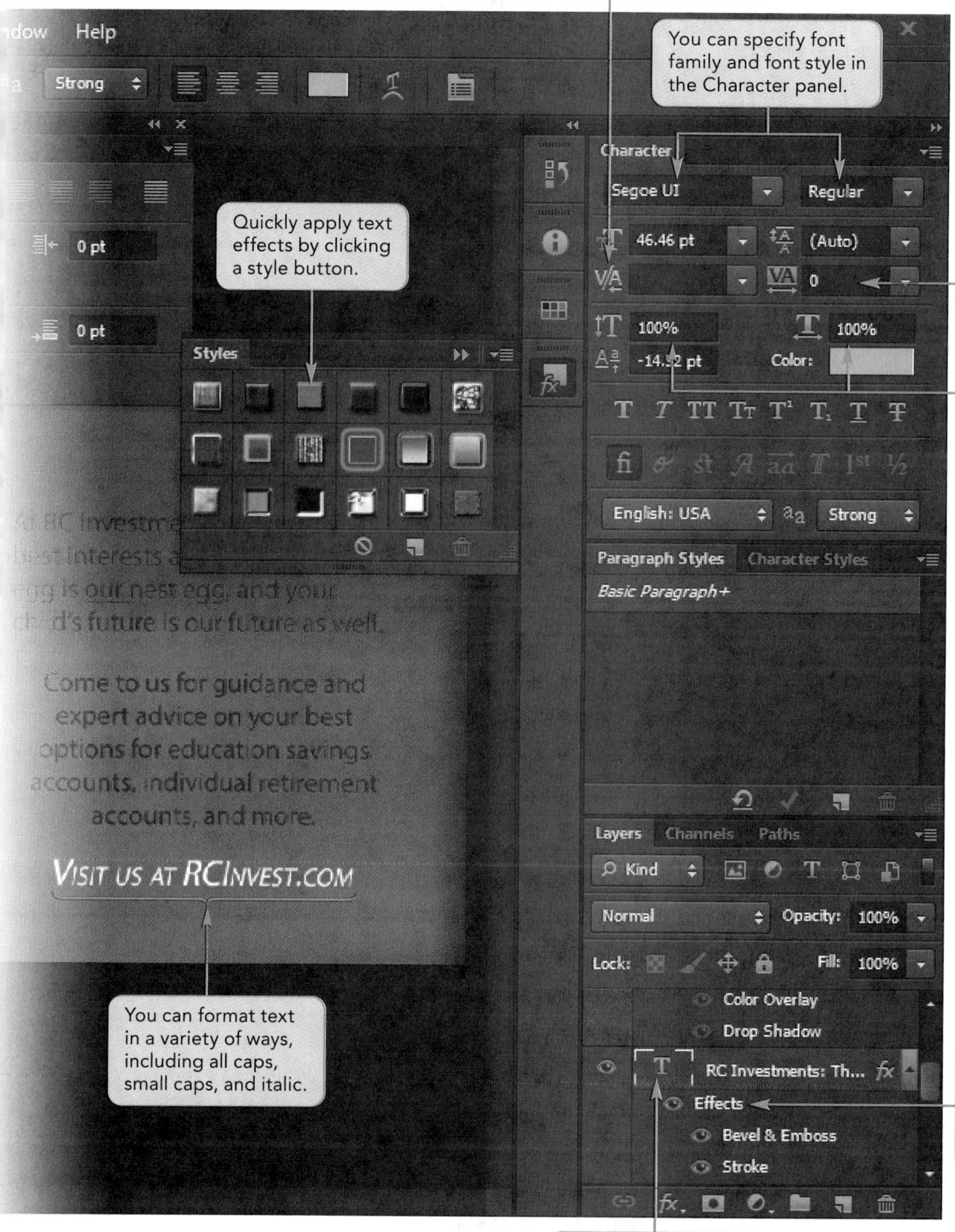

You can format text in a variety of ways, including all caps, small caps, and italic.

Text effects change the appearance of text and are listed in the Layers panel grouped with the layer to which they apply.

Text in Photoshop is stored on **text layers**.

Introducing Text Layers

Photoshop is first and foremost a digital image-editing tool, but it also provides a variety of text tools that let you format and arrange text in a document in much the same way you would format text in a page layout application. In fact, new features in Photoshop CS6, including the new Character Styles and Paragraph Styles panels, make it easier than ever to achieve the text effects you want in your compositions. When you add text to a Photoshop image, it is added as a vector object. This means that you can resize it, rotate it, stretch it, change its color, or apply a style to it without affecting its resolution. You can also stroke vector text to add an outline that makes it stand out. However, if you want to use the full set of image-editing tools available in Photoshop, you need to rasterize text to change it to a bitmap object. This gives you the flexibility to fill the text with an image, apply filters, and use other image-editing features; however, once you rasterize text, you can no longer edit it as text.

The Photoshop interface uses the terms *text* and *type* interchangeably. The tools you use to add text are called **Type tools**, but text is stored on text layers. See Figure 6-1.

Figure 6-1 **Text layers in a composition**

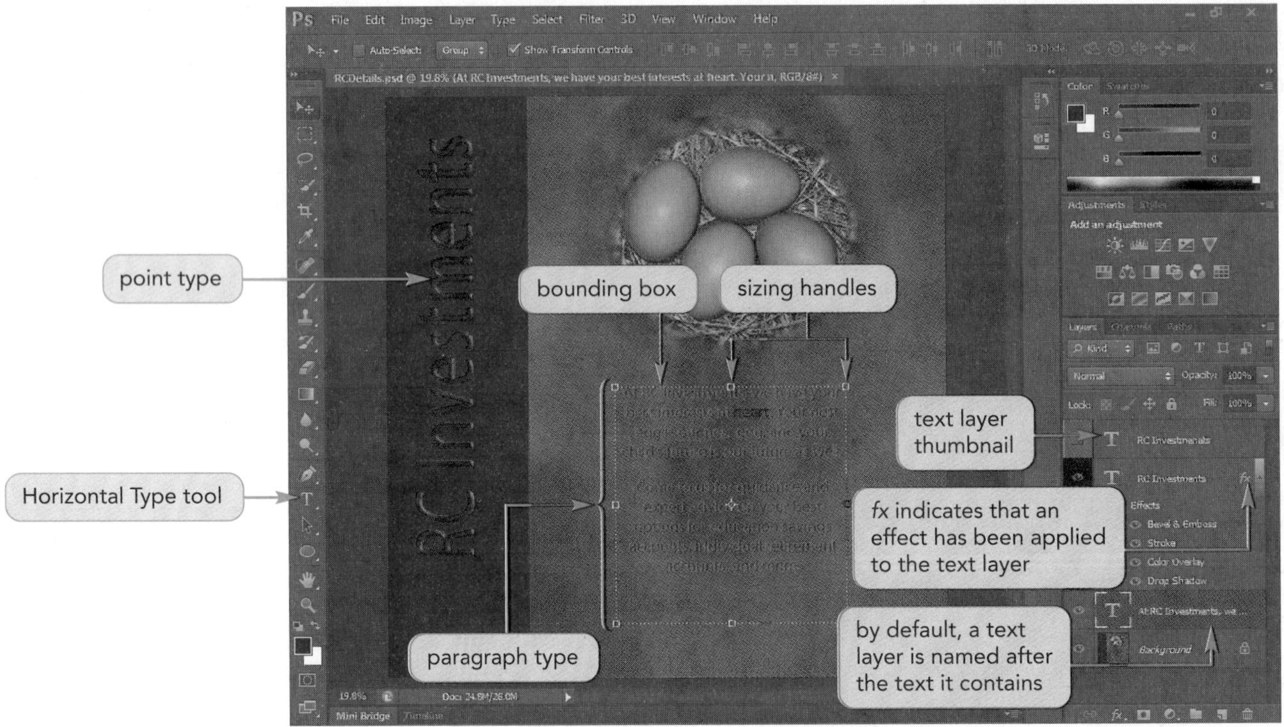

Steven Russell Smith Photos/Shutterstock.com

Text layers follow the same hierarchy rules as other layers in the Layers panel. A text layer on the canvas appears on top of any layers that it is on top of in the Layers panel. You can clip adjustments to text layers and set their opacity and blending modes. You can also select text layers, and move, group, copy, merge, and delete them.

A text layer is distinguished in the Layers panel by a Text thumbnail, which is a square with the letter *T* in it. By default, a text layer takes as its name the text that is included in the layer, but you have the option to rename the layer just as you can rename any other layer. When you apply an effect to a text layer, an *fx* appears to the right of the layer name in the Layers panel, and the details of the effect are listed beneath the layer name.

If you show transform controls when a text layer is selected, you will see that the text is contained in a bounding box. You can manipulate the bounding box in the same way you manipulate any other object. You can drag a handle to resize it, or use the rotate pointer to rotate it. When you resize a bounding box that contains text, you also resize the text.

Photoshop lets you enter two kinds of text: point type (also called character type) and paragraph type. **Point type** or **character type** is text you type after selecting one of the Type tools and clicking directly on the canvas to type. At the point you click, Photoshop adds a **baseline**, which is the line on which the text will rest as you type. The baseline extends with each new character. You can move to a new line by pressing the Enter key, and Photoshop will add a new baseline on the new line. When you have finished entering point type and move to a new task, Photoshop encloses the point type in a bounding box that you can see if you select the layer again and turn on transform controls or layer edges.

Paragraph type is text that is contained in a bounding box whose dimensions you specify by activating a Type tool and then clicking on the canvas and dragging. Once you define the dimensions of the bounding box, you can start to type, and the text will appear in the box. As you type, text wraps to a new line when it reaches the border of the bounding box. If you type more text than can fit in the bounding box, it is hidden unless you change the dimensions of the bounding box by dragging a transform control.

After you select a Type tool, you can use the options bar to define the font, font style, font size, and anti-aliasing method for the text, as well as its alignment. See Figure 6-2.

Figure 6-2 Type tool options

Icon	Tool	Description
	Toggle text orientation	Switches between the Horizontal and Vertical Type tools
Myriad Pro	Set the font family	Lets you preview and choose from a list of fonts installed on your computer; the font name in the box varies depending on the most recent font selection
Regular	Set the font style	Applies styles such as bold, italic, and bold condensed
12 pt	Set the font size	Allows you to select from a list of font sizes or type a custom size in the text box
Sharp	Set the anti-aliasing method	Sets the anti-alias setting, which determines the smoothness of text; settings include None, Sharp, Crisp, Strong, and Smooth
	Left align text, Center text, and Right align text	Aligns text within a text bounding box on the canvas
	Set the text color	Opens the Color Picker (Text Color) dialog box where you can use the color ramp and color field to select a color or enter color values; the color of this icon varies depending on the most recent text color selection
	Create warped text	Opens the Warp Text dialog box, where you can apply a style and/or horizontal and vertical distortions
	Toggle the Character and Paragraph panels	Toggles between the Character and Paragraph panels

INSIGHT

Using the Typography Workspace

When you are working with a lot of text in a composition, you'll find that the Typography workspace has many of the tools you'll need. The Typography workspace provides character formatting tools in the Character panel and paragraph formatting tools in the Paragraph panel. The Character and Paragraph panels appear in the Typography workspace in their own tab group, stacked with some of the panels you are already familiar with, including the Layers, Channels, and Paths tab group. In addition, the History, Info, Swatches, and Styles panels are collapsed to icons to the left of the Character panel. You can switch between the Character and Paragraph panels depending on whether you are formatting individual characters, words, or entire paragraphs. The Typography workspace also includes a Paragraph Styles panel and a Character Styles panel, where you can store any styles that you create. Using the many tools available in the Typography workspace will streamline your workflow whenever you work with text-heavy documents or want an easy way to apply consistent formats across a composition.

You'll use both point type and paragraph type to work on the compositions you'll submit to Rose for the new RC Investments marketing campaign.

Adding and Modifying Point Type

In Photoshop, you can add two different kinds of point type: horizontal and vertical. **Horizontal type** flows from left to right along a horizontal line. You create horizontal type using the Horizontal Type tool in the Tools panel. **Vertical type** runs from top to bottom along a vertical line. You can rotate horizontal type 90 degrees so it has a vertical orientation in your composition, but when you do so, the characters themselves are also rotated 90 degrees. If you want the characters in vertical type to have a horizontal orientation, you need to enter the type using the Vertical Type tool. See Figure 6-3.

Figure 6-3 Horizontal and vertical type

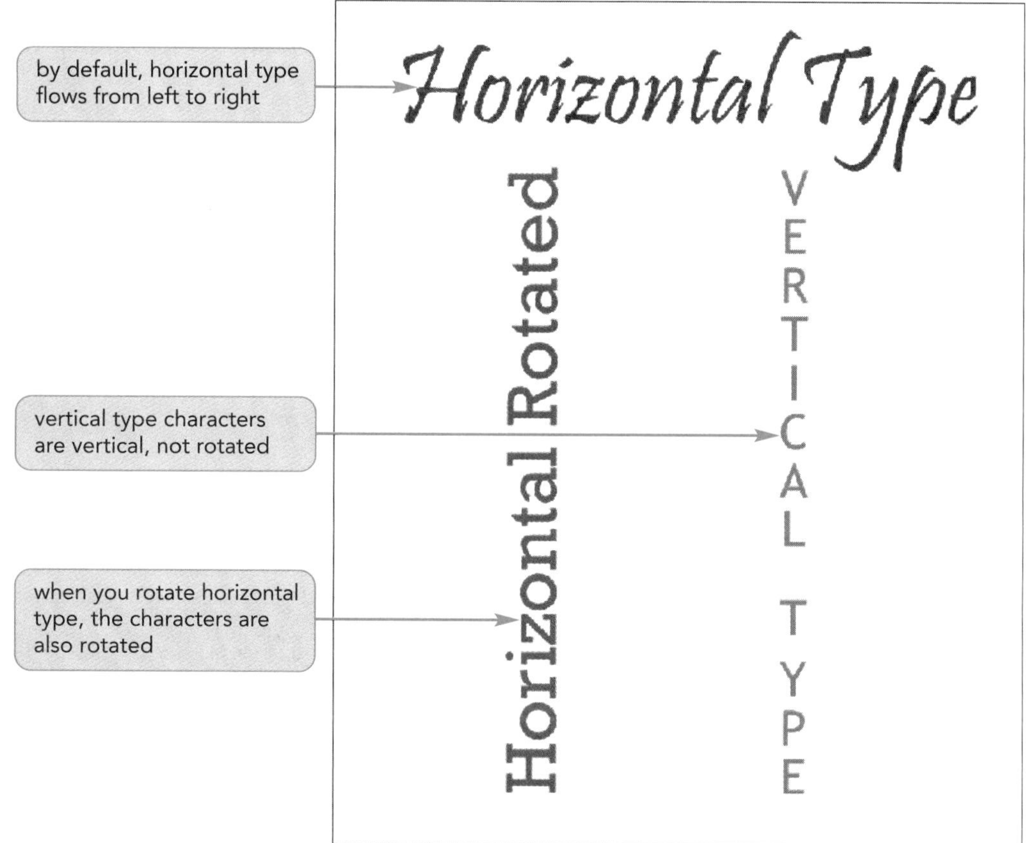
by default, horizontal type flows from left to right
Horizontal Type
Horizontal Rotated
VERTICAL TYPE
vertical type characters are vertical, not rotated
when you rotate horizontal type, the characters are also rotated

When you add point type, you are in text mode. In **text mode**, a blinking **cursor**, or vertical line, appears at the end of the text that you type, indicating that you can continue to type with the same settings. A horizontal baseline also appears under the text as you type. The type rests on that line unless you specify a baseline shift, which you will do later in this tutorial.

Once you add a point type layer, you can modify it. For example, you can change its font, font size, color, or style. Styles include Regular, Italic, Bold, and Bold Italic. If a font family doesn't include a style that you want to apply, you can apply a **faux style**, which is a style generated by Photoshop when an attribute, such as bold, is unavailable in a font family. For example, the Pristina font includes only regular characters. If you want to make a Pristina character bold, you have to use the Faux Bold button in the Character panel to have Photoshop generate a bold version of the character.

REFERENCE

Adding Point Type to an Image

- In the Tools panel, click the Horizontal Type tool or the Vertical Type tool.
- On the options bar, specify the font, font style, font size, anti-aliasing method, alignment, and color.
- Click the canvas at the location you want the text to appear, and type the text.
- On the options bar, click the Commit button.

You'll use a photograph of robin's eggs as the basis for the ad you'll present to Rose, and you'll add point type to it.

To add point type to a file:

1. Start Photoshop while pressing the **Ctrl+Alt+Shift** keys, and click **Yes** to delete the Settings File when prompted. Reset Photoshop to the default Essentials workspace layout, and then reset all tools.
2. Navigate to the Photoshop6\Tutorial folder included with your Data Files, and open **Right Choice.psd**. Press the **Ctrl+0** keys to fit the image in the window.
3. Display the rulers, and then add vertical guides at 1 1/4 inches and 2 inches on the horizontal ruler. Add two horizontal guides at 3/4 inches and 1 1/2 inches on the vertical ruler.
4. In the Tools panel, click the **Horizontal Type Tool** button T. The options bar displays settings for the Horizontal Type tool.
5. On the options bar, click the **Set the font family** button Myriad Pro. Photoshop lists the fonts available on your system. To the right of the font name, you can see a preview of the font. See Figure 6-4.

Figure 6-4 Available fonts

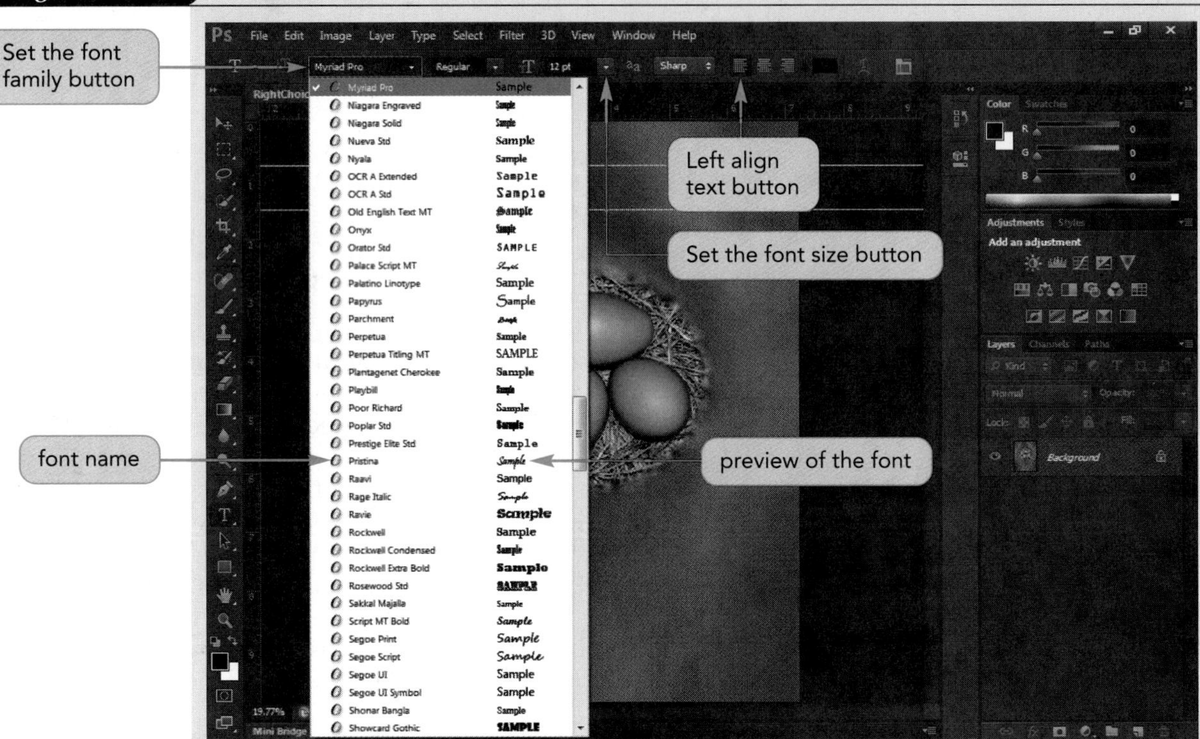

Steven Russell Smith Photos/Shutterstock.com

6. In the font family list, click **Pristina**, and on the options bar, click the **Set the font size** button 12 pt, and then click **48 pt**. Click the **Left align text** button, if necessary.

   Trouble? If you don't have Pristina, choose a different font.

7. Click the **Set the text color** button to open the Color Picker (Text Color) dialog box, and enter the following values: R=**0**, G=**102**, B=**102**. Click the **OK** button to close the dialog box.

   You are now ready to type text that will have the settings you specified.

8. Click at the intersection of the top horizontal guide and the left vertical guide, and type **Who's**. See Figure 6-5.

Figure 6-5 Adding point type

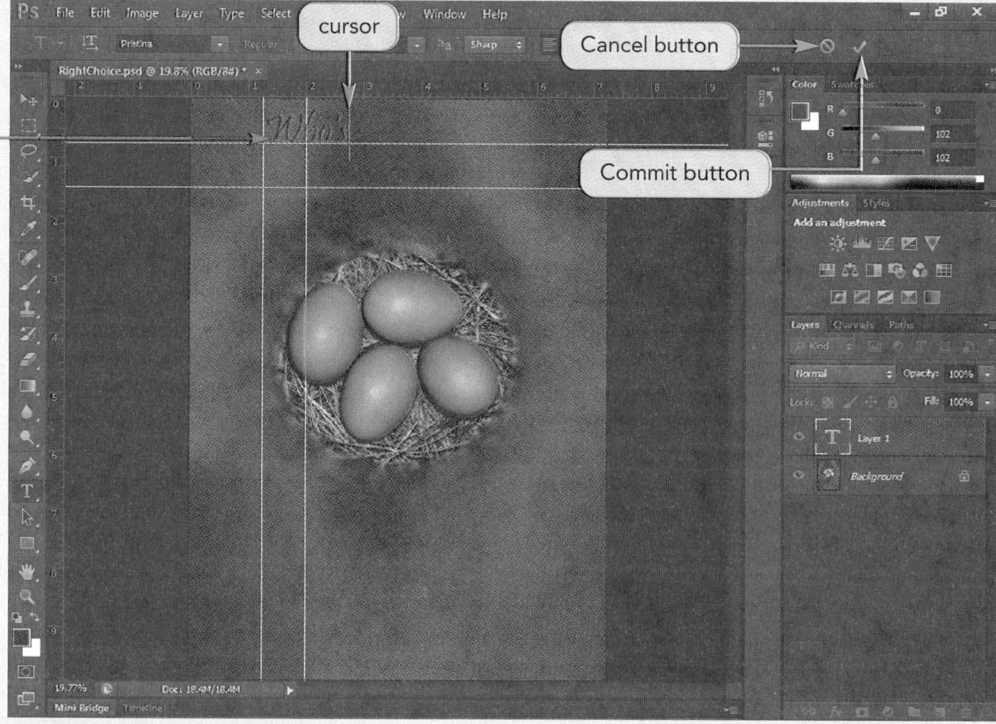

Steven Russell Smith Photos/Shutterstock.com

Because the text is left-aligned, it starts where you clicked with the mouse. If you look closely, you can see the baseline running along the bottom of the text. Photoshop adds the text on its own layer. Any new text you enter will be added to that text layer until you click the Commit button ✓, which tells Photoshop that you have finished entering text.

TIP

You can click the Cancel button on the options bar to delete the text entry rather than committing it.

9. Press the **Spacebar**, and then type **watching over**, and then on the right side of the options bar, click the **Commit** button ✓.
10. Click at the intersection of the second horizontal guide and the right vertical guide, type **your nest egg?**, and then click the **Commit** button ✓.
11. Click **View** on the menu bar, and then click **Clear Guides** to get a better view of your work.

    Because you didn't change any of the options on the options bar, the new text has the same formatting and size as the first text you entered.

Working in the Typography Workspace

When you are working extensively with text in Photoshop, you might find it helpful to switch to the Typography workspace, which provides easy access to many tools for working with text. The Character panel is particularly useful, and it appears at the top of the dock in the Typography workspace. See Figure 6-6.

Figure 6-6 Character panel formatting options

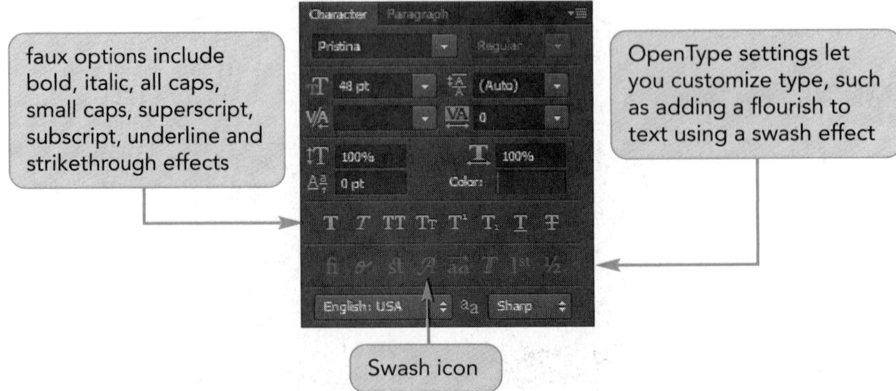
faux options include bold, italic, all caps, small caps, superscript, subscript, underline and strikethrough effects
OpenType settings let you customize type, such as adding a flourish to text using a swash effect
Swash icon
Character Paragraph
Pristina
Regular
48 pt
(Auto)
0
100%
100%
0 pt
Color:
English: USA
Sharp

The Character panel includes options for generating faux styles, such as bold or italic. Options for working with OpenType fonts also appear in the Character panel. OpenType fonts are scalable, modifiable fonts that you can use in either a PC or a Mac environment. OpenType fonts provide a great deal of flexibility to a designer because they can be scaled to almost any size, and modified to include characters found in languages other than English. They also let you add artistic effects to type, such as a swash, which is an italic embellishment that extends a character beyond the baseline. If you've ever received a fancy wedding invitation, you've probably seen a swash or two.

You'll be making a lot of changes to the text you enter in your new composition, so you'll switch to the Typography workspace.

To switch to the Typography workspace and modify the point type:

1. On the menu bar, click **Window**, point to **Workspace**, and then click **Typography** to display the Typography workspace.
2. In the Layers panel, double-click the **your nest egg?** text thumbnail. The text is highlighted on the image. Double-clicking the thumbnail is a quick and efficient way to select the text on a layer.

   You'll change the color of the *your nest egg* text so it stands out more than it did with the color you originally assigned.
3. In the Character panel, click the **Color** button, change the color of the text to white by typing RGB values of R=**255**, G=**255**, and B=**255** in the Color Picker (Text Color) dialog box, click the **OK** button, and then click the **Commit** button on the options bar. The text is now white.
4. On the canvas, double-click within the word ***your***. Double-clicking within a word selects it. See Figure 6-7.

Figure 6-7 **Double-clicking a word to select it**

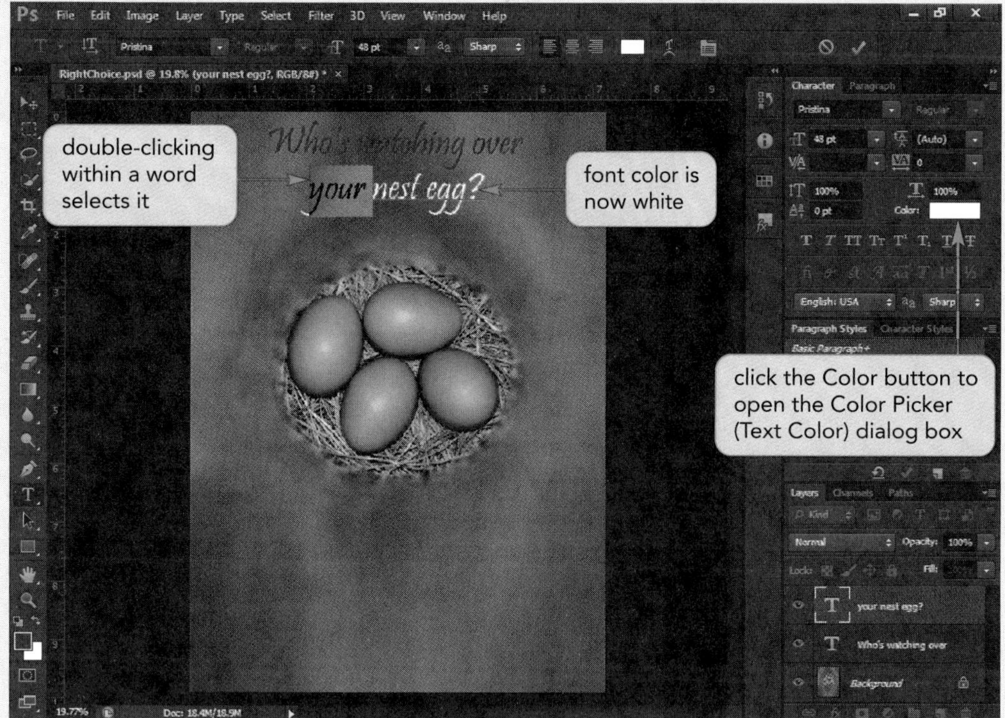

Steven Russell Smith Photos/Shutterstock.com

When a word is selected, you can edit it by typing new text, or you can change its format using the options bar or the Character panel.

5. In the Character panel, click the **Faux Bold** button, and then click the **Commit** button. The word *your* is now bold.
6. In the Layers panel, double-click the **Who's watching over** text thumbnail to select the words *Who's watching over.*
7. Click the **Swatches panel** icon to expand the panel, and then click the **White** swatch in the Swatches panel to change the text to white. Collapse the Swatches panel, and then click the **Commit** button.

   You could have also clicked the Color button in the Character panel to select the new color, but the Swatches panel provides an easier way to assign a standard text color because it avoids the dialog box.

You can also use the Character panel to format the text as all caps or small caps. The **all caps** format changes any text you type, whether you type it as uppercase or lowercase, to all capital letters in the current point size. The **small caps** option formats all letters as capital letters. The letters you type in uppercase are taller than the letters you type in lowercase, but all are capitalized. You'll add some additional text, and then change the formatting of that text to add interest to the composition.

To center text and format it as small caps:

1. Add guides at 3 1/2 inches on the horizontal ruler and at 7 inches and 9 inches on the vertical ruler. At the intersection of the top horizontal guide and the vertical guide, click to make the insertion point active, and then, on the options bar, change the font size to **60 pt** and click the **Center text** button. Type **RC Investments**.

   When the Center text option is selected on the options bar, any text that you type spreads out from the center point, which is the point where you click the mouse. See Figure 6-8.

Figure 6-8 Adding centered point type

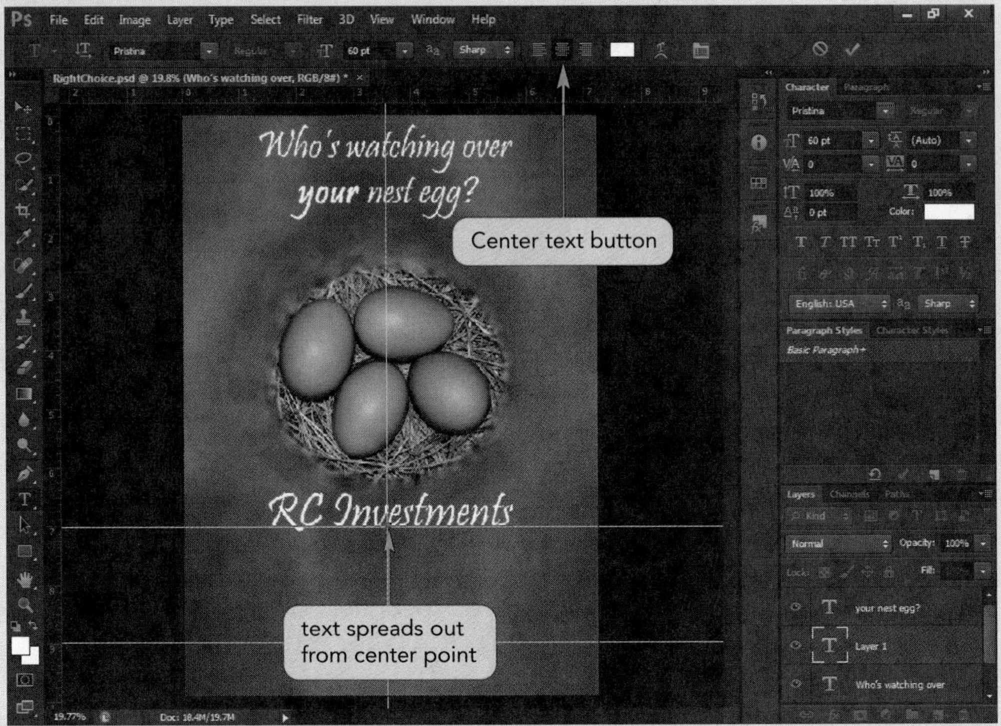

Steven Russell Smith Photos/Shutterstock.com

You can use small caps in a layout to add sophistication to your text, or to make it stand out from the other text. You'll apply it to the word *Investments* in the company name.

2. Highlight ***Investments*** by dragging the mouse over the word. In the Character panel, click the **Small Caps** button, and then click the **Commit** button. The capital *I* in the word is the same size as the capital *R* and capital *C*. However, the letters you typed as lowercase (*nvestments*) are formatted not as lowercase, but as small capital letters.
3. Using the same settings, type **The Right Choice** beneath RC INVESTMENTS at the intersection of the guides, and then click the **Commit** button.

Scaling Text Using the Character Panel

Using the Character panel, you can also scale text on a text layer. Scaling has an effect similar to changing the font size, but scaling gives you the flexibility to scale width and height separately.

REFERENCE

Scaling Text Using the Character Panel

- In the Layers panel, click the text layer you want to scale.
- If necessary, select individual words on the canvas.
- In the Character panel, in the Vertically scale box, type a scaling percentage.
- In the Character panel, in the Horizontally scale box, type a scaling percentage.
- Click outside the scale box, or press the Enter key to apply the new size.

Next, you'll scale the letters *R* and *C* in RC investments to add flair to the text on the canvas.

To scale the RC Investments text:

1. In the Layers panel, click the **RC Investments** layer, select *RC* on the canvas, and then in the Character panel, double-click in the **Vertically scale** box and type **110**. Double-click in the **Horizontally scale** box, type **120**, and then press the **Enter** key. The selected text is now 10 percent taller and 20 percent wider.
2. Click to the right of the letters *RC* and then press the **Enter** key. Photoshop adds a line break, and the *Investments* text moves to a new line below *RC*.

   Pressing the Enter key while the Text tool is active adds another line with the same point text settings as the current line. Notice that the *Investments* text is still centered at the vertical guide because the Center text button is still selected on the options bar.
3. Select the *I* in *Investments* and change the Vertically scale setting to **110%** and the Horizontally scale setting to **120%**. Select the last *s* in *Investments* and change both the Vertically scale setting and the Horizontally scale setting to **120%**, and then click the **Commit** button.

   See Figure 6-9.

Figure 6-9 Adding a line break and increasing scale

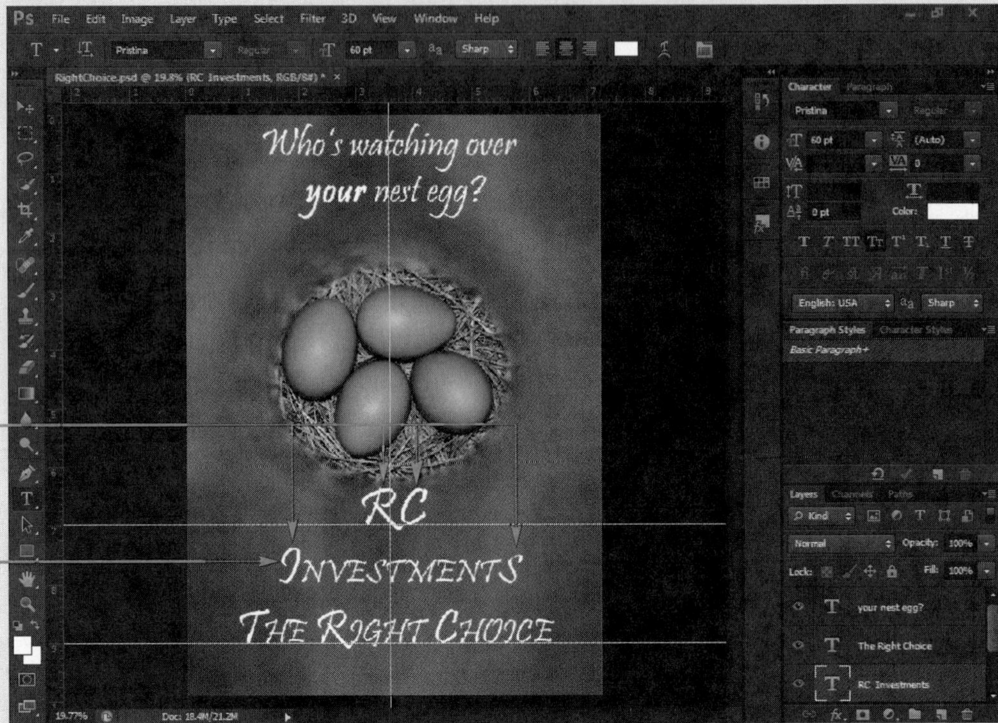
Who's watching over
your nest egg?
RC
INVESTMENTS
THE RIGHT CHOICE
RC, I, and S are all wider and taller
text on new line is still centered

Steven Russell Smith Photos/Shutterstock.com

4. Save the file as **RCI.psd** in the Photoshop6\Tutorial folder, and leave it open for the next set of steps.

Scaling Text Using the Move Tool

You can also use the Move tool to scale text using the transform controls. The transform controls, also called selection handles, let you resize the contents of the selected layer by dragging. You drag a side control to make the text wider or narrower, and you drag a top or bottom control to make the text taller or shorter. You can maintain the width-to-height ratio by pressing the Shift key while dragging a corner handle. After you click a transform control, you can also use the W (width) and H (height) boxes on the options bar to scale text by increasing or decreasing its width and height percentages. To constrain the scaling so that it's uniform, click the Maintain aspect ratio button on the options bar before changing a percentage.

REFERENCE

Scaling Text Using the Move Tool

- In the Layers panel, click the text layer you want to scale.
- In the Tools panel, click the Move Tool button.
- On the options bar, select the Show Transform Controls check box.
- Press and hold the Shift key, and drag a corner handle to scale text uniformly.

or

- Drag any handle to change the size of the text in the direction you drag.
- Press the Enter key, or on the options bar, click the Commit button.

You'll use the Move tool and the Shift key to scale the text on the The Right Choice layer uniformly.

TIP

After you click a transform control, you can use the Width and Height boxes on the options bar to scale text by increasing or decreasing its width and height percentages. To constrain the scaling so that it's uniform, click the Maintain aspect ratio button on the options bar before changing a percentage.

To use the Move tool to scale text:

1. In the Layers panel, click **The Right Choice** layer.
2. In the Tools panel, click the **Move Tool** button, if necessary, and then on the options bar, click the **Show Transform Controls** check box to select it, if necessary.
3. Press and hold the **Shift** key, click the **lower-left transform control**, and then drag the lower-left transform control up and to the right until it touches the horizontal guide. Release the mouse button, and then the Shift key. See Figure 6-10.

Figure 6-10 Resizing text by dragging transform controls

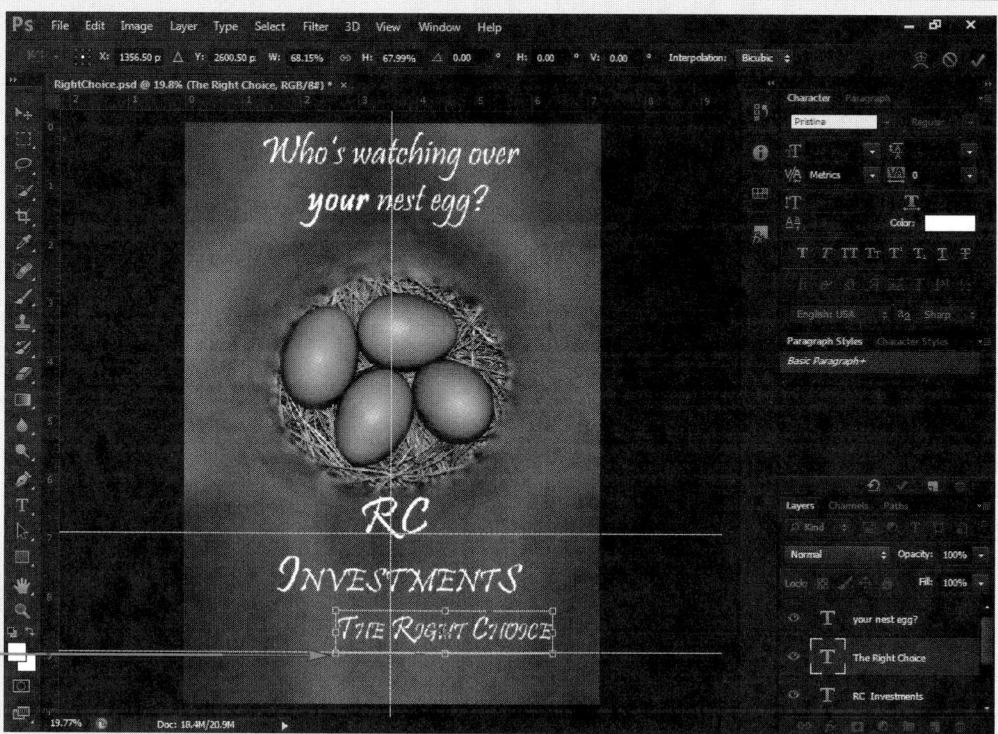

Steven Russell Smith Photos/Shutterstock.com

Trouble? If the text doesn't have similar proportions to Figure 6-10, you released the Shift key before releasing the mouse button. Cancel the transformation by clicking the Cancel button on the options bar, and then repeat Step 3.

4. Click the **Commit** button.
5. With the **The Right Choice** layer still selected, move the text to the left so it is centered beneath the word *INVESTMENTS*.
6. Save the RCI.psd file and close it.

You can emphasize text in a composition by typing it using a vertical orientation, so it is read from top to bottom. Next, you'll experiment with adding vertical text to a variation of the image you used for the previous composition.

Working with Vertical Point Type

Using vertical instead of horizontal type is another way to draw attention to a word or words in a composition. Obviously, you wouldn't apply vertical text to entire paragraphs. That would just frustrate your audience. However, a company name or catch phrase running vertically in a composition is an excellent way to make it stand out.

You will create another sample RC Investments ad for Rose using vertical type for the company name to add interest to the layout. You'll work with two kinds of vertical text. First, you'll enter horizontal type and rotate it 90 degrees to see if you like that effect. Then, you'll enter text using the Vertical Type tool, which adds the text from top to bottom.

To rotate horizontal type to a vertical position:

1. Open **RCVertical.psd**, located in the Photoshop6\Tutorial folder, size it to fit the window, and then save it as **RCDetails.psd** in the same folder.
2. Extend the canvas so you add an additional 2 1/2 inches to the left side of the canvas. Use black as the canvas extension color. (*Hint*: Click the Relative check box and anchor the existing image on the right.) The canvas now includes a 2 1/2 inch wide black bar along the left side. This is where you'll place the company name.
3. In the Tools panel, click the **Horizontal Type Tool** button, and then use the Character panel to set the font to **Myriad Pro** and the font size to **72 pt**. Click the **Small Caps** button to deselect it. Leave the other settings in the Character panel as they are.
4. On the options bar, click the **Left align text** button.
5. Click the canvas at about 8 inches on the vertical ruler and 1 inch on the horizontal ruler, and then type **RC Investments**. See Figure 6-11.

Figure 6-11 Entering font settings for horizontal type

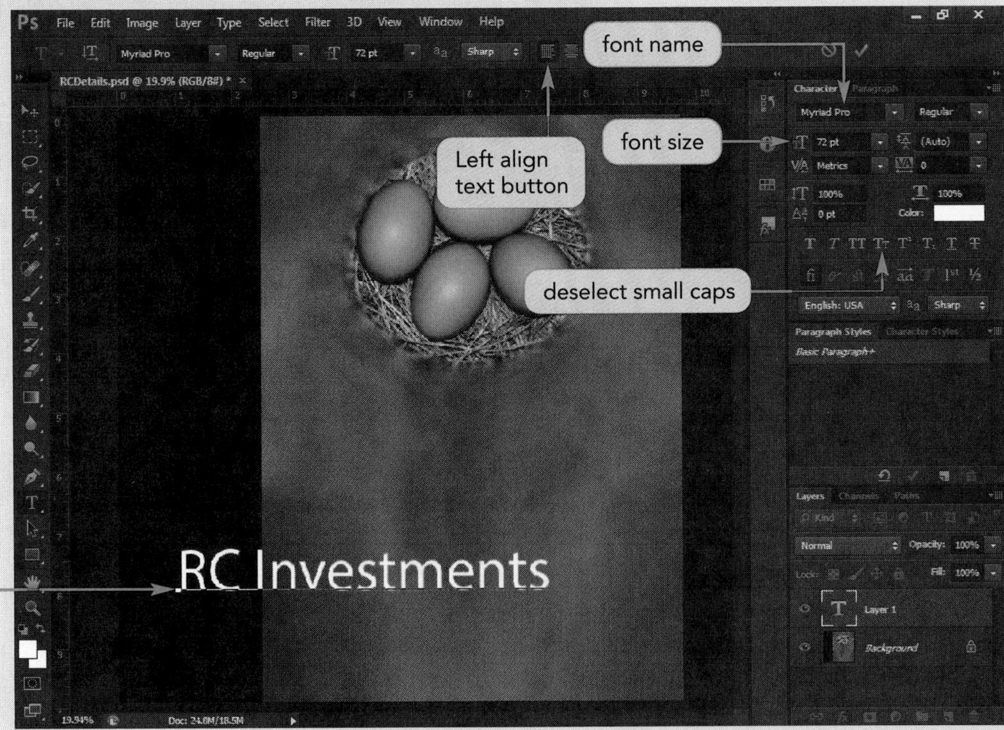

Steven Russell Smith Photos/Shutterstock.com

6. Click the **Commit** button . The text appears near the bottom of the image.
7. Press the **V** key to activate the Move tool , show the transform controls if necessary, and then position the mouse pointer near the upper-right transform control so it appears as a curved double-headed arrow .
8. Drag the control up and to the left until the text is at a – 45-degree angle. As you drag, the text rotates counterclockwise. See Figure 6-12.

TIP

Pressing the Shift key while rotating the text constrains the rotation to increments of 15 degrees.

Figure 6-12 **Rotating horizontal type**

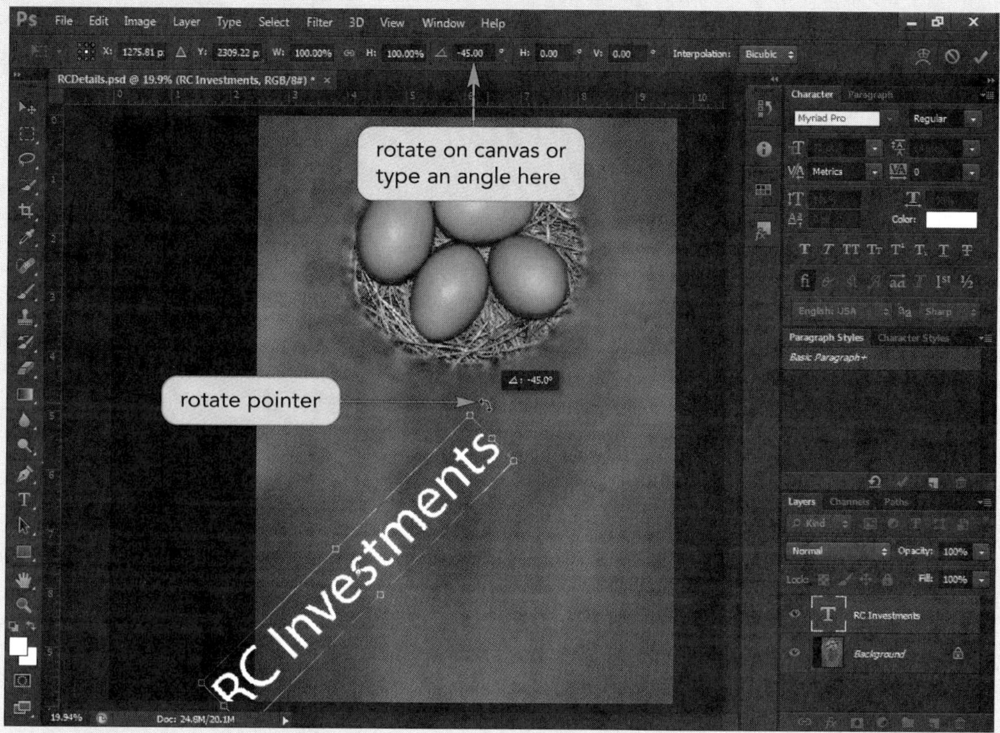

Steven Russell Smith Photos/Shutterstock.com

There will be times when you'll want to eyeball an angle of rotation until you're happy with how it looks in the image. However, if you know the angle of rotation that you want, it is easier to type it on the options bar or use the Shift key to rotate in increments.

9. On the options bar, type **-90** in the Rotate box .

   Specifying a negative number rotates the text in a counterclockwise direction. Typing a positive number rotates the text in a clockwise direction.

10. On the options bar, click the **Commit** button , and then drag the text until it appears centered in the black bar.
11. On the options bar, deselect the **Show Transform Controls** check box so you can see the full effect of the text rotation. See Figure 6-13.

Figure 6-13 **Horizontal text rotated to vertical position**

Steven Russell Smith Photos/Shutterstock.com

12. In the Layers panel, right-click the **RC Investments** layer, and then click **Red**. This layer color change will help you distinguish this layer from a similar layer you'll create next.
13. In the Layers panel, click the **Eye** icon to the left of the RC Investments layer to hide that layer.

To have some different options to present to Rose, you'll create another RC Investments layer that has vertical text in the black bar, only this time, you'll use the Vertical Type tool.

To use the Vertical Type tool to enter vertical type:

1. In the Tools panel, click the **Vertical Type Tool** button.

   Trouble? If you can't find the Vertical Type Tool button, right-click the Horizontal Type Tool button, and then click the Vertical Type Tool button.

2. On the options bar, select **Times New Roman** as the font. Click in the **Set the font size** box, highlight the current value, and then type **54**.
3. Click the canvas at about 1 inch on the horizontal ruler and ½ inch on the vertical ruler, and then type **RC Investments**. As you type, Photoshop enters subsequent letters beneath the previous letters, so the text has a vertical orientation. It also centers the letters along a vertical baseline. Click the **Top align text** button, if necessary. See Figure 6-14.

Figure 6-14 **Entering vertical type**

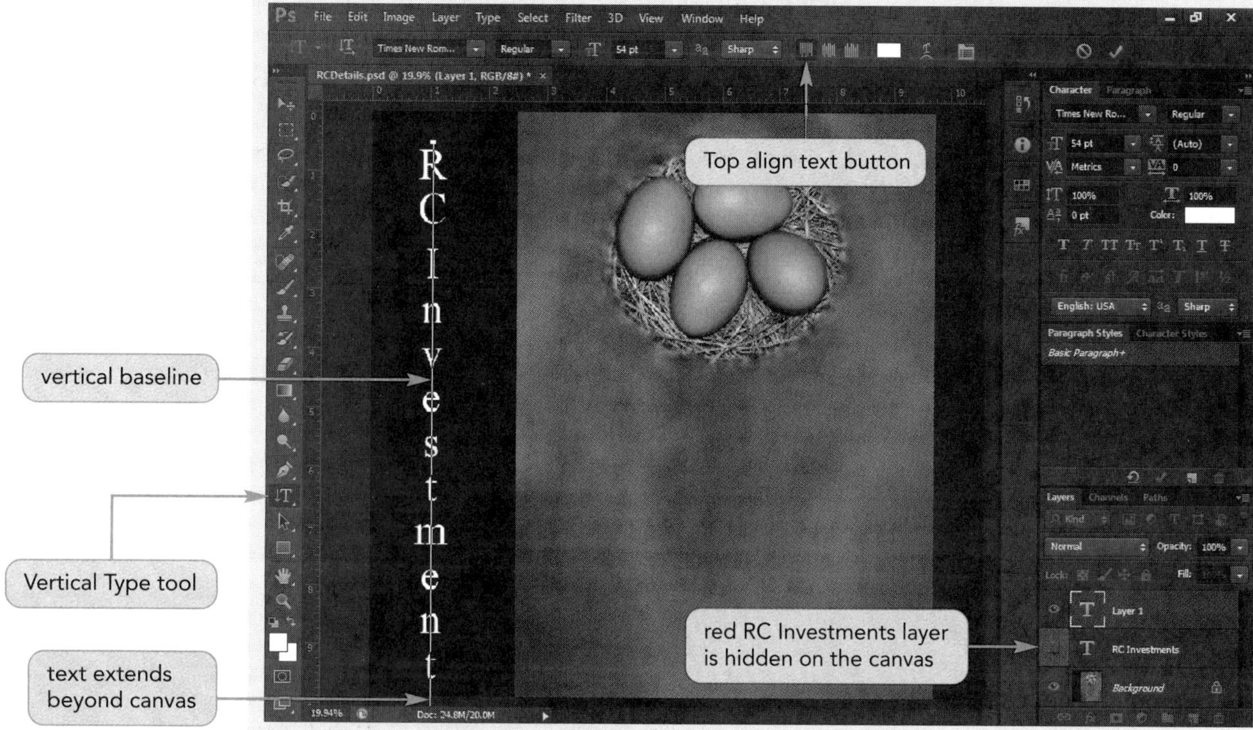

Steven Russell Smith Photos/Shutterstock.com

4. On the options bar, click the **Commit** button.

   Notice that the text has extended beyond the canvas. You'll adjust the tracking of the text to fix this problem.

Adjusting the Tracking of Vertical Text

In Photoshop, you can modify text tracking, which is the spacing between characters. The settings in the Character panel allow you to increase or decrease the spacing between the characters in selected text.

The RC Investments text is too spread out, so you will adjust the tracking so it all fits on the canvas. You'll also adjust the scaling of one of the characters so the characters line up better vertically.

To adjust the tracking and the scaling of the RC Investments text:

1. In the Layers panel, right-click the new **RC Investments** layer, and then click **Green** to change the layer color.
2. Double-click the **RC Investments** text thumbnail for the green text layer, and then in the Character panel, double-click the **Set the tracking for the selected characters** icon, and then type **-100** in the box. All of the characters now fit on the canvas, but the result still isn't satisfactory because it appears as if there is no space between *RC* and *Investments*.

3. Select the *C* and the *I*, and then in the Character panel, click the **Set the tracking for the selected characters** arrow, and then click **-50**. There is now more space between the words.

   The text now fits on the canvas, but the letter *m* seems out of place because it's much wider than the other letters in *Investments*.

4. Select the ***m***, and then in the Character panel, type **75** in the Horizontally scale box to make it narrower, and then on the options bar, click the **Commit** button.

   The text still needs work because the *I* in *Investments* is now too far from the *n*. You'll adjust the tracking between the *I* and the *n*.

5. Select the letters ***In*** within the word *Investments*, click the **Set the tracking for the selected characters box** arrow, and then click **-100**. The *I* and the *n* move closer together. Commit the change.

6. If necessary, use the Move tool to drag the text layer so it is centered in the black bar, as shown in Figure 6-15.

Figure 6-15 Centering the vertical text

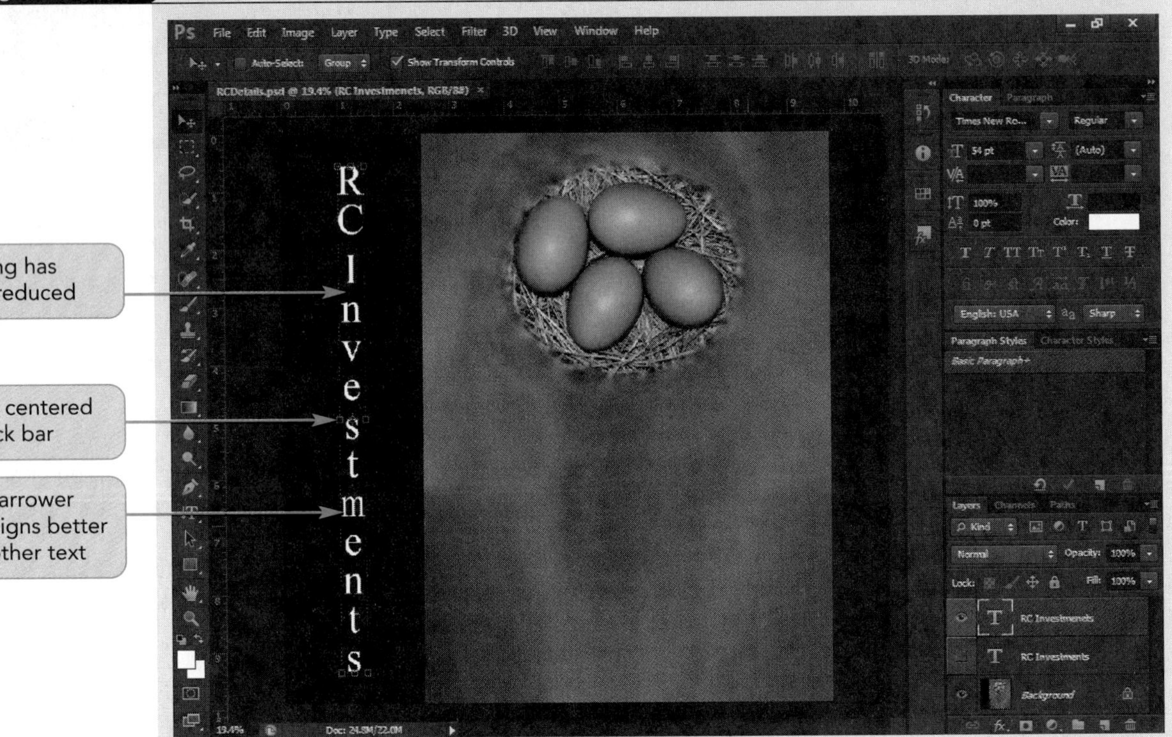
tracking has been reduced
text is centered in black bar
m is narrower and aligns better with other text
RC Investments

Steven Russell Smith Photos/Shutterstock.com

7. In the Layers panel, hide the green RC Investments layer, and display and select the **red RC Investments** layer. In the Tools panel, click the **Horizontal Type Tool** button, and then on the canvas, select the ***RC Investments*** text.

8. In the Character panel, increase the vertical scale of the RC Investments text to **150%**, and increase the tracking to **60**. See Figure 6-16.

Figure 6-16 **Changing the vertical scale and tracking**

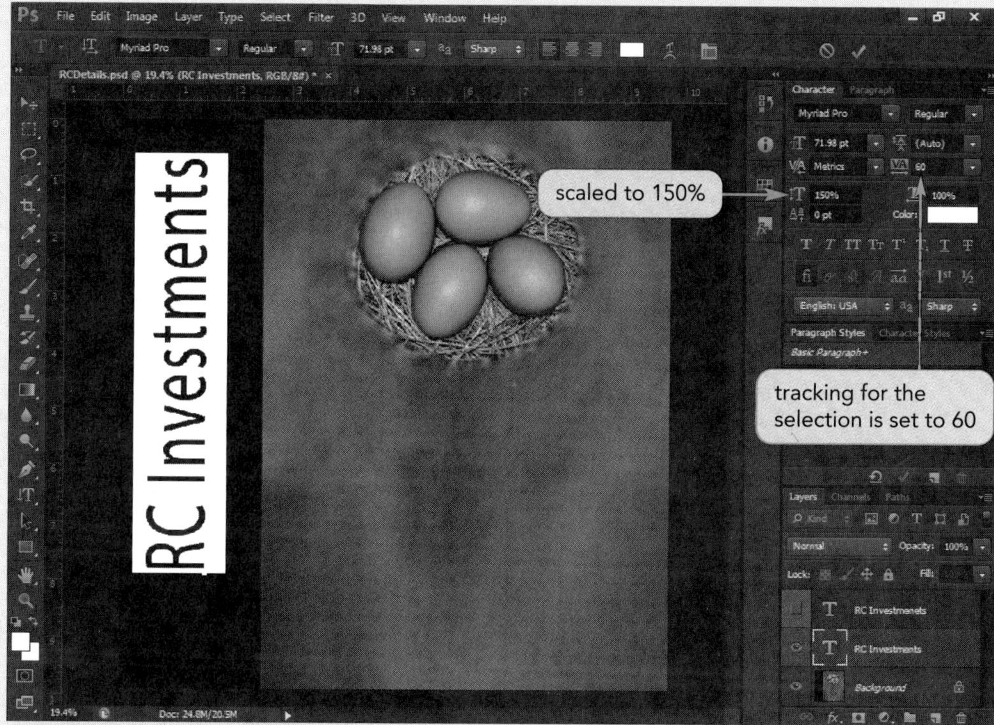

Steven Russell Smith Photos/Shutterstock.com

9. Commit the change, and then open the Layer Comps panel, and save the current view as a new layer comp called **Rotated**. Base it on Visibility and Position.
10. Hide the **red RC Investments** layer, display the **green RC Investments** layer, and save the current view as a new layer comp called **Vertical**, based on Visibility and Position. Minimize the Layer Comps panel group.
11. Save RCDetails.psd, and leave the file open.

Working with Paragraphs

TIP

You can add guides to help position a bounding box. As you drag the borders of the bounding box toward the guides, the borders snap to the guide location.

You can also work with paragraphs in a Photoshop composition. Paragraph text lets you predefine the size of the text box before you type, which is often essential when you are working with a fixed layout. To create paragraph text, select the Horizontal Type tool, and then drag on the canvas to create the bounding box that will hold the text. When you first enter it, Paragraph text behaves differently than point text. For example, if you type beyond the edges of the bounding box, the text will not appear, although as you'll see in the following steps, it's still being recorded by Photoshop.

REFERENCE

Adding Paragraph Text

- In the Tools panel, click the Horizontal Type Tool button, and on the options bar, specify the formatting options for the paragraph text.
- Click on the canvas, and drag to create a bounding box to hold the paragraph.
- Type the text in the bounding box.
- When you have finished entering text, click the Commit button on the options bar.

To enter paragraph type in a bounding box:

1. Position guides at about 5 inches and 6 1/2 inches on the vertical ruler and 4 inches and 8 inches on the horizontal ruler. Zoom the display to **25%**, and in the Layers panel, click the **Background** layer.
2. In the Tools panel, click the **Horizontal Type Tool** button T, and reset all of the tools.
3. Click the canvas at the upper-left intersection of the guides, and then drag a bounding box down to the lower-right intersection, as shown in Figure 6-17.

Figure 6-17 **Creating a bounding box**

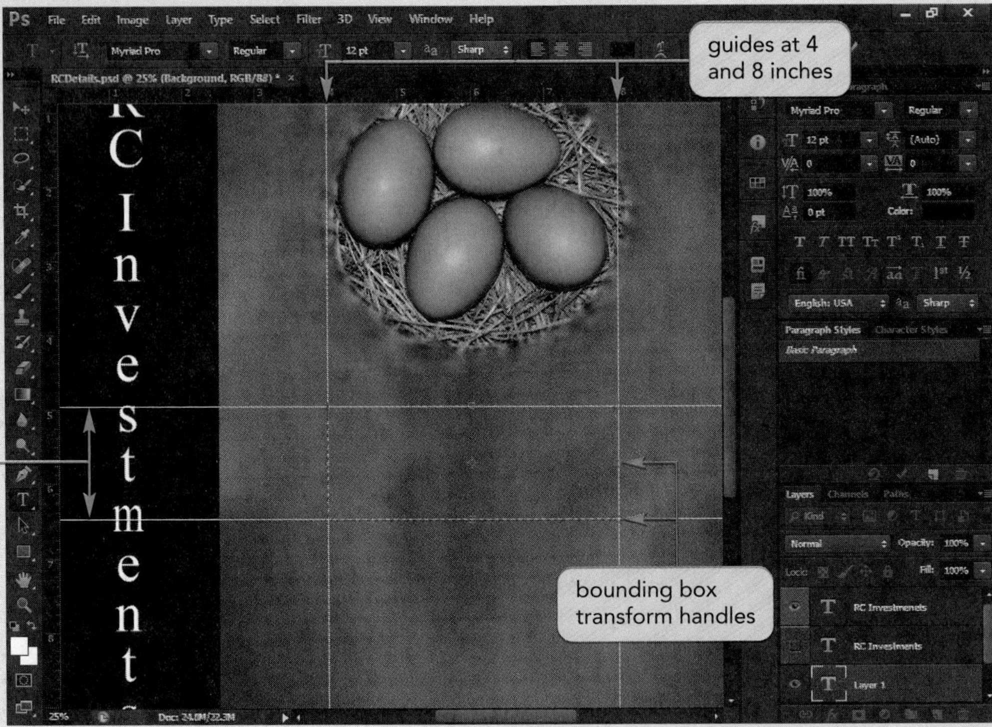

Steven Russell Smith Photos/Shutterstock.com

The bounding box has transform handles like other objects in Photoshop. An insertion point appears in the upper-left corner of the bounding box, although it might be difficult to see.

Trouble? If your bounding box doesn't fit in the guides exactly, press the Escape key and repeat Step 3. If it still doesn't fit the guides, your text might wrap differently than the text shown in the figures.

4. In the Character panel, set the font to **Myriad Pro**, if necessary, click the **Set the font size arrow**, and then click **18 pt**. If necessary, set the vertical scale to **100%**.
5. Click the **Swatches panel** icon to expand it, and then click the **Darker Cyan** swatch in the middle of the second-to-last visible row. The Color boxes in the Character panel and on the options bar display the new text color. Darker Cyan is also the new foreground color in the Tools panel.

   Trouble? If you can't find the Darker Cyan swatch, click any blue swatch in the panel.
6. Type **At RC Investments, we have your best interests at heart.** As you type, notice that the text wraps to fit in the bounding box you drew.
7. Press the **Spacebar**, and then type **Your nest egg is our nest egg, and your child's future is our future as well.**
8. Press the **Enter** key. Pressing the Enter key starts a new paragraph and moves the cursor to a new line, just as it does in a word-processing program.
9. Type **Come to us for guidance and excellent advice on your best options for** in the bounding box. The word *excellent* is hyphenated, and the rest of the text is hidden. See Figure 6-18.

Figure 6-18 **Text beyond bounding box is hidden**

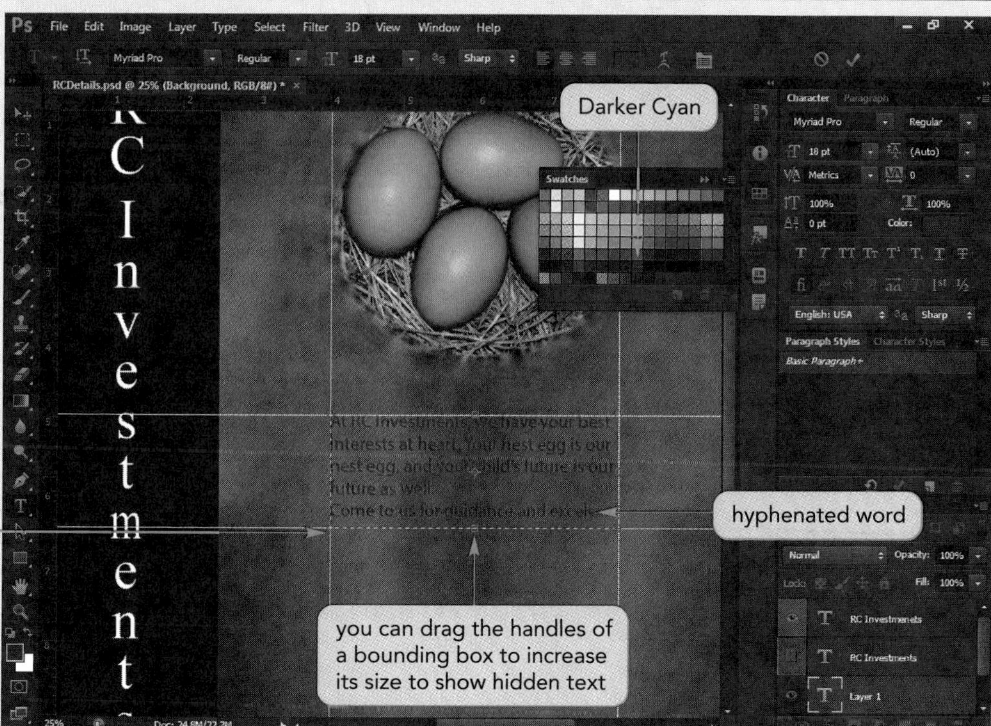
Darker Cyan
text flows to next line and out of bounding box
hyphenated word
you can drag the handles of a bounding box to increase its size to show hidden text

Steven Russell Smith Photos/Shutterstock.com

Trouble? If your text wraps differently, or fits the text box differently, don't worry. If there is even a slight difference in the size of the bounding box, line breaks will vary.

When you enter point type, the bounding box expands to fit the text as you add it to the canvas. However, with paragraph type, the text you type must fit in the bounding box to show up on the canvas. To display more text, you need to change the size of the bounding box.

10. Position the mouse pointer over the center-bottom handle of the bounding box, and then drag the handle down to about the 9-inch mark on the vertical ruler. The rest of the text that you typed is now visible.

    You'll continue to type, and will intentionally misspell the word *education* as *edcuation* so you can correct it when you check spelling later.

11. Press the **Spacebar**, type **edcuation savings accounts, individual retirement accounts, and more.**

12. On the menu bar, click **View**, point to **Show**, and then click **Guides** to hide the guides. Collapse the Swatches panel.

13. Select all of the text and change the font size to **20 pt**, and then commit the change. See Figure 6-19.

Figure 6-19 **Paragraph text after the bounding box has been extended**

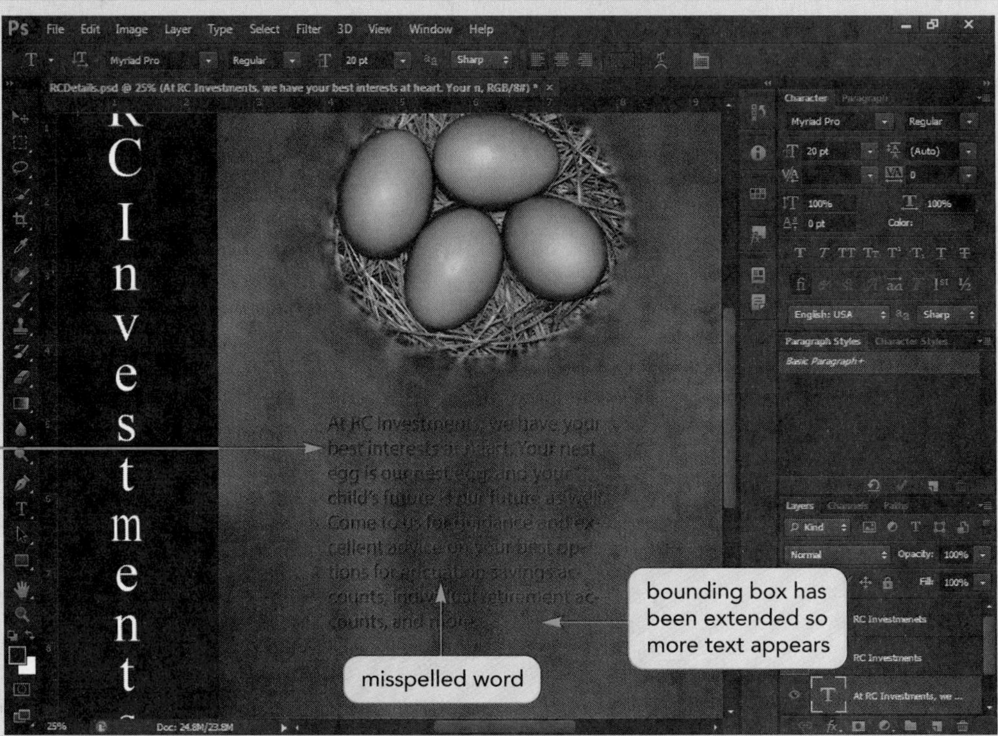

text is left aligned
bounding box has been extended so more text appears
misspelled word

Steven Russell Smith Photos/Shutterstock.com

PROSKILLS

Decision Making: Knowing When to Justify

When formatting paragraph text, you can choose to left-align, right-align, center, or justify it. When you left-align a paragraph, text appears **flush left**, or straight along the left margin, and has a ragged right edge, like the paragraphs in this book. In Photoshop, and in word-processing programs, text is left-justified by default. When you right-align text, it appears **flush right** along the right margin, and has a ragged left edge. When you center text, both the left and right edges are ragged, and each line is centered, resulting in lines of different lengths. When you **justify** text, it is aligned flush along both the left and the right margins. This gives your paragraphs neat, symmetrical margins, but it can introduce other problems, such as loose or tight lines. In a **loose line**, text is so spread out that it is distracting to the eye because of all of the white space. White space flowing from line to line, called a **river**, can draw a reader's attention away from the content. In a **tight line**, some words are so close together that they are difficult to distinguish. In general, justifying text in a narrow column results in a great number of loose lines and is, therefore, not advised. Photoshop and most word-processing programs provide tools that let you fix the tracking and kerning of loose lines to reduce the white space between words and characters in justified text, but making adjustments line by line can be very time consuming.

So when do you use justified text, and when do you use some other alignment option? In fact, there's no simple answer. You need to determine your needs on a case-by-case basis. In general, justified text is considered formal, while unjustified text is less so. Other considerations are column width and page design. For example, how do the graphics on the page look next to justified or unjustified text? As you become more experienced working with text, you'll develop a sense of what works best in a given situation. You'll also need to weigh other factors, such as the time it takes to adjust tracking, kerning, and hyphenation in a particular design. Once you have weighed all of these factors, you'll have the information you need to make the right decision for a given project.

Next, you'll use the Paragraph panel to adjust the alignment of the paragraphs and the space between paragraphs to see if that improves the layout. You'll also turn off hyphenation to see how different line breaks affect the readability of the text.

To use the Paragraph panel to adjust alignment and hyphenation:

1. Click the **Paragraph panel** tab to display the Paragraph panel.
2. On the canvas, click in the first line of the first paragraph, and then in the Paragraph panel, click the **Center text** button. The text in the first paragraph is centered, and both the left and right margins are ragged. Notice that clicking the Center text button only affects the current paragraph.
3. Click in the second paragraph, and in the Paragraph panel, click the **Justify last left** button. See Figure 6-20.

Figure 6-20 Adjusting text alignment

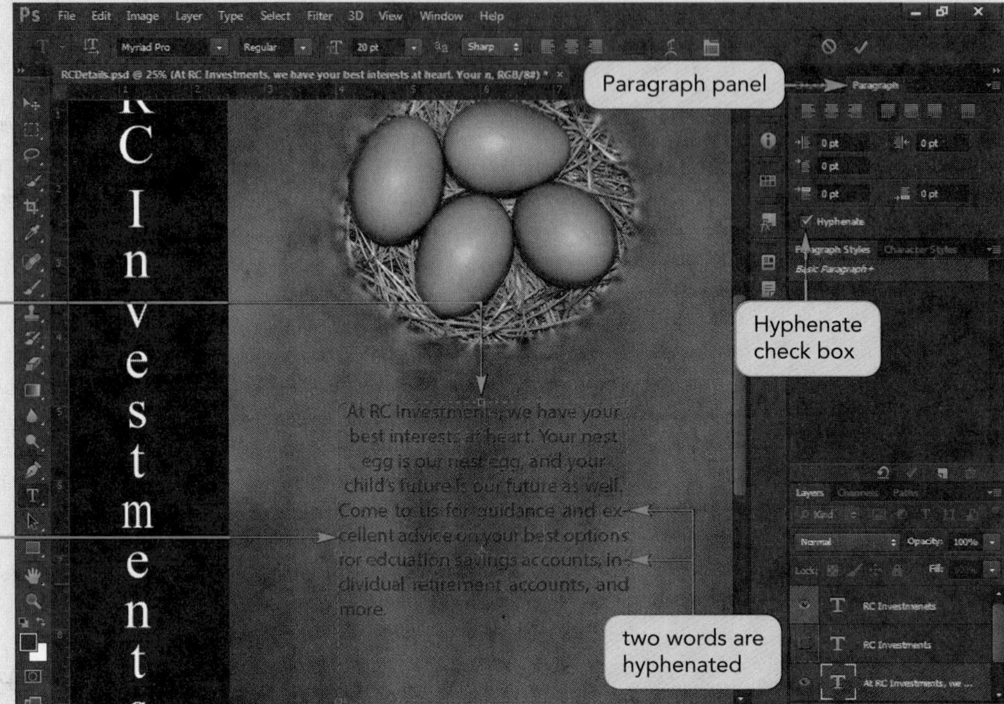

Steven Russell Smith Photos/Shutterstock.com

The text is justified, or evenly spread between the margins of the bounding box, with the last line aligned at the left margin. Two of the words in the second paragraph are hyphenated.

Trouble? If you don't see two hyphenated words, your bounding box is a different size. Continue with the remaining steps.

4. In the Paragraph panel, click the **Hyphenate** check box to deselect it. The words that were hyphenated in the second paragraph have now moved to the next line of text, without hyphenation, and the remaining text spreads out to maintain the justification. Notice that there are now more loose lines and rivers of blank space.
5. In the Paragraph panel, click in the **Add space before paragraph** box, and type **20**. Photoshop adds a 20-point vertical space before the second paragraph.

   Even with the space before the second paragraph, the text doesn't work well as it is currently formatted. Some of the words are too spread out, which makes the paragraph look sloppy. You'll use the center align option for the second paragraph so the characters and words are spaced for easier reading and so it matches the formatting of the first paragraph.
6. Click in the second paragraph, if necessary, and then in the Paragraph panel, click the **Center text** button. The text is centered, without hyphenation.
7. Commit the changes to the paragraph text. See Figure 6-21.

Figure 6-21 Paragraphs centered and separated by space

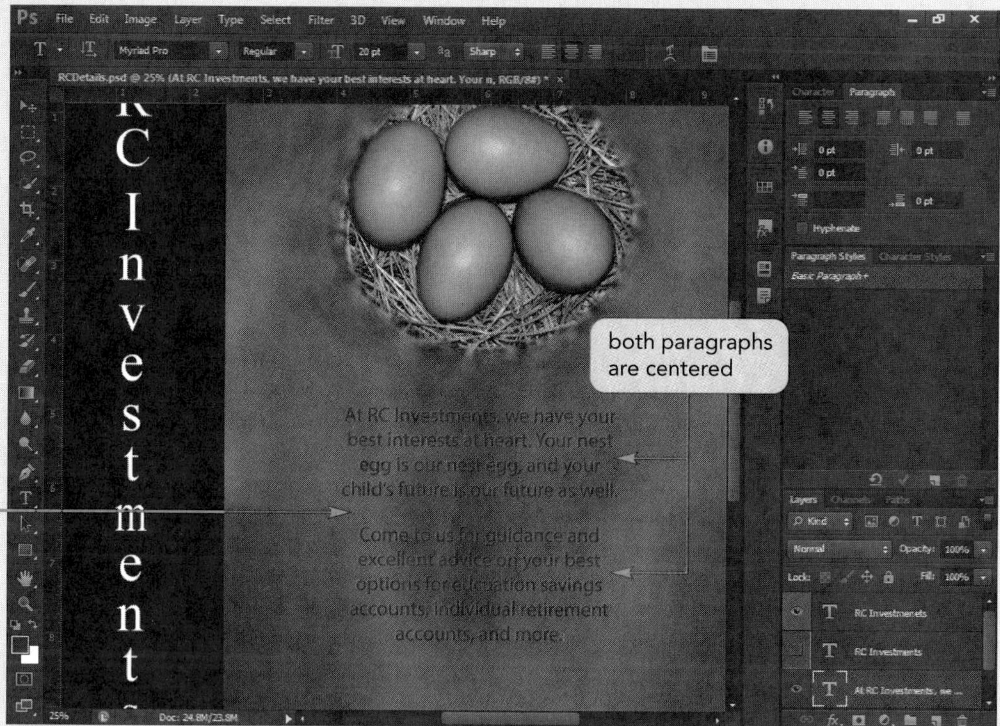

Steven Russell Smith Photos/Shutterstock.com

INSIGHT

Using Advanced Justification Settings

You can access advanced justification settings by selecting Justification from the Paragraph panel menu. Advanced justification settings let you specify Minimum, Desired, and Maximum values for word and letter spacing, as well as glyph scaling. The **Word Spacing** setting determines the space between words. You typically add space between words by pressing the Spacebar. Using advanced justification settings, you can adjust the width of that space. The **Letter Spacing** setting controls the distance between letters. A setting of 100% puts the width of a regular space between letters; 0% packs letters tightly together with no space between them. The **Glyph Scaling** setting determines the width of individual characters. Each font family has predetermined widths for characters, but you can override that setting by specifying a value between 50% and 200%. **Auto Leading** sets the leading—or the vertical space between lines of text—to 120% of the font size by default. You can change the space between lines by changing the value in the Auto Leading box.

Next, you'll format individual words in the paragraphs to make them stand out from the rest of the paragraph. You'll do this using the Character panel and the Swatches panel.

To format the paragraph text:

1. Double-click the word ***heart*** in the first paragraph.
2. Expand the Swatches panel, click any **red swatch**, and then commit the change. Collapse the Swatches panel. The word *heart* is formatted in a red font.

3. In the third line of the first paragraph, double-click the word ***our***, display the Character panel, click the **Set the font style** button Regular, and then click **Italic**.
4. Near the bottom of the Character panel, click the **Underline** button, and then click outside the word *our* to deselect it. The word *our* is italicized and underlined, while the rest of the words retain their original formatting.

Even though you entered the text you just formatted as paragraph type, you can format it the same way you format point type. In fact, after you commit either paragraph type or point type, they behave in the same manner.

Checking Spelling and Replacing Text

When you enter a lot of text in a bounding box, you'll sometimes find that you've made typing errors. You might be used to word-processing programs that mark misspelled words as you type. Photoshop doesn't have that feature, so you need to use the Check Spelling option on the Edit menu. You can also replace one word or phrase with another using the Find and Replace feature in Photoshop. This command is also on the Edit menu.

To check spelling in the paragraph text:

1. Click at the beginning of the first paragraph, to the left of the word *At*.
2. On the menu bar, click **Edit**, and then click **Check Spelling**. The Check Spelling dialog box opens, indicating that *edcuation* is not in the dictionary. Photoshop suggests that you replace the word with the correctly spelled version, *education*.

   Trouble? If the spelling suggested in the Check Spelling dialog box is not the spelling you want, or is not the word you intended, you can either type the correct spelling in the Change To box, or scroll down the list of suggestions and select one of the alternate words.

   Trouble? If a dialog box with a "Spell check complete." message appears, you either have no errors in your text, or you have not clicked at the beginning of the first paragraph. When checking spelling, Photoshop starts at the insertion point and goes to the end of the bounding box. If the insertion point is in the middle of the text, it checks only the second half of the text entry.
3. Click the **Change** button. Photoshop corrects the spelling of *education* and indicates that the spelling check is complete.

   Trouble? If Photoshop finds additional misspelled words, correct them as necessary before closing the dialog box.
4. Click the **OK** button to end the spelling check.

You can also replace text using the Find and Replace Text command on the Edit menu, which opens the Find And Replace Text dialog box. See Figure 6-22.

Figure 6-22 Find And Replace Text dialog box

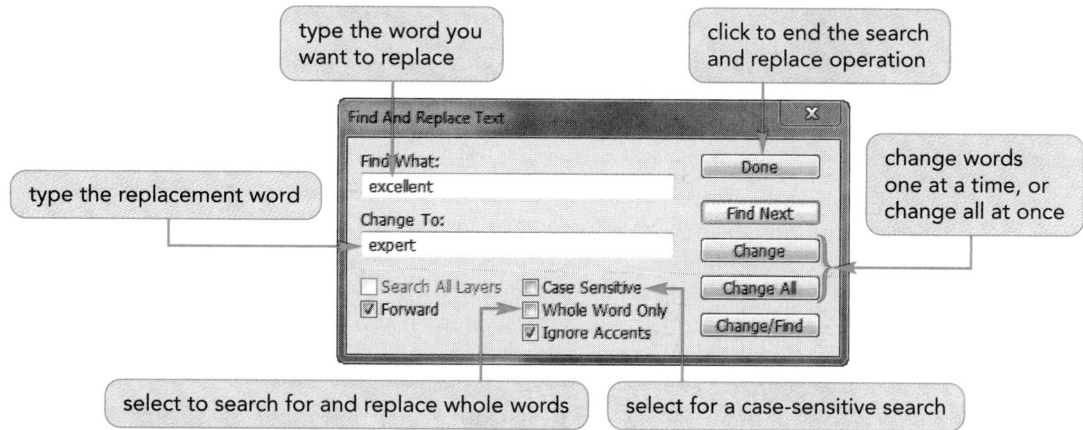

You can type the word you want to replace in the Find What box, and then type the new word in the Change To box. The Find Next button finds the next instance of the word you want to replace. The Change button replaces the word. The Change All button replaces all instances of the Find What word in one step. To change one instance of the word you want to replace and then move to the next, click the Change/Find button. You can also specify whether you want to search forward through the text, whether you want to search all layers, and whether the search should be case sensitive and should look for whole words. For example, if you specify *day* as the word to find, Photoshop will find *today*, *Monday*, and *daylight* in addition to *day*. If you specify Whole Word Only, Photoshop will only find *day*.

While the Find and Replace feature is most useful in situations in which you are working with large segments of text, you will experiment with it by replacing the word *excellent* with the word *expert* in the ad you are working on for Rose.

To find and replace text:

1. Click at the beginning of the first paragraph. On the menu bar, click **Edit**, and then click **Find and Replace Text**. The Find And Replace Text dialog box opens.
2. In the Find What box, type **excellent**, and then in the Change To box, type **expert**.
3. Click **Find Next**. Photoshop highlights the instance of *excellent* in the paragraph.
4. Click the **Change** button to change *excellent* to *expert*.
5. Click the **Done** button, and then in the Layers panel, click the **Background** layer to deselect the paragraph text.
6. Save RCDetails.psd. If you are not taking a break before the next session, leave the file open.

INSIGHT

Creating Paragraph and Character Styles

If you plan to use the same format for multiple paragraphs, it's a good idea to create and save a paragraph style so you can use it again in the future. Photoshop CS6 has a new panel, the Paragraph Styles panel, that lets you do just that. To save a paragraph style, click the Create new Paragraph Style icon at the bottom of the panel, and then double-click the new style in the list to open the Paragraph Style Options dialog box. In this dialog box, you can set character formats, indents, spacing, justification, and hyphenation, among other things. When you save the style, it is saved as a choice in the Paragraph Styles panel and can be applied to other paragraphs in your document. Because the paragraph style is saved with the document, it can also be used in future sessions. To access the style, display the Paragraph Styles panel, and select the style from the list.

You can also save character styles using the new Character Styles panel. To do so, format the text in the style you want to save, and then double-click the new style in the list to open the Character Style Options dialog box. In this dialog box, you can set character formats, including font, font style, font size, and leading, tracking, and kerning options. You can also create special styles that use all caps or small caps, among other settings.

Because you can also load styles into one document from another by selecting Load Character Styles or Load Paragraph Styles from the panel menu, using paragraph and character styles is a good way to streamline your work flow and achieve a consistent look across compositions.

In this session, you learned about text layers, and you worked with horizontal point type, vertical point type, and paragraph type. You explored the Typography workspace, and experimented with a variety of text formatting and alignment options. You also learned about character styles and paragraph styles. In the next session, you'll work with some more advanced text formatting options, including applying text styles, specifying baseline shifts, and bending text to a path. You'll also fill text with an image, a pattern, and a gradient.

REVIEW

Session 6.1 Quick Check

1. What is the difference between the way you enter paragraph type and the way you enter point type?
2. Point type is entered along a(n) ____________ that expands to accommodate new text.
3. The ____________ workspace is designed for text editing and formatting.
4. True or False. Vertical type entered with the Vertical Type tool has the same appearance as text that is entered with the Horizontal Type tool and then rotated counterclockwise 90 degrees.
5. Which setting in the Paragraph panel lets you adjust the space between words and characters?
6. What does it mean to justify the text in a paragraph?

SESSION 6.2 VISUAL OVERVIEW

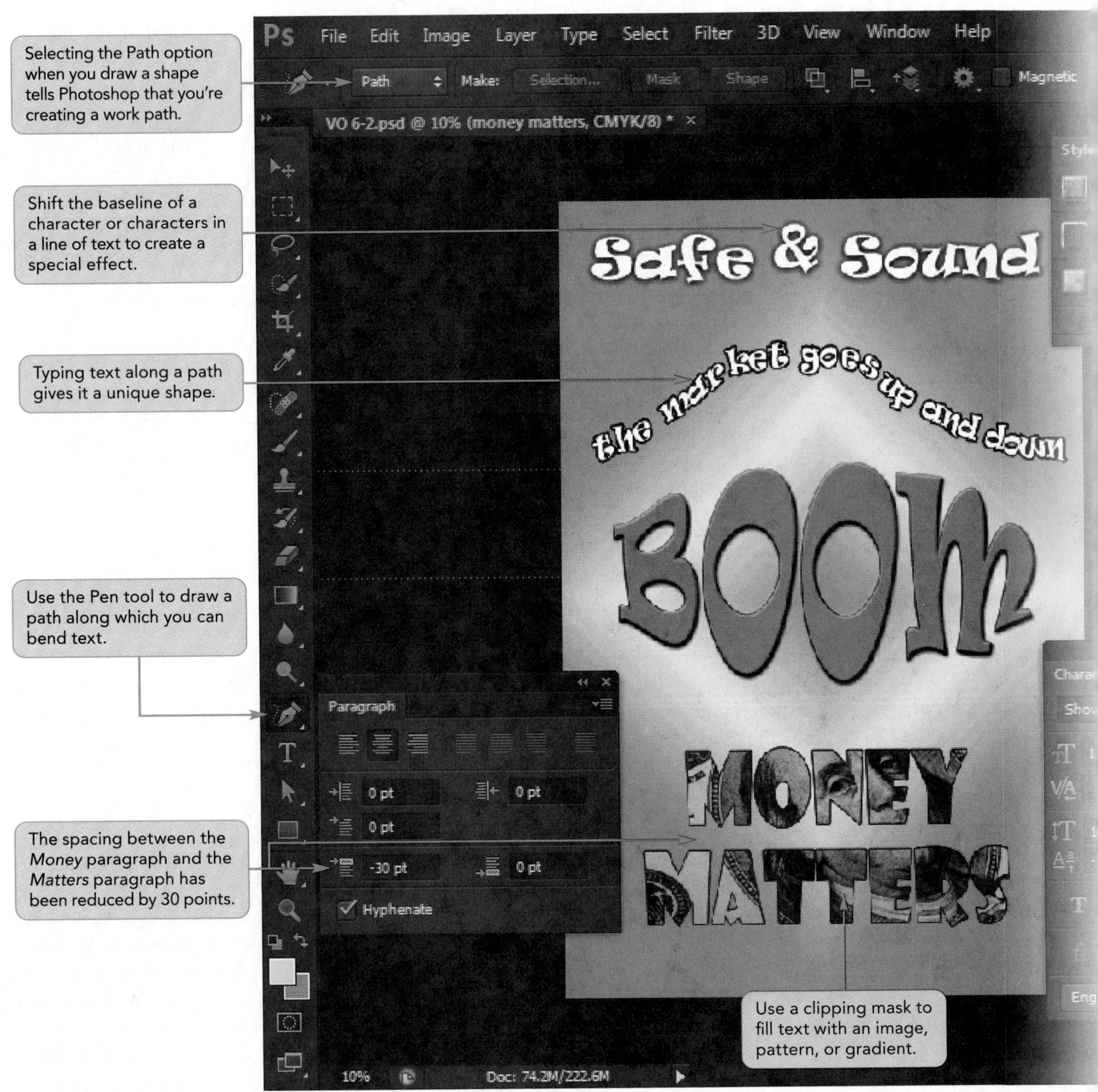
Selecting the Path option when you draw a shape tells Photoshop that you're creating a work path.
Shift the baseline of a character or characters in a line of text to create a special effect.
Typing text along a path gives it a unique shape.
Use the Pen tool to draw a path along which you can bend text.
The spacing between the *Money* paragraph and the *Matters* paragraph has been reduced by 30 points.
Use a clipping mask to fill text with an image, pattern, or gradient.
Ps File Edit Image Layer Type Select Filter 3D View Window Help
Path
Make:
Selection...
Mask
Shape
Magnetic
VO 6-2.psd @ 10% (money matters, CMYK/8) *
Safe & Sound
the market goes up and down
BOOM
MONEY
MATTERS
Paragraph
0 pt
0 pt
0 pt
-30 pt
0 pt
Hyphenate
10%
Doc: 74.2M/222.6M

Helder Almeida/Shutterstock.com

CREATING UNIQUE TEXT

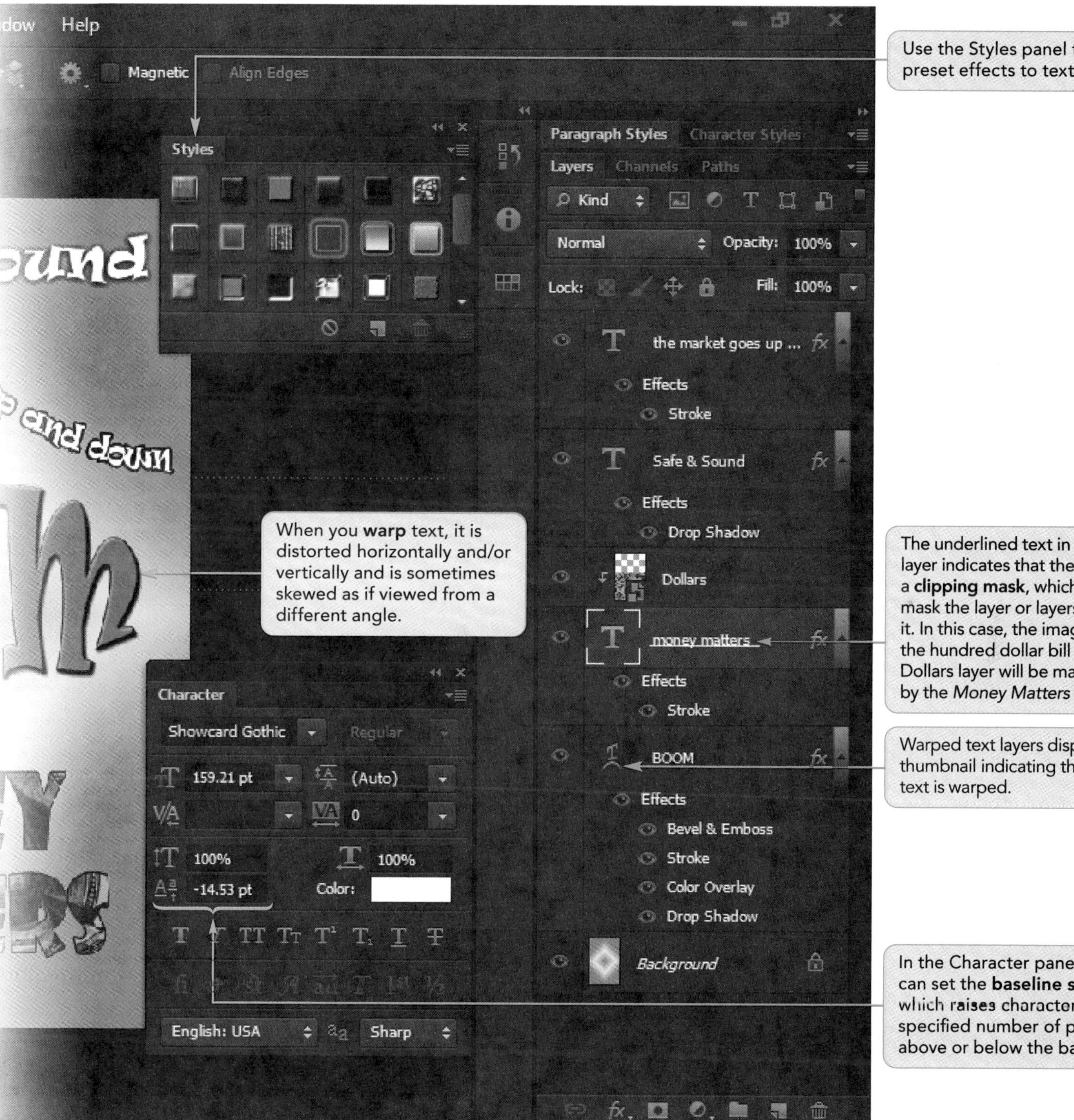

Use the Styles panel to apply preset effects to text.
When you **warp** text, it is distorted horizontally and/or vertically and is sometimes skewed as if viewed from a different angle.
The underlined text in this layer indicates that the layer is a **clipping mask**, which will mask the layer or layers above it. In this case, the image of the hundred dollar bill in the Dollars layer will be masked by the *Money Matters* text.
Warped text layers display a thumbnail indicating that the text is warped.
In the Character panel, you can set the **baseline shift**, which raises characters a specified number of points above or below the baseline.

Creating Unique Text

When you enter text in Photoshop, you can combine formatting options such as font, color, and alignment to get the look you want. However, there might be times when you want a unique look that isn't possible using the standard formatting tools. With the options available in the Styles panel, the baseline shift feature, and the text warping and bending capabilities of Photoshop, you have more powerful tools to work with to achieve interesting and unique results for your text. In addition, the ability to rasterize text and treat it as a digital or bitmap image opens up countless other possibilities as you use Photoshop's digital image-editing tools to create eye-catching text in your compositions.

Applying a Style to Text

The Styles panel has dozens of formatting presets that you can apply with the click of a button. In fact, Photoshop has style presets designed specifically for text, which are accessible via the Styles panel menu. Using the style presets allows you to experiment with different looks for the text in your composition without having to set a variety of individual effects such as shadow, bevel and emboss, and gradient fills.

The RC Investments text is too plain to draw attention to the company name in the layout you've been working on. You'll apply a text style to the company name, and then see if formatting the paragraph text with preset styles makes the layout more interesting.

To apply a style to the text:

1. If you took a break after the last session, start Photoshop while pressing the **Ctrl+Alt+Shift** keys, and click **Yes** to delete the Settings file when prompted. Switch to and reset the Typography workspace, and then reset all tools. Press the **D** key to restore the default foreground and background colors if necessary.
2. Navigate to the Photoshop6\Tutorial folder, open **RCDetails.psd**, if necessary, and fit the image on screen. Clear the guides and hide the rulers, if necessary. Double-click the Paragraph Styles tab to minimize the panel group so you can see all of the layers in the Layers panel.
3. In the Layers panel, hide the green RC Investments layer, if necessary. Display and select the **red RC Investments** layer.

   Trouble? If you are prompted to save changes to the current set of styles, click No.
4. Expand the Styles panel, click the panel menu button, and then click **Text Effects 2**. Click the **OK** button to replace the current styles. Click the **Swamp Bevel with Shadow** icon (the first effect). This effect gives the text a raised, three-dimensional look.
5. Click the **Dented Metal with Shadow** icon (third row, fourth column). This effect gives the text a shiny, metallic look.
6. Click the **Bright Red Bevel** icon (the third effect in the first row). This style adds four effects: a bevel and emboss effect, a stroke, a color overlay, and a drop shadow. Each effect in the style is listed beneath the RC Investments layer in the Layers panel. See Figure 6-23.

Figure 6-23 Applying a style

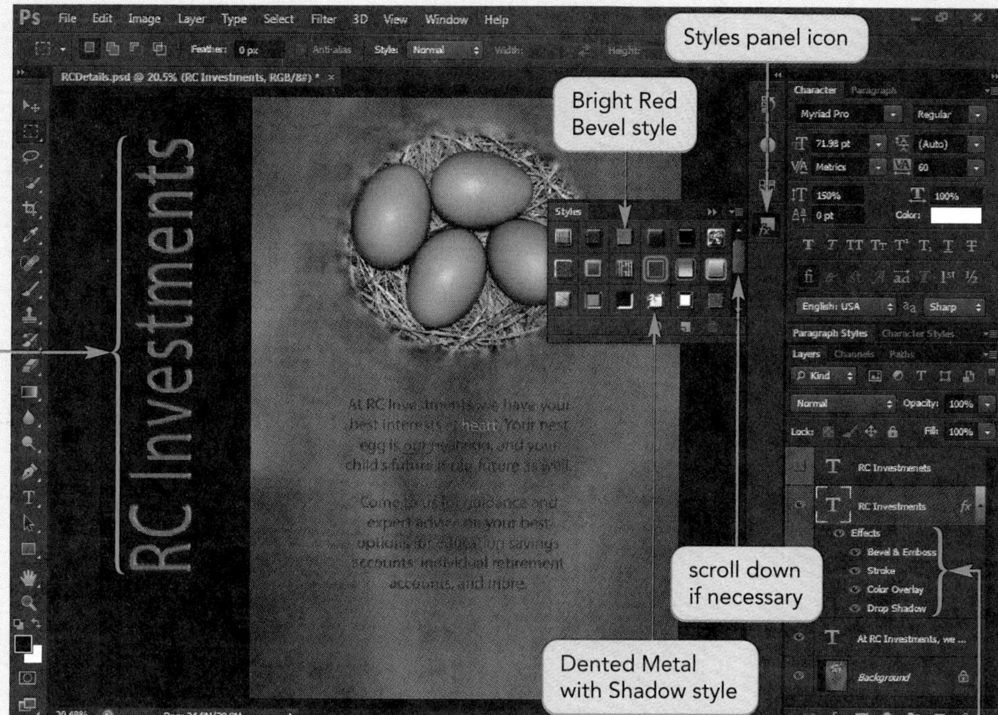

Steven Russell Smith Photos/Shutterstock.com

7. In the Layers panel, select the **At RC Investments...** layer, and then apply the **Bright Red Bevel** style to both paragraphs. Although the style made the company name stand out well on the black background, when it is applied to the paragraph, it makes the text difficult to read.
8. Apply the **Dented Metal with Shadow** style to the paragraphs. See Figure 6-24.

Figure 6-24 **Style applied to paragraphs**

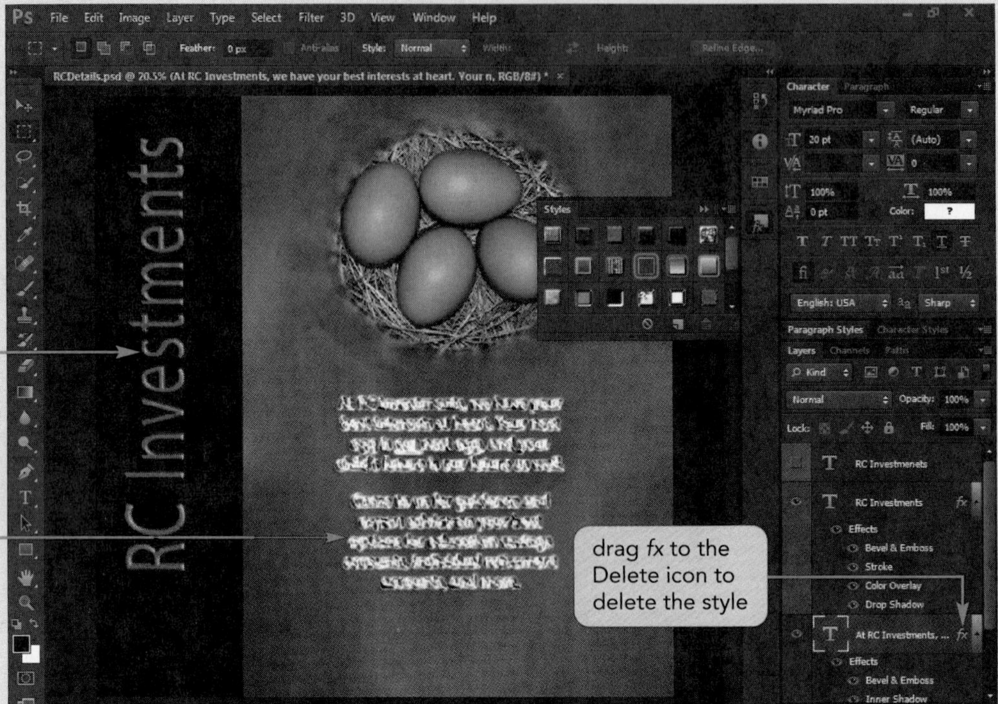
the Bright Red Bevel style works well with limited text
the Dented Metal with Shadow style makes the paragraphs difficult to read
drag fx to the Delete icon to delete the style
RC Investments

Steven Russell Smith Photos/Shutterstock.com

The Dented Metal style also makes the paragraph text difficult to read. For paragraphs with a lot of text, the simpler the better. You can get a message across much more effectively if the text itself takes center stage rather than its formatting.

9. Delete the paragraph text style you added by dragging the ***fx*** symbol at the right of the At RC Investments… text layer name to the **Delete** icon at the bottom of the Layers panel. The text returns to the formatting you applied earlier.
10. Collapse the Styles panel, save RCDetails.psd, and close it.

Scaling and Tracking Text to Achieve Balance

You can also create unique text by scaling individual characters to give words and phrases different shapes, and to achieve balance in a layout. When you adjust the tracking between characters, text shifts left or right in the text layer, changing its relation to the center point. When you change the horizontal scale of a letter or letters, you're not only changing the shape of the word, you're also shifting the text on either side as you widen or narrow the selected characters.

To adjust scaling and tracking to add shape and balance a text object:

1. Open **RCPath.psd**, located in the Photoshop6\Tutorial folder, and save it as **RightPath.psd** in the same folder; then press the **Ctrl+0** keys to fit the image on screen. Display the rulers, if necessary. This file includes an image and text.

TIP

If a text tool is active, you can also triple-click text on a selected layer directly on the canvas to select all of the text in the text object.

Trouble? If your system doesn't have the font provided in the file, accept the suggested font substitution.

2. Double-click the **Safe & Sound** text thumbnail to select all of the text, and then click on the canvas to the left of the ampersand (&) to place the insertion point.
3. Double-click the **&** to select it. See Figure 6-25.

Figure 6-25 Single character selected in text-editing mode

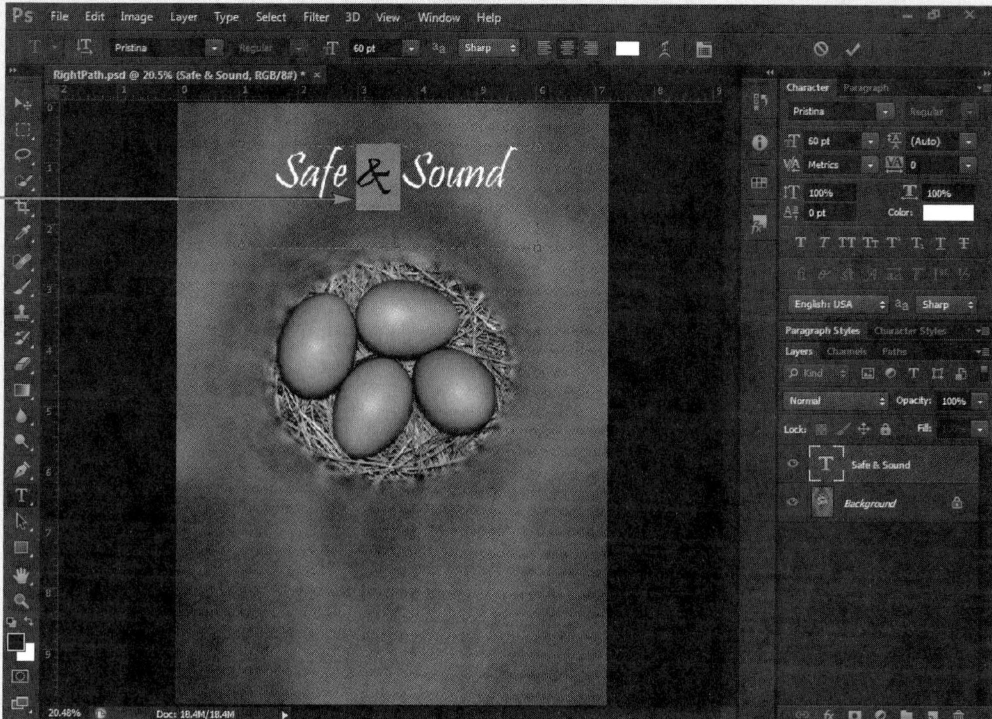

Steven Russell Smith Photos/Shutterstock.com

The & and the space after it are selected. You'll make the ampersand larger to give the text a unique shape.

4. Change the font size of the & from 60 points to **72** points, and then commit the change. See Figure 6-26.

Figure 6-26 Mixed font sizes

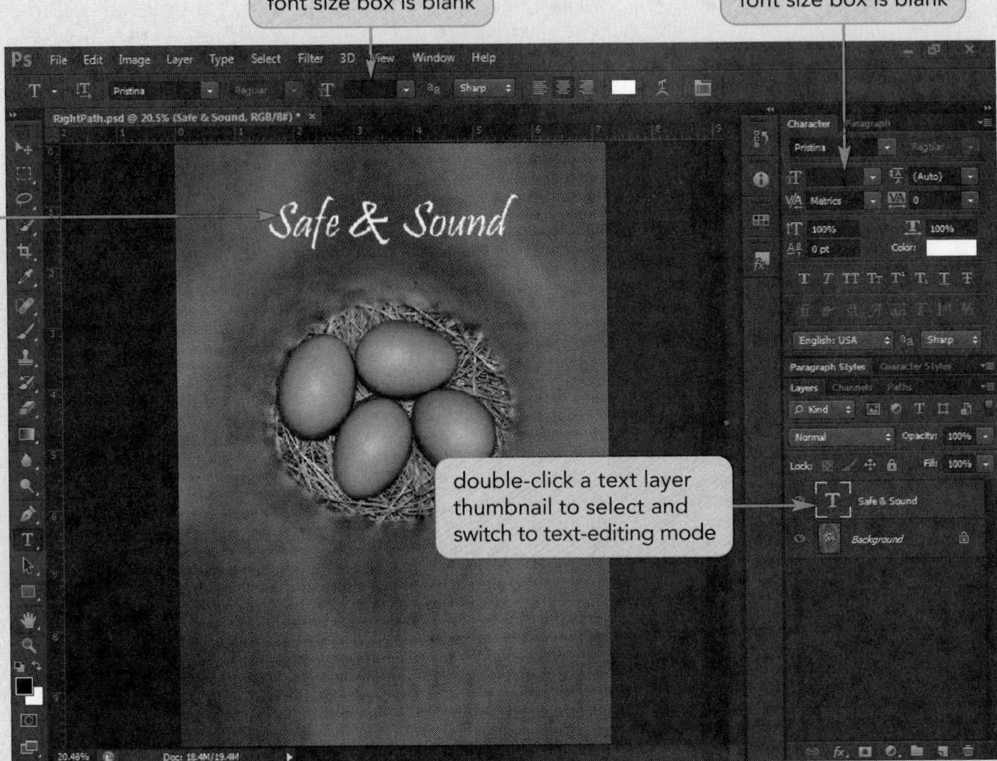
font size box is blank
font size box is blank
selected text layer has two different font sizes
Safe & Sound
double-click a text layer thumbnail to select and switch to text-editing mode

Steven Russell Smith Photos/Shutterstock.com

Because this text layer now has more than one font size applied, the Set the font size boxes are blank in the Character panel and on the options bar.

Trouble? If you can't see the Set the font size box on the options bar, make sure the Horizontal Type tool is still selected in the Tools panel.

5. Press the **V** key to activate the Move tool, and then show the transform controls, if necessary. See Figure 6-27.

Figure 6-27 **Centering text**

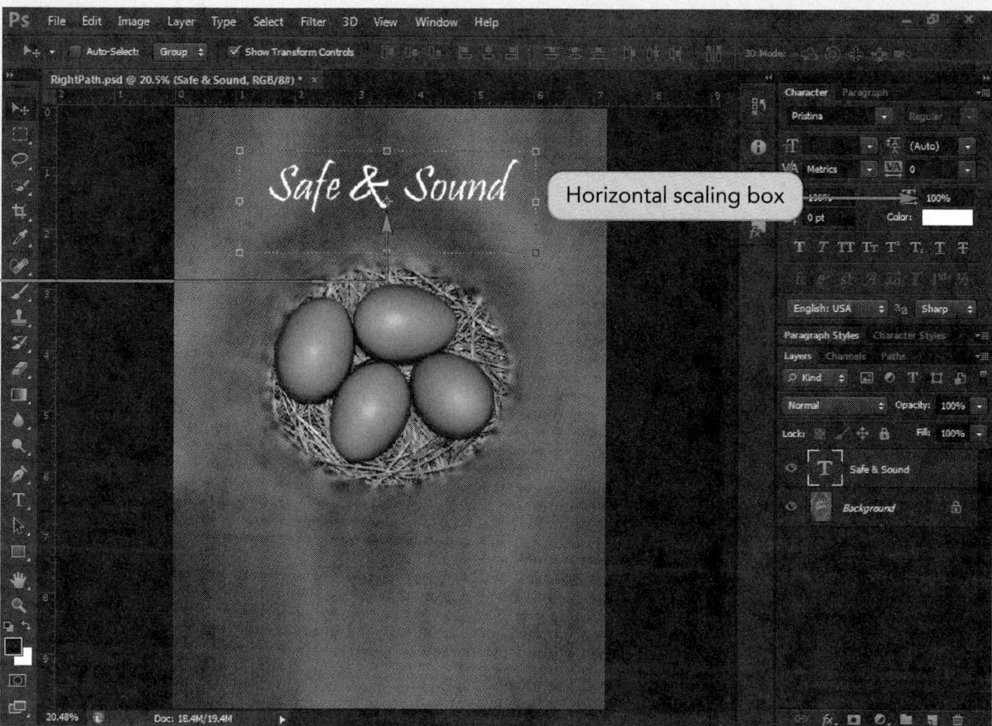

Steven Russell Smith Photos/Shutterstock.com

Notice that the center transform control, which marks the center of the text, is to the right of the ampersand. You'll change the horizontal scaling of the word *Safe* and change the tracking of individual letters and spaces to make the text more balanced around the center point.

6. In the Layers panel, double-click the **Safe & Sound** text thumbnail, and then drag on the canvas to select all of the letters in the word *Safe*.
7. In the Character panel, horizontally scale the word *Safe* to **120%**.
8. On the canvas, select the ***e*** in *Safe* and the space after the word *Safe*, and set the tracking to **60**.
9. Select the space after the & and select the ***S*** in *Sound*, and decrease the tracking to **-75**. Click the **Commit** button. The text is now more evenly balanced around the center point. See Figure 6-28.

TIP

You can also scrub the Set the tracking for the selected characters icon in the Character panel to adjust the tracking value by increments of 20.

Figure 6-28 **Balanced text**

tracking is increased between the *e* and the space

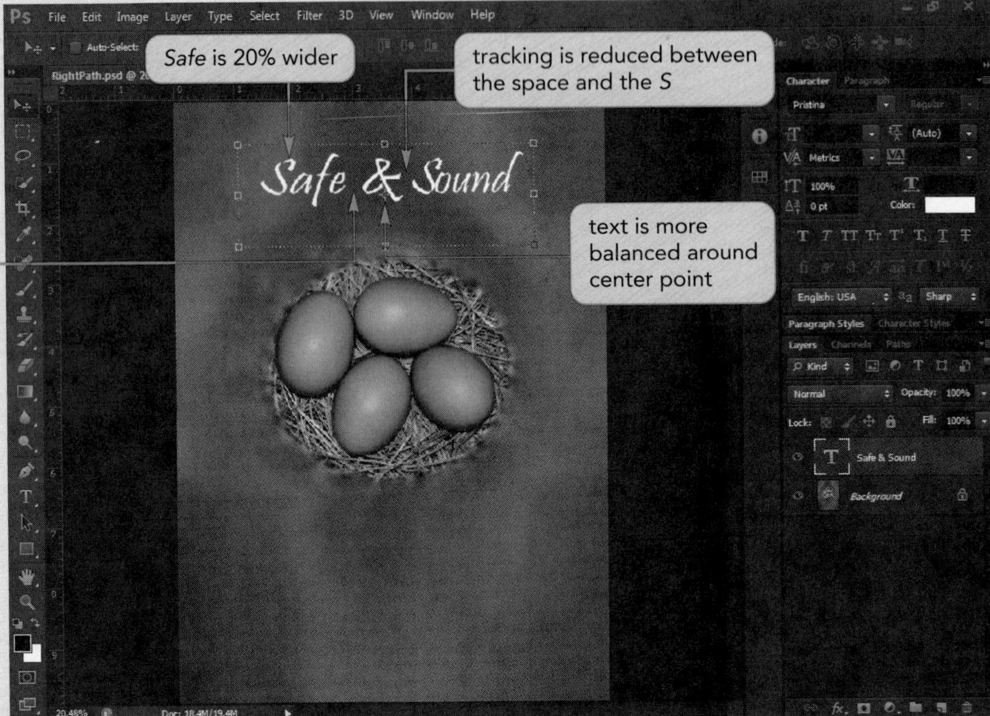

Steven Russell Smith Photos/Shutterstock.com

10. Save RightPath.psd, and keep the file open.

INSIGHT

Understanding Optical and Metrics Kerning

Kerning makes text easier to read by adding or subtracting space between pairs of characters. Just looking at the text on this page, you can probably see that some character pairs are closer together than others based on the shapes of the characters. Many of the font families you'll work with come with predefined kern pairs that handle letter pairings that might otherwise be problematic—for example, the letter *W* might be kerned differently when paired with the letter *o* than when paired with the letter *i* simply for readability. When this kerning is built in to a font family, it's called **metrics kerning**. However, some fonts don't have built-in kerning, or they have kerning for some character pairs but not others. When this is the case, you can choose the **optical kerning** option in Photoshop, and Photoshop will adjust the spacing between character pairs based on the shapes of the characters. To work with metrics and optical kerning, you can choose either Metrics or Optical, rather than a number setting, from the "Set the kerning between two characters" list in the Character panel.

Next, you'll change the baseline shift of the ampersand in the *Safe & Sound* text to give the text in the composition a more interesting shape.

Specifying a Baseline Shift

So far, all of the point text you have entered has been placed on the default baseline, indicated by *0 pt* in the Set the baseline shift box in the Character panel. However, you can assign a positive number to the baseline to shift characters above the baseline by the specified number of points. Assign a negative number to shift characters so they sit beneath the baseline.

To specify a baseline shift for the ampersand:

1. Press the **T** key to activate the Horizontal Type tool, and then select the **&** on the Safe & Sound layer.
2. In the Character panel, type **10** in the Set the baseline shift box. The ampersand moves above the rest of the text, 10 points above the baseline. You'll try a different setting to see how the ampersand looks below the baseline.
3. In the Character panel, set the baseline shift to **-15**. See Figure 6-29.

Figure 6-29 **Baseline shift**

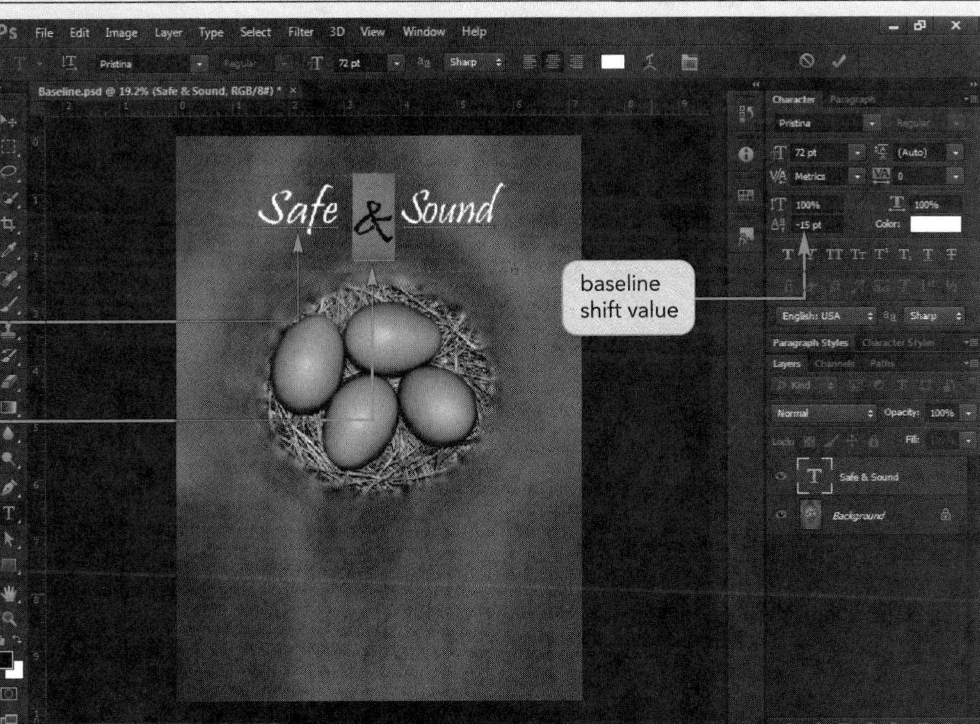

Steven Russell Smith Photos/Shutterstock.com

A negative baseline shift value moves the selection below the baseline of the other characters.

4. Commit the change, save the file as **Baseline.psd** in the Photoshop6\Tutorial folder, and keep the file open.

Warping Text

You can warp text to give it a unique shape. When you warp text, characters fill the shape of the warp style you specify. Characters no longer have a consistent font size, and depending on the warp, they might also be slightly skewed in perspective—for example, they might look as if they are being squashed or stretched vertically, horizontally, or diagonally. See Figure 6-30, which shows some of the default warp styles available in Photoshop, including Flag, Squeeze, and Bulge.

Figure 6-30 Warping text

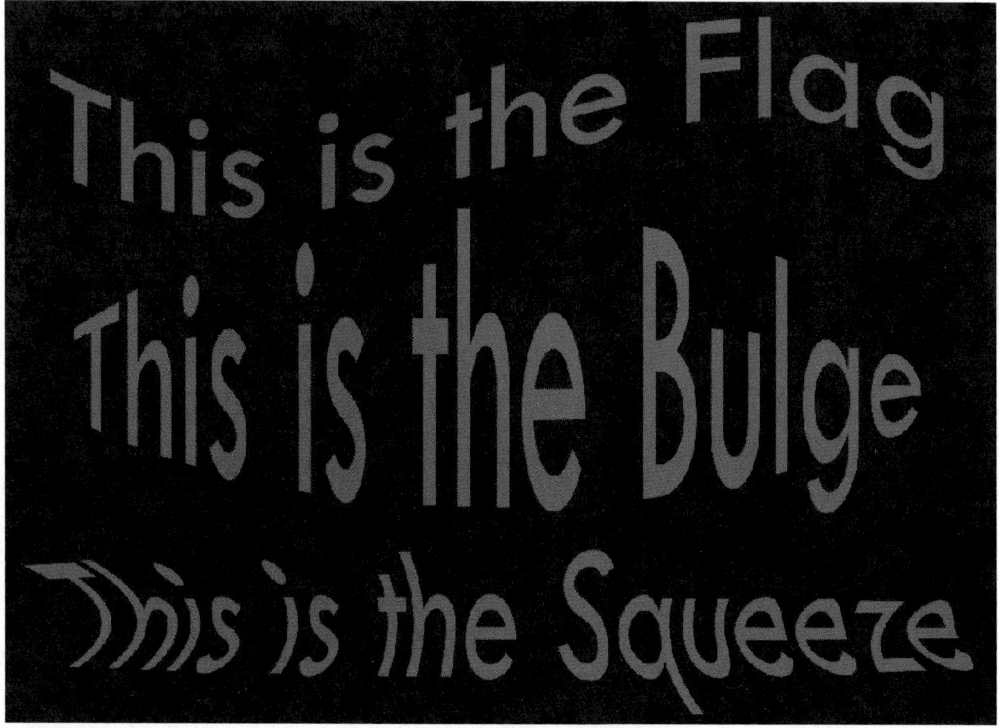

When you warp text, you can use the default settings for the specified warp, or you can modify the extent of the warp by changing the Bend percentage, or the Horizontal or Vertical Distortion. As you change the values in the Warp Text dialog box, you can see them being applied on the canvas.

REFERENCE

Warping Text

- In the Layers panel, click the text layer you want to warp, and in the Tools panel, click the Horizontal Type Tool button or the Vertical Type Tool button.
- On the options bar, click the Create warped text button.
- In the Warp Text dialog box, select the style for the warp.
- Specify a direction for the warp, and change the Bend, Horizontal Distortion, and Vertical Distortion percentages to change the warp effect, as desired.
- Click the OK button to warp the text.

You'll warp the Safe & Sound text to see if the effect works in your composition.

TIP

You can also click Layer on the menu bar, point to Type, and then click Warp Text to open the Warp Text dialog box.

To warp the Safe & Sound text:

1. In the Layers panel, click the **Safe & Sound** text layer to select it, if necessary.
2. On the options bar, click the **Create warped text** button. The Warp Text dialog box opens.
3. Drag the **Warp Text** dialog box to the right so you can see all of the canvas.
4. In the Warp Text dialog box, click the **Style** arrow, and then click **Arc Lower**. See Figure 6-31.

Figure 6-31 Arc Lower warp applied to text

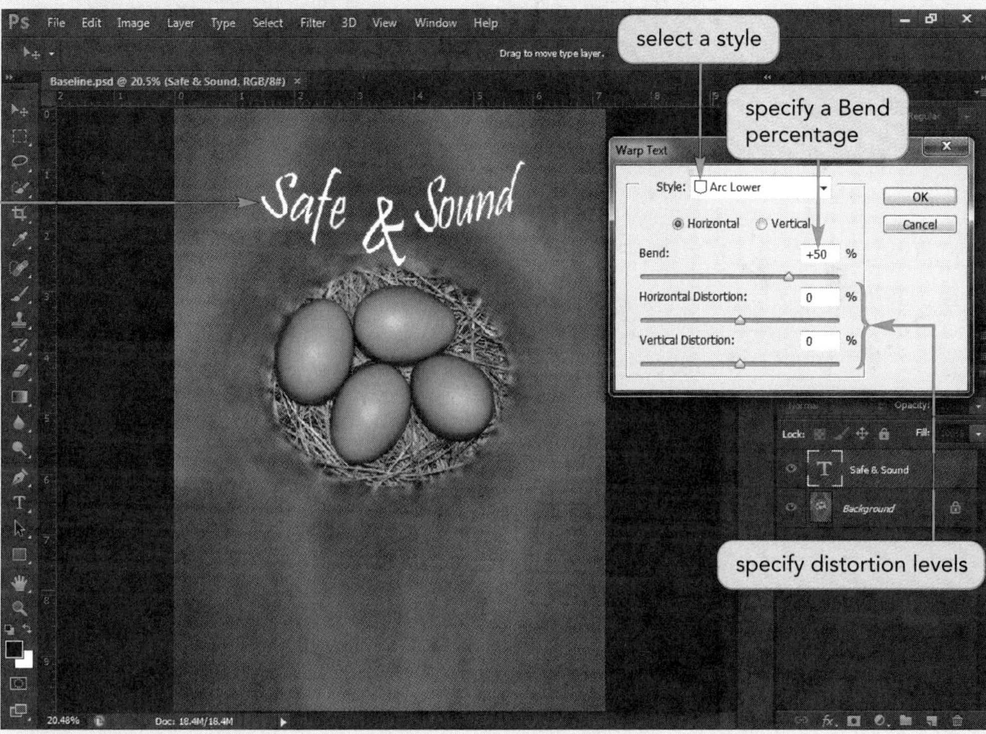

Steven Russell Smith Photos/Shutterstock.com

5. Change the Bend to -**20** and the Horizontal Distortion to -**60**. The Bend setting determines the amount of distortion applied to the text. By specifying a negative number, you reduced the distortion. The Horizontal Distortion setting changes the perspective of the warp.
6. Press and hold the **Alt** key and then click the **Reset** button in the Warp text dialog box. Photoshop removes the warp, and the settings go back to their defaults. You'll try a different warp setting to see if it works better in the composition.
7. Click the **Style** arrow, and then click **Rise**.
8. Change the Bend setting to **0**. A Bend setting of 0 applies no distortion, so the text is not affected by the warp.
9. Drag the **Bend** slider to change the Bend setting to **+55**.

   As you experiment with warp effects, you can move the text around the image without closing the dialog box. This feature lets you get the effect you want in the most efficient way.

10. On the canvas, drag the text up and to the left. See Figure 6-32.

Figure 6-32 Rise warp applied to text

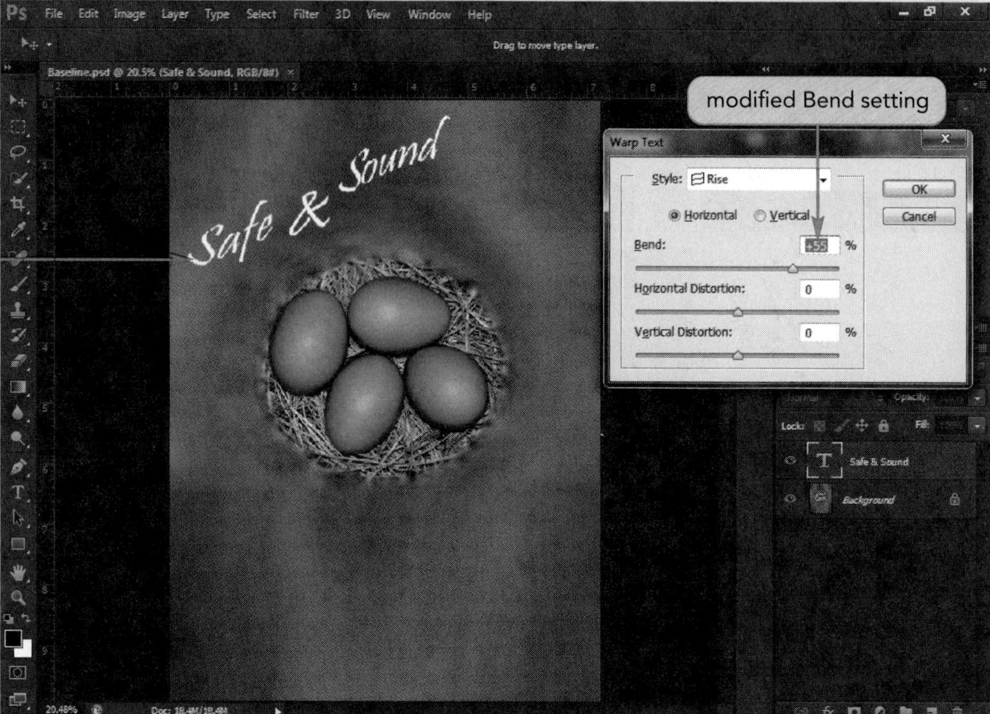

Steven Russell Smith Photos/Shutterstock.com

Trouble? If your Bend setting does not have a plus sign in front of the 55, you typed the value rather than dragging the Bend slider. Either method achieves the same result.

11. Press and hold the **Alt** key and then click the **Reset** button in the Warp Text dialog box. You'll try one more warp setting and reposition the text so it flows around the nest.

12. Click the **Style** arrow, and then click **Arc Upper**. Increase the Bend setting to **+100%**, and then change the Horizontal Distortion to **0%** and the Vertical Distortion to **0%**, if necessary. Then drag the text so it is positioned as shown in Figure 6-33.

Figure 6-33 Arc Upper warp applied to text

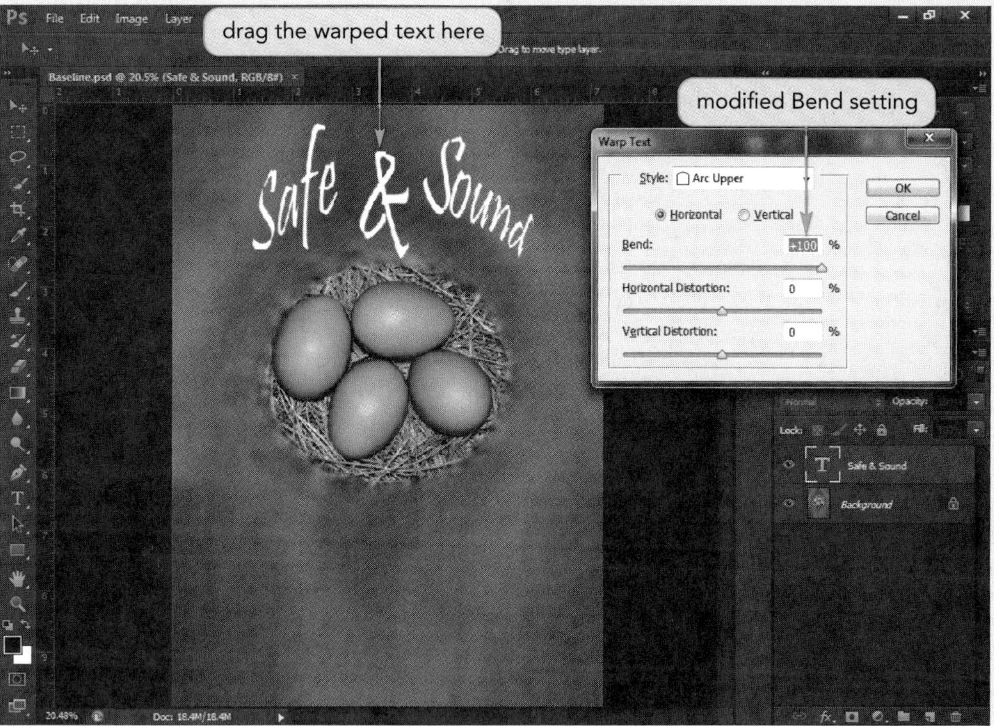

Steven Russell Smith Photos/Shutterstock.com

13. Click the **OK** button to close the Warp Text dialog box. The warp is applied to the text, and in the Layers panel, the text layer now has a different icon, indicating that the text is warped.
14. In the Layers panel, position the pointer over the **Safe & Sound** text thumbnail. Photoshop displays an "Indicates warped text layer" tip.
15. Save the file as **ArcUpper.psd** in the Photoshop6\Tutorial folder, and leave it open.

INSIGHT

Working with Placeholder Text

If your Photoshop comp includes text, you might not be the one who writes the text. Instead, you might need to get the text for your piece from some other department, such as editorial or marketing. If this is the case, and the text is not readily available, consider using **placeholder text** or **dummy text**, which lets you work with fonts and font sizes in text boxes to plan your layout. Many compositors use *lorem ipsum* text as placeholder text in templates. **Lorem ipsum** text is a standard series of Latin words. Oddly enough, if you do use lorem ipsum text, what you are doing is called **greeking**. Photoshop CS6 includes a new Paste Lorem Ipsum command on the Type menu. To fill a text box with lorem ipsum text, simply click Type on the menu bar, and then click Paste Lorem Ipsum. Photoshop fills the text box with text using the paragraph and character settings you have selected. The first sentence of the text is "This is Photoshop's version of Lorem Ipsum." The rest of the sentences are in Latin.

Adding Text Along a Path

TIP

To add and delete anchor points, you use the Add Anchor Point and Delete Anchor Point tools, which are hidden beneath the Pen tool in the Tools panel.

If the warp options in Photoshop aren't what you need for your composition, you can draw a path on the canvas and then add text to it so the text follows the path. When you create text on a path, the path becomes the baseline for any text you enter. Photoshop provides a number of tools for creating paths. You can use the Pen tool or the Freeform Pen tool to create an **open path** with a separate start point and endpoint and then manipulate individual points on the path until it takes the shape you need. Using the Pen and Freeform Pen tools often creates an initial path that is inexact. Getting the path to conform to the shape you want can be tedious, as it requires adding, deleting, and moving **anchor points**, the points that define the path.

Drawing tools like the Ellipse tool, the Rectangle tool, and the Custom Shape tool provide an easier way than the Pen tools to create interesting paths for text. When you draw a path with the Ellipse or Rectangle tool, you are creating a **closed path**, or a path in which the start point and the endpoint are one and the same. You can use the drawing tools individually, or you can combine them to create a complex path shape. In Figure 6-34, the elliptical path was created using the Ellipse tool, and the other two paths were drawn with the Pen tool.

Figure 6-34 Sharp angles and curves in a path

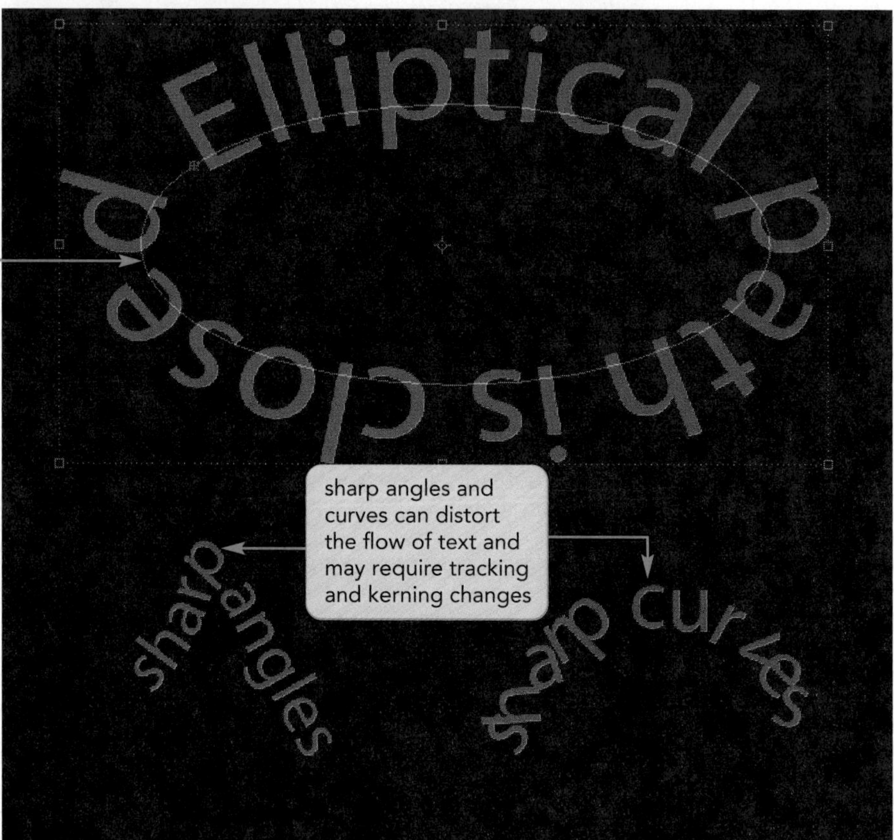
Elliptical path is closed
closed paths can be created with the drawing tools
sharp angles and curves can distort the flow of text and may require tracking and kerning changes
sharp angles
sharp curves

Figure 6-34 shows two of the pitfalls of aligning text to a path. Typing text along a path with a sharp angle or a sharp curve can distort the flow of text and throw characters on top of each other. Typing text along a curved or angled path often requires tracking and kerning adjustments so the text flows smoothly.

Rose would like you to try a different promotional phrase on the image of the nest. In addition, she'd also like you to wrap the text completely around the nest. You'll use the Ellipse tool to create a closed path along which you'll enter the new text.

To create the closed path and add text to it:

1. In the Layers panel, select and hide the Safe & Sound layer.
2. In the Tools panel, click the **Ellipse Tool** button.

   Trouble? If you don't see the Ellipse Tool button, right-click the Rectangle Tool button and then click the Ellipse Tool button on the context menu.
3. On the options bar, click the **Shape** button, and then click **Path**. Selecting the Path option ensures that the shape you draw will be a path rather than a shape on a new layer.
4. Click near the center of the nest. The Create Ellipse dialog box opens. Set both the width and height to **1500** pixels, verify that the **From Center** check box is selected, and then click the **OK** button.

   Photoshop adds a path in the shape of a circle around the image of the nest.
5. To ensure that the path is centered over the nest, in the Tools panel, click the **Path Selection Tool** button, point to the path, and then drag it to the location shown in Figure 6-35.

Figure 6-35 Closed path for text

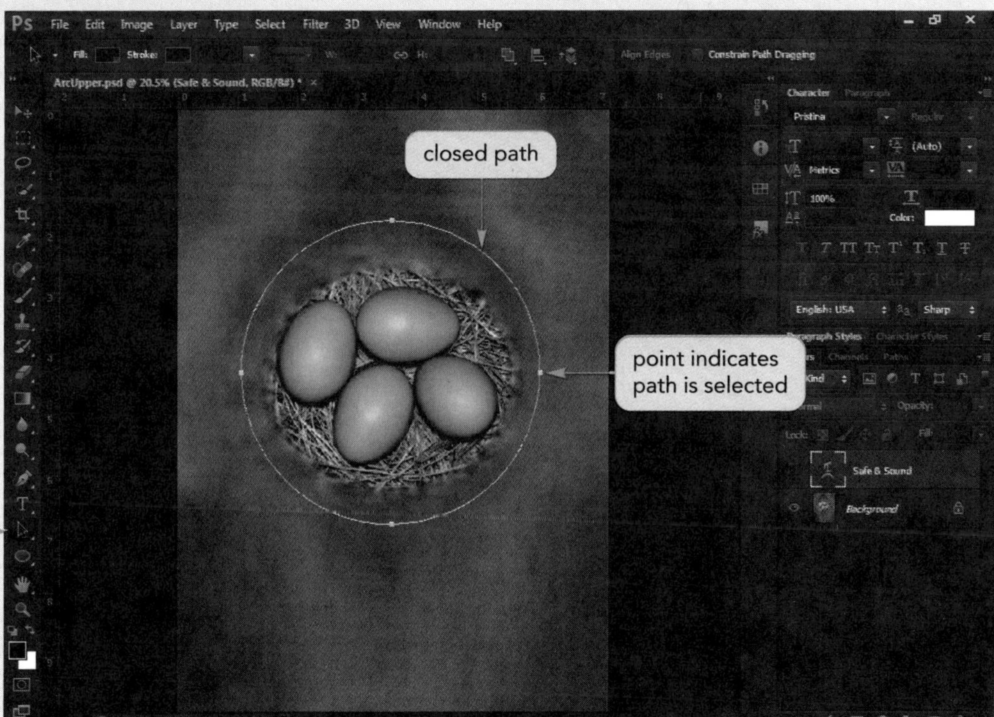

Steven Russell Smith Photos/Shutterstock.com

6. Click the **Horizontal Type Tool** button, and on the options bar, select **Segoe UI** as the font, set the font style to **Regular**, set the font size to **48** points, set the anti-aliasing Sharp to **Strong**, left-align the text, and on the options bar, set the color to any **blue**.
7. Click the left side of the path, just under the anchor point, and then type **RC Investments: The Right Choice for Your Nest Egg**. The text follows the shape of the path you drew. See Figure 6-36.

Figure 6-36 Text along a closed path

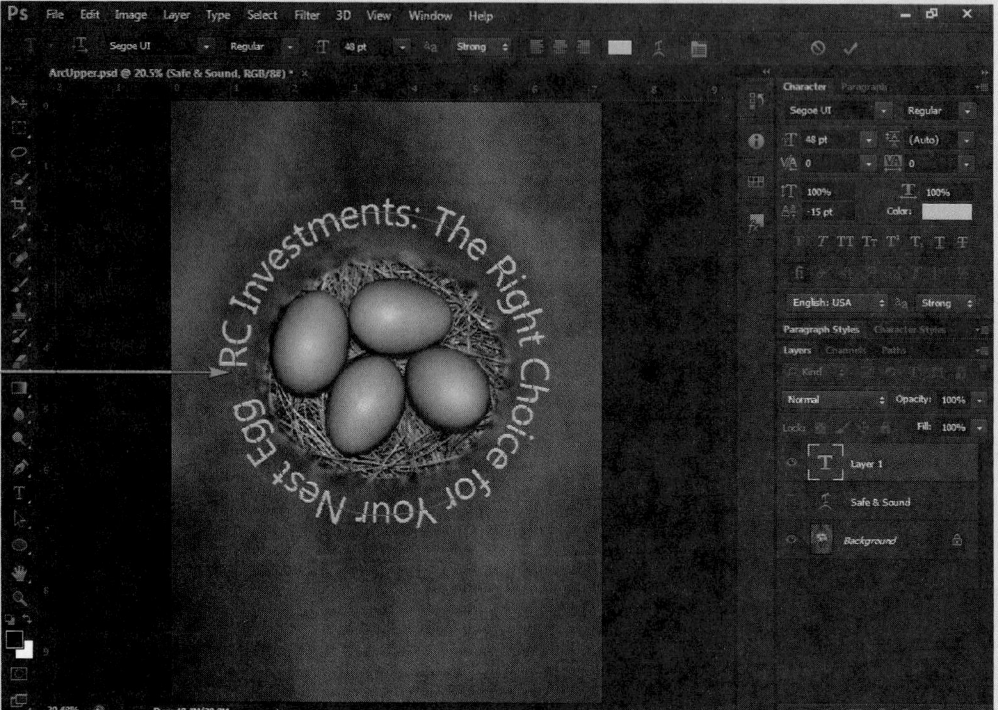

Steven Russell Smith Photos/Shutterstock.com

8. In the Layers panel, click the **Background** layer to deselect the path and commit the text. Save the file as **CirclePath.psd** in the Photoshop6\Tutorial folder, and close it.

PROSKILLS

Written Communication: Adding Copy to a Composition

If it is your responsibility to write the text in a layout yourself, you need to gather the information and details you'll need for the copy ahead of time. To do so, you can discuss the copy with managers or subject matter experts in other departments. Or, if the piece is for an external customer, contact the customer for details about their product or service. Once you have written the copy, you'll most likely need to get it approved by the department responsible for external communications, such as the Public Relations Department or the Marketing Department. You'll also need to have someone edit the text, and when the composition is complete, you should have someone proofread the copy to check it for errors.

You need to consider the context in order to make decisions about text layout and formatting. Will your composition appear in a newsletter that uses a particular font set? If so, you'll need to use a font from that set—unless, of course, your goal is to draw attention to the image in a way that is out of the ordinary. You also need to consider the nature of the brand you're writing about. If your piece is an ad, is there a specific font that the company always uses in its advertisements so the text itself is recognizable as part of the brand? Once you understand what the expectations are for written communication in your organization, you can use your image- and text-editing skills to create impressive, attention-grabbing layouts.

Rose would like to eventually work with a Web developer to create an ad that appears along the right side of some of the more popular search engines. Her idea is that three words, "Money Changes Everything," will appear one by one to grab the viewer's attention. She wants each word to have a different effect, and has asked you to create a comp that shows her some options.

Filling Text with an Image, Pattern, or Gradient

Another way you can give text a unique look is to fill it with an image, pattern, or gradient. To fill text with an image, you apply a clipping mask to the image you want the text to display. A clipping mask lets you define a mask for a layer based on the shape of another layer. When you fill text with an image, pattern, or gradient, you are actually specifying that everything *except* the text should mask the underlying image. As a result, the graphic or pattern shows through the letter shapes.

To fill text with an image:

1. Open **Money.psd**, located in the Photoshop6\Tutorial folder, and save it as **MoneyClip.psd** in the same folder. Reset the background and foreground colors to the default colors.

   Right now, only the Sunrise layer is visible. Two of the text layers are hidden, and the Money and Background layers are covered on the canvas by the Sunrise layer. You'll use the Sunrise layer to fill the first word, *Money*, with an image. First you'll add a stroke to the Money layer so that the fill is more dramatic.

2. In the Layers panel, hide the **Sunrise** layer, double-click the **Money** layer to open the Layer Style dialog box, and then add a **10-pixel**, **Outside**, **Normal**, **black** stroke to the text, as shown in Figure 6-37.

Figure 6-37 Stroke added to text

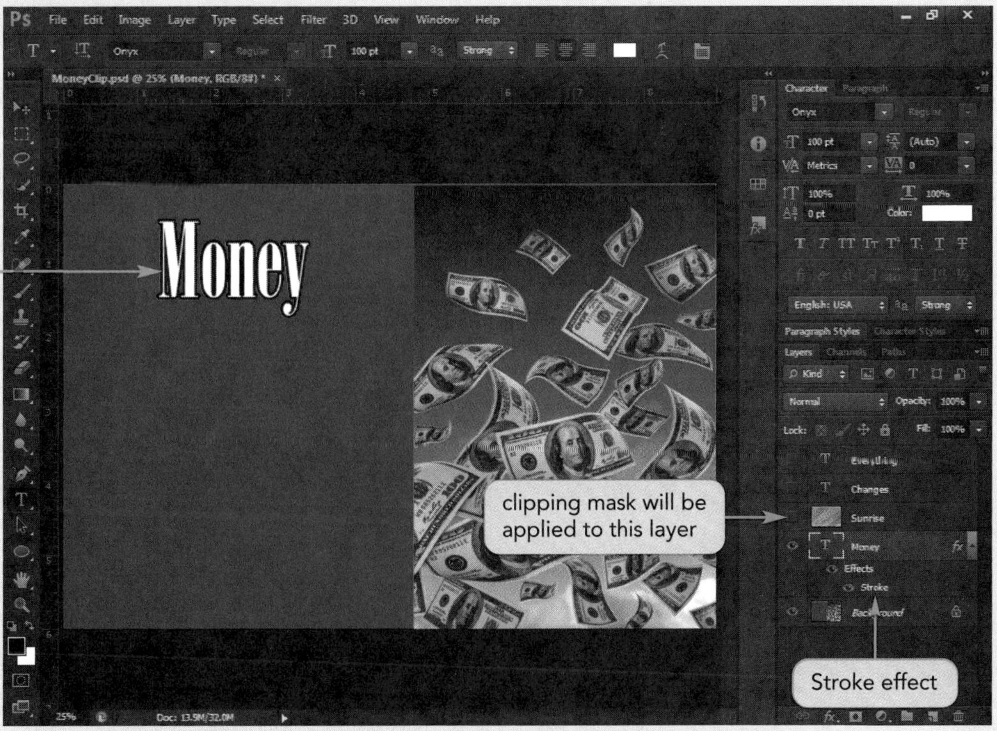

the Stroke effect will add emphasis to the image you will place within the letters

clipping mask will be applied to this layer

Stroke effect

Helder Almeida/Shutterstock.com; Jane Hosie-Bounar

TIP

You can also press the Alt+Ctrl+G keys to create a clipping mask.

3. In the Layers panel, display the **Sunrise** layer and select it.
4. On the menu bar, click **Layer** and then click **Create Clipping Mask**. Photoshop uses the Sunrise image layer to fill the *Money* text. See Figure 6-38.

Figure 6-38 **Clipping mask applied to text**

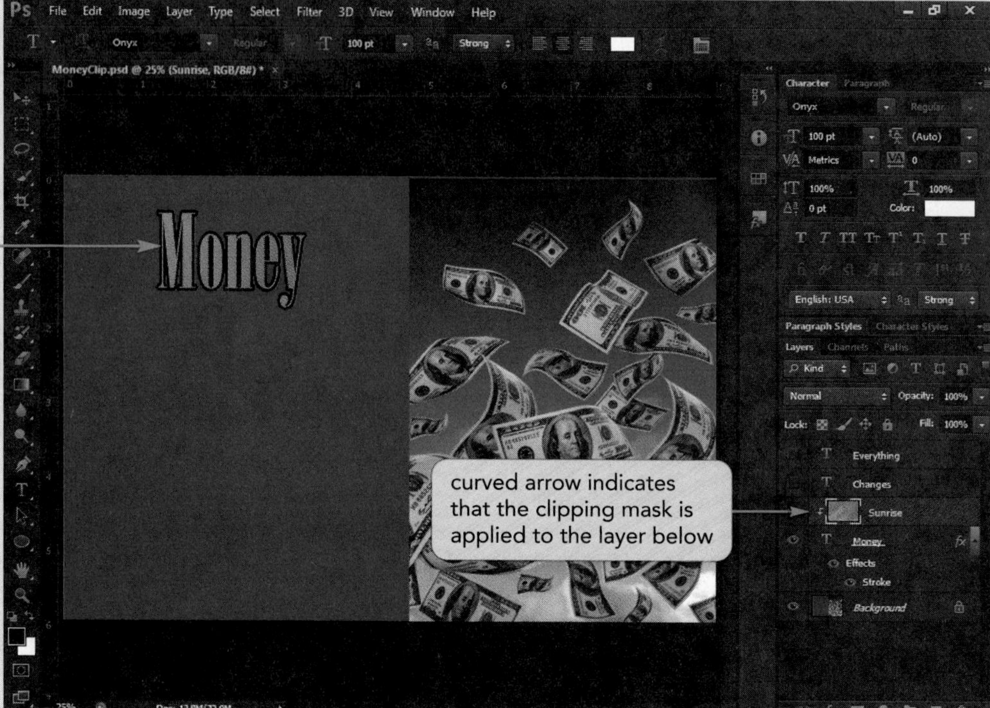
the Sunrise image is contained by text outlines
Money
curved arrow indicates that the clipping mask is applied to the layer below
Everything
Changes
Sunrise
Money
Effects
Stroke
Background

Helder Almeida/Shutterstock.com; Jane Hosie-Bounar

5. Right-click the **Sunrise** layer, and then click **Release Clipping Mask**. The image you used to mask the text now appears on top of the canvas, covering everything beneath it in the Layers panel, including the text and the background.
6. Press the **Ctrl+Z** keys to undo Step 5. The mask is reapplied.
7. Save the file, and keep it open.

You can also use a clipping mask to fill text with a gradient or a pattern. To do so, add a gradient or pattern layer above the text you want to fill, and then create the clipping mask. You'll experiment with pattern and gradient clipping mask effects to see which one will work best for RC Investments.

To fill the text with a pattern and a gradient:

1. In the Layers panel, display the **Changes** layer. You'll copy the layer style you applied to the Money layer and apply it by pasting it on the Changes layer.
2. Right-click the **Money** layer, and click **Copy Layer Style**. The layer style is copied to the Clipboard.
3. Right-click the **Changes** layer, and then click **Paste Layer Style**. The Changes layer now has a 10-pixel black stroke.

4. At the bottom of the Layers panel, click the **Create new fill or adjustment layer** icon, and then click **Pattern**.
5. In the Pattern Fill dialog box, click the **pattern** thumbnail to open the Pattern Fill preset picker, click the **More options** button to display the list of available preset libraries, click **Nature Patterns**, and then click the **Append** button to append the new presets to the current set of patterns.
6. Select the **Yellow Mums** preset (the third preset in the second row), change the Scale to **60%**, and then click the **OK** button. The layer is now filled with a pattern of yellow flowers.

   Trouble? If the Yellow Mums preset is not in the second row, position the mouse pointer over the preset thumbnails until you see *Yellow Mums*.
7. Right-click the **Pattern Fill 1** layer, and then click **Create Clipping Mask**. The *Changes* text is filled with the pattern you selected. See Figure 6-39.

Figure 6-39 Pattern-filled text

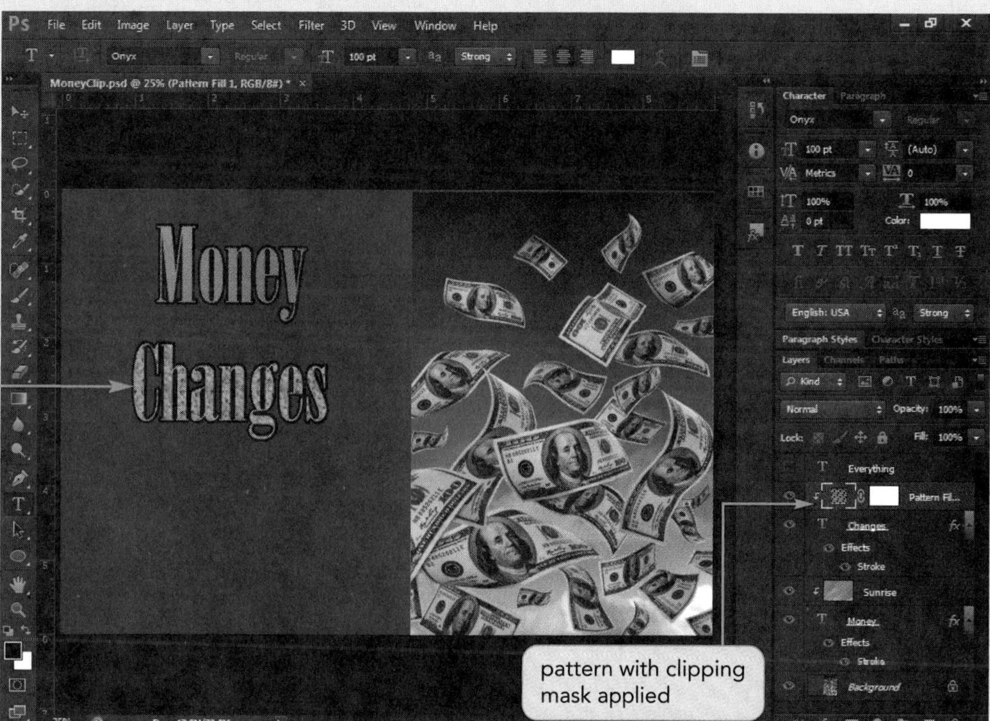

Helder Almeida/Shutterstock.com; Jane Hosie-Bounar

8. Display and then right-click the **Everything** layer, and then click **Paste Layer Style**. The Everything layer now has a 10-pixel black stroke.
9. At the bottom of the Layers panel, click the **Create new fill or adjustment layer** icon, and then click **Gradient**.
10. In the Gradient Fill dialog box, click the **Gradient** arrow, click the **Transparent Rainbow** gradient (the second gradient in the last row), change the angle to **30** degrees, and then click the **OK** button to add a gradient fill layer above the Everything layer.

Trouble? If you don't see the Transparent Rainbow gradient, click the More options button, click Reset Gradients, click the OK button, and then click the No button if you are asked if you want to save changes to the current gradients. Repeat Step 10.

11. Right-click the **Gradient Fill 1** layer, and then click **Create Clipping Mask**. The *Everything* text is filled with the gradient you selected. See Figure 6-40.

Figure 6-40 Gradient mask applied to text

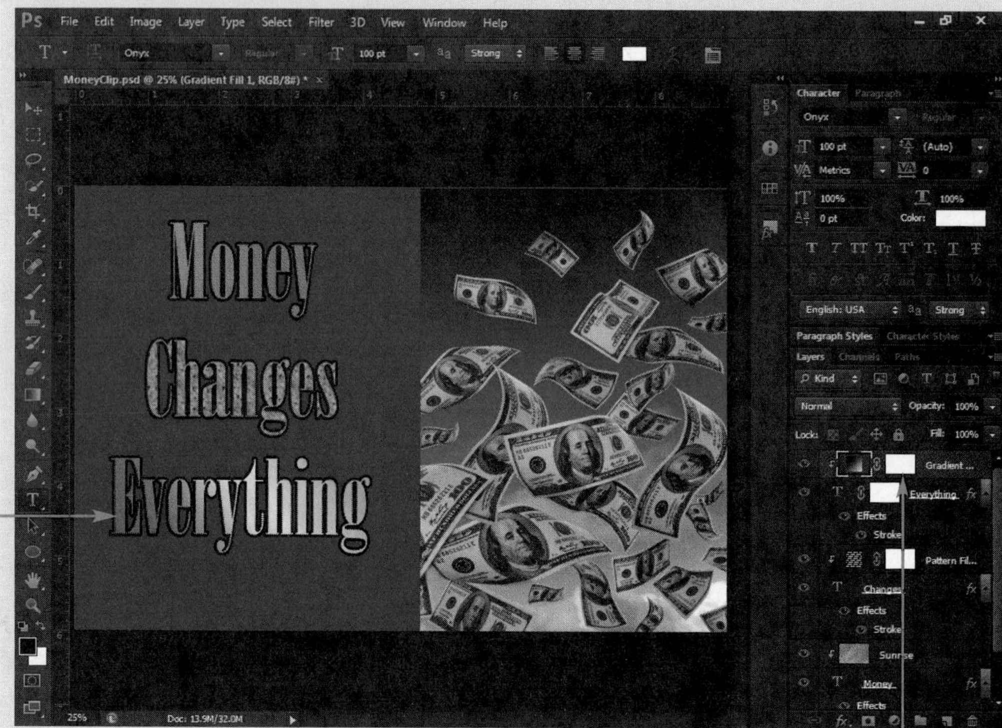

Helder Almeida/Shutterstock.com; Jane Hosie-Bounar

12. Save the MoneyClip.psd file, close it, and then exit Photoshop.

Rose is satisfied with the options you provided her for the Web ad and will send it to a Web developer for her input.

In this session, you learned how to further customize and enhance text by applying different styles using the Styles panel. You also set tracking and scaling for individual characters, specified a baseline shift, and added text to a closed path. You applied clipping masks so you could fill text with an image, a pattern, and a gradient.

REVIEW

Session 6.2 Quick Check

1. In which panel can you adjust the horizontal and vertical scale of text?
2. What is a baseline shift?
3. When you change the shape of text by applying a predefined style with bend and distortion settings, you are ____________ the text.
4. A path that has the same beginning and ending point is called a ____________ path.
5. True or False. A path can be used as the baseline for text typed on a layer.
6. The individual points along a path are called ____________ points.
7. When you fill text with a gradient, pattern, or image, you are using a(n) ____________ mask.

Practice the skills you learned in the tutorial using the same case scenario.

PRACTICE

Review Assignments

Data Files needed for the Review Assignment: RCRetire.psd

Rose wants you to create an ad directed specifically at baby boomers and their retirement accounts. She has provided you with an image and has asked you to add text that will capture the attention of potential customers and educate them about RC Investment opportunities. Complete the following steps:

1. Start Photoshop while pressing the Ctrl+Alt+Shift keys, and click Yes to delete the Settings File when prompted. Switch to and reset the Typography workspace, and then reset all tools.
2. Open **RCRetire.psd**, located in the Photoshop6\Review folder provided with your Data Files, and save it as **RCRetirement.psd** in the same folder.
3. Using the Horizontal Type tool, drag a bounding box that is about 6 1/2 inches wide and 4 inches high starting in the upper-left corner of the canvas. Use a Papyrus, Regular, 18 pt, Strong, left-aligned black font, and type the following two paragraphs (*Note*: The three spelling errors—*liesure*, *conselors*, *carreer*—are intentional):

   At RC Investments, we believe that retirement is not an end, but a beginning, a time to spread your wings and take flight, or to settle in to a life of liesure and relaxation--a life you and your investment firm have worked hard to achieve.

   Our investment conselors were there for you when you started your carreer, and we're here for you now. RC Investments. The Real Choice. The Right Choice.

4. Format both paragraphs with no hyphenation, and justify them so the last line of each paragraph is centered.
5. Add a 10-point space before the second paragraph to separate it from the first paragraph.
6. Put each of the last three phrases in its own paragraph. (*Hint*: You can press the Enter key to add a paragraph break.)
7. Adjust the tracking of the text if necessary to improve its appearance by avoiding loose and tight lines and rivers of white space. Determining when the paragraphs are acceptable will be an individual choice.
8. Use the Move tool to change the dimensions of the bounding box and reposition it on the canvas. Adjust the size of the bounding box so it is about 6 inches wide and 3 1/2 inches tall, and place it so the bounding box is centered near the top of the document.
9. Add a new text layer but change the font to 60 point and the color to white. Type **Dreams Take Flight** on the canvas as point type. Apply the Rise warp style and change the bend to 80%. Reposition the text layer so it starts just above the water on the left and rises above the sun on the lower-right side of the canvas.
10. Select the Dreams Take Flight text, and format it with an underline. Add a 2-pixel stroke effect in the Layer Style dialog box.
11. Check the spelling in the document, and correct any misspelled words.
12. Add a vertical type layer using Verdana, Italic, 24-point black font, and type **RC Investments** down the left edge of the canvas. Increase the horizontal scale of the text to 145%. Increase the vertical scale of the text to 120%. Reduce the horizontal scale of the letter *m* to 115%, and then increase the tracking between the letter *C* and the letter *I* to about 80.
13. Use a clipping mask to apply a Leaf pattern fill to the company name. (*Hint*: Use the Color Paper presets.)

14. Apply a Drop Shadow and a Bevel & Emboss effect to the RC Investments layer text using the default settings.
15. Save RCRetirement.psd, and exit Photoshop.
16. Submit the results of the preceding steps to your instructor either in printed or electronic form, as requested.

Use your skills to create special effects with text.

APPLY

Case Problem 1

Data Files needed for this Case Problem: Shuttle.jpg, Fireworks.jpg

Concord High School You've recently been hired as a teaching assistant at Concord High School in Ohio. You'll be working with the school's physics teacher, Dr. Marie Cash. She has asked you to create a series of slides meant to pique students' interest in physics. You'll add text with different special effects to an image and save a series of layer comps to see which options will work best in the slide show. Complete the following steps:

1. Start Photoshop while pressing the Ctrl+Alt+Shift keys, click Yes to delete the Settings File when prompted. Switch to and reset the Typography workspace layout, and then reset all tools.
2. Open **Shuttle.jpg**, located in the Photoshop6\Case1 folder provided with your Data Files.
3. Switch the foreground and background colors so the foreground color is white. Using the Horizontal Type tool, choose a font that you think is appropriate for a clipping mask—with a font size that is at minimum 200 points. For example, Showcard Gothic is a heavy, wide font that would work well for a clipping mask. Type **E = MC2** near the bottom of the image.
4. Apply a superscript effect to the *2* in the *E = MC2* text.
5. Scale the text horizontally so it fills the width of the image, but not the bar on the left side.
6. Add a new layer at the top of the Layers panel, and place **Fireworks.jpg**, located in the Photoshop6\Case1 folder, on the new layer.
7. Fill the $E = MC^2$ text with the Fireworks image you just added. You may need to drag the Fireworks layer to get the effect you want. Add a stroke of any color and size to the text.
8. Add any adjustment to the composition, if desired, and then save a layer comp called **Fireworks**, and hide any adjustment layers and the Fireworks layer.
9. Duplicate the E = MC2 layer. (*Hint*: Right-click the E = MC2 layer in the Layers panel, and select Duplicate Layer.) Reapply the original clipping mask, if necessary. Move the copy beneath the original in the Layers panel. Change the layer color of the original E = MC2 layer to red and change the color of the copy layer to green. Then, hide the red E = MC2 layer and the Fireworks layer.
10. Warp the green E = MC2 layer using the style of your choice. Fill the warped text with a pattern from the Rock Patterns preset group. Create a layer comp, and save it as **PhysicsRocks**.
11. Hide all layers except the Background layer, and then type **Physics** so it runs vertically on the left side of the canvas. (*Hint*: Use the Vertical Type tool and choose any font and any font size.) Fill the word with a gradient.

12. Type the following paragraphs at the bottom of the canvas in 24 point, Times New Roman in any color you choose:

    You might not believe it yet, but physics is fun! Or should we say phun? What other disciplines have put a man on the moon and the shuttle into orbit? And who would argue that gravity doesn't keep us grounded?

    So put on your space suits, your x-ray specs, and your thinking caps and get ready for the ride of a lifetime!
13. Check the spelling of the text you typed, but leave the spelling of *phun*.
14. Format *physics is fun!* in small caps.
15. Adjust the alignment and the paragraph spacing until you're satisfied with the results.
16. Save the file as **Physics.psd** in the Photoshop6\Case1 folder, and exit Photoshop.
17. Submit the results of the preceding steps to your instructor either in printed or electronic form, as requested.

Use your skills to create a logo and an online ad for a catering business.

CREATE

Case Problem 2

Data File needed for this Case Problem: Gourmet.jpg

No Fuss Gourmet You've recently started your own catering business. You specialize in intimate parties, and you treat food as an art form. You are going to start advertising online, and you need to create a logo and an online ad for your business. You'll experiment with the text features of Photoshop to come up with the best look for your logo, and then you'll place the logo with an image to see the full effect. Complete the following steps:

1. Start Photoshop while pressing the Ctrl+Alt+Shift keys, click Yes to delete the Settings File when prompted. Switch to and reset the Typography workspace layout, and then reset all tools.
2. Create a new file of any size, with any background color. Make sure you have enough space to experiment with at least two different logo ideas. Because you are creating the logo for the Web, you can work with a file that is 72 ppi.
3. Create two possible logos with the name of the company—No Fuss Gourmet—using different fonts, styles, fills, and effects. Adjust character spacing, font, and styles as necessary to come up with the best effect. Combine text with shapes to achieve the effect you want. Change layer order as necessary to build the logo, and then merge the layers in each logo so that the file consists of only the Background layer and the two logo layers.
4. Save the file as **Logos.psd** in the Photoshop6\Case2 folder provided with your Data Files.
5. Open **Gourmet.jpg**, located in the Photoshop6\Case2 folder, and save it as **NoFuss.psd** in the same folder.
6. To create a mock-up for an online ad, choose your favorite logo from Logos.psd, and copy it to the NoFuss image. Resize it as necessary to achieve the best effect. You can use Figure 6-41 as an example, but your composition should be unique.

Figure 6-41 Sample No Fuss Gourmet ad

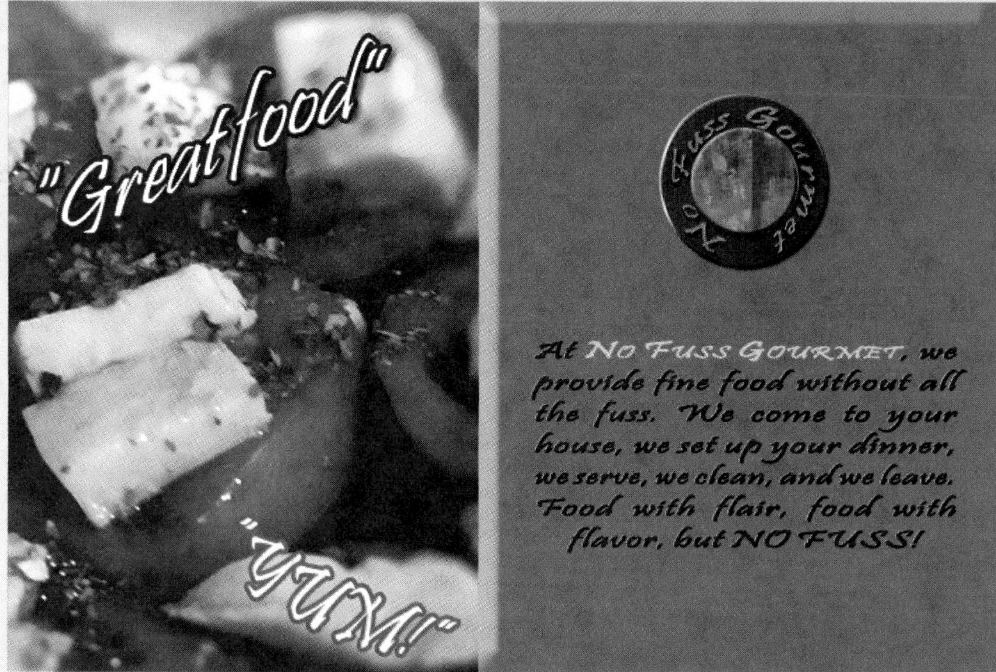

Jane Hosie-Bounar

7. Create a rectangle of any color on the right side of the image and format it with any effects you want. Move the logo so it appears on top of the rectangle, and then type the following paragraph text over the rectangle:

   At No Fuss Gourmet, we provide fabulous food without all the fuss. We come to your house, we set up your dinner, we serve, we clean, and we leave. Food with flair, food with flavor, but no fuss!

8. Format *No Fuss Gourmet* as small caps, and change the font color. In the last sentence, format *no fuss* as all caps.
9. Check the spelling in the paragraph, and replace *fabulous* with *fine*.
10. Turn off hyphenation, and justify the paragraph settings as desired.
11. On the left side of the composition, add short sample quotes from customers using warped text. Format the text with any style or stroke.
12. Save NoFuss.psd and Logos.psd, and exit Photoshop.
13. Submit the results of the preceding steps to your instructor either in printed or electronic form, as requested.

Use your skills to add text to an image for an ad campaign.

APPLY

Case Problem 3

Data File needed for this Case Problem: Luxury.jpg

Goldilocks Inn Goldilocks Inn is a small bed-and-breakfast in Ripton, Vermont. The proprietor Betsy Hemmings, hoping to attract both tourists and the parents of local college students, has asked you to create an ad for a page in the college calendar. Complete the following steps:

1. Start Photoshop while pressing the Ctrl+Alt+Shift keys, click Yes to delete the Settings File when prompted. Switch to and reset the Typography workspace layout, and reset all tools.

2. Open **Luxury.jpg**, located in the Photoshop6\Case3 folder provided with your Data Files, and save it as **Goldilocks.psd** in the same folder.
3. Extend the canvas so it measures 11 inches wide and 12 inches high. The canvas extension should be a color that you think works well with the image supplied. Anchor the image in a corner when you extend the canvas.
4. Using a font or fonts of your choosing, type the name of the inn on two different layers. For one layer, use the Vertical Type tool and for the other, use the Horizontal Type tool, but rotate the text 90 degrees. You'll save layer comps so you have a couple of choices to show to Betsy. Save the composition that shows the rotated text as a layer comp named **Horizontal** and the vertical composition as a layer comp named **Vertical**.

EXPLORE

5. Using the Vertical layer comp, apply a style to the text. Modify the style by changing at least one of its attributes. (*Hint*: Double-click an individual effect in the Layers panel to open the Layer Style dialog box with the settings for that effect displayed.)
6. Use the Type tools to type the word **Comfort** three times, one time on each front pillow, and once on the carpet. Each instance should use a different text effect. For example, warp the text, type it along a path, apply a style to it, or change its scale in some way. Rotate individual instances until you have the effect you want for each pillow and for the carpet.
7. At the bottom of the image, type the following paragraph text:

   At Goldilocks Inn, we offer all the comforts of home, with none of the hassles. Dine in our four-star dining room and enjoy the company of other guests. Or request a table in a romantic corner. Sip cognac by the common fireplace in the evening or relax in our outdoor hot tub year-round. Take a cooling dip in our pool, or heat up in the sauna.

   Goldilocks Inn is all about comfort. Comfort, comfort, and affordability. And oh, did we mention comfort?

8. Check the spelling of the paragraph text.
9. Format the inn name in small caps in the paragraph text.
10. Format the second paragraph in a way that distinguishes it from the first paragraph, and adjust the alignment and justification for each paragraph as desired.
11. Type the word **AHH!** somewhere on the composition, and fill it with a pattern.
12. Display and hide layers until you are happy with the comp, and then save the new layer comp as **Favorite**.
13. Save the file, and then convert the image to CMYK mode, rasterize it, and flatten it.
14. Save the flattened file as **Goldilocks.tif** in the Photoshop6\Case3 folder, using the default TIFF settings.
15. Submit the results of the preceding steps to your instructor either in printed or electronic form, as requested.

Extend your skills to create a logo and a poster for a soccer academy.

CHALLENGE

Case Problem 4

Data File needed for this Case Problem: Soccer.jpg

Soccer Academy You are a recent college graduate who played soccer in college. You had trouble finding a job, so you have decided to start your own business using the assets and skills you have: a degree in marketing, experience in soccer, and a flair for Photoshop. Your "soccer academy" offers classes for women who are interested in playing in recreational leagues. You'll go to their homes or to a soccer field of their choice and teach them shooting, dribbling, and strategy skills. You need to create a logo for your new business, as well as a poster that you'll hang at local community and child-care centers. Complete the following steps:

1. Start Photoshop while pressing the Ctrl+Alt+Shift keys, click Yes to delete the Settings File when prompted. Switch to and reset the Typography workspace layout, and then reset all tools.
2. Open **Soccer.jpg**, located in the Photoshop6\Case4 folder provided with your Data Files, and save it as **Academy.psd** in the same folder.
3. Extend the canvas size to add 1 ½ inches on the left side. Use black for the canvas extension color.
4. Add white vertical text along the left side of the image using the Raavi, Regular, 30-point font. Type **Soccer Academy**, and position the text so it is centered in the black bar.
5. Increase the tracking between the *r* in *Soccer* and the *A* in *Academy*.
6. Decrease the horizontal scale of the *m* in *Academy*, and increase the vertical scale of the *S* in *Soccer* and the *A* in *Academy*. Adjust the tracking between individual characters as you see fit.
7. Create a duplicate layer of the Soccer Academy layer and name it **Soccer Academy copy**. Hide the original layer.

EXPLORE

8. Change the vertical alignment so the text runs sideways from top to bottom. (*Hint*: Click the Character panel menu button, and deselect Standard Vertical Roman Alignment.) Reposition and resize the text to your liking and change settings in the Character panel as required, and then rename the layer **Sideways**.
9. Hide the Sideways layer, select and display the Soccer Academy layer, click the Character panel menu button, and select Change Text Orientation. Reposition and resize the text so it fits over the turf along the bottom of the image. Adjust the tracking so the letters aren't crowded.
10. Shift the baseline of *cc* down and shift the baseline of *de* up. Add a 10-pixel black stroke to the text.
11. Extend the canvas height by 3 inches using black, and anchor the image on the top. Using any character or paragraph settings, type the following text in a paragraph:

    New to soccer? Call us for a fun workout while learning the fundamentals of the most popular sport in the world.

    You name the place and the time and we'll be there. If you don't have access to a field in your neighborhood, no problem! We'll arrange a meeting place.

EXPLORE

12. Explore the other Paragraph panel settings, as well as the options on the panel menu, while aligning and/or justifying the text to your liking. If you don't like an effect, use the History panel to undo your change.
13. Add **555-555-5555** as a phone number somewhere on the poster. Type it along a path that you specify.
14. Type **Have a ball!** on the image so it follows the curve of the soccer ball.

EXPLORE

15. To create a logo, select the soccer ball in the Background layer and copy it to a new layer. Rearrange the layers so the Have a ball layer is on top of the new layer, and then merge the two layers. (*Hint*: Select both layers, right-click, and then click Merge Layers.) Create a new file with any color background and drag the new logo layer you just merged into the file. See Figure 6-42 for an example.

Figure 6-42 **Sample Soccer Academy logo file**

Dmitriy Shironosov /Shutterstock.com

16. Save the new file as **FinalLogo.psd** in the Photoshop6\Case4 folder.
17. Save Academy.psd, and exit Photoshop.
18. Submit the results of the preceding steps to your instructor either in printed or electronic form, as requested.

ENDING DATA FILES

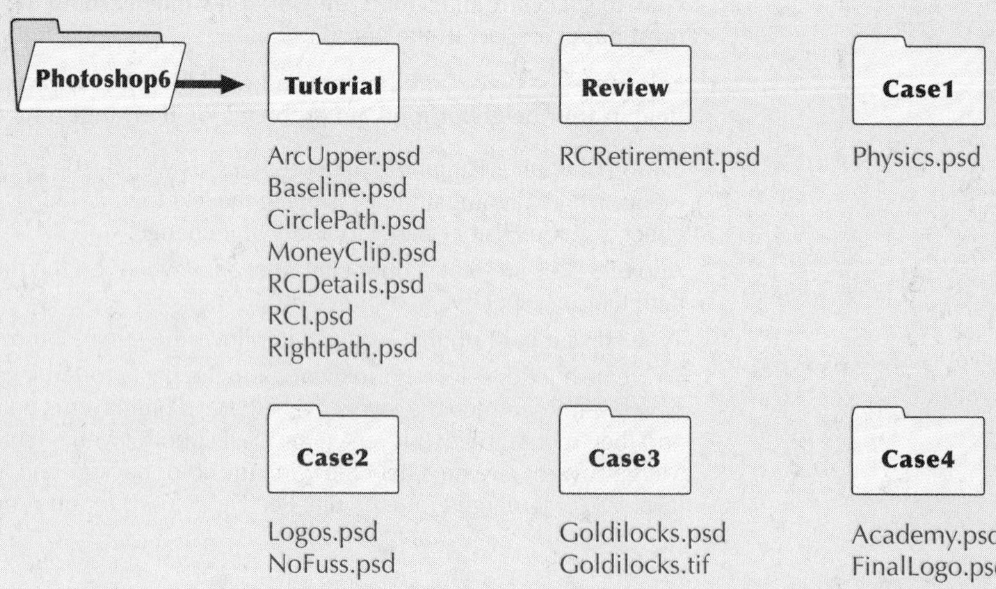

Teamwork

Working with a Team to Create a Campaign

Teamwork is the collaborative process by which team members work together to achieve a common goal. Often, you may find that you need to reach out to managers, to fellow employees, and to people in other departments within your organization to achieve a goal. You might also need to collaborate with a customer or with organizations outside of your company.

Knowing how to be a team player is a critical skill because many organizations rely heavily on teams to complete work tasks. Learning the different roles team members play, how they complement each other for efficient task completion, and how to lead and motivate a team toward achieving a goal can mean the difference between success and failure. Whether your team is ad hoc and short-lived, or ongoing and strategic, the ability to work effectively on a team is a professional skill you need to develop.

What Is a Team?

The Web sites of this country's most desirable employers tell potential employees they'll be working on teams from the start. At Google, the Advertising Sales team members "collaboratively shape solutions that drive their [clients'] strategic initiatives." Apple's corporate retail team is "the backbone behind Apple's retail revolution." For KPMG, one of the world's leading professional services organizations, you may be part of a multidisciplinary team or on a team that is "at the heart of our organization." But what exactly is a team?

More than just people thrown together, a team consists of individuals who have skills, talents, and abilities that complement each other and, when joined, produce synergy—results greater than those a single individual could achieve. It is this sense of shared mission and responsibility for results that makes a team successful in its efforts to reach organizational goals.

Types of Teams

In organizations, there are a variety of team types. Some are formal, while others are more informal. Some meet in person; others have members who have never met face-to-face. Depending on the work, the type of teams you work on will vary.

Formal teams are organized within the company as part of its official structure. These teams can be either horizontal or vertical. A horizontal team has members from roughly the same level in the organization. When people on a team come from different functional areas of the company—finance, information systems, sales—they are often called a cross-functional team, project team, special-purpose team, or task force because they usually have a specific problem to solve within a limited time frame. After the problem is solved, the team disbands. A vertical team, sometimes called a functional team, has a manager and subordinate workers from the same department in the company's hierarchy. The manager is in charge and directs the workers as they complete their tasks. This type of team has a much longer life because the work is not single-goal oriented. Functional teams work together to accomplish their everyday tasks.

Informal groups sometimes form in the workplace when the members choose to join forces to solve a problem, work on a task, or simply meet to talk over lunch. Because they are not appointed by management and their duties are not specifically outlined in job descriptions, there is little or no direct accountability or reporting of results to the organization. For example, a group that organizes to clean up a stretch of highway outside a company's office building won't have management directing its efforts.

A virtual team is one whose members rarely, if ever, meet in person to work on team tasks. Instead, technology makes it possible for members to be geographically distant yet work as if everyone was in the same room. Some common examples of technologies used in virtual teamwork include the following:

- Corporate networks, such as intranets, as well as File Transfer Protocol (FTP) sites
- Teleconferencing—both audio and video
- Groupware and collaboration software tools, such as those found in Adobe Creative Suite and Microsoft Office 2010
- Social networks, blogs, and wikis
- Email, voice mail, and fax

Virtual teams often must work rapidly to accomplish tasks, so knowing how best to use these technologies is critical. Some virtual teams also have high turnover because members will join when their expertise is needed and then leave upon completion of their contribution. The leader may change as well, depending on the stage of work the team is completing.

The Importance of Technology in Teamwork

Each time you work in a group, decide at the outset how the team will use different technologies to communicate and document work activities. Determine how the team will organize and combine deliverable documents or presentation materials. Use whatever technology tools make the most sense for your team, your task, and your skills.

The Roles of Team Members

If a team is to be successful, individual members must see the value in their respective contributions and what the team as a whole gets out of each member's contribution. This means two important requirements must be met: task performance and social satisfaction. Task performance usually is handled by one or more members who are task specialists. Task specialists spend a lot of time and effort ensuring that the team achieves its goals. They initiate ideas, give opinions, gather information, sort details, and provide motivation to keep the team on track. Social satisfaction is handled by individuals who strengthen the team's social bonds through encouragement, empathy, conflict resolution, compromise, and tension reduction. Have you ever been on a team where the tension was high, and someone stepped in to tell a joke or tried to soften the blow of criticism? That person held the role of managing social satisfaction. Both the task specialist and social satisfaction specialist are important roles on teams. These are not the only roles, however. Other roles include team leaders, work coordinators, idea people, and critics. The roles of individual team members are not always mutually exclusive. For example, the task specialist might also be the team leader, and the idea person might also fill the social satisfaction role. As you begin working with your team in this exercise, watch how these roles are filled and how they change as your team completes its work. Perhaps you'll want to discuss up front which role each member is comfortable filling to see how complementary your collective skill sets turn out to be. What if a role is not being filled on your team? Then you'll need to figure out, as a team,

ProSkills

how to move forward so you can complete your work successfully. The following are tips that everyone should respect as work on a team begins:

- Remember that everyone brings something of value to the team.
- Respect and support each other as you work toward the common goal. When criticism or questions arise, try to see things from the other person's perspective.
- If someone needs assistance, find ways to encourage or support that person so the team is not affected.
- Deal with negative or unproductive attitudes immediately so they don't damage team energy and attitude.
- Get outside help if the team becomes stuck and can't move forward.
- Provide periodic positive encouragement or rewards for contributions.

PROSKILLS

Create a Campaign for a Business

Many organizations use Photoshop for both internal and external publications, including Web and print pieces. In this exercise, you'll work with other team members to design a logo as well as print and Web marketing pieces for a fictional business. As you decide on your business, keep the following in mind: Your main tool for this exercise will be Photoshop; therefore, the business should lend itself to striking visuals so that you have photographs and other images to manipulate for the exercise. In other words, a travel agency would probably be a better candidate than a company that provides typing services.

As a group, you'll create the following three pieces: a company logo consisting of both text and a drawing or photograph; a Web banner with text and graphics for the company's home page; and a magazine ad that includes point text and paragraph text, as well as a digital image that has been modified using special effects, adjustment layers, and the Brush tool. The ad will consist of multiple layer comps, with the goal of each team member presenting his or her comps to the group so you can come to a consensus on the best design. To create and design these pieces, your group will use the Photoshop skills and features presented in Tutorials 1 through 6.

1. Meet with your team to brainstorm and come to a consensus on what your business will be. Coming to a consensus is a necessary part of any work a team undertakes, so make sure everyone is happy with the choice. Once you have chosen a business, discuss what products and/or services it provides.
2. As a group or individually, use the Web to research businesses similar to the one your group chose. Print the home pages of the similar businesses you find, and, if you can find banner ads in other Web pages, print those. What kinds of logos do the businesses use? What kind of language do they use in their ads? Do they use a particular font and color scheme? Do you think their branding is effective?
3. As a group, discuss what color scheme might work best to promote your business and create a recognizable brand. Do you want complementary, monochromatic, analogous, or neutral colors? Any member who proposes a color scheme should begin a group discussion on the reasons for that color scheme, and what kind of audience might respond to the scheme.

4. Have each team member create a logo for the business, and set a deadline for its completion. The logo should include both text and graphics, and to create it, team members should use the Drawing tools, the Type tools, special effects, warped text or text along a path, and multiple layers. The logo should be created in the RGB color mode at 300 ppi. It will be saved at lower resolutions and in different color modes later in the exercise. The logo can include a digital image, but it must be either your own image, in the public domain, or available for commercial, royalty-free use.
5. In a team meeting, have each member present his or her logo. Spend time discussing the effectiveness of each one. At the end of the discussion, choose the two logos (we'll call them Logo1 and Logo2) that best represent the products, services, and perceived brand of the company.
6. Split the team into two groups. Team members in Group 1 will work with Logo1, and those in Group 2 will work with Logo2. Every team member should leave the meeting with a digital copy of the logo their group will be using.
7. Each team member should create a new file based on one of the Photoshop Web presets. The new file should include the placed logo and any supporting text for a Web banner for the company's home page. It can be a horizontal or vertical banner, and can include horizontal or vertical type. The final version of the file should be saved using the RGB color mode in JPEG format and should have a resolution of 72 ppi.
8. Each group should meet separately so the individual team members can present their banners to each other. Each group should then create one file and place each member's banner JPEG on a separate layer in the file. Each layer will comprise its own layer comp, which means that all other layers must be hidden when the layer comp is created. The name of the layer comp should be the name of the team member who created that particular banner. The layer comp Comment field should list what the group considered the strengths of each banner design.
9. Each group should choose its favorite banner and save the combined banner file with the favorite banner layer on top and visible, and all of the other layers hidden. To preserve the individual layers, the file should be saved in PSD format.
10. As a final step, the two groups should rejoin and all the team members should combine their efforts to lay out a magazine ad using one of the logos, point text, and paragraph text. The ad should include text along a path and/or warped text. The paragraph text can be placeholder text or can be written specifically for the ad. Either the point text or the paragraph text should include at least one character that uses a baseline shift. The ad should demonstrate knowledge of how to adjust colors; how to use fill layers, blending modes, opacity, masks, and filters; and how to use the Brush tool and the History Brush tool. Team members can work together to come up with the best design. When there is a consensus, save the ad in PSD format at 300 ppi for a CMYK print piece, and then save it in Grayscale at the appropriate resolution and as the appropriate file type for a newspaper ad.
11. Submit your team's completed files to your instructor as requested. Files should include the two logo files in digital format, the Web banner file in digital format with the multiple Web banner layers, and the magazine ad in CMYK PSD format and Grayscale JPEG format. The team should also provide written documentation that describes the role of each team member and his or her contributions to the team. This documentation should include descriptions of any challenges the team faced while completing this exercise and how the team members worked together to overcome those challenges.

TUTORIAL 7

Correcting, Adjusting, and Retouching

Adjusting and Retouching Photographic Images

OBJECTIVES

Session 7.1

- Crop and straighten images using the Crop tool
- Move, patch, and stretch using the Content Aware Move, Extend, and Patch tools
- Adjust images with the auto correction tools
- Make nondestructive corrections using the Levels, Threshold, and Curves adjustments in the Adjustments panel

Session 7.2

- Retouch images with Spot Healing Brush and Healing Brush tools
- Correct images using the Dodge, Burn, and Sponge tools
- Create focus in an image with the Blur Gallery filters and the Sharpen tool
- Adjust color and luminosity using Curves in Lab color mode

Case | ***Hooked***

Hooked, a small ecoadventure company, based in New Braunfels, Texas, provides guided zip line tours that enable adventurers to experience the canopy of the hill country of central Texas from a whole new perspective. Every tour is led by an experienced guide who is an expert in finding and explaining the local ecosystems to guests.

You have been hired by Dayne Brenneman, the owner of Hooked, to create a new promotional brochure. In this tutorial, you'll crop, straighten, and change the perspective of some of Dayne's images using the Crop tool. You'll experiment with the Content-Aware Move tool's settings and the Patch tool. You'll correct images with Photoshop's adjustments and auto correction tools. You'll retouch images using the Dodge, Burn, Sharpen, Sponge, and Healing tools and some Blur Gallery filters. Finally, you'll explore the Lab color mode.

STARTING DATA FILES

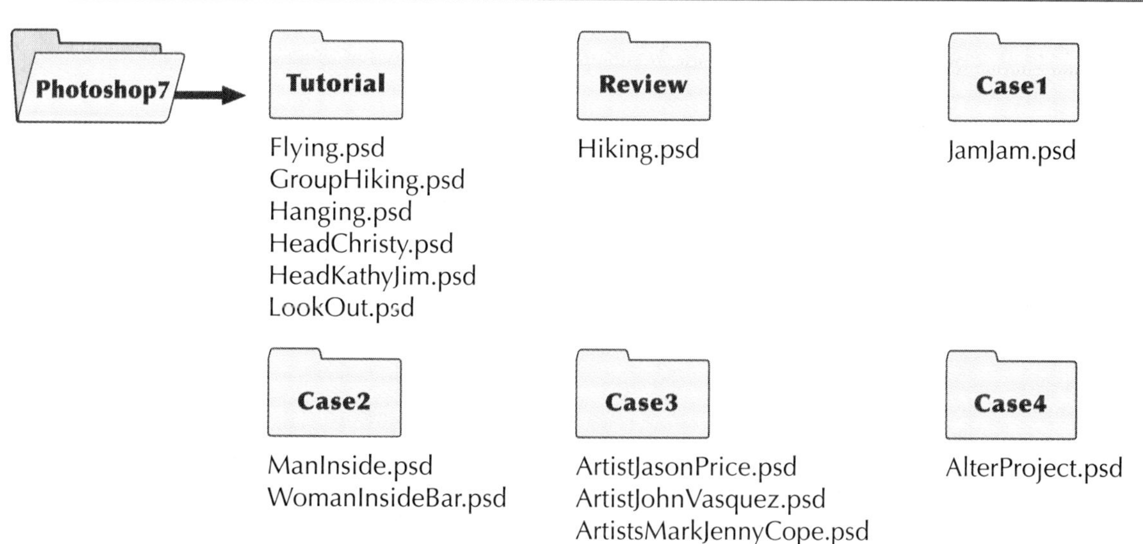

SESSION 7.1 VISUAL OVERVIEW

Using the Image menu, you can access **auto correction tools**, which use mathematical algorithms and preset values to adjust images.

The Aspect Ratio Preset button lets you choose from several commonly used aspect ratios when you are cropping an image; the Unconstrained option is the default setting. Aspect ratio is the proportional relationship between image width and height.

The Crop tool enables you to crop your image using the Rule of Thirds grid.

When the Crop tool is selected, you adjust the crop area by moving the selection handles that are positioned around the edges of the crop area.

The **Rule of Thirds** suggests that you should divide every image into nine equal parts, using two vertical lines and two horizontal lines. To achieve the greatest visual interest, energy, and tension, position significant elements along the lines or, for even more power, where they intersect.

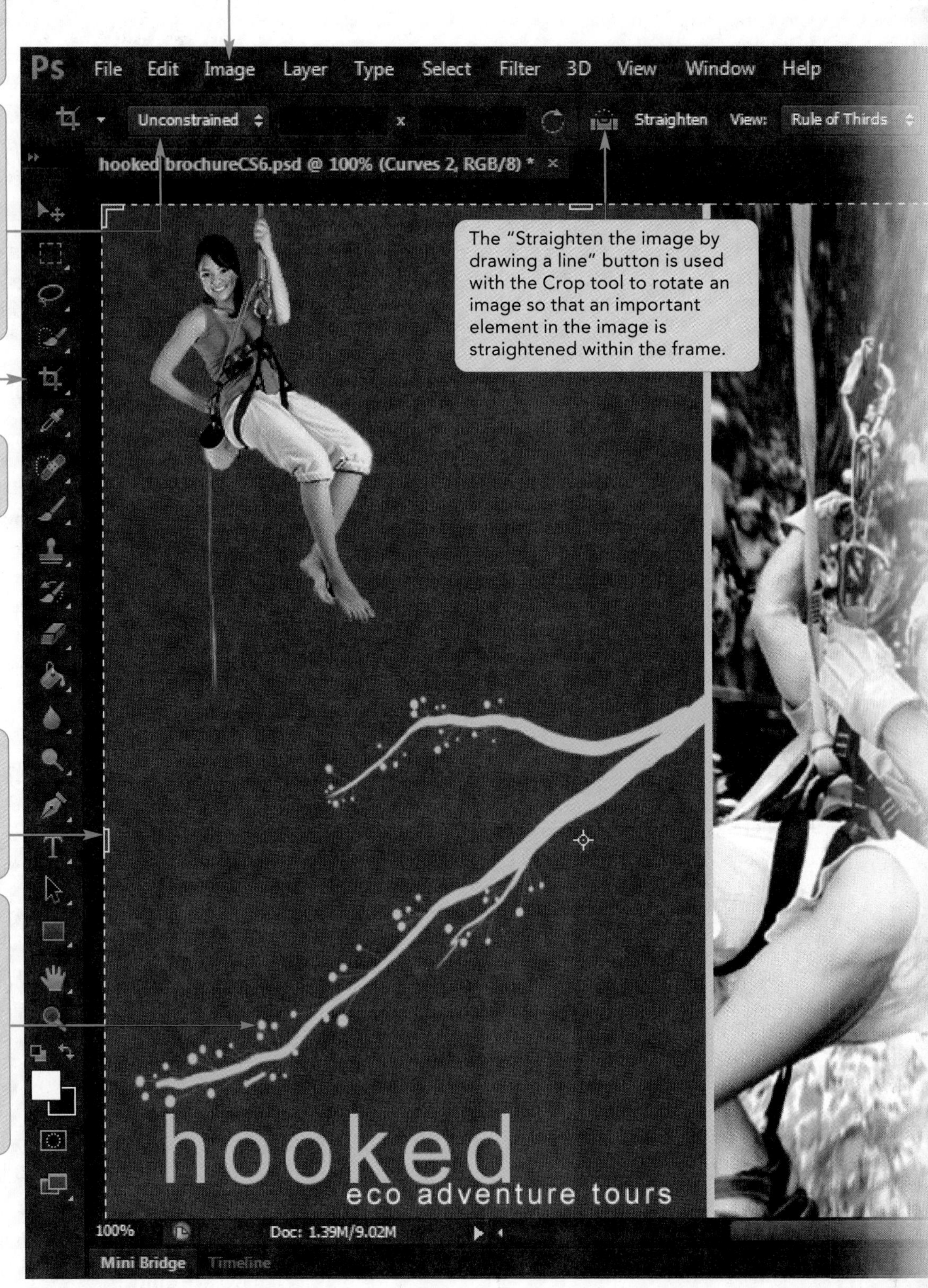

The "Straighten the image by drawing a line" button is used with the Crop tool to rotate an image so that an important element in the image is straightened within the frame.

CROPPING AND CORRECTION TOOLS

The Adjustments panel provides an easy way to create adjustment layers.

Clicking the Auto button is the same as selecting Auto Color from the Image menu, but it is applied to the adjustment layer so it is nondestructive.

The **Curves adjustment** alters image contrast and tone by taking selected input tones and stretching or compressing them using anchor points.

The **Threshold adjustment** changes an image to high-contrast black-and-white output by specifying a threshold level at which lighter pixels are changed to white and darker pixels are changed to black.

Adjustment layers are displayed above the layer, or layers, they affect.

Because each adjustment is on its own layer, the adjustments are nondestructive and can be changed at any time.

Photoshop as Digital Darkroom

One of Photoshop's most powerful applications is as a darkroom that enables you to digitally correct, enhance, and retouch your photographic images. Just as traditional photographers adjusted their images when they were developing film and printing photographs, modern photographers use Photoshop to optimize the composition, color, contrast, and tone of photographic images. In this section, you'll explore a range of Photoshop tools that enable you to correct your compositions and photographs.

Straightening and Cropping

The first step in creating a breathtaking photo is to frame the image in a way that is visually appealing. **Framing** is the process of cropping an image to create an interesting composition that draws the viewer's eye to the subject, or focal point, and removes distracting elements. This process takes some thought. First, you need to identify which elements you want to include in the front—or foreground—of the final photo, and then you must determine how much of the background you want to include in your final product. Determining the position of the main elements within the photo is also an important part of creating a good photographic composition.

When working with images in Photoshop, look at the original image and determine which elements you would like the viewer's eye to focus on, and then try to remove any distracting elements from the image. You can often do this easily by cropping those elements from the image. You can also use the selection handles to rotate the image to perform cropping rotation. By making calculated decisions regarding what is included in your photographs, you can control the message that you are creating. Framing your composition so that foreground elements are grouped together instead of being randomly placed usually creates a more visually appealing composition.

INSIGHT

Archiving Original Photos

Remember that many of the changes that you make in Photoshop are destructive and alter an image permanently. Having an archival file of original artwork ensures that you can find and use the original, unaltered image again in the future. In addition, many photographers and graphic design professionals use tools such as Adobe Bridge to keep track of photographs and to create identifying information, such as tags and metadata, that make it easier to search for those images. Maintaining organized archives of your original work should become a regular part of your work routine.

Cropping with the Crop Tool

Using the Crop tool, you can drag a grid, called the Crop Guide Overlay, over an image and then adjust the visible area of the overlay to determine where you will crop the image. The portion of the image that falls in the darkened area outside the Crop Guide Overlay will be cropped. By default, the Crop Guide Overlay is divided into three equal horizontal sections and three equal vertical sections. This creates a grid with nine sections that you can drag and reposition over the image. The amount of flexibility you will have in adjusting the Crop Guide Overlay is dependent on the aspect ratio setting you select. Aspect ratio describes the proportional relationship of the width of an image to its height. Photoshop provides presets for several commonly used aspect ratios, including the following:

- **Unconstrained**—The default setting; this option enables you to move the Crop Guide Overlay in any direction.

- **Original Ratio**—This setting constrains adjustment of the Crop Guide Overlay to the aspect ratio of the original image.
- **1 × 1 (Square)**—This option constrains adjustment of the Crop Guide Overlay to a square.
- **4 × 5 (8 × 10); 8.5 × 11; 4 × 3; 5 × 7; 2 × 3 (4 × 6); and 16 × 9**—These settings constrain adjustments of the Crop Guide Overlay to the specified aspect ratio.

In addition to the aspect ratio presets, Photoshop allows you to input a custom aspect ratio in the Set a custom aspect ratio boxes on the options bar for the Crop tool. We will use the default setting, Unconstrained, because it enables you to easily use the Rule of Thirds when making cropping decisions.

The Rule of Thirds grid provides guidance in helping you achieve good photographic composition. The Rule of Thirds suggests that you should imagine every image as being divided into a grid of nine equal parts. To achieve the greatest visual interest, energy, and tension, you should position significant elements along these lines or, for even more power, where they intersect. You can also select other grid layouts to help you crop your image, including Grid, Diagonal, Triangle, Golden Ratio, and Golden Spiral.

Employing the Rule of Thirds prevents designers from making the common mistake of placing the main object in a photograph directly in the center of the composition, which can be less visually interesting. The rule is like a set of training wheels; it enables you to create reasonably good compositions even before you have fully developed your skills. However, there is more to good composition than just following the rules. To consistently create exceptional compositions, you need to understand why the rules work, and you need to take some time to think about each composition as an independent creation. It is also important to recognize when you need to break the rules.

Examining the compositions that you create using the Rule of Thirds can provide you with insight into what a well-framed composition looks like. Take some time with each image you create and think about how the image makes you feel. Then, try to identify what elements in the image reinforce that feeling and which elements are distractions. Examining the compositions of successful artists can also provide you with insights. The understanding you develop from these exercises will enable you to develop your design muscles and to create your own personal style.

REFERENCE

Cropping an Image

- In the Tools panel, click the Crop Tool button.
- On the options bar, click the View button, and then click Rule of Thirds to select it, if necessary.
- Using the side and corner selection handles, adjust the Crop Guide Overlay until the areas of the image that you want to crop are in the darkened area outside the Crop Guide Overlay.
- Using the Rule of Thirds to optimize the composition, further adjust the placement of the grid to ensure that important items are located on the grid lines and intersection points.
- Press the Enter key or click the Commit button on the options bar to crop the image.

Dayne has provided you with another image that he wants to use in the brochure. In this image, the employee is centered in the frame surrounded by a great deal of background imagery; consequently, the composition is not that interesting. You will examine the image aspect ratio, and then you'll employ the Rule of Thirds and the Crop tool to create a more interesting composition that focuses on the employee rather than on the background.

To crop the image with the Crop tool:

1. Start Photoshop while pressing the **Ctrl+Alt+Shift** keys, and click **Yes** to delete the Settings File when prompted. Reset Photoshop to the default Essentials workspace layout, and then reset all tools.
2. Open **LookOut.psd**, located in the Photoshop7\Tutorial folder provided with your Data Files.
3. Save the file as **LookOutCrop.psd** in the Photoshop7\Tutorial folder, and then press the **Ctrl+0** keys to fit the image on screen. Press the **X** key to switch the default background and foreground colors.
4. In the Tools panel, click the **Crop Tool** button. The crop box is now visible around the border of the image, and when you move the pointer over the image, it changes to the crop pointer.
5. On the options bar, click the **Aspect Ratio Preset** button and click **Unconstrained**, if necessary.
6. On the options bar, click the **View** button, click **Rule of Thirds**, if necessary, and then click the **Delete Cropped Pixels** check box to deselect it, if necessary. Click in the image to select it. See Figure 7-1.

TIP

You can also activate the Crop tool by pressing the C key.

Figure 7-1 Crop Guide Overlay displayed over an image

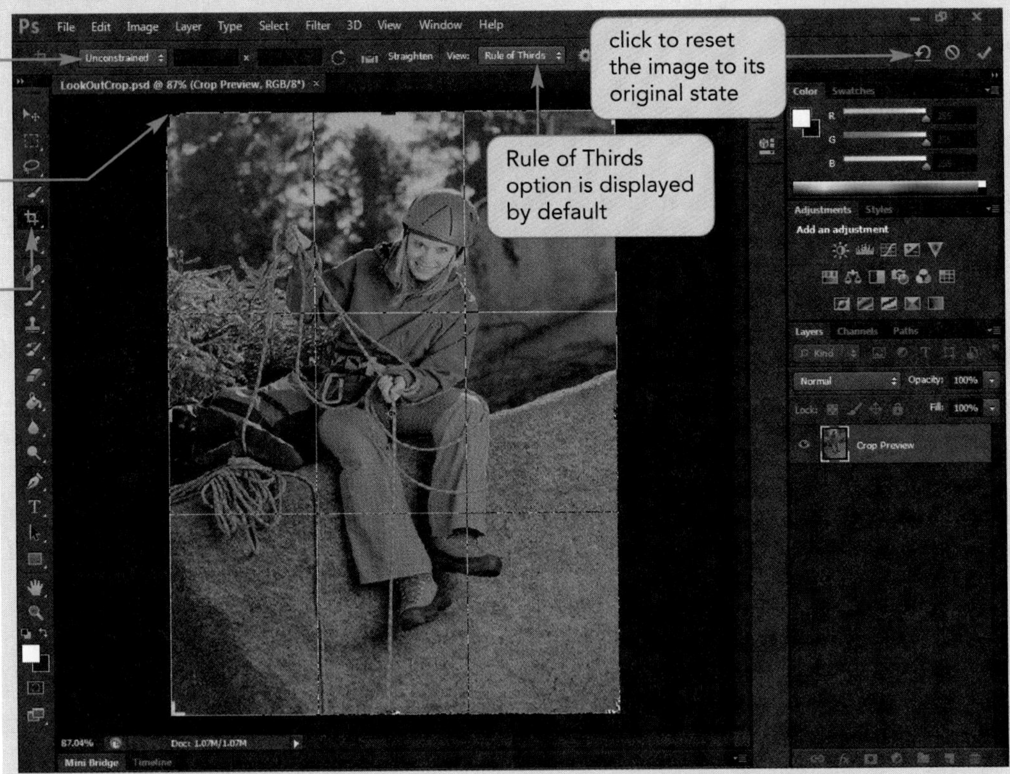

CandyBox Images/Shutterstock.com

7. Drag the upper-left corner selection handle down and to the right until the lower-right corner of the upper-left rectangular grid square is over the center of the woman's chest. This places the woman, who is the focus of this image, at an optimum focal point according to the Rule of Thirds. See Figure 7-2.

Figure 7-2 **Grid positioned to place subject at an optimum position**

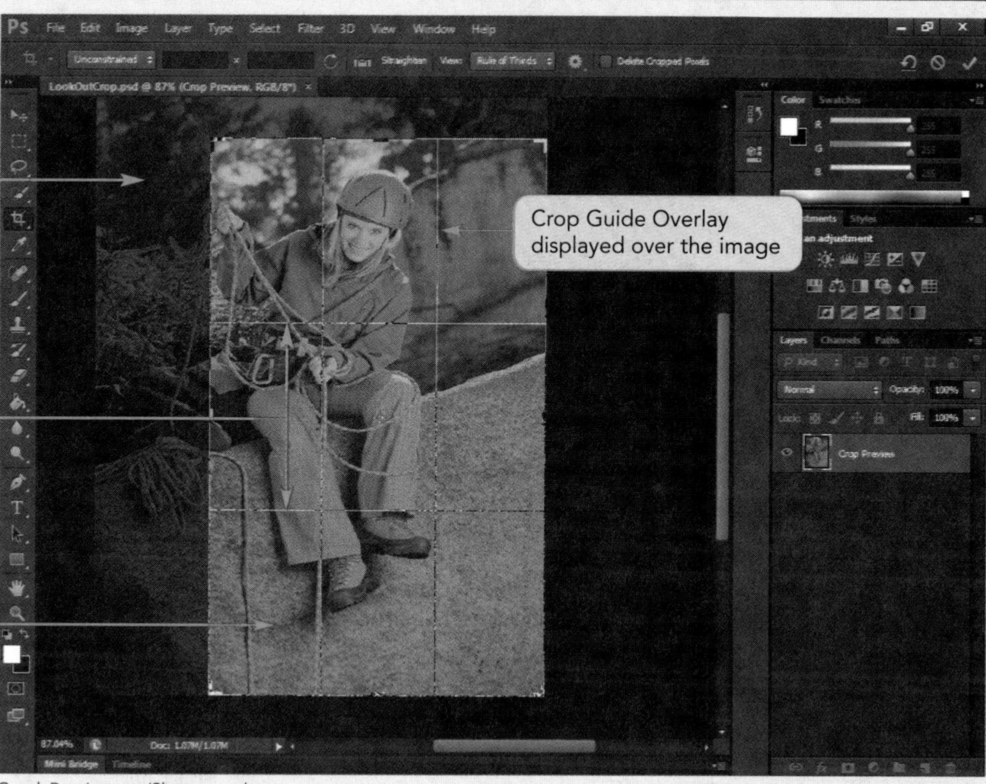
the darkened area of the image will be cropped
optimum positions are along the grid lines, especially where two grid lines cross
the lighter area, enclosed by the Crop Guide Overlay, will be the new image
Crop Guide Overlay displayed over the image

CandyBox Images/Shutterstock.com

8. Place the pointer inside the highlighted grid area and drag the image to the right until the woman's chest is aligned with the lower-right corner of the center-top rectangle.

   This placement is even better because the woman and her gear are now in the frame, creating a more interesting image. By including more foliage and the woman's gear, you create an image that conveys a more dramatic story about the Hooked experience. This will be a more powerful image for the brochure.

9. On the options bar, click the **Commit** button or press the **Enter** key to crop the image. See Figure 7-3.

Figure 7-3 Cropped image

the area that was outside of the Crop Guide Overlay has been cropped
Photoshop changes the layer name to Layer 0

CandyBox Images/Shutterstock.com

10. Save the file, and then click the image. Notice that, because you unchecked the Delete Cropped Pixels check box, the crop is nondestructive, enabling you to return to the Crop tool and change the crop in the future.
11. On the options bar, click the **Cancel** button, and close the file.

By cropping the image, you have made the young woman the focus of the composition. Placing her on a grid line with trees in the background and her equipment in the composition creates visual interest and energy. Dayne likes what you have done with this image, and he plans to use it in the brochure.

Straightening an Image

TIP

When you use the Straighten feature, the image is also cropped to remove any blank areas from the composition.

Photoshop CS6 has a new Straighten feature on the options bar of the Crop tool. You can use this feature to straighten an image by quickly aligning key elements of the image with a horizontal or a vertical line that you draw. This enables you to rotate an image to create a composition that is oriented around elements you would like the viewer to focus on. For example, if you have an image of a building that is positioned at an angle, you can use the Straighten feature to draw a line that is parallel to the roofline of the building, and Photoshop will rotate the photograph so the roofline of the building is parallel to the top of the image.

REFERENCE

Straightening an Image

- In the Tools panel, click the Crop Tool button, and then on the options bar, click the "Straighten the image by drawing a line on it" button.
- On the canvas, draw a line that is parallel to the key element to which you want to orient the image.
- On the options bar, click the Commit button.

Dayne has an image of one of his employees hanging from a zip line that he would like to use in the brochure. However, the employee is positioned at an angle that might not work well in the brochure. You'll use the Straighten feature of the Crop tool to straighten and crop the image, thus creating a more dramatic and focused composition.

To use the Straighten feature to straighten the image:

1. Navigate to the Photoshop7\Tutorial folder, and open **Hanging.psd**.
2. Save the file as **HangStraight.psd** in the Photoshop7\Tutorial folder, and then press the **Ctrl+0** keys to fit the image on screen.
3. Make sure the Crop tool is still selected, and then on the options bar, click the **Straighten the image by drawing a line on it** button. The pointer changes to the straighten pointer. Place the pointer at the right corner of the platform on which the people in the background are standing.
4. Click and drag the mouse to the left to create a line parallel to the top of the platform. Release the mouse button after the line exits the image.

   Photoshop rotates the image to make the line you drew (and the platform) parallel to the top of the image. In addition, the crop grid is automatically reduced in area to ensure that when you crop the image there is no blank canvas inside of the cropped area. See Figure 7-4.

Figure 7-4 Ruler line drawn parallel to the rope

"Straighten the image by drawing a line" button
when you release the mouse button, Photoshop rotates the image and adjusts the crop grid
image has been rotated to place the line you drew parallel to the top of the image
Commit button

© iStockphoto.com/Devon Stephens

5. On the options bar, click the **Commit** button ✓. The image is cropped to eliminate any blank areas of the canvas that appeared when the image was rotated. See Figure 7-5.

Figure 7-5 Straightened and cropped image

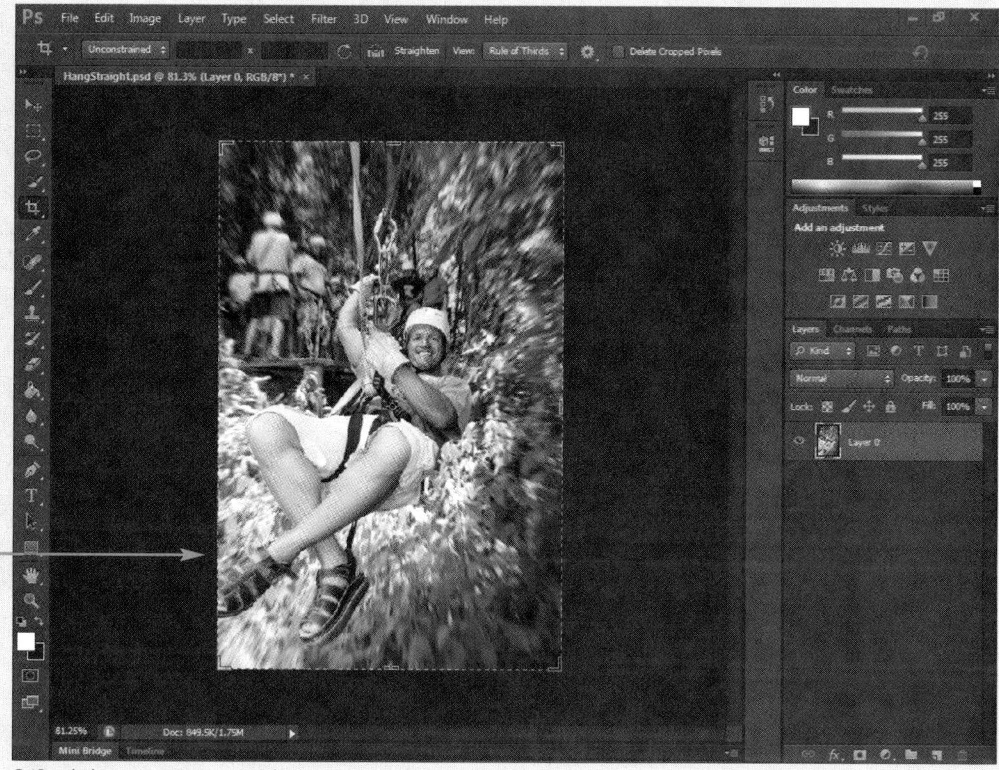
any areas showing the blank canvas have been cropped

© iStockphoto.com/Devon Stephens

When Photoshop crops the composition area of a straightened image, it does not delete the areas of the image that lie outside the cropped area. This enables you to move the straightened image around slightly if you feel that different positioning will create a better composition.

Dayne thinks this image would work better in the brochure if the man, who is the focus of the composition, is slightly higher in the frame and the image is cropped a little tighter. You will adjust the cropping on the image first by dragging the crop grid and then by moving the image under the grid.

To recrop an image:

1. Click inside the image to reveal the crop grid, and then click the right border of the crop grid. The pointer will change to the resize pointer ↔. Drag the grid to the left until the man's nose is positioned under a vertical line.
2. Next, click on the image inside the grid, and drag the image up until the lower-right corner of the crop grid is touching the bottom of the image. See Figure 7-6.

Figure 7-6 Image repositioned to focus attention on the person

repositioning the image enables you to place the man in a more powerful position
make sure that the background is not displayed at the corners
drag the image up until the lower-right corner of the crop grid is touching the bottom of the image

© iStockphoto.com/Devon Stephens

3. Press the **Enter** key to crop the image, and then save and close the file.

This straightened and cropped image will work well in the new Hooked brochure. Dayne would also like to use the Hanging image as a mailer. For the mailer, he would like you to alter the perspective of the image. You will use the Perspective Crop tool to change the perspective of the image, and then you'll save a version of the image that can be used in the mailer.

Cropping and Altering the Perspective of an Image

Perspective is a technique for representing volume and spatial relationships on a two-dimensional surface, such as a drawing or a photograph. One example of the use of perspective is when an artist draws a road as though it is getting smaller as it approaches the edge of the canvas, creating the illusion that the road is extending off into the distance. Photoshop's Perspective Crop tool enables you to adjust the perspective of an image while you crop it. You will use the Perspective Crop tool to change the perspective of the Hanging image to make it appear that the man on the zip line is zooming toward the viewer and the background is getting smaller behind him.

To use the Perspective Crop tool to change the perspective of the image:

1. Navigate to the Photoshop7\Tutorial folder, and open **Hanging.psd**.
2. Save the file as **HangingPerspective.psd** in the Photoshop7\Tutorial folder, and then press the **Ctrl+0** keys to fit the image on screen.

3. In the Tools panel, click the **Perspective Crop Tool** button, which is located under the Crop Tool button.
4. Click at the upper-left corner of the image, and drag down and to the lower-right corner of the image to select the entire image. A grid is displayed over the image.
5. Drag the center-right selection handle to the left until it touches the man's shirt and then drag the upper-right selection handle back to the upper-right corner of the image. See Figure 7-7.

Figure 7-7 Adjusting perspective with Perspective Crop tool

Perspective Crop tool is selected
upper-right selection handle moved back to the upper-right corner of the image
center-right selection handle

© iStockphoto.com/Devon Stephens

6. On the options bar, click the **Commit** button to complete the crop. The perspective changes and the image are cropped. See Figure 7-8.

Figure 7-8 Image perspective changed

the perspective of the image changed and the image was cropped

© iStockphoto.com/Devon Stephens

7. Save the file, and close it.

Moving and Removing Objects in an Image Using Content-Aware Tools

As you have seen in earlier tutorials, you can sometimes create a more pleasing composition—and one that draws the viewer's eye to the focal point—by adjusting the position of a few of the objects within the image. The new Content-Aware Move tool was added to Photoshop in CS6 to respond to this need. Because the Content-Aware Move tool is "content-aware," it blends the edges of the selection with its new location, and it uses the surroundings to blend the hole left by the moved object so the area looks natural. However, because of the complexity of this task, Photoshop sometimes produces results that aren't satisfactory. The Content-Aware Move tool's Adaptation settings give you some control over the amount of blending that will be performed, which can help you achieve professional-looking results. Adaptation settings include: Very Strict, Strict, Medium, Loose, and Very Loose. The Adaptation setting determines how much of the existing image background will be retained as Photoshop blends the selection in to its new location. A setting of Very Strict will cause the selection area to retain more of its background characteristics when it is blended into the new area of the image while a setting of Very Loose will cause the selection to blend more fully into the new area. Medium is a good place to start, but you may need to adjust the Adaptation setting to optimize your results.

Dayne has an image of a group hiking that he would like to use at the vertical fold of the inside of the brochure, but he would like to move the front-most hiker down and to the left to optimize his placement within the image. When the hiker is moved to the new location, the layout of the image will follow the Rule of Thirds, creating a more aesthetically pleasing composition.

To move an object and adjust the Content-Aware Move tool Adaptation setting:

1. Navigate to the Photoshop7\Tutorial folder, and open **GroupHiking.psd**.
2. Save the file as **HikingMoved.psd** in the same folder, and then press the **Ctrl+0** keys to fit the image on screen.
3. In the Tools panel, right-click the Spot Healing Brush Tool button, and then click the **Content-Aware Move Tool** button. On the options bar, confirm that **Move** is selected as the Mode and that **Medium** is selected as the Adaptation. Drag a selection marquee around the hiker in the foreground of the image. See Figure 7-9.

Figure 7-9 **Hiker selected with Content-Aware Move tool**

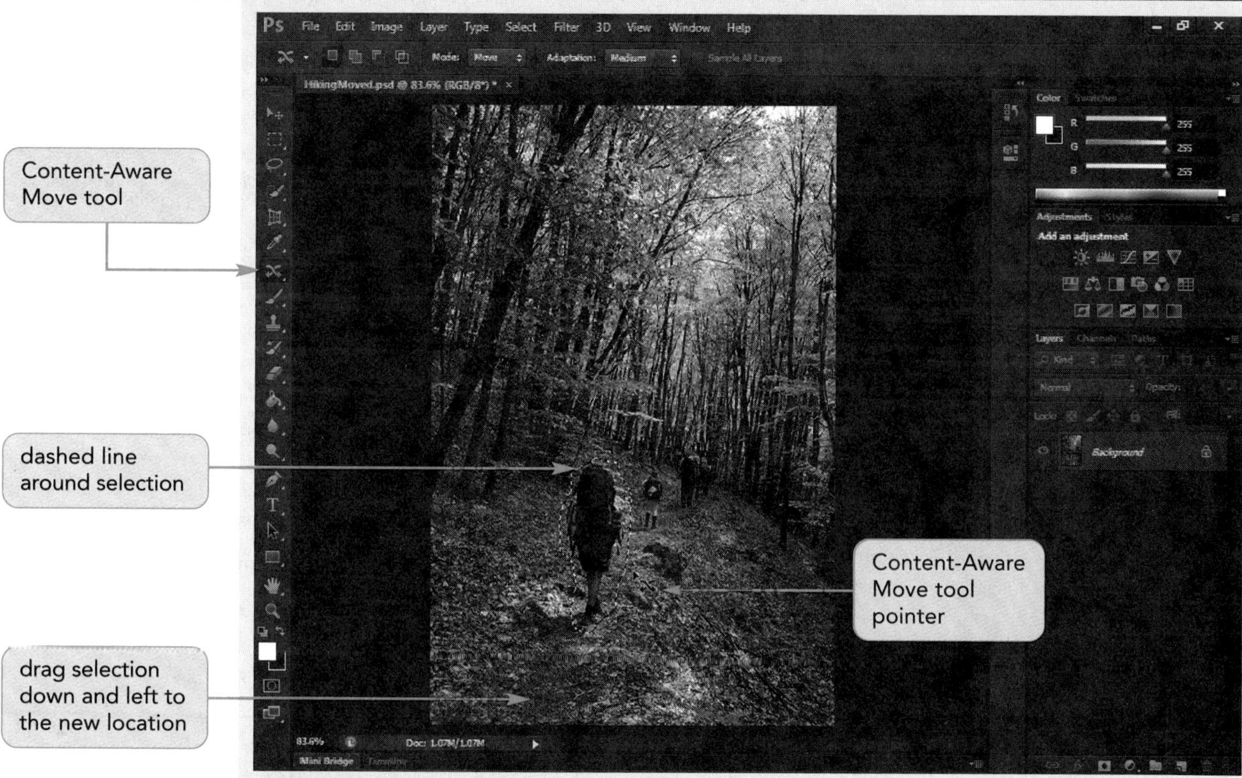

Maslov Dmitry/Shutterstock.com

4. Click and drag the selection down and to the left so it is positioned at the bottom of the photograph and roughly over the spot where the left, vertical grid line would appear if the Rule of Thirds grid was displayed. Release the mouse button after the selection has been repositioned. Photoshop shows a progress indicator while it performs the operation.
5. Click outside of the selection, and then zoom in to get a better look at the changes.

   Photoshop moves the hiker but with the Medium Adaptation setting, the selection does not blend well with its new location. See Figure 7-10.

Figure 7-10 **Hiker moved with Content-Aware Move tool**

change Adaptation settings to adjust blending
selection moved to new location
the blend is not smooth

Maslov Dmitry/Shutterstock.com

The hiker looks odd because the background from original location of the selection is brighter than the background of the new location. You'll undo your move, and adjust the Adaptation setting to achieve a better result.

6. Press the **Ctrl+Alt+Z** keys twice to undo the move.
7. On the options bar, click the **Adaptation** button, and then click **Very Loose**. Move the selection again.
8. Repeat Steps 6 and 7, changing the Adaptation setting as necessary and moving the hiker to different positions until you achieve a realistic effect. Click outside of the selection when you are finished. See Figure 7-11.

Figure 7-11 **Adaptation adjustment makes hiker blend with new background**

Adaptation setting of Very Loose provides a better blend
moved forward slightly for better blend with background

Maslov Dmitry/Shutterstock.com

In addition to moving objects in your composition, the Content-Aware Move tool can be used to stretch objects to extend them over a larger area of the composition. This is done by selecting only the portion of the object that you would like to stretch and then selecting Extend as the Mode setting on the options bar. Extending an object produces the best effect when the object is repetitive and structured, like an architectural element, and when the background is fairly uncluttered. For example, Extend is often used to increase the height of a building to make a skyline more interesting. Next, you will use the Extend Mode to increase the height of the hiker that you just repositioned—giving him more visual weight in the composition.

TIP

You can also use Content-Aware Move with the Extend Mode selected to copy a selection to another place in the image.

To extend an object in an image:

1. Draw a selection around the top part of the hiker, starting just above the horizontal gray line on the backpack.
2. On the options bar, click the **Mode** button, and then click **Extend**.
3. Click and drag the selection up, making sure that the straps on the left of the backpack are still connected, and then click outside the selection. The hiker appears larger and has more visual weight in the image. See Figure 7-12.

Figure 7-12 **Extend Mode used to stretch backpack**

Maslov Dmitry/Shutterstock.com

Next, you'll use the Patch tool—with its Content-Aware setting—to remove a hiker from the image.

Patching an Image

Sometimes you need to remove an object from an image or patch a distracting part of the background so the image can be used for a project. The new Content-Aware setting for the Patch tool enables you to remove an element from an image and patch the hole all in one step—without creating multiple layers or spending a great deal of time. When you remove objects or portions of the image using the Patch tool with the Content-Aware setting, you first draw a selection around the element you want to remove, and then you select another portion of the image to use to patch the original selection area. Photoshop blends the selections so the original area looks natural, as though the object or distracting elements were never there. To take advantage of the new functionality, you must select Content-Aware from the Patch mode list when the Patch tool is selected.

REFERENCE

Moving an Object and Patching the Hole with the Patch Tool

- In the Tools panel, click the Spot Healing Brush Tool button, and then click the Patch Tool button.
- On the options bar, click the Patch button, and then click Content-Aware to select it as the patch mode.
- On the canvas, drag a selection around the element you would like to remove.
- Click in the selection, drag it to the area you would like Photoshop to use to patch the hole and release the mouse button.

Dayne would like you to remove the center hiker from the image. Because the image will be used at the vertical fold of the brochure, the center hiker may be located in the fold, creating a distraction for viewers. Removing the hiker from the image will create more open space and will enable the image to work as intended in the brochure.

To use the Content-Aware Patch tool to remove an object and patch the image:

1. In the Tools panel, right-click the **Content-Aware Move Tool** button, and then click the **Patch Tool** button.
2. On the options bar, click the **Patch** button, and then click **Content-Aware** to select it as the patch mode. Click the **Adaptation** button, and then click **Very Loose**.
3. When you move the pointer over the image, it changes to the patch pointer. Drag a selection around the hiker located closest to the center of the screen, and then place the pointer over the selected area. The pointer changes to the patch move pointer, indicating that the selection is ready to move. See Figure 7-13.

Figure 7-13 Content-Aware Patch tool

Content-Aware Patch tool
drag the selection to the area of the image you want to use as the sample for the patch
patch move pointer
move selection to this area to sample it for for patch

Maslov Dmitry/Shutterstock.com

4. Click in the selection, and drag it down and to the right slightly, examining the patch area as you drag, until you find a background area that you think will create a natural-looking patch. Release the mouse button after the selection has been repositioned and click outside of the selection.
5. Press the **Ctrl+0** keys to view the entire image.

   Photoshop removes the hiker and patches the background. See Figure 7-14.

Figure 7-14 Content-Aware Patch tool

Maslov Dmitry/Shutterstock.com

6. Save the image and close it.

Dayne has some additional images that he needs your help with, so next, you'll adjust an image using auto adjustments.

Auto Correction Tools

The Auto Tone, Auto Contrast, and Auto Color tools in Photoshop allow you to quickly correct the color, contrast, and tone in an image, using the tools alone or in combination. The auto correction tools use mathematical algorithms and preset values to adjust images. The following is a summary of the three tools:

- **Auto Tone**—Adjusts the black-and-white points in an image; portions of the shadows and highlights in each channel are clipped, and the lightest pixels in each color channel are mapped to pure white while the darkest pixels in each color channel are mapped to pure black. The remaining colors are redistributed proportionally.
- **Auto Contrast**—Adjusts the contrast of an image as a whole, without adjusting individual color channels; contrast is created by clipping shadow and highlight values of the image and then mapping the lightest pixels to pure white and the darkest pixels to pure black.
- **Auto Color**—Adjusts the color and contrast of an image by adjusting highlights, midtones, and shadows; highlights and shadows are clipped by .5 percent and midtones are neutralized. You can use Auto Color to neutralize color casts created by the Auto Tone correction.

TIP

To prevent the auto correction tools from taking large blocks of color, such as an image border, into account when calculating correction values, first select the area of the image you want to correct and then apply the auto correction.

The values and settings for each auto correction tool can be adjusted in the Auto Color Correction Options dialog box, but it is a good idea to use the default settings until you have a good understanding of how these tools work. The obvious shortfall in this, and any general approach to correction, is that the character and details of specific images are not factored into the corrections. Because of this, you are sometimes left with average-looking images, or worse yet, images that look odd due to an auto adjustment that looks unnatural or jarring. The other problem with using the auto correction tools is that the adjustments are destructive. However, the auto correction tools are a great place to start, especially when you are trying to develop an understanding of what an image with good color, contrast, and tone looks like.

INSIGHT

Understanding Components of Color

Understanding some of the components of color will help you to adjust and manipulate photographic images. **Hue** is essentially what we think of or perceive as the color of an object. Generally, when you refer to an object as being red, or blue, you are referring to the hue of an object. Hue is expressed as the measurement, in degrees, of the location of a color around the standard color wheel. **Saturation** is the expression of purity or strength of a color. If a color has 0 percent saturation, it is gray, whereas a pure color has a saturation of 100 percent. Colors that have a 100 percent saturation value are located at the outer edge of the color wheel, and saturation decreases as the pure color is blended or diluted while you move toward the middle of the wheel. **Brightness** is a measurement of the lightness or darkness in a color and is also measured as a percentage. A brightness value of 0 percent is black and a brightness value of 100 percent is white.

The third image that Dayne would like to use in the brochure needs some adjustment to its color, contrast, and tone. You'll use the auto correction tools in an attempt to quickly improve the image.

To correct the image with the auto correction tools:

1. Open **Flying.psd**, located in the Photoshop7\Tutorial folder.
2. Save the file as **FlyingAuto.psd** in the Photoshop7\Tutorial folder, and then press the **Ctrl+0** keys to fit the image on screen.
3. In the Layers panel, click the **Background** layer to select it, if necessary, and create three duplicate layers of the Background layer. Name the new layers **Fly Girl Tone**, **Fly Girl Contrast**, and **Fly Girl Color**. See Figure 7-15.

Figure 7-15 Duplicate layers created and renamed

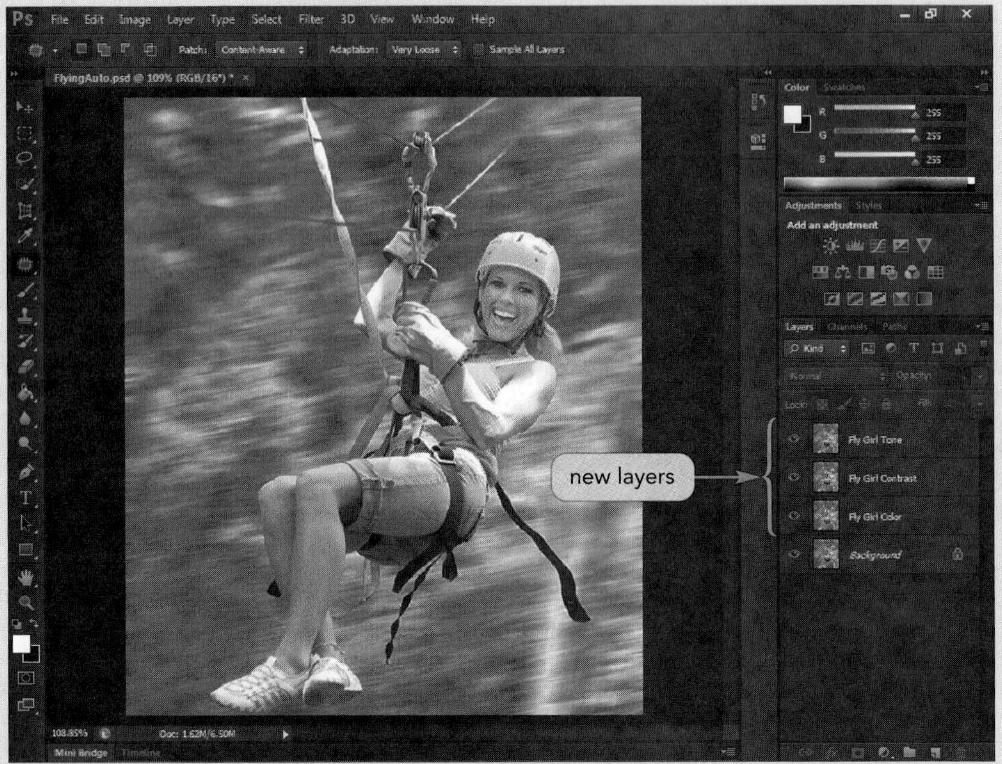

© iStockphoto.com/Devon Stephens

4. In the Layers panel, click the **Fly Girl Tone** layer, and on the menu bar click **Image**, and then click **Auto Tone** to apply the tone adjustment. The image now has deeper blacks, brighter whites, and greater contrast. See Figure 7-16.

Figure 7-16 Auto Tone correction applied

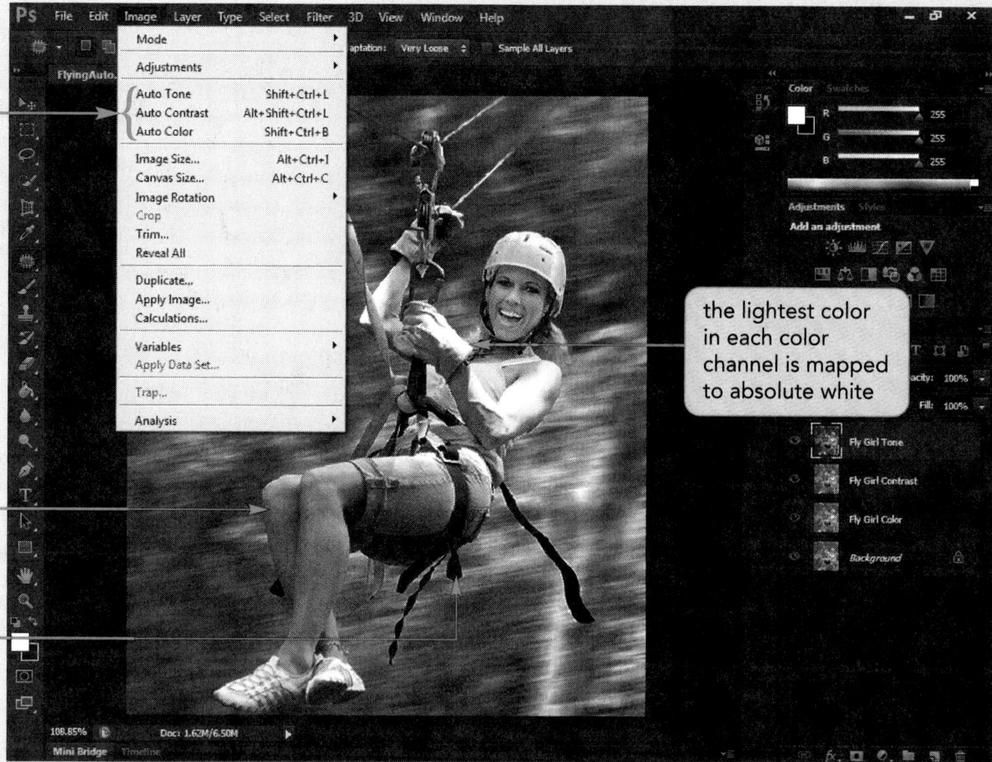

5. In the Layers panel, click the **Eye** icon in the Show/Hide column next to the Fly Girl Tone layer to hide that layer.
6. Click the **Fly Girl Contrast** layer, and on the Image menu, click **Auto Contrast** to apply the contrast adjustment. The contrast of the entire image is increased compared with the original image. See Figure 7-17.

Figure 7-17 **Auto Contrast correction applied**

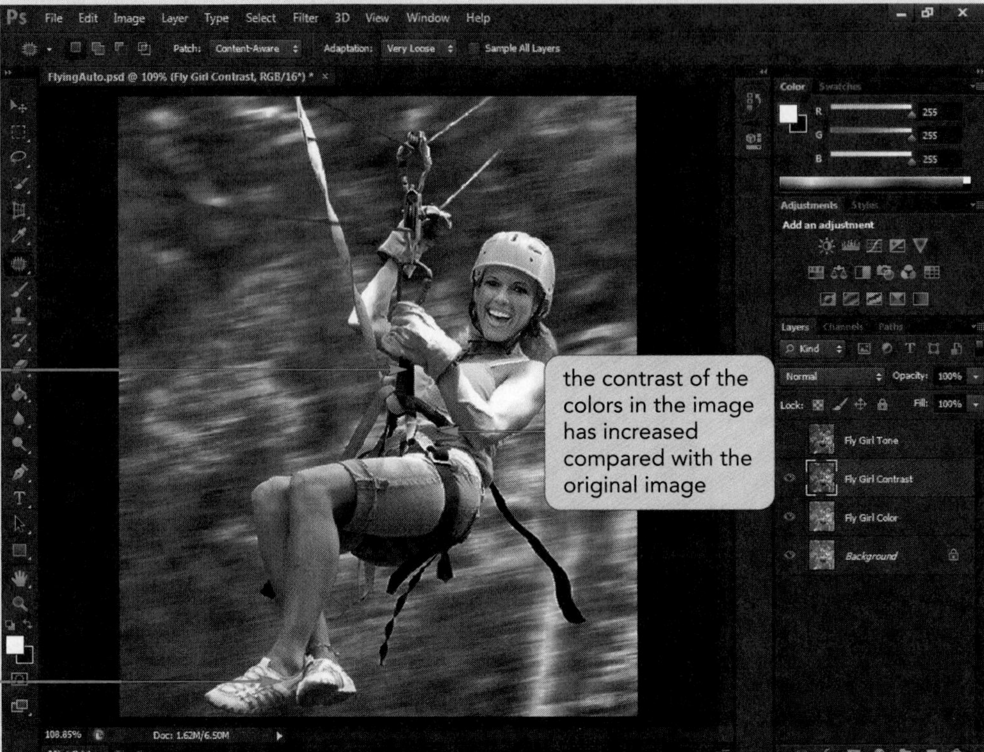
the darkest color in the image is mapped to absolute black
the lightest color in the image is mapped to absolute white
the contrast of the colors in the image has increased compared with the original image
File Edit Image Layer Type Select Filter 3D View Window Help
FlyingAuto.psd @ 109% (Fly Girl Contrast, RGB/16*)
Fly Girl Tone
Fly Girl Contrast
Fly Girl Color
Background

© iStockphoto.com/Devon Stephens

Compare the Fly Girl Contrast layer with the Fly Girl Tone layer. Although the Auto Tone and Auto Contrast corrections often produce very different results, in this case the results of the two corrections are similar. You'll try the Auto Color correction next to see if it produces different results.

7. In the Layers panel, click the **Eye** icon in the Show/Hide column next to the Fly Girl Contrast layer to hide that layer.

8. Click the **Fly Girl Color** layer, and on the Image menu click **Auto Color** to apply the color adjustment. The green color cast is removed from the image, but now there is too much red visible in the skin tones. See Figure 7-18.

Figure 7-18 **Auto Color correction applied**

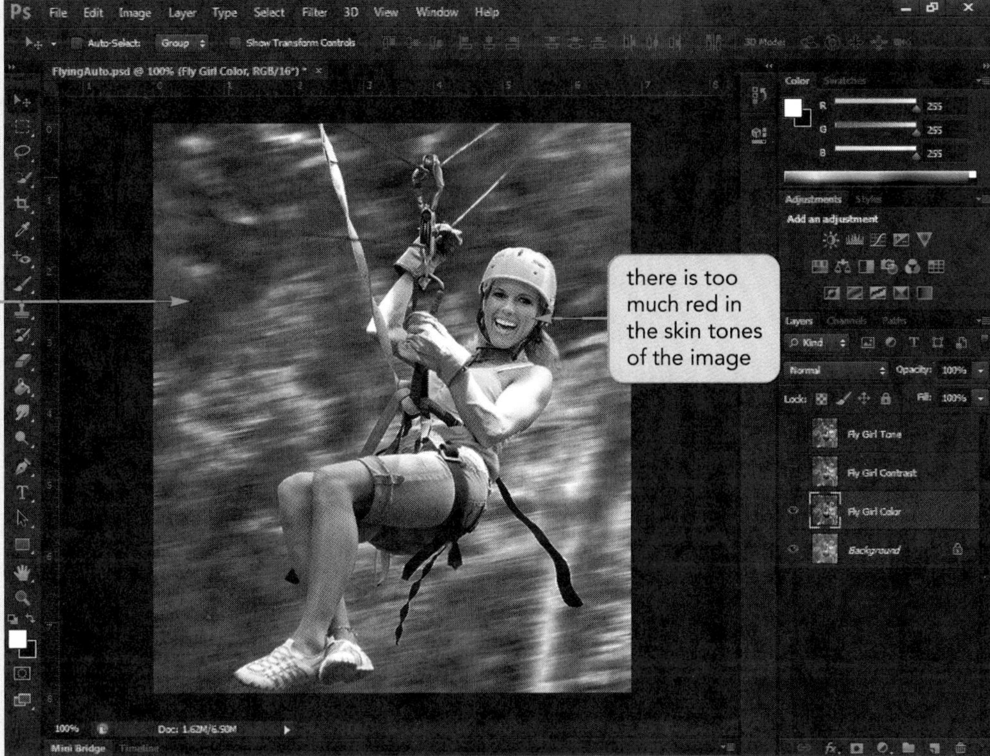
the green color cast has been removed from the image
there is too much red in the skin tones of the image

© iStockphoto.com/Devon Stephens

9. Compare the changes made to each layer, and then save the file.

INSIGHT

Using the Image/Adjustments Menu to Correct Your Images

The Image menu provides access, via the Adjustments submenu, to several other methods for improving your images—in addition to the auto correction tools. The Shadows/Highlights adjustment allows you to make changes that only affect an image's shadows or highlights. This adjustment lets you quickly correct exposure issues that affect only certain elements in an image. You can use the Desaturation adjustment to remove all color saturation from an image. And the Match Color and Replace Color options on the Adjustments menu help you to match, mix, and replace specific colors in an image. As with the auto correction tools, the changes you make using these tools are destructive; however the options available on the Image/Adjustments menu are powerful tools that you can use to quickly improve the color and exposure of your images.

None of the auto corrections were perfect. Auto Tone and Auto Contrast left a green color cast to the image, and Auto Color made the skin tones too red. Dayne has decided that he would like you to use the Levels adjustment to achieve a better result.

PROSKILLS

Problem Solving: Displaying Color Accurately

Before you can accurately adjust or correct the color in your projects, you must create an environment in which you can reliably evaluate compositions in the context of their intended output. You do this by creating a work flow process that integrates color management into every phase.

The first step in creating an effective color management work flow is to calibrate and profile your monitors for accurate display. **Calibrating** a monitor adjusts the display to conform to known specifications, and creating a color profile enables you to save those settings so your monitor display is consistent over time. Although all monitors display images using RGB color, every monitor is calibrated to display colors slightly differently. This fact becomes evident when you look at a wall of monitors in a department store. In addition, to inherit color display differences, users can make adjustments to the brightness and contrast of most monitors. Because of these variables, it can be difficult to know how the adjustments you make to images will affect your final product. Both the Windows and Mac OS operating systems provide a basic monitor calibration utility; however, for professional results, you can purchase third-party calibration software with additional measuring devices for greater accuracy. By making use of high-quality color calibration tools, you can ensure that throughout your design process, your decisions regarding color will be based on accurate input and output information.

Next, you'll explore how adjustment layers enable you to create remarkable, precise, nondestructive adjustments to the tone, contrast, and color of your images.

Correcting Images with the Adjustments Panel

The Adjustments panel provides an array of powerful tools that enable you to correct images nondestructively by making corrections on adjustment layers rather than to the image itself. As with the auto adjustment tools you just used, you can use adjustment layers alone or in combination, but each adjustment creates its own independent adjustment layer, which you can tweak repeatedly until you get the look you desire. In addition, changing the order in which adjustment layers are stacked will also change their effect on the image because layers that are lower in the stacking order are applied before layers that are higher in the stacking order.

Now that you have a basic understanding of tone, contrast, and color, it is a good time to take a deeper look at how you can use the power and precision of the adjustments in the Adjustments panel to create spectacular images. Figure 7-19 provides a description of all the available options in the Adjustments panel.

Figure 7-19 **Major tools in the Adjustments panel**

Adjustment	Use To
Brightness/ Contrast	Quickly adjust the brightness and contrast of the image.
Levels	Manipulate the intensity level of shadows, midtones, and highlights using sliders and histograms.
Curves	Adjust the contrast and tone of images using curve controls.
Exposure	Adjust the tonal range of 32-bit High Dynamic Range (HDR) images (this tool also works, but is less effective, with 8-bit and 16-bit images); the Exposure tool uses a linear color space, not the image's current color space, to make adjustments. When used with HDR images, this can uncover details that would otherwise be lost in shadow or highlight.
Vibrance	Adjust the saturation or intensity of color in an image (not available in CMYK).
Hue/Saturation	Adjust the hue, saturation, and lightness of an entire image or individual colors.
Color Balance	Alter the range of colors used in an image.
Black & White	Convert color images to grayscale and control how individual colors convert; this tool can also be used to add a color tint to a grayscale image (not available in CMYK).
Photo Filter	Reproduce the effects of various camera lens filters.
Channel Mixer	Adjust the amount of information to include from each channel when creating a grayscale image.
Color Lookup	Adjust image color by loading 3D LUT (look-up table) files, Abstract profiles, or DeviceLink profiles.
Invert	Invert image colors to their opposites on the color wheel or invert values in noncolor images.
Posterize	Specify the number of tonal (or brightness) levels for each channel of an image to create a special effect where the image contains large, flat areas of color.
Threshold	Change an image to high-contrast black-and-white output by specifying a threshold level where lighter pixels are changed to white and darker pixels are changed to black.
Selective Color	Target specified colors, and adjust the amount of cyan, magenta, yellow, and black in the specified color.
Gradient Map	Convert an image to grayscale by mapping the image colors to a specified gradient fill.

Using Auto Adjustments in Adjustment Layers

Several of the adjustments in the Adjustments panel have Auto buttons that enable you to adjust your image using an algorithm or set of algorithms that are known to produce generally good results based on the effect that the adjustment is intended to create. Like the Auto Tone, Auto Contrast, and Auto Color adjustments that you just worked with, these Auto buttons provide you with a good place to start while you are learning how to correct your images. In addition, many of the adjustments have a list of presets that enable you to achieve results that are better than the basic Auto settings. You will use the Auto button and the presets in the Levels adjustment to achieve better results with the FlyingAuto image.

To correct the image with the Auto button and a preset in the Levels adjustment:

TIP

You can also access the Levels adjustment from the Image menu, and you can use the Auto button to apply default corrections; however any adjustments applied that way will be destructive.

1. In the Layers panel, click the **Eye** icon in the Show/Hide column next to the Fly Girl Color layer to hide that layer.
2. Click the **Background** layer, and in the Adjustments panel, click the **Levels** icon.

   An adjustment layer titled Levels 1 is added to the Layers panel, and the Properties panel opens to display the properties of the Levels adjustment. See Figure 7-20.

Figure 7-20 Properties panel showing the properties of the Levels adjustment

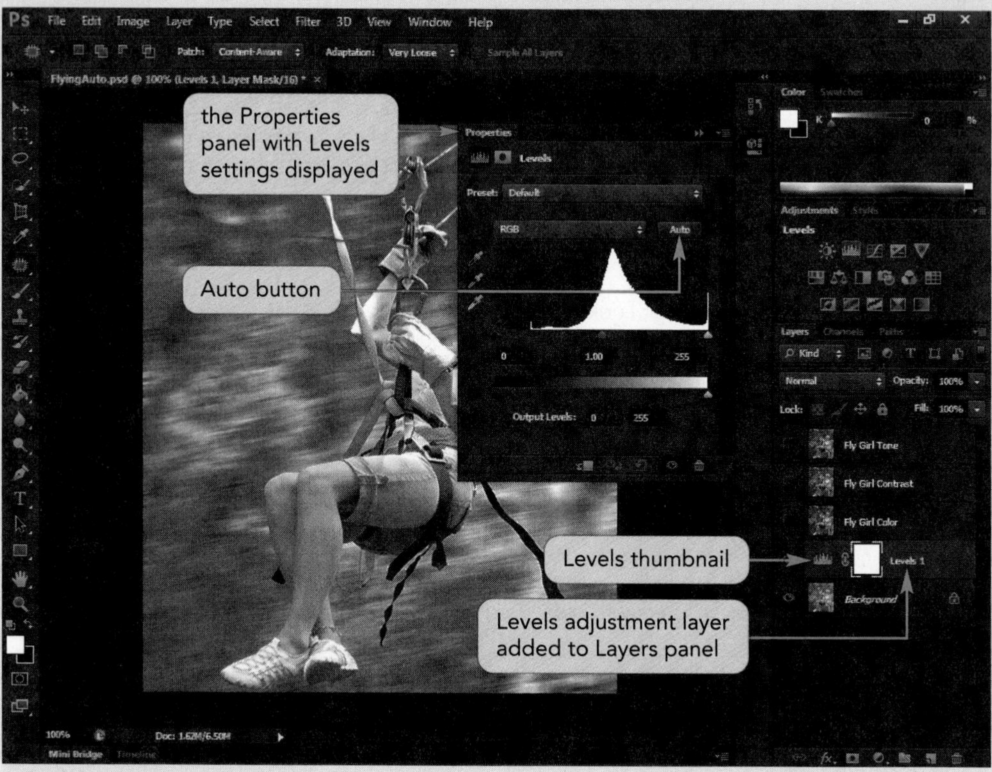

3. In the Properties panel, click the **Auto** button. The intensity of the shadows, midtones, and highlights of the image is adjusted.
4. Close the Properties panel to view the image.
5. In the Layers panel, click the **Eye** icon in the Show/Hide column next to the Levels 1 adjustment layer to hide that layer. Notice that the adjustments were made in the adjustment layer and that the Background layer remains unchanged.
6. In the Layers panel, double-click the **Levels** thumbnail for the Levels 1 adjustment layer to reopen the Properties panel.
7. In the Properties panel, click the **Preset** button and then click **Midtones Darker** to override the Auto adjustment you just made. Close the Properties panel to view the image.
8. Click the empty **Eye icon** box next to the Levels 1 adjustment layer to show that layer. See Figure 7-21.

Figure 7-21 **Midtones Darker preset Levels adjustment**

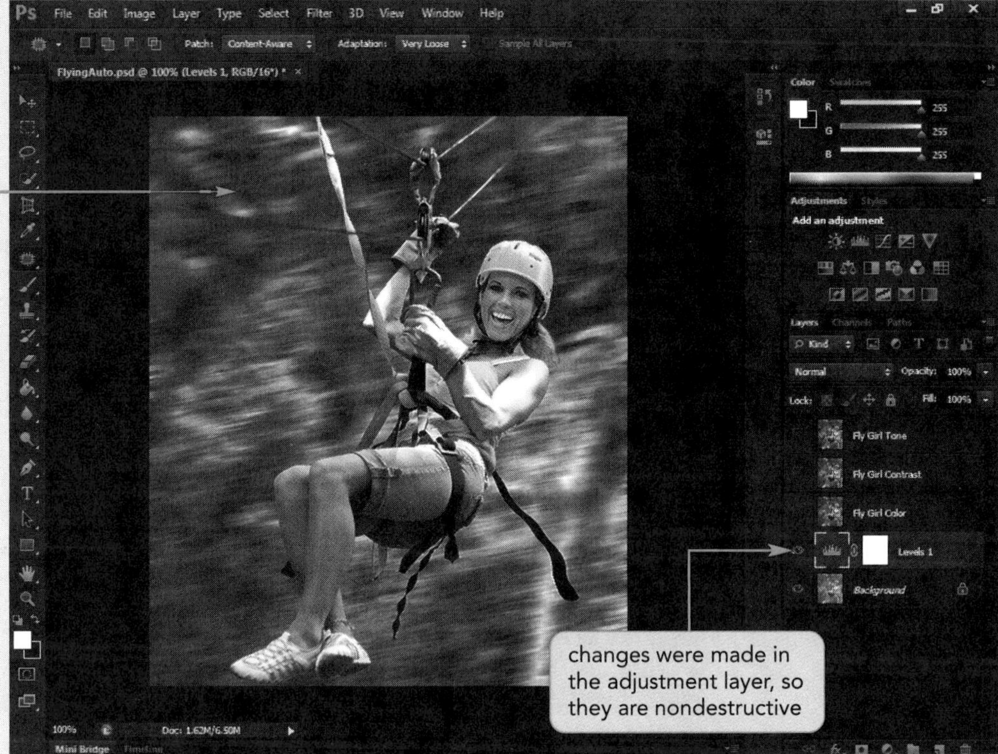
the shadows, midtones, and highlights were adjusted separately, creating better results
changes were made in the adjustment layer, so they are nondestructive
Fly Girl Tone
Fly Girl Contrast
Fly Girl Color
Levels 1
Background

© iStockphoto.com/Devon Stephens

Compare this layer with the Fly Girl Tone layer. The Levels adjustment produces better results than any of the other auto corrections because it provides you with more control by adjusting the shadows, midtones, and highlights of the image separately.

9. Save and close the image.

Dayne likes the results that you were able to achieve using the Levels adjustment and he has decided to include the image in the brochure. Next, you will make some changes to another image using manual adjustments in the Adjustments panel.

Using the Threshold Adjustment

As explained in Figure 7-19, the Threshold adjustment changes an image to a high-contrast black-and-white image. The Threshold Level slider enables you to adjust the **threshold level**, which is the pixel value above which all lighter pixels are changed to white and below which all darker pixels are changed to black. Moving the slider all the way to the right changes all pixels to white and moving the slider all the way to the left changes all pixels to black.

Primarily, this adjustment is used to create special effects. For example, you might change a photograph, which has millions of colors, to a two-color black-and-white image and then adjust the threshold level to create a dramatic composition. You could then use the Selective Color adjustment to change white and black to different colors, as shown in Figure 7-22.

Figure 7-22 Image with Threshold and Selective Color adjustments

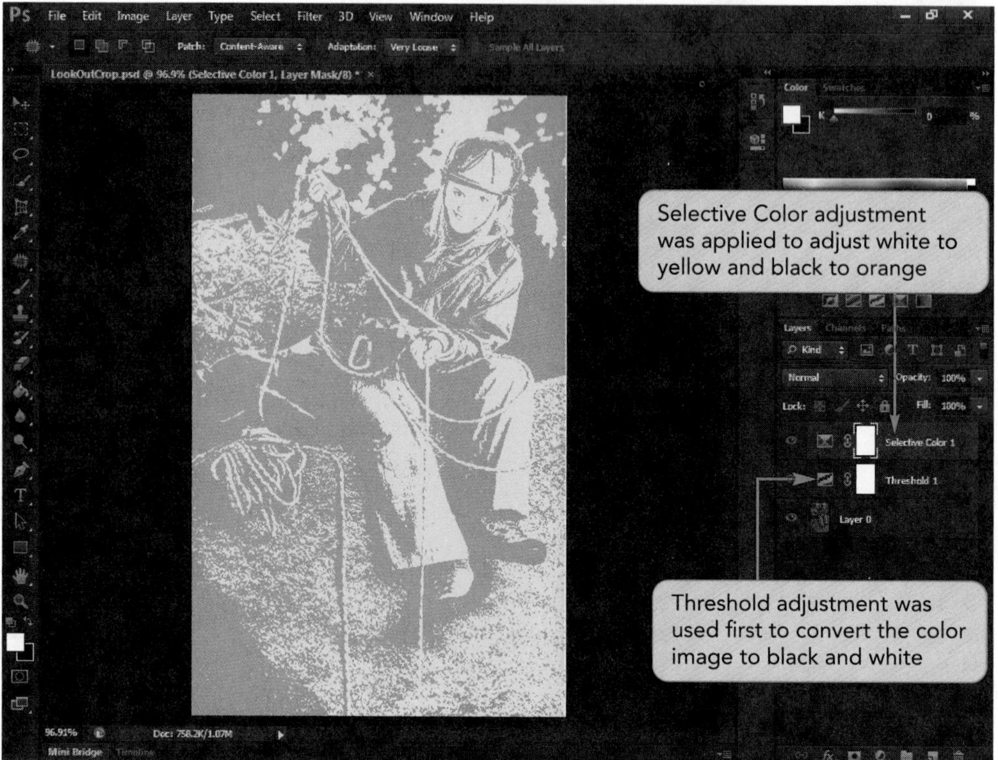
Selective Color adjustment was applied to adjust white to yellow and black to orange
Threshold adjustment was used first to convert the color image to black and white

CandyBox Images/Shutterstock.com

You can also use the Threshold adjustment to locate the darkest and lightest points in an image. To find the darkest pixels in your image, move the slider all the way to the left. Then, move it slightly toward the middle until some black pixels are displayed on the white background. The first points to appear are the darkest points in the image. To find the lightest pixels in the image, reverse the process, moving the slider all the way to the right and then back to the left until the first white pixel appears.

Once you have located the darkest or lightest pixels in an image, you can use the Color Sampler tool to add color markers to your image that will enable you to locate those points in the future. **Color markers** are identifiers that are only visible in Photoshop and that enable you to locate specific areas of color while you are adjusting your image. When you select a pixel with the Color Sampler tool, the Info panel opens; however, you might find it helpful to open the Info panel prior to selecting a pixel. As you move the tool over the image in the Document window, the Info panel displays the RGB values, CMYK values, and the X and Y values (the values that correspond to placement along the x- and y-axes of a graph) of the pixels over which you are moving the pointer.

Although Dayne was happy with the way you cropped the image of the young woman in climbing gear, he noted that the image looks a bit dull. He would like you to do some additional work to make the photo more vibrant and dynamic. Your first step in creating a more dramatic image is to locate the darkest and lightest points in the image. You'll use the Threshold adjustment to locate these points. Then, you'll use the Color Sampler tool with the Threshold adjustment to create color markers that enable you to identify the darkest and lightest pixels in your image. Finally, you'll increase the contrast of the image using the Curves adjustment by setting the darkest pixels to absolute black and setting the lightest pixels to absolute white.

REFERENCE

Marking Lightest and Darkest Pixels with the Threshold Adjustment

- In the Layers panel, click the layer you want to adjust.
- In the Adjustments panel, click the Threshold icon.
- In the Properties panel, move the Threshold Level slider all the way to the left and then slide it back toward the middle until some black pixels are displayed.
- In the Tools panel, click the Color Sampler Tool button, and then click the black pixels to create a marker over those pixels that will enable you to locate them again.
- Move the Threshold Level slider all the way to the right, and then slide it back toward the middle until some white pixels are displayed.
- Click the white pixels to create a marker over those pixels.

To locate the lightest and darkest points in the image:

1. Open the **LookOutCrop.psd** file that you saved in the Photoshop7\Tutorial folder, and then press the **Ctrl+0** keys to fit the image on screen.
2. In the Layers panel, click the **Layer 0** layer to select it, if necessary.
3. In the Adjustments panel, click the **Threshold** icon. The image is converted to black and white, and an adjustment layer named Threshold 1 is added above the Layer 0 layer in the Layers panel. The Properties panel opens to display the properties of the Threshold adjustment.
4. In the Properties panel, slide the **Threshold Level** slider to the left until the Threshold Level value reads **1**. The image is now entirely white. See Figure 7-23.

Figure 7-23 Image with Threshold at Level 1

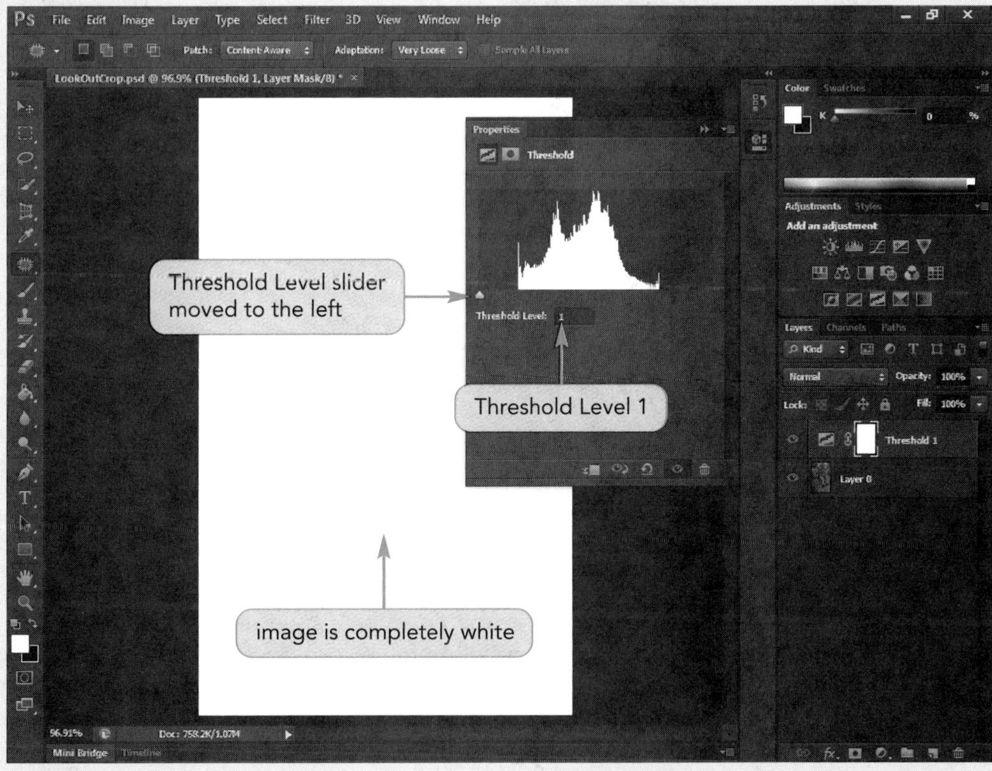

5. Slowly move the **Threshold Level** slider back to the right until several pixels of black are displayed together.
6. On the menu bar, click **Window**, and then click **Info** to open the Info panel.
7. In the Tools panel, click the **Color Sampler Tool** button, which is hidden beneath the Eye Dropper Tool button. Place the bottom edge of the Eye Dropper tool over the black pixels, make sure that a value of 0 is displayed beside R, G, and B in the 8-bit section of the Info panel, and click to add color marker 1 to the image. See Figure 7-24.

TIP

To remove a color marker, click the Color Sampler Tool button, if necessary, place the pointer over the color marker, and Alt-click the marker to delete it.

Figure 7-24 Threshold adjustment with color marker 1 inserted

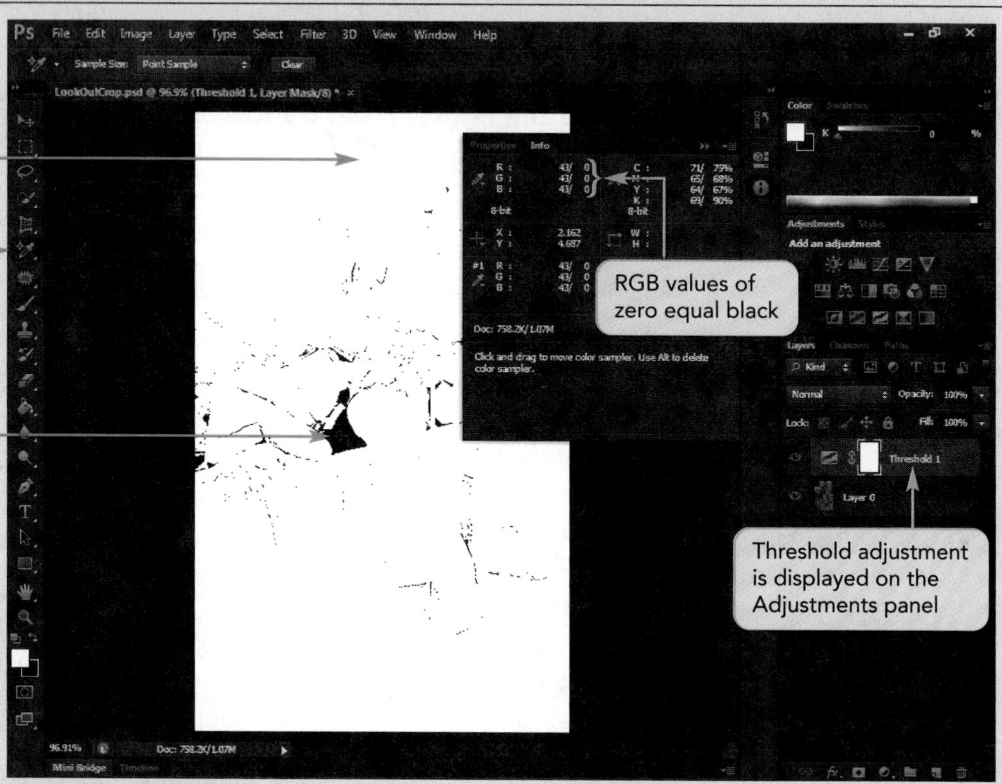
most of the image is white at this threshold level
Color Sampler tool selected
color marker 1 has been inserted over the darkest pixels in the image
RGB values of zero equal black
Threshold adjustment is displayed on the Adjustments panel

CandyBox Images/Shutterstock.com

Trouble? If the layout of your Info panel does not match that shown in Figure 7-24, click the panel menu button at the top of the Info panel, and then click Panel Options. In the Info Panel Options dialog box, click the Mode arrow, click Actual Color, and then click the OK button.

8. Click the **Properties** tab to display the Properties panel, slide the **Threshold Level** slider all the way to the right, and then slide it back to the left to display some white pixels.
9. Click the white pixels to place color marker 2 to mark the lightest pixels in the image. This time, the RGB values in the Info panel should all be **255**.
10. Close the Properties panel, and then in the Layers panel, drag the **Threshold 1** layer to the **Delete layer** icon to delete it. The color markers remain on the image. Notice that they are located over the darkest and lightest pixels in the image. See Figure 7-25. The location of your color markers might vary.

Figure 7-25 **Color markers 1 and 2 inserted**

color marker 2 marks the lightest pixels in the image
color marker 1 marks the darkest pixels in the image

CandyBox Images/Shutterstock.com

Now that you have identified the darkest and lightest pixels in the image, you'll use the Curves adjustment to correct the contrast, tone, and colors of the image.

Enhancing Images with the Curves Adjustment

The Curves adjustment is a robust adjustment that alters image contrast and tone by taking selected input tones and stretching or compressing their values using anchor points. Initially, the tonal range of any image is represented by a straight diagonal line that is displayed in the center of the Curves graph in the Adjustments panel. In this graph, the values of **Input tones** (the original value of the tones in the image when the Curves adjustment layer is first created) are represented horizontally, and the values of **Output tones** (the values of the same tones after adjustments are made) are represented vertically. The initial representation is a diagonal line because the original Input tones are equal to the Output tones—indicating that no adjustments have yet been made. As you alter the tones, anchor points are added to the line, and the line changes to a curve to visually represent the altered Output values of the tones you stretch or compress. The line is displayed over a histogram, which is a simple bar graph with two axes. The horizontal x-axis represents all of the possible brightness (also called luminance) values that can be displayed in an image starting at 0 (complete darkness) on the left and running to 255 (the brightest white) on the right. This means that the center of the x-axis represents the midtones of the image. The vertical y-axis represents the number of pixels in the image that display a particular luminance value, starting with 0 pixels at its lowest point and moving upward. There are several different ways to adjust an image using the Curves adjustment. See Figure 7-26.

Figure 7-26 Curves adjustment

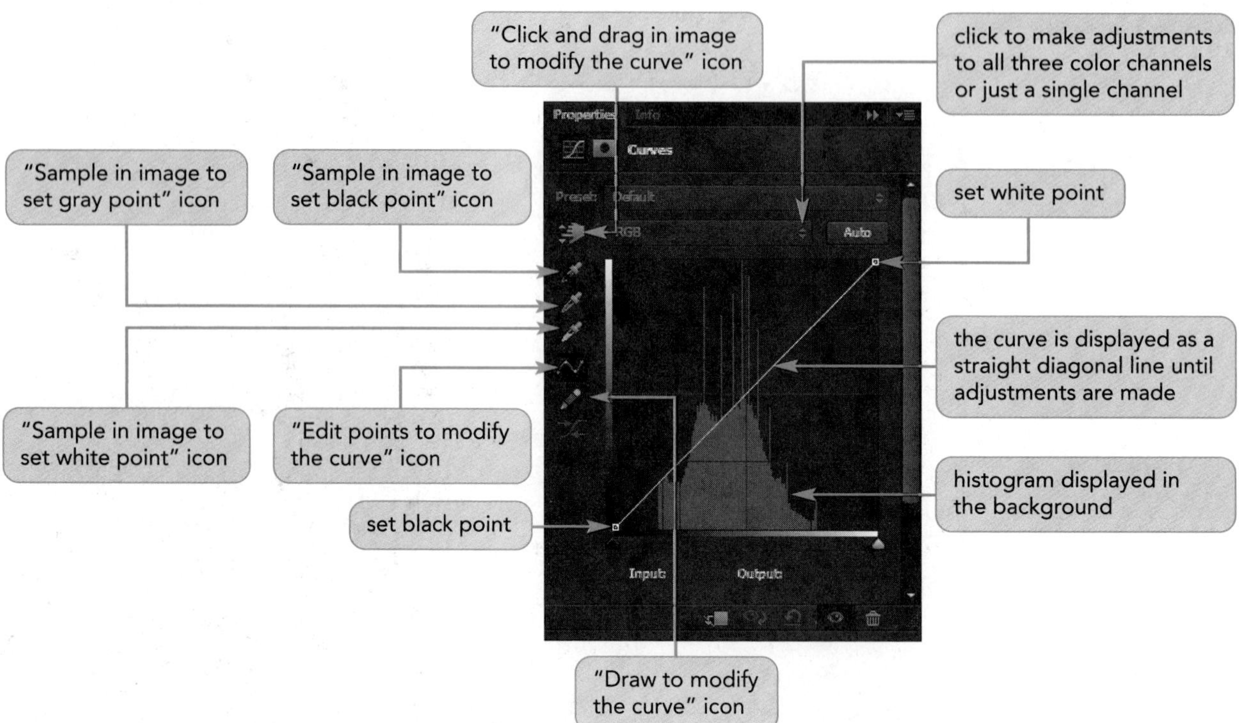

You'll add a Curves adjustment to enhance the LookOutCrop.psd image. First, you'll use the eyedropper icons in the Adjustments panel to set the white point and the black point of the image. When you set the white point, you click on a point in the image (in this case, you'll click in color marker 2), and that point changes to absolute white. When you set the black point, you click on a point in the image (in this case, you'll click in color marker 1), and that point changes to absolute black. The remaining pixels in the image adjust proportionately and the contrast in the image is increased. If an image is dull or flat, this adjustment produces a more rich and vibrant image.

REFERENCE

Setting the White and Black Points of an Image

- In the Layers panel, click the layer you would like to adjust.
- In the Adjustments panel, click the Curves icon.
- In the Properties panel, click the "Sample in image to set black point" icon, and click the darkest point in the image to change the value of that point to absolute black.
- Click the "Sample in image to set white point" icon, and click the lightest point in the image to change the value of that point to absolute white.

To set the white point and black point of the image:

1. In the Adjustments panel, click the **Curves** icon. An adjustment layer is added above the Layer 0 layer in the Layers panel, and the Properties panel opens.

2. Drag the bottom edge of the Properties panel down until the Input and Output labels are visible, click the **Sample in image to set black point** icon, and then click in the image in color marker 1. The darkest pixels are now set to absolute black. You will notice a dramatic change in the image as the darkest pixels are set to black. Toggle the Properties panel closed and open, if necessary, to better see the change in the image.
3. In the Properties panel, click the **Sample in image to set white point** icon, and then click in color marker 2 in the image. The lightest pixels are set to absolute white, and the contrast of the image is increased, creating a more vibrant composition.

   The new blue diagonal line in the Curves graph in the Properties panel reflects the changes that you have made to the image. See Figure 7-27.

Figure 7-27 Image with white point and black point adjusted

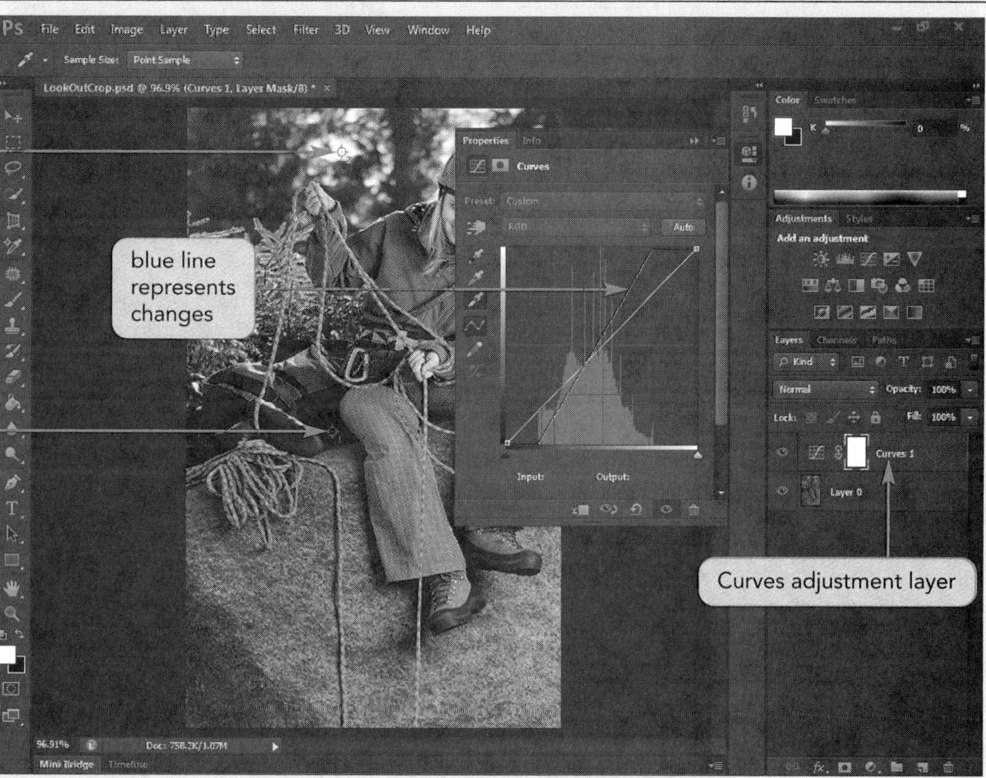
whites are brighter and the image has increased contrast
blue line represents changes
the darkest pixels are much darker
Curves adjustment layer

CandyBox Images/Shutterstock.com

Trouble? If, in addition to the new blue line, you see red and green lines in the Curves panel, it means that the red, green, and blue values are slightly different. This will not affect the outcome of your adjustments.

You can also use the Curves adjustment to change the highlights, midtones, and shadows of an image. The midtones of the image are represented by the center area of the Curves grid, and making adjustments to that area of the line will have the strongest effect on the midtones of the image. Highlights are represented by the area above the center of the grid, and making adjustments to that area of the line will have the strongest effect on the highlights of the image. Finally, the shadows are represented by the area below the center of the grid, and making adjustments to that portion of the line will have the strongest effect on the shadows of the image. See Figure 7-28.

Figure 7-28 Highlights, midtones, and shadows on the Curves graph

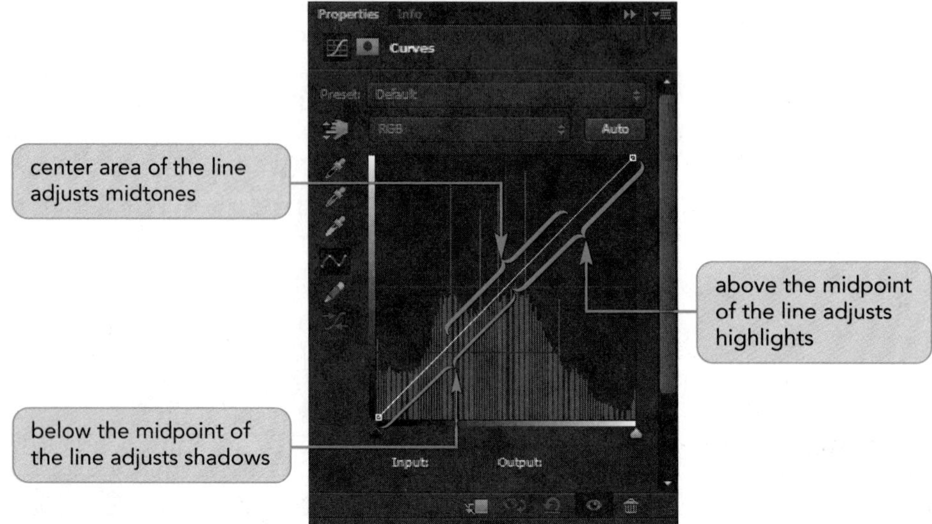
center area of the line adjusts midtones
above the midpoint of the line adjusts highlights
below the midpoint of the line adjusts shadows
Properties
Curves
Auto
Input:
Output:

Note that there is not a cutoff point between where highlights end and midtones begin, or between where midtones end and shadows begin. The areas of overlap, shown in Figure 7-28, demonstrate that the high midtones are also the low highlights. This way of thinking is in line with the way your eyes view things. Most people do not distinguish a specific point at which shadow begins; rather, when you look at something, you see a range of tonalities that flow subtly from lighter to darker.

One way to locate the tones that fall into a certain area of the grid is to click the "Click and drag in image to modify the curve" icon in the Curves panel. The pointer changes to an eyedropper, and as you move the pointer over the image, a circle is displayed over the diagonal line. When the circle is displayed over the midpoint of the line, located at the center of the grid, you have located the center of the midtones in the image. When the circle is displayed on the line over the third vertical grid line, you have located the center of the highlights. If you click in the image and drag up and down, you can adjust the value of the tones represented by that point on the line. The line will become curved to reflect the changes you make. The curve represents the change in value between the original input value of the tones and the new value of the adjusted tones.

> **TIP**
> A good point for adjusting highlights is the middle of the highlights—halfway between the midpoint and top of the line, where the grid lines intersect.

To further enhance the LookOutCrop.psd image, you'll lighten the highlights in the image slightly to give the image more fullness. To maximize the effect of your adjustment across the range of highlight tones, you'll select the center point of the highlights. This is the point located halfway between the center of the line and the top of the line, where the vertical and horizontal grid line intersect under the line.

To adjust the highlights of the image:

1. In the Properties panel, click the **Click and drag in image to modify the curve** icon.
2. Place the pointer in the image, over the young woman's right hand, and then move the pointer around on her hand until the circle is located over the third vertical grid line in the Curves panel. (Remember that her right hand is the hand that is on the left when you are looking at the image.) The Input and Output values at the bottom of the Properties panel should both be about 192 when the pointer is over the middle of the highlights. See Figure 7-29.

Figure 7-29 **Modify the curve by dragging in the image**

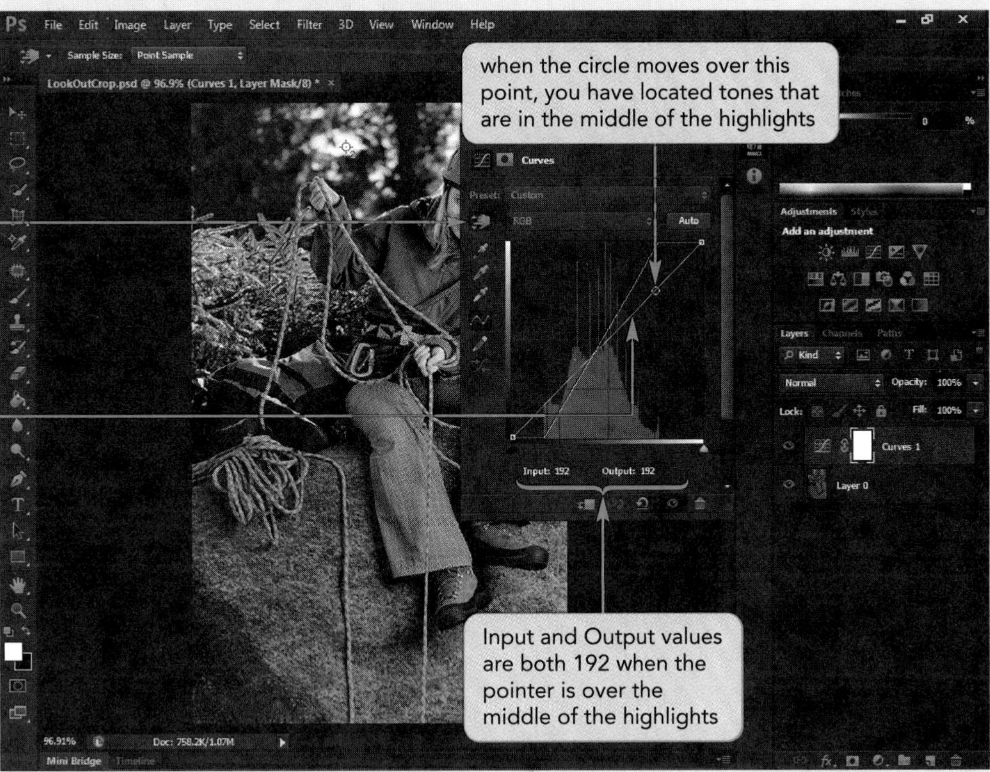

when the circle moves over this point, you have located tones that are in the middle of the highlights
"Click and drag in image to modify the curve" icon
the circle moves over the line as you move the pointer over different areas in the image to reflect the value of the tones being sampled
Input and Output values are both 192 when the pointer is over the middle of the highlights

CandyBox Images/Shutterstock.com

3. Click in the image and then drag the pointer up slightly until the Output value shown below the Curves graph on the Adjustment panel is **210** and the Input value is **192**, and then release the mouse button.

   Trouble? If you have difficulty getting these exact values by dragging the pointer in the image, enter 192 in the Input box and 210 in the Output box.

   As the curve is stretched upward on the Properties panel, the tones of the image, especially the highlights where the anchor is located, become lighter. See Figure 7-30.

Figure 7-30 **Highlights of the image adjusted**

image is lighter, especially in the highlight areas
new anchor point has been added, and the line has been stretched into a curve
at the anchor point, the Input of 192 has been stretched to an Output value of 210

CandyBox Images/Shutterstock.com

4. Close the Properties panel, and in the Layers panel, click the **Eye** icon beside the Curves 1 layer to make the layer invisible. Notice how this affects the way the image looks.
5. In the Layers panel, click the empty **Eye icon** box to make the Curves 1 adjustment layer visible.

You can also create and edit anchor points to modify the curve. You'll create a new anchor point at the center of the grid, which is the center of the midtones, and you'll move the anchor point down to darken the midtones of the image. By selecting the center point of the midtones to create your adjustment point, you ensure that your adjustments will have an effect on the lighter and darker midtones in the image. If you were to select a point that was in the darker range of the midtones, your adjustments would affect the deepest midtones and the lightest shadows. Making this adjustment will give some balance and richness to all of the midtones in the image.

To create and modify anchor points:

1. Open the Properties panel, click the **Edit points to modify the curve** icon to select it, if necessary, and then click on the curve where it crosses the center vertical grid line. Photoshop adds an anchor point to the curve where you clicked.
2. Drag the anchor point down until the Output is **128** and the Input is **128**. Notice how making this slight change adds balance to the image. See Figure 7-31.

Figure 7-31 New anchor point added to adjust midtones

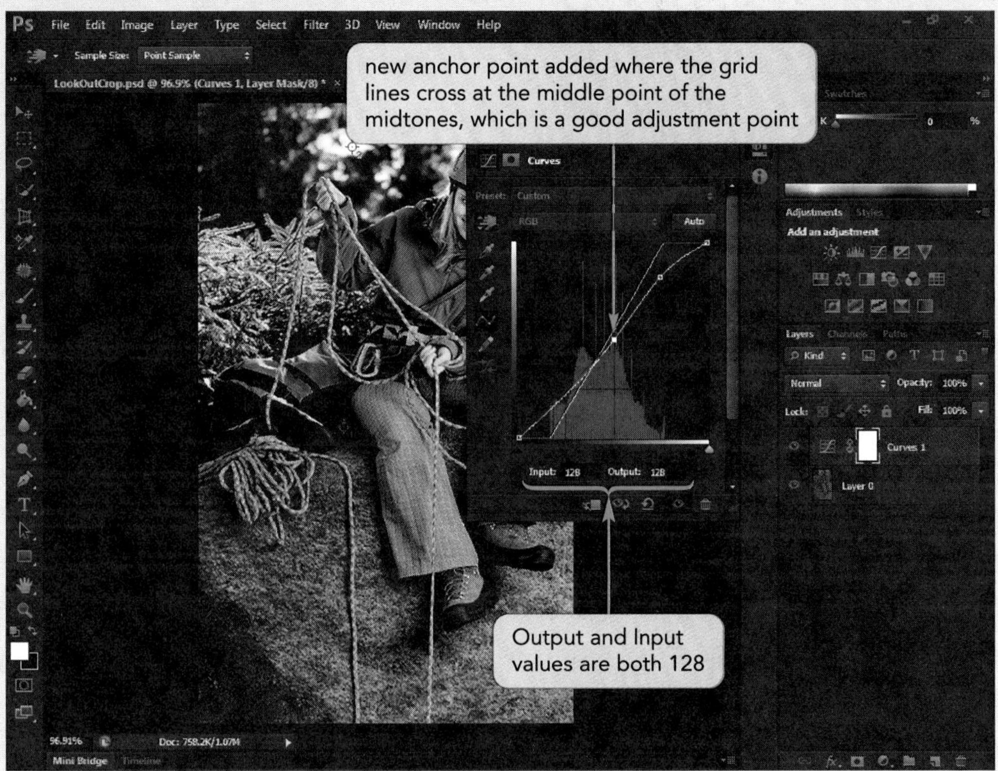
new anchor point added where the grid lines cross at the middle point of the midtones, which is a good adjustment point
Output and Input values are both 128

CandyBox Images/Shutterstock.com

3. Save the image, and close the Properties panel. See Figure 7-32.

Figure 7-32 Image with darker midtones

darkening the midtones adds depth and richness to the image

CandyBox Images/Shutterstock.com

4. Close the file, and then exit Photoshop.

Dayne is thrilled with the images that you have corrected thus far and with the progress of the project. He has approved the adjusted images for use in the brochure.

In this session, you learned that the first step in creating a professionally corrected image is to rotate and crop the image. You learned how to rotate and crop images, and you learned how to use the Rule of Thirds. As you explored how to frame an image to focus a viewer's eye on the most important elements, you also learned how to adjust the the Content-Aware Move tool's settings and use the Patch tool to move and remove objects in an image, with professional-looking results. The next step in the image-correction process is to perform color and tonal corrections. In this session, you adjusted images with the auto correction tools and went on to perform more complex corrections with the Levels, Threshold, and Curves adjustment tools. The final step in image correction is to use retouching tools to correct smaller imperfections and flaws in the image. In the next session, you'll retouch some of the images for the brochure.

REVIEW

Session 7.1 Quick Check

1. What is the Rule of Thirds?
2. What is the quickest way to adjust the contrast, tone, and color of an image?
3. True or False. The Auto Tone, Auto Contrast, and Auto Color correction tools make nondestructive edits to your images.
4. ______________ are layers in which you can make nondestructive edits to images and compositions.
5. The Threshold adjustment enables you to create ______________ images.
6. The ______________ adjustment enables you to alter contrast and tone by taking selected input tones and stretching or compressing them using anchor points.
7. What is hue?

SESSION 7.2 VISUAL OVERVIEW

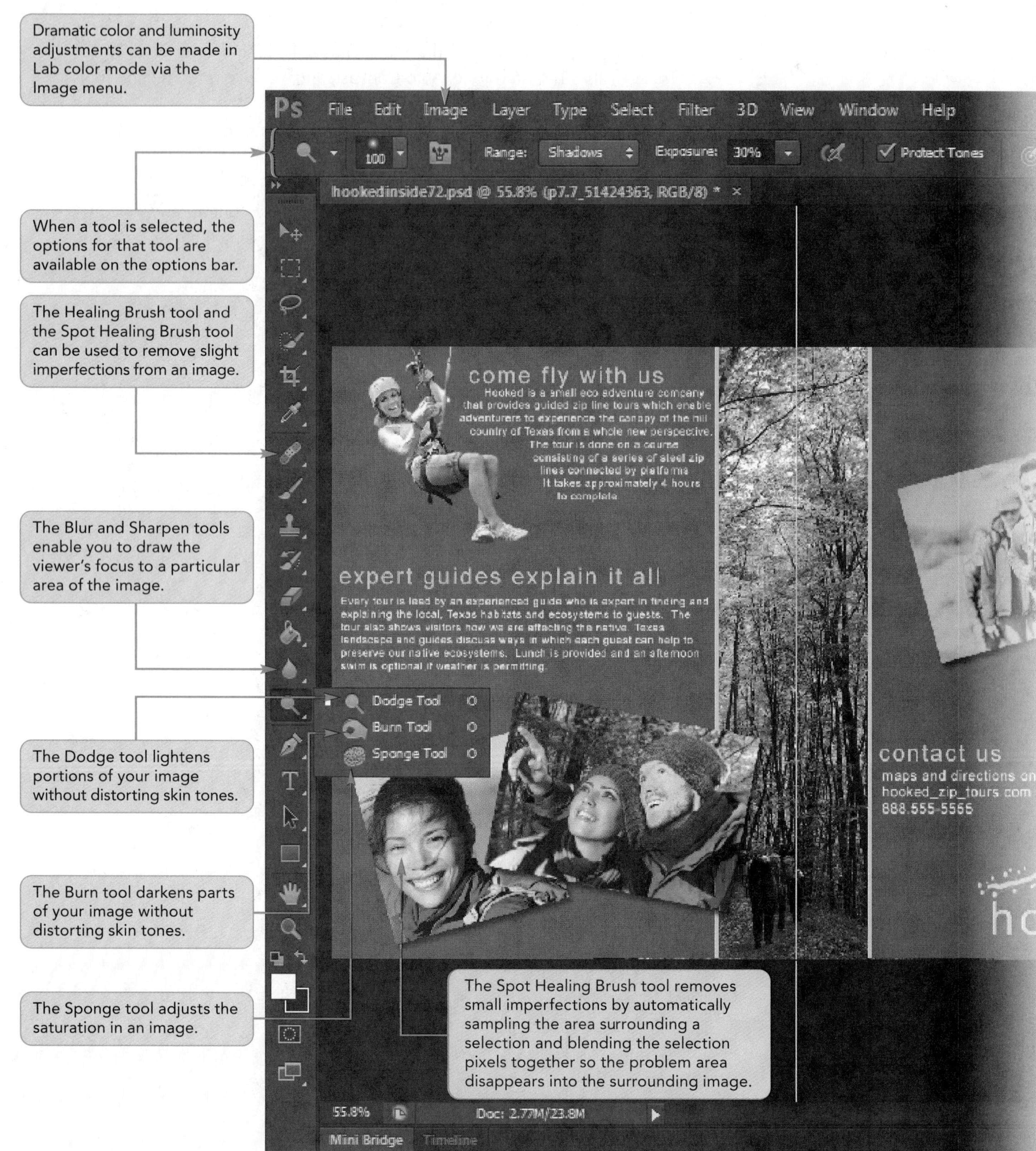
Dramatic color and luminosity adjustments can be made in Lab color mode via the Image menu.
When a tool is selected, the options for that tool are available on the options bar.
The Healing Brush tool and the Spot Healing Brush tool can be used to remove slight imperfections from an image.
The Blur and Sharpen tools enable you to draw the viewer's focus to a particular area of the image.
The Dodge tool lightens portions of your image without distorting skin tones.
The Burn tool darkens parts of your image without distorting skin tones.
The Sponge tool adjusts the saturation in an image.
The Spot Healing Brush tool removes small imperfections by automatically sampling the area surrounding a selection and blending the selection pixels together so the problem area disappears into the surrounding image.
File Edit Image Layer Type Select Filter 3D View Window Help
Range: Shadows
Exposure: 30%
Protect Tones
hookedinside72.psd @ 55.8% (p7.7_51424363, RGB/8) *
come fly with us
expert guides explain it all
Dodge Tool O
Burn Tool O
Sponge Tool O
contact us
888.555-5555
55.8%
Doc: 2.77M/23.8M
Mini Bridge
Timeline

RETOUCHING TOOLS

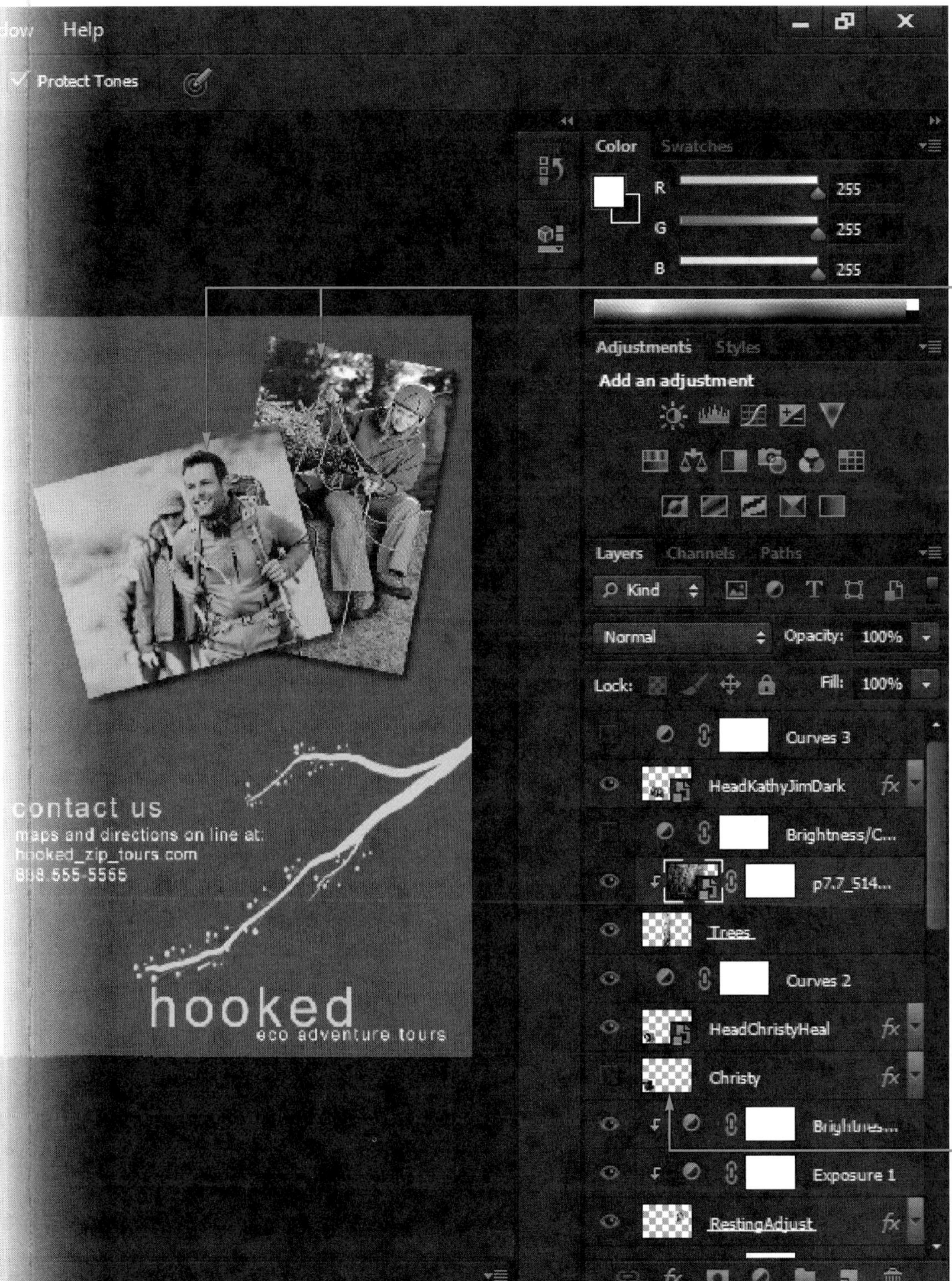

Retouching tools are used to remove small imperfections from an image or to correct areas of the image that still need help after color and tonal corrections are made to the entire image.

When you can use the Healing or Spot Healing Brush tool on a blank layer above the layer you would like to affect, the adjustments are nondestructive.

Repairing and Retouching Images

Almost any photograph can benefit from a little retouching, and Photoshop offers a virtual first aid kit full of tools that enable you to smooth backgrounds, perform localized color correction, fix blemishes, and patch problems. There are also tools for red-eye correction and tools that help you adjust skin tone and sharpness. In this section, you'll use Photoshop's retouching tools to improve some photographs of the tour guides that Dayne provided for the Hooked brochure.

Repairing Images with the Spot Healing Brush Tool

TIP

The Spot Healing Brush tool is not a good tool for correcting large areas in an image because the tool produces artificial looking results in large areas.

The Spot Healing Brush tool is used to remove slight imperfections or problems from an image by automatically taking samples from the area surrounding the part of the image that is being retouched and blending them together so texture and tone cause the problem area to disappear into the surrounding image. This brush is frequently used to fix blemishes and other small imperfections. You can apply the Spot Healing Brush tool directly to the image that you want to correct; however, this creates a destructive edit. A better choice is to create a blank layer above the image that you want to retouch and then apply the brush to that layer with the Sample All Layers check box checked. In this scenario, the alteration is created in the blank layer and is nondestructive. The settings on the options bar for the Spot Healing Brush tool include the following:

- **Brush**—The brush you select determines the shape and size of the area that will be affected. It is best to select a round brush that is slightly larger in diameter than the area you would like to repair.
- **Mode**—The Mode setting controls the painting mode, which determines how pixels in the image are affected by the tool. The blending modes available with the Spot Healing Brush tool are a subset of those available when you are blending layers.
- **Type**—The Type setting enables you to determine how the pixels used to heal the problem area will be selected. The Proximity Match option uses the pixels just outside the edges of the brush area to heal the brush area. The Create Texture option creates texture by examining the pixels within the brush area; this option is often used when the problem area is surrounded by a great deal of detail. The Content-Aware option is a good starting point. The Content-Aware Type setting takes information into account using intelligent algorithms that give you the best shot at a clean fix.
- **Sample All Layers**—This setting enables you to gather healing information from all of the layers in the document. If you want to use this setting, it must be checked when you apply the Spot Healing Brush tool to an empty layer above the image.

Dayne would like to use some shots of the Hooked tour guides in the brochure. You'll use the Spot Healing Brush tool to fix a shiny spot on the headshot of Christy, one of the Hooked tour guides.

REFERENCE

Applying the Spot Healing Brush Tool to an Image

- Create an empty layer above the layer that you would like to adjust.
- Click the empty layer, and in the Tools panel, click the Spot Healing Brush Tool button.
- On the options bar, select a brush size that is slightly larger than the area you would like to alter, select a painting mode, select a type, and click the Sample All Layers check box to select it. Confirm that the empty layer is the active layer.
- Place the brush over the area of the image you would like to heal, and press the Enter key.

To correct an imperfection with the Spot Healing Brush tool:

1. Start Photoshop while pressing the **Ctrl+Alt+Shift** keys, and click **Yes** to delete the Settings File when prompted. Reset Photoshop to the default Essentials workspace layout, and then reset all tools.
2. Navigate to the Photoshop 7\Tutorial folder, open **HeadChristy.psd**, and save the file as **HeadChristyHeal.psd** in the same folder.
3. Press the **Ctrl+0** keys to fit the image to the screen, and then in the Layers panel, click the **Background** layer to select it, if necessary. Press the **X** key to switch the default background and foreground colors.
4. In the Layers panel, click the **Create a new layer** icon to add a new layer above the Background layer; name the new layer **Heal Shine**.
5. In the Tools panel, click the **Spot Healing Brush Tool** button.
6. On the options bar, click the **Brush picker** button, and set the brush size to **30 px**. Click the **Mode** button, and select **Normal** as the painting mode, if necessary. Select **Content-Aware** as the Type, and click the **Sample All Layers** check box to select it.
7. Place the pointer over the shiny circular spot on the tip of Christy's nose and click. The image is corrected. See Figure 7-33.

   Trouble? If your selection does not produce results you like, undo the adjustment by pressing the Ctrl+Z keys, and repeat Step 7.

Figure 7-33 Spot Healing Brush tool applied to image

8. Save the image, and keep it open for the next set of steps.

Repairing Images with the Healing Brush Tool

The Healing Brush tool is like the Spot Healing Brush tool's bigger, tougher brother. It has all of the capabilities of the Spot Healing Brush tool, and it enables you to select the pixels that will be used as a sample to create the healing effects. This is a better choice when you are working with larger or more complex areas because it provides you with more control.

The Healing Brush tool can be found in the Tools panel under the Spot Healing Brush tool. Additional options for the Healing Brush tool include the following:

- **Source**—You can select the source for the sample pixels that you will use to heal your image. With the Sampled option, you Alt-click in the image, or in any image that is open in Photoshop, at the point where you would like your pixel sample to begin. The Pattern option allows you to select one of the patterns in the Pattern picker as the source for your brush.
- **Aligned**—When the Aligned check box is selected, your sample point stays aligned to your pointer even if you release the mouse and move to a different area. If the Aligned check box is not checked, the original sample point is used each time you start to paint with your healing brush.
- **Sample**—The Sample options enable you to select the layer, or layers, that the tool will use when sampling pixels; choices include Current Layer, Current & Below, or All Layers.

First, you'll experiment with using a pattern as the source for the Healing Brush tool so you can get a sense of how you can use this brush option. Then, you'll use the Healing Brush tool to smooth some of the wrinkles under Christy's eyes.

To add a pattern using the Healing Brush tool:

1. In the Layers panel, add a new layer above the Heal Shine layer and name the new layer **Fix Squint Wrinkles**.
2. In the Tools panel, click the **Healing Brush Tool** button.
3. On the options bar, use the Brush picker to select a brush size of **138 px**. Set the Mode to **Multiply**, select **Pattern** for the Source, and then click the **Pattern** thumbnail to open the Pattern picker.
4. In the Pattern picker, click the **Bubbles** pattern (the first pattern) to select it.

   Trouble? If you do not see Bubbles in your list of patterns, you might have a different Pattern group open. On the right side of the Pattern picker, click the More options button, click Patterns in the context menu, and click the OK button to replace the current patterns. Do not save changes to the current patterns.
5. On the options bar, click the **Aligned** check box to select it. Click the **Sample** button, and then click **Current & Below**.
6. Ensure that the Fix Squint Wrinkles layer is active, and paint over Christy's forehead area. Although the pattern is very visible as you paint, when you release the mouse button, the Healing Brush tool uses the settings you specified to blend the pattern with the layers below it, creating a unique, translucent effect. Congratulations—you have turned Christy into an alien. See Figure 7-34.

Figure 7-34 Pattern applied using the Healing Brush tool

Patterns can be useful and sometimes fun. However, in this case, the effect is not suitable for the Hooked brochure. Next, you'll remove the Bubble pattern from the image, and use the Healing Brush tool to remove the slight puffiness under Christy's eyes.

To retouch the image using the Healing Brush tool:

1. On menu bar, click **Edit**, and then click **Step Backward** until the bubble pattern is removed from Christy's face.
2. On the options bar, use the Brush picker to change the brush size to **20 px**. Set the Mode to **Normal**, and select **Sampled** for the Source. Now, you'll select a pixel source.
3. Zoom the image to **100%**, and pan the image, if necessary, so that Christy's right eye is displayed in the Document window. (Note that Christy's right eye appears on the left side of the image.)
4. On the Tools panel, click the **Healing Brush Tool** button again, if necessary. Place the pointer at the inner edge of Christy's right eye, below the puffy area, and then Alt-click to select the pixels for your source.
5. Place the pointer over inner edge of the puffy area of the right eye and paint over the puffiness and wrinkles to smooth them. Remember that your source pixels started at the inner edge of the eye, so when you paint, you need to start at the inner edge of the eye and move outward making one long stroke. Make a second pass with the brush, if necessary. See Figure 7-35.

TIP

Select pixels as close as possible to the area you want to heal to provide the most realistic and accurate results.

Figure 7-35 **Wrinkles and puffiness under right eye smoothed with the Healing Brush tool**

Source is set to Sampled
retouched area
pixel sample as source
nondestructive repair is added to this layer

Trouble? If your result does not look like the figure, step backward, and try again. This process takes some practice and finesse, especially when there is an obstacle, like a strand of hair, in the way.

Now you'll use the Healing Brush tool to remove some of the shadow under Christy's left eye.

6. Reposition the image in the Document window so that Christy's left eye is displayed.
7. Make sure the Healing Brush tool is still selected, and place the pointer at the inner edge of Christy's left eye, below the darker area, and then Alt-click to select the pixels for your source.
8. Place the pointer over the darker area at the inner edge of the left eye and paint over it. Make a second pass if necessary but this is a more subtle fix, so don't be heavy-handed.

Finally, you will remove the strand of hair that is lying across Christy's face near her left eye. Don't get discouraged if you make a pass that produces weird results, just undo the pass and try again. Fixing more complex problems will give you the practice you need to perfect your skill with this tool.

9. Place the pointer to the left of the bottom of the strand of hair and Alt-click to select the pixels for your source.
10. Place the pointer over the bottom of the strand of hair and follow it upward stopping below the eye.

11. Repeat Steps 9 and 10 as necessary, using source pixels close to the area that you are adjusting, until you are happy with the results, and then move above the eye and continue until you are happy with the results. (In some places, you might get better results with long strokes, whereas short strokes might work better in other spots. You may also need to vary the size of your brush.) See Figure 7-36.

Figure 7-36 **Puffiness smoothed and hair removed with the Healing Brush tool**

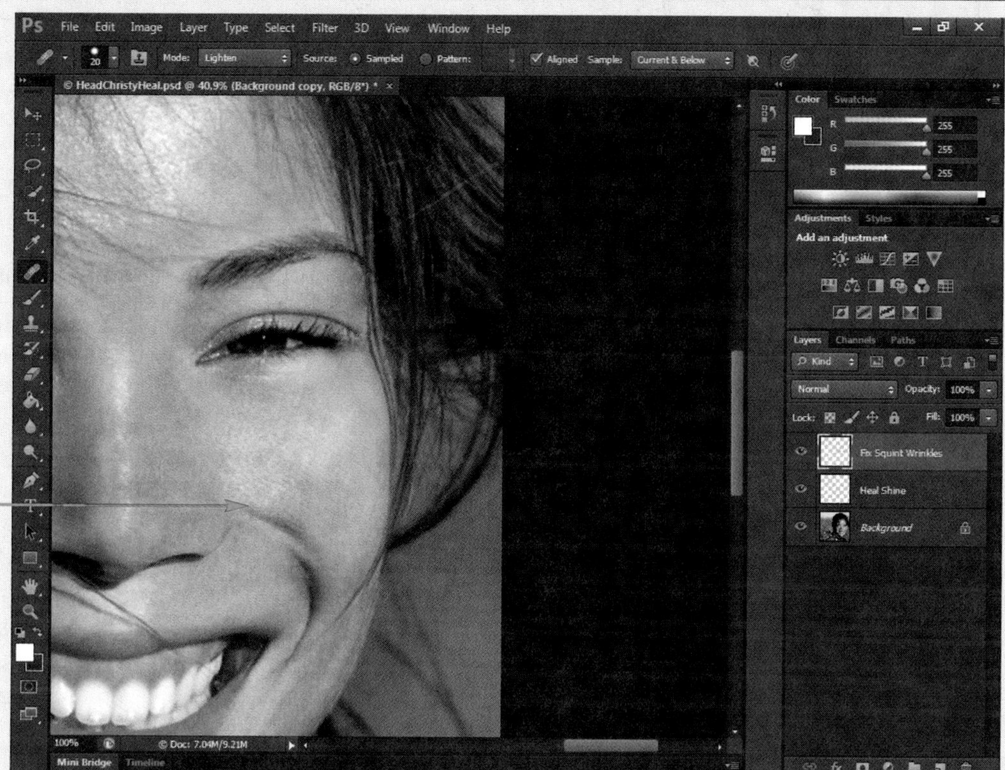

© iStockphoto.com/Maridav

Notice that a few wrinkles and stray hairs are left on Christy's face to maintain a realistic feel.

12. Save the image, and keep it open for the next set of steps.

INSIGHT

Retouching and Repairing Images of People

Photoshop offers some tools that can be particularly helpful when you are working with images of people. For instance, you can use the Color Range tool on the Select menu to help you select a subject's skin to make adjustments to skin tone. In the Color Range dialog box, set the Select option to Skin Tones, and select the Detect Faces check box to increase the tool's reliability in detecting facial features. The Red Eye tool is another useful tool for repairing images of people. As its name implies, the Red Eye tool is used to retouch red eyes, which are caused by the reflection of a camera flash. The Red Eye tool is in the same tool group as the Spot Healing Brush tool and the Healing Brush tool. After selecting the Red Eye tool, click in each affected eye. You can adjust the Pupil Size and Darkness settings on the options bar to fine-tune the effect of the tool. Photoshop's wide array of retouching tools provide you with many ways to improve your images, and tools such as these, along with the Spot Healing Brush and Healing Brush tools, are especially effective at improving images of people.

Next, you'll use the Dodge and Burn tools to adjust the brightness and darkness of specific areas in an image.

Retouching with the Dodge Tool

The Dodge tool allows you to perform localized color correction by brightening small areas of an image, such as areas that are in a shadow. When the Protect Tones option for this tool is selected, shadow clipping is minimized, and the Dodge tool attempts to brighten without shifting the hue of affected colors. This produces more realistic and subtle adjustments, especially when working with skin tones. The Dodge tool allows you to select the tonal region to which changes are applied. You can brighten the highlights, midtones, or shadows of an image discreetly, and that provides you with added control. When painting with the Dodge tool, you can also adjust the exposure of the brush, which has the effect of adjusting the opacity of the changes.

Although it is an effective tool, the Dodge tool is a destructive tool. When using it, you should make a copy of the layer you will adjust and apply the changes to that copy, preserving the original layer in case the changes go awry. When you paint with the Dodge tool, each time you pass over an area with the brush, it increases the effect of the dodge.

Because there are other, nondestructive tools that enable you to adjust the brightness of an image, a good rule to use is: If the area you want to brighten is more than 25 percent of the image, you should consider using a nondestructive tool. For example, you could use a Brightness/Contrast adjustment layer with a mask that prevents it from affecting the areas you want to remain unchanged.

REFERENCE

Brightening an Image with the Dodge Tool

- In the Layers panel, click the layer you would like to adjust, if necessary.
- Duplicate the layer, and then click the duplicate layer to make it active.
- In the Tools panel, click the Dodge Tool button, and on the options bar, select a brush and a brush size. Select the range and exposure, and then click the Protect Tones check box to select it.
- Paint the areas of the image that you would like to lighten until you achieve the desired effect.

You'll use the Dodge tool to brighten some of the shadows on Christy's face and hair.

To lighten shadows in the photograph:

1. In the Layers panel, duplicate the **Background** layer, and use the default layer name, Background copy.
2. In the Layers panel, click the **Background copy** layer to select it, if necessary, and then press the **Ctrl+0** keys to fit the image on screen.
3. In the Tools panel, click the **Dodge Tool** button.
4. On the options bar, click the **Brush picker** button, and set the brush size to **100 px**.
5. On the options bar, click the **Range** button, and then click **Shadows**. Set the Exposure to **30%**, and then click the **Protect Tones** check box to select it, if necessary.
6. Paint the top of Christy's head and the right side of her face (which is on the left side of the image) to lighten the shadows in her hair and along the edge of her face. Target the darker areas, so you do not end up with too much artificial lightness in the lighter areas. Decrease the size of the brush to reach smaller areas, if necessary, and decrease the Exposure setting on the options bar to decrease the opacity of changes.
7. Save the file, and close it.

TIP

Each pass over an area increases the effect of the tool, so use multiple passes only in areas that need additional lightening.

When you compare Christy's initial headshot photograph with the final retouched photograph, you can see significant improvement in the final product. See Figure 7-37.

Figure 7-37 **Compare starting image with retouched image**

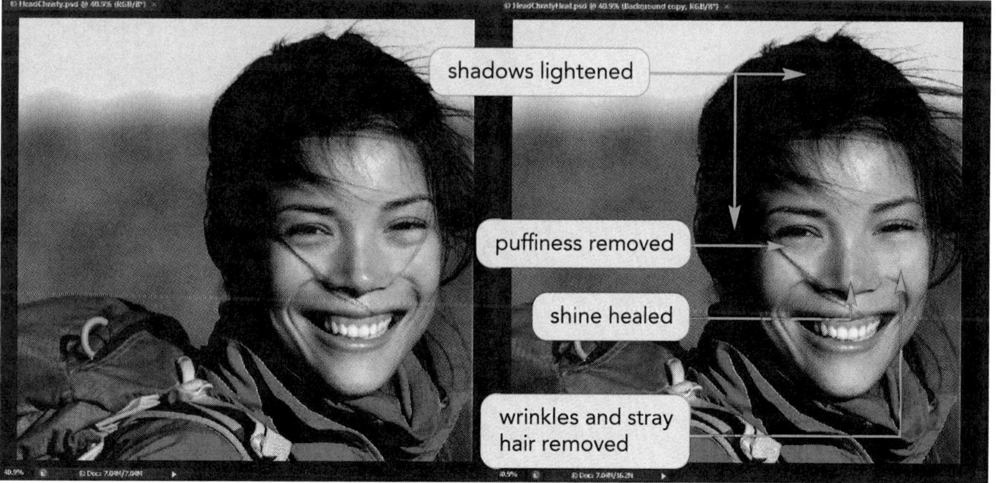

Next, you'll use the Burn tool to darken an image background to draw focus to the subject of the photo.

Retouching with the Burn Tool

The Burn tool allows you to perform localized color correction by darkening small areas of an image in the same way that the Dodge tool allows you to brighten them. The Burn tool can be found in the Tools panel under the Dodge tool, and it has all of the features and limitations of the Dodge tool. Although it produces the opposite outcome, darkening instead of brightening, it works in the same way.

INSIGHT

Making Small Changes with Big Results

When using tools such as Dodge and Burn, keep in mind that the effects of the changes you make are cumulative and, therefore, making several subtle changes can create a big impact on the final image. For example, if you are correcting an image of a person, darkening the highlights of the image might make only a small change. However, once you have darkened the highlights, the midtones, and the shadows as needed, and you have brightened the highlights, midtones, and shadows, as needed, the photo will usually have a much different look. For this reason, it is a good idea to make small changes to all of the areas that need retouching, then, once you have examined the image, you can repeat the process until you achieve the look you desire.

Dayne has provided another headshot of two tour guides; however, the image is flat because the shadows of the image are not very different from the midtones. You'll add depth to the image by creating more dramatic shadows. Because it is an excellent tool for darkening areas of an image, while maintaining skin tones, you'll use the Burn tool.

To darken areas of the photograph:

1. Open **HeadKathyJim.psd**, located in the Photoshop7\Tutorial folder, and save it as **HeadKathyJimDark.psd** in the same folder.
2. In the Layers panel, duplicate the **Background** layer, and use the default layer name, Background copy. You'll work in the Background copy layer.
3. On the menu bar, click **View**, and then click **Fit on Screen**.
4. In the Tools panel, click the **Burn Tool** button, which is hidden under the Dodge Tool button.
5. On the options bar, click the **Brush picker** button, and set the size to **50 px**.
6. Click the **Range** button, and then click **Highlights**. Set the Exposure to **10%**, and then click the **Protect Tones** check box to select it, if necessary.
7. Paint Jim's face and neck to darken the highlights.
8. On the options bar, click the **Range** button, and then click **Shadows**. Paint both faces in areas where you would like to darken the shadows, such as on the sides of the faces. See Figure 7-38.

Figure 7-38 **Burn tool used to darken an image**

9. Turn the visibility of the Background copy layer off and on to see how your changes have affected the image.
10. Save the file, and keep it open for the next set of steps.

Although the changes that you have made to the image are subtle, they have created a better photographic composition by removing the highlights that caused the viewer to focus more on Jim than on Kathy and by creating more depth in the image by intensifying the shadows. As you continue to retouch the image, the effects of the small changes will add up to create big results. Next, you'll use the Sponge tool to increase the saturation of the image.

Retouching with the Sponge Tool

The final tool in the Dodge tool family is the Sponge tool. The Sponge tool has the same settings and nuances as the Dodge and Burn tools, and it is used to perform localized color correction by increasing or decreasing saturation in a small part of an image. This is helpful because adjusting image brightness can sometimes wash the color out of an image. When this happens, you can use the Sponge tool to add a little saturation where needed. You'll use the Sponge tool to add some saturation to the headshot.

To add saturation to areas of the image:

1. In the Layers panel, ensure that the Background copy layer is selected and visible.

2. In the Tools panel, click the **Sponge Tool** button, which is currently hidden under the Burn Tool button.
3. On the options bar, set the brush size to **75 px**, click the **Mode** button, and then click **Saturate**. Set the Flow to **15%**, and click the **Vibrance** check box to select it, if necessary.
4. Paint Jim's clothing and the forest background to create a more vibrant and dramatic image.
5. Change the Flow setting to **5%**, paint Kathy's scarf, paint Jim's jacket and hat, and, finally, paint the trees in the forest background to make the shot look more vibrant.
6. Now that the color in your image is saturated, examine your image, and use the Dodge and Sponge tools on any small areas that still need work. See Figure 7-39.

Figure 7-39 The Sponge tool increases the saturation in washed-out areas

the Sponge tool is used to increase or decrease image saturation

© iStockphoto.com/Izabela Habur

Turn the visibility of the Background copy layer off and on to see how your changes have affected the image. Notice how the addition of this subtle change has increased the overall intensity of the changes to the image.

7. Save the file, and keep it open for the next set of steps.

You'll continue retouching this image using the Sharpen tool to draw focus to Kathy and Jim's eyes.

INSIGHT

Keeping Up with New Developments

Designers constantly push the limits of what technology can accomplish, and new techniques for using the current design tools are in a state of continuous development. As a result, what is considered contemporary and fresh in aesthetic design is constantly shifting and evolving. Designers have a responsibility to continue to grow and develop their craft. This does not mean that you should simply mimic the latest trends, but rather that you should be aware of new developments and be able to incorporate current techniques and best practices into your design intelligently. One way to continue your development is to dedicate a few hours, each week, to reading design-related trade magazines and Web sites. The Adobe Design Center (*http://adobe.com/designcenter*) is Adobe's community forum for designers. The design center provides resources such as tutorials, opinions, training, articles, and design galleries. Another method for furthering your professional development is to occasionally take a class or attend a seminar. Whatever steps you take, remember that you are responsible for your continuing development as a design professional.

Retouching with the Sharpen Tool

The Sharpen tool can be used to retouch images and redirect focus within compositions. The Sharpen tool is primarily used to intensify detail in an area of an image where you would like to draw the viewer's eye or to sharpen areas of the image that have a soft focus. For example, a common, industry technique is to use the Sharpen tool over the eyes of a subject to increase clarity and detail. This technique can produce stunning results by adding depth and drama to your images. The Sharpen tool can also be used nondestructively, in an empty layer above the image, or it can be applied directly to the image, creating a destructive edit. The Sharpen tool is found under the Blur tool in the Tools panel, and is a good choice if you only want to alter small areas of your image. You'll use the Sharpen tool to sharpen Jim's and Kathy's eyes in the headshot.

To sharpen an area of the image using the Sharpen tool:

1. In the Layers panel, create an empty layer above the Background copy layer, and name the layer **Sharpen**. Position the image so that Jim's and Kathy's eyes are visible in the Document window.
2. In the Tools panel, click the **Sharpen Tool** button, which is currently hidden under the Blur Tool button.
3. On the options bar, set the brush size to **10 px**, set the Mode to **Normal**, if necessary, and set the Strength to **50%**. Click the **Sample All Layers** check box and the **Protect Detail** check box to select them both.
4. Zoom in to **150%**, and make sure the Sharpen layer is selected in the Layers panel. In the image, paint Jim's and Kathy's eyes until they become sharp enough to be slightly dramatic.
5. To check your progress, show and hide the Sharpen layer as you go so you can view the changes you have made to the look of the image. When you feel you have achieved the desired effect, stop. See Figure 7-40.

TIP

You can use the Darken mode to increase the intensity of the Sharpen tool.

Figure 7-40 Eyes sharpened using Sharpen tool

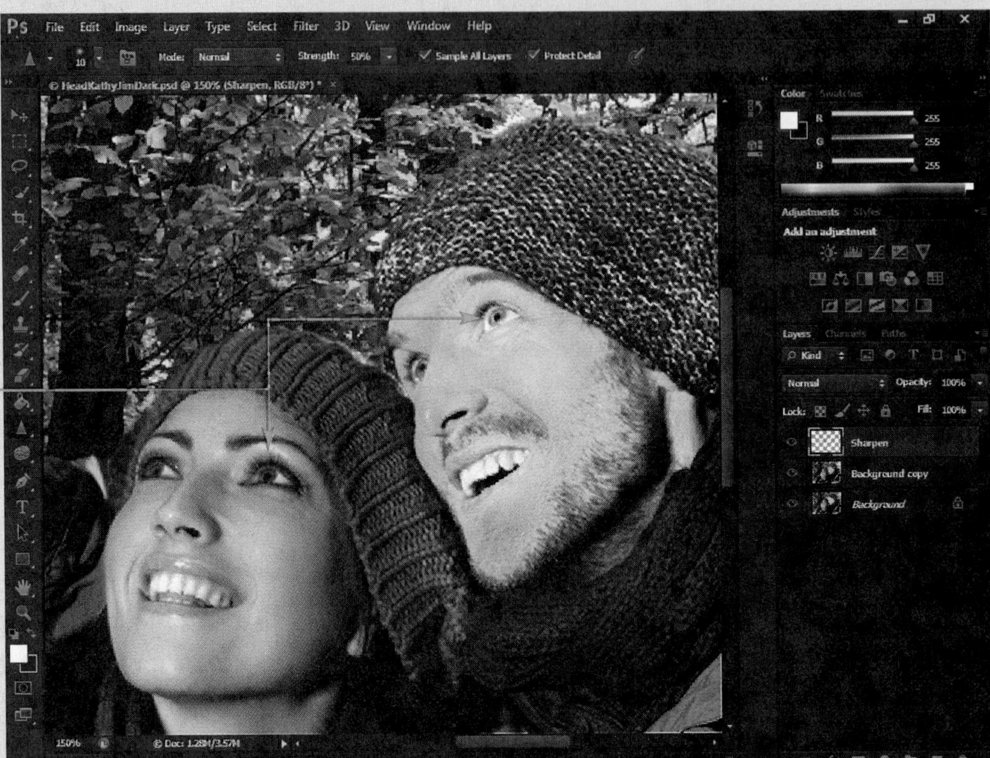

The sharpness of Kathy and Jim's eyes draws attention to them

© iStockphoto.com/Izabela Habur

6. Save the image, and leave it open for the next set of steps.

Next, you'll use the Blur Gallery of filters to diffuse the background of the image so Kathy and Jim remain the focus of the composition.

Transforming an Image using the Blur Gallery of Filters

The Blur Gallery is a set of three filters you can use to create varying blur effects that enable you to alter an image's **depth of field**, which is the range of distances in the image that appears acceptably sharp. Blur filters are often used to change the depth of field to redirect focus within a composition. You can use blur to blend areas of an image, to soften imperfections, or to create a soft focus around an object on which you would like the viewer's eye to focus. The Blur Gallery of filters includes a head's up display, which is an intuitive, onscreen set of controls that are overlaid on the image, enabling you to adjust images quickly and easily while previewing the changes that you make on screen. Another interesting note is that you can move between the filters in the Blur Gallery to combine the effects of the different filters in your selection. Finally, the Blur Gallery provides a Blur Effects panel, which enables you to create a Bokeh effect in your images. The Bokeh effect creates round circles of light in areas of the image. The effect works well to create a diffuse background, but it does not always produce the desired effect when added to an image. As with most tools in Photoshop, the possibilities that can be achieved with the Blur Gallery filters are as endless as your imagination.

While the Blur Gallery filter effects are created using masks, after you accept the changes, the effects are applied directly to the selected layer, creating a destructive edit. Because of this, it is a good idea to copy the layer that you want to work on and make the changes to the duplicate layer. The Blur Gallery filters are a good choice if you plan to adjust the entire image or a large portion of the image. The Blur tool is a better choice if you only want to blend small areas of your image. Another useful blending tool, the Smudge tool, is in the same tool set as the Blur tool, and it works in a similar manner to enable you to blend small portions of your image by smudging details, as if you were working with wet paint.

The following paragraphs provide a description and a figure showing each of the three filters in the Blur Gallery:

- **Field Blur**—Without adjustment, Field Blur applies a uniform, soft blur to the entire selected layer, which is good for layering behind other objects to create a shallow depth of field to focus the viewer's eye on the object in the unblurred layer. This filter is particularly useful because with it you can add additional pins to the layer that is being blurred. Each additional pin creates an additional blur effect area that can be controlled separately, and the effects of each pin area interact with the other pin areas. Because you can adjust each pin separately, you can create an image that has different amounts of blur in different areas. When multiple pins are used, this filter can produce very precise and powerful results. See Figure 7-41.

Figure 7-41 **Blur Gallery filters with Field Blur displayed**

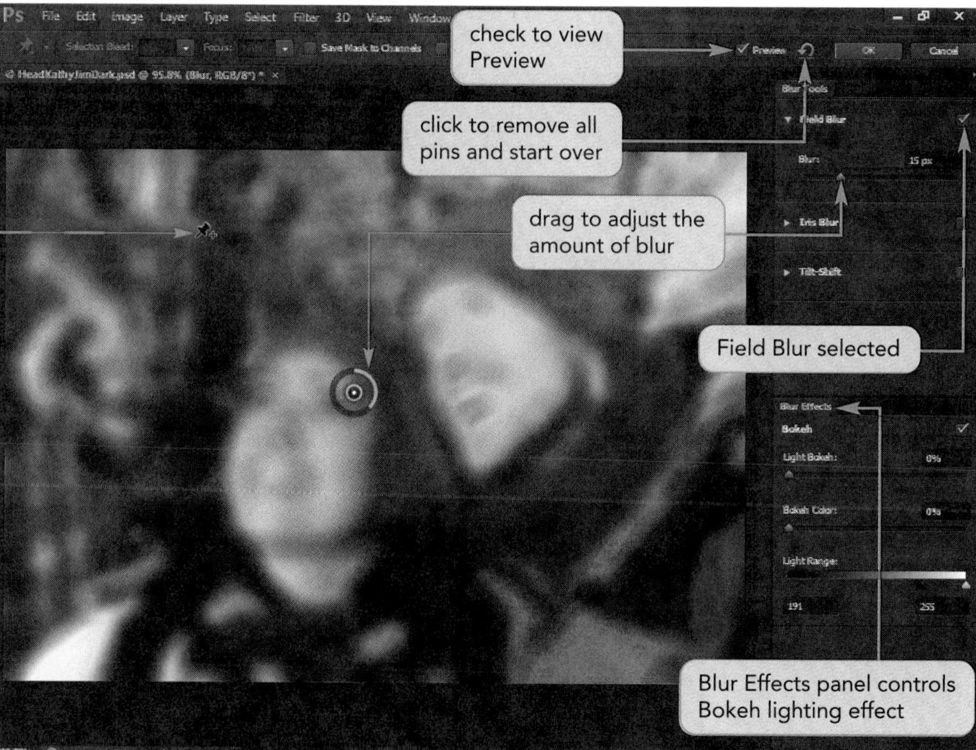

- **Iris Blur**—The Iris Blur filter produces a blur with a circular perimeter and a non-blurred point of focus at the center of the pin. With this filter, you can adjust the location of the center pin in the image as well as the size and shape of the outer perimeter. You can also adjust additional points that control where the blur effect starts within the circle. Like Field Blur, you can add multiple pins to a layer creating multiple Iris Blurs that interact with one another. See Figure 7-42.

Figure 7-42 Blur Gallery filters with Iris Blur displayed

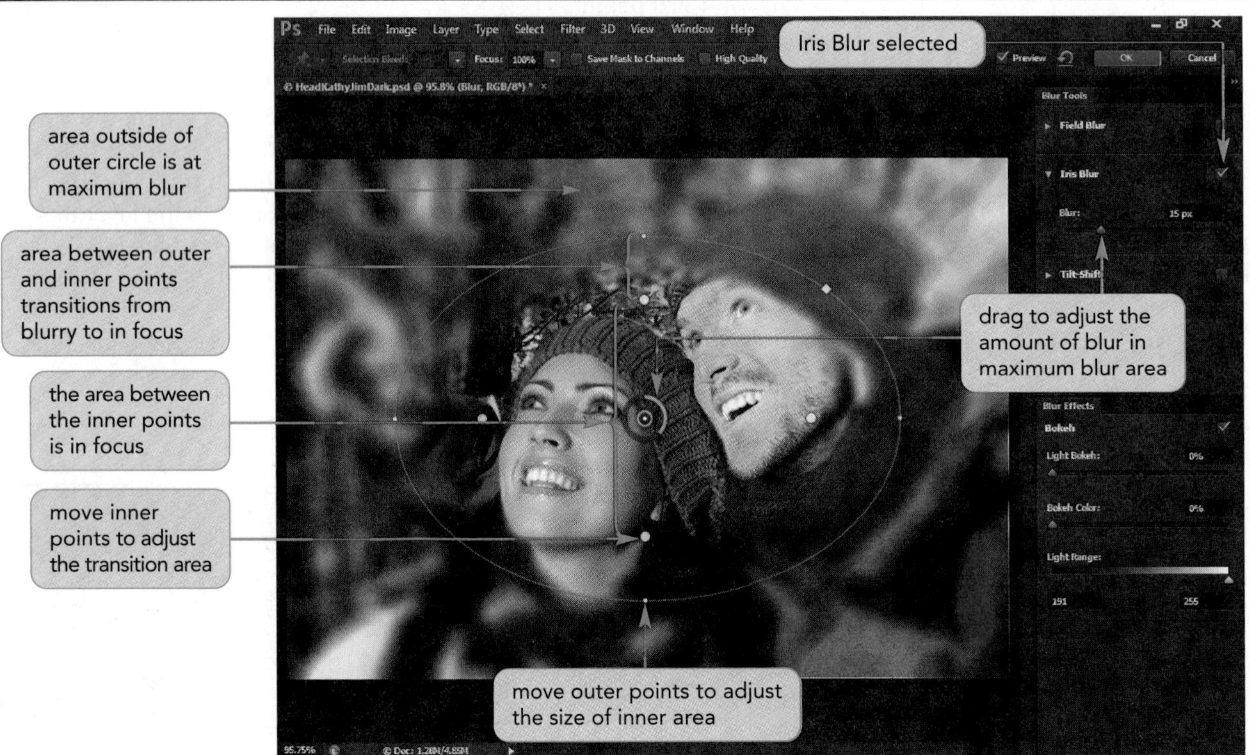

© iStockphoto.com/Izabela Habur

- **Tilt-Shift**—The Tilt-Shift is blur filter is most often used to create a special effects blur. The filter creates a linear blur area that is, by default, placed horizontally across the screen. The pin creates a center line of focus in the image, and perimeter lines enable you to adjust the outer edges of the filter. This filter also has inner lines that enable you to adjust the amount of space between the center nonblur and the beginning of the blur effect. See Figure 7-43.

Figure 7-43 Blur Gallery filters with Tilt-Shift blur displayed

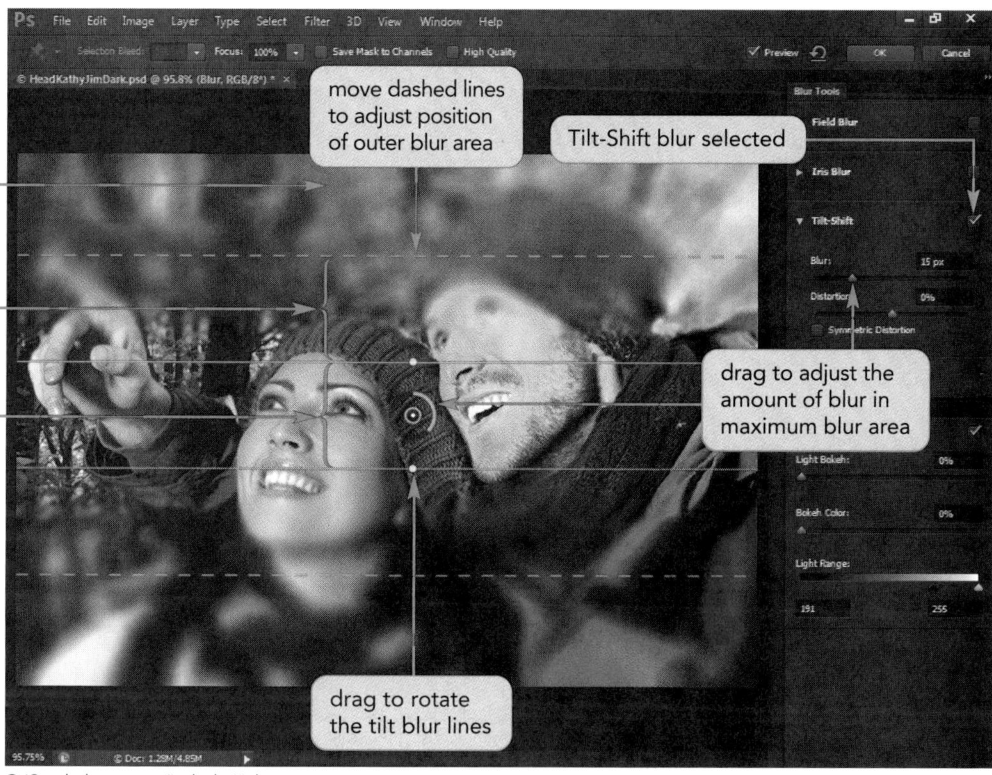
the area outside of top and bottom dashed lines is at maximum blur
the area between outer and inner lines transitions from blurry to in focus
the area between inner lines is in focus
move dashed lines to adjust position of outer blur area
Tilt-Shift blur selected
drag to adjust the amount of blur in maximum blur area
drag to rotate the tilt blur lines

© iStockphoto.com/Izabela Habur

You will use the Iris Blur filter to create a soft focus around Kathy and Jim. This will allow the viewer to focus on the couple rather than the busy forest background.

REFERENCE

Blurring an Area of an Image Using a Blur Gallery Filter

- In the Layers panel, duplicate the layer you would like to adjust, and then select the duplicate layer.
- On the menu bar, click Filter, point to Blur, and then click one of the top three filters to open the Blur Gallery.
- Adjust the position of the pin on the screen, and then adjust the inner and outer selection points and the amount of blur to create the desired effect.
- Press the Ctrl+H to keys toggle the onscreen display on and off to view the effects of your adjustments.
- Add additional pins, and make adjustments as desired.
- Click the OK button to accept the adjustments, and make the changes to the layer.

To adjust depth of field and create focus in the image using the Iris Blur filter:

1. In the Layers panel, duplicate the Background copy layer, and name the new layer **Blur**. Hide the **Background** and **Background copy** layers, and click on the **Blur** layer to select it, if necessary.

2. On the menu bar, click **Filter**, point to **Blur**, and then click **Iris Blur**. The Blur Gallery opens. Click the **Ctrl+0** keys to fit the image on screen. On the right side of the options bar, click the **Remove all pins** button to remove the pin from the image then place the pointer in the center of the image and click to add a new pin with default setting. See Figure 7-44.

   Trouble? If you have trouble interacting with the Blur Gallery controls or seeing the image, you may not have a compatible graphics card or you may not have the functionality enabled. The onscreen controls and some of the features of the Blur Gallery filters use your computers graphics card to speed up processing and to increase functionality. Click Cancel to close the Blur Gallery, and on the menu bar, click Edit. Point to Preferences, and then click Performance. In the Preferences dialog box, click the Use Graphics Processor check box to select it if it is unchecked. Then close the Photoshop, and reopen it to enable the advanced functionality. If the Blur Gallery controls still do not work, repeat the steps above, and write down the name of the graphics processor displayed in the Preferences dialog box under Detect Graphics Processer. Then, go to Adobe Help online (*http://helpx.adobe.com/photoshop/kb/photoshop-cs6-gpu-faq.html*) for advanced help and information. If you are unable to enable the functionality, or if the Use Graphics Processor check box is grayed out, read but do not perform the rest of the steps in this section, and then save your document.

Figure 7-44 **Blur Gallery filters with Iris Blur displayed**

Remove all pins button
eyes are on the Sharpen layer above the Blur layer so they are not affected by the filter
new pin in image

© iStockphoto.com/Izabela Habur

3. Drag the white line around the center circle until the Blur setting in the Blur Tools panel is **8 px**. Then, drag the outer points of the circle until it becomes more of an oval, with the top and bottom edges just inside the top and bottom edges of the image and the left and right points positioned a bit outside of Kathy's and Jim's faces. When you are finished, you should have an oval that incircles Kathy's and Jim's heads. Finally, move the inner points of the circle until the faces are mostly in focus and the blur transition is smooth. See Figure 7-45.

Figure 7-45 Adjusted pin settings

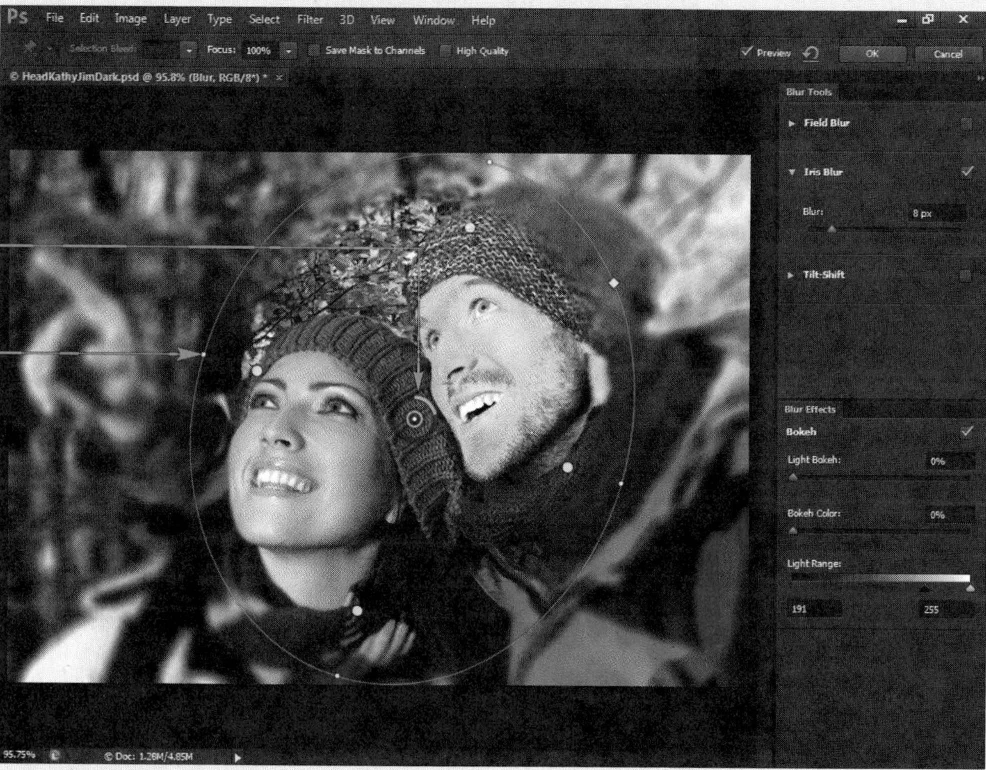

© iStockphoto.com/Izabela Habur

4. Click on the thumb of the hand that Jim is pointing with to add a second pin to the image. Adjust the outer points to form an oval outside of the hand, and drag the white line around the inner circle until the Blur setting is **4 px**. Adjust the inner points so Jim's hand is in focus and the background surrounding the hand fades from focus.

5. Press and hold the **Alt** key, and drag the upper-left inner point to move that point out so that Jim's extended finger is inside the focus area. See Figure 7-46.

Figure 7-46 Second pin added

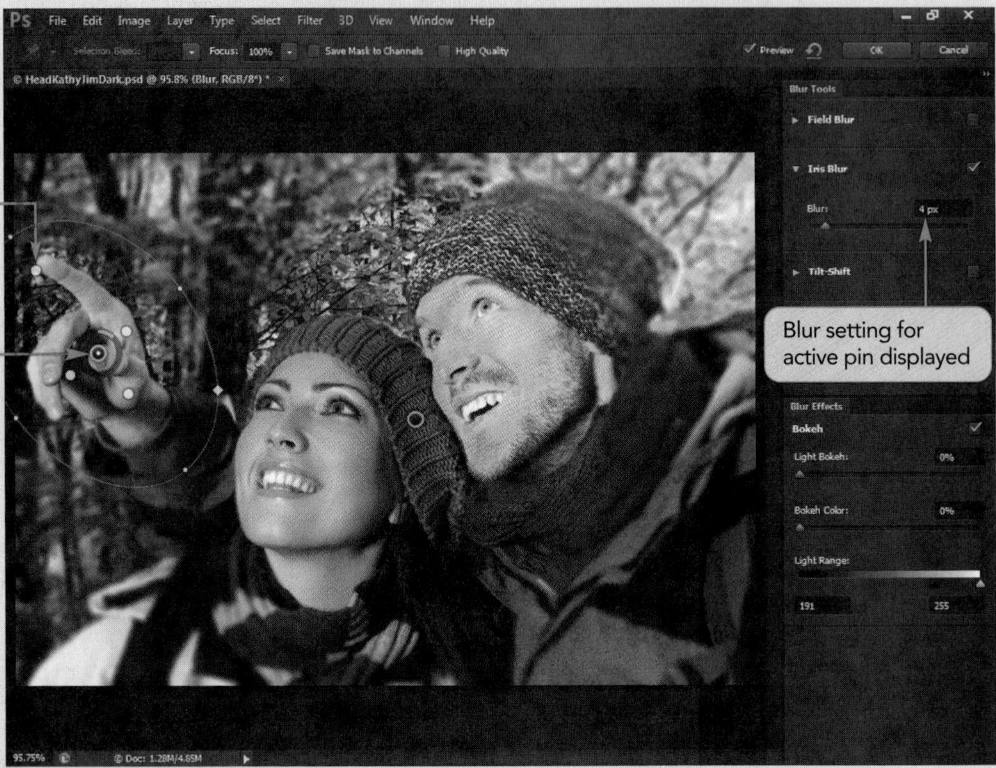

© iStockphoto.com/Izabela Habur

6. Press the **Ctrl+H** keys to hide the onscreen controls so that you can see the entire image, and then press the **Ctrl+H** keys again to display the controls. Make any final adjustments to the two pins in your image, as necessary. If your transitions are too harsh, adjust the points individually (by pressing the Alt key) or decrease the blur slightly. See Figure 7-47 to compare your starting image with your finished product.

Figure 7-47 **Comparing the original image with the final image**

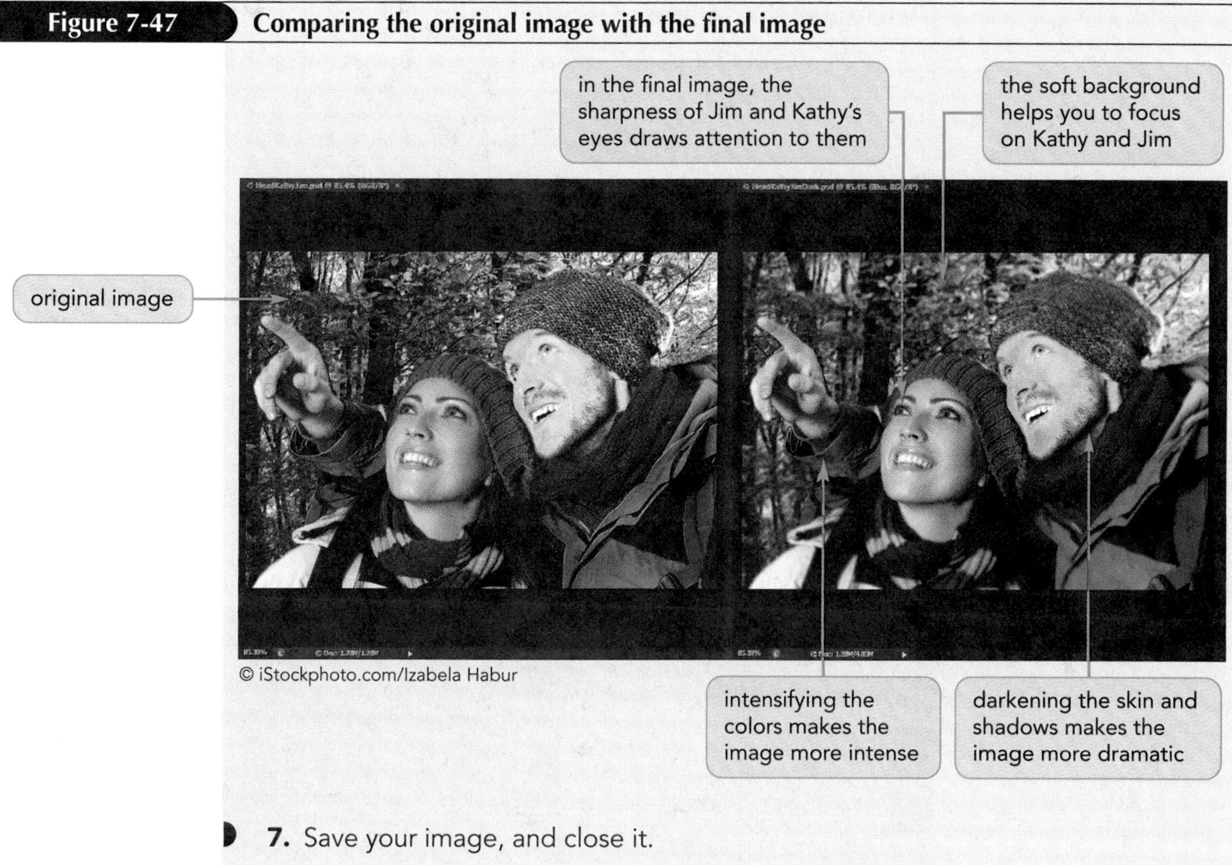
in the final image, the sharpness of Jim and Kathy's eyes draws attention to them
the soft background helps you to focus on Kathy and Jim
original image
intensifying the colors makes the image more intense
darkening the skin and shadows makes the image more dramatic

© iStockphoto.com/Izabela Habur

7. Save your image, and close it.

Working with the Lab Color Mode

As you learned in Tutorial 4, Lab (Luminosity, A and B channels) is another color mode that, like RGB and CMYK, can be used in Photoshop. Lab color is based on human color perception, and it contains values for the range of color that can be seen with the average human eye. It is unique because it is considered to be a device-independent color model that describes how color looks rather than how much of each pure color a device must mix to achieve the color. Lab color separates color into three channels:

- The Luminosity channel contains all of the lightness and darkness information for the image. In fact, with a few adjustments, you can use the Luminosity channel to create an amazing black-and-white image.
- The A channel contains the red and green color information for the image.
- The B channel contains the yellow and blue color information for the image.

Because of the way Lab color interprets color, you can use it to create remarkable color and luminosity adjustments to your images. For instance, you can adjust the lightness and darkness values in an image without affecting the colors, or you can adjust a color value without affecting the brightness. You can move in and out of Lab color mode without damaging your images, but Photoshop merges adjustment layers when you move from Lab to another color mode. Because of this, it is especially important to work with a copy of your original images when you are working in Lab.

Dayne thinks the cropped and adjusted version of the LookOut.psd image looks so good he would like to use it on a promotional postcard he is creating. Because the cropped version of the image does not have the right dimensions for use in a postcard layout, Dayne would like you to adjust the original image so the person creating the postcard can crop it for use in her layout. You will use the Lab color mode to adjust the image.

To adjust the image using Lab color mode:

1. Open **LookOut.psd**, located in the Photoshop7\Tutorial folder. (Do not use the LookOutCrop.psd file that you have already changed.)
2. Save the file as **LookOutLAB.psd** in the same folder, and change the view to **Fit on Screen**.
3. On the menu bar, click **Image**, point to **Mode**, and then click **Lab Color**.
4. In the Layers panel, click the **Create new fill or adjustment layer** icon, and then click **Curves**. Photoshop adds a Curves 1 adjustment layer above the Background layer, and the Properties panel opens. Drag the bottom of the Properties panel down to reveal the Input and Output labels.
5. In the Properties panel, click **Lightness** from the channel list, if necessary. Then, use the **black point** slider below the Curves grid to drag the bottom point of the curve to the right until the right edge of the point is against the left edge of the histogram and the Input value is **14**. See Figure 7-48.

TIP

The Lightness channel controls the Luminosity in Lab color mode in the Curves adjustment.

Figure 7-48 Adjusting an image in Lab color mode

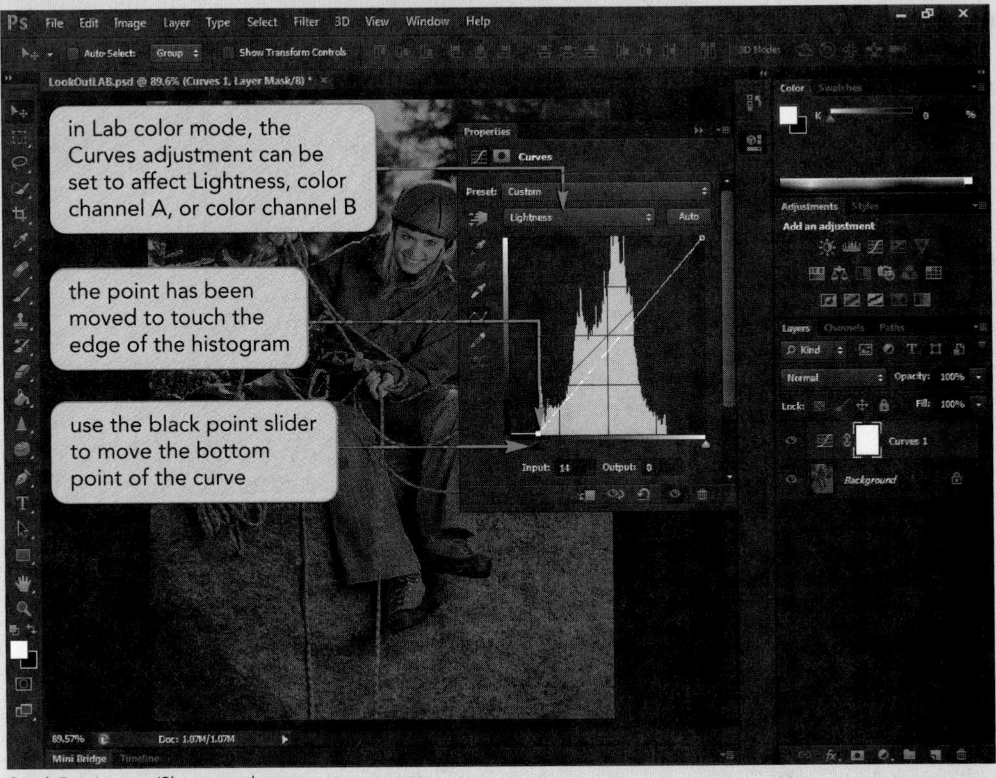

CandyBox Images/Shutterstock.com

6. Click the **white point** slider below the Curves grid, and drag it to the left until the slider meets the right edge of the histogram, and the Input is 81 and the Output is 100.

   Turn the visibility of the adjustment layer on and off to see how you have affected the brightness of the image.

   See Figure 7-49.

Figure 7-49 Image in Lab color mode with Lightness adjusted

the white point slider touches the edge of the histogram

CandyBox Images/Shutterstock.com

7. In the Properties panel, click **b** from the channel list.
8. Click the bottom point of the curve, and drag it to the right until it is located over the first vertical grid line. The Input value should now be **-65** and the Output value should be **-128**. See Figure 7-50.

Figure 7-50 **Image in Lab color mode with the B channel adjusted**

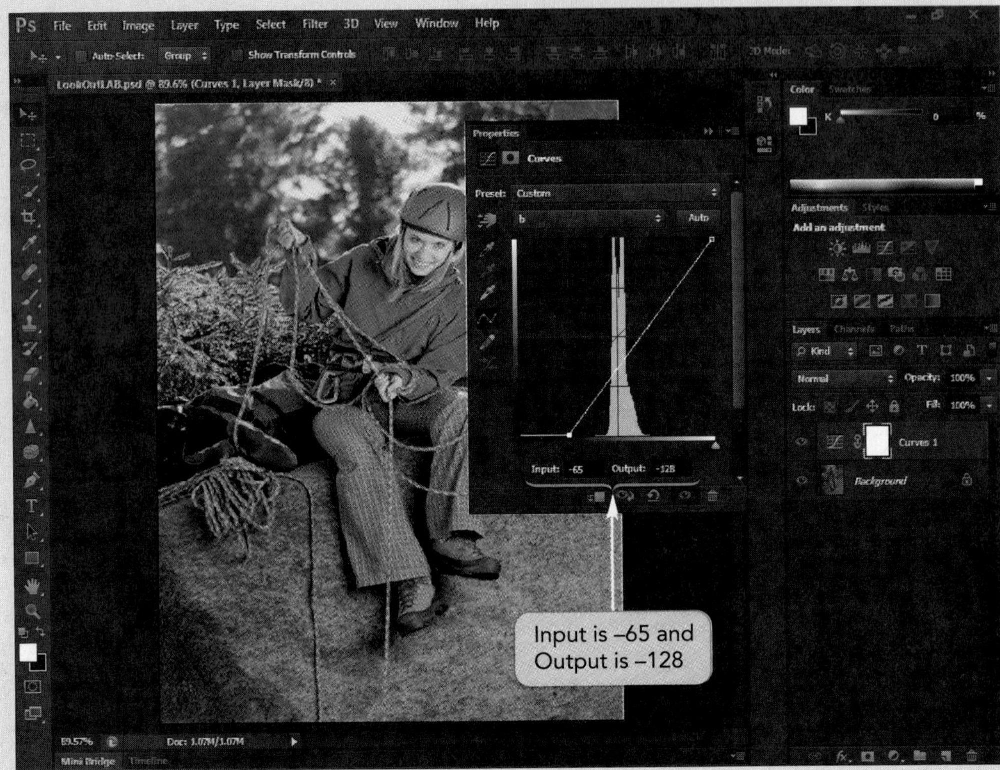
Input is –65 and
Output is –128

CandyBox Images/Shutterstock.com

9. Click the top point of the curve, and drag to the left until it is located over the first vertical grid line it meets. The Input value should now be **62** and the Output value should be **127**. Turn the visibility of the Curves 1 layer off and on to see how you have affected the image. Notice how vibrant the colors are.
10. In the Properties panel, click **a** from the channel list, and repeat Steps 8 and 9.
11. Close the Properties panel, click **Image**, point to **Mode**, and then click **RGB Color**. Click the **Flatten** button in the dialog box to merge the adjustment layer.

    The image is flattened, and Photoshop converts it back to RGB color mode. See Figure 7-51.

Figure 7-51 **Final image with adjustments**

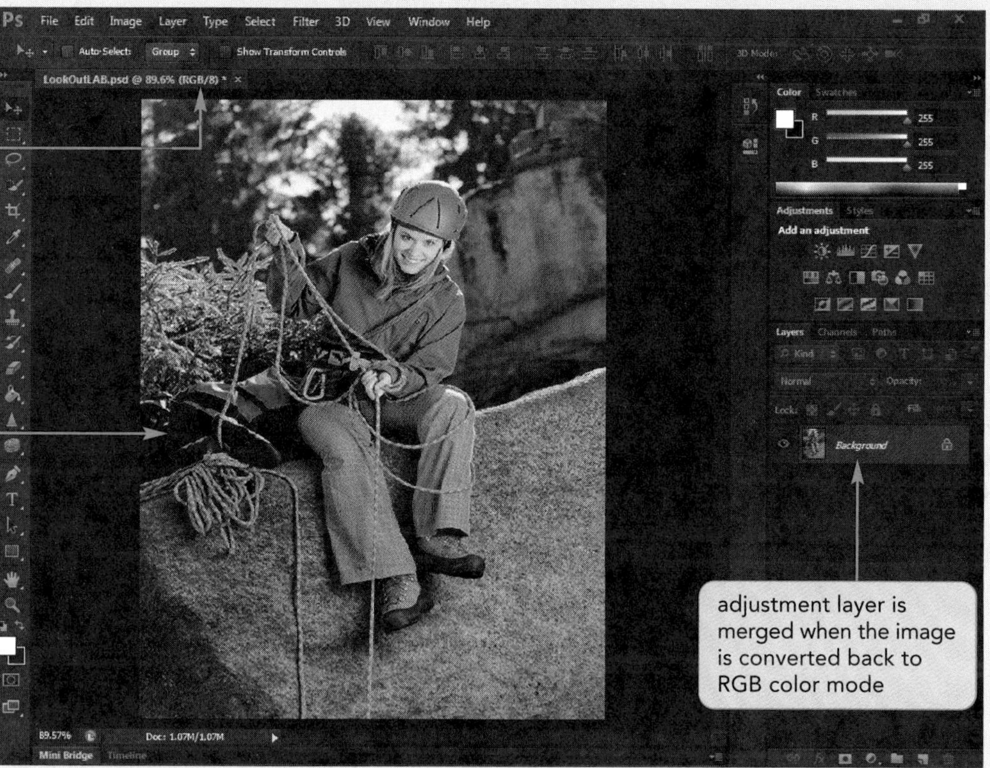
image is back in RGB color mode
simple Lab adjustments can create dramatic images
adjustment layer is merged when the image is converted back to RGB color mode

CandyBox Images/Shutterstock.com

12. Save the image, close it, and exit Photoshop.

Now that the images have been corrected, you will be able to use them in the Hooked brochure. Once they are in place, additional small adjustments might be necessary, but all of the hard work is finished.

In this session, you worked on the final phase of image adjustment: retouching. You learned to correct blemishes and small image problems with the Spot Healing Brush tool and the Healing Brush tool. You used the Dodge, Burn, and Sponge tools to adjust areas of relative lightness, darkness, and saturation within an image. You used the Sharpen tool and the Blur Gallery filters to create areas of focus, and you used Lab color mode to create dynamic color and luminosity adjustments.

PROSKILLS

Decision Making: Making It Real

Once you learn the tricks for making images look perfect, it is easy to fall into the trap of needing to create a perfect-looking world where every chin is sharp, and every flaw has been neatly removed. But that perfect world does not exist, and images or compositions that look "too perfect" have the artificial feel that manufactured reality can produce. To serve your client's interest, you must use a light touch in creating aesthetically pleasing, yet interesting and believable imagery. Remember that the product you create should be driven by the client's desired goals for the campaign. The end product is only a success if it serves your client's interest.

REVIEW

Session 7.2 Quick Check

1. Why would you use the Spot Healing Brush tool?
2. True or False. The Dodge tool can be used to make areas of an image darker.
3. The ______________ tool is used to increase or decrease saturation in a small area of an image.
4. You use the Burn tool to make areas of an image ______________.
5. ______________ color mode is used to adjust color and luminosity in images.
6. What tools and filters can you use to draw focus to an area of an image?

Practice the skills you learned in the tutorial using the same case scenario.

PRACTICE

Review Assignments

Data File needed for the Review Assignments: Hiking.psd

Your design team will be adding more images to the brochure and other collateral materials that have been created for Hooked. Dayne would like you to crop, adjust, and retouch the remaining images. Remember that retouching is an art. Use discretion when cleaning up flaws to ensure that the images retain an authentic look. Complete the following steps:

1. Start Photoshop while pressing the Ctrl+Alt+Shift keys, and click Yes to delete the Settings File when prompted. Reset Photoshop to the default Essentials workspace layout, and then reset all tools.
2. Open **Hiking.psd**, located in the Photoshop7\Review folder provided with your Data Files, save it as **HikingAdjust.psd** in the same folder, and set your view to Fit on Screen.
3. Use the Crop tool to add a Crop Guide Overlay that covers the entire image, and set the View to Rule of Thirds. Notice that the man is currently in the center of the image. You will crop the image to a closer shot of the man using the Rule of Thirds to guide your crop.
4. Drag the edges of the Crop Guide Overlay until the right vertical line is over the man's zipper, the bottom of the grid touches the bottom of his green jacket, and the top horizontal line is under the man's chin, and then crop the image.
5. Create a Curves Adjustment layer, and use the Auto button in the Curves adjustment to see if it will correct the contrast and tone of the image. For this image, the Auto button does not make a significant correction, so you'll use the Burn tool to correct the image instead.
6. Duplicate the Background layer, and title the new layer **Hiking with Changes**. Hide the Background layer.
7. Zoom in on the man's face, and use the Burn tool with a 20-pixel brush in the Highlights Range at 10% Exposure, with the Protect Tones option selected. Paint the overexposed areas of the man's cheeks, nose, and forehead so the image has consistent color over the entire face.
8. Repeat Step 7 with the Burn tool to correct the midtones.
9. Create a new blank layer above the Hiking with Changes layer, and name the layer **Healing**.
10. Select the Healing Brush tool with a 5-pixel brush in Screen Mode, with the Sample option set to All Layers. Zoom in and remove the squinting wrinkles and puffiness from the below the man's eyes.
11. Create a new blank layer above the Healing layer, and name the layer **Sharpen**.
12. Select the Sharpen tool with a 5-pixel brush in Normal Mode at 50% Strength, with the Sample All Layers and Protect Detail options selected. Paint over the man's eyes to sharpen them.
13. In the Hiking with Changes layer, use the Patch tool with Content-Aware and Very Loose settings selected and patch any areas of the background that are distracting.
14. Save the file, and exit Photoshop.
15. Submit the results of the preceding steps to your instructor either in printed or electronic form, as requested.

Use your skills to add some interest to images in a poster.

APPLY

Case Problem 1

Data File needed for this Case Problem: JamJam.psd

The Jam Jam Every April, the spring thaw brings hundreds of competitors out to Washington Park in Portland, Oregon, for a funky day of jamming and jamming. The Jam Jam started as a way to teach Portland residents to use locally grown, seasonal fruits in new and interesting ways. Jenny Conn, the event organizer, was quoted as saying, "By encouraging people to jam, we are showing them how to use fruit that is in season in a way that will enable them to enjoy it at other times of the year." Since its inception, the jam has become something of a local event promoting local gardening, local bands, and local art. This year, your firm has volunteered to create marketing materials for the Jam Jam. The Art Department has created a poster and, after review, Jenny has asked you to create a little drama by punching up some of the images in the poster. Complete the following steps:

1. Start Photoshop while pressing the Ctrl+Alt+Shift keys. When you are prompted to delete the Adobe Photoshop Settings File, click Yes. Reset Photoshop to the Essentials workspace, and then reset all tools.
2. Open **JamJam.psd**, located in the Photoshop7\Case1 folder provided with your Data Files, and save it as **JamJamAdjust.psd** in the same folder. (*Hint*: If a dialog box appears stating that you need to replace missing fonts, click the OK button; this will not affect the end result.)
3. Select the Jam 3 layer, change the image to the Lab color mode, and do not flatten the layers when prompted.
4. In the Channels panel, ensure that all of the channels are visible so you can effectively adjust the lightness of the Jam 3 layer.
5. Add a Curves adjustment layer, and clip the adjustment layer to the Jam 3 layer only. (*Hint*: Use the "This adjustment affects all layers below" icon in the Properties panel to clip the adjustment layer to the Jam 3 layer.)
6. Expand the Properties panel to reveal the Input and Output labels at the bottom. Drag the black point slider under the Curve graph to the right until the Input value is 15.
7. Click in the center of the curve to add a new anchor point, and then drag the point down and to the left until the Input value is 56 and the Output value is 44.
8. In the Layers panel, select the new Curves 1 layer and the Jam 3 layer, and from the Layer menu, select Merge Layers to merge the new adjustment layer with the Jam 3 layer. Rename the newly merged layer **Jam 3**. (Remember that adjustment layers created in the Lab color mode are lost when you move from Lab color mode to RGB color mode.)
9. Select the Jam 2 layer, add a Curves adjustment layer, and clip the adjustment layer to the Jam 2 layer only.
10. Select the bottom point of the curve and drag it to the right until it is halfway between the outside of the grid and the first vertical line. The Input value should be 11. Then, select the top point of the curve, and drag it down until it is over the first horizontal grid line. The Input value should now be 100, and the Output value should be 76.
11. Select channel a from the channel list on the Properties panel, and then select the top point of the curve and drag it straight down until it is over the first horizontal grid line. The Input value should be 127, and the Output value should be 65. Merge the Curves 2 adjustment layer and the Jam 2 layer, and rename the newly merged layer **Jam 2**.
12. Change the image back to RGB color mode, and choose not to flatten the layers when prompted.

13. Select the Jam 1 layer, and add a new Brightness Contrast adjustment layer with the Brightness set to -40 and the Contrast set to 36. Clip the adjustment layer to the Jam 1 layer only.
14. Select the Jar Left layer, and create a new Posterize adjustment layer with the Levels set to 8. Clip the adjustment layer to the Jar Left layer only.
15. Create a Hue/Saturation adjustment layer above the Posterize layer, and set the adjustment layer to affect only the Jar Left layer. Set the Hue to -27, and set the Saturation to 21.
16. Select the Jar Right layer and repeat Step 14 and Step 15, substituting the following settings in Step 15: Hue 158, Saturation 20.

EXPLORE

17. Select the Jam2 layer, and add a Tilt-Shift blur from the Blur Gallery filters. Move the pin over the guitarist's chest, and then rotate the filter so the lines are vertical. Move the inner lines so they are located at the left and right of the man's hat. Then, adjust the left and right outside dotted lines so they are at the left edge of the composition and the right side of the guitarist image, respectively. Use a Blur setting of 5 px.

EXPLORE

18. Select the Jam3 layer, and apply a Tilt-Shift blur that mimics the one you created in the Jam2 layer.
19. Save the file, and exit Photoshop.
20. Submit the results of the preceding steps to your instructor either in printed or electronic form, as requested.

Use your skills to adjust images for a media campaign for a new restaurant.

APPLY

Case Problem 2

Data Files needed for this Case Problem: ManInside.psd, WomanInsideBar.psd

The Cell The Cell is probably the only restaurant in Chicago where customers don't get dirty looks for talking on their phones. This new Asian-fusion restaurant and lounge actually encourages its patrons to talk it up. The concept for a restaurant that caters to cell phone junkies is the brainchild of Denise Duke. Duke was an executive at a local marketing firm, and she spent her days tied to the phone. "One day, I was at lunch and realized that half the restaurant was working, like me, and the other half was annoyed. It occurred to me that, in downtown Chicago, you could create a cell phone friendly restaurant that would solve everyone's problem." Your company is working on a media campaign for The Cell. Your job is to take the images that Denise gave you and make them pop by adding color and some dramatic flair. Complete the following steps:

1. Start Photoshop while pressing the Ctrl+Alt+Shift keys. When you are prompted to delete the Adobe Photoshop Settings File, click Yes. Reset Photoshop to the Essentials workspace, and then reset all tools.
2. Open **ManInside.psd**, located in the Photoshop7\Case2 folder provided with your Data Files, and save it as **ManInsideCrop.psd** in the same folder.
3. Use the Straighten feature of the Crop tool to draw a line across the image that runs parallel to the top edge of the table, and then straighten the image.
4. Using the Crop tool with the View set to Rule of Thirds, crop the image by dragging the top of the grid down to the 1-inch mark on the vertical ruler.

EXPLORE

5. Create a Vibrance adjustment layer above the Man Inside Table layer, and increase the Vibrance and the Saturation settings so the image does not appear to be washed out. (*Hint*: Remember that because this adjustment is done in an adjustment layer, you can change the settings as many times as you would like. Play with the adjustment until you achieve the look you want.)
6. Save the image.

7. Open **WomanInsideBar.psd** located in the Photoshop7\Case2 folder, and save it as **WomanAdjusted.psd** in the same folder.

EXPLORE

8. Examine the image and compare it with the ManInsideCrop.psd image that you just corrected. In the WomanAdjusted.psd file, create an Exposure adjustment layer and adjust the image so it will complement the image of the man sitting by himself when the images are used together in marketing materials. (*Hint*: Remember that image adjustment takes thought and judgment. Your images should have similar or complementary colors, tones, and saturation, and they should have a similar look and feel.)
9. Create a copy of the Background layer, and hide the original layer.
10. Select the Burn tool with a 200-pixel brush in the Highlights Range at 10% Exposure. Paint any highlights on the Background copy layer that are overexposed. Change the brush to 100 pixels. Change the Range to Midtones, and paint the woman, the cell phone, and the sushi to add contrast that will draw focus to them. Repeat this using the same brush settings in the Shadows Range.
11. Select the Sponge tool with a 150-pixel brush in Saturate Mode at 10% Flow with Vibrance checked. Paint the woman, the cell phone, and the sushi to draw the viewer's focus to the subject of the composition.
12. Select the Background copy layer. Using the Content-Aware Move tool, select the light fixture on the ceiling, and move it slightly to the right. Then, switch the Mode to Extend, and move the selection to the left to create a second fixture. If your selection is noticeable, undo the move and select a bigger area, or try using the Very Loose Adaptation setting.
13. Save your image, close both files, and exit Photoshop.
14. Submit the results of the preceding steps to your instructor either in printed or electronic form, as requested.

Extend your skills to adjust images to fit with a Web site's stylized look.

CHALLENGE

Case Problem 3

Data Files needed for this Case Problem: ArtistJohnVasquez.psd, ArtistsMarkJennyCope.psd, ArtistJasonPrice.psd

Graffiti Street Graffiti Street is a section of East Hardmon Street in Detroit, Michigan, that has opened its walls as a canvas for local graffiti artists. It is the concept of urban planner and local artist, David Galvan. As an urban planner, David was looking for a cost-effective way to revitalize the dilapidated walls of East Hardmon Street when he happened upon an amazing graffiti mural painted by local artist Daryl Huffington. The project solved several problems: It provided local artists with a legal space to create; it provided the city with an inexpensive way to revitalize a rundown area of town; and it created a sense of pride and ownership in the community.

You are part of a team creating a Web site that will provide information about the project. David has provided several images of the artists with their artwork. He has selected a very stylized urban look for the photography that will be used on the Web site. The imagery is slightly overexposed and oversaturated, mimicking the look of some contemporary magazine imagery. This is a look that will appeal to the target audience of the site. You'll adjust and retouch the artist images so they fit with that look. Complete the following steps:

1. Start Photoshop while pressing the Ctrl+Alt+Shift keys. When you are prompted to delete the Adobe Photoshop Settings File, click Yes. Reset Photoshop to the Essentials workspace, and then reset all tools.
2. Open **ArtistJohnVasquez.psd**, located in the Photoshop7\Case3 folder provided with your Data Files, and save it as **ArtistJohnVasquezFix.psd** in the same folder.

3. Show and hide the Exposure 1 layer to view the adjustments and the original image. Notice the settings that were used in the adjustment layer to achieve the desired look. The Exposure adjustment was used to create a stylized look, rather than to make a necessary correction.
4. Create a new a new blank layer under the Exposure 1 layer, and name the layer **Heal**. The stylized adjustments have created a harsh brown shadow under John's chin. You'll retouch the image to blend the shadow.
5. Use the Healing Brush tool to retouch the area under John's chin. (*Hint*: Make sure Current & Below is selected as the Sample method, and do not overcorrect the image.)
6. Save the image, and leave it open.
7. Open **ArtistsMarkJennyCope.psd**, located in the Photoshop7\Case3 folder, and save it as **ArtistsMarkJennyCopeFix.psd** in the same folder.

EXPLORE

8. Create an Exposure adjustment layer above the Background layer, and adjust the Exposure, Offset, and Gamma Correction values to match the Graffiti Street style. Switch between this image and the ArtistJohnVasquezFix.psd image to evaluate the changes to the ArtistsMarkJennyCopeFix.psd image.
9. Use your judgment to evaluate the image and locate any problem areas. Add a new layer above the Exposure adjustment layer, name the new layer **Heal**, and use the Spot Healing Brush tool to make any necessary adjustments. Then, add a new layer named **Burn and dodge** below the Exposure layer, and make any final adjustments using the Burn tool and the Dodge tool.
10. Save the image, and leave it open.
11. Open **ArtistJasonPrice.psd** located in the Photoshop7\Case3 folder, and save it

and, then in the Document window, fill the selected area with black. The white T-shirt in the image remains unaffected by the adjustments. (*Hint*: Any area that is filled with black in the mask for your adjustment layer will not be affected by the adjustment layer.)

14. Create a new layer above the Background layer, and name the layer **Heal**.
15. Use the healing brushes to retouch any problem areas in the image.
16. Duplicate the Background layer, and then hide the original layer.
17. Use the Dodge and Burn tools to correct any remaining problem areas in the image.
18. Save the image, close all three files, and exit Photoshop.
19. Submit the results of the preceding steps to your instructor either in printed or electronic form, as requested.

Use your skills to create something that expresses your point of view.

CREATE

Case Problem 4

Data File needed for this Case Problem: AlterProject.psd

The Digital Alter The Digital Alter project is a collective art project that provides artists with a group of images and asks each artist to combine, adjust, and alter the images so the final artwork has some sort of personal meaning that reflects the artist's point of view. You have been invited by project coordinator Juana Lewis to participate in the project. The images have been broken into four categories, each of which has been placed in a group in the AlterProject.psd file, so the file is organized and easy to use. Groups include Backgrounds, Fruits, Stars, and Birds. Examine the images that have been provided and use one image from each group to create something new. See Figure 7-52 for an example, but remember that the final artwork is supposed to reflect your personal point of view. This example is also included in the AlterProject.psd file on the Example layer.

Figure 7-52 Digital Alter project example

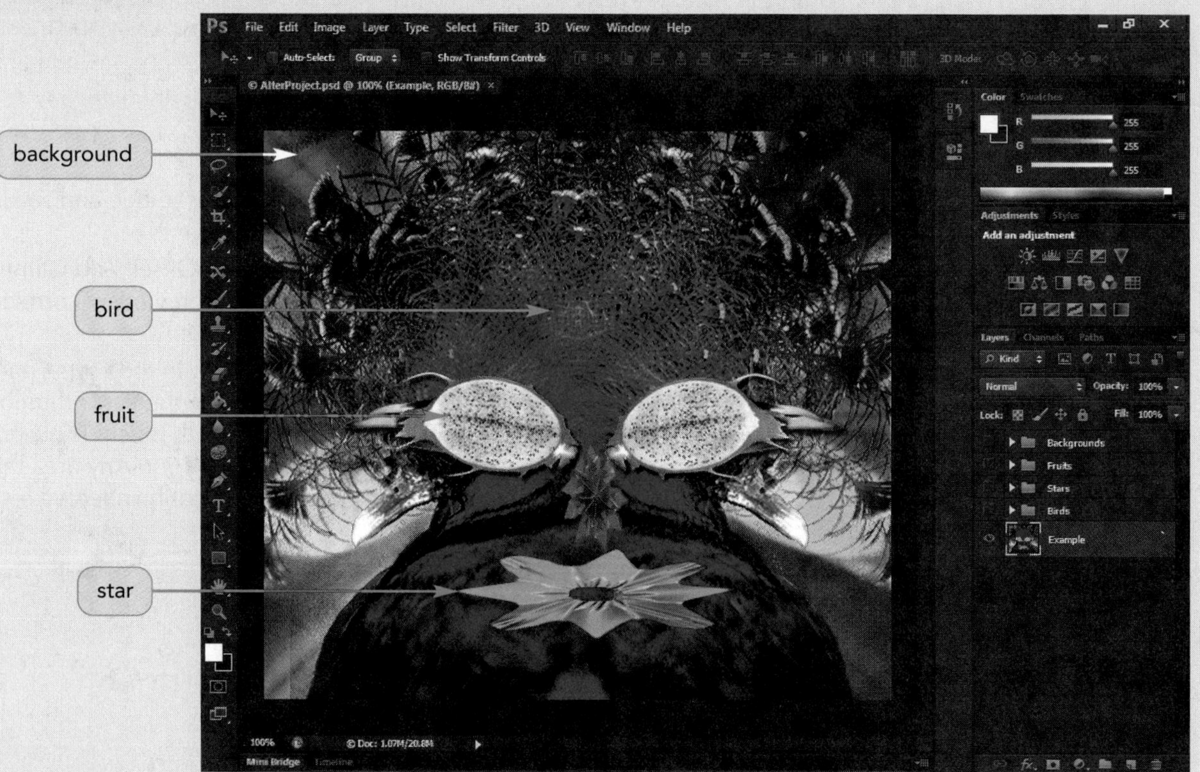

HAKKI ARSLAN/Shutterstock.com; Murat Subatli/Shutterstock.com; © 2012 Oksana Shufrich, Photos.com, a division of Getty Images. All rights reserved.; © 2012 John Foxx, Photos.com, a division of Getty Images. All rights reserved.

Complete the following steps:

1. Start Photoshop while pressing the Ctrl+Alt+Shift keys. When you are prompted to delete the Adobe Photoshop Settings File, click Yes. Reset Photoshop to the Essentials workspace, and then reset all tools.
2. Open **AlterProject.psd** located in the Photoshop7\Case4 folder, and save it as **MyAlterProject.psd** in the same folder.
3. Open the Backgrounds group folder, and examine the images provided by Digital Alter.
4. Repeat Step 3 for the Fruits, Stars, and Birds folders.

5. Think about the images in each folder, how they look, what they represent to you, and how you might combine them together to create something unique.
6. Hide all of the group folders, and examine the image on the Example layer to get an idea of how you might work with the individual images to create a new composition, and then hide the Example layer.
7. Select one image/layer from each group. Copy each layer, and then move the copy out of its folder group to the main area of the Layers panel below all of the folder groups.
8. Move the Back layer that you selected to the bottom of the Layers panel, and then hide the other layers.
9. Switch to Lab color mode, and use a Levels or Curves adjustment layer to alter the look of your Back layer.
10. Merge the adjustment layers with the Back layer, and switch back to RGB color mode.
11. Rename the newly merged layer, if necessary, and then continue to adjust and manipulate the background until you achieve the look you desire.
12. Select the Bird layer, and alter the layer as needed to achieve the look you desire. Use at least one adjustment layer and either a Blur Gallery filter, the Sharpen tool, or the Blur tool. Rename the layer, if necessary, as you work to ensure your work flow is not confusing.
13. Select the Star layer, and alter the layer as needed to achieve the look you desire. Use at least one adjustment layer and either the Healing Brush tool, the Content-Aware Patch tool, or the Spot Healing Brush tool. Rename the layer, if necessary,

electronic form, as requested.

ENDING DATA FILES

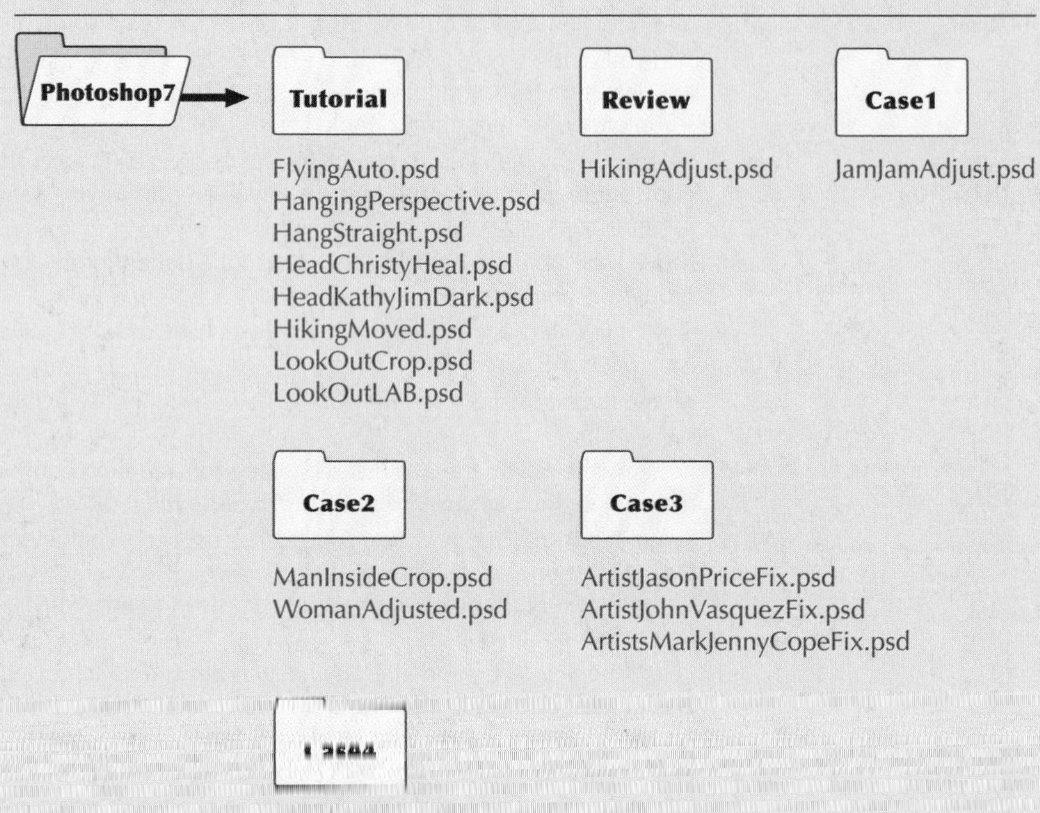
Photoshop7
Tutorial
FlyingAuto.psd
HangingPerspective.psd
HangStraight.psd
HeadChristyHeal.psd
HeadKathyJimDark.psd
HikingMoved.psd
LookOutCrop.psd
LookOutLAB.psd
Review
HikingAdjust.psd
Case1
JamJamAdjust.psd
Case2
ManInsideCrop.psd
WomanAdjusted.psd
Case3
ArtistJasonPriceFix.psd
ArtistJohnVasquezFix.psd
ArtistsMarkJennyCopeFix.psd
MyAlterProject.psd

TUTORIAL 8

Advanced Input/ Output and Color Management

Working with the Camera Raw Plug-In and Color Management Tools

PHOTOSHOP

OBJECTIVES

Session 8.1

- Work with camera raw files and the Camera Raw plug-in
- Explore Camera Raw retouching tools
- Set Camera Raw workflow options
- Create Smart Objects from camera raw files
- Examine a histogram and understand pixel clipping
- Adjust white balance, tone, clarity, vibrance, and saturation

Session 8.2

- Understand color management basics and calibrate a monitor
- Set up soft proofing, and explore color models, color

and graphics for use in video

Case | *FW Museum Store*

The FW is a Western art museum located in the heart of Fort Worth, Texas. The Museum Store is situated in the FW lobby, enabling visitors to commemorate their visit by purchasing a variety of collection reproductions and items created by local artisans.

Sadie Downing, the FW Museum Store administrator, has asked

You'll also learn about the parameters and requirements for files to be printed locally, printed professionally, and used on the Web. Finally, you'll learn about preparing content for video output.

STARTING DATA FILES

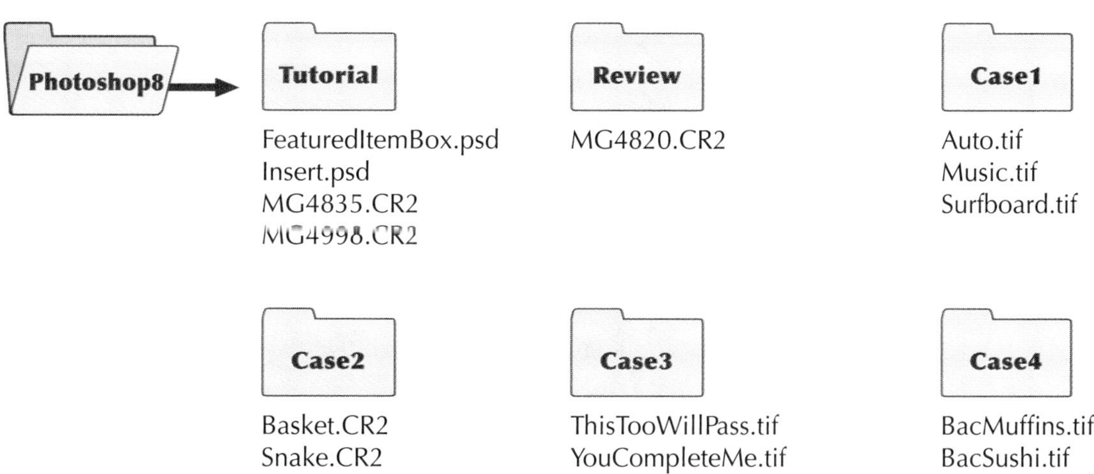

SESSION 8.1 VISUAL OVERVIEW

The Document window tools in the Camera Raw dialog box enable you to move, resize, rotate, and perform slight retouching to an image.

You can zoom, pan, and crop an image in the Camera Raw Document window; you can also preview changes that you make using the Camera Raw tools.

A **Smart Object layer** is a layer in a Photoshop file that contains either vector or raster image data and that preserves a link to the image's source content, enabling you to open and edit the image source.

Open a camera raw file from Mini Bridge by right-clicking the file and selecting Open in Camera Raw.

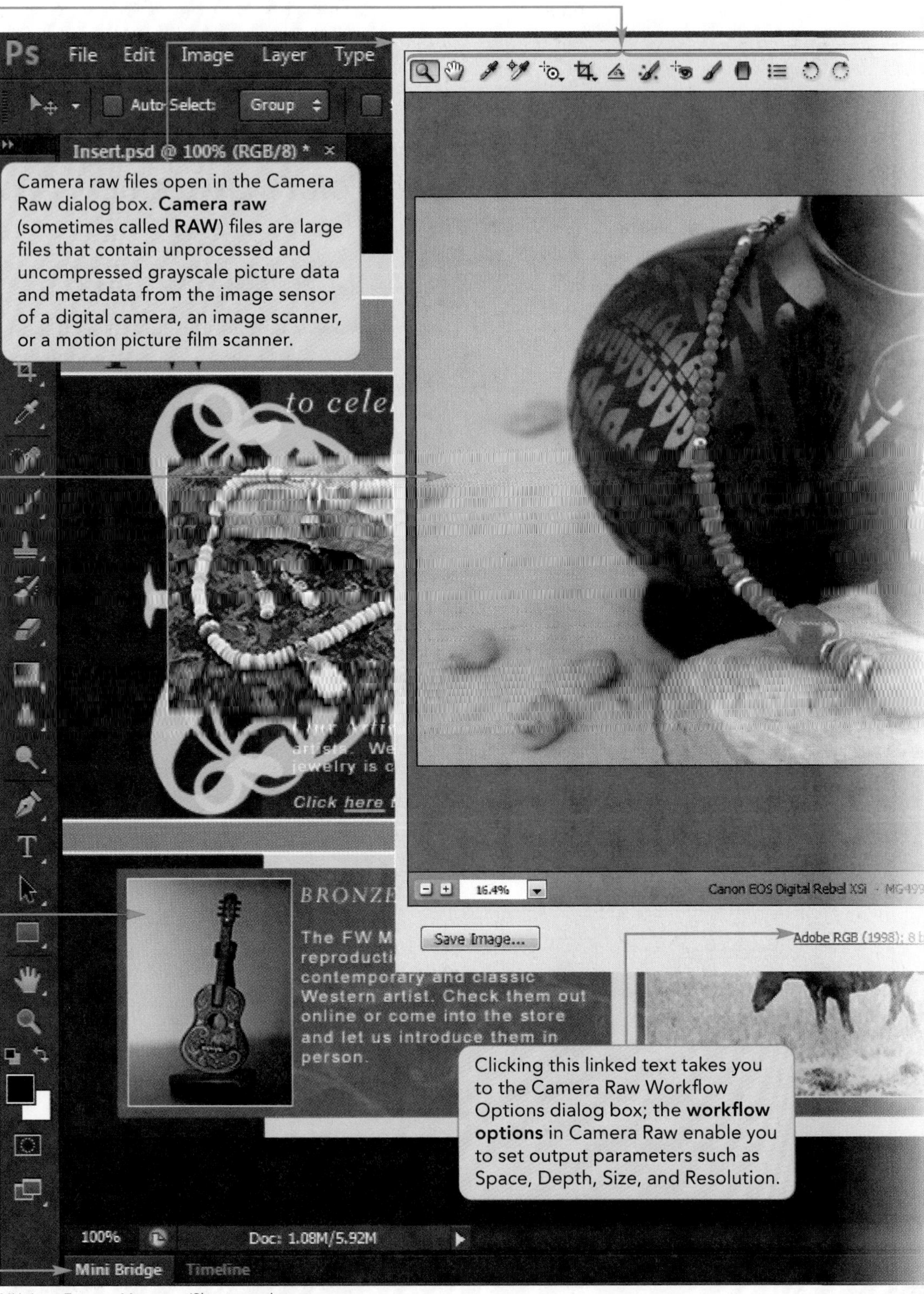

Camera raw files open in the Camera Raw dialog box. **Camera raw** (sometimes called **RAW**) files are large files that contain unprocessed and uncompressed grayscale picture data and metadata from the image sensor of a digital camera, an image scanner, or a motion picture film scanner.

Clicking this linked text takes you to the Camera Raw Workflow Options dialog box; the **workflow options** in Camera Raw enable you to set output parameters such as Space, Depth, Size, and Resolution.

NU, Inc.; Eugene Moerman/Shutterstock.com; © iStockphoto.com/1234567890987654321

WORKING WITH CAMERA RAW

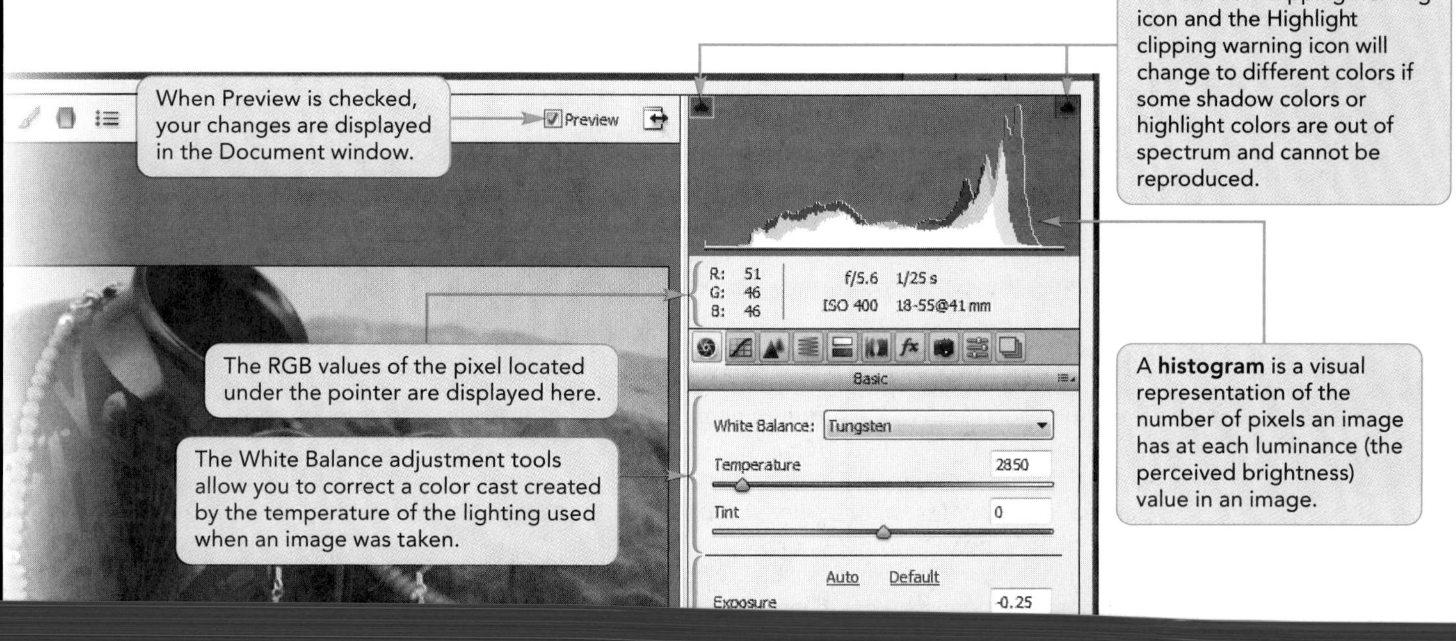
The Shadow clipping warning icon and the Highlight clipping warning icon will change to different colors if some shadow colors or highlight colors are out of spectrum and cannot be reproduced.
When Preview is checked, your changes are displayed in the Document window.
Preview
R: 51
G: 46
B: 46
f/5.6 1/25 s
ISO 400 18-55@41 mm
The RGB values of the pixel located under the pointer are displayed here.
Basic
A histogram is a visual representation of the number of pixels an image has at each luminance (the perceived brightness) value in an image.
White Balance: Tungsten
Temperature 2850
Tint 0
The White Balance adjustment tools allow you to correct a color cast created by the temperature of the lighting used when an image was taken.
Auto Default
Exposure -0.25

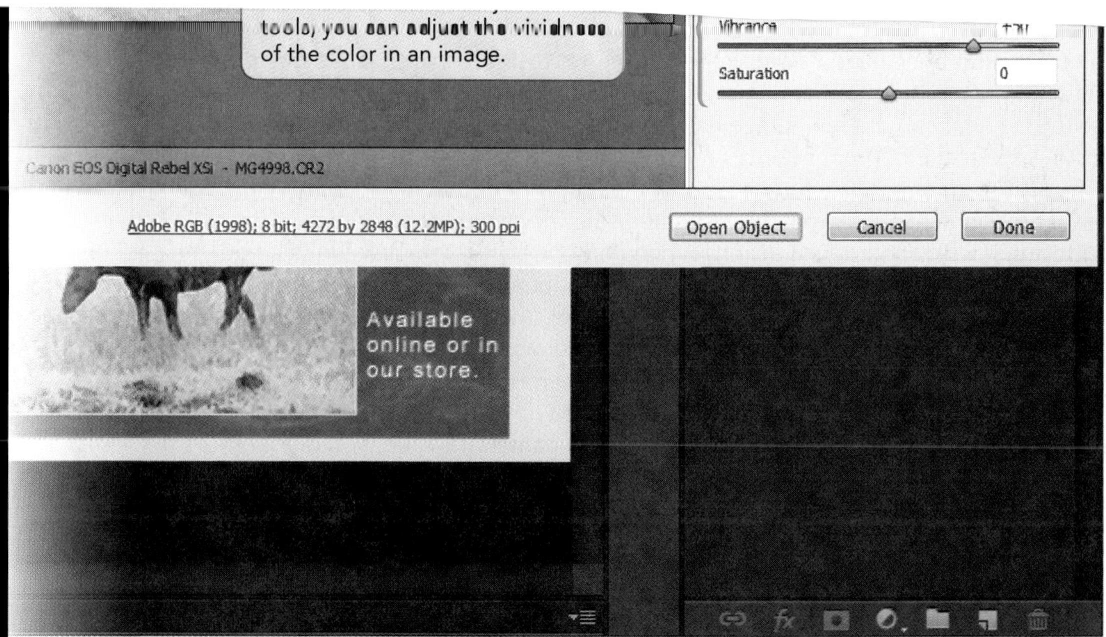
tools, you can adjust the vividness of the color in an image.
Vibrance
Saturation 0
Canon EOS Digital Rebel XSi - MG4998.CR2
Adobe RGB (1998); 8 bit; 4272 by 2848 (12.2MP); 300 ppi
Open Object
Cancel
Done
Available online or in our store.

Working with Camera Raw Files

When you take pictures with a high-end digital camera, you can specify that the images be saved in the camera's RAW format. A camera raw file is the digital equivalent of a photo negative. Because the major camera manufacturers have each developed their own proprietary processes for creating camera raw files, there are actually hundreds of different camera raw formats and file extensions that vary between manufacturers and sometimes even between camera models. In the past, this made working with camera raw files somewhat difficult unless you used the software that came with your camera to process the images and to save them in other, usable image formats. Fortunately, Adobe provides the Camera Raw plug-in, which is a third-party software that works with Photoshop to allow you to open and process many different camera raw files. You can find a list of cameras and camera raw files that Camera Raw supports at *www.adobe.com/go/learn_ps_cameraraw*.

The Photoshop Camera Raw Plug-in

The Photoshop **Camera Raw plug-in** enables Photoshop users to construct images from camera raw file data and to adjust and process those images. Each type of camera raw file saves image information in a slightly different way, and with the Camera Raw plug-in you can open and adjust all supported types of camera raw image files. However, you cannot use the Camera Raw plug-in to save images in a camera raw format. Instead, when you use Camera Raw to make adjustments to camera raw images, you can specify that the adjustment data is saved outside of the camera raw file, in one of two ways:

- **In the Camera Raw database**—A Camera Raw database file is located by default in the folder titled Documents and Settings/[*your username*]/Application data/Adobe/CameraRaw. When you choose the Camera Raw database option, all of the adjustment data for a file (such as data related to cropping or changes in contrast and brightness) is stored in the database, enabling you to move the camera raw file to different locations on your computer. If you need to move the image file to a storage location outside your computer, such as a CD or another computer, you must export the information from the database to an XMP file. Therefore, this option is a poor choice if you are working in a team or from more than one computer.
- **As a companion file called a sidecar XMP file**—An **XMP file** is a separate file that is saved in the same folder as the camera raw file and holds all of the image adjustment data. The original camera raw image data is not altered; rather, the adjustment data is saved outside of the original file. This means that all of the edits are nondestructive, and you can continue to use the camera raw file as your digital negative or as an archival file. Camera Raw saves the XMP file using the name of the original camera raw file along with an .xmp extension. When you open a camera raw file that you have adjusted, all of your adjustment data is automatically pulled from the XMP file and applied to the camera raw file. If you delete the XMP file, you will lose all of the adjustment data, and when you next open the camera raw file, it will appear as it did before you made any changes. When you move a camera raw file to another storage location, you must remember to move the XMP file with it or you will not be able to view any adjustments. To create another file from a camera raw file, you output the file to Photoshop where you must save it in a different file format, such as a JPEG or TIFF. Saving changes to a camera raw file in an XMP file is a good option whenever you might need to work on a file on more than one computer; because of this, it is the preferred option for people who work in teams.

To get set up before you begin working on the catalog image files, you'll adjust your Photoshop settings to specify that Camera Raw adjustment data will be saved in a sidecar XMP file.

TIP

When Camera Raw is open, you can access the Preferences dialog box by clicking the Open preferences dialog button on the toolbar or by pressing the Ctrl+K keys.

To adjust Camera Raw preferences:

1. Start Photoshop while pressing the **Ctrl+Alt+Shift** keys, and click **Yes** to delete the Settings File when prompted. Reset Photoshop to the default Essentials workspace layout, and then reset all tools.
2. On the menu bar, click **Edit**, point to **Preferences**, and then click **Camera Raw**. The Camera Raw Preferences dialog box opens. See Figure 8-1.

Figure 8-1 Camera Raw Preferences dialog box

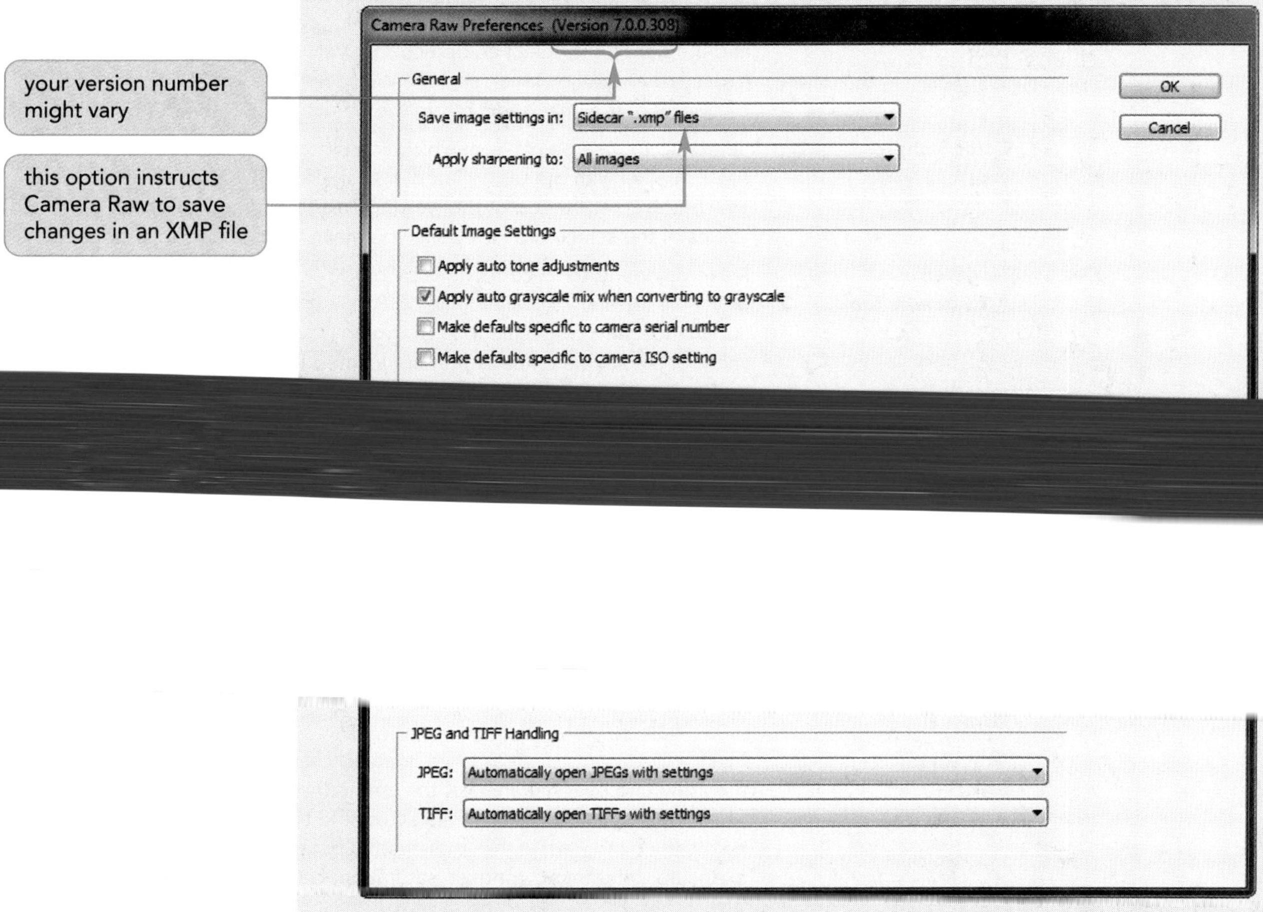

Make sure you click the Sidecar ".xmp" files option, or your adjustments will not be saved in the same folder as your Data Files.

3. In the "Save image settings in" box, click **Sidecar ".xmp" files**, if necessary.
4. Click the **OK** button to close the dialog box, and save the changes.

Exploring the Camera Raw Workspace

When you open a camera raw image, the image is displayed in the Camera Raw dialog box, which is divided into a Document window and an Adjustments panel. The Document window is where the image is displayed and, when the Preview check box is selected, where your adjustments are displayed. Above the Document window, you'll find a toolbar with a variety of viewing and retouching tools that enable you to manipulate the way you see the image and to correct small blemishes and problems in your image. For an overview of these tools, see Figure 8-2.

Figure 8-2 **Viewing and retouching tools in the Camera Raw dialog box**

Button Name	Icon	Use To
Zoom Tool		Control how much of an image is displayed in the Document window; clicking in the viewing area zooms in to the next higher zoom preset value while Alt-clicking zooms out. Dragging in the viewing area with the Zoom tool enables you to zoom in on an area of an image so it fills the screen.
Hand Tool		Pan an image to display a different area of the image when the entire image is not visible in the viewing area.
White Balance Tool		Adjust the colors in an image to correct for color cast created by flash and ambient light; select an object from your image that should be displayed as gray or white, and the White Balance tool will correct the color cast of the image and return the object to true white or gray.
Color Sampler Tool		Select up to nine points from which you can sample color; when you select a pixel with the Color Sampler tool, the RGB values for that point are displayed at the top of the viewing area, enabling you to see the values of the selected pixels while you make adjustments to your photo.
Targeted Adjustment Tool		Make color and tonal corrections by dragging on the image rather than using the sliders; you can adjust the Parametric Curve, Hue, Saturation, Luminance, and Grayscale Mix. Dragging down in an area decreases the value of colors in the image that are located in that area, while dragging upward increases their value.
Crop Tool		Adjust the borders of the image created from the Camera Raw file; because this does not affect the original file, you can readjust the image at any time.
Straighten Tool		Adjust the horizontal and vertical orientation of an image based on a line you drag in the viewing area; anything outside of the newly created borders of the image will be cropped.
Spot Removal		Repair a selected area of an image with sample pixels from another area of the image.
Red Eye Removal		Darken the red pupils that sometimes occur when a flash is used in photography.
Adjustment Brush		Make adjustments to areas of an image by setting the brush options and then painting over the areas of the image that you would like to alter; when the Adjustment Brush is selected, the tool options are displayed below the histogram in the Adjustments panel. Options include exposure, brightness, contrast, saturation, clarity, sharpness, and color.
Graduated Filter		Adjust a region of your image by setting filter options and then dragging across the image to select the region that the filter will affect; options include exposure, brightness, contrast, saturation, clarity, sharpness, and color.
Open preferences dialog box		Open the Camera Raw Preferences dialog box.
Rotate image 90° counter clockwise		Rotate the image displayed in the viewing area 90° in a counterclockwise direction; each time you click, the image rotates 90°.
Rotate image 90° clockwise		Rotate the image displayed in the viewing area 90° in a clockwise direction; each time you click, the image rotates 90°.
Preview check box		View the image with changes; uncheck it to view the original image.
Toggle full screen mode		View the Camera Raw dialog box in Full Screen mode.

REFERENCE

Opening a File in Camera Raw

- On the menu bar, click File, click Open, navigate to the camera raw file, and double-click the file to open it in the Camera Raw dialog box.

or

- Open Bridge, navigate to the camera raw file, right-click the file, and select Open in Camera Raw.

Next, you'll open a camera raw file provided by the catalog photographer and examine the Document window in the Camera Raw dialog box. Then, you'll crop the image using the Camera Raw Crop tool.

To open the camera raw file:

1. On the menu bar, click **File**, click **Open**, navigate to the Photoshop8\Tutorial folder provided with your Data Files, and open **MG4835.CR2**. The file opens in the Camera Raw dialog box.
2. On the toolbar located above the Camera Raw Document window, click the **Toggle full screen mode** button. See Figure 8-3.

Figure 8-3 **Camera Raw dialog box**

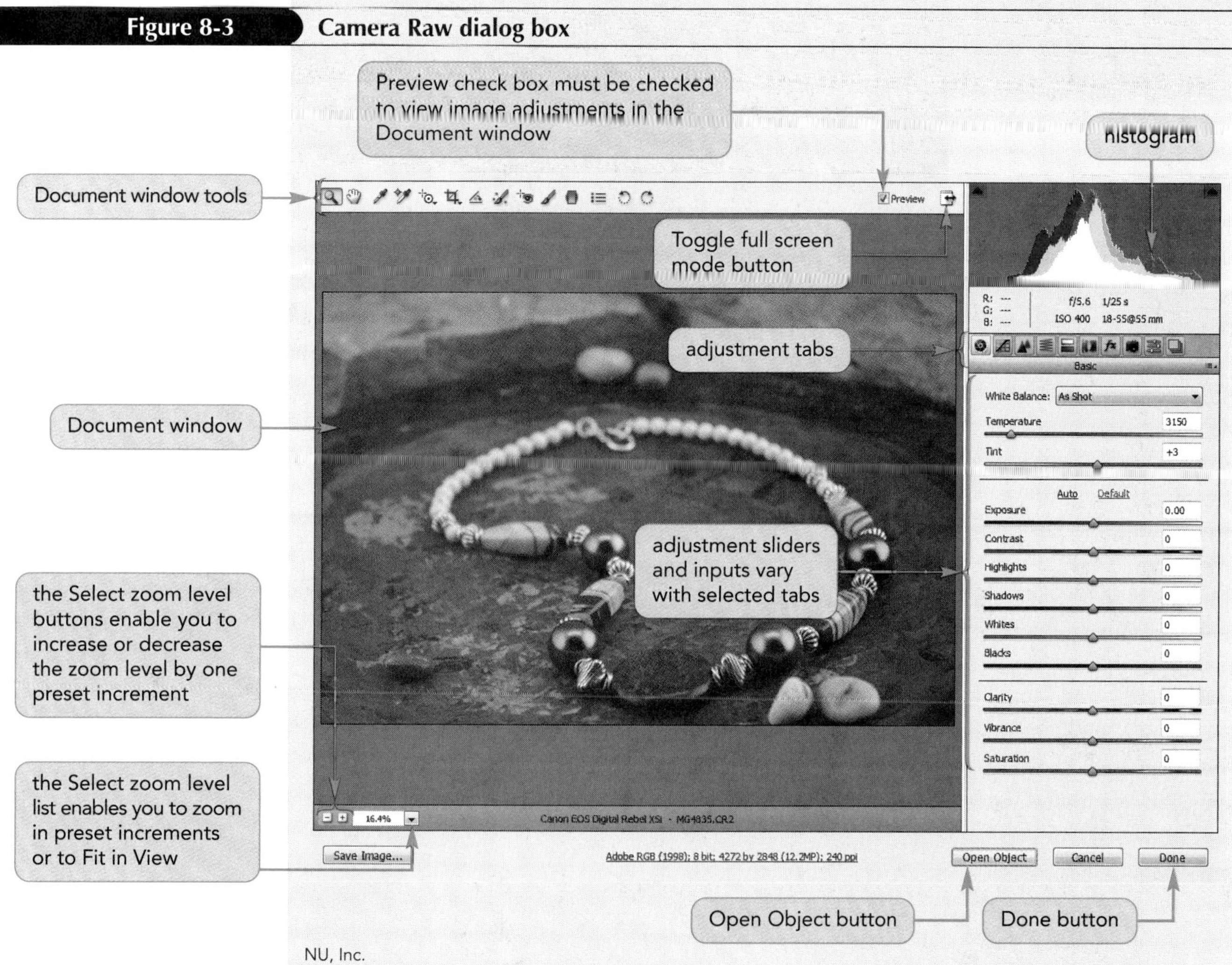

NU, Inc.

3. On the toolbar, click the **Zoom Tool** button, if necessary, and then click in the Document window to increase the magnification of the image to **25%** (which is one of the preset values).
4. Click in the Document window, and drag to select the front of the necklace. The selected area expands to fill the Document window, as shown in Figure 8-4.

Figure 8-4 **Selected area of the image fills the Document window**

use the Zoom tool to select an area of the image to magnify

the selected area of the image fills the Document window

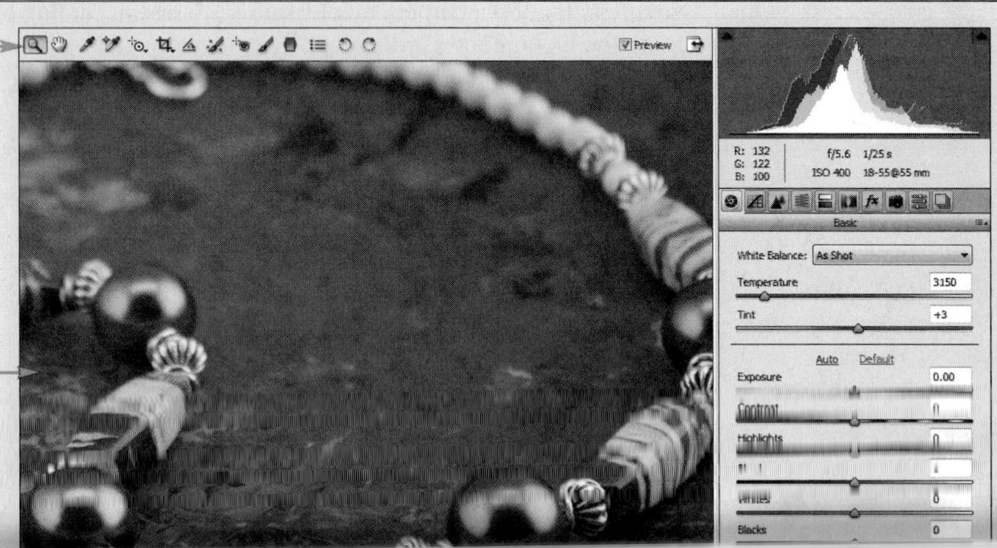

NU, Inc.

5. On the toolbar above the Document window, click the **Hand Tool** button, click in the image, and then drag the image to the right, so you can see how to pan the image within the Document window.
6. Click the **Select zoom level** button below the Document window, and then click **Fit in View**. The entire image is displayed in the Document window.
7. On the toolbar, click and hold the **Crop Tool** button to display its context menu, and then click **Custom**. The Custom Crop dialog box opens.

8. In the Crop list, click **Ratio** to select it, if necessary. Type **1** in the first box and **.8** in the second box, and then click the **OK** button.

   The crop ratio is now set for the Crop tool. Next, you'll crop the image.

9. In the Document window, place the pointer at the upper-left corner of the necklace, and click and drag the mouse down and to the right until the front of the necklace is in the area that will not be cropped. Release the mouse button. See Figure 8-5.

Figure 8-5 **Crop tool in the Document window**

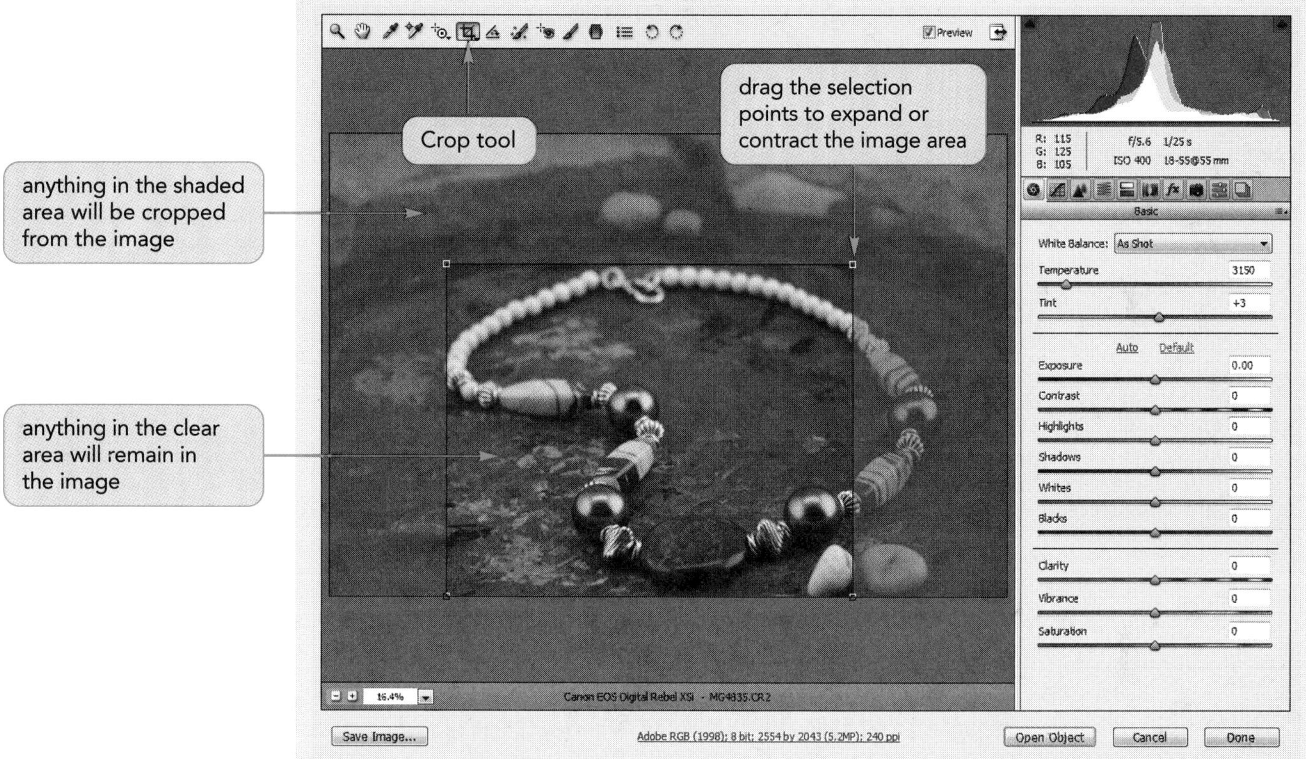

Crop tool

drag the selection points to expand or contract the image area

anything in the shaded area will be cropped from the image

anything in the clear area will remain in the image

NU, Inc.

10. Drag the upper-right selection handle up and to the right until the entire necklace is in the image area. See Figure 8-6.

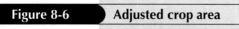

Figure 8-6 **Adjusted crop area**

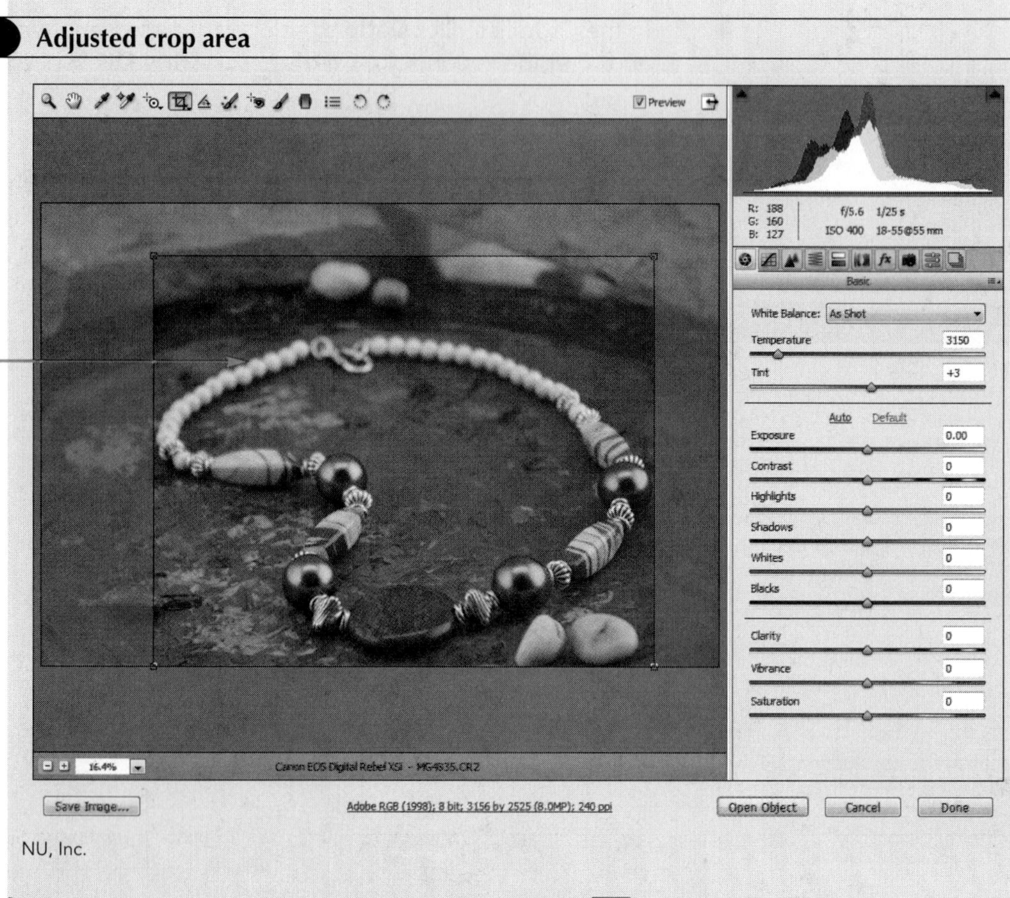

the entire necklace is now included in the clear area of the image; the rest of the image will be cropped

NU, Inc.

11. On the toolbar, click the **Hand Tool** button to view the newly cropped image.

Specifying Workflow Options

As noted previously, the way you work in the Camera Raw plug-in is slightly different from the way you work in Photoshop and other graphics programs because any adjustments that you make in Camera Raw are stored outside of the original file, in an XMP file or the camera raw database, and are only applied when you create other files from your original camera raw file by outputting the file to Photoshop. Once you output your file to Photoshop, the adjustments you made in Camera Raw are incorporated into the file, and you must save the file as a different file type, such as PSD, PDF, TIFF, or JPEG.

Another difference is that images are always opened in Camera Raw with the full size, resolution, color specifications, and bit depth with which your digital camera captured them, and because you do not make destructive adjustments to camera raw files, there is never a need to adjust these settings while you are working in Camera Raw. You can, however, use the Workflow Options dialog box in Camera Raw to adjust these parameters for files you output from the Camera Raw plug-in. You access the Workflow Options dialog box by clicking the linked text below the Document window. The workflow settings are very similar to the settings you input when you create a new document in Photoshop, and they are applied when a file is output from Camera Raw to Photoshop. The Camera Raw workflow options include the following:

- **Space**—RAW files usually use camera-native specifications for color; however, Camera Raw enables you to specify a target color profile for image output. Selecting Space settings is like selecting a color mode and color profile when you create a new document in Photoshop.
- **Depth**—You can set the bit depth for an image in Camera Raw, as you have already done in Photoshop. You can choose to open a file in Photoshop as an 8Bits/Channel or a 16 Bits/Channel image.
- **Size (or Crop Size)**—With this setting, you can select the pixel dimensions of images you import into Photoshop. By default, the size is set to the dimensions of the image. Once you have cropped an image in Camera Raw, the label changes to Crop Size, indicating that the image will be output at the cropped size. This is similar to setting the width and height of a new document in Photoshop.
- **Resolution**—You can adjust the resolution at which an image is printed. This setting does not affect the pixel dimensions; it is the same as setting Resolution for a document in Photoshop.
- **Sharpen For**—This option allows you to specify sharpening settings for output to Screen, Glossy Paper, or Matte Paper. Typically, this setting is left to the default option—None.
- **Open in Photoshop as Smart Objects**—When this box is checked, camera raw images opened in Photoshop will open as Smart Object layers.

PROSKILLS

Decision Making: Determining Project Parameters

To make good work flow decisions during a project, you must have a clear understanding of what you need to provide as a final product. Decisions regarding color model, size, resolution, file type, delivery method, and so forth should be determined during the planning phase of the project. Get input from all of the people who will receive versions of the final product to ensure that you create an end product that will satisfy all of your client's needs. For example, if your project includes professional print output, ask the printer to specify the required image size, resolution, and file type. If you are creating a Web version of the materials, ask the Web designer similar questions. It is a good idea to create a complete project plan prior to beginning any work on your project. Even if you are just retouching an image, take a few moments to make sure you understand exactly what you need to provide as an end product. Taking the time to make decisions regarding project parameters prior to beginning work will enable you to streamline your process and to provide superior final results.

When Sadie hired your team to create this project, she contacted her printer who provided all of the parameters for the catalog insert project. You'll use that information to set the Camera Raw workflow options before you save your adjustments.

REFERENCE

Setting Workflow Options in Camera Raw

- In the Camera Raw dialog box, click the linked text at the bottom of the Document window.
- In the Workflow Options dialog box, set the Space, Depth, Size (Crop Size), Resolution, and Sharpen For settings, as desired.
- Click the Open in Photoshop as Smart Objects check box to select it so that camera raw images opened in Photoshop will open as Smart Object layers.

To set workflow options in Camera Raw:

1. At the bottom of the Document window, click the linked text (as called out in the Session 8.1 Visual Overview). The Workflow Options dialog box opens.
2. In the Space box, click **Adobe RGB (1998)** to select it, if necessary, and in the Depth box select **8 Bits/Channel**. In the Resolution box, type **300** and make sure the **pixels/inch** setting is selected. Click the **Open in Photoshop as Smart Objects** check box to select it, if necessary. See Figure 8-7.

Figure 8-7 Camera Raw Workflow Options dialog box

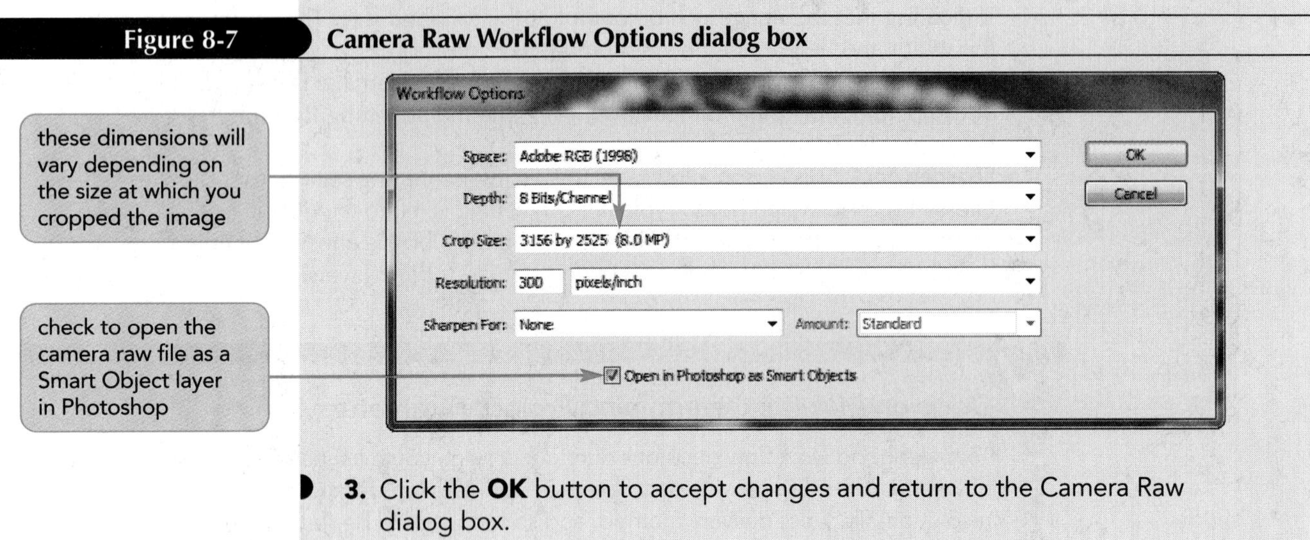

3. Click the **OK** button to accept changes and return to the Camera Raw dialog box.

Saving Adjustments to a Camera Raw File

After you make adjustments to a camera raw file, you can save the adjustments by clicking either the Done button or the Open Object button at the bottom of the Camera Raw dialog box. When you click Done, the changes are saved in an XMP file (based on the option you chose in the Camera Raw Preferences dialog box), and the Camera Raw dialog box closes without a copy of the image being opened in Photoshop. If you click Open Object, the adjustments are saved in an XMP file, the Camera Raw dialog box closes, and a copy of the image is opened as a Smart Object layer in a Photoshop document. To save a copy of the image that opened in Photoshop, you must save the file as a PSD in Photoshop. This will not affect the original camera raw file, which can only be accessed via the Camera Raw plug-in, but it will make your image accessible for other uses.

Unlike most Smart Objects, which are linked to an original source file, a Smart Object that is created from a camera raw file is linked to a copy of the camera raw file that is embedded in the Photoshop file. When you double-click the Smart Object layer, it will open the embedded camera raw file in the Camera Raw dialog box. You can make edits to the embedded camera raw file and when you exit Camera Raw the adjustments will flow through to your Smart Object in your PSD file, but they will not affect the original camera raw file. Further, additional adjustments to your original camera raw file will not affect the Smart Object or its embedded camera raw file. As with regular Smart Objects, you can make nondestructive adjustments to the Smart Object layer from within Photoshop. However, if you would like to make pixel-altering adjustments, like dodging or burning, you must convert the Smart Object into a regular layer by rasterizing it. (Note that if you leave the Open in Photoshop as Smart Objects check box unchecked in the Camera Raw Workflow Options dialog box, the Open Object button would say Open Image, and clicking it would save the adjustments in an XMP file, the Camera Raw dialog box would close, and a copy of the image would open as the Background layer in a Photoshop document.)

Next, you'll save your adjustments and open a copy of the image of the necklace as a Smart Object layer in a document in Photoshop so you can create versions of the image that you will use for print and for the Web. You'll save the document as a PSD file, and then you'll open the embedded camera raw file in Camera Raw to ensure that the Smart Object is linked to the embedded camera raw file. Finally, you'll open the folder where your Data Files are stored, and you'll locate the XMP file, which is created when you click the Open Object button.

TIP

When you click the Open Object button, the camera raw file opens in Photoshop, but the image will still need to be saved in Photoshop.

To open the camera raw file as a Smart Object:

1. In the Camera Raw dialog box, click the **Open Object** button, and then press the **Ctrl+0** keys to fill the screen.

   Trouble? If you see an Open Image button instead of the Open Object button, you did not check the Open in Photoshop as Smart Objects check box in the Camera Raw Workflow Options dialog box. Open the Workflow Options dialog box, check the Open in Photoshop as Smart Objects check box, and then click the OK button to save your change. Then click the Open Object button. Or, simply Shift-click the Open Image button to open the file as a Smart Object.

   The adjustments to the camera raw file are saved in an XMP file, and a copy of the image is opened as a Smart Object layer in a document in Photoshop. See Figure 8-8.

Figure 8-8 **Image opened as a Smart Object**

image opened as a Smart Object layer in Photoshop
the filename does not have a file extension, indicating that it has not yet been saved
a small portion of a rock is visible in the frame; you will crop this later
icon indicates that the layer contains a Smart Object
File Edit Image Layer Type Select Filter 3D View Window Help
MG4835 as Smart Object-1 @ 21.6% (MG4835, RGB/8*)
Color Swatches
Adjustments Styles
Add an adjustment
Layers Channels Paths
Normal
Opacity: 100%
Fill: 100%
MG4835
Doc: 22.8M/22.8M
Mini Bridge

NU, Inc.

2. Save the file as **MG4835SO.psd** in the Photoshop8\Tutorial folder.
3. In the Layers panel, double-click the thumbnail for the Smart Object layer. The embedded camera raw file opens in the Camera Raw dialog box.
4. Click the **OK** button to return to Photoshop.

   The Progress dialog box opens, indicating that Photoshop is updating the Smart Object to synchronize it with the embedded camera raw file and display any changes that you made to the original files. You must save the PSD file again even if you have not made changes.
5. On the menu bar, click **File**, and then click **Save**.
6. On the Windows 7 taskbar, click the **Windows Explorer** icon, and navigate to the Photoshop8\Tutorial folder. Locate the MG4835.xmp file; this is the sidecar file where the adjustments to your original camera raw file are stored.
7. Close the folder window.

TIP

Deleting the XMP file would delete all of the adjustments that you made to the camera raw file.

Sadie would like to use this image in the insert, but she feels that the small portion of the brown rock that appears at the left of the cropped image is distracting. She would like you to adjust the cropping so that the rock is removed from the frame. This will require cropping a portion of the necklace from the frame, but it will create a less cluttered and, therefore, more aesthetically appealing composition.

When you adjust the size of the camera raw file embedded in the Smart Object layer of your PSD file, the width and height of your PSD canvas do not change; therefore, a portion of the canvas will not be filled by your image. To fill the document area with the image, you can either reduce the size of the canvas so it is the same size as the image or you can stretch the image to fill the canvas.

You'll open the Smart Object in Camera Raw and adjust the cropping to remove the portion of the rock that is displayed at the left of the frame. Then, you'll return to Photoshop and use Free Transform to stretch the cropped image to fill the canvas. Finally, you'll examine your original camera raw file to see if the changes you made to the embedded document affect the original file.

To crop the image in the camera raw file embedded in the Smart Object:

1. In the Layers panel, double-click the thumbnail for the Smart Object layer to open the embedded camera raw file in the Camera Raw dialog box.
2. On the toolbar located above the Document window in the Camera Raw dialog box, click the **Crop Tool** button to display the entire image and the adjustable cropping area.
3. In the Document window, click and drag the upper-left selection handle down and to the right until the brown rock, located at the left of the visible area, is no longer within the cropped area of the image.
4. Click the **OK** button to save the adjustment and update the Smart Object. See Figure 8-9.

Figure 8-9 Updated Smart Object

asterisk indicates that changes have been made to the document since it was last saved
the cropped Smart Object no longer fills the canvas

NU, Inc.

You'll use Free Transform to stretch the image to fill the canvas. When you make adjustments to the Smart Object in Photoshop, it does not affect the embedded camera raw file.

5. On the menu bar, click **Edit**, and then click **Free Transform**. Photoshop adds selection handles to the image in the Document window.
6. Click and drag the upper-right selection handle up and to the right until it is in the upper-right corner of the canvas.
7. Click and drag the lower-left selection handle down and to the left until it is in the lower-left corner of the canvas.
8. Press the **Enter** key. Notice that the cropped area has not changed but the image now fills the canvas. See Figure 8-10.

Figure 8-10 Cropped Smart Object transformed to fill the canvas

canvas is no longer visible
the cropped area remains the same, but it now fills the canvas
File Edit Image Layer Type Select Filter 3D View Window Help

NU, Inc.

9. Save the image, and close the file.
10. On the menu bar, click **File**, click **Open**, and then navigate to the Photoshop8\Tutorial folder, and open **MG4835.CR2**, which is the file you originally worked with.

    The file opens in the Camera Raw dialog box. Notice that the crop adjustment you made in Camera Raw is still applied to this file, but the last adjustment you made to crop out the brown rock in the embedded camera raw file in the MG4835SO.psd document was not applied to this file.
11. Click the **Cancel** button to close the Camera Raw dialog box.

INSIGHT

Using Mini Bridge (or Bridge) with Camera Raw

You can use Mini Bridge (or Bridge) to view and manage your camera raw files, just as you would with other image files. Camera raw files are displayed in the same way your other image files are displayed, and in Bridge, you can open a camera raw file without opening Photoshop by right-clicking the file and selecting Open in Camera Raw or you can double-click a camera raw file to open the image in the Camera Raw plug-in and also open Photoshop. Bridge also enables you to apply, copy, and clear settings between files and to see file metadata. It enables you to batch process your files and to apply settings to files without opening the Camera Raw dialog box. In Mini Bridge, you can open a file in Camera Raw by right-clicking it, pointing to Open with, and then clicking Camera Raw.

Before you can use Camera Raw to create a professional image, you must understand the Camera Raw retouching and adjustment tools, and you need to learn a bit about the language photographers use so you will understand how your adjustments will affect your photographic image. Next, you'll spend some time exploring the Adjustments panel in the Camera Raw dialog box.

Making Basic Adjustments to RAW Images

The Camera Raw Adjustments panel is located on the right side of the Camera Raw dialog box, and it provides a robust array of tools for adjusting your RAW images. The Adjustments panel in Camera Raw is set up a bit differently than the Adjustments panel in Photoshop, but it enables you to create some similar adjustments. The histogram, which is displayed above the Adjustments panel, provides a visual representation of how the adjustments you make are affecting the image. Because camera raw files contain so much more data than image files that you work with in Photoshop, and because the Camera Raw plug-in was created specifically to enable you to make the fine adjustments necessary for correcting professional photographic images, you can usually achieve better results adjusting images in Camera Raw rather than in Photoshop. Using the information provided by the histogram and the adjustment tools available in Camera Raw provides you with a great deal of control over image output. For an overview of the tabs in the Adjustments panel, see Figure 8-11.

Figure 8-11 Adjustments panel tabs

Tab	Icon	Description
Basic		General adjustments to white balance, tone, and saturation are performed using the Basic tab; the other tabs are used for fine-tuning images.
Tone Curve		Like the Curves Adjustment in Photoshop, the Tone Curve tab is used to fine-tune tonal adjustments.
Detail		The Detail tab contains the Sharpening and Noise Reduction adjustments. Sharpening adjusts the edge definition of images, and Noise Reduction adjusts the artifacts (or distortions) that are sometimes visible in digital photographic images.
HSL/ Grayscale		Fine adjustments to hue, saturation, and luminance, as well as conversion to grayscale, are adjusted on the HSL/Grayscale tab.
Split Toning		Fine adjustments to the highlights, shadows, and balance of an image are adjusted on the Split Toning tab.
Lens Corrections		Perspective and lens flaws can be corrected automatically or manually on the Lens Corrections tab.
Effects		The Grain and Vignette effects are located on the Effects tab. The Grain effect creates artifacts that simulate film grain, and Vignette effects create dark or light edges around images, creating a circular frame that is used to draw the viewer's eyes toward an object of focus located near the center of the frame.
Camera Calibration		The Camera Calibration tab enables you to adjust how Camera Raw will process the colors of your camera raw images.
Presets		The Presets tab allows you to create and name custom presets, which you can use to adjust images.
Snapshots		The Snapshots tab enables you to record the state of an image at any point while you are in Camera Raw. Once you have created a snapshot of an image, you can restore the image back to the settings that were applied when the snapshot was taken, at any time during the editing process.

The Basic tab is displayed on the Adjustments panel by default when a file is opened in the Camera Raw dialog box because its controls enable you to make general adjustments to your image, including white balance, tone, and saturation adjustments. Almost all images benefit from Basic tab adjustments. Once you have cropped an image so that the composition is appealing, your next step should always be to make adjustments to the image using the adjustments on the Basic tab. All of the images that you are working on for the catalog insert will need basic adjustments. In the next section, you'll examine the histogram and the Basic tab to see how your adjustments affect your images.

Understanding the Histogram

The histogram that appears above the Adjustments panel displays a great deal of useful information, but it can be a bit tricky to interpret what you see. It is important to remember that the histogram is a simple bar graph that has two axes. Recall from Tutorial 7 that the horizontal x-axis of a histogram represents all the possible brightness (also called luminance) values that can be displayed in an image, starting at 0 (complete darkness) on the left and running to 255 (the brightest white) on the right. The center of the x-axis represents the midtones. The vertical y-axis represents the number of pixels in the image that display a particular luminance value, starting with 0 pixels at the bottom of the axis and moving upward. Understanding this information can tell you a lot. For example, when a large number of high Y values in an image are concentrated at the left of the x-axis, the image is probably underexposed and, therefore, looks dark. If a large number of high Y values in an image are concentrated at the right of the image, it is probably overexposed, and looks blown out—or white.

The histogram also has three channels of color: red, green, and blue. White is displayed when all three of the channels overlap. Yellow, magenta, or cyan appears when two channels overlap.

A histogram that displays a fairly wide curve or arc for each channel is representative of an image that uses the full tonal scale; for such an image, the histogram shows the highest number of pixels at the midtone values, along with some pixels that display shadows and some pixels that display highlights. When making adjustments to images, designers often try to spread out pixel values fairly evenly across the histogram. A histogram that has wide areas of zero value across channels is an image that does not use a full tonal range. Images that display this type of histogram are often dull. Finally, a histogram that displays tall spikes is likely to produce clipping.

Clipping occurs when the pixel values fall outside of the range that can be reproduced in the color space in which you are working. Areas that are overly bright are clipped to output white, whereas areas that are overly dark are clipped to output black. Whenever clipping occurs, detail is lost in areas of the image containing the clipped color values.

Now that you understand how to interpret a histogram, you can see that when spikes occur at the left of the histogram, there is potential for shadow clipping because the spikes are occurring on the side of the x-axis that displays darker values. Conversely, spikes at the right of the histogram indicate potential highlight clipping.

Clipping warnings are displayed in the upper corners of the histogram. The Shadow clipping warning icon is displayed at the left of the histogram and the Highlight clipping warning icon is displayed at the right. When pixel values fall outside of the reproducible range, the black clipping warning triangles in the histogram change in color to correspond with the color(s) being clipped. The clipping warning icons display red, green, or blue if only red, green, or blue values are being clipped. White is displayed when all three of the channels are being clipped, and yellow, magenta, or cyan appears when two channels are being clipped. If you click on a clipping warning triangle icon, the clipped pixels will be colored in the Document window—highlights in red and shadows in blue—enabling you to identify problems and to adjust your image more effectively.

TIP

Toggling a clipping warning icon off and on can help you identify the pixels that may be affected by clipping.

You'll select the Highlight clipping warning icon to display pixels in your image that will be clipped.

TIP

In images that contain a lot of red, you will need to examine the image closely to differentiate the pixels that will be clipped from those that are naturally red.

To display clipped pixels:

1. Click the **Mini Bridge** panel tab to open it, click the Launch Bridge button, and navigate to the Photoshop8\Tutorial folder. Right-click the **MG4998.CR2** file, point to **Open with**, and then click **Camera Raw**. The file opens in the Camera Raw dialog box.
2. On the Basic tab of the Adjustments panel, drag the **Highlights** slider to the right until **+83** is displayed as the Highlights value and the red Highlight clipping warning is displayed in the upper-right corner of the histogram.
3. Click the red **Highlight clipping warning** icon. The pixels that will be clipped are displayed in red in the image. See Figure 8-12.

Figure 8-12 **Highlight clipping displayed in red**

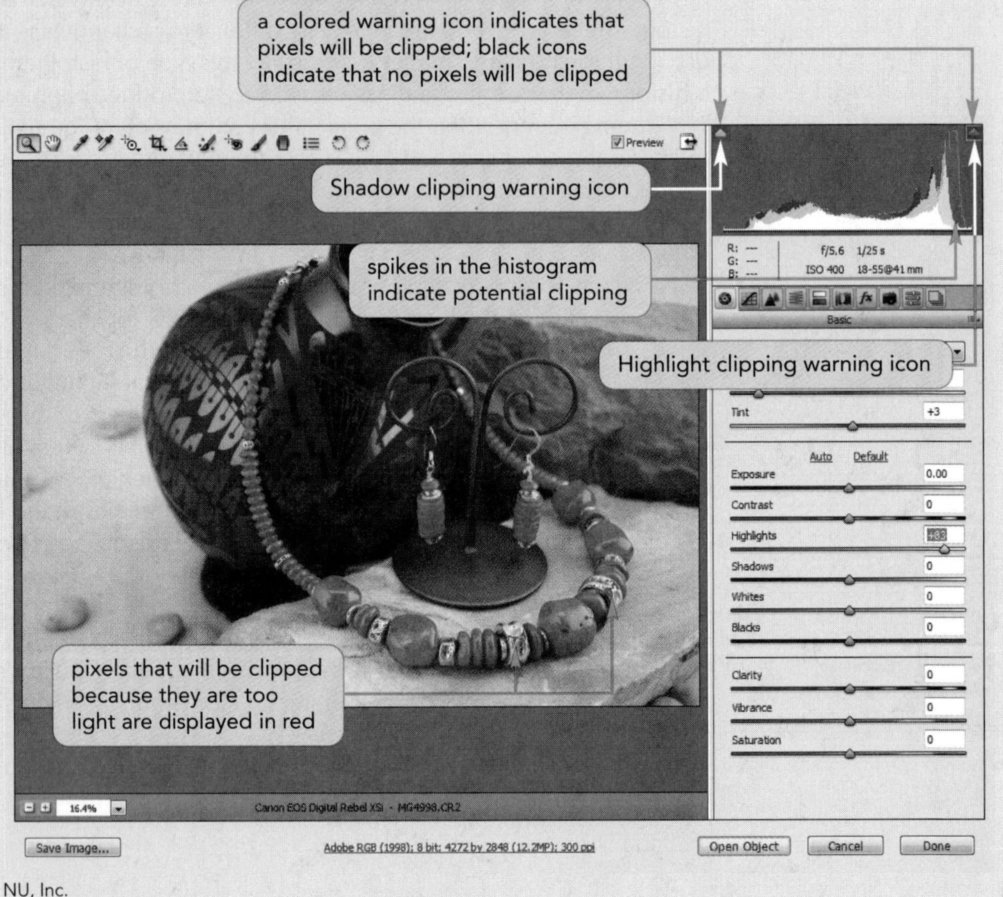

NU, Inc.

4. Click the **Highlight clipping warning** icon again. The red is removed from the display.

INSIGHT

Working with the Histogram Panel in Photoshop

The Histogram panel in Photoshop (as well as the histogram that is displayed in the Photoshop Properties panel when you make a Level or Curves adjustment) can be interpreted in the same way that you interpret the histogram in Camera Raw. You can use histograms in Photoshop to help you make better adjustments in the same way you use the Camera Raw histogram. When you use the Histogram panel to examine an image, you can choose Compact View, which is similar to what you see in Camera Raw, or you can select Expanded View, which provides additional information about your image and allows you to view a histogram for the entire composition or to select a single layer and view the histogram information for only that layer. In addition, in the Histogram panel, you can select All Channel View, which shows the combined histogram as well as separate histograms for each of the color channels used in the color mode your image is using (either red, green, and blue or cyan, magenta, yellow, and black). This view enables you to more closely examine how your adjustments are affecting your image. The Histogram panel does not provide the clipping warning buttons that are provided in Camera raw.

Lighting Concepts

Lighting is an important factor in taking a good photograph, and one of the important components of light that can affect your photographs is color temperature. Every light source has a color temperature that is measured in Kelvins (K). High color temperature measurements (5000K or more) produce light that is considered to have a cool color because it has a bluish tint. Florescent lights, found in many office buildings, are a good example of cool-colored light. Lower color temperature measurements (2700K to 3000K) produce light that is considered to have a warm color because it has a yellowish or reddish tint. The sun and fire are good examples of warm-colored light. Tungsten lights, often used by photographers when lighting in a studio, also have a warm color.

The color temperature of lights has a minimal effect on us in our daily lives because our eyes do an excellent job of recognizing what we are supposed to see, making things look fairly normal to us. However, the sensor that interprets light on a digital camera does not do as good of a job dealing with color temperature. Because of this, photographs often have a color cast. A **color cast** is a tint that affects an entire photograph. For example, a photograph that was taken in the sun might have a yellowish color cast; a photograph taken under florescent lighting might have a bluish color cast.

White Balancing an Image

Camera Raw enables you to correct the color cast created by the color temperature of lighting by white balancing your images. When you **white balance** an image, you locate objects in the image that should be white or gray and then make corrections that account for the color temperature of the lighting and that remove color casts from the image. In Camera Raw, the White Balance list has several preset options you can use to make general white balance corrections to your images, including the following:

- **As Shot**—Uses a camera's white balance settings
- **Auto**—Uses image data to calculate white balance adjustments
- **Daylight, Cloudy, and Shade**—Adjusts white balance to compensate for a specified lighting condition
- **Tungsten, Florescent, and Flash**—Adjusts white balance to compensate for the color temperature of the lighting used when a photograph was taken
- **Custom**—Enables you to create custom white balance settings

TIP

It is a good idea to make white balance corrections before you make any other tonal corrections.

In addition, you can create small adjustments by moving the Temperature and Tint sliders in the Adjustments panel in the Camera Raw dialog box.

Next, you'll adjust the white balance settings to compensate for the tungsten lighting that the photographer used while shooting the image for the catalog insert. Remember that tungsten lights have a color temperature of around 3200K, which produces a warm color. You'll experiment with white balance settings, and then you'll adjust to compensate for tungsten lighting. By white balancing the image, you'll remove the yellowish color cast from the photograph.

REFERENCE

White Balancing an Image

- In the Adjustments panel in the Camera Raw dialog box, click the White Balance button, and then click the option for the type of lighting that was used when the photograph was taken.
- At the top of the Camera Raw dialog box, click the Preview check box to uncheck it, and then click it again to check it, to see the effects of the White Balance option you selected.
- If the White Balance option you selected did not remove the color cast from the image, select a different White Balance option.

To white balance the image:

1. On the Basic tab of the Adjustments panel in the Camera Raw dialog box, click the **White Balance** button, and then click **Flash**. See Figure 8-13.

Figure 8-13 **Image with white balance adjusted to compensate for flash**

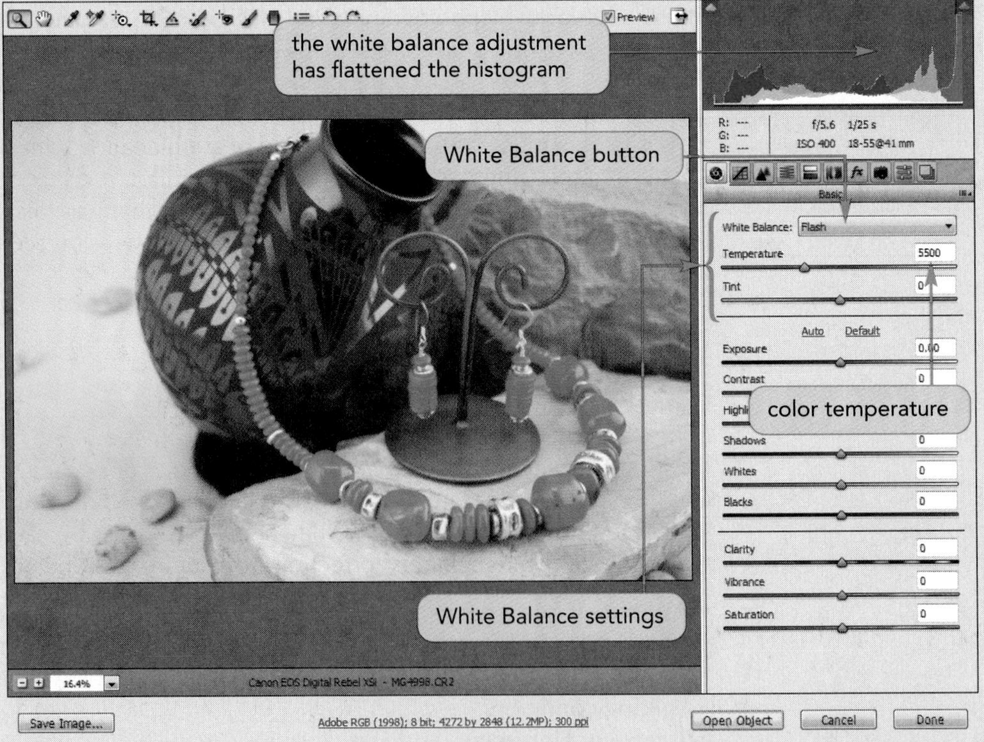

NU, Inc.

Because the color temperature of flash lighting is cool, the white balance adjustment made the image warmer, which has a poor effect on your image because it was shot with warm-colored tungsten light. The correction created a very yellow image.

2. In the Adjustments panel, click the **White Balance** button, and then click **Tungsten**. See Figure 8-14.

Figure 8-14 Image with white balance adjusted to compensate for tungsten

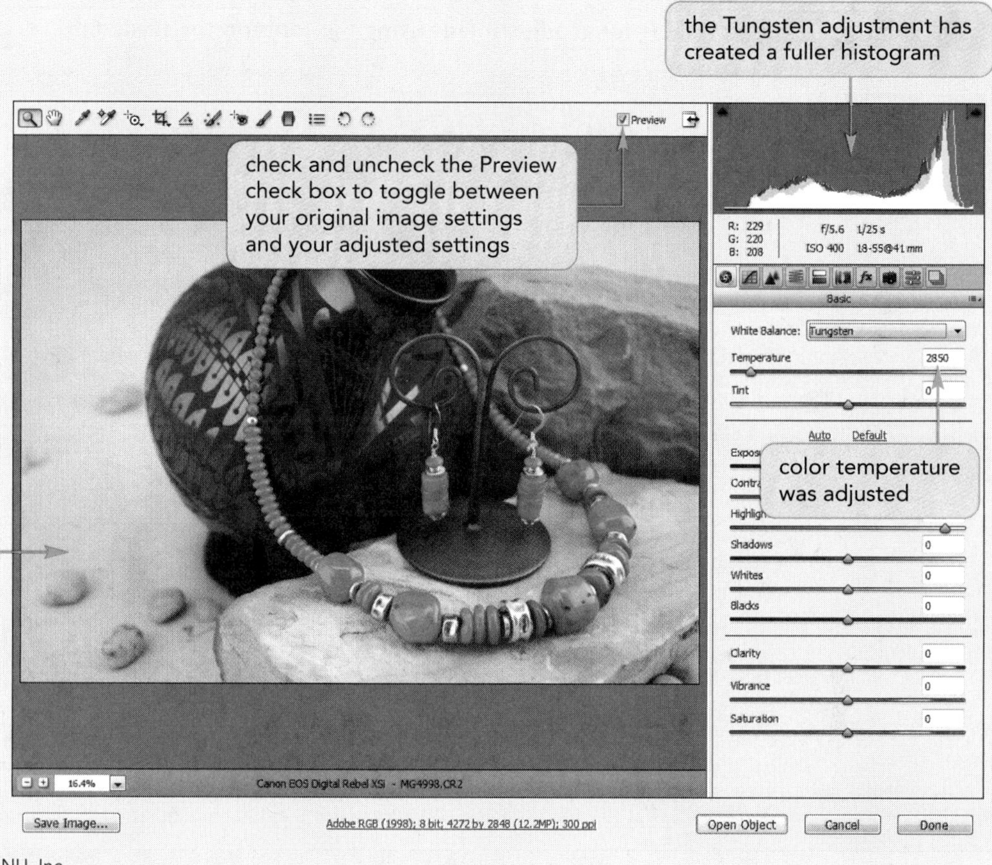

NU, Inc.

3. Click the **Preview** check box to uncheck it and see your original image settings.

4. Click the **Preview** check box again to check it and see your adjusted image settings. Notice how the yellowish color cast has been removed from the image.

Once you have adjusted the white balance of an image, you should make tonal corrections to the image. Tonal adjustments enable you to create a more dynamic and professional looking image. If the image is too bright, you can create a richer image by adding shadows and darker midtones. If the image is too dark, you can lighten the image to see more detail in areas of shadow. If an image is flat, you can increase contrast to create a more dynamic range of colors in the image.

Next, you'll make tonal adjustments to the image you just white balanced.

Making Basic Tonal Adjustments

Like Photoshop, Camera Raw has an Auto adjustment option, located at the top of the tonal adjustments section of the Basic tab, which analyzes the camera raw data and makes adjustments based on generalized rules of best practice. The Auto adjustment can be a good place to start, but, as with Photoshop's Auto adjustments, the Auto adjustments in Camera Raw are often too general. It is a better idea to become familiar with the tonal adjustment tools on the Basic tab, which allow you to make changes by dragging the sliders, entering values in the boxes, or selecting the numbers in the box and pressing the up or down arrow. See Figure 8-15.

Figure 8-15 **Making tonal adjustments using the tools on the Basic tab**

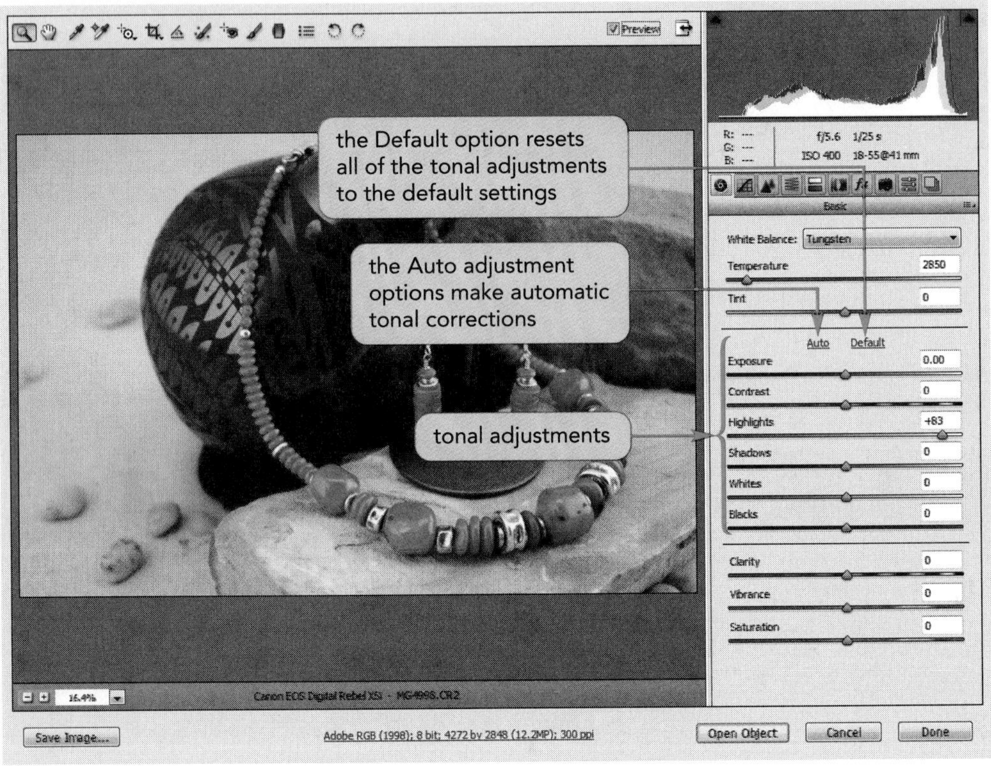

NU, Inc.

The Basic tab includes the following tonal adjustment tools:

- **Exposure**—Exposure adjusts the overall brightness/darkness of the image and has a greater effect on the image highlights. (Increments are equivalent to a camera's f-stop adjustments.) Because the tonal adjustment tools have a cumulative effect on your image, it is best to start with Exposure adjustments and then work your way through the Basic tab, as needed.
- **Contrast**—Contrast enables you to adjust the image by increasing or decreasing the opposition of relative lightness to relative darkness in the midtones of your image. An image with higher contrast has brighter light values and deeper dark values in the midtones of the image. Increasing the difference between the lightest tones and the darkest tones creates a more visually dynamic composition.
- **Highlights**—The Highlights tool is used to recover highlight details by bringing highlight values down; it enables Camera Raw to reconstruct some detail in areas where some color channels were clipped to white.

- **Shadows**—The Shadows tool is used to recover shadow details by bringing shadow values up without brightening blacks. Like the Highlights tool, the Shadows tool enables Camera Raw to reconstruct some detail, in this case, in areas where some color channels were clipped to black.
- **Whites**—Like the Exposure tool, the Whites tool is used to adjust the brightness/darkness of an image; however, the Whites tool creates the changes by compressing highlights while expanding shadows, when you move the slider right—or the reverse, when you move it left.
- **Blacks**—Concentrating its effects on the shadows in an image, this tool adjusts the input levels that are mapped to black. When you increase the Blacks value, you increase the range of dark colors in the image that are set to black. It is similar to setting and adjusting the black point in Photoshop. Increasing the Blacks value can be used to create the illusion that an image has greater contrast.

INSIGHT

Image Style

Before you begin making tonal adjustments to images you will use in a project, identify the look you are trying to create. It is not enough to create beautiful images. To produce a strong final project, all the images in a project must work well together. You should make general decisions about cropping, lightness, darkness, and color saturation before you begin adjusting images. Consider how you want objects to appear within the frame of the image. Cropping an image tightly around an object gives the object an exaggerated importance, whereas making an object a small part of a large composition can provide a sense of environment. Decide what you want to accomplish with the images in your project, and then make decisions regarding the cropping with those goals in mind. Consider how you would like the images to make the viewer feel and consider what styles are popular with your target audience. Also, consider the color of your composition background. For example, lighter images will pop on a dark background and may blend into a lighter background.

After you have taken all of these elements into account, make decisions about the lightness and darkness of your images. Image lightness and darkness can affect the drama and intensity of your composition as well as how the image looks in the overall composition. Saturation can be used to create a stylized look. Images that have heavily saturated colors look full and rich. Christmas catalogs often use images with oversaturated colors to create a festive look. Reducing image saturation also creates a stylized look. Western landscape photographers sometimes reduce the saturation of their images to intensify the vast openness of their photographic compositions. When making saturation decisions, think about the subject matter of your photographs. How will saturation affect the look of the images in your composition? What will be most effective in creating the look you are trying to achieve? Once you have an overall plan in place, you can adjust the images that you will use in your project. When you are finished, you should also compare the final images to ensure that when combined they will create a cohesive composition.

For the FW Museum Store project, your team has decided to crop all of the images fairly closely to emphasize the details of the jewelry. Images must be cropped with a 1 to .8 ratio to fit into the layout created by other members of your team. (The current image has already been cropped to reflect these dimensions.) The images for the insert should be light, and earth tones should be juxtaposed with vibrant, saturated colors. Next, you'll make tonal adjustments to your image.

To make basic tonal adjustments to the image:

1. In the Adjustments panel, click the **Auto** link. Notice that the adjustments are fairly heavy-handed and that the image is now fairly dark. In the histogram, the Highlight clipping warning is off, but now some shadow clipping is occurring.
2. Click the **Shadow clipping warning** icon. Pixels in the image that will be clipped are now displayed in a dark blue. See Figure 8-16.

Figure 8-16 Auto adjustment with shadow clipping visible

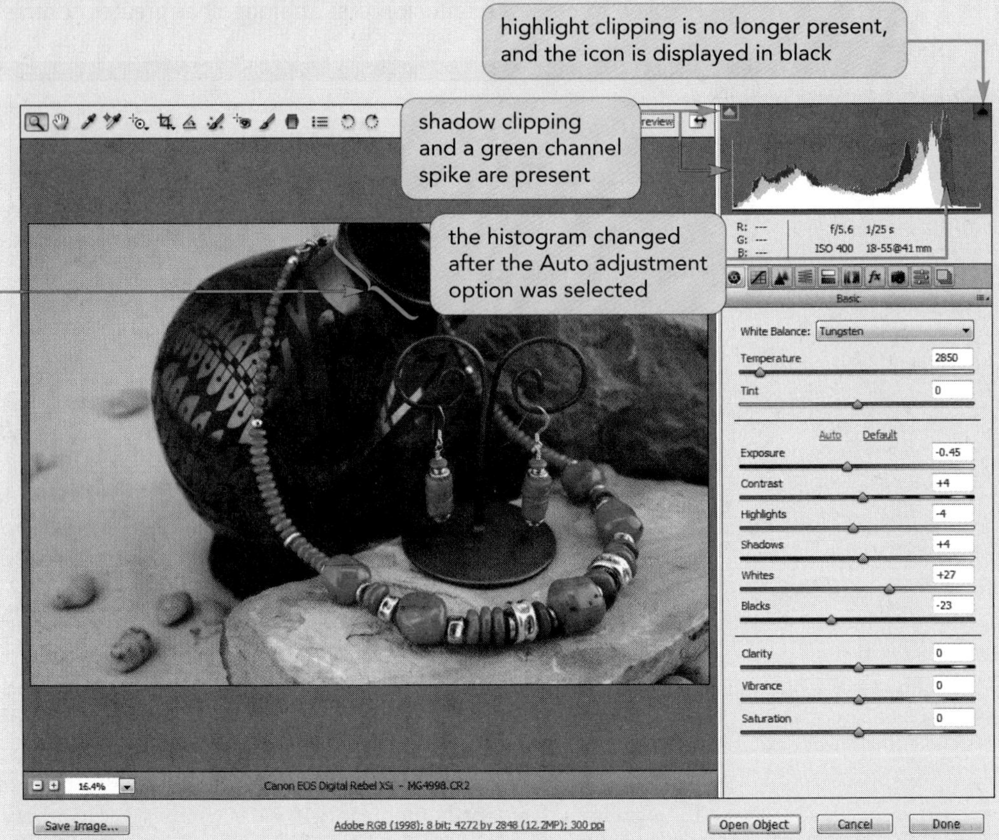

NU, Inc.

3. Press the **Ctrl+Z** keys to undo the Auto adjustment, and then drag the **Exposure** slider in the Adjustments panel left until **−0.25** is displayed in the box. This adjustment darkens the image in a less dramatic way than the Auto correction. Notice how the histogram changes as you drag the slider.

   You do not want to decrease the exposure of the entire image any further because it will make the image too dark, but it would be nice to see some of the detail that is currently lost in the highlights of the image, especially on the silver beads. To accomplish this, you'll decrease the Highlights value. This will darken only the highlight tones of the image, so you will be able to see more of the details in those areas.
4. To recover some of the detail in the silver beads, drag the **Highlights** slider to the left until **20** is displayed in the box. See Figure 8-17.

Figure 8-17 **Image with Highlights decreased**

highlight clipping is not present
new Highlights value
the Highlights adjustment has increased the level of detail in the silver beads where highlights were being clipped

NU, Inc.

5. Click the **Preview** check box to uncheck it and view your original settings, and then click it again to recheck the box.
6. Drag the **Shadows** slider to the left to decrease the Shadows value to **−25**, which increases shadows without changing the Blacks level.
7. Drag the **Blacks** slider to the right, to increase the Blacks value to **+10** to decrease the number of colors in the image that are displayed as black and to remove the clipping warnings.

Your image is looking better, but it is not perfect. Next, you'll adjust the clarity, vibrance, and saturation of your image to enhance the look of the final image.

Clarity, Vibrance, and Saturation Adjustments

The remaining controls on the Basic tab all affect the saturation of color in your images. As you learned in Tutorial 7, the saturation is the vividness or purity of the color. Adjustments to the Clarity value have the greatest effect in the midtones of an image. Increasing the Clarity value increases the sharpness and detail of an image by increasing local contrast of the image, especially in the midtones. Decreasing the Clarity value can make an image seem smoother and less detailed. Adjustments made using the Vibrance tool change the saturation of all of the lower-saturated colors in an image and have a small effect on colors that are already high in saturation. Finally, the Saturation tool adjusts the saturation of all colors equally. Next, you'll work with the Clarity and Vibrance settings to adjust the saturation of your image.

To adjust the color saturation of the image:

1. In the Adjustments panel, type **−100** in the Clarity box. Notice that some of the detail has been removed from the image. See Figure 8-18.

Figure 8-18 Clarity decreased to soften the image

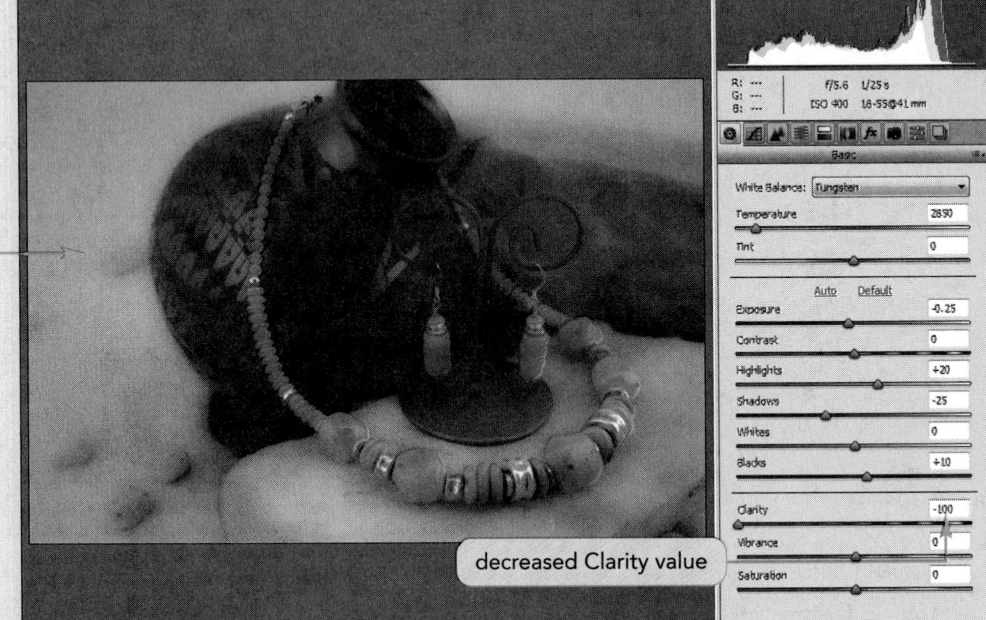

NU, Inc.

Adjusting the clarity has made the image too soft; some of the details have been lost.

2. Double-click the **Clarity** slider to return the Clarity value to **0**.
3. Increase the Vibrance value to **+50**. Although the increase has a minimal effect on the saturated red beads, it increases the saturation of the more neutral earth tones of the rock and background. Notice that shadow clipping has returned.

4. Increase the Blacks value to **+88** to remove shadow clipping, and then decrease the Shadows to **−30** to add some depth. See Figure 8-19.

Figure 8-19 **Image with the Vibrance and Blacks values adjusted**

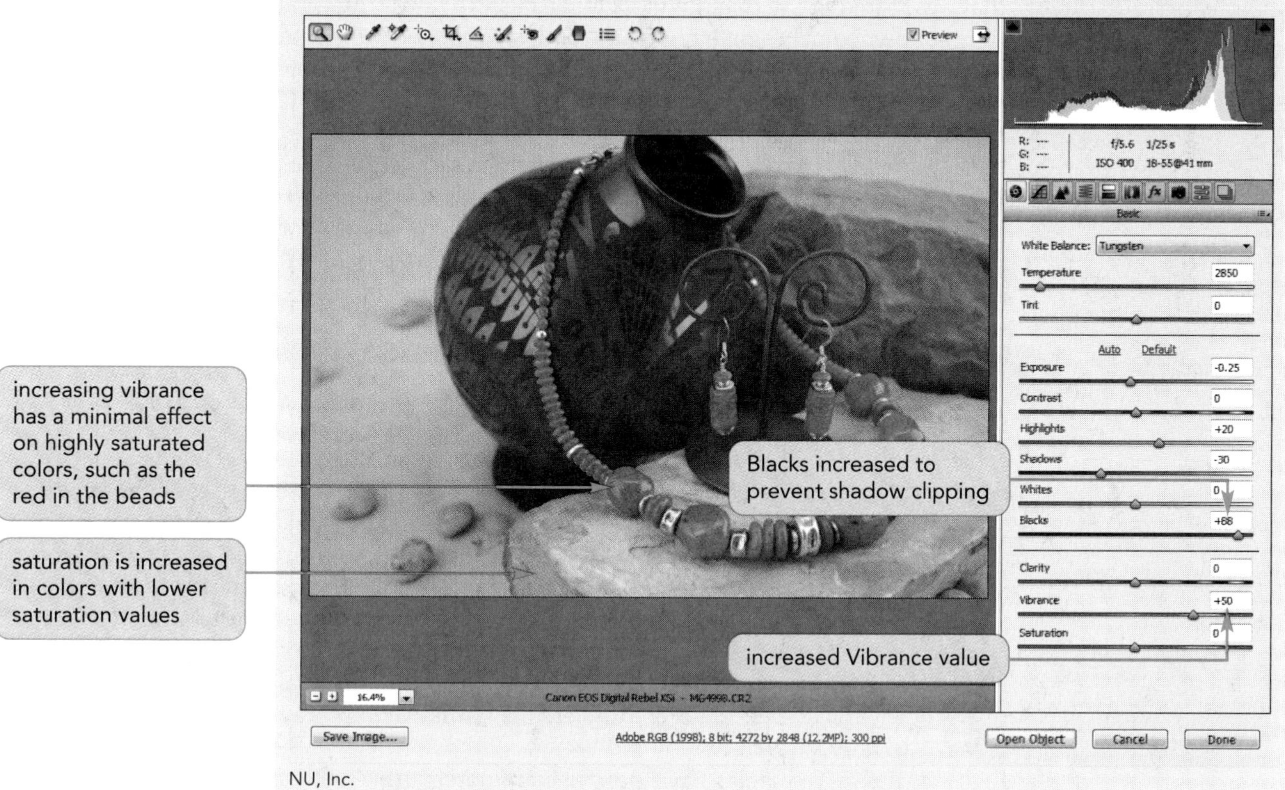

NU, Inc.

5. Click the **Done** button to save your adjustments and close the Camera Raw dialog box, and then exit Photoshop.

Opening JPEG and TIFF Files in Camera Raw

You can also open and work with JPEG and TIFF files in the Camera Raw plug-in with Mini Bridge (or Bridge). In Bridge, you open the image by right-clicking the image and selecting Open in Camera Raw. In Mini Bridge, you right-click, point to "Open with", and then select Camera Raw. In CS6, Photoshop has improved how well Camera Raw works with JPEG and TIFF images. The changes are all under the hood, but you will notice improvement in the effects the tools have on your images. When you open these files in Camera Raw, you have access to all of the tools and controls you have when you work with camera raw files; however, some of the settings are different. For example, the White Balance options only include As Shot, Auto, and Custom because JPEG and TIFF files, unlike camera raw files, do not include metadata about how the images were shot. The biggest drawback with using these file types in Camera Raw is that you cannot achieve the same effect with adjustments because the files do not have as much image data as uncompressed and unprocessed camera raw files. This is especially true with JPEG images because JPEG is not a lossless format.

Saving Camera Raw Files as DNG files

The **Digital Negative (DNG)** file format was created by Adobe as a potential solution to the problems introduced by all of the competing proprietary camera raw formats. DNG files contain all of the uncompressed raw data that proprietary raw files contain, and when you save a camera raw file as a DNG, it does not lose any of the information that was stored in the original file. Unlike camera raw formats, DNG is nonproprietary (it is not owned by a single company) and is publicly documented; the code is available for free to the general public, and it is widely supported. This means that software does not need camera-specific knowledge to read DNG files, and because of this, it is more likely that DNG files will be usable in the future. DNG files are often used as archival files, but you can also use them for working files. You work with DNG files in Camera Raw just as you work with camera raw files, and the adjustment data can be embedded nondestructively within the file, so you do not need multiple files for an image. The point at which you will convert camera raw files to DNG files depends upon the work flow process that you or your team has selected.

INSIGHT

Understanding Digital Camera Settings

To create good photographic images, you need to understand a few things about your digital camera. Digital cameras capture images in pixels. Because digital cameras can now capture huge amounts of image data, we typically measure image size in megapixels. A megapixel is equal to one million pixels. The size and resolution of the photographs you can output from a digital camera are directly related to the number of megapixels your camera can capture. Digital cameras typically have a variety of settings relating to the file format in which they capture images. If possible, capture images using your camera's raw file format to get the best quality images. TIFF is the next best choice because it is a lossless file format; JPEG should be avoided if you have another alternative.

Most digital cameras have internal light meters that enable them to measure lighting conditions, including temperature, and to compensate for those lighting conditions; however, cameras often do not do a good job of correcting for lighting conditions. As a result, many photographs come out under- or overexposed, or with a color cast. This is true especially when you use a flash to produce more light. It is a good idea to learn how your camera handles internal metering so you can use its settings to create better images.

Digital cameras usually provide manual and automatic focus settings. Automatic focus settings often work best when you are shooting quickly moving subjects, such as when you are taking pictures at sporting events, but manual focus settings can provide you with finer control when you are setting up a staged shot. For example, the photographer who shot the necklace in Figure 8-3 used manual focus settings to focus on the front portion of the necklace while letting the back portion of the necklace drop out of focus, creating a more dramatic effect. Finally, Bridge enables you to import images from most digital cameras or a memory card using the Get Photos from Camera button located on the Bridge menu bar. Once your images are in Bridge, you can open them in Photoshop or in Camera Raw in the same way that you would open any other image.

In this session, you learned about the camera raw file format, and you used the Camera Raw plug-in to crop and adjust camera raw files. You also saved adjustments to your camera raw files, and you opened images as Smart Object layers in Photoshop. In addition, you worked with a histogram and made several adjustments on the Basic tab in the Camera Raw dialog box to enhance your image and eliminate pixel clipping.

REVIEW

Session 8.1 Quick Check

1. __________ files are large files that contain unprocessed and uncompressed grayscale picture data and metadata from the image sensor of a digital camera, an image scanner, or a motion picture film scanner.
2. True or False. There is only one type of camera raw file, and it has the file extension .raw.
3. What is the name of the software plug-in that enables you to open and adjust camera raw files?
4. What file type accompanies a camera raw file and contains image adjustment data?
5. What is a histogram?
6. True or False. You can measure the temperature of light.
7. DNG stands for__________ file format.

SESSION 8.2 VISUAL OVERVIEW

From the View menu, you can access Proof Setup options that allow you to specify output settings to simulate color blindness or a particular type of output, such as CMYK. Select Proof Colors from the View menu to view a **soft proof**, which simulates the way your project will look when output.

The Optimized tab on the Save for Web & Devices dialog box displays an image as it will appear with the compression settings you have selected.

The Save for Web & Devices dialog box enables you to optimize and save a copy of an image for display on the Web.

As you change the file type and the compression quality, you can see how the file size and the Web download time are affected.

Change your working space color profiles and adjust your color management policies by selecting Color Settings from the Edit menu.

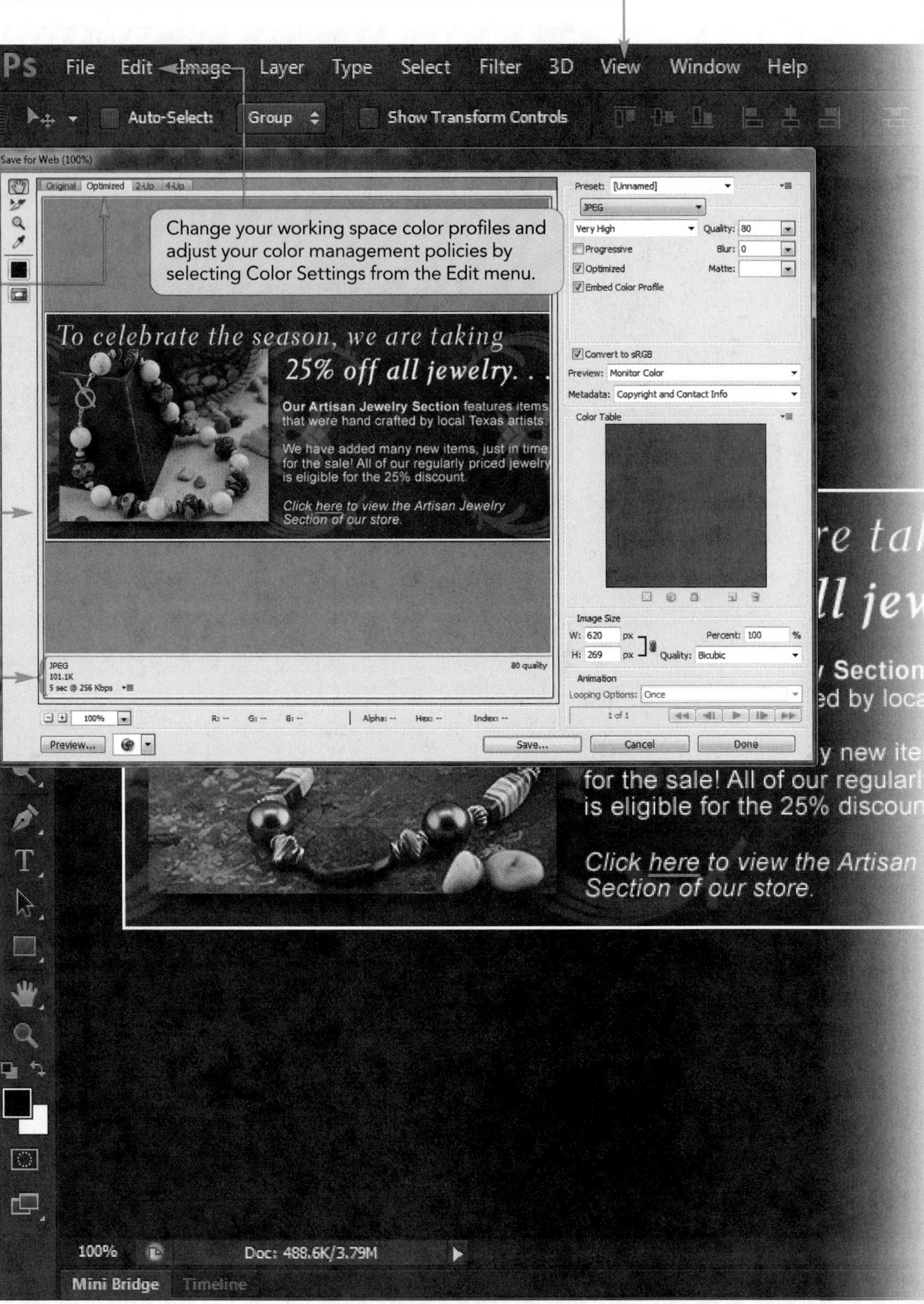

NU, Inc.

COLOR MANAGEMENT AND OUTPUT

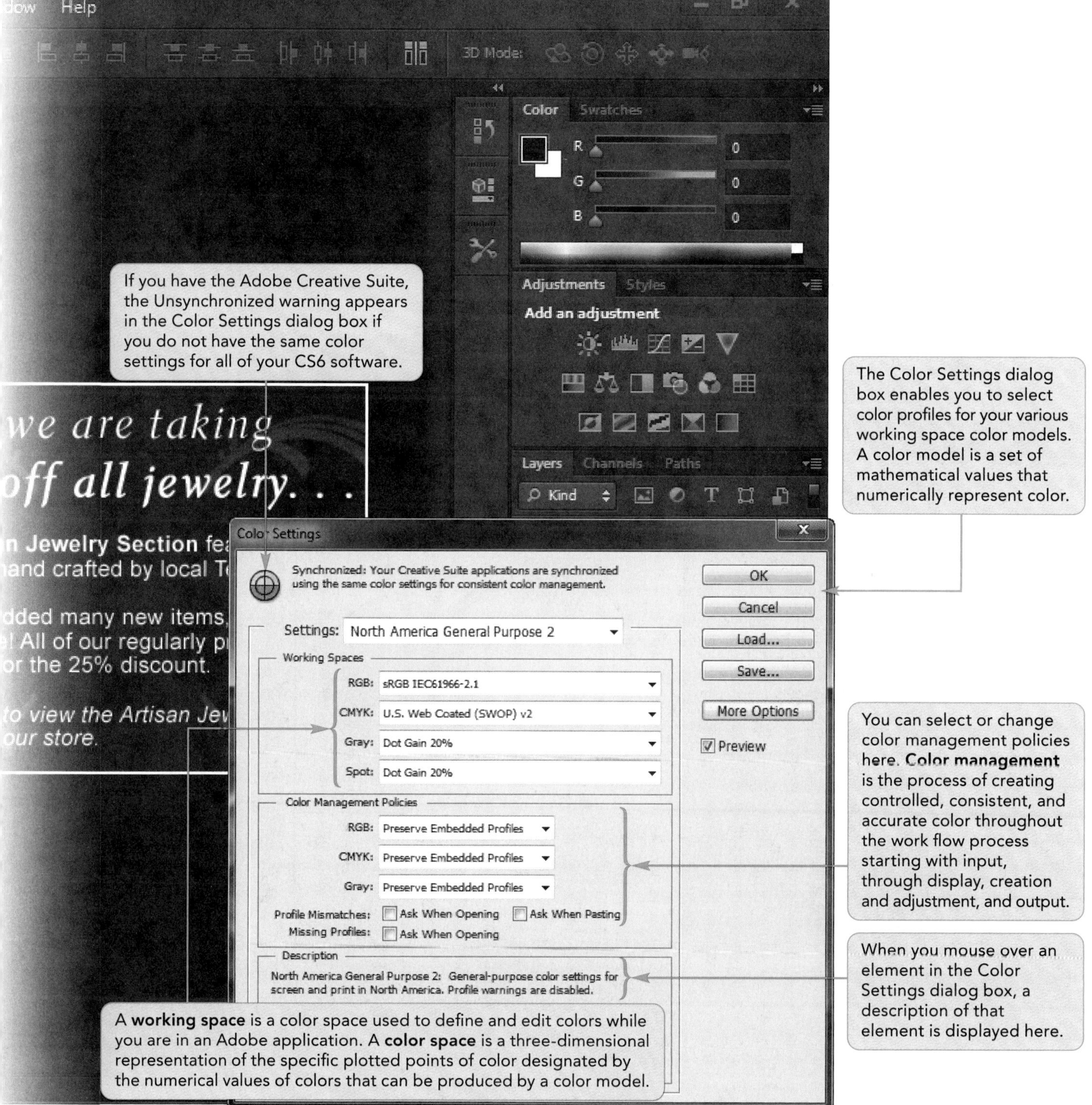
If you have the Adobe Creative Suite, the Unsynchronized warning appears in the Color Settings dialog box if you do not have the same color settings for all of your CS6 software.
The Color Settings dialog box enables you to select color profiles for your various working space color models. A color model is a set of mathematical values that numerically represent color.
You can select or change color management policies here. **Color management** is the process of creating controlled, consistent, and accurate color throughout the work flow process starting with input, through display, creation and adjustment, and output.
When you mouse over an element in the Color Settings dialog box, a description of that element is displayed here.
A **working space** is a color space used to define and edit colors while you are in an Adobe application. A **color space** is a three-dimensional representation of the specific plotted points of color designated by the numerical values of colors that can be produced by a color model.
Color Settings
Synchronized: Your Creative Suite applications are synchronized using the same color settings for consistent color management.
OK
Cancel
Load...
Save...
More Options
Preview
Settings: North America General Purpose 2
Working Spaces
RGB: sRGB IEC61966-2.1
CMYK: U.S. Web Coated (SWOP) v2
Gray: Dot Gain 20%
Spot: Dot Gain 20%
Color Management Policies
RGB: Preserve Embedded Profiles
CMYK: Preserve Embedded Profiles
Gray: Preserve Embedded Profiles
Profile Mismatches: Ask When Opening Ask When Pasting
Missing Profiles: Ask When Opening
Description
North America General Purpose 2: General-purpose color settings for screen and print in North America. Profile warnings are disabled.

Creating Successful Output

Photoshop enables you to create artwork for output to a variety of media, including desktop printers, professional printers (both offset and digital), and the Web. In addition, because Photoshop is not primarily used as a layout program, the artwork you create and manipulate in Photoshop is often output to other programs that are used to create the final product. For example, for one project you might get photographic images of products from a digital camera and manipulate those images in Camera Raw and Photoshop. Then, you might output a high-resolution version of the images to use in a print catalog that will be created in InDesign (Adobe's layout program) and a low-resolution version of the images to use in a site created in Dreamweaver (Adobe's Web design program). The path that a project travels from original input through final output is called the **design chain**. It is important to understand the design chain so you can create a work flow process that intelligently controls variables and maximizes the potential for professional output. See Figure 8-20.

Figure 8-20 The design chain

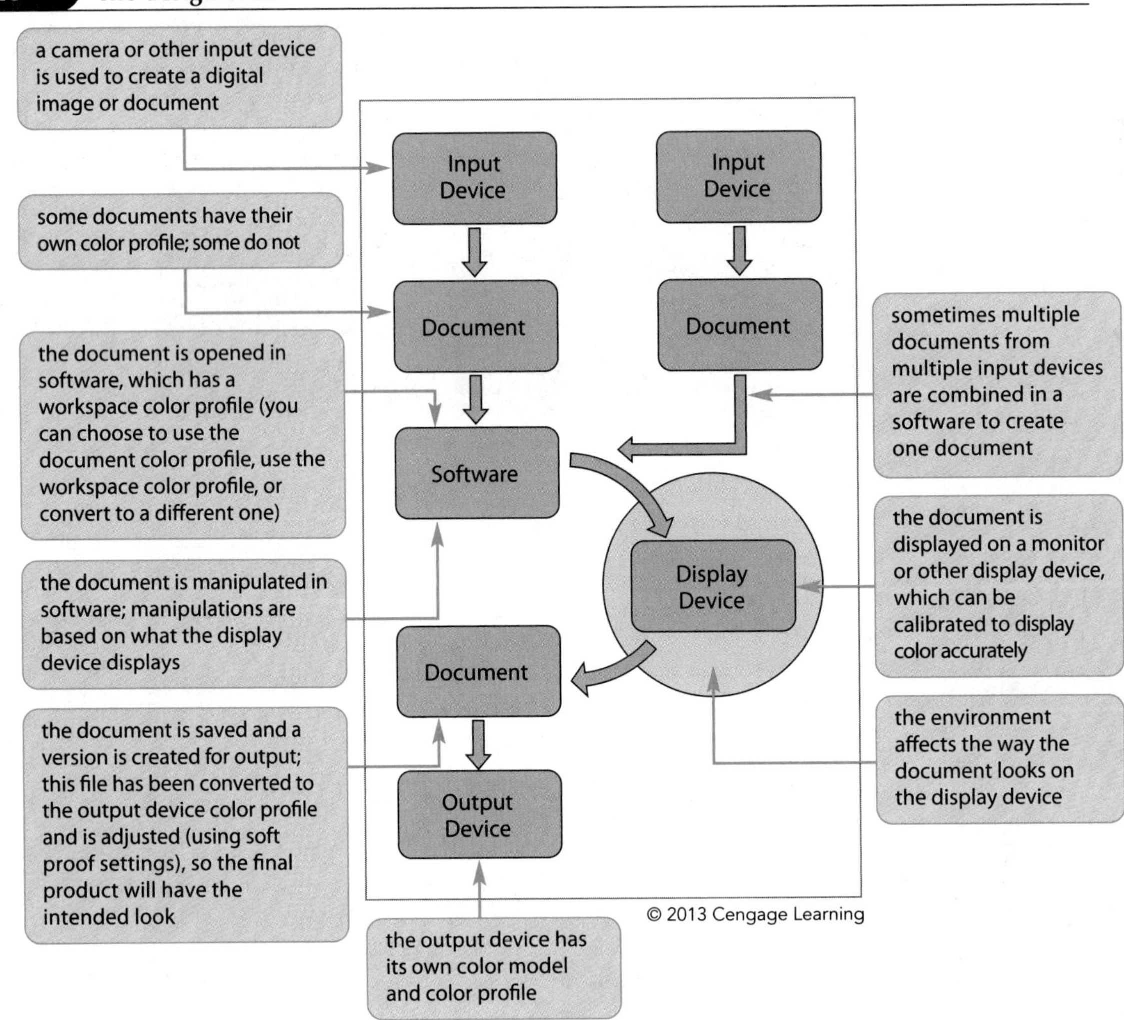
a camera or other input device is used to create a digital image or document
some documents have their own color profile; some do not
the document is opened in software, which has a workspace color profile (you can choose to use the document color profile, use the workspace color profile, or convert to a different one)
the document is manipulated in software; manipulations are based on what the display device displays
the document is saved and a version is created for output; this file has been converted to the output device color profile and is adjusted (using soft proof settings), so the final product will have the intended look
the output device has its own color model and color profile
Input Device
Input Device
Document
Document
Software
Display Device
Document
Output Device
sometimes multiple documents from multiple input devices are combined in a software to create one document
the document is displayed on a monitor or other display device, which can be calibrated to display color accurately
the environment affects the way the document looks on the display device

To understand the effect the links in a design chain have on the end product, think of the children's game, telephone. In this game, people stand in a line and the first person in the line whispers a message to the person to her right. As the process is repeated and the message moves down the chain of people, the original information becomes distorted as the message is reinterpreted and "output" by each person in the chain. Finally, when the message reaches the end of the line, the person at the end of the chain "outputs" the end product, which is usually nothing like the original message. If the design chain is not carefully managed, you can experience the same distortion in your project output. Some of the links in your design chain, such as your monitor, affect every project; while other links, such as print profiles, are specific to a particular output.

Because you are working on professional projects, it is important that you learn about color management. In this session, you'll learn to manage all of the links in your design chain so you can create high-quality output.

PROSKILLS

Problem Solving: Gathering Important Information

To maximize your chances for creating professional output, it is critical that you obtain all relevant specifications and parameters for your final output before you even get started. Problems can often be anticipated and avoided when you have the information you need to make informed decisions before you start your project. If you are working with a professional printer, you should ask for information regarding color profiles and output preferences. It is also important to decide when in your process you will move between color spaces. Each time you move between RGB and CMYK, you degrade your files during the conversion. For this reason, you should try to make conversion your final step, and you should keep a copy of the files with the working color space so you can return to your original working environment to make changes. Finally, your entire team should be aware of the requirements so you are all working with the same settings in place. Gathering all of the relevant information before you begin your project will enable you to avoid many common problems and will enable you to create a better end product.

Basic Color Management

Color management is the process of creating controlled, consistent, and accurate color throughout the work flow process—from input, through display, creation, adjustment, and, finally, output. The goal of color management is to display accurate color that matches across different media and display devices—regardless of color mode, color gamut capabilities, or output limitations. Whenever your creative process includes at least one device that attempts to reproduce or interpret the color output from another device, you can benefit from some color management.

At the professional level, color management can be quite complex, but there are some simple things you can control on any level that will enable you to better manage your colors and create more professional output.

Calibrating Your Monitor

The first step in creating an effective color management work flow is to calibrate your monitor by adjusting the display to conform to known specifications. Next, you should create a color profile, which enables you to save those settings so your monitor display is consistent over time. Remember that all monitors display images using RGBcolor, but every monitor is calibrated to display colors slightly differently. In addition, users can complicate things by making additional adjustments to the brightness and contrast of their monitors. Professional calibration results are usually only obtained by purchasing and using a third-party calibration software that provides additional measuring devices and greater accuracy, such as the Datacolor Spyder3 (*www.datacolor.com*) or the Pantone hueyPRO (*www.pantone.com*). However, Windows provides a basic monitor calibration utility that provides a baseline calibration.

INSIGHT

Adjusting Ambient Lighting

Ambient lighting levels and reflections on your monitor can have a significant impact on your perception of color. For instance, red objects look blacker in blue light. It is important to consider the ambient lighting and color in your work environment and adjust it before making calibration adjustments to your monitor. For optimum results, you should work in a neutrally colored room, under subdued lighting, and no strong direct light should reach the screen. It is ideal to have the overall ambient illumination lower than the brightness output of the screen, with light sources positioned away from the screen, and windows covered completely to maintain consistent illumination. The purpose of this is to ensure that dark areas of the screen appear dark to the eye. If you have trouble working in such low lighting, you can install daylight-balance fluorescent or filtered halogen lights to a color temperature of 5000 degrees Kelvin. You should make these changes before you calibrate, and you should calibrate your monitor under your regular working conditions. When your working conditions change, recalibrate your monitor.

You'll calibrate your monitor using the Windows calibration tool, which walks you through the steps for setting the gamma, brightness, contrast, and the color balance for your monitor. Before you begin, you should understand what you are adjusting:

- **Gamma**—Gamma is a measure of the nonlinear relationship between red, green, and blue color values that are sent to the monitor and the luminance (or light energy) that is actually emitted from the monitor. Gamma generally affects midtones and has no effect on black or white. When gamma is set too high, the midtone display is too dark, and when it is set too low, the midtone display is too light. You'll adjust the gamma of your monitor using an on-screen slider provided in the Windows calibration tool.
- **Brightness**—Some monitors have a brightness control, whereas others do not. The brightness control might be a physical button that is located on the monitor, or it might be located in an on-screen menu. The icon for the brightness control is a circle with lines around it that looks like a sun. In most cases, the brightness control actually adjusts the black level of the monitor by adjusting the red, green, and blue signals. When brightness is adjusted properly, black objects are displayed as true black on the monitor. To adjust the brightness of your monitor, you must locate the brightness control on your monitor and use it to adjust an image that is displayed in the Windows calibration tool. If your monitor does not have a brightness control, you will need to skip this step when calibrating your monitor.

- **Contrast**—Some monitors have a contrast control, whereas others do not. The icon for the contrast control is a circle that is divided in half vertically with black filling the left half of the circle and white filling the right half of the circle. The contrast control might be a physical button that is located on the monitor, or it might be located in an on-screen menu. Adjusting the contrast control affects the luminance that is produced for a white input signal. When contrast is set correctly, the highlight values on your monitor will be bright but not unpleasant to look at. To adjust the contrast of your monitor, you must locate the contrast control on your monitor and use it to adjust an image that is displayed in the Windows calibration tool. If your monitor does not have a contrast control, you will need to skip this step when calibrating your monitor.
- **Color balance**—When you adjust the color balance of your monitor, you are actually adjusting the color temperature to remove any color cast that might be visible on your monitor. As with images, monitors with a lower color temperature will have a warm color cast to their display, whereas monitors with a higher color temperature will have a cool color cast to their display. Although some monitors have color settings, it is a good idea to leave those set to the factory default and to use the sliders in the Windows calibration tool to adjust the color balance of your monitor.

You'll use the Windows 7 Display Color Calibration Wizard to adjust your monitor. If you have a professionally calibrated monitor, do not complete the following steps; instead, read the steps and move to the next section.

REFERENCE

Calibrating a Monitor

- On the Windows 7 taskbar, click the Start button, click Control Panel, click Appearance and Personalization, and then click Display.
- In the Display window, click Calibrate color.
- Follow the directions provided by the Display Color Calibration Wizard.
- Click Finish to save the new calibration settings.

To calibrate your monitor:

1. On the Windows 7 taskbar, click the **Start** button, and then click **Control Panel**.
2. In the Control Panel window, click **Appearance and Personalization**, and in the Appearance and Personalization window, click **Display** to open the Display window.
3. In the Display window, click **Calibrate color** from the list on the left to open the Display Color Calibration Wizard. If necessary, click the **Maximize** button to maximize the window. See Figure 8-21.

   Trouble? If a User Account Control dialog box appears asking if you want to allow the program to make changes to your computer, enter an administrator password in the Password box, and then click Yes.

Figure 8-21 **Windows Display Color Calibration Wizard**

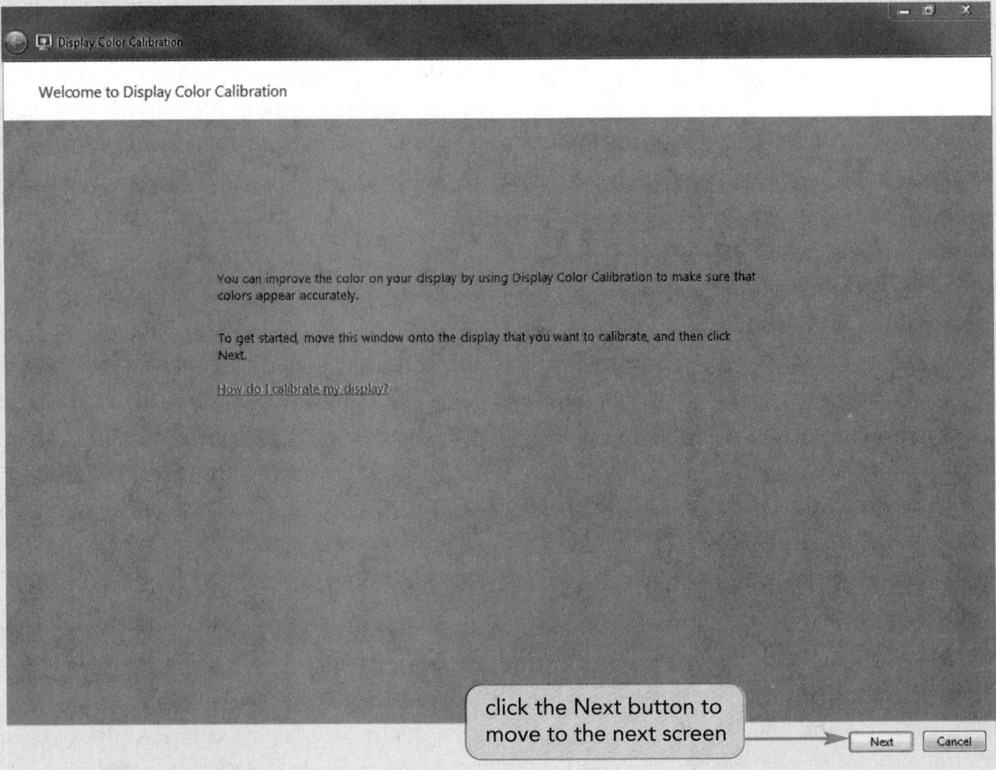

Used with permission from Microsoft Corporation

4. Click the **Next** button to move to the next screen, and then read the on-screen information, which instructs you to locate the menu button on your monitor.
5. Once you have located the physical menu button, click it to display the menu on your monitor screen. What you see and what you can control from the on-screen menu will vary from monitor to monitor. If necessary, move the position of the menu so it does not cover the Next button at the bottom of the screen.

   Trouble? If you cannot locate the button that opens the on-screen menu, look for buttons located on the side or bottom edge of your monitor. If you still cannot locate the button, ask your instructor or technical support staff, look through the documentation that came with your monitor, or search online for documentation for your monitor.

   Trouble? If your on-screen menu covers the Next button and you are unable to move the menu, close the menu to access the Next button, and then reopen the menu in Step 8.
6. Set your monitor display to the factory default color settings, and click the **Next** button to move to the next screen.
7. Read the information explaining how to adjust the gamma for your monitor. Take a careful look at the Good gamma image, as shown in Figure 8-22.

Figure 8-22 Good gamma as displayed by the Windows Display Color Calibration Wizard

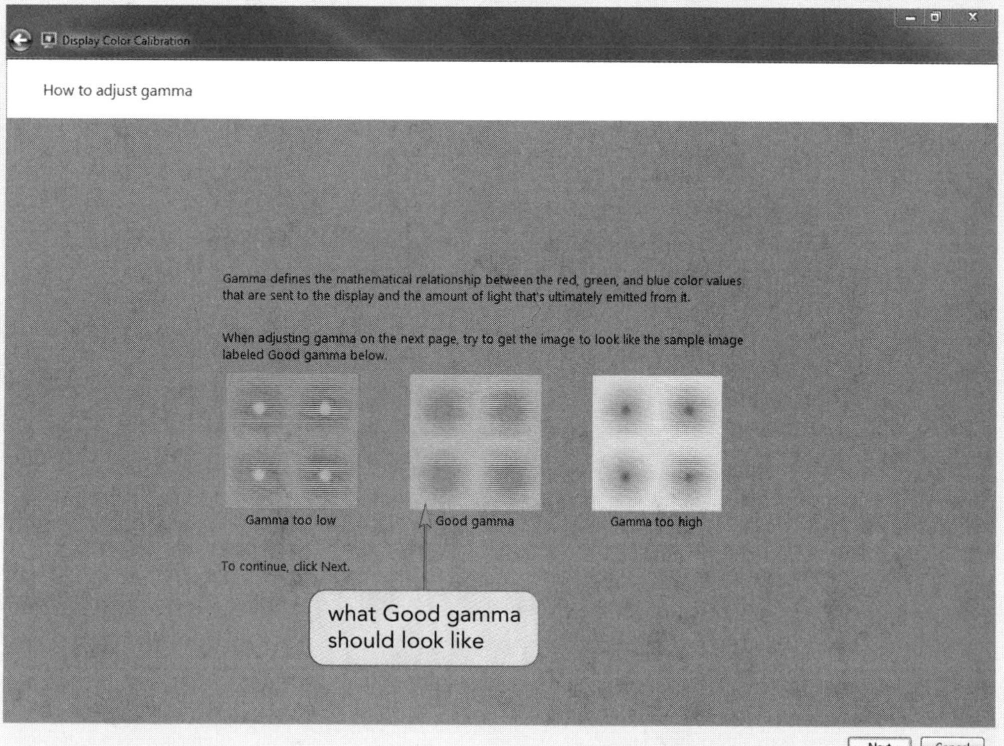

Used with permission from Microsoft Corporation

8. Click the **Next** button, and open your on-screen menu, if necessary.
9. Adjust the on-screen slider until the image on your screen looks like the Good gamma image from Step 7, close the on-screen menu, if necessary, and then click the **Next** button.
10. Read the on-screen information explaining how to locate the brightness and contrast controls, and then locate the brightness and contrast controls for your monitor. Click the **Next** button.

    Trouble? If you cannot find brightness or contrast controls for your monitor, click the Skip brightness and contrast adjustment button, and move to Step 17.
11. Take a careful look at the Good brightness image, as shown in Figure 8-23.

Figure 8-23 Good brightness as displayed by the Windows Display Color Calibration Wizard

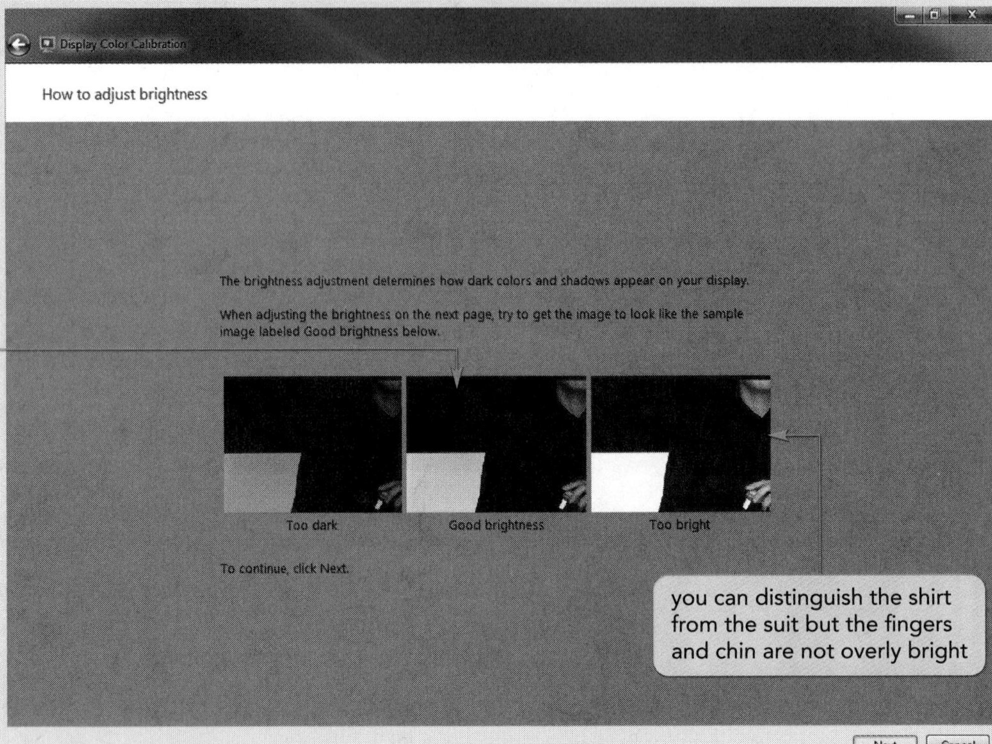

Used with permission from Microsoft Corporation

12. Click the **Next** button, and open your on-screen menu, if necessary.
13. Use the brightness control on your monitor to adjust the image on your screen so it matches the Good brightness image from Step 11, close the on-screen menu, if necessary, and then click the **Next** button.

    Trouble? If your screen does not match the image, do the best you can. Some monitors will not be able to match the image exactly.
14. Read the on-screen information to learn more about contrast, and take a careful look at the Good contrast image, as shown in Figure 8-24.

Figure 8-24 Good contrast as displayed by the Windows Display Color Calibration Wizard

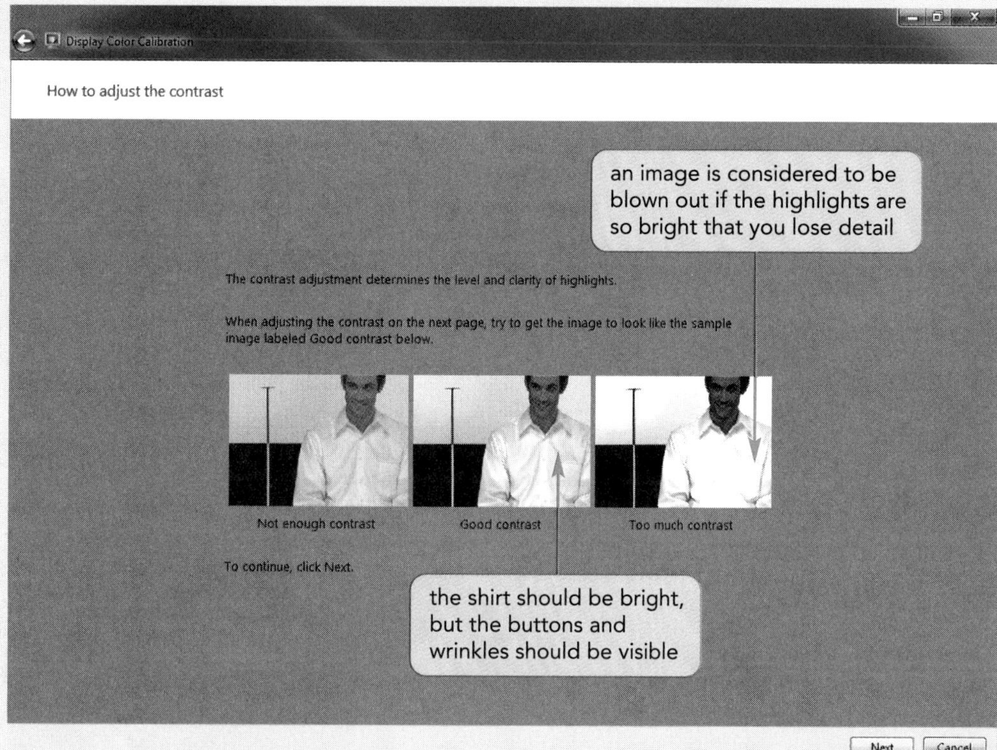

Used with permission from Microsoft Corporation

15. Click the **Next** button, and open your on-screen menu, if necessary.
16. Use the contrast control on your monitor to adjust the image to match the Good contrast image from Step 14, and click the **Next** button.

    Trouble? If your screen does not match the image, do the best you can. Some monitors will not be able to match the image exactly.

    Trouble? If your monitor does not have a contrast control, skip Step 16, and move to Step 17.
17. Read the on-screen information to learn more about color balance, and take a close look at the neutral grays image, as shown in Figure 8-25.

Figure 8-25 Good color balance as displayed by the Windows Display Color Calibration Wizard

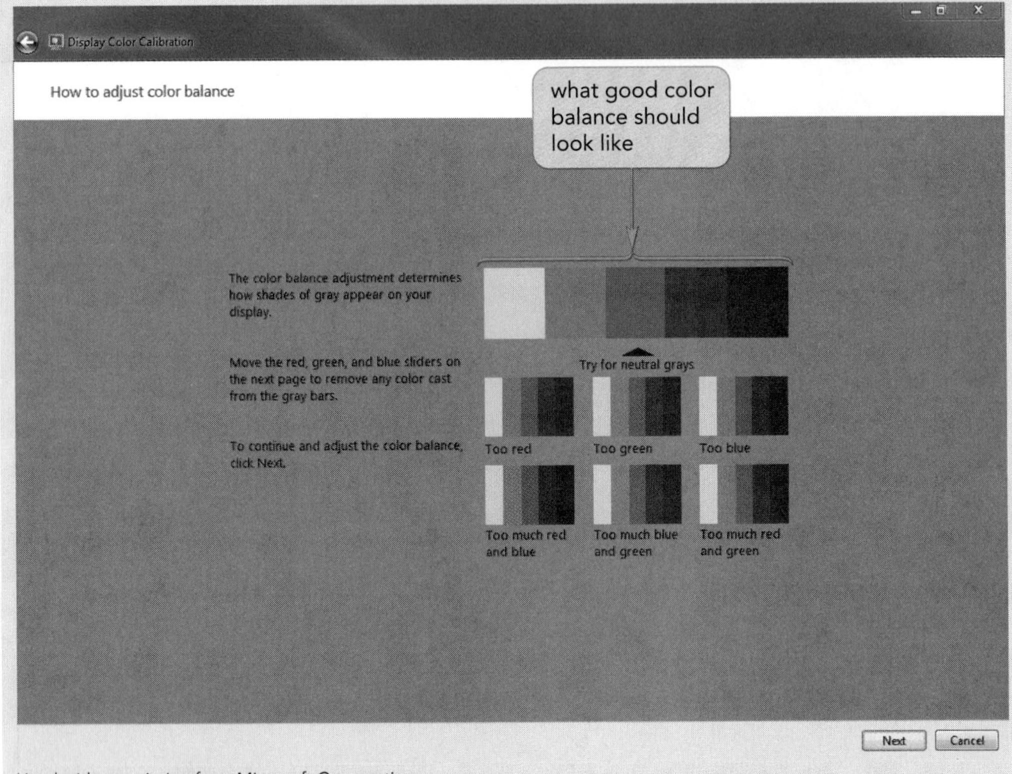

18. Click the **Next** button.
19. Adjust the red, green, and blue on-screen sliders to adjust the image to match the neutral grays, and then click the **Next** button.
20. Toggle between the **Previous calibration** button and the **Current calibration** button to see how your monitor's display has changed.
21. Click **Finish** to save your changes, and close any open windows.

Next, you'll learn about color profiles, which are an important part of color management.

Setting Your View for Soft Proofing

Because you will often work in one color mode and then output to another color mode, Photoshop provides a view that enables you to see your artwork as it will appear when output to another color mode. Simulating output settings is called soft proofing. Although the changes to output that you see when soft proofing are often small, it is still very important to make sure that you do not skip this step because even small changes in the display of color can make the difference between an amateur or professional looking composition.

You can also create a soft proof that enables you to see your artwork as a person who is color blind would see the work. This is a great feature because you can ensure that someone with color blindness will be able to view all of the important information you are trying to convey. Photoshop has settings that simulate the two most common forms of color blindness: protanopia (reduced sensitivity to red) and deuteranopia (reduced sensitivity to green).

A member of the FW Museum Store project team created the insert that will be printed for placement in catalogs and that will also be displayed on the Web. You'll open that file, which was created in RGB, and you'll adjust your Proof Settings to specify output settings that simulate protanopia color blindness. Then, you'll view a soft proof of the file. You'll also specify output settings that simulate CMYK output, and you'll view a soft proof with those settings.

To view a soft proof:

1. Start Photoshop while pressing the **Ctrl+Alt+Shift** keys, and click **Yes** to delete the Settings File when prompted. Reset Photoshop to the default Essentials workspace layout, and then reset all tools.
2. Navigate to the Photoshop8\Tutorial folder provided with your Data Files, and open **Insert.psd**.

   Trouble? If you get a message about missing fonts, click the OK button, and let Photoshop make the substitution.
3. Save the file as **InsertCMYK.psd** in the Photoshop8\Tutorial folder, and then press the **Ctrl+0** keys to fit the image on screen.
4. On the menu bar, click **View**, point to **Proof Setup**, and then click **Color Blindness - Protanopia-type** to select it. This tells Photoshop to simulate the way someone with protanopia will see the artwork.
5. On the menu bar, click **View**, and then click **Proof Colors** to check it, if necessary, and view a soft proof of the document. See Figure 8-26.

Figure 8-26 Soft proof that simulates protanopia color blindness

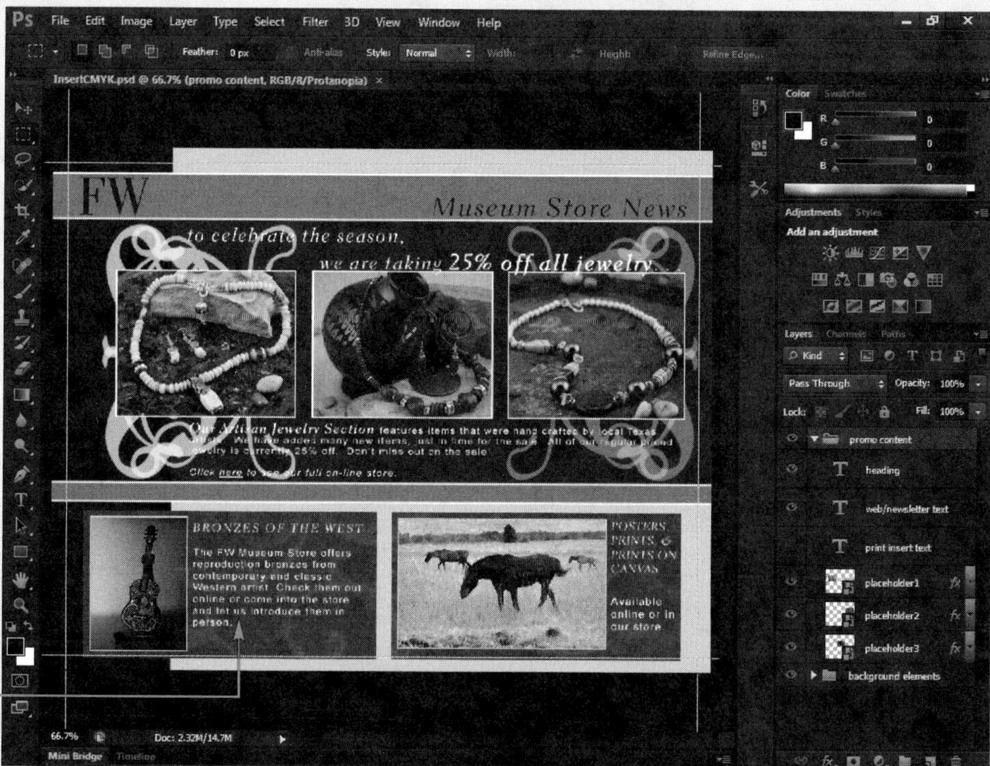

check to make sure that text does not disappear into the background

NU, Inc.; Eugene Moerman/Shutterstock.com; © iStockphoto.com/1234567890987654321

Although the results of the soft proof are not pretty, they are acceptable because they show that users who have Protanopia-type color blindness will be able to see the product images and read the text. Next, you'll adjust your settings to proof for CMYK output.

6. On the menu bar, click **View**, point to **Proof Setup**, and then click **Working CMYK**. The document is now displayed as a soft proof for CMYK output. See Figure 8-27.

Figure 8-27 Soft proof that simulates CMYK output

indicates that the document is RGB and is being viewed as a CMYK soft proof

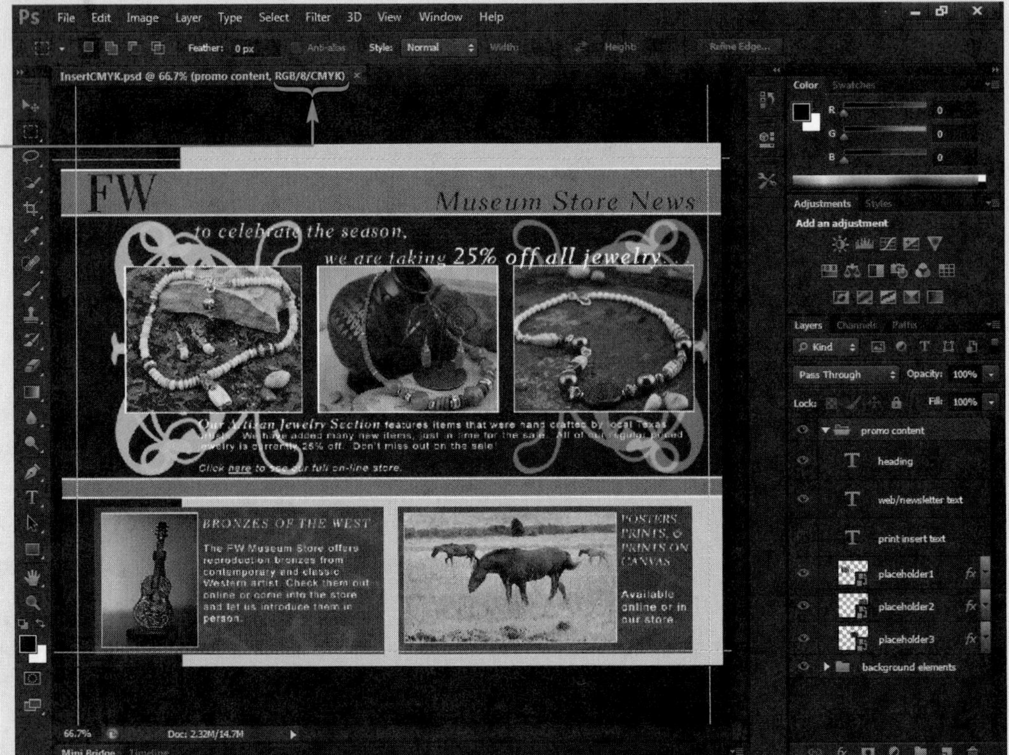

NU, Inc.; Eugene Moerman/Shutterstock.com; © iStockphoto.com/1234567890987654321

The soft proof shows that CMYK output will not change the colors drastically, and the insert will look good when it is printed.

You should check your View settings every time you open a document in Photoshop because these settings affect the way your compositions look and, therefore, affect your output. It is a good idea to get into the habit of unchecking Proof Colors on the View menu when you first view a document so you can see the document displayed with its own settings or with the workspace settings if it has no profile of its own.

The soft proof presets that Photoshop provides use the color profiles specified in your Color Settings to create the soft proof you view.

Understanding Color Profiles

The **International Color Consortium (ICC)** is a group of industry professionals who are dedicated to the development of cross-platform standards for color communication and consistency. The ICC color profile is the vehicle they have created to communicate color information across platforms and devices that support ICC standards. An **ICC profile** (or just **color profile**) is a data file that characterizes an input, display, or output device and provides color management systems with the information needed to intelligently convert color data between native device color spaces and device-independent color spaces using ICC standards.

To clearly understand what color profiles do, it is important to understand a few industry terms that remain frequent sources of confusion:

- **Color model**—Color models, such as RGB, CMYK, and Lab, are sets of mathematical values that numerically represent color. When a color model is device dependent, different devices interpret the exact numeric values differently. Most devices can reproduce or display only portions of a device-dependent color model.
- **Color space**—A color space is a three-dimensional representation of the specific plotted points of color designated by the numerical values of colors that can be produced by a color model. A color space enables you to map the values of a color in a color model to a specific, concrete color in the real world. The standards we use for colors that correspond to a specific coordinate in a color space are those created by the ICC.
- **Gamut**—The range of color that a device can produce or display, or the range of color a color model can represent is called the gamut. The gamut of a device or process is the portion of the color space that can be represented or reproduced. When a color cannot be displayed or reproduced, it is said to be "out of gamut."
- **Color profile**—To create consistent color across devices, a color profile maps the color model to an absolute color space. A color profile communicates information about the portion (or gamut) of the color model a device can reproduce or display as well as how to most accurately translate from one color model to another so your image's colors are as consistent and accurate as possible.
- **Color mode**—In Photoshop, you can specify a color mode in which to work. Examples of modes include Grayscale, RGB, and CMYK. When you select a specific color mode in Photoshop, you are selecting a color model, and, where applicable, you are selecting a color profile that is associated with that color model. Color profiles are specified in the Color Settings dialog box.

To sum it up, ICC profiles use the standards created by the ICC to create data files that specify a color model, mapped to a specific color space with concrete values that are defined by ICC standards. This enables users to reproduce and display accurate specific colors. Furthermore, profiles specify additional information, which enables accurate and consistent translation, display, and reproduction of color—across software, between color models, and between devices.

Setting Profiles and Color Management Policies

ICC profiles are used across the design chain. You can create monitor profiles, working space profiles, input profiles, document profiles, and output profiles. The file formats that support ICC profiles include JPEG, PDF, Photoshop EPS, PSD, and TIFF. In addition to selecting a file format that supports profiles, you must make sure the Embed Color Profile or ICC Profile check box is checked when you save the file. When you calibrated your monitor, Windows saved a profile that enables your monitor to provide a more accurate display.

Photoshop provides some color setting presets that enable you to set your working space profiles and color management policies for general purposes. Using preset settings is a good place to start. In the Color Settings dialog box, you can select a working space color profile for each color model. When you create a new document

TIP

It is a good idea to preserve embedded profiles when opening documents.

in Photoshop, it will have the color profile you have associated with the color model you select for the document. If you open a document in Photoshop and that document has an embedded color profile that does not match your working space color profile, or if it does not have a color profile at all, Photoshop relies on your color management policy settings to decide how to handle the color data for that file.

You can also save your own custom settings, which will then appear in the Settings list along with the preset Adobe settings. This becomes important when you start working with professional printers who often provide custom color profiles.

Next, you'll examine the Color Settings dialog box, and you'll adjust your settings.

To adjust color settings in Photoshop:

1. On the menu bar, click **Edit**, and then click **Color Settings** to display the Color Settings dialog box.
2. Click the **Settings arrow**, click **North America Prepress 2** from the Settings list, if necessary, and then click the **More Options** button to expand the dialog box, if necessary. See Figure 8-28.

Figure 8-28 Color Settings dialog box

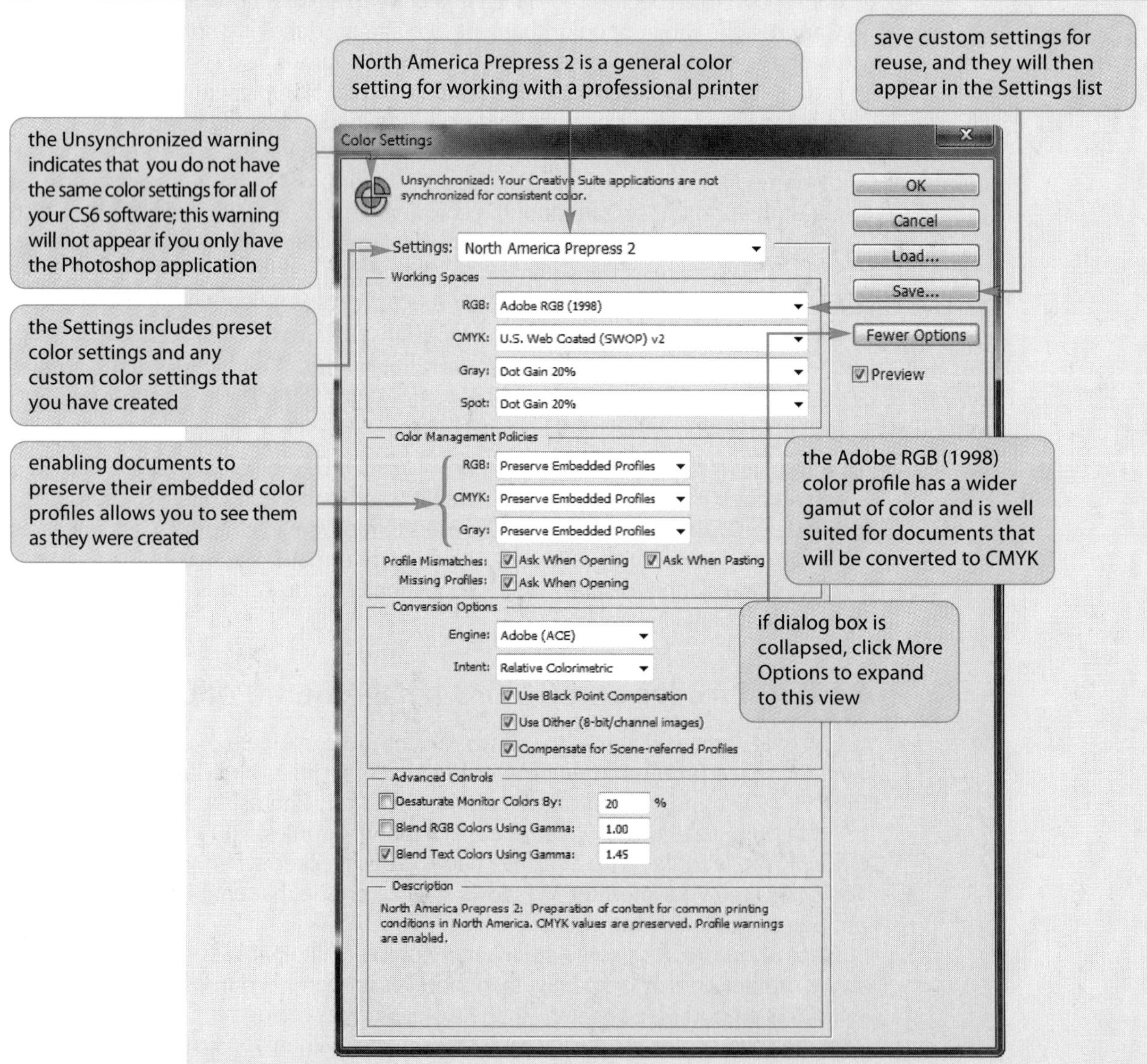
North America Prepress 2 is a general color setting for working with a professional printer
save custom settings for reuse, and they will then appear in the Settings list
the Unsynchronized warning indicates that you do not have the same color settings for all of your CS6 software; this warning will not appear if you only have the Photoshop application
the Settings includes preset color settings and any custom color settings that you have created
enabling documents to preserve their embedded color profiles allows you to see them as they were created
the Adobe RGB (1998) color profile has a wider gamut of color and is well suited for documents that will be converted to CMYK
if dialog box is collapsed, click More Options to expand to this view
Color Settings
Unsynchronized: Your Creative Suite applications are not synchronized for consistent color.
OK
Cancel
Load...
Save...
Fewer Options
Preview
Settings: North America Prepress 2
Working Spaces
RGB: Adobe RGB (1998)
CMYK: U.S. Web Coated (SWOP) v2
Gray: Dot Gain 20%
Spot: Dot Gain 20%
Color Management Policies
RGB: Preserve Embedded Profiles
CMYK: Preserve Embedded Profiles
Gray: Preserve Embedded Profiles
Profile Mismatches: Ask When Opening Ask When Pasting
Missing Profiles: Ask When Opening
Conversion Options
Engine: Adobe (ACE)
Intent: Relative Colorimetric
Use Black Point Compensation
Use Dither (8-bit/channel images)
Compensate for Scene-referred Profiles
Advanced Controls
Desaturate Monitor Colors By: 20 %
Blend RGB Colors Using Gamma: 1.00
Blend Text Colors Using Gamma: 1.45
Description
North America Prepress 2: Preparation of content for common printing conditions in North America. CMYK values are preserved. Profile warnings are enabled.

Selecting this preset changes the color profiles associated with your working spaces to the profiles that are most often used by professional printers in North America.

3. Click the **OK** button to accept the changes.

Using Bridge to Synchronize Color Settings

If you have Adobe's Creative Suite 6, you can synchronize the color settings for all of the Creative Suite 6 applications using Bridge. If you only have Photoshop, you will not have this option, but it is important to understand that you should maintain consistent color management policies across all of the software you use. Keeping applications synchronized helps you to maintain consistent color and color management policies. The icon and message displayed at the top of your Color Settings dialog box tells you if all of your applications are in sync. When applications do not have synchronized color settings, a warning message is displayed at the top of the Color Settings dialog box.

If you have the entire suite of applications, your colors settings are not synchronized because you have just changed the Photoshop settings. You'll open Bridge and synchronize the color settings for all of your applications. If you do not have the entire Adobe Create Suite, do not open Bridge. Instead, read the following steps, and then skip to Step 3.

To synchronize color settings in Bridge:

1. Open Bridge, and on the menu bar, click **Edit**, and then click **Creative Suite Color Settings**.

   The Suite Color Settings dialog box is displayed. See Figure 8-29.

   Trouble? If a dialog box opens stating that Suite Color Management requires that a qualifying product has been launched at least once to enable this feature, then you have not yet opened all the applications included in your creative suite. You must open each product once to enable color management. Open each application, close it, and then repeat Step 1 or skip to Step 3.

Figure 8-29 Setting Creative Suite color settings from Bridge

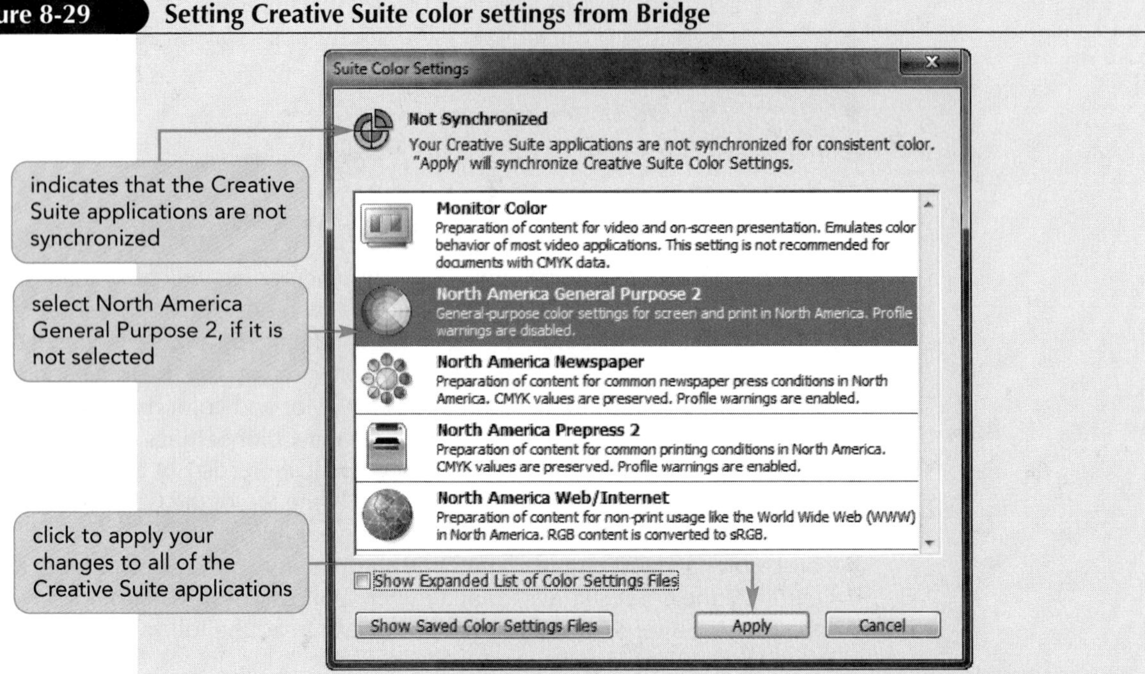

2. Click **North America General Purpose 2** to select it, if necessary, click the **Apply** button, and then close Bridge.
3. On the menu bar in Photoshop, click **Edit**, and then click **Color Settings**.

   The color setting has been changed back to North America General Purpose 2.

   Trouble? If you do not have the entire Adobe Creative Suite, click the Settings arrow, and then click North America General Purpose 2 to select it.
4. Click the **OK** button to close the Color Settings dialog box.

Converting a Color Profile

You should keep documents in their native color space while you work with them and convert them to the output color model and profile, if necessary, only when you are finished with adjustments. This ensures that your composition is not degraded by moving between color models. Save the converted composition with a new name to ensure that you have a copy of the composition with its original profile. In the future, if you need to make changes, you should go back to the original composition, make changes, and repeat the process. To change the color profile, use the Convert to Profile option on the Edit menu. This is the preferable method because Photoshop converts the colors to the color space of the new profile by shifting the color numbers. This is done to preserve the original appearance of the document as much as possible. The Convert to Profile dialog box is broken into three sections:

- **Source Space**—The Source Space profile is the color profile that is currently attached to the document.
- **Destination Space**—When you click the Advanced button, the Convert to Profile dialog box allows you to select the color model to which you will convert the document, and then you can select the color profile for the selected color model.

- **Conversion Options**—The Convert to Profile dialog box also provides you with additional conversion options. It is a good idea to leave these alone until you have a solid understanding of color management.

You can assign a new profile by selecting a different color model from the Mode menu, but this is not recommended. When this method is used, the color numbers in the document stay the same and, because of this, the new profile may change the appearance of a document dramatically.

You'll convert the InsertCMYK.psd document to the CMYK color model, and you'll select a new color profile.

To convert the document to a new color profile:

1. On the menu bar, click **Edit**, and then click **Convert to Profile**.
2. In the Convert to Profile dialog box, click the **Advanced** button.

   Trouble? If you see a Basic button rather than an Advanced button on the right side of the Convert to Profile dialog box, then the Advanced options are already displayed. Skip Step 2.
3. Under Destination Space, click the **CMYK** option button, if necessary, to select it, click the **Profile arrow** next to the CMYK option, and then click **Working CMYK - U.S. Web Coated (SWOP) v2**, if necessary. See Figure 8-30.

Figure 8-30 Convert to Profile dialog box with Advanced Options displayed

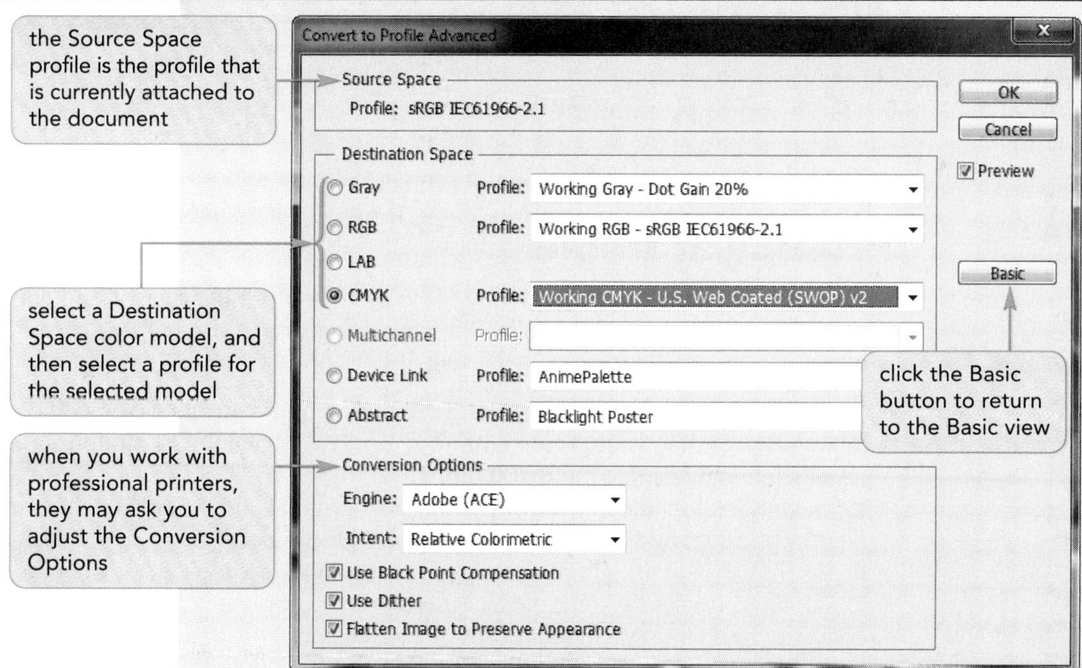

4. Click the **OK** button to convert the profile of the document. See Figure 8-31.

Figure 8-31 **Insert CMYK.psd document with new profile**

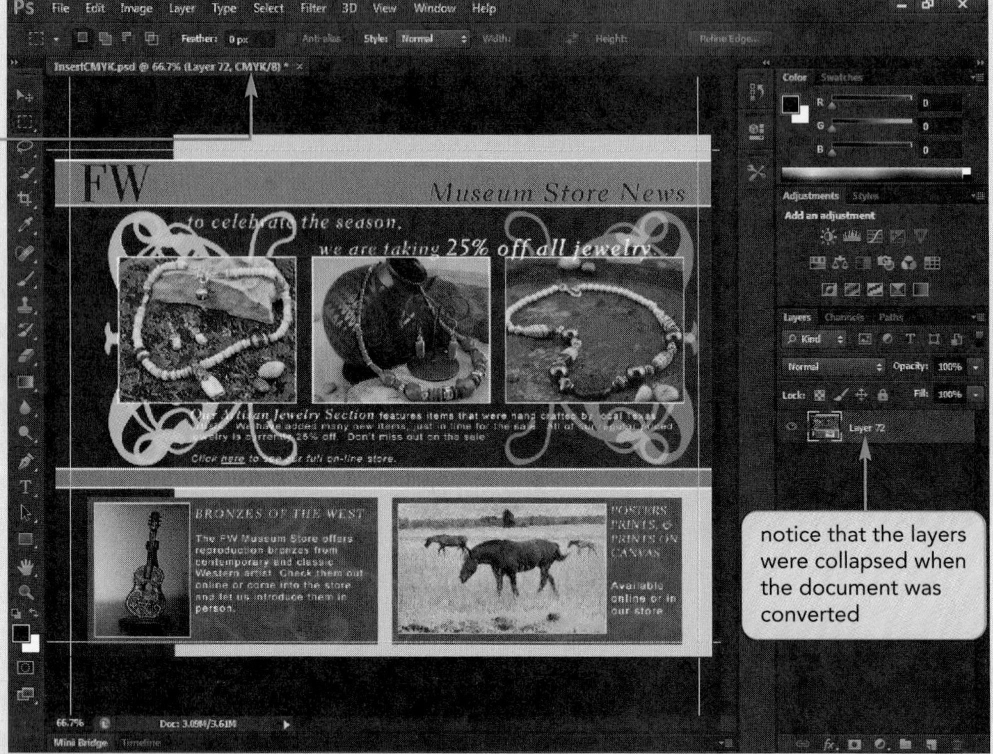
the new color model is displayed here
notice that the layers were collapsed when the document was converted
FW
Museum Store News

NU, Inc.; Eugene Moerman/Shutterstock.com; © iStockphoto.com/1234567890987654321

5. Save the file, and close the document.

Printing at Home

Most users typically print their documents to a desktop printer, such as an inkjet, laser, or dye sublimation printer. The following are a few tips that can help you achieve better results with your desktop prints:

- Crop, edit, and resize your image or composition before printing. You will do a better job of resizing than your printer will. Also, remember that the resolution should be somewhere between 200 and 400 ppi.
- Work with lossless file formats whenever possible. PSD, PDF, and TIFF files are good files for printing, and they can all be tagged with profiles.
- If you are working in RGB, do not convert your document to CMYK when printing to a desktop printer because most of these printers apply a built-in RGB-to-CMYK converter to all images automatically. If your images are already CMYK, they will be converted a second time, and you can end up with very unpredictable results.
- As always, ensure that your monitor is calibrated and that you have color management in place.
- Research your printer online, and download the printer profile recommended for your printer and the paper on which you are printing. Paper does matter when printing because different papers have slightly different brightness and the paper's finish affects the way in which the toner is absorbed into the paper. You should consider changing your printer profile when you change the type of paper on which you are printing.

TIP

Often, you can find specific printer profiles at the Web sites of paper manufacturers.

- Create a custom Color Settings profile for your printer, using the printer profile you downloaded, and remember to select your new profile in the Proof Setup. Then, check the Proof Colors command on the View menu to preview how your image will look when printed on a specific printer.
- In the Print dialog box, do the following:
  - For the Color Handling setting, select Photoshop Manages Color to enable Photoshop—rather than the printer—to control the color management process, and then select the Printer Profile that matches the printer and paper you are using.
  - Select Normal Printing unless you are printing a **hard proof**. A hard proof is a print that simulates what you will see when you print at a professional printer. Very few home printers have the resolution that is necessary to create a hard proof.
  - Select a Rendering Intent option. The **rendering intent** determines how conversion from one color space to another is handled by your color management system. Each rendering intent setting uses different rules, which can produce very different results:
    - Perceptual preserves the visual relationship of the colors to make the image appear natural to the human eye.
    - Saturation produces vivid colors in the image at the expense of accurate color conversion.
    - Relative Colorimetric compares the highest highlights of the source color space with those in the destination color space and shifts all of the colors based on that information.
    - Absolute Colorimetric leaves colors that fall inside the destination gamut alone and clips out-of gamut colors.
  - Check the Black Point Compensation check box to select it, if necessary. (This is usually checked by default.) **Black Point Compensation** preserves the shadow detail in the image.

It is also a good idea to check your printer's settings to ensure that color management in the printer is turned off so no conflicts occur. By following these tips—and with a little practice—you will achieve consistent, high-quality printing on your home printer.

Printing at a Professional Print Shop

Most of the time, you will not send files from Photoshop straight to a professional printer; instead, you will use the images you adjust in Photoshop as part of a layout you create in Illustrator or InDesign. However, even in these cases, you will often convert the color profile for these images prior to placing them in another program. The best thing you can do to achieve professional output when working with a service bureau is to contact the printer and ask them questions. Every printer is different, and most are extremely happy to provide you with all of the information that you will need to create professional output. Following are some of the questions you should ask your printer:

- How will your document be printed? Because digital presses use toner and commercial offset presses use ink, it is a good idea to know what type of press will be used.
- Should you convert to CMYK, or should you leave your files in RGB? Some RIP (Raster Image Processor) programs do a better job of converting files to CMYK than you could do, whereas others do better when starting with a CMYK file.
- What color profile should you use? Do they have one for you to download? This may change with every job because it is partially dependent on the paper on which you will be printing.
- What file format would the printer prefer to receive? Today, many printers prefer to receive a PDF file, and most printers have preferences for specs for compatibility, compression, output, and so forth. The preferences vary from printer to printer so it is important to ask.

- What resolution should your files be? Most often 300 ppi is fine, but sometimes a printer will ask you to provide images at a slightly higher resolution. The required resolution will depend on the line screen frequency the printer uses to create halftones, which are used to print continuous tone images, such as photographs and gradients. Halftones are actually composed of small dots that vary in size with the lightness or darkness of the area being printed. Dark areas use larger dots, and light areas use smaller dots. Halftones simulate continuous tone images while using less ink. **Line screen frequency** refers to the number of halftone dots in a linear inch. The resolution of a digital image must be high enough to create the halftones at the specified line screen frequency.
- Do I need to add a bleed around the edge of my document and if so, how large should it be? Documents printed at a professional printer often have color that goes all the way to the edge of the page. To achieve this look, you create a document that is slightly larger than the size you need the final document to be, and the printer trims the outside edge off of the final document. If any color or part of an image in your layout will go to the edge of the document, the printer will ask you to create a bleed—to extend the color or image into the area that will be trimmed from the final document. This is done because the cutting process is not exact. By extending anything that should go to the edge of your document, you can be sure that, regardless of slight variations due to the cutting process, your final documents will appear as you intended. Usually the bleed will extend an eighth of an inch or a quarter of an inch on all sides of the document. In addition to requesting you create a bleed, the printer may provide additional guidelines. For example, they may ask you to keep all text and important elements a certain distance from the finished edge of the document to ensure that nothing important gets cut from your document when they trim the bleed from the outside edge and they may ask you to add guides or crop marks to the document so that they will know where to cut the final document.

Remember that in order for all of this information to help you produce professional output, you must first have your monitor calibrated, and you must have color management built in to your internal work flow. Because most print files are so large when viewed on a computer screen, it is easy to forget to stop occasionally and look at the document in a different view. Flaws that can be seen in print are often not visible when you view the entire document on a computer screen. Therefore, it is a good idea to periodically switch your view to Print Size and to Actual Pixels while you are working.

Creating Images for the Web

Unlike images created for print, the name of the game when creating images for the Web is balance; you must find the right balance between image quality and file size. Because of this, the file formats used for the Web are all compressed file formats. The most common image formats used on the Web are GIF, JPEG, and PNG. Because all of these image formats are compressed, you should save your image in its original uncompressed file format, and then make a copy of the image to use on the Web. This allows you to return to your original image to make changes and prevents the possibility of degrading the images over time. Because size matters, for some projects, you might decide to cut a large image into pieces to decrease the size of the image. For example, if you create a layout design for a Web page in Photoshop, you would not save the entire image as a background for your Web page. Instead, you would create an image for the logo and an image for each button and for each image on the page. This approach will create several images that will load quickly, and it will enable a Web designer to add interactivity to some of the graphics in the page. The easiest way to create graphics in Photoshop for use on the Web is use the Save for Web dialog box to save a Web version of your image. To create a high-quality Web version of an image, do the following:

- **Use RGB**—Screens display in RGB, so it is a good idea to create artwork that will end up on the Web, in RGB.
- **Resample the image**—Images are displayed in pixels on screen, and 72 ppi is the standard resolution for Web images. You can adjust the width and height dimensions of the image in pixels at 72 ppi, or you can set the resolution to 72 ppi and then visually adjust your image size to resize the image by resampling it. Although the exact physical size of the image on the screen will vary with the size and resolution of the screen, it is important to consider the size of the average screen on which your image will be displayed when creating Web graphics. Common sizes for Web pages are 1024 × 768 and 760 × 480. A common size for tablets is 772 × 475, and common sizes for smartphones are 480 × 800 and 320 × 480.
- **Select a file format**—Decide which file format you would like to use to compress the image. Remember that each format has pros and cons. For example, JPEG is a good choice for photographic images, and PNG supports gradient transparency.
- **Save a copy**—Use Save for Web to save a copy of your image for use on the Web. Using this dialog box to save a copy will provide you with adjustment options for optimizing your compressed image. It is very important to balance image quality and file size because this will affect users' experiences with the Web site. Your goal should be to create the smallest possible file size while maintaining good quality in your image.

TIP

Decisions regarding Web page size should be based on research regarding target audience and the goals of the site.

You will use the Save for Web dialog box to save a copy of the new banner for use in the FW Museum Store Web site. You will save the banner as a JPEG because there is a photographic image in the file. Once you select JPEG, you will set the quality to Low. If you can see blurriness or artifacts (distortions) in the image, you will raise the quality to Medium; you'll continue this process until you find the lowest image quality that still displays a professional looking image.

REFERENCE

Saving a JPEG Image Using Save for Web

- On the menu bar, click File, and then click Save for Web.
- In the Save for Web dialog box, click the Optimized tab to select it, if necessary. Select JPEG from the Optimized file format list, and check the Embed Color Profile check box to include the color profile with the image. Click the Compression quality button, and then click Low.
- In the Save for Web dialog box, zoom in on the image to check for artifacting. Select a higher compression quality, if necessary, to remove the artifacting—balancing image quality with file size and download time.
- At the bottom of the Save for Web dialog box, click the Save button to open the Save Optimized As dialog box. Navigate to the folder where you want to save the file, and then click the Save button.

To save a copy of the image for the Web banner using the Save for Web dialog box:

1. Open **FeaturedItemBox.psd**, located in the Photoshop8\Tutorial folder, and set the View to **Fit on Screen**.

   Trouble? If you get a message about some text layers containing fonts that are missing, click the OK button and let Photoshop make the substitution. You will not adjust the text, so this will not affect you.

2. On the menu bar, click **File**, and then click **Save for Web**. The document is displayed in the Save for Web dialog box.

3. Select the **Optimized** tab, if necessary, select **JPEG** from the Optimized file format list, and check the **Embed Color Profile** check box to include the color profile with the image. Click the **Compression quality** button, and then click **Low**.
4. Click the **Select download speed** button below the image, and then click **Size/Download Time (256Kbps Cable/DSL)**.
5. Using the zoom controls at the lower-left corner of the Save for Web dialog box, zoom the image to **200%** to get a better look. Notice the artifacting around letters and around the beads. See Figure 8-32.

Figure 8-32 Low-quality JPEG with artifacting

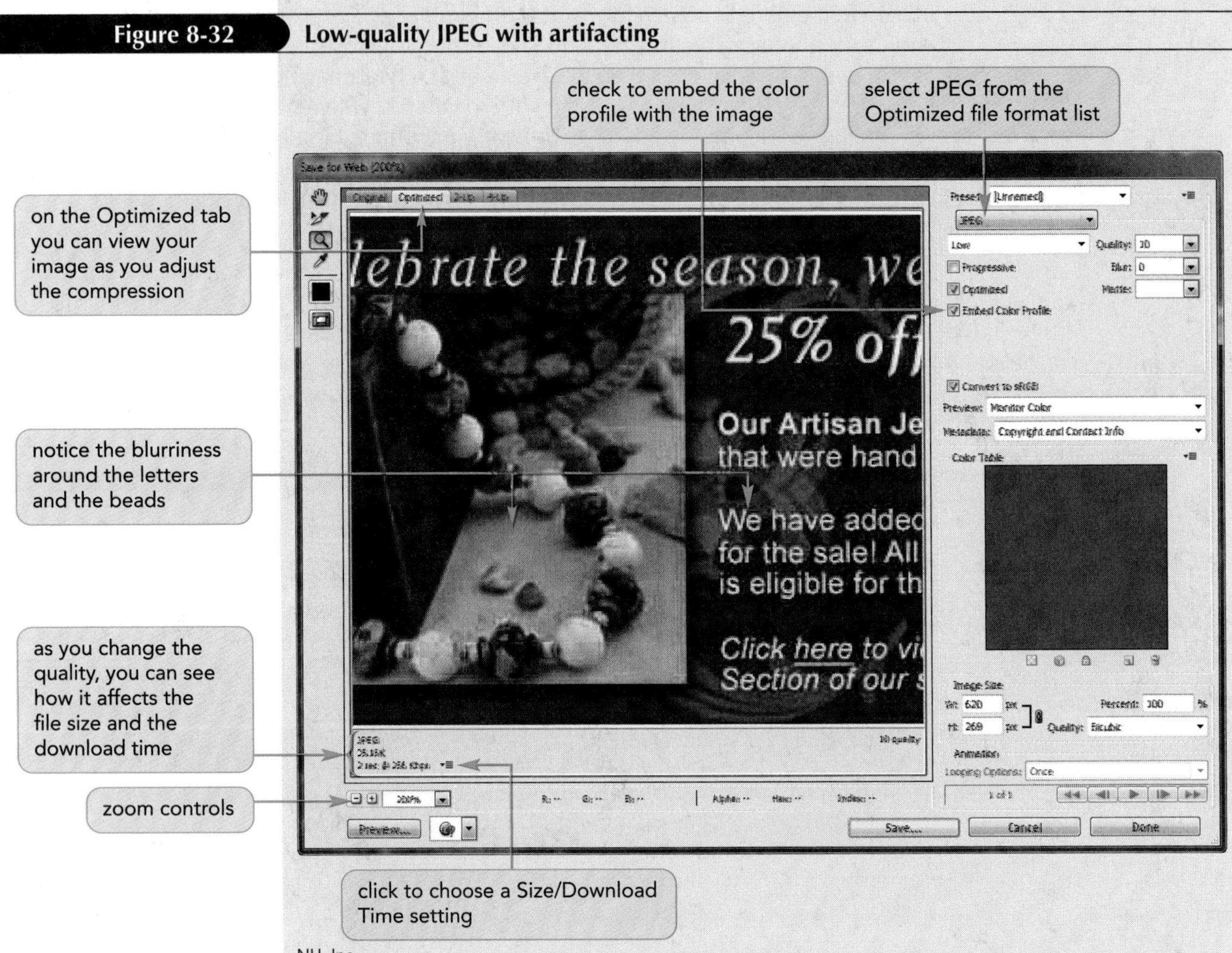
check to embed the color profile with the image
select JPEG from the Optimized file format list
on the Optimized tab you can view your image as you adjust the compression
notice the blurriness around the letters and the beads
as you change the quality, you can see how it affects the file size and the download time
zoom controls
click to choose a Size/Download Time setting

NU, Inc.

6. Click the **Compression quality** button, and then click **Medium**.

   Some of the artifacts disappear, but there are still some pixelated spots in the image.
7. Click the **Compression quality** button, and then click **High**. Examine the image, and then select **Very High**. Leave the quality at Very High, and zoom out to **100%** to see the entire image. See Figure 8-33.

Figure 8-33 High-quality JPEG with larger file size

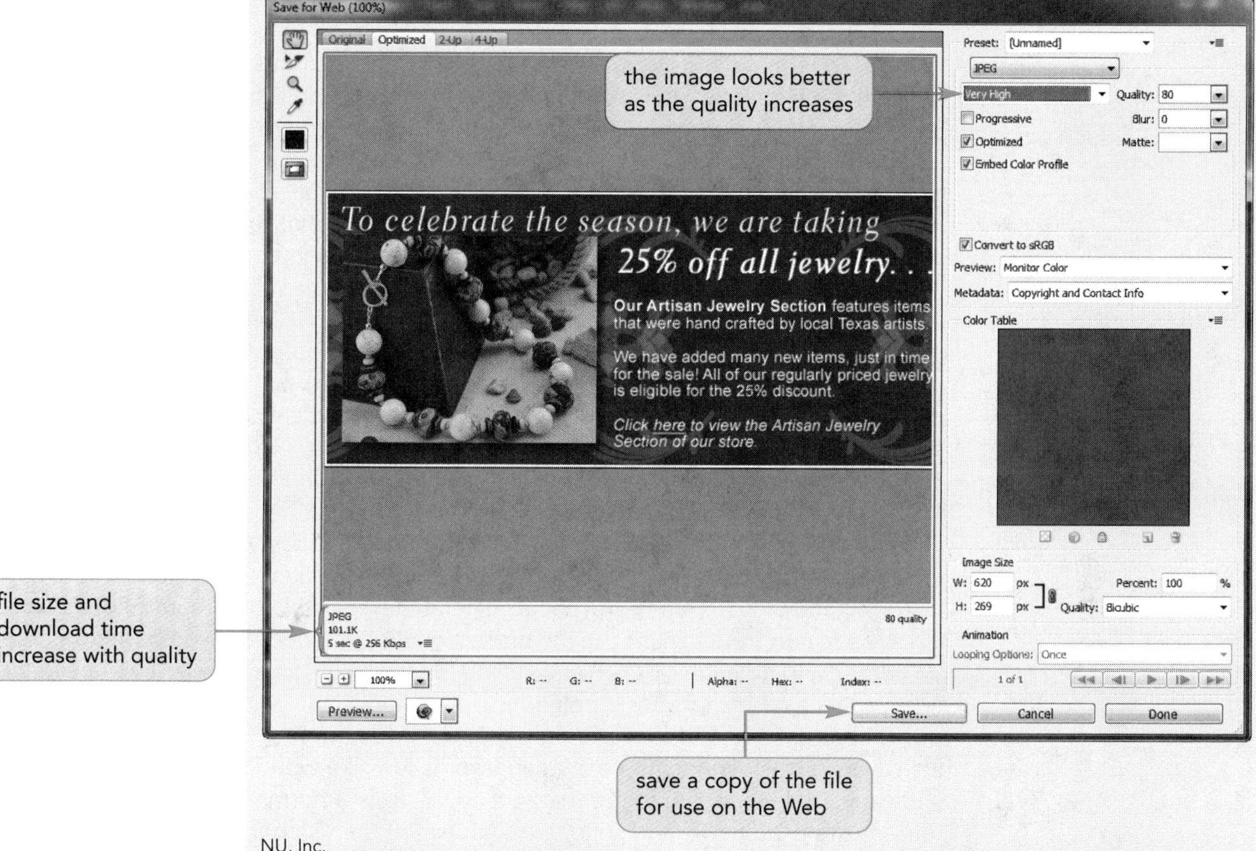

NU, Inc.

8. At the bottom of the Save for Web dialog box, click the **Save** button to open the Save Optimized As dialog box. Navigate to the Photoshop8\Tutorial folder, and then click the **Save** button.

   It is not necessary to rename the image because it will be saved with a different file extension (.jpg), and it will not save over your Photoshop document.

9. Close FeaturedItemBox.psd without saving it, and exit Photoshop.

Creating Video Output and Preparing Images for Video

In Photoshop CS6, importing, opening, editing, and exporting video files are easy tasks. You should keep in mind the following when creating files that you will output as video and when creating text, images, and graphics that you will use in video files:

- Video files can be saved in a variety of different formats. A **video format** is a set of standards that define a video file's display characteristics and limitations. Some video standards are tied to a specific country's broadcast standards (such as the NTSC – SD format, which was the standard for U.S. standard-definition television broadcast for many years), while others are more universal. Digital video formats include a video file type (which is a container such as AVI and MPEG-4) and a **codec**, (such as enCOder/DECoder, x264, or DivX), which defines how the information is stored and processed within the container and may provide options for adjusting resolution, compression, and stream. This can be confusing because video formats are sometimes referred to by the file type and sometimes by the codec. In addition, some file types are only used with one codec, while other file types can be used with several different codecs.

- Each video format has its own width and height specifications. Recall that the ratio of width to height of a file is called the aspect ratio. In addition, different formats use different pixel aspect ratios. A **pixel aspect ratio** is the width to height ratio of a single pixel. The video format you select will determine the pixel aspect ratio. Many computer video formats use a 4:3 ratio for the frame. A 4:3 ratio produces a frame size, such as 640 pixels wide by 480 pixels high, that results in square pixels. Some video formats have a pixel aspect ratio that results in nonsquare pixels. When nonsquare pixels are displayed on a square-pixel monitor without correction, images appear distorted. Photoshop provides a Pixel Aspect Ratio Correction preview setting that compensates for nonsquare pixel ratio and allows you to preview a video (and images or graphics you create for use in a video) as they will be displayed on the output device. This will help you achieve better results when using Photoshop tools such as the movie paint feature.
- To open a video clip that you shot with a video camera in Photoshop, you must first transfer the file to your computer. Then, you can drag the clip to the Document window and add it to the Timeline panel (where you can apply various effects and create transitions between clips) using the Add New Media to Track button or by importing individual frames of video to separate layers using the Import Video Frames to Layers feature. You should use the highest quality of video clip you have available for editing and then create compressed versions of the clip for output if you need the final product to be a smaller file size.
- Video clips open in a video layer that is displayed in the Timeline panel as well as the Layers panel. Working with a video layer is just like working with regular layers, and you can do all of the things that you could do to a normal layer, including masking, adjusting, painting, and so forth, regardless of the video format specifications because Photoshop now has nonsquare pixel support for video files. Note that the Properties panel does not provide information about video layers.
- Video files and images and graphics that you will use in video files should use the RGB color mode with a resolution of 72 ppi. Some video formats provide a color profile that you can use. Photoshop provides a Film & Video preset that you can select when creating a new image for use in a video file. The Film & Video preset enables you to easily create a file that is optimized for film/video format display so you can create graphics and images to layer over video clips. You can use Photoshop to layer images over a video, or you can save the image file and add it to your video using another video-editing program. When you select the format you are using from the Size list in the New dialog box, Photoshop fills in the other parameters including Width, Height, Color Mode, Resolution and Pixel Aspect Ratio. When you use the Film and Video preset, the document will include guides that indicate the area of the image that is title-safe (safe for displaying text) in formats that are intended for display on devices that sometimes obfuscate the edge of the video from view. You should use the preset settings as a guide to optimize existing graphic and image files for use in your video.
- Once you have created video, you must export it in the formats that are appropriate for the devices—and playback conditions—on which you will be viewing the final video. To do this you render the video file. Rendering is different than saving a file. While working on a video file, you should save it periodically, just as you would save an image file. However, the video files you work with in Photoshop are large files, with many layers of video and audio information that remain separate so you can edit them while you work. To create a video file that is ready for playback,

you render the file. Rendering is the process of generating all the individual frames, which are combined and compressed to form the final video. Check the playback conditions or read the device specifications to determine the appropriate video formats for your project, and render the video using the Adobe Media Encoder as the rendering engine. Adobe Media Encoder allows you to simply select a format and a preset, and then it fills in all of the remaining specifications for the final video output.

In this session, you learned about color management and how it impacts every aspect of your design. You calibrated your monitor, examined your color settings, and synchronized the color setting for all of your Adobe Creative Suite 6 software. You set your soft proof parameters and learned to soft proof documents. You also converted the color profile of a document, and you saved a copy of an image for use on the Web. Finally, you learned some important information about creating video output and preparing images and graphics for use in video.

REVIEW

Session 8.2 Quick Check

1. The path that a project travels from original input through final output is called the ________.
2. You can use the Windows ________ Wizard to calibrate your monitor.
3. Name at least three file formats that can include ICC color profiles.
4. _______ is the process of creating controlled, consistent, and accurate color throughout the work flow process—from input, through display, creation and adjustment, and, finally, output.
5. When should you convert your document's color profile?
6. _________ is a three-dimensional representation of the specific plotted points of color designated by the numerical values of colors that can be produced by a color model.
7. What are the two things that you must balance when saving a copy of an image for use on the Web?

Practice the skills you learned in the tutorial using the same case scenario.

PRACTICE

Review Assignments

Data File needed for the Review Assignments: MG4820.CR2

In addition to the FW Museum Store catalog insert, Sadie would like you to create a version of the insert to place on the Web and to send to customers as a newsletter. You'll adjust images of some new products to add to the Web version of the insert, and then you'll soft proof the insert and correct it for Web distribution. Finally, you'll need to provide Sadie with a file that can be distributed on the Web. Complete the following steps:

1. Start Photoshop while pressing the Ctrl+Alt+Shift keys, and click Yes to delete the Settings File when prompted. Reset Photoshop to the default Essentials workspace layout, and then reset all tools.
2. Set your color settings to North America General Purpose 2, if necessary, and then select Internet Standard RGB (sRGB) from the Proof Setup menu, if necessary.
3. Navigate to the Photoshop8\Review folder provided with your Data Files, and open **MG4820.CR2**.
4. Select the Crop tool in the Camera Raw dialog box, and then create a custom ratio of 1 to .8. Crop the image closely around the necklace.
5. Change the White Balance setting to Tungsten, and then adjust the tonal controls until you create a clear, vibrant image that will work well with the other product images you adjusted in the tutorial. (*Hint*: View the other product images, if necessary, and notice that all of the images are filled with neutral earth tones and only one or two vibrant colors.)
6. Make sure that neither the Highlight nor Shadow clipping warning is displayed at the top of the histogram. If warnings appear, adjust the image until they are gone.
7. Increase the clarity of the image so that the parts of the necklace that have a softer focus become clearer.
8. Make any other adjustments that you feel are necessary, and click the Open Object button to save your changes and open the image as a Smart Object in Photoshop.
9. Change the View to Fit on Screen, and then save the image as **MG4820.psd** in the Photoshop8\Review folder.
10. Using the Proof Setup options and the Proof Colors command on the View menu, view the image as it will appear when displayed in a Web page. If you see problems, open the Smart Object in Camera Raw, adjust it, and view it again as a soft proof. Repeat this process as needed until your soft proof looks the way you think it should, and then save the file.
11. In the Image Size dialog box, set the Resolution to 72 ppi image, using a 300-pixel width. Use the settings in the Save for Web dialog box to optimize the image and to save a copy as **MG4820.jpg** in the Photoshop8\Review folder.
12. Close the MG4820.psd file without saving the changes because you do not want to change the resolution of the original image.
13. Open the **MG4820.psd** file again, select Working CMYK under Proof Setup, and then check Proof Colors, if necessary. Notice the difference in the vibrancy of the colors in the image.
14. Open the MG4820 Smart Object. Adjust the image in Camera Raw, and then click the OK button to go back to Photoshop. View the soft proof of the image. Repeat as necessary to achieve the look you desire, then save the file, and exit Photoshop.
15. Submit the results of the preceding steps to your instructor either in printed or electronic form, as requested.

Use your skills to correct, adjust, proof, and convert images.

APPLY

Case Problem 1

Data Files needed for this Case Problem: Music.tif, Auto.tif, Surfboard.tif

Old School Based in the Dotty Lynn Recreation Center in Sacramento, California, the Old School offers unconventional evening classes that pair adult and youth students who have similar interests in student-led classes. The classes are structured so the first four weeks are taught by older members of the class who share their experiences, techniques, and historical perspective on the subject. The last four weeks are taught by the younger members of the class who present current trends, technologies, and techniques. The Old School has been very well received in the greater Sacramento community. The school's most popular classes include music appreciation, automotive and motorcycle repair, and surfing.

Matthew Palmer, the founder of the Old School, has hired your firm to create posters to promote the fall class schedule. When you adjust photographs that will be used in the poster, you'll use the color profiles provided to your team by the printer. You'll also need to convert the files for print. Complete the following steps:

1. Start Photoshop while pressing the Ctrl+Alt+Shift keys, and click Yes to delete the Settings File when prompted. Reset Photoshop to the default Essentials workspace layout, and then reset all tools.
2. Set your color settings to North America General Purpose 2, if necessary.
3. Open Mini Bridge, navigate to the Photoshop8\Case1 folder provided with your Data Files, and open **Music.tif** in Camera Raw.
4. Select Auto from the White Balance list, and then adjust the other settings on the Basic tab until you have created an image that you find aesthetically pleasing.
5. If necessary, click the Shadow and Highlight clipping warning icons located above the histogram to view pixels in the image that are out of gamut, and make further adjustments to remove clipping.
6. **EXPLORE** Use the HLS/Grayscale tab or the Tone Curve tab to adjust the hue, saturation, or luminance, if necessary. (*Hint*: The Tone Curve tab works in the same way that the Curves adjustment works in Photoshop.) Remember that small adjustments are usually enough to create big results.
7. Open the image as a Smart Object in Photoshop, and then view a soft proof of the image.
8. If the soft proof does not have the desired look, open the Smart Object in Camera Raw, adjust the image, and view the image in Photoshop again.
9. Repeat Step 8 until the image has the desired look when you view it as a soft proof.
10. Save the image as **MusicAdjust.psd** in the Photoshop8\Case 1 folder, and then use Convert to Profile to convert the image to CMYK, and save a copy as **MusicAdjust.tif** in the same folder. Uncheck the Layers check box in the Save As dialog box, and make sure that the ICC Profile check box is checked to ensure that the image is tagged with a color profile. Use the following settings in the TIFF Options dialog box: Image Compression: None, Pixel Order: Interleaved, Byte Order: IBM PC, Layer Compression: Discard Layers and Save a Copy. This is the image you will provide to the team that is laying out the posters.
11. Close the MusicAdjust.psd file without saving it.
12. Repeat Steps 3–11 for the Auto.tif image and the Surfboard.tif image. Use **AutoAdjust** and **SurfboardAdjust** as the filenames for the PSD and TIFF files that you create.
13. Submit the results of the preceding steps to your instructor either in printed or electronic form, as requested.

Use your skills to adjust images in Camera Raw and save copies for the Web.

APPLY

Case Problem 2

Data Files needed for this Case Problem: Snake.CR2, Basket.CR2

Tom Little, Ferrier/Artisan Tom Little is a farrier and artisan who has lived in Sedona, Arizona, for the past 19 years. Using old lariats, he creates baskets, which he shapes by hand, joining them together by melting the rope with an electric soldering iron. No glue is involved in his unique process. Tom also creates snakes from old blacksmith tools called rasps, which he heats on his forge and twists to shape and beat with a hammer to form realistic scales.

Tom has had some photographs of his work taken by a professional photographer, and he has asked you to crop, adjust, and correct the images so he can use them in online newsletters that he sends to collectors, festivals, and stores that might be interested in his unique works of art. Because the images will be used online, you will create a compressed JPEG copy of each image that he will use in the newsletter. For an example of a corrected image, see Figure 8-34.

Figure 8-34 **Snake image adjusted and cropped**

NU, Inc.

Complete the following steps:

1. Start Photoshop while pressing the Ctrl+Alt+Shift keys, and click Yes to delete the Settings File when prompted. Reset Photoshop to the default Essentials workspace layout, and then reset all tools.
2. Navigate to the Photoshop8\Case2 folder provided with your Data Files, and open **Snake.CR2** in Camera Raw.
3. In the Camera Raw dialog box, select the Crop tool, and then select 1 to 1 from the Ratio list (use the 2 to 3 ratio option for the Basket.CR2 image). Draw a square around the snake and the baskets, and make sure that you do not include any of the edges of white tent in the square. (*Hint*: In the Snake.CR2 image, it is okay to crop some of the tips of the plants from the shot; in the Basket.CR2 image, you may need to crop some of the basket edges.)
4. Select the Hand tool to view your cropped image.
5. Select Tungsten from the White Balance list, and then adjust the tonal adjustments, clarity, and vibrance on the Basic tab until you are satisfied with the look of the image.
6. Zoom in on the image, and locate any debris located within the image area. (*Hint*: In the Snake.CR2 image, there are a few pieces of dirt to the right of the snake; in the Basket.CR2 image, there is a little dirt on the canvas in the left foreground.)
7. **EXPLORE** On the Document window toolbar in the Camera Raw dialog box, select the Spot Removal tool, and select Heal from the Type list in the Adjustments panel. You'll use this tool to remove the debris in the image. Using a Radius of 5 and an Opacity setting of 100, place the pointer in the image area over the spot you would like to clean up, and click. Two circles are drawn in the image area.
8. **EXPLORE** Drag the red circle so it is over the spot that you would like to remove, and then drag the green circle to an area of the background that is similar to the area where the spot is located, but which is spot free. The spot disappears from the image. (*Hint*: If the circles are too large, place the pointer over the edge of a circle, then drag in to make the circles smaller, or drag out to make the circles larger.)
9. Repeat Steps 7–8 until all of the debris is removed from the image. Select Fit in View from the Select Zoom Level list, and use the Hand tool to pan and view the image.
10. Make any adjustments you feel are necessary, and then open the image as a Smart Object in Photoshop.
11. Save the image as **Snake.psd** in the Photoshop8\Case2 folder. Then, adjust the image size so the image is 400 pixels by 400 pixels, with a resolution of 72 ppi. Use the settings in the Save for Web dialog box to optimize and save a JPEG copy of the image as **Snake.jpg** in the Photoshop8\Case2 folder. (For the Basket.jpg, use a width of 600, a height of 400, and a resolution of 72 ppi.)
12. Close Snake.psd without saving.
13. Repeat Steps 2–12 for the Basket.CR2 image, saving the image as **Basket.psd** and **Basket.jpg**.
14. Submit the results of the preceding steps to your instructor either in printed or electronic form, as requested.

Extend your skills to explore some other Camera Raw tools.

CHALLENGE

Case Problem 3

Data Files needed for this Case Problem: ThisTooWillPass.tif, YouCompleteMe.tif

Petcentric Petcentric is a line of greeting cards for pets. Have you ever wanted to say "I'm sorry" to your parrot or "I'm thinking about you" to your boxer? Now you can with Petcentric cards. Owner Bobby May came up with the idea when her bull dog, Nicky, was in the hospital with a virus. "She looked so sad. I just wanted to bring her something to say get well, and there was nothing out there. I thought if I feel this way, there are surely other crazy pet owners who are feeling the same thing." One year later, her first line of cards hit the shelves, and Petcentric cards have been a success from the start.

The Petcentric line of cards uses humorous images of animals with bold bursts of color, and tongue-in-cheek sentiments to distinguish it from other lines of cards. You will adjust some images that will be used by another member of your team to create final cards. For an example of a Petcentric card image, see Figure 8-35.

Figure 8-35 **ThisTooWillPass image adjusted**

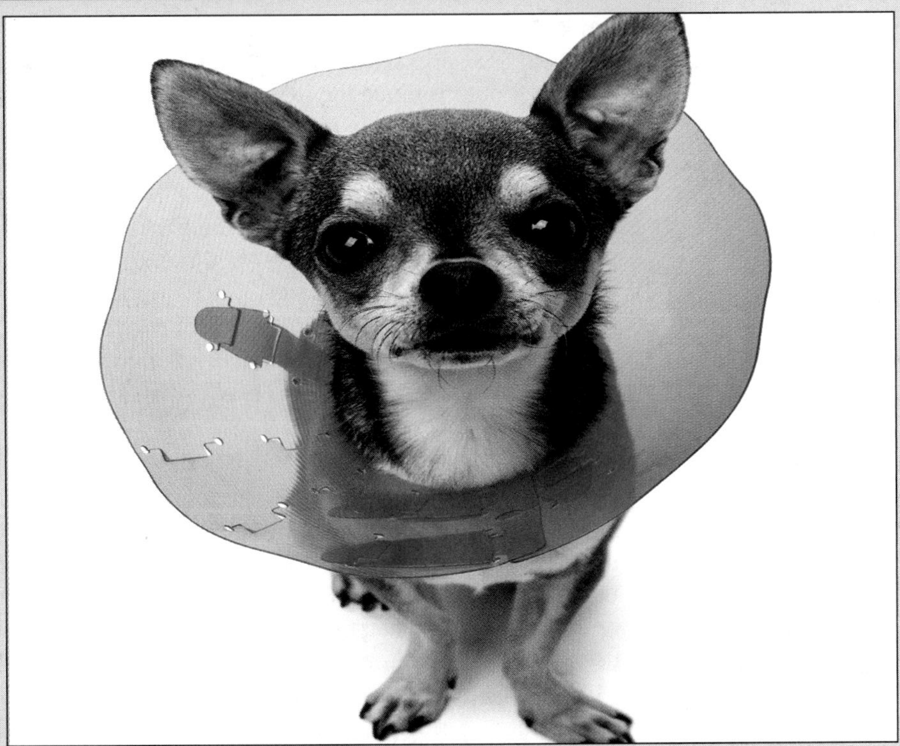

Eric Isselée /Shutterstock.com

Complete the following steps:

1. Start Photoshop while pressing the Ctrl+Alt+Shift keys, and click Yes to delete the Settings File when prompted. Reset Photoshop to the default Essentials workspace layout, and then reset all tools.
2. Use Mini Bridge, navigate to the Photoshop8\Case3 folder provided with your Data Files, and open **ThisTooWillPass.tif** in Camera Raw.
3. EXPLORE To raise the saturation values of the collar, select the Targeted Adjustment tool on the toolbar, and select Saturation from the Targeted Adjustment Tool list. Place the pointer over the plastic collar and drag upward until the blue in the collar has increased significantly. Then, to lower the saturation values in the rest of the image, place the pointer over the dog's face or body, and drag down until the dog appears to be grayscale, leaving only the collar in color. You may need to repeat the desaturation process over the white on the dog's neck, to remove the purple color cast from his neck.
4. EXPLORE Select Luminance from the Targeted Adjustment Tool list, and decrease the luminance of the collar by dragging down on the collar, as needed, to intensify the color. Then, decrease the luminance of the dog as needed to create a more dramatic image.
5. Use the Adjustment tabs to make any other necessary adjustments. (*Hint*: Increasing the clarity and vibrance will enhance the intensity of the color-saturated areas.)
6. Open the image as a Smart Object in Photoshop, save the image as **ThisTooWillPass.psd** in the Photoshop8\Case3 folder, and close the image. Another member of the team will now be able to convert the image and place it in a layout program to create the final card.
7. EXPLORE Open **YouCompleteMe.tif** from the Photoshop8\Case3 folder in Camera Raw, and use the Hue setting in the Targeted Adjustment Tool list to change the background color to turquoise.
8. On the Basic tab, decrease the clarity of the image to give the image a soft glow. Use the sliders on the Basic tab to make any additional corrections to the image. Remember that you are creating a humorous image with a bold burst of color.
9. Open the image as a Smart Object in Photoshop, and save the image as **YouCompleteMe.psd** in the Photoshop8\Case3 folder. Close the file, and exit Photoshop.
10. Submit the results of the preceding steps to your instructor either in printed or electronic form, as requested.

Using Figure 8-36 as a guide, create images that have a similar look and feel.

CREATE

Case Problem 4

Data Files needed for this Case Problem: BacMuffins.tif, BacSushi.tif

Baconality Baconality is a restaurant located in Atlanta, Georgia, that is dedicated to all things bacon. The concept for a bacon-centric restaurant was created by two frat brothers, John Waynes and Bob Hansel, after a late-night breakfast where they agreed that bacon was a food that almost every person loves. From that after-hours epiphany, Baconality was born.

John has hired your firm to create an online version of the menu for Baconality, and he has provided you with a few professional photographs of menu items. Although the images have come from different sources, it is important that you create a unified look and feel when you adjust them to give the online menu a cohesive look. Take some time before you begin editing to determine what unifying elements you will emphasize to ensure that the images work together. Consider the following items:

- Number of items in the shot
- Relative closeness of items in the shot
- Space around items in the shot
- Focus and depth
- Color and saturation of each image

For some examples of images that would work well in the online menu, see Figure 8-36.

Figure 8-36 **Sample Baconality images**

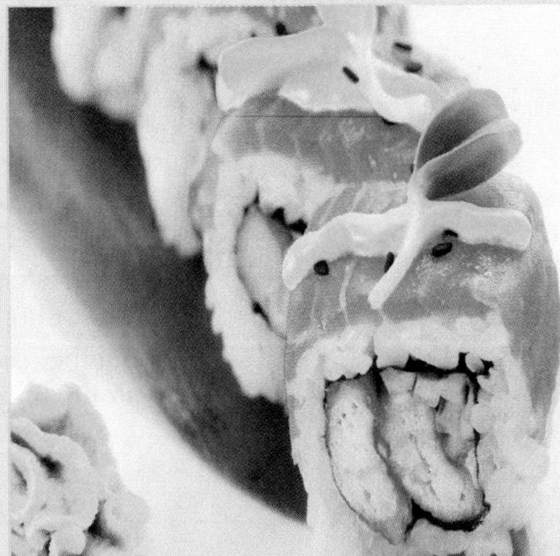

© iStockphoto.com/Ivan Mateev; Ouh_Desire/Shutterstock.com

Complete the following steps:

1. Start Photoshop while pressing the Ctrl+Alt+Shift keys, and click Yes to delete the Settings File when prompted. Reset Photoshop to the default Essentials workspace layout, and then reset all tools.
2. Use Mini Bridge to navigate to the Photoshop8\Case4 folder provided with your Data Files, and examine both images in the folder.
3. Consider which elements are similar in each image, and which elements are unique to an individual image. Then, write a short paragraph outlining your findings and your plan for creating a cohesive look for the online menu.
4. Determine how you will adjust the images to create a unified look and feel.
5. Use Mini Bridge to open one of the images in Camera Raw.
6. Adjust the image as needed according to your plan. Then, open the image as a Smart Object in Photoshop, and save a copy as a PSD file, using the same filename, in the Photoshop8\Case4 folder.
7. Adjust the image size so the image is 400 pixels × 400 pixels at 72 ppi. (*Hint*: Do not save the original image at this size in case you need to make adjustments later.)
8. Use the settings in the Save for Web dialog box to create an optimized and compressed JPEG copy of the image for use in the online menu, using the same filename, and save the image in the Photoshop8\Case4 folder.
9. Repeat Steps 5–8 for the remaining image.
10. Submit the results of the preceding steps to your instructor either in printed or electronic form, as requested.

ENDING DATA FILES

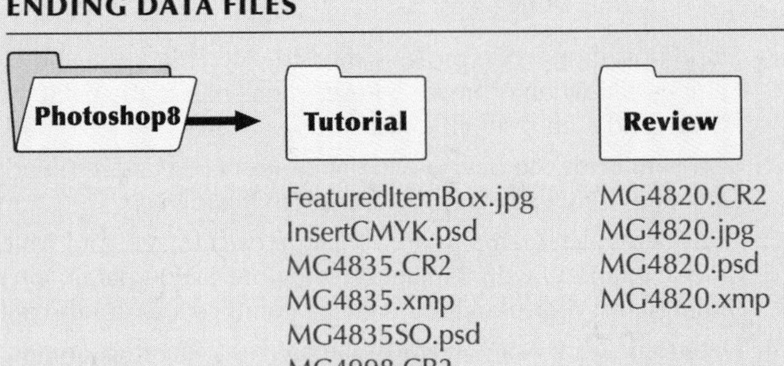

Tutorial

FeaturedItemBox.jpg
InsertCMYK.psd
MG4835.CR2
MG4835.xmp
MG4835SO.psd
MG4998.CR2
MG4998.xmp

Review

MG4820.CR2
MG4820.jpg
MG4820.psd
MG4820.xmp

Case1

AutoAdjust.psd
AutoAdjust.tif
MusicAdjust.psd
MusicAdjust.tif
SurfboardAdjust.psd
SurfboardAdjust.tif

Case2

Basket.CR2
Basket.jpg
Basket.psd
Basket.xmp
Snake.CR2
Snake.jpg
Snake.psd
Snake.xmp

Case3

ThisTooWillPass.psd
YouCompleteMe.psd

Case4

BacMuffins.jpg
BacMuffins.psd
BacSushi.jpg
BacSushi.psd

TUTORIAL 9

Planning, Creating, and Delivering a Complete Project

Creating a Web Banner Ad Campaign

OBJECTIVES

Session 9.1

- Define project scope, goals, phases, and deliverables
- Create a viewer profile and identify the target audience
- Research audience interests, competition, branding, and identity
- Identify output specifications

Session 9.2

- Gather materials and develop a concept and metaphor
- Understand layout theories and create a layout
- Select a color palette, typographical style, typeface, and fonts
- Decide on a graphic style and create graphics
- Determine a photographic style
- Create output files and archive project files

Case | *FlashFlock*

FlashFlock is a nonprofit organization made up of nature photographers, activists, artists, and flash mob enthusiasts. The group started when George Lemming and Rick Loon created the FlashFlock Web site to publicize an exhibition of photos showing animal flash mobs staged in urban settings.

FlashFlock now hosts an annual nature photography festival, and George has asked your firm to create collateral materials for this year's event. Your team, led by Jessica Tate, will work with George and Rick to plan, develop, create, and execute the Web banner campaign advertising the FlashFlock Festival.

STARTING DATA FILES

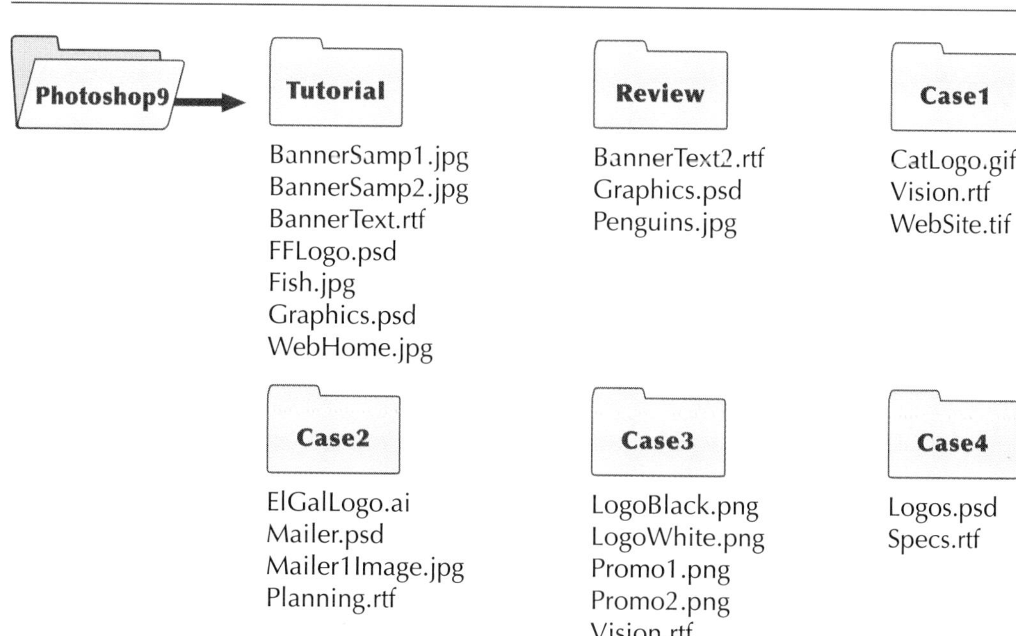

SESSION 9.1 VISUAL OVERVIEW

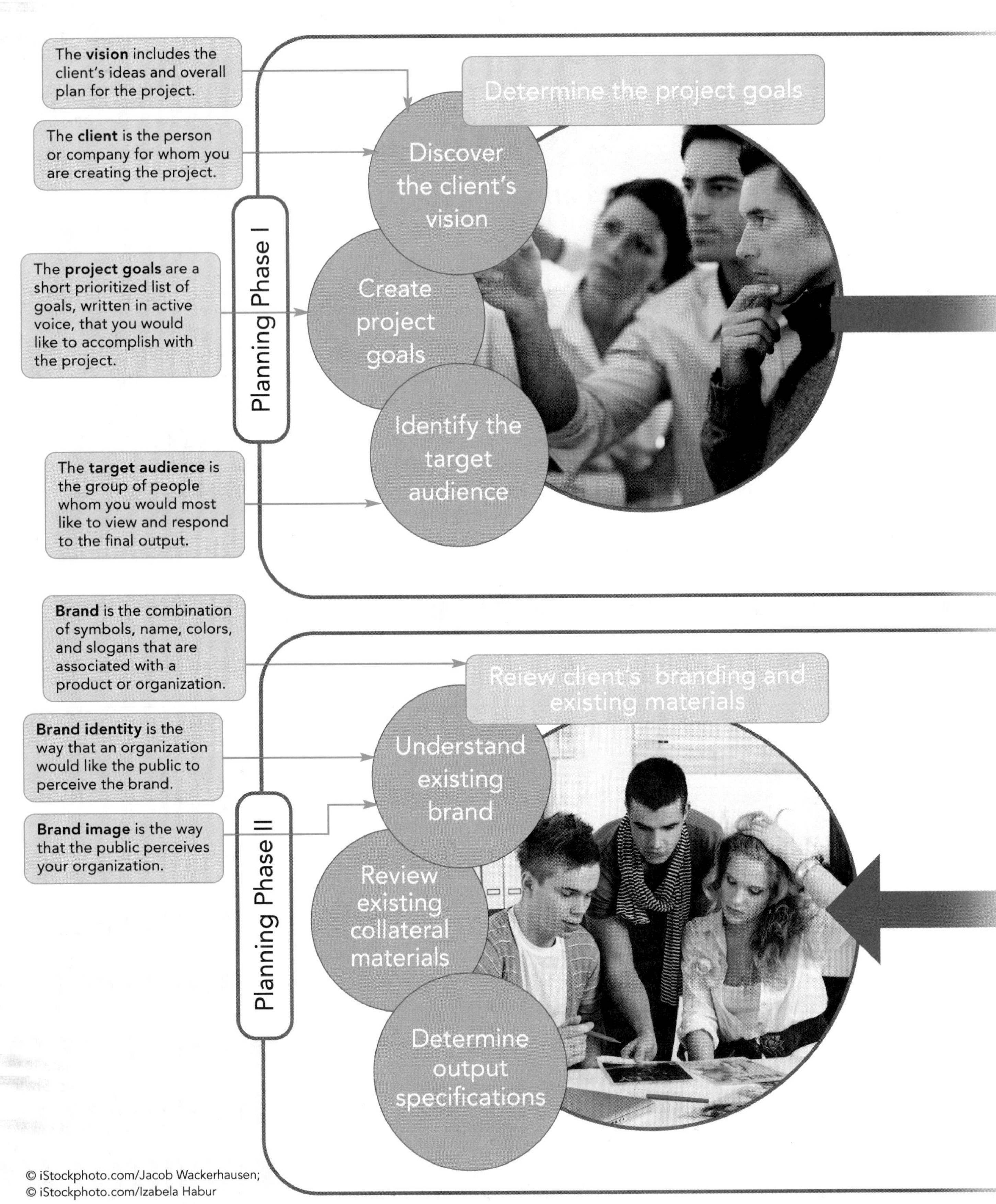
The **vision** includes the client's ideas and overall plan for the project.
The **client** is the person or company for whom you are creating the project.
The **project goals** are a short prioritized list of goals, written in active voice, that you would like to accomplish with the project.
The **target audience** is the group of people whom you would most like to view and respond to the final output.
Planning Phase I
Determine the project goals
Discover the client's vision
Create project goals
Identify the target audience
Brand is the combination of symbols, name, colors, and slogans that are associated with a product or organization.
Brand identity is the way that an organization would like the public to perceive the brand.
Brand image is the way that the public perceives your organization.
Planning Phase II
Reiew client's branding and existing materials
Understand existing brand
Review existing collateral materials
Determine output specifications

PLANNING A PROFESSIONAL PROJECT

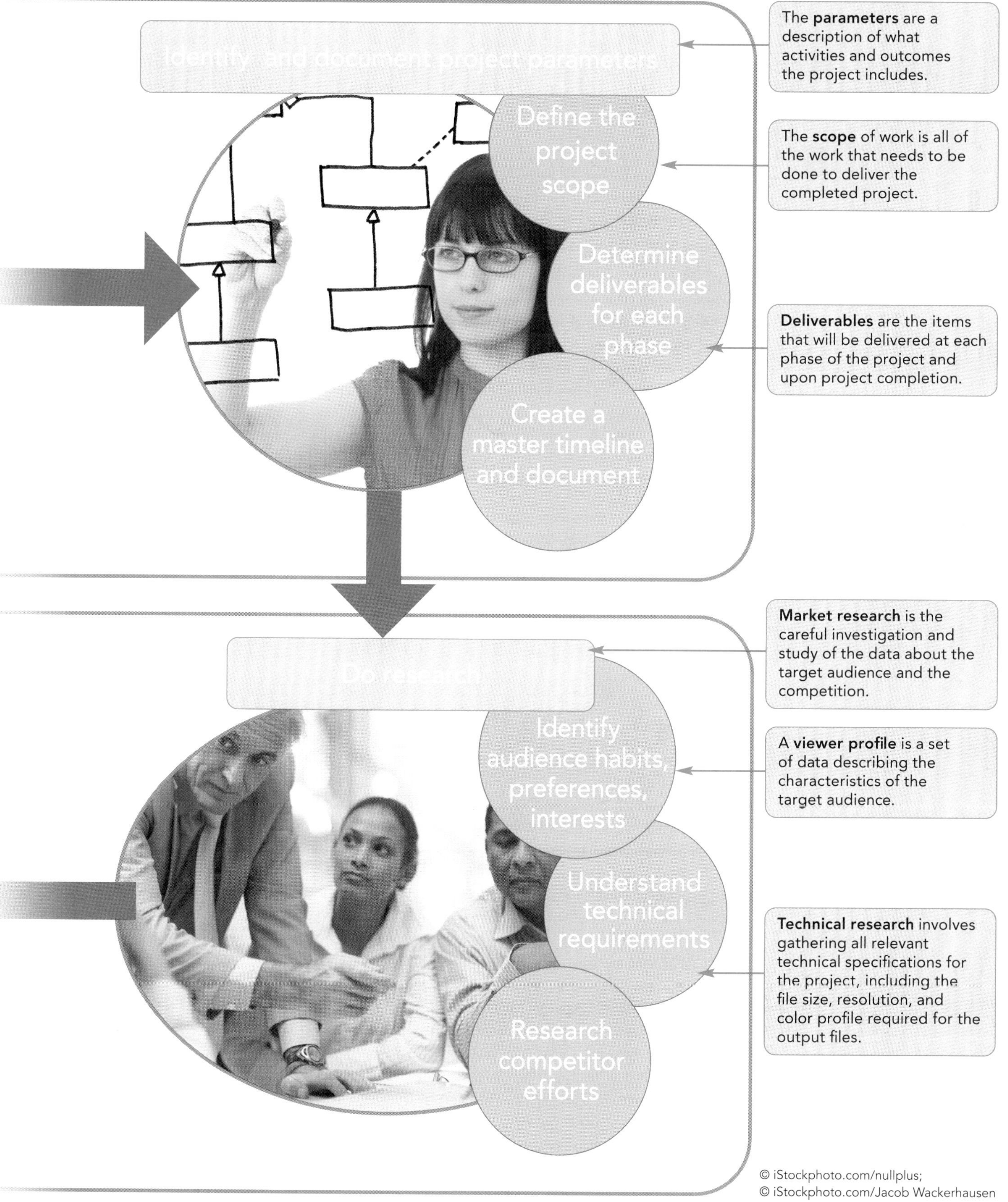
Identify and document project parameters
Define the project scope
Determine deliverables for each phase
Create a master timeline and document
Do research
Identify audience habits, preferences, interests
Understand technical requirements
Research competitor efforts

The **parameters** are a description of what activities and outcomes the project includes.

The **scope** of work is all of the work that needs to be done to deliver the completed project.

Deliverables are the items that will be delivered at each phase of the project and upon project completion.

Market research is the careful investigation and study of the data about the target audience and the competition.

A **viewer profile** is a set of data describing the characteristics of the target audience.

Technical research involves gathering all relevant technical specifications for the project, including the file size, resolution, and color profile required for the output files.

Planning and Delivering a Professional Project

A **project** is an endeavor with an explicit beginning and endpoint that is undertaken to meet specific goals—including producing predefined deliverables—using limited, identified resources for a predetermined cost. Creating a professional project involves much more than just opening Photoshop and using its tools to make a composition. In the real world, defining and creating a graphic design project is a process that has many important steps or phases. The first part of the process—the planning phase—is where you learn about the client's vision for the project and make all of the major decisions regarding project parameters, such as determining what the project will include, how long it will take to complete, what you will provide to the client at each step of development, what resources the project will use, and how much the project will cost. The planning phase also includes all of the marketing and technical research that needs to be done prior to starting the design phase of the project. Below is an outline of the planning phase:

- Planning Phase I (Create a Plan)
  - Understanding the client's vision
  - Establishing goals for the project
  - Ascertaining the target audience
  - Defining the project scope and determining the project deliverables
  - Creating a master planning document
- Planning Phase II (Research)
  - Studying the target audience and the competition
  - Reviewing the client's branding, identity, and marketing materials
  - Determining output specifications

When the planning process is complete, you are ready to move to the design phase of the project. In this tutorial, you will start by planning a project, and then you'll move on to learn more about each step of the process as you work to create a finished project. Understanding the entire process will provide you with the knowledge and skills you need to create successful professional projects.

Now that you have an overview of the process, your team will begin planning the FlashFlock banner ad campaign.

Planning a Design Project

The design process usually starts with a series of meetings with a client. (If you are working on an internal company project, the person for whom you are creating the project is your client.) During the meetings, you must ascertain your client's vision for the project. You should also help the client develop specific goals, define a target audience, articulate his or her aesthetic preferences, and define the scope of the project. Once you have made general decisions, you need to break down the project into logical phases, decide exactly what you will deliver to the client at the end of each phase, and designate one member from the client's team as the person who will approve and sign off on each phase of the project. It is a good idea to create a project overview document outlining all of your preliminary decisions and agreements. Include a timeline or schedule with this document so everyone is clear on what will happen before you start working on the project. Once that document is complete, you can begin the research phase of the project.

Client meetings are a crucial part of the planning process because it is impossible to design a project that will effectively meet a client's needs until you determine exactly what those needs are. It is important to communicate with your client at every step of the project and to include them in your decision-making process. You should explain clearly to the client what information you will need and how his or her contributions will add value to the final project. Throughout the project, be sure to show your work to the client and other team members for feedback, evaluation, and sign-off.

There are many possible paths in any creative process. As you gain experience in planning, designing, and creating projects, you will find that some things work better than others. As part of your training, Jessica has asked you to come up with your own ideas about the FlashFlock banner project goals, target audience, and so on. You'll then compare them with those approved by George. You'll evaluate how your findings, proposed goals, and project plan are similar to and different from the final FlashFlock project plan; you'll then consider the benefits and drawbacks of each option.

INSIGHT

Developing Your Professional Design Skills

Becoming an expert on Photoshop and other design software is an important first step in becoming a successful designer. Just as a successful carpenter must be able to use the tools of her trade, a designer must have expert skills in working with the software that is one of the tools of his trade. However, expert use of tools is not enough to make you an expert designer. To become a professional, you must also develop expertise in additional areas, including project management, marketing principles, and aesthetic/art theory. To extend the carpenter metaphor—a carpenter building a table for someone's home must understand how the size and shape of the room, the style of the house, and the aesthetic preferences and lifestyle of the client will affect what design would work best for that client.

A designer must understand how to lead a project from inception to completion as well as how to create a project that will fulfill the client's vision and goals, reach and connect with the target audience, and produce the desired results when the project is output to its final format. In addition, a good designer understands classic design theory and current aesthetic trends and is able to create solid designs that effectively communicate with the target audience. An effective designer is also able to use her own sense of aesthetics to create successful, original projects. For example, without an understanding of the effective use of white space, a designer might create layouts filled with graphic elements that do not give the composition a sense of space and flow. Without an understanding of what styles are popular with a particular age group, a designer might not be able to create a composition that catches the attention of people in that group. You develop these skills by taking classes in classic art theory, reading trade magazines, working for professional designers, and using what you learn to create new projects.

Understanding the Client's Vision

When a client comes to you with a project, that client has a need that he wants to address. Usually, the client has an idea of what the project should look like, communicate, and achieve. However, there are often many details that the client has not considered. Clients seek your expert skills and knowledge, and they rely on you to know what questions to ask and to guide them in making decisions throughout the design process. Your first task is to discover the client's vision for the project by asking him to explain, in detail, what he would like you to create.

George and Rick have provided your team with a document that explains their initial vision of the project. Read the statement shown in Figure 9-1.

Figure 9-1 FlashFlock vision statement

FlashFlock Banner Ad Project Vision Statement

We would like your firm to create a series of banner ads that will advertise our annual fall FlashFlock Festival. Below, we have provided some information about the festival along with our ideas and parameters for the campaign.

FlashFlock Festival

This is a juried online festival that is open to the general public. This year we would like to increase participation among younger viewers—specifically targeting college students and artists age 18–25. There is no charge for entry, and people will be able to fill out an online form to enter.

There are several categories of photographs that can be entered, including:

- Organized flash flock—Photographs of organized animal flash mobs
- Organic flash flock—Photographs taken of herds/flocks/gaggles of animals in their natural environment
- Staged flash flock—Photographs that have been digitally altered to produce a flash flock with real or synthetic animals

All photographs will be judged on artistic composition, humor, social commentary, and audacity. Winners will be featured on the FlashFlock Web site and will receive a $200 cash prize and a package of photographic equipment worth $500. Artists may enter up to three photographs in each category. The above information, as well as additional details, will be posted on our Web site.

Banner Ads

Banner ads will be used in the body of our Web site, on other Web sites, and in advertisements on our social media pages. Banners should contain the FlashFlock logo and one of the following taglines:

- Come fly with us
- Get your flock on
- We let the cows out
- Murders in numbers
- Gaggle your tail off

The ads should contain one or more photos that we will provide, and they should generate interest in the festival—causing the viewer to click on the banner to get more information. Banner ads do not need to provide in-depth information about the festival because that will be provided on the site. All of the banners should look good on our Web site and should be consistent with the FlashFlock look.

Although the vision statement provides a good deal of information, it does not contain all of the information your team will need from George and Rick. For example, they do not mention what size the banner ads should be, and they have not clearly articulated their goals for the project. This information is probably missing simply because George and Rick did not think of these questions.

Establishing Goals for the Project

After your client has explained the initial vision for a project, you'll need to pose questions that he or she must answer—with your guidance—to fill in the necessary project details. One of the first questions you should ask when guiding a client through the planning process is: What are the primary goals and purpose of the project? A design project can have one goal or many goals. The goals should be in alignment with the client's vision for the project. If a client's goals do not fit with the original project vision, you should help the client work to envision a project that will accomplish his goals. It is a good idea to brainstorm with the client to create a list of all of the possible goals you can think of for the project. For example, the goals of a commercial project might include the following:

- Provide information about a product.
- Sell a product.
- Increase brand recognition.
- Provide help or operational instructions.

These examples are very general; the list of goals for an actual project should be much more specific. For example, the first two bullets should state what the product is and the third bullet should include a specific measurement of brand recognition and what the targeted increase is.

After you have a list of possible goals, review the list and place the goals in order of importance from most important to least important. For example, the commercial project goals might be reordered as follows:

- Sell a product.
- Increase brand recognition.
- Provide information about a product.
- Provide help or operational instructions.

Review your list again. Combine goals, if possible, and then reprioritize as needed. Your final list for a given project should include no more than five goals. You might be able to combine some of the lower-priority goals with some of the higher-priority goals. For example, providing help or operational instructions might be incorporated into the general goal of providing information about the product. There is a limit to the number of goals that a project can effectively achieve; therefore, you will probably want to focus on the top two or three goals for any given project. Remember that goals are most effective if they are the result of collaboration with the client. After all, just as you are an expert on design, the client is an expert on his or her business. Also remember that what you can accomplish with a project varies with the size and scope of the project. For example, you can communicate much less information with a banner than you can with a printed brochure.

PROSKILLS

Written Communication: Writing Effective Goals for Your Project

Creating a strong list of project goals requires careful thought. Keep in mind the following guidelines as you develop the list of goals for a project:

- Write goals in active voice rather than passive voice, using verbs that move the action along and that identify you, your team, or the client as the actors. For example; *increase sales* rather than *product sales will increase.*
- Use action verbs to help you select achievable goals rather than concepts. For example, *brand recognition* is a concept, not a goal; *increase brand recognition* is a goal. Action verbs include words such as *achieve*, *increase*, and *provide.*
- Be specific when you are creating goals. Identify specific products, programs, or outputs, and when possible, specify an identifiable and measurable amount of change. For example: *Increase sales of "Widget A" by 10 percent.* With specific goals, you are able to evaluate your success in the future.
- Create individual goals that touch on different aspects of the product or service or event that you are promoting. For example, in addition to selling products, you might want to advertise reliable support.

Learning to write clear, achievable, and specific goals will enable you to guide your clients through the process of creating a project that accomplishes their most important goals. As you gain experience in project management and design, your ability to identify and articulate goals will continue to improve.

After your list of goals is final, review the list, and develop a one-sentence statement of purpose for the project. A **statement of purpose** is a precise statement that articulates the vision and aspirations for the project. This is your chance to help the client hone his or her original vision of the project by drafting a statement that speaks to the core purpose of the project and the stated purpose of the content. For example, a good statement of purpose for a banner ad campaign for an e-commerce Web site might be: "With this banner ad campaign, we intend to increase public awareness of our site and our brand by 10 percent, to drive customers to our site, to increase our sales of quality widgets by 5 percent, and to connect with new clients with the intention of building lifelong customer relationships."

Next, using the information from the initial vision statement, you'll develop a list of goals and a statement of purpose for the FlashFlock banner ad campaign.

To create a list of goals and a statement of purpose for the project:

1. Review the initial FlashFlock vision statement, and then, using WordPad, which is available from the Accessories menu of the All Programs menu in Windows 7, create a new document and generate 10 to 15 possible goals. Save the document as **Goals.rtf** in the Photoshop9\Tutorial folder provided with your Data Files.
2. Review the list to be sure that all statements are in active voice and use action verbs.
3. Prioritize the goals in order of importance, based on your understanding of the vision statement.
4. Review your list, combining goals, if possible, and reprioritizing them, as necessary.
5. Review the top five goals. Make sure that your list of goals will help FlashFlock fulfill its vision for the project.
6. Write a brief statement of purpose for the FlashFlock project based on your final list of goals, and add it to the Goals document.

   Jessica worked with George to create a list of goals for the banner ad campaign, and then she prioritized and combined them. From her list of goals, she developed a statement of purpose, using the top five goals for the project.
7. Compare your goals and statement of purpose with Jessica's, which are shown in Figure 9-2. Consider how her list and statement are similar to and different from yours. Also, consider how this might affect the project.

Figure 9-2 **Approved FlashFlock project goals and statement of purpose**

Goals

1. Enhance FlashFlock's brand identity by 5% as measured by our marketing polls and surveys.
2. Increase FlashFlock's brand recognition by 5% as measured by our marketing polls and surveys.
3. Promote the FlashFlock Festival.
4. Boost participation in the FlashFlock Festival by 3%.
5. Direct viewers to additional festival information.
6. Promote the animal flash mob movement.
7. Promote social commentary, awareness, and activism.
8. Increase traffic to the FlashFlock Web site by 5%.
9. Encourage viewers to participate in animal flash mobs.
10. Inspire an increased sense of humor and joy throughout the world.

Statement of Purpose

With this banner ad campaign, we will promote the FlashFlock brand and festival. With humor and audacious photographs, we will increase viewer interest in the animal flash mob movement, and we will drive viewers to learn more about the festival and the movement at *FlashFlock.com*.

8. Save the Goals.rtf file, and close it.

You'll use the goals developed by George and Jessica to make decisions about the project layout and design. The top two goals are to enhance brand identity and increase brand recognition—in other words, to make people aware of FlashFlock and its Web site and to associate FlashFlock with the animal flash mob movement. The project will be designed to create a buzz about the festival and to emphasize the FlashFlock name and logo. The banners will include at least one photograph of an animal flash mob and some information about the festival. The banners will be designed to drive people to find more information on the FlashFlock Web site. The FlashFlock logo and a tagline will appear prominently on each banner.

The priority of each of the goals helps to determine the banner layout. If the first and fourth goals were switched, for example, making the primary goal to boost participation in the festival, the banner layout might be organized differently. The festival information could be featured, and the festival logo could be deemphasized. Text could be focused to encourage artists to sign up rather than to drive viewers to the site to get more information.

When you start to examine how the goals and purpose can affect the layout of the final project, you can see how important it is to carefully consider what you want to accomplish. Taking the time to establish goals and expectations from the very beginning will make a world of difference in the final output.

Ascertaining the Target Audience

TIP

The word *viewer* usually refers to the target group of viewers, rather than an individual viewer.

The target audience for a design project is the group of people whom you would *most* like to view and respond to the final output. You identify the target audience by creating a viewer profile, which is a set of data describing the viewer you are trying to reach. The data is gathered from a list of questions, such as those shown in Figure 9-3. Creating a viewer profile helps you define the characteristics of your target audience.

Figure 9-3 General viewer profile questions

1. **What is the age range of the viewer?**
   - You can create a project that appeals to any range of ages. The age range will depend on the project goals. Generally, the group members are linked because they share a commonality such as a habit, a characteristic, or a developmental stage.
2. **What is the gender of the viewer?**
   - Projects can be targeted to males only, females only, or males and females. Not all projects are targeted to a specific gender.
3. **What is the education level of the viewer?**
   - Education level will be a range. Designate education level either by the current year in school (e.g., senior in high school) or the degree earned (e.g., associate's degree).
4. **What is the economic situation of the viewer?**
   - Economic situation refers to the annual income level of the viewer, as well as other extenuating economic factors, such as parental support or student loan debt. For example, the viewer may be a student who has only a part-time job. As a student, the viewer may have a lower income bracket, earning only $20,000 a year, but extenuating economic factors, such as parental support, may affect the viewer's buying power. When the viewer is employed, information about the viewer's occupation should also be included here.
5. **What is the geographic location of the viewer's residence?**
   - Projects can be targeted at users in a specific city, a specific region, or a specific country.
6. **What is the primary language of the viewer?**
   - It is important to know the primary language of the viewer so you can make an intelligent decision about what language the project will be created in—if the project includes text elements. There are times when it will make sense to create a project in a language other than that of the viewer—for example, when a foreign brand wants to maintain its identity or when the viewer might be attracted to the allure of another language and culture.
7. **What is the ethnic background of the viewer?**
   - Most projects that you will create are targeted at a viewer group with diverse ethnic backgrounds; however, sometimes ethnicity is a factor in your target audience. For example, ads in *Jet* magazine are typically targeted at African-American viewers.
8. **Are there other unifying characteristics that are relevant to the viewer?**
   - If you know that the target group has a common characteristic that may be of use in designing the project, list it here. Unifying characteristics are useful if they are related to the topic or purpose of the project or if they could affect the goals of the project. Unifying characteristics could include things such as target viewers have diabetes (for an educational diabetes disease-management brochure), target viewers ride dirt bikes (for a Web banner advertising motorcycle helmets), target viewers listen to club music (for an advertisement in *Rolling Stone*), and so on.

Jessica asks you to create a profile that identifies the target audience of the FlashFlock banner ad campaign.

To identify the target audience for the project:

1. Using WordPad, create a new document, and answer the viewer profile questions included in Figure 9-3. Review your answers to ensure that the target audience you identified reinforces FlashFlock's project vision, final goals, and purpose, as shown in Figure 9-1 and Figure 9-2. If it does not, adjust either your target audience or your goals (depending on which is more flexible) so the two are compatible and so the project will produce the best possible outcome.
2. Compare your answers to the user profile questions with those compiled by Jessica and George, as shown in Figure 9-4.

Figure 9-4 **FlashFlock banner ad target audience**

1. Age: 18 to 25
2. Gender: Male and female
3. Education level: Some college, especially art school and liberal arts
4. Economic situation: One-and two-income households (with incomes ranging from $35,000 to $90,000+) or college students who have financial support; households with enough disposable income or financial support to afford a computer with high-speed, home Internet access, preferably those who have access to photographic equipment and digital-editing software; any occupation
5. Geographic location: United States, but we hope to encourage participation internationally
6. Primary language: English
7. Ethnic background: No specific ethnicity targeted
8. Other unifying characteristics: Primary target viewer is an adult who enjoys art and who appreciates social satire-preferably people who appreciate wry and silly humor

3. Save the document as **Target.rtf** in the Photoshop9\Tutorial folder, and close the file.

TIP

When a project is being created for use on the Web, the *viewer* becomes a *user* because she will interact with the final output by clicking, buying, and so on.

Sometimes clients and designers are hesitant to identify the target audience because they think it will limit the reach of the project. However, a very broad target audience can be even more restrictive than a very narrow target audience. A project that must appeal to many different groups of people must be more generic in some ways. For example, if the new FlashFlock banner ad campaign was intended to appeal to an older audience (50 to 60 years of age) as well as to a college-aged audience (18 to 29 years of age), it should only include elements that will be attractive and communicate effectively to both age groups. This might exclude some stylistic options, such as graphics, wording, and colors that would be appropriate for a project with a target audience that includes only a college-aged group.

Some projects must appeal to a broad target audience. Consider the Internal Revenue Service (IRS) Web site, *www.irs.gov*. The IRS site and much of its collateral material, such as brochures, are designed for a very diverse target audience. Because the target audience for the IRS Web site and collateral materials is broad and the goal of the various materials is to dispense information, designers working on these projects must create text-based materials with few graphic elements that will be accessible to the broadest possible group of users. IRS materials are very effective at achieving their goals. However, the primarily text-based designs would not be effective if the main goal was entertainment because although rich in informational content, the materials are not particularly entertaining.

After you have identified a target audience, you can use the information from the viewer profile as a basis to research—and eventually make more advanced decisions about—viewer wants, needs, and so on. For example, you can use the information to form a hypothesis about the computer literacy of the target audience. When used appropriately, the viewer profile is a great tool for focusing a design project so it achieves the project goals and communicates effectively with the target audience. However, be careful with stereotypes. It is easy to draw general conclusions about a target audience without backing up those assumptions with research. This can lead to an output that does not actually appeal to your intended audience, or worse yet, offends them. For example, think about a television commercial you've seen that is supposed to appeal to your gender and/or age group. What was your reaction to a commercial that had the right look but underestimated your intelligence or misinterpreted your styles and habits? Use the target audience information as a starting point for your research so you can create a project that will communicate effectively with your audience.

Defining Project Scope and Determining Project Deliverables

After you have an understanding of the client's vision, have developed goals, and have ascertained your target audience, the next step is to write a project overview that defines the project parameters and scope and determines the project deliverables. The parameters of the project provide a description of what activities and outcomes are included in the project. The scope of work is all of the work that needs to be done to deliver the completed project, and project deliverables are the items that will be delivered at each step or phase of the project and upon completion of the project. If something is not specifically mentioned in the documentation that details the project parameters, scope, and deliverables, it is not part of the project. Creating a project overview ensures that everyone, including the client and other team members, will have a clear understanding of what they are agreeing to. If the client does not have the same understanding of what will be included in the project, it will usually come up at this time and you can work together to revise the project overview document before the project begins. Defining the project scope—and detailing that in a project overview document—can also help you avoid a problem that large projects often encounter—scope creep. **Scope creep** occurs when additional elements and requirements are added to a project, causing it to grow in size, complexity, cost, and so on. When a project is not clearly defined, new project elements can easily be added as the project progresses. A project overview document that defines the scope and parameters of the project keeps the project on point and prevents scope creep.

Creating a Master Planning Document

After you and the client have agreed to everything included in the project overview document, you will create a master planning document that details every part of the project. With a small project, this might be a one-page document, but, when the project is complex, the document might be fairly large. The master planning document might include the following:

- The project overview document detailing the project parameters, scope, and deliverables
- The vision statement, list of project goals, and statement of purpose
- The viewer profile and a paragraph explaining any other important insights about the target audience
- A breakdown of the project budget and resource allocation
- A breakdown of the resources that will be used (this includes your team and any outside contractors)
- A description of each team member's role and responsibilities, including specific tasks and deliverables, and due dates
- A schedule or timeline that includes the various phases of the project, such as planning and analysis, designing, building, testing, implementing, or publishing, among others
- A detailed description of deliverables, including technical specifications and so forth
- Any additional technical specification
- Any aesthetic parameters and requirements
- A sign-off sheet stating that the client and every member of the team understand and agree with the document

The exact information, specifications, and phases included in the master planning document will depend on the type of project you are working on. If you are designing the interface for a Web site, you would need to include a build phase, a test phase, and an implementation phase. If you are creating a brochure, you would probably include a print and production phase in the master project plan.

After the project begins, the project manager will continue to add to the master planning document so it is always a current, living embodiment of the project. For example, once you do your research, you will create a one- or two-page summary of your findings, insights, and conclusion and those pages will be added to the document. This ensures that all major project decisions are documented and clearly available to all team members and the client. After the project is complete, the master planning document serves as a project history that can be archived and used in the future.

INSIGHT

Effective Project Management

Different project management approaches work for different people, in different circumstances. Some projects require that the project manager focus on timeline and budget, while others benefit from a focus on teamwork and deliverables. Keeping a project on schedule and on budget—while ensuring that each team member's time is fully utilized and that the project produces a quality end product or result—is the ultimate responsibility of the project manager. As long as those duties are accomplished and the project is successful, there are really no specific project methods and approaches to avoid.

In addition to monitoring scope and parameters and managing the project deadlines and deliverables, a project manager must specify the responsibilities of each team member to ensure the project progresses smoothly through its various phases. A project manager must keep up with the progress, deadlines, and deliverables of each member of the team because one team member's work is often dependent on the completion of another member's tasks. For example, when creating an ad campaign that includes print and online elements, a delay in the creation of the client's logo can affect the timeline for both print and online deliverables. This type of relationship is referred to as a dependency. Complex projects often have many layers of dependencies, which means that one missed deadline can cause a cascading effect that can push the end date of the project beyond an acceptable point. In addition to project management software—which can help the project manager track various aspects of the project, including deadlines and dependencies—the most powerful tool in the project manager's arsenal is effective and consistent communication. Because of this, project managers often hold short but regular meetings to ensure that all team members on the same page and are aware of the latest developments. Meetings also enable members to work together to identify and preempt potential problems.

To effectively manage a project, a project manager must identify problems and opportunities, keep track of the schedule and budget, and communicate clearly and consistently with all the team members. Developing your project management skills will make you a valuable team member for any project. To further cultivate your project management skills, you can pursue training and certification in the field of project management.

Once everything is clearly documented and the client and all the team members understand the scope of the project and their roles in the team, the second phase of planning—the research phase—can begin.

Conducting Research

Market research is the careful investigation and study of data about a target audience's preferences, needs for a particular product or service, and personal habits. Market research also involves evaluating the products and services of competitors, as well as the marketing efforts they put behind those products and services. Remember that the viewer profile provides information that enables you to identify your target audience. After you have created the viewer profile and you understand who you are targeting, you need to investigate the habits, interests, likes, and dislikes of that group of people as well as what competitors are doing to attract them.

Research on technical information—such as the average screen size and speeds of the computer and Internet connection used by the target audience—can help you determine the technical limitations for an effective banner ad campaign, for example. In a commercial campaign, information about the spending habits of the target audience tells you the potential profitability of the campaign. In campaigns for other types of organizations, such as nonprofit groups, spending habits sometimes help you to identify need. Information on the interests of the target audience tells you what will appeal to the target audience and what elements you might include in the campaign to draw in viewers. Information on the needs of the target audience tells you what you can do to provide value to the target audience. Information about the culture and the customs of the target audience tells you what colors, symbols, fashions, and styles will be effective in communicating with the target audience. Finally, information about what the competition is doing tells you what the competition believes effectively attracts and communicates with the target audience, which can be useful in your decision making. Large advertising and design agencies spend a substantial amount of money subscribing to services (such as *www.ipsos-asi.com* and *www.marketresearch.com*) that provide in-depth market analysis of products or services and their target audiences, but the average individual designer has to rely on his or her own research.

Studying the Target Audience and the Competition

TIP

Three common search engines are Google (*www.google.com*), Yahoo! Search (*www.yahoo.com*), and Bing (*www.bing.com*).

The fastest way to obtain information about the habits, interests, and likes of a target audience is to use a search engine to locate Web sites with statistics and other data about the target audience's lifestyle, needs, and preferences. A **search engine** is a Web site or program whose primary function is to retrieve Web pages based on a search for specified keywords or phrases. Jessica and George spent some time using search engines to gather information online and compiled the data shown in Figure 9-5 about FlashFlock's target audience.

Figure 9-5 Statistics and information about the FlashFlock target audience

- 71.1 percent of U.S. households use computers with Internet access (68.2 percent of all households use high-speed broadband connections and 2.8 percent have 56Kbs or less narrowband connectivity.). In the target income range 63.4 percent to 80.8 percent of people use broadband Internet service, and in the target age range 73.7 percent to 80.5 percent of people use broadband Internet service (*http://www.ntia.doc.gov/files/ntia/publications/ntia_internet_use_report_february_2011.pdf*).
- Artists and designers held about 673,500 jobs in 2010; about 60 percent were self-employed (*www.bls.gov/ooh/arts-and-design/home.htm*).
- Median annual wages of salaried photographers were $29,130 in 2010 (*www.bls.gov/ooh/media-and-communication/photographers.htm*).
- Data underscore the relationship between having had arts lessons and participating in all modes of arts activities as an adult. Specifically, having had any arts lessons increases the likelihood of arts creation by 32 percent, increases the likelihood of media-based arts participation by 33 percent, and increases the likelihood of arts attendance by 29 percent, after controlling for demographics variables (*www.nea.gov/research/2008-SPPA-BeyondAttendance.pdf*).
- Approximately 15 percent of adults in the United States participate in the arts via electronic media only (*www.nea.gov/research/2008-SPPA-BeyondAttendance.pdf*).
- As virtually all research on participation has demonstrated, educational attainment is the strongest predictor of cultural engagement (DiMaggio and Ostrower 1992; Peterson et al. 2000).

The information that Jessica and George compiled gives you some understanding of the target audience's habits and likes. Now, you'll move your focus from the habits of FlashFlock's target audience to what you can do with your design to attract the target audience. Because this is a Web-based project, you'll investigate Web sites that the target audience might frequent as well as Web sites of FlashFlock competitors. Jessica has selected some sites based on the information gathered about the target audience, including its habits and preferences. For future projects, you can use the information you gather about a project's target audience to make assumptions about which sites to explore. By exploring sites that are popular with the target audience—as well as the sites of competitors—you can familiarize yourself with graphic styles to which the target audience is accustomed. You can get a better understanding of what colors, symbols, fashions, styles, and slang terms have been effective in communicating with the target audience.

TIP

For nonprofit organizations, competitors are other organizations that target your viewers.

While you are exploring the Web sites, pay close attention to their designs. What colors do the sites use? Is there anything unique about a particular site? What aspects of each site might appeal to the target audience? How is the space used? Is the content presented using straightforward language or using slang specific to the target audience? Is there a lot of text on each page, or is the text broken into smaller segments?

If you were creating a magazine ad, you would still use the Web to research your target audience, but you would also need to look at other ads in the magazine in which you would be advertising, as well as other magazines and print materials that might appeal to your target audience. You would also need to spend time reviewing magazine ads of competitors. The same principles are true for brochures and other forms of output.

You'll examine some sites that might attract the FlashFlock target audience as well as the Web sites of competitors. For each piece of information you find, note the name and URL of the Web page in case you need to refer to that source in the future.

To use a search engine to research the target audience and the competition:

1. Create a new document in WordPad, and name the document **Research.rtf**. Save the document in the Photoshop9\Tutorial folder.
2. Start your Web browser, type **bing.com** in the Address bar, and then press the **Enter** key. The Bing home page opens.

   Trouble? If the Bing search engine is unavailable for some reason, type the URL for another search engine in the Address bar, and then press the Enter key.
3. In the Enter your search term box at the top of the page, type **art activism**, and then click the **Search** button to start the search.
4. Review the list of Web sites, click the link for a Web site that you think looks promising, and then explore that site.
5. In the Research.rtf document, type **Art activism** as a heading, and then create a bulleted list of the pertinent information you find, especially information regarding aesthetics and use of language. Make sure to include the name and URL of the Web page in case you need to refer to that source in the future.

   Trouble? If the site does not seem relevant, continue with Step 6.
6. On the browser toolbar, click the **Back** button to return to the search results.
7. Repeat Step 4 through Step 6 to gather information from other Web sites until you have documented at least three distinct insights, statistics, or facts.
8. Repeat Step 3 through Step 6—using the phrase **art as social commentary**—until you have gathered three new insights, statistics, or facts.
9. In your browser, go to the Web site, *www.thisridiculousworld.com*. This is a competing site, which has produced satirical social commentary in China since 2007.
10. Explore the site, and in the Research.rtf file, type **www.thisridiculousworld.com** as a heading then make note of any pertinent information. You should have at least one short paragraph of information about this site.
11. Repeat Step 9 and Step 10 for the following sites:
    - *www.californiaphotofest.com*
    - *www.guerrillagirls.com*
12. Save the Research.rtf file, and close it.

Next, you'll review some of the FlashFlock marketing materials to familiarize yourself with the group's current branding efforts.

Reviewing the Client's Branding, Identity, and Marketing Materials

Like all people, businesses, and organizations, FlashFlock has a public image. In marketing and design, brand image is the way that the public, especially your target market, perceives your organization and its products or services. Originally, a brand was a symbol that enabled people to distinguish one person's cattle from another's. As the marketing industry grew, the term *brand* was used to describe the symbol, name, colors, and slogans associated with an organization, product, or service. An organization's brand also includes a separate component referred to as *identity*. Brand identity refers to the way that an organization would like the public to perceive the brand. It includes everything that the organization creates, presents, and cultivates as an outward expression of the brand. Organizations usually spend a great deal of time, energy, and money to create a brand identity that is in line with the goals, mission, and ideals they want the public to associate with their brand; however, organizations do not have complete control over how they are viewed. Everything that a company does contributes to the public's perception of who that company is and what they stand for. When the public's brand image is in line with the organization's brand identity, the organization's marketing efforts are considered successful.

Maintaining a well-planned brand image helps an organization in many ways. It helps the public to remember the organization and to associate it with specific goals, ideas, products, and/or services. This enables the organization to spend marketing dollars on focused campaigns instead of having to continually remind the public who they are and what they do. When a focused campaign reinforces brand identity, it increases the strength of the brand, creating even more bang for the buck.

When an organization sends mixed or unclear messages, or when they change what they are trying to be too often, the organization can suffer from a lack of identity. When this occurs, the public either does not have an image of the organization, or they have an image that is muddy and unclear. In either case, an organization is forced to increase the amount of marketing funds spent just reminding the public of who they are and what they do. Because of this, organizations that maintain a strong brand and brand identity have an advantage.

Before you create a project for an organization, you need to understand the organization's brand, brand identity, and brand image. The layout, colors, fonts, and graphic style that you select when you create your project should reinforce the organization's brand and brand identity. In other words, your project should look like it goes with the design, colors, and graphic style of the materials used by the organization, and your project should support the brand identity. If the organization has not spent time creating a strong, consistent brand and brand identity, it is your job to explain the importance of brand identity, to help your client make brand and identity decisions, and then to create a project that will reinforce those decisions. As you can see, a lot of work goes in to creating a professional project.

FlashFlock has a logo and a set of taglines they use across all of their materials. Their marketing materials and their Web content have a witty, tongue-in-cheek style, and their designs have a consistent graphic style. George has provided a few of the organization's existing marketing materials for you to examine. You'll look at the materials and consider the look, style, and colors to provide you with ideas that you'll use when you start to create the banner ad campaign.

To examine the materials that George provided:

1. Start Photoshop while pressing the **Ctrl+Alt+Shift** keys, and click **Yes** to delete the Settings File when prompted. Reset Photoshop to the default Essentials workspace layout, and then reset all tools.
2. Navigate to the Photoshop9\Tutorial folder included with your Data Files, and open **BannerSamp1.jpg**. See Figure 9-6.

Figure 9-6 Existing FlashFlock banner ad 1

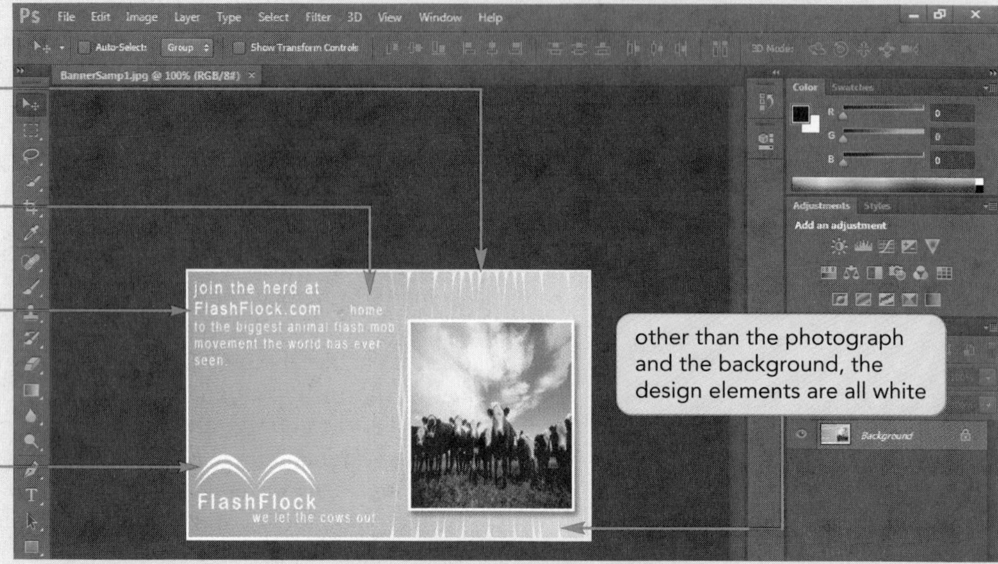
background graphic elements match the style of the logo
banner uses a gradient jewel tone for a background
the text is white and fonts are all sans serif
the FlashFlock logo is a simple, flat, graphic style
other than the photograph and the background, the design elements are all white
join the herd at FlashFlock.com
home
to the biggest animal flash mob movement the world has ever seen.
FlashFlock
we let the cows out

3. Notice the colors used and the graphic style of the banner ad and the logo.
4. Examine the layout. Is the banner filled with text and images, or is it open and airy?
5. Consider the photograph. Is there a style to the image? Is the image saturated with color, or is it washed out? Are a few items close to the screen, or are you viewing an entire scene?
6. Repeat Step 2 through Step 5 using **BannerSamp2.jpg**, which shows another of FlashFlock's current banner ads. See Figure 9-7.

Figure 9-7 Existing FlashFlock banner ad 2

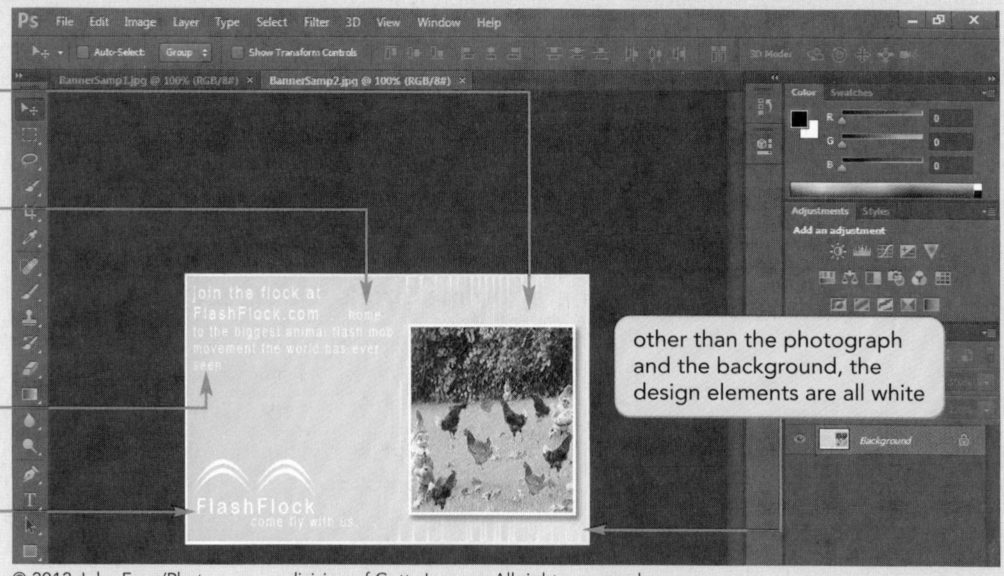
background graphic elements match the style of the logo
banner uses a gradient jewel tone for a background
the text is white and fonts are all sans serif
the FlashFlock logo is a simple, flat, graphic style
other than the photograph and the background, the design elements are all white
join the flock at FlashFlock.com
home
FlashFlock
come fly with us

7. Repeat Step 2 through Step 5 using **WebHome.jpg**, which shows the existing FlashFlock Web site home page.
8. To see the entire Web page at full size, which enables you to read the text, press the **Ctrl+1** keys to view Actual Pixels, click **View** on the menu bar, click **Screen Mode**, click **Full Screen Mode**, and then click the **Full Screen** button in the dialog box. The FlashFlock Web site image fills the screen. See Figure 9-8.

Figure 9-8 Existing FlashFlock Web site home page

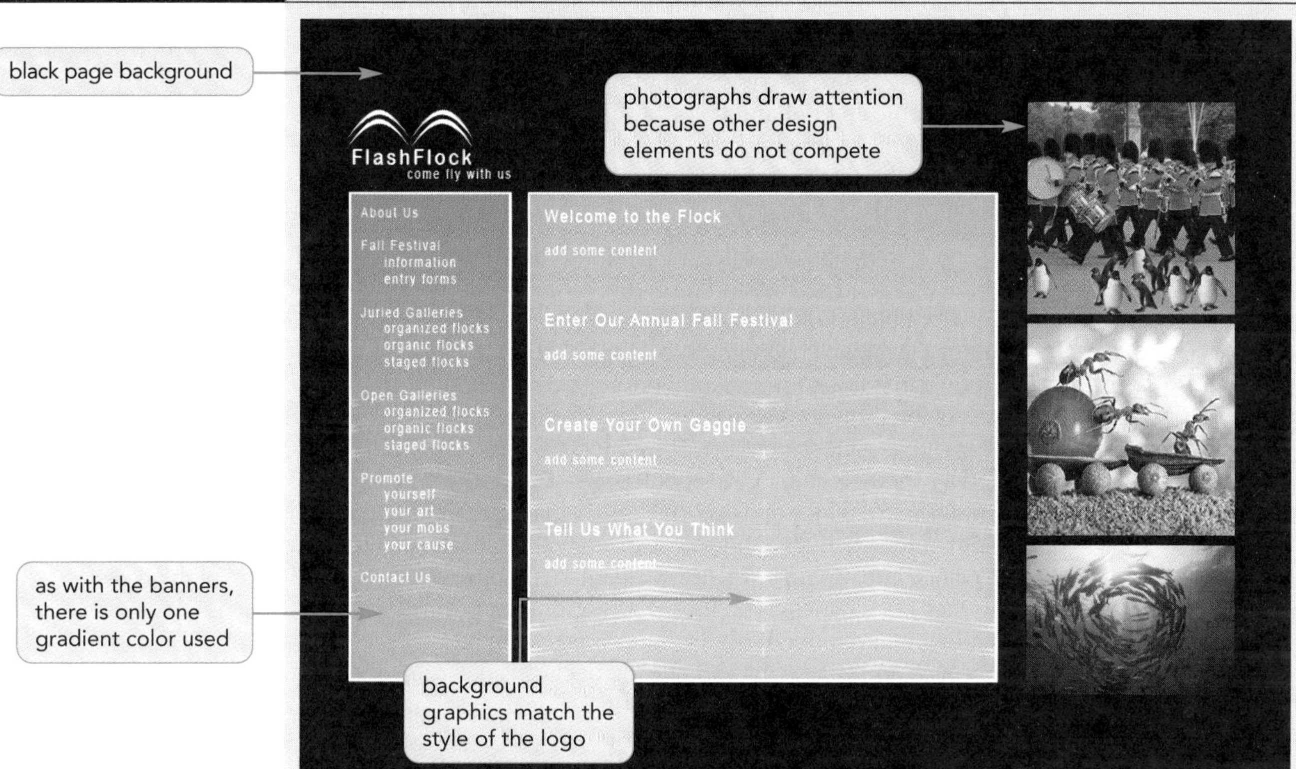

9. Press the **Esc** key to return Photoshop to the normal display.
10. Now that you have seen several existing pieces of FlashFlock marketing material, write a paragraph describing the materials that FlashFlock is currently using to create its brand and identity. Open WordPad, create a new document, and save the document as **CurrentBrand.rtf** in the Photoshop9\Tutorial folder.
11. What are the unifying elements that you notice? Are any elements unique to only one of the pieces that you examined? Describe how the materials make you feel about the FlashFlock brand, and identify design elements that work well for you, as well as any elements that you don't think work.
12. Indicate what layout and design elements you think would work well in the new banner campaign, and explain how you might make the new banners different from the old banners while maintaining a consistent brand identity.
13. Close all three images, and then save and close the WordPad document.

Now that you have spent time setting goals, identifying your target audience, and doing research, it is time to make decisions regarding your final output files for the project.

Determining Output Specifications

You already know what deliverables are required for the project, but before you can begin designing the project, you must flesh out the technical details of your deliverable files. The final step before you can begin to create your project is to do some research to determine how you should deliver the final files. You should answer the following questions:

- What file type, size, and resolution should be used?
- What color model and color profile are needed for final output?
- What delivery method should be used for the final output files?
- Should the final working files (probably PSD files) also be included with the final output files?

You need to make these decisions prior to beginning work to ensure that you create files that have adequate size and resolution and to ensure you soft proof using the correct color model and profiles so you can produce accurate colors. In this case, you'll be producing FlashFlock banner ads for display on the Web.

You can make some assumptions regarding output files, based on the technical parameters of the project. Web resolution is 72 ppi, and that is the resolution at which you'll create the FlashFlock project. The banners will be displayed on Web sites and on social media pages—including Facebook pages. Currently, the maximum width at which you can display graphics on Facebook is 480 pixels; therefore, you will use 480 pixels as the width of your banners. Your color space will be RGB because the Web is displayed on monitors, and as you have already learned, monitors use red, green, and blue pixels to produce color. Finally, you'll use the sRGB color profile because it defines the color space of the standard monitor used to view images on the Web.

Jessica and George have made the decisions regarding the remaining output specifications. The height of the banner will be 275 pixels, and the images will be compressed and delivered as JPEGs because that file format will create small files that can be displayed on the Web; the JPEG format will also do a good job of compressing the photographic images that will be included in the banners.

Next, you'll create a new Photoshop file with the correct size, resolution, color model, and color profile.

To create a Photoshop document for the project:

1. On the menu bar, click **File**, and then click **New**.
2. In the New dialog box, type **FFBanners** in the Name box.
3. In the Width box, type **480**, and then click **Pixels** from the drop-down list. In the Height box, type **275**, and then click **Pixels**, if necessary.
4. In the Resolution box, type **72**, if necessary, and then select **Pixels/Inch**. Select **RGB Color** and **8 bit** from the Color Mode list to select the RGB color model. In the Background Contents box, select **White**.
5. Click the **Advanced** arrow to expand the dialog box to show the advanced settings, and then in the Color Profile box, select **sRGB IEC61966-2.1**. See Figure 9-9.

Figure 9-9 New dialog box

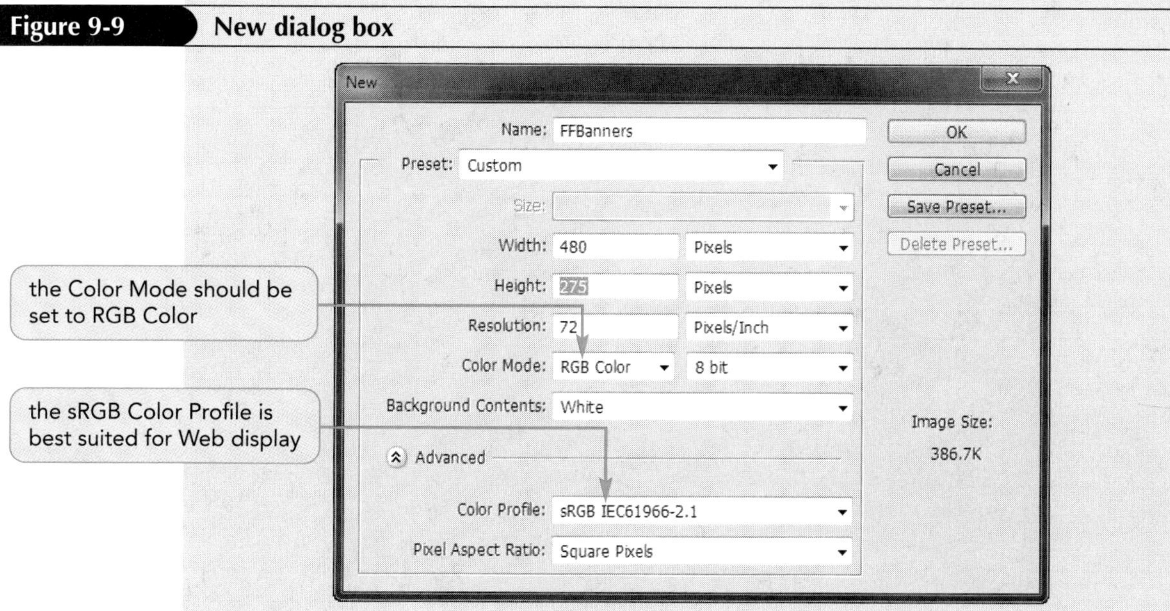

6. Click the **OK** button to create the new document.
7. On the menu bar, click **File**, and then click **Save As**.
8. In the Save As dialog box, confirm that the ICC Profile check box is checked.
9. Save the file as **FFBanners.psd** in the Photoshop9\Tutorial folder.
10. Close the file, and exit Photoshop.

The ICC Profile check box in the Save As dialog box must be checked to save the document with a color profile.

Your team has completed the planning phase of the project. You have defined project goals and written a statement of purpose. You created a viewer profile, identified your target audience, and researched your target audience and the competition. You've also started the Photoshop document that you'll use to create your composition for the project. Now you are ready to begin creating the banners. In the next session, you'll work through the creation and delivery process.

REVIEW

Session 9.1 Quick Check

1. True or False. You should create a plan before you begin to create a design for a project.
2. What is the purpose of listing project goals?
3. How many goals can a project achieve effectively?
4. What is a target audience?
5. What happens if you draw general conclusions about the target audience without backing up those conclusions with research?
6. Why should you conduct market research?
7. What is a brand?

SESSION 9.2 VISUAL OVERVIEW

The **concept** is the general underlying theme that unifies the various elements of a composition to create a cohesive look and feel.

Layout is the position of elements in a composition.

Create layout

Balance is the feeling of equilibrium that is felt when looking at a composition as a whole.

Create a concept & metaphor

FlashFlock
gaggle your tail off. . .

hey old school, swim on by
www.flashflock.com ...

jump in the bowl with the
other contestants

...you might win or you might
get schooled

A **project metaphor** is a visual extension of the project concept.

Gather materials

FlashFlock
murders in numbers. . .

hey you in the tuxedo. . .

loosen up and dive in to
www.flashflock.com

. . . enter the contest and you
might just be the next emperor

Organize & archive files

Design is an exacting form of art that has a specific and defined purpose.

Review design & create output

CREATING A PROFESSIONAL PROJECT

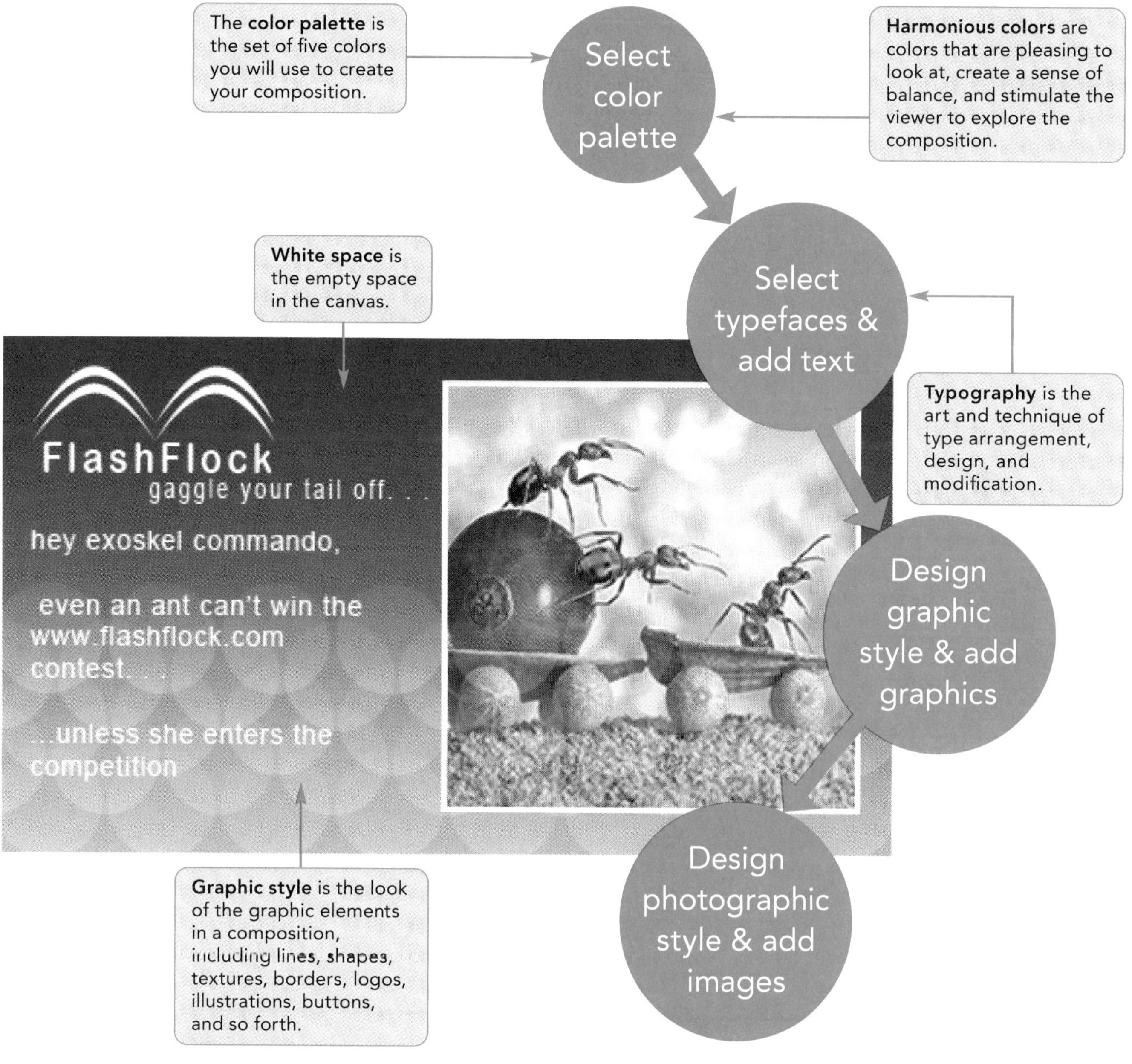
The **color palette** is the set of five colors you will use to create your composition.
Select color palette
Harmonious colors are colors that are pleasing to look at, create a sense of balance, and stimulate the viewer to explore the composition.
White space is the empty space in the canvas.
Select typefaces & add text
Typography is the art and technique of type arrangement, design, and modification.
FlashFlock
gaggle your tail off. . .
hey exoskel commando,
even an ant can't win the www.flashflock.com contest. . .
...unless she enters the competition
Design graphic style & add graphics
Design photographic style & add images
Graphic style is the look of the graphic elements in a composition, including lines, shapes, textures, borders, logos, illustrations, buttons, and so forth.

Designing a Project

After you have completed the planning phases of the project, you begin the design phase. Design is a form of art that has a specific and defined purpose. The phrase **look and feel** is used to describe the overall impact of the characteristics of the design of a graphic project. It refers to the way that all the elements of the design interact to create an experience for the viewer. The look and feel of a particular design is achieved from a mixture of many smaller choices, including which colors, typefaces, graphic style, and layout are selected for the design. Jessica will make all of the choices regarding the aesthetic design elements in the project. You'll create the project and, as you did in the planning phase, you'll create alternative designs as part of your training. As you make decisions, consider how each element impacts the design and the target audience. To combine all these elements effectively, you'll need to create a concept and metaphor for the project, but first you must gather all of the materials that you will use in the project.

Gathering or Acquiring Materials

It is a good idea to assemble all of the content and materials that you will use in a project before you jump into the layout process. You need to know what you have to work with so you can determine the best layout and design options. For example, if you need to include a large quantity of text in a composition, you will need to create a different layout than you would for a composition containing only a small amount of text.

TIP

When possible, request high-quality, uncompressed files so you can do any compression or conversion yourself to ensure the best possible output quality.

When you are assembling materials, ask the client to provide any text content in a digital format, such as a Word document. You'll also need any photographic images and logos the client already has that will be used for the project. Make sure that the images and graphic elements you'll be using in the project are of adequate size and resolution and, if possible, get a version that is in the same color model.

Jessica has helped George collect all of the materials that he has available for the project. They have gathered the existing files, which you have already reviewed to gain an understanding of FlashFlock's branding and identity. George has provided a copy of the FlashFlock logo as a PSD file and a copy of the photographs as JPEG files (these were the best files they had available). Jessica has provided you a document containing the text that George would like to include in the banner. You'll examine the new image files and read the text George has created so that you'll have an understanding of the elements that will be included in the new campaign. See Figure 9-10 to review the photographs that George has selected for the campaign.

Figure 9-10 **Images that will be used in the new campaign**

To review the tagline and text that George would like to use with each image in the campaign, see Figure 9-11.

Figure 9-11 Text for the new FlashFlock campaign

Banner 1

Tagline: gaggle your tail off. . .

Content:

hey old school....swim on by www.flashflock.com ... jump in the bowl with the other contestants....you might win or you might get schooled

Image: Fish.jpg

Banner 2

Tagline: murders in numbers. . .

Content:

hey you in the tuxedo...loosen up and dive in to www.flashflock.com. . . enter the contest and you might just be the next emperor

Image: Penguins.jpg

Banner 3

Tagline: we let the cows out. . .

Content:

yo exoskel commando ...even an ant can't win the www.flashflock.com contest ...unless she enters the competition

Image: Ants.jpg

Now that you have what you need to start, you can begin creating a concept and metaphor for the composition.

Developing a Concept and Metaphor

A good concept is the basis for developing an aesthetically cohesive composition or campaign. A concept unifies the various elements of a composition and contributes to the cohesiveness of the look and feel. To develop a concept, review some of the artwork and Web sites that appeal to the target audience and look for common underlying themes. Next, make a list of words that describe what you would like the banners to convey. Try to think of words that will reinforce the project goals and communicate something to the target audience. Finally, write down the concept. Examples of a possible concept for a project include *growth*, *speed*, or *stability*.

After you have developed a concept, you need to create a metaphor for the project. A **metaphor** is a comparison in which one object, concept, or idea is represented as another. For example, the expression "at that moment, time was molasses" and Shakespeare's famous observation that "all the world's a stage" are metaphors. A project metaphor should be a visual extension of the project's concept, which reinforces the vision and the site goals. The metaphor helps to create a unified design.

The metaphor you choose for your project does not have to be concretely represented in the composition. For example, if the concept is fluidity, the metaphor might be a river. The actual composition does not need to be designed to look like a river, but instead could integrate elements that are commonly identified with rivers, such as a series of small, partially transparent, wavy lines in the background, a flowing theme in the graphic design, and cool colors such as muted blues and silvers. The river metaphor is an instrument to focus all of the aesthetic choices.

For the FlashFlock banner campaign, Jessica came up with a list of words to describe FlashFlock and the campaign: *fun, underground, campy, organic, technical, creative, human, artificial, sarcastic, playful, intelligent, hip, outsider*, and *enlightening*. Some words apply to a look that is popular with the target audience (*campy, underground*, and *outsider*); other words apply to the undertone George would like to create (*playful, enlightening, artificial*, and *organic*).

Next, Jessica reviewed the research and spent some time considering how to pull it all together to create a campaign that will accomplish the stated goals, reinforce FlashFlock's branding and identity, and appeal to the target audience. Finally, she worked with George to develop the concept—*artistically motivated scientific experimentation fostering artificially engineered, temporary, symbiotic, interspecies habitats for the purpose of enlightenment and fun*. Based on that concept, they chose a metaphor of "mashups." In later sections, you'll see how the mashups metaphor helps to shape the site design by providing a foundation for color choice, font choice, graphics choice, and layout.

To continue your training, Jessica asks you to develop an alternate concept and metaphor for the project.

To develop an alternate concept and metaphor for the project:

1. Open WordPad, create a new document, and save the document as **Concept.rtf** in the Photoshop9\Tutorial folder.
2. In the WordPad document, list at least five words that describe FlashFlock and the banner campaign.
3. Review your notes regarding artwork and imagery that appeal to the target audience.
4. Choose a project concept, and then write a short description of the concept and why you selected it.
5. Choose a project metaphor, and then write a short description of the metaphor and why you selected it.
6. Write a paragraph that explains how you could integrate the concept and the metaphor into the banner campaign.
7. Save the Concept.rtf file, and close it.

Now you have a foundation that will help you create a cohesive project; you can make design choices that support the project metaphor. You have also experimented with creating a metaphor of your own. This experience will help you when you create a project on your own. Next, you'll begin working on the layout for the FlashFlock banner ad.

Creating a Layout

The term *layout* comes from traditional print design. Layout is the position of elements in a composition—in this case, on the computer screen. Most elements in two-dimensional artwork are created using lines or shapes—or a combination of both. A **line** is a mark that spans the distance between two points in space, and a **shape** is an area of two-dimensional space, defined by edges, that sets one portion of space apart from another; a circle is an example of a shape. Shapes can be geometric or organic, and lines can be straight or nonstraight paths. When a shape is created to look as if it has depth and occupies a three-dimensional space, it is called a **form**. Even text elements are created by combining lines and shapes (and sometimes forms, when the text is three-dimensional) into recognizable characters. Part of creating an aesthetically cohesive design is choosing the best way to combine shapes, lines, and forms to create elements such as the text, logo, artwork, and so on, and then deciding where in the composition to place those elements. The layout should support the project goals and metaphor. It should be easy for a viewer to interpret, and it should appeal to the target audience. Finally, it should be consistent. For example, the logo should be located in the same place in all of the banners to create a unified look across the compositions in your campaign. Most important, layout should conform to the basic tenets of sound artistic design by employing balance, unity, and rhythm. You need to consider the space as a whole—in addition to the individual elements in the composition.

Balance and Space

Balance is achieved by arranging objects, or groups of objects, so that their visual weight is balanced in the overall composition. The two main approaches to balance are symmetrical and asymmetrical. **Symmetrical balance** evenly distributes the visual weight of objects in a composition around the central horizontal and vertical axes of the canvas. See Figure 9-12.

Figure 9-12 **Symmetrical balance**

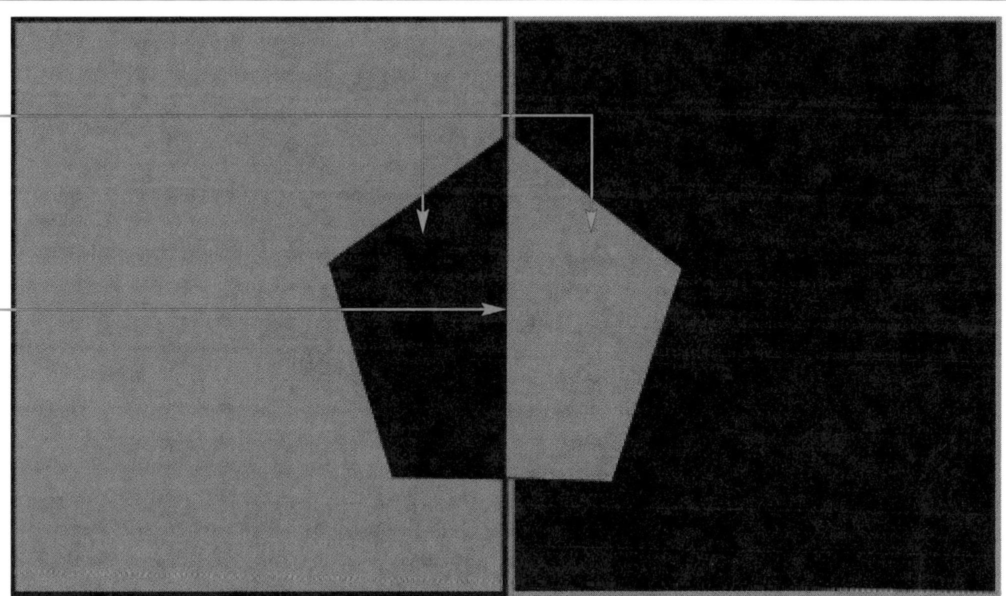
the left side is a mirror image of the right side
objects are centered around the horizontal and vertical axes

Radial symmetry creates balance in a composition by distributing objects around one center point. See Figure 9-13.

Figure 9-13 Radial symmetry

objects are distributed around the imaginary center point of the composition

In juxtaposition, **asymmetrical balance** (also referred to as *informal balance*) is created by distributing visually disproportionate objects in the composition so that the visual weight of the various groupings of objects achieves balance with respect to one another instead of with the canvas axes. Informal balance is often more visually compelling than symmetrical balance because it better incorporates the white space (or negative space) of the canvas into the design. In addition, informal balance enables you to create balance by offsetting the visual weight of a large object in one area of the composition with a grouping of smaller objects placed in close proximity to each other in another area of the composition. See Figure 9-14.

Figure 9-14 Asymmetrical balance

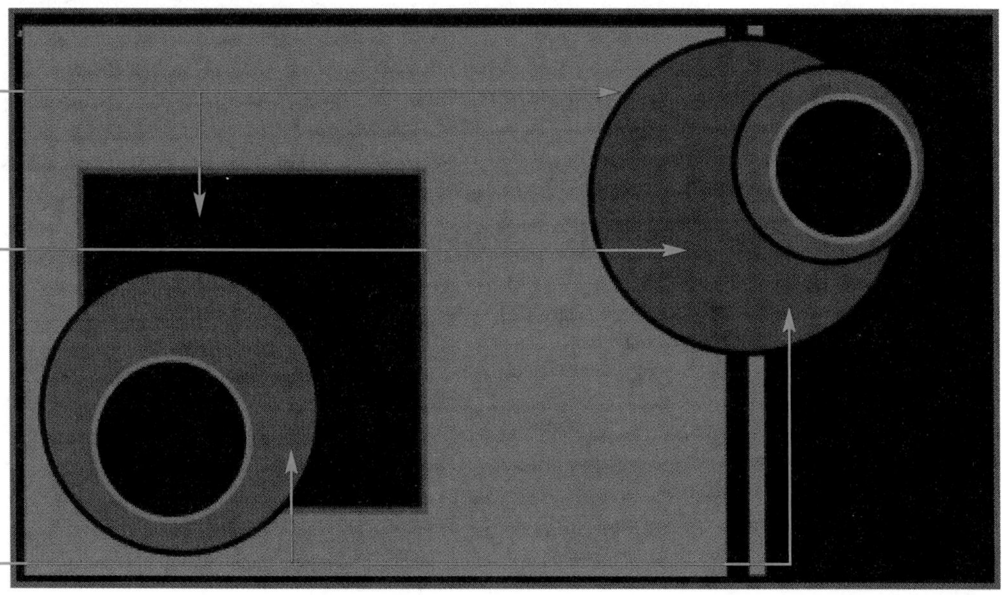
objects are scattered around the image
in this layout, objects are laid out using the Rule of Thirds
balance is achieved because total visual weight of each group of objects is equal

White space is the empty space in the canvas, and it is an important part of a well-designed composition. (White space doesn't have to be white; it can be filled with the background color.) If graphic elements, text, and images fill every inch of the canvas, viewers can become disoriented. Visually, they may not be able to move easily through the composition or to ascertain the meaning or emotion that the artist was trying to convey. Including white space in a layout opens up the composition and enables the viewer to more easily navigate the canvas. White space can also be used to draw attention to important components of a composition. Separating important elements, such as headings or taglines, from other page content with a little white space helps the viewer to distinguish those elements more quickly.

One tool for achieving an open design that integrates white space into the layout is a frequently used design concept you are already familiar with—the Rule of Thirds. Remember, the Rule of Thirds states that the most interesting compositions are those in which the strongest element is off center. You can implement this technique in compositional design in a way that is similar to the technique you used to crop images. For instance, the composition in Figure 9-14 was created following the Rule of Thirds to produce a composition that has energy and visual interest. To use the Rule of Thirds when designing a composition, divide the page into thirds both horizontally and vertically, and then place the objects in the composition on the lines. No object should take up more than two-thirds of the canvas. For example, in most advertisements the logo takes up no more than one-third of the canvas, leaving the other two-thirds of the canvas for the remaining content.

Rhythm and Unity

Rhythm is a sense of order achieved in a composition by repeating or alternating objects or elements on the canvas. For example, a color that is repeated in different places in the canvas helps create a sense of rhythm or flow. **Unity** is a quality achieved by ordering elements in a design so that each contributes to an overall unified composition. **Harmony** is achieved when the unity of all of the visual elements in a composition is soothing or pleasing to the viewer, and **contrast** is created when the elements conflict with one another, creating an unsettling feeling for the viewer. Contrast can also be used to create emphasis on specific content or on a visual component. The same concept applies across a campaign. See Figure 9-15.

Figure 9-15 Rhythm and unity in a composition

white space is used to open the composition
repetition of colors and shapes as well as a consistent graphic look creates a sense of unity and harmony in the compositions and across the campaign
patterns and shapes are repeated, but altered slightly across the campaign
contrast between the dark black and the color will catch the attention of the viewer
colors are repeated within the canvas

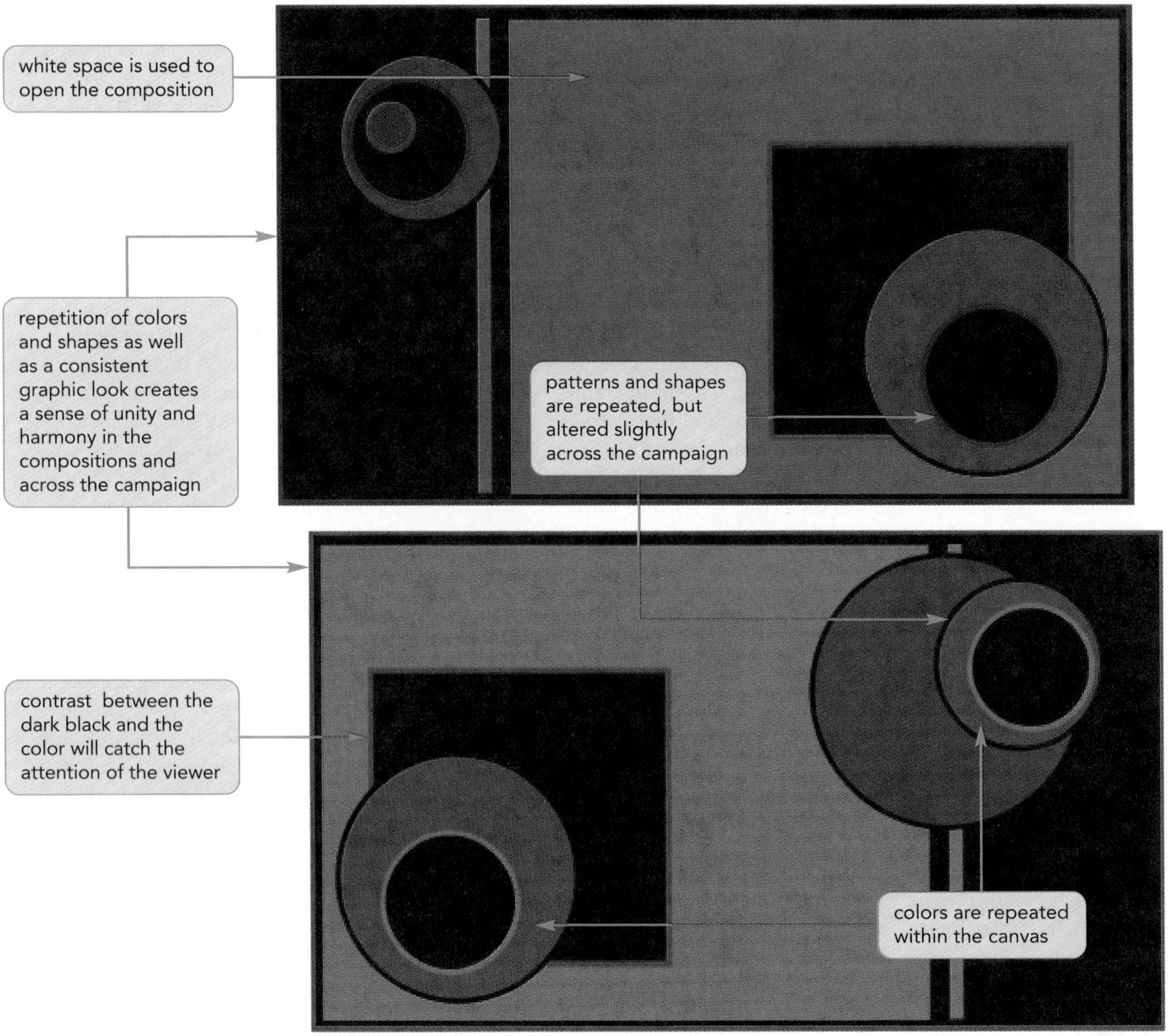

Repeating or alternating objects or elements across a campaign helps unify the individual compositions into a cohesive project. Using one graphic style throughout the project, repeating colors throughout the project, and creating balance and symmetry between objects in the compositions all help to create unity in the design.

Creating a Wireframe of Your Layout

> **TIP**
> For large amounts of placeholder text, you can use lorem ipsum text. Insert lorem ipsum text using the new Paste Lorem Ipsum option on the Type menu.

Often, two or three effective layouts are possible for a given project. Initially, designers create rough sketches of possible layout designs. Sometimes designers create wireframes of the layout. A **wireframe** is a bare-bones mock-up that is created in a graphics program instead of being drawn by hand. Wireframes include only rough placeholder images, such as boxes with text, to indicate where a graphic or image will be placed. The purpose of creating a wireframe is to show placement of the logo, images, text, and other elements to the client before creating the actual artwork.

Jessica has developed a rough wireframe of the layout for the FlashFlock banner campaign that she will present to George and Rick for their approval. See Figure 9-16.

Figure 9-16 Wireframe for the FlashFlock banner campaign

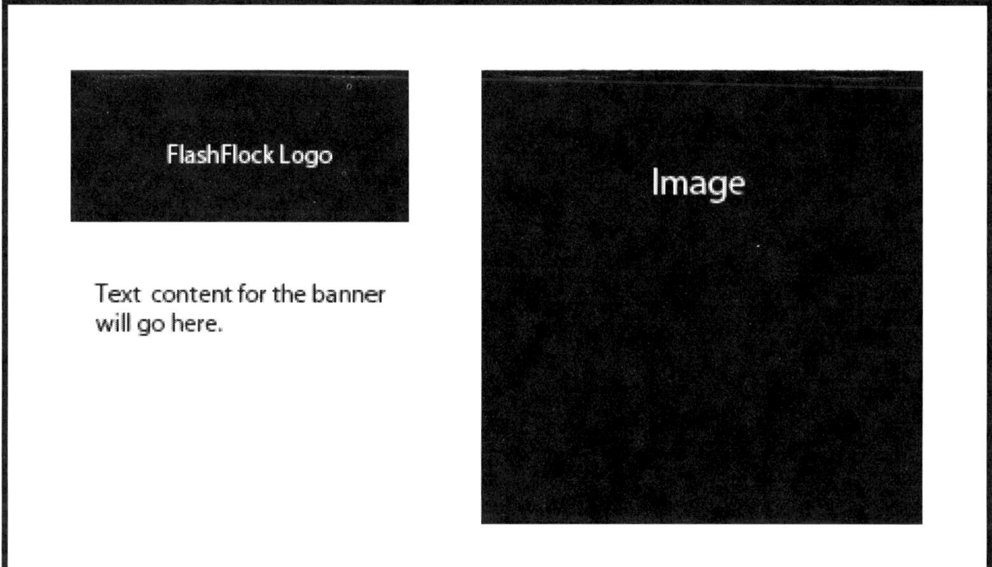

Jessica used asymmetrical balance when creating the sketch, and she placed the logo in the upper-left corner of the page, where the viewer's eye usually focuses first. This was done to support the top two goals of the campaign: Enhance brand identity and increase brand recognition. The text content will be located below the logo, and a photograph will be located at the right center of the page.

Based on the alternate concept and metaphor you created, you will create a wireframe of another possible layout. You'll use the Rectangle tool in Photoshop to create shapes that represent the logo and the image you will include in your composition. You'll use placeholder text to designate where the text will be placed. If Jessica likes your layout, both layouts will be presented to George and Rick at the next meeting. You'll create the wireframe in the Photoshop composition that you created and saved in the first session. Remember to consider the goals, target audience, and research as well as the current FlashFlock marketing materials. Also remember to employ the concepts that you have learned regarding space, balance, and harmony.

To create a wireframe of your layout:

1. Start Photoshop while pressing the **Ctrl+Alt+Shift** keys, and click **Yes** to delete the Settings File when prompted. Reset Photoshop to the default Essentials workspace layout, and then reset all tools.
2. Navigate to the Photoshop9\Tutorial folder included with your Data Files, and open **FFBanners.psd**, which is the new file you created at the end of the first session. Make sure it is displayed at **100%**, and then save the file as **Wireframe.psd** in the same folder.
3. On the Tools panel, click the **Rectangle Tool** button, and draw a black rectangle that is 2.25 inches wide by 1 inch high; this shape will represent the FlashFlock logo and tagline. Move it where you want it within the composition. Use the Type tool to type **FlashFlock Logo** in the rectangle to label the shape.
4. Repeat Step 3 for the photographic image and any additional elements that you would like to include in the banner. Include appropriate labels for the all of the elements in the layout.

5. Because the banners include only a small amount of text, it is not necessary to use lorem ipsum text to mark where the content will be placed. Instead, in the location where you would like to display text in the banner, type **Text content for the banner will go here**.
6. Once all of the elements are on the canvas, review your layout. Does it follow the Rule of Thirds? Identify the type of balance that your composition uses and locate the white space in the composition. Finally, consider how effective this layout will be at communicating with your target audience and achieving the goals you have set for the campaign. Consider how it works with FlashFlock's current materials to reinforce branding and identity.
7. Make any necessary adjustments that you identified in your review, and then save and close your file.

Once you and your client have narrowed down the options to one or two layouts, you'll need to create comps (comprehensive drawings, or in this case digitally created comprehensive compositions) from the sketch or wireframe. Comps are the fully developed, detailed compositions from which you'll eventually create your final output files.

TIP

The exact number of layouts, comps, and rounds of changes should be specified in the proposal that you submit to win a project as well as in the master project plan.

There are usually several rounds of creation and client feedback built into the design process. In the first round of design, you'll create a comp for each selected layout to show to the client at a meeting where you review the work. During the review process, you'll work with the client to select elements that are working. Often, you will end up combining elements that the client likes from different layouts in this round. In the second round of design, you'll create a single comp based on the input and discussion from your first review. Again, you'll present the comp to the client and you'll work together to fine-tune the composition. This process may occur one or two more times while you make slight changes to achieve sign-off on your finished product.

INSIGHT

Using Focus Groups, User Studies, and Surveys

It is often a good idea to get additional feedback from outside viewers who are a part of the target audience to ensure that your design works as you have intended. Focus groups, usability testing, and surveys are tools that designers can use to get additional information about the effectiveness of their work. These tools can be used at any time during the design process. For example, you could use a focus group before you begin to create a campaign to find out how viewers feel about the client's brand, or you could use a focus group after you have created a new Web site design to see if the new Web site is intuitive for users to navigate. Focus groups are a selected group of people who are asked questions about the product, design, and so forth in an interactive group setting. Questions are usually asked by a trained moderator in an interview style that is informal and unstructured, enabling respondents to express their views casually. Focus groups work well for gathering marketing information and for gathering information about the usability of designs that the viewer will be interacting with, such as Web site or software interface designs.

User studies are another means of collecting information about how end users will interact with your designs. In a usability study, you create a working model of the product you have designed and you evaluate the design by testing the product, often a Web site or software, on a group of users. This type of testing can provide you with information about how easy it is for users to understand and navigate through the product. It also allows you to determine if the product provides value to the user. Having this information enables you to create more successful and useful products. Surveys are another tool that designers use to ask an audience for information about their design. Surveys work well because viewers can take a survey online or on the phone enabling the designer to get information from a wider range of people than other tools that require in-person contact. Surveys are also valuable because the respondent can remain anonymous, enabling her to be more candid about things that are off-putting or that do not work in the design.

Next, you'll continue the creation process by selecting colors for the composition.

Selecting Colors

Color is an interesting component of design because it sets the tone for a composition. The colors you choose affect the emotional response that a viewer has to the composition. To effectively select colors for a project, you need a basic understanding of color theory as it applies to design. You have already learned about the concepts of additive (RGB) and subtractive (CMYK) color, and you have learned about color management, color profiles, and out-of-gamut color. You have also learned that the three components of color are brightness (or luminosity), saturation, and hue.

The Kuler panel is a tool that Adobe provides to help you select color palettes. You will work with the Kuler panel to learn more about how colors work in relation to each other and within the framework of a composition. You'll use the Kuler panel and your new insights to select a color scheme for the FlashFlock project. The selection of good color is not a science, so remember to take the rules you have learned as guidelines; use them along with your judgment and experience to select a color scheme for your projects. See Figure 9-17 to view the Kuler panel.

Figure 9-17 **The Kuler panel**

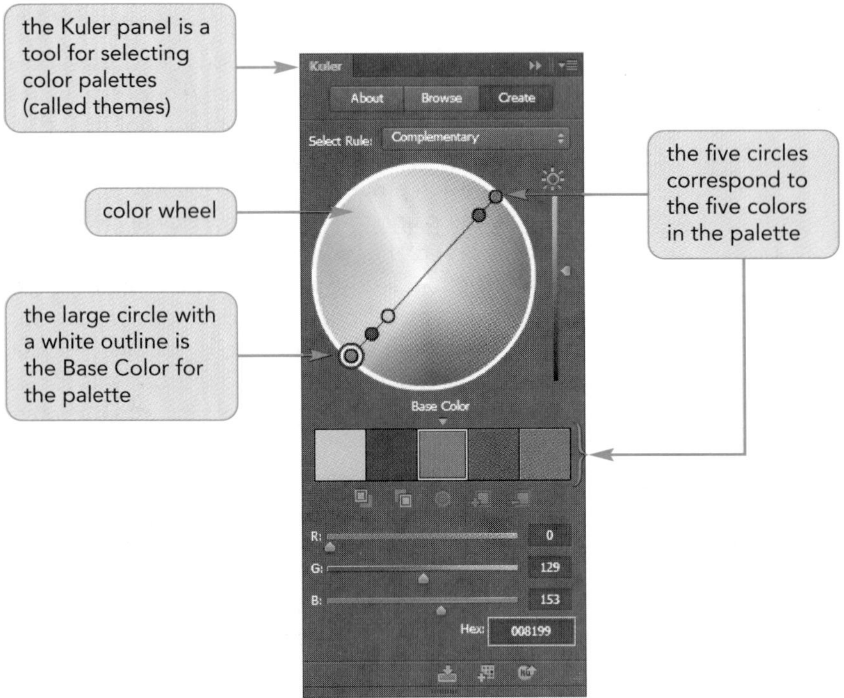
the Kuler panel is a tool for selecting color palettes (called themes)
color wheel
the large circle with a white outline is the Base Color for the palette
the five circles correspond to the five colors in the palette
Kuler
About
Browse
Create
Select Rule:
Complementary
Base Color
R:
0
G:
129
B:
153
Hex:
008199

Selecting Harmonious Colors

One of the goals of color selection is to create a harmonious composition. As noted earlier, harmony is a pleasing arrangement or combination of parts that creates an engaging end product that is balanced and filled with dynamic equilibrium. The term *harmony* can be used to refer to anything from the parts in a musical composition to the flavors of ice cream in a banana split. Harmonious colors are pleasing to look at. They create a sense of balance and are engaging, stimulating the viewer to explore the composition. Harmony is subjective, but there are some rules or formulas that can help you to select color combinations that are considered by experts and scholars to be harmonious. All of these formulas are based on the location of colors on a standard artistic color wheel.

Remember that complementary colors are colors that are located directly across from each other on the standard color wheel, such as red and green. See Figure 9-18.

Figure 9-18 Complementary colors on the Kuler panel

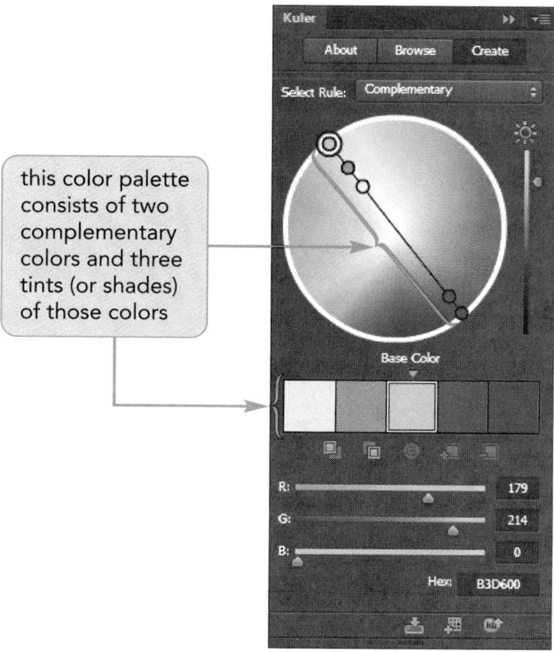

Colors that are opposite one another on the color wheel have the maximum amount of contrast. Creating a composition with complementary colors maximizes the contrast in the composition, which creates a vibrant, visually stimulating composition. The maximum number of colors you should use when creating a composition is five. In addition to two complementary colors, the additional three colors in a complementary color palette should be tints (lightened by mixing with white) or shades (darkened by mixing with black) of the two complementary colors, as shown in Figure 9-18.

Because they produce vibrant effects, color schemes based on complementary colors are frequently seen in advertising. The potential danger with these color schemes is that they can be jarring; the colors must be employed intelligently to produce a visually appealing composition. For example, a color scheme of red and green is often used over a white or black canvas so the colors do not overwhelm the viewer. Another approach is to select one color as the dominant color and use the other color sparingly, as an accent. As you work with color, you will develop a sense of how to use complementary colors in your compositions.

When selecting a color for small text, avoid selecting the color that is the complement of your background because the stark contrast of the text against the background can make it difficult for the viewer to read the text. When using vibrant colors, high contrast sometimes creates excessive brightness at the edges of the text and sometimes very high contrast can cause fine lines to disappear against the background. For an example, see Figure 9-19.

Figure 9-19 Complementary colors and text

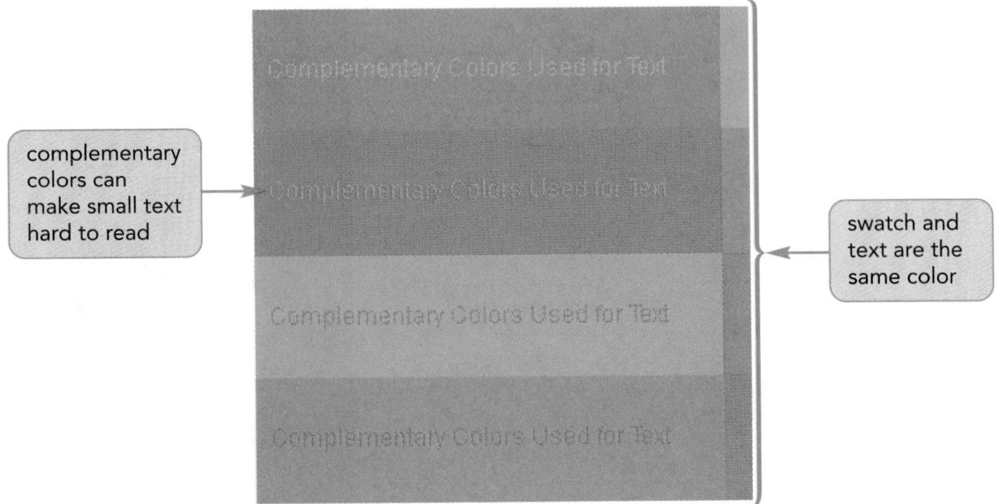

A **triad color palette** divides the color wheel into three sections, enabling you to select three colors that are spaced at an equal distance from each other on the color wheel from each other. See Figure 9-20.

Figure 9-20 Triad color palette with warm colors as the dominant colors

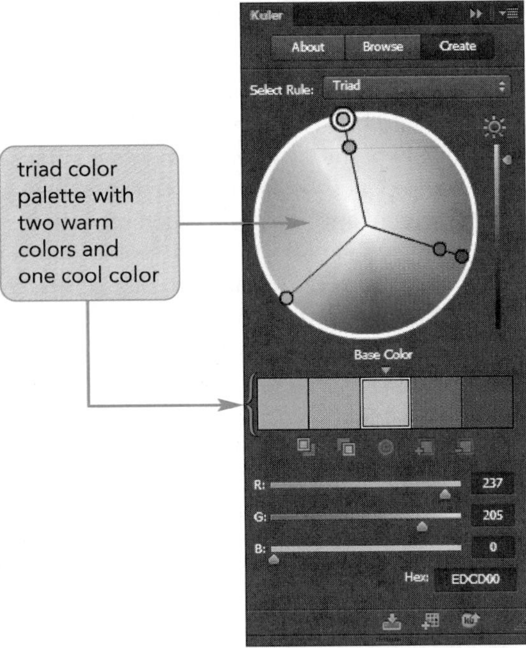

A triad color palette provides you with three colors for your palette; the other two colors in your five-color palette should be selected from the tints, shades, and tones of the original three colors. The triad color scheme provides less contrast than a complementary color scheme, but it still has balance because the colors are equidistant from each other on the color wheel. Again, there is a danger when you use this type of color scheme that the colors will not be harmonious because they are all competing for the viewer's attention. It is a good idea to select one or two dominant colors for this color scheme and to use the other color or colors as accents. A nice way to use this type of color scheme is to select two warm colors (colors that have higher color temperatures—such as reds, oranges, and pinks) to be your dominant colors, and then select one cool color (colors that have lower color temperatures—such as greens, blues, and purples) to be your accent color. This will create a warm, active composition that uses cool accents to provide a bit of contrast and visual interest. You can also do the opposite by selecting two cool colors as dominant colors and one warm color as an accent. This will create a cool, flowing composition that uses warm accents to add contrast and visual interest. See Figure 9-21.

Figure 9-21 **Triad color palette with cool colors as the dominant colors**

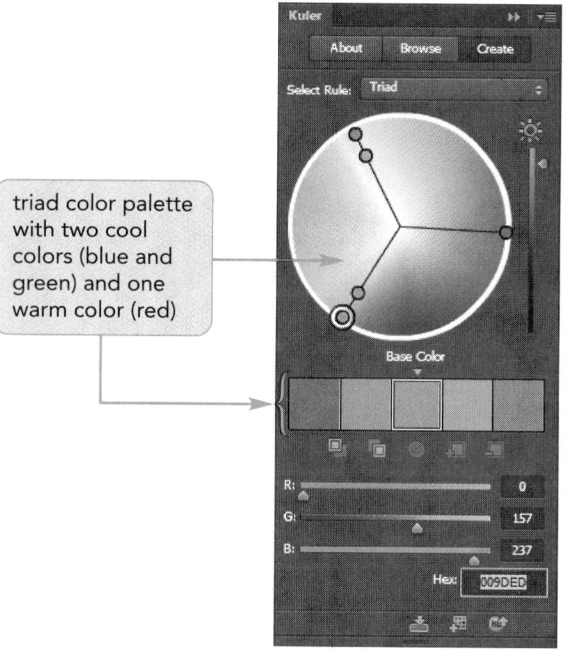

You may recall that analogous color palettes have at least three colors that are located beside each other on the color wheel, with an identifiable common hue, such as yellow, yellow-orange, and orange. See Figure 9-22.

Figure 9-22 **Analogous color palette**

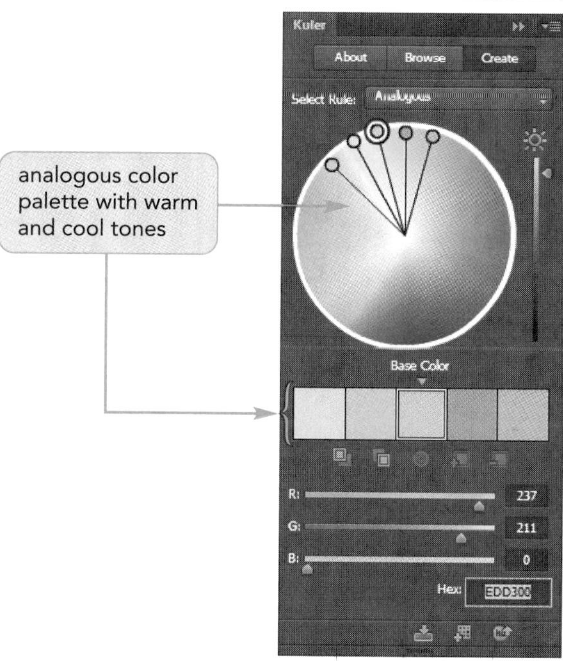

The additional two colors in an analogous color palette can be other colors that are located next to the colors you selected on the color wheel, or they can be tints or shades of those colors. Analogous color schemes are harmonious because the colors blend with each other. When the colors in an analogous color scheme are all tints or shades of the same hue, it is referred to as a monochromatic color scheme. See Figure 9-23.

Figure 9-23 **Monochromatic color palette**

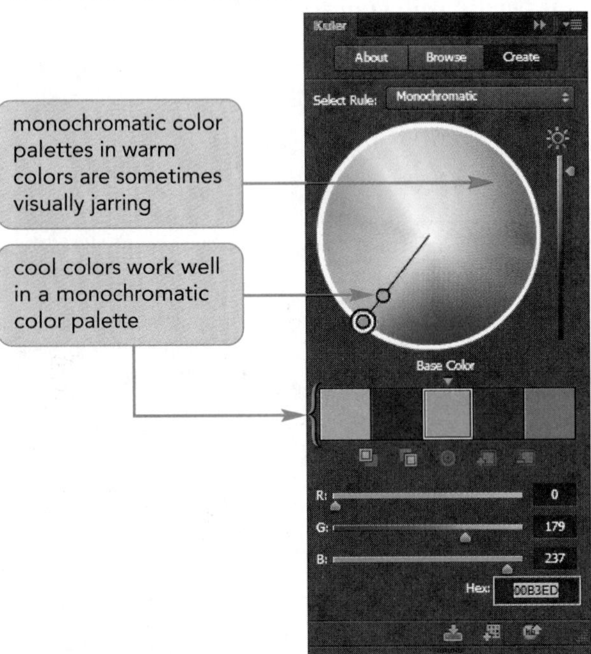

When designing with an analogous color scheme, one of the colors is usually used as the dominant color in the composition, while the other two or more colors are used as accents. When using an analogous color scheme, you need to ensure that your composition does not become bland and visually uninteresting. To avoid this, you should step back from your composition frequently during the design process and take a fresh look. Try to visualize the composition as though you are seeing it for the first time and consider how a viewer will feel when looking at the composition. Because analogous color schemes tend to blend together, designers often use black or white in the composition to make the analogous colors pop. See Figure 9-24.

Figure 9-24 Monochromatic color palette with black

dominant color

black adds drama to the composition

There are many other techniques for selecting color combinations. Once you are comfortable using complementary and analogous color schemes, try researching other ways to use color.

Additional Guidelines for Color Selection

In addition to selecting a color scheme for your project, you need to consider how to use the colors within the composition. Here are a few guidelines that will provide some guidance:

TIP

Photographic images can contain thousands of colors. These do not count as part of the color palette, but you should consider how your images look with your selected palette.

- **Keep it simple**—With color choice, more is definitely not better. Everyone has seen a Web site or flyer that looks as if it erupted from a rainbow. Too many competing colors cause the eye to race around the page, leaving the user dazed and confused. Remember that you want to create a harmonious composition that conveys a sense of balance.
- **Remember branding, identity, and project goals**—Your color palette must reinforce the organization's branding and identity. It also must work with the project goals and metaphor you selected for the composition.
- **Consider the mood you want to create**—Colors create a mood. Studies show that colors have certain psychological effects on people. For example, blue is calming; red is hot or intense. Think about what your target audience might associate with a color when choosing your palette.
- **Keep the target audience in mind**—Different cultures do not always have the same psychological associations with specific colors. For example, people in the United States associate white with purity and red with danger, whereas some countries associate white with death and red with marriage. If a composition has a global or foreign target audience, you might need to research the customs and symbols of the target culture(s).
- **Examine your colors in the composition**—When two colors are placed side by side, they interact with one another. This is called **simultaneous contrast**, and it affects the way you interpret what you see when you look at a composition. This is especially true if you are using a warm color and a cool color because warm colors—such as red, yellow, and orange—are active. They seem to advance out into space, and an object that is colored with a warm color will appear to be larger than the same object that is colored with a cool color. Cool colors—such as blue or green—are passive. They seem to recede from view and appear to fall back in space. To identify potential problems

with color interaction, look at your composition as a whole to see how the colors are affecting each other and how they are affecting the balance of the composition.

By creating different versions of the same layout using different accent colors, you can visualize the way that different color combinations affect the composition. See Figure 9-25 for examples.

Figure 9-25 Color interactions affect the composition

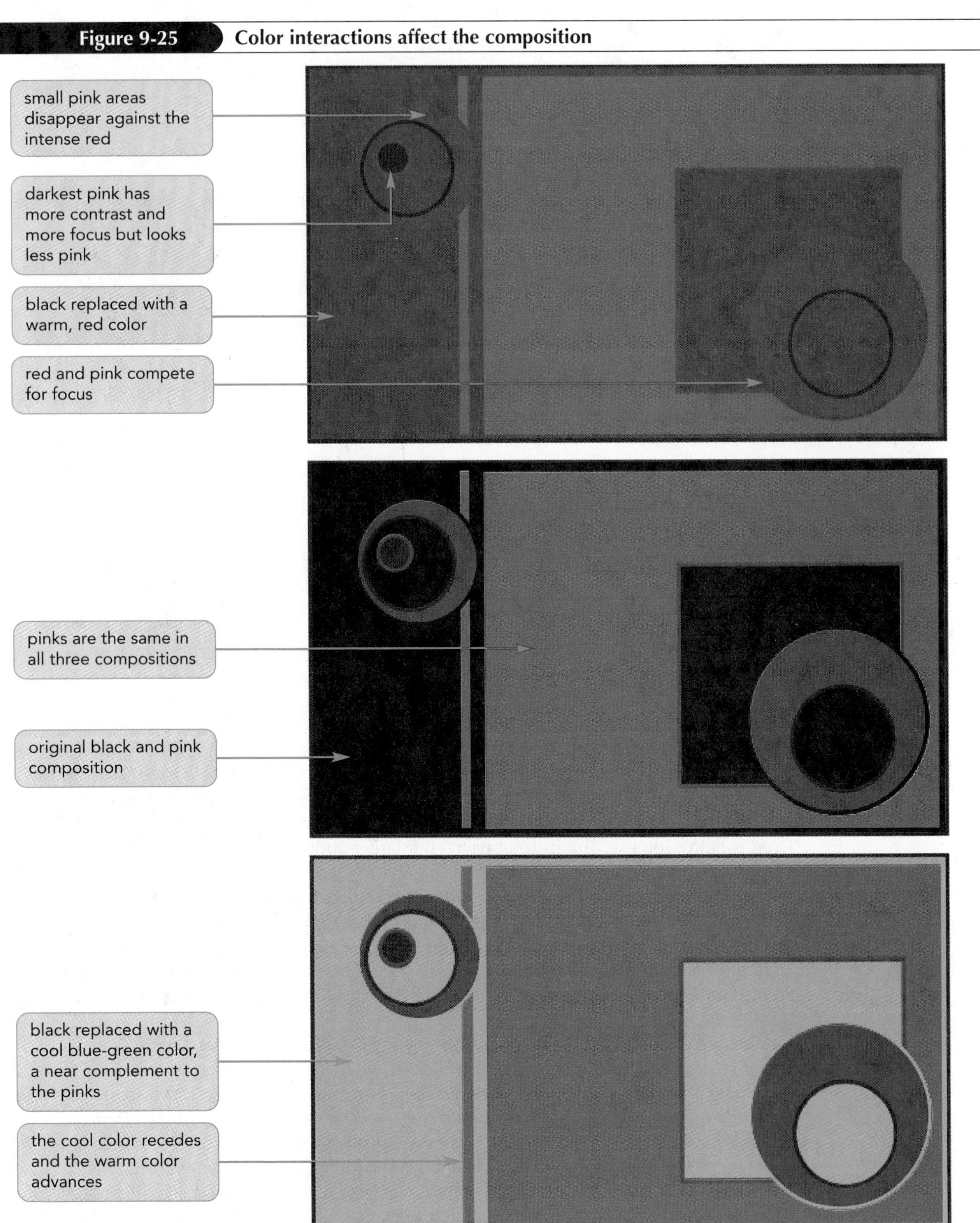
small pink areas disappear against the intense red
darkest pink has more contrast and more focus but looks less pink
black replaced with a warm, red color
red and pink compete for focus
pinks are the same in all three compositions
original black and pink composition
black replaced with a cool blue-green color, a near complement to the pinks
the cool color recedes and the warm color advances

INSIGHT

Using Art as an Inspiration When Choosing a Color Palette

Another way to develop an effective color palette is to look to works of art for inspiration. Think of what emotions and feelings you want to evoke with the composition, and then find a painting, photograph, or other work of art that stirs those feelings in you. Evaluate the colors the artist used. Consider how the colors interact. Try to pinpoint colors that are causing the emotion. Consider how that color palette would work with your metaphor. Think about how you might use that color palette in your composition.

Using the Kuler Panel

Adobe provides the Kuler panel to help you create harmonious color schemes, which Kuler refers to as themes. The Kuler panel is an add-on piece of software—like Camera Raw—that is included with Photoshop. From the Kuler panel, if you have an Internet connection, you can use the Browse tab to view color themes that were created by other artists and then uploaded to the Kuler Web site (*kuler.adobe.com*). In the default view, the Browser tab displays the Highest Rated themes. These are the themes that members of Kuler's online community have given the highest aggregated ratings, using a five-star rating system. See Figure 9-26.

Figure 9-26 Kuler panel with the Browse tab displayed

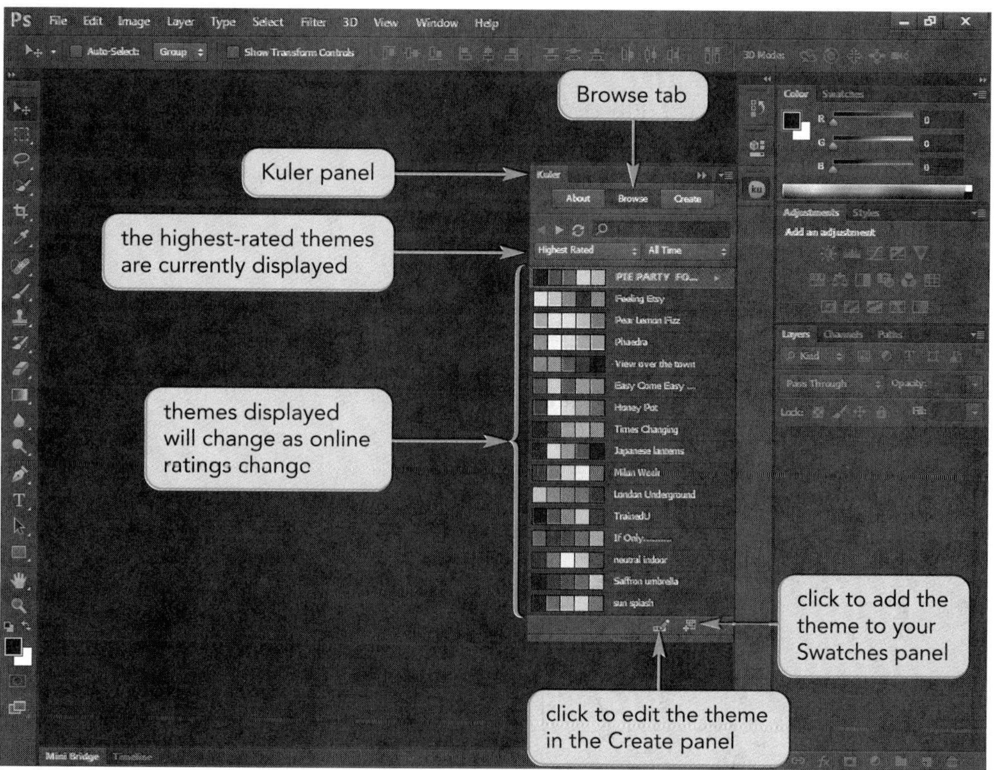

If you find a theme in the Browse tab that you like, you can add the palette to your Swatches panel, or you can edit the theme in the Create tab where you can adjust the colors to create your own custom theme. See Figure 9-27.

Figure 9-27 **Kuler panel with Create tab displayed**

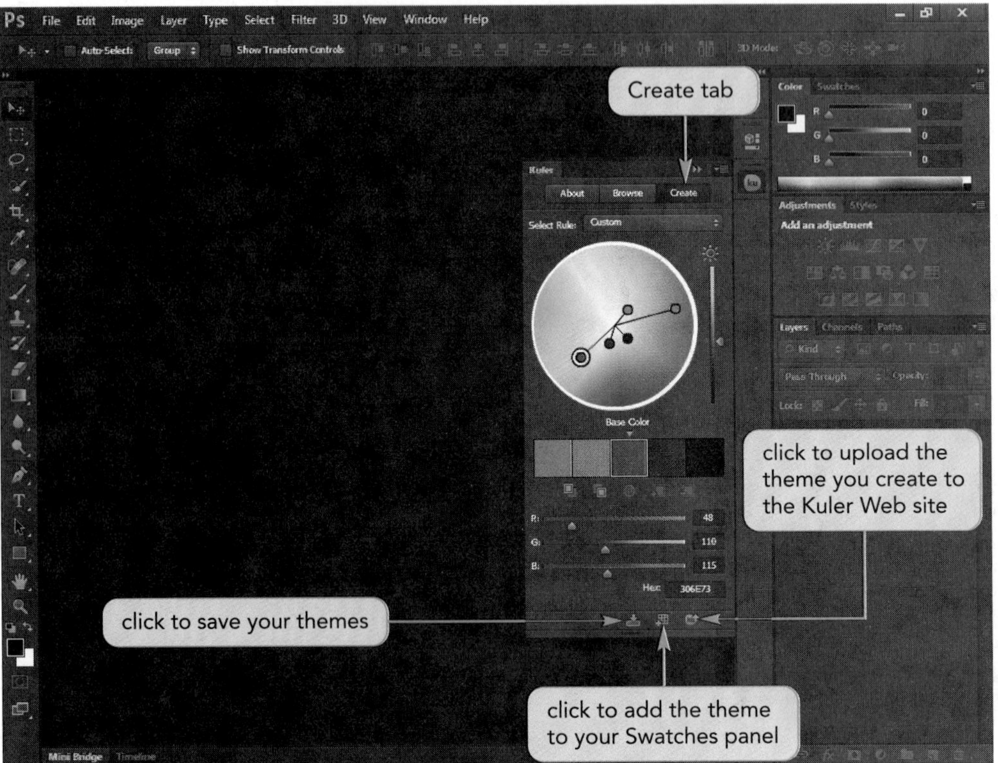

From the Create tab, you can adjust themes that were created by other artists, you can create and save your own themes using the color theory rules that you just learned, and you can adjust themes that you have previously created. You can also upload the themes you create to the Kuler Web site where other artists can view them and comment on them. One drawback of the Kuler panel is that it uses RGB colors, so it sometimes creates themes with colors that are out of gamut for printing.

To gain experience in creating color schemes, you'll open the Kuler panel and use the Browse tab to view color themes created by other artists. Then, you'll use the Create tab to experiment with the different rules that you learned about creating color palettes. If you do not have Internet access, you will not be able to complete the steps that include the Browse tab but you can still create your own color palettes using the Create tab. If you cannot complete the steps, read them and examine the figures.

REFERENCE

Using the Kuler Panel

- On the menu bar, click Window, point to Extensions, and then click Kuler.
- In the Kuler panel, click the Browse tab, select Highest Rated from the Choose which themes you wish to display list, and select All Time from the Limit themes by their creation date list.
- Select a theme that you like, and then click the Add selected theme to swatches icon.
- Click a theme's arrow, and then click Edit This Theme to open the Create tab and edit the selected theme.

Before you begin working with color, it is a good idea to check your Color Settings to ensure that they are set to display color using the color profile you selected when you did your planning. This will ensure that colors are displayed as accurately as possible, regardless of your Color Management Policies settings.

To explore the Kuler panel:

1. On the menu bar, click **Edit**, and then click **Color Settings**. Select **North America General Purpose 2** from the Settings list, if necessary, and then click the **OK** button to close the dialog box.
2. On the menu bar, click **Window**, point to **Extensions**, and then click **Kuler**. The Kuler panel opens in the Photoshop window.
3. In the Kuler panel, click the **Browse** tab, select **Highest Rated** from the Choose which themes you wish to display list, and select **All Time** from the Limit themes by their creation date list.

   The Browse tab is connected to the Kuler Web site, which is constantly updated with new styles. If you are connected to the Internet, the list displayed on your screen will probably change each time you use the tab to browse for new color themes.

   Trouble? If you are not connected to the Internet, you might see the list of themes that was displayed the last time the computer was connected to the Internet or you might not see any themes at all. You might also see a message indicating that no Internet connection was detected. Click the OK button to acknowledge the message, and then read but do not keystroke the following steps.
4. Select a theme that you like, and then click the **Add selected theme to swatches** icon at the bottom of the Browse tab.
5. Click the **Swatches** panel to display it. Notice that the colors from the theme you selected have been added to the end of your swatches. See Figure 9-28.

Figure 9-28 Theme added to Swatches panel

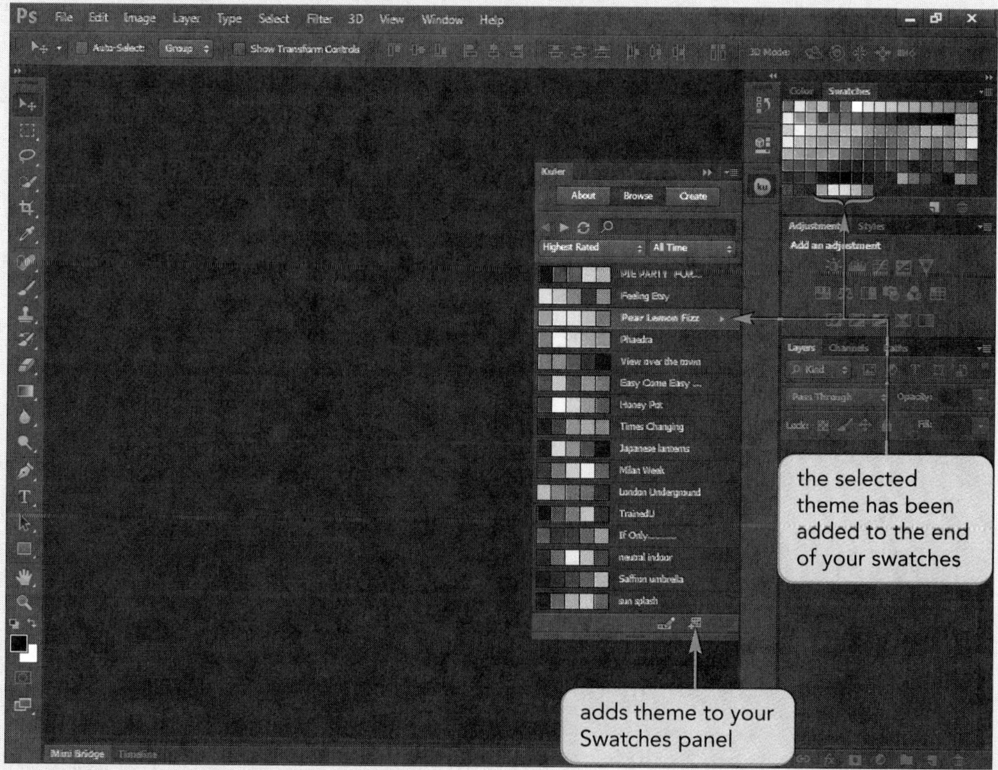

the selected theme has been added to the end of your swatches
adds theme to your Swatches panel

6. Select another theme on the Browse tab, click its arrow, and then click **Edit This Theme**. The Create tab opens, and the theme you selected is displayed.

Next, you'll customize this theme to create your own custom color theme. When creating a custom theme, you can start with an existing theme or you can simply open the Create tab and start experimenting, using the rules you have learned.

REFERENCE

Creating a Theme in the Kuler Panel

- On the Create tab of the Kuler panel, select a rule from the Select Rule list.
- Click the Base Color swatch located below the color wheel, if necessary.
- Click the Base Color circle and drag it around the color wheel until you find the base color you want to use.
- Select the other circles on the color wheel, and move them around to select the four other colors for your theme.
- Adjust the shade of any color by dragging the Control brightness by increasing or decreasing black slider located at the right of the color wheel up or down.
- Click the Name and save this theme icon at the bottom of the Create tab, and in the Name box, type a name for the theme.
- Click the Save button.

To create your own themes:

1. In the Kuler panel, select **Analogous** from the Select Rule list, and then click the **Base Color** swatch located below the color wheel, if necessary.

   The Base Color indicator on the color wheel of the Kuler panel is a circle that is surrounded by a white border.

2. Drag the **Base Color** circle around the color wheel until a shade of red is displayed in the circle.
3. Select one of the circles, other than the Base Color circle, and drag it until all of the circles are fairly close together. See Figure 9-29.

TIP

You can also select the Base Color by typing a specific hexadecimal color code in the Hex box at the bottom of the Kuler panel.

Figure 9-29 Adjusted analogous color palette

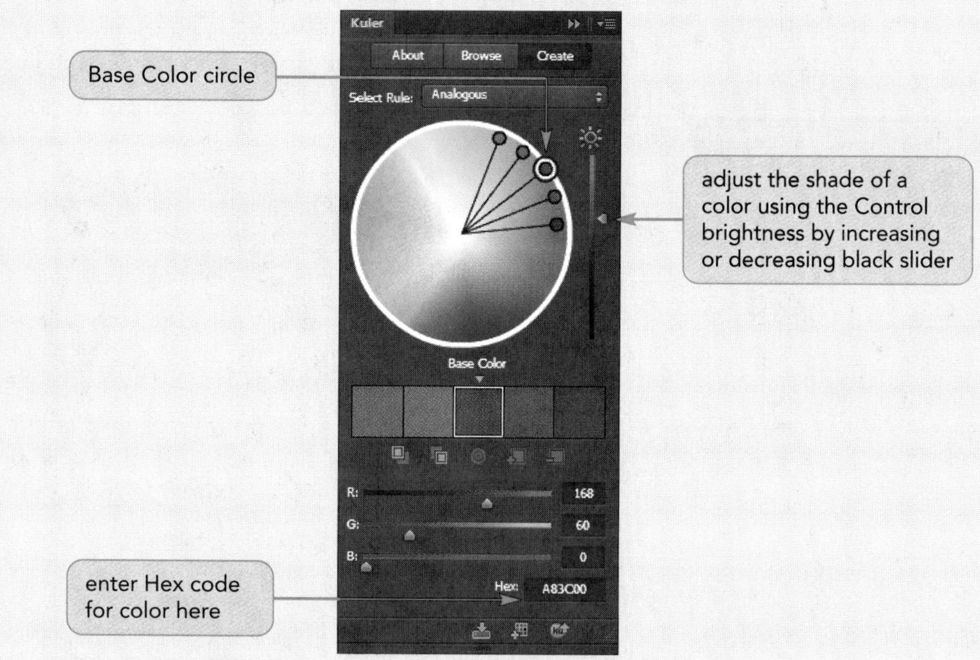
Kuler
About
Browse
Create
Base Color circle
Select Rule: Analogous
adjust the shade of a color using the Control brightness by increasing or decreasing black slider
Base Color
R: 168
G: 60
B: 0
enter Hex code for color here
Hex: A83C00

4. Adjust the shade of all of the colors by clicking the **Base Color** swatch, and then clicking and dragging the **Control brightness by increasing or decreasing black** slider located at the right of the color wheel to the top.
5. Drag the bottom color circle about halfway toward the center of the color wheel to lighten the tint of this color swatch. See Figure 9-30.

Figure 9-30 Adjusted analogous color palette

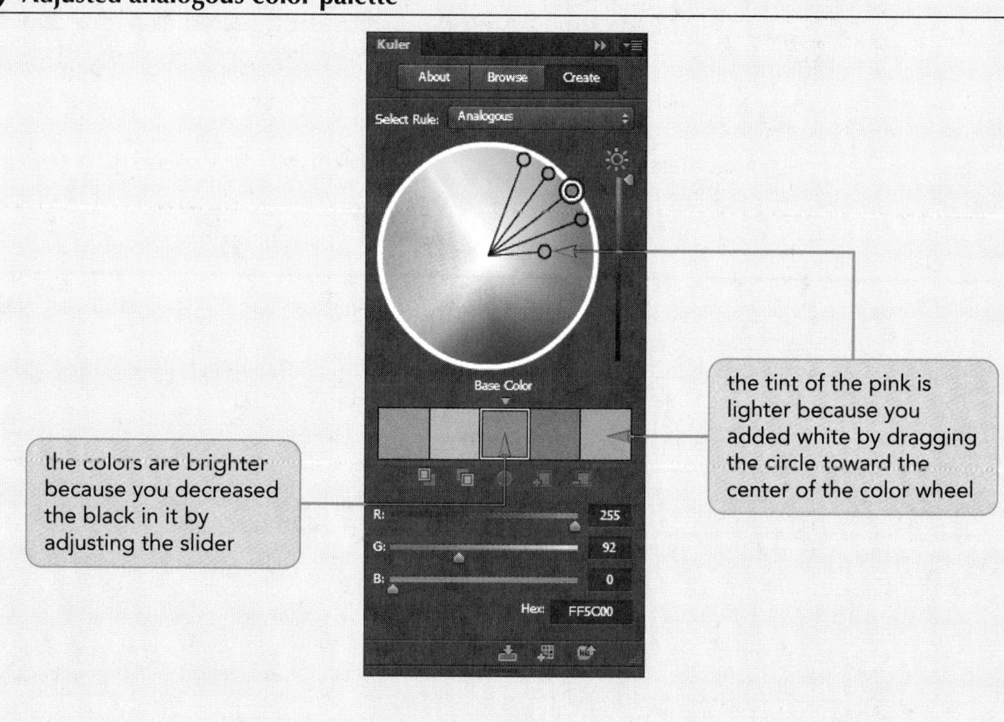
Kuler
About
Browse
Create
Select Rule: Analogous
Base Color
the tint of the pink is lighter because you added white by dragging the circle toward the center of the color wheel
the colors are brighter because you decreased the black in it by adjusting the slider
R: 255
G: 92
B: 0
Hex: FF5C00

6. Select **Triad** from the Select Rule list, and then drag the **Base Color** circle around the color wheel until the Base Color circle and one of the other color circles are displaying cool colors (blue and green) and one is displaying a warm color (red); then adjust the shades and tints as you like. See Figure 9-31.

Figure 9-31 **Triad color theme**

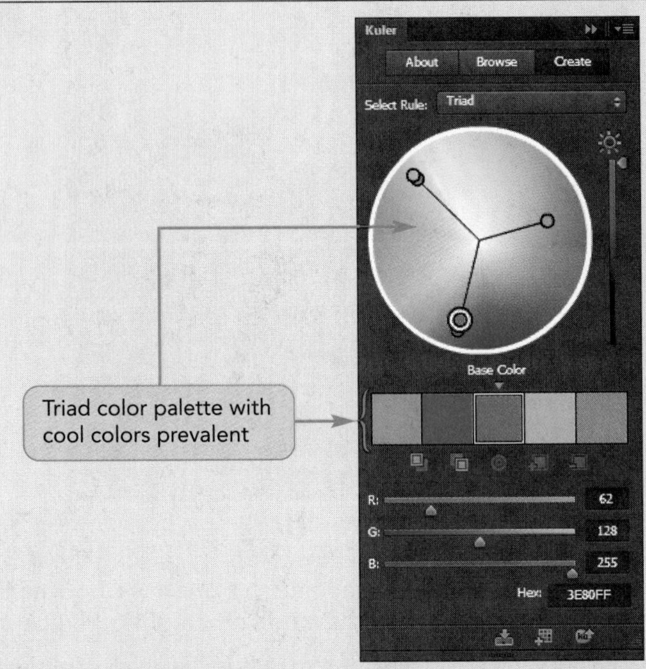

7. Click the **Name and save this theme** icon, and in the Name box, type **Test**. Click the **Save** button.

8. Click the **Browse** tab, and select **Saved** from the Choose which themes you wish to display list. Your new theme is displayed in the tab so you can access it later.

Jessica used the Kuler panel to choose the colors shown in Figure 9-32 for the new FlashFlock banner ad campaign.

Figure 9-32 FlashFlock banner ad campaign color theme

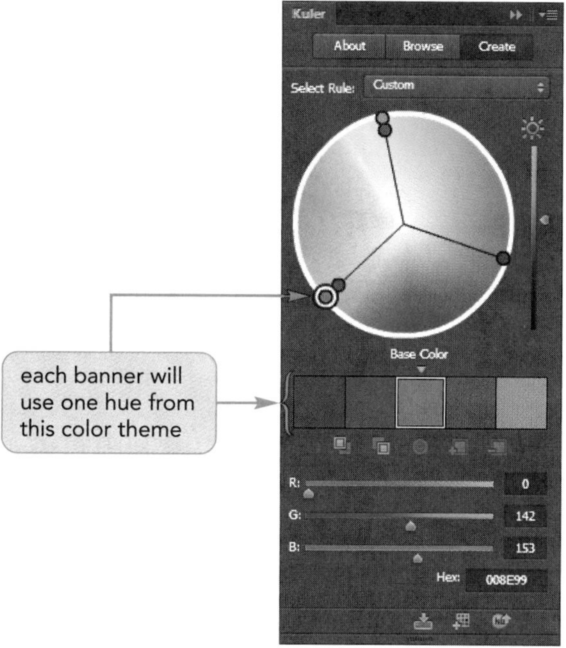

This color palette fits nicely into the mashup metaphor because each of these colors is created by mixing other colors together. They are not normal primary or secondary colors that are frequently used in advertising. Instead, they are slightly odd versions of the colors you might expect to see. This provides the synthetic, outsider feel that Jessica wants to evoke. Each banner in the campaign will use one hue of the colors from the palette along with white for the text and graphic elements. This color scheme will allow the new banners to reinforce the current FlashFlock branding and identity without repeating the current look exactly. Finally, the colors are fun and they will work well with other graphic elements in the banners.

Now that you have had a chance to experiment with the Kuler panel and create some color themes using the rules that you learned, you'll create an alternate color palette for the FlashFlock banner ad campaign.

To create an alternate color palette for the FlashFlock campaign:

1. Using the rules you have learned, decide on the type of color scheme you'll create as an alternate FlashFlock color palette.
2. Envision a set of colors that will work with your alternate concept and metaphor. If you have trouble, use the Browse tab of the Kuler panel to look at themes other artists have created.
3. On the Create tab of the Kuler panel, select the type of color theme you would like to create from the Select Rule list.
4. Move the **color** circles on the color wheel and the **Control brightness by increasing or decreasing black** slider until you have a color theme that you like.
5. Examine the theme and consider the psychological associations of the colors. Do these fit with your goals? Do the colors work with the concept and metaphor, the FlashFlock branding and identity, and the project goals? Make any adjustments that you think are necessary.

6. When you are finished making adjustments, click the **Name and save this theme** icon, and save the theme as **FlashFlockAlt**.
7. Open WordPad, create a new document, and save the document in the Photoshop9\Tutorial folder as **Color.rtf**.
8. Write a paragraph explaining how the palette you selected works with FlashFlock's current branding and identity and how it supports the project goals, and your alternate concept and metaphor. Describe where and how you intend to use the colors in the project, and then save and close the document.
9. On the menu bar, click **Window**, point to **Workspace**, and then click **Reset Essentials** to close the Kuler panel and return the workspace to its default view.

Adding Colors to Your Composition

You are ready to add colors to your composition, using the FFBanners.psd file that you created in the first session. You'll create a new layer group for the first banner, and then you'll create a gradient background using white and one color from the color palette. Before you begin working with color in your composition, it is a good idea to check your Color Settings to ensure that the Working Spaces setting displays RGB color using the color profile that you selected when you did your planning. This will ensure that colors are displayed as accurately as possible, regardless of your Color Management Policies settings. This is also the point at which you would normally adjust your Proof Setup setting, so you can soft proof your work, if necessary. In this case, that step is overkill because you are working in RGB and you know that your document color profile is the same as your Working Spaces color profile, so we will skip that step.

To create gradient banner backgrounds:

1. Press the **Ctrl+Shift+K** keys to open the Color Settings dialog box and select **North America General Purpose 2** from the Settings list, if necessary. This changes the Working Space setting for RGB to sRGB IEC61966-2.1, which is the color profile you selected when you created the document. Click the **OK** button to close the dialog box.
2. Open the **FFBanners.psd** file that you saved in the Photoshop9\Tutorial folder, and set the document to display at **100%**, if necessary. Display the rulers, and collapse the Adjustments panel group.
3. In the Layers panel, click the **Create a new group** icon, and name the new group **Banner 1**.
4. With the Banner 1 group selected on the Layers panel, click the **Create a new layer** icon to create a new layer inside of the Banner 1 folder, and name the new layer **Banner Background**.
5. In the Color panel, click the **Set foreground color** icon, and type **9c005e** in the # box at the bottom of the Color Picker (Foreground Color) dialog box. Click the **OK** button. The new foreground color is the berry color from Jessica's color palette.
6. In the Tools panel, click the **Gradient Tool** button, and then on the options bar, click the **Gradient picker** button.
7. In the Gradient picker, double-click the first option, **Foreground to Background**, to select it and close the Gradient picker.

8. On the options bar, click the **Linear Gradient** icon, click the **Mode** button, and click **Normal**, if necessary. Set the Opacity to **100%**, and click the **Dither** and **Transparency** check boxes to select them, if necessary.
9. With the Gradient tool still selected, click at the top of the canvas and drag the mouse straight down the canvas, past the bottom edge to around the 5-inch mark on the ruler. Release the mouse button. The background is now a gradient. See Figure 9-33.

Figure 9-33 **Gradient background of Banner 1**

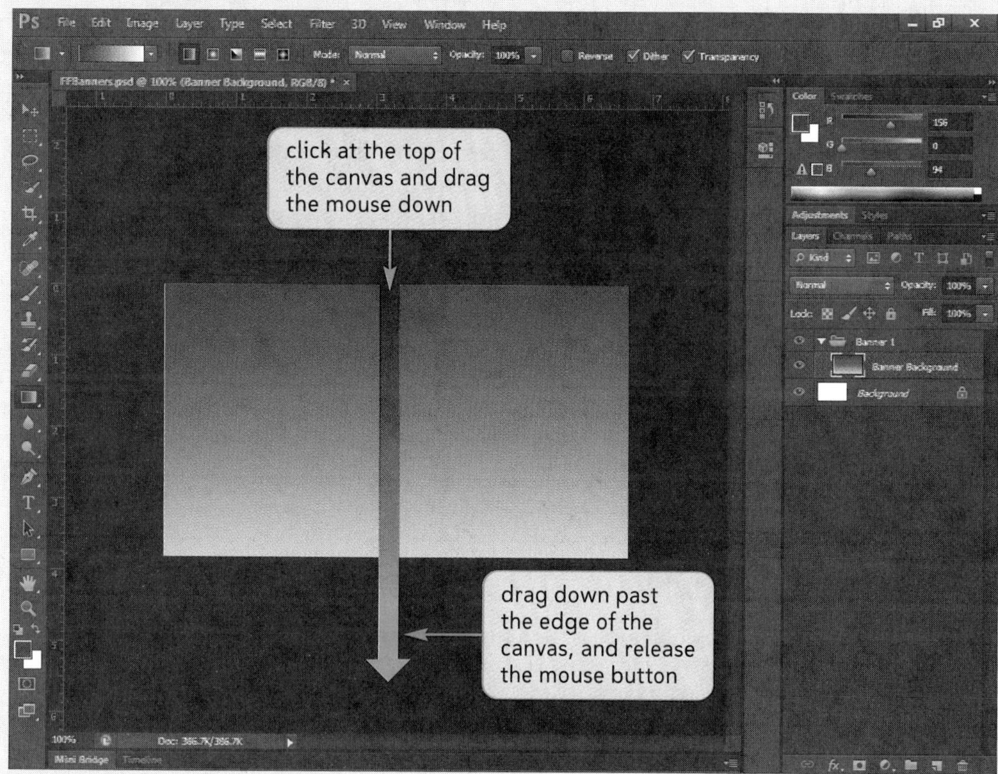
click at the top of the canvas and drag the mouse down
drag down past the edge of the canvas, and release the mouse button

10. Save the document.

With color added to your composition, you're ready to select typefaces and add the text to the composition.

Selecting Fonts and Adding Text

Typography is the art and technique of arranging, designing, and modifying type. From the time of the first printing press, designers and typographers have used text as part of aesthetic design. You have learned the basics skills of type arrangement, including adding text to a canvas; adjusting text colors; selecting point sizes; and adjusting line spacing, leading, tracking, kerning, and so forth. Now, you'll learn how to use text effectively as part of your composition.

Selecting the Appropriate Typographical Style

In traditional **text typography**, the goal of text design and layout is to create a cohesive, readable, and visually pleasing document, using an unobtrusive typographical style that is designed to create a logical and ordered visual hierarchy that will guide the reader through the document. This approach to working with text is appropriate when your project is a traditional printed work with a large amount of text, or when the goal of your project is to communicate information efficiently, such as in an IRS pamphlet. It is also an approach you should consider when adding paragraph text to a composition. For example, in a magazine article, this style would be appropriate for the text in the main body of the article, so it is easy for the viewer to read, but it would probably not be the first choice for the title text. When you employ the text typography approach, you use typeface, color, and text size to create a logical, hierarchical structure that helps the viewer move through the content. This approach can be used to distinguish relative importance of content or to categorize content. Using this approach, text is usually left aligned, or placed in columns, and font size and color are used to indicate hierarchical importance.

Another approach to typography is **display typography**. When using this approach, a designer is less concerned with the readability of a large body of text, and more concerned about using the text in an artistic manner to communicate a succinct, potent message to the viewer. Designers often employ the display typography approach along with images when creating a composition. With this approach, it is important to keep in mind that a background image and other graphic elements affect text readability by causing visual interruptions and alignment issues. Because of this you should step back from your composition and check for text readability, alignment, and so forth. Both approaches are appropriate in different circumstances, and you can combine the approaches to create a more effective and well-rounded composition.

Now that you understand how your approach affects your design, you'll select typefaces for the FlashFlock project.

Selecting Typefaces and Font Styles

A **typeface** is a unified set of alphanumeric symbols that are designed with stylistic unity. Most typefaces include letters, numerals, punctuation, and symbols—sometimes in multiple languages. Typefaces are usually grouped together into a collection or family of fonts. A **font** actually refers to a designated set of letters, numbers, and symbols in a single size and style in one typeface. For example, the Helvetica typeface might include 12-point Helvetica bold font and 9-point Helvetica italic font, among many other fonts. However, in the modern age, people often use the words *typeface* and *font* interchangeably. In fact, digital typeface designers are often referred to as font designers.

Because of this blurring of the traditional lines, Photoshop refers to the typeface as the *font family* and to the font as the *font style*. And, in some instances, such as certain articles within Help, Photoshop uses the general term *font* to refer to all aspects of the font, including font family and font style. We will use Photoshop's terminology for the remainder of this tutorial.

Selecting the font is the most important typographical decision you will need to make for a project. Selecting the right font family and font style is important in creating an effective design because a font conveys a wealth of subtle information and often creates an impression about the content before it is even read. Just think about the different fonts that might be used on designs that present current news and events, offer Far East travel information, or advertise science fiction movies. Font selection also has an effect on the readability of the text. Because of this, different fonts are appropriate for different applications and in different circumstances. In fact, some industries have specific standards and specifications for selection of appropriate fonts. You should be sure you understand font characteristics—and the project requirements—when selecting a font for your project.

The three general categories of font are serif, sans serif, and mono. **Serif fonts** are fonts in which a delicate, horizontal line called a serif finishes the main strokes of each character; an example would be the horizontal bars at the top and bottom of an uppercase M. The most common serif font is Times New Roman. Serif fonts are often used in traditional printing for body text in books, newspapers, and magazines because historically, people believed that serif fonts were easier to read. Recent studies have disproven this fact, but the history and perception still persist.

Sans serif fonts are those in which the serifs are absent. (*Sans* means *without* in French, so *sans serif* means *without serif*.) The most common sans serif font is Helvetica. Sans serif fonts are commonly used on Web sites and in other digital media, even for body text. Because of their prevalence in contemporary digital design, they have also become popular for headlines and headings in contemporary print.

A third category, mono, is sometimes used. *Mono* is short for *monospaced*. A **monospaced font** is one in which each letter takes exactly the same width in the line; for example, the letter *i* (a thin letter) takes the same amount of space as the letter *m*. A common monospaced font is `Courier`. Monospaced fonts are serif fonts, but they are considered a separate font family because of their unique characteristic. Fonts that are not monospaced are **proportional fonts** because each letter takes up a different width on the line, proportional to the width of each letter. For example, the letter *i* takes less space than the letter *m*. Both the serif font Times New Roman and the sans serif font Helvetica are proportional.

The font selection for the FlashFlock banner campaign was fairly simple because FlashFlock has a very minimalist approach to design. In addition, because FlashFlock is primarily a Web-based organization, they have traditionally used sans serif fonts. The FlashFlock logo font family (typeface) is **Arial Rounded MT Bold** and the font style (font) is Regular. All other text is always displayed using the Arial font family, and all text is displayed in white (hexadecimal color #ffffff). See Figure 9-34.

Figure 9-34 Font family and font style used by FlashFlock

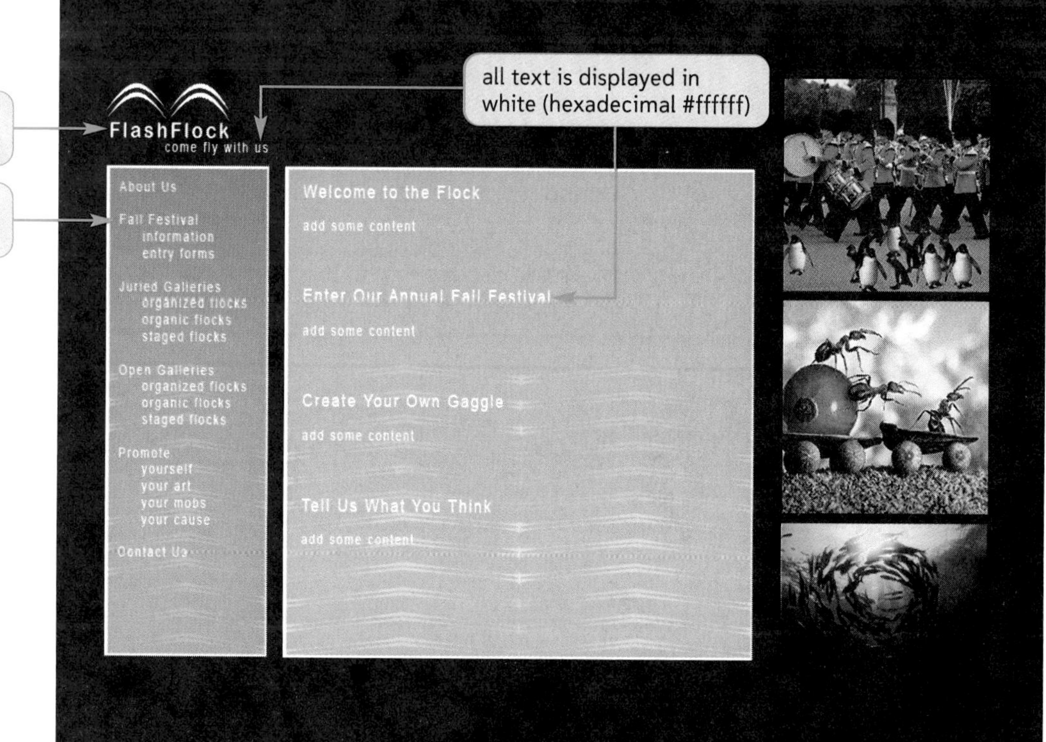

Jessica has decided that for the purposes of branding and identity, you will follow those guidelines for the banner ad campaign. This style also supports the mashup metaphor because it is contemporary and minimalist.

INSIGHT

Selecting Fonts for Use as Text on the Web

When you are creating a design for a Web page, remember that although you are creating a picture of what the Web page will look like, the actual page will be made using a combination of graphic images, text, and computer code. In a Web page, a font must be installed on the end user's computer for the page to be displayed using that font. If you use a font that is not found on a user's computer, the page will be displayed in the default font the end user has chosen for his or her browser (unless you use new HTML code that allows you to add Web fonts to a page). To avoid possible font substitutions, you can create a graphic that is a picture of the text; you place the graphic in the Web page as you would any other image. For example, many logos that you see displayed on Web pages are actually images that change appearance when the user drags the mouse over the image. This technique works for a small amount of text, such as a title or heading. However, you cannot change all text to graphic images because it would make the pages slow to load in a browser, and it would prevent the text from wrapping to accommodate the size of the viewer's screen.

Web design programs, such as Adobe Dreamweaver, arrange fonts into groups, as shown here:

Verdana, Geneva, sans-serif
Georgia, Times New Roman, Times, serif
Courier New, Courier, monospace
Arial, Helvetica, sans-serif
Tahoma, Geneva, sans-serif
Trebuchet MS, Arial, Helvetica, sans-serif
Arial Black, Gadget, sans-serif
Times New Roman, Times, serif
Palatino Linotype, Book Antiqua, Palatino, serif
Lucida Sans Unicode, Lucida Grande, sans-serif
MS Serif, New York, serif
Lucida Console, Monaco, monospace
Comic Sans MS, cursive

These groups provide designers with the best chance for achieving the desired look for a page. Each group contains the most common names for the selected font; these include the most common PC name, the most common Mac name (when different), and the generic font family name.

When you apply a font grouping to text, you actually apply computer code that contains all three choices, ensuring maximum potential for aesthetic continuity across all platforms and all computers. When a browser displays a page, it checks the user's computer for the first font in the group. If the computer doesn't have that font, the browser checks for the second font in the list, and then, if necessary, the third font.

Once you have selected your font family and font style and you have set the font size and font color, you can fine-tune the text by making small adjustments to spacing, kerning, line spacing, indentation, and so forth, as needed. Because you will be using FlashFlock's existing font family, font style, and font color, there is no need to make an alternate font selection, just remember to use what you have learned here when you select fonts for projects in the future. Next, you'll add text to Banner 1.

To add text to your composition:

1. Drag a vertical guide ¼ inch from the left side of the canvas and a horizontal guide ¼ inch from the bottom of the canvas.
2. In the Tools panel in Photoshop, click the **Horizontal Type Tool** button and starting at the left guide, approximately one-third of the way down the page, draw a box that is 2 ¾ inches wide with the bottom of the rectangle against the bottom guide. See Figure 9-35.

Figure 9-35 **Text box in the new banner**

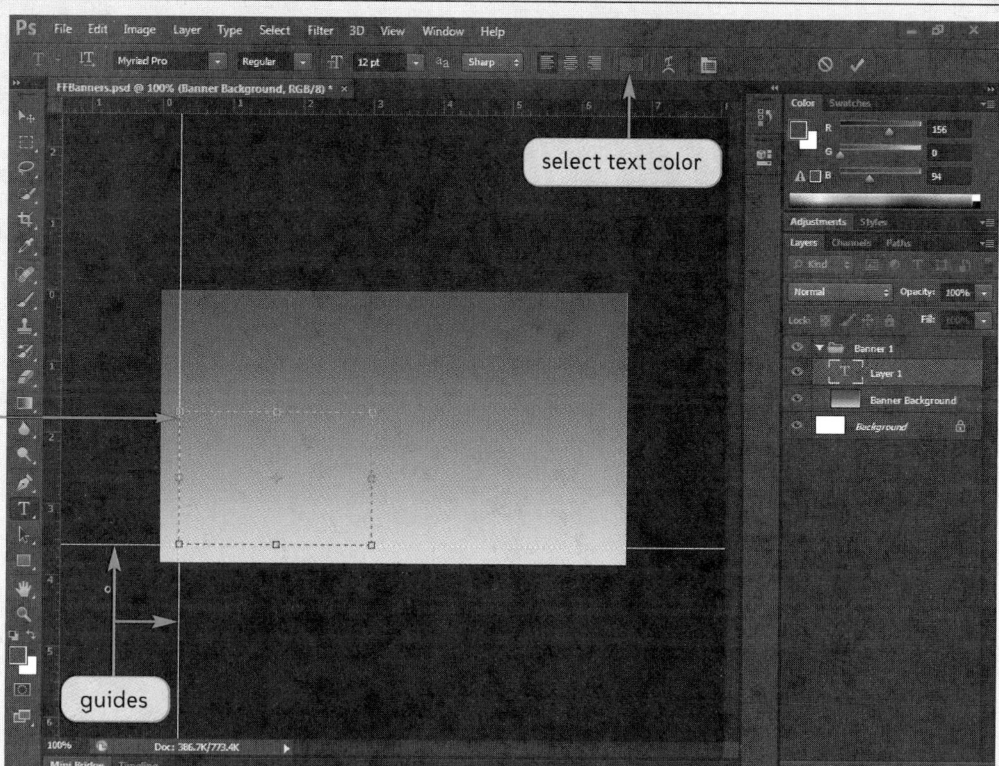

3. Double-click the text layer in the Layers panel, change the layer name to **Content**, and then double-click the **Content** text thumbnail to select the text box again.
4. On the options bar, click the **Set the font family** button Myriad Pro, and then click **Arial**. Select **Regular** from the font style list, select **14 pt** from the font size list, and set the anti-aliasing method to **Sharp**. Click the **Left align text** icon, and click the **Set the text color** button to open the Select text color dialog box. Type **ffffff** in the # box at the bottom of the dialog box, and then click the **OK** button.
5. Using WordPad, open **BannerText.rtf**, located in the Photoshop9\Tutorial folder, and copy the text from the Content section for Banner 1.
6. In Photoshop, paste the text into the box, and add a line break between each chunk of text by clicking at the end of the line and pressing the **Enter** key. See Figure 9-36.

Figure 9-36 Text content in the new banner

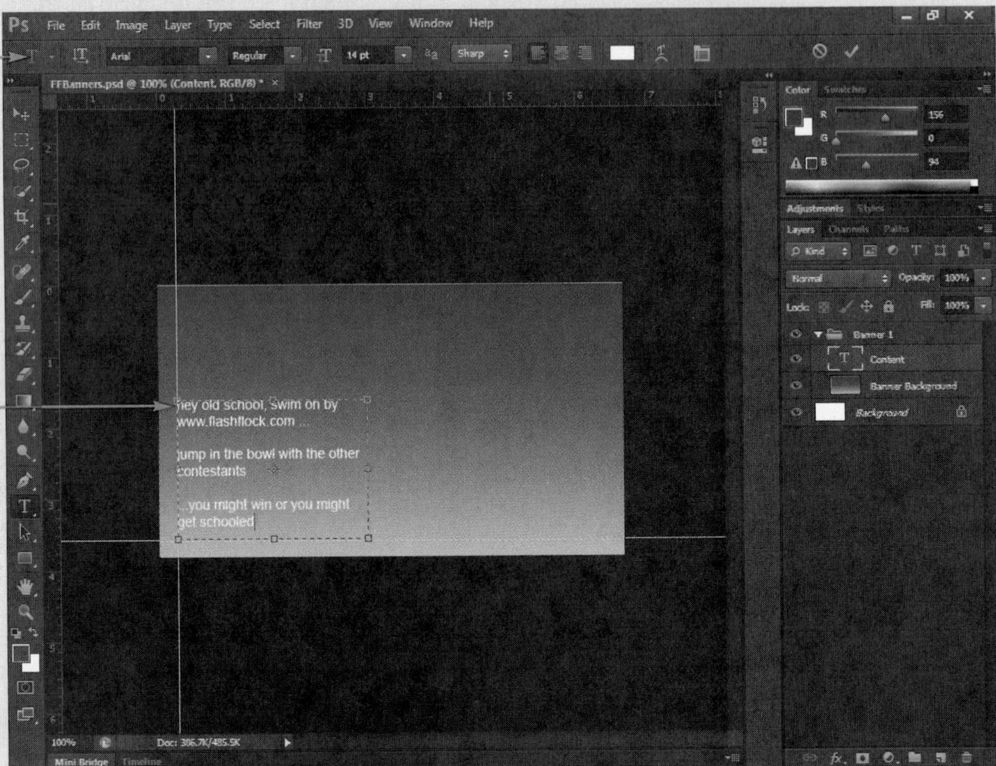

7. On the menu bar, click **Window**, and then click **Character** to open the Character panel. In the Document window, select all of the text, and then in the Character panel click the **Set the tracking for the selected characters list** icon, and type **50** in the box. This will add more space between characters.
8. On the menu bar, click the **Commit** button.
9. Save the FFBanners.psd file, and then close the Character tab group.
10. Close the BannerText.rtf file.

Next, you'll select a graphic style, create any graphics that you need, and add graphics to the composition.

Creating a Graphic Style

Now it is time to determine the graphic style for your project. The graphics in a composition provide the personality of the project. They are like accessories that either pull the composition together or detract from its overall look. Graphic style refers to the look of the graphic elements in the project, including lines, shapes, textures, borders, logos, illustrations, buttons, and any other elements you draw or create digitally that are not text or photographs. There are several elements to consider when you are creating the graphic style for your composition. Here are a few questions you can ask yourself to get the creative juices flowing and to help you decide upon a graphic style for your project:

- Will the graphics be flat like a two-dimensional drawing you see in magazine ads or comics, or will they have depth that is created using shadows, highlights, gradient colors, and perspective? Remember that a simple graphic style can be as sophisticated and powerful as a complex graphic style, and it can be just as successful if it reinforces your goals and works with your metaphor.
- Will the graphic elements be flowing—like wavy lines, swirls, and circles—or will they have sharp angles and breaks?
- Will you use flat colors, gradients, textures, or some combination?
- Will your graphics look realistic—like they are attempting to re-create something from the real world, or will they look artificial, like they are symbolic of real-world objects?
- Are there other words that you can use to describe what you would like the graphic style to convey to the viewer—such as *grungy* or *crisp*?

Finally, remember that the choice not to use any graphic elements in your composition is a stylistic choice as well, and it can be just as powerful a choice if it helps you to accomplish your goals.

After you have decided upon a graphic style, you are ready to create the graphic elements that you'll use in your composition. Graphics can be helpful in many ways. They can reinforce the organization's branding, identity, project goals, and metaphor. You can use graphics (such as symbols) to communicate information, you can use graphics (such as those used in the background of FlashFlock's current ads) to break up space, and you can use graphics (such as customized bullet points or stylized backgrounds for featured content) to add logic to the composition. You can also use graphics to help the flow of the composition by guiding the viewer's eye from one element to the next. The possibilities are endless.

Based on the FlashFlock banner ad goals, color palette, typeface choices, layout, and metaphor, Jessica selected a graphic style that includes flat, white, stylized graphic elements that will be inserted into the background of the composition to add movement to the composition, which is otherwise very static. The elements will be stylized or manufactured representations of organic elements, which will reinforce the mashup metaphor and will work with the current FlashFlock aesthetic. Although the older FlashFlock banners and marketing materials used linear elements, this campaign will use curved elements repeated with varying opacities to soften the composition and to add some repetition to the composition by mimicking the lines of the logo. Each banner will include a slightly different graphic repeated as a background element layered over the gradient background. The curves will guide the viewer's eye up to the FlashFlock logo in each banner to help reinforce the goals for the project. This will provide unity to the campaign while maintaining visual interest in the individual compositions. See Figure 9-37 for a sample of the three graphic background elements.

Figure 9-37 Graphics patterns created for the FlashFlock campaign

Jessica is also considering adding a thin white border around the outside of the banners. She would like you to create two versions of the banner—one with the border and one without it—so that she can present both to George and Rick. However, first you'll design an alternate graphic style to go with your alternate concept/metaphor, layout, and color palette for the FlashFlock banner ad campaign. You'll answer the above questions and write a paragraph explaining the style and how it works with your alternate project metaphor and goals as well as FlashFlock's branding and identity.

To design an alternate graphic style:

1. Review the alternate concept, metaphor, layout, and color palette that you developed for the banner ad campaign. Also, review the research that you gathered about what appeals to the target audience.
2. Open WordPad, create a new document, and save the document as **AltGraphics.rtf** in the Photoshop9\Tutorial folder. Consider how you would like to use graphics in the campaign, and answer the questions in the bulleted list presented earlier in this section regarding graphic style.
3. Write a few sentences that describe the graphic style you have selected for the campaign. Explain how this graphic style supports your metaphor, works with the FlashFlock aesthetic, and reinforces the campaign goals.
4. Save and close the AltGraphics.rtf document.

Once you have designed a graphic style, you will create graphics and add them to your composition. You should examine and prepare graphic files before you add the graphics to your composition. It is a good idea to convert your graphics to the correct color model and, when possible, the correct color profile, before you add them to your composition so you can access the colors of the converted graphic. In addition, if the converted graphic needs color correction because of the way the converter compensated for out-of-gamut colors, you can return to the original graphic to make any necessary color adjustments, and then create a new converted version of the graphic file before you add it to the composition. Following this work flow will allow you to achieve the best possible results because you will be able to adjust the colors of the converted graphic without affecting the other elements in the final composition.

When possible, you should add the graphics to your composition as Smart Objects to enable you to continue to edit them at their original size and in their original format. This is especially helpful if you have created the graphics in another Adobe software program, such as Illustrator. Adding the file as a Smart Object enables you to open, edit, and save the file in the original program (assuming you have that program installed on your computer), and to view the alterations in your composition.

Now, you'll add the graphic element that Jessica created to the FlashFlock banner and you'll add the other graphic element, the FlashFlock logo, to the banner. Once you do this, you might need to adjust the text slightly to create an aesthetically pleasing composition.

To add graphics to your composition:

1. In Photoshop, open **Graphics.psd**, located in the Photoshop9\Tutorial folder, and set the document to display at **100%**, if necessary.
2. On the menu bar, click **Edit**, and then click **Convert to Profile**. Review the Source Space profile for the document. This document already has the color profile that you decided to use when you were planning (sRGB IEC61966-2.1) because Jessica created the graphic specifically for this project.

3. Now that you have confirmed that the color profile is correct, click **Cancel** to close the Convert to Profile dialog box without making any changes.
4. On the menu bar click **Window**, point to **Arrange**, and then click **2-up Horizontal** . The file containing the graphics for the banners opens in one pane, and the FFBanners document is displayed in the other. See Figure 9-38.

Figure 9-38 **Graphics.psd and FFBanners.psd open in the Document window**

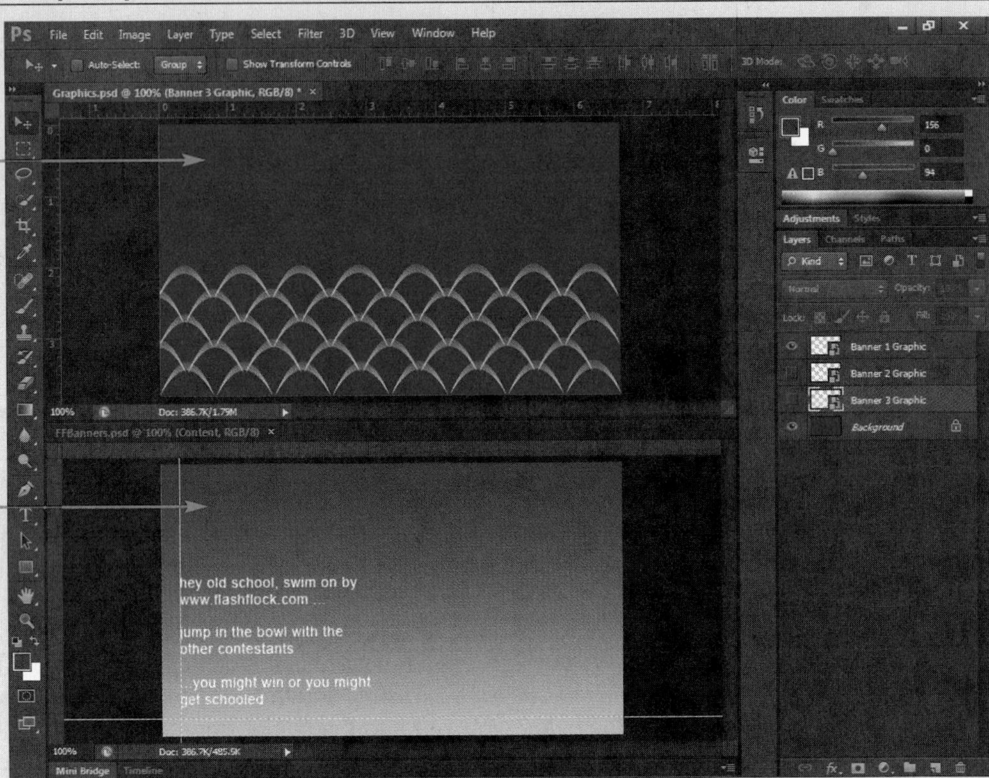

5. Select the **Graphics.psd** document, if necessary, and then drag the **Banner 1 Graphic** layer from the Layers panel to the FFBanners.psd Document window.

   A copy of the Banner 1 Graphic layer is added to the FFBanners.psd document. It appears at the top of the Layers panel for the FFBanners.psd document.
6. In the Tools panel, click the **Move Tool** button , and move the graphic in the FFBanners.psd Document window until it is centered at the bottom of the document (it should appear in essentially the same position as it does in the Graphics.psd document). See Figure 9-39.

Figure 9-39 Graphic in the new banner

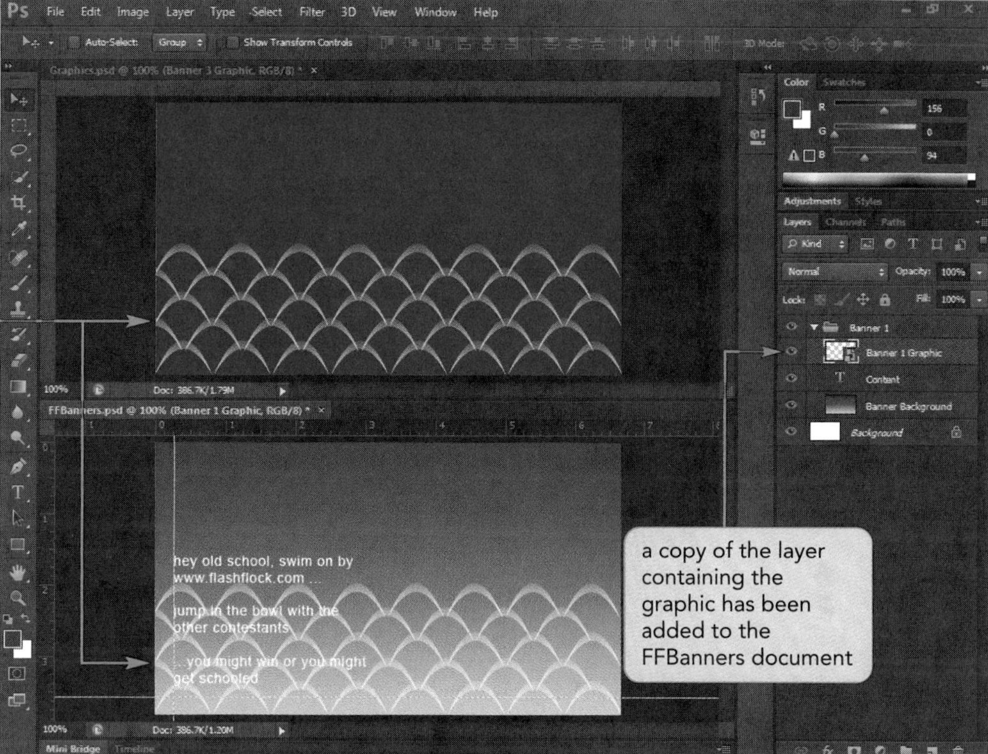
the graphic is positioned in the same place in both documents
a copy of the layer containing the graphic has been added to the FFBanners document
hey old school, swim on by
www.flashflock.com ...
jump in the bowl with the other contestants
...you might win or you might get schooled

7. In the Layers panel, reduce the opacity of the new layer to **40%** to ensure that the graphic does not compete with the text for the viewer's attention.

8. Save the FFBanners.psd document, and close the Graphics.psd document without saving it.

   Now you'll add the FlashFlock logo to the FFBanners document as a Smart Object.

9. In a Windows Explorer window, navigate to the Photoshop9\Tutorial folder, select the **FFLogo.psd** file, drag it over the FFBanners.psd Document window in Photoshop, and release the mouse button. Press the **Enter** key to place the object.

   The entire Photoshop file is placed as a Smart Object in the banner. See Figure 9-40.

Figure 9-40 FFLogo.psd document added to the banner as a Smart Object

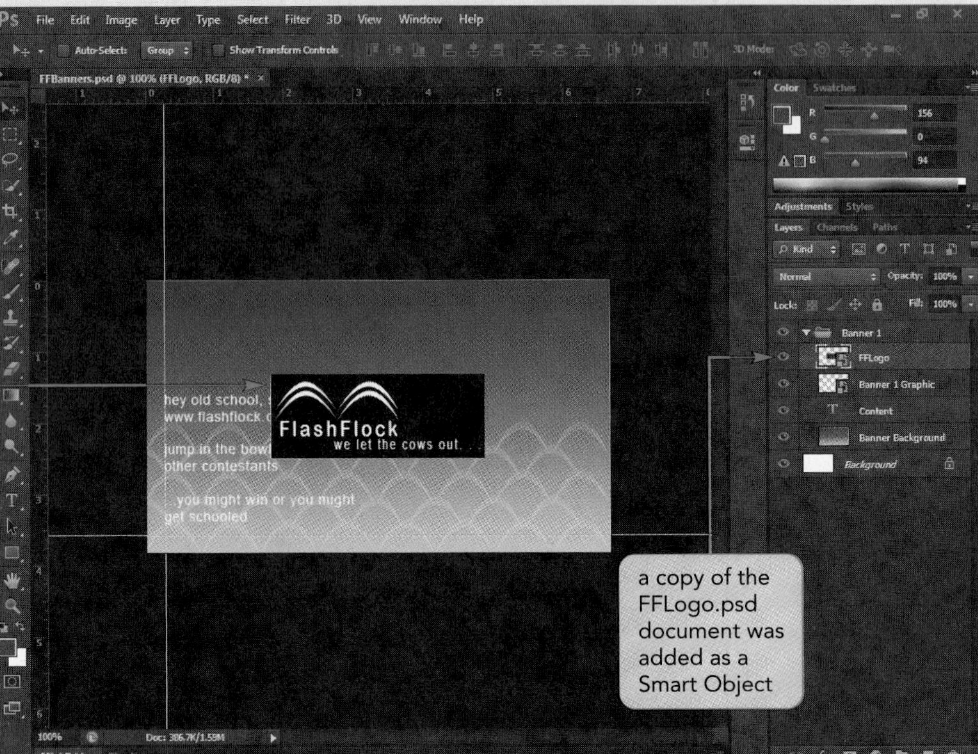
the graphic is placed in the document
a copy of the FFLogo.psd document was added as a Smart Object
FlashFlock
we let the cows out. . .
hey old school,
www.flashflock
jump in the bowl
other contestants
you might win or you might get schooled

10. In the Layers panel, double-click the **FFLogo** layer thumbnail to open the FFLogo.psd document in a new Document window.

    Trouble? If a dialog box appears with information regarding saving the file, click the OK button.

    Trouble? If a message about missing fonts appears, click the OK button.

11. In the Layers panel for the FFLogo.psd file, show the **Gaggle Your Tail Off** layer and hide the We Let The Cows Out layer and the Background layer. See Figure 9-41.

Figure 9-41 **FFLogo.psd document with changes**

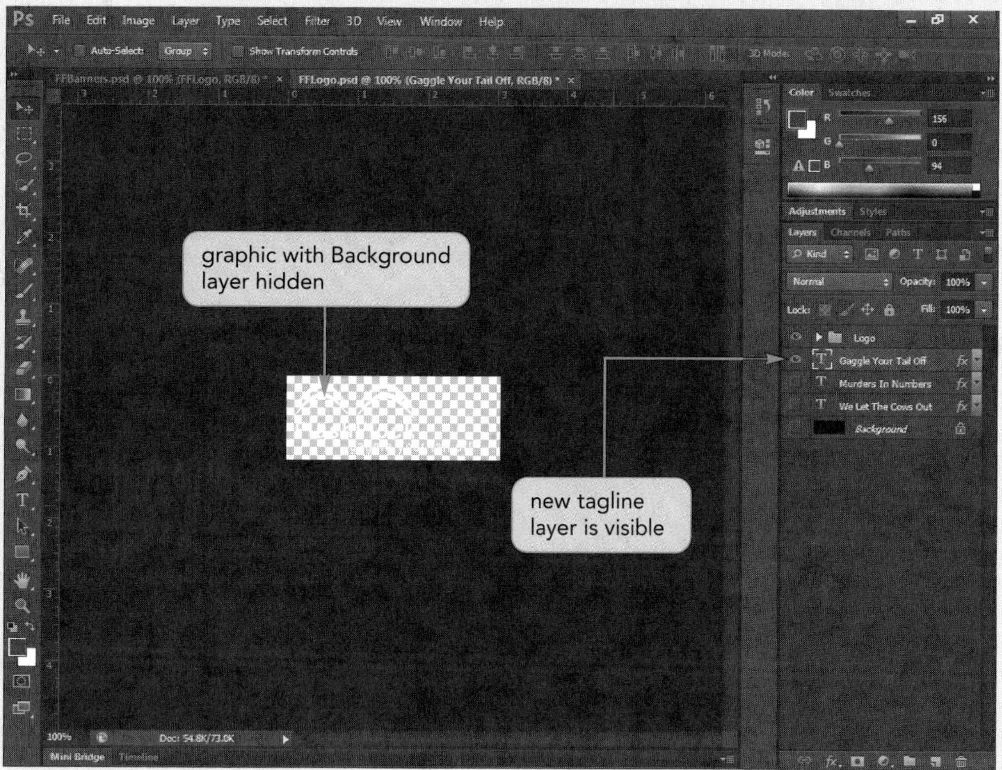

12. Save the FFLogo.psd file, and close it.

The Smart Object is now displayed in the FFBanners.psd document with the changes made; the tagline has changed, and the black background color is no longer visible.

13. In the FFBanners Document window, drag a horizontal guide ¼ inch from the top of the canvas, and then drag the logo so that the left tip of the wings are positioned against the left guide and the top of the wings are positioned against the top guide. See Figure 9-42.

Figure 9-42 **Logo positioned correctly in the composition**

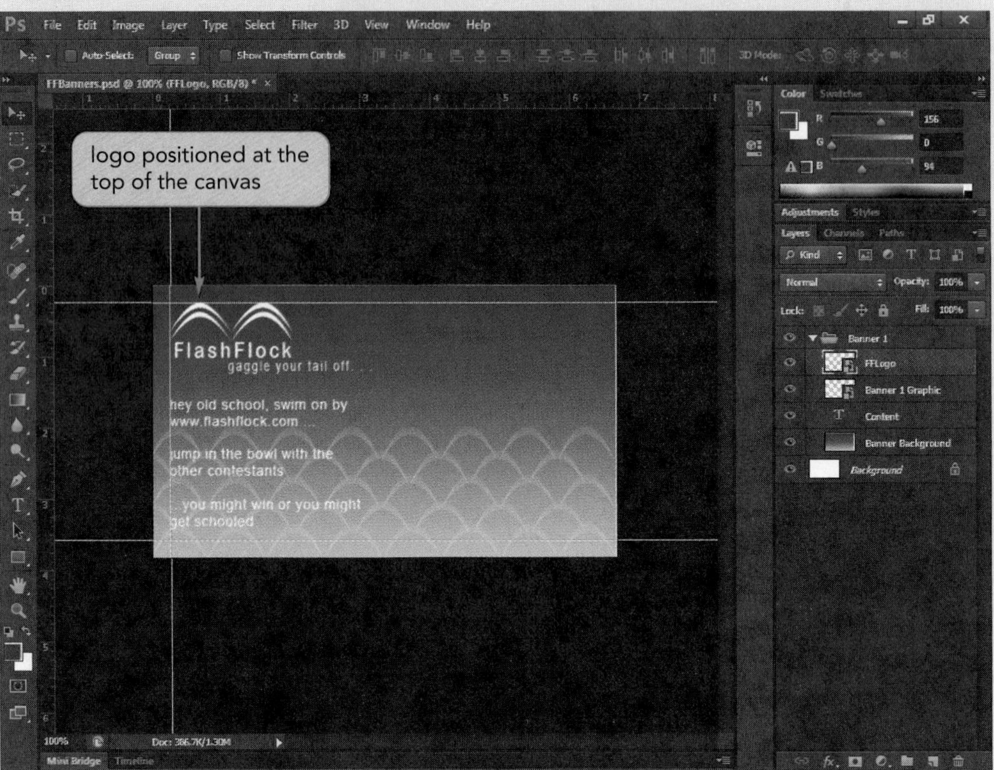

14. In the Layers panel, duplicate the Banner Background layer, name it Banner Background A, and drag it directly above the original, if necessary.
15. Double-click the **Banner Background A** thumbnail to open the Layer Style dialog box, and in the Styles list, click **Stroke**.
16. In the Stroke settings in the right side of the dialog box, type **3** in the Size box, select **Inside** from the Position list, and select **Normal** from the Blend Mode list. Set the opacity to **100%**, and the fill type to **Color**. Click the **Color** box, change the color to **white** (#ffffff), and press the **Enter** key.
17. In the Layer Style dialog box, click the **OK** button, and then save the document. See Figure 9-43.

Figure 9-43 **Banner with alternate background**

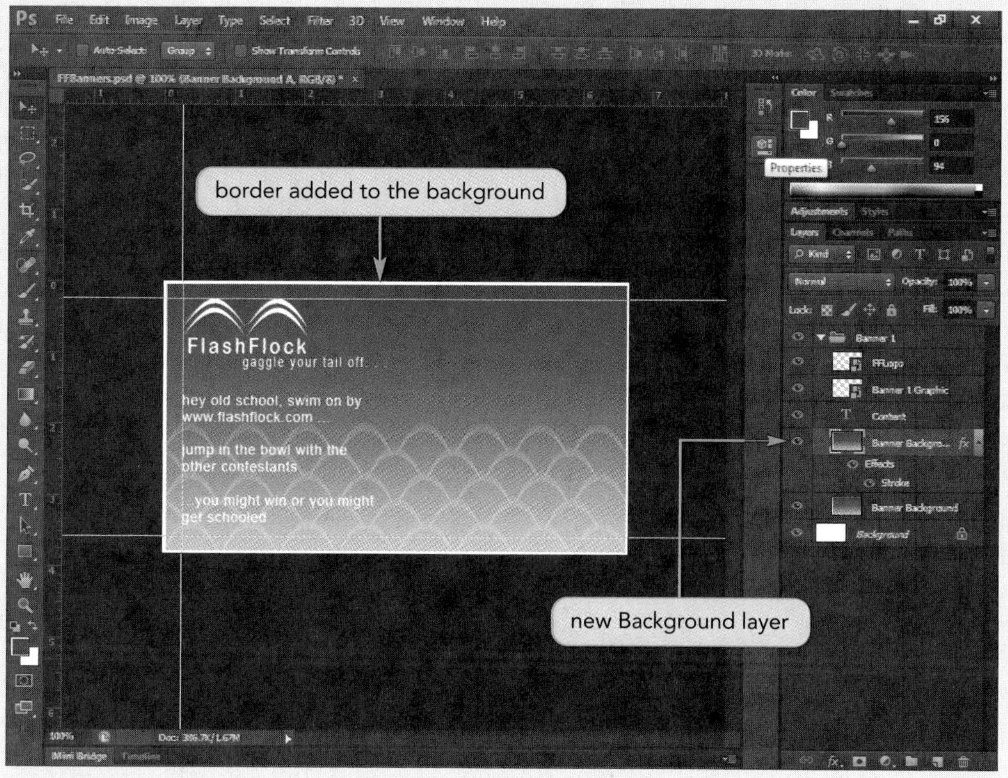

Now that the graphic elements have been added to the composition, you are ready to select your photographic style, retouch an image, and add it to your composition.

Selecting a Photographic Style

Photographic images are the final element that you add to a composition. As you have seen in previous tutorials, photographs can be blended or combined with other elements as part of a composition, or they can be placed in a composition as individual elements. When you adjusted and retouched photographs, you learned about image brightness, contrast, saturation, cropping, and exposure. All of those elements can be used to create a style for all of the photographs in a composition to give a unified, cohesive look to the project. Answering the following list of questions will help you to develop an intelligent photographic style for the project:

- What would you like to communicate with the photographs in the composition, and how can you accomplish those communication goals with the images you have?
- What looks will appeal to your target audience and reinforce your brand identity and project metaphor?
- Will you cut elements from the images, or will you use the entire image?
- How will images be cropped? Will they be cropped tightly, like product shots? How will you adjust and retouch your images? Will you process your images to create a distinct artificial look, possibly by oversaturating the color or overexposing the images? Or, will you use digital adjustments to enhance the natural look of the photos?
- Will images have borders?

Images are a very important part of the FlashFlock brand and identity because the Web site is devoted to photography. Although some of the animal flash mobs are artificially created using digital software, the images attempt to maintain the look of realistic professional nature photos. This is a major contributing factor to the underlying humor of the FlashFlock brand. Because of this unique circumstance, Rick and George have provided the final versions of all of the photographs you will use in the banner campaign. The photographs support your metaphor because they are depicting collisions of nature and the urban environment or urban concepts. Some of the images are even digital mashups of real photographic elements.

Jessica has already made some aesthetic decisions regarding how you will use the images in the banners. You'll add a border around all of the images to frame them and separate them from the background elements of the banners. The photographs will be the single largest element in the banners. This signifies their importance to the brand and identity. By positioning the photos to the right of the banner and making it the largest element, Jessica is reinforcing the campaign goals visually by using the viewer's natural tendency to first look at the upper-left portion of a composition and then to move right and then down (like the motion of reading). The viewer first sees the logo (which is fairly large in scale), then the photograph, and finally the text.

Because FlashFlock already has a specific photographic style, you will not need to create an alternate style for this project. You should use what you have learned from the decisions that Jessica, George, and Rick have made when you create projects in the future.

TIP

Remember to create a copy of your original file before you convert the color profile to ensure that you do not alter your original image.

Even though you do not need to adjust, resize, crop, or retouch the photographs, you should prepare them before you add them to your composition. When possible, you should add the images to your composition as Smart Objects to enable you to continue to edit the images at their original size. This is especially helpful if you have high-quality camera raw images because those files enable you to achieve better results than you can achieve by adjusting compressed images. Regardless of the file type of the photograph, it is a good idea to convert your images to the correct color model and the correct color profile (for file formats that support color profiles) before you add them to your composition. This will allow you to make any necessary color adjustments to the original image file before you add it to the composition and will enable you to achieve the best possible results with the final composition.

To convert the image and add it to your working document:

1. Open **Fish.jpg**, located in the Photoshop9\Tutorial folder, and save the image as **FishAdjust.jpg** in the same folder, using Maximum quality for compression.
2. On the menu bar, click **Edit**, and then click **Convert to Profile**.

   The Source Space Profile for this image is Adobe RGB (1998) D65 WP 2.2 Gamma. Although this is in the RGB color model, it does not use the color profile that you selected when planning the project, so you'll select the correct color profile and convert the document.
3. In the Convert to Profile dialog box, select **sRGB IEC61966-2.1** from the Destination Space Profile list, and click the **OK** button.

   In this case, the changes to the document are so slight that they might not be perceptible, but the change is necessary to maintain consistency with color profiles across all of the documents in your project.

   Next, you'll convert the layer to a Smart Object, and you'll add a copy as a Smart Object to a layer of the FFBanners.psd document.
4. On the menu bar, click **Window**, point to **Arrange**, and then click **2-up Horizontal** to display both images in the Document window. Click in the **FishAdjust.jpg** Document window to select it, if necessary.

5. In the Layers panel, right-click the **Background** layer of the FishAdjust.jpg document, and click **Convert to Smart Object** on the context menu. In the Layers panel, rename the layer **Fish**. See Figure 9-44.

Figure 9-44 Color Profile converted with layer converted to a Smart Object

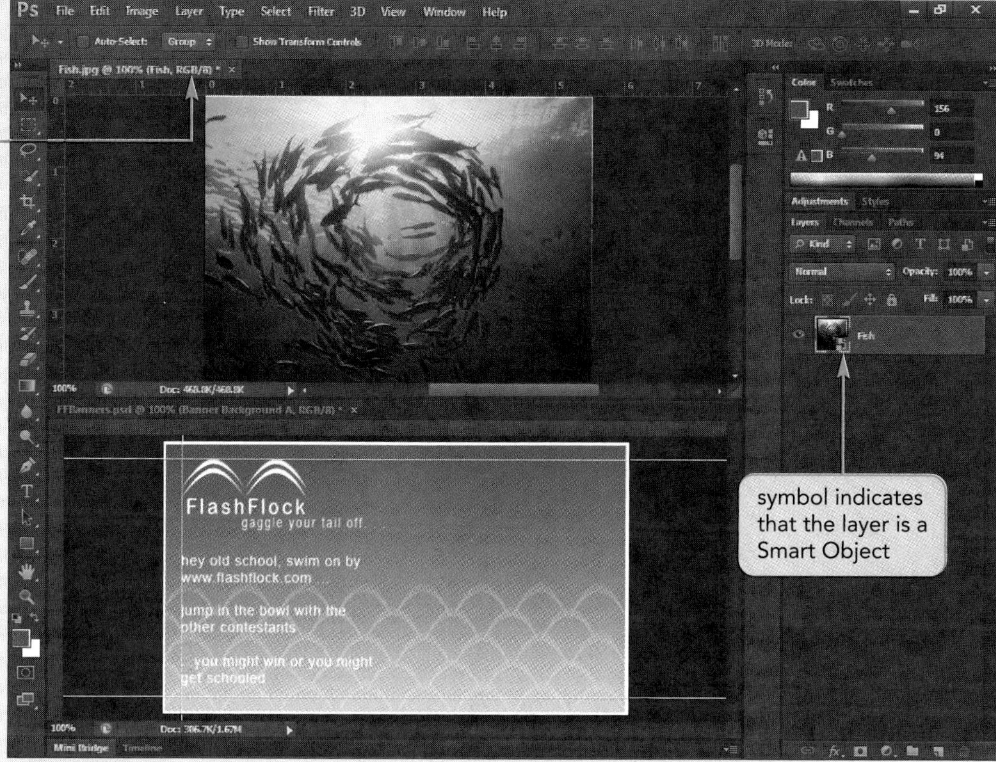

TIP

Documents containing Smart Objects must be saved as Photoshop documents.

6. Save the FishAdjust.jpg document as **FishAdjust.psd** in the Photoshop9\Tutorial folder.
7. In the Layers panel, click the **Fish** layer, and drag it over the FFBanners.psd document in the Document window. Release the mouse button to add the image to the document as a Smart Object, and then close the FishAdjust.psd file. See Figure 9-45.

Figure 9-45 Fish layer added to the composition as a Smart Object

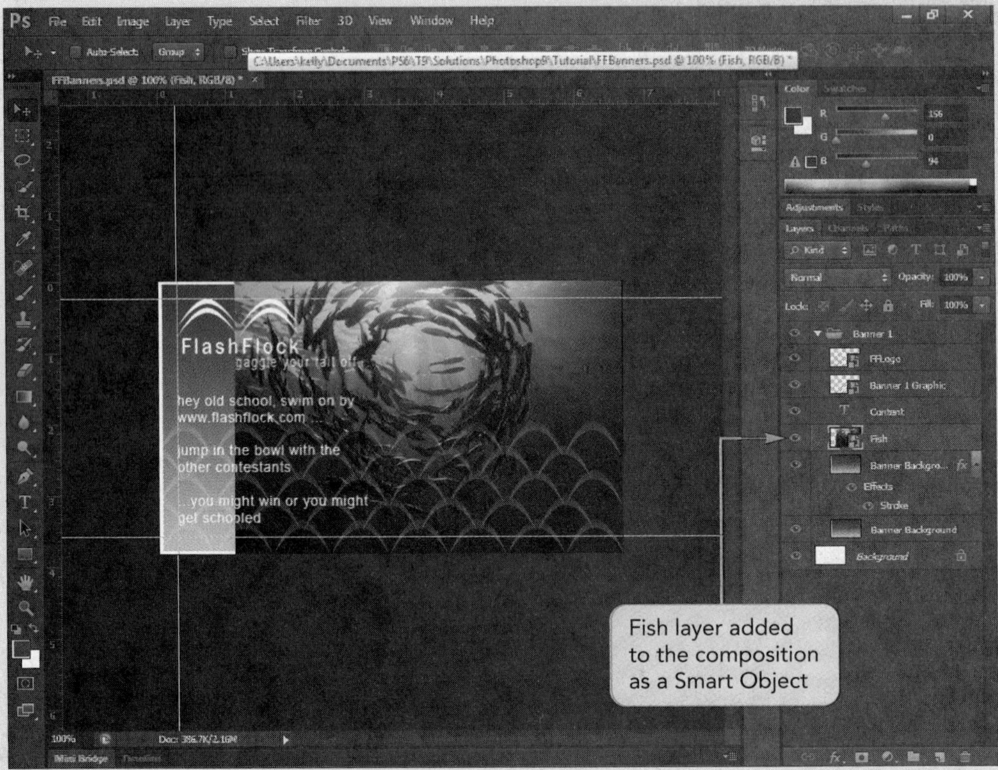

8. In the Layers panel, drag the Fish layer above the Banner 1 Graphic layer, if necessary, and then drag a vertical guide ¼ inch from the right border of the canvas.
9. Place the mouse pointer inside the image and drag the image down and to the left until the top border of the image is aligned to the top guide and the right border of the image is aligned to the right guide.
10. Press the **Ctrl+T** keys to activate Free Transform so that you can adjust the size of the image. See Figure 9-46.

Figure 9-46 Fish layer selected with Free Transform

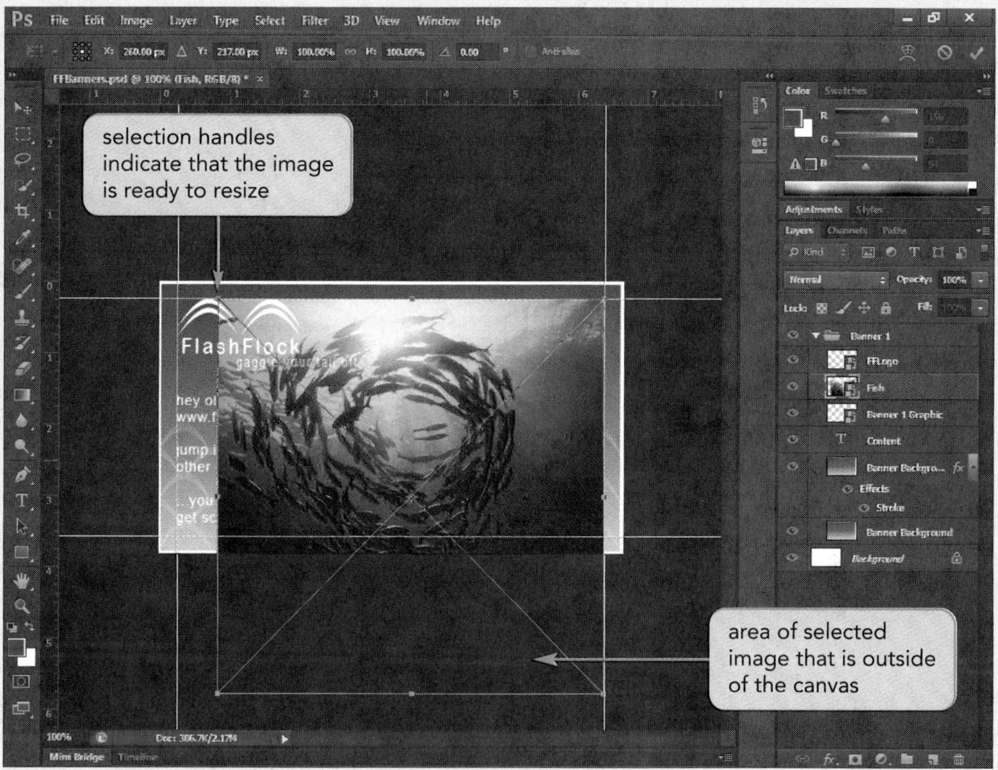
selection handles indicate that the image is ready to resize
area of selected image that is outside of the canvas

11. Press and hold the **Shift** key while dragging the lower-left selection handle until the image is resized so that the bottom border of the image is at the bottom guide. Press the **Enter** key to accept the changes. Notice that the logo tagline text overlaps the image slightly. See Figure 9-47.

Figure 9-47 **Resized image**

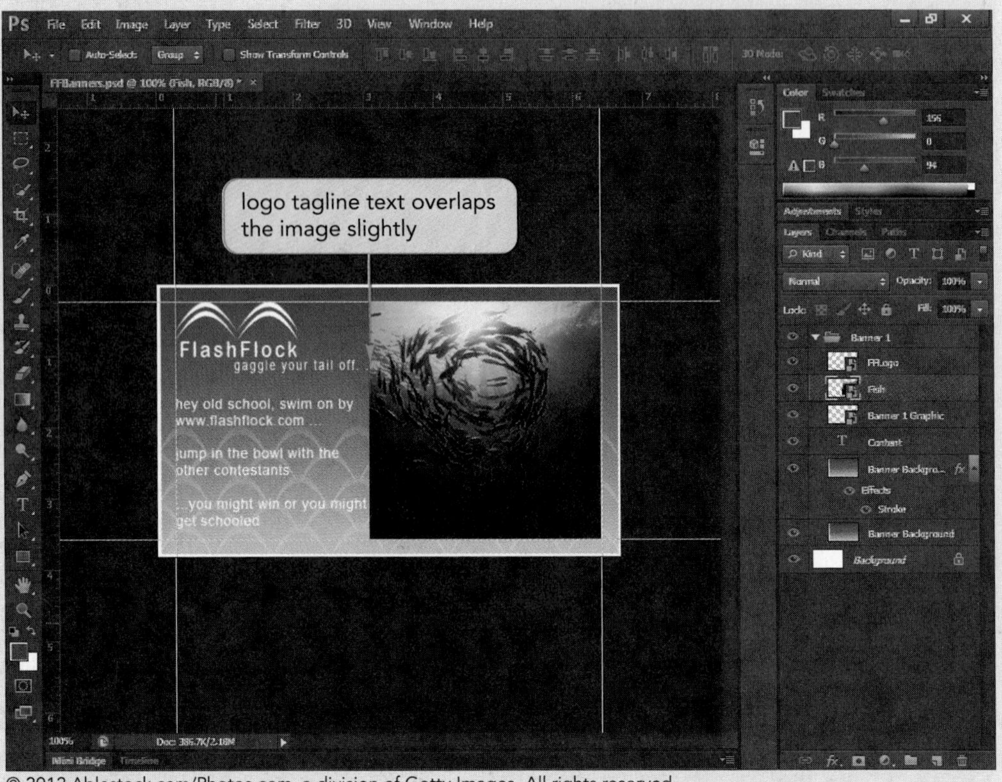

Now that all of the elements are in the composition, you can make your final adjustments and corrections. You'll add a border around the image, and you'll adjust elements in the composition so the image and tagline text do not overlap. You could accomplish this by shrinking the size of the logo or by shrinking the size of the image. Because your top goals for the campaign involve brand and identity recognition, you'll shrink the image and not the logo. Then, you'll reposition the resized image so it is centered between the guides. Finally, you'll hide the guides and examine your completed composition.

To make final adjustments:

1. In the Layers panel, double-click the **Fish** layer to open the Layer Style dialog box. In the Styles list, click **Stroke**, and use the following settings: Size: **3**, Position: **Inside**, Blend Mode: **Normal**, Opacity: **100%**, and Fill Type: **Color**. Double-click the **Color** box, and change the color to **white** (#ffffff). Click the **OK** button to close the Select stroke color dialog box, and then click the **OK** button to close the Layer Style dialog box.
2. Press the **Ctrl+T** keys, and then press and hold the **Shift** key while dragging the upper-left selection handle down until there is approximately ⅛ inch of space between the last period in the tagline and the edge of the image. Press the **Enter** key to accept the transformation.
3. Move the image until it is equal distance between the top and bottom guides. Press the **Ctrl+;** keys to hide the guides. See Figure 9-48.

Figure 9-48 Completed Banner 1

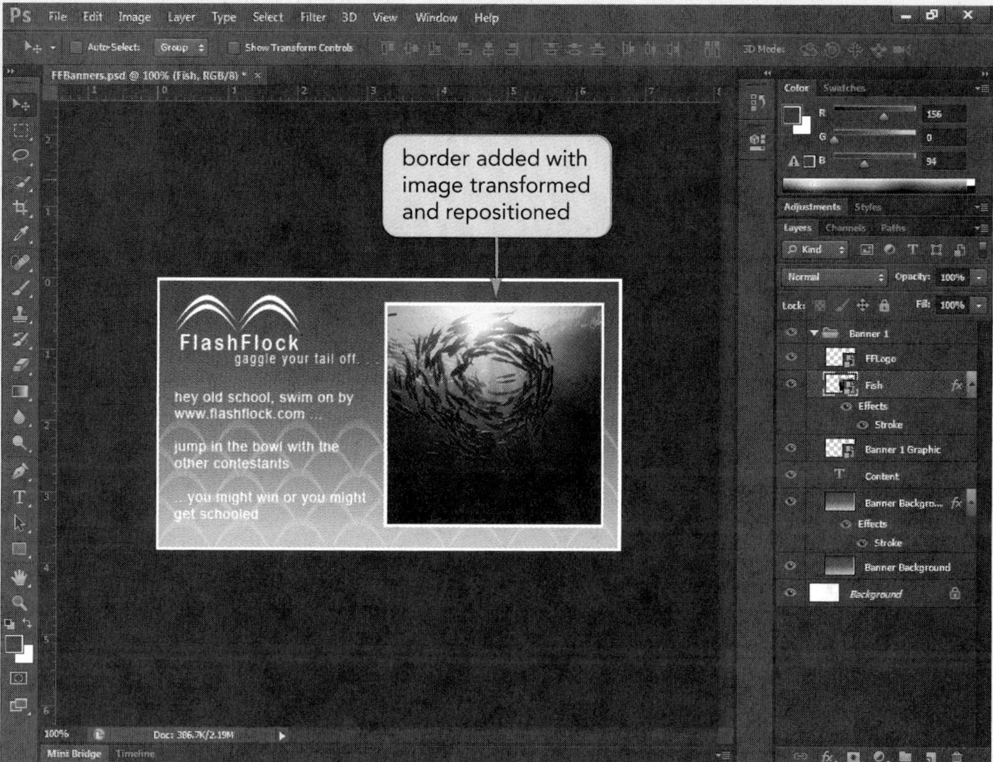

4. Save the FFBanners.psd file, close it, and then exit Photoshop.

Creating Output Files and Wrapping Up

You have completed your first composition, but you have not finished your work on the campaign. Once you have presented the comps to the client and you have made any necessary changes based on that review, the client will need to approve the project. At this point, you can create all of the output files you will need. You can look back at your plan to see the exact size, resolution, color model, color profile, and file formats required for your output files. When all of the files have been created, you will provide them to the client or to the person who was specified in the plans, such as the printer. Then, you should gather all project working files from the members of your team into one folder. Make sure that everything is labeled in a way that will make sense in the future, and then you can archive the project. Every company has its own way of archiving files from projects that are no longer active. Follow your company's guidelines to ensure that anyone who needs these files in the future can locate and understand them.

Jessica plans to present both versions of Banner 1 to George and Rick. Once they approve the first banner, you'll create two additional banners for the campaign. Because the campaign is still in progress, you will not create output files or archive your working files.

PROSKILLS

Teamwork: Broadening Your Understanding to Strengthen Your Team

It is a good idea to gain a general understanding of all the components involved in completing a successful project. No matter what your role is, understanding the project as a whole and understanding what is required of your teammates makes you better equipped to do your job, and makes you a more valuable member of the team.

Employers look for people who can understand the big picture and can contribute to the project in ways that may move beyond the scope of their current position. For example, if you design projects that will be displayed on the Web, it is a good idea to gain a basic understanding of HTML, even if you are not a programmer. Graphic designers benefit from this knowledge because they are better able to create useful Web site and banner ad designs when they understand the breadth and limits of HTML code. Project managers are better able to facilitate successful projects when they understand the various steps involved in creating a graphic design and the time it takes to complete each activity. The possibilities are endless; the more you know, the more valuable you become to the team.

REVIEW

Session 9.2 Quick Check

1. What is design?
2. What is the purpose of selecting a concept and metaphor?
3. Name two types of balance.
4. ______________ is the empty space in the canvas.
5. ______________ is the art and technique of type arrangement, design, and modification.
6. ______________ colors are pleasing to look at, creating a sense of balance and engagement.

Practice the skills you learned in the tutorial using the same case scenario.

PRACTICE

Review Assignments

Data Files needed for the Review Assignments: FFBanners.psd, BannerText2.rtf, Graphics.psd, Penguins.jpg

George and Rick have signed off on Banner 1, and they are excited to see the other banners for the campaign. They selected the version that has the white border. You'll create an additional banner for the campaign using all of the aesthetic guidelines Jessica already set. Jessica is also considering making some additional materials to go with this banner, and she would like you to use the Kuler panel to select a monochromatic color palette using the background color from the new banner as the Base Color. Complete the following steps:

1. Start Photoshop while pressing the Ctrl+Alt+Shift keys, and click Yes to delete the Settings File when prompted. Reset Photoshop to the default Essentials workspace layout, and then reset all tools. Collapse the Adjustments panel group.
2. Navigate to the Photoshop9\Tutorial folder included with your Data Files, and open **FFBanners.psd**, which is the file in which you created Banner1. Save the document in the Photoshop9\Review folder as **FFBanners2.psd**.
3. Unhide the guides that you previously added to the file. (*Hint*: To view guides, press the Ctrl+; keys.) Drag an additional horizontal guide to the top of the photograph, drag another to the bottom edge of the photograph, drag a third to the top of the text, and then drag a fourth to the top of the graphic element in the background. You will now have a total of six horizontal guides and two vertical guides, which will enable you to place the objects in the same positions in the other banners.
4. Create a new layer group, drag it above the Banner 1 folder, and name it **Banner 2**. Drag the FFLogo layer above the Banner 2 group because it will be used in both banners. Hide the Banner 1 group.
5. Create a layer in the Banner 2 group and name it **Banner Background B**; use the color picker to set the foreground color to #b29a00 and to set the background color to #ffffff, if necessary.
6. Select the Gradient tool, with the following settings: Gradient: Foreground to Background, Linear Gradient, Mode: Normal, and Opacity: 100%. Check Dither and Transparency, and uncheck Reverse, if necessary. Drag the mouse straight down the canvas to create the gradient banner background. (*Hint*: The logo and tagline will be visible once the background has been created.)
7. Copy the layer style from the Banner Background A layer in the Banner 1 group, and paste it on to the Banner Background B layer in the Banner 2 group.
8. Double-click the thumbnail image in the FFLogo layer, and then click the OK button in any dialog boxes that appear to open up the original logo Smart Object file.
9. Show the Murders In Numbers layer to make it visible, and hide the Gaggle Your Tail Off layer. Save and close the FFlogo.psd document, and view the updated logo in the FFBanners2 file.
10. Duplicate the text layer in the Banner 1 group using the default layer name, and drag the copied layer above the Banner Background B layer in the Banner 2 group. Double-click the thumbnail image for the copied layer to select the text in the Document window, and then delete the text. (Copying the Banner 1 layer ensures that the text area in Banner 2 is the exact same size as the text area in Banner 1; you'll add the new text in the next step.)
11. Open **BannerText2.rtf**, located in the Photoshop9\Review folder, and copy the text in the Content section for Banner 2. Paste the text into the text box in the Photoshop window, and add a line break between each chunk. If any word breaks

over two lines and is hyphenated, press the Enter key to create a line break and move the word to the next line. Close the BannerText2.rtf file.

12. Open **Graphics.psd**, located in the Photoshop9\Review folder. Arrange the Document windows using the 2-up Horizontal option, and drag the Banner 2 Graphic layer into the FFBanners2.psd file. Then, in the Layers panel for the FFBanners2.psd file, drag the Banner 2 Graphic layer into the Banner 2 group, above the Banner Background B layer, if necessary.
13. Use the Move tool to position the graphic using the guides, so it appears in the same position as it did in the Graphics document. Close the Graphics.psd document, and set the Banner 2 Graphic layer to display at 60% opacity. (You do not need to check the color profile because you did that when you created Banner 1.)
14. Open **Penguins.jpg**, located in the Photoshop9\Review folder, and convert the color profile to sRGB IEC61966-2.1, if necessary. Then, convert the layer to a Smart Object, and name it **Penguins**. Save the file as **Penguins.psd** in the same folder.
15. Arrange the Document windows using the 2-up Horizontal, drag the Penguins layer into the FFBanners.psd document, and then close the Penguins.psd document. Move the Penguins layer above the Banner 2 Graphic layer, if necessary.
16. Transform the image, and shrink it to the correct dimensions. (*Hint*: Remember to hold down the Shift key while you move the selection handle to keep the same image proportions while you shrink it.)
17. Copy the layer style from the Fish layer in the Banner 1 group, and paste the layer style in the Penguins layer.
18. Save the FFBanners2.psd document, and close it.
19. Open the Kuler panel to the Create tab. Select the Base Color swatch, type **b29a00** into the Hex text box, and then select Monochromatic from the Select Rule list.
20. Adjust the colors in the color palette by adjusting the position of the color circles on the color wheel and by adjusting the Control brightness by increasing or decreasing black slider until you have a color palette with which you are satisfied.
21. Save the theme as **FF Additional**.
22. Submit the results of the preceding steps to your instructor either in printed or electronic form, as requested.

Use your skills to plan a design project for an indie record label.

APPLY

Case Problem 1

Data Files needed for this Case Problem: Vision.rtf, CatLogo.gif, WebSite.tif

Catalyst Records Catalyst Records is an indie record label founded in 2000 by Sara Lynn. Catalyst is based in Washington, D.C., and most of the bands affiliated with the label originated as part of the underground D.C. music scene, which centers around low-fi dub music (a genre of music that uses low-fidelity recording equipment to achieve interesting sounds) and post punk discord. Since the label created a Web site, some of its bands have developed a national following. Sara believes that this success is due in part to exposure from the Catalyst Web site. She would like to take this momentum to the next level by creating a banner ad that will be displayed on other sites that cater to the indie music scene. She has asked your company to create the banner, and you have been selected as the project manager. Your first task is to research and plan the project. Once your planning and research are complete, you will meet with Sara to get her input before you begin the design phase of the project. Complete the following steps:

1. Open **Vision.rtf**, located in the Photoshop9\Case1 folder provided with your Data Files, and read the document to gain insight into Sara's vision for the project.
2. Open WordPad, create a new document, and save the document as **CatPlan.rtf** in the Photoshop9\Case1 folder.

3. In the CatPlan document, create a list of 10 goals for the project, in order of importance. Write the goals in the active voice. Combine goals where possible, and narrow your list to five goals for the ad.
4. Use what you have learned about Catalyst from Sara's Vision.rtf document, as well as the goals you wrote, to write a statement of purpose summarizing what you would like to accomplish with the ad.
5. Identify your target audience, and develop a viewer profile by answering the list of questions from Figure 9-3 in the tutorial. Write each question followed by your answer.
6. Use a search engine to locate statistics and additional information about Catalyst's target audience and its competitors. Search for the terms *low-fi music* and *dub music*. For each term, record at least two statistics or insights you gather from the search results. Include the URL next to each statistic so you can locate the information again in the future. Also, find at least two statistics or findings about Catalyst's target audience, aesthetics that may appeal to the target audience, and Catalyst's competitors.
7. Start Photoshop while pressing the Ctrl+Alt+Shift keys, and click Yes to delete the Settings File when prompted. Reset Photoshop to the default Essentials workspace layout, and then reset all tools.
8. Open **CatLogo.gif**, located in the Photoshop9\Case1 folder. Examine the logo, and then close it.
9. Open **WebSite.tif**, located in the Photoshop9\Case1 folder. Examine the file, and then close it.
10. Write a few sentences about Catalyst's branding and identity, and indicate how you will incorporate the current aesthetic into the banner ad design.
11. Use a search engine to determine the standard size for horizontal banner ads, and then determine the exact height, width, resolution, color space, and file format that you will use for your final output files. Document those specifications in the CatPlan document.
12. Save your work, and exit Photoshop, if necessary.
13. Submit the results of the preceding steps to your instructor either in printed or electronic form, as requested.

Using Figure 9-49 as a guide, create a mailer for a boutique.

CREATE

Case Problem 2

Data Files needed for this Case Problem: Planning.rtf, Mailer1Image.jpg, Mailer.psd, ElGalLogo.ai

El Gallinero El Gallinero is a boutique located in the quaint harbor town of Portland, Maine. The shop imports and sells a stunning array of Mexican art and handcrafts. The owner, Tika, has long been known as the *Chicken Goddess*, a name she got when she started raising specialty breed show chickens. "I have a love of all things Mexican and all things chicken, so calling the store El Gallinero, which means *the roost*, was a natural choice." Tika would like you to create a postcard-sized mailer that she can print out on her color laser printer and mail as part of her store marketing campaign. She has worked with a consultant who planned the project extensively and has provided all of the information that you will need to design and create the mailer. See Figure 9-49 for an example of a possible mailer design.

Figure 9-49 El Gallinero mailer

sisqopote /Shutterstock.com

Complete the following steps:

1. Open **Planning.rtf**, located in the Photoshop9\Case2 folder provided with your Data Files. Read the document and visit the Web sites listed in the Research – Competitors section to familiarize yourself with the planning and research for the project.
2. Start Photoshop while pressing the Ctrl+Alt+Shift keys, and click Yes to delete the Settings File when prompted. Reset Photoshop to the default Essentials workspace layout, and then reset all tools.
3. Open **Mailer1Image.jpg**, located in the Photoshop9\Case2 folder to see the image that Tika has provided for you to use in the mailer.
4. Open **Mailer.psd**, located in the Photoshop9\Case2 folder, and save it as **ElMailer1.psd** in the same folder. Hide the guides, examine the Background layer, and then show the guides. (*Hint*: The term *bleed* is a printing term that defines the area outside of the borders of the final composition, into which the background extends. Standard bleed is ¼ inch around each edge. This area provides the printer with a small amount of space to move around paper and account for slight deviations when cutting print materials. Cuts are generally made at the inside border of the bleed area, and the area just inside the bleed is usually reserved for noncrucial print elements, such as backgrounds. Print is usually not allowed in the outside ¼ inch bordering the bleed to ensure that slight deviations in cutting do not affect important design components.)
5. Arrange the Documents windows using the 2-up Horizontal option so you can view the image and the mailer document while you are making aesthetic decisions for the composition.
6. EXPLORE Open a Windows Explorer window, and navigate to the **ElGalLogo.ai** file located in the Photoshop9\Case2 folder. Drag the ElGalLogo.ai file over the ElMailer1.psd document in the Photoshop Document window. Click the OK button in the Place PDF dialog box, and press the Enter key to insert the logo as a Smart Object in the ElMailer1 document.
7. Examine the El Gallinero logo to help you settle on a look and feel for the mailer.
8. Create a concept and metaphor for the mailer, and then look up the term *bleed* in a search engine if you need additional insight on how this should be laid out.

9. Create a layout for the mailer, and create a wireframe of the layout.
10. Open the Create tab of the Kuler panel, and create a color theme for the mailer. Save the theme as **Mailer**. Add the theme to your Swatches panel, and then close the Kuler panel. (*Hint*: Consider the colors in the logo and image when creating your theme. You can enter the hexadecimal code for a color from the image or logo as the Base Color to get started.)
11. Add colors to the background and anywhere else that they are needed. (*Hint*: Once you have added a background, you can use the guides to show you where the bleed area is and where it is safe to place text.)
12. Develop a graphic style, and then create graphic elements and add them to your composition; transform and adjust the logo graphic as necessary so it works in your composition.
13. Add layer styles, adjustment layers, and masks as needed to create the look you have envisioned.
14. Add the Mailer1Image.jpg image to your composition and adjust it as necessary to make it work with your layout and design.
15. Add the copy text from the Planning document to the composition, and then adjust the color and style of the text to fit your composition.
16. Review your composition, and make any necessary adjustments.
17. Save your image, close all open files, and exit Photoshop.
18. Submit the results of the preceding steps to your instructor either in printed or electronic form, as requested.

Use your skills to plan a project for a small pub.

APPLY

Case Problem 3

Data Files needed for this Case Problem: Vision.rtf, Promo1.png, Promo2.png, LogoBlack.png, LogoWhite.png

The Rookery The Rookery is a small, English-style pub in Nashville, Tennessee, that specializes in traditional fish and chips. The owner, Brian Botan, has decided to run a special on the pub's famous fish and chips, and he would like your company to create the insert that he can place in the menu. If this first promotion works well, Brian would like your company to provide a new insert once a month. You have been selected to head the project, and your first job is to read Brian's vision and to create a plan, which you will present to Brian. Complete the following steps:

1. Open **Vision.rtf**, located in the Photoshop9\Case3 folder provided with your Data Files, and read the document to gain insight into what Brian would like to accomplish with the project.
2. Start Photoshop while pressing the Ctrl+Alt+Shift keys, and click Yes to delete the Settings File when prompted. Reset Photoshop to the default Essentials workspace layout, and then reset all tools.
3. Open the following images from the Photoshop9\Case3 folder: **Promo1.png**, **Promo2.png**, **LogoBlack.png**, and **LogoWhite.png**. Examine the files to get an idea of the Rookery's style, and then close the files and exit Photoshop.
4. Open WordPad, create a new document, and save the document in the Photoshop9\Case3 folder as **Plan.rtf**.
5. In the Plan document, create a list of 10 goals for the insert, and put them in order of importance. Combine goals where possible, make sure they are in active voice, and narrow your final list to five goals for the insert.
6. Use the goals you wrote and what you have learned about the Rookery from Brian's Vision document to write a statement of purpose summarizing what you would like to accomplish with the insert.

7. Identify your target audience and develop a viewer profile by answering the list of questions from Figure 9-3 in the tutorial. Write each question followed by your answer.
8. Use a search engine to locate statistics and additional information about your target audience, their interests, and your competitors. Search for the following terms: *English pubs*, *pub food*, and *English pub advertisements* (try searching for images on this one). Write down at least two statistics or findings about each term. Include the URL by each statistic, so you can locate the information again in the future. Also, find at least two statistics or findings about your target audience, about aesthetics that may appeal to them, and about the Rookery's competitors.
9. Write a few sentences about the Rookery's branding and identity and how you will incorporate the current aesthetic into the insert design, and save your work.
10. Submit the results of the preceding steps to your instructor either in printed or electronic form, as requested.

Using Figure 9-50 as a guide, create something that expresses your point of view.

CREATE

Case Problem 4

Data Files needed for this Case Problem: Specs.rtf, Logos.psd

Montana Science and History Museum The Montana Museum of Science and History is a medium-sized museum in Billings, Montana, run by director Andy Hall. Andy has decided that to stay relevant and to engage a contemporary adult audience, the museum needs to embrace current technologies and social media. In an effort to meet this goal, Andy has asked your firm to develop an iPad application that will enable patrons to use technology to explore and engage with the artifacts and exhibits in a different way. He hopes this will forge new frontiers in the area of inquiry-based learning. You are leading the team that will design the interface for the application. You will follow the specs provided by the programming team, and you'll manage the interface design project from start to finish. Before you get started, look at a sample interface in Figure 9-50.

Figure 9-50 iPad interface for Montana Museum of Science and History

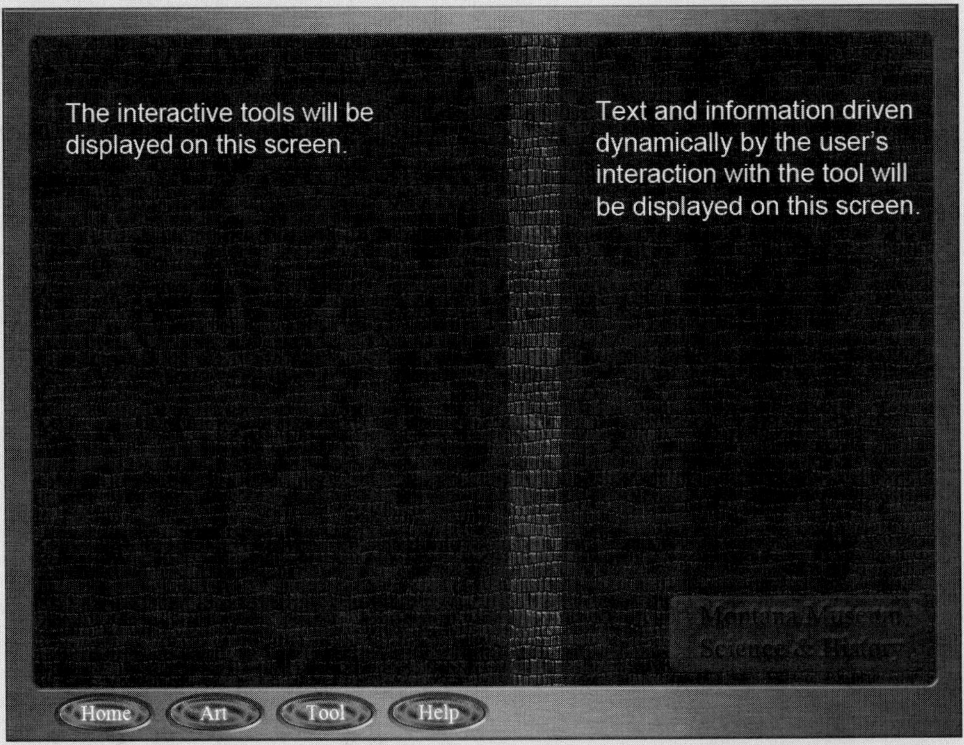

Complete the following steps:

1. Start Photoshop while pressing the Ctrl+Alt+Shift keys, and click Yes to delete the Settings File when prompted. Reset Photoshop to the default Essentials workspace layout, and then reset all tools.
2. Open **Specs.rtf**, located in the Photoshop9\Case4 folder provided with your Data Files, and read Andy's vision statement and the programming team's specifications and requirements for the interface project.
3. Open WordPad, create a new document, and save the document in the Photoshop9\Case4 folder as **PadPlan.rtf**.
4. Create a list of potential goals for the project, prioritize the list, and combine goals when possible. Narrow the list to five goals, and then write a statement of purpose for the project.
5. Based on what you have been told, identify the target audience and create a viewer profile.
6. Use a search engine to research audience interests and find out what the museum's competitors are doing. Provide three insights about your audience and three insights about the competition. Include URLs that support your findings.
7. In Photoshop, open **Logos.psd**, located in the Photoshop9\Case4 folder, to view two versions of the museum's logo (on two different layers) to gain insight into the museum's current branding and identity.
8. Based on your research and insights, create a concept and metaphor for the project and add them to your PadPlan document.
9. Use Photoshop to create a wireframe for the composition, and save the file in the Phtoshop9\Case4 folder as **Wireframe.psd**. (Use the information in the Specs document to determine the document size, color model, and resolution and to see a list of the components that the interface must include, as well as applicable dimensions.)
10. In the PadPlan document, write a short paragraph explaining how your layout supports your metaphor and project goals. Also, explain how your layout is balanced and how you use white space in the composition.
11. Use the Kuler panel to create a color theme for the project. Save your theme as **Museum iPad**, and add the theme to the Swatches panel. Answer the questions from the "Creating a Graphic Style" section of the tutorial. Select a graphic style, and then write a short paragraph in your PadPlan document explaining your style choice. Save the PadPlan document, and close the file.
12. Create a new Photoshop document using the information in the Specs document regarding size, resolution, and so forth. Save the document as **IPadInterface.psd** in the Photoshop9\Case4 folder.
13. Create each of the following graphic elements on its own layer, and name the layer with the element name. Or, if your style dictates that you use multiple layers for an element, create a layer group with the element name and place all of the layers for the element in the file group. Elements should include the following:
    - Background and border (You can create the border as one object, or you can create each side of the border on its own layer.)
    - Help button
    - Tool button
    - Art button
    - Home button
    - Screen – Right
    - Screen – Left

    Remember that each element should have the style that you selected and explained above.

14. Add the museum's logo to the composition. You can use one of the versions included in the Logos.psd file, or you can create a new version of the logo that will work with your design.
15. Using the font, color, and size that you will use for the general body text in the project, add the following text on the left screen: **The interactive tools will be displayed on this screen.** On the right screen, add the following text: **Text and information driven dynamically by the user's interaction with the tool will be displayed on this screen.** (Adding text will help the client identify the various components, and it will provide an example of what text will look like in the project.)
16. Examine what you have created and adjust elements as needed to create a cohesive, harmonious composition that reinforces goals, metaphor, organization branding, and identity and that will appeal to the target audience.
17. Save the file, and exit Photoshop.
18. Submit the results of the preceding steps to your instructor either in printed or electronic form, as requested.

ENDING DATA FILES

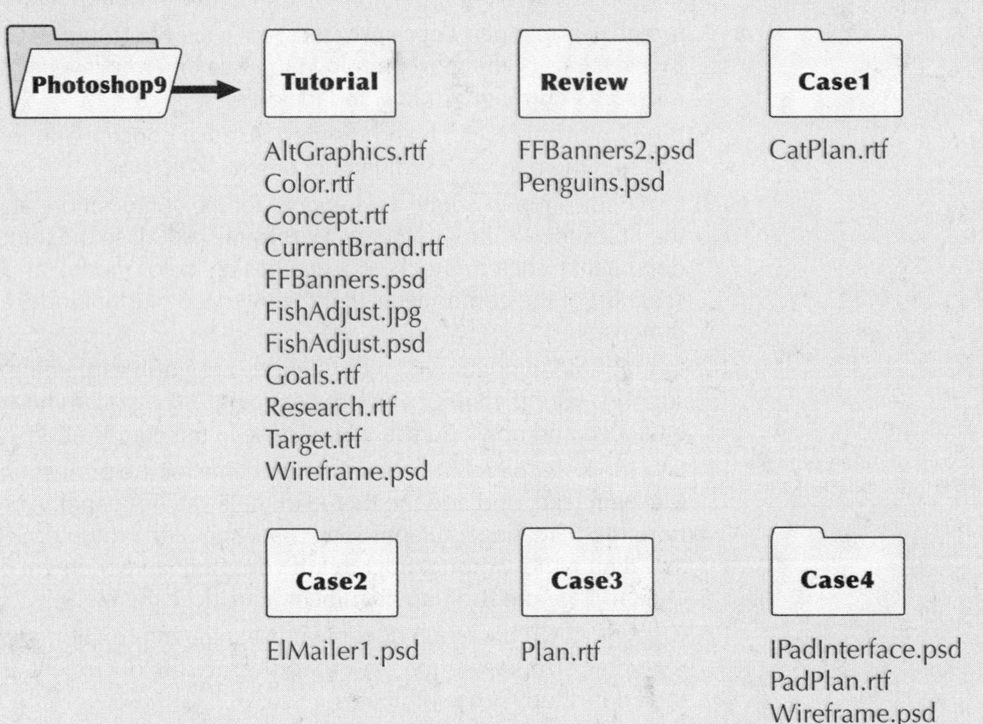

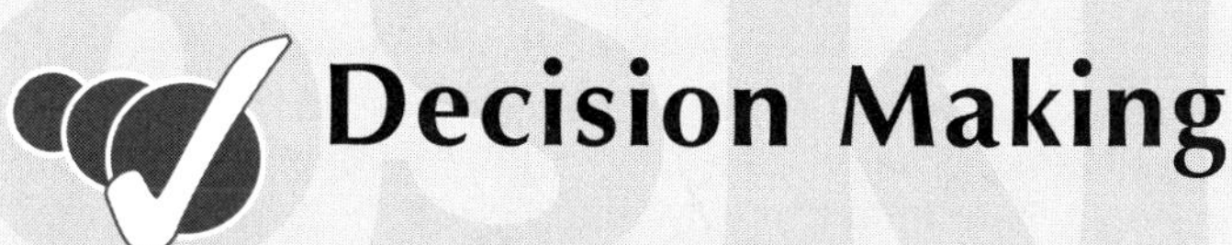

Decision Making

Making Design Decisions

Decision making is the process of choosing the best option among possible alternative courses of action. Decision making is a crucial skill because business people at all organizational levels must make decisions. Understanding the decision-making process will enable you to make better decisions and will give you greater confidence in implementing your decisions.

Typically, when you make a decision, you should complete the following steps:

1. Gather relevant information.
2. Make predictions about factors outside of your control.
3. Select the best alternative.
4. Prepare an action plan to implement your decision.
5. Take action and monitor results.
6. Evaluate the consequences of your decision, and take corrective action, if needed.

Complex decisions—especially those that affect other people and those that could have a significant monetary impact—should be made in a systematic way, following the above steps. This will increase the chances that the decision you make will be the right one. Less complex decisions may require only some of the steps.

Gather Relevant Information and Make Predictions

In order to effectively evaluate a potential course of action, you need to gather information and data. The relevant information may include quantitative factors, such as the required resolution for a Web banner ad, and qualitative factors, such as the concept and metaphor upon which a design decision must be based. You should also make predictions about relevant factors outside of your immediate control, such as how the target audience might respond to a particular color scheme or layout.

Select the Best Alternative

After gathering information and making predictions about outside factors, selecting the best alternative may require asking additional questions, such as:

- Do you have the time and resources to implement each alternative?
- Will each alternative be acceptable even if the outcome is not perfect or if some unconsidered factors emerge after implementation?
- How comfortable are you (and/or your client) with the decision?

If none of the alternatives you have considered appear to be the correct choice, continue to develop and analyze alternatives until one emerges as the best option.

Prepare an Action Plan

Once you have made a decision, prepare an action plan that accounts for all the steps and resources required to implement the decision. Make a list of the specific tasks that must be completed. Develop a schedule that takes into consideration how long it will take to complete each task, as well as what tasks must be completed before others can be started. Determine the key milestones in your action plan, and decide who is accountable for those milestones.

ProSkills

Take Action and Monitor Results

After you develop an action plan, you are ready to take action. Monitor the results of your action plan as you move forward. As progress is made, check off completed tasks and compare your progress to your schedule. Occasionally, even the best-laid plans can veer off course. In this case, determine why, when, and where the tasks fell behind schedule to help get back on course.

Evaluate Your Decision and Take Corrective Action

Once you have completed your action plan, evaluate your decision to determine if it was the correct course of action. If necessary, take corrective action to improve the results. To wrap up, document your experiences in case a similar decision needs to be made in the future. By reflecting on the decision-making process and its implementation, you can learn from the experience and make better decisions down the road.

PROSKILLS

Design a Logo and a Brochure

Photoshop is the industry-standard tool for professional graphic design and photo manipulation, and it has a wide array of uses within the industry. In this exercise, you will use Photoshop to design a logo and a brochure for a fictional company. The brochure should include at least three photographic images that you will crop, correct, and retouch.

1. Decide on a business that you will use for this project. Select a name for the business, and determine what products and/or services the business provides.
2. Based on the business you have selected, determine an appropriate vision for the branding and identity of the company. Decide on goals, a statement of purpose, and a target audience for the brochure project. (Develop a viewer profile to help you determine the characteristics of the target audience.)
3. Use the Internet and a search engine to do research into the target audience and the competition. Develop specifications for output, including size, resolution, color space, color profile, and file type. Call a local printer, if necessary, to get the information you need to develop the specifications.
4. Create a concept and metaphor for the project, and decide how you will integrate both to create a unified theme.
5. In Photoshop, create a wireframe of the layout for the brochure (including a spot for the logo), using the specifications you finalized above. Review the wireframe, and decide if any additional changes need to be made.
6. Calibrate your monitor using Windows Color Calibration tool, if necessary. Then, in Photoshop, double check your color settings, create a new document, and set up a soft proof using your specifications.
7. Using the information you gathered about the target audience, and keeping in mind the project's goals and statement of purpose, use the Kuler panel to decide on a color palette. Your color selections should also reflect the decisions you made about the project's concept and metaphor.

ProSkills

8. Select fonts, design a graphic style, and create graphics—including a logo for the business. Then, add colors, text, and the graphics to the composition using layers, shapes, masks, tools, and adjustments.
9. Select at least three photographic images for the brochure; the original images should be in a camera raw format, if possible. Decide on a photographic style, and crop, adjust, and retouch the photos, as necessary. Convert the photographs to the correct color profile, if necessary, and add them to the composition as Smart Objects. Finally, use Free Transform to make any small adjustments to the images in the composition, and add layer styles, as needed.
10. Review the composition as a whole and make any small changes that are necessary to ensure that the composition has a harmonious balance and flow. Create a layer comp that you could use to present your final composition.
11. Using WordPad, create a document in which you provide details on the business you chose. Discuss your vision for the branding and identity of the company, as well as the project goals, statement of purpose, target audience, and project concept and metaphor. Explain how your design choices reinforce the company's identity and the project goals, purpose, concept, and metaphor.
12. Submit your completed files to your instructor, as requested.

GLOSSARY/INDEX

A

Absolute Colorimetric, PS 503

accessibility for the color blind, PS 187

actions, undoing and redoing, PS 262–275

active layer The layer that is currently selected in the Layers panel. PS 117

active selection A selection on the canvas enclosed by an animated series of dashed lines or curves called a marquee. PS 240

adding
- anchor points, PS 358
- color markers, PS 406
- colors to compositions, PS 566–567
- colors to Swatches panel, PS 190
- content to canvas, PS 47–49
- empty layers, PS 125–126
- fill layers, PS 200–206
- gradient layers, PS 204–205
- guides, PS 39–41
- metadata to files, PS 74
- pattern layers, PS 205–206
- patterns, PS 422–423
- pixels to selections, PS 250
- point type, PS 318–321
- to selections, PS 254
- shape layers vs. filling pixels on layers, PS 206–219
- solid color fill layer, PS 200
- strokes to selections, PS 294–295
- text along paths, PS 358–360
- text to compositions, PS 571–572
- vector layer, effects layer, PS 126–127

additive color mode A color mode, such as RGB, that adds colors together to create a different color. PS 76

adjusting
- selected pixels, PS 243
- selections, PS 251–254

adjustment A Photoshop feature that allows you to easily manipulate an image and preview a change as you make it. PS 91
- and compositing, PS 240
- destructive, nondestructive, PS 92
- making image, PS 92–96
- making to RAW images, PS 469–481
- making tonal, PS 476–479
- saving to camera raw files, PS 464–469

adjustment layer A layer in the Layers panel that changes the look of an image in a nondestructive way. PS 91
- adding, PS 118
- display of, PS 379
- positioning, PS 119–120

Adjustments and Styles panel group, PS 27

Adjustments panel, PS 92
- correcting images with, PS 402–416
- described, PS 379
- major tools in (fig.), PS 403
- tabs, PS 469–470

Adobe Bridge, managing image files with, PS 72–73. *See also* Bridge

Adobe Community Help An online forum for information about Adobe Creative Suite features. PS 2, PS 11, PS 12

Adobe Creative Suite, Unsynchronized warning, PS 485

Adobe Design Center, PS 431

Adobe Illustrator, PS 6

Adobe Media Encoder, PS 509

Adobe Photoshop. *See* Photoshop CS6

Adobe Product Activation dialog box, PS 7

algorithm In Photoshop, a mathematical formula that determines how part of an image is displayed; blending modes use algorithms to determine how the colors on one layer will blend with the colors in the layers beneath it. PS 149

align To line up objects along their centers or edges, or to line up text along a margin or center line. PS 116, PS 314

Align options, PS 209

Aligned setting, Healing Brush tool, PS 422

aligning
- layers, PS 138–139
- objects, PS 42–43
- paragraphs, PS 337–339

all caps A text format that changes any text you type, whether it is typed in uppercase or lowercase, to all capital letters in the current point size. PS 323

alpha channel A feature that stores selections as masks on the Channels panel. PS 276

ambient lighting, adjusting, PS 488

analogous A term used to refer to colors that are next to each other on a color wheel. PS 175

anchor A setting in the Canvas Size dialog box that determines whether the existing content on a canvas will remain in the center or whether it will be aligned with an edge or a corner of the canvas when the canvas is extended. PS 97
- extending canvas, PS 98

anchor points Points that determine the shape of a work path. PS 358, PS 414–416

anti-aliased A technique used by Photoshop to add pixels to the edges of a brushstroke or text in order to blend it into the background, creating a smooth rather than a jagged or pixelated edge. PS 220, PS 245

append To add a library to the current library of swatches or presets. PS 188

arbitrary angle An angle that you specify when rotating a canvas; other rotation angles are provided as presets. PS 90

archiving original photos, PS 380

Arial Rounded MT Bold, PS 569

Arrange Documents menu, PS 19

arranging file windows, PS 17–20

art, using as inspiration, PS 559

Art History Brush tool, PS 274

aspect ratio The relationship between the width and the height of an image. PS 145, PS 380–381

Aspect Ratio Preset button, PS 378

asymmetrical balance The distribution of visually disproportionate objects in a composition so that the visual weight of the objects achieves a balance with respect to one another instead of with the canvas axes; also called informal balance. PS 546

attribution A credit to a copyright owner of a work, such as an image, that appears in another work. PS 52

Auto buttons, PS 379, PS 403–405

Auto Color An auto correction tool that adjusts the color and contrast of an image by adjusting highlights, midtones, and shadows. PS 396

Auto Contrast An auto correction tool that adjusts the contrast of an image as a whole, without adjusting individual color channels. PS 396

auto correction tools Tools that use mathematical algorithms and preset values to adjust images; include Auto Contrast, Auto Color, and Auto Tone. PS 378, PS 396–401

Auto leading A setting that determines the vertical space between lines of text, with a default setting of 120% of the font size. PS 339

Auto Tone An auto correction tool that adjusts the black-and-white points in an image. PS 396

B

background color The color used to extend the canvas or to create a gradient. PS 172
- changing, PS 185–187
- generally, PS 176
- selecting in new documents, PS 59

backing up, and using layers, PS 118

balance The feeling of equilibrium that is felt when looking at a composition as a whole. PS 540

banner ads, PS 535–536

baseline The line on which text rests as you type. PS 317

baseline shift A feature that raises characters a specified number of points above or below the baseline. PS 345
- specifying, PS 353

Basic Drop Shadow style, PS 123
Bevel & Emboss effect, PS 223
bevel effect An effect that appears to give an object a third dimension. PS 192
bit depth The amount of color information each pixel in an image has access to. PS 59
  and color mode affects file size, PS 80
  and color mode (fig.), PS 81
bitmap A graphic that consists of closely spaced rows of pixels, the smallest element in a digital image; also called a raster graphic. PS 5
  drawing shapes, PS 218–219
Black Point Compensation A Photoshop printing feature that preserves the shadow detail in a printed image. PS 503
Black & White adjustment command, PS 82
Black & White adjustment layer preset, PS 96
Blanket (Texture) style, PS 193
bleeds, adding, PS 504
blend The way in which the colors in a layer interact with the colors in the layers beneath that layer. PS 149
blending mode A setting that determines how the colors in a layer blend, or interact, with the colors in the layers beneath that layer. PS 149
  in Layer Style dialog box, PS 194
  working with, applying, PS 155–158
Blur and Sharpen tools, PS 418
Blur Gallery of filters, using, PS 432–439
Boken effect, PS 432–439
borders, adding around images, PS 98–99
bounding box A box showing the borders of a layer on the canvas; appears when the layer is selected. PS 121
  around point type and paragraph type, PS 317
  creating, PS 334
  extending, PS 336
  positioning, PS 333
brand The combination of symbols, name, colors, and slogans associated with a product, service, or organization. PS 520, PS 535
brand identity The way an organization would like the public to perceive a brand. PS 520
brand image The way that the public perceives an organization and its products or services. PS 520, PS 534–537
Bridge, PS 380
  importing images from digital cameras, PS 482
  managing image files with, PS 72–73
  metadata options, PS 74
  synchronizing color settings for Creative Suite 6 applications, PS 499–500
  using with Camera Raw, PS 469
brightening images, PS 427
brightness A measurement of the lightness or darkness in a color, measured as a percentage. PS 397
  histograms, PS 470–471
Brightness/Contrast adjustment, PS 91, PS 93–94, PS 426
Brightness setting, monitor calibration, PS 488
browser file-loading options, PS 60
Brush panel, rearranging, PS 29–30
Brush Preset picker, PS 46, PS 221–222
Brush Presets
  creating from images, PS 231
  loading other presets, PS 226–227
  stroking paths using, PS 227–229
  working with, PS 225–226
Brush Presets panel (fig.), PS 199
Brush setting, Image menu, PS 420
Brush tool
  options (fig.), PS 221
  using, PS 220–224
brushstrokes, creating, PS 199
Burn tool
  described, PS 418
  retouching with, PS 428–429

C

calibrate To adjust the display of a monitor to conform to known specifications. PS 402
calibrating your monitor, PS 488–494
camera raw (RAW) An image file format that contains unprocessed and uncompressed grayscale picture data and metadata from the image sensor of a digital camera, an image scanner, or a motion picture film scanner; RAW files are large files. PS 456
  adjusting preferences, PS 456–457
  Adjustments panel tabs, PS 469–470
  Auto adjustment option, PS 476
  cameras, camera raw files supported, PS 456
  clarity, vibrance, saturation adjustments, PS 479–481
  Mini Bridge, using with, PS 469
  opening files in, PS 459–462
  opening JPEG and TIFF files in, PS 481
  tonal adjustment tools, PS 476–477
  visual overview (fig.), PS 454–455
  workflow options, PS 462–464
Camera Raw dialog box, PS 454
  viewing, retouching tools in (fig.), PS 458
camera raw files
  opening, PS 454
  saving adjustments to, PS 464–469
  saving as DNG files, PS 482–483
  working with, PS 456–457
Camera Raw plug-in A software plug-in that enables Photoshop users to construct images from camera raw file data and to adjust and process those images. PS 456
Camera Raw Workflow Options dialog box, PS 454–455
cameras
  digital camera settings, PS 482
  supported by Camera Raw, PS 456
canvas The blank area in the middle of the Photoshop Document window, on which you can "paint" with bitmap images, vector graphics, and text. PS 83
  extending with background color, PS 186
  repositioning layers on, PS 137–138
  working with, PS 97–101
Canvas Size command, PS 97
Caps options, PS 209
cases
  Cooking the Books Publishing, PS 115
  Food for Change, PS 239
  GreenHouse Construction, PS 59
  Mirabeau Media, PS 1
  RC Investments, PS 313
  ReCycle Bike Shop, PS 171
center align To align text by balancing each line of text using an imaginary vertical line through the center of a bounding box. PS 314
center point The point around which a placed image will rotate if you change its angle of rotation on the canvas. PS 144
centering
  text, PS 324
  vertical text, PS 332
Channels panel, PS 296
Character panel, PS 30–31, PS 318
  all caps, small caps, PS 323
  formatting options (fig.), PS 322
  scaling text, PS 323–332, PS 325–326
character styles, PS 342
Character Styles panel, PS 342
character type Text that you type after selecting one of the Type tools and clicking on the canvas; also called point type. PS 317
Check Spelling dialog box, PS 340–341
checkerboard pattern around shapes, PS 119
clearing guides, PS 41
client The person or company for whom you are creating a project. PS 520, PS 523
client meetings, PS 522
clip To assign an adjustment to the layer directly beneath the adjustment layer so that other layers are unaffected by the adjustment. PS 91
Clipboard, PS 243
clipping The process by which pixels that are overly bright are changed to output white and pixels that are overly dark are change to output black; occurs automatically when pixel values fall outside of the range that can be reproduced in the color space in which you are working. PS 471
clipping mask A layer that masks the layer or layers above it. PS 345, PS 361–362
closed path A path for which the start point and the end point are the same. PS 358, PS 359–360
closing, PS 30–31
  files, PS 20–21
  panels, panel groups, PS 31–32
CLUT. *See* color lookup table

CMYK (cyan, magenta, yellow, key) A color mode specifically meant for printed output; the CMYK mode assigns only cyan, magenta, yellow, and black in varying percentages. PS 77, PS 78, PS 180, PS 295, PS 496

codec A computer program that defines how the information is stored and processed within a video file container; may provide options for adjusting resolution, compression, and stream. PS 507

collaboration using layer comps, PS 155

collection A feature in Adobe Bridge that allows you to access photos stored in multiple locations. PS 72

Color and Swatches panel group, PS 27

Color Balance adjustments, PS 252

Color balance setting, monitor calibration, PS 489

color blind The inability to see certain colors in the same way the majority of the population see them. PS 187, PS 494–496

color cast A tint that affects an entire photograph. PS 473

color channel A channel that appears on the Channels panel and stores information about the colors in an image. PS 276, PS 297

Color Dodge blending mode, PS 157

color field An area in many of the color selection tools that displays shades of a selected color. PS 173

color lookup table (CLUT) A Photoshop table created by analyzing the colors in an image and converting them to 256 colors. PS 79

color management The process of creating controlled, consistent, and accurate color throughout the work flow process. PS 485
- basic, PS 487–494
- setting policies, PS 497–498
- setting view for soft proofing, PS 494–496
- and output, visual overview (fig.), PS 484–485

color marker An identifier that is only visible in Photoshop and that enables you to locate specific areas of color while you are adjusting your image; set using the Color Sampler tool. PS 406
- removing, PS 407–409

color mode A setting in Photoshop that is based on one of a variety of industry-standard color model. PS 75, PS 497
- and intensities, PS 75–83

color model A set of mathematical values that numerically represent color; each color model consists of a few primary, or starting colors that can be combined in different intensities create hundreds of thousands, or even millions of other colors. PS 75, PS 497

color palette The set of colors used to create a composition. PS 541, PS 565–566

Color panel
- described, PS 172
- setting foreground color in, PS 180–185

Color Picket (Foreground Color) dialog box, PS 183

color profile A data file that characterizes an input, display, or output device and that provides color management systems with the information needed to intelligently convert color data between native device color spaces and device-independent color spaces using ICC standards. *See also* ICC profile. PS 497
- converting, PS 500–502
- setting, PS 497–498

color ramp An area in a color selection tool where you can click to choose a color whose shades will then be displayed in the color field. PS 173

Color Range dialog box, PS 257

color ranges, selecting, PS 257–262

color scheme A combination of colors that work well together. PS 175

color selection tools, PS 176–191

Color Settings dialog box, PS 485, PS 498–499

Color settings, Edit menu, PS 484

color slider A tool on the Color panel that you drag to fine-tune the selected color selected on the color ramp. PS 172

color space A three-dimensional representation of the specific plotted points of color designated by the numerical values of colors that can be produced by a color model. PS 485, PS 497

color value A combination of numbers and letters that specify the current foreground or background color; based on the selected color mode. PS 76, PS 173

color wheel A diagram used to the show the relationships between colors. PS 174, PS 175

Colorimetric, Relative and Absolute, PS 503

colors
- adding to Swatches panel, PS 187, PS 190
- adding to your composition, PS 566–567
- adjusting image saturation, PS 479–481
- applying adjustments, PS 252
- background. *See* background color
- blending modes, applying to layers, PS 155–158
- changing layer, PS 131–133
- changing standard screen, PS 25
- components of, PS 397
- controlling content (visual overview), PS 172–173
- correcting, PS 396–402
- displaying accurately, PS 402
- dithering, PS 182
- effects of, PS 174–175
- fill, PS 48–49
- filling selections with, PS 285–286
- foreground. *See* foreground color
- harmonious, PS 541, PS 552–557
- histogram channels, PS 471
- indexed, PS 78–79
- intensities, PS 75
- Kuler panel, PS 551–552, PS 553
- Lab color mode, working with, PS 439–443
- managing. *See* color management
- matte, PS 64
- modes and intensities, PS 75–83
- psychology of, PS 175
- selecting, PS 551–567
- settings in new documents, PS 59
- synchronizing color settings for Creative Suite 6 applications, PS 499–500
- Web-safe, PS 182

combining shapes, PS 213, PS 217–218

commands
- alignment and distribution (fig.), PS 139
- on menu bar (fig.), PS 10
- workspace, PS 8

comp A mock-up or sketch of what a final design will look like. PS 152. *See also* layer comp

Compact View, Histogram panel, PS 473

complementary A term used to refer to colors that are on opposite sides of a color wheel. PS 175

composite To make adjustments to an image or combine different image files (or parts of image files) and/or vector objects in a single file. PS 240
- selecting content for, PS 242–243

compress To reduce the file size of an image. PS 60

concept The general underlying theme that unifies the various elements of a composition to create a cohesive look and feel. PS 540
- creating, PS 543–544

conducting research, PS 532–537

Content-Aware fill A Photoshop feature that allows you to remove an object from a photograph and replace it with similar versions of the surrounding pixels. PS 278

Content-Aware Move tool A Photoshop feature that combines a typical move action with the Content-Aware fill feature so that when you move a selection, the empty space behind is automatically filled with pixels copied from the surrounding area. PS 280
- Adaptation settings, PS 390–393
- moving selections using, PS 280–283
- stretching (extending) objects, PS 393–394

contrast A quality created when the visual elements in a composition conflict with one another, creating an unsettling feeling for the viewer. PS 547
- adjusting image, PS 399–401

Contrast setting, monitor calibration, PS 489

Convert to Profile dialog box, PS 500–502, PS 582–583

converting
- color mode to Grayscale, PS 80
- colors, degradation costs, PS 487
- documents, files to color profiles, PS 582–583
- documents to color profiles, PS 500–502
- images to Grayscale mode, PS 81–82

Copy command, PS 121

copying
- and pasting selections, PS 128–129, PS 253–254
- selected pixels, PS 243

copyright, PS 52

Create Shape dialog box, PS 212

creating
- anchor points, PS 414–416
- bounding box, PS 334
- brushstrokes, PS 199
- complex selections, PS 245–246, PS 254–257
- concept and metaphor, PS 543–544
- custom document presets, PS 86–88
- custom presets, PS 229–230
- documents from current state, PS 241
- gradient layers, PS 203–205
- graphic style, PS 572–575
- images for the Web, PS 504–507
- layer comps, PS 152–154
- layer groups, PS 159–160
- layers by copying, cutting and pasting selections, PS 128–129
- layouts, PS 544–551
- master planning documents, PS 530–531
- new documents, PS 59, PS 83–88
- new layers, PS 125
- output files, PS 587–588
- pattern layers, PS 205–206
- professional project, visual overview (fig.), PS 540–541
- snapshots, PS 267
- solid color fill layer, PS 202–203
- successful output, PS 486–487
- themes in Kuler panel, PS 562–564
- unique text, PS 344–357
- unique text (visual overview), PS 344–345
- video output, PS 507–509
- wireframes of layouts, PS 548–550
- work paths, PS 228–229

crop To decrease the dimensions of an image by cutting out image data. PS 101

Crop Guide Overlay, PS 380

Crop tool
- in Document window, PS 461
- using, PS 378, PS 380–384

cropping
- and altering perspective of images, PS 388–390
- images with Crop tool, PS 380–384
- vs. trimming, PS 101

cropping and correction tools, visual overview (fig.), PS 378–379

cursor A blinking white vertical line that indicates that you can continue to type with the current type settings. PS 319

Curves adjustment An adjustment tool that alters image contrast and tone by taking selected input tones and stretching or compressing them using anchor points. PS 379
- enhancing images with, PS 409–416

custom document presets, PS 86–88

custom presets, PS 83–84

Custom Shape picker, PS 48

Custom Shape Tool, PS 47–48

custom workspace A saved workspace that displays the panels and tools you have selected to improve your workflow when completing specific tasks, such as working on a photograph for a brochure or designing a poster. PS 38. *See also* workspace.

customizing Swatches panel display, PS 188

cutting and pasting selections, PS 247

D

data files
- opening, PS 9
- starting, PS 1

Deep Red Photo Filter adjustment, PS 120

Define Brush Preset command, PS 231

deleting
- adjustment layers, PS 94–95
- anchor points, PS 358
- colors from Swatches panel, PS 191
- custom document presets, PS 88
- custom workspaces, PS 38
- guides, PS 41
- layer comps, PS 154
- layers, PS 143
- tool presets, PS 51

deliverables The items that will be delivered at each phase of a project and upon project completion. PS 521, PS 530

Dented Metal style, PS 346–348

depth of field The range of distances in an image that appears acceptably sharp. PS 432
- adjusting, PS 435–439

Depth workflow option, Camera Raw, PS 463

Desaturation adjustment, PS 401

deselecting layers, PS 121–125

design An exacting form of art that has a specific and defined purpose. PS 540

design chain The path that a project travels from original input through final output. PS 486

design projects, planning, PS 522–531

designer resources at Adobe Design Center, PS 431

designer skills, developing, PS 523

designing
- alternative graphic styles, PS 575
- projects, PS 542

destination file Any currently open file or a new file into which you copy a duplicate layer. PS 129

destructive editing An edit that permanently changes the pixels in an image and cannot be undone once a file is saved. PS 80, PS 207

destructive image adjustment An adjustment that changes the pixels in the image and cannot be undone once a file is saved. PS 92

deuteranopia, PS 494

device independent A term used to describe a color mode that ensures that a color will look the same to the human eye no matter which device it is displayed on. PS 183

diameter The width of the Brush tool brush tip. PS 199

DICOM tab, medical images, PS 74

Diffuse Glow effect, PS 276–277

digital camera settings, PS 482

digital image A photograph or drawing in electronic form; can be displayed on a computer monitor or the LCD screen of a camera or mobile device. PS 4

Digital Negative (DNG) A nonproprietary file format created by Adobe as a potential solution to the problems introduced by the many competing proprietary camera raw formats. PS 482

display typography An approach to typography in which the designer is less concerned with the readability of a large body of text, and more concerned about using the text in an artistic manner to communicate a succinct, potent message to the viewer. PS 568

displaying
- clipped pixels, PS 472
- and closing panels, PS 29–32
- colors accurately, PS 402
- custom workspaces, PS 38
- hidden tools, PS 10
- layer edges, PS 133–134
- layers, PS 141–143
- Tools panel in two columns, PS 10

distribute To spread selected objects evenly across or down the canvas along an invisible horizontal or vertical axis. PS 117

distributing layers in compositions, PS 139–140

distribution, icons and commands (fig.), PS 139

dithering The process of replacing the discarded colors from a lossy compression using colors from a new, smaller color palette. PS 63, PS 182

Divide blending mode, PS 156

DNG files, saving camera raw files as, PS 482–483

dock A group of complementary panels or panel groups displayed one on top of the other using tabs. PS 23

Document window The area of the Photoshop application window where Photoshop displays the images you open or create. PS 2–3
- floating, PS 17–18
- overview, PS 11

Document window tools, PS 454

documents
- adding guides, PS 39–41
- converting to new color profile, PS 500–502
- creating master planning, PS 530–531
- creating new, PS 59, PS 538–539
- presents, nonstandard size, PS 86

Dodge tool, PS 418, PS 426–427

downsample To decrease the resolution of an image by throwing out pixels to keep the document the same physical dimensions. PS 69

dpi A measurement that uses dots per inch. PS 69

dragging to hide and redisplay layers, PS 142–143

drawing
- bitmap shapes, PS 218–219
- vector shapes, PS 210–212

Dreamweaver, PS 486

Drop Shadow settings, Layer Style dialog box, PS 195–196

dummy text Text that lets you work with fonts and font sizes in text boxes to plan your layout, but doesn't include the final text; also called placeholder text. PS 357

duplicating layers, PS 129–130

E

editing
- anchor points, PS 414–416
- destructive, PS 80
- images, PS 64

effects
- adding to inverse selections, PS 268–269
- gradient (fig.), PS 203
- in Layer Style dialog box, PS 195

effects layer A layer created by applying a style to an existing layer. PS 125

ellipses, drawing, PS 358

Elliptical Marquee tool, PS 244–248

Encapsulated Postscript (EPS) A file format that supports both vector and bitmap graphics; contains a great deal of data and can be used to output high-quality print pieces. PS 63

enlarging bitmaps vs. vector images, PS 6

EPS. *See* Encapsulated Postscript

Eraser tool, PS 45–46

Essentials workspace, PS 27, PS 35, PS 36

excluding from shapes, PS 213

exiting Photoshop, PS 21

expanding selections, PS 249

exporting video, PS 508–509

extending canvas, PS 98–99

Eye Dropper Tool, PS 408

Eyedropper tool
- described, PS 172
- setting foreground color with, PS 177–180

F

Facebook, PS 538

fastening point One of a series of dots that define a selection marquee based on a specified frequency. PS 276

faux style A style generated by Photoshop when an attribute, such as bold, is unavailable in a font family. PS 319

feathering, PS 245

Field Blur filter, PS 433

file format The way the information (or data) in a file is organized when it is stored on a storage device, such as a camera's memory card, a hard drive, or a flash drive. PS 60
- Digital Negative (DNG), PS 482
- types of, PS 60–61

file size The measurement of a digital Image, usually in megabytes or gigabytes; dependent both on its resolution and on its physical dimensions. PS 6
- bit depth and color modes affects, PS 80

files
- adding point type to, PS 320–321
- applying layer comps to, PS 153–154
- closing, PS 20–21
- creating new, PS 83–88
- creating output, PS 587–588
- cycling through open, PS 15–16
- metadata, adding, PS 74
- opening, PS 8–9
- opening in Camera Raw, PS 459–462
- opening in Mini Bridge, PS 74
- placing images in new, PS 83–86
- Preferences, setting, PS 26
- previewing in Full Screen mode, PS 73
- saving with new names, PS 14–15
- stepping backward, forwards through, PS 263–264
- working with multiple, PS 13–14

Fill color palette, PS 48–49

fill layer A layer filled with a solid color, a pattern, or a gradient. PS 198
- adding, PS 200–206
- visual overview (fig.), PS 198–199

fill pixels vs. adding shape layers, PS 206–207

filling
- selections, PS 241, PS 278–283
- text with images, PS 361–362

filter A search feature that hides all files except those specified by the certain criteria. PS 72
- Blur Gallery, PS 432–439
- visual overview (fig.), PS 276–277
- working with, PS 295

Filter Gallery
- folders, PS 277
- working with, PS 301–305

filtering layers, PS 124–125

finalizing layers, PS 160–162

Find and Replace Text dialog box, PS 340–341

fixed ratio selections, PS 246–247

fixed size selected, PS 248

flat format A file format such as GIF, PNG, or JPEG that consists of a single layer. PS 63

flattening images, PS 162

flipping images, PS 107–109

floating Document windows, PS 17–18

flush left Text that appears straight along the left margin, with a ragged right edge. PS 337

flush right Text that appears straight along the right margin, with a ragged left edge. PS 337

focus groups, PS 551

font A designated set of letters, numbers, and symbols in a single size and style in one typeface. PS 568

font family, PS 568, PS 569

font size The height of text measured in points. PS 314

font style, PS 568, PS 569

fonts, selecting, PS 567–570

foreground color The color Photoshop uses when you work with the drawing tools. PS 172
- generally, PS 176
- setting in Color panel, PS 180–185
- setting with Eyedropper tool, PS 177–180

form A shape created to look as if it has depth and occupies a three-dimensional space. PS 544

framing The process of cropping an image to create an interesting composition that draws the viewer's eye to the subject, or focal point, and removes distracting elements. PS 380

free transform To rotate an image in any direction using the mouse. PS 146

Freeze Mask tool, PS 297, PS 299

frequency A setting that determines the distance between fastening points in a selection. PS 276

Full Screen mode, PS 73

Fuzziness setting, color range, PS 258

fx A designation that appears in the Layers panel next to a layer that has been modified by an effect. PS 126

G

Gamma setting, monitor calibration, PS 488

gamut The range of colors allowed by the CMYK color mode. PS 180

GIF. *See* Graphics Interchange Format

Glyph Scaling A setting that determines the width of individual characters. PS 339

gradient fill A gradual blending of the foreground and background colors or of other colors determined by a gradient preset. PS 176, PS 363–364

Gradient Fill dialog box, PS 198, PS 200–201

gradient fill layers, PS 198, PS 200–201

gradient layers, creating, PS 203–205

graphic style The look of the graphic elements in a composition, including lines, shapes, textures, borders, logos, illustrations, buttons, and so forth. PS 541, 572–575

Graphics Interchange Format (GIF) A lossless file format for bitmap images that consists of a single layer; often used on the Web. PS 63

graphics
- adding to compositions, PS 575–580
- introduction to, PS 4

Grayscale color mode, PS 79–80

greeking The method of using lorem ipsum (Latin) text as placeholder text. PS 357

grid A series of lines that divide a document into squares that can be used as guides when drawing, moving, and placing objects in a document. PS 23
- Crop Guide Overlay, PS 380

displaying, PS 38
showing, hiding, aligning objects, PS 42–43
Snap To feature, PS 44

groups, panel, PS 23

growing selections, PS 249

guide Line dragged from the horizontal and vertical rulers into the Document window to aid in aligning and moving objects in a document or drawing objects with specific dimensions or alignments. PS 23
adding, PS 39–41
Smart Guides, PS 38
Snap To feature, PS 44

H

Hand tool, PS 45, PS 104

hard proof A print that simulates what you will see when you print at a professional printer. PS 503

hardness A setting that determines the amount of anti-aliasing applied to a brushstroke. PS 220

harmonious colors Colors that are pleasing to look at, create a sense of balance, and stimulate a viewer to explore a composition. PS 541
selecting, PS 552–557

harmony A pleasing arrangement or combination of parts that creates an engaging end product that is balanced and filled with dynamic equilibrium. PS 547, PS 552

HDR. *See* high dynamic range image

Healing Brush tool
described, PS 418
options, using, PS 422–426

Help
Adobe Community Help, PS 2, PS 11
Adobe online, PS 436
Photoshop, PS 11–13

hexadecimal color values A series of numbers and letters that specify a Web-safe color; can be used to specify color in the RGB color mode for an HTML file. PS 173

hidden layer A layer that is not visible on the canvas; indicated by the lack of an Eye icon next to it in the Layers panel. PS 117

hiding
layers, PS 118, PS 404
panels, PS 32–33

high dynamic range (HDR) image A 32-bit image typically used in 3D imagery or in a computer graphics scene that requires great contrast between dark and light areas and a high level of detail. PS 81

highlights, PS 411–412
clipping warning icon, PS 455
decreasing, increasing, PS 479
recovering details, PS 476

Histogram panel, working with, PS 473

histogram A visual representation of the number of pixels an image has at each luminance value. PS 455, PS 470–471

History and Properties panel group, PS 27

History Brush tool, PS 240, PS 241, PS 270–274

History panel
described, PS 241
reverting to previous state using, PS 265–269

history state A previous version of a file; you can return to a history state using the History panel. PS 241

horizontal type Type that flows from left to right along a horizontal line. PS 318, PS 319

Horizontal Type tool, PS 47, PS 122

HTML. *See* HyperText Markup Language

HyperText Markup Language (HTML) A programming language used to create Web pages. PS 183

hue What we think of or perceive as an object's color; expressed as the measurement, in degrees, of the location of a color around the standard color wheel. PS 397

Hue/Saturation adjustment, PS 94–95, PS 118

hyphenation, adjusting, PS 337–339

I

ICC profile A data file that characterizes an input, display, or output device and that provides color management systems with the information needed to intelligently convert color data between native device color spaces and device-independent color spaces using ICC standards. PS 497. *See also* color profile.

icons
collapsed panels, PS 3
Type tool options (fig.), PS 317

Illustrator, PS 125

image rotation options (fig.), PS 107

Image Size dialog box (fig.), PS 60, PS 68, PS 70

Image/Adjustments menu, PS 401

image-editing program Software that lets you manipulate a digital image and then save it with the changes you have made. PS 4

images
adding point type to, PS 319
adjusting, viewing, rotating, PS 90–91
adjusting using Lab color mode, PS 440–443
adjustments, making, PS 92–96
blending, PS 159
blurring areas of, PS 435–439
brightening, PS 427
changing resolution, PS 68–71
converting to Grayscale mode, PS 81–82
correcting, adjusting, retouching, PS 377–380
correcting with Adjustments panel, PS 402–416
correcting with auto correction tools, PS 397–401
creating Brush Presets from, PS 231
creating for the Web, PS 504–507
cropping, PS 380–384
cropping and altering perspective of, PS 388–390
digital, PS 4
editing, PS 64
filling text with, PS 361–362
enhancing with Curves adjustment, PS 409–416
filling text with, PS 361–362
finding available, PS 52
flattening, PS 162
making tonal adjustments, PS 476–479
managing files with Adobe Bridge, Mini Bridge, PS 72–74
marking darkest, lightest pixels, PS 407–409
moving, PS 390–393
optimizing, PS 63–68
panning, PS 103–104
panning in Navigator, PS 91
patching, PS 394–396
of people, retouching and repairing, PS 426
permissions for using, PS 52, PS 284
placing, resizing, positioning on layers, PS 143–147
placing in new files, PS 83–86
preparing for video, PS 507–509
RAW. *See* RAW images
recropping, PS 387–388
repairing with Healing Brush tool, PS 422–426
repairing with Spot Healing Brush tool, PS 420–421
resampling, PS 70–71
retouching, PS 423–425
retouching with Dodge tool, PS 426–427
returning to previous state, PS 270–274
rotating, flipping, PS 107–109
rotating placed, PS 146–147
Rule of Thirds, PS 378
saving using Save for Web dialog box, PS 505–507
setting black, white points of, PS 410–411
sharpening areas of, PS 431–432
straightening, PS 384–387
style, PS 477
transforming using Blur gallery of filters, PS 432–439
scanner-acquired, PS 97
upsampling, PS 68
white balancing, PS 473–475
zooming, PS 102–103

Indexed color model, PS 78–79

input tones The original value of the tones in an image when a Curves adjustment layer is first created. PS 409

intensity The value assigned to one of the primary colors in a color mode; in Photoshop there are 256 intensities for each primary color. PS 75

International Color Consortium (ICC) A group of industry professionals who are dedicated to the development of cross-platform standards for color communication and consistency. PS 497

interpolation method The method Photoshop uses to determine how pixels will be added or subtracted when it resamples an image. PS 60, PS 69

intersecting shapes, PS 213

Iris Blur filter, PS 434–439

J

Joint Photographic Experts Group (JPEG) A lossy file format for bitmap images that consists of a single layer; often used on Web pages. Sometimes written as JPG. PS 63

JPEG. *See* Joint Photographic Experts Group

JPEG files
- saving PSD files as, PS 161
- vs. TIFF files, PS 67–68

JPEG Options dialog box (fig.), PS 60, PS 64

justification
- advanced settings, PS 339
- setting and adjusting, PS 337–339

justify To align text flush along both the left and the right margins. PS 337

K

kerning The space between a pair of characters. PS 315
- metrics, and optical, PS 352

Lab color mode, working with, PS 439–443

Lasso tools
- described, PS 278
- using, PS 278–280
- visual overview (fig.), PS 276–277

key plate The plate in the printing process used to print the details in an image. PS 77

keyword A word used to categorize or describe an image in some way to allow for filtering or searching. PS 72

L

Lab color mode A color mode that describes colors as most people actually see them, rather than as they are interpreted by a device such as a monitor or a printer. PS 183

layer A separate element of an image file that allows you to make changes to one part of a composition while leaving the other parts intact. PS 63
- adding empty, PS 125–126
- adjustment, PS 379
- aligning, PS 138–139
- blending and finalizing (visual overview), PS 148–149
- blending modes, applying, PS 155–158
- changing properties, PS 131–133
- changing visibility, PS 135–137
- coloring, PS 131–133
- creating by copying, cutting and pasting selections, PS 128–129
- deleting, PS 143
- displaying edges, PS 133–134
- duplicating, PS 129–130
- filtering, PS 124–125
- finalizing, PS 160–162
- grouping, ungrouping, PS 159–160
- hiding, showing, PS 118, PS 141–143
- locked, PS 121
- merging, PS 160–161
- overview, PS 118–119
- placing images on, PS 143–145
- positioning, PS 119–120
- repositioning on canvas, PS 137–138
- selecting, deselecting, PS 121–125
- similar, PS 124
- stamping, PS 161
- working with multiple (visual overview), PS 116–117

layer comp A snapshot of layer visibility, position, and appearance settings that is saved in the Layers Comps panel. PS 148
- deleting, PS 154
- working with, PS 152–153

Layer Comps panel, PS 148

layer edges Borders that indicate where a layer begins and ends on the canvas. PS 116

layer group A set of related layers organized in the Layers panel in a way that makes sense to you. PS 117
- creating, PS 159–160

layer mask A feature that hides part of a layer so it does not show through on the canvas. PS 200

layer styles, modifying, PS 194–196

Layers panel, PS 122, PS 133
- moving layers in, PS 135–137
- text layers in, PS 316–317

layout The position of elements in a composition. PS 540
- workspace (fig.), PS 36

leaderboard An advertising banner at the top of a Web page. PS 85
- creating files using, PS 85–86

left align A setting that lines up text along the left edge of a text box. PS 314

Letter spacing An advanced justification setting that controls the distance between letters. PS 339

library A palette of Color swatches. A library can also contain other presets. PS 188
- changing in Styles panel, PS 192
- deleting colors from, PS 191
- loading preset, PS 226–227

lighting, adjusting ambient, PS 408

line A mark that spans the distance between two points in space. PS 544

line screen frequency The number of halftone dots in a linear inch. PS 504

Linear Light blending mode, PS 157

links, clicking, PS 11

Liquify filter, using, PS 297–301

Liquify tools (fig.), PS 297

loading selections, PS 289

lock icons, PS 148

locked layer A layer that you cannot move or resize. PS 121

locking layer content, PS 150–152

look and feel A term used to describe the way all the elements of a design interact to create an experience for a viewer. PS 542

loose line Text that is so spread out it is distracting to the eye because of all of the white space. PS 337

lorem ipsum Placeholder text that uses a standard series of Latin words. PS 357

lossless compression A type of compression that does not discard data but rather reduces file size by storing data more efficiently; for example, by mapping all colors to a color table instead of storing each pixel's color information with the pixel itself. PS 63

lossless file format A file format that uses lossless compression. PS 63, PS 482, PS 502

lossy compression A type of compression that reduces file size by throwing out, or "losing" some of the original data in an image. PS 63

lossy file format A file format that uses lossy compression. PS 63
- saving files in, PS 64–66

M

Mac OS monitor calibration utility, PS 402

Magic Wand tool, PS 249–250

Magnetic Lasso tool, PS 276, PS 284–288

managing image files with Adobe Bridge, Mini Bridge, PS 72–74

market research The careful investigation and study of data about the target audience and the competition for a particular project. PS 521

mask The inverse of a selection; an area protected from any image-editing performed on a selection. PS 252
- overview, PS 296
- working with, PS 295

matte The color that will appear in the background of an image as it downloads while a user is trying to view it on the Web. PS 64

maximizing floating Document windows, PS 18

megapixel Millions of pixels (mega means millions). Because resolution is usually measured in millions of pixels, the term megapixel if often used when discussing resolution. PS 6

menu bar, PS 10

merging
- layers, PS 160–161
- shapes, PS 215–217

metadata Data about data; for example, information describing how data is formatted, or how it was collected. PS 72
- adding to files, PS 74

metaphor A comparison in which one object, concept, or idea is represented as another. PS 543
- creating, PS 543–544

metrics kerning Kerning that is built into a font family. PS 352

Mini Bridge, PS 73–74, PS 469

minimizing
- floating Document windows, PS 18
- panels, PS 32–33

Mode command, Image menu, PS 81
Mode setting, Spot Healing Brush tool, PS 420
monitor calibration utility, PS 402
monitors, PS 489
  adjusting, PS 402
  calibrating, PS 488–494
monochromatic Consisting of different shades of a single color. PS 175
monochromatic color palette, PS 556
monospaced font A font in which each letter takes exactly the same width in the line. PS 569
moods created by colors, PS 557
Move tool, PS 43, PS 123, PS 326–327
moving
  images, PS 390–393
  layers to change visibility, PS 135–137
  objects and patching holes, PS 394–396
  panels, panel groups, PS 33–34
  selections using Content-Aware Move tool, PS 280–283
  tabs, PS 16–17

N

naming files, PS 14–15
native A term used to describe a file format that is created in and can only be edited in its proprietary program; for example, PSD files are native to Photoshop and can only be edited in Photoshop and other Adobe products. PS 63
navigating file windows, PS 15–20
Navigator
  panning images in, PS 91
  zooming, panning images, PS 105–106
neutral A term used to describe colors, such as browns and grays, that are not on a color wheel. PS 175
New Adjustment command, Layer menu, PS 93
New dialog box (fig.), PS 59, PS 83
New Layer Comp dialog box, PS 153
nondestructive editing
  with adjustment layer, PS 118
  vs. destructive editing, PS 207
nondestructive image adjustment An adjustment that is stored as a layer on top of the original image and does not affect the pixels in an image. PS 92
Normal blending mode, PS 156

O

objects
  aligning, PS 42–43
  removing with Content-Aware Patch tool, PS 394–396
one-click method, shape tools, PS 212
online Help, PS 436
opacity, setting layer's, PS 149
Opacity setting
  blending layers using, PS 158–159
  of layers, PS 155
Open in Photoshop as Smart Objects option, Camera Raw, PS 463
open path A path with separate start and end points. PS 358
OpenGL, PS 102, PS 103
opening
  camera raw files, PS 454
  camera raw files as Smart Objects, PS 465–466
  files, PS 8–9
  files in Camera Raw, PS 459–462
  files in Mini Bridge, PS 74
  multiple files, PS 13–14
  video clips, PS 508
OpenType fonts, PS 322
optical kerning A setting used by Photoshop to adjust the spacing between character pairs based on the shapes of the characters. PS 352
optimization The process of finding the right balance between image quality and file size. PS 63
optimizing images, PS 63–68
options bar The area in the Photoshop window that displays the settings for the currently selected tool; appears beneath the Application bar. PS 2
  changing tool settings, PS 45–47
  overview, PS 11
organizing layers, PS 133
origin The point on the on-screen ruler where the number zero appears. PS 41
out of gamut A color that will not print properly. PS 173
  color correction, PS 181
Outer Glow effect, PS 256–257
output, determining specifications, PS 538–539
output files, creating, PS 587–588
output tones The values of the tones in an image after adjustments are made using a Curves adjustment layer. PS 409

P

Paint Bucket tool, PS 172
painting, visual overview (fig.), PS 198–199
Painting workspace, PS 35, PS 36
pan To move an image within the Document window so that a different part of the image is visible. PS 91
panel A group of related tools. PS 3. *See also specific panels*
  displaying and closing, PS 29–32
  managing, PS 12
  text layers and (fig.), PS 314–315
  working with, PS 27–35
panel group An organized group of complementary or related panels. PS 23
  customizing, moving, PS 33–34
panel tab The area at the top of a panel that you click to display and access the tools in a panel. PS 2
panning images, PS 103–106
paper, printing, PS 502
Paragraph panel, PS 318
paragraph type Text that is contained in a bounding box whose dimensions you specify by activating a Type tool and then clicking on the canvas and dragging. PS 317
paragraphs
  creating styles, PS 342
  spell-checking, PS 340–341
  working with, PS 333–337
parameters A description of what activities and outcomes a particular project includes. PS 521
pasting selections, PS 247, PS 253–254
Patch tool, PS 394–396
patching images, PS 394–396
Path operation options, PS 213
paths
  adding text along, PS 358–360
  stroking using Brush Presets, PS 227–229
  for unique text, PS 344
Pattern Fill dialog box, PS 201, PS 206
pattern fill layers, PS 201
pattern layers, creating, PS 205–206
patterns, adding, PS 422–423
Pencil tool, PS 220
permissions
  for using images, PS 284
  for using photos, PS 52
Perspective Crop tool, PS 388–390
perspective of images, altering, PS 388–390
photographic styles, selecting, PS 581–587
photographs
  archiving original, PS 380
  darkening areas of, PS 428–429
  enhanced (fig.), PS 4–5
  lightening shadows, PS 427
  permissions, PS 52
Photoshop
  communicating visual data with, PS 244
  default resolution, PS 6
  Document window (fig.), PS 2–3
  exiting, PS 21
  Help, PS 11–13
  rearranging interface, PS 28
  role in professional production, PS 4–5
  starting, PS 7–8
Photoshop CS6
  exploring, PS 8–11
  Help, PS 11–13, PS 436
  new panels, PS 36
Photoshop document (PSD) The default Photoshop format, which can store both vector and bitmap data and which stores multiple image components and enhancements on separate elements called layers so that you can make changes to one part of a composition while leaving the other parts intact. PS 63
Photoshop Format Options dialog box, PS 15
Photoshop Preferences, setting, PS 24–26

pixel A square that defines a color; short for picture element. PS 5
adding to selections, PS 250
displaying clipped, PS 472
locking, positioning, PS 150–152
marking darkest, lightest, PS 407–409
selecting, copying, adjusting selected, PS 243
upsampling images, PS 68
pixel aspect ratio The width to height ratio of a single pixel. PS 508
Pixels tool mode, PS 218–219
place To import a copy of an image file, which is still linked to the original image file, into another image file. PS 83
placeholder text Text that lets you work with fonts and font sizes in text boxes to plan your layout, but doesn't include the final text; also called dummy text. PS 357
placing images, PS 143–145
planning design projects, PS 522–531
planning professional projects, visual overview (fig.), PS 520–521
PNG. *See* Portable Network Graphics
point A measurement, abbreviated as pt, that is 1/72 of an inch; used to describe the size of text. PS 314
point sample A sample selection method that uses the color of a single pixel to set the color sampled by the Eyedropper tool. PS 172
point type Text that you type after selecting one of the Type tools and clicking on the canvas; also called character type. PS 317
adding and modifying, PS 318–321
Polygon tool, PS 216
Portable Network Graphics (PNG) A lossless file format for bitmap images that consist of a single layer; suitable for use on the Web. PS 63, PS 505
positioning
bounding box, PS 333
layer content, pixels, PS 150–152
layers, PS 119–120
subject at optimum position, PS 382–384
Posterize adjustments, PS 91
ppi A measurement that determines screen resolution (pixels per inch). PS 69
Preferences, setting, PS 24–26
Preferences dialog box (fig.), PS 25
presets
See also specific type
creating and saving custom, PS 83–84, PS 229–230
saving modified swatches as, PS 191
zooming images using, PS 103
previewing
files before saving, PS 64
JPEG files, PS 60
primary color A color, such as red, green, or blue, that serves as a starting color for a color model; primary colors can be combined in different intensities to create hundreds of thousands, or even millions, of other colors; primary colors vary by color model. PS 75
Print dialog box, PS 503
printer resolution, PS 69
printers and color modes, PS 78
printing
at home, PS 502–503
at professional print shop, PS 503–504
project An endeavor with an explicit beginning and endpoint that is undertaken to meet specific goals—including producing predefined deliverables—using limited, identified resources for a predetermined cost. PS 522
conducting research, PS 532–537
creating graphic style, PS 572–575
creating layout, PS 544–550
creating output files, wrapping up, PS 587–588
creating professional, visual overview (fig.), PS 540–541
designing, PS 542
determining output specifications, PS 538–539
determining parameters, PS 463
developing concept, metaphor, PS 543–544
gathering, acquiring materials, PS 542–543
planning design, PS 522–531
rhythm, and unity, PS 547–548
selecting colors, PS 551–567
selecting fonts, PS 567–570
selecting photographic style, PS 581–587
project goals A short prioritized list of goals, written in active voice, that you would like to accomplish with a project. PS 520, PS 524–527
project management, PS 531
project metaphor A visual extension of a project concept. PS 540
property A setting for an adjustment layer. PS 91
See also specific property
changing layer properties, PS 131–133
Properties panel A new feature in Photoshop CS6 that lists the properties or settings of the adjustment layer selected in the Layers panel. PS 91, PS 93
proportional font A font in which each letter takes up a different width on the line, proportional to the width of a letter. PS 569
proprietary A term used to describe a file format that can only be edited in the program in which it was created. PS 63
protanopia, PS 494, PS 495–496
PSD. *See* Photoshop Document
public domain A term used to describe some government images and older works that are not protected by copyright law and can be used however you want; an image copyright holder may choose to release an image into the public domain. PS 52

Q

Quick Selection tool, PS 289–293

R

radial A gradient style in which the colors emanate out like a bull's eye. PS 198
radial symmetry The distribution of objects around one center point in a composition to create balance. PS 198
raster A graphic that consists of closely spaced rows of pixels, the smallest element in a digital image; also called a bitmap graphic. PS 5
raster objects, PS 218–219
rasterizing vector shapes, PS 210
RAW files, PS 454
RAW images, making adjustments to, PS 469–470
Reconstruct tool, PS 300
recropping images, PS 387–388
Rectangle tool, PS 48
Rectangular Marquee tool, PS 104–105, PS 128, PS 244–248
Red Eye tool, PS 426
redisplaying
layers, PS 141–143
panels, PS 32–33
redoing actions, PS 262–275
reference point The point, located at the (0,0) point on invisible x- and y-axes, from which Photoshop will measure any change in position. PS 145
Relative Colorimetric, PS 503
reloading selections, PS 288–289
removing
color markers, PS 407–409
objects, PS 394–396
renaming layers, PS 131–132
rendering intent A Photoshop printing feature that determines how conversion from one color space to another is handled by your color management system. PS 503
replacing text, PS 340–341
repositioning
layers on canvas, PS 137–138
placed images, PS 145–146
resample To change the number of pixels in an image by changing its resolution. PS 60
resampling images, PS 68, PS 70–71
research, conducting, PS 532–537
resetting
tools to default settings, PS 24
workspace(s), PS 37
resizing placed images, PS 145–146
resolution The level of detail in an image, measured in pixels per inch. PS 5
changing, and resampling images, PS 60, PS 68–71
deciding which is best, PS 71
decreasing image's, PS 81–83
printer, PS 69
Resolution workflow option, Camera Raw, PS 463

restoring
- Photoshop Preferences, PS 26
- Photoshop's default settings, PS 7–8

retouching
- with Burn tool, PS 428–429
- with Dodge tool, PS 426–427
- images, PS 423–425
- with Sharpen tool, PS 431–432
- with Sponge tool, PS 429–430
- tools in Camera Raw dialog box (fig.), PS 458

retouching tool A tool that can be used to remove small imperfections from an image or to correct larger areas of an image that still need help after color and tonal corrections are made to an entire image. PS 419

Review mode, PS 73

RGB (red, green, blue) A color mode most often used for Web images; the RGB color mode assigns only red, green, and blue in varying intensities to create approximately 16.7 million color choices. PS 76

RGB color model, PS 75, PS 180, PS 295, PS 442, PS 505

rhythm A sense of order in a composition achieved by repeating or alternating objects or elements on a canvas. PS 547

river A term used to describe white space flowing from line to line in loose text. PS 337

Rotate View tool, PS 107

rotating
- horizontal type to vertical position, PS 328–330
- images, PS 90–91, PS 107–109
- placed images, PS 146–147

royalty A fee paid each time an image is used. PS 52

royalty-free An image that does not require a per use fee; a payment may be required in the form of a one-time fee. PS 52

Rule of Thirds A design rule that suggests you divide every image into nine equal parts, using two vertical lines and two horizontal lines; to achieve the greatest visual interest, energy, and tension, position significant elements along the lines or where they intersect. PS 378, PS 381

ruler A screen element that displays the measurement of a document in pixels, inches, centimeters, or other units. PS 22
- origin, PS 41
- showing, PS 38–39

S

sample To copy the color of pixels in an image using the Eyedropper tool; the color can then be applied to another part of the image or to another image. PS 172
- colors with Eyedropper tool, PS 177–180

Sample All Layers setting, Image menu, PS 420, PS 421

Sample options, Healing Brush tool, PS 422

sans serif font A font in which serifs are absent. PS 569

saturation The expression of purity or strength of a color, measured as a percentage. PS 397, PS 401

Save As dialog box, PS 14

saving
- custom document presets, PS 87
- custom workspaces, PS 38
- files with new names, PS 14–15
- images in different formats, PS 63
- JPEG files, PS 64–66
- modified swatches as presets, PS 191
- PSD files in JPEG format, PS 161
- selections, PS 288–289
- styles, PS 196
- tool presets, PS 50

scaling text
- adjusting, PS 331–333, PS 348–352
- using Character panel, PS 325–326
- using Move tool, PS 326–327

scan A state or stage of a JPEG image that a viewer sees as the image is being loaded for viewing on the Web; each subsequent scan increases the detail in the image. PS 64

scope All of the work that needs to be done to deliver a completed project. PS 521, PS 530

scope creep The process by which additional elements and requirements are added to a project, causing it to grow in size, complexity, cost, and so on. PS 530

scripted pattern A special effect you can apply to a pattern fill, such as a spiral or a weave. PS 284
- filling selections with, PS 286–287

scrub To use the mouse pointer to drag over a setting to increase or decrease its value. PS 158

Search box, searching Help, or the Web, PS 13

search engine A Web site or program whose primary function is to retrieve Web pages based on a search for specified keywords or phrases. PS 532

searching Help, or the Web, PS 13

selecting
- all text in text objects, PS 349
- color ranges, PS 257–262
- content (visual overview), PS 240–241
- content for compositing, PS 242–243
- content with Magnetic Lasso tool, PS 284–288
- inverse of selections, PS 292–293
- layers, PS 23, PS 121–125
- pixels, PS 243
- with Quick Selection tool, PS 289–293
- with Rectangular or Elliptical Marquee tool, PS 244–248
- tools, PS 44–45
- words, PS 323

selection handles, PS 326

selection marquee An animated series of dashed lines or curves that indicates the area of a selection; a marquee can be used to zoom in on an area on which you want to focus or to select part of an image. PS 103

selection tools (fig.), PS 242

selections
- applying adjustments to, PS 251–254
- creating complex, PS 254–257
- filling using Content-Aware Fill feature, PS 278–283
- modifying, PS 249–250
- moving, PS 280–283
- restarting, PS 285
- saving, PS 288–289
- specifying fixed ratio, PS 246–247
- specifying fixed size, PS 248
- stroking, PS 293–295

serif font A font in which a delicate, horizontal line called a serif finishes the main strokes of each character. PS 569

shape An area of two-dimensional space, defined by edges, that sets one portion of space apart from another; a circle is an example of a shape. PS 544

shape fills, PS 208

shape layer A layer with a fill and a shape outline ; also known as a vector layer, a shape layers is a form of nondestructive editing because it can be overlaid on an image without altering the pixels in the layer or layers beneath it. PS 207
- adding, PS 209–214

shape options bar buttons (fig.), PS 209

Shape tool mode, PS 207

shapes
- adding to layers, PS 126
- visual overview (fig.), PS 198–199

shortcut keys, PS 10

Show Transform Controls check box, PS 116, PS 122

showing rulers, PS 38–39

similar layers Layers with common characteristics. PS 124

simultaneous contrast The interaction of two colors placed side by side; affects the way you interpret what you *see* when looking at a composition. PS 557

sizing canvas, PS 97

Sketch filters, PS 302

small caps A text format in which all text appears in capital letters; the letters you type in uppercase are taller than the letters you type in lowercase, but all are capitalized. PS 323

Smart Guides Lines that appear automatically in the Document window as you move an object on one layer to align it with an object on another layer. PS 38

Smart Object A Photoshop feature that lets you transform a placed object in some way, such as by rotating or distorting it. PS 83

Smart Object layer A layer that contains either vector or raster image data and that preserves a link to an image's source content, enabling you to open and edit the image source. PS 454

Snap To A Photoshop feature that lets you easily align objects using gridlines or guides by "magnetizing" the lines so that when you drag a selection or shape, or move an object, the object aligns to the closest gridlines or guides. PS 44

snapshot A thumbnail picture of what a composition looks like at any given history state; appears in the History panel. PS 241
  creating new, PS 267
  using as source for History Brush tool, PS 273

Soft Life blending mode, PS 156

soft proof Display settings that enable you to simulate the way a composition will look when output. PS 484

solid color fill layer, creating, PS 202–203

source In the History panel, an earlier state of the current image. You can set the source for the History Brush and then use the brush to paint over your composition and uncover part of the history state that is saved as the source. PS 241
  using snapshot as, PS 273

spell-checking paragraph text, PS 340–341

stack A collection of panels or panel groups joined top to bottom. PS 22

stacking panels, PS 33–35

Stained Glass effect, PS 276

Stained Glass filter, PS 304

stamp A composite layer with all selected or visible layers merged. PS 161

stamping layers, PS 161

starting
  Mini Bridge, PS 73
  Photoshop CS6, PS 7–8

state. *See* history state

statement of purpose A precise statement that articulates the vision and aspirations for a project. PS 526

status bar An area at the bottom of the Photoshop window that displays information about the current file, such as magnification, size, and resolution. PS 2

stroke (n.) An outline drawn around an object to make it stand out in an image. PS 194
  of Brush tool, PS 220
  options, PS 208

stroke (v.) To make a selection stand out by drawing a border around it. PS 293
  selections, PS 293–295

style A preset grouping of effects that are applied together. PS 126
  applying to text, PS 346–348
  creating paragraph, character, PS 342
  saving, PS 196
  using, PS 192–193

Styles panel, PS 127
  described (fig.), PS 345
  working with, PS 192–197

stylus A tool that lets you write or draw directly on a monitor screen. PS 220

subtracting from shapes, PS 213–217

subtractive color mode A color mode in which each color subtracts the light from the white page on which it is printed. PS 77

Sunset Sky (Text) style, PS 193

Swatches panel
  adding sampled colors to, PS 190
  deleting colors from, PS 191
  working with, PS 187–189

Switch Foreground and Background Colors button, Tools panel, PS 185

symmetrical balance The even distribution of visual weight of objects in a composition around the central horizontal and vertical axes of the canvas. PS 545

T

tab order, changing, PS 16–17

Tagged Image File Format (TIFF) A bitmap image file format that contains a great deal of data and is used to output high-quality print pieces; supports layers in Photoshop, but not in other applications. Sometimes written as TIF. PS 63

target audience The group of people whom you would most like to view and respond to the final output of a project. PS 520, PS 532–534, PS 557

technical research The gathering of all relevant technical specifications for a project, including the file size, resolution, and color profile required for the output files. PS 521

text
  adding along paths, PS 358–360
  adding to compositions, PS 360, PS 571–572
  adjusting tracking of vertical, PS 331–333
  alignment, PS 337–339
  applying style to, PS 346–348
  baseline shift, PS 345, PS 353
  centering, PS 324
  creating paragraph, PS 333–336
  creating unique, PS 344–357
  filling with patterns, gradients, PS 362–364
  finding and replacing, PS 340–341
  justification, PS 337
  kerning, PS 315, PS 352
  placeholder, PS 357
  rotating horizontal to vertical, PS 328–330
  selecting fonts for use on Web, PS 570
  vertical orientation, PS 327
  warping, PS 354–357

text effect A setting that changes the appearance of text; appears in the Layers panel grouped with the layer it applies to. PS 315

text layer A Photoshop layer that stores text. PS 315
  introduction to, PS 316–318
  visual overview (fig.), PS 314–315
  warped, PS 345

text mode A Photoshop mode in which you can add point type to the canvas. PS 319

text typography An approach to typography in which the goal is the creation of a cohesive, readable, and visually pleasing document, using an unobtrusive typographical style. PS 568

text-edit mode A Photoshop mode in which you can modify text by changing the font style and color, among other things. PS 122

text-editing mode, PS 349, PS 350

Thaw Mask tool, PS 298, PS 299

Threshold adjustment An adjustment tool that changes an image to high-contrast black-and-white output by specifying a threshold level at which lighter pixels are changed to white and darker pixels are changed to black. PS 379, PS 405–409

threshold level The pixel value above which all lighter pixels are changed to white and below which all darker pixels are changed to black, when using the Threshold adjustment tool. PS 405

Tie-Dyed Silk style, PS 127

TIFF. *See* Tagged Image File Format
  vs. JPEG format, PS 67–68
  opening files, PS 65

tight line A line of text with words so close together that they are difficult to distinguish. PS 337

Tilt-Shift filter, PS 434–435

tonal adjustments, making to images, PS 476–479

tone A shade of a color; for example, when Photoshop translates an image from color to grayscale mode, each shade of every color is translated to a different shade, or tone, of gray. PS 79
  adjusting color, PS 399–400

tool group A set of additional tools hidden beneath a tool that is visible in the Tools panel. PS 44

tool preset A set of custom settings for a Photoshop tool—such as a brush, gradient, shape, or type tool—that you can save and use again and again. PS 47
  deleting, PS 51
  saving, PS 50

Tool Preset picker, PS 51

tools
  Bridge, PS 72
  color selection, PS 176–191
  defining custom settings, PS 45–47
  hidden, PS 10
  selecting and using, PS 44–45
  Selection (fig.), PS 242
  Shape, PS 22
  in Tools panel, PS 44–52
  Type, PS 316
  vector, PS 6

tooltip On-screen text that appears when you point to a tool; includes the name of the tool plus any shortcut key for selecting the tool. PS 10

Tools panel The panel that includes tools for zooming, panning, selecting, and working with colors and bitmap and vector objects. PS 2
  overview, PS 10
  using tools in, PS 44–52

tracking The spacing between all of the characters in selected text or a paragraph. PS 315

  adjusting, PS 348–352
  adjusting vertical text, PS 331–333

transform To make a selection larger or smaller, or to distort or warp a selection. PS 83

transform control The squares at each corner of a selection's bounding box that let you change the shape and size of an object. PS 116, PS 326, PS 327

transform perspective To remove the distortion produced by taking a photograph at an angle. PS 101

transforming images using Blur gallery of filters, PS 432–439

transparent A term used to describe pixels on a layer that you can see through. PS 119

triad color palette A color palette created by dividing divide the color wheel into three sections, enabling you to select three colors that are spaced at an equal distance from each other on the color wheel. PS 554, PS 555

trimming
  canvas, PS 99–101
  vs. cropping, PS 101

tungsten lights, white balancing, PS 475

TWAIN plug-in, PS 97

Twirl Clockwise tool, PS 297

Type setting, Image menu, PS 420

Type tools The tools used to add text to a Photoshop composition. PS 316
  options (fig.), PS 317

typeface A unified set of alphanumeric symbols that are designed with stylistic unity. PS 568

typography The art and technique of type arrangement, design, and modification. PS 541

Typography workspace, PS 35, PS 36, PS 318, PS 321–324

U

undoing, redoing actions, PS 262–275

unhiding layers, PS 161

unity A quality achieved by ordering of elements in a design so that each contributes to an overall unified composition. PS 547

unlocking layer content, PS 150–152

upsample To increase the resolution of an image by adding pixels to an image so there are more pixels per inch. PS 68

V

vector A graphic that is a collection of points, lines, curves, and shapes stored as a set of mathematical instructions. PS 6

vector layers, adding, PS 126–127

vector objects, adding, PS 209–214

vector shapes
  drawing, PS 210–212
  rasterizing, PS 210
  specifying fill and stroke options for, PS 207–209

verbal communication, PS 225

vertical point type, working with, PS 328–333

vertical type Type that runs from top to bottom along a vertical line. PS 318

Vertical Type tool, PS 330–331

video format A set of standards that define a video file's display characteristics and limitations. PS 507

video output, creating, PS 507–509

view box A feature in the Navigator panel that outlines the area of the image that is displayed in the Document window. PS 91

viewer profile A set of data describing the characteristics of a target audience. PS 521

viewers, and users, PS 527, PS 529

viewing
  images, PS 90–91
  soft proofs, PS 495–496
  tools in Camera Raw dialog box (fig.), PS 458

visibility, changing layer, PS 135–137

vision The client's ideas and overall plan for a project. PS 520, PS 523–524

vision statement, PS 524

W

warm colors, PS 554

warnings, clipping, PS 471

warp To distort text horizontally and/or vertically or skew it as if it is being viewed from a different angle. PS 345

warping text, PS 354–357

Web, the
  creating images for the, PS 504–507
  selecting fonts for use as text on, PS 570

Web presets, PS 85–86

Web-safe color A color that will always be displayed properly in a Web browser. PS 182, PS 184

white balance To locate objects in an image that should be white or gray and make corrections that account for the color temperature of the lighting used when a photograph was taken; removes color casts from an image. PS 473

white balancing images, PS 473–475

white space The empty space in a canvas. PS 541, PS 547

windows
  arranging file, PS 17–20
  managing, PS 12
  navigating open file, PS 15–16

Windows, monitor calibration utility, PS 402

Windows calibration tool, using, PS 488–494

Windows Display Color Calibration Wizard, PS 489–494

wireframe A bare-bones mock-up that is created in a graphics program instead of being drawn by hand. PS 548

Word spacing An advanced justification setting that determines the space between words on a text layer. PS 339

work path A temporary outline on a layer that can be used to define the shape of text or a brushstroke. PS 227

workflow options Camera Raw setting options that enable you to set output parameters such as Space, Depth, Size, and Resolution. PS 462–464

working space A color space used to define and edit colors while you are in an Adobe application. PS 485

workspace All the elements of the Photoshop window, including the Document window, panels, and menus; the default workspace is the Essentials workspace. PS 7
  commands, PS 8
  layouts (fig.), PS 36
  touring, PS 10–11

Workspace Switcher button, PS 3

workspaces
  choosing preset, PS 35–38
  custom, PS 38

writing project goals, PS 525

XMP file A separate file that is saved in the same folder as a camera raw image file and that holds all of that image's adjustment data. PS 456

Z

zoom level, changing, PS 45, PS 91

Zoom tool
  described, PS 44–45
  options (fig.), PS 102

zooming
  images, PS 102–103
  with Navigator, PS 105–106

TASK REFERENCE

TASK	PAGE #	RECOMMENDED METHOD
Adjustment layer, add	PS 93	In the Layers panel, select a layer to adjust, click the desired adjustment in the Adjustments panel, change the settings in the Properties panel as desired
Adjustment layer, delete	PS 95	In the Layers panel, drag the adjustment layer to the lower-right corner of the Layers panel to
Auto button, correct an image using	PS 404	In the Layers panel, click to select the layer to be corrected; in the Adjustments panel, click an icon to apply an adjustment; click the Auto button in the Properties panel
Background color, change	PS 185	In the Color panel or in the Tools panel, click to open the Color Picker (Background Color) dialog box to select a color or click to sample a new background color
Baseline shift, specify	PS 353	Select the text, type a baseline shift value in the box in the Character panel, click
Blending mode, apply	PS 157	In the Layers panel, select the layer, click the Set the blending mode for the layer button, click the desired blending mode
Blur Gallery filter, use	PS 435	*See* Reference box: Blurring an Area of an Image using a Blur Gallery Filter
Brush preset library, load	PS 226	In the Brush Presets panel, click , click a preset library
Brush preset picker, open	PS 46	In the Tools panel, click , click on the options bar
Brush preset, create	PS 230	In the Brush panel, select a brush and specify the settings, click in the Brush Presets panel, click New Brush Preset; in the Brush Name dialog box, type a name for the preset in the Name box, click the Capture Brush Size in Preset check box to select it, click OK
Brush tool, activate	PS 222	Press the B key
Brush tool, use	PS 222	In the Tools panel, click , set the options on the options bar or click to set the brush size and hardness, drag on the canvas to create a brushstroke
Brush tool, use to draw straight line	PS 223	In the Tools panel, click , set the options on the options bar or click to set the brush size and hardness; click on the canvas at the starting point for the line, press and hold the Shift key, click at the end point for the line
Burn tool, use	PS 428	In the Tools panel, click ; on the options bar, select brush type, set brush diameter, select Range, adjust Exposure, click Protect Tones; paint the area in the image to be adjusted
Camera Raw preferences, adjust	PS 457	On the menu bar, click Edit, point to Preferences, click Camera Raw, adjust settings, click OK
Camera Raw, adjust saturation in an image	PS 480	On the Basic tab of the Adjustments panel in Camera Raw, drag the Clarity, Vibrance, and Saturation sliders
Camera Raw, adjust zoom level in	PS 460	On the toolbar located above the Document window in the Camera Raw dialog box, click , click in the Document window to increase zoom in preset increments

TASK	PAGE #	RECOMMENDED METHOD
Camera Raw, crop image in	PS 460	On the toolbar located above the Document window in the Camera Raw dialog box, click [crop tool button], click in the Document window, drag to draw a rectangle that covers the area of the image you want to crop to
Camera Raw, display clipped pixels	PS 472	In the Camera Raw dialog box, click [button] or [button]
Camera Raw, make tonal adjustments	PS 476	On the Basic tab of the Adjustments panel in Camera Raw, adjust the sliders for Exposure, Recovery, Fill Light, Blacks, Brightness, and Contrast
Camera Raw, open a file in	PS 459	*See* Reference box: Opening a File in Camera Raw
Camera Raw, reposition image in	PS 460	On the toolbar located above the Document window in the Camera Raw dialog box, click [hand tool button], drag the image in the Document window to reposition it
Camera Raw, save adjustments and close file	PS 464	In the Camera Raw dialog box, click Done to save adjustments, close the file
Camera Raw, save adjustments and open image as a Smart Object in Photoshop	PS 465	In the Camera Raw dialog box, click Open Object to save adjustments and open a copy of the Camera Raw file as a Smart Object in Photoshop
Camera Raw, set workflow options	PS 463	*See* Reference box: Setting Workflow Options in Camera Raw
Camera Raw, white balance an image	PS 474	*See* Reference box: White Balancing an Image
Canvas, extend	PS 98	*See* Reference box: Extending the Canvas
Canvas, trim	PS 100	*See* Reference box: Trimming the Canvas
Clipping Mask, create	PS 362	In the Layers panel, select a layer to serve as the clipping mask, click Layer on the menu bar, click Create Clipping Mask
Clipped pixels, display in Camera Raw	PS 472	In the Camera Raw dialog box, click [button] or [button]
Color, adjust using Auto Color	PS 400	On the menu bar, click Image, click Auto Color
Color Balance adjustment, apply to a selection	PS 252	Make a selection in an image, click [button] in the Adjustments panel, drag the color sliders to achieve the desired color balance
Color mode, change	PS 81	On the menu bar, click Image, point to Mode, click a mode
Color picker, open	PS 183	In the Color panel or the Tools panel, click [foreground color button] or [background color button], click a color on the color ramp, click a shade of that color in the color field, click OK
Color profile, convert	PS 501	On the menu bar, click Edit, click Convert to Profile, select the desired settings in the Convert to Profile dialog box, click OK
Color range, select localized	PS 259	On the menu bar, click Select, click Color Range; in the Color Range dialog box, select Sampled Colors, if necessary, click the Localized Color Clusters check box, click part of the image that includes the desired color range, click OK
Color, sample using the Eyedropper tool	PS 178	*See* Reference box: Using the Eyedropper Tool
Color settings, adjust	PS 498	On the menu bar, click Edit, click Color Settings; in the Color Settings dialog box, select the desired settings, click OK
Color settings, synchronize in Bridge	PS 499	Open Bridge, click Edit on the menu bar, click Creative Suite Color Settings, click the desired setting, click Apply

TASK	PAGE #	RECOMMENDED METHOD
Color, specify using the Color Panel	PS 181	*See* Reference box: Specifying a Color in the Color Panel
Color, specify using the Color Picker dialog box	PS 183	In the Color panel or the Tools panel, click ■ or ▫, click a color on the color ramp, click a shade of that color in the color field, click OK
Color, specify Web-safe colors using the Color Picker dialog box	PS 182	In the Color Picker dialog box, click the Only Web Colors check box to select it
Complex selection, create	PS 254	*See* Reference box: Adding to a Selection to Create a Complex Selection
Content-Aware Fill, use	PS 278	Make a selection in an image, click Edit on the menu bar, click Fill; in the Fill dialog box, select Content-Aware from the Use drop-down menu, set the Blending Mode and the Opacity, click OK
Content-Aware Move tool, use	PS 281	Make a selection in an image, click [icon] in the Tools panel, drag the selection to its new location
Content Aware Move tool, use to extend an object	PS 393	Make a selection in an image; click [icon] in the Tools panel; click the Mode button on the options bar, click Extend, drag the selection to extend the object as desired
Contrast and tone, adjust using the Curves adjustment	PS 409	In the Adjustments panel, click [icon], click on line in the Curves grid, drag to adjust contrast and tone
Contrast, adjust using Auto Contrast	PS 399	On the menu bar, click Image, click Auto Contrast
Crop Guide Overlay, use to crop an image	PS 381	*See* Reference box: Cropping an Image
Crop tool, activate	PS 382	In the Tools panel, click [icon]; or press the C key
Curves adjustment, apply	PS 410	In the Adjustments panel, click [icon], click on line in the Curves grid, drag to adjust contrast and tone
Custom document preset, delete	PS 88	*See* Reference box: Deleting a Custom Document Preset
Custom document preset, save	PS 87	*See* Reference box: Saving a Custom Document Preset
Custom Shape picker, open	PS 48	In the Tools panel, click [icon], click Shape: [icon] on the options bar
Darkest point in an image, mark using the Threshold adjustment	PS 407	*See* Reference box: Marking Lightest and Darkest Pixels with the Threshold Adjustment
Document, navigate to an open	PS 15	Click the Document window tab of the desired document
Document preset, delete a custom	PS 88	*See* Reference box: Deleting a Custom Document Preset
Document preset, save a custom	PS 87	*See* Reference box: Saving a Custom Document Preset
Document window, float	PS 17	Point to a Document window tab, press and hold the mouse button, drag the tab to the middle of the workspace, release the button
Documents, arrange in Document window	PS 19	On the menu bar, click Window, point to Arrange, click the desired arrangement option
Dodge tool, use	PS 426	*See* Reference box: Brightening an Image with the Dodge tool
Eyedropper tool, use	PS 178	*See* Reference box: Using the Eyedropper Tool
File, close	PS 20	On the menu bar, click File, click Close
File, create using a preset	PS 84	*See* Reference box: Creating a New File Using a Preset
File, navigate to an open	PS 15	Click the Document window tab of the desired file
File, open	PS 8	On the menu bar, click File, click Open, navigate to the folder containing the file, click the file, click Open
File, open recent	PS 15	On the menu bar, click File, click Open Recent, click the filename

TASK	PAGE #	RECOMMENDED METHOD
File, save as	PS 14	On the menu bar, click File, click Save As, select a file type in the Save As dialog box, type the new filename in the File name box, click Save
Files, close all	PS 21	On the menu bar, click File, click Close All
Files, display a list of open	PS 15	In the Document window, click >>
Filter Gallery, use	PS 302	On the menu bar, click Filter, click Filter Gallery, click a folder, click a filter, adjust the settings as desired, click OK
Filter layers	PS 124	Click the desired filter icon at the top of the Layers panel
Font size, set	PS 320	Select the text, type a new font size in the T 12 pt box in the Character panel
Foreground and background colors, switch	PS 185	In the Tools panel, click ; or press the X key
Foreground color, change	PS 183	In the Color panel or in the Tools panel, click to open the Color Picker dialog box to select a color or click to sample a new foreground color
Freeze Mask tool, use	PS 298	*See* Reference box: Using the Liquify Filter
Gradient fill layer, create	PS 204	At the bottom of the Layers panel, click , click Gradient, click in the Gradient Fill dialog box, click a gradient, click OK; in the Layers panel, adjust the Opacity setting as needed
Grid, show or hide	PS 42	On the menu bar, click View, point to Show, click Grid
Guides, add	PS 39	On the menu bar, click View, click New Guide, click the Vertical or Horizontal option button, type a value in the Position box, click OK
Guides, add by dragging	PS 39	Drag down from the horizontal ruler to place a horizontal guide; drag over from the vertical ruler to place a vertical guide
Hand tool, use	PS 104	In the Tools panel, click , click in the image, drag in the desired direction
Healing Brush tool, use	PS 422	In the Tools panel, click , Alt-click to select source pixels for repair, place pointer at edge of problem area, paint the area in the image to be retouched
Help, access	PS 11	On the menu bar, click Help, click Photoshop Online Help, click the link for a topic, click the subtopic hyperlink
Help, access	PS 11	Press the F1 key
Help, search	PS 13	In Adobe Community Help Search box in the Photoshop Help window, type a search term, press Enter, click the topic link
History Brush tool, activate	PS 272	Press the Y key
History Brush tool, use to return part of an image to a previous state	PS 270	*See* Reference box: Using the History Brush Tool to Return Part of an Image to a Previous History State
History panel, use to revert to a previous state	PS 266	*See* Reference box: Reverting to a Previous History State Using the History Panel
History state, delete	PS 266	In the History panel, click the history state, click
Horizontal point type, add	PS 319	*See* Reference box: Adding Point Type to an Image

TASK	PAGE #	RECOMMENDED METHOD
Horizontal type, rotate	PS 329	Select text with the Move tool, click the Show Transform Controls check box on the options bar, place the mouse pointer at the corner of the bounding box, drag clockwise or counterclockwise to achieve the desired rotation, click [✓] on the options bar
Image resolution, change using resampling	PS 70	*See* Reference box: Changing Image Resolution Using Resampling
Image, adjust saturation in Camera Raw	PS 480	On the Basic tab of the Adjustments panel in Camera Raw, drag the Clarity, Vibrance, and Saturation sliders
Image, adjust saturation, using the Sponge tool	PS 429	In the Tools panel click [Sponge tool], on the options bar, select brush type, set brush diameter, select Mode, adjust Flow, paint the area in the image to be adjusted
Image, adjust using Lab color mode	PS 440	On the menu bar, click Image, point to Mode, click Lab Color; in the Layers panel, click to select the layer to be adjusted; in the Adjustments panel, click an icon to apply an adjustment
Image, blur using a Blur Gallery filter	PS 435	*See* Reference box: Blurring an Area of an Image using a Blur Gallery Filter
Image, brighten shadows, highlights, or midtones using the Dodge tool	PS 426	*See* Reference box: Brightening an Image with the Dodge tool
Image, correct using Auto Color	PS 400	On the menu bar, click Image, click Auto Color
Image, correct using Auto Contrast	PS 399	On the menu bar, click Image, click Auto Contrast
Image, correct using Auto Tone	PS 398	On the menu bar, click Image, click Auto Tone
Image, crop	PS 381	*See* Reference box: Cropping an Image
Image, crop in Camera Raw	PS 460	On the toolbar located above the Document window in the Camera Raw dialog box, click [Crop tool], click in the Document window, drag to draw a rectangle that covers the area of the image you want to crop to
Image, crop using the Rule of Thirds	PS 381	*See* Reference box: Cropping an Image
Image, darken shadows, highlights, or midtones using the Burn tool	PS 428	In the Tools panel, click [Burn tool], on the options bar select brush type, set brush diameter, select Range, adjust Exposure, click Protect Tones, paint the area in the image to be adjusted
Image, display and pan in the Navigator	PS 105	On the menu bar, click Window, click Navigator, drag the view box in the Navigator to pan the image
Image, fit on screen	PS 382	Press the Ctrl+0 keys
Image, flatten	PS 162	On the menu bar, click Layer, click Flatten Image
Image, pan	PS 104	In the Tools panel, click [Hand tool], click in the image, drag in the desired direction
Image, place	PS 84	On the menu bar, click File, click Place; in the Place dialog box navigate to and select the image you want to place, click Place, press Enter
Image, remove imperfections using the Spot Healing Brush	PS 420	*See* Reference box: Applying the Spot Healing Brush Tool to an Image

TASK	PAGE #	RECOMMENDED METHOD
Image, repair using the Healing Brush tool	PS 422	In the Tools panel, click [icon], Alt-click to select source pixels for repair, place pointer at edge of problem area, paint
Image, reposition in Camera Raw	PS 460	On the toolbar located above the Document window in the Camera Raw dialog box, click [icon], drag the image in the Document window
Image, resample	PS 70	*See* Reference box: Changing Image Resolution Using Resampling
Image, rotate by a preset amount	PS 107	On the menu bar, click Image, point to Image Rotation, select a rotation option
Image, rotate by an arbitrary amount	PS 108	On the menu bar, click Image, point to Image Rotation, click Arbitrary, type an angle in the Angle box, select a direction option button, click OK
Image, save adjustments and close file in Camera Raw	PS 464	In the Camera Raw dialog box, click Done to save adjustments and close the file
Image, save adjustments and open image as a Smart Object in Photoshop	PS 465	In the Camera Raw dialog box, click Open Object to save adjustments and open a copy of the Camera Raw file as a Smart Object in Photoshop
Image, sharpen using the Sharpen tool	PS 431	In the Tools panel, click [icon]; on the options bar, select brush type, set brush diameter, select Mode, adjust Strength, check Protect Detail, paint the area in the image to be adjusted
Image, straighten using the Crop Tool's Straighten feature	PS 385	*See* Reference box: Straightening an Image
Image, white balance in Camera Raw	PS 474	*See* Reference box: White Balancing an Image
Image, zoom	PS 44	In the Tools panel, click [icon] or press the Z key, click the image
Image, zoom to 100%	PS 45	Press the Ctrl+1 keys
Image, zoom to a specified percentage	PS 45	On the status bar, double-click the current zoom percentage, type a new percentage value, press Enter
Image, zoom to fit on screen	PS 45	Press the Ctrl+0 keys
Image, zoom using a preset	PS 103	In the Tools panel, click [icon], click a zoom preset on the options bar
JPEG file, open in Camera Raw	PS 481	In Mini Bridge, right-click the image, click Open in Camera Raw
JPEG, save a file as	PS 65	On the menu bar, click File, click Save As, click the Format arrow, click JPEG (*.JPG; *.JPEG; *.JPE), click Save; in the JPEG Options dialog box, click the desired Quality setting, click the desired Format Option, click OK
Kuler panel, add a selected theme to the Swatches panel	PS 561	On the Browse tab of the Kuler panel, select a theme, click [icon]
Kuler panel, create theme	PS 562	*See* Reference box: Creating a Theme in the Kuler Panel
Kuler panel, open	PS 560	*See* Reference box: Using the Kuler Panel
Kuler panel, view and edit themes	PS 560	*See* Reference box: Using the Kuler Panel
Lab color mode, adjust image using	PS 440	On the menu bar, click Image, point to Mode, click Lab Color; in the Layers panel, click to select the layer to be adjusted; in the Adjustments panel, click an icon to apply an adjustment
Lasso tool, use	PS 278	In the Tools panel, click [icon], drag to make a selection
Layer comp, apply	PS 153	In the Layer Comps panel, click to the left of the layer comp

TASK	PAGE #	RECOMMENDED METHOD
Layer comp, create	PS 153	On the menu bar, click Window, click Layer Comps, click [icon] at the bottom of the Layer Comps panel; in the New Layer Comp dialog box, type a layer comp name in the Name box, type a comment in the Comment box, click OK
Layer comp, delete	PS 154	In the Layer Comps panel, click the layer comp, click [icon]
Layer edges, display	PS 134	On the menu bar, click View, point to Show, click Layer Edges
Layer edges, hide	PS 134	On the menu bar, click View, point to Show, click Layer Edges to deselect it
Layer Style dialog box, open	PS 195	In the Layers panel, double-click fx or double-click the layer thumbnail, select the desired settings in the dialog box, click OK
Layer style, apply	PS 127	In the Layers panel, select a layer, click a style in the Styles panel
Layer style, copy and paste	PS 211	In the Layers panel, right-click a layer, click Copy Layer Style, right-click the layer you want to copy the style to, click Paste Layer Style
Layer(s), deselect	PS 123	On the menu bar, click Select, click Deselect Layers
Layer, add empty	PS 126	At the bottom of the Layers panel, click [icon]
Layer, add new by copying and pasting	PS 128	In the Layers panel, select a layer; in the Tools panel, click a selection tool; drag to make a selection on the canvas; on the menu bar, click Edit, click Copy, click Edit again, click Paste
Layer, change color in the Layers panel	PS 132	In the Layers panel, right-click the layer, click a color
Layer, change opacity of	PS 159	In the Layers panel, drag the scrub mouse pointer over the word Opacity to the right to increase the opacity and to the left to decrease it
Layer, create a gradient fill	PS 204	At the bottom of the Layers panel, click [icon], click Gradient, click the Gradient arrow in the Gradient Fill dialog box, click a gradient, click OK; in the Layers panel, adjust the Opacity setting as needed
Layer, create a pattern fill	PS 205	At the bottom of the Layers panel, click [icon], click Pattern, click the pattern thumbnail in the Pattern Fill dialog box, click a pattern, click OK; in the Layers panel, adjust the Opacity setting as needed
Layer, create a solid color fill	PS 202	At the bottom of the Layers panel, click [icon], click Solid Color, select a color in the Color Picker (Solid Color) dialog box, click OK; in the Layers panel, adjust the Opacity setting as needed
Layer, delete	PS 143	In the Layers panel, select the layer, press the Delete key
Layer, hide and redisplay	PS 141	In the Layers panel, click [icon] to the left of the layer
Layer, lock all	PS 150	In the Layers panel, select the layer, click [icon]
Layer, lock image pixels	PS 150	In the Layers panel, select the layer, click [icon]
Layer, lock position	PS 150	In the Layers panel, select the layer, click [icon]
Layer, lock transparent pixels	PS 150	In the Layers panel, select the layer, click [icon]
Layer, move to change position on canvas	PS 137	In the Layers panel, select a layer, point to the layer on the canvas, click and drag the layer to a new position
Layer, move to change visibility	PS 135	*See* Reference box: Moving a Layer in the Layers Panel to Change Its Visibility
Layer, redisplay	PS 141	In the Layers panel, click [icon] to the left of the layer

TASK	PAGE #	RECOMMENDED METHOD
Layer, rename	PS 132	In the Layers panel, click the layer, double-click the current layer name, type a new name, press Enter
Layer, select	PS 122	Click the layer in the Layers panel
Layers, align	PS 139	*See* Reference box: Aligning Layers in a Composition
Layers, distribute	PS 140	*See* Reference box: Distributing Layers in a Composition
Layers, filter	PS 124	Click the desired filter icon at the top of the Layers panel
Layers, group in the Layers panel	PS 159	*See* Reference box: Grouping Layers
Layers, hide all but selected layer	PS 142	In the Layers panel, select a layer, press and hold the Alt key, click [icon] on the selected layer
Layers, merge selected	PS 160	Select the layers, click Layer on the menu bar, click Merge Layers
Layers, merge visible	PS 160	On the menu bar, click Layer, click Merge Visible
Layers, select multiple	PS 123	*See* Reference box: Selecting Multiple Layers
Layers, stamp selected	PS 161	Select the layers, press the Ctrl+Alt+E keys
Layers, ungroup in the Layers panel	PS 160	In the Layers panel, select the group, click Layer on the menu bar, click Ungroup Layers
Lightest point in an image, mark using the Threshold adjustment	PS 407	*See* Reference box: Marking Lightest and Darkest Pixels with the Threshold Adjustment
Liquify Filter, use	PS 298	*See* Reference box: Using the Liquify Filter
Magic Wand tool, use to add pixels to a selection	PS 250	In the Tools panel, click [icon]; on the options bar, specify a Tolerance setting, and select or deselect Anti-alias and Contiguous as desired, click [icon], click the pixels to be added to the selection
Magnetic Lasso tool, use	PS 285	*See* Reference box: Using the Magnetic Lasso Tool
Mini Bridge, launch	PS 73	At the bottom of the Photoshop window, click the Mini Bridge tab, click Launch Bridge
Monitor, calibrate	PS 489	*See* Reference box: Calibrating a Monitor
Move tool, activate	PS 43	Press the V key
Multiple files, open at once	PS 13	*See* Reference box: Opening Multiple Files at Once
Navigator, display and use to pan an image	PS 105	On the menu bar, click Window, click Navigator, drag the view box in the Navigator to pan the image
New file, create using a preset	PS 84	*See* Reference box: Creating a New File Using a Preset
Opacity, change for a layer	PS 159	In the Layers panel, drag the scrub mouse pointer over the word Opacity to the right to increase the opacity and to the left to decrease it
Panel dock, expand	PS 32	Click [icon]
Panel dock, minimize	PS 32	On the right side of the title bar for the docked panels, click [icon]
Panel tab, select	PS 28	Click the desired panel tab in a panel group
Panel, close	PS 31	On the title bar for the panel, click [icon], click Close
Panel, close from Window menu	PS 32	On the menu bar, click Window, click the panel name to remove the check mark
Panel, display	PS 29	On the menu bar, click Window, click the desired panel
Panel, move	PS 33	Point to the panel bar to the right of the panel tab, press and hold the mouse button, drag the panel group to the desired location, release the mouse button
Panels, hide all	PS 33	Press the Tab key

TASK	PAGE #	RECOMMENDED METHOD
Panels, redisplay all	PS 33	Press the Tab key
Panels, stack	PS 34	Point to a panel bar to the right of the last panel tab, press and hold the mouse button, drag the panel group under another panel group until a blue bar appears, release the mouse button
Paragraph text, add	PS 334	*See* Reference box: Adding Paragraph Text
Patch tool, use to move an object and patch the hole	PS 394	*See* Reference box: Moving an Object and Patching the Hole with the Patch Tool
Pattern fill layer, create	PS 205	At the bottom of the Layers panel, click , click Pattern, click the pattern thumbnail in the Pattern Fill dialog box, click a pattern, click OK; in the Layers panel, adjust the Opacity setting as needed
Perspective Crop tool, use to change the perspective of an image	PS 388	In the Tools panel, click ; click the upper-left corner of the image, drag down to the lower-right corner to display the grid over the image; drag a selection handle to adjust the perspective as desired
Photoshop preferences, set	PS 24	*See* Reference box: Setting Photoshop Preferences
Photoshop settings file, reset	PS 7	Click , click All Programs, click Adobe Photoshop CS6 while pressing and holding the Ctrl+Alt+Shift keys; when prompted to delete the Adobe Photoshop settings, click Yes
Photoshop, exit	PS 21	On the menu bar, click File, click Exit
Photoshop, start	PS 7	Click , click All Programs, click Adobe Photoshop CS6
Placed image, reposition using relative positioning	PS 146	On the options bar, click , right-click the X or Y box, click the desired units on the context menu, highlight the current value in the X box, type a new value, press Enter, repeat for the Y box
Placed image, resize and maintain aspect ratio	PS 145	On the options bar, click , highlight the current value in the W box, type a new value, press Enter
Placed image, rotate	PS 146	Place the mouse pointer at the corner of the placed image on the canvas, drag clockwise or counterclockwise
Placed image, rotate in 15-degree increments	PS 146	Place the mouse pointer at the corner of the placed image on the canvas, press and hold the Shift key, drag clockwise or counterclockwise to achieve the desired rotation
Point type, add to an image	PS 319	*See* Reference box: Adding Point Type to an Image
Preferences, set	PS 24	*See* Reference box: Setting Photoshop Preferences
Resolution, change using resampling	PS 70	*See* Reference box: Changing Image Resolution Using Resampling
Rule of Thirds, use to crop an image	PS 381	*See* Reference box: Cropping an Image
Rulers, show or hide	PS 38	On the menu bar, click View, click Rulers
Selection, complex	PS 254	*See* Reference box: Adding to a Selection to Create a Complex Selection
Saturation, adjust in Camera Raw	PS 480	On the Basic tab of the Adjustments panel in Camera Raw, drag the Clarity, Vibrance, and Saturation sliders
Saturation, adjust using the Sponge tool	PS 429	In the Tools panel click ; on the options bar, select brush type, set brush diameter, select Mode, adjust Flow, paint the area in the image to be adjusted
Save for Web & Devices	PS 505	*See* Reference box: Saving a JPEG Image Using Save for Web

TASK	PAGE #	RECOMMENDED METHOD
Selection, copy and paste	PS 253	Make a selection in an image, click Edit on the menu bar, click Copy, click Edit again, click Paste
Selection, create using a color range	PS 259	On the menu bar, click Select, click Color Range; in the Color Range dialog box, select Sampled Colors, if necessary, click the Localized Color Clusters check box, click the part of the image that includes the desired color range, click OK
Selection, expand or grow	PS 249	*See* Reference box: Expanding or Growing a Selection
Selection, fixed ratio	PS 246	*See* Reference box: Specifying a Fixed Ratio Selection
Selection, fixed size	PS 248	*See* Reference box: Specifying a Fixed Size Selection
Selection, save and load	PS 289	*See* Reference box: Saving and Loading a Selection
Selection, select inverse of	PS 268	Make a selection, click Select on the menu bar, click Inverse
Selection, stroke	PS 294	Make a selection in an image, click Edit on the menu bar, click Stroke; in the Stroke dialog box, specify a width, color, location, blending mode, and opacity, click OK
Selection, use Magic Wand tool to add pixels to	PS 250	In the Tools panel, click ; on the options bar, specify a Tolerance setting, and select or deselect Anti-alias and Contiguous as desired, click , click the pixels to be added to the selection
Shape layer, create	PS 210	In the Tools panel, click a shape tool, ensure that Shape is selected as the Pick tool mode on the options bar; draw the shape on the canvas
Shape, add to	PS 218	In the Tools panel, click a shape tool, click , click on the options bar, draw a shape on the canvas over an existing shape
Shape, draw	PS 210	In the Tools panel, click a shape tool, ensure that Shape is selected as the Pick tool mode on the options bar; draw the shape on the canvas
Shape, draw a bitmap	PS 219	In the Tools panel, click a shape tool, ensure that Pixels is selected on the options bar, draw the shape
Shape, exclude overlapping	PS 213	In the Tools panel, click a shape tool, click , click on the options bar, draw the shape on the canvas
Shape, subtract from	PS 214	In the Tools panel, click a shape tool, click , click on the options bar, draw the shape on the canvas over the existing shape you want to subtract from
Sharpen tool, use	PS 431	In the Tools panel, click ; on the options bar select brush type, set brush diameter, select Mode, adjust Strength, check Protect Detail, paint the area in the image to be adjusted
Soft proof, view	PS 495	On the menu bar, click View, point to Proof Setup, click the desired proof setting; on the View menu, check Proof Colors
Solid color fill layer, create	PS 202	At the bottom of the Layers panel, click , click Solid Color, select a color in the Color Picker (Solid Color) dialog box, click OK; in the Layers panel, adjust the Opacity setting as needed
Spelling, check	PS 340	Click at the beginning of the text, click Edit on the menu bar, click Check Spelling; in the Check Spelling dialog box, select the correct spelling for the first highlighted word, click the Change button, click OK when the spelling check is complete

TASK	PAGE #	RECOMMENDED METHOD
Sponge tool, use	PS 429	In the Tools panel click , on the options bar, select brush type, set brush diameter, select Mode, adjust Flow, paint the area in the image to be adjusted
Spot Healing Brush, use	PS 420	*See* Reference box: Applying the Spot Healing Brush Tool to an Image
Step backward	PS 264	On the menu bar, click Edit, click Step Backward
Step forward	PS 264	On the menu bar, click Edit, click Step Forward
Straightened image, recrop	PS 387	Click in the image to reveal the crop grid, click a crop grid border, drag the border to a new position
Style, apply	PS 192	In the Layers panel, select a layer, click a style on the Styles panel
Swatches panel, add sampled color to	PS 190	Sample a color, move the mouse pointer to a blank (gray) area at the bottom of the Swatches panel, when the mouse pointer changes to , click, type a swatch name in the Name box, click OK
Swatches panel, change palette preset	PS 188	On the Swatches panel, click , click a palette preset
Swatches panel, customize display	PS 188	On the Swatches panel, click , click a display option
Swatches, delete a color from	PS 191	Press the Alt key to change to the pointer, point to the color swatch and click
Swatches, load	PS 191	On the Swatches panel, click ,click Load Swatches, click the desired swatches preset, click Load
Swatches, reset to default	PS 189	On the Swatches panel, click , click Reset Swatches
Swatches, save as a preset	PS 191	On the Swatches panel, click , click Save Swatches, type a name for the swatches, click Save
Tab group, close	PS 31	On the title bar for the panel, click , click Close Tab Group
Tab order, change	PS 16	Point to a Document window tab, press and hold the mouse button, drag the tab to the new location, release the mouse button
Text, add along a closed path	PS 359	Select a drawing tool, ensure that Path is selected on the options bar as the Pick tool mode; draw a closed path on the canvas; in the Tools panel, click , specify type settings, click the path, type to add text along the path
Text, apply style to	PS 346	Select the text, click a style on the Styles panel
Text, center	PS 324	With a text tool active, click on the options bar, click
Text, find and replace	PS 341	Click at the beginning of the text, click Edit on the menu bar, click Find and Replace Text; in the Find And Replace Text dialog box, type a word in the Find What box, type a word in the Change To box, click Find Next, click Change, click Done when finished
Text, format as small caps	PS 324	Select the text, click on the Character panel, click
Text, scale using Character panel	PS 325	*See* Reference box: Scaling Text Using the Character Panel
Text, scale using Move tool	PS 326	*See* Reference box: Scaling Text Using the Move Tool
Text, warp	PS 354	*See* Reference box: Warping Text
Threshold, adjust	PS 407	*See* Reference box: Marking Lightest and Darkest Pixels with the Threshold Adjustment

TASK	PAGE #	RECOMMENDED METHOD
TIFF file, open in Camera Raw	PS 421	In Mini Bridge, right-click image, click Open in Camera Raw
Tone, adjust using Auto Tone	PS 398	On the menu bar, click Image, click Auto Tone
Tool options, set	PS 45	In the Tools panel, select a tool, select the settings on the options bar
Tool preset, delete	PS 51	On the options bar, click , click the preset, click , click Delete Tool Preset
Tool preset, save	PS 50	On the options bar, click , click , type a preset name in the Name box, select any other desired options, click OK
Tool, reset	PS 46	On the eft side of the options bar, right-click the tool, click Reset Tool
Tracking, adjust	PS 331	Select the text, click in the box in the Character panel, select any existing value, type a new value
Vertical point type, add to an image	PS 319	*See* Reference box: Adding Point Type to an Image
Web-safe colors, specify in the Color Picker dialog box	PS 183	In the Color Picker dialog box, click the Only Web Colors check box to select it
White and Black Points, set using the Curves adjustment	PS 410	*See* Reference box: Setting the White and Black Points of an Image
Work path, create and stroke with brush	PS 228	In the Tools panel, select a drawing tool, click Path on the options bar, draw the path, right-click the path, click Stroke Path; in the Stroke Path dialog box, click the Tool arrow, click Brush, click OK
Workflow options, set in Camera Raw	PS 463	*See* Reference box: Setting Workflow Options in Camera Raw
Workspace, choose a preset	PS 36	On the menu bar, click Window, point to Workspace, click the desired workspace name; or click the Workspace switcher and then click the desired workspace name
Workspace, reset	PS 8	On the menu bar, click Window, point to Workspace, click Reset [*workspace name*]
Workspace, switch	PS 36	On the menu bar, click Window, point to Workspace, click the desired workspace
Zoom level, adjust in Camera Raw	PS 460	On the toolbar located above the Document window in the Camera Raw dialog box, click , click in the Document window to increase zoom in preset increments
Zoom tool, access	PS 44	Press the Z key or click in the Tools panel